EP 2.1.5 Advance human rights and social and economic justice:
 a. Understand the forms and mechanisms of oppression and discrimination
 b. Advocate for human rights and social and economic justice
 c. Engage in practices that advance social and economic justice

EP 2.1.6 Engage in research-informed practice and practice-informed research:
 a. Use practice experience to inform scientific inquiry
 b. Use research evidence to inform practice

EP 2.1.7 Apply knowledge of human behavior and the social environment:
 a. Utilize conceptual frameworks to guide the processes of assessment, intervention, and evaluation
 b. Critique and apply knowledge to understand person and environment

EP 2.1.8 Engage in policy practice to advance social and economic well-being and to deliver effective social work services:
 a. Analyze, formulate, and advocate for policies that advance social well-being
 b. Collaborate with colleagues and clients for effective policy action

EP 2.1.9 Respond to contexts that shape practice:
 a. Continuously discover, appraise, and attend to changing locales, populations, scientific and technological developments, and emerging societal trends to provide relevant services
 b. Provide leadership in promoting sustainable changes in service delivery and practice to improve the quality of social services

EP 2.1.10 Engage, assess, intervene, and evaluate with individuals, families, groups, organizations and communities:
 a. Substantively and affectively prepare for action with individuals, families, groups, organizations, and communities
 b. Use empathy and other interpersonal skills
 c. Develop a mutually agreed-on focus of work and desired outcomes
 d. Collect, organize, and interpret client data
 e. Assess client strengths and limitations
 f. Develop mutually agreed-on intervention goals and objectives
 g. Select appropriate intervention strategies
 h. Initiate actions to achieve organizational goals
 i. Implement prevention interventions that enhance client capacities
 j. Help clients resolve problems
 k. Negotiate, mediate, and advocate for clients
 l. Facilitate transitions and endings
 m. Critically analyze, monitor, and evaluate interventions

For more information about the standards themselves, and for a complete policy statement, visit the Council on Social Work Education website at www.cswe.org.

Adapted with permission from the Council on Social Work Education

Social Work and Social Welfare
An Introduction

Empowerment Series

Social Work and Social Welfare

An Introduction

EIGHTH EDITION

ROSALIE AMBROSINO

University of Texas at San Antonio

ROBERT AMBROSINO

University of Texas at San Antonio

JOSEPH HEFFERNAN

Emeritus, University of Texas at Austin

GUY SHUTTLESWORTH

Emeritus, University of Texas at Austin

CENGAGE
Learning·

Australia · Brazil · Mexico · Singapore · United Kingdom · United States

CENGAGE
Learning®

Empowerment Series: *Social Work and Social Welfare: An Introduction,* **Eighth Edition**
Rosalie Ambrosino, Robert Ambrosino, Joseph Heffernan, and Guy Shuttlesworth

Product Director: Jon-David Hague

Product Manager: Lee Gordon

Content Developer: J. L. Hahn Consulting Group-Theodore Knight

Product Assistant: Stephen Lagos

Media Developer: John Chell

Marketing Manager: Shanna Shelton

Art and Cover Direction, Production Management, and Composition: Lumina Datamatics, Inc.

Manufacturing Planner: Judy Inouye

Cover Image: © iStockphoto.com/ARTQU

Unless otherwise noted, all items
© Cengage Learning

Library of Congress Control Number: 2014954893

Student Edition:

ISBN: 978-1-305-10190-6

Cengage Learning
20 Channel Center Street
Boston, MA 02210
USA

Cengage Learning is a leading provider of customized learning solutions with office locations around the globe, including Singapore, the United Kingdom, Australia, Mexico, Brazil, and Japan. Locate your local office at **www.cengage.com/global**

Cengage Learning products are represented in Canada by Nelson Education, Ltd.

To learn more about Cengage Learning Solutions, visit **www.cengage.com**

Purchase any of our products at your local college store or at our preferred online store **www.cengagebrain.com**

Printed in China
2 3 4 5 6 7 19 18 17 16

Brief Contents

Contents

PART 2   Social Work Practice: Methods of Intervention

Preface

The eighth edition of this book is written at a critical time for the United States and the entire world. The United States faces many challenges both at home and abroad. An often-debated topic is what the role of the United States should be in fostering relationships around the world as a means of promoting the social well-being of world citizens. Civil wars stemming from ethnic conflicts and the human rights violations they bring about, coupled with famines and other natural disasters, impact the United States daily. These global challenges raise critical issues regarding how to balance our need to address important domestic issues against our leadership role in an increasingly complex world.

Current domestic policy issues that cannot be ignored or swept under the rug include the state of the economy and the increasing national debt, how to successfully implement reforms in health care to best help the millions of Americans who are either uninsured or underinsured to meet their health care needs, how to reduce poverty, how to address the growing homeless population, what to do about the increasing lack of support for those who need mental health care, how to guarantee the fair and equitable treatment of the country's rapidly growing immigrant population, what commitment should be made to keeping the nation's children free from harm, how to implement and sustain juvenile and criminal justice reforms, and how to create a civil society in which *all* persons are appreciated and valued. Should we devote considerable resources to helping those who are struggling throughout the world when we can't provide well for those within our own country? What should the balance be?

At the dawn of the 20th century, the roots of social work were just beginning to take hold. It was one of the most prolific eras for social and economic justice in the history of the social work profession. The settlement house movement was in full force. Social workers (mainly women) were making significant contributions to the development of social welfare policy that affected the lives of immigrants, the poor, the homeless, delinquent youth, the medically indigent, individuals in need of mental health services, and many others. It was a time of massive social and economic change. Social workers sought to bring order out of chaos, to connect private troubles to public causes, and to help the disenfranchised create better lives for themselves. Most of all, it was a period of hope—hope for a better future for all of humanity.

The 21st century has gotten off to a rocky start. The time is more critical now than ever before for social workers to advocate for policies and programs they believe will address these issues most effectively, as well as to provide services and support to the vulnerable populations most likely to be affected by world events. This book is about the many social welfare issues facing the United States and the world today and the many roles that social work professionals play in responding to those issues.

Although approaches to social welfare have changed over the decades, the needs to which the social work profession responds remain much the same—not because the social work profession has been ineffective in addressing these needs but, rather, because the response to social welfare needs is tied closely to the prevailing social values. It can be argued that there is a rhythm of social responses to social welfare problems. This rhythm is affected by the events of history, the state of the economy, the prevailing political ideology, and the will of the people.

At this time in history, the social welfare needs of the United States have taken a back seat to other issues, such as waging a global war on terrorism, the spread of life-threatening infectious diseases, natural disasters across the globe, and a worldwide economic downturn. Yet the problems of poverty, homelessness, AIDS, addiction to alcohol and other drugs, child abuse and neglect, teen pregnancy, youth violence, immigration, and an inadequate and unjust health-care system remain and will not simply disappear by ignoring or trying to eliminate programs that try to address them. Because these problems tear at the very fabric of our society, they once again will stand high on the country's social agenda and receive the bulk of public attention.

Approach

This text takes a generalist practice perspective in addressing social welfare issues within the context of the ecological/systems framework, the overarching framework used by social workers as they intervene to address social welfare needs at the individual, family, group, organization, community, and societal levels.

Part 1 of the text, Understanding Social Work and Social Welfare, provides an introduction to the nature of social welfare and the profession of social work. In Chapter 1, we focus on the historical context of social welfare to show how the past has shaped present-day social welfare problems, the evolution of society's views of people in need, and the roles of social workers in responding to those needs. Chapter 2 explores the social work profession, contrasting social work with other helping professions and showing the importance of collaboration in working with individuals, families, groups, and communities. In Chapter 3, we introduce key underpinnings of the social work profession, including the ecological/systems framework, the concept of generalist practice, and the strengths perspective, all used by social workers in assessing client needs and working with clients and other helping professionals to develop appropriate strategies of intervention. In Chapter 4, we highlight key social justice issues such as the impact of racism, sexism, homophobia, and other forms of oppression on individuals and the ways the allocation of resources reinforces these forms of oppression and injustice.

In Part 2, Social Work Practice, you will develop a beginning understanding of micro- and macro-levels of practice and learn intervention methods that social workers use. In Chapter 5, you will learn about methods that social workers use in working with individuals, families, and groups. Chapter 6 focuses on social work at the macro-level, including work in the community and in policy, administration, and research.

In Part 3, Fields of Practice and Populations Served by Social Workers, you will study a number of fields of practice and populations with which social workers are involved. You will be considering the issues discussed within each chapter from the broad perspective of social welfare, the nature of the social work profession, the ecological/systems framework, and the impact of oppression and social and economic injustice on at-risk populations. Chapter 7 focuses on poverty and income assistance. Because homelessness is primarily a result of poverty and economic conditions, a discussion of homelessness is also included. Chapter 8 explores health care, including a discussion of who is more likely to be in good health and why and critical issues in current health care delivery, including implementation of the Affordable Care Act.

In Chapter 9, you will learn about mental health, alcoholism and other substance misuse, and disabilities and policies and programs intended to address impacted individuals and their families. Chapters 10 and 11 focus on needs of and services to children, youth, and families, focusing on family issues such as divorce, child maltreatment, and problems associated with adolescence, and policy and program responses to address these concerns. In Chapter 12, you will learn about the needs of and services to older adults and the critical need for social workers as our population continues to age. Chapter 13 explores the criminal justice system, including differences in the adult and juvenile justice systems. Chapter 14 focuses on social work in different environmental contexts, with a focus on rural and urban settings as well as the impact of the natural environment on vulnerable populations and the role of social workers in protecting the natural environment. Social workers increasingly must consider the impact of work on their clients, as discussed in Chapter 15. In this chapter you will also learn about social work opportunities in the workplace.

In addition, because social workers must incorporate a global worldview into their interventions wherever they practice, and because social workers are playing ever more important roles in international circles, discussion of international social work has been incorporated into Chapter 16. Finally, content on immigration is also included in this chapter because immigration issues are central to the social and economic future of the United States and because the 2,000-mile border shared with Mexico is a major entry point into the United States for immigrants from Mexico and Central and South America.

In keeping with the current Council on Social Work Education's Educational Policy and Accreditation Standards, the text focuses on competencies and practice behaviors needed to be an effective social worker. "Helping hands" icons within the chapters and end-of-chapter competency notes spotlight text coverage of the required core competencies and recommended practice behaviors detailed by the Council on Social Work Education's (CSWE) new (2008; revised 2010) Educational Policy and Accreditation Standards. Social work graduates are expected to master these competencies and practice behaviors upon completion of their bachelor of social work (BSW) degrees or foundation coursework at the master's of social work (MSW) level. In addition, case examples throughout the text help readers understand how chapter concepts are put into action by social work practitioners.

New to the Eighth Edition

In this text we hope to help students develop a frame of reference to understand social welfare and an approach to address social issues that will serve them well in times of commitment as well as retrenchment. We have reworked much of this eighth edition to reflect changes in the social work profession, as well as in the social welfare policy arena. Content on race, gender, and sexual orientation in the chapter on social justice has been updated, and additional content added that focuses on classism, ageism, ability, and religious discrimination. The chapter on health care has been moved to an earlier place in the text to highlight the importance of the Affordable Care Act, and the chapter on mental health, substance use, and disability has been updated with new content on biological implications for understanding these issues. The chapter on rural social work has been expanded to include content on urban social work as well as the natural environment and environmental racism. Finally, content on looking to the future has been moved from the global chapter to an epilogue at the end of the text.

Features

We also have included a number of additional features to help students and instructors get the most out of the book. At the end of each chapter is a list of key terms and discussion questions that can be used in the classroom or individually to help students strengthen their critical-thinking skills. We also include a list of Internet sites by which to locate additional information on subjects of interest.

Joining a Collaborative Venture

This text is a collaborative effort among colleagues. Where consensus was possible, we sought it; where it was not possible, we sought to identify the diverse views about the established wisdom of social work. Each of us contributed to the book from the perspectives of our own education and professional experience in addition to social work: educational psychology, policy, and administration in the case of Robert Ambrosino; child development, education, human behavior, and psychology in the case of Rosalie Ambrosino; political science and economics in the case of Joe Heffernan; and sociology and history in the case of Guy Shuttlesworth. We also want to acknowledge our newest collaborator, recent BSW graduate Caitlyn Counihan, who gave us invaluable feedback throughout the revision process and served as a co-author for Chapter 9. Although the text reflects our diverse interdisciplinary perspectives, it is disciplined by the continuity and the certainty of unresolved social issues to which social work skills are relevant.

We hope that a number of you using this text will be persuaded, or have your choices reinforced, to join the social work profession. We urge those of you considering a career in social work to talk with your course instructors about getting a BSW and/or an MSW degree. We also recommend that you visit social agencies and undertake some volunteer experiences in conjunction with your course. Most important, however, we hope this book in some way contributes to your social conscience no matter what career you choose and encourages you to recognize social work as a dynamic, challenging profession whose values, principles, and practices intersect with a wide variety of other professions.

As we continue to struggle with social welfare issues that have existed in various forms for centuries, we urge you to look back on the early roots of social work—to remember the profession's significant contributions to making the world a better place to live. We urge you to build on the many accomplishments of the social work profession that took root at the turn of the last century and to translate what was learned there into the very different and ever-changing world of today. We urge you to rekindle the flame of hope that burned so brightly in those early days of the profession. We urge you to seek to advance what the social work profession stands for in everything you do. Finally, regardless of what profession you choose, we urge you to leave a legacy, no matter how large or small, for others who will follow you into the future to build on to continue to make the world a better place to live.

Rosalie Ambrosino
Robert Ambrosino
Joe Heffernan
Guy Shuttlesworth

Acknowledgements

Four "referent" groups played an important role in strengthening this book: our families, our students and faculty colleagues in Austin and San Antonio, and our colleagues in the profession. We owe our gratitude to our families—Megan, Will A., Chris, Will C., Catie, Coleman, and Jimmy for their support and understanding when the book took priority over them. A special note of thanks goes to our children and grandchildren who have enriched our lives immeasurably with their open minds and zest for life—and ultimately for whom this book was written, as they are the inheritors of the world we leave behind.

We also thank the diverse group of reviewers whose comments contributed significantly to the quality of this eighth edition:

Donna Aguiniga, Western Illinois University; Paul Baggett, East Tennessee State University; Sheli Bernstein-Goff, West Liberty University; Patricia Carlson, University of Nebraska at Omaha; Michel Coconis, Wright State University-Dayton; Wilma Cordova, Stephen F. Austin State University; Rosalyn Deckerhoff, Florida State University; Christy Fisher, Iowa Western Community College; Roy Fowles, Purdue North Central; Darron Garner, Prairie View A & M University; Gail Grabczynski, Malcolm X College; Andrea Horigan, Ventura College; Diane Loeffler, University of Kentucky; Donna McElory, Atlantic Cape Community College; Thomas Oles, Skidmore College; Yolanda Padilla, University of Texas at Austin; Joan Pendergast, Concord University; Becky Scott, Baylor University; Jeanne Sokolec, Loyola University-Chicago; Allen Stata, Judson College; Susan Vorsanger, Mount Saint Mary College; Linda Wells-Glover, University of Missouri-St. Louis; and Lisa Zerden, University of North Carolina-Chapel Hill.

We very much appreciate the thoughtful guidance they provided in our making revisions for the eighth edition.

The referent group of greatest relevance has been our students. We owe special appreciation to them for helping us frame the issues in the text by asking the "hard questions" and challenging us to remember that social welfare issues are timeless and complex. Their comments in classes over our collective years of teaching have helped to shape our views of what they want and need to know to become better social workers and citizens in our complex society. The most rewarding part of teaching is watching our students begin to see connections between the past and the present, as well as the many complex factors that shape social welfare issues and their impact on the diverse populations within the United States. We have incorporated many of their ideas into this eighth edition.

Last but not least, we express our gratitude to our acquisition editor, Gordon Lee, for his persistence and encouragement in the book preparation and publication. Also, a special thanks to the production guidance and abilities—and the patience—of Ted Knight, Sharib Asrar, and all others who helped with this publication along the way.

PART **1**

Understanding Social Work and Social Welfare

Key Concepts and Perspectives

AP Photo/The Times Argus, Jeb Wallace-Brodeur

Part 1 of this book is an introduction to the nature of social welfare and social work—what social welfare encompasses and what social workers who function in social welfare settings do. The information in these four chapters constitutes an historical and theoretical framework for understanding subsequent chapters.

Chapter 1, Social Welfare, Past and Present, provides the historical context of social welfare—how the past has shaped present-day social welfare problems and society's views toward people in need. The chapter begins with a discussion of early welfare policies and legislation and traces these influences to contemporary social welfare institutions.

Chapter 2, Social Work and Other Helping Professions, explores the relationships between social welfare as a broad system intended to maintain the well-being of individuals within a society and the profession of social work. The discussion covers the diverse roles and functions of social work professionals, contrasting the profession of social work with other helping professions and examining ways in which they can work together. For those who are interested in careers in one of the helping professions, the chapter indicates educational pathways and credentialing for various roles.

Chapter 3, The Ecological/Systems Perspective, suggests a theoretical framework for understanding subsequent chapters. An ecological/systems perspective is the basis for considering individuals within the broader environment. This framework encompasses a broad societal perspective, a community perspective, a family perspective, and an individual perspective. Examples are provided to show how social work practitioners apply the framework and its concepts. The chapter also covers generalist social work practice and the strengths perspective, explaining how these perspectives fit within an ecological/systems context.

Chapter 4, Diversity and Social Justice, addresses the ways in which racism, classism, sexism, homophobia, and other forms of oppression and discrimination disenfranchise vulnerable groups in our society. Specific examples illustrate the long-range effects of social injustice at the individual, family, group, organizational, community, and societal levels related to color, gender, class, age, sexual orientation, ability, and religion. The promotion of social and economic justice and work toward eliminating oppression at all levels of the environment are implicit roles of the social work profession.

Together, these chapters comprise an overview of the major concepts upon which the profession of social work is based, and they lay the groundwork for the remaining chapters. Concepts introduced in these chapters also provide the foundation for understanding content in later chapters. For those majoring in social work, these concepts and their application will become second nature. You will use them daily, probably without even realizing it.

The focus of these chapters is on those competencies and practice behaviors needed to become a social worker that relate to: (1) identifying as a professional social worker, (2) developing a beginning understanding of the ethical principles that guide social work practice, (3) becoming aware of the links between diversity and social and economic justice, and (4) understanding how history has shaped U.S. social welfare policy and services provided by social workers.

As you read the chapters in this section and engage in classroom discussions about the material, note that from the beginning of time, our society has been shaped by the discussion of conflicting ideas. These initial chapters present multiple perspectives about many social welfare issues—for example, poverty and welfare reform, diversity, reproductive rights of women, and same-sex marriage. You also will find that social workers have multiple perspectives about these issues. Social work is a diverse profession, and like members of the broader society, social workers do not always agree on the ways these issues are framed and the best approaches to address them. We hope that you will consider the ideas presented in this text and those of your student colleagues and your professor—and listen to these different voices with an open mind. More important, we hope that you will treat clients you serve with dignity and respect, even though their values and other perspectives may differ from yours.

CHAPTER 1

Social Welfare, Past and Present

EP 2.1.8a

Consider what your life would be like if you were living in an earlier time or at a future time. What would be the same? What would be different? Why? How would personal and religious values and beliefs of the time, the economy, and the group in power shape your life and the choices available to you? Have you ever thought about how the personal and religious values and beliefs, the economy, and groups in power in earlier years of the United States impact your life now and the choices available to you?

Social welfare policy in the United States has undergone tremendous change since the time of the early settlers. Yet, much of social welfare as we know it today reflects the mainstream belief system in place during colonial American times—a system borrowed from Elizabethan England—which in turn largely reflects the English Poor Laws of the early 1600s. Many of the provisions of the English Poor Laws—such as an emphasis on personal responsibility, local control over decision making, promotion of family values, limited government involvement in social welfare programs, the equating of work to religious salvation, and a distinction between the "deserving" poor and the "undeserving" poor—are embedded in contemporary social welfare policies.

The landmark welfare reform legislation passed in 1996 and reauthorized as part of the Deficit Reduction Act of 2005 with even more stringent provisions created a burgeoning underclass of working poor. In spite of the fact that many Americans still cannot find sustainable employment since the economic downturn of 2007, it is unlikely that Congress will ease up on welfare eligibility requirements or increase funding to states for welfare benefits, which have been flat for 16 years (Shott & Pavetti, 2013). Implementation of the Affordable Care Act, stabilizing the economy, extending unemployment benefits for millions of Americans who are unable to find employment following the economic downturn of 2007, and reducing the federal debt have taken priority over further welfare reform in recent years.

For many, working at a job, even two jobs, no longer guarantees a life free from poverty and even a small share of the American dream. Can this trend be reversed, or is the fundamental belief system about social welfare in the United States so entrenched that limited incremental change is the best we can expect? What lessons can be learned from the American social welfare experience? What are the implications of failing to meet the basic needs of a large segment

3

of the population? Resolving these and similar questions is central to the social work profession. Failing to resolve them is simply not an option.

There is no consensus regarding the nature, focus, and development of social policy or the responsibility—if any—of government in developing programs to assist those in need. In the following discussion, we identify some of the more salient factors involved in developing a comprehensive approach to social welfare in the United States. But first, a few basic questions are in order: What is social welfare? Who gets it? Who pays for it? Does it create dependency? Why is our social welfare system organized as it is?

Social welfare in our society has long been a matter of dispute and controversy. Often, the controversy results from a misunderstanding of the policies that govern social welfare, as well as misinformation about people who should receive social welfare benefits. Many people view those who receive public assistance (commonly called "welfare") as lazy, unwilling to work, and content to live off government aid. This perspective presumes that poverty, mental illness, and unemployment signify personal failure. Others view recipients of public assistance as victims of a rapidly changing society that provides little help in enabling people to become self-sufficient. It is understandable, then, that people with divergent views would have different opinions about the nature and scope of social welfare programs and the people they serve.

Determining who is in need represents one of the fundamental decisions involved in developing any public social welfare program. This judgment is almost always based, at least in part, on how much we think a person deserves help. Frequently, a distinction is made between the deserving poor and the undeserving poor. Many people are more accepting of the needs of older people and those with disabilities and chronic illnesses (deserving poor) than of the needs of seemingly able-bodied persons (undeserving poor).

Today, the term "deserving" is defined more often than not by whether the person is able to work. Many times, we assume that people who are poor have chosen that lifestyle, are lazy, or lack motivation to rise out of poverty. Stereotypes such as these fail to consider how changing social systems contribute to outcomes that result in poverty for a substantial portion of the population. Increasingly, even those who work at two or more jobs can be poor.

Why does poverty in the United States persist? What can and should be done about it, and who should be responsible for addressing the problem? What resources should be brought to bear, and who should pay for them?

A Definition of Social Welfare and Its Relationship to Social Work

EP 2.1.3a

What is social welfare? Although social welfare is viewed by many as services provided to the poor, government expenditures and tax breaks for members of the upper and middle classes could also be included (Gilbert & Terrell, 2012; Jansson, 2012). In fact, the term *welfare* is derived from the phrase "getting farewell," which means to travel, to go, and to be well (Midgley & Livermore, 2008). A broad definition of social welfare could incorporate all organized societal responses that promote the social well-being of a population: education, health, rehabilitation, protective services for adults and children, public assistance, social insurance, services for those with physical and mental disabilities, job-training programs, marriage counseling, psychotherapy, pregnancy counseling, adoption, and numerous other related activities designed to promote social well-being. In short, social welfare incorporates what is needed to provide people with resources to lead satisfying and productive lives (Day & Schiele, 2012; Karger & Stoesz, 2013; Stern & Axinn, 2012).

The term **social welfare**, then, refers to the full range of organized activities of public and voluntary agencies that seek to prevent, alleviate or contribute to solving a selected set of social problems. For some who view social welfare broadly—from the concept that a society pools its resources for the general welfare of all—it encompasses public facilities such as libraries, public parks, and hospitals. Others include social support to corporations, sometimes called "corporate welfare," or the extensive investment that some countries such as the United States make in businesses in addition to investment in people in need. Still others view social welfare more narrowly, to consist of programs that address issues such as poverty and child maltreatment.

The length and breadth of the list of social problems typically depend on the values perspective of the person compiling the list, the historical time in which the list is developed, and the perceived economic resources available to meet the social welfare problems listed. As you read on, consider how individual and professional values shape one's views about what constitutes social welfare.

EP 2.1.1a

Social work is the primary profession that works within the social welfare system and with those the system serves. Social workers implement planned social change activities prescribed by social welfare institutions. They facilitate change by working with individuals, families, groups, organizations, and communities and at the societal level to improve social functioning. Social workers advocate for social and economic justice within the social welfare system, making needed resources available to members of vulnerable populations—children, elderly people, those with disabilities, and those living in poverty (Dubois & Miley, 2013).

Social workers within the social welfare system assist abused and neglected children and their families, pregnant and parenting teens, the homeless and others living in poverty, individuals with health and mental health problems, youth and adults within the criminal justice system, employees in the workplace, refugees across the world, and individuals with a multitude of other needs. They organize neighborhoods and communities to strengthen or create programs and policies to better meet human needs and advocate for change in a variety of roles at state, national, and global levels. Individuals involved in other helping professions work closely with social workers in planned change at all levels. The roles of social work professionals and other helping professions in the social welfare system are discussed in Chapter 2.

The Value Base of Social Welfare

EP 2.1.3a
EP 2.1.8a

Values are assumptions, convictions, or beliefs about what is good and desirable or the way things ought to be. A person's values are shaped by her or his socialization experiences. Many values are dominant and supported by the majority of the population (Reamer, 2013). For example, most people agree that life is sacred. Nearly everyone believes that killing another person with wanton disregard for that person's life is a criminal offense. Other values related to the sanctity of life, however, are not shared so readily. For example, our society differs on issues such as abortion, physician-assisted suicide, and capital punishment.

The development of social welfare over time reflects differences in values as they relate to social responsibility for those in need. Values alone, however, do not determine social policy. Availability of resources, coupled with economic, religious, and political influences, results in ever-evolving policies of social responsibility for vulnerable members of a society.

One dominant value that has guided the development of our social welfare system is **humanitarianism**, derived largely from Judeo-Christian philosophy and teachings (Day & Schiele, 2012). Our society also is influenced by the economic doctrine of **laissez-faire**, based on limited government involvement, individualism, and personal responsibility (Stern & Axinn, 2012). From a laissez-faire perspective,

1. problems of the poor and the disenfranchised are perceived as a matter of personal failure that government welfare programs would only perpetuate,
2. work is considered to be the only justifiable means of survival because it contributes to the productive effort of society, and
3. social responsibility for vulnerable members of society would be carried out through volunteerism aimed at encouraging personal responsibility and self-sufficiency rather than formal government intervention.

A different perspective maintains that we all are members of society and, by virtue of that membership, are entitled to share in its productive effort. Those who hold this belief argue that people become poor or needy as a result of changing social institutions such as economic globalization or the shift from a manufacturing economy to a service-based economy. Individuals are not the cause of these conditions but, rather, are swept along and victimized by them. For example, members of some ethnic groups face barriers such as inferior educational resources, limited (and usually menial) job opportunities, poor housing, and inadequate health resources. An analysis from this perspective would not blame these conditions on individual group members but, instead, identify factors such as institutional discrimination and oppression.

Those who conceptualize social welfare have differing values perspectives. Some focus on whether one's view is liberal or conservative or on a continuum somewhere in between. From a conservative perspective, individuals are responsible for taking care of themselves, with little or no government intervention. This perspective suggests that government should provide a safety net only for those with the greatest need. From the liberal perspective, government is responsible for ensuring the availability of social and economic structures, including equitable access to support for those who cannot meet their own needs (Karger & Stoesz, 2013).

Another perspective contrasts residual and institutional social welfare. The residual perspective views social welfare as serving only those with the most problems or greatest needs. This perspective often is associated with a values system that supports individualism and an expectation that people can, and should, take care of themselves and that those who are unable to care for themselves are deficient in some way. In contrast, an institutional perspective holds that everyone has needs throughout the life cycle and that society is responsible for supporting those needs by providing services and benefits (Dinitto & Johnson, 2012).

Thus, perspectives regarding societal responsibility for vulnerable members of society vary widely. As you follow the discussion of historical influences that have converged to shape our present social welfare structure, see whether you can identify the values positions that have contributed to the formulation of social policy.

Historical Influences That Shape Social Welfare Today
Our English Heritage

In England, before mercantilism, care for the poor was a function primarily of the Church. By extending themselves through charitable efforts to those in need, parishioners fulfilled a required sacred function. The Church's resources usually were sufficient to provide the relief that was made available to the poor.

The feudal system itself provided a structure that met the needs of most of the population. The only significant government legislation during this time was passed as a result of the Black Death—bubonic plague—which began in 1348 and killed approximately two-thirds of the English population within 2 years. In 1351, King Edward III mandated the Statute of Laborers Act, which required all able-bodied individuals to accept any type of employment within their parish. Furthermore, it laid the groundwork for residency requirements by forbidding able-bodied persons from leaving their parish. (This later became an intrinsic part of American social welfare legislation.)

Some 150 years later, with the breakdown of the feudal system and the division of the Church during the Reformation, organized religious efforts could no longer cope with the increasing needs of the poor. Without the Church or the feudal manor to rely on in times of need, the poor were left to fend for themselves. This change frequently led to malnutrition, transience, poor health, broken families, and even death.

As Europe struggled with the transition from an agricultural society to an industrial one, the numbers of dislodged persons increased. Many of the poor found their way into cities, lured by the prospect of work in manufacturing facilities. The Industrial Revolution, however, was still in its early stages, and the number of jobs was insufficient to accommodate the growing population. Further, most of those who were seeking jobs were illiterate and lacked the skills necessary to work in a manufacturing environment. Turned away by the cities, large bands of poor, unemployed people wandered the countryside begging for whatever meager assistance they could get. A sense of lawlessness often accompanied them. Local officials were pressed to find suitable solutions for the homeless, the poor, and dependent children. Unable to address the problems on their own, local officials turned to Parliament for a solution (Stern & Axinn, 2012).

Parliament responded by passing the **Elizabethan Poor Law** (Elizabeth 43) in 1601. This legislation is significant because it attempted to codify earlier legislation as well as establish a national policy regarding the poor (Lees, 2007). The Elizabethan Poor Law delineated "categories" of assistance, a practice retained in our current social welfare legislation.

1. *Individuals considered to be "worthy."* These were individuals for whom impoverishment was not viewed as a fraudulent attempt to secure assistance. They included the aged, the chronically ill, individuals with disabilities, and orphaned children. The worthy poor typically were placed in almshouses (poorhouses), where they received minimal care. This practice was called "indoor relief" because it provided services to the poor within institutions. In some instances, children were placed with families and often were required to work for their keep.
2. *The able-bodied poor.* For those classified in this way, programs were less humane. Some of the able-bodied were placed in prisons, others were sent to workhouses, and still others served as indentured servants in local factories or as slave laborers on local farms. Unlike the worthy poor, the able-bodied poor were assumed to be malingerers who lacked the motivation to secure gainful employment. The treatment they received was designed to deter others from following in their footsteps, as well as to punish them for their transience and idleness.

The Elizabethan Poor Law was enacted primarily to standardize the way the poor were to be managed, not because of altruism and concern for them (Lees, 2007). This law is significant because it established the guiding philosophy of public assistance legislation in England until 1834 and in the United States until the Social Security Act was passed in 1935 (Jansson, 2012). Its influence also can be seen in the Personal Responsibility and Work Opportunity Act of 1996 (commonly called "welfare reform"). The important components of the Elizabethan Poor Law (Day & Schiele, 2012) in relation to U.S. policies toward the poor are the establishment of:

- clear (but limited) government responsibility for those in need,
- government authority to force people to work,
- government enforcement of family responsibility,
- the principle of local responsibility, and
- strict residence requirements.

More than 200 years after the passage of the Elizabethan Poor Law, the Poor Law Reform Act of 1834 was passed in reaction to concerns that the earlier law was not being implemented as intended. The prevailing belief then was that liberalized supervision of the programs for the poor had served as a disincentive for work and, in effect, had created dependency on the program. The Poor Law Reform Act mandated that all forms of outdoor relief (assistance to people in their homes) be abolished and that the full intention of the provisions of the Poor Law of 1601 be rigidly enforced. Furthermore, the act established the "principle of least eligibility," which prescribed that no assistance be provided in an amount that left the recipient better off than the lowest-paid worker (Lees, 2007). This principle also served as a basic tenet of early American social welfare legislation and public welfare programs today.

The social welfare system in the United States has in many cases actually harmed rather than improved the lives of the people it was intended to serve (e.g., women, people of color, the elderly, persons who are mentally ill, persons who are homeless, immigrants, and other populations that are not part of the dominant group). In addition, because the focus is often exclusively on the problems these groups face, the assets they could contribute are often ignored (Jansson, 2012).

Social Welfare in Colonial America

Early American settlers brought a religious heritage that emphasized charity and the mutual interdependence of people. They also brought with them the heritage of the Elizabethan Poor Law. America in colonial times was an undeveloped and often hostile land that required early settlers to work hard to survive. The country had no formal government network for providing any significant assistance. Those in need were aided by their neighbors or by members of religious organizations. As the population increased, many colonies passed laws requiring new arrivals to demonstrate their ability to sustain themselves or, in the absence of such ability, locate sponsors who were willing to pledge their support for them. For the most part, transients were "warned out" and returned to their place of residence or back to England (Stern & Axinn, 2012). Times were difficult, the Puritan work ethic was embedded deeply, and little surplus was available to distribute to those in need. The names of habitual paupers were posted routinely at the townhouse in many towns and villages. Women during this time were considered to be the property of their husbands, and were accorded few legal protections against cruelty, lack of support, or desertion. They were largely uneducated and had limited social and economic roles. They could not own land and were not allowed to work outside the home unless they were poor, in which case they were forced to work in almshouses or workhouses to obtain the meager resources provided to them (Shiele & Day, 2012).

Because much of colonial America was based on a feudal system, with indentured servants in the mid-colonies (more than half of all colonists came to this country as indentured servants) and slavery in the southern colonies, the pauper class clearly lacked freedom. Often overlooked, however, was a set of harsh laws—reasonably enforced up until the time of independence—requiring masters to meet the basic survival needs of servants and slaves. Ironically, in the transition from a plantation to a pre-industrial economy, economic uncertainty also increased. Consequently, public relief was the largest expenditure in the public budgets of most major cities at the time of the American Revolution (Stern & Axinn, 2012).

The rigid restraint of the Poor Law philosophy was consistent with the extreme scarcity in the colonial economy. Colonial law stressed **indoor relief**, placing those who could not care for themselves in settings other than their own homes. Although the intent may have been to provide care in the homes of others, usually in exchange for work as in the case of indentured servants, in effect, the truly poor (paupers) often were segregated within almshouses as punishment for being poor and were given tasks that at least paid for their meager keep. The apprenticeship of children reflected a belief in family controls for children and emphasized work and training for productive employment. Also, the deification of the work ethic and the belief that pauperism was a visible symbol of sin permitted a harsh response to those in need as a means of saving their souls.

Changing Patterns After the Revolution

Between the time of the American Revolution and the Civil War, several broad patterns of welfare emerged, all of which were consistent with the basic tenets of the Elizabethan Poor Law. The American doctrine of separation of church and state forced the connection between parish and local welfare office to be severed. Nevertheless, most states retained a religious connection, with the requirement that at least one member of the welfare board be a "licensed preacher." Local governments accepted grudgingly the role of welfare caretaker and adopted rigid residency requirements.

The most important shift in this period was from indoor relief to **outdoor relief**—providing cash assistance that allowed individuals to remain in their own homes. Outdoor aid, with its reliance on in-kind aid and work-relief projects, was more adaptable to the volatile economics of the first half of the 19th century.

Another significant movement during this period was the shift away from public-sector to private-sector welfare. The responsibility for welfare, therefore, was left to charitable institutions rather than remaining a public concern.

It is interesting to note that references to women were conspicuously absent from the Declaration of

Independence. The rights and protections guaranteed by the Constitution were considered by most to be exclusively the purview of males. Women's right to vote would not be incorporated into the Constitution until a much later time. Also, the seeds for the enslavement of nearly one million Africans were sown during early colonial times, due in large part to the need to support the burgeoning agrarian economy of the south. While the Emancipation Proclamation officially ended the practice of slavery, one could argue that the legacy of those dark days has lingered throughout American history, as evidenced by the continued oppression of African Americans and the roles that they play in society.

Caring for the Urban Poor

As the new nation grew, cities began to appear on the Eastern Seaboard. The immigrants who arrived regularly often had difficulty finding jobs that paid a living wage, and a large population of displaced poor began to emerge. People who were interested in the welfare of these individuals sought avenues for meeting their needs. Attaching the poor to subsistence-level employment usually was the goal, but concern arose over meeting their basic needs until they could derive income through employment. While almshouses often were used to care for the chronic poor, outdoor relief was increasingly accepted as a suitable way to care for the poor.

Before moving to a discussion of early organizations that emerged to address the needs of the rapidly-growing urban poor, it is important to point out that the majority of those efforts were funded by wealthy philanthropists and well-to-do workers (mostly women) who imposed their values on those they served, with little attention to their cultural norms, practices, and traditions. The informal, and often intricate, support networks that once flourished among the struggling immigrants gave way to formal services, albeit limited in supply, and thus, a "we know best" philosophy of services was born (Katz, 2013).

One of the earliest organizations to seek a formal solution to the problems of poverty was the New York Society for the Prevention of Pauperism, established in 1817. Following the precedent established by Thomas Chalmers in England, the society divided the city into districts and assigned "friendly visitors" to work in each district to assess and respond to the

needs of the poor (Stern & Axinn, 2012). In 1843, the Association for Improving the Conditions of the Poor was established in New York City to coordinate relief efforts for the unemployed. One significant technique the association introduced—and which the social work profession widely practices today—was the requirement that relief could not be dispensed until the individual's needs were assessed so that agencies providing relief could do so more effectively.

EP 2.1.8b
EP 2.1.9b
Perhaps the most effective relief organization for the poor was the Charity Organization Society (COS) of Buffalo, New York, a private organization modeled after the COS in London. The COS sought to infuse efficiency and economy into programs serving the poor, as well as to organize charities in an effort to prevent duplication of services and reduce dependency on charitable efforts (Stern & Axinn, 2012). Like the Association for Improving the Conditions of the Poor that preceded it, the COS emphasized the necessity of assessing the conditions of the poor and added the dimension of engaging "friendly visitors" with clients in an effort to guide, rehabilitate, and help prepare for self-sufficiency. The COS had little sympathy for chronic beggars, viewing them essentially as hopeless derelicts. Some would argue that this practice spelled the beginnings of the marginalization of homeless individuals that has permeated American history to the present time (Jansson, 2012).

Caring for Specific Populations

Many other private charities emerged during the 1800s to address special problem areas such as care of orphan children, and those who were mentally ill or had visual or hearing impairments (referred to as "blind" or "deaf" at that time). For the most part, these services were sponsored by state or local governments and provided largely in institutional settings that were physically removed from the community. A growing number of socially active citizens expressed grave concern over the treatment that residents of these institutions received (Stern & Axinn, 2012).

Dorothea Dix, a philanthropist and social reformer, traveled throughout the United States observing the care given to the "insane" and was appalled by what she saw. She sought to convince President Franklin Pierce to allocate federal and land-grant monies for establishing federal institutions to care for individuals with mental illness. Although she initially was unsuccessful in changing the system, Dix was successful in raising public awareness about the problems of people with mental illness, and her work set the tone for an era of significant reform during the mid- to late 1800s.

Toward the latter part of the 19th century, several states developed centralized agencies to oversee the activities of charitable institutions. State charity agencies sought better quality of care for those who were institutionalized, as well as greater efficiency and economy in providing relief to the poor. With the federal government assuming only limited responsibility for selected groups (veterans, for example), state agencies became the primary public resource for addressing the problems of the poor and debilitated (Day & Schiele, 2012).

A new wave of immigrants from southern Europe entering the United States in the late 1800s and early 1900s added to the burden of unemployment, homelessness, and poverty. **Jane Addams**, a social worker, was instrumental in creating the settlement house movement as a resource for preparing immigrants to live in a new society. Patterned after Toynbee Hall in London, Addams established **Hull House** in 1889 in one of the worst slum neighborhoods of Chicago. By addressing the problems of deficient housing, low wages, child labor, juvenile delinquency, and disease, Hull House and other settlement houses became major social action agencies (Day & Schiele, 2012).

Here we must point out the ideological conflict between the COS movement and the settlement house movement, as well as the contributions of each to contemporary social work practice. COS proponents believed that urban poverty was rooted in moral and character deficiencies and that poverty could be abolished by helping poor people recognize and correct their flawed characters. The COS movement embraced social Darwinism as its theoretical underpinning for helping (or not helping) the poor, and labeled this process "scientific charity." The focus of COS workers was on clients' self-support, but only after a thorough investigation and determination of their worthiness. The primary emphasis of COS agencies was on helping the poor find social and economic salvation through work (Day & Schiele, 2012).

The settlement house movement was guided by a completely different set of principles. Clients of settlement houses were viewed as able, "normal" individuals. No effort was made to separate the "worthy" poor from the "unworthy" poor. The emphasis was on providing neighborhood services and community development. The settlement house movement embraced a philosophy that combined individual achievement with satisfying social relations and social responsibility. Settlement house workers took a holistic perspective of the person in society. The overall mission of the settlement house movement was social reform (Day & Schiele, 2012; Slavicek, 2011; Stern & Axinn, 2012).

Both the COS and the settlement house movements left an indelible mark on contemporary social work practice. The COS movement was the forerunner of clinical social work, with its concentration on individuals and families, scientific methods to determine need, and specialized training of social service providers. The settlement house movement was the forerunner of nonclinical social work, with a primary emphasis on individuals as part of their community, social needs assessment, community organizing, social reform and political action, understanding and appreciating the strengths of cultural diversity, and research on the community (Day & Schiele, 2012).

The current debate in social work circles about whether nonclinical social work is legitimate social work has its roots in the ideological differences inherent in these two early approaches to social welfare (see for example, Specht & Courtney, 1995). You should be aware of these differences because of their direct impact on how social welfare policy is formulated and carried out.

The period of time between the mid- to late 1800s when the COS and settlement houses flourished is commonly referred to as the Progressive Era (Day & Schiele, 2012). Major trends that occurred during this time period included:

- economic growth, industrialization, and large-scale immigration;
- continued population growth in urban areas;
- wealth concentrated in the hands of a few;
- wide disparity between the "haves" and "have-nots"; and
- poverty prevalent among industrial workers, immigrants, and rural southern African Americans.

Change was rapid and dramatic. Middle-class, white married women during this time did not work outside of the home. Those women who did work outside the home were primarily young and single, widows or divorcees, poor married women, women of color, or some combination thereof, who worked in deplorable conditions for little pay (Day & Schiele, 2012). Many of those at the forefront of Progressive Era reforms were middle- and upper-class women like Jane Addams and Mary Richmond. Although they worked tirelessly and passionately with immigrants and the poor, they incorporated their values and worldview in their efforts, focusing on assimilating those with whom they worked.

Another social welfare policy issue debated in the 1800s—and still debated today—is whether social welfare services should be provided by public or by private entities. During the 1800s, the parameters of public versus private welfare programs were defined more clearly. Public welfare benefit programs relied on taxation for funding. Private welfare programs were funded through the voluntary contributions of individuals or philanthropic organizations. No clearly defined limits determined what types of benefits either public or private (voluntary) agencies would offer. As a result, services often overlapped. Public agencies were administered by local or state governments. Private agencies often had religious or philanthropic sponsorship or received contributions from citizens. Public and private agencies alike provided a diverse range of services throughout the 1800s and into the 1900s.

Because these agencies focused almost exclusively on immigrants and other urban poor who were most often white, African Americans created their own agencies and services, including settlement houses and orphanages, in addition to well-organized informal support systems in both rural and urban areas. Native Americans were also left to fend for themselves, primarily in poverty-stricken rural areas, as were Mexican Americans in the southwest as the United States expanded its territory for the benefit of its white citizens (Jansson, 2012). The roots of disparities in education and health and human services for these groups began during the colonization of the United States, with the marginalization continuing today.

Post–World War I and the Great Depression

Following World War I, the nation entered a period of significant social change and prosperity which ended abruptly in 1929 with the economic downturn that led to the **Great Depression**. In short order, conditions

became grave. Businesses that had been considered stable ceased production, banks declared bankruptcy, and millions of workers lost their jobs. Savings were depleted as banks collapsed and businesses failed, and a large portion of the American population was left penniless, homeless, and without resources as levels of unemployment increased.

As jobs became scarce, the unemployed had nowhere to turn. Organized charities quickly exhausted their limited resources. Pessimism and despair were rampant, and many felt hopeless. Unemployment insurance was nonexistent, and no federal guarantees existed for monies lost in bank failures. The economic disaster resulted in a state of chaos never experienced before on American soil. As conditions worsened, homes were lost through foreclosed mortgages.

The New Deal

 Although state and local governments attempted to respond to the fallout from the Great Depression, many of the poorer states lacked the resources to provide even temporary relief. In New York, an Emergency Relief Act passed, providing public employment, in-kind relief (food, clothing, and shelter), and limited cash benefits. This act later served as a model for federal relief programs.

EP 2.1.8a
EP 2.1.8b
EP2.1.9b

Although he sympathized with those victimized by the Depression, President Herbert Hoover was convinced that the most effective solution to the Depression and its consequences would be to offer incentives for business to regain its footing, expand, and provide jobs for the jobless. In 1932, Hoover was swept from office by public discontent over his policies and was replaced by Franklin Delano Roosevelt, former governor of New York.

One of President Roosevelt's first actions was to institute emergency legislation that provided assistance for the jobless and poor. This legislation, coined the **New Deal**, marked the first time in history that the federal government became engaged directly in providing relief. It also provided an interpretation of the health and welfare provisions of the Constitution that established a historical precedent in mandating the federal government to assume health and welfare responsibility for its citizens (Hiltzik, 2011). The statement was clear: Citizens were, first and foremost, citizens of the United States and, second, residents of specific

Courtesy of the Franklin D. Roosevelt Library and Museum, #53227

The Great Depression created immense hardship for millions of Americans. Families who became homeless formed tent cities in many areas of the country, supporting each other to survive.

states. This policy opened the door for later federal legislation in the areas of civil rights, fair employment practices, school busing, public assistance, and a variety of other social programs.

One of the first attempts to supply relief for depression victims was the Federal Emergency Relief Administration (FERA). Modeled after New York's Emergency Relief Act, FERA provided food, clothing, and shelter allowances for the homeless and displaced. In a cooperative relationship with states, the federal government made monies available to states to administer the relief programs. States were responsible for establishing agencies for that purpose and also were required to contribute state funds, when possible, to broaden the resource base available to those in need (Stern & Axinn, 2012). This established the precedent for "matching grants," which later became an integral requirement of public assistance programs.

Additional federal emergency legislation was enacted to provide public employment for those who were out of work. The Works Progress Administration (WPA), created in 1935 to provide public service jobs, ultimately employed approximately 8 million workers over the duration of the Depression. States and local governments identified needed projects and supplied necessary materials for laborers, who were paid by the WPA. Many public schools, streets, parks, post office buildings, state college buildings, and related public projects were constructed under the auspices of the WPA.

Youth programs also were established. Perhaps the most noteworthy was the Civilian Conservation Corps (CCC), designed to protect natural resources and to improve and develop public recreational areas. Primarily a forest camp activity, the CCC provided young men between the ages of 17 and 23 with jobs, food, clothing, and shelter. Wages were nominal (about $25 per month), and the major portion of the wages ($20 per month) was sent home to help support families. CCC workers improved and developed many national parks. The National Youth Administration (NYA), gave work-study assistance to high school and college youths as an incentive to remain in school and provided part-time jobs for out-of-school students to learn job skills and increase their employability (Hiltzik, 2012). Also, FERA programs extended low-interest loans to farmers and small business operators. These programs enabled those activities to survive and become sources of employment for the jobless.

The New Deal legislation offered a temporary solution to the crisis generated by the Great Depression. The jobless found jobs, the hungry were fed, and the homeless received shelter. Perhaps of more importance, the nation felt the full impact of system changes. The issue of blaming poverty on idleness and laziness was put to rest—at least temporarily (Hiltzik, 2011).

The Social Security Act

EP 2.1.8a
EP2.1.9b

Congress passed, and President Roosevelt signed into law, the **Social Security Act** on August 4, 1935. This act remains the most significant piece of social legislation ever enacted in the United States. It also paved the way for greater federal involvement in health and welfare (American Bar Association, 2013).

The act reflected a realization that our economic system was subject to vacillations that invariably would leave many people without resources because of unemployment. It also acknowledged that older adults needed income security as an incentive to retire. This act was designed to be a permanent resource system administered by the federal government. Its provisions were outlined under three major categories (covered in more depth in Chapter 7): social insurance, public assistance, and health and welfare services (American Bar Association, 2013).

Social Insurance

Social insurance, commonly referred to as **Social Security**, is based on the premise that individuals and their families cannot always provide the financial resources necessary to meet their needs. Social insurance became the basis for financial support to the elderly, persons in poor health or with serious disabilities, individuals injured on the job, and dependents whose primary breadwinners were deceased.

Social insurance under the Social Security Act initially included two important benefit programs (American Bar Association, 2013):

1. Old Age, Survivors, and Disability Insurance (see Chapter 7); these three programs were based on taxes deducted from employees' wages and matched by employer contributions, and eligibility was based on participation earned through employment.
2. Unemployment insurance, in which employers contributed the funds, with the purpose of providing a source of income security for covered workers who had lost their jobs.

Benefits derived from these programs were considered to be a matter of right in that the recipients and their employers had paid "premiums" for the benefits they would receive. In many ways, social insurance was similar to private insurance, for which entitlement to benefits is directly related to beneficiary participation through contributions.

Public Assistance

The category of **public assistance** was based on "need" and was not established as a right earned through employment. It was administered by states with monies made available by states and matched by the federal government (matching grants). When the Social Security Act was first passed, public assistance incorporated three components (American Bar Association, 2013):

1. Old Age Assistance,
2. Aid to Dependent Children, and
3. Aid to the Blind.

In 1955, the Permanently and Totally Disabled component was added. Benefits under each of these programs were invariably limited and varied among the states according to each state's willingness to match federal funds.

Eligibility requirements were rigid and enforced rigorously. Participation was based on a "means test," requiring applicants to demonstrate that they were hopelessly without resources. Recipients' private lives were opened to the scrutiny of welfare workers in an attempt to minimize fraud and to ensure that benefit levels did not exceed budgeted needs.

Perhaps the most controversial assistance program was Aid to Dependent Children (ADC) (Day & Schiele, 2012). This program made limited funds available to mothers with dependent children when no man was present in the home. Because benefit levels were adjusted for family size (to a maximum of four children), concern arose that promiscuity and illegitimacy would be rewarded by increasing benefits as family size increased. Rigid cohabitation policies were instituted, mandating that mothers who were guilty of cohabitation would lose their grant funds entirely. Because most ADC recipients were able-bodied, there was added concern that welfare payments would be a disincentive for meeting financial needs through gainful employment. In many ways, ADC recipients were treated as the "unworthy" poor of the time and, as a consequence, often were dealt with in a punitive manner. It has been argued that ADC was the precursor to the **feminization of poverty** (a term used to emphasize the fact that families living in poverty are most often headed by single mothers because of income disparities for women) that has played out since the implementation of this program and its variants until the present (Day & Schiele, 2012).

The public usually refers to public assistance as "welfare." Because benefits are based on impoverishment and not earned through employment, participation in the program carries a stigma of personal imprudence, ineptness, or failure.

Health and Welfare Services

Programs authorized under **health and welfare services** provided for maternal and child-care services, vocational rehabilitation, public health, and services for children with physical disabilities. These services are discussed more fully in later chapters.

In the ensuing years, amendments to the Social Security Act extended each of these titles to cover more people (American Bar Association, 2013). Social insurance later added health insurance for the elderly (Medicare), and a health assistance program (Medicaid) was instituted for recipients of public assistance. The ADC assistance category was redefined as Aid to Families with Dependent Children (AFDC), and an AFDC-Unemployed Parent (AFDC-UP) provision was added so states could assist families under limited circumstances when an employable unemployed male was in the home. Only a few states opted to implement the AFDC-UP provisions. As requirements for participating in these programs became less stringent in the 1960s and 1970s, welfare rolls increased dramatically.

Social Welfare: The Post–Social Security and Welfare Reform Eras

The time since passage of the Social Security Act has been tumultuous, with significant U.S. military involvement in several major wars, a longstanding cold war followed by the fall of communism, periods of increasingly persistent inflation and recession, the emergence of a global economy, an unprecedented terrorist attack on the United States, and increasing civil unrest throughout the world that has resulted in the displacement of millions of individuals who have been forced to live in overcrowded, unsafe refugee camps in countries that are ill-prepared or politically unmotivated to receive them (U.N. High Command on Refugees, 2013). The economic downturn in the United States that began in 2007 has resulted in persistent unemployment for all age groups, especially older workers. Many individuals have simply given up on looking for a job and face a life of hardship and uncertainty (U.S. Bureau of Labor Statistics, 2013). Nearly half of marriages today end in divorce. Single-parent families, typically headed by females, have become a prominent family constellation. The general population is growing older at a rapid rate, fueled by a longer life span and aging "baby boomers." The country is woefully short of affordable housing, and incentives (financial or otherwise) to create such housing have been limited or nonexistent. Also, the country has become increasingly polarized over the merits of the Patient Protection and Affordable Care Act of 2010, and the early rollout of the provisions of that legislation has been fraught with problems. Meanwhile, the health care needs of many individuals continue to be unmet (Kaiser Family Foundation, 2014).

While the Social Security Act is viewed by many as the most significant piece of social welfare legislation ever passed in the United States, many believe that changing demographics, needs, and economic factors require a reevaluation of what is needed to best meet today's social welfare needs. We now turn to a discussion of some of the more significant social welfare programs that have been instituted since the Social Security Act was passed in 1935. As you read about them, ask yourself if they are still relevant and if not, what changes need to be made so they can adequately meet the needs of those living in the United States today.

The Great Society Programs

EP 2.1.8a
EP 2.1.8b
EP 2.1.9b

Attempts to broaden the activities of government in securing the rights of citizens and providing for personal, social, and economic development were introduced through social reform measures enacted during the Lyndon Johnson administration (1963–1968). This administration based many of its social programs on the premise that the environment in which an individual lives significantly influences personal outcomes. The so-called **Great Society** legislation promoted maximum opportunities for those in need, extending benefits of many existing programs and services designed to help the poor, the disabled, and the aged (Day & Schiele, 2012).

The Social Security Act was amended to provide for health-care benefits to the aged under the Health Insurance Program (Medicare) and to public assistance recipients through the Health Assistance Program (Medicaid). Several pieces of new legislation designed to meet needs not specifically addressed through existing resources also were passed. The Older Americans Act (1965) established a legal base for developing luncheon programs, health screening, transportation, meals-on-wheels programs, and recreational activities for older Americans. The Civil Rights Act (1964) sought to end discrimination in employment, the use of business facilities, and extension of credit. Education bills were passed that sought to rectify many of the educational disadvantages experienced by children of the poor.

Perhaps the most significant—and controversial—effort to achieve social reform came through the Economic Opportunities Act of 1964, commonly referred to as the **War on Poverty** (Bailey & Danziger, 2013). The objective of this act was to eliminate poverty through institutional change. Poverty traditionally was viewed as an individual matter, and its causes generally were thought to be the result of personal failure, lack of motivation, or personal choice. Those who designed the War on Poverty program came to a different conclusion. They considered poverty to be the result of inadequate social institutions that failed to provide opportunities for all citizens, and they concluded that traditional approaches to solving the problems of poverty were unsuccessful.

Changing the status of the poor would come not through working with them on an individual basis but, rather, through modifying institutions within a person's environment that produced the problems in the first place. Hence, programs under the Economic Opportunities Act were structured to offer the poor a greater likelihood of success by creating opportunities for their decision making and participation. Educational programs such as Head Start sought to extend relevant learning experiences to educationally disadvantaged children. Community Action Agencies encouraged the poor to become more vocal in community affairs and to organize efforts for community betterment.

Special employment incentives were generated to teach job skills. Youth Job Corps programs provided public service jobs contingent on youths remaining in school, thereby offering greater potential for employment upon graduation. Job Corps centers taught employment skills to teenage dropouts. Small-business loans were made to individuals with potential for developing businesses. Rural programs extended health and social services for the poor in rural areas.

In a nation boasting the highest standard of living in the world, it was believed that the scourge of poverty could be eliminated forever. The euphemism "war on poverty" was selected to rally the population to a full-scale commitment to overcome the enemy—poverty. Social action advocates found the climate produced by the Economic Opportunities Act favorable for their efforts. It was a heyday for the expansion of social programs. But social legislation is invariably affected by the political climate. As government resources and attention were diverted to the Vietnam War, the domestic "war" soon was neglected and terminated before its benefits could be fully realized (Bailey & Danziger, 2013).

Conservatism in the Mid-1960s and Early 1970s

The period from the mid-1960s through the mid-1970s was one of both domestic and foreign conflict. The antiestablishment movement in the United States was galvanized by the highly unpopular Vietnam War; rioting was occurring in the Watts section of Los Angeles; in Detroit, Martin Luther King, Jr., was championing the cause of disenfranchised Americans; and inflation was depleting the buying power of those who were working, especially the working poor (households with combined incomes of 200% or less of the federal poverty level).

In reaction to these disconcerting changes, a wave of conservatism emerged in the American public, leading to an effort to dismantle many of the social programs enacted during the New Deal and expanded through the Great Society programs. The welfare "establishment" was viewed as costly, ineffective, and counterproductive. The conservatives maintained that the federal government was much too large and cumbersome and that states could, and should, assume many functions (Sanderman, 2014).

Although federal involvement in public welfare programs had emerged largely because states lacked sufficient resources to provide needed supports, conservatives were convinced that states and localities were better suited to determine social welfare policies and administer social programs. One result was the reorganization—and eventual termination—of the federal antipoverty program. Several popular programs, such as Head Start and job training, were transferred to other government agencies. Under the Richard Nixon administration, a major welfare reform measure, the Family Assistance Program (FAP), was submitted for congressional approval. This measure, which was not enacted into law, would have eliminated the public assistance program and substituted workfare, a program designed to provide incentives for recipients to work without losing all of their government benefits. The expectation is that activities, such as job training, coaching, and work experience either as a volunteer or for limited pay, will improve job prospects and retention once a person is hired, leading to reductions in welfare rolls. Although many variations of "workfare" have been tried, few have worked well because full-time jobs that pay a living wage and provide health-care benefits are limited, even if a recipient completes all of the required work-related programs (Brodkin & Marston, 2013). The proposed legislation did not pass because the level of defined need was far below the benefit levels already in place in the higher-paying states but higher than the benefits in more than half the states.

Countering this conservative trend, public assistance programs for the aged, disabled, and blind were combined by enactment of the Supplemental Security Income (SSI) Act in 1974. SSI increased benefit levels for millions of recipients. AFDC continued to be funded and implemented under the federal–state arrangements already in effect.

Welfare Reform in the Late 1970s

Social welfare policymakers of the mid-1970s inherited a welfare system that had no positive constituency. Recipients, social workers, public officials, and tax-conscious groups agreed only on the inadequacy of the existing system. Each of the four constituencies had initiated a **welfare reform** effort, and each constituency had failed to achieve its reform, largely because of the others' opposition (Schram, Soss, & Fording, 2013). The problems that had drawn such negative attention in earlier decades persisted. The rapidly expanding welfare costs in the years of Presidents Richard Nixon and Gerald Ford, in juxtaposition to the intractability of poverty, made welfare reform an urgent but unpleasant necessity.

Welfare reform continued to be an issue during the Jimmy Carter administration, which proposed that $8.8 billion be appropriated to create as many as 1.4 million public service jobs (Caputo, 2011). It was expected that 2 million persons would hold the jobs in a given year, as individuals were processed through these jobs on their way to regular employment.

Carter's proposal, however, was not adopted, and debate about the most effective way to overhaul the welfare system continued.

Cutbacks in the Reagan and Bush Years

The 1980s were characterized by **welfare devolution**, or relentless efforts to reduce and eliminate government social entitlement programs (Beland & Wadden, 2012). Public expenditures for welfare were viewed as antithetical to economic progress. Mounting inflation was considered to be the result of federal domestic spending. The precarious state of the U.S. economy was thought to be the work of social progressives who had engineered the expansion of welfare programs and, as a result, caused the economy to falter. Many social support programs were either reduced dramatically or eliminated altogether (Jansson, 2012).

As part of his State of the Union message in 1982, President Reagan proposed his version of welfare reform, "New Federalism" (Obinger, Leibfried, & Castles, 2005). The centerpiece was a plan whereby the states would assume financial and administrative responsibility for food stamps and AFDC, while the federal government would assume responsibility for the Medicaid program. This reform was dubbed the "welfare swap." The plan went through a number of variations before the administration dropped it as politically infeasible.

Following his reelection in 1984, President Reagan again began to push for reshaping welfare responsibilities among the various layers of government. A presidential task force was appointed, which was to issue its report after the congressional elections in 1986. That election resulted in a Democratic landslide, and the responsibility for welfare reform shifted from the White House to Capitol Hill (Caputo, 2011).

President George H.W. Bush's administration continued to be influenced by a conservative view of welfare. As the Cold War wound down, progressives hoped that monies appropriated for defense spending would be directed toward domestic programs. Meanwhile, welfare costs continued to escalate. In 1988, the Democratic Congress passed the **Family Support Act**, which mandated that states provide job opportunities and basic skills (JOBS) programs for most AFDC recipients (some, such as those with very young children and those with health problems, were exempted from participation).

The act also provided as many as 12 months of Medicaid (health care) and child care after recipients found jobs, to ease the transition from welfare to work without loss of income. The act also mandated that states provide AFDC-UP benefits for a limited time to families with previously employed males who were unable to find employment. The act further required stronger enforcement of child support payments by absent parents. States were not required to implement some parts of the act until 1992.

The promise of the Family Support Act was never fulfilled, as federal funding for its programs was inadequate, jobs that paid a living wage for former welfare recipients failed to materialize and attempts to mobilize the private sector to support the program proved more difficult than anticipated. In short, the program was doomed to failure before it even got off the ground (Jansson, 2012).

The Clinton Years

By 1992, the political landscape of welfare reform had shifted again. Bill Clinton, the Democratic presidential candidate, was a "New Democrat" who had been instrumental, as governor of Arkansas, in advocating for passage of the Family Support Act of 1988. Clinton sought a wider role for the states in the design of federal welfare programs. More significantly, as a "political centrist," he aimed to distance himself from "liberal Democratic reform" that also had been instrumental in passing the 1988 legislation. Clinton promised to "end welfare as we know it." The goal of the reform was to make welfare "a second chance, not a way of life" (Clinton, 1997). The cornerstones of Clinton's reform agenda were portrayed as employment readiness, parental responsibility, and state discretion (Caputo, 2011).

Lawmakers at all levels of government and of both parties now were demanding that welfare recipients be required to take more responsibility for ending, or at least easing, their dependence on public support. The clamor for change was being driven by a significant shift to the right in public mood and a much-increased effort to reduce the federal deficit (Katz, 2013).

Republicans won both houses of Congress in the 1994 national elections. Various coalitions and individual members of Congress introduced many reform measures in the 104th congressional session. Nearly all reform measures proposed limiting the length of stays on welfare, restricting the right to welfare of unmarried mothers under the age of 18, and imposing far more stringent work requirements (Schram, Soss, & Fording, 2013). Perhaps most disturbing to members of the social work community were the efforts to end AFDC as a national government entitlement program.

The landmark welfare reform legislation enacted in 1996 did precisely that. Under the **Personal Responsibility and Work Opportunity Budget Reconciliation Act of 1996 (PRWOA)**, each state was provided with a block grant from the federal government and charged with administering various assistance programs, including AFDC, with a change in name to Temporary Assistance for Needy Families (TANF), at the direction of state legislatures with minimal federal guidelines (Karger & Stoesz, 2013). The thrust of the reform measures was to move recipients off the welfare rolls by engaging in work, work training, or educational programs designed to enable them to develop skills essential for employment (Caputo, 2011).

Many states, however, implemented "work first" programs, moving recipients into jobs without training (Brodkin & Marston, 2013). Although these programs reduced the welfare rolls because the economy was strong, most recipients who moved off TANF entered "dead-end," minimum-wage jobs without health care or other benefits. Recipients were allowed a maximum of 2 years to find employment. Those who failed to do so faced a significant reduction in or termination of their benefits. This approach presumes that mandatory work requirements would reduce, if not eliminate, dependence on welfare benefits. The PRWOA was reauthorized by Congress as part of the Deficit Reduction Act of 2005, with even stricter work requirements for TANF recipients. The PRWOA was scheduled for reauthorization a third time in 2010; however, Congress turned its attention to other domestic priorities such as health-care reform and a flagging economy, and the reauthorization never took place. Instead, the act has been renewed annually through a series of continuing resolutions (the latest expiration for which is September 30, 2014), enabling the legislation to remain in effect. As of the time of this writing, reauthorization of the PRWOA has yet to take place.

The George W. Bush Years

When he became President of the United States in 2000, George W. Bush ushered in a new era of social welfare policy. He argued that government cannot solve every problem, but it can encourage people and communities to help themselves and to help one another. He asserted that the truest kind of compassion is to help citizens build lives of their own. He termed his philosophy and approach **compassionate conservatism:** It is compassionate to actively help fellow citizens in need, yet conservative to insist on responsibility and results (Norman & Ganesh, 2014; Olasky, 2010).

Bush's campaign of compassionate conservatism resonated well with a broad range of Americans who were strongly influenced by the antiwelfare rhetoric of the late 1990s but who also believed in the need to reach out and help those less fortunate. In many ways, the principle of compassionate conservatism reflected the social welfare principles of colonial America: limited government intervention, personal responsibility, family values, and the role of the faith community and the private sector in addressing the social welfare needs of the citizenry.

Some opponents have argued that the notion of compassionate conservatism was a carefully disguised cover for a much more punitive approach to addressing the social welfare needs of the country—driven by a conservative religious element, a new Puritanism, and the interests of big business (Katz, 2013). The search for truth in this matter was interrupted abruptly by

the terrorist attacks on America in September 2001, the ensuing global war on terrorism, dissension among world leaders about the war in Iraq, and the search for a solution to peace in the Middle East (Webel & Arnaldi, 2011).

Social workers are left with the compelling question, "How can we operate within the framework of such an agenda—which is still strong today—to ensure that the social welfare system in the United States is not dismantled to the point at which it no longer is responsive to the needs of the country's citizens and incapable of being rebuilt without a huge investment in public funds?" (Schram, Soss, & Fording, 2013).

The Obama Years

EP 2.1.8a
EP 2.8.1b
EP 2.1.9b

The election of Barack Obama to the presidency of the United States in 2008 ushered in a new sense of hope by many that the government would renew its commitment to addressing the social welfare needs of underserved populations. President Obama expressed a strong commitment to social and economic justice during his campaign for the presidency. Such hopes were dashed, however, at least in the short term, by the string of events that faced President Obama soon after he assumed office in January 2009.

As the second decade of the 21st century began, the United States was in the throes of a major economic crisis caused in large part by the collapse of the home mortgage industry, after a period of unprecedented growth fueled by low mortgage-interest rates and questionable lending arrangements, some of which bordered on the criminal (Lewis, 2010). The collapse of the home mortgage industry resulted in severe liquidity problems for the country's largest and most-venerated financial institutions, as investors fled the home mortgage scene in large numbers. The economic collapse in the United States had worldwide impact, and there was concern that other countries would also face economic collapse if immediate action were not taken. In response, the U.S. federal government launched a broad-scale economic stimulus package that cost upward of $1 trillion to jump start the country's faltering economy (Lewis, 2010). Defense expenditures related to continued U.S. military involvement in Iraq and Afghanistan contributed to the federal deficit as well (Institute for International Studies, 2013).

President Obama officially ended American military involvement in Iraq in December, 2011; however, the ability of the Iraqi government to ensure the safety of its people against a renewal of insurgency in that country is in serious question. President Obama has also made a commitment to end U.S. military involvement in Afghanistan by the end of 2014, although like Iraq, there is growing pessimism among American military leaders that the government of Afghanistan will be able to protect its citizens from a renewal of insurgency in that country. It is projected that costs associated with U.S. military involvement in Iraq and Afghanistan alone will amount to $4 trillion through federal fiscal year 2014. Billions of additional dollars will be required to provide treatment for the health and mental health needs of American soldiers who were deployed to war zones in these two conflicts (Institute for International Studies, 2013).

The economic downturn of 2007 has resulted in significant cuts in education, transportation, and social and other public services (Sorkin, 2010). As will be discussed in detail in the chapter on health care, the country's health-care system is at a tipping point, as businesses, medical providers, and the insurance industry struggle to implement the complex, and by some reports, onerous provisions of the Affordable Care Act of 2010. While this legislation will enable millions of Americans previously not covered by health insurance to have access to comprehensive and affordable health care, the program still falls short of the original goal of providing affordable health care to all Americans. Also, the political fallout from early implementation problems, coupled with a relentless attack on the philosophical underpinnings of the legislation by conservative politicians and special interest groups, threatens the very future of the legislation.

EP 2.1.3a
With the economic downturn in recent years and attention—and funds—devoted to the wars in Iraq and Afghanistan, government spending for domestic social welfare programs has taken a back seat (see Figure 1.1). Because President Obama and his administration believed that health care was a critical factor for many U.S. citizens that also impacted other social problems, they made health care reform a top priority. The rest of the country's social welfare agenda has remained at a stalemate because of the economic and international issues with which Obama has been

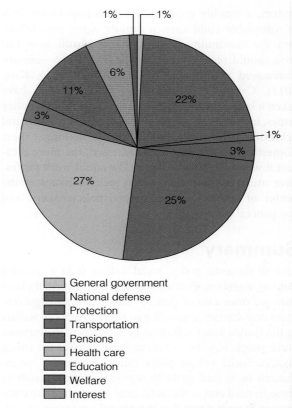

FIG 1.1 Federal Government Expenditures, Fiscal Year 2014
SOURCE: Government Consumption Expenditures and Gross Investment by Function. (Washington, DC: *Bureau of Economic Analysis*, 2014).

confronted, as well as conflicts among political parties about what our domestic agenda should be and how it should be implemented. The question remains: At what point will the government turn its attention to other domestic social welfare problems?

There is another important side to this story when considering what our U.S. domestic priorities should be. A rapidly growing underclass of individuals in the United States, even though they work at one and often two jobs, are unable to lift themselves and their families out of poverty. These families no longer qualify for government assistance, yet they are unable to move out of poverty. Children born into these families are at high risk for repeating this pattern for themselves and their families.

Other controversial social welfare issues—such as ensuring the solvency of the country's social security system, a steadily growing homeless population, lack of affordable child care, a rapidly aging population, and the continuing rising costs of health care and who should receive what at whose expense,—remain unresolved (Abramsky, 2013; Edelman, 2013; Katz, 2013). Critical domestic social welfare issues have taken a back seat to increasingly volatile foreign policy issues, including waging a global war on terrorism and achieving peace in the Middle East. The longer these domestic social issues go unaddressed, the more difficult it will be to resolve them. The social work profession must put domestic social welfare issues at the center of attention of legislators, policymakers, and the general public.

Summary

Like all domestic policy, social welfare is in a constant state of evolution. Policies and practice historically have emerged from a set of choices—national or state, government or voluntary, expanding or restrictive. Social welfare in the United States will never be satisfactory to everyone. Some people will always believe we have made the wrong choices. Social welfare policy cannot escape the contradictions in its dual goals: to respond compassionately to those in need and at the same time to structure the compassion in such a way that the natural tendencies of people to work, save, and care for their own are not eroded.

Competency Notes

EP 2.1.1a: Advocate for client access to the services of social work (p. 5). Social work is the primary profession that works with and advocates for clients within the social welfare system.

EP 2.1.3a: Distinguish, appraise, and integrate multiple sources of knowledge, including research-based knowledge and practice wisdom (pp. 5, 19). Critical thinking involves the ability to distinguish, appraise, and integrate multiple sources of knowledge, including research-based knowledge and practice wisdom. Social workers use critical thinking in understanding how history shapes current social welfare policies and client services.

EP 2.1.8a: Analyze, formulate, and advocate for policies that advance social well-being (pp. 3, 5, 11, 13, 15, 18). Social workers must have an understanding of the ways that history has shaped our social welfare system to be able to analyze, formulate, and advocate for policies that advance social well-being.

EP 2.1.8b: Collaborate with colleagues and clients for effective policy action (pp. 9, 11, 15). Collaboration with colleagues and clients is an important requisite for effective policy action.

EP 2.1.9b: Provide leadership in promoting sustainable changes in service delivery and practice to improve the quality of social services (pp. 9, 15, 18). Social workers engage in leadership roles within the social welfare system to promote sustainable changes in service delivery and to improve the quality of social services.

Key Terms

The terms below are defined in the Glossary.

compassionate conservatism
Dorothea Dix
Elizabethan Poor Law
Family Support Act
feminization of poverty
Great Depression
Great Society
health and welfare services
Hull House
humanitarianism
indoor relief
Jane Addams
laissez-faire
New Deal
outdoor relief
Personal Responsibility and Work Opportunity Budget Reconciliation Act of 1996 (PRWOA)
public assistance
social insurance
social security
Social Security Act
social welfare
social work
values
War on Poverty
welfare devolution
welfare reform

Discussion Questions

1. Compare the various values perspectives discussed in this chapter: institutional and residual, liberal and conservative. Give examples of how these different perspectives shape social welfare programs. What are your perspectives?
2. Identify the conditions that led to enactment of the Elizabethan Poor Law. Which aspects of that law can be found in the U.S. social welfare system today?
3. Discuss the differences between indoor relief and outdoor relief. Give an example of each. Which do you think is the better approach for assisting the poor? Why?
4. What effect did passage of the Social Security Act have on the federal government's role in health and welfare? What components of the Social

Security Act can be seen in today's social welfare programs?

5. In various forms, "workfare" has been attempted as a means of reducing welfare rolls. What is workfare? Why has it not been entirely effective in reducing welfare rolls? What approach do you suggest to reduce the number of individuals on public assistance? Why do you suggest that approach?

6. Compare the values perspectives upon which the War on Poverty and compassionate conservatism are based. Does the point of time in history shape the values perspectives existing at that time and, in turn, the proposed outcomes to deal with social problems such as poverty?

7. Social welfare policy decisions made at one point in time may be based on assumptions that do not hold up in later years. What were the assumptions upon which the Personal Responsibility and Work Opportunity Budget Reconciliation Act of 1996 (PRWOA) were based? Are these assumptions realistic in times of economic downturn?

8. Compare the Obama administration's stimulus plan to the New Deal. How did the economic conditions and mood of the country shape each?

9. Why do you think the Obama administration made health care its top domestic priority? Do you agree with this decision? Why?

10. What do you consider to be the most pressing major social welfare issue facing the United States today and why?

On the Internet

www.aecf.org
www.clasp.org
http://www.cswe.org/
www.financeprojectinfo.org/WIN
http://www.socialworkers.org/
http://www.naswfoundation.org/pioneer.asp
www.urban.org

References

Abramsky, S. (2013). *The American way of poverty: How the other half still lives.* New York: Nation Books.

American Bar Association. (2013). *The Social Security Act sourcebook.* Washington, DC: ABA Publishers.

Beland, D., & Waddem, A. (2012). *The politics of policy change: Welfare, medicare, and social security reform in the United States.* Washington, DC: Georgetown University Press.

Bailey, M., & Danziger, S. (Eds.). (2013). *Legacies of the war on poverty.* New York: Russell Sage Foundation.

Brodkin, E., & Marston, G. (2013). *Work and the welfare state: Street-level organizations and workforce politics.* Washington, DC: Georgetown University Press.

Caputo, R. (Ed.). (2011). *Policy transitions from 1981 to the present.* New York: Springer.

Clinton, B. (1997). *Between hope and history: Meeting America's challenges for the 21st century.* New York: Random House.

Day, P., & Schiele, J. (2012). *A new history of social welfare* (7th ed.). Boston: Pearson.

DiNitto, D., & Johnson, D. (2012). *Essentials of social welfare: Politics and public policy.* Boston: Pearson.

Dubois, B., & Miley, K. (2013). *Social work: An empowering profession* (8th edition). Boston, MA: Pearson.

Edelman, P. (2013). *So rich, so poor: Why it's so hard to end poverty in America.* New York: New Press.

Gilbert, N., & Terrell, P. (2012). *Dimensions of social welfare policy* (8th edition). Boston: Pearson.

Hiltzik, M. (2011). *The New Deal: A modern history.* New York: Free Press.

Institute for International Studies. (2013). *Estimated dollar costs of wars, in billions.* Providence, RI: Brown University Watson Institute for International Studies.

Jansson, B. (2012). *The reluctant welfare state: Engaging history to advance social work practice in contemporary society* (7th ed.). Belmont, CA: Brooks/Cole Cengage.

Kaiser Family Foundation. (2014). *Health coverage and care in the South in 2014 and beyond.* Menlo Park, CA: Author.

Karger, J., & Stoesz, D. (2013). *American social welfare policy: A pluralist approach* (6th ed.). Boston: Pearson.

Katz, M. (2013). *The undeserving poor: America's enduring confrontation with poverty* (2nd ed). New York: Oxford University Press.

Lees, L. H. (2007). *The solidarities of strangers: The English Poor Laws and the people, 1700–1948.* New York: Cambridge University Press.

Lewis, M. (2010). *The big short: Inside the doomsday machine.* New York: W.W. Norton & Company.

Midgley, J., & Livermore, M. (2008). *The handbook of social policy.* Thousand Oaks, CA: Sage.

Norman, J., & Garresh, J. (2014). *Compassionate conservatism: What it is—why we need it.* Buckingham, UK: University of Buckingham Press.

Obinger, H., Leibfried, S., & Castles, F. (Eds.). (2005). *Federalism and the welfare state: New World and European experiences*. New York: Cambridge University Press.

Olasky, M. (2010). *Compassionate conservatism: What it is, what it does, and how it can transform America*. New York: Free Press.

Reamer, F. (2013). *Social work values and ethics* (4th ed.), New York: Columbia University Press.

Sanderman, P. (Ed.). (2014). *The end of welfare as we know it?: Continuity and change in Western welfare state settings and practices*. Leverkusen, Germany: Barbara Budrich Publishers.

Schram, S., Soss, J., & Fording, R. (2013). Welfare and welfare reform in the age of Neoliberalism. In M. Reisch (Ed.), *Social policy and social justice*. Thousand Oaks, CA: SAGE, pp. 377–404.

Shott, L., & Pavetti, L. (2013). *Changes in TANF work requirements could make them more effective in promoting employment*. Washington, DC: Center on Budget and Policy Priorities. Retrieved from www.cbpp.org.

Slavicek, L. (2011). *Jane Addams: Humanitarian*. Bel Air, CA: Chelsea House Publishers.

Sorkin, A. (2010). *Too big to fail: The inside story of how Wall Street and Washington fought to save the financial system—and themselves*. New York: Penguin Press.

Specht, H., & Courtney, M. (1995). *Unfaithful angels: How social work has abandoned its roots*. New York: Simon & Shuster Digital Media.

Stern, M., & Axinn, J. (2011). *Social welfare: A history of the American response to need* (7th ed.). Boston: Allyn & Bacon.

U.N. High Command on Refugees. (2013). *Military intervention in Afghanistan following the terrorist attack on September 11, 2001*. Geneva: Author.

U.S. Bureau of Labor Statistics. (2013). *The unemployment situation—November 2013*. Washington, DC: Author.

Webel, C., & Arnaldi, J. (Eds.). (2011). *The ethics and efficacy of the global war on terrorism: Fighting terror with terror*. New York: Palgrave Macmillan.

Suggested Readings

Blau, J. & Abramovitz, M. (2010). *The dynamics of social welfare policy* (3rd ed.). New York: Oxford University Press.

Collins, J. & Mayer, V. (2010). *Both hands tied: Welfare reform and the race to the bottom in the low-wage market*. Chicago: University of Chicago Press.

Ehrenreich, B. (2002). *Nickel and dimed: On (not) getting by in America*. New York: Owl Press.

Popple, P.R., & Leighninger, L. (2010). *Social work, social welfare, and American society* (8th ed.). Boston: Pearson.

Seccombe, K. (2010). *"So you think I drive a Cadillac?": Welfare recipients' perspectives on the system and its reform* (3rd ed.). Boston: Allyn & Bacon.

Selker, H., & Wasser, J. (Eds.). (2014). *The Affordable Care Act as a national experiment*. New York: Springer.

CHAPTER 2
Social Work and Other Helping Professions

- In a community drug treatment center, social worker Jimmy Johnson is leading a group of teenage boys, helping them develop skills that will counter peer pressure from friends who are still using drugs.
- In another part of the city, Tony Gonzalez, a medical social worker, assists clients and their families in coping with the effects of illness and in developing resources that will provide support while family members are in the hospital or recovering after a hospital stay.
- Just down the street, Charlotte Ray, a school social worker, is working with a group of pregnant teenagers on issues of health care, relationships, and decision making surrounding their pregnancies, including ways that they can continue their education.
- Candace McNabb is a social worker employed by the local United Way, where she assists community groups in identifying community needs and developing resources to meet them. Currently she is working with a community coalition on homelessness.
- Maria Herrera, a social worker with the adult probation department, helps clients find employment and educational resources so they can choose a life path that doesn't involve crime.
- Amy Lu, a social worker for a women's shelter, aids women who have experienced interpersonal violence and their children in locating safe havens while they develop coping skills that will enable them to live lives free from threats and attacks.
- In a rural area several hundred miles away, Jackson Lee is a social worker for the Department of Human Services. His generalist skills in social work are helpful in dealing with a wide variety of problems with few organized resources to address them.
- Peter Thacker and Jean Reeves, social workers at a senior center serving three counties, oversee a group of volunteers who are preparing lunches for the meals-on-wheels program that will be delivered to homebound elderly adults.
- At a large military hospital not too far away, Captain Lorenzo Vasquez, a military social worker, provides counseling to a soldier gravely injured

while in combat in Iraq who, in addition to his physical injuries, is experiencing posttraumatic stress.

- Across the globe, Jason Stewart, a social worker with an international development group, finds his generalist social work skills helpful in aiding refugees from a war-torn village begin to rebuild their lives and homes.

These social workers are representatives of the broad and diverse positions held by social workers throughout the world who engage individuals, families, groups, organizations, and communities in seeking solutions to unmet needs.

Social work practice demands from its practitioners the utmost in passion, intellect, creativity, skill, and knowledge. It is an exciting, challenging profession. Students who have the aptitude and desire to prepare for a career in the helping professions may find social work well suited to their interests. In this chapter, we explore the professional culture, tasks, knowledge base, and skills that incorporate social work practice. First, though, we examine why people have unresolved needs and why they often need professional assistance in seeking solutions to meet them.

Why Do People Experience Challenges in their Lives?

EP 2.1.3a

Social workers deal with challenges that inhibit optimal functioning for individuals, families, groups, organizations, and communities. The many challenges that professional social workers help people address include mental/behavioral health, health, poverty, interpersonal conflicts between adults as well as between parents and children, delinquency, abuse and neglect, and substance use.

Why do individuals face challenges to the extent that they need outside assistance? No rational person deliberately plans to have debilitating problems. No child plans to spend a life in poverty, nor does an adolescent choose a life of mental illness. What newly married couple, in love and looking forward to a joyful future together, plans for continuous conflict, family violence, or divorce? Why, then, do these problems

and challenges emerge? Why do some individuals have happy, satisfying relationships while others move from relationship to relationship without finding satisfaction? Why do some people prosper and climb the occupational and income ladders readily while others remain deeply enmeshed in poverty? Are these situations a matter of personal choice? Of course not! Challenges that jeopardize individual and family functioning result from a mix of many factors. We will briefly examine some of them.

Genetics and Heredity

From a biological standpoint, people are born with many of the physiological characteristics of their ancestors. Some individuals have a tendency to be tall, others short; some are lean, others heavy; and so on. Some presumably have greater intellectual potential than others; some are more agile, others less so. To an extent, these characteristics affect how well we adapt to the world around us and, indeed, opportunities throughout life. For example, regardless of desire or ability, a 5-foot, 6-inch male would have extreme difficulty becoming a professional basketball player. Regardless of desire or skill, opportunity clearly is affected by physical characteristics. We encourage you to think of other examples in which genetic or hereditary factors might impose limitations on social behavior or opportunities.

The Human Genome Project and other major scientific advances suggest that biological factors play a much more extensive role in human functioning than previously believed, particularly when coupled with the impact of the environment. **Psychobiological** approaches to understanding behavior focus on identifying anomalies in body chemistry and studying how environmental stress converges with those anomalies to produce specific behavioral outcomes. For example, conditions such as schizophrenia, mood disorders such as depression, and chronic anxiety are widely believed to be genetically linked.

Socialization

Whatever limits heredity may impose, individuals develop as social beings through the process of **socialization**. Social behavior is learned behavior, acquired through interactions with other human beings. Parents are most often the primary sources of early socialization experiences, and family culture has a significant impact on the development of values, priorities, and role prescriptions. Families are not the only source of social development, though. Neighbors, playmates, and acquaintances from school and other community institutions also play a part.

Lower-income parents and wealthy parents, for example, may socialize their children in different ways because of access to resources and opportunities. The society in which people live also influences their socialization. Thus, as children develop, their behaviors are shaped by the learning opportunities available to them. Our thoughts and mental attitudes are as much a product of learning as the skills we develop. For example, children who grow up in at-risk families, in which violence or substance abuse are present, often learn inappropriate techniques of problem solving, as well as negative perspectives about themselves and those around them.

Cultural Differences

Culture plays a major role in shaping norms and expectations. Behaviors that seem to conflict with broader societal norms and expectations sometimes can be attributed to cultural differences. Traditional customs and behaviors of some groups differ considerably from the expectations of the majority group and create dissonance, which sometimes results in behavior that may be interpreted as dysfunctional by members of the dominant group. The United States takes pride in, and has been enriched by, immigrants from around the world. Many of our social institutions expect immigrants to adapt and assimilate to the dominant culture, but trying to meet these expectations may be difficult for them. Language differences and cultural traits often result in stereotyping, categorizing individuals as "out-group" members, and imposing barriers to social opportunities. How to balance celebrating and maintaining individual cultures with collective contributions to the common good of all requires further exploration of environmental factors.

Environmental Factors

Geography, climate, and resources all affect quality of life and opportunities available for satisfactory growth and development. These factors vary widely throughout the world. Added to the environmental factors are the economic and political forces that largely determine the availability of opportunities and resources around which people seek to organize their lives. Smog-infested, polluted areas contribute to various health problems. Unpredictable economic trends may result in loss of jobs for certain segments of the population. Discrimination limits opportunities for career development and impedes adequate employment.

A person's environment is a major element in the availability of opportunities. It can serve as a stimulus for producing life's satisfactions or become a major source of the challenges that people experience.

The Opportunity Structure

Clearly, genetics and heredity, socialization and cultural differences, and environmental factors are important in understanding why people face challenges. All of these factors shape an individual's **opportunity structure**—the accessibility of opportunities for an individual within that individual's environment. For example, a person may have physical traits and characteristics upon which society places a high value, a strong educational background, a stable and supportive family, work-oriented values, and a desire to work, yet be without a job because of an economic recession or depression. In spite of suitable preparation, this person may remain unemployed for some time, with all of the problems associated with lack of income.

In another case, an individual may be born into a family living in extreme poverty, be severely abused as a child, lack encouragement or incentives from parents and teachers to complete school and drop out at an early age, and have limited social skills because of inadequate parenting. Even if jobs were plentiful, this person likely would be able to compete for only the lowest-paying positions.

Other factors also play a major role in one's access to the opportunity structure. Gender, race, and ethnicity often result in discrimination and unequal treatment in job opportunities as well as the income a person will receive from the job. Women, African Americans, Native Americans, and Latinos, for example, are not afforded equal opportunity in the job market even when all other factors are equal.

What are some of the possible outcomes you can think of that might result if a person's environment has failed to provide opportunities to meet even the most basic human needs? Which groups in society might be most and least likely to have their needs met by the environment?

Social Work Defined

EP 2.1.1a
EP 2.1.1c

In the minds of many, **social workers** are identified as "welfare" workers who are employed in public assistance programs. This is a false and limited premise because social workers are involved in many different practice settings that offer a wide range of services. Recall from Chapter 1 that *social welfare* literally means "social well-being." In the United States, this generally refers to providing institutional programs for those in need. The profession of social work—the topic of this chapter—is one of the professions that is instrumental in enhancing the well-being of individuals, families, groups, organizations, communities, and the broader society.

The opportunity structure consists of more than what is available in the environment. It includes inner resources such as cognitive development and personality structure. Furthermore, many challenges faced by individuals, families, groups, organizations, and communities result from the way society is organized and the limited choices available to some people.

One of the advantages about the profession of social work is its diversity of both roles and career opportunities. However, because social workers are actively involved in wide-ranging tasks, it is difficult to devise a specific, all-inclusive definition of social work. According to the National Association of Social Workers (NASW), the largest social work professional

organization in the world, the primary mission of **social work** is to

> *enhance human well-being and help meet the basic needs of all people, with particular attention to promoting social justice, addressing the needs and empowerment of people who are vulnerable, oppressed, or living in poverty.... [Social workers help people] identify and manage the environmental forces that create, contribute to, and address problems in living. (National Association of Social Workers (2008). NASW Code of Ethics. Washington, DC: Author).*

Most discussions about social work focus on key concepts that include individual and community well-being, diversity, social justice, an emphasis on both the person and the broader environment, and working with and advocating on behalf of vulnerable populations. Box 2.1 delineates the purpose of the social work profession developed by the Council on Social Work Education, the national organization that accredits social work education programs in colleges and universities. Compare this statement with the preamble to the Code of Ethics established by the National Association of Social Workers in Box 2.2. What similarities can you identify that help you understand more about the definition and purpose of social work?

Social work is a profession that seeks to help individuals, families, organizations, groups, and communities engage resources that will enhance social well-being and alleviate human problems. Social work is concerned, too, with enabling clients to develop internal capacities and strengths that will improve their social functioning. As the NASW definition indicates, social work is an active, "doing" profession that brings about positive change in individuals, families, groups, organizations, communities, and ultimately, the broader society, through problem solving or prevention.

Box 2.1   Purpose of the Social Work Profession

The purpose of the social work profession is to promote human and community well-being. Guided by a person and environment construct, a global perspective, respect for human diversity, and knowledge based on scientific inquiry, social work's purpose is actualized through its quest for social and economic justice, the prevention of conditions that limit human rights, the elimination of poverty, and the enhancement of the quality of life for all persons.

SOURCE: Council on Social Work Education (2010) Educational Policy and Accreditation Standards (p. 1). Washington, DC: Author.

A primary focus of the social work profession is its commitment to the promotion of social and economic justice, effecting changes in societal values and policies that limit or prohibit the free and full participation of individuals. Social workers have a professional responsibility to work for changes in discriminatory or otherwise restrictive practices that limit opportunities and prevent maximum social functioning.

The Early Years of Social Work

Professional social work developed slowly over the years as a result of efforts to refine and improve its knowledge and skill base. As discussed in Chapter 1, early administration of relief to the needy was accomplished by a diverse group of individuals—overseers of the poor, friends and neighbors, church members, the clergy, philanthropists, and friendly visitors, among others. As early as 1814 in Scotland, the Reverend Thomas Chalmers expressed concern over the wasteful and inefficient approaches of relief programs and encouraged the development of a more humane and effective system for providing services and support.

Chalmers emphasized the need for more personalized involvement with the needy. He devised a system wherein his parish was divided into districts, with a deacon assigned to investigate each case to determine the causes of the problems people were experiencing. If the resulting analysis indicated that self-sufficiency was not possible, an attempt was made to engage family, friends, neighbors, or wealthy citizens to provide the necessary assistance for those in need. As a last resort, the congregation was asked to provide assistance (Day & Schiele, 2013).

Later, in the United States, the Association for Improving the Conditions of the Poor (New York City) and the Charity Organization Society (Buffalo, New York City, and Philadelphia) took similar approaches when organizing efforts to help the poor. The **Charity Organization Society (COS)** had a profound effect on establishing social work as a specialized practice. It promoted "scientific philanthropy," emphasizing that charity was more than almsgiving. Furthermore, the COS stressed the importance of individual assessment and a coordinated plan of service.

The COS was the first relief organization to pay personnel to investigate requests for assistance and to refer eligible applicants to one or more existing agencies for intensive aid and supervision. Special emphasis was placed on "following up" on the recipients of assistance, and making efforts to secure someone to establish friendly relationships with them (Stern & Axinn, 2012).

Just as "friendly visiting" was encouraged, attention was directed to data collection and assessment. It was believed that a more structured, informed, and skillful approach would increase efficiency, discourage dependence on charity, lead to personal development and self-sufficiency, and reduce the practice of providing relief for chronic beggars.

As discussed in Chapter 1, the **settlement house** movement emerged during the late 1800s as another viable means to provide a variety of community-based services and advocacy for the poor and disenfranchised. This movement contributed significantly to the beginning of the social work profession in the United States. Perhaps the most noteworthy of the settlements was Hull House, established in Chicago in 1889 by Jane Addams, a pioneer social worker. The success of this venture was immediate, and the programs offered by Hull House captured the imagination of philanthropic helpers and the poor alike. The settlements maintained a strong family focus, provided socialization experiences, and, through advocacy efforts, sought to influence the community to improve the dismal social conditions under which the poor were living.

This structured approach to managing charitable efforts quickly resulted in the need for trained workers. **Mary Richmond**, a major contributor to the COS movement who had a long-lasting impact on the profession, inaugurated the first training program for social workers at the New York School of Applied Philanthropy, forerunner of schools of social work.

Richmond, considered by many to be the founder of the professional clinical social work movement, also formulated the concept and base for **social casework**, a practice method designed to "develop personality through adjustments consciously effected, individual by individual, between [persons] and their environment" (1922, p. 9).

In addition, Richmond maintained a keen interest in personality and family development, emphasizing influence of the environment within which interpersonal interactions transpire. Believing that environmental factors are significant contributors to personal as well as family problems, she maintained a strong interest in social reform that would promote a better quality of life for individuals (Stern & Axinn, 2012).

Jane Addams, one of the first social workers in the United States and the founder of Hull House in Chicago, the first settlement house in the United States, advocated for social reforms to improve the lives of immigrants.

Richmond was convinced that this task should be included in the social worker's sphere of responsibility. In her classic work *Social Diagnosis* in 1917, Richmond laid the framework for social casework practice.

Women of color also played key roles in elevating the status of service to individuals and communities. African Americans Janie Porter Barrett and Sarah Collins Fernandis began settlement houses in Hampton, Virginia, and Washington, DC and developed community-based programs in those areas. Modeled after Hull House, these were the first settlement houses located in African American communities. Barrett later founded a rehabilitation center for African American girls; its treatment model was adopted by many other social work programs. Fernandis became the first African American social worker employed by the Baltimore Health Department. African American Dorothy Height, mentored by Jane Addams and other women leaders of the progressive era, was the head of the Young Women's Christian Association (YWCA) and a founder of the National Council of Negro Women (NASW, 2014). Under the impetus provided by these leaders, Richmond, Addams, and other early social work pioneers, a profession was born.

Schools of social work began to emerge along the Eastern Seaboard and in large cities of the Midwest, emphasizing direct social work practice (then called *casework* based on Richmond's work). Many were influenced by newly developing psychological perspectives, most notably those of Sigmund Freud and Otto Rank. Schools adopting Freudian psychology were more prevalent and became identified as "diagnostic" schools. Schools incorporating Rankian theory were known as "functional" schools. Shaping of curriculum around psychological theories increased the scientific knowledge base for social work practice.

By the late 1920s, **group work** also had gained visibility as a method of social intervention. Learning and social development were believed to be enhanced through structured group interactions. This technique soon was popularized in settlement houses and in work with street gangs, participants in organized recreational programs, and residents of institutions. Social group work became well entrenched as a viable helping method and later was adopted as a social work method.

Community organization had its roots in the New York Society for the Prevention of Pauperism, the Association for Improving the Conditions of the Poor, and the settlement house movement. By the late

1930s, community organization was prominent as a social work method. Dealing largely with community development and emphasizing the importance of citizen participation and environmental change, community organizers used their skills to identify unmet human needs and develop community resources to meet those needs. Among the prerequisites for community organizers were skills in needs assessment, planning, public relations, organizing, influencing, and resource development.

By the 1950s, social casework, group work, and community organization all were considered methods of social work practice. In 1955, the various associations established to promote and develop each separate method merged and became known collectively as the **National Association of Social Workers (NASW)**. NASW continues to serve as the main professional organization for social workers today, with 56 chapters throughout the world, and some 150,000 members. It seeks to promote quality in practice, stimulates political participation and social action, maintains standards of eligibility for membership in the association, and publishes several journals, including *Social Work*. Each state has a NASW chapter with a designated headquarters, and local membership units are active in all major cities. In addition, many college and university social work programs have student units of NASW.

Although the majority of social workers today are involved in direct practice with individuals and families, many facilitate groups or are involved in community organization efforts. As the profession has diversified to meet human needs as they arise, there has been less emphasis on distinctions between these three social work methods and greater emphasis on fields of practice, although all social work education programs offer coursework that emphasizes knowledge and skills needed to work with individuals and families, groups, and communities. NASW, for example, has 13 specialized practice areas that members can subscribe to, with social workers in almost all areas providing a range of direct practice, group, and community organization efforts. Areas include adolescent health; aging; behavioral health; bereavement/end of life care; children, youth, and families; clinical social work; diversity and equality; health; HIV/AIDS; international social work; peace and social justice; school social work; and violence. As discussed later, many social work education programs offer courses and sometimes specializations in these areas.

Underpinnings of the Profession

Social work professional practice is based on values, ethics, a common body of knowledge that builds on a liberal arts base, and planned change. Each attribute is important to professional social workers. The Council on Social Work Education (CSWE) has incorporated these attributes into a curriculum policy statement and specific content areas that social work education programs must address at the bachelor's (BSW) and master's (MSW) levels (discussed later in the chapter).

Values

EP 2.1.2a
EP 2.1.2b

All of us have values, or a set of beliefs that shape the ways we view others and the world around us. Our values serve as the basis for the way we live our lives and the decisions that we make. The profession of social work is also guided by a set of values that shape the way social workers view their clients and guide the decisions that they make. Social workers are committed to the dignity, worth, and value of all human beings regardless of social class, race, ethnicity, gender, sexual orientation, gender identity, age, religion, or ability. The value of human life transcends all other values, and the best interest of human beings merits a humane and helpful response from society. People with problems and unmet needs, regardless of the nature of those problems and needs, are not to be judged, condemned, or demeaned. Social workers emphasize that nonjudgmental attitudes are essential for maintaining clients' dignity and privacy and that clients must be accepted as they are, with no strings attached.

Furthermore, clients (or the **client system**, which may include more than one individual, such as a family or a group of adults with disabilities) have the right to autonomy—the right to determine courses of action that will affect their lives. Likewise, groups and communities hold these fundamental rights.

Ethics

Organizations, communities, and societies, in turn, operate within formal (stated) or informal (unstated but expected to be understood by members) ethical principles that are based on the shared values of their members. **Ethics** can be seen as a set of rules by which a society, community, or organization operates, while values are individually held. Thus, ethics (sometimes referred to as *moral duty*) is a product of values.

The concept of professional ethics, therefore, relates to the moral principles of practice. Social work values form the basis for social workers' beliefs about individuals and society, while ethics defines the framework for what should be done in specific situations. Both provide the basis for decision making, and both create dilemmas for individuals as well as larger entities. Both values and ethical dilemmas and conflicts are common.

NASW has established a code of ethics (see Box 2.2) for its members, incorporating the values of the profession. A strong professional culture has developed and is expressed through the state and national associations of social work practitioners. Social work incorporates a strengths perspective, too, acknowledging that individuals, families, groups and communities are more likely to change when helping professionals build on their strengths rather than emphasize their deficiencies (see Chapter 3). As you read the excerpt from the Code of Ethics in Box 2.2, you will see how both the concepts of values and ethical principles discussed earlier in this chapter serve as a core foundation of the social work profession.

Social workers, like their clients, have personal reference groups whose values frequently conflict with those of others. For example, a client may belong to a religious group that forbids and censures the use of professional medical intervention in cases of illness. The social worker may strongly favor medical intervention in those cases. Noting the value differences, what is the social worker's moral (ethical) duty in such cases? How can the client's best interests be served when value conflicts are present? Do clients have the right to self-determination in these cases?

Client confidentiality is an important social work value emphasized in the Code of Ethics. Clients need assurance that they can trust social workers with often very personal information. A social worker in a mental health clinic, for example, cannot disclose specific information to a family member or another helping professional without the written consent of the client under most circumstances. There are guidelines that help social workers determine when information should be shared: for example, when clients disclose a plan to physically harm themselves or others or when a youth reports being abused. What would you do if you were a social worker working with a client with HIV who told you that she was in a sexual relationship with someone else, was not using protection, and her partner was not aware that she had HIV?

The Code of Ethics also specifies other guidelines that protect clients, including those that could create a conflict of interest with a client. Having a sexual relationship with a client clearly violates the Code of Ethics. If you are a social worker who has a client that is unemployed and desperate for work, and you need your house painted, would it be appropriate to hire your client to do the work?

As you consider these questions, ask yourself what you would do. You will discover that responses to these types of situations are seldom achieved easily. Review the excerpt from the NASW Code of Ethics in Box 2.2 again and access the link to the entire Code to see whether it helps you arrive at appropriate ethical behavior for such situations.

Liberal Arts Base

EP 2.1.3a

Social workers at all levels must obtain a college education with a strong liberal arts base on which to build as they gain additional knowledge about human behavior, social welfare policy, research, and practice and earn one or more social work degrees. Courses in composition and literature; language; government, history, and economics; sociology and psychology; mathematics and science; and culture and the fine arts all provide students with connections to the past and a broad perspective on social and human conditions. These courses also strengthen critical thinking and problem-solving skills and foster a more holistic understanding of our world.

Knowledge That Builds on the Liberal Arts Base

What do you need to be able to know to be a competent social worker? Social work practice is derived from a common body of knowledge that encompasses theories of human behavior as well as theoretical and experiential knowledge related to practice. Research is integrally important in understanding individual, family, group, organizational, and community behavior. Research also identifies more effective intervention techniques. Students of social work are expected to have knowledge of the life cycle and developmental processes, as well as personality development, social functioning, group and organizational dynamics, social justice and the effects of discrimination, social policy formation, research methods, and community environments.

Schools of social work expect students to become familiar with a wide range of social and behavioral

Box 2.2   NASW Code of Ethics

Preamble

The primary mission of the social work profession is to enhance human well-being and help meet the basic human needs of all people, with particular attention to the needs and empowerment of people who are vulnerable, oppressed, and living in poverty. A historic and defining feature of social work is the profession's focus on individual well-being in a social context and the well-being of society. Fundamental to social work is attention to the environmental forces that create, contribute to, and address problems in living.

Social workers promote social justice and social change with and on behalf of clients. "Clients" is used inclusively to refer to individuals, families, groups, organizations, and communities. Social workers are sensitive to cultural and ethnic diversity and strive to end discrimination, oppression, poverty, and other forms of social injustice. These activities may be in the form of direct practice, community organizing, supervision, consultation administration, advocacy, social and political action, policy development and implementation, education, and research and evaluation. Social workers seek to enhance the capacity of people to address their own needs. Social workers also seek to promote the responsiveness of organizations, communities, and other social institutions to individuals' needs and social problems.

The mission of the social work profession is rooted in a set of core values. These core values, embraced by social workers throughout the profession's history, are the foundation of social work's unique purpose and perspective:

- service
- social justice
- dignity and worth of the person
- importance of human relationships
- integrity
- competence.

This constellation of core values reflects what is unique to the social work profession. Core values, and the principles that flow from them, must be balanced within the context and complexity of the human experience.

Ethical Principles

The following broad ethical principles are based on social work's core values of service, social justice, dignity and worth of the person, importance of human relationships, integrity, and competence. These principles set forth ideals to which all social workers should aspire.

Value: *Service*

Ethical Principle: *Social workers' primary goal is to help people in need and to address social problems.*

Social workers elevate service to others above self-interest. Social workers draw on their knowledge, values, and skills to help people in need and to address social problems. Social workers are encouraged to volunteer some portion of their professional skills with no expectation of significant financial return (pro bono service).

Value: *Social Justice*

Ethical Principle: *Social workers challenge social injustice.*

Social workers pursue social change, particularly with and on behalf of vulnerable and oppressed individuals and groups of people. Social workers' social change efforts are focused primarily on issues of poverty, unemployment, discrimination, and other forms of social injustice. These activities seek to promote sensitivity to and knowledge about oppression and cultural and ethnic diversity. Social workers strive to ensure access to needed information, services, and resources; equality of opportunity; and meaningful participation in decision making for all people.

Value: *Dignity and Worth of the Person*

Ethical Principle: *Social workers respect the inherent dignity and worth of the person.*

Social workers treat each person in a caring and respectful fashion, mindful of individual differences and cultural and ethnic diversity. Social workers promote clients' socially responsible self-determination. Social workers seek to enhance clients' capacity and opportunity to change and to address their own needs. Social workers are cognizant of their dual responsibility to clients and to the broader society. They seek to resolve conflicts between clients' interests and the broader society's interests in a socially responsible manner consistent with the values, ethical principles, and ethical standards of the profession.

Value: *Importance of Human Relationships*

Ethical Principle: *Social workers recognize the central importance of human relationships.*

Social workers understand that relationships between and among people are an important vehicle for change. Social workers engage people as partners in the helping process. Social workers seek to strengthen relationships among people in a purposeful effort to promote, restore, maintain, and enhance the well-being of individuals, families, social groups, organizations, and communities.

Value: *Integrity*

Ethical Principle: *Social workers behave in a trustworthy manner.*

(continued)

Box 2.2   NASW Code of Ethics *(continued)*

Social workers are continually aware of the profession's mission, values, ethical principles, and ethical standards and practice in a manner consistent with them. Social workers act honestly and responsibly and promote ethical practices on the part of the organizations with which they are affiliated.

Value: *Competence*

Ethical Principle: *Social workers practice within their areas of competence and develop and enhance their professional expertise.*

Social workers continually strive to increase their professional knowledge and skills and to apply them in practice. Social workers should aspire to contribute to the knowledge base of the profession.

SOURCE: NASW Code of Ethics (2008) reprinted with permission from the National Association of Social Workers, Inc.

NOTE: The full Code of Ethics is available at www.socialworkers.org/pubs/code/code.asp.

---

science theories that serve as a basis for knowing how client systems adapt and cope with client needs, and how theory guides planned social intervention. This knowledge serves as the foundation for competent social work practice.

Practice Skills

Social workers are familiar with techniques related to direct practice with individuals, families, and groups, as well as practice in organizations and communities, commonly referred to as **generalist practice**. Organizing, planning, administration, and policy analysis and advocacy are included as areas of focus for many social work practitioners. Research skills are essential for identifying unmet needs, developing human service programs, and evaluating practice effectiveness. The **Council on Social Work Education (CSWE)**, the organization that oversees social work education programs and accredits them at the bachelor's and master's levels so they can award social work degrees, requires students to demonstrate mastery of practice behaviors identified by each social work program that are relevant to the populations typically served by its graduates. These are discussed in more detail later in this chapter.

Planned Change

EP 2.1.9b

Professional social work intervention is based on a process of **planned change**. Change is indicated when clients present needs and problems that are unresolved.

Planned change is an orderly approach to addressing clients' needs and is based on assessment, knowledge of the client system's capacity for change, and focused intervention. The social worker functions as a change agent in this process.

Planned change is characterized by purpose and a greater likelihood of predictable outcomes derived from the change effort. Social workers play many different roles in facilitating client change depending on the type of client/client system and the needs being addressed (see Box 2.3). For example, Jimmy Johnson, the social worker introduced at the beginning of this chapter who works with teens who have problems with use of alcohol and other drugs, advocates for his clients to help them get needed resources, serves as a broker as he identifies possible resources, enables his clients to focus on goals that will help them be successful, facilitates groups of youth to help them support each other, mediates conflicts between youth and their parents, and evaluates the effectiveness of his work with his clients. Think about a type of social work in which you are interested. What roles might you play as a social worker focusing on planned change with clients you would be likely to serve?

Social Work Methods

EP 2.1.1a
EP 2.1.1c
EP 2.1.8a

In their roles as change agents, social workers attempt to improve the conditions that adversely affect the functioning of clients (or client systems). Change efforts may be geared toward assisting individuals, families, groups, organizations, or communities (or any combination of these), and entail appropriate methods of intervention to achieve solutions to problems. Practice methods incorporate social work: values, principles, and techniques in

- helping people obtain resources,
- providing counseling and psychotherapy to individuals or groups,

Box 2.3 Roles Played by Generalist Social Workers

Advocate: a social worker who fights for the rights and dignity of people in need of help.

Analyst or evaluator: a social worker whose role is to gather information to assess the effectiveness of work with clients or client systems and to make recommendations for change as needed.

Broker: a social worker who links client systems with existing resources, while ensuring that those resources treat client systems in a humane and effective way.

Educator: a social worker whose main task is to convey information and knowledge with the goal of developing skills—a role that can be played in many situations in addition to a classroom.

Enabler: a social worker who provides encouragement, offers hope, helps clients identify and focus on goals, and enables clients to make choices that improve their functioning.

Facilitator: a social worker who facilitates change by bringing together groups of people and helping them use their own talents as well as other resources to create positive change.

Manager: a social worker who assumes administrative responsibility for a specific project, program, or agency.

Initiator: a social worker who calls attention to an unaddressed problem or need.

Integrator or coordinator: a social worker who is tasked with bringing together various components of a system into a unified whole to create positive change.

Mediator: a social worker who helps resolve conflicts between client systems at one or more levels of the environment while playing a neutral role.

Mobilizer: a social worker who assembles, energizes, and organizes new or existing groups.

Negotiator: a social worker who advocates on behalf of a client system.

Outreach worker: a social worker who identifies specific client systems and reaches out to provide assistance.

SOURCE: Adapted from Kirst-Ashman, K., & Hull, G. (2015). *Generalist Practice with organizations and communities* (6th ed., pp. 6, 21–27). Belmont, CA: Cengage.

- helping communities or groups provide or improve social and health services, and
- participating in relevant legislative processes that affect the quality of life for all citizens.

The social work practice methods introduced next are discussed more extensively in Part 2 of this text.

Social Work with Individuals and Families (Direct Practice)

When the social worker's effort is aimed at working directly with individuals or families, the process is called **direct practice** (or sometimes casework). This method is geared toward helping individuals and families identify solutions to personal or other problems related to difficulty with social functioning. In many instances, problems related to social inadequacy, emotional conflict, interpersonal loss, social stress, or the lack of resources prevent individuals from functioning adequately. Social work practitioners are skilled in assessment and know how to intervene strategically to ameliorate these problems. Direct practice can include referral to resources and case management to ensure that they are effective in addressing a client's needs as

well as counseling and therapy. Direct practice often is considered to be therapeutic in nature.

Social work with Groups

Many social workers use groups to enrich individuals' lives through planned group experiences. These planned experiences stress the value of self-development through structured interactions with other group members. This process, based on theories of group dynamics, encourages personal growth and change through active participation as a group member. Groups may be natural (already formed), such as street gangs, or formed purposefully, such as support or therapy groups. Whatever the composition, groups facilitated by social workers emphasize the value of participation, democratic goal setting, freedom of expression, acceptance, and the development of positive attitudes through sharing. Not all groups are considered to be therapy groups; some groups are recreational or educational, for example. Group therapy is designed to be therapeutic in that it seeks to alter or diminish dysfunctional behavior through the dynamic use of group interaction. Members of a therapeutic group often share emotionally distressing experiences (e.g., a group of recent divorcees or survivors of sexual abuse) and develop options for more adaptive behaviors through focused discussion. Groups can be extremely powerful in facilitating client change, as the shared experiences of other members can help participants understand that they are not the only ones with the problem, learn from the experiences of other members, and develop a support system that extends beyond the social worker.

Community Organization

Social workers who practice at the community level draw on techniques of community organization to promote change. Recognizing that citizen awareness and support are vital to the development of resources in generating a more healthy and constructive environment for all citizens, community organizers work with established organizations within the community (such as chambers of commerce, Lions and Kiwanis Clubs, city governments, cultural groups, welfare organizations, the Junior League, political groups, social action groups, and other citizens' organizations) to gain support for needed services and secure funding to maintain them. Social workers who practice at this level typically are employed by city governments, planning agencies, councils of social agencies, or related community agencies.

Social Work Research

Although all social workers use research constantly, many social workers specialize in social work research. Research increases the knowledge base of practice as well as the effectiveness of intervention. In addition, it provides an empirical base on which to formulate more specific policies. Social research is essential in establishing a scientific framework for solving problems and refining social work practice methods. Evaluative research enables agencies and practitioners to better understand the effectiveness of efforts designed to meet the goals and objectives of their practice. Competent social work practitioners keep abreast of professional research and use research findings in their practice.

Social Work Administration and Planning

Administration and planning is a social work method that seeks to maximize the effective use of agency resources in problem solving. Administrators must be skilled in organizing, planning, and employing management techniques and be knowledgeable about social work practice. Many social agency administrators begin their careers as direct practitioners, subsequently become supervisors, and then move into administrative roles. Social planning also is seen as a social work role, which is discussed in Chapter 6.

Professional Issues in Social Work

By now you are aware that social work is a multifaceted profession and that social workers are employed in a variety of roles and settings. One of the exciting aspects of social work is the continuous growth of the profession and the opportunities provided as individual, family, organizational, community, and societal needs change. This text will discuss many of the issues that the social work profession is facing in more detail in later chapters. However, three key issues will be touched on in this section:

1) the impact of economic and technological changes on people across the globe as well as the social work profession;
2) the impact of expanding fields of practice on the profession's historical emphasis on social justice and vulnerable populations; and
3) increased demands on social agencies as more people need services.

Impact of Economic and Technological Changes

With economic and technological changes erupting rapidly during the past century, the nature of needs and problems experienced by the population has mirrored those changes. At the same time, the knowledge base of social, behavioral, and biological sciences has expanded and generated more insightful theories of human behavior. Technology and social media bring new challenges, such as an increased gap in opportunities for learning and employment between those who have access to technology and those who don't, Internet addiction, cyber bullying, and increased risk for obesity. At the same time, technology and social media present important opportunities, such as access to a wealth of information and instant communication, online therapy and medicine, and use of social media for advocacy and public awareness campaigns. New technologies have also led to an expansion of the knowledge base of the social and behavioral sciences and generated more insightful theories of human behavior. The genome mapping project, for example, has led to new discoveries in the role the brain plays in addiction and exposure to violence and other types of trauma and cellular changes that result in various types of cancer.

Impact of Expanding Fields of Practice on the Profession's Emphasis on Social Justice

In spite of the progress made over the past 100 years, a substantial number of people in the United States continue to be poor and disenfranchised. However, an increasingly complex society and the disappearance of the middle class have resulted in problems experienced by individuals, families, and communities regardless of socioeconomic status. As discussed earlier in this chapter, fields of practice offer almost limitless opportunities for social workers, ranging from prenatal health care to end-of-life care with a focus on individuals, families, groups, organizations, communities, or the broader society. Social workers provide direct services, community outreach, policy advocacy, and research. Most social workers today engage in direct practice with individuals and families. Although many work with vulnerable clients who have limited resources, social workers also serve the middle class and the wealthy, and a number of them are engaged in private practice.

Some people argue that the social work profession has abandoned the poor, oppressed, and disenfranchised (Specht & Courtney, 1995) in favor of the more esoteric practices of counseling and psychotherapy. Proponents of this belief believe that the profession, once identified as a bulwark and vanguard for the oppressed, has turned its back on social justice and community action in favor of a case-by-case approach. Others argue that social workers are effective in efforts that range from "case to cause," as their multidimensional approach makes valuable contributions in multiple arenas at all levels of the environment, ranging from clinical practice with individuals to social action. They argue that collaboration of social workers working at all levels of the environment is essential to effect positive change. Social workers providing clinical services to individuals need to be aware of macro level policies and how they impact their clients and make sure that social workers who work at organizational, community, and societal levels of the environment receive this information. In turn, social workers who work at broader levels of the environment cannot make effective decisions without knowledge of how

those decisions impact individuals and families. The debate over the appropriate role of the social work profession is not likely to end soon. We invite you to review the definition of social work and its history and consider the stance you deem most appropriate for the profession in the future.

Increased Demands on Social Agencies

Most social workers perform their professional functions through the auspices of a social agency. **Social agencies** are organizations that have been formed by states and communities to address the social needs and problems of their citizens. Agencies may be public (funded by taxes), voluntary (funded through contributions), proprietary (profit-oriented), or increasingly, a combination of all three. The typical community social agency is headed by a board of directors of local citizens and meets regularly to review the agency's activities and establish policy that governs the agency's services. Most larger agencies have an administrator who has sole responsibility for supervising the agency's activities. In smaller agencies, the administrator may be involved in assisting clients with their needs, as well.

Local agencies are community resources that stand ready to address needs that make day-to-day functioning difficult for a segment of people. Social workers are employed to carry out the agency's mission. Many agencies do not charge fees for the services they provide. In some instances, however, agencies have a "sliding-fee scale," adjusting the fee to the client's ability to pay. All clients, regardless of their economic resources, are afforded the same quality of service.

Many social workers are employed at state agencies providing child welfare, health care, mental health, or income assistance, while some work for federal agencies providing services to refugees or persons in the criminal justice system. State and federal offices are often established in local communities to increase access to their services. Still other social workers are employed at social agencies that provide international services such as the United Nations or the Red Cross.

Regardless of whether it is nonprofit or for profit or a community, state, federal, or international agency, all social agencies face increased demands on their services, staff, and finances as more and more people need services across the globe.

Typically, agencies cooperate with each other in meeting human needs. They readily make referrals when clients have needs that another agency can address more effectively. Interagency coordination is vital, maximizing resources and the strengths of different professional viewpoints to respond to unmet needs.

Education and Levels of Social Work Practice

EP 2.1.1e

Professional social workers assist clients with a wide variety of unmet needs. As a consequence, the nature and extent of skills necessary for addressing unmet needs vary with the complexities of the needs encountered. Recognizing that professional competence is a right of clients in seeking assistance, regardless of how difficult meeting their needs might be, the social work profession has developed three education levels of practice for meeting these differing needs. And the profession has established the Council on Social Work Education (CSWE), which, through its division of standards and accreditation, serves as the accrediting body for professional educational programs at the bachelor's and master's levels. There are about 490 accredited undergraduate programs and 230 accredited master's programs in the United States, with about 30 programs in candidacy to establish new programs (CSWE, 2014).

Bachelor of Social Work (BSW)

The entry level for professional social work practice is the BSW degree. Social work practitioners entering practice at this level must complete the education requirements for an undergraduate social work program accredited by the CSWE. Professional social work education programs offered by colleges and universities vary. However, CSWE mandates that, as a minimum requirement for meeting accreditation standards, each program must build on a liberal arts foundation and provide classroom and field education that enables its graduates to demonstrate mastery of 10 core competencies. The CSWE (2008) *Educational Policy and Accreditation Standards* outlines the core **competencies**, or applied knowledge and skills, that undergird social work practice. A social work practitioner must:

1. Identify as a social worker and conduct oneself accordingly;
2. Apply social work ethical principles to guide professional practice;

3. Apply critical thinking to inform and communicate professional judgments;
4. Engage diversity and difference in practice;
5. Advance human rights and social and economic justice;
6. Engage in research-informed practice and practice-based research;
7. Apply knowledge of human behavior and the social environment;
8. Engage in policy practice to advance social and economic well-being and to deliver effective social work services;
9. Respond to contexts that shape practice; and
10. Engage, assess, intervene, and evaluate with individuals, families, groups, organizations, and communities (pp. 3–6).

Social work education programs assess student mastery of these competencies through documentation of completion of practice behaviors delineated for each competency (see Box 2.4 for a description of the 41 practice behaviors suggested by CSWE for adoption or modification by individual social work programs). All students who graduate from an accredited BSW program must complete a minimum of 400 clock-hours of field experience in a social work or related setting under the supervision of a social work practitioner. Typical field placements include mental/behavioral health agencies, family violence programs, child welfare agencies, residential treatment centers, juvenile and adult probation programs, corrections facilities, public schools, substance abuse treatment programs, health clinics, hospitals, hospice programs, programs for seniors, programs for persons with disabilities, and programs for the homeless.

The education curriculum for baccalaureate-level practice is developed around a model of generalist practice, which incorporates basic social work skills used to invervene with individuals, families, groups, organizations, and communities. Typically, the generalist practitioner is knowledgeable about the ecological/systems approach (see Chapter 3 for a complete discussion) to practice and is skillful in needs assessment, interviewing, resource development, case management, use of community resources, establishment of intervention objectives with clients, and problem solving.

Entry-level social workers are employed by agencies that offer a wide spectrum of services. As generalist social workers, they may perform professional activities as eligibility workers for state human services

Box 2.4   The Social Work Curriculum and Professional Practice

The Council on Social Work Education sets forth 10 core competencies BSW and MSW graduates must master. Mastery of competencies prepares BSW graduates for generalist practice; mastery of competencies enhanced by knowledge and practice behaviors specific to a concentration prepares MSW graduates for advanced practice. Core competencies for both foundation and advanced practice and practice behaviors for foundation practice are delineated here. Note that some social work programs have modified foundation practice behaviors to fit with populations served by their graduates. Additionally, each MSW program must have specific practice behaviors for each competency that fit with each concentration its program offers.

2.1.1—Identify as a professional social worker and conduct oneself accordingly.

Social workers serve as representatives of the profession, its mission, and its core values. They know the profession's history. Social workers commit themselves to the profession's enhancement and to their own professional conduct and growth. Social workers

- advocate for client access to the services of social work;
- practice personal reflection and self-correction to ensure continual professional development;
- attend to professional roles and boundaries;
- demonstrate professional demeanor in behavior, appearance, and communication;
- engage in career-long learning; and
- use supervision and consultation.

2.1.2 Apply social work ethical principles to guide professional practice.

Social workers have an obligation to conduct themselves ethically and to engage in ethical decision making. Social workers are knowledgeable about the value base of the profession, its ethical standards, and relevant law. Social workers:

- recognize and manage personal values in a way that allows professional values to guide practice;
- make ethical decisions by applying standards of the National Association of Social Workers Code of Ethics (NASW, 2008) and, as applicable, of the International Federation of Social Workers/International Association of Schools of Social Work Ethics in Social Work, Statement of Principles

(International Federation of Social Workers and International Association of Schools of Social Work, 2004).

- tolerate ambiguity in resolving ethical conflicts; and
- apply strategies of ethical reasoning to arrive at principled decisions.

2.1.3—Apply critical thinking to inform and communicate professional judgments.

Social workers are knowledgeable about the principles of logic, scientific inquiry, and reasoned discernment. They use critical thinking augmented by creativity and curiosity. Critical thinking also requires the synthesis and communication of relevant information. Social workers

- distinguish, appraise, and integrate multiple sources of knowledge, including research-based knowledge, and practice wisdom;
- analyze models of assessment, prevention, intervention, and evaluation; and
- demonstrate effective oral and written communication in working with individuals, families, groups, organizations, communities, and colleagues.

2.1.4—Engage diversity and difference in practice.

Social workers understand how diversity characterizes and shapes the human experience and is critical to the formation of identity. The dimensions of diversity are understood as the intersection of multiple factors including age, class, color, culture, disability, ethnicity, gender, gender identity and expression, immigration status, political ideology, race, religion, sex, and sexual orientation. Social workers appreciate that, as a consequence of difference, a person's life experiences may include oppression, poverty, marginalization, and alienation as well as privilege, power, and acclaim. Social workers:

- recognize the extent to which a culture's structures and values may oppress, marginalize, alienate, or create or enhance privilege and power;
- gain sufficient self-awareness to eliminate the influence of personal biases and values in working with diverse groups;
- recognize and communicate their understanding of the importance of difference in shaping life experiences; and
- view themselves as learners and engage those with whom they work as informants.

(continued)

Box 2.4   The Social Work Curriculum and Professional Practice (continued)

2.1.5—Advance human rights and social and economic justice.

Each person, regardless of position in society, has basic human rights, such as freedom, safety, privacy, an adequate standard of living, health care, and education. Social workers recognize the global interconnections of oppression and are knowledgeable about theories of justice and strategies to promote human and civil rights. Social work incorporates social justice practices in organizations, institutions, and society to ensure that these basic human rights are distributed equitably and without prejudice. Social workers:

- understand the forms and mechanisms of oppression and discrimination;
- advocate for human rights and social and economic justice; and
- engage in practices that advance social and economic justice.

2.1.6—Engage in research-informed practice and practice-informed research.

Social workers use practice experience to inform research, employ evidence-based interventions, evaluate their own practice, and use research findings to improve practice, policy, and social service delivery. Social workers comprehend quantitative and qualitative research and understand scientific and ethical approaches to building knowledge. Social workers:

- use practice experience to inform scientific inquiry and
- use research evidence to inform practice

2.1.7—Apply knowledge of human behavior and the social environment.

Social workers are knowledgeable about human behavior across the life course; the range of social systems in which people live; and the ways social systems promote or deter people in maintaining or achieving health and well-being. Social workers apply theories and knowledge from the liberal arts to understand biological, social, cultural, psychological, and spiritual development. Social workers:

- use conceptual frameworks to guide the processes of assessment, intervention, and evaluation; and
- critique and apply knowledge to understand person and environment.

2.1.8—Engage in policy practice to advance social and economic well-being and to deliver effective social services.

Social work practitioners understand that policy affects service delivery, and they actively engage in policy practice. Social workers know the history and current structures of social policies and services; the role of policy in service delivery; and the role of practice in policy development. Social workers:

- analyze, formulate, and advocate for policies that advance social well-being; and
- collaborate with colleagues and clients for effective policy action.

2.1.9—Respond to contexts that shape practice.

Social workers are informed, resourceful, and proactive in responding to evolving organizational, community, and societal contexts at all levels of practice. Social workers recognize that the context of practice is dynamic, and use knowledge and skill to respond proactively. Social workers:

- continuously discover, appraise, and attend to changing locales, populations, scientific and technological developments, and emerging societal trends to provide relevant services; and
- provide leadership in promoting sustainable changes in service delivery and practice to improve the quality of social services.

2.1.10(a)–(d)—Engage, assess, intervene, and evaluate with individuals, families, groups, organizations, and communities.

Professional practice involves the dynamic and interactive processes of engagement, assessment, intervention, and evaluation at multiple levels. Social workers have the knowledge and skills to practice with individuals, families, groups, organizations, and communities. Practice knowledge includes identifying, analyzing, and implementing evidence-based interventions designed to achieve client goals; using research and technological advances; evaluating program outcomes and practice effectiveness; developing, analyzing, advocating, and providing leadership for policies and services; and promoting social and economic justice.

(continued)

Box 2.4   The Social Work Curriculum and Professional Practice (continued)

2.1.10(a)—Engagement
Social workers:

- substantively and affectively prepare for action with individuals, families, groups, organizations, and communities;
- use empathy and other interpersonal skills; and
- develop a mutually agreed-on focus of work and desired outcomes.

2.1.10(b)—Assessment
Social workers:

- collect, organize, and interpret client data;
- assess client strengths and limitations;
- develop mutually agreed-on intervention goals and objectives; and
- select appropriate intervention strategies.

2.1.10(c)—Intervention
Social workers:

- initiate actions to achieve organizational goals;
- implement prevention interventions that enhance client capacities;
- help clients resolve problems;
- negotiate, mediate, and advocate for clients; and
- facilitate transitions and endings.

2.1.10(d)—Evaluation
Social workers critically analyze, monitor, and evaluate interventions.

Professional practice involves the dynamic and interactive processes of engagement, assessment, intervention, and evaluation at multiple levels. Social workers have the knowledge and skills to practice with individuals, families, groups, organizations, and communities. Practice knowledge includes identifying, analyzing, and implementing evidence-based interventions designed to achieve client goals; using research and technological advances; evaluating program outcomes and practice effectiveness; developing, analyzing, advocating, and providing leadership for policies and services; and promoting social and economic justice.

Educational Policy 2.1.10(a)—Engagement
Social workers:

- substantively and affectively prepare for action with individuals, families, groups, organizations, and communities;
- use empathy and other interpersonal skills; and
- develop a mutually agreed-on focus of work and desired outcomes.

Educational Policy 2.1.10(b)—Assessment
Social workers:

- collect, organize, and interpret client data;
- assess client strengths and limitations;
- develop mutually agreed-on intervention goals and objectives; and
- select appropriate intervention strategies.

Educational Policy 2.1.10(c)—Intervention
Social workers:

- initiate actions to achieve organizational goals;
- implement prevention interventions that enhance client capacities;
- help clients resolve problems;
- negotiate, mediate, and advocate for clients; and
- facilitate transitions and endings.

Educational Policy 2.1.10(d)—Evaluation
Social workers critically analyze, monitor, and evaluate interventions.

SOURCE: Council on Social Work Education (2010). *Educational Policy and Accreditation Standards* (p. 1). Washington, DC: Author.

departments; work with children, families, and the elderly as protective services (protecting children and the elderly from abuse and neglect) workers; serve as youth or adult probation workers; work in institutional care agencies that provide services for children or adults, especially the elderly; engage in school social work; work with persons who are homeless in shelters and outreach programs; act as program workers or planners for areawide agencies on aging; work in behavioral/mental health outreach centers or institutions; assist refugees in war-torn countries; and perform professional tasks in many other agencies providing human services. Baccalaureate-level professionals with experience and demonstrated competence frequently are promoted to supervisory and administrative positions.

Professional activities performed by BSW social workers to help their clients are challenging and rewarding. Many social workers prefer to practice at this level throughout their careers. For others, an advanced degree in social work is desirable and opens up areas of practice that typically are not in the domain of BSW practitioners.

For those who have completed their undergraduate social work education from an accredited college or university, the school of social work to which they apply may grant advanced standing. Although not all graduate schools accept advanced-standing students, CSWE provides a listing of those that do. When admitted to a graduate program, advanced-standing students are able to shorten the time required to secure a master's degree in social work without diluting the quality of their educational experience.

Master of Social Work (MSW): Advanced Practice

Advanced practice in social work is predicated upon receiving the master's degree in social work (MSW). Students in master's degree programs in social work programs are engaged in an education curriculum that is more specialized than the BSW curriculum. Most programs offer foundation coursework that focuses on generalist practice knowledge, skills and values, with courses then completed in one or more concentrations that build on foundation coursework. Some programs offer concentrations organized by method of practice, while others offer concentrations organized by field of practice. Although the most common concentration by method of practice offered is direct practice/clinical social work, others include community organization, social policy, and program evaluation. Concentrations offered by field of practice include children, youth and families; mental health; aging/gerontology; school social work, health; substance abuse/addiction; criminal justice; disabilities; housing; international/global/immigration; military social work; research, and occupational social work. Some programs focus on advanced generalist practice or organize their curriculum around thematic areas such as social justice or cultural competence.

Many graduate social work programs offer dual degree programs in law, public health, theology, public policy, public administration, or business, while others offer certificate programs in aging/gerontology, school social work, play therapy, substance abuse, and nonprofit management. CSWE's website (http://www.cswe.org) provides information on all accredited BSW and MSW programs in the United States, including concentrations and certificate programs offered (CSWE, 2014).

The master's degree program is typically a two-year program, balanced between classroom learning and field practice. Graduates seek employment in specialized settings such as Veterans Administration and other hospitals; mental/behavioral health agencies and child guidance clinics; family and children's service agencies, including military programs for troops and their families; legislative committees; government research units; policy advocacy organizations; and related settings that require specialized professional education. MSW graduates must master the same basic core competencies and similar practice behaviors as those expected of BSW level social workers (see Box 2.4), as well as a set of advanced practice behaviors determined by each social work program that fit with the mission of its respective university and program and the populations likely to be served by its graduates.

Doctorate in Social Work (DSW and PhD)

Professional social workers who are interested in social work education, highly advanced clinical practice, research, planning, or administration often seek advanced study in doctor of social work (DSW) or doctor of philosophy in social work (PhD) programs. Approximately 50 schools of social work in the United States offer education at this level. Students who are admitted are often seasoned social work practitioners, although this is not a prerequisite for admission to all schools. However, because knowledge of social work practice is a critical aspect of social work education, social work faculty who teach practice courses must have a minimum of 2 years of practice experience after completing their MSW.

Education at the PhD level stresses research, advanced clinical practice, advanced theory, administration, and social welfare policy. Graduates usually seek employment on the faculty of schools of social work, in the administration of social welfare agencies, or, with increasing frequency, in private clinical practice.

Licensure and NASW Membership

Social work professionals with BSWs, MSWs, and PhDs or DSWs are strongly encouraged to maintain membership in the NASW as well as social work licensure in the state in which they practice. In fact, in many states, it is illegal to call yourself a social worker if you are not licensed or certified. Regulation of professional practice to ensure that social workers practice ethically and competently is critical for the protection of clients as well as the profession (ASWB, 2014). Social work practice is regulated by state law, with requirements and titles for licensure or certification varying by state.

Social work professionals at the BSW level are eligible for full membership in NASW and can be licensed in many states if they take and pass state BSW-level credentialing exams. In most states, MSW graduates may be licensed as LMSW social workers (licensed MSW) or CMSW (certified MSW) after taking and passing a test administered by a state oversight board. After working under the supervision of an advanced social worker for a specified amount of time (often 2 years), MSW-level social workers in many states can take an advanced social work exam and then be licensed at the advanced-practitioner level. In some states, two types of advanced licensing can be obtained, advanced clinical social worker (licensed clinical social worker) and advanced practitioner for those engaged in macro practice. A number of jobs, including those as military social workers, require clinical social work licensure. Some states have reciprocity and honor licensure from other states. All states have a designated state agency that oversees social work licensure or certification. The Association of Social Work Boards (ASWB) is owned and operated by state regulatory agencies that oversee social work licensure and provides state licensing examinations. Information about ASWB can be found at http://www.aswb.org/. Licensed social workers must maintain licensure by completing a number of continuing education credits in a variety of topic areas, including ethics, each year.

NASW also has a number of certification programs for which MSW social workers can qualify, including advanced hospice and palliative care (care focused on reducing pain and suffering of persons who are seriously ill); clinical and macro social work practice in gerontology; advanced work with children, youth, and families; advanced work in health care; clinical alcohol, tobacco, and other drugs social worker; advanced social work case manager; and school social work specialist. BSW graduates can seek certification in hospice and palliative care, gerontology, children youth and families,

and case management. NASW also offers continuing education programs at the local, state, and national level in which many social workers participate to maintain licensure (2014).

Careers in Social Work

EP 2.1.1c

Social workers held about 607,300 jobs in the United States in 2012 (U.S. Bureau of Labor Statistics, 2014b). Social work is a growing profession; employment for social workers is expected to grow much faster than the average for all occupations through 2022. All occupations are expected to grow by 11%, while social work is expected to grow by 19%, with 114,100 positions added. New positions are being created in addition to the vacancies created through attrition. Areas that are experiencing growth include health care and social services.

Social work is an ideal profession for individuals who are interested in working with people and helping them address their needs. These broad interests are the heart of the social work profession. Positions in a wide variety of areas continue to attract social workers at all levels of practice, such as child welfare, health, corrections, developmental disabilities, family counseling, substance abuse, and public assistance programs (see Box 2.5 to learn more about the diverse settings in which social workers practice). There has been a marked increase in the number of social workers employed by the military, as either active-duty officers or as a civil service or contract employee. Most of these social workers are required to have advanced clinical certification that enables them to work with the thousands of soldiers who have returned from Afghanistan and Iraq with traumatic brain injury, posttraumatic stress disorder, severe depression, or some combination of the three.

Wages in social work are becoming more competitive than they have been in the past, with increases based on skill and experience. According to the U.S. Bureau of Labor Statistics (2014a; 2014b), the median annual income of all social workers in the United States in 2012 was $44,200, ranging from a median income of $39,980 for those employed in mental health and drug and alcohol settings to $50,000 for those employed in medical and public health settings. The *Occupational Outlook Handbook* (available at http://www.bls.gov/ooh/community-and-social-service/social-workers.htm) gives data on current median incomes of social workers employed in various settings. Median entry salaries vary,

Box 2.5   The Power of Service

Everywhere, social workers provide practical and compassionate guidance to individuals confronting and resolving personal dilemmas. Every day, over half a million professional social workers bring hope, help, and opportunity for success into people's lives.

Community: To increase the capacity of individuals to address their own needs, social workers frequently connect people with critical community resources. They are skillful at providing the right tools to help their clients cope with and solve most severe challenges.

NASW members assist people of all ages in many different situations, and can be found working in a variety of settings:

Elementary, middle and high schools
Public health agencies
Family service agencies
Community action agencies
Child and adult care centers
Private clinical practices
Foundations
Armed Forces
Policy making organizations
Corporate employee assistance programs

Disaster relief organizations
Veterans services
Local, state, and national government Hospitals
Domestic violence centers
Child welfare agencies
Psychiatric facilities
Rehabilitation facilities
Emergency assistance organizations
Drug treatment clinics
Home care agencies
Community mental health centers
Senior citizen centers
Developmental disabilities centers
Jails and prisons
Colleges and universities
Career centers
Legal service agencies
Homeless shelters
Hospices and nursing homes

SOURCE: National Association of Social Workers (2002). *The power of social work.* Washington, DC: Author, p. 4. Available from http://www.naswdc.org/nasw/nasw.pdf.

depending on experience, degree, location, and place of employment. For example, schools, hospitals, and government agencies are more likely to pay higher salaries than local nonprofit agencies, and social workers with graduate degrees are more likely to earn higher salaries than BSW graduates. Many social workers in high-level administrative jobs earn upward of $100,000 annually.

Mobility often is a valuable asset to the social worker who is looking for an initial social work job. Rural areas have a shortage of social workers, whereas metropolitan areas tend to have a tighter employment market. Being bilingual is also an advantage in many geographic locations. Employment vacancies sometimes are listed with college placement services, state employment commissions, professional associations, state agencies, local newspapers, or Internet sites. Many social work students are hired just prior to graduation because of the network that exists among students, universities, and field practicum agencies. In recent years, more social workers with advanced degrees in social work have engaged in **private practice**. Unlike more traditionally employed social workers, private practitioners must rely on fees from their

clients to support their practices. Social workers in private practice often spend most of their time employed by a social agency and see clients in private practice on a part-time basis. Others practice full-time. Generally, private practice is directed to clients in need of counseling or group therapy. Private practitioners are governed by the NASW Code of Ethics and the social work value base. They extend their services to clients who may not seek assistance through traditional agency networks. Many private practitioners provide some services **pro bono** (meaning "for the public good" and at no cost) to clients who otherwise could not afford them.

Collaboration with Other Helping Professions

EP 2.1.8b

Social workers are not alone in assisting people who face challenges. The unique skills of other helping professionals can be beneficial in addressing needs outside the realm of the social worker's skill and knowledge base or inappropriate for social work intervention. One key role of social workers is to refer clients to other resources. Thus, social workers have to be aware of the different types of helping professionals and the roles they typically play in working with people.

Frequently, social workers are part of a collaborative effort with other professionals who assist individuals, families, groups, or communities in finding solutions to problems or in establishing prevention programs. For example, a school social worker, school counselor, clinical psychologist, and school nurse might combine their professional expertise in developing a program to prevent teenage pregnancy. Or a social worker might work with a pastoral counselor and a psychiatrist to help a former client with emotional problems become reestablished into community life.

Social workers often facilitate or participate in case staffings as members of **multidisciplinary teams**. At these staffings, professionals and sometimes the client meet to determine what the client's strengths and needs are, how best to maximize the strengths to address the identified needs, and who should be involved in addressing which needs. Multidisciplinary teams maximize the strengths and expertise of each professional on the team to avoid duplication of effort, divergent interventions that might be at cross-purposes, and gaps in service to clients. Although professional teamwork in many instances enhances the opportunities for clients and furthers the opportunities for successful intervention, it is the social workers' responsibility to guard the integrity of the referral process when seeking the expertise of resources to which they refer their clients.

Other Professionals Likely to Collaborate with Social Workers

Other community professionals who practice in the area of human services include psychiatrists, psychologists, sociologists, licensed professional counselors, school counselors, rehabilitation specialists, chemical dependency counselors, pastoral counselors, employment counselors, nurses, and attorneys. Most of these professionals have their own educational requirements, mandated licensing or certification standards, and professional organization.

Psychiatrists   **Psychiatry** is a field of medical practice that specializes in behavioral health, addressing mental and emotional problems experienced by individuals. Psychiatrists are physicians with a concentration in mental and emotional disorders. Unlike other professionals who assist with psychological and emotional problems, as well as those of social dysfunction, psychiatrists can provide medications in cases when symptoms indicate the need for them. Because psychiatrists have a medical degree, they have at their disposal a wide array of medical interventions as well as expertise in treating problems of a mental and emotional nature. Social workers in mental health and health-care settings often work with psychiatrists collaboratively to assess a client and identify issues to be addressed, with the psychiatrist prescribing and monitoring medication and the social worker providing therapy to the client.

Psychologists   **Psychologists** often work with social workers in assisting clients. Unlike psychiatrists, professional psychologists are not physicians. Psychologists who assist with clients' psychological and emotional problems generally are referred to as clinical or counseling psychologists. While social workers use many of the same approaches in their work with clients, psychologists are more likely to focus on the intrapsychic and behavioral aspects of a client. A social worker is more likely to take a person-in-environment approach, working with the client to identify problems in relationships, work, school, or family or other aspects of the client's environment that are impeding the person's ability to function successfully. Many individuals who have been clients of both psychologists and social workers say there is often little difference between the two, and it is the quality of the relationship with the helping professional that is important and not the degree. In fact, many social workers and psychologists work together in school, mental health, health, and private clinics, sometimes with the same clients. For example, two clinicians may see individual members of a family in counseling sessions, while a third may provide family counseling.

Some psychologists use **psychometric instruments** (testing) to help diagnose problems and provide helpful information to social workers and other professionals about clients and their functioning, which may not be readily observable during a client interview. Results of the tests provide a basis for establishing a personality profile for including client strengths, and to gain insights into a client's ability to handle stress and areas in which the client is vulnerable. This service frequently is helpful in gaining insights into clients and establishing appropriate treatment and intervention plans. For example, a school psychologist may test a child to identify possible learning or emotional disabilities, while a school social worker might work with the teacher and the parent in implementing suggested recommendations to improve the child's ability to learn successfully or refer the family to other needed community resources.

Sociologists   **Sociologists** engage in the study of society, its organization, and the phenomena arising out of group relations. As such, professionals in this area contribute much to the awareness of human interaction, including establishment of norms, values, social organization, patterns of behavior, and social institutions. Sociologists are skilled in research techniques and methods. Most are employed at institutions of higher education and related educational institutions, although a growing number of them are entering the field of clinical, or applied, sociology. Clinical or applied sociologists work in criminal justice or child welfare settings, often in concert with social workers. Rather than provide direct counseling services to clients, they are more likely to be involved in community organization, conflict resolution, and administration.

Pastoral Counselors   Perhaps no other single source of contact by people with problems is sought more often than religious leaders. Priests, pastors, ministers, rabbis, and others in positions of spiritual leadership are called on readily by members of their congregations and others in trouble. Pastoral counselors frequently serve as members of multidisciplinary teams with social workers. As spiritual leaders, they tend to be trusted by their congregations and are presumed to have an extraordinary understanding of human frailty and a special ability to communicate with spiritual powers. Professional **pastoral counselors** typically are educated at schools of theology that offer a specialization in counseling. Social workers work collaboratively with pastoral counselors in many settings. Some religious organizations like Methodist Ministries, Lutheran Social Services, and Catholic Charities employ both social workers and persons with degrees in theology and counseling. Many hospice programs also provide teams of helping professionals that work with individuals and families, including a social worker and a pastoral counselor.

School and Rehabilitation Counselors   School counselors and rehabilitation counselors are valuable allies of social workers. School counselors are vital on teams of professionals who work with school-age children and their families. If they are employed in public schools, school counselors may be required to have classroom teaching experience in addition to graduate education before they are eligible for certification as counselors by state education agencies. Counselors in school settings assist students with education-related problems and in locating education resources that are best suited to their individual interests. Many students with behavioral problems, as well as those with academic difficulties, are referred to the school counselor for assistance. In many instances, counselors work with teachers to address specific classroom behavior issues, although social workers in some school settings also perform these tasks. Social workers also link children and families to community resources and collaborate with school personnel to bring these resources to the school setting, for example, facilitators that provide groups on grief and loss or educational programs on bullying.

Counselors also are employed in correctional systems, where they help inmates assess the attitudes and skills they need to obtain productive employment after they are released from prison. This type of intervention benefits from collaboration with other members of the correctional team, including social workers, who often network with the inmates' families as well as community social service agencies.

Social workers, especially those involved with individuals with disabilities and their families, often work with rehabilitation counselors. Most states have established agencies to help individuals with physical or mental disabilities identify competencies and secure academic or vocational training that will enable them to find employment. Counselors from these agencies also help clients obtain specialized medical treatment to enhance their physical, mental, and social capacities. Rehabilitation counselors are heavily involved in teamwork and networking with social workers and other human and vocational service workers to secure resources for clients that will enable them to achieve their productive potential.

Nurses   Social workers, particularly those who are employed in health and mental health settings, work closely with nurses on many occasions. In recent years, the role of nurses has changed dramatically, and they frequently have administrative roles in mental health programs that serve clients with substance abuse and mental health problems. Traditionally viewed as "doctors' helpers" or as pseudoprofessionals whose primary responsibility was to make sure that doctors' orders were dutifully carried out, contemporary nurses have emerged as professionals in their own right. Nurse practitioners, who have advanced training similar to that required to be a physician's assistant, also can prescribe medication.

Schools of nursing now incorporate the psychosocial aspects of services to impaired or hospitalized clients along with mastery of the basic skills related to patient care. Nurses specialize in a variety of areas such as pediatrics, gerontology, psychiatry and mental health, and oncology.

Attorneys-at-Law   Social workers work with lawyers in civil and criminal matters with clients and as key members of state and local agencies, ensuring that the agency is meeting its legal mandate in serving clients. Lawyers engage in both civil and criminal matters to assist individuals in securing their rights under the law.

Many communities have established legal aid clinics that offer legal counsel to the poor or near-poor, addressing problems such as divorce, child custody, citizenship and immigration issues, tenants' rights, and adequate defense in a court of law. These clinics are an invaluable resource for the poor. Many lawyers are employed as full-time legal counselors at the clinics, and others work part-time or volunteer their time. Legal aid clinics promote justice for the poor as well as for those in better financial circumstances. Typically, law firms assign a portion of their staff time to pro bono efforts, representing indigent clients.

Other Helping Professionals   Social workers interact with many other helping professionals. Those who work in health-care settings are likely to be involved with physicians, nutritionists, physical and occupational therapists, cardio-care specialists, and transplant specialists, depending on the nature of the health-care area in which they work. Those who work with clients who need help finding jobs are likely to work with employment counselors, who assist clients in assessing skill levels, in determining appropriate education and job training options, and in finding and maintaining employment successfully. Social workers in schools, juvenile and adult criminal justice programs, and child protective services programs are likely to work with law enforcement officers, judges, and others, besides attorneys, who are involved with the legal system. Social workers who are involved with children are likely to work with teachers and school administrators, child-care providers, and early childhood intervention specialists. Indeed, to serve clients effectively, social workers rely heavily on other professionals from various disciplines.

The Need for Professional Diversity

Although the brief discussion of selected professions involved with social workers is by no means complete, it does encompass the primary disciplinary areas in the human services field. Social workers and others in the helping professions must develop awareness of the expertise available in their practice area. The issues that many clients face require the attention of helping professionals from diverse areas of practice to move toward resolution. If clients are to receive maximum benefit from those who assist them, professionals must develop an awareness of their own limitations as practitioners as well as their strengths.

In our complex, highly technological society, specialization is necessary. With the explosion of knowledge and our understanding of human needs fostered by advances in technology, no one person can master it all. Just as society is complex, so are human beings. Values differ, as do the diverse groups with whom we hold an identity. In response to these diverse needs, specialty areas have emerged to help professionals understand and apply the theoretical explanations of behavior. Invariably, all of us will encounter problems for which no ready solutions seem apparent. Often, the friendly advice of a neighbor, spouse, or confidant is sufficient to provide the perspective that will lead to an acceptable solution. At other times, professional assistance is essential.

One frequently asked question relates to how the professions are alike and different. With a specific client, for example, what does a psychiatrist do that is different from what a psychologist would do? Or a social worker? Or a pastoral counselor?

Several specialties might engage, for example, in marriage counseling or assist a family struggling with the behavioral problems of an adolescent. To an uninformed observer, the professional response to those problems might seem to be about the same. The client sees the professional for an hour or so each week, the interaction consists primarily of verbal interaction, and the client typically is assigned specific tasks to work on before the next visit. The professional may contact other social systems, such as the school or the employment system, related to the client's functioning. What then, constitutes the difference?

In part, although not exclusively, the difference may lie in the theoretical perspective that the professional brings to address the problem. The specialized emphasis on individual psychodynamics as reflected in psychiatry and psychology often varies with the emphasis of social work on the ecological/systems framework and the relationship between the person and the environment within which the person functions. Also, the emphasis of social work on using community resources is distinct from the approaches typically used in psychiatry and psychology.

Social work advocates a holistic approach with a goal of enhancing the client's strengths (see Box 2.6). Recognizing that stress may be generated by a lack of resources as well as intrapsychic conflict, social workers may offer their clients concrete resources, such as locating a job, adequate housing, health-care services, childcare, or other needed services. Once those resource issues are addressed, a social worker could then provide therapy to focus on any identified intrapsychic conflicts, or, depending on the field of practice, make a referral to another social worker or helping professional. The different roles that the generalist social work practitioner plays, such as advocate, broker, enabler, case manager, and intervener, may be essential to creating an environment in which individual clients as well as families and communities eventually can address their own needs.

Social workers may be the ones who provide the links to other professionals involved with a case and often are more attuned than professionals in other disciplines to the need for collaboration. Social work takes a systemic approach to intervention, and the importance of collaboration and case management is emphasized at all levels of professional training. One of the first questions social workers ask the client prior to developing an intervention strategy is: "Who else is involved?" followed by, "Who is not involved and who should be?"

Some individuals are seen by a helping professional in isolation, and it is left to them to consider who else they might want to ask for help. Or they might receive a suggestion for a referral but are too overwhelmed, intimidated, or concerned about issues such as cost to follow up. Social workers play key roles in suggesting possible resources and linking clients to other helping professionals who can best meet their needs. In still other situations, clients may be working with multiple resources but those resources are unaware that others are involved. This could represent duplication of services and place undue strain on clients if they receive conflicting information or suggestions from different service providers.

One of the authors worked for an agency that received a referral about a family that had moved to the area. The family was about to be evicted from housing because of failure to adhere to housing policies. Also, the children were enrolled in multiple schools, and most were having difficulty. Some were in special education classes, two older children had come to the attention of the juvenile court, and a number of child neglect reports had been registered with the local child protection agency.

When the author called a meeting of the staffs from the six agencies she knew were involved with the family, 26 different personnel from 19 different agencies arrived at the meeting! The helping professionals present immediately realized how many personnel were involved and the different messages they had been giving the family, and they were not surprised when they were told that the family had resorted to keeping the shades drawn and refused to answer the door to any outsiders. Fortunately, with coordinated case management from a social worker charged with overseeing the case, agreed-upon goals by the family and the agencies involved, and fewer personnel working with the family, trust was established with the family and its members made significant gains.

Social workers frequently coordinate case staffings of those involved with a case, including the client(s), when appropriate. To address the needs of one family, a social worker might participate in a staffing that includes the client and extended family members and personnel from schools, hospitals, law enforcement, the court system, child protective services, and religious organizations.

An atmosphere of cooperation and respect among the helping professions is necessary to attain the optimal helping environment. Social workers often have clients who need psychiatric treatment or the special

Box 2.6   The Power of Relationships

Social workers are trained to make a positive impact in difficult situations. They do it because they want to improve lives. And they know that when social work succeeds, a lot of good things can happen:

Problems get solved
Prevention outweighs treatment
Families function
Children find parents
Sex becomes safer
Lights stay on
Stress is managed
Communities unite
Neighbors compromise
Life gets manageable
Homes stay heated
Homes are restored
Education is valued
Fears shrink
Sympathy becomes empathy
Prisoners don't go back
Exceptional people live normally
Battered people find shelter
Children are immunized
Doors are opened
Houses become homes
Teens come off the streets
Marriages are restored
Beliefs are respected
People learn to love
Children are adopted

Children play safely
Anxiety decreases
Homeless people find shelter
Immigrants are welcomed
Self-esteem increases
Friends are made
People help themselves
Families reunite
Barriers are hurdled
Emotions are healed
People die with dignity
Differences are valued
Violence stops
Hammers build houses
Health care is accessible
Disabilities are surmounted
Jobs get filled
Drugs aren't abused
Kids get clothes
Abuse is exposed
Goals are accomplished
Justice is served
Seniors find companions
Loneliness is lifted
People stay sober
Relationships work

Source: National Association of Social Workers (2002). *The power of social work.* Washington, DC: Author, p. 7. Available from http://www.naswdc.org/nasw/nasw.pdf.

services available from a clinical or counseling psychologist or pastoral counselor. Other clients are assisted by referral to an employment counselor. Students who are having difficulty in school can benefit from referral to a school counselor. At the community level, social workers, church leaders, and medical practitioners might collaborate to organize health fairs or immunization clinics, while attorneys might join in a collaborative effort to assist immigrants in establishing citizenship. Social workers are at the forefront across the globe collaborating with diverse groups when some type of crisis occurs such as a hurricane or act of human violence. Professionals who work together and look at the situations through different lenses can achieve more positive

outcomes for clients and communities than if their services were provided independently. For example, a law enforcement officer involved in a situation of alleged child abuse would try to determine whether a crime had been committed and what legal steps might be necessary to ensure the child's safety. A social worker in the same case would be interested in the child's safety but would not be involved directly in arresting a perpetrator. A medical professional would attend to the child's physical and mental health and would provide medical treatment. A social worker would be concerned about the child's physical and mental health but would not provide direct medical treatment. The social worker would focus on the holistic strengths and needs of the child and his or her family, working closely with both law enforcement officers and medical professionals. All of these professionals might collaborate together to organize community-wide efforts to provide education about abuse and neglect and advocate for additional prevention and intervention programs.

Clearly, the professions discussed in this section overlap, but the specific characteristics of each ultimately should result in positive benefits to clients served. Each profession has its own distinct professional culture, and being aware of these differing cultures should promote more appropriate referrals and foster collaboration rather than isolation or competition. Positive interaction and collaboration among professionals enrich the service systems and improve intervention with clients and communities in need.

The Baccalaureate Social Worker and Other Professions

Baccalaureate social workers (those holding the BSW degree) typically function as generalist practitioners and hold a unique position in the professional community. Their attention to a wide variety of human needs demands skills as counselors, resource finders, case managers, evaluators, advocates, brokers, enablers, and problem solvers. The BSW social worker's awareness of community resources and the ability to use them skillfully in problem solving are valuable tools in securing the needed assistance for clients. These social workers are employed in various social service agencies and community settings.

In a case that presents multiple problems and requires intervention by a number of different helping professionals, the BSW social worker may become engaged as a case manager, with primary responsibility for securing referrals to appropriate resources. The social worker, too, may become involved in providing the necessary supports to ensure that the client uses the services. In this role, the BSW social worker would continue to monitor and coordinate the intervention effort, with the cooperation of all components of the intervention system.

The BSW social worker may serve as a vital link among community professionals. The knowledge related to individual, family, group, organizational, and community functioning within the context of the ecological/systems framework helps this social worker identify the appropriate referral resources, engage them, and become an essential component in the helping process.

The Graduate-Degreed Social Worker and Other Professions

While a social worker with an MSW degree may provide many of the same functions in working with other community professionals as a social worker with a BSW, as an advanced practitioner they can provide additional services. MSW level social workers are less likely to be engaged in case management and resource referral than BSW social workers. They are typically more skilled in assessment and intervention strategies and can specialize by providing individual, group or family therapy; serving as administrators of multidisciplinary agencies; conducting evaluative research to help all professionals become more effective in service delivery; and organizing community programs and projects.

Social workers with PhDs often collaborate with other professionals in teaching and research though many also provide high level clinical or macro services to clients and communities. Because social work draws on multiple sources of knowledge, social workers are adept at bridging various perspectives and bring a holistic approach to collaborative efforts. This approach is critical in generating new knowledge through teaching and research as well as work with clients. Regardless of whether social workers hold BSW, MSW, or PhD degrees, they are respected members of the helping profession who bring a unique and important perspective to their work with individuals, families, groups, organizations, communities, and the broader society.

The Importance of Self-Care for Social Workers and Other Helping Professionals

EP 2.1.1c

Although social work is a rewarding profession, it brings many challenges. Many social workers serve clients who are survivors of painful life experiences and/or must respond to crisis situations. Social workers often experience large client caseloads, time constraints and deadlines, and limited resources. The need to take care of themselves is critical if social workers and other helping professionals are to be effective in working with their clients. NASW has issued a statement emphasizing the importance of professional **self-care** "... in promoting the practice of professional self-care, a repertoire of self-care strategies is essential to support the social worker in preventing, addressing, and coping with the natural, yet unwanted, consequences of helping" (Lopez, 2007, cited in NASW, 2009, p. 269). Self-care strategies include attention to diet, exercise, and sleep patterns; engaging in stress-management techniques; "having a life" beyond the job, and taking adequate time off. Workplaces can also support self-care through supportive supervision, staff retreats and team-building efforts, and policies that support social workers' abilities to do their jobs effectively. "Professional self-care is an essential component in competent, compassionate, and ethical social work practice, requiring time, energy, and commitment" (NASW, 2009, p. 269). Some individuals are drawn to social work because they have experienced their own painful life experiences. It is important for social workers to address those issues, often done through counseling, so that their own issues and experiences do not interfere with their ability to work effectively with clients.

Summary

Social work is a complex profession, relying on a strong value base and clearly defined code of ethics. The social worker has to develop skills in direct practice, community organization, and research, as well as in administration and planning. All social work practice is based on knowledge of human behavior and social organizations.

Clients' problems and needs stem from factors including heredity and genetics, socialization, cultural differences, environmental factors, and gaps in the opportunity structure. Social workers use a holistic approach to enhance the well-being of individuals, families, groups, organizations, communities, and the broader society, gathering information about these factors that they then draw upon to determine appropriate intervention strategies.

Social work is the primary profession that is instrumental in administering planned change within the social welfare system. Change can occur with individual clients, their families, groups, organizations, and communities, as well as at the societal level. Social workers are engaged at all levels of the environment to address the social welfare needs identified in Chapter 1, including poverty, mental health, and child welfare.

Social work as a profession draws on early work of the Charity Organization Society and its emphases on individual assessment and coordinated plans of service, and the settlement house movement and its emphases on community-based services and advocacy for members of vulnerable populations. Three major practice methods of social work have emerged over the years: social casework, social group work, and community organization. In 1955, proponents of these three practice methods merged to form the National Association of Social Workers (NASW), the major professional organization for social workers, which promotes quality in practice and advocates for the profession and the members of society it serves. NASW maintains a Code of Ethics to which all members of the profession are expected to adhere.

The Council on Social Work Education (CSWE) is the national organization that oversees social work education. In collaboration with NASW, CSWE has worked to ensure that social work education incorporates the values and ethics of the profession, a common body of knowledge that builds on a liberal arts base, and planned change. Regardless of which social work program students attend, CSWE mandates that all BSW and MSW students complete coursework that results in demonstrated mastery of competencies and practice behaviors to receive their respective social work degrees.

Social workers are known for their roles as problem-solvers, collaborators and case managers. Using a holistic approach that focuses on the relationship between the client and the broader environment in which the client functions, social workers collaborate with other helping professionals, including psychiatrists, psychologists, sociologists, pastoral counselors, school and rehabilitation counselors, employment counselors, nurse practitioners, and attorneys. Social workers often serve as case managers, coordinating services to ensure that the client receives what is needed. They also facilitate case staffings as members of multidisciplinary teams, in which all professionals and often clients and their families participate to determine clients' strengths and needs and how best to maximize resources to address the identified needs. In our complex society, many professionals with specialized knowledge often are needed to best serve a client. Across the globe, social workers are often at the forefront of collaborative efforts to provide and enhance services to individuals, families, groups, organizations and communities.

Competency Notes

EP 2.1.1a: Advocate for client access to the services of social work (pp. 26, 32). One important social work role is advocacy for client access to services on behalf of individuals, families, groups, and communities.

EP 2.1.1c: Attend to professional roles and boundaries (pp. 26, 32, 41, 48). Social workers engage in multiple professional roles and attend to professional boundaries across all levels of the environment in their work with individuals, families, groups, organizations, and communities.

EP 2.1.1e: Engage in career-long learning (p. 36). Social workers engage in career-long learning, committing themselves to personal and professional growth throughout their careers.

EP 2.1.2a: Recognize and manage personal values in a way that allows professional values to guide practice (p. 29). Social workers are aware of the impact of personal values on their work with individuals, families, groups, organizations, and communities, and manage these values in a manner that allows professional values to guide their practice.

EP 2.1.2b: Make ethical decisions by applying standards of the National Association of Social Workers Code of Ethics and, as applicable, of the International Federation of Social Workers/International Association of Schools of Social Work Ethics in Social Work, Statement of Principles (p. 29). Social workers make ethical decisions by following the NASW Code of Ethics and applying ethical standards when working with clients across all levels of the environment.

EP 2.1.3a: Distinguish, appraise, and integrate multiple sources of knowledge, including research-based knowledge and practice wisdom (pp. 24, 30). Effective social workers distinguish, appraise, and integrate multiple sources of knowledge, drawing on information received from clients as well as research-based knowledge and practice wisdom.

EP 2.1.8a   Analyze, formulate, and advocate for policies that advance social well-being (p. 32).

Social workers recognize the impact that policies have on clients and service delivery and advocate for policies that enhance client and community well-being.

EP 2.1.8b: Collaborate with colleagues and clients for effective policy action (p. 42). Social workers collaborate with clients and colleagues across disciplines to provide effective services and to advocate for needed changes in policies.

EP 2.1.9b: Provide leadership in promoting sustainable changes in service delivery and practice to improve the quality of social services (p. 32). Social workers engage in leadership roles within their organizations and communities and the social work profession to improve client well-being.

Key Terms

The terms below are defined in the Glossary.

Charity Organization Society (COS)	pastoral counselors
client system	planned change
community organization	private practice
competencies	pro bono
Council on Social Work Education (CSWE)	psychiatry
direct practice	psychobiological
ethics	psychologists
generalist practice	psychometric instruments
group work	self-care
Mary Richmond	settlement house
multidisciplinary teams	social agencies
National Association of Social Workers (NASW)	social casework
	social work
	social workers
opportunity structure	socialization
	sociologists

Discussion Questions

1. What does the term opportunity structure mean? What are the characteristics of the opportunity structure? How might an individual's level of access to the opportunity structure shape outcomes for that individual?

2. What are social work values? How do values relate to ethics? Can you think of a values dilemma that a social worker might face when working with a client?

3. How important is a code of ethics for a profession? Why? Why would a code of ethics be particularly important for the profession of social work?

4. What constitutes direct practice? Community organization? Research? Administration and planning? How are they similar, and how are they different? In which are you most interested? Why?

5. Compare and contrast the major contributions of the Charity Organization Society and the settlement house movement to social work practice.

6. What skills should the generalist-level (BSW) social worker have? How do these skills compare with those of the MSW social worker? The PhD social worker?

7. In which areas of social work practice are you most interested and why? What roles do you think a social worker might play in that area?

8. How do you think the roles of a social worker today would compare to roles played by early pioneers like Jane Addams and Mary Richmond? Do you think the profession should focus more on direct practice with individuals, advocating for social justice, or both? Explain the rationale for your response.

9. How does social work differ from other professions that also function in the human services arena? Compare how you think a social worker and another helping professional discussed in this chapter might differ in approach. Why do you think the differences would arise?

10. Why do you think that self-care is especially important to social workers and those in other helping professions? What self-care strategies will be most effective for you as you take this course and learn about the profession and the challenging issues that impact clients and the profession?

On the Internet

www.aswb.org
www.bls.gov
www.cswe.org
www.nasw.org
www.uic.edu/jaddams/hull/hull_house.html

References

Association of Social Work Boards. (2014). *About ASWB*. Retrieved from aswb.org

Council on Social Work Education. (2008, revised 2010). *Educational policy and accreditation standards*. Washington, DC: Author.

Council on Social Work Education. (2014). *Directory of accredited social work degree programs*. Washington, DC: Author. Retrieved from www.cswe.org

Day, P., & Schiele, J. (2013). *A new history of social welfare* (7th ed.). Boston: Allyn & Bacon.

International Federation of Social Workers and International Association of Schools of Social Work. (2004). *Ethics in social work, statement of principles*. Retrieved from http://www.ifsw.org

Kirst-Ashman, K., & Hull, G. (2015). *Generalist practice with organizations and communities* (6th ed.). Belmont, CA: Cengage.

Maslow, A. (1943). A theory of human motivation. *Psychological review*, 50(4), 370–396. Retrieved from http://psychclassics.yorku.ca/Maslow/motivation.htm

National Association of Social Workers. (2002). *The power of social work*. Washington, DC: Author.

National Association of Social Workers. (2008). *NASW code of ethics*. Washington, DC: Author.

National Association of Social Workers. (2009). Professional self-care and social work. In *Social work speaks* (9th ed., pp. 267–271). Washington: DC: Author.

National Association of Social Workers. (2014). *Specialty practice sessions*. Retrieved from http://www.socialworkers.org/sections/

National Association of Social Workers Foundation. (2014). *Social work pioneers*. Retrieved from http://www.naswfoundation.org/pioneers/default.asp

Richmond, M. (1917). *Social diagnosis*. New York: Russell Sage Foundation.

Richmond, M. (1922). *What is social casework?* New York: Russell Sage Foundation.

Specht, H., & Courtney, M. (1995). *Unfaithful angels*. New York: Free Press.

Stern, M., & Axinn, J. (2012). *Social welfare: A history of the American response to need* (8th ed.). Boston: Pearson.

U.S. Bureau of Labor Statistics. (2014a). *Employment and earnings*. Retrieved from http://www.bls.gov/oes/current/oes_nat.htm

U.S. Bureau of Labor Statistics. (2014b). *Occupational outlook handbook, 2014–2015.* Retrieved from http://www.bls.gov/ooh

Suggested Readings

Dolgoff, R., Lowenberg, F., & Harrington, D. (2012). *Ethical decisions for social work practice* (8th ed.). Belmont, CA: Cengage.

Dubois, B., & Miley, K. K. (2014). *Social work: An empowering profession* (8th ed.). Boston: Allyn & Bacon.

Grobman, L. (Ed.). (2005). *More days in the lives of social workers: 35 "real life" stories of advocacy,* *out-reach and other intriguing roles in social work practice.* Harrisburg, PA: White Hat.

Johnson, L. C., & Yanca, S. J. (2011). *Social work practice: A generalist approach.* (10th ed.). Boston: Allyn & Bacon.

LeCroy, C. *The call to social work: Life stories* (2nd ed.). Thousand Oaks, CA: Sage.

Ritter, J., Halaevalu, F. V., & Kiernan-Stern, M. (2008). *101 careers in social work.* New York: Springer.

Segal, E. A., Gerdes, K. E., & Steiner, S. (2013). *An introduction to the profession of social work* (3rd ed.). Belmont, CA: Cengage.

CHAPTER 3
The Ecological/Systems Perspective

Juan, a 12-year-old Mexican American male, is in the seventh grade in an urban school in California. He has recently returned to school after a week's suspension for smoking marijuana in the courtyard during school hours and threatening to stab a classmate during a fight in the lunchroom. His teachers are concerned about him and are recommending to Christina Herrera, the school social worker, that he be enrolled in an anger-management program and the school's dropout-prevention program. Juan has been socializing during school with a group of much older students who are members of a local gang. He has been skipping classes, not completing class assignments, fighting with other students, and arguing with his teachers when they confront him about his behavior.

Ms. Herrera has talked with both Juan and his mother, and Juan has signed a contract agreeing to specific conditions he must meet if he is to remain in school. Ms. Herrera also has suggested that Juan participate in a school support group and has referred Juan and his mother to the local teen–parent outreach center for counseling as soon as a counseling slot is available. Juan's mother is extremely concerned about him, but she also has indicated to Ms. Herrera that she is under a great deal of stress and is angry that Juan is adding to it.

Juan lives in a one-bedroom apartment with his mother and his younger brother, who is 5 years old. Juan's parents divorced 6 months ago, and his father moved to a neighboring state 300 miles away. Juan always had a fairly close relationship with both of his parents. Although he knew that they fought a lot and that his father drank and lost his job, Juan was surprised when his parents told him that they were getting a divorce.

When Juan's father moved out, his mother had to get an extra job to make ends meet, and the family had to move into a small apartment in another part of the city. Juan's mother's relatives and friends, all devout Catholics, were adamantly against the divorce and have not been supportive at all. When she is not working, Juan's mother spends much of her time crying or sleeping. At first, Juan tried hard to be supportive of his mother—cooking meals, cleaning the house, and taking care of his little brother—but at times he doesn't cook or clean exactly the way his mother wants him to. When his brother is too noisy, Juan gets in trouble for not keeping him quiet. Lately, Juan's mother has begun yelling at or hitting Juan when this happens. Because she was abused as a child, Juan's mother feels guilty when she gets so angry at Juan, but she doesn't understand why he can't be more supportive when she is trying so hard to keep the family together.

Since the divorce, Juan has felt abandoned by everyone. His mother is usually angry at him, and his two longtime friends, who come from two-parent families, seem less friendly to him. When they do ask him to do things with them, Juan usually can't anyway because he has to take care of his younger brother or he doesn't have any money. Transportation is another problem, because Juan's friends live across town in his former neighborhood.

Although he used to do well in school, Juan has lost interest in his classes. He can't get used to the new school, and he doesn't know any of the teachers there. He does have several new friends who seem to accept him. They are older, and their interest in him makes him feel important. Juan is excited that they want him to be a member of their gang. As long as school is so boring, he can spend time with them during the day and still take care of his brother after school. However, he is seriously considering running away from home and moving in with one of the gang members, who lives with an older brother. The friend's older brother recently got out of prison and has promised that Juan can make a lot of money as a drug runner for him.

Juan's case illustrates the many factors that influence how people react to what is going on in their lives. Juan's present situation is affected by:

- his developmental needs as he enters adolescence;
- his relationships with his mother, father, younger brother, friends, and school personnel;
- his father's alcoholism and unemployment;
- his parents' divorce;
- his mother's abuse as a child;
- his family's tenuous economic situation;
- the lack of positive social support available to Juan's family from relatives, friends, the workplace, the school, the church, and the neighborhood;
- the lack of programs available to divorced parents and teens in Juan's community;
- Juan's cultural and ethnic background; and
- community and societal attitudes about divorce, female-headed households, and intervention in family matters.

From Juan's perspective, the family system, the economic system, the political system, the religious system, the education system, and the social welfare system have failed to meet his needs. Still, Juan is forced to interact continually with all of these individuals, groups, and social structures regularly, and he depends on all of them in some way.

In this chapter, we explore frameworks that social workers use to understand social problems and issues that individuals and families face in today's world. The **ecological/systems framework** is an umbrella framework used by generalist social work practitioners to understand both social welfare problems and individual needs and to guide the various interventions that social workers use when helping clients.

Using Theoretical Frameworks to Guide Intervention

EP 2.1.3a
EP 2.1.3b
EP 2.1.7a

Everyone perceives what is going on in their lives and in the world somewhat differently. For example, an argument between a parent and a teenager over almost any topic usually is perceived quite differently by the parent and by the teenager. People view their environments and the forces that shape them differently, depending on many things: biological factors, such as their own heredity and intelligence; personal life experiences, including their childhood; ethnicity and culture; and level and type of education.

How people perceive their world determines to a great extent how involved they are in it and how they interact with it. For example, women who perceive themselves as unimportant and powerless may continue to let their partners beat them and may not believe that they can be successful if they leave their batterers. In contrast, women in the same situation who perceive that they have some control over their lives and feel better about themselves may enter counseling programs and get jobs.

Professionals from different disciplines also view the world somewhat differently. A physicist, for example, will offer a different explanation from that of a philosopher or a minister about how the world began. A law enforcement officer and a social worker may disagree about how best to handle young teens who join gangs and harass elderly people. A physician may treat a patient who has headaches by meeting the patient's physical needs, whereas a psychologist may treat the person's emotional needs through individual counseling to ascertain how the individual can better cope. The way professionals who work with people perceive the world—their **worldview**—largely determines the type of intervention they choose in helping people.

Worldview is an important concept to social workers for two reasons. They must be continually aware of their own worldviews and how they affect their choices of intervention in helping people, and they also must be aware of the worldviews of others. Some worldviews have more influence than others on world, national, state, and local policies and the ways in which our society at all levels is structured. One key to being an effective social worker is to understand those influences, and how they have shaped current policies and systems and how those influences have affected at-risk and diverse populations. According to Shriver (2011), an important aspect of social work is to help individuals find their voices to advocate for themselves and to be allies for them when they cannot. Shriver, a social work educator, suggests the following questions as criteria for analyzing worldviews, or ways of thinking:

1. Does this perspective contribute to preserving and restoring human dignity?
2. Does this perspective recognize the benefits of, and does it celebrate, human diversity?
3. Does this perspective assist us in transforming ourselves and our society so that we welcome the voices, the strengths, the ways of knowing, the energies of us all?
4. Does this perspective help us all (ourselves and the people with whom we work) to reach our fullest human potential?
5. Does the perspective … reflect the participation and experiences of males and females, economically well-off and poor; white people and people of color; gay men, lesbians, bisexuals, transgender persons, and heterosexuals; old and young; and temporarily able-bodied people and people with disabilities? (p. 10).

Worldviews sometimes are called "paradigms" or "frameworks." In our society, many individuals currently are rethinking ways to view critical social issues such as poverty and health care. The profession of social work requires a framework to understand how

and why views are changing and how to work for social change during this shift.

The Difference between Causal Relationships and Association

In the past, many professionals who dealt with human problems tended to look at those problems in terms of cause and effect. A **cause-and-effect relationship** suggests that if x causes y, then by eliminating x, we also eliminate y. For example, if we say that smoking is the sole cause of lung cancer, eliminating smoking would mean eliminating lung cancer. This limited worldview presents problems for many reasons. We know that smoking does not always cause lung cancer, and sometimes people who do not smoke get lung cancer.

Further, the relationship between smoking and developing lung cancer is not always one-dimensional. Other intervening variables or factors, such as living in a city with heavy pollution, also increase a person's chances of getting lung cancer. The chances of getting lung cancer are more than twice as great for a person who smokes and lives in a city with heavy smog than for someone who does neither. The causal-relationship viewpoint usually is not appropriate when examining social welfare problems.

Juan's case definitely cannot be discussed in terms of a cause-and-effect relationship. Are the situations he is experiencing caused by the abuse his mother suffered as a child, by the divorce, by his father's drinking too much, by his mother's worries about money, by his use of marijuana, by his association with gang members, by the limited social support system available, or by discrimination because he and his family are Mexican American? It is unlikely that one of these factors caused Juan's current situation, but they all probably contributed to it in some way. In looking at factors related to social welfare problems, it is more appropriate to view them in **association** with the problem—meaning that all factors are connected to or are related to the problem, rather than saying that one isolated factor, or even several factors, directly causes a social problem.

A Conceptual Framework for Understanding Social Welfare Problems

EP 2.1.3a
EP 2.1.3b
EP 2.1.7a

Because many factors are associated with, or contribute to, social welfare problems, we need a broad theory or framework to understand them. First, it is useful to define *theory* and to discuss why theories are important.

A **theory** is a way of clearly and logically organizing a set of facts or ideas. All of us use theories daily. We continually are taking in facts, or information, from our environment and ordering them in some way to make sense of what is going on around us. Although some of our theories may be relatively unimportant to everyone else, they are useful to us in being able to describe, understand, and predict our environment.

Most important, theories are useful in helping us change either the environment or the ways in which we relate to it. For example, a college student has a roommate who always turns up the music she is listening to, to full volume whenever the student gets a phone call. During the year that they have shared a room, the student has gathered a great deal of information as to when this happens. She now is able to articulate a theory based on this information to describe the situation, to understand why it happens, and to be able to predict when her roommate will exhibit this behavior. Making sense of the facts in this situation has made it easier for her to deal with this trying behavior and attempt to change it. What theories might you suggest to understand why this roommate situation is happening? A theory can be relatively insignificant, such as the one just described, or it can have major importance to many people.

A theory can be used to describe something, such as Juan's family situation; to explain or to understand something, such as why a family in crisis would exhibit some of the behaviors of Juan's family; to predict something, such as what behaviors another family in a similar situation might experience; or to change something, such as Juan's ability to get his needs met from his environment in a healthier way.

The same set of facts can be ordered in different ways, depending on who is doing the ordering and the worldview of that person or group. If we think of facts as individual bricks and a theory as a way of ordering the bricks so they make sense, we can visualize several different theories from the same set of facts, just as we can visualize a number of different structures built from the same set of bricks.

If a theory is to be widely used, it must have three attributes:

1. A good theory must be **inclusive**, or able to explain consistently the same event in the same way. The more inclusive a theory is, the better it explains facts the same way each time an event occurs. For example, if the person in the roommate situation could describe, explain, or predict the roommate's behavior exactly the same way every single time the

telephone would ring, she would have a highly inclusive theory.
2. A good theory must also be **generalizable**, which means that a general conclusion about what happens in one situation must be able to be transferred to other, similar situations. Even though the person may be able to explain the facts about her roommate in a highly inclusive way, the same situation would not likely occur with all roommates at the same university, much less in the same city, the United States, or the world. The more a theory can be generalized beyond the single situation it is describing or explaining, the better it is as theory.
3. A good theory must be **testable**, which means that we must be able to measure it in some way to ensure that it is accurate and valid. This is the major reason that theory in understanding and predicting social welfare problems and human behavior is somewhat limited. To develop accurate ways of measuring what goes on inside people's minds, their attitudes, and their behaviors is difficult. How do we measure, for example, behavior change such as child abuse, particularly when it happens most often behind closed doors? Can we administer psychological tests to measure attitudes that would lead to abuse, or can we measure community factors such as unemployment to predict child abuse?

Any time we try to measure human behavior or environmental influences, we have difficulty doing so. This does not mean we should stop doing research or trying to develop higher-level theories. Actually, this is an exciting area of social work, and the problems merely point out the need to develop skilled social work practitioners and researchers who can devote more attention to developing good social work theory.

Because social work draws its knowledge base from many disciplines, many theories are applicable to social work. These include psychological theories such as Freud's theory of psychoanalysis and its derivatives, economic and political theories, sociological theories such as Emile Durkheim's theory relating to suicide, and developmental theories such as Erik Erikson's. All of these theoretical perspectives are relevant to social work and an understanding of social welfare problems, but looking at only one of them limits understanding and, in turn, intervention. Thus, we are presenting a framework or perspective that allows us to view social problems and appropriate responses that incorporate a multitude of factors and a multitude of possible responses.

The Ecological/Systems Framework

Social workers, more than any other group of professionals, have directed their profession to the individual and beyond the individual to the broader environment, ever since the professional casework of the Charity Organization Society and the settlement house reform movements of Jane Addams (Germain & Gitterman, 2008). Consider the definitions of *social work* presented in Chapter 2. All emphasize enhancing social functioning of the individual or in some way addressing the relationships, interactions, and interdependence between people and their environments.

This perspective is exemplified by the many roles that social workers play within the social welfare system. True generalists, they advocate for changing living conditions of persons who are mentally ill and obtaining welfare reform legislation that enables the poor to obtain employment and economic self-sufficiency; empower clients to advocate for themselves to reduce violence in their communities; lead groups of children who have experienced divorce; educate the community about parenting, AIDS, and child abuse; and provide individual, family, and group counseling to clients.

This broad framework allows for identifying all of the diverse, complex factors associated with a social welfare problem or an individual problem; understanding how all of the factors interact to contribute to the situation; and determining an intervention strategy or strategies, which can range from intervention with a single individual to an entire society and can incorporate a variety of roles. Such a framework must account for individual differences, cultural diversity, and growth and change at the individual, family, group, organizational, community, and societal levels.

The generalist foundation of social work is based on a framework that incorporates both ecological and systems perspectives. We choose to use the term ecological/systems *framework* rather than *theory* because the ecological/systems perspective is much broader and more loosely constructed than a theory. This framework is most useful in understanding social welfare problems and situations and determining which specific theories are the basis for appropriate interventions.

In addition, although various systems (see, for example, works by Talcott Parsons, Max Siporin, Allen Pincus, and Anne Minahan) and ecological approaches (see, for example, works by Urie Bronfenbrenner, James Garbarino, Carel Germain, Alex Gitterman, and Carol Meyer) have been described extensively in the literature, they have not been tested or delineated with enough specificity to be considered theories. A number of advocates of the ecological/systems framework, in fact, refer to it as a *metatheory,* or an umbrella framework that can be used as a basis for incorporating additional theories. Note that in past editions, we referred to this framework as the *systems/ecological* framework. Although the concepts and discussion of the framework remain the same, we have reversed the order of the two terms, because it is our perspective that social work emphasizes the *ecological* concepts—the interactions within and between systems—more than the *systems* concepts, which focus more on the structure of systems.

For many years, a general systems framework has been discussed in the literature of many disciplines—medicine, biology, anthropology, psychology, economics, political science, sociology, and education—and it has been used somewhat differently in each discipline. Its principles, as well as similar principles associated with *social systems,* or systems associated with living things, have been incorporated into the social work literature since the beginning of social work.

Mary Richmond, the social work pioneer discussed in Chapter 2, wrote in 1922, "The worker is no more occupied with abnormalities in the individual than in the environment, is no more able to neglect the one than the other" (pp. 98–99). Since then, many social work proponents (for example, Gordon Hearn, Allen Pincus and Anne Minahan, Max Siporin, Helen Harris Perlman, and Harriet Bartlett) have developed specific approaches or explored various aspects of social work from within the boundaries of the ecological/systems framework.

More recently, other social work theorists, including Carel Germain, Alex Gitterman, and Carol Meyer, have advocated an ecological perspective that incorporates many of the same concepts as the systems framework. Some social work theorists (see, for example, Rothery, 2008) clearly separate the systems perspective and the ecological perspective, considering them as two distinct frameworks. These theorists view the systems framework as relating largely to the *structure,* or the systemic properties of cases, which helps us focus on how variables are related and to order systems within the environment according to complexity. They view the ecological perspective, in contrast, as directed more to *relationships* of person and environment, with more emphasis on interactions and transactions than on structure.

Others (Compton & Galaway, 2004; van Wormer, 2010) incorporate concepts that are similar in both perspectives and refer to one framework. Although one can make distinctions between the two perspectives, we have chosen to use the combined approach in this text. Rather than getting confused over semantics, readers should pay attention to the broad definitions and principles of the various frameworks discussed and their commonalties rather than their differences. We emphasize these points in understanding an ecological/systems perspective and its significant contributions to social work.

Systems Theory: Perspectives and Major Concepts

EP 2.1.3a
EP 2.1.3b
EP 2.1.7a

Systems theory was used initially to explain the functioning of the human body, which was seen as a major system incorporating a number of smaller systems: the skeletal system, the muscular system, the endocrine system, the circulatory system, and so on. Medical practitioners, even ones in ancient Greece, realized that when one component of the human body fails to function effectively, it affects the way that other systems within the body function and, in turn, affects the way the human body as a whole functions. This led to further exploration of the relationships among sub-parts of living organisms. Aided by technology, more contemporary biological research has allowed scientists to focus on not only living cells, but also the intricate proteins and other components that comprise them. (For example, the Human Genome Project articulates the intricate interrelations among the many complex parts of a single cell that result in various DNA sequences that enable cells to reproduce. The Project has been instrumental in determining how various types of cancer and other diseases occur, leading to improved strategies for prevention and treatment.)

Systems theory has also gained increased attention in fields other than medicine and social work. Consider the tenuous balance between the various ecosystems as our world becomes increasingly populated and resulting concerns about global climate change and the availability of resources such as water. Engineering and business are among the disciplines that use various derivations of systems theory, specifically the interactions between complex technological and manufacturing components. Major concepts used to understand and apply systems theory include system, synergy, boundaries, open and closed systems, interactions and interrelations, steady state, and equifinality.

System

One early proponent of systems theory, Ludwig Von Bertalanffy (1968), defined a **system** as "a set of units

with relationships among them" (p. 38). A system also can be defined as a whole, an entity composed of separate but interacting and interdependent parts. The early Greek physicians, for example, viewed the body as the larger system and the body's various smaller systems as interacting and interdependent parts. Similarly, a family can be viewed as a system composed of separate but interdependent and interacting individual family members. From a global perspective, the world can be viewed as a system composed of separate but interdependent and interacting nations. One advantage of the ecological/systems framework is that it is a conceptual framework and can be applied in many different ways to many different situations.

Synergy

The contribution of biology to systems theory is its emphasis on the concept that the whole is greater than the sum of its parts; that is, when all of the smaller systems or subsystems of an organism function in tandem, they produce a larger system that is far more grand and significant than the combination of those smaller systems working independently. The larger system, when it functions optimally, is said to achieve **synergy**, the combined energy from the smaller parts that is greater than the total if those parts were to function separately.

Imagine for a moment that your instructor for this course will ask the class to take an exam on the chapters covered thus far in this text. Each student takes the exam separately, and the scores of each student are listed. The lowest score is 50; the highest is 85. Now suppose that your instructor decides to let the entire class take the exam together. Each person in the class now functions as part of the total group, together solving each exam question. As a class, your score on the exam is 100. The class has demonstrated the concept of the whole being greater than the sum of its parts, or synergy.

Boundaries

An important aspect of any system is the concept of **boundary**. A system can be almost anything, but, by its definition, it has some sort of boundary, or point at which one system ends and another begins. The system's environment encompasses everything beyond this boundary. For example, the human body can be seen as a system, as discussed earlier, with the skin as a boundary and the various body subsystems as smaller components of the larger system. From a different perspective, the human mind can be seen as a system, with Freud's id, ego, and superego as components within that system interacting to form a whole that is greater than any of the three components alone—the human mind.

An individual, too, can be part of a larger system. For example, a family system might include one or two parents, a child, and the family dog. We might wish to expand the boundaries of the family system and include the grandparents, the aunts and uncles, and the cousins. We can establish larger systems, such as school systems, communities, cities, states, or nations, and study their interactions and interdependence with each other. We can look at a political system, an economic system, a religious system, and a social welfare system and the ways that those broader systems interact with one another.

When using a systems perspective, the important thing to remember is that the systems we define and the boundaries we confer on those systems are conceptual. We can define them in whatever ways make the most sense in looking at the broad social welfare or the narrower individual problem we are addressing.

For example, if we were to conceptualize Juan's family as a social system, we could include within its boundaries his mother, his younger brother, and Juan. We could choose to include Juan's father as part of his family system (even though he is out of the home, he is still part of Juan's life, and his absence is a major emotional issue for Juan). We could include grandparents and other extended family members because, although they are not actively involved either physically or emotionally in supporting the family, they are a possible source of support because they have been heavily involved in the past (see Figure 3.1). If we were looking at another family system, however, we might well include more members. The ecological/systems framework is a useful way to organize data to help understand a situation, and its flexibility allows us to define systems and their boundaries in many ways.

Open and Closed Systems

We can draw boundaries wherever it seems appropriate when using an ecological/systems framework, but we must be able to ascertain how permeable those boundaries are. Some systems have easily permeated boundaries between units (such as people) in the system and those outside. We call these **open systems**. Some families exemplify open systems, readily incorporating other people. When someone rings the doorbell at dinnertime, the family adds a place setting. A cousin or a friend may live with the family temporarily or longer, so it may be difficult to know exactly who is a family member and who is not. Systems have internal boundaries as well, such as boundaries between parents and their children.

The systems/ecological framework helps social workers and their clients determine who should be included in the family system when identifying potential strengths within the client's environment.

Yellow Dog Productions/The Image Bank/Getty Images

FIG 3.1 Using an Eco-Map to Understand Juan's Family Situation

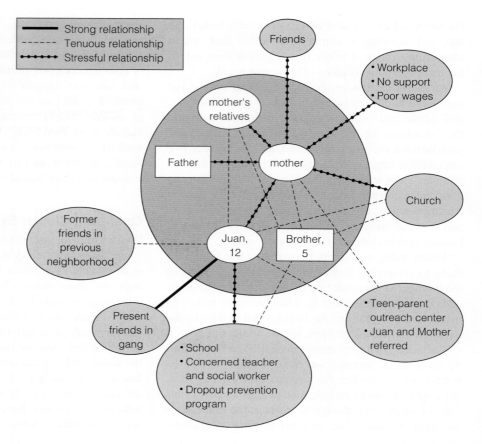

Strong relationship
Tenuous relationship
Stressful relationship

Friends

• Workplace
• No support
• Poor wages

mother's relatives

Father   mother

Church

Former friends in previous neighborhood

Juan, 12   Brother, 5

• Teen-parent outreach center
• Juan and Mother referred

Present friends in gang

• School
• Concerned teacher and social worker
• Dropout prevention program

Sometimes boundaries can be too open. For example, in some families, members become overly involved in each other's lives. In other families, parents do not set consistent limits for their children, and no clear boundaries are established between the parents and the children. Unclear boundaries within systems can lead to family problems such as incest. However, healthy open systems with clear boundaries are likely to achieve synergy because of their members' willingness to accept new energy from their interactions with the broader environment.

In contrast, some families represent **closed systems**. They have rigid boundaries and are tightly knit within. They may have special traditions for family members only. Although they might get along well with each other, they sometimes are isolated and rarely incorporate other individuals into their system. Sometimes boundaries can be too closed. For example, an abusive husband may not allow his wife to go anywhere unless he goes along.

Before Juan's father began drinking heavily, his family was a fairly open system. While his family engaged in many activities together just as a family, they also socialized a great deal with friends and relatives. If Juan's friends were playing at his house, they frequently were invited to have dinner or to participate in family activities. When Juan's father's drinking increased, his family system became more closed. Juan's mother tried to limit his father's drinking by limiting the family's social activities. When relatives became more critical of his drinking, Juan's family stopped socializing with them to avoid being confronted about the problem. Because Juan's father lost his temper easily when he drank, Juan stopped inviting his friends to his home and began playing at their houses instead. The family became more isolated. The isolation continued, and the family system remained closed when Juan's father left and his parents divorced.

Organizations, too, may be open or closed systems. Some organizations welcome new members and readily expand their activities to meet new interests. Others are extremely closed and do not encourage new ideas or new members, making those who try to enter the organization feel unwelcome. Communities and other social structures can be viewed as open or closed as well. Juan's new school, for example, is a somewhat closed system, which has made making friends and fitting in difficult for him.

Usually, the more closed a system is, the less able it is to derive positive energy from other systems. Over time, closed systems tend to use up their own energy and develop **entropy**, which means that they tend to lose their ability to function and eventually can stagnate and die. The more isolated Juan's family becomes, the less energy it takes in from the environment, so it has less energy for family members and is less able to function. The family system becomes more and more lethargic and eventually will either change or die, with the family separating and its members becoming part of other family systems. If, for example, Juan's mother were to become extremely abusive and Juan were to become heavily involved in the gang and serious criminal activities, his brother might be placed in foster care, and Juan in a correctional facility for youth.

Interactions and Interrelations

Boundaries and open and closed systems are structural aspects of systems. An additional feature of the ecological/systems framework is its emphasis on the *interactions* and *interrelations* between units rather than on the systems or subsystems themselves. This lends itself well to the need to identify associations among many factors rather than on cause-and-effect relationships between two factors. The interactions and interrelatedness between systems suggest constant motion, fluidity, and change.

The relatedness and interactions incorporate the concept that a change or movement in one part of the system, or in one system, will have an impact on the larger system, or on other systems. Imagine a room full of constantly moving ping-pong balls, each representing a system or a subsystem of a larger system. Hitting one ping-pong ball across the room will change the movement of the other balls.

Similarly, the recent downturn in the economy has resulted in changes in systems other than the economic system. The educational system has been affected because many states have had to cut back on funding for public education, resulting in larger classrooms, fewer remedial and enrichment opportunities for students, and reduced services, including social work services; and higher education, resulting in tuition increases, faculty and staff layoffs, and fewer students who can afford to go to college. The social welfare system has been affected because many more people are unemployed, cannot pay their mortgages, and need food, housing, public assistance, social services, and health care; the criminal justice system has been affected because more people are turning to crime; and the political system has been affected because dissatisfied voters have not reelected the party in office or in some instances, regardless of party, incumbents.

The results of interactions and interrelatedness between systems can be seen when viewing Juan's family. Juan's father's drinking led to his job loss, which led to his increased drinking. Both of these factors affected Juan's parents' relationships with each other, or the marital system; the parents' relationships with Juan and his younger brother in the parent–child system; the communication patterns between the family as a system; and relationships between Juan's family system and other systems beyond the family, such as his father's workplace, his family's church, and Juan's school.

Interactions and interrelatedness occur continually, with a constant flow of energy within and across systems. This creates natural tensions that are viewed as healthy if communication is open, because the energy flow creates growth and change. Feedback among systems is important in the ecological/systems perspective, which emphasizes communication. Social workers and others who work within and across various systems must understand those systems' goals and communication patterns. In unhealthy systems, for example, the various members of the system may be communicating in certain ways and may have certain unspoken goals that maintain the system because its members are afraid to change the system or the system is productive for them in some way.

In a family such as Juan's, in which a parent is an alcoholic, the other parent or an older child may perpetuate the alcoholism and unconsciously try to keep the family system as it is because the nonalcoholic sees his or her role as one of caretaking—keeping the family together and protecting the younger children from the alcoholism. If the family system changes, the nonalcoholic parent or the older child no longer will be able to maintain that role and thus may try to force the system back to the way it once was.

Steady State

Another integral concept in the ecological/systems framework is **steady state**, in which systems are not static but are steadily moving. The system is adjusting constantly to move toward its goals while maintaining a certain amount of order and stability, giving and receiving energy in fairly equal amounts to maintain equilibrium. A healthy system, then, may be viewed as one that is not in upheaval but is always ebbing and flowing to achieve both stability and growth.

If Juan and his family receive counseling and other support from the broader environment, his family system might well achieve equilibrium. The system will not stop changing but, instead, will move toward its goals in a less disruptive manner.

Equifinality

A last concept in the ecological/systems framework is **equifinality**, the concept that the final state of a system can be achieved in many different ways. Because a given situation may be interpreted in many ways, many options usually are possible for dealing with it.

When working with Juan and his family, a number of alternatives can be considered to help them function better as individuals and as a family unit. Options might be individual and family counseling, support or therapeutic groups for Juan and his mother, a child-care program for his younger brother, increased interactions between Juan and his father, enrollment in a chemical-dependency program for Juan's father, enrollment in a job-training program for Juan's mother or father (or both), involvement in positive recreational programs for Juan, and membership in a supportive church. Although not all of these options might be realistic for Juan and his family, various combinations could lead to the same positive results. The concept of equifinality is especially important to social workers because their role is to help clients determine what is best for them, and clients' choices are as diverse as the clients themselves.

Incorporating an Ecological Perspective

EP 2.1.3a
EP 2.1.3b
EP 2.1.7a

One criticism of the ecological/systems framework in social work is that it encompasses the broad environment, yet ignores the biological, intrapsychic, and psychosocial aspects of the individual. **Intrapsychic aspects** include internal psychological processes, while **psychosocial aspects** include the impact of interactions between internal psychological processes and the environment. Proponents of the ecological/systems framework argue, however, that the individual is perceived as a highly valued system itself and that biological, intrapsychic and psychosocial aspects, which incorporate the individual's capacity and motivation for change, are parts of any system involving individuals that cannot and should not be ignored. The framework's inclusiveness encompasses the biological, psychological, sociological, and cultural aspects of

developing individuals and their interactions with the broader environment. In fact, the ecological/systems framework often is referred to as a biopsycho-social-cultural framework. Ecomaps, tools that social workers use to "map out" interactions within and between clients/client systems, incorporate this framework and most often have the individual at the center of the "map." (See Figure 3.1.)

Another criticism of the ecological/systems framework is that, because it incorporates everything, it is too complicated, so important aspects of a situation are easily overlooked. The ecological perspective articulated by social scientists Urie Bronfenbrenner and James Garbarino attempts to address this concern. While Bronfenbrenner and Garbarino incorporate individual developmental aspects into the systems perspective of the broader environment, they divide the system into different levels, or layers of the environment. Note that even though not all social work texts use the same terminology as this text in referring to layers of the environment (some use three layers—micro, mezzo, and macro), they all adhere to the same conceptual perspective that each layer impacts other layers. We like the Bronfenbrenner and Garbarino model because it specifically emphasizes intervention at the community level, which is often overlooked when facilitating planned change.

Bronfenbrenner and Garbarino suggest that for all individuals, each of these environmental levels has both **risks** and **opportunities**. Opportunities within the environment encourage individuals to meet their needs and to develop as healthy, well-functioning people. Risks are either direct threats to healthy development or the absence of opportunities that would facilitate healthy individual development. Social workers, then, assess risks and opportunities at each level of the environment, working with the client (or client system, such as a family) to achieve positive change by promoting or increasing the environmental opportunities and reducing or eliminating the environmental risks.

Levels of the Environment

EP 2.1.3a
EP 2.1.3b
EP 2.1.7a

Bronfenbrenner (1979; 2009) and Garbarino (1992; 2009) suggest that risks and opportunities can be found at all levels of the environment. They describe these levels as being like a series of Russian eggs, with a large egg cut in half that opens to reveal a smaller egg, which opens to reveal a still smaller egg, which opens to reveal a still smaller egg (see Figure 3.2 and Table 3.1).

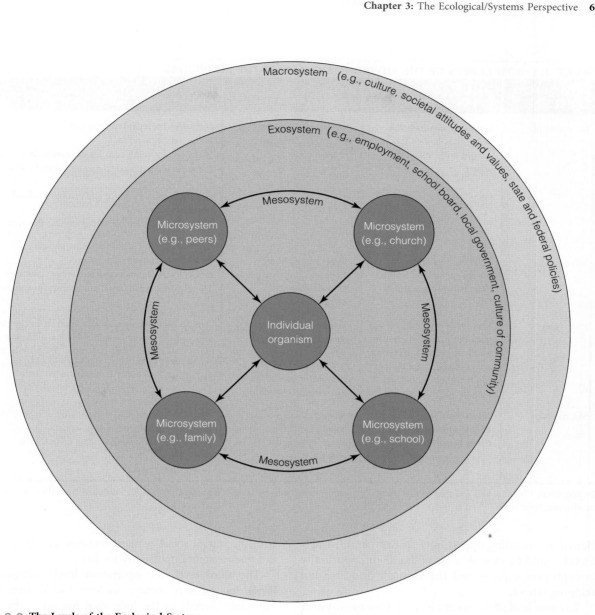

FIG 3.2 The Levels of the Ecological System
SOURCE: Adapted from Children and Families in the Social Environment, 2nd ed., by James Garbarino, pp. 29–30. Published by Aldine de Gruyter, Hawthorne, NY.

They suggest that we consider the tiniest egg to be the **microsystem level** (individual level), which includes the individual and all persons, groups, and activities that incorporate the individual's day-to-day environment. This level incorporates the individual's level of functioning, intellectual and emotional capacities, and motivation; the impact of culture and life experiences; and the interactions and connections between that individual and others in the immediate environment.

The social worker's focus at this level would be on identifying strengths within the individual and the environment, and then drawing on those strengths to try to reduce or eliminate environmental risks. Social workers would consider whether the messages and regard for the individual are consistent across individuals and groups, and whether the individual is valued and respected. Juan's microsystem level incorporates all of his own personal characteristics, such as his biological makeup and intelligence; his culture and gender; and his interactions and connections with his mother, brother, father, teachers, and friends. His mother and his old friends, as well as the social worker, could be

TABLE 3.1 HOW LEVELS OF THE ENVIRONMENT AFFECT THE INDIVIDUAL

ECOLOGICAL LEVEL	DEFINITION	EXAMPLES	ISSUES AFFECTING PERSON
Microsystem	Situations in which the person has face-to-face contact with influential others	Family, school, workplace, peer group, church, or synagogue	Is the person regarded positively? Is the person accepted? Is the person reinforced for competent behavior? Is the person exposed to enough diversity in roles and relationships? Are the person's culture and ethnicity valued and positively affirmed? Is the person given an active role in reciprocal relationships?
Mesosystem	Relationships between microsystems; the connections between situations	Home-school, home-workplace, home-religious institutions, school-neighborhood	Do settings respect each other? Are cultural factors respected between settings? Do settings present basic consistency in values?
Exosystem	Settings in which the person does not participate but in which significant decisions are made affecting the person or others who interact directly with the person	Place of employment of others in the person's microsystem, school board, local government, peer groups of others in the person's microsystem	Are decisions made with the interests of the person and the family in mind? How well do supports for families balance stresses for parents and children? Is diversity considered when decisions are made?
Macrosystem	"Blueprints" for defining and organizing the institutional life of the society	Ideology, social policy, shared assumptions about human nature, the "social contract"	Are some groups valued at expense of others? Are some groups oppressed (e.g., sexism, racism)? Is there an individualistic or a collectivistic orientation? Is violence a norm?

SOURCE: From Children and Families in the Social Environment. 2nd ed., by James Garbarino, pp. 29–30. Published by Aldine de Gruyter, Hawthorne, New York.

viewed as providing opportunity to Juan, and his new friends could be viewed as providing both opportunity through peer support and risk through drug use and skipping school.

The next level of the system is termed the **mesosystem level.** A mesosystem involves the relationship between two microsystems that are linked by some person or activity present in both microsystems. Because Juan is part of his family and his school, he provides the link between these two microsystems. The interactions in one microsystem influence the interactions of the others. For example, the conflicting messages to Juan from his school and family settings versus his peer setting had an influence on Juan and can be seen as environmental risks. While his mother and school personnel advocated against his skipping school and experimenting with marijuana, his new peers encouraged him to become involved in these activities. His mother's involvement

with the school social worker, however, can be viewed as a mesosystem opportunity for Juan.

The third level, the **exosystem level** (community level), incorporates community-level factors that may not relate directly to the individual but affect the way the individual functions. This level includes factors such as the workplace policies of the parents (if they cannot take sick leave when the child is sick, for example, this policy has an impact on the child), school board and community policies, community attitudes and values, and economic and social factors within the neighborhood and community. For Juan's family, exosystem risk factors include the lack of jobs that pay well for employees with his mother's skill level, the unavailability of affordable child care for Juan's younger brother, and community attitudes toward divorce, Mexican Americans, and single parenting. The teen–family outreach center provides an exosystem opportunity for Juan, if it is not too overloaded with other clients.

The final level, the **macrosystem level** (societal level), consists of societal factors such as the cultural attitudes and values of the society (for example, attitudes toward women, people of color, the poor, and violence); the role of the media in addressing or promoting social problems (some suggest, for example, that the media promote violence and teen pregnancy); and federal legislation and other social policies that affect a given individual. Contributing to Juan's current life situation are a lack of government programs for single parents and potential school dropouts, societal attitudes toward divorce and single parents, discrimination toward Latinos, and the media's glamorizing of gangs and violence. These factors all can be viewed as environmental risks. In spite of these risks, however, opportunities for Juan include democracy, freedom of religion, and education, which might not be found within other macrosystems.

Bronfenbrenner adds an additional dimension to this framework, the **chronosystem**. This dimension focuses on changes, or ecological transitions, that take place over time (the prefix *chrono* means "time") or during the life cycle of an individual. Chronosystem changes would include starting school, a new baby in the family, graduating from college, getting a job for the first time, and retiring. Chronosystem changes also include historical events, such as an economic downturn or boom or a war. For Juan, chronosystem changes would include his parents' divorce, moving, changing schools, and challenges for his family economically given the fact that the change in his family structure occurred during an economic downturn. How these changes impact an individual like Juan depend on a number of factors, including the person's age, physical and intellectual capabilities, and risks and opportunities in the person's environment (Bronfenbernner, 2005; Gardiner & Kosmitzki, 2011; Berk, 2014).

Many advocates of the ecological framework as conceptualized by Bronfenbrenner and Garbarino agree that it is a derivation of systems theory and another way of defining boundaries of systems. They suggest that its use is advantageous because it allows us to see the interdependence and interaction across levels from the microsystem level to the macrosystem level as well as historical context over time while also allowing us to target intervention at a variety of levels to address social problems and individual needs. In Juan's case, we could do the following:

1. at the microsystem level, provide individual counseling to Juan, counsel his family, and help him develop a new network of friends;

2. at the mesosystem level, work with Juan's mother, teachers, and peers to help them become more consistent in the messages they are conveying to Juan;

3. at the exosystem level, advocate for the establishment of a community program to assist teens who are having family problems, as well as low-cost child care for working parents; and

4. at the macrosystem level, advocate for legislation to develop national media programs that educate the public about gangs, drugs, and the working poor.

Note that this framework is a guide to understand how systems interact with and are shaped by the broader environment. It may not always be clear at which level of the environment a factor fits, and some factors may fit at more than one level of the environment. In Juan's situation, religion and the church can fit all levels, depending on how they are conceptualized. If Juan has an individual relationship with a higher power or spiritual being, that relationship could be viewed as a microsystem relationship.

Juan's interactions with individual members of his church—his priest, for example—could be viewed as microsystem relationships as well. The church and Juan's family could be viewed as a mesosystem relationship because Juan is part of both of these microsystems. The church could be viewed at the exolevel of the environment, too, because its attitudes, values, and policies at the community level have a definite impact on how Juan and his family are perceived in the community, especially after the divorce. Likewise, the church plays a major role in shaping the norms, attitudes, and values about divorce and other issues at the societal level, and it can be a macrolevel factor that shapes Juan's development. Deciding where in the environment each factor fits is not as important as the interdependence and interactions between and among the different levels of the environment and how they influence and are influenced by the developing system being viewed (Garbarino, 1992).

Problems in Living

Social workers Carel Germain and Alex Gitterman (2008) consider the ecological perspective somewhat differently in their approach, adding still another significant way of viewing individuals within their environments. They suggest that everyone has problems at some point—what they term "problems in living." They differentiate three common types of problems in living that may require intervention by a social worker:

1. problems associated with life transitions, such as marriage/entering a long-term partnership, birth of

a first child or movement of a child out of the family, or movement into middle age or retirement. Juan's family is experiencing the transitions of divorce and a child moving into adolescence. (Note that this is similar to Bronfenbrenner's concept of the chronosystem.)

2. problems associated with tasks in using and influencing elements of the environment. Juan's mother has had difficulty locating affordable child care for her youngest son, and Juan is having difficulty adjusting to a new school. The limited social networks available to Juan and his family suggest the need for intervention in this area.

3. interpersonal problems and needs in families and groups. Juan's family has developed some of the unproductive communication patterns typically found in families in which alcoholism is a problem. Even though these patterns maintained the family as an intact unit for many years, they will continue to stifle individual and family growth unless they change.

Developmental Niche

A final concept that helps social workers apply the ecological/systems framework in their work with clients and client systems is **developmental niche** (Super and Harkness, 1994; Gardiner & Kozmitzki, 2011). This concept, borrowed from biology, incorporates the idea that everyone has a unique cultural world that differs from everyone else's, even other family members living in the same household. Super and Harness use the example of a robin and a pigeon living in the same yard. Even though they both share the same environment, they eat different foods, use different materials to build their nests, and create a distinct niche for themselves to meet their needs. Individuals do the same. Developmental niche is shaped by the layers of the environment laid out by Bronfenbrenner and Garbarino. However, this concept is important for social workers because it helps us understand that each person's story and worldview are unique, even if circumstances and experiences are similar to others in the same environment.

In summary, an ecological/systems framework emphasizes that our lives are shaped by the choices we make, that the environment shapes our choices, and that our choices in turn shape the way we interact with our environment. This continual interaction and cyclical perspective suggest that we cannot discuss the individual without including the environment, or the environment without considering the strong forces of individuals in its formulation. The individual and the environment are adapting to each other constantly. The social worker's primary role is to ensure that this adaptation is supportive of both the individual and the environment.

Utility of the Ecological/Systems Framework

The ecological/systems framework is intended to be used as a mechanism to order facts about social welfare problems or individual needs in such a way that appropriate theories can be identified to explore the problems and needs further or to determine interventions. This framework can be thought of as a way to "map the territory" or gather and fit together pieces of a puzzle to understand a situation.

When dealing with a problem such as poverty, for example (addressed in Chapter 7), many individuals have one-dimensional ways of explaining the problem such as "because people are lazy" or "they are the victims of their own circumstances." An ecological/systems perspective would identify many factors—a large, complex territory and a puzzle with many pieces. Individual factors, family factors, community factors, and societal factors, such as the impact of the economic system and of unemployment, racism, sexism, and so forth—all contribute to poverty in some way. Table 3.2 lists some of the factors that shape the interactions between individuals and their environments.

Once the territory is mapped out or all of the puzzle pieces (or as many as possible) are obtained, the ecological/systems framework allows for further exploration of certain factors, parts of the terrain, or pieces of the puzzle. This perspective, too, allows for individualization and diversity, which means that cultural and gender differences are readily accounted for (see Table 3.2). After obtaining the larger picture, we can better ascertain where to direct our attention; whether more information is needed and in what areas; what aspects of the environment create risks or opportunities; and, if intervention is required, how risks can be minimized and opportunities promoted, and at what level and within which system or systems within the environment. One or more additional theories or frameworks can then be applied to obtain more

TABLE 3.2	FACTORS THAT SHAPE INDIVIDUAL FUNCTIONING AND RELATIONSHIP WITH THE ENVIRONMENT	
FACTORS	**EXAMPLES**
Personal	Level of prenatal care received Intellectual capacity or ability Emotional capacity or mental health Level of social functioning Physical health Age Ethnicity and culture Motivation Life stage or transitional period Crisis level
Family	Support systems and availability of significant others Family patterns, structure, and values Economic level and employment Level of functioning or family crisis
Community	Social class compared to rest of community Ethnic, cultural, and class diversity; attitudes and values Social roles available within community Community support Economic conditions Employment opportunities Educational opportunities Environmental stress
Societal	Societal attitudes and values Racism, sexism, poverty levels Supportive or lack of supportive legislation, programs, and policies Media role

information or to guide intervention. The advantage of the ecological/systems perspective is that we are less likely to overlook a major aspect of a situation and, as a result, intervene inappropriately.

The Utility of Other Theories and Frameworks

EP 2.1.3b
EP 2.1.7a

In their professional practice, social workers call upon other, more limiting theories and frameworks under the umbrella of the ecological/systems framework. Two useful types of frameworks are psychosocial

frameworks and cognitive behavioral frameworks (Coady & Lehmann, 2007). These and other frameworks that social workers commonly use are discussed in greater depth in Chapter 5.

Psychosocial Frameworks

Psychosocial frameworks include psychoanalytic theory, ego psychology, and life-span development frameworks. These frameworks often are used together and are not always viewed as mutually exclusive.

Psychoanalytic Theory Psychoanalytic theory, based largely on the works of Sigmund Freud, is built on the premise that children are born with biologically rooted functions, termed "drives," that dictate individual functioning. These drives are related primarily to sexual expression and aggression. Psychoanalytic theory also is a stage or developmental framework because its premise is that individuals cope with different changes in biological, psychological, and social functioning at different stages of their lives. This framework includes both conscious and unconscious drives and internal interactions within an individual among the id, ego, and superego.

The emphasis on interaction between the individual and the broader environment is more limited than it is in many other theories, although psychoanalytic theory does include attention to the impact of life experiences, primarily during early childhood, on later functioning; and on the development of internal defense mechanisms, such as denial and rationalization, to cope with the environment. If Juan's situation were to be viewed from this framework, his sexual drives during preadolescence and the impact of his father's leaving during this time would be major focal points.

This framework is complex and is based largely on individual psychopathology, or emotional illness. In applying this framework to individuals with problems, the suggested intervention is individual psychoanalysis to work through intrapsychic conflicts.

Ego Psychology and Life-Span Development Frameworks Ego psychology stems from psychoanalytic theory, with a major concentration on the development of a strong ego as opposed to interactions among the id, ego, and superego. The ego psychology perspective also focuses more on the transactions between the person and the environment and the impact of the environment in shaping the development of a healthy ego (Erikson, 1994). From this perspective for Juan and his family, intervention would involve determining the impact of his family situation during his childhood and ways to help him feel better about himself and increase his self-esteem.

Psychoanalytic and ego psychology are both life-span development frameworks. They suggest that individuals interact with their environments in different ways to meet different needs at different points in the life cycle, and the ways that needs are met in previous stages shape individual functioning and later development. Like psychoanalytic theory, this approach emphasizes ways that early life experiences shape later behavior. The emphasis, however, is much more on the ways that the environment shapes the resolution of these issues.

For example, using a life-span development framework developed by Erik Erikson (1950), an individual addresses issues of basic trust versus basic mistrust during the first year of life. If an infant is placed in an environment in which his or her basic needs (such as feeding or nurturing) are not met or are met inconsistently, the child does not develop a sense of trust. If trust is not developed later, the child is likely to have difficulty in other stages of life—for instance, in developing intimate relationships during young adulthood. Within this framework, Juan's developmental needs involve developing a sense of identity, primarily through peer relationships. Thus, for example, the gang members are filling a major developmental need for Juan that he does not feel can be met in other ways.

Although important and useful to social workers, these frameworks are more limiting than the ecological/systems framework. They place more emphasis on early life experiences than later experiences and less emphasis on interactions and transactions among broader levels of the environment and the impact on the individual. Finally, they suggest intervention primarily at the individual level.

Cognitive Behavioral Frameworks

Cognitive behavioral frameworks place little emphasis on an individual's life experiences or biological factors. Their premise is that environment, and not heredity, is what largely determines behavior. These frameworks focus primarily on the present and on

shaping individual thinking and behavior within the person's immediate environment. The goal is to shape behavior, not to change personality. In Juan's case, he may have developed a series of self-messages that suggest to him that he is not competent. These repeated messages have led to his poor schoolwork and his attempts to seek competence in other areas, such as drug use and illegal activities. If Juan is helped to change his self-messages to positive affirmations about himself, he will begin to see himself as competent and reengage in school.

The interventions within these frameworks are largely at the individual level, with much greater emphasis on the present and the environment. Cognitive behavioral frameworks are extremely useful to social workers. They can help individuals understand ways that unproductive thought patterns shape behaviors and, knowing this, help the person develop new thought patterns and behaviors leading to healthier functioning.

Political and Ideological Frameworks

Social workers often use political and ideological frameworks, as well as others, in a variety of ways and often in tandem with one another. In a political sense, people may adhere to perspectives that are considered liberal, conservative, libertarian, or radical. Although people often label themselves as fitting one category, their perspectives often fit more than one category, depending on the issue. Someone may be liberal in policies about child welfare and education and conservative about policies related to crime. Ideologies shape how we vote, our attitudes about social welfare programs and policies, and our beliefs about whether people are capable of change.

The ecological/systems framework can help us understand how environment shapes the development of a person's ideologies and political perspectives, as well as what might be likely to persuade someone to change a point of view. Understanding why someone holds a certain perspective is helpful for social work with clients and also in engaging in community action and legislative and political advocacy.

When addressing social welfare issues, an understanding of a person's worldview, as opposed to a more traditional approach based only on facts, has gained attention in recent years. Many social workers adhere to a constructivist perspective (Granvold, 2007), which holds that each individual constructs his or her own reality based on his or her perceptions and belief systems. Social workers with this perspective try to see the world from their client's perspective rather than from their own perspective, or use a more global concept of reality. Because a social worker must understand the person's interactions with the environment to understand his or her reality, one can see how this perspective is consistent with the ecological/systems framework.

Although the ecological/systems perspective also can be used when intervening with an individual or the broader environment, social workers almost always use it as the major framework for understanding a given situation or problem. Once the problem is understood, however, and the broad terrain is mapped out using this framework, other frameworks may be added for further assessment as well as intervention.

The Ecological/Systems Framework in Professional Practice

EP 2.1.3a
EP 2.1.3b
EP 2.1.7a

Because the generalist model of social work incorporates all levels of the environment and the interactions and interdependence within and between levels, the ecological/systems framework is especially useful as an organizing framework for professional practice. Specifically, the framework:

1. enables social workers to identify strengths of the individual as well as the person's environment and draw on those strengths to reduce or eliminate barriers;
2. allows the social worker to deal with large amounts of information from many different areas and to bring order to that information;
3. includes concepts that are applicable to the full range of clients served by social workers, including individuals, couples, families, groups, organizations, communities, and broader societal systems;
4. incorporates not only the structures of the social units involved but also the interrelatedness and interactions within and between units;
5. shifts attention away from the characteristics of units to the transactions and interactions between them;

6. views individuals as active participants in their environments, capable of change and adaptation, including shifting to new environments;
7. incorporates the concept of client self-determination and recognizes that multiple approaches can be effective in facilitating change;
8. focuses social workers on the need to provide and maintain continual transactions between people and their environments for all populations and to monitor social systems heading for isolation;
9. provides a constant reminder to social workers that change is healthy and necessary for systems to grow but that systems often resist change;
10. places both the social worker and the agency within the client's environment; and
11. reminds social workers that because a change at one level of the system creates changes at other levels, interventions must be thought through and chosen with care (Compton & Galaway, 2004).

Applying the Ecological/Systems Framework

EP 2.1.3b
EP 2.1.7a

The ecological/systems framework is especially useful in understanding the complexities of large systems within our environment, such as the social welfare system. The social welfare system in place at any given moment is the product of the interactions and interrelatedness of historical, economic, and political forces. As a large system, it is reshaped constantly by changes in societal values and events beyond its boundaries. Changes in societal values, for example, result in increased public acceptance of programs for battered women and child care for children of working mothers. An economic recession results in extensive cutbacks in social welfare services.

The scope of social welfare systems in the United States is neither as broad, comprehensive, and integrated as most social workers would like nor as constrained and limited as some contend. In a sense, it is not a formal system at all but, rather, a collection of ad hoc programs developed in diverse and often unique political circumstances. Thus, although we have programs for the aged, individuals with physical disabilities, and dependent children, each program has its own political history and its own political constituency.

Target populations of social service agencies are groups that are not served adequately by the primary social systems in our society (the economic system, the political system, the family system, the religious system, the health system, and the educational system). Typically, the social welfare system comes into play as a result of family breakdown, problems in income distribution, and institutional failure in the religious, education, health, and/or business sectors.

Although each of us probably would offer a somewhat different mission statement for an ideal social welfare system, at a minimum we probably would agree that such a system should guarantee to each person a socially defined minimum standard of well-being. To attempt to meet this standard, the social welfare system interacts with primary social systems within our society: the family system, the economic system, and the political system. Each of these primary systems has a principal function, as illustrated in Table 3.3. The social welfare system is most often seen as a residual social system that comes into play when the primary

system either fails in some way or generates undesirable consequences.

The organized social welfare system, composed of numerous and varied social services and institutions, is designed to help individuals and groups attain satisfactory standards of life and health. This view implies recurring failure in other social systems. It assumes that individuals sometimes need outside help in coping with a complex social order. Social welfare institutions that make up the social welfare system assist in meeting the needs of individuals when primary resources are not available or adequate to address them. A structured set of social agencies must stand ready to respond to personal crises and system failures—to overcome the crisis; to enhance problem-solving and coping skills of communities, groups, organizations, families, and individuals; and to empower these entities to create social change that will result in less frequent crises.

In this view, the social welfare system is seen as the structured set of responses developed to deal with the dysfunction of other systems. For example, the family system is intended to meet children's physical and emotional needs. But at times, the primary family system fails and is unable to serve this function. At that point, the social welfare system provides services such as respite child care, foster care, and counseling. When the social welfare system functions to assist or replace the family in its child care roles, this exemplifies a social welfare system response to a primary system failure. A second example of a social welfare system response to a primary system dysfunction can be seen in relation to the economic system. We know that in the economic system, income is uneven, leaving some people poor. Thus, we have generated an income-assistance system to provide various types of financial help to specific classes of people in need.

An overview of American social welfare institutions and social work practice reveals an incredible range of public and voluntary agencies seeking to respond to social problems. For some areas of need, the response is well conceptualized and generous. In other areas, the response is poorly conceptualized and scant. Still other social needs invoke no response at all. A major problem with our social welfare system is that each need usually is treated as a separate issue rather than as an interactive and interdependent part of a larger issue. Seldom, for example, is attention given to how a response to need A is related to its impact on need B.

The federal welfare reform legislation enacted in 1996 serves as a good example. One of the highly

TABLE 3.3 SOCIAL SYSTEMS AND THEIR FUNCTIONS

SYSTEM	FUNCTIONS
Primary	
Family	The primary personal care and mutual assistance system between parents and children and between adults and the elderly
Political	The authoritative allocation of public social goals and values
Economic	The allocation and distribution of scarce resources to competing entities
Secondary	
Other goal-specific systems (e.g., education system, health-care system, defense system)	The list and functions of secondary systems are dependent on individual choice. What would you include?
Social welfare system	To respond to failure or dysfunction in primary and secondary systems

publicized outcomes of passage of this legislation has been that more former welfare recipients have obtained jobs. In reality, most public-assistance recipients receive benefits for only a short time, but they often have to move back and forth between welfare and work because they cannot make ends meet with the low-paying jobs they are forced to take because of their limited education and training. Thus, while more former welfare recipients are employed now, the legislation has failed to address their other needs, such as child care, transportation, health-care benefits, and affordable housing. As a result, many of these individuals are in worse circumstances than when they were receiving the public assistance benefits.

These additional unmet needs are overloading local social service government agencies and private-sector entities such as religious institutions. Child advocates also are worried about the increase in cases of spouse abuse, child abuse, substance abuse, homelessness, malnutrition, and other problems that are likely to arise when the time limit ends for individuals who are unable to make it without public assistance. The legislation, unfortunately, did not allow for the allocation of additional resources to meet these needs.

Health care also exemplifies the interrelatedness between systems and social problems. In recent years, state legislators, concerned about the high costs of health care for the poor, reduced the funds allocated for health care rather than raise taxes. In doing so, they ignored the fact that state dollars are matched by federal dollars to provide health care for the poor. For every dollar that a state contributes, the federal government matches the amount with federal money. The reduction in dollars by the states limits the amount of federal money coming into the states, which seriously reduces the number of clients who can be served by state public-assistance health programs. No longer served by these health programs, the states' poor do not seek health care until they are desperate, and when they do, they come to local hospitals as indigent (nonpaying) patients. This means that local hospitals have to foot these bills, which now are higher than they might have been if the poor had sought care earlier. It also means that the higher costs in these states are footed by local taxpayers who pay local taxes to support hospitals. Thus, what the legislators ultimately intended as a money-saving measure for their states' citizens has turned out to be far more costly in the long run. Projections show that the Affordable Care

Act of 2010 (commonly referred to as "Obamacare") will not only provide access to health care for the many Americans who could not afford health insurance, but will also reduce the current high expenditures of health care made by state and local governments (Dorn & Boettinger, 2010). The negative response to this legislation underscores the need to understand the impact of policy decisions at all levels of the environment.

The ecological/systems framework can be used to help understand issues at every level of the environment and across levels. The framework further can be used to determine types of intervention at all levels of the environment once the complex issues are understood.

The Generalist Model

EP 2.1.3a
EP 2.1.3b
EP 2.1.7a

As we discussed in Chapter 2, the generalist model of social work practice suggests the use of multiple interventions in working with clients at the individual, family, group, organizational, community, or societal level. Generalist practice focuses on the interface between systems, with equal emphasis on the goals of social justice, humanizing systems, and improving the well-being of people. It uses a multilevel methodology that can be applied to varying levels of the environment, depending on the needs of the client system (Johnson & Yanca, 2009).

The central theme of most generalist practice is the ecological/systems framework. Generalist practice is based on the need for congruency, or a positive fit, between the person and his or her environment, and the premise that the role of social work is to promote, strengthen, and restore—if necessary—that positive fit. **Person–environment** is the actual fit between the person's or group's needs, rights, goals, and capacities and the physical and social environment within which the person or group operates. The fit can be favorable, adequate, or unfavorable. When exchanges with the environment over time are inadequate, the individual's healthy development might be affected negatively, or the environment might be damaged (Germain & Gitterman, 2008, p. 817).

The Strengths Perspective

Generalist social work practice is aimed at identifying a system's strengths and using them to modify the

> ## TABLE 3.4 COMPARISON OF GENERALIST SOCIAL WORK STRENGTHS PERSPECTIVE AND MEDICAL MODEL

GENERALIST PRACTICE OR STRENGTHS PERSPECTIVE	MEDICAL MODEL
Lack of goodness of fit between person and environment; needs not being met	Problem with individual or weakness of individual; person labeled as sick or deviant, given diagnosis
Client and environment present strengths or opportunities and barriers or risks; building on strengths can motivate clients to change themselves, their perceptions, or their environment.	Client has problems or needs; sick clients need help in changing their worldviews to fit the norm.
Client is expert about his or her life and needs; social worker is a facilitator to help client discover needs and identify possible resources to get them met.	Helper is expert who diagnoses client and prescribes treatment; expert is in charge of treatment; client is expected to cooperate.
Client can be empowered to get needs met/use or learn new skills and resources.	Client needs expert helper to help change; needs to be dependent on experts for help.

SOURCE: Adapted from The Integration of Social Work Practice, by R.J. Parsons, J.D. Jorgensen, and S.H. Hernandez. Published by Brooks/Cole Publishing Company, 1994.

environment with which that system interacts to increase the level of person–environment fit. Generalist practice requires knowledge of social work, as well as knowledge and skills in working with individuals, families, groups, organizations, and communities, including advocacy, to empower individuals to change their environments. In this view, the client is the expert, the one who is most knowledgeable about his or her needs, and the social worker builds on the strengths of individuals to facilitate their ability to change their environment, or their coping mechanisms for interacting with it.

The generalist social work **strengths perspective** can be contrasted with what commonly is referred to as the "medical model," which considers the client as having some type of illness or weakness and the helper as the expert who determines and provides the treatment. Table 3.4 compares the generalist social work strengths perspective and the medical model.

All individuals have strengths, and they are much more likely to grow and change when these strengths, rather than the deficiencies, are emphasized. In his book *The Strengths Perspective in Social Work Practice,* Dennis Saleeby (2013), a social work educator at the University of Kansas, delineates six basic principles on which the strengths perspective is based:

1. *Respecting clients' strengths*—Social work practice is guided first and foremost by a profound awareness of, and respect for, clients' positive attributes and abilities, talents and resources, desires and aspirations....

2. *Clients have many strengths*—Individuals and groups have vast, often untapped and frequently unappreciated reservoirs of physical, emotional, cognitive, interpersonal, social and spiritual energies, resources and competencies....

3. *Client motivation is based on fostering client strengths*—Individuals and groups are more likely to continue autonomous development and growth when it is funded by the coin of their capacities, knowledge, and skills....

4. *The social worker is a collaborator with the client*—The role of "expert" or "professional" may not provide the best vantage point from which to appreciate client strengths....

5. *Avoiding the victim mindset*—Emphasizing and orienting the work of helping around clients' strengths can help to avoid "blaming the victim." ...

6. *Any environment is full of resources*—In every environment there are individuals and institutions [that] have something to give, something that others may desperately need ... and for the most part, they are untapped and unsolicited. (pp. 9–13)

The ecological/systems framework enables the social worker and the client to identify strengths at all levels of the environment. This assessment includes the client's personal characteristics, individuals within the client's immediate environment who can be of support to the client, and neighborhood and community resources. The social worker can play a key role in helping the client and those within the client's environment reframe a quality so it can be seen as a strength and be used to address the client's needs.

A school social worker may reframe how school personnel view a mother who has been deemed overly persistent and someone to be avoided because she comes to the school every day to complain angrily about how school personnel are treating her children. The social worker can help school personnel see that this mother cares about her children deeply and wants the best for them as a parent, pointing out the quality of persistence as a strength. The school social worker then can mediate with the mother and school personnel to help the parent use this strength in more appropriate ways so her concerns are heard.

Often, when strengths are identified and reinforced in positive ways, behaviors can go beyond change to even exceed expectations. For example, this mother could become an advocate for the school and use her persistence to obtain support for school bonds in the community. Contrast this approach with a deficit model, which would label the mother's persistence as negative, may anger the parent, and possibly eliminate the persistent behavior rather than help her learn how and when to use persistence effectively.

A goal of social work is to build on client and environmental strengths so clients can reduce barriers and increase opportunities. A strengths-based perspective supports the concept of **resilience**, the ability to recover or adapt successfully to adversity. Juan has many strengths that reveal his resilience. When he felt rejected by his family, he tried to find others in his environment for support. Although he initially found acceptance from gang members, his ability to establish relationships with peers and adults helped him reach out to receive the help he needed and ultimately end his relationship with those who erected barriers to his success. Instead, he began to seek opportunities in his environment that would promote his success, building on his strengths as he saw the success that came with his new behaviors and relationships.

Social workers and other helping professionals are capitalizing on research that identifies characteristics of resilience, such as being more likely to seek out others (teachers, neighbors, parents of friends, grandparents) in an environment for support when the usual resources (parents) are unavailable for some reason. Clients can learn resiliency skills, making them better able to capitalize on opportunities in their environments and to avoid or reduce risks.

School social workers such as Ms. Herrera are working with Juan and other students to build on their strengths and ultimately become more resilient when interacting with their environment. Box 3.1 identifies resiliency factors that she and other helping professionals can encourage in youth to help prevent juvenile delinquency and other problems.

Empowerment

Another key aspect of generalist social work practice is **empowerment**, the "process of increasing personal, interpersonal, or political power so individuals can take action to improve their life situation" (Gutierrez, 1990, p. 149). Many of the individuals with whom social workers interact are members of at-risk populations who face barriers at all levels of the environment, which often limits their functioning. They often lack the power and resources to change their environments, or they may be in situations in which they perceive themselves as powerless, incompetent, or lacking in resources. Rather than "fixing" problems, which often reinforces such feelings, social workers help clients see that they can create change. People who are empowered can make changes at the individual, family, group, neighborhood, organizational, community, state, national, or international level.

Juan's situation illustrates how the strengths perspective and empowerment are used effectively. As Ms. Herrera continued to emphasize Juan's strengths, he realized that he had more power over his life than he had thought. He was able to talk with his mother and negotiate more time with friends. He also felt empowered to say no to his peers who were pressuring him to join the gang. Realizing that other teens were in situations similar to his, he became active in a school leadership program and a key member of a community group that helped to establish a youth center.

Empowering clients like Juan gives them hope and helps them see that they have control over their lives. Empowerment leads to continual growth and change and increased feelings of competence.

Social and Economic Justice

The ecological/systems framework is useful in committing the social work profession to promote **social and economic justice**, which includes fairness and equity in regard to basic civil and human rights, protections, resources and opportunities, and social benefits.

Box 3.1 Resiliency Factors That Reduce Juvenile Delinquency and Other Problems Associated with Youth

- Competence—being able to do something well
- Usefulness—having something to contribute
- Belonging—being part of a community and having relationships with caring adults
- Power—having control over one's future
- Responsiveness—ability to elicit positive responses from others
- Communication—ability to assert oneself without violating others
- Empathy and caring—ability to know how another feels and understand another's perspective
- Compassion—desire and will to care for and alleviate another's suffering
- Altruism—doing for others what they need, not what you want to do for them
- Forgiveness—ability to cease to feel resentment against self and others, including one's abusers
- Problem solving—ability to plan and use identified resources effectively
- Positive identity—sense of one's internal, relatively stable self, apart from others
- Internal locus of control and initiative—sense of being in charge, of having personal power; being motivated from within to direct attention and effort toward a challenging goal (initiative)

- Refusal to accept negative messages about one's gender, culture, or race (resistance)
- Goal direction, achievement motivation, and educational aspirations—relentless effort, persistent inner drive, or unshakable determination to survive
- Special interests, creativity, and imagination—interests and hobbies that bring a sense of task mastery (special interests); ability to create rather than imitate (creativity); ability to form a mental image of something not present to the senses or never before perceived in reality (imagination)
- Optimism and hope—choosing to see the glass half-full and not half empty (optimism); confidence that the odds can be surmounted (hope)
- Faith, spirituality, and sense of meaning—having a belief system that allows you to attribute meaning to misfortune and illness (a form of reframing the situation)

SOURCE: Adapted from U.S. Department of Health and Human Services Administration for Children and Families, Family and Youth Services Bureau (2004). *Four pillars of the positive youth development model.* Washington, DC: Author; and U.S. Department of Justice, Office of Juvenile Justice and Delinquency Prevention (2003). *Risk and protective factors of child delinquency.* Washington, DC: Author.

How resources are distributed at every level of the environment, who has access to those resources and opportunities, and how policies at all levels of society affect human development shape social work practice and types and levels of intervention. Juan and his family, because they are Mexican American, poor, and in a family situation involving divorce, face social and economic injustice at all levels of the environment.

Social workers advocate for social and economic justice by working to expand individual access to resources and opportunities at all levels of the environment, including adequate education; food, clothing, and shelter; employment; health care; and participation in local, state, and national political processes. Further, social workers have a commitment to alleviate social and economic injustice and its resulting oppression and discrimination. Some of

the possible types of oppression that can result from social and economic injustice are shown in Table 3.5.

The Helping Process

EP 2.1.3b
EP 2.1.10a
EP 2.1.10b
EP 2.1.10c

The beginning generalist social work professional is seen as a "change agent" who can assist client systems in identifying needed change, developing strategies to make the change with those client systems, empowering and assisting client systems to implement those strategies, and monitoring and evaluating throughout the process to ensure that the desired change is happening. Note that the term *client system* is used rather than *client*, because social work intervention often is directed at a level of the environment beyond the

TABLE 3.5 COMMON FORMS OF OPPRESSION	
INSTITUTIONAL OPPRESSION	CULTURAL OPPRESSION
Housing	Values and norms
Employment	Language
Education	Standards of behavior
Media	Holidays
Religion	Roles
Health services	Logic system
Government	Societal expressions
Legal services	The arts
Transportation	
Recreation	

SOURCE: Interdependence: The Route to Community, by A. Condeluci (Delray Beach, FL: St. Lucie, 1996), p. 18. Reprinted with permission of the author.

individual. A **client system** can encompass individuals, families, groups, organizations, communities, or larger social entities at which intervention is directed.

Social workers with a bachelor of social work degree are trained to follow a generalist approach that can be applied to individual needs that are part of everyday life, as well as to larger client systems. No matter what level of the environment the social worker selects as an intervention point, the generalist approach can be a useful tool in bringing about planned change. Social workers with a master's degree in social work also draw on the generalist approach as they work with clients. Whether providing clinical services to an individual or a family or macro services at the community level, social workers need to take into account the interaction of the various levels of the environment and their impact on the social issue being addressed.

Although many variations can be chosen when delineating the stages of the helping process from a generalist social work perspective, all have the ecological/systems framework as a base. In their identification of three stages, Miley, O'Melia, and DuBois (2013) incorporate the framework with a strengths/empowerment perspective.

Dialogue

- Build partnerships based on acceptance, respect, and trust
- Define respective roles
- Discuss clients' experiences with challenging situations
- Define the purpose of working together
- Activate client motivation for change
- Address crisis needs

Discovery

- Explore clients' strengths as resources for change
- Examine resource possibilities in clients' environments
- Assess capabilities of available resource systems
- Specify outcome goals and concrete objectives
- Construct a plan of action
- Negotiate a contract for change

Development

- Operationalize the plan of action
- Increase the experience of power within client systems
- Access resources necessary to achieve goals
- Create alliances among persons and organizations to accomplish the plan
- Enhance opportunities and choices by creating additional resources (pp. 111–114)
- Social work educators Compton and Galaway (2004) and others take a somewhat more traditional view, delineating what is referred to as a problem-solving approach, but they suggest similar stages when working with client systems:

Contact or Engagement

- Develop a relationship with the client system
- Define the problem(s) to be addressed
- Identify preliminary goals
- Obtain as much information as possible to develop intervention strategies

Contract

- Assess and evaluate the strengths and needs of the client system
- Formulate an action plan
- Determine what resources are needed for the plan to be successful

Action

- Carry out the plan
- Monitor and adjust the plan as needed
- Terminate
- Evaluate

Note the similarities between these stages and those with more emphasis on the strengths and empowerment of the client system. In moving through these stages with a client system, regardless of the specific model used, the social worker and the client address the following issues together:

- Who has the power?
- What connections does the client have?
- What connections are working?
- What connections are not working?
- What connections are missing?
- Is this the way things should be? What would the client like to see changed?
- What connections can be used as resources to facilitate the change?
- What about the big picture? How do all the pieces of the system fit together? (Miley, O'Melia, & Dubois, 2013, pp. 271–276)

As you can see from the phases and issues addressed, the ecological/systems framework is the organizing framework, and intervention is from a generalist practice perspective, which incorporates the client's strengths and the broader environment, empowerment, and promotion of social and economic justice. A large part of generalist social work practice often involves mediating between systems to strengthen their connections to each other.

After reviewing the phases of the helping process, it is easy to see the "goodness of fit" between this process and the ecological/systems framework and the many ways in which the two are related. Ms. Herrera's involvement with Juan and his family illustrates how this framework can be applied to understand or to intervene at various levels of the environment.

Applications with Juan and His Family

During the *contact and engagement,* or dialogue, phase of the helping process, Ms. Herrera, the school social worker, applied all of the concepts of the ecological/systems framework. In developing an initial relationship with Juan and his mother, she called upon her preliminary knowledge about 12-year-old boys and their developmental needs during this preadolescence stage, single-parent women and their special needs, the Mexican American culture, and ways in which preadolescents and parents might view a professional from an authoritative organization such as a school. She empathized with Juan and his mother as she realized how they might view life in their day-to-day reality. As she continued to get to know Juan, Ms. Herrera allowed him to be the "expert," telling her what his life was like and what his needs were. She emphasized his strengths and helped him realize that he had many on which to draw.

As Juan and Ms. Herrera began the *contract,* or discovery, phase, Ms. Herrera gathered information about Juan from his mother, his teachers, his friends, and others within his environment who could help in obtaining a holistic picture of Juan and his needs. Ms. Herrera and Juan looked at the characteristics of Juan, his mother, his teachers, and his friends and also at their interactions with Juan and with each other. They considered both needs and strengths. They realized that both Juan and his mother were motivated to change and that his teachers were committed to helping him.

Ms. Herrera incorporated information she learned about Juan's family with her knowledge about the dynamics of a family in which substance abuse had been a problem, about long-term effects of child maltreatment on parents, about gangs and peer relationships when adolescents feel lonely and isolated, and about Juan's family's church, Juan's mother's jobs, and the community and its attitudes toward Juan and his family. She was especially concerned about the lack of resources in the community and the lack of support for young adolescent males and single-parent mothers.

As she discovered more about Juan's situation, Ms. Herrera and Juan began to explore possible resources that would be available to help meet Juan's needs. Ms. Herrera set up a meeting with Juan and his mother to clarify their needs and to establish preliminary goals based on the information they had gathered. The three of them agreed that three initial needs were to: (1) reduce Juan's responsibility at home, (2) address his sense of loss over his father's leaving and anger because he had left, and (3) help Juan create a positive peer support group.

They identified goals to reduce the pressure from Juan's mother for him to take care of his brother and do so much at home, to help Juan deal with his feelings about the divorce, and to help him develop a positive peer support group. The three of them agreed that, although the initial referral related to Juan's school behavior and performance, these underlying needs were more critical and would, in fact, most likely improve his school performance if they were addressed.

After these three goals were identified, Juan and Ms. Herrera began meeting, sometimes separately and sometimes with his mother. They considered all possible options regarding how these goals might be met, listing potential resources that might be helpful. Some resources, such as more financial help from Juan's father or Juan's mother quitting her job and going on public assistance, were rejected for various reasons. Finally, the three of them developed a contractual agreement specifying how Juan's needs would be addressed.

During the *action*, or development, phase, Ms. Herrera referred Juan's mother to the local human services agency, where she was able to qualify for low-income child care for her younger child. Juan's mother also asked for information about a job-training program to upgrade her skills so she could obtain a higher-paying job and be able to have only one job instead of two. This would allow her to spend more time with Juan and his brother.

With Ms. Herrera's help, Juan and his mother negotiated specific tasks that Juan would do at home and agreed that he would have 2 hours after school every day to spend time with friends. They also agreed to rules regarding how he could spend his time with them. Juan and his mother also agreed that if Juan were to follow the rules and complete his chores, he could spend time weekly with his friends in his old neighborhood. In addition, Juan agreed to participate in a school support group for seventh-grade boys whose parents have divorced. Ms. Herrera believed that this approach would help Juan work through some of his feelings about the divorce and also develop a new set of peers with whom he could become socially involved.

Juan and his mother also began counseling at the local teen–parent center, and the counselor and Ms. Herrera conferred regularly about his progress there. Ms. Herrera, while maintaining confidentiality about Juan's specific family issues, communicated with Juan's teachers. They agreed to help Juan feel more accepted in his new school and to provide opportunities for him to get to know other students.

After 3 months, Juan's teachers reported that he was coming to class, participating in class discussions, handing in his homework, and no longer exhibiting behavior problems. His grades also improved significantly. Juan began to feel more empowered, and he dropped his friends who were gang members and formed several solid friendships with classmates at his new school. Two of his friends were from the support group. Although the group was terminated after 8 weeks, Ms. Herrera still met with Juan every 2 weeks or so to be sure that he was doing well.

Juan spent a great deal of time in the group talking about the divorce and his feelings about his father. He had visited his father twice and was looking forward to seeing him during spring vacation. Juan and his mother, and sometimes his younger brother, participated in family counseling sessions at the teen–parent center. Juan's mother developed a new set of friends and a support system through her youngest son's child-care center, to which many other single parents brought their children. The mother enrolled in a computer-programming training course and was looking forward to the opportunity to upgrade her skills.

As positive changes in one system took place, they had a positive impact in other systems as well. The fact that Juan's mother was able to obtain child care, for example, reduced her stress and enabled her to interact more positively with Juan. Ms. Herrera's talking with Juan's teachers and helping them understand his needs for acceptance enabled them to view Juan more positively. This, in turn, reduced some of the pressure on him, increased his self-esteem, and gave him the needed confidence to seek new friendships and find more positive ways to gain acceptance. Juan became involved in a school leadership program and helped develop an outreach program for new students.

Although she believed that she was able to make a difference when helping Juan and his mother, Ms. Herrera was increasingly frustrated about many other of her students who were like Juan. She had referrals on her desk for 12 more students in similar situations. She decided that, as a more productive use of her time, she would develop additional resources at other levels of the environment rather than deal with each student on an individual basis. Ms. Herrera contacted the director of the counseling center and other individuals in the community who were concerned. A group of 15 community representatives, including Juan as the teen representative from the school, began to develop plans for a comprehensive program that would help teens and their families. The plan called for staff members from the counseling center to come to the school weekly to lead additional support groups, for outreach efforts to be made to local businesses to locate adult mentors to work one-to-one with teens in need of additional adult support, and for the development of a teen center with after-school, evening, and weekend recreational programs. Finally, the group decided to work with a state legislative group to advocate for additional funding for adolescent services and for single-parent families.

Summary

Social welfare needs involve many interrelated factors. These factors may be ordered in many ways to describe social welfare needs, to understand them, and to predict when they will occur and under what conditions. Because the needs are so complex and involve human behaviors and environmental influences that are difficult to measure, as well as a variety of disciplines, no one theory can address all social welfare or human needs. The ecological/systems framework, however, is a framework of choice for social workers because it incorporates the concept that an individual is part of a larger environment with which he or she continually interacts and is an interdependent part of that environment. This framework is useful in organizing information to determine what else is needed and to develop an appropriate intervention strategy.

The framework incorporates factors at the individual, family, group, organizational, community, and societal levels and allows for a variety of interventions at one or more levels. The framework is congruent with the generalist practice approach and its emphasis on client strengths, empowerment, and the promotion of social and economic justice.

Competency Notes

EP 2.1.3a: Distinguish, appraise, and integrate multiple sources of knowledge, including research-based knowledge and practice wisdom (pp. 54–55, 58, 62, 69, 71). Social workers use the ecological/systems framework as a guide to organize and assess multiple sources of knowledge and, drawing on that knowledge, make informed judgments in their work with clients and service delivery systems.

EP 2.1.3b: Analyze models of assessment, prevention, intervention, and evaluation (pp. 54–55, 58, 62, 67, 69, 71, 74). Social workers use the ecological/systems framework and models of assessment, prevention, intervention, and evaluation, applying critical thinking to assess frameworks and models used to ensure that they are most appropriate with the diverse clients they serve.

EP 2.1.7a: Use conceptual frameworks to guide the process of assessment, intervention, and evaluation (pp. 54–55, 58, 62, 67, 69, 71). Social workers use the ecological/systems framework, incorporating other frameworks as appropriate, to guide the processes of assessment, intervention, and evaluation.

EP 2.1.10a: Substantively and affectively prepare for action with individuals, families, groups, organizations, and communities (p. 74). Social workers incorporate the ecological/systems framework and emphasize strengths and empowerment in engaging individuals, families, groups, organizations, and communities in the helping process.

EP 2.1.10b: Use empathy and other interpersonal skills (p. 74). Social workers incorporate the ecological/systems framework and other relevant frameworks assessing client strengths and limitations, developing mutually agreed-on intervention goals, and selecting appropriate intervention strategies.

EP 2.1.10c: Develop a mutually agreed-on focus of work and desired outcomes (p. 74). Social workers incorporate the ecological/systems framework when helping clients solve problems; negotiating, mediating and advocating with and on behalf of clients, and implementing interventions that enhance client and community well-being.

Key Terms

The terms below are defined in the Glossary.

association
boundary

cause-and-effect
    relationship
chronosystem

client system
closed systems
developmental niche
ecological/systems
  framework
empowerment
entropy
equifinality
exosystem level
generalizable
inclusive
intrapsychic aspects
macrosystem level
mesosystem level
microsystem level

open systems
opportunities
person-environment fit
psychosocial aspects
resilience
risks
social and economic
  justice
steady state
strengths perspective
synergy
system
testable
theory
worldview

Discussion Questions

1. Why is it difficult to develop a good theory to address social welfare needs?
2. Briefly identify the key components of the ecological/systems perspective. Compare and contrast open and closed systems, and static and steady-state systems, and offer examples to exemplify your discussion.
3. From an ecological/systems perspective, identify the social systems that currently affect Juan's life. Which aspects of each system you identified seem to be barriers and which are opportunities?
4. Using the ecological/systems perspective as conceptualized by Bronfenbrenner and Garbarino, identify at least one strategy you might use as a social worker to help Juan and his family at each of the four levels of the environment: microsystem, mesosystem, exosystem, and macrosystem.
5. What are at least four advantages of using the ecological/systems perspective to understand social welfare needs?
6. Briefly describe the helping process and its advantages to social workers within social welfare institutions. What type of intervention plan would you suggest if you were the school social worker assigned to work with Juan? Why?
7. How are the concepts of empowerment, client strengths, resilience, and social and economic justice congruent with the ecological/systems framework?
8. Identify two people (you and a sibling, for example) who were raised in the same household. Apply the concept of developmental niche to show how these two people differ and why.

On the Internet

www.clasp.org
www.jcpr.org
www.who.int/violenceprevention/approach/ecology/en/index.html

References

Berk, L. (2014). *Development through the lifespan* (6th ed.). Boston: Pearson.

Bronfenbrenner, U. (1979). *The ecology of human development*. Cambridge, MA: Harvard University Press.

Bronfenbrenner, U. (2005). *Making human beings human: Bioecological perspectives on human development*. Thousand Oaks, CA: Sage.

Coady, N., & Lehmann, P. (Eds.). (2007). *Theoretical perspectives for direct social work practice: A generalist-eclectic approach* (2nd ed.). New York: Springer.

Compton, B., & Galaway, B. (2004). *Social work processes* (8th ed.). Florence, KY: Cengage Learning.

Condeluci, A. (1996). *Interdependence: The route to community*. Delray Beach, FL: St. Lucie.

Dorn, S., & Buettgens, M. (2010). *Net effects of the Affordable Care Act on state budgets*. Washington, DC: Urban Institute.

Erikson, E. (1950). *Childhood and society*. New York: Norton.

Erikson, E. (1994). *Identity and the life cycle*. New York: Norton.

Garbarino, J. (1992). *Children and families in the social environment*. New York: Aldine de Gruyter.

Garbarino, J. (2009). *Children and the dark side of human experience: Confronting global realities and rethinking child development*. New York: Springer.

Gardiner, H., & Kozmitzki, C. (2011). *Lives across cultures: Cross-cultural human development* (5th ed.). Boston: Allyn & Bacon.

Germain, C., & Gitterman, A. (2008). *The life model of social work practice: Advances in theory and practice* (3rd ed.). New York: Columbia University Press.

Granvold, P. K. (2007). Constructivist theory and practice. In N. Coady & P. Lehmann (Eds.), *Theoretical perspectives for direct social work practice: A generalist and eclectic approach* (pp. 401–427). New York: Springer.

Gutierrez, L. M. (1990). Working with a woman of color. *Social Work*, 35, 135–153.

Johnson, L. C., & Yanca, S. J. (2009). *Social work practice: A generalist approach* (10th ed.). Upper Saddle River, NJ: Prentice-Hall.

Miley, K., O'Melia, M., & DuBois, B. (2013). *Generalist social work practice: An empowering approach* (7th ed.). Boston: Allyn & Bacon.

Parsons, R., Jorgensen, J., & Hernandez, S. (1994). *The integration of social work practice*. Belmont, CA: Brooks/Cole.

Richmond, M. (1922). *What is social casework?* New York: Russell Sage Foundation.

Rothery, M. (2008). Critical ecological systems theory. In N. Cody & P. Lehmann (Eds.). *Theoretical perspectives for direct social work practice: A generalist-eclectic approach* (2nd ed., pp. 89–118). New York: Springer.

Saleeby, D. (2013). *The strengths perspective in social work practice* (6th ed.). Boston: Allyn & Bacon.

Shriver, J. (2011). *Human behavior and the social environment: Shifting paradigms in essential knowledge for social work practice* (4th ed.). Boston: Allyn & Bacon.

Siporin, M. (1975). *Introduction to social work practice.* New York: Macmillan.

Super, S., & Harkness, C. M. (1994). The developmental niche: A theoretical framework for analyzing the household production of health. *Social Science Medicine*, 38(2), 217–226.

U.S. Department of Health and Human Services Administration for Children and Families, Family and Youth Services Bureau. (2004). *Four pillars of the Positive Youth Development Model.* Washington, DC: Author.

U.S. Department of Justice, Office of Juvenile Justice and Delinquency Prevention (2003). *Risk and protective factors of child delinquency.* Washington, DC: Author.

van Wormer, K., Besthorn, F., & Keefe, T. (2010). *Human behavior and the social environment: Macro level: Groups, communities and organizations.* New York: Oxford University Press.

Von Bertalanffy, L. (1968). *General system theory.* New York: Braziller.

Suggested Readings

Ashford, J.B., LeCroy, C.W., & Lortie, K.L. (2009). *Human behavior in the social environment: A multidimensional perspective.* Florence, KY: Cengage Learning.

Butts, J., Mayer, S., & Ruth, G. (2005). *Focusing juvenile justice on positive youth development.* Chicago: Chapin Hall Center for Children.

Day, P., & Schiele, J. (2013). *A new history of social welfare* (7th ed.). Boston: Allyn & Bacon.

Hepworth, D.H., Rooney, R.H., Rooney, G.D., Strom-Gottfried, K., & Larsen, J. (2012). *Direct social work practice: Theory and skills.* (9th ed.). Florence, KY: Cengage Learning.

Mullis, R., & Davis, M. (2005). An ecological model approach to childhood obesity. Available from http://www.csrees.usda.gov/nea/food/pdfs/roundtable_presentations_mullis.pdf

Orren, D., Smith, R., Norlin, J., & Chess, W.A. (2008). *Human behavior and the social environment: Social systems theory* (6th ed.). Boston: Allyn & Bacon.

Zastrow, C., & Kirst-Ashman, K. (2013). *Understanding human behavior in the social environment* (9th ed.). Belmont, CA: Cengage Learning.

CHAPTER 4

Diversity and Social Justice

Jackson Dupree, a 22-year-old African American male, is a student at a small university in the Midwest. Growing up in a large city on the East Coast, he enjoyed a relatively easy childhood until he started high school. From the time Jackson and his friends began driving, the city police stopped them routinely for various reasons. They were told that they "looked like suspects" in some recently reported crime or that they seemed to be "cruising" a neighborhood and were asked why they were there. On several occasions, Jackson and his friends were stopped by clerks or security guards at city malls and questioned about their activities. Jackson's parents had taught him to be respectful, especially when relating to police, so he always answered their questions politely. These events took a toll on Jackson, who was an honors student in school and active in his church. As a result of these experiences, he had trouble sleeping at night and became much more cautious around adults.

Hoping he would fit in better if he were to go to a university in an area that seemed more accepting of African Americans, he decided to attend college out of state. During his sophomore year, Jackson developed an intense relationship with another male and came out, declaring to his friends that he was gay. Jackson was a well-respected student leader on campus and his sexual orientation didn't seem to matter to those with whom he interacted on the small university campus. This past year, however, Jackson had two negative experiences indicating that sexual orientation clearly matters to some. At the suggestion of one of his professors, he applied for a summer job at a local youth center. After an interview, he did not hear back from the center in spite of having phoned them several times. He later learned that he hadn't been hired because the center was worried about ruining its image and angering parents if it were to hire a gay person.

Later in the year, Jackson went to a local club with a group of friends, both gay and straight. When he decided to leave his friends early to study for an exam, he was attacked in the parking lot by two men and beaten with a tire iron while his assailants called him names relating to his sexual orientation. Now physically recovered from the beating, Jackson wonders where he fits in a world that doesn't seem to support either his race or his sexual orientation.

Situations such as those experienced by Jackson are not rare. Many individuals seek fulfillment and opportunities only to find that social barriers hamper their ability to achieve these goals. Jackson represents only one case in millions of Americans who find that social and economic justice is not necessarily achieved through hard work, dedication, and quality performance. All too often, social mobility and opportunity are not equally available to all who seek to attain the American Dream. People of color; those who are lesbian, gay, bisexual, or transgender; women; people who are living in poverty; those with disabilities; older adults; and other members of diverse groups historically have been denied opportunities in business, religious, political, and social life, while white males have come to expect fair treatment and take it for granted. Because of micro and institutional racism, classism, sexism, ageism, ableism, religious discrimination, and heterosexism and homophobia, the right to free and full participation in our social and economic institutions is denied to those who fail to meet dominant-group criteria. In Jackson's case, the fear that he would influence young people at the recreation center to "become gay" was sufficient justification for denying him the opportunity for a job. And often, being a member of a marginalized group makes one an easy target for racial profiling or the type of hate crime that Jackson experienced. Stereotypes, once institutionalized, are difficult to overcome.

In this chapter we will explore the concepts of social and economic justice and examine the characteristics of social injustice implicit in racism and ethnic discrimination, classism, sexism, heterosexism and homophobia, ageism, religious discrimination, and ableism. The impact of social injustice is not always the same for people of color, women, those who are poor, those who have a disability, persons who are elderly, persons whose religious beliefs differ from the dominant group, or those who are lesbian, gay, bisexual, or transgender. It is somewhat ironic, for example, that white women, the targets of gender inequality, often discriminate against people of color, or that people of color discriminate against individuals because of their sexual orientation. To better understand the strengths of groups marginalized by society as well as the differential effects of institutional racism, sexism, classism, heterosexism and homophobia, ableism, ageism, and religious discrimination, we review these separately. Keep in mind that social and economic injustices and their consequences lead to a life of second-class citizenship in our society for members of all groups who are impacted and that being a member of more than one minority group may further marginalize an individual. Note that not all disparities are discussed in this chapter, as more detailed information is provided in later chapters.

The promotion of social and economic justice and efforts to reduce prejudice and discrimination against all groups are key components of the social work profession. Like everyone, all social workers participate in a society where some groups have more opportunities and privileges than others and have reaped the benefits of opportunity, while others have experienced oppression and discrimination. Because we are members of multiple groups, most of us have experienced opportunity and privilege as well as oppression and discrimination at some points in our lives. As you read this chapter, keep in mind that all of us have received messages about those groups in which we hold membership as well as groups other than our own, and that all of us have biases and stereotypes. This chapter provides an overview of aspects of social and economic justice and differential outcomes of various social groups based on the ways they are viewed by the dominant groups in power. The focus of the chapter is to get students to think about the issues raised, rather than to provide full coverage of each issue. Those of you continuing in social work education will take at least one course that provides much more depth about issues of social and economic justice and injustice and their impact on various social groups. Regardless of whether you continue in social work courses or not, learning about your own biases and the ways that your experiences have shaped your views of yourself and others, as well as the experiences of others and the impact on their world views, is a life-long journey.

Social and Economic Justice

EP 2.1.5a
EP 2.1.8a

Although much has been written about the concepts of social and economic justice, many works talk more about social and economic injustice than justice. The term **social justice** was first used by a Sicilian priest in 1840, and then by philosophers in discussions about how society should be structured to best meet the needs of its citizens. The concept of social justice gained additional attention in 1861 in John Stuart Mill's essay "Utilitarianism." Mill advocated that all resources and other benefits of living in a society should be distributed according to recognizable principles of justice. His writings were intended to appeal to the aristocracy in Europe to address the needs of uprooted peasants who had relocated to cities seeking jobs. Mill called for decision makers to attend to the "common good," whereby citizens would work collaboratively to build communities and programs that would contribute to the "good" of others.

Mill and other philosophers debated the question: What is a just society? Their writings covered a continuum of perspectives, from allowing members of society to create their own lives and use resources as they wished, as long as they didn't infringe on the rights of others, to the idea that resources generated by all members of society should be distributed to all, first meeting the needs of those members who were the worst off (Novak, 2000).

Today, social justice is viewed from both political and philosophical perspectives. This concept is imbedded in many religious teachings as well, including principles set forth in Judeo-Christian teachings. The goal of social justice is full participation of all groups in a society that is mutually shaped to meet their needs and ensures that all of its members are psychologically safe and secure (Adams, Bell, & Griffin, 2007). Social justice focuses on how individual rights are protected and supported in day-to-day interactions as well as within the fabric of society.

Advocates for social justice want all members of society, regardless of background or status, to have basic human rights and equal opportunities to access the benefits of the society. Although this concept sounds reasonable, particularly when talking about basic freedoms such as freedom of thought, the right to humane treatment, and other general principles, the concept of **economic justice**, which relates to fair allocation of resources, becomes more complicated. A basic problem with the perspective of economic justice is that few of us want to surrender our economic freedom if it means that ultimately we will have less so that others can have more (Capeheart & Milovanovic, 2007; Garcia & Van Soest, 2006; Rawls, 2005). The social work profession has as one of its core values the promotion of social and economic justice, in which social workers are called upon constantly to assess how their actions support these principles in all of their interactions and at all levels of the environment.

Prejudice, Discrimination, and Oppression

EP 2.1.2a
EP 2.1.4a
EP 2.1.4c

Social injustice and **social inequality** are products of prejudice and discrimination. **Prejudice** is a value learned through the process of socialization. Once internalized, prejudice becomes part of an individual's value system. People who are prejudiced rarely consider themselves to be so. Objects of negative prejudice are presumed to have behavioral characteristics that those who are prejudiced find objectionable. Through negative stereotyping, women, people of color, lesbians and gays, and members of other diverse groups are presumed to hold behavioral traits that justify their exclusion from free and full participation in the social roles of society.

Stereotypes are beliefs that members of certain groups behave in specific ways. Hence, some in our society hold beliefs that women are not as astute as men at decision making; that African Americans are less intelligent and are prone to idleness and crime; that Latinos prefer the slower pace of agrarian life; and that gays and lesbians encourage heterosexuals to become homosexual. These are among the many negative stereotypes associated with each of these groups. In contrast, positive stereotypes—that women are nurturing and supportive; that African Americans gain strength from religion and their churches; and that Latinos place considerable value on their large, extended families—are just as liable to lead to false presumptions as are negative stereotypes. To illustrate how prejudice affects decision making, consider the following:

> A conservative EuroAmerican (white, of German and English ancestry) couple had an older daughter who graduated from college and moved to Florida to work for a well-known national corporation. While there, she fell in love with an attorney who also worked for the corporation. At first her family was happy about the reported relationship, but became extremely upset when they learned that the attorney was African American. In spite of family pressure, she married the attorney and joined the Baptist church. As a consequence, her parents, two of her four siblings, and one set of grandparents discontinued contact with her. Because there were also strong differences of opinion within the family about whether the marriage was desirable, in effect, interracial marriage tore this family apart.

In this situation, the older daughter violated strong in-group values and traditions that had become institutionalized and affirmed as a matter of family beliefs and faith. There was little doubt that her husband was of impeccable character, a hard worker, an outstanding citizen, a man of faith, and a loving and caring husband. Those qualities from the family's perspective were necessary but not sufficient for their blessing and acceptance of the newlyweds. Indeed, from the parents' perspective, any male who was not white would have been unacceptable as a marriage partner for their daughter.

Although most people hold deep respect for traditions and strongly held values, one can readily understand how prejudgment can ensue. Like the family just described, dominant-group members in society have long-standing values, attitudes, customs, and beliefs related to women, people who are poor, lesbians and gays, and people of color. These beliefs often result in social barriers that preclude or limit members of these groups from living in a socially just society.

Social distance is invariably a mirror of prejudice, just as discrimination is a vehicle to ensure social distance. Prejudice is the presumption, without the benefit of facts, that certain behaviors are characteristic of all members of a specific group. As a consequence, members of the dominant group may demean members of a minority group by assuming that assigned behaviors are true and by then relating to individual members of that group through the filter of prejudice.

Although the target of prejudice may vary, the paradox is that virtually no one is free from prejudice. For example, prejudice may not be directed toward gender, race, ethnicity, or creed. It may be directed toward people who themselves are prejudiced!

Prejudice is a psychological construct that may result in discrimination. Although prejudice can exist without discrimination (and discrimination without prejudice, for that matter), the two usually coexist. Prejudice fuels the fires and provides the justification for discrimination. If individuals hold the false belief (prejudice) that people of certain groups are less intelligent, are incapable of equal participation, or would threaten traditional practices, those individuals may practice differential treatment (discrimination), thereby placing the erroneously feared threat at some distance. Denying women, people of color, the poor, the elderly, lesbians and gays, and other social groups the right to equal social participation limits the opportunity structures through which the desired behavioral characteristics could be acquired. A vicious, self-perpetuating cycle then is set in motion.

Discrimination is the action that maintains and supports prejudice. It involves actions toward selected individuals or groups because of prejudicial beliefs: denying equal access to education, community services, employment opportunities, residential housing areas, and membership in certain religious and social organizations. Although everyone has prejudices, the people who are most damaged by prejudice and

discrimination are those who are not members of the dominant group. Individuals who are members of the group that has the most power are the least likely to suffer from the repercussions of prejudice and discrimination.

Over time, the impact of prejudice and discrimination becomes part of the everyday fabric of society. Members of both dominant and minority groups are not always aware that what they take for granted is discriminatory to some social groups.

Institutional discrimination is discrimination that results from accepted beliefs and behaviors and is codified in societal roles and policies. It is thereby "intrinsic" to the mores of a society. Institutional discrimination is reinforced through the social practices of dominant-group members, who may be oblivious to the effects of their actions. Examples of institutional discrimination include lack of access to housing in specific geographic areas where ethnic groups have settled over time (see Box 4.1); the resulting ethnic composition of schools based on housing patterns; the location of freeways and storage units for dangerous chemicals; access and participation in higher education; access to certain types and levels of employment; and pay differentials among white males, women, and people of color who are doing the same type of job. Whereas institutional racism is based on a person's color, institutional sexism results in the denial of rights or opportunities for participation on the basis of gender. In both instances, free and full participation is denied on the basis of membership in some group.

Members of the dominant societal group with prejudices against other groups have the power to use their prejudices against those groups. These prejudices coupled with power result in **oppression,** unjust uses of power against nondominant groups by the dominant group. This power restricts the actions of the nondominant groups and also allows the dominant group to exploit these groups to its advantage. Examples of oppression include the placement of tank farms and other dangerous environmental hazards in poor neighborhoods populated largely by people of color and restricted access of certain groups to educational and employment opportunities.

Even if individuals who are members of the dominant social group do not demonstrate overt prejudice toward other groups, they have advantages that members of nondominant groups are less likely to enjoy. Peggy McIntosh of the Wellesley College Center for Research on Women has written about

Box 4.1   The Intergenerational Web of Institutional Discrimination

Institutional discrimination is often a difficult concept to understand. Most people would agree that using the "n" word to refer to someone who is African American, or a business owner denying a job to a woman because the firm only hires men, is discriminatory. But it is harder to identify discrimination that is ingrained in the very fabric of our society. One example of institutional discrimination can be seen in by looking at how federal policies and funding have impacted housing markets, using the housing development Levittown, in Long Island, New York, as a case study (California Newsreel, 2003).

After World War II, returning soldiers had difficulty finding places to live, as housing was scarce and often expensive. At that time, most mortgage companies required a down payment of about 50% of the value of a home to buy it. Although the Federal Housing Administration (FHA) was created in 1930, it changed its system after the war to allow people to buy homes with down payments that were only 10–20% of the value of a home, as is common practice today. This new practice and funding for loans available for veterans from the Veteran's Administration resulted in booms in housing construction across the United States, particularly in the suburbs. One new planned development of 17,000 new homes, Levittown, in Long Island, New York, became home to many military personnel and their families. However, Levittown did not sell homes to African Americans.

Another practice in place during this time was a national appraisal system that rated housing areas with a color-coded system based on a number of factors, including the race of individuals living in a given area. The logic of this approach was that areas that were predominantly white would result in well-kept-up neighborhoods, low crime rates, and few foreclosures. All-white suburbs far away from areas with high numbers of people of color received "green" ratings, while inner-city areas populated largely by non-whites received "red" ratings. It was difficult for developers and interested home owners alike to receive authorization for funds in areas with "red" ratings. This practice was commonly referred to as "redlining." Between 1934 and 1962, $120B in new housing funds were made available; less than 2% went to nonwhites (California Newsreel, 2003).

When the Fair Housing Act was passed under the leadership of President Lyndon Johnson in 1968, developments like Levittown could no longer deny selling a home to someone based on race. However, because of "redlining," as soon as a nonwhite family moved into a neighborhood that was all white, unscrupulous realtors quickly moved in with a practice called "block busting." They went door to door, telling white families that if they didn't sell their homes quickly, their housing values would drop significantly and they would lose any equity that they had established. The realtors then turned around and sold those homes to people of color at inflated values. Many developments became predominantly African American within a year or two. Beverly Tatum, president of Spelman College and author of a number of well-known publications on race relations, makes the point that it was not people of color moving into neighborhoods that changed housing values, but whites moving out of them.

Because of long-term results of redlining and block busting practices, housing values in predominantly non-white neighborhoods were and remain much less than those found in predominantly white neighborhoods. The net worth of a nonwhite-owned house in a predominantly nonwhite neighborhood might be worth $60,000, while the exact same white-owned home in the suburbs might be worth as much as $320,000. Since many middle-class families in the United States accrue wealth through real estate, one can see how race and class intersect to create inequities because of government policies. Primarily as a result of inequities in real estate value, the median net worth of whites in the United States was 20 times greater than it was for blacks in 2012 (Brown, 2012).

These inequities also create inequities in neighborhood tax bases. The resulting segregation thus has resulted in an intergenerational "web" effect, impacting neighborhood schools, access to jobs and services, street repairs, and environmental and public safety. As Dr. Tatum notes,

> So if you can get a government loan with your GI Bill, your newly earned college degree and buy a house in an all-white area, that then appreciates in value, that then you can pass on to your children, then you're passing on wealth. That has all been made more available to you as a consequence of racist policies and practices. To the child of that parent, it looks like my father worked hard, bought

(continued)

Box 4.1   The Intergenerational Web of Institutional Discrimination *(continued)*

a house, passed his wealth on to me, made it possible for me to go to school, mortgaged that house so I could have ... a relatively debt-free college experience, and has financed my college education. How come your father didn't do that? You know ... there are some good reasons why maybe your father had a harder time doing it if you're African-American, or Latino, or Native American. (California Newsreel, 2003)

Sources: California Newsreel. (2003). *Race: The power of an illusion.* Available at http://www.pbs.org/race/000_General /000_00-Home.htm. Brown, D. (2012). *How home ownership keeps blacks poorer than whites.* Forbes. Available at http:// www.forbes.com/sites/forbesleadershipforum/2012/12/10/how -home-ownership-keeps-blacks-poorer-than-whites/.

You might want to view the PBS special *Race: The Power of an Illusion* developed by California Newsreel for additional information on housing patterns as well as other examples of race and racism in the United States.

"white privilege," noting that white males and females alike, regardless of whether they are personally prejudiced against nonwhite groups, have taken-for-granted privileges not always available to members of other groups. Her list includes privileges such as being fairly certain that one can rent or purchase a home in an area of choice if it's affordable; being exposed to educational materials that don't exclude their group; being assured that skin color won't be a barrier when making financial transactions with either checks or debit or credit cards; easily finding foods, music, and hair products that are part of one's culture; not having to educate one's children about physical safety, even from those who are supposed to protect them; not being expected to speak for all the members of one's group; and being fairly certain that mistakes made will not be attributed to one's racial group (McIntosh, 1988).

Groups that experience prejudice, discrimination, and oppression from the dominant group are considered to be **populations at risk**. Because of their treatment, both historically and presently, members of at-risk populations are more likely to experience serious health and mental health problems, to live shorter lives, and to be victims of hate or other serious crimes. Before going into more detail in this chapter about commonly marginalized groups (members of nonwhite racial and ethnic groups; those who are in the bottom class economically; women; lesbians, gays, bisexuals, and transgender persons; persons with disabilities; persons who are elderly; and persons who are not members of mainstream religious groups), we point out that each group has many strengths as well as disadvantages because of marginalization and oppression. In

addition, although large numbers of individuals within a group may have similarities (i.e., income level, education), members also show much diversity. Therefore, it is inappropriate to stereotype and assume that all members of a group exhibit the characteristics held by the majority of group members. Actually, there is more diversity *within* a group of individuals (e.g., a group of African Americans) than *between* groups (e.g., between African Americans and whites/ EuroAmericans or between African Americans and Asian Americans).

Cultural Competence

Social workers use the terms **cultural competence** or cultural sensitivity to emphasize the need to work with clients and client systems within the context of their culture. Culture is viewed within a broad sense, incorporating race, ethnicity, gender, class, sexual orientation, religious perspective, ability and age. Other attributes, such as whether the person is a current member of the military, a veteran, or is in a family with military affiliation, can also shape a person's identity as well as the way that other individuals, the community, and the broader society view that person. Some attributes typically provide advantage (being male, heterosexual, able-bodied, EuroAmerican/white, and Christian in the United States, e.g.), while others create risk for historical and current oppression and discrimination.

Social work frameworks, including the ecological/systems framework, incorporate a constructionist perspective (Lum, 2011). This perspective views clients/client systems as the "experts" about their lives, experiences, and needs, with the role of social worker to develop positive relationships with their clients that facilitate an understanding of the clients' world views. One aspect of being culturally competent is to learn as much as possible about the groups to which a client belongs to understand the strengths of the groups as well as typical power, privilege, or historical and current oppression experienced by group members. Relevant information that fits with their clients is then drawn upon as social workers get to know more about them, as not all the information learned about a group will be applicable to a person who is a member of the group. For example, although research and literature suggests that family and religion are important to Mexican Americans, not all Mexican Americans are Catholic, or highly religious, and not all view family as a key factor in their lives. To stereotype that all Mexican Americans fit information found to be valid about a group in general not only jeopardizes the social worker-client relationship, but can lead to inappropriate intervention that can be harmful to a client. Thus, a client becomes a "cultural guide" for the social worker, helping to provide an understanding of the client's day-to-day experiences and the ways that membership in various cultural groups shape their lives (Leigh, 1998).

Social work students are often surprised that the most important aspect of being culturally competent is not knowing as much as you can about populations you are likely to work with, but knowing yourself—your own belief systems, values, biases, and how your own life experiences have shaped who you are as a person and what you as an individual bring to a relationship with clients. Lum (2011) stresses that cultural competence is relational, with three components: (1) self-awareness and self-knowledge on the part of the social worker; (2) awareness and knowledge about the client and the groups to which the client belongs and an ability for the social worker to look at the world from the client's perspective; and (3) the interaction (shared space) between the social worker and the client that facilitates open communication. Most social work programs require courses on diversity and cultural competence where these concepts are explored in much more depth. Learning about yourself and the cultural experiences of others is a life-long process, and it is impossible to be perfectly culturally competent when working with all groups. The key is learning how to learn about a client or a group and how to use the information learned sensitively and constructively when working with diverse clients.

Social and Economic Justice for People of Color and the Impact of Racism

EP 2.1.2a
EP 2.1.4a
EP 2.1.5a

Race and ethnicity are personal attributes that often result in social and economic injustices. People who are distinguished by specific physical or cultural traits are often singled out for differential or unequal treatment. In the United States, the dominant racial group is EuroAmerican, often referred to as white, and people of color—African Americans, Latinos, Asian Americans, Iranians, Native Americans, and Vietnamese, among others—are considered by many members of the dominant (majority) group to have lower status. Note that racial and ethnic groups are referred to using many different terms: For example, Black and African American (which leaves out Blacks who are not from Africa); Hispanic (a term first used by whites); Latino/Latina (which leaves out those not from Latin America); Native American or First People; Caucasian, EuroAmerican (which leaves out whites not from Europe), and white. We will use words sometimes interchangeably in this text. The important consideration is to ask someone who is a member of a specific racial or ethnic group what term she or he prefers, realizing that another member of the same group may prefer a different term.

The terms race and ethnicity are often used interchangeably. The concept of race suggests the presence of marked, distinct genetic differences. The term actually is a socially constructed definition, because few genetic differences are found among *Homo sapiens*. Race commonly is used to classify members of groups who have similar physical characteristics, such as skin color or facial features. Behavioral traits frequently are attributed incorrectly to physical differences rather than to socialization experiences. In contrast to racial groups, ethnic groups tend to be classified by language differences or cultural patterns that differ from those of the dominant group. As the concepts of race and ethnicity are socially constructed, it is important to consider how individuals self-identify regarding their own race and ethnicity, as well as how others identify them. Both racial and ethnic groups not part of the dominant group are viewed as "different" by the group in power, and prejudice and discrimination are often the result.

Many people argue that too much time is spent focusing on racial and ethnic differences, and that we should take a "color blind" approach and work toward the assimilation of all groups in society, what is sometimes referred to as a "melting pot" concept. However, total assimilation of all groups in society would result in the loss of racial or ethnic identity. Many find this prospect objectionable. In recent years, ethnic and racial pride has received considerable attention from groups of color, and to ignore one's ethnic and/or racial identity would mean denying an important part of person's identity. Although complete **assimilation** (the expectation that members of a nondominant group will adopt the values and behaviors of the dominant group) theoretically would result in the erosion of racial and ethnic discrimination patterns, it probably will not happen. Many people argue that the contributions of our divergent ethnic and racial groups enrich our culture.

An alternative to assimilation is **cultural pluralism**, or **cultural diversity**, the coexistence of various ethnic groups whose cultural differences are respected as equally valid. Cultural pluralism, however, is difficult to achieve within the matrix of prejudice, discrimination, and cultural differences. While people of color are creating and promoting cultural pride, less than equal coexistence continues to characterize their relationship with the dominant group.

Ironically, most immigrant populations have been subjected to prejudice and discrimination as each new group settled in the United States—Irish, Italians, Swedes, Germans, French, and others. The irony is, of course, that, with the exception of Native Americans (also often referred to as First Americans), all of us are descendants of immigrants. How quickly groups move from the role of the persecuted to that of persecutors!

Even more ironic, prejudices and discrimination persist and become institutionalized by members of a society that values its Judeo-Christian heritage and provides equal constitutional rights and privileges for all. Some progress has been seen in opening up avenues for social and economic participation, but nonwhite racial and ethnic groups still must cope with differential treatment and limited opportunities.

In the following discussion, we identify some of the issues and problems that confront racial and ethnic groups and examine antidiscrimination efforts designed to neutralize racial, cultural, and ethnic prejudices. As we discuss these groups, keep in mind that although each group shares a common history and other characteristics, each group enjoys a rich diversity within itself.

The groups we will consider here are African Americans, Latinos, Asians and Pacific Islanders, Native Americans, and Middle Easterners/Arabs.

Blacks and African Americans

All nonwhite racial and ethnic groups have been subjected to discrimination, but perhaps none more visibly than those who are Black/African American. Emerging from slavery, in which they were considered chattel (property) and nonpersons, Blacks/African Americans continue to find that societally imposed constraints impede their progress toward achieving social equality.

During the "Jim Crow" days in the South, for example, Blacks/African Americans could not dine at public restaurants used by whites, could use only specially marked public restrooms and drinking fountains, had to ride in the rear of buses, were required to attend segregated schools, faced expectations of subservient behavior in the presence of whites, and could get only lower-paying domestic or manual-labor jobs. Few could achieve justice before the law or gain acceptance as equals to even the lowest-class whites. Although the prescribed behaviors that characterized "Jim Crowism" represent an extreme manifestation of discrimination, all groups of color have experienced social inequality, at least in its more subtle forms.

Persons who identify as only Black/African Americans represent about 13% of the total U.S. population; when those who identify as Black/African American and a member of another racial group are considered, the percentage increases to 14.2%. This figure is expected to increase to 18.4% by 2060. About 55% live in the South, and regardless of geographic region of the United States, slightly more than half live in inner-city metropolitan areas. They earn only 65% as much as whites, are unemployed in greater numbers than their white counterparts, and are almost three times more likely than whites to have incomes below the federal poverty line (Centers for Disease Control and Prevention, 2014; Rastogi, Johnson, Hoeffel, & Drewery, 2011). Numerically, more whites receive public assistance than Blacks/African Americans; however, Blacks/African Americans are proportionally overrepresented on welfare rolls (U.S. Department of Health and Human Services, 2012).

Although one has to be careful about stereotyping, Blacks/African Americans as a group have many strengths. They are known for their resilience, emphasis on extended family, respect and care for elderly family members, and emphasis on religion as a source of strength and as a catalyst for community-building and change.

Whites are more likely than Blacks/African Americans to complete high school, and Blacks/African Americans are underrepresented in the fields of law, medicine, dentistry, and business and overrepresented in occupations that require hard manual labor. These data reflect the differential opportunity structure available to the African American population in this country. While the middle-class and upper-middle-class Black/African American population in the United States is increasing, income levels for Blacks/African Americans overall are still lower than for whites; the median household income for Blacks/African Americans in 2012 was only 58% of what it was for whites: $33,321 compared to $57,009 (DeNavas-Walt, Proctor, & Smith, 2013).

Blacks/African Americans have long demonstrated resilience in the face of oppression from many fronts. Hurricane Katrina raised awareness about disparities in income, economic opportunities, housing, education, and treatment from the justice system. The recent deaths of two young African Americans, Trayvon Martin and Michael Brown, have raised additional questions about the lingering effects of racism in America, particularly toward Blacks/African Americans.

Latino/Hispanic Populations

People from Mexico, Puerto Rico, Cuba, Central and South America, or other Spanish culture or origin are referred to as being of Hispanic or Latino origin. In 2011, this group constituted slightly over 16.7% of the total population and, as the fastest growing population group in the United States, is expected to reach 30% by 2050 (Centers for Disease Control and Prevention, 2013). The Latino (the preferred term) population has come to the United States from 26 nations. By far the largest group is Mexican Americans (see Table 4.1), but increasing numbers of Latinos are coming to the United States from South and Central America, often replacing Mexican Americans and Puerto Ricans in some poverty neighborhoods and low-wage jobs as Mexican Americans and Puerto Ricans become more upwardly mobile.

Although there is considerable diversity among Hispanics/Latinos, and one has to be careful about stereotyping and assuming that all Hispanics/Latinos

TABLE 4.1 HISPANIC/LATINO POPULATIONS IN UNITED STATES

GROUP	PERCENTAGE OF HISPANIC/ LATINO POPULATION
Mexican	63
Puerto Rican	9.2
Central American (excluding Mexicans)	7.9
South American	5.5
Cuban	3.5
Dominican Republic	2.8
Spaniards	1.3
All others	6.8

SOURCE: Ennis, S., Rios-Vargas, M., & Albert, N. (2011). *The Hispanic population: 2010.* Washington, DC: U.S. Census Bureau. Retrieved from http://www.census.gov/prod/cen2010/briefs/c2010br-04.pdf.

David S. Holloway/Getty Images

Immigration policy and the treatment of undocumented citizens are important social justice issues that many Latinos feel passionate about.

have the same characteristics, as a group they are known for their emphasis on hard work, patriotism, emphasis on extended family, respect and care for elderly family members, religion as an important part of their lives, and valuing children as members of their group.

People of Mexican descent constitute the second largest group of color in the United States. Although most live in major urban areas of the West and Southwest, with over half living in California, Texas, and Florida, many continue to reside in rural areas throughout the country (Ennis, Rios-Vargas, & Albert,

2011). Because employment often is limited in those areas, many Mexican Americans work in low-paying jobs, such as those available in the agricultural and meat-processing industries.

The Mexican American population is a diverse group. The urban Mexican American population tends to be better educated, and the effects of acculturation are more visible among them. Those living in rural areas are more apt to be less acculturated and continue to use Spanish as a primary language.

Cultural pride among Mexicans and Mexican Americans is best reflected in their retaining Spanish as a first language, although many second and third generation Mexican Americans have not learned it because their parents, punished for speaking Spanish when they attended school, did not want their children to face the same plight. Bilingual and English as a second language (ESL) education programs are in place in many public school systems to enable Mexican American children to progress educationally, although dropout rates continue to be much higher for them than for the dominant-group population.

In general, people of Mexican ancestry have experienced the consequences of discrimination in that they hold lower-paying jobs, are underrepresented in politics, live in de facto segregated neighborhoods, and are viewed as being "different" by the dominant group. Many, even those who are third and fourth generation citizens, are assumed to be undocumented. Upward mobility has been slow in coming for this group as a whole, in spite of their growing numbers. Increasingly, however, Mexican Americans have moved into visible government and corporate positions, and media and other entities have realized the group's economic power and targeted it for advertising and other forms of outreach. Organizations such as La Raza and LULAC (League of United Latin American Citizens) have sought to unite Spanish-speaking populations to promote favorable social change and to give more visibility to the issues that impede their achievement of social equality.

Puerto Ricans and Cubans constitute the largest non-Mexican Hispanic population. Most of the Puerto Rican population in the United States resides in the metropolitan New York area or in eastern seaboard cities such as Newark, New Jersey, and New Haven, Connecticut. The Cuban population has settled primarily in the Miami area of Florida (Ennis, Rios-Vargas, & Albert, 2011). The social and economic progress of these groups is similar to that of the Mexican American

group. Housing often is inferior, jobs tend to be menial and low-paying, the school dropout rate is high, and access to services and support systems is difficult. Social progress has been considerably greater for the Cuban population due, in part, to the higher educational level of the first waves of Cuban immigrants to the United States.

As has been the case with newly migrated Mexicans, other Latinos come to the United States with the hope of being able to achieve a higher-quality life, only to find that prejudice and discrimination present barriers to achieving that dream. Cultural and language barriers continue to make them "different," and more visible targets for differential treatment. In 2014, large numbers of undocumented youth came to the United States from Guatemala, Honduras, and El Salvador, fleeing violence and oppression with the belief that their lives would be short-lived if they remained in their native countries (see Chapter 16 for further discussion). The strong negative feelings that exist among many in this country about immigration and the belief that most immigrants, particularly those who are Latino, are here illegally, has increased negative stereotyping and oppression of all members of this group.

Language is a barrier for many Latinos, even in communities where they make up the majority of the population. Many social service agencies, for example, do not have Spanish-speaking staff or required forms in Spanish, making access to effective services a challenge.

Asians and Pacific Islanders

Asian and Pacific Islanders have distinct cultural traits and physical characteristics that separate them from the dominant group in the United States but represent one of the most diverse ethnic groups within the United States—Chinese, Japanese, Korean, Asian Indian, Vietnamese, and Pacific Islanders. "Asian" refers to those with origins in the Far East, Southeast Asia, or India. These countries include Cambodia, China, Japan, Korea, Malaysia, Pakistan, the Philippine Islands, Thailand, India, and Vietnam, among others. "Pacific Islander" refers to those with origins in Hawaii, Guam, Samoa, and other Pacific Islands. Although they represent 5.6% of the U.S. population, Asian Americans are one of the fastest growing groups in the United States. Nearly three-fourths of all Asian Americans in the United States live in ten states: California, New York, Texas, New Jersey, Hawaii, Illinois, Washington, Florida, Virginia, and Pennsylvania (Hoeffel, Rastogi, Kim, & Shahid, 2012).

Chinese immigration dates back to the mid-19th century, and the Chinese represent the largest percentage of Asian immigrants (see Table 4.2). Japanese immigration began around the turn of the 20th century, the Korean population in the mid-20th century, and the Vietnamese population in the 1960s and 1970s.

The U.S. Census Bureau has begun distinguishing Asians from Pacific Islanders, which include Native Hawaiians, Samoans, and Guanamians. Pacific Islanders comprise 26% of the population of Hawaii but less than 1% of the population in the remainder of the U.S. states and the District of Columbia (Centers for Disease Control and Prevention, 2013b).

Even though all of the nationalities constituting the Asian American population have experienced differential treatment, many have been able to achieve a relatively high standard of living despite the social barriers. The Chinese have been noted for their in-group living patterns. The "Chinatowns" in San Francisco, Los Angeles, New York, and other large cities encourage preservation of the Chinese cultural heritage. Still, prejudice and discrimination continue to impede significant social and economic progress. Because of their physical characteristics, language, and cultural heritage, they are viewed by many as

TABLE 4.2 ASIAN POPULATION IN THE UNITED STATES BY NATIONALITY

GROUP	PERCENTAGE OF ASIAN IMMIGRANTS IN UNITED STATES
Chinese	22.8
Filipino	17.4
Asian Indian	19.4
Vietnamese	10.6
Korean	9.7
Japanese	5.2
All others—including those who are members of two groups	15

Source: Hoeffel, E., Rastogi, S., Kim, M. O., & Shahid, H. (2012). *The Asian population: 2010.* Washington, DC: U.S. Census Bureau. Retrieved from http://www.census.gov/prod/cen2010/briefs/c2010br-11.pdf.

"foreigners." Internment of the Japanese population in camps during World War II is one example of how the Japanese, many of whom were native-born, were viewed as foreigners with presumptive allegiance to Japan rather than the United States. Ironically, Germans and Italian Americans were not treated in this manner even though Germany and Italy, along with Japan, constituted the Axis powers.

More recently, the Vietnamese and Bhutanese refugees have been the target of discrimination, as reflected in their difficulty in securing housing, employment, and acceptance in American communities. In addition to physical characteristics, language barriers have intensified the "differences," resulting in closed avenues for social and economic participation for these groups.

The number of Asian Indian immigrants has increased in recent years because of political turmoil in their countries, as well as the demand in the United States for highly trained personnel in technology and health care. Despite the fact that many are highly educated, they experience discrimination.

Asian Americans have many strengths, and as a group they are unfairly stereotyped as "the model minority." Their median household income ($68,636) and levels of educational attainment are higher than for any other group, including whites (Centers for Disease Control and Prevention, 2013b). The perspective that all groups should fare as well as Asian Americans not only pits them against other groups of color, but also overlooks their needs and limits availability of services that are culturally sensitive to their needs. As a group, keeping in mind that there is extensive diversity within the group, Asian Americans are known for their emphasis on education and hard work, respect for family and for the elderly and their wisdom, and collective emphasis as opposed to an emphasis on individualism.

First (Native) Americans

Numerically the smallest group of color in the United States, making up 1.7% of the U.S. population (Centers for Disease Control and Prevention, 2013a), First Americans (American Indians or Native Americans) have experienced severe oppression over the years. A diverse group, First Americans comprise 565 tribes and a number of groups that are not officially recognized by the federal government. Prior to colonization, they were free to establish their villages and roam the countryside but lost all their rights and privileges once they were conquered. Early white settlers and the military considered them to be savages, and most First Americans were relegated to reservations, where they encountered oppressive limits on their behaviors and freedom of movement. The responsibility for overseeing these reservations was relegated to the Bureau of Indian Affairs (now the Administration for Native Americans), a government agency that more often was a barrier rather than a help. Some First American tribes have never lived on a reservation, and today more First Americans live in urban areas than on reservations. Their lack of access to services for which they are eligible creates a unique set of social justice issues about which social workers must be concerned.

Valuing cultural traditions is an important part of one's identity. Too often, Native Americans and other groups have been given the message that they must reject their traditions to be accepted and viewed as successful. Fortunately, today many young people are learning to have pride in themselves and their heritage.

Although they were the first "Americans," First Americans seldom have been able to experience free and full involvement in society. Those who continue to live on reservations have limited interaction with the dominant group, which in turn limits their opportunity structure. Reservations represent the most overt form of purposeful discrimination. Although the status of First Americans has improved somewhat in recent years (with higher levels of education and commercial development on the reservations), many barriers remain to their free and full social participation.

Like other racial and ethnic groups, not all First Americans have the same values and traditions. Lifestyles, as well as opportunities, vary among the many tribes in the United States. Almost 75% of persons surveyed in the 2010 census who indicated that they were Native American reported themselves as members of a tribe or tribal grouping, with the largest tribes being the Cherokee, Navajo, Latin American Indian groups, Choctaws, Sioux, and Chippewa. In the Alaska Native tribal grouping, the Eskimo was the largest group. States with the largest First American and Alaska Native populations in 2010 were California, Oklahoma, Arizona, Texas, New York, New Mexico, Washington, North Carolina, Florida, and Michigan (Norris, Vines, & Hoeffel, 2012).

Many Native Americans have migrated to urban centers in search of employment and better resources. New York and Los Angeles have the largest urban populations of Native Americans, and large populations also are found in Chicago, Houston, Philadelphia, Phoenix, San Diego, Dallas, San Antonio, and Detroit (Norris, Vines, & Hoeffel, 2012). The migration of Native Americans to urban areas has created identity problems for many. Discriminated against, they don't always fit in well in city environments. Yet, because they left their reservation, they also have difficulty being accepted if they return to their homeland (McLemore & Romo, 2005).

Although there is much diversity among First American groups, many First Americans have come together across affiliations to celebrate their First American identity, particularly in areas where there may not be large numbers of a given tribe. Many older First Americans are serving as mentors and spiritual leaders to younger First Americans in an attempt to instill a sense of identity in each new generation. Powwows and other celebrations bring First Americans of all age groups together to share traditions. Although each tribal group has its own religious beliefs,

David W. Hamilton/The Image Bank/Getty Images

traditions, language, and symbols, some common themes are shared and First Americans from across the United States often attend and support each other's celebrations. First Americans are known for their collective identity, emphasis on family, respect for elderly members of their families and their tribes, and a strong connection with the natural environment.

Arab Americans

Although Arab Americans are considered by many to be white, they are not EuroAmerican and are a marginalized group in the United States, particularly since the terrorist attacks on September 11, 2001. Arab households in the United States are comprised of individuals who are Algerian, Bahraini, Egyptian, Emirati, Iraqi, Jordanian, Kuwaiti, Lebanese, Libyan, Moroccan, Omani, Palestinian, Qatari, Saudi Arabian, Syrian, Tunisian, and Yemeni (Asi & Beaulieu, 2013). A small population estimated to be about 1.5 million in 2010, Arab Americans make up about .5% of the total U.S. population. About one in three Arab Americans is Lebanese. Arab Americans have a median income that is higher than the median income for all U.S. citizens ($56,433 compared to $51,914), with Lebanese having the highest average income and Iraqi the lowest. Their levels of education are higher than for other groups, with most employed in the private sector. Most Arab Americans live in metropolitan areas, with the largest population in Dearborn and the Detroit, Michigan, area, followed by New York City, Los Angeles, Chicago, and Washington, DC (Asi & Beaulieu, 2013).

While the stereotype is that most Arab Americans are Muslim, 63% are Christian, with 24% Muslim, though the population of Muslims is increasing. The majority of Arab Americans were born in the United States; 82% are U.S. citizens (Asi & Beaulieu, 2013). Like other groups discussed, Arab Americans are an extremely diverse group. They value family, education, and hard work. However, they are often stereotyped as being terrorists, wealthy oil tycoons, patriarchal and disrespectful of women. Since 2001, they have been subject to racial profiling and hate crimes including the desecration of mosques. The Southern Poverty Law Center, a southern civil rights group established during the civil rights era to fight for rights for Blacks/African Americans, has worked with Arab American groups and other advocates to try to eradicate stereotypes and reduce discrimination directed toward Arab Americans (Arab American Institute, 2014).

Social and Economic Justice: Class and the Impact of Classism

EP 2.1.2a
EP 2.1.4a
EP 2.1.5a

Too often, when discussing social justice and equality, people ignore issues of class. Regardless of one's color, gender, or sexual orientation, people at the lower end of the economic structure in the United States are treated differentially by the dominant group. The stratification of individuals and groups according to their social and economic assets and power is termed **class**. Discrimination toward members of a group because of their economic status is termed **classism**. Labeling those who are poor as inferior gives justification to oppress this group.

Like other forms of discrimination, classism can be seen at the individual level, such as making disparaging comments or jokes about the poor or treating those who are poor in derogatory ways. At the institutional level, classism is shown by structuring policies and practices in ways that marginalize or exclude people at the bottom of the class structure from opportunities afforded to others. Examples of institutional classism are lack of access to safe neighborhoods and good schools, and the ability to influence politicians and government officials through political contributions (Pascale, 2006).

Obviously, race, ethnicity, and gender play significant roles in determining the class to which one is likely to belong. Because of the oppression of these populations at risk, women and people of color are less likely to have access to superior educational opportunities, gainful employment that allows for upward mobility, adequate health care, and opportunities for their children to move into a higher economic class. Thus, members of these groups are likely to remain in the lower class for multiple generations. Interestingly, members of marginalized groups who are in higher-income groups advocating for changes for that group often fail to see how those in their group at the bottom of the class structure experience additional oppression because of classism.

Lahiri and Jensen (2002) provide a checklist to facilitate discussion about how we inadvertently may exhibit classist behavior:

- treatment of executives and managers in workplaces in comparison to lower-level clerical staff and custodians;

- recruiting personnel from Ivy League colleges instead of other universities;
- requiring personnel in lower levels of an organization to purchase uniforms at their own expense; and
- scheduling work hours without taking into consideration the availability of affordable transportation and child care.

Debate is increasing in the United States about the impact of class on individual and social well-being. African American scholar William Julius Wilson (1997) and others write about what they call the **underclass**, those outside the economic mainstream who remain chronically in poverty and who are, for the most part, dependent on government welfare of one kind or another (Marger, 2005, p. 60). When talking about discrimination, class is discussed far less often than gender and race. Those with privilege often either feel guilty because they have advantage or believe that those who are less well-off are in those circumstances by their own volition: If they would just work harder and be more motivated, they, too, could be better off financially.

In 2011, advocacy groups across the globe united to protest the continuous control of wealth by a limited minority of the population. Called the 99% Movement, based on the fact that 1% of the population held the majority of world's wealth, with little change in recent decades, the movement called for economic justice and fair distribution of wealth (see Chapter 7 for additional discussion of income disparities in the United States). The initial protest in the United States began with a movement called Occupy Wall Street during the same time period that protests in other countries also called for changes in economic disparity. Protesters occupied a New York City park, and through social media, protests grew to 951 cities in 82 countries, including over 500 cities in the United States. The movement splintered over time because various groups had different agendas in what specifically they wanted changed and how best to advocate for it. However, Occupy Movement was still advocating for economic change in 2014, calling for the following: eliminating corporate influence in political campaigns; eliminating student debt; eliminating wrongful foreclosures; focusing on helping individuals in debt rather than financial institutions; protesting profits of private hospitals, insurance companies, and pharmaceutical companies at the expense of consumers; advocating for a living wage; and calling for an end to any budget cuts in schools (Occupy Movement, 2014).

Economic disparities continue to exist in the United States today, and it is increasingly difficult for individuals, even those considered middle class, to improve their economic status. As skill in technology has become a necessity for successful employment, the number of individuals with limited access to education who are left out of the U.S. economic structure has risen significantly (Pierson, 2009). This growth has impacted not only the poor but those in other classes as well. For example, if an additional 630,000 Texans do not attend college (330,000 more than projected if current trends in college participation continue), the average income of Texans in the year 2015 will be less than it was in 1991 because businesses are more likely to move to areas with educated workforces (Murdock, Hogue, Michael, White, & Pecote, 1997; Texas Higher Education Coordinating Board, 2014). Put more positively, if Texas achieves established college participation and graduation rates, the state's economy will "experience estimated increases of $489 billion in total spending, $194 billion in gross state product, and $122 billion in personal income as well as the creation of over 1 million new jobs by the year 2030 (Texas Higher Education Coordinating Board, 2014, p. 3). Other states and the nation as a whole are in similar circumstances, with U.S. companies outsourcing research and production to countries with greater numbers of educated personnel, such as India and China.

Social and Economic Justice for Women and the Impact of Sexism

EP 2.1.2a
EP 2.1.4a
EP 2.1.5a

In a grievance against her employer, a female staff member with a college degree charged that her male boss had touched her inappropriately on numerous occasions, pressured her to come to his hotel room while they were attending a conference, hired males for comparable positions at much higher salaries than hers, and told her when she applied for a transfer to a different division of the organization that she should either quit her job and stay at home with her children or go to work as a checker at a local grocery store.

Throughout recorded history, women have faced various forms of social inequality and discrimination.

Invariably, inequality was—and is—justified on the basis of the biological superiority of men, despite no evidence to support that premise. Notwithstanding advances made during the past several decades, women in our society experience discrimination. Gender-based discrimination is more visible in the occupational market and economic areas than in other aspects of social participation. Some progress has been made, but many male-dominated job positions have remained virtually unobtainable by qualified women. Males still primarily hold positions such as pilots, military officers, and construction supervisors.

Although many women have successfully entered and moved up in male-dominated careers, they tend to be concentrated in lower-paying, lower-status positions such as secretaries and administrative assistants; nursing,

psychiatric, and home health aides; retail salespersons and first line supervisors in retail settings; receptionists and clerks; waiters and waitresses; child care workers; and maids and housekeeping staff. Of the top thirty positions most commonly held by women, social work ranked 24th (U.S. Department of Labor, 2014). Men tend to be concentrated in higher-paying positions, including lawyers, judges, engineers, accountants, college instructors, physicians, and dentists, as examples. Even in lower paying positions typically held by women, they are paid less than men in those same positions. Management and administrative positions at the upper levels continue to be held mostly by men, even in the social work profession. (See Table 4.3 for a listing of the top 30 positions, as well as the average pay both men and women in those positions receive.)

TABLE 4.3 **THIRTY LEADING OCCUPATIONS FOR EMPLOYED WOMEN BY SELECTED CHARACTERISTICS (2013 ANNUAL AVERAGES)**

OCCUPATION NAME	TOTAL NUMBER OF WOMEN EMPLOYED (IN THOUSANDS)	WOMEN AS A PERCENT OF TOTAL EMPLOYED IN THE OCCUPATION[1]	WOMEN'S MEDIAN WEEKLY EARNINGS (IN DOLLARS)	MEN'S MEDIAN WEEKLY EARNINGS
All occupations	46,268	47	706	860
Elementary and middle-school teachers	2,138	81	937	1.025
Secretaries and administrative assistants	2,113	94	677	772
Registered nurses	2,023	90	1,086	1,236
Nursing, psychiatric, and home health aides	1,207	89	450	499
Customer service representatives	1,068	66	616	639
First-line supervisors of retail sales workers	981	43	612	778
Accountants and auditors	945	62	1,029	1,268
Cashiers	932	72	379	426
Managers, all others	905	34	1,105	1,399
First-line supervisors of office and administrative support workers	828	70	748	846
Receptionists and information clerks	828	92	527	600
Retail salespersons	737	50	485	719
Office clerks, general	734	84	596	620
Bookkeeping, accounting, and auditing clerks	702	89	670	751

(Continued)

TABLE 4.3 THIRTY LEADING OCCUPATIONS FOR EMPLOYED WOMEN BY SELECTED CHARACTERISTICS (2013 ANNUAL AVERAGES) (CONTINUED)

OCCUPATION NAME	TOTAL NUMBER OF WOMEN EMPLOYED (IN THOUSANDS)	WOMEN AS A PERCENT OF TOTAL EM-PLOYED IN THE OCCUPATION[1]	WOMEN'S MEDIAN WEEK-LY EARNINGS (IN DOLLARS)	MEN'S MEDIAN WEEKLY EARNINGS
Financial managers	613	55	1,064	1,518
Maids and housekeeping cleaners	605	88	406	467
Waiters and waitresses	558	70	400	449
Personal care aides	539	84	445	470
Secondary-school teachers	529	57	986	1,093
Social workers	507	80	818	978
Teacher assistants	501	89	475	501
Preschool and kindergarten teachers	484	98	624	—
Education administrators	450	64	1,130	1,543
Postsecondary teachers	424	50	1,100	1,338
Janitors and building cleaners	421	33	418	517
Cooks	418	40	382	411
Childcare workers	410	95	418	—
Licensed practical and licensed vocational nurses	404	92	732	—
Counselors	391	69	884	889
Billing and posting clerks	380	92	629	—

NOTES: 1. All data (unless otherwise noted) are 2013 annual averages for full-time wage and salary workers only, from the Bureau of Labor Statistics, Current Population Survey, http://www.bls.gov/cps/cpsaat39.htm.

2. Women as a percent of total employed are 2013 annual averages for all people employed (includes part-time and self-employed), from the Bureau of Labor Statistics, Current Population Survey, http://www.bls.gov/cps/cpsaat11.htm.

3. Dash indicates no data available or base is less than 50,000.

SOURCE: Bureau of Labor Statistics, Current Population Survey, U.S. Department of Labor. (2014). *30 leading occupations for women by selected characteristics.* Washington, DC: Author. Retrieved from http://www.dol.gov/wb/stats/leadoccupations.htm.

Income and Employment

From 1900 to 2012, the proportion of women in the U.S. labor force increased from 19% to 57.7% (U.S. Bureau of Labor Statistics, 2014). This increase ushered in a number of conflicts and issues related to women's participation in the labor market. Chief among the issues is the concept of **comparable worth**, often best understood by the phrase "equal pay for equal work." Much of the income disparity

between men and women, however, is attributable largely to differences in occupational positions, which have changed little over the past decade. Income differences exist primarily because men are employed in positions of leadership or in technical fields, whereas women are employed disproportionately in the lower-paying clerical and service fields. Even when women hold positions similar to those of men, their income is lower. Seniority or related factors

Box 4.2   Facts About Working Women and Gender Equity

- Percentage of women who participated in the labor force in 2012: 57.7[1]
- Percentage of the workforce in 2012 who were women: 46.9[1]
- Percentage of women who worked full-time year-round in 2011: 60[2]
- Earnings of women in the labor force in 2012 by ethnicity compared to their male counterparts: blacks $599/week, earned 90% of black men; whites $710/week, earned 81% of white men; Latinas/Hispanics $521/week, earned 88% of Latino/Hispanic men; Asians $770/week, earned 73% of Asian men; all groups of women $691/week, earned 81% of all men[2]
- Percentage of women veterans: 10[2]
- Percentage of women workers living below the poverty level by ethnicity: blacks 15.6; Latinas/Hispanics 13.6; whites 6.7; Asians 5.4[2]
- Percentage of median income for full-time, year-round women workers as compared with men in 2013: 82[1]
- Percentage of mothers in the workforce in 2011 with children under 1 year of age: 55.8[1]
- Percentage of mothers in the workforce in 2011 with children under age 18: 70.6; fathers: 93.5[1]
- Amount of income working families in the United States lose annually because of the wage gap: $200 billion[3]
- Amount of income an average 25-year-old working woman will lose due to unequal pay during her work life: $316,160[3]
- Hourly salary of female high school graduates compared to male high school graduates: males earn $1 an hour more on average[4]
- Hourly salary of females with 4-year college degrees compared to males with 4-year college degrees: males earn almost $4 more an hour on average[4]
- Occupations with the highest median weekly earnings among women who worked full-time in 2012: pharmacists, chief executives, and lawyers[2]
- Percentage of executive officer positions held by women in Fortune 500 companies in 2013: 14.6[1]

SOURCES:
[1]Catalyst. (2014). *Statistical overview of women in the workplace.* New York: Author. Retrieved from http://www.catalyst.org/knowledge/statistical-overview-women-workplace.
[2]Bureau of Labor Statistics. (2014). *Women in the labor force: A databook.* Washington, DC: Author. Retrieved from http://www.bls.gov/cps/wlf-databook-2013.pdf.
[3]National Employment Lawyers Association. (2003). *Fact sheet: Why we still need affirmative action.* San Francisco: Author. See also www.nela.org.
[4]Berman, J. (2014). "Congratulations, graduates! Equal pay is already out of your reach." *Huffington Post.* Retrieved from http://www.huffingtonpost.com/2014/05/01/young-gender-pay-gap_n_5246893.html.

do not always account for these differences, and employers generally concede that, for a given type of position, men receive a higher income than women (see Table 4.3). In 2013, median weekly pay earned by women who were full-time employees in the United States was 82% of the median weekly pay earned by men (U.S. Bureau of Labor Statistics, 2013).

Researchers note that this gap is closing because women are more likely to graduate from college and have more years of work experience than women did in the past, rather than because of less discrimination in hiring and retaining women in the workforce. The discrepancy in pay between males and females, however, is increasing for one group—those with 4-year college degrees. Female high school graduates earn on

average a dollar an hour less than males, while female graduates with 4-year degrees earn almost $4 an hour less on average (Berman, 2014). Analysts note that this difference is most likely because of both gender discrimination and the fact that many women in this group are more likely to choose to stay at home with children rather than earn high salaries. Box 4.2 gives characteristics of women in the labor force. Not only are there discrepancies between what men and women earn, but women of color overall earn less than white women.

The practice of channeling women into lower-level positions, with the resulting limited career choices and lower incomes, represents an institutionalized policy of gender-based discrimination. Although efforts are being made to provide equal employment opportunities for women, social roles continue to be gender-typed and are passed down from generation to generation through the process of socialization. Women choose careers for many reasons, and there are interactive effects between careers chosen, salaries, and gender. For example, women traditionally have been socialized to be nurturers and find value in those roles. Because they also have been socialized to value relationships, they tend to enter careers that involve relating to people in some way, such as teaching, nursing, and social work. Even from a values standpoint, these careers should pay more than they do, but they remain at the lower end of the salary range because those positions historically have been filled by women.

Women continue to be less well represented in engineering and the sciences, law, transportation and utilities, mining, and construction, and overrepresented in the fields of financial activities, education, health services, and leisure and hospitality. When women are excluded or limited from participating in job arenas, educational preparation programs also are affected because women are forced to make career (and consequently, educational) choices on the basis of opportunities for employment and advancement.

Education   Ironically, men hold leadership positions in professions that employ predominantly women, such as public education and social work. A career-oriented woman entering the education system often has more difficulty than a similarly qualified man in securing promotion to an administrative position. Meanwhile, women are more likely to be in lower-paying, less prestigious positions as classroom teachers throughout their careers.

Even though nondiscrimination policies are in place, qualified women educators who seek promotion to administrative positions are confronted with the task of penetrating a gender-biased tradition of assigning men to those roles in the public school system. Some evidence points to changes in the numbers and percentages of women who hold administrative positions. Women are more likely to hold administrative positions as elementary and middle school principals, while men are more likely to be principals of high schools and district superintendents. Opening the opportunity structure to accommodate all qualified professionals, regardless of gender, is a slow process.

The first step in widening the doors for women in these areas is higher education, and more women are pursuing degrees than in previous years. In fact, their participation in higher education overall is now greater than it is for men. Women earned 57.4% of all bachelor's degrees, 62.6% of all master's degrees, and 53.3% of all doctoral degrees in 2009–2010 (National Center on Educational Statistics, 2014).

Social Work   Historically, most social work professionals have been women—in 2013, 80% of all social work practitioners. In a field that has championed equal rights for women (as well as a field that is predominantly female), median salaries, ironically, are higher for males and leadership roles are more often held by men. Men are represented disproportionately in administrative and managerial roles, and, as a group, receive higher salaries than women ($978 weekly compared to $818 weekly for women) (U.S. Bureau of Labor Statistics, 2014). To that extent, the social work profession—despite its advocacy of women's rights—reflects the tendency of other professions as well as the business community.

Religion   In organized religion, in which women are more active participants than men, only 17.7% of those in clergy roles are women, though this number has increased in recent years (U.S. Bureau of Labor Statistics, 2014). Women are much less likely to hold primary leadership positions in churches and synagogues, and women are employed in religious associations even less often. In recent years, a number of religious organizations have embraced female leaders, including some Jewish, Methodist, and Episcopal congregations. In other religious organizations, including some of those that have women leaders, on-going controversy exists about whether to allow them to participate in leadership roles, and if so, what levels. Some religious groups have left the larger organization and formed their own separate groups as a result of the controversy, either because they want to involve women and their religious group opposes it or because they don't want to involve women and their group has voted to include them. Many religious groups base their male-only religious leadership roles on the "holy writ," thereby effectively excluding women from appointments to significant leadership responsibilities in those bodies.

Politics The majority of members of Congress are men, as are U.S. governors. Of the members of the 113th Congress (2013–2015), 79 women were members of the House of Representatives (18.2%) and 20 women were members of the Senate (20%). Only 5 of the 50 governors were women in 2014 (Center for American Women and Politics, 2014). Although these figures reflect the subordinate role that women continue to play in the legislative process, some women have played major leadership roles in recent years: Nancy Pelosi (D-California) served as the first female Speaker of the House and then served as the minority leader when Republicans gained control of that body. At the state level, nearly 25% of the members of state legislatures were women in 2014 (Center for American Women and Politics, 2014).

The first woman elected to Congress, Jeanette Rankin, who served as a member of the House of Representatives from 1917 to 1919 and again from 1941 to 1942, was a social worker. In spite of the increase of women in politics, male bias often is present in legislative debates about proposed laws that directly affect women. Although both men and women are on opposing sides in debates about many issues, recent debates about women's reproductive rights, rape, and interpersonal violence have included comments made by male elected officials that have resulted in outcries from women (and men) from both political parties because of their sexist nature, as well as the misinformation provided.

Many women's advocates believed that federal legislation strengthening policies personal bankruptcy enacted by the 110th Congress was detrimental to women because the law allowed credit card companies to charge high interest charges and late fees to credit card holders. This legislation had a disproportionate impact on low-income people, particularly single-parent women, who often use credit cards to help pay for regular living expenses because they do not generate enough income to cover living costs. Making good on one of his campaign promises to strengthen consumer protection in the credit card market, President Barack Obama signed the Credit Card Accountability, Responsibility, and Disclosure (CARD) Act of 2009 into law on May 22, 2009. This legislation helps protect credit card holders from unfair and deceptive practices by card-issuing institutions that had resulted in financial hardship for millions of Americans, particularly single-parent

women who use credit cards as a source of immediate cash to pay their bills.

Institutional Sexism

The discussion and examples just presented indicate the strong gender bias that exists in our society. Women are treated differently in the professions, in business, and in other areas that impact their daily lives. Their status as women negatively influences their opportunities to survive economically and to move into prominent roles regardless of their competence or ability. In effect, women are discriminated against solely because they are women. This practice, called **sexism**, is a result of the values and practices embodied in our social institutions.

Although males and females are born with different anatomy, gender differences—what it means to be male and what it means to be female—are socially constructed. Regardless of our gender, we receive messages about gender from birth from our environment—families, school, peers, community, and the media. Most children learn through socialization that boys are to be aggressive and dominant and that girls are to be nurturing and submissive. Parents often model these attributes in family interactions, in which the father assumes the roles of rule maker, disciplinarian, primary provider, and decision maker and the mother assumes responsibility for the nurturing roles of caring for the children and the household. Although many parents rear their children in nonsexist ways, children are exposed to sexist views in interactions outside their families including the media.

Performance differences between men and women invariably reflect societal attitudes and values far more than any inherent physical or psychological variances in maleness or femaleness. In modern society, few roles could not be performed by either men or women, although throughout the life cycle, gender-role distinctions are made and differences are emphasized. These distinctions become entrenched in societal values, hindering women from "crossing over" into roles considered masculine and men from "crossing over" into roles considered feminine. Hence, an aggressive, goal-oriented, intelligent woman may be viewed as masculine and censured for departing from prescribed female role behavior, while an emotional, nurturing, free-spirited male may be viewed as feminine.

Societal values and practices continue to result in a gender-segregated division of labor. Although some progress has been made in identifying roles as "nongender-based" (neither male nor female), roles in general are gender-typed. Women have great difficulty gaining access to roles identified as appropriate for men only. In 2013, the Pentagon announced that women can now serve in combat positions, which had previously been disallowed. The Chiefs of each military division have until January of 2016 to develop standards required to fill each combat-related position and to justify if there are any combat positions that women will not be able to fill. For example, women presently are barred from becoming Navy Seals. As the military develops standards, it must also work to ensure that sexual assaults and harassment do not take place as combat is opened to women. Gender differentiation, too, is observed in other arenas besides the military; for example, in opportunities to secure credit, purchase homes, negotiate contracts, and obtain credit cards, in which men typically have the advantage.

Over the past decade, the issue of sexual harassment has received considerable attention as a problem that women must contend within the workplace. **Sexual harassment** is a form of sex discrimination that violates Title VII of the Civil Rights Act of 1964. "Unwelcome sexual advances, requests for sexual favors, and other verbal or physical conduct of a sexual nature constitute sexual harassment when this conduct explicitly or implicitly affects an individual's employment, unreasonably interferes with an individual's work performance, or creates an intimidating hostile or offensive work environment" (U.S. Equal Employment Opportunity Commission, 2014, p. 1).

Sexual harassment includes graphic comments about a person's body, sexually suggestive pictures or other objects in the workplace, or threats that failing to submit sexually will affect adversely a person's job or salary. A person also may file charges of sexual harassment if she or he is affected by the behaviors of others (e.g., a boss and a coworker involved in a sexual relationship). It is highly likely that much sexually harassing behavior goes unreported by employees for fear that it might place their jobs in jeopardy. Although some progress has been made in reporting and eradicating these behaviors, it continues to pose a significant problem for working women.

Both sexual harassment and sexual assault are ignored or downplayed at individual, organizational, and societal/cultural levels. One example that has significant received recent national attention is the military. A report by the U.S. Commission on Civil

Rights (2013) indicated that 23% of all women and 4% of all men in the military reported unwanted sexual contact since enlistment. In 2012, 26,000 members of the military were survivors of sexual assault; however, 89% did not report it because of fear of reprisal, including a reduction in rank, loss of privileges, or being discharged from the military, as well as a strong sense of duty. Reports indicate that many were threatened by superiors with reprisal when they made initial outcries so did not pursue them further (King et al., 2013).

Fear of reprisal, including discharge, has been validated in a number of recent reports. One study found that 62% of those who reported a sexual assault experienced retaliation. A survey of 1,200 service members who sought help because of sexual assault since 2003 showed that 90% of those who reported them were involuntarily discharged. A significant number of them were labeled as having pre-existing psychiatric illnesses (and thus, unfit for military duty), even though their mental health symptoms did not surface until after the assault. Advocates for these individuals testified that many of their symptoms were identical to those of post-traumatic stress disorder, often experienced by survivors of sexual assault regardless of where it occurred (King et al., 2013). When official reports were made, the alleged perpetrators were seldom prosecuted. Of the 2,900 who faced charges in fiscal year 2012, half were allowed to remain in the military. Court-martial proceedings were initiated for 594, 302 faced trials, 238 were convicted, 177 went to jail, and 133 cases were dismissed (U.S. Commission on Civil Rights, 2013).

As media attention increased, with editorials and other calls for reform among advocates, the military made a number of reforms. A special unit, the Sexual Assault Prevention and Response Office, now handles every case of sexual assault for all military branches. Additional training, removal of perpetrators and commanders who did not take reported incidents of assault seriously, and other safeguards have been put in place. For example, after extensive publicity, Lackland Air Force Base in San Antonio, Texas, investigated 33 instructors for illicit conduct with 63 trainees, resulting in convictions and discharges from the military for many and removal of leaders at the base. Efforts by the military to address these problems appear to be having an impact, as reports increased by 50% in 2013. However, there is still work to be done: of the 5,061 reports received, only 484 went to trial and 376 resulted in convictions (U.S. Commission on Civil Rights, 2013). Congress has also attempted to mandate reforms to address this issue. After a series of Congressional hearings, one bill that focuses on access to treatment for military survivors of assaults was pending in 2014. However, a bill introduced in 2013 by Kirsten Gillibrand (D-NY), requiring among other mandates that decisions of military members convicted of assault be made outside of the chain of military command, has been met with resistance by the Pentagon and had been referred back to committee as of September, 2014.

Sexism is reinforced on a day-to-day basis, often unintentionally, in many ways, including language. The American Psychological Association, which has published guidelines for writing that many university social work programs have adopted, includes specific guidelines for nonsexist language (APA, 2010). Guidelines suggest using plural ("they" instead of "he") when possible, and being careful about examples that may appear sexist (e.g., women when talking about physical attractiveness, and men when talking about success). See the American Psychological Association website at http://www.apastyle.org/manual/related/nonhandicapping-language.aspx its policies on use of nonsexist language.

Issues Relating to Reproductive Rights

One of the more emotionally charged issues that epitomizes conflicts in values for men and women alike is reproductive rights. Issues relating to reproductive rights can be discussed from legal, medical, and values perspectives. While early issues relating to reproductive rights focused on abortion, recent reproductive rights debates have included issues relating to contraception and other methods of family planning; sterilization; privacy issues involving pregnancy, such as whether minors should have to notify or receive permission from parents or legal guardians when making decisions that relate to reproduction; and who should be notified regarding sexually transmitted infections. Advances in technology have resulted in issues relating to who has rights to embryos and decisions regarding embryos and births involving surrogate mothers.

Legal Issues   Early legal issues relating to reproduction centered on abortion, with the legal precedent for abortion established in 1973 by the *Roe v. Wade* decision. In effect, the U.S. Supreme Court maintained

that a woman has the constitutional right to seek an abortion if she so desires. This decision defined abortion as a personal decision rather than one to be determined by government policy. Although the Court's interpretation was straightforward and clear, issues surrounding abortion are being revisited in many state courts, and policy attitudes have shifted considerably at the federal level. Much of the controversy involves philosophical and scientific issues about when life begins. Breakthroughs in biotechnology have escalated the debate, which is framed by some as a conflict between the status of the human embryo and a woman's right to privacy. These issues extend beyond the abortion debate to the use of stem cells and fetal tissue in research and whether the fetus should be protected legally before birth.

Who should obtain reproductive health services and under what conditions is also being debated in state legislatures across the United States. Legislation passed in a number of states limits the right of minors to obtain confidential health services, which many health providers fear will limit minors' access to health care to obtain family-planning information and contraceptives, to be tested and receive treatment for sexually transmitted infections, and to receive pregnancy testing and prenatal care. A major change has been to limit federal funding for family planning for any agency that performs abortions or provides counseling or referrals to clients about abortions. This policy change has severely limited the services of programs such as Planned Parenthood that offer affordable family planning and gynecological services to low-income women and men who otherwise might not be able to afford them. Other proposed legislation would make it a federal crime for anyone other than a parent to help a minor travel out of state to obtain an abortion if the woman is not following the relevant laws regarding compliance in her own state. Hundreds of bills have been introduced in state legislatures in the past few years aimed at either increasing or restricting access to family planning services and reproductive rights. Many states have adopted laws limiting abortion. Some states prohibit third-trimester abortions for any reason, and others limit abortions to situations involving very young teens, rape, or cases in which a woman's health is severely jeopardized.

The U.S. Supreme Court upheld the use of what is commonly termed "partial birth" abortions in 2000 in *Stenberg v. Carhart,* stating that language in a Nebraska law was vague. Congress passed the Partial Birth Abortion Ban Act of 2003, crafting language that took into account criticisms used in earlier court decisions. The U.S. Supreme Court upheld the ban in 2013 in a 5–4 decision. As of January, 2014, about half the states had passed laws mandating counseling and other procedures, such as requiring a waiting period prior to obtaining an abortion, which often means a return trip to a clinic; being given a verbal description of the fetus during a mandatory sonogram prior to an abortion; requiring parental notification or consent before a minor obtains an abortion; and imposing strict regulations on clinics that perform abortions, resulting in the closure of some. In 2000, 13 states had at least four types of major restrictions on abortion; this number had increased to 27 by 2013, while the number of states considered supportive of abortions fell from 17 to 13 (Guttmacher Institute, 2014). Public opinion on abortion remains mixed. In May 2014, the Gallop poll reported that 47% of persons surveyed were prolife, while 46% were prochoice. Nineteen percent of those surveyed indicated that abortion views play a major role in determining which candidates they vote for in state and federal elections (Saad, 2014). Information about state initiatives related to reproductive rights and sexual health can be found at the Guttmacher Institute, a reproductive health policy and research organization (www.guttmacher.org). Both pro-choice and pro-life advocates expect the controversy over abortion and related issues to escalate in government policy and the courts over the next few years.

Medical Issues   From a medical perspective, abortion during the first trimester of a pregnancy is a relatively simple, uncomplicated procedure. Although any medical intervention entails risk, abortion generally is not considered a high-risk procedure, even during the second trimester. Most abortions are performed during the first trimester. Assessing women's psychological preparedness for an abortion can be difficult. Most medical facilities require a psychological assessment and counseling as prerequisites for an abortion. Few studies have attempted to assess post-abortion adaptation, and the methodology of those that have been conducted has often been flawed. A recent study conducted in Denmark (Munk-Olsen et al., 2011) that drew from a sample of 84,620 women focused on the number of visits to mental health facilities made by those who had first trimester abortions, comparing the number of visits made the 12 months

prior to the procedure to the number made in the 9 months following. No significant differences were found.

The availability of drugs that can be taken to prevent a pregnancy from occurring after intercourse or to terminate a possible pregnancy is also controversial. A pregnancy prevention option is the so-called morning-after pill, EC (emergency contraception) that can be taken up to 5 days after unprotected intercourse. EC interacts with hormones to keep the ovaries from releasing eggs and thickens the uterus to block the joining of sperm and egg. Mifepristone (RU-486), which was approved by the Food and Drug Administration (FDA) in 2000, ends a pregnancy by blocking activity of progesterone, a substance needed to continue a pregnancy.

In 2005, the Center for Reproductive Rights sued the FDA over the agency's decision to limit over-the-counter access to the emergency contraceptive EC to women over 18. In March 2009, a federal court ruled that the FDA had put politics before women's health when it decided to limit coverage of the drug. The U.S. District Court for the Eastern District of New York ordered the agency to reconsider its decision. It also ordered the FDA to act within 30 days to extend over-the-counter access to 17-year-olds. Today, some types of emergency contraception are available without a prescription for women of all ages, while others require a prescription for women under 17 (Kaiser Family Foundation, 2014).

Controversy about reproductive rights has moved beyond abortion to other forms of pregnancy prevention. A controversial portion of the Affordable Care Act requires insurance providers to cover various types of birth control as part of their health-care plans. Hobby Lobby and Wheaton College both appealed through the courts, indicating that certain kinds of birth control served as forms of abortion and thus violated their religious freedom in requiring coverage. The Obama administration had proposed a compromise, which would have allowed those organizations that did not want to provide coverage for religious reasons to request an exception, and then allowed their employees who wanted the birth control to obtain it directly from their insurance provider, thus bypassing the organization. In both instances, the Supreme Court ruled 5–4 in favor of the organizations. Advocates for women's reproductive rights believe that these decisions allow corporations to take precedent and make decisions about women's health-care needs that should be left to women and their health-care providers. In an unprecedented move, the three women Supreme Court justices wrote a sharp rebuke stating their opposition to the Wheaton College decision, indicating that it opened the door to other unintended limitations. It was clear during deliberations that they viewed the case from the perspective of female employees as opposed to their employers. These decisions as well as recent proposed and passed state and federal legislation are indicative of the divided opinions on whose rights prevail when considering reproductive rights.

Values Issues and the Social Work Perspective

Perhaps the most emotionally charged aspect of abortion involves values. On the one hand, members of the anti-abortion (right-to-life) movement base their resistance to abortion on the conviction that life begins at conception. Consequently, they view abortion as murder. Members of pro-choice groups, on the other hand, argue that life begins at birth, and they further insist that a woman has the constitutionally granted right to decide whether she wishes to continue her pregnancy or terminate it. Anti-abortion groups seek the government's protection of the life (and rights) of the fetus in the same sense that children and adults merit protection of the law from injury or injustice.

Within each of the groups is some variance in value positions. For example, while arguing that life begins at conception, some anti-abortion groups take the position that abortion is acceptable and justified in instances of rape or when the mother's health would be seriously jeopardized. Other anti-abortion groups oppose abortion under any circumstances, arguing that taking the life of the fetus is never acceptable.

Abortion is not solely a women's issue, but only women become pregnant and have the legal right to decide whether a pregnancy will be carried to full term or terminated. The law remains unusually silent concerning the role of men in matters of conception and pregnancy. Fathers are referred to as "alleged fathers," and they have no legal right to affect a woman's decision to terminate a pregnancy.

We have included this discussion to illustrate the differential treatment of women in our society. Although the topic of abortion is difficult to discuss, because of differing values issues, social work professionals must be willing to listen to different points of view and to remain informed about facts as well as values positions. Social workers, like everyone else, have differing personal values, and this is certainly true regarding reproductive rights.

Regardless of personal beliefs, social work professionals must follow the values of the profession in treating with dignity and respect those who have values and points of view that differ from their own. Social workers must be especially attuned to the impact of unplanned pregnancy and abortion on women and to the views surrounding abortion. If social workers have personal views that would preclude their participation in abortion counseling, they have a professional responsibility to work with clients in a nonjudgmental way that supports client self-determination and to make referrals to protect the rights of the client. The National Association of Social Workers (NASW) clearly outlines the profession's position (see Box 4.3).

Social Reform: The Feminist Movement

 Ever since this nation's inception, women have pursued equal social treatment. Early leaders include

EP 2.1.5b
EP 2.1.5c

- Elizabeth Stanton (1815–1902), who petitioned for a property-rights law for women in New York (1845);
- Lucretia Mott (1793–1880), who organized the first women's rights convention in New York;
- Susan B. Anthony (1820–1906), who helped to form the National Women's Suffrage Association in 1869; and
- Lucy Stone (1818–1893), who formed the National American Women's Suffrage Association.

Carrie Catt (1859–1947), a political activist, founded the International Women's Suffrage Alliance and, later, following World War I, the League of Women Voters, an organization that today wields significant political influence. Catt's efforts were largely responsible for enactment of the 19th Amendment to the U.S. Constitution, which extended voting rights to women in 1920 (Stern & Axinn, 2012).

In more recent times, women's groups have intensified their efforts to secure equal rights. The **Civil Rights Act** of 1964 addressed the problems of discrimination in gender as well as race. A major attempt to secure women's rights was embodied in the **Equal Rights**

Box 4.3   Social Work Speaks

National Association of Social Workers (NASW) Policy Statement on Family Planning and Reproductive Choice

The NASW position concerning family planning, abortion, and other reproductive health services is based on the bedrock principles of self-determination, human rights, and social justice:

- Every individual, within the context of her or his value system, must have access to family planning, abortion, and other reproductive health services.
- The use of all reproductive services, including abortion and sterilization services, must be voluntary and preserve the individual's right to privacy.
- The nature of the reproductive health services that a client receives should be a matter of client self-determination in consultation with the qualified health-care provider furnishing them.
- Public policies and legislation, nationally and internationally, must support a woman's authority over her sexual life and reproductive capacity, free from coercion, violence, and discrimination.
- Lesbians, gay men, and both male-to-female and female-to-male transgender people, as well as those who feel more comfortable living androgynously, are as capable as any other people of being good parents and should have equal access to parenting support services.
- Social workers who choose to restrict their services to clients and the community in a way that deprives their clients or community of a comprehensive consideration of all legal reproductive health options have a responsibility to disclose the limited scope of their services and to assist clients in obtaining comprehensive services elsewhere.

NASW supports the fundamental right of each individual throughout the world to manage his or her own fertility and to have access to a full range of effective family planning and reproductive health services, regardless of the individual's income, marital status, age, race, ethnicity, gender, sexual orientation, national origin, or residence; these services include, but are not limited to, contraception and emergency contraception; fertility enhancement; prevention and treatment of HIV/AIDS, STIs, and the human papillomavirus (HPV); prenatal, birthing, and postpartum care; sterilization, abortion services, and adoption rights.

Policy statement is approved by the NASW Delegate Assembly, August 2008.

SOURCE: National Association of Social Workers (2009). *Social work speaks* (8th ed.). Washington, DC: Author, pp. 127–133.

Amendment (ERA). Bitterly opposed by organized labor, the John Birch Society, the Christian Crusade, and the Moral Majority, and over the protest of Senator Sam Ervin (D-North Carolina), who castigated the proposed amendment, the bill was passed by Congress in 1972 and remanded to the states for ratification.

Pro-ERA forces, including the National Organization for Women (NOW), the League of Women Voters, and the National Women's Political Caucus, lobbied the states to seek ratification of the amendment. Anti-ERA spokespersons lobbied the states against ratification, arguing that all women would be sent into combat, subjected to unisex public facilities, and required to secure jobs (Francis, 2003). The amendment passed. The Carter administration, favorable to passage of the ERA, had little influence on the states in encouraging its adoption. The Reagan administration opposed the measure. The amendment was never ratified and died in June 1982.

Since that time, efforts to achieve **gender equity** have met with some success. Active efforts by NOW and related women's rights groups and public sentiment have coalesced to remove some of the barriers that historically had subjugated women in their pursuit of social equality. Earlier efforts to achieve gender equity were led primarily by white upper- and middle-class women, failing to involve women of color or to highlight issues of importance to them. More recent efforts have focused on the inclusion of women of color and those who are lesbian, bisexual, and transgender, valuing difference and advocating for rights for all women. During the Clinton administration, a precedent was set in naming both women and people of color to key roles in government offices, a practice that was extended by the Obama administration.

Although the profession of social work has advocated for the abolition of societal barriers that deny equal treatment of women, it has not been in the forefront in providing leadership for the more significant feminist movements. However, a number of social work activists made significant individual contributions to women's rights, including Jane Addams, founder of Hull House (see Chapter 1) and Dorothy Height, who served as the president of the National Council of Negro Women for 40 years and helped integrate the YWCA. Addams was awarded the Nobel Peace Prize in 1931; Height was awarded the Presidential Medal of Freedom in 1994. During the 1960s, women's equality was established as a major priority for the profession of social work. Both the NASW and the Council on Social Work Education (CSWE) initiated policies committing the profession to promoting social and economic equality for women.

Social and Economic Justice: Sexual Orientation and the Impact of Heterosexism and Homophobia

EP 2.1.5b
EP 2.1.5c

In the past decade, increased attention has been focused on the prejudice and discrimination experienced by individuals who are lesbian, gay, bisexual, or transgender (often referred to as persons who are LGBT, sometimes with a Q added for "queer" or "questioning"). Transgender individuals are those who either are born anatomically as one gender but have a psychological identity with the other or are born with a combination of male and female physiology (Nangeroni, 2006). Transsexuals, whether they have or have not had sex-change surgery, are considered to be transgender persons. Transgender persons are particularly oppressed, sometimes even by gays and lesbians.

Although a person's **sexual orientation** is considered to be a personal and private matter not related to free and full participation in our society, this has not been the case for those who are not heterosexual. The intense negative emotional reaction to homosexuals, a result of fear and hatred of homosexual lifestyles, is a state of psychological conditioning termed **homophobia**. Even if a person's immediate environment is supportive, our society is organized around those who are heterosexual. The system of unearned advantages afforded to heterosexuals based on societal norms and standards, while excluding the needs and life experiences of persons who are LGBTQ, is termed **heterosexism** (Blumenfeld, 2013). Homophobia and heterosexism can be seen when discussing a number of issues, including HIV/AIDS, military service, legal benefits, and same-sex marriage. Examples of heterosexism include school personnel who assume that all students and their parents are heterosexual, parents who assume that their children will marry a person of the opposite sex, and workplace policies that provide benefits only to those partners in a legal marriage. Examples of homophobia include constant jokes and name-calling, including use of the term "that's so gay"; assumptions that HIV/AIDS is a gay condition, despite the fact that the fastest-growing groups of persons with AIDS now are heterosexual women and heterosexual people of color; believing that persons who are LGBTQ are all pedophiles who will prey on children or will "come on" to anyone who is a member of the same sex that they are; and violence, including the tragic deaths of Matthew Shepard and James Byrd (Blumenfeld).

The rejection of rights for persons who are LGBTQ, with the accompanying prejudice and discrimination, has been bolstered by many fundamentalist religions, and until not that long ago, some traditional psychologists. In his classic work, *Homosexuality*, Irving Beiber (1962), a psychoanalyst, clearly described the view that homosexuality is abnormal and that it can be cured through psychotherapy. These and other "authoritative" sources reinforce the biases and prejudices that have long existed in the general population. In 1952, the American Psychological Association's *Diagnostic and Statistical Manual of Mental Disorders* (*DSM*) listed homosexuality as a sociopathic personality disorder. The diagnosis was changed to sexual deviance in 1968 and eliminated altogether in the *DSM-IV*, released in 1974. The American Psychological Association (APA), like many other entities, has changed its viewpoints considerably about LGBTQ: in 2009, the APA took a stand against reparative therapy, therapy provided to persons who are LGBT with a focus on changing them to become heterosexual, claiming that this kind of therapy not only was not successful, but could be extremely harmful to clients. In 2011, the APA unanimously approved its support of full marriage equality for persons who are LGBTQ (American Psychological Association, 2014).

Many persons who are LGBTQ have become more vocal and have sought legal redress for discriminatory practices, whereas others, fearing rejection from families, loss of jobs, intimidation, and harassment, have opted to remain "in the closet." Although debate continues as to whether sexual orientation is determined by genetics, is a product of socialization, or a combination of both, many people continue to believe that sexual orientation is a matter of choice. Those who say it is definitely not a matter of choice ask if there is a point when heterosexuals "choose" to be heterosexual and how easily it would be for them to change their minds and "choose" to become LGBT or Q.

Recent Legislation and Court Decisions: Progress and Uncertainty

Although some progress has been made in securing legal rights for members of the LGBTQ community, discrimination and prejudice continue to characterize responses to them. Ambivalence surrounding this issue is best expressed by the "don't ask, don't tell" policy for members of the military enacted by the Clinton administration in the mid-1990s but reversed by Congress in 2010 after extensive debate. Presumably this policy was designed to provide guarded protection to gay and lesbian military personnel (Lum, 2011).

In some instances, protections for those who are LGBTQ have required decisions by the U.S. Supreme Court. In 2003, laws prohibiting sodomy existed in 14 states. Ten states plus Puerto Rico had sodomy laws that applied to both heterosexuals and homosexuals. Four states—Kansas, Missouri, Oklahoma, and Texas—had sodomy laws that applied only to homosexuals. Penalties for violating sodomy laws in the United States ranged from $500 to life imprisonment. In late June 2003, in what some gay rights activists called a landmark legal victory, the U.S. Supreme Court ruled in a 6–3 vote that sodomy laws are unconstitutional. The 2003 decision, based on privacy rights, bans all states from "regulating private sexual expression between consenting adults regardless of whether the laws apply to homosexuals or both heterosexuals and homosexuals" (U.S. Supreme Court, 2003b). The ruling added private sexual expression to the list of constitutional protections under the 14th Amendment to the Constitution relating to privacy protections. The Supreme Court decision was viewed as a major step forward in legal protections for persons who are LGBT because sodomy laws had been used to prohibit persons who are LGBT from obtaining custody of or adopting children.

Hate Crime and Antidiscrimination Legislation

According to the Federal Bureau of Investigation (2014), there were 5,796 incidents of single-bias hate crimes throughout the United States in 2012. Nearly 17% of these incidents related to sexual orientation, most notably gay males. Although many states and localities have introduced legislation to protect against discrimination due to sexual orientation and gender identity, attempts have not always been successful. After the senseless murders of Matthew Shepard, a gay male in Wyoming, and James Byrd, an African American in Texas, over 200 advocacy groups such as the American Civil Liberties Union, Human Rights Campaign, Anti-defamation League, National Association for the Advancement of Colored People, and NASW succeeded in winning passage of a new, strong law on **hate crimes** that now includes crimes committed because of bias against people of any race, color, religion, national origin, ethnicity, gender, disability or sexual orientation. This law, passed in 2009, was the first federal legislation that included protections for persons who are transgender (American Civil Liberties Union, 2014). Hate crimes impact not only the targeted person and his or her family but also send a threatening message to all members of a particular group. Twenty-one states, the District of Columbia, and Puerto Rico have passed laws outlawing discrimination based on sexual orientation and 17 states, the District of Columbia, and Puerto Rico have outlawed discrimination based on gender identity or expression.

Same-Sex Marriage

More recent attention throughout the world has been on laws either allowing or prohibiting same-sex couples to marry. The first country to allow same-sex marriage was the Netherlands, in 2007. As of August, 2014, **same-sex marriage** is recognized in 16 countries, including Canada, Belgium, Norway, South Africa, Spain, and Sweden. The federal government of the United States was prohibited from doing so by the Defense of Marriage Act (DOMA) enacted in 1996. However, President Obama advocated for its repeal, expressing particular concern over the section that allowed states that did not support same-sex marriage to disallow federal benefits afforded to same-sex persons legally married in states that allowed it.

Proponents of same-sex marriages argue that lesbian and gay couples are denied access to health care, retirement and death benefits, inheritances, and other benefits that heterosexual married couples take for granted. Opponents argue that marriage is to be a religious union between a male and female for purposes of procreation. In 2013, the Supreme Court ruled that the portion of DOMA, which allows states that do not recognize same-sex marriage to refuse to recognize those performed in other states was unconstitutional. The Court ruled that regardless of a state's law, individuals in same-sex marriages were entitled to all allowable federal benefits available to spouses, including insurance benefits if a federal employee, eligibility for the Family Medical Leave Act, veteran's benefits, bankruptcy, filing joint tax returns, and social security benefits for survivors.

Attitudes toward same-sex marriage are changing, with approximately one-third of persons in the United States supporting it, another one-third supporting some type of civil agreement that offers the same protections as marriage but not marriage, and one-third opposing any type of recognition of same-sex relationships whatsoever. Same-sex marriage is now recognized in 19 states and the District of Columbia and by the federal government, while other states recognize civil unions or other types of legal benefits and protections. However, 66% of persons in the United States still reside in areas where those who are LGBTQ cannot choose to marry, and members of some religious groups that oppose same-sex marriage are pushing for a Supreme Court ruling that prohibits it completely. It is anticipated that the Supreme Court will make additional rulings on this issue sometime in 2015 (American Civil Liberties Union, 2014).

Persons who are LGBT have had a number of strong advocates. One of the earlier groups to support their rights was the Chicago Society for Human Rights, established in 1924. In 1950, the Mattachine Society was founded to further rights for, and acceptance of, same-sex-oriented individuals. Currently, groups that established themselves as advocates of persons who are LGBTQ include the American Civil Liberties Union (ACLU), the National Center for Lesbian Rights, the Human Rights Campaign, PFLAG National, and the Gay and Lesbian Advocates and Defenders (GLAD). NASW, too, is a strong advocate for LGBT rights. In 2006, NASW joined the Maryland Chapter of NASW in filing a brief in a suit brought by the ACLU relating to claims that same-sex couples should

be prevented from marrying because they cannot be effective parents (see Chapter 11 for further discussion on this issue).

Stereotypical thinking based on erroneous information guides most heterosexuals' reactions to those with nonheterosexual orientations. Thus, individuals who are LGBTQ are often denied freedom of expression and access to the opportunity structure that is available for heterosexuals. Adolescents who may be labeled LGBTQ face special challenges. In 2010, a rash of suicides among LGBTQ teens led to a national media campaign against bullying of LGBTQ youth. "It Gets Better" features a number of well-known figures from a variety of fields, including President Barack Obama, calling for an end to bullying but urging LGBTQ youth not to take their lives (see www.itgetsbetter.org).

Clearly, social work and related professions must address more forcefully the prejudices and biases toward homosexuality that remain pervasive within our professions as well as the broader society. Accreditation standards for social work programs require that course content address the needs of diverse populations, including those who are LGBTQ. Advocacy on behalf of this and other vulnerable populations subject to oppression and discrimination is a priority of the profession. Until the fear and apprehension about those who are LGBTQ are dispelled through public education and enlightenment, however, prejudice and discrimination will continue to be barriers to social and economic justice for members of this group.

Social and Economic Justice for Persons with a Disability and the Impact of Ableism

EP 2.1.2a
EP 2.1.4a
EP 2.1.5a

The largest group of marginalized individuals in the United States consists of persons with disabilities. Disabilities include those that are physical (i.e., chronic illness, visual, hearing, mobility) as well as mental (i.e., depression, attention deficit disorder, learning disability). While disabilities are wide-ranging and can have virtually no impact to significant impact on one's ability to complete daily tasks, they result in stigma and oppression for many members of this population. Our culture is organized around what we term **ableism** at the individual, institutional, and societal levels. Unfair advantage is afforded to persons who are able-bodied with a tendency to either blame or ignore those who are not able to keep up physically, cognitively, or emotionally with cultural expectations (Castaneda, Hopkins, & Peters, 2013). Persons with a disability are discussed extensively in Chapter 9, but we would be remiss not to point out in this chapter the fact that they are a marginalized group that receives much of the same unfair treatment as other groups discussed here.

Social and Economic Justice Based on Age and the Impact of Ageism

EP 2.1.2a
EP 2.1.4a
EP 2.1.5a

A person's age often results in discrimination and oppression, most often either because someone is too young or too old. While one's actual age is a reality, attitudes toward age are socially constructed, with children and the elderly revered in some cultures and marginalized because they are not viewed as productive members of society in others. Ageism, or stereotyping and discrimination against people because of their age, is discussed in Chapter 12, which focuses on older adults.

Recent attention has also been given to discrimination against persons at the other end of the age spectrum, those who are young. **Adultism** refers to the process of stereotyping and discrimination against those who are young, although some use the term "ageism" to refer to both (DeJong & Love, 2013).

Although clearly youth need guidance and protection from their parents and other adults, they are often treated disrespectfully. Being treated in a demeaning manner, having opinions devalued, not being respected in the workplace by those older than they are (especially when in a supervisory role), and being told they are "immature" when they become emotional are examples of adultism. Systematic treatment of this type results in low self-esteem, feelings of powerlessness, and often either acting out behavior or withdrawal (Bell, 2013). Many adults treat children and teens in ways that they would never treat another adult. As seen in other groups that are oppressed, those who are continually marginalized because they are either too young or too old often internalize these beliefs, becoming incapable of making decisions on their own and needing constant care and supervision.

Social and Economic Justice Based on Religion and the Impact of Religious Oppression

EP 2.1.2a
EP 2.1.4a
EP 2.1.5a

Religion and religious institutions play major roles in society, and in the United States freedom of religion is a well-guarded principle of democracy upon which our country was founded. However, not only in the United States but globally, religion both honors freedom and denies it, and religious organizations can be both oppressive and oppressed.

Religious organizations have long fought for social and economic justice for vulnerable populations, provided services and support for the poor and other groups in need, and provided an organizing framework for social cooperation and collaboration. Jewish organizations, for example, partnered with the NAACP and other civil rights groups in fighting against segregation, while many Christian organizations have worked tirelessly to provide for persons who are homeless and refugees and disaster relief across the globe. Although religious groups are often stereotyped as being conservative ("the religious right"), many have advocated for same-sex marriage, nondiscrimination legislation for persons who are LGBTQ, reproductive rights for women, and expanded health care and other services for those who are poor.

At the same time, dominant religious groups hold power that gives them advantage and marginalizes members of other religious groups as well as those who choose not to participate in organized religion and/or to adhere to a belief system that does not include religion. The dominant religious group in the United States is Christianity, with the predominant Christian group Protestant. Often unintentionally, persons who are Jewish, Muslim, Buddhist, or Hindu, members of other religious groups, or those who don't incorporate religious beliefs in their lives are marginalized by a culture that is organized around Christian privilege (Adams & Joshi, 2013). Which first amendment protections and how they can be interpreted have been addressed by the U.S. Supreme Court over the years, with many still pending. First amendment protections do not require that religion be entirely separate from public life, but they do require that the federal government cannot mandate a single official religion or legislate for or against a specific religion (Adams & Joshi). Thus, issues regarding specific prayers in public schools and celebration of specific religious holidays while ignoring others have to be considered within the context of first amendment rights.

Even so, the United States is organized around Christianity, with unintended privileges for those who are Christian. In most locations, public school and university vacations are organized around Christian holidays. Music and television specials most often celebrate Christian holidays, store hours are for the most part organized around Sunday church services, bumper stickers and jewelry with Christian symbols are usually not questioned, foods at grocery stores and restaurants are consistent with dietary rules, worship places are easily located when traveling within the United States, history courses value the Christian religion and cover its historical significance, Christian literature is not banned from schools or reading lists, and Christians can remain ignorant about other religions and their language and customs without feeling the need to understand them to fit in (Schlosser, 2013).

In contrast to Christianity, because of stereotypes and targeting, members of some groups, particularly those who are from the Middle East, have been unfairly oppressed. Mosques have been vandalized, Muslims have experienced violence, and even those who are not Muslim (the majority of Middle Easterners in the United States are actually Christian) have been assumed to be Islamic terrorists. Anti-semitism, oppression against those who are Jewish, also is not uncommon, and many Native American groups have experienced discrimination when attempting to hold religious ceremonies on their sacred ground, in spite of laws intended to protect them from this unfair treatment. Increased pluralism in the United States as it becomes more diverse and the collaborations of many religious leaders and their organizations offer hope that religious oppression will decrease and organized religion will escalate its efforts to promote social and economic justice.

Historically, although many early social workers and social service agencies were faith-based, social workers were educated to avoid focusing on religion and spirituality with their clients. Recent thinking takes a different perspective: if religion and/or spirituality are important parts of a person's identity, social workers need to respect their client's beliefs and incorporate that information into their work with the client and an intervention plan. However, social workers may not impart their own personal religious beliefs in their work with clients.

Efforts to Produce Social Justice for Populations at Risk

EP 2.1.5b
EP 2.1.5c

Bringing an end to institutional racism and other forms of oppression is not an easy task. Longstanding prejudices that have lingered over many generations are difficult to extinguish, despite efforts to enlighten the public about the consequences of maintaining false beliefs and practices. Little progress was made in dismantling segregation until the government decreed it. Before President Harry Truman ordered the integration of the armed forces in 1948, most government agencies supported racial segregation. Although racism and discrimination still are found in the armed forces, its desegregation has resulted in employment and educational opportunities for people of color that are inaccessible to them elsewhere in the United States. Many successful people of color attribute the opportunities afforded to them to their early military experiences. Significant gains in the military, government, and other primary social institutions have been made in recent years in improving the civil rights of persons who are LGBTQ. Advocates have also continued to press for changes that would improve the quality of life for persons of color, women, those with disabilities, those who are poor, older adults, and those experiencing religious oppression. While you can't read this text, or any media today for that matter, without realizing that there is still significant oppression directed toward all of these groups and that much still needs to be done to eradicate it, gains are being made on many fronts, with social workers involved in the majority of them in some way.

School Desegregation

The catalyst for ending separate public school education was the Supreme Court decision *Brown v. Board of Education* in 1954, which mandated an end to segregation in public schools. Ruling that "separate is not equal," the Court ordered public schools to be integrated and opened to children of all races and ethnic groups. Because of de facto housing patterns, members of minority groups lived in segregated neighborhoods and their children attended neighborhood schools.

To implement the Court's decision, busing became necessary. Many communities required students of color to be bused to schools in predominantly white neighborhoods, which resulted in strong resistance by the dominant white population. White citizens' councils emerged in the South and Midwest to resist school integration.

Many state governments questioned the constitutionality of the Court's decision and resisted taking appropriate action to hasten the integration process. Evidence was sought to support the position that integration of schools would have catastrophic effects on the educational achievement of children of all races. In an article that appeared in *The Harvard Educational Review* in 1969, Arthur Jensen, an educational psychologist from the University of California at Berkeley, concluded that white Americans were more intelligent than African Americans, and cited this fact as the reason why Head Start programs designed to improve African American IQ scores had failed. Release of the article resulted in a huge furor among scholars, civil rights groups, and countless others from across the world. Jensen's work was largely discredited by the research community, and his reputation suffered irreparable harm as a result. Jensen's work faded from view as a result of this event. Racist and supremacist groups, such as the Ku Klux Klan, joined in efforts to prevent school integration.

In time, school busing became common and school integration a technical reality. Universal public acceptance of desegregation through busing, however, was never achieved. In the 1980s and 1990s, the movement to return to neighborhood schools was strong. Charles Murray's (1994) book *The Bell Curve* was a rallying point for many, urging the elimination of busing and returning to neighborhood schools. Although advocates for neighborhood schools argued that these schools could be more culturally relevant to students and their families, in many instances schools in non-white neighborhoods experienced a significant loss of resources when busing was eliminated.

Author and educator Jonathan Kozol has written about the state of U.S. public schools for a number of years. His book *The Shame of the Nation: The Restoration of Apartheid Schooling in America* (2005), based on a study of public schools across the United States, makes the case that conditions in schools where the majority of children are nonwhite are actually worse than they were before the *Brown v. the Board of Education* ruling outlawing segregation. Recent data support Kozol's findings, indicating that U.S. schools are actually more segregated than they were in the 1950s. This raises concern about inequitable resources for nonwhite students, who are more likely to live in areas with more limited tax bases than their white counterparts, as well as the inability of children educated separately to be able to function in diverse workplaces and a diverse society.

Civil Rights Legislation

During the 1960s, significant progress was made in eliminating segregationist policies and controlling the effects of discrimination. President Lyndon Johnson's Great Society programs sought to eradicate segregation entirely and to make discrimination an offense punishable under the law. In 1964, the **Civil Rights Act** was passed. Amended in 1965, this act sought to ban discrimination based on race, religion, color, or ethnicity in public facilities, government-operated programs, and employment. A similar act, passed in 1968, made illegal the practice of discrimination in advertising and the purchase, financing, or rental of residential property.

Under the new legal sanctions for desegregation, a groundswell of support mounted among disenfranchised people of color and sympathetic dominant-group members. The Reverend Martin Luther King, Jr., and organized freedom marchers sought to raise the consciousness of society regarding the obscenities of segregationist policies. King's nonviolent movement provided high visibility to the injustices of discrimination and served to stimulate and influence policies for change. During this period, other significant organizations, including the Southern Christian Leadership Conference (SCLC), the National Urban League, the National Association for the Advancement of Colored People (NAACP), La Raza, and the League of United Latin American Citizens (LULAC), actively pursued social and economic justice for people of color.

As the new civil rights legislation was implemented, an air of hope prevailed that discrimination would soon become a matter of history. School busing facilitated public-school integration, public facilities were opened to people of color, and the employment market became more accepting of minority applicants. Further advances were made under the influence of the Economic Opportunities Act of 1964. Neighborhoods were organized, and their residents registered to vote. This movement was furthered by the Voting Rights Act of 1965, which prohibited the imposition of voting qualifications based on race, color, age, or minority status. The impact of the **civil rights movement** was far-reaching in the struggle for full and equal participation by minorities in the social and economic areas of our society.

Uneven Progress

The rapid pace of the change effort was short-lived. By the late 1970s, racial polarization had increased with a new wave of conservatism. Discussions of race, as they often are today, were centered most often on whites and blacks, ignoring other groups of color. Whites were much more prone to attribute the "lack of progress" among the black population to blacks themselves rather than to discrimination—thus supporting the position that discrimination was no longer a problem for "motivated" blacks. By the late 1970s, racial and minority issues were replaced by national defense, energy, and inflation as the top priorities for the white majority.

Although the *Brown v. Board of Education* court decision to end school desegregation was hailed as a major breakthrough in 1954, public schools throughout the United States are segregated today, not because of laws prohibiting attendance but, rather, because of housing patterns, a result of institutional discrimination. Thus, much of the progress gained during desegregation has been lost. Central cities throughout the United States have become mostly nonwhite and economically poor, resulting in largely segregated schools.

Tax bases in rural and urban school districts alike in economically disadvantaged areas produce limited funding in comparison to wealthier districts. This raises issues in many states about the best way to fund public education so all students will receive a quality education. Funding is limited to provide resources to children who are less likely to speak English, more likely to have parents who work long hours and cannot be involved in their children's education as much as they would like or are unfamiliar with the education system and how to guide their children through it, and often need additional resources beyond the classroom to be successful.

Affirmative Action

Affirmative action programs, which once mandated the selection of qualified members of oppressed groups for publicly operated business and education, have been downgraded and, in many instances, dismantled. The concept of affirmative action was derived from the civil rights acts of the 1960s and was, in part, an attempt to initiate actions that would equalize the social and economic playing field for all people and ultimately break the barriers of discrimination for those who had long been oppressed by established values, policies, and practices.

Compensatory justice, an underlying axiom for affirmative action directives, provided the impetus for eliminating institutionalized barriers to employment, education, and social parity in general. It required that women and people of color be hired, or admitted to educational institutions and professional schools, on a basis equal to that of white males. Public reaction to what was considered a "quota system" resulted in cries of "reverse discrimination." Many of these cries have come from white women—the group that has benefited the most from affirmative action programs. In the late 1990s, the U.S. Supreme Court ruled on a number of cases that reversed parts of affirmative action.

Affirmative action programs clearly have opened up opportunities for the oppressed. Although "tokenism" has been a major concern, many women, African Americans, Latinos, and other members of nonmajority groups have been able to achieve higher educational status, secure jobs, and achieve vertical mobility in the employment arena as a result of efforts to right historical wrongs. Critics of the downgrading of government efforts in the area of affirmative action argue that such actions will result in a return to past discriminatory practices. Proponents of downgrading these programs believe that they have not been effective, and, in the final analysis, all populations will be better served if positions are awarded on competency and merit rather than arbitrarily mandated by social legislation.

In this regard, one arena receiving more attention has been higher education. In the late 1990s, a court ruling in district federal courts prohibited Texas and other states in its region from using race as a criterion in admitting students or awarding scholarships. Many advocates for social justice viewed the ruling as discriminatory because it indicated that admissions decisions could be based on athletic or musical ability or legacy (meaning that a family member had attended the institution) but not race. Two subsequent lawsuits, *Grutter v. Bollinger* and *Gratz v. Bollinger,* filed against the University of Michigan regarding its admissions selection process for undergraduate and law students, were appealed to the U.S. Supreme Court. Many organizations, including the military and Fortune 500 companies, filed briefs in support of the university, concerned that limiting access to higher education would jeopardize diversity in the workplace and the military.

In a divided decision, the Court ruled in June 2003 that instituting racial quotas and assigning points based on one's race could not be used in admissions decisions, but that race could be considered as one of many factors. The Court noted that limited forms of affirmative action were reasonable because the value of diversity extends beyond the college campus. In the decision, Sandra Day O'Connor, stated that

> the diffusion of knowledge and opportunity through public institutions of higher education must be accessible to all individuals regardless of race or ethnicity. Effective participation by members of all racial and ethnic groups in the civic life of our nation is essential if the dream of one nation is to be realized. (U.S. Supreme Court, 2003a)

The University of Michigan ruling was hailed as the most significant regarding affirmative action in some time. Opponents of the ruling, however, worked to organize the Michigan Civil Rights Initiative, also known as Proposal 2, a proposed amendment to the state constitution prohibited state and local government from "discriminating against or granting preferential treatment to any individual or group based on race, sex, color, ethnicity, or national origin in the areas of public employment, public contracting and public education" (Michigan Proposal 2, 2006). The amendment passed and was upheld by the U.S. Supreme Court in 2013. In a second ruling, the Court referred a University of Texas case back to the lower court for additional scrutiny. In 2014, the lower court ruled in favor of the University of Texas, indicating that its process of using race as one of many factors in considering admissions decisions, but not the only factor, was allowable.

Universities and other institutions are working to develop other ways to try to ensure diversity in their populations. Approaches that universities have taken include recruitment efforts targeted at high schools with large numbers of students of color and including criteria associated with race or ethnicity, such as being a first-generation college student or a student from a disadvantaged background. Workplaces are recruiting at schools and other sites that reflect the populations of employees they hope to hire. Nevertheless, ways to ensure that members of marginalized groups have access to education and employment are becoming limited by court and voter decisions.

Law Enforcement and Profiling

EP 2.1.2a
EP 2.1.4a
EP 2.1.5a

Another area receiving increased attention has been the relationship between law enforcement and people of color. Several high-profile cases involving white law enforcement officers beating or killing nonwhite civilians have led to concerns about the increasingly negative relationships between law enforcement agencies and communities of color. A recent case involved 18 year old Michael Brown of Ferguson, Missouri, a St. Louis suburb, who was shot multiple times by a white policeman, reportedly by some who observed the shooting while walking away from the officer with his hands in the air. The U.S. Department of Justice is conducting an investigation of both the shooting and the practices of the all-white Ferguson Police Department. This shooting as well as others have called attention to the shift in philosophy among many law enforcement agencies across the United States, that have adopted a more militaristic perspective, as opposed to community policing approaches that incorporate dialogue, training, and involving law enforcement officers in activities at the neighborhood level, including citizens' efforts to strengthen their communities.

Although people of color have indicated for years that they have been stopped by police, arrested, and jailed more often than whites, documentation in many cities indicates that **racial profiling** (sometimes called "DWB"—"driving while black or brown"), the practice of law enforcement officers stopping and searching people not otherwise engaged in suspicious behavior but, because of their race, is practiced in many areas. Racial profiling also can involve stopping pedestrians, shoppers at malls, voters on their way to the polls, employees at sites where immigrants are likely to be working, and airport passengers (American Civil Liberties Union, 2014) (see Box 4.4).

In many locations, African Americans and Latinos, particularly males, are stopped and searched at much higher rates than their white counterparts, and also are much more likely to be subjected to the use of force when being arrested. In many areas, racial profiling also includes young Asians and Asian Americans, immigrants, and Middle Easterners.

The outlook for a well-articulated and well-implemented program to eliminate prejudice and discrimination is mixed. Efforts to creatively and forcefully address this issue have waned since the mid-1970s, and race continues to be a sensitive topic that many individuals at

Box 4.4   Reported Incidents of Racial Profiling in the United States

- *While driving:* A young African American school-teacher reports being routinely pulled over in his suburban neighborhood in San Carlos, California, where only five other African American families live.

  Native Americans in Oklahoma report being stopped routinely by police because of the tribal tags displayed on their cars.

  In Texas, a Muslim student of South Asian ancestry is pulled over and asked by police if he is carrying any dead bodies or bombs.

- *While walking:* In Seattle, Washington, a group of Asian American youths are detained on a street corner by police for 45 minutes on an allegation of jaywalking. A sergeant ultimately ordered the officer in question to release them, but the young people say they saw whites repeatedly crossing the same street in an illegal manner without being stopped.

- *While traveling through airports:* An 8-year-old Muslim boy from Tulsa, Oklahoma, reportedly was separated from his family while airport security officials searched him and dismantled his Boy Scout pinewood derby car. He now is routinely stopped and searched at airports.

- *While shopping:* In New York City, an African American woman shopping for holiday presents was stopped by a security guard at a major

department store. Even though she showed the guards her receipts, she was taken to a holding cell in the building where every other suspect she saw was a person of color. She was subjected to threats and a body search. Three hours later she was allowed to leave without being charged, but was not allowed to take her purchases with her.

- *While at home:* On the day after Father's Day, a Latino family in a Chicago suburb reportedly was awakened at 4:50 a.m. by nine building inspectors and police officers, who prohibited the family from getting dressed or moving about. The authorities reportedly proceeded to search the entire house to find evidence of overcrowding. Enforcement of the zoning ordinance, which was used to justify the search, reportedly was targeted at the rapidly growing Latino population.

- *While traveling to and from places of worship:* A Muslim imam from the Dallas area reports being stopped and arrested by police upon leaving a mosque after an outreach event. Officers stopped him, searched his vehicle, arrested him for expired vehicle tags, and confiscated his computer.

SOURCE: Adapted from Amnesty International. (2004). *Threat and humiliation: Racial profiling, national security, and human rights in the United States.* New York: Author. Retrieved from www.amnestyusa.org/racial_profiling/index.do.

all levels of society choose to avoid. Current efforts at both federal and state levels to balance the budget by scaling down government programs and services, with an increased emphasis on enforcement of laws through power instead of community-building and collaboration, tend to overshadow concerted efforts to dismantle the institutional barriers that result in differential treatment for groups of color.

Social Work and the Promotion of Social and Economic Justice

EP 2.1.4c

Inherent in the identity of social work is its commitment to social action directed toward eliminating barriers that deny equal rights and full participation to all members of society. Since the early days, when social workers assisted in assimilating new immigrants into our

culture and sought to improve social conditions for them, the profession has engaged the citizenry in working toward social equality and an equal opportunity structure. The National Association of Social Workers and the Council on Social Work Education have placed high priority on incorporating content about vulnerable populations—including women; gays, lesbians, bisexuals, and transgender persons; the poor; and people of color—into professional social work practice and social work education. NASW has developed specific standards for culturally competent social work practice that address key areas, including values and ethics, cross-cultural knowledge and skills, service delivery, empowerment and advocacy, language diversity, and leadership. The standards were developed to:

- Maintain and improve the quality of services provided by social workers, and programs delivered by social service agencies.

- Establish professional expectations so social workers can monitor and evaluate their practices.
- Provide a framework for social workers to assess culturally competent practices.
- Inform consumers, governmental regulatory bodies, and others, such as insurance carriers about the profession's standards for practice.
- Establish specific ethical guidelines for social work practice in agency or private practice settings.
- Provide documentation of professional expectations for agencies, peer review committees, state regulatory bodies, insurance carriers and others (National Association of Social Workers, 2001).

Social work practitioners strive to be familiar with the racial and cultural backgrounds of their clients, including strengths and the impact of oppression, when assisting them in achieving solutions to problems. Through social action, efforts are made to change community attitudes, policies, and practices that disadvantage members of at-risk populations. As advocates, social workers seek to modify rules and regulations that deny equal treatment to those accorded at-risk status. As organizers, they work with leaders from at-risk populations in identifying priorities, gaining community support, and facilitating change through the democratic process.

As citizens (as well as professionals), social workers are active in organized public efforts to abolish discriminatory practices. They support political candidates who are openly committed to working for social equality. They are involved in public education to dispel prejudice and to promote productive interactions among divergent racial and ethnic groups. In a public climate in which the pursuit of social and economic equality has lessened, social workers have a responsibility to maintain a vigilant pursuit of equality.

Social workers should view the concept of *social justice* as more than just rhetoric. Ever since the inception of the profession, social justice has been a basic axiom for practice. Social justice—achieving a society in which all members have access to the same rights and privileges without regard to gender, race, ethnic affiliation, creed, age, sexual orientation, or physical and mental capacities—is essential for the establishment of a nondiscriminatory society. Only when that goal is achieved can social and economic equality prevail.

A fundamental avenue through which social justice is achieved is by empowering disenfranchised and oppressed individuals and groups. **Empowerment** is both a process and a goal, through which individuals and groups gain mastery over their lives, become active participants, and make decisions that will enable them to gain control over their lives and the environment in which they interact. Disempowered populations can only react to the norms and mandates of others, which can perpetuate discriminatory practices.

Summary

Few observers would deny that the United States has seen a major gender revolution during the past few decades. As part of the human rights movement, many advances have been made in reducing sexism in our society. Opportunities for economic and social participation of women are now greater than ever. Despite some reversals, such as the failure to ascertain comparable worth/pay equity for women, societal pressures to ensure equal treatment and opportunities continue.

Social inequality has characterized the treatment of racial and ethnic groups, the poor, and persons who are lesbian, gay, bisexual, transgender, or questioning in the United States. Although some progress has been made toward more favorable treatment, these groups have not achieved full participation rights. Discrimination and differential treatment of women, people of color, those who are LGBTQ, those with disabilities, those who are poor, those who are elderly, and those who are not part of the Christian majority continue to restrict their achieving social and economic progress. Social work has a long tradition of promoting social equality, and the commitment of the profession to continue in this role will increase as the societal thrust to do so declines.

Over the past decade the euphemism "politically correct" has gained popularity among those who question the validity of certain attitudes or practices directed toward oppressed or disenfranchised groups. Politically correct responses have become, for many, substitutes for "correct" responses. The concept of political correctness invokes negativism for positive actions taken. For example, a person may behave in a certain manner because it is the politically correct thing to do—not necessarily the right (or decent) thing to do. In reality, many politically correct responses are socially responsible ones. Prejudiced persons can behave in a socially responsible manner even though their intentions are simply to be politically correct.

Unfortunately, some may use the guise of political correctness out of fear that a true and honest response may place them in jeopardy of losing an advantage they treasure. Social workers should not be overly concerned with being politically correct. The value base of the profession and commitment of social work practitioners to genuineness always should be paramount when intervening with clients or serving as advocates on their behalf.

This chapter is intended to make you aware that prejudice, institutional discrimination, and oppression have long existed, and that the targets of these practices continue to suffer the consequences of differential treatment and limited opportunity. While advocacy groups have been able to bring about positive political changes and public attitudes have improved, much remains to be accomplished if we are to achieve social equality for all groups in the United States. Prejudice and discrimination are the products of social interaction. As social constructs, they can be replaced by values that respect the dignity and worth of all human beings and result in a society that promotes equal treatment for all.

Competency Notes

EP 2.1.2a: Recognize and manage personal values in a way that allows professional values to guide practice (pp. 83, 87, 93–94, 107–108, 112). Social workers are aware of their own personal values and manage them in ways that enable them to work effectively with diverse client groups.

EP 2.1.4a: Recognize the extent to which a culture's structures and values may oppress, marginalize, alienate, or create or enhance privilege and power (pp. 83, 87, 93–94, 107–108, 112). Social workers demonstrate an understanding that prejudice, oppression, and personal and institutional discrimination marginalize some individuals, families, groups, organizations, and communities, while power and privilege give advantages to others.

EP 2.1.4c: Recognize and communicate their understanding of the importance of difference in shaping life experiences (pp. 83, 113). Social workers understand the dimensions of diversity, including race, gender, class, ethnicity, and sexual orientation, and the ways that the intersectionality of these dimensions shapes life experiences.

EP 2.1.5a: Understand forms and mechanisms of oppression and discrimination (pp. 82, 87, 93–94, 107–108, 112). Social workers can articulate the many forms of oppression and discrimination that exist across all levels of the environment and their impact on clients.

EP 2.1.5b: Advocate for human rights and social and economic justice (pp. 103, 105, 109). Social workers advocate for policies and engage in practices that promote human rights and social and economic justice.

EP 2.1.5c: Engage in practices that advance social and economic justice (pp. 103, 105, 109). Social workers engage in practices with individuals, families, groups, organizations, and communities that advance social and economic justice.

EP 2.1.8a: Analyze, formulate, and advocate for policies that advance social well-being (p. 82). Social workers analyze, formulate, and advocate for policies that advance social well-being, with special attention to the impact of policies on diverse groups and to social and economic justice.

Key Terms

The terms below are defined in the Glossary.

ableism	hate crimes
adultism	heterosexism
affirmative action	homophobia
assimilation	institutional
Civil Rights Act	discrimination
civil rights movement	oppression
class	populations at risk
classism	prejudice
comparable worth	racial profiling
cultural competence	same-sex marriage
cultural diversity	sexism
cultural pluralism	sexual harassment
discrimination	sexual orientation
economic justice	social inequality
empowerment	social injustice
Equal Rights	social justice
Amendment (ERA)	stereotypes
gender equity	underclass

Discussion Questions

1. How do you explain the presence of prejudice and discrimination in a society whose values are based in Judeo-Christian ideology?
2. Discuss early efforts to eradicate discriminatory practices against women, people of color, and

persons who are lesbian, gay, bisexual, transgender, or questioning.

3. Why is social justice difficult to achieve in a society characterized by cultural pluralism?

4. Give an example of institutional discrimination and show how it has impacted the group(s) discriminated against.

5. Assume that you are a member of an oppressed group. What would your reaction be to the watering down of affirmative action programs?

6. What is the role of social work in breaking down institutional barriers of discrimination?

7. How do you explain that some white women, who historically have experienced gender discrimination, discriminate against women of color?

8. What privileges in society are you afforded that you take for granted? What privileges are less available to you because of groups to which you belong?

9. What role, if any, do you think that race should play in deciding who should be admitted to colleges and universities and why? How important do you think diversity should be on a college campus?

10. Choose one social justice issue that is important to you. What population(s) does it most impact and why? What do you think is the best way to address this issue? What role could social workers play in addressing this issue?

On the Internet

www.socialworkers.org
www.aflcio.org
www.pflag.org
www.amnestyusa.org
www.census.gov
www.aclu.org
www.cesj.org
www.nela.org
www.sjti.org
www.guttmacher.org
www.itgetsbetter.org

References

Adams, M., Bell, L. A., & Griffin, P. (2013). *Teaching for diversity and social justice: A sourcebook* (2nd ed.). New York: Routledge.

American Civil Liberties Union. (2014). *Lesbian and gay rights*. Retrieved from https://www.aclu.org/lgbt-rights

American Psychological Association. (1992). *Guidelines for nonhandicapping language in APA journals*. Washington, DC: Author. Retrieved from http://www.apastyle.org/manual/related/nonhandicapping-language.aspx

American Psychological Association. (2010). *Publication manual of the American Psychological Association* (6th ed.). Washington, DC: Author.

American Psychological Association. (2014). *LGBT pride 2014: Much to be proud of at APA*. Washington, DC: Author.

Amnesty International. (2004). *Threat and humiliation: Racial profiling, national security, and human rights in the United States*. Retrieved from www.amnestyusa.org/racial_profiling/index.do

Arab American Institute. (2014). *About Arab Americans*. Retrieved from http://aaiusa.org/

Asi, M., & Beaulieu, D. (2013). Arab households in the United States: 2006–2010. Washington, DC: U.S. Census Bureau. Retrieved from http://www.census.gov/prod/2013pubs/acsbr10-20.pdf

Beiber, I. (Ed.). (1962). *Homosexuality*. New York: Basic Books.

Berman, J. (2014). Congratulations, graduates! Equal pay is already out of your reach. *Huffington Post*. Retrieved from http://www.huffingtonpost.com/2014/05/01/young-gender-pay-gap_n_5246893.html

Blumenfeld, W. (2013). Heterosexism: Introduction. In M. Adams, W. Blumenfeld, C. Castaneda, H. Hackman, M. Peters, & X. Zuniga (Eds.), *Readings for diversity and social justice* (3rd ed., pp. 373–378). London: Routledge.

Brown, D. (2012). How home ownership keeps blacks poorer than whites. *Forbes*. Retrieved from http://www.forbes.com/sites/forbesleadershipforum/2012/12/10/how-home-ownership-keeps-blacks-poorer-than-whites/

Bureau of Labor Statistics. (2014). *Women in the labor force: A databook*. Washington, DC: Author. Retrieved from http://www.bls.gov/cps/wlf-databook-2013.pdf

California Newsreel. (2003). *Race: The power of an illusion*. Retrieved from http://www.pbs.org/race/000_General/000_00-Home.htm

Capeheart, L., & Milovanovic, D. (2007). *Social justice: Theories, issues, and movements*. New Brunswick, NJ: Rutgers University Press.

Castaneda, C., Hopkins, L., & Peters, M. (2013). Ableism: Introduction. In M. Adams, W. Blumenfeld, C. Castaneda, H. Hackman, M. Peters, & X. Zuniga

(Eds.), *Readings for diversity and social justice* (3rd ed., pp. 461–467). London: Routledge.

Catalyst. (2014). *Statistical overview of women in the workplace.* New York: Author. Retrieved from http://www.catalyst.org/knowledge/statistical-over view-women-workplace

Center for American Women and Politics. (2014). *Women in elective office.* New Brunswick, NJ: Author.

Centers for Disease Control and Prevention. (2013a). *American Indian and Alaska Native heritage.* Retrieved from http://www.cdc.gov/features/aianheritagemonth/

Centers for Disease Control and Prevention. (2013b). *CDC Celebrates Asian and Pacific Islander heritage.* Retrieved from http://www.cdc.gov/features/aapi heritagemonth/

Centers for Disease Control and Prevention. (2013c). *Observances September 15–October 15: Hispanic/ Latino heritage month.* Retrieved from http://www .cdc.gov/minorityhealth/observances/HL.html

Centers for Disease Control and Prevention. (2014). *Black or African American populations.* Retrieved from http://www.cdc.gov/minorityhealth/populations /REMP/black.html

DeNavas-Walt, C., Proctor, B., & Smith, J. (2013). *Income, poverty, and health insurance in the U.S.: 2012.* Washington, DC: U.S Census Bureau. Retrieved from http://www.census.gov/prod/2013pubs/p60-245.pdf

Ennis, S., Rios-Vargas, M., & Albert, N. (2011). *The Hispanic population: 2010.* Washington, DC: U.S. Census Bureau.

Federal Bureau of Investigation. (2014). *2012 hate crime statistics.* Retrieved from http://www.fbi .gov/about-us/cjis/ucr/hate-crime/2012/topic-pages /incidents-and-offenses/incidentsandoffenses_final

Garcia, B., & Van Soest, D. (2006). *Social work practice for social justice.* Alexandria, VA: Council on Social Work Education.

Guttmacher Institute. (2014). *Fact sheet: Induced abortion in the United States.* Retrieved from http://www .guttmacher.org/pubs/fb_induced_abortion.html

Hoeffel, E., Rastogi, S., Kim, M. O., & Shahid, H. (2012). *The Asian population: 2010.* Washington, DC: U.S. Census Bureau.

Jensen, A. R. (1969). How much can we boost I.Q. and scholastic achievement? *Harvard Educational Review, 33,* 1–123.

Kaiser Family Foundation. (2014). *Fact sheet: Emergency contraception.* Menlo Park, CA: Author. Retrieved from http://kff.org/womens-health-policy /fact-sheet/emergency-contraception/

King, K., Krantz, L., Owen, B., Sheppard, D., Rios, L., Hui, K. M., et al. (2013). *Twice betrayed.* San Antonio, TX: San Antonio Express News.

Kozol, J. (2006). *The shame of the nation: The restoration of apartheid schooling in America.* New York: Three Rivers Press.

Lahiri, I., & Jensen, K. (2002). *Uncovering classism: A checklist for organizations.* (The Gil Deane Group). Retrieved from http://www.globalinclusionstrategies .com/popup/articles_uncovering-classism.html

Leigh, J. (1998). Communicating for cultural competence. Long Grove, ILL: Waveland Press.

Lum, D. (2011). *Culturally competent practice: A framework for understanding diverse groups and justice issues* (4th ed.). Florence, KY: Cengage Learning.

Marger, M. N. (2005). *Social inequality: Patterns and processes* (4th ed.). New York: McGraw-Hill.

McIntosh, P. (1988). *White privilege: Unpacking the invisible knapsack.* Wellesley, MA: Wellesley College Center for Research on Women.

McLemore, S. D., & Romo, H. D. (2005). *Racial and ethnic relations in America* (6th ed.). Boston: Allyn & Bacon.

Michigan Proposal 2. (2006). *Voter guide to Proposal 2.* Retrieved from www.michiganpro-posal2.org

Mill, J. S. (1861). Utilitarianism. In J. S. Mill & J. Gray (1998). *On liberty and other essays* (pp. 74–112). Oxford, England: Oxford Press.

Munk-Olsen, T., Laresn, T., Pedersen, C., Lidegaard, O., & Mortensen, P. (2011). Induced first-trimester abortion and risk of mental disorder. *New England Journal of Medicine, 364,* 332–339.

Murdock, S., Hogue, N., Michael, M., White, S., & Pecote, B. (1997). *The Texas challenge: Population change and the future of Texas.* College Station: Texas A & M University.

Murray, C. (1994). *The bell curve.* Washington, DC: New Republic.

Nangeroni, N. (2006). Transgenderism: Transgressing gender norms. *GenderTalk.* Retrieved August 3, 2010, from www.gendertalk.com

National Association of Social Workers. (2001). *NASW standards for cultural competence in social work practice.* Washington, DC: Author. Retrieved August 3, 2010, from www.nasw.org

National Association of Social Workers. (2012). Public policy statement on family planning and reproductive choice. *Social Work Speaks.* Washington, DC: Author.

National Center on Educational Statistics. (2014). *Fast facts: Degrees conferred by sex and race.* Washington,

DC: Author. Retrieved from http://nces.ed.gov/Fast Facts/display.asp?id=72

National Employment Lawyers Association. (2003). *Fact sheet: Why we still need affirmative action.* San Francisco: Author. Retrieved August 3, 2010, from www.nela.org

Norris, T., Vines, P., & Hoeffel, E. (2012). *The American Indian and Alaskan Native population: 2010.* Washington, DC: U.S. Census Bureau. Retrieved from http://www.census.gov/prod/cen2010/briefs/c2010 br-10.pdf

Novak, M. (2000). Defining social justice. *First Things.* Retrieved from www.firstthings.com

Occupy Together. (2014). *Issues.* Retrieved from http://www.occupytogether.org/

Pascale, C. (2006). *Making sense of race, class, and gender: Common sense, power, and privilege in the United States.* London: Routledge.

Pierson, J. (2009). *Tackling social exclusion* (2nd ed.). London: Routledge.

Rastogi, S., Johnson, T., Hoeffel, E., & Drewery, M. (2011). *The Black population: 2010.* Washington, DC: U.S. Census Bureau. Retrieved from http://www.census.gov/prod/cen2010/briefs/c2010br-06.pdf

Rawls, J. (2005). *A theory of justice.* Cambridge, MA: Belknap Press.

Saad, L. (2014). *U.S. still split on abortion: 47% pro-choice; 46% pro-life.* Princeton, NJ: Gallop. Retrieved from http://www.gallup.com/poll/170249/split-abortion-pro-choice-pro-life.aspx

Stern, M., & Axinn, J. (2011). *Social welfare: A history of the American response to need* (8th ed.). Boston: Allyn & Bacon.

Tatum, B. D. (2008). *Can we talk race? And other conversations in an era of school resegregation.* Boston: Beacon Press.

Texas Higher Education Coordinating Board. (2014). *Closing the gaps: Participation and success—2014 progress report.* Retrieved from www.thecb.state.tx.us

U.S. Commission on Civil Rights. (2013). *Sexual assault in the military.* Washington, DC: Author. Retrieved from http://www.usccr.gov/pubs/09242013_Statutory_Enforcement_Report_Sexual_Assault_in_the_Military.pdf

U.S. Department of Health and Human Services. (2012). *Characteristics and financial circumstances of TANF recipients: FY 2010.* Washington, DC: Author. Retrieved from http://www.acf.hhs.gov/programs/ofa/resource/character/fy2010/fy2010-chap10-ys-final

U.S. Department of Labor. (2014). *30 leading occupations for women by selected characteristics.* Washington, DC: Author. Retrieved from http://www.dol.gov/wb/stats/leadoccupations.htm

U.S. Supreme Court. (2003a, June 23). *Gratz et al. v Bollinger et al.* Washington, DC: Author.

U.S. Supreme Court. (2003b, June 26). *Laurence v. Texas.* Washington, DC: Author.

Wilson, W. J. (1997). *When work disappears: The world of the new urban poor.* New York: Vintage.

Suggested Readings

Adams, M., Blumenfeld, W., Castaneda, C., Hackman, H., Peters, M., & Zuniga, X. (Eds.). (2013). *Readings for diversity and social justice* (3rd ed.). New York: Routledge.

Anderson, M. L., & Collins, P. H. (2009). *Race, class, and gender: An anthology.* Florence, KY: Cengage Learning.

Appleby, G., Colon, E., & Hamilton, J. (2011). *Diversity, oppression, and social functioning: Person-in-environment assessment and intervention* (3rd ed.). Boston: Allyn & Bacon.

Barak, G., Leighton, P., & Flavin, J. (2006). *Class, race, gender and crime: The social realities of justice in America.* Lanham, MD: Bowman and Littlefield.

Davis, K., & Bent-Goodley, T. (Eds.). (2005). *The color of social policy.* Alexandria, VA: Council on Social Work Education.

Diller, J. (2006). *Cultural diversity: A primer for the human services* (3rd ed.). Pacific Grove, CA: Brooks/Cole.

Fong, R. (Ed.). (2004). *Culturally competent practice with immigrant and refugee children and families.* New York: Guilford Press.

Garcia, B., & Van Soest, D. (2006). *Social work practice for social justice.* Washington, DC: Council on Social Work Education.

Gardella, L. G., & Haynes, K. (2004). *A dream and a plan: A woman's path to leadership in human services.* Washington, DC: NASW Press.

Healey, J. F. (2009). *Diversity and society: Race, ethnicity, and gender.* Newbury Park, CA: Pine Forge Press.

Heuberger, B. (2005). *Cultural diversity: Building skills for awareness, understanding, and application* (3rd ed.). Dubuque, IA: Kendall Hunt.

Hooks, B. (2000a). *Feminism is for everybody: Passionate politics.* Cambridge, MA: South End Press.

Hooks, B. (2000b). *Where we stand: Class matters.* New York: Routledge.

Hunter, S., & Hickerson, J. (2003). *Affirmative practice: Understanding and working with lesbian, gay, bisexual, and transgender persons.* Washington, DC: NASW Press.

Journal of Gay and Lesbian Issues in Education. Binghamton, NY: Haworth Press.

Logan, S. (2005). *Social work with people of African descent.* Alexandria, VA: Council on Social Work Education.

Martin, E., & Martin, J. (2003). *Spirituality and the Black helping tradition in social work.* Washington, DC: NASW Press.

Martin, J., & Hunter, S. (2005). *Lesbian, gay, bisexual, and transgender issues in social work.* Alexandria, VA: Council on Social Work Education.

Ortega, R., Gutierrez, L., & Yeakley, A. (2006). *Latinos and social work education.* Alexandria, VA: Council on Social Work Education. (bibliography)

Sengstock, M. C. (2009). *Voices of diversity: Multiculturalism in America.* New York: Springer.

Sullivan, N., Mesbur, E., & Lang, N. (2003). *Social work with groups: Social justice through personal, community, and social change.* Binghamton, NY: Haworth Press.

Van Wormer, K. (Ed.). (2004). *Confronting oppression, restoring justice.* Alexandria, VA: Council on Social Work Education.

Wing, S. D., & McGoldrick, M. (2006). *Multicultural social work practice.* Hoboken, NJ: Wiley.

PART 2

Social Work Practice: Methods of Intervention

Andersen Ross/Photodisc/Getty Images

Part 2 of this text presents methods of intervention used by generalist social workers. Chapter 5, Social Work Practice With Individuals, Families, and Groups, explains the most prevalent method in professional social work practice—intervention with individuals and families who are having difficulty interacting within their environment. Included are theories and techniques that social workers use in helping individuals and families build on their strengths, along with strategies to meet their needs and improve their social functioning and the environment in which they function.

In Chapter 5 we also examine methods used in working with clients in groups. Group work is an effective method of intervention that is receiving increasing attention, both because of its effectiveness with many populations and because it often is seen as more cost-effective than working with clients individually. The chapter reviews relevant theories related to working with groups and identifies a variety of groups in which individuals interact. Finally, the chapter brings up important factors to consider when social workers form groups, the importance of group process when working with groups, and various methods that social workers use when working with groups.

Chapter 6, Social Work Practice With Agencies and the Community, points out the importance of the community and community agencies in working with clients and describes various methods of community organization and community intervention that social workers typically use to create individual and social change. Because the exosystem—or community—level of the environment has had such a significant impact on individual and family functioning, one of the major ways in which social workers can address client needs is by working within the community to develop or strengthen programs and policies, advocate for client needs, and empower community members to advocate for themselves and develop interventions that address their needs.

In Chapter 6 we also describe the relationships between social welfare policy and practice and approaches that social workers can take to evaluate proposed and existing social welfare policies. The chapter suggests administrative, leadership, and management strategies that social workers can use to gather resources and opportunities to create and maintain efficient and effective social services agencies. As social welfare needs continue to expand while resources to address these needs are shrinking, the management of social welfare programs is increasingly critical for an agency's survival.

Because sound practice and policy decisions should be based on research, this chapter also includes discussion of the interdependence of social work practice and research and the use of social research as integral in problem solving. The vital role of research in policy and practice is emphasized to continually buttress practice with data from research findings. This role is essential so that we can continue to conceive ways in which to address social welfare issues and work with client systems more effectively and so that we can demonstrate our effectiveness in garnering the resources to deal with the many social welfare needs of today.

This section focuses on competencies needed to become a skilled generalist social work practitioner, providing a beginning understanding of the stages of the helping process—engagement, assessment, intervention, and evaluation—when working with individuals, families, groups, organizations, and communities. Social work roles and relevant knowledge needed in policy and research are also explored.

As you learn about the methods of intervention used by social work generalist practitioners in Part 2, ask yourself the following questions that draw from what you learned in Part 1:

- How do past and present social welfare perspectives and policies shape the ways people view individuals and families today, the types of needs that individuals and families might be likely to have, and the methods of intervention that might be used in working with individuals, families, and groups to deal with these needs?
- How can the ecological/systems framework help us understand issues relating to individuals and families and the impact of the broader environment on their functioning?
- How might these issues be addressed using the methods of intervention discussed in Part 2?
- What are the relationships among factors such as race and ethnicity, gender, age, class, and sexual orientation on individual and family functioning, and how would social workers consider these factors when working with individuals, families, and groups in practice settings?

CHAPTER 5

Social Work Practice with Individuals, Families, and Groups

EP 2.1.1a

At age 42, Patrice Dillon moved with her four children from Nebraska to Illinois. Later, she was joined by her mother, Susan. One of her children, Bill, age 18, is a school dropout who works sporadically as an automobile mechanic. Laura, 19, completed high school and works at a clerical job while living at home. Robert, 11, has a physical disability and attends school now and then. Beatrice, 8, goes to school at times but often stays at home to help with chores around the house. Patrice's mother, who is functionally illiterate, tries to manage the household while Patrice works.

In Nebraska, Patrice had a job as a waitress and also received SNAP (food stamp) benefits. After moving to Illinois, she found a job she liked but was laid off recently because she began to have health problems. She went to the county health center, but her diagnosis remained a mystery.

Patrice has come to the local social services agency seeking help with her "down feelings." She says she is "about ready to give up" because she never seems to be able to "get on top of my problems." Even though she feels reasonably strong now, she has not heard from her most recent employer, who told her, according to Patrice, "You can have your job back as soon as you're well enough to handle it." She has considered applying for SNAP and TANF benefits but would prefer to work, and with all the changes in welfare reform, she's not sure she is eligible, especially for TANF benefits.

Because Beatrice has missed so much school, Patrice is concerned that child welfare officials might remove her daughter from her home. Patrice is too depressed to get Beatrice up and ready in the morning and to do the laundry, so the girl has no clean clothes to wear. Patrice says she needs money for food and rent and has come to the agency as a last resort.

Patrice's family is best classified as one having multiple needs. She and the social worker she sees at the agency identify some immediate objectives on which to work together. First, the social worker will help Patrice contact the food bank to arrange for food for the family. After being reassured that child welfare workers will not remove Beatrice from the home for not going to school unless there are other problems of abuse or neglect, Patrice agrees to go with the social worker to the school to discuss how to help Beatrice get caught up in her schoolwork.

The social worker also agrees to help Patrice contact her landlord and arrange for rent support until Patrice can find a job or establish her eligibility for TANF. In addition, Patrice and the social worker agree to meet weekly and develop options to deal with her needs, and Patrice agrees to join a group to gain emotional support and strengthen her employment skills. The social worker and Patrice also determine that enrolling Robert in a program at the local rehabilitation center will be beneficial. This program provides physical therapy and also group socialization experiences and skill building that will help Robert learn self-care and self-sufficiency skills. As Patrice builds her relationship with the social worker and gains self-confidence, her health problems diminish and she finds a job with the local hospital food service. Patrice's problems are neither rare nor unusual. Thousands of people like her are coping with similar problems and are turning to social agencies for help. Social workers often represent the only hope that many people have in finding avenues to resolve their problems.

In this chapter we identify the components and characteristics of generalist practice methods that are used with individuals, families, and groups. Chapter 6 continues the topic with generalist practice in the community and policy, administration, and research. These chapters will acquaint you with social work processes and methods, as well as with the theories that undergird generalist practice. As you progress through the social work curriculum, you will examine methods, processes, and theories in more depth.

Generalist Practice: Background

EP 2.1.10a-l

The society and world in which we live are characterized by rapid transition, change, and uncertainty. The technological revolution and globalization have contributed to sweeping modifications in lifestyle, increased mobility, and changing values. Along with the growing capacity to create new products, the shifting job market is requiring new skills and more adaptable employees. Relationships among individuals have become more tenuous and short-lived.

As a result, many people have difficulty achieving a sense of roots in the community. Increases in the cost of living, more tenuous job security, and rapid social changes have affected family life. Single parent and blended families have become more commonplace, and many grandparents have become primary care givers for their grandchildren. Children with special needs, addiction to alcohol and other drugs of both

adults and children, an increasing number of individuals caring for older adults, higher costs of housing and other necessities, and families with all adult members working have placed demands on individuals and families that too often leave them disrupted, confused, angry, frustrated, and overwhelmed.

At one time or another, virtually all of us have experienced at least one of these and many other social pressures generated by our rapidly changing society. To seek professional help with alleviating stress and its **dysfunctional** consequences is neither an unusual response nor a sign of weakness for individuals and families in stressful situations. All of us have needed the steady guidance of a respected friend or professional at some time. When problems become stressful and self-help efforts fail to produce desired solutions, professional assistance may be needed. **Generalist** social work practice offers that assistance.

As described in Chapter 2, generalist practice with individuals and families, traditionally called **casework**, is the oldest social work practice. Another form of generalist practice is **group work**, a method that fosters personal development through the mechanism of group process.

Generalist Practice: A Definition

EP 2.1.7a

A social work generalist practitioner assists clients in attaining a higher level of social functioning. **Generalist practice** is both a process and a method. As a process, it involves a more or less orderly sequence of progressive stages in engaging the client (or client system, such as a family) in activities and actions that promote agreed-on goals. As a method, generalist practice entails the creative use of techniques and knowledge that guide intervention activities determined by the client and the social work practitioner. Generalist practice, too, is an art that applies scientific knowledge about human behavior and the skillful use of relationships to enable the client to activate or develop interpersonal and, if necessary, community resources to achieve a more positive balance with his or her environment. Generalist social work practice seeks to improve, restore, maintain, or enhance the client's social functioning.

The most significant converging elements in social work practice are that it:

- is an art—involving a skill that results from experience or training;
- applies knowledge about human behavior;
- is based on client involvement in developing options to resolve problems;
- emphasizes using the client's resources (psychological and physical), as well as those available in the community, to meet client needs;
- is based on an orderly helping process;
- is based on planned change efforts; and
- is focused on solutions.

Social work generalist practice with individuals and families is grounded in the philosophy and wisdom of early social work pioneers such as Mary Richmond, Gordon Hamilton, Helen Harris Perlman, Florence Hollis, and others, but practice has seen significant changes over the years. With emerging knowledge of human development, ecology, economics, organizational behavior, stress management, social change, and more effective intervention techniques, social work practice with individuals, families, and groups has been enriched and offers a more scientifically buttressed model for intervention.

The face-to-face relationship between the social worker and the client has maintained its integrity as a fundamental prerequisite for intervention, as has the emphasis on process (study, assessment, intervention objectives, intervention, evaluation, and follow-up). Democratic decision making and belief in the dignity, worth, and value of the client system continue to undergird the philosophy of social work practice. The client's right to self-determination and confidentiality are fundamental practice values in the helping process.

Generalist social workers practice in many settings. Here, a social worker in a university counseling center talks with a student to determine how to best meet her needs.

These values and practice principles form the fundamental concepts and practice techniques identified with generalist practice with individuals, families, and groups.

Key Components of Generalist Practice with Individuals, Families, and Groups

EP 2.1.7a
EP 2.1.7b
EP 2.1.10a

Generalist practice requires knowledge and skill needed to work effectively with diverse clients. The following are the key components, which provide the foundation for all work with clients: the social worker-client relationship, an emphasis on strengths and empowerment, an intervention process with planned stages, and learned practice skills.

The Social Worker–Client Relationship

EP 2.1.10c

Professionals use various tools in their work: for example, a carpenter uses a hammer and a saw. The most important tool that you as a social worker bring to a relationship is yourself. The relationship between a social worker and a client (or client system) is the conduit through which assistance is extended by the social worker and received and acted on by the client. The principles and values underpinning the relationship are much more than a mere catechism for the social worker to learn. The client must experience them in interacting with the social worker. Practitioners must be genuine and approachable if clients are to feel enabled to share their problems and to develop confidence and trust in the social worker and the helping process. As the client invests time and energy in the problem-solving process, trust (an underlying axiom for an effective helping relationship) will be established only if the relationship principles and values are a distinctive aspect of client–social worker interaction.

The principles of social work practice are derived from the profession's value base and reflected in its code of ethics (see summary of the code in Chapter 2). Historically, professional social workers have been committed to the following principles as the basis for establishing a helping relationship with client systems:

- *Self-determination:* Social work practitioners respect their clients' rights to make choices that affect their lives. On occasion, when those choices do not seem to be in the client's best interests, the practitioner's role is to point out the potentially negative or dysfunctional aspects of the choices. Of course, this does not preclude or limit the practitioner's effort to assist the client in making more appropriate choices, but it does indicate that exerting undue influence or belittling the client is unacceptable in "bringing the client around" to more appropriate choices. Social work is based on a democratic process in which self-determination is fundamental.

- *Confidentiality:* The client's right to privacy is guarded by the principle of confidentiality, the notion that information shared between the client and practitioner is privileged. The practitioner must not compromise the client by making public the content of information disclosed during the intervention process. Confidentiality ensures that the client's feelings, attitudes, and statements expressed during intervention sessions will not be misused. This principle also commits the practitioner to using client information only for professional purposes in working with the client.

- *Individualization and acceptance:* Regardless of the nature of the client's problems, each client has the right to be treated as an individual with needs, desires, strengths, and weaknesses that are different from those of anyone else. Acceptance means the ability to recognize the dignity and value inherent in all clients, in spite of the complex array of problems and needs that characterize their behavior.

- *Nonjudgmental attitude:* Recognizing that all human beings have strengths and weaknesses, experience difficult problems, make improper choices, become angry and frustrated, and often act inappropriately, the practitioner maintains a neutral attitude toward the client's behavior. To judge clients and their behaviors is to implicitly erect a barrier that may block communication with them. The client may view a social worker who is judgmental as just another person who is making negative judgments about her or him. The social worker does have a responsibility to confront the clients about inappropriate behaviors but must not condemn clients because of those behaviors.

- *Freedom of expression:* The practitioner encourages clients' need to express their feelings and emotions. Often, pent-up emotions become disabling to the client, resulting in more problematic behaviors. The client is encouraged to engage in open and honest self-expression within the safety of the social worker–client relationship.

A Focus on Strengths and Empowerment

Regardless of whether a social worker is working with an individual, a family, or a group, the approach used will incorporate the strengths and empowerment perspectives discussed in Chapter 3. Clients are often unaware of their strengths and need reinforcement in understanding how they can draw on them as they work to address their needs and problems. Even a negatively perceived characteristic, such as a parent becoming angry at a teacher when her child is singled out for disciplinary action, can be reframed as a strength because the parent is protective of her child. Acknowledging this strength is likely to make it easier to work with the parent on how her behavior might be different in the future. All clients have strengths on which social workers can build as they work together on identifying and implementing strategies to address problems and needs. As they work with their clients and progress is made in achieving goals, social workers can reinforce these strengths and help clients identify new ones they are developing.

Drawing on the strengths of their clients, social workers also empower clients so they can become more adept at making positive choices that enable them to achieve their goals. The process of empowerment is both an art and a science, as social workers need to "start where the client is" and step the client through learning needed skills. Some clients may know how to get to a referral and be perfectly capable of calling to make an appointment and getting to the location themselves the first time. Others may not know how to use a directory, call to make an appointment, or take a bus to get there. Social workers don't do tasks for clients they can do for themselves, but rather guide them so they learn to do them independently. Through role modeling and reinforcement, clients then are able to advocate for themselves and complete other tasks on their own as they realize their strengths and find their voices.

Knowledge Needed for Generalist Practice

As we indicated earlier, a requisite for generalist social work practice with individuals, families, and groups is knowledge of factors that affect human behavior. The practitioner must be armed with an understanding of personality theory and knowledge of the life cycle, and also must be able to assess the effects of the social systems context within which behavior occurs. Factors such as race, gender, ethnicity, religion, social class, sexual orientation, physical and cognitive ability, occupation, family structure, health, age, income, and educational achievement are among many contributing variables that converge to account for behavior within different social contexts. Although practitioners obviously cannot master all knowledge related to behavior, theories allow us to make guided assumptions about behavior from which we can infer possible factors associated with the client's unmet needs. The generalist social work practitioner is able to arrive at probable causes of problems and to establish theoretically plausible interventions that will assist client systems in addressing needs.

Stages of Generalist Practice

Generalist practice at all levels is based on social work values, which are at the core of the profession. Interventions incorporate the dignity and strengths of the client/client system and emphasize self-determination and empowerment. The orderly process of social work generalist practice consists of social study, assessment, goal setting, contracting, intervention, and evaluation. Each step in this process is guided by the application of theory and knowledge of human behavior.

Social Study   The process begins with the **social study**, which consists of obtaining relevant information about the client system and perceived needs. Important to the social study is the client's perception of his or her needs and problems, antecedents, ways these are affecting life satisfaction and performance, attempts at life management, and outcome goals. The practitioner also obtains information regarding the client's ability to function in a variety of roles and collects data that enhance the practitioner's ability to form initial judgments about probable causes and potential actions that might lead to resolution.

The social study responds to questions such as the following (DuBois & Miley, 2013):

- Who is the client?
- What is the nature of the needs and problems as the client sees and experiences them?
- What has the client done to alleviate these needs and problems?
- How effective were the efforts?
- What other individuals or groups are affected by the needs and problems, and how is the client related to or associated with them?
- What are the client's strengths and weaknesses?
- How motivated is the client to work toward solutions to address these needs and problems?

Assessment   **Assessment** is the process of making tentative judgments about how the information derived from the social study affects the client system in its behaviors as well as in the meaning of those behaviors. DuBois and Miley (2013) suggest that assessment is designed to help the client and the practitioner work together to identify the issues identified by the client and the factors that have contributed to their existence so that they can then determine how to address those issues. As such, assessment provides the basis for initiating and establishing intervention objectives and formally engaging the client system in the intervention process. This is the stage of the generalist practice process at which the perceived reality of client behaviors is filtered through the matrix of practice theory and a basic understanding of human behavior to arrive at potential sources of the problem(s).

EP 2.1.10e

Accurate assessment is the catalyst for working with the client to jointly establish goals and objectives and is an essential precursor to focused intervention. For that reason, assessment is a dynamic process that is modified and updated as the practitioner and the client gain more insight, information, and experience in working together, including estimates of how the client is using the helping process to address identified needs. In addition, a meaningful assessment reflects the ethnic, gender, racial, and cultural context of the client system.

At the most rudimentary level, assessment seeks to answer questions such as:

- What factors are contributing to the client's unmet needs?
- What systems are involved?
- What is the effect of the client's behavior on interacting systems (and vice versa)?
- What is the potential for initiating a successful change effort?

Goal Setting   In **goal setting**, the client and the practitioner work together to identify intervention options that have the potential to address identified needs based on the client's abilities and capacities. After reviewing all options and determining which are most appropriate for the client, need, and situation, they develop short- and long-term goals.

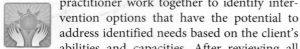

EP 2.1.10f

The responsibility for goal setting evolves as a product of mutual exploration between the social worker and the client. Effective goal setting can serve as a therapeutic "jump-start" for the client as an initial commitment to engage in the change process. Goals should be realistically achievable, organized around specific targets for change, and related to the client's capacity to engage in behaviors that will move in the direction of positive change. As a practical matter, the least emotionally charged goals should be addressed first because they are more likely to be achieved. As a consequence of successfully achieving goals, the client's confidence is bolstered and she or he will likely be more enthusiastic about the change effort.

Contracting   In **contracting**, the practitioner and the client (or client system, as in a family or a group) agree to work toward the identified intervention goals. To facilitate and clarify the commitment implied by the contract, the practitioner's role is identified explicitly and the client agrees to perform tasks that address identified needs and problems. The contract makes visible the agreement both parties have reached and serves as a framework from which they may assess intervention progress periodically. During the course of intervention, contracts may be renegotiated or altered as more viable strategies to address agreed-upon goals or even new goals become apparent. Contracts also help maintain the focus of intervention.

Intervention   Generalist practice **intervention** with individuals, families, and groups is derived from the social study and assessment and is sanctioned by the contract between the practitioner and the client. The implementation phase of intervention is directed to meeting established goals and may involve activities such as

EP 2.1.10g
EP 2.1.10i

- counseling;
- role playing;
- engaging other community resources;
- establishing support groups;
- developing resources;
- finding alternative-care resources;
- encouraging family involvement;
- offering play therapy; or
- employing related strategies.

The goal of intervention is to assist clients toward acceptable resolution of their problems and to address their unmet needs. The practitioner must skillfully involve the client throughout the intervention process by empowering the client to make the identified changes, providing regular feedback and support and as well as an honest appraisal of the problem-solving efforts.

Evaluation   Clients are not likely to remain in the intervention process unless they perceive some positive movement toward meeting their needs. **Evaluation** is an ongoing process in which the practitioner and client review intervention activities and assess the impact on the client's problem situation. Both the practitioner and the client must intensively examine their behavior, with the goal of understanding the impact on intervention goals.

EP
2.1.10d
EP
2.1.10m

- What has changed?
- What has not changed? Why?
- How does the client view identified needs and problems at this time?
- Has social functioning improved?
- Has the client become less functional?
- What is the overall level of progress?
- Are different strategies to achieve goals needed? Do goals need to be changed or new goals added?

Evaluation within this context becomes both a self-assessment and a joint assessment process. Based on the evaluation, intervention may continue along the same lines or be modified as implied by the evaluative process (DuBois & Miley, 2013).

The Development of Practice Skills

EP
2.1.10a

Social workers can develop competency in the generalist practice method with individuals, families, and groups through study, role playing, and supervised practice. Because generalist practice involves the application of knowledge, it is an effective method of problem solving only if it is used skillfully.

As in other applied professions, the application of skill is an "art" that is enriched and refined continually through controlled and thoughtful interaction with clients. Just as you might expect the skills of a surgeon to increase with time and experience, that same principle applies to the development of social work practice skills. We now examine some of the more significant skill areas that are essential for effective social work practice with individuals, families, and groups.

Conceptual Skills   The ability to understand the interrelationships of various dimensions of the client's life experiences and behaviors and to place them within an appropriate perspective provides a framework within which to establish intervention goals. Conceptual skills enable the worker to view the client's many incidents and interactions not as discrete entities within themselves but, rather, as interacting parts of the client's behavioral repertoire within the context of the environment within which the client interacts. Without conceptual skills, social study data have little meaning and assessment may become less accurate. Conceptual skills also involve an ability to place the client's needs within a theoretical framework and to arrive at appropriate intervention strategies to address those needs.

Interviewing Skills   The interview is more than just a conversation with the client. It is a focused, goal-directed activity to assist clients in identifying and addressing their needs and problems. Communication skills are essential in ensuring that the interview will be productive. The practitioner must assume the responsibility for maintaining the professional purposes of the interview. Sensitivity to both the client's statements and feelings is necessary. Putting the client at ease, asking questions that enable the client to share observations and experiences, and being a sensitive listener enhance the productivity of the interview. The social worker's sensitivity to the client's feelings and ability to communicate an awareness of those feelings strengthen the helping relationship and encourage and support the client.

Empathy, the ability to "put oneself in the client's shoes," is a benchmark quality of the helping relationship. Clients who conclude that the social worker really understands their needs are more relaxed and hopeful that they will be able to work together and find ways to address their needs.

Interviews are conducted for different purposes. Zastrow (2013) has identified three types of interviews that facilitate the helping process in social work:

1. *Informational interviews* are used primarily to obtain a client history that relates to the client's current needs and problems. The history-collecting process should not be concerned with all of the client's life experiences but, instead, only with selected information that may be influencing his or her current social functioning.

2. *The diagnostic (assessment) interview* has a more clinical focus in that it elicits responses that clarify

the client's reactions to her or his needs and problems and establishes some sequential ordering of events that enables the practitioner to make initial judgments about events that affect the client's behaviors.

3. *Therapeutic interviews* are designed to help clients make changes in their life situations that will enable them to function more effectively. The client shares her or his feelings and emotions in these interviews. Also, problem-solving options are developed and efforts at change are reviewed.

Recording   Maintaining case records that provide insightful information into the client's background (social study data), judgments about the nature of needs and problems (assessment), and client–social worker activity is essential. Practitioners typically carry a large caseload with many clients over a long time. Properly maintained records enable the social worker to review the nature of the situation, objectives, and progress in each case prior to appointments with clients. In many instances, cases are transferred both inside and outside the agency, or an individual or family may participate in more than one activity within the same agency—e.g., individual counseling and group therapy. The case record facilitates coordination by giving everyone involved an up-to-date accounting of the client's problems and activities directed toward their resolution. Case records also are useful for research purposes. Properly maintained records strengthen the process of social work practice. If viewed within this context, record keeping becomes less of an irrelevant chore and more of a vital tool for effective service delivery.

Beginning social workers should be informed that not all client systems are equally motivated to engage in a process designed to help them resolve their problems. Even voluntary clients (those who take the initial steps to seek help) are not always strongly committed, although they are motivated to some extent. Involuntary clients (those who are mandated to seek help, such as criminal offenders) may or may not be motivated to engage in the change effort. Practitioners must be aware that even if they cannot motivate their clients (motivation comes from within), they may provide the incentives that will cause clients to become motivated to work on their problems.

Practice Theories and Skills: Individuals and Families

EP 2.1.7a

Over the years, social workers have adopted a number of theoretical approaches in their work with individuals and families. Some theories are used primarily to understand human behavior and others are used primarily for intervention. Many practitioners take an eclectic approach—integrating elements of several theories as a framework for understanding human behavior and for practice. They may find that a specific model is viable in one type of situation and another model may have greater utility in other situations. For example, a social worker may use behavior therapy with children and ego psychology with adults. The point is that many different approaches to social work practice are possible, each offering the practitioner a theoretical framework for intervention. Following are brief synopses of some of the theories that generalist practitioners typically use. We include them here to help you see how they might be applied in work with clients and the different outcomes that can take place depending on the practice theory applied. Note that if theories are not included in this discussion, it does not mean that they are not important or well suited to generalist practice. Social work students will engage in more in-depth discussion and application of a number of theories in later courses.

Ecological/Systems Framework

The ecological/systems framework is based on the perspective that individuals and their environment are continually interacting and that problematic behavior is the result of disequilibrium between these entities (the individual and the environment). The ecological/systems framework, discussed extensively in Chapter 3, is the overriding framework that generalist practitioners use to understand human behavior and how it is impacted by the environment, although this framework also is used as a practice model. Most other practice models can be incorporated within this broad framework.

Because people live in a constantly changing environment, adaptive skills are necessary to maintain coping abilities that are consonant with environmental demands. Adequate coping skills are predicated on the abilities of individuals, families, and groups to integrate the consequences of environmental forces into their adaptive response repertoires and to influence (and change) the environmental factors that are producing dysfunctional stress. The individual and the environment shape each other. Styles of coping with the demands of the environment emerge based on the person's perceptions of those demands and his or her capacity to respond.

The ecological/systems framework directs the social worker's attention to the interacting systems within which the client system lives, and it provides a theoretical basis for understanding the rationale underlying the system's adaptive responses. As an assessment tool, this framework enables the social worker to identify both functional and dysfunctional responses to environmental demands and stresses. Once these have been identified, the social worker can focus on the processes of social work intervention and goal setting with the client system.

Ego Psychology

Often referred to as psychosocial treatment theory, **ego psychology** stresses the interplay between the individual's internal state and the external environment. The individual's developmental experiences, fears, hostilities, failures, successes, and feelings of love and acceptance all converge to form an estimate of self through which life experiences are filtered and responded to. A main feature of this theory is that it deals with the individual's ability to cope with external pressures and to respond in such a way as to produce satisfaction and feelings of security and self-worth. Often, internal stress results from the inability to solve problems of a mental or physical nature. Inappropriate or underdeveloped coping skills aggravate and intensify the problems, causing the person to become apprehensive, insecure, unwilling to risk, anxious, or, in extreme cases, mentally ill.

Ego psychology also is concerned with environmental factors that affect the individual's adaptive abilities. Among many potentially stressful conditions that may overextend coping capacities are job loss, immobility, death, divorce, poverty, discrimination, and parenting children with special needs. Because stress is experienced individually, practitioners must give individualized consideration to the client and his or her specific situation. Knowledge of stress management, personality organization, and effective coping mechanisms is essential in the assessment process. Ego psychology is an "insight" therapy. Thus, clients are helped by developing an awareness of their unmet needs and problems

and their reactions to them, then developing more adaptive coping skills.

Perhaps the key principle associated with ego psychology as a treatment therapy is that it can enable the individual to develop more adaptive coping skills. The result should be reduction of internal stress, more satisfactory role performance, and greater life satisfaction.

Problem-Solving Approach

One of the more widely used approaches in social work practice with individuals and families is the **problem-solving approach**. Developed by Perlman (1959), this approach holds that successful intervention is based on the motivation, capacity, and opportunity of the client systems for change. Recognizing that problems often immobilize the client, that the client's abilities then are neutralized or applied inappropriately, and that opportunities for problem solutions are not engaged, this approach emphasizes the need to "free up" the client system so the client can work toward solving the problem.

The problem-solving approach requires that the client do more than just identify and talk about problems—although both are necessary. The client must move toward taking action (within her or his capacity to do so) to resolve or alleviate the discomfort produced by those problems. Often, this requires that resources (the opportunity structure) be tapped to achieve these goals. Generally, opportunity resources include those of the client, the client's family, and the agency involved in the helping process, although they may extend to other community resources as well.

Motivation Conceptually, the problem-solving approach is based on the premise that without *motivation* (the will or desire to change), the client can make only limited progress. Motivation frequently is stymied as a result of stress experienced through dysfunctional or unresolved problems. Social workers often hear the client's doubts through statements such as, "I know it won't do any good to try," "It hasn't worked out in the past," or "Nothing ever turns out right for me." In such instances, the social worker must provide inducements, such as encouragement, that will motivate the client to risk taking steps toward resolution of the problem, with the social worker's assistance. Groups can be a powerful tool in motivating clients because the same messages conveyed by the social worker can be conveyed by other group members. Successful problem solving likely will be accompanied by increased motivation.

Capacity   In the problem-solving process, the social worker must be aware of other issues, too. *Capacity* addresses the client's limits (or ability) to change, and includes physical as well as psychological characteristics. For example, a client functioning at a sixth-grade level probably could not become an electrical engineer, but he or she might attend a vocational training program and thereby develop skills to enhance job opportunities.

Opportunity   *Opportunity* relates to possibilities within the environmental milieu in which the client interacts daily. A client might attend a vocational school if one is available within the client's locale. If the client has to travel 50 miles, however, transportation and finances might well serve as deterrents, and the client thus might not have the opportunity to participate. Optimal problem solving can be achieved only if the three components—motivation, capacity, and opportunity—are engaged in the process.

Cognitive-Behavioral Approaches

Cognitive-behavioral theories fall into the general category of behavioral intervention, which emphasizes the client's responsibility to actively engage in behaviors that should reduce or eliminate problems. These include behavior modification and reality therapy.

Behavior Modification   Social learning theory undergirds behavior modification therapy. Based on the assumption that all behavior (adaptive as well as maladaptive) is learned, **behavior modification** is an "action" therapy. Developmental processes that contribute to the acquisition of positive human responses also are responsible for the development of inappropriate or dysfunctional responses. Because behavior is learned, the client possibly can be assisted in discarding faulty behaviors and acquiring new and more appropriate response patterns.

Recognizing that external events and internal processing result in specific behaviors, change is effected by modifying one's actions, which will result in changing thought patterns. Any attempt to change the internal process (that is, helping the client develop insight into the problem apart from addressing behavior changes directly) is considered largely ineffective.

Based on these general principles, the practitioner using behavior modification approaches intervention with the following organizing framework:

- In a social study, only information that is related directly to the current problem is essential for

intervention, not past life experiences. Antecedent factors are pertinent, such as when the problem began, the circumstances that contribute to the problem behavior, and the client's efforts at problem resolution.

- Intervention must focus on specific needs and problems, not the entire range of needs and problems, that the client experiences. The practitioner assists clients in addressing each need or resolving each problem one at a time, or using a process called partialization, rather than treating them all at once.

- Although the client's "feelings" are considered an important factor, the behavioral act is the target, not intrapsychic dynamics. The practitioner assists the client in developing specific techniques and learning more appropriate behavioral responses, as opposed to altering thought processes related to the problem and its effect. Thought processes are considered to be the results, not causes, of behaviors.

Behavior modification treats the objective, definable dimensions of human response patterns. To facilitate the intervention process, the practitioner and the client must agree on the problem to be addressed, contract to work on that problem, agree on the responsibility that each will assume in the change effort, specify goals and objectives, discuss the techniques to be used, and commit themselves to the treatment effort. As with other therapies, monitoring and evaluation are important. As more functional and acceptable behavior evolves, it is reinforced by more adaptive functioning. Dysfunctional responses are discarded as they become less functional and less rewarding for the client.

Reality Therapy   **Reality therapy** is based on the assumption that individuals are responsible for their behavior. Dysfunctional behavior is viewed as the product of a negative self-identity. Identity—a basic psychological need of all human beings—is achieved by experiencing love and a sense of self-worth. Individuals who have been deprived of love fail to gain a sense of worth and, as a consequence, develop a poor self-concept. Change is effected by confronting clients with their irresponsible behaviors and encouraging them to accept responsibility for their behavior. It is assumed that clients cannot develop a sense of self-worth while they are engaging in irresponsible behaviors.

Because **self-concept** is a person's internal reaction to the perception of how others see him or her, the practitioner's role in establishing a warm, friendly, accepting relationship becomes an important factor in the intervention process. As with behavior modification, the focus of intervention is on the client's actions rather than feelings. Reality therapy emphasizes confronting the client about inappropriate behavior when it occurs, along with rejection of rationalizations (excuses). Many practitioners elect reality therapy as an intervention framework because of its straightforward application and the therapist's more informal, relaxed role. Reality therapy also is used effectively with groups of youth, particularly in schools, substance abuse treatment programs, and groups involved with the criminal justice system.

Task-Centered Social Work

The **task-centered method**, which builds on the problem-solving approach, exemplifies a short-term therapeutic approach (Reid, 2000; Marsh & Doel, 2006). It stresses the selection and establishment of specific tasks to be worked on within a limited time. Although different models of intervention may be used (such as the ones discussed previously), the emphasis on setting brief time limits for problem solutions is an integral therapeutic ingredient. By "compacting" the agreed-on time limits to work on problems, the client must concentrate his or her attention and energy on the problem and quickly adopt tasks to achieve resolution. The task-centered approach is an action model designed to engage the client quickly and meaningfully in identifying, confronting, and acting on problems.

Social Work Intervention with Families

Social workers long have recognized that the family unit provides physical and emotional support for its members and shapes their identity. Socialization of the young is a basic task of the family, and when problems arise, all family members are affected. As an example, when a husband/father loses his job, the income available for food, clothing, shelter, and family recreation becomes limited, which alters the family's daily patterns. He may become depressed, which affects relationships with his partner and children. Or a teenager may develop emotional problems, have difficulty with schoolwork, and in turn resist completing household responsibilities. Again, this problem affects all

family members. Families experience changes in structure and roles, life transitions, patterns of communication, conflict, and crisis. We can all identify with family problems of some sort, recalling when our family life has been disrupted and the resulting stress and tension.

Social workers often focus on the family as a unit of intervention. Recognizing that all members of a family are affected by the problems of any one member, intervention is directed to treating the family system. This approach recognizes that the attitudes and emotions of each family member are significant components in moving the family toward healthier functioning. Family therapy (or intervention) does not preclude any individual member from specialized treatment. Ideally, however, all members agree to be included in the intervention process because all family members both contribute to and are affected by ongoing problems within the unit. If one family member is left out of the intervention process, he or she can, consciously or unconsciously, sabotage the progress of other family members and the family as a whole.

Work with families involves the same planned change process that takes place when working with individuals. The social worker has to engage family members, gather information about each person's perspectives about problems and needs, assess family dynamics and needs, work with the family to develop appropriate intervention strategies, and then evaluate those strategies and adjust them as needed during the intervention process. While work with families can be challenging because the social worker has to incorporate differing perspectives and ensure that all voices are heard, more than one person giving feedback can be extremely powerful. Family therapy can involve confrontation, support, healing, and unity.

Social workers incorporate strengths-based and empowerment perspectives with other theories, just as they do when working with individuals. They also help the family identify current and intergenerational patterns that impact communication, roles, and decision-making within the family, just as they would when working with an individual client. Most of the theories and practice approaches that can be used with individuals can also be used when working with families. For example, cognitive behavioral therapy can help family members identify and understand distortions in expectations and beliefs about each other and the ways that this impacts individual and family behavior. Solution focused therapy can help families jointly come up with solutions to problems they have identified. A number of theoretical approaches used in family ther-apy are based on systems theory. Because families are systems, each with their own subsystems (i.e., parents, children, older siblings, younger siblings, mother and daughter), one of the goals of family therapy can be to strengthen or realign subsystems that exist within the larger family system. Structural family therapy, for example, focuses on identifying subsystems, align-ments, and boundaries within the larger family system and then working with the family to change identified patterns, coalitions, and conflicts. For example, getting a father to discipline or spend special time with a child when those roles have previously been the domain of the mother can be one way to change family commu-nication patterns that occur within family subsystems (Hepworth, Rooney, Rooney & Strom-Gottfried, 2013). Family sculpting, where each family member is asked to physically position the other family members to show both body and spatial perceptions can be a pow-erful way for everyone to learn how each views the family system. Noted family therapy pioneer Virginia Satir also drew on systems theory in developing con-joint family therapy, based on the idea that family members shared each other's pain but could learn how to understand the impact of the pain and nurture and support each other in the process (1983).

Other Approaches

In addition to the theoretical approaches identified, social work practitioners may elect to use other approaches. *Rational emotive therapy* emphasizes "self-talk" as a target for change, getting individuals to focus on changing the messages that they give them-selves when something happens, with the expectation that more positive self-talk will result in behavior change. *Role therapy* examines both prescriptive and descriptive roles played by clients and identifies incon-gruities in role expectations as well as dysfunctional role behaviors. Its purpose is to guide the client toward more functional and appropriate role performance. Other approaches are briefly described below.

- **Client-centered therapy**, based on the perspective that clients know most about their problems and needs, seeks to provide an accepting emotional climate in which clients can work out their own solutions with support and reflection from the therapist.
- **Feminist therapy**, which many also view as client-centered, empowers individuals who have been

members of an oppressed group to find their own voices and view themselves as equals as they make decisions about their lives.
- **Solution-focused therapy** focuses on identifying solutions to problems rather than the problems themselves. This approach is short-term, often consisting of only a few sessions, during which the therapist guides the client through a series of questions such as: "When does this problem you are talking about *not* occur?" "If you could wave a magic wand and make this problem go away dur-ing the night, when you wake up in the morning, how will things be different?" "On a scale of 1 to 10, how serious is this problem for you now?" "What would it take for you to move from where you are on the scale now up one notch?" Clients are assigned "homework" between sessions, and report on their success during the next session.

Other approaches focus on dealing with individuals who have experienced trauma in their lives. Trauma-informed interventions help practitioners and clients understand the impact of previous traumas experienced by clients and the roles that traumas have played in their lives, while other approaches help clients by setting up a safe environment that allows them to process previous traumas. Some of these approaches sound fairly simplis-tic, while others are clearly more complex and require extensive training. Any approach, regardless of how sim-ple it may seem, requires a highly skilled practitioner to know when and how to use it. In working with indivi-duals and families, many additional methods of inter-vention can be used. The more advanced methods require additional training and are studied in MSW (master of social work) programs with a clinical special-ization. Throughout their careers, social workers develop deeper and more complete awareness of intervention theories. As new knowledge and understanding of human behavior evolve, social workers must remain vig-ilant and open to incorporating new theoretical concepts into their practice methods.

Practice Theories and Skills: Groups

EP 2.1.7a

Many of the problems that clients or client systems encounter can be addressed and resolved more effectively through group intervention. As a generalist practitioner, the social worker recognizes, first, the importance of groups in achieving intervention goals and, second, the utility of group methods in effective problem solving. We will examine group work as a social work method that assists individuals and groups in problem solving.

Social groups are formed for many purposes. The most common is the **natural group**, in which members participate as a result of common interests, shared experiences, similar backgrounds and values, and personal satisfactions derived from interacting with other group members. A street gang or a group of neighbors who hang out together is a natural group. Members of natural groups are characterized further by face-to-face interactions, and they share an emotional investment in the group. Natural groups seldom are formed purposefully to meet specific objectives.

All of us are members of natural groups, and seldom is our membership in those groups the result of a planned effort to become involved. In natural groups, a leader often emerges without premeditation or election by group members but, rather, because one member possesses behavioral attributes or resources that the other group members highly value. Like all groups, natural groups tend to be transitory, with old members exiting and new ones entering throughout the group's life cycle.

Some of the most effective interventions that social workers undertake are with groups. Members of indigenous groups—such as street gangs, youth who have run away from home, teen mothers living in the same apartment complex, or persons who are homeless—can begin to trust the efforts of a social worker who interacts with them and listens nonjudgmentally to their stories and concerns. Once trust develops, the social worker may be able to provide assistance and convince group members to go to a local agency to receive services and other types of assistance (see Box 5.1).

Other groups are formed purposefully for a specific reason. As examples, apartment residents organize to seek building repairs and better living conditions, and a church or synagogue organizes a softball team. Established agencies, such as the YMCA and Boys and Girls Clubs, organize recreational groups within the city. A common characteristic of each of these groups is that they are developed to fulfill a specific purpose.

Before attempting to understand the components and process of generalist practice with groups, a basic understanding of what is meant by **group** will be helpful. Norlin, Dale, Smith, Chess, and Norlin (2008) define a group as a form of social organization whose members identify and interact with one another on a personal basis and also have a shared sense of the group as a social entity. The type of group with which the generalist practitioner works is called a primary *group*—a group with face-to-face interaction among group members. Regardless of the reasons for forming a group (a natural group or a planned group), the group work method may be used to assist group members in achieving personal growth through the democratic process.

Group work is a process and an activity that seeks to stimulate and support more adaptive personal functioning and social skills of individuals through structured group interaction. The goal of the group work experience is to develop effective skills in communication, coping skills, and effective problem-solving techniques (Toseland & Rivas, 2012). Toseland and Rivas point out a number of advantages of group intervention: Empathy and feedback are received from multiple sources with diverse view points, members offer mutual support and hope to each other, stigma is reduced and validation occurs when members realize others have had the same experiences or share the same feelings that they do, and members can learn how others have coped and practice new behaviors and ideas in a safe environment (2012, p. 17).

Group work techniques can be used more effectively when goals and objectives are related to the needs of group members. Effective group work capitalizes on the dynamics of interaction among members of the group. Members are encouraged to participate in making decisions, questioning, sharing, and contributing toward achievement of the agreed-upon goals and objectives.

Group Focus

Social workers engage in practice with groups to accomplish a variety of tasks. Generally, groups may be classified in terms of a specific purpose. Several of the more common types of groups are identified and discussed in Box 5.2.

Effective Group Development

Achieving the desired outcomes of the group process depends on several key considerations—purposefulness, leadership, selection of group members, and size.

Box 5.1   The Impact of Group Work

Harry, Charlie, John, Manuel, Frank, and Oscar were all teenagers who grew up in a lower-income area of a large city. Although they were not related, from very early in their lives they had played with each other, gone to school together, and now "hung out" together. None of them did very well in school. Three were from single-parent families, two had fathers who were alcoholics, and one had a father in the state penitentiary.

Often considered to be a "gang," this small group had several brushes with the law for theft, fighting, and malicious mischief. They spent most of their hours after school roaming the streets, often late into the night. Although, as individuals, each of the boys appeared to be somewhat compliant (if not shy), as a group they represented a threat to be reckoned with. None of the boys had developed adaptable social skills, and they all had difficulty coping with peers who had.

Tyrone Jones, a social worker at a nearby settlement house, had, on occasion, discussed with his supervisor and the nearby high school the possibility of enrolling these boys in a socialization group at the agency. Initially, it was decided that Tyrone would work with the six boys as a small group. Tyrone met with the boys as a group (and later, individually), identified the group leader (Oscar), and was able to enlist Oscar's interest in

settlement house activities. Tyrone identified the strengths that each of these individuals brought to the group, as well as the dynamics guiding their group activities. Using this knowledge and the strengths of each group member, he was able to assist group members in developing more adaptive social skills. As the group engaged in activities through the center, including a neighborhood cleanup project, a summer camping trip, and weekly group sessions during which they discussed a wide range of topics, the boys became motivated to achieve goals that were more socially productive and less threatening to the community.

As Tyrone worked with the group, he also became involved in a community network on working effectively with at-risk youth. Tyrone and the other members of the network developed close ties with school, law enforcement, and juvenile probation personnel and secured state funding for a community-wide prevention program. Tyrone and two of the boys in his group served as members of the task force and its committees, and this past year one of the boys was honored for his work in preventing youth gangs. In an interview with the press when he received the award, he said he wanted to be a social worker like Tyrone and work to help other kids see that there are other ways than gangs to meet important needs.

Purposefulness   Purposefulness, an essential characteristic for maximum effectiveness of the group work process, involves establishing specific goals and objectives and access to their achievement by the group. It provides the direction or intent for each group session and a framework for monitoring and evaluating the group's progress.

Leadership   Leadership is essential in helping the group maintain its focus and in encouraging maximum participation. The social worker may play an active or a passive role in the group, depending on the needs of the group as it moves toward its established goals and objectives. The leader must be skilled in group processes and able to fill a variety of roles in supporting the accomplishment of tasks necessary to maintain group integrity and continuing progress. A wide range of role responses may be required of a group leader—for instance, director, policymaker, planner, expert, external group representative,

facilitator, nurturer, disciplinarian, cheerleader, mediator, and scapegoat (Zastrow, 2003; Toseland & Rivas, 2012).

Effective leadership is essential to achieve the group's purposes. The methods a leader may use to accomplish group goals should be consistent with the values and purposes of social work practice. Although leaders of groups have diverse leadership styles, the style most compatible with social work encourages empowerment of group members; helping members assume responsibility for the life of the group, including planning; developing skills and values; and making their own decisions about the group's goals and activities. The empowerment method fully embraces the principles of democratic process and encourages individual responsibility and risk sharing as products of group interaction and decision making. The success of group process and goal attainment is related, to a great extent, to effective group leadership. Needless to say, the group leader is accountable for group

Box 5.2   Different Types of Groups, Their Focus, and Membership

- *Recreation group.* Purpose: to provide for participants' entertainment, enjoyment, and experience, and allow opportunities for shared interaction, interdependence, and social exchange; also can serve as constructive outlets for individuals in a monitored environment. Examples: community centers, YMCAs and YWCAs, settlement houses, senior centers for older adults organizing sports teams and table games.

- *Recreation-skill groups.* Purpose: to promote development of a skill within a recreational context. Skills are often taught by a resource person with expertise; participants develop competency in a craft, game, or sport. Task development is emphasized, and mutual interaction is encouraged in the learning process. Examples: school district and college extension programs, settlement houses, YMCAs, YWCAs, senior centers offering sessions on current events, pottery-making, learning a sport, or creative writing.

- *Educational groups.* Purpose: to transmit knowledge and enable participants to acquire more complex skills; to provide opportunities for interaction. Leaders have professional expertise in the area of interest. Examples: can range from learning about the aging process and coping with aging parents, to parenting skills, to substance abuse or other health or mental health issues, to English as a second-language.

- *Socialization groups.* Purpose: to help participants strengthen their social skills and develop socially acceptable behavior; to stimulate behavior change and increase self-confidence, focusing on cooperation and personal decision making. Examples: anger-management group for youths, groups for youths that include games and other activities fostering socialization through democratic participation and personal decision making.

- *Self-help groups.* Purpose: to provide support and reassurance to group members in dealing with specific issues, with the goal of facilitating behavior change. Participation may be either voluntary or involuntary (abusive parents or persons charged with driving while intoxicated may be required by the court to participate in groups). Groups emphasize mutual aid and interdependence and playing an active role in responding to the needs of other group members. Members often select their own convener, or the group is facilitated by a person that has personal experience with the issue being addressed. Professional group workers often do not facilitate these groups, although they may serve as a resource to the group. Examples: Alcoholics Anonymous; Parents Anonymous.

- *Therapeutic groups.* Purpose: to facilitate behavior change in individuals with intensive personal or emotional problems such as interpersonal loss (death, divorce, or abandonment), physically disabling injuries, terminal illness, marital or family conflict, or mental illness. Therapeutic groups require skilled professional leadership from a well-trained professional such as an MSW social worker or a clinical psychologist. Groups may be supplemented by individual counseling. Examples: Therapeutic groups for individuals who have difficulty dealing with emotional problems associated with divorce, interpersonal loss, alcohol- and drug-related problems, sexual assault and other forms of violence, mental health problems, parent–child relationships, or other areas in that impact a person's ability to function.

- *Personal growth groups.* Purpose: to assist individuals in developing more self-awareness and interpersonal skills in an atmosphere that encourages trust, open expression, candid feedback, and sensitivity to one's own and others' emotions (sometimes called "sensitivity" or "encounter" groups). Examples: group organized by local service agency to help young women who lack assertiveness, are self-deprecating, and feel inadequate; groups facilitated by professionals to encourage self-exploration and personal growth.

maintenance and the success (or failure) of the group in achieving its purposes.

Selection of Group Members   The selection of group members is an important factor in achieving group cohesion, as is a determination about whether the group will be open-ended or closed. Some groups meet for a set number of sessions, and membership is closed to new members after the first or second session. Other groups, such as Alcoholics Anonymous groups, are open-ended, with no set start or end point, welcoming anyone at any point in the group's life. In open-ended groups, "old timers" help the leader welcome and socialize "newcomers" to the group's purpose, structure, and patterns of interaction.

In composing groups, the group worker must accurately assess each individual's needs, capacity for social functioning, interests, and willingness to assume an active role as a group member. Although diversity of background and experience may enhance the alternatives for achieving the group's purposes, homogeneous (similar) motives are essential to formation of the group and identification as a group member.

Members with few interests in common often have more difficulty in becoming involved in group activities. Age, ethnicity, and/or gender may be critical factors, depending on the group's purposes and the activities designed to achieve those purposes. Individuals with severe emotional problems or behavior disorders may need additional support so they are not disruptive to the group process depending on the nature of the group; therefore, careful consideration should be given to how they are incorporated into a group.

Members should have the ability to attend to group tasks. Systematic disruptive behavior is disconcerting and may even cause group disintegration. The type of group being formed (e.g., recreational or educational) will determine the criteria for selecting members. In all instances, selection should be based on the "principle of maximum profit" (individuals with specific needs who would be most likely to achieve the greatest benefit from the group). Assessment of individuals for group membership is enhanced by a personal interview prior to their being included in the group.

Size   The size of a group is determined largely by its purposes. To determine in advance that 4, 6, or 15 members is the "ideal" size of a group has little validity. Examining the goals and purposes of the proposed group is more effective in determining group size. If, for example, anonymity (the ability to "lose" oneself) is a desirable end, a larger membership may be indicated, to ensure more limited interaction and group fragmentation (through the emergence of subgroups). Smaller groups, by definition, demand more intimate interaction, so group pressures typically are intensified. Absenteeism affects group process and task accomplishment more in small groups than in large ones. Small groups may function more informally than larger ones, which usually require a structured format.

The role of the group leader also varies with the size of the group. The democratic process can be achieved in both large and small groups, although it is more difficult in the former. The principles and techniques of social group work are effective with large and small groups alike.

The number of members selected for the group depends on the desired effect on its individual members, their needs, and their capacity to participate in and support group purposes. Generally, a small group is composed of 4 to 9 members, whereas a large group may consist of 10 to 20 members.

Theory for Group Work Practice

EP 2.1.7a

Group work is a social work practice method requiring the social worker to be familiar with theories related to group behavior. Group theory provides a framework for promoting guided change through group interaction. The discipline of social psychology has contributed much to our understanding of group formation, roles, norms, values, group dynamics, and cohesion (Baron & Byrne, 2006). Early social group work pioneers also contributed valuable experiential and theoretical insights that added to the knowledge base from which an informed approach to working with groups can be used (Toseland & Rivas, 2012).

Social group work can be distinguished as a professional social work method by the informed application of theory in helping groups achieve their objectives and goals. Because groups vary extensively in composition, types, and purposes, the practitioner also must have a broad-based understanding of the life cycle, emotional reactions to stress, and diverse behavior. Group workers must be skilled in working with the group and sensitive in helping the group move toward achieving its goals.

Just as social workers use different theoretical approaches when working with individuals and families, the same is the case when working with groups. The ecological/systems framework and systems theory focus on understanding the group as a system, with subsystems that impact the group as a whole. Concepts of boundaries, feedback, synergy, and goal attainment all can be applied to groups of various types. Psychodynamic and psychosocial theories, focusing on insight about early life experiences and their impact on functioning in later life, can also be applied to groups. Many groups are guided by social learning and cognitive behavioral theories, focusing on learned behavior and behavior change. Many groups are based on narrative and constructivist theories that focus on the ways that individuals create and perpetuate life stories based on their experiences, and how those stories can impact self esteem and restrict ability to identify possible options for change (Toseland & Rivas, 2012). Again, just a few theories have been discussed briefly here to give readers an idea of the diversity of approaches that can be used when working with groups, not to highlight those that are most effective.

Group Work as a Practice

As indicated previously, group work is directed toward the enrichment of an individual's life through a group. Although group members are unlikely to derive equal benefit from the group experience, all can be expected to show some measure of growth. Positive group work is a planned change effort in which change is predicated on benefits derived from group process and interaction. The social worker is responsible for incorporating the following principles governing social work practice in the process (National Association of Social Workers [NASW], 2008):

- ensuring the dignity and worth of all members;
- developing an articulated understanding of the group's purpose and the roles that group members agree to follow (e.g., exercising confidentiality; treating each other with respect);
- assessing the problems and needs of individual group members and the group as a whole and offering support as needed;
- helping the group develop its own identity, which reflects its unique character, relationships within the group, and needs;
- facilitating the development of communication among group members, which permits the expression of feelings and emotions;
- facilitating the planning and implementation of relevant group activities that promote constructive interaction, assessment of group process, and the advancement of the group's purpose; and
- preparing for termination.

Each group also has its own life cycle, characterized by developmental stages. Within this context, the stages of a group's development often follow this pattern:

1. *Beginning:* basic orientation and getting acquainted; "honeymoon period"
2. *Norm development:* establishing ground rules for operation; beginning level of trust among members
3. *Conflict phase:* members asserting individual ideas; as members get to know each other better, the resulting conflict often leads to members questioning the group's purpose and suggesting that they leave the group or that the entire group disband
4. *Relationship phase:* replacing initial conflicts with acceptance of others; members working through the conflict and deepening their relationship with each other; sharing of leadership, tasks, and trust; appreciation for the group and a strong sense of group identity; flexibility, consensus, and decision making
5. *Termination:* ending of the group, with recognition of the loss that the group experience is ending, along with acknowledgment of personal growth

Awareness of these stages is helpful in monitoring the group's progress as it moves toward greater cohesion and effectiveness. Dysfunctional "blocking" at any stage, once identified, can be addressed and resolved by the group, and the developmental progress can continue. If allowed to continue unchecked, the unresolved blockage may result in dissolution of the group.

Groups involve both cyclical and progressive processes. While groups navigate the stages of development from beginning to end, they also come back to revisit or address certain basic process issues in a cyclical stage (Toseland & Rivas, 2012). Skill in working with groups is an important aspect of social work practice. The efficiency and effectiveness of the group work process may result in personal enhancement, skill development, and reduction of problems.

Group Settings

Traditionally, social group work was practiced in recreational settings, such as the YWCA or YMCA, settlement houses, and community centers. With the growing popularity of group work, along with redefinition of the scope of social work practice, group work has become a valuable practice method within most social service agencies. For example, a family service agency might form a group of prospective adoptive parents to orient them to the adoptive process. A treatment center might organize a group of adolescent substance users to assist them in becoming sober and maintaining sobriety and to manage their stress and interpersonal problems. A recreational center might sponsor athletic teams for middle-school youths. Older adults living in a long-term–care facility could constitute a group that focuses on how to lead meaningful lives in their final life stage. Increasingly, because of the fast pace of life, agencies are providing short-term groups that meet for a limited time, sometimes only once. Agencies may provide one or more bereavement sessions for individuals who have lost a family member or a psychoeducational group session for parents experiencing conflict with their teenage children.

Working with groups promotes growth and change through interactions of the members and also enables the agency and workers to serve more clients. Although some group members may need individual counseling in addition to the group experience, in most instances, the group activity is sufficient for personal change. When the agency offering the group does not work individually with clients, it makes referrals to an appropriate agency, and a cooperative relationship between the service providers assures the client of maximum assistance with problems.

Group Termination

EP 2.1.10I Groups are terminated when the purposes for which they were established are achieved. Although many groups are initiated with a predetermined expiration period, termination usually is related to meeting group goals and members' personal goals. Occasionally, a group is aborted when it becomes obvious that its goals are unattainable or when dysfunctional behavior of one or more group members continually disrupt the group's activities. Most often, however, conflict within the group is typical in group development, and how conflicts are addressed is an important contributor to individual and group growth and how well the group handles termination.

The practitioner must be sensitive to the needs of group members at the time of termination, and assist them in phasing out their attachment to the group. Often, resistance to termination becomes highly emotional and vocal. Among the more common reactions to the loss of the close ties that have developed among members throughout the life of the group are frustration, anger, withdrawal, and grief. By helping the group assess its accomplishments and plan alternatives, the practitioner can assist members in a more adaptive transition.

Practice Effectiveness with Individuals, Families, and Groups

EP 2.1.10a-l Like all professionals who are engaged with clients in efforts to strengthen their ability to function and improve their quality of life, social workers have a profound interest in assessing the effectiveness of their work. In social work practice with individuals, families, and groups, the concept of accountability relates to the social workers' ongoing monitoring, feedback, and evaluation of their efforts in assisting clients and client systems toward the resolution of issues and problems for which they sought professional help.

Professional practice with individuals, families, and groups must include an evaluative process. Evaluation is done to determine the extent to which the client or client system is achieving its objectives. This may be an ongoing process as well as an assessment of the total intervention process upon termination of the social worker or group. The social worker continually monitors the intervention process to enable the client or client system to concentrate on its goals. Monitoring also may help redefine its purpose and goals if it becomes evident that the original goals are unachievable. Monitoring consists of critical assessment of the client's output.

Evaluation involves assessing all activities and behaviors related to the client system's performance. Factors including attendance and participation in individual or group sessions, resources, changes in behavior, and agency support, among others, are all reviewed in relation to achievement of the goals and objectives. Evaluation must also take into account cultural factors, as social workers must often adapt intervention strategies to ensure that they are a good fit with their clients' worldviews. Evaluation has the potential of providing a basis for answering questions such as:

- What could have increased clients' growth and change?
- What were the positive achievements of the clients or client systems?

- What implications for change are suggested?

Efficiency and better quality of service are likely when rigorous evaluative standards are maintained. Various methods have been developed (see Chapter 6) to provide an empirical framework for making this assessment. Practice evaluation is essential for viewing movement in cases, and it also provides a basis for reviewing the effectiveness of various techniques the social worker uses to address specific problems, as well as provide an impetus for updating skills. On the broader scene, social work researchers have been engaged continually in reviewing practice effectiveness, using differing intervention methods, and found that outcomes vary, given the nature of the problem, the individuals or groups involved, and projected outcome goals.

Issues related to the practitioner's technique and/or personality, in terms of positive outcomes, are generally considered to be invalid. Like all professions, some social workers are more personable, skilled, engaging, and effective than others, and provide good role models for all who desire to become helping professionals.

Research on the whole has been encouraging with respect to the effectiveness of social work practice with individuals, families, and groups. As techniques are refined through practice and as knowledge accrues through research, social workers are expected to become even more effective in helping individuals and families meet their needs.

Supervision of Generalist Practitioners

EP 2.1.1f

Supervision typically is thought of as a management function—that of overseeing and ensuring that employees are fulfilling the purpose and goals of an agency or organization. Although this function may be one of the responsibilities of social work supervisors, they must do much more. They provide enrichment to practitioners by helping them develop practice skills through periodic feedback and discussion of cases. They regulate the flow of cases assigned to social workers and use their unique skills through selective case assignment. They are at different times educators, listeners, enablers, and resources for identifying alternative techniques for addressing problems.

In their management functions, supervisors present the need for resources to agency executives and maintain standards for excellence in the performance of the social workers they supervise. Supervisors play a vital role in helping an agency achieve its purposes.

Social Work Practice and the MSW Social Worker

EP 2.1.1c

Most social workers interact directly with individuals, families, or groups, although contemporary practice requires that the social worker become involved in other aspects of social work practice as well. MSW practitioners may specialize in community organization, social policy, research, social planning, or social administration, as well as practice with individuals, families, and groups. At the master's level, the **specialization** builds on generalist practice knowledge and skills. Many MSW workers are employed in highly clinical environments such as psychiatric or family service settings, in criminal justice settings, in centers serving AIDS clients, in programs working with military personnel who have been in combat and their families, in hospitals and other health-care settings, and in related fields of practice requiring specialized knowledge and skill. Others work in agencies such as a department of human resources, serving people with less specialized problems.

Competence in all social work methods enhances the social worker's effectiveness in helping client systems seek solutions to problems at all levels of the environment. As discussed in Chapter 2, private practice has increased in recent years. This kind of practice typically calls for competence in psychotherapeutic and intensive counseling skills. Most states require that private practitioners be licensed at an advanced level, often mandating 2 years of practice experience beyond the MSW under the supervision of a state board–approved advanced practitioner in order to sit for the licensing exam. Practitioners continue to develop resources that will enable clients to attain a more satisfactory level of adaptation, regardless of the setting in which social work is practiced.

Social Work Practice and the BSW Social Worker

Education for social work at the BSW (bachelor of social work) level is geared toward enabling the student to become skilled in generalist social work practice. Guidelines for curricula content are established by the Council on Social Work Education, which also serves as the accrediting body for undergraduate social work programs.

As generalist social workers, practitioners at the baccalaureate level typically find employment in social agencies specializing in direct practice with individuals, families, and groups. Appreciation of the nature of client needs and problems in these settings is enhanced by a generalist background and focus.

Direct practice with individuals, families, and groups does not always demand in-depth psychotherapeutic treatment. Although interviewing and assessment skills are essential in establishing intervention goals, the BSW social worker need not be concerned with skills required for intensive psychotherapy. Social work practice with individuals, families, and groups extends far beyond psychotherapeutic involvement.

The case presented at the opening of this chapter is a good example. The BSW social worker could be involved as a **case manager** in helping identify needed resources for reducing stress and linking with other appropriate resources to ensure that needs are being addressed. His or her interviewing and counseling skills would be useful in providing opportunities to identify needs and problems and explore resources necessary for resolving them. The BSW social worker also could facilitate the support group in which Patrice was involved or the skills group in which her son participated.

The skill of the BSW practitioner in articulating community resources in the problem-solving process must not be underestimated. Knowledge of resources and preparation of clients to use those resources are paramount in resolving problems.

BSW practitioners are employed in a variety of direct practice settings that offer services to individuals, families, and groups. Among the many opportunities are agencies such as state departments of human resources (or public welfare), mental health and substance-abuse programs, programs that serve children and adults with disabilities, children's service agencies (child welfare and child-care institutions), halfway houses, nursing homes and other long-term–care facilities, areawide agencies on aging, agencies serving battered women, rape crisis centers, schools, and child-care centers.

Summary

Social work is a multifaceted profession requiring its practitioners to be familiar with theories of human behavior and social intervention. Social workers also must understand the logic of the social work process.

Professional values serve as the underpinning for the relationship that social workers establish with their client systems. These values also are the catalyst for promoting societal change designed to enrich the lives of the populace. The goal of generalist social work practice with individuals, families, and groups is to empower client systems to take charge of their lives and to act on their environment so as to produce positive change for themselves and those with whom they interact.

To be an effective change agent, a social work practitioner must have far more than counseling skills. Generalist social workers engage a variety of social systems to facilitate positive change for their clients. This requires interpersonal skills as well as conceptual, planning, and evaluative skills. To become effective, social work practice requires the skillful application (an art) of scientific knowledge in the problem-solving process. Regardless of whether they work with individuals, families, or groups, social workers apply generalist practice skills and adhere to the stages of the helping process: engaging the client, conducting the social study as they gather information about the client/client system, assessment, goal setting, contracting, intervention, and evaluation.

Competency Notes

EP 2.1.1c: Attend to professional roles and boundaries (p. 141). Social workers engaged in direct practice maintain professional boundaries and engage in appropriate roles when working with individuals, families, and groups.

EP 2.1.1f: Use supervision and consultation (p. 141). Social workers engaged in direct practice with individuals, families, and groups effectively use supervision and consultation to inform and guide their work.

EP 2.1.7a: Use conceptual frameworks to guide the process of assessment, intervention, and evaluation (pp. 125–126, 130, 134, 138). Social workers engaged in direct practice with individuals, families, and groups use the ecological/systems framework and other conceptual frameworks to guide the social work processes of assessment, intervention, and evaluation.

EP 2.1.7b: Critique and apply knowledge to understand person and environment (p. 126). As they work with individuals, families, and groups, social workers demonstrate an understanding of human behavior and development and the ways these dimensions are shaped by the environment.

EP 2.1.10a: Substantively and affectively prepare for action with individuals, families, groups, organizations, and communities (pp. 124, 126, 129, 140). Social workers substantively and affectively are prepared when engaging with individuals, families, and groups.

EP 2.1.10c: Develop a mutually agreed-on focus of work and desired outcomes. (pp. 124, 126, 140). Social workers in direct practice collaborate to develop a mutually agreed-on focus of work and desired outcomes in their work with individuals, families, and groups.

EP 2.1.10d: Collect, organize, and interpret client data (pp. 124, 129, 140). Social workers in direct practice draw on client data when working with individuals, families, and groups.

EP 2.1.10e: Assess client strengths and limitations (pp. 124, 128, 140). Social workers in direct practice assess the strengths and limitations of the individuals, families, and groups with whom they work.

EP 2.1.10f: Develop mutually agreed-on intervention goals and objectives (pp. 124, 128, 140). Social workers in direct practice with individuals, families, and groups work collaboratively to develop mutually agreed-on intervention goals and objectives.

EP 2.1.10g: Select appropriate intervention strategies (pp. 124, 128, 140). Social workers in direct practice select appropriate intervention strategies when working with individuals, families, and groups.

EP 2.1.10i: Engage, assess, intervene, and evaluate with individuals, families, groups, organizations, and communities (pp. 124, 128, 140). Social workers in direct practice implement prevention strategies that enhance the capacities of the individuals, families, and groups with whom they work.

EP 2.1.10l: Facilitate transitions and endings (pp. 124, 140). Social workers in direct practice facilitate transitions and endings in their work with individuals, families, and groups.

EP 2.1.10m: Critically analyze, monitor, and evaluate interventions (p. 129). Social workers in direct practice critically analyze, monitor, and evaluate their interventions with individuals, families, and groups.

Key Terms

The terms below are defined in the Glossary.

assessment	group work
behavior modification	intervention
case manager	natural group
casework	problem-solving
client-centered therapy	approach
contracting	reality therapy
dysfunctional	self-concept
ego psychology	social study
evaluation	socialization groups
feminist therapy	solution-focused therapy
generalist	specialization
generalist practice	task-centered method
goal setting	therapeutic groups
group	

Discussion Questions

1. Define generalist social work practice. What components are essential in generalist practice intervention?
2. What skills are necessary to become a generalist practitioner? How do the skills used by generalist practitioners differ from those used by advanced specialist social workers?
3. What is the importance of theory in social work intervention?
4. What is the relationship between social work values and effective social work intervention?

5. Identify the components of the problem-solving process used in social work practice. Using a case example, show how these would be used in working with a client/client system.
6. Review the vignette at the beginning of the chapter. Which practice approaches discussed in this chapter would be effective in working with the family members? How might the outcomes differ depending on the approach used?
7. What are some of the primary considerations that a social worker must take into account when working with families?
8. What are some of the primary considerations that a social worker must take into account when forming groups?
9. What are the basic principles governing group work practice? Explain how those principles would be applied to the different types of groups delineated in Box 5.2.
10. Why is it important for social workers to evaluate their practice with clients and client systems?

On the Internet

http://eserver.org/feminism
http://www.planet-therapy.com/
http://www.clinicalsocialworkassociation.org/
www.asgw.org
www.socialworkers.org
http://www.socialworktoday.com/

References

Baron, R. A., & Byrne, D. (2008). *Social psychology* (12th ed.). Boston: Allyn & Bacon.

Dale, O., Smith, R., Norlin, J., & Chess, W. A. (2008). *Human behavior and the social environment* (6th ed.). Boston: Allyn & Bacon.

DuBois, B., & Miley, K. K. (2012). *Social work: An empowering profession* (8th ed.). Upper Saddle River, NJ: Prentice-Hall.

Hepworth, D. H., Rooney, R., Rooney, G., & Strom-Gottfried, K. (2012). *Direct social work practice: Theory and skills.* Belmont, CA: Cengage.

National Association of Social Workers. (2008). *NASW code of ethics.* Washington, DC: Author.

Perlman, H. H. (1959). *Social casework: The problem solving process.* Chicago: University of Chicago Press.

Reid, W. J. (2000). *The task planner.* New York: Columbia University Press.

Satir, V. (1983). *Conjoint family therapy.* Palo Alto, CA: Science and Behavioral Books.

Toseland, R., & Rivas, R. (2012). *An introduction to group work practice* (7th ed.). Boston: Allyn & Bacon.

Zastrow, C. (2013). *The practice of social work.* Belmont, CA: Cengage Learning.

Suggested Readings

Bentovim, A., Cox, A., Bingley, M., & Pizzy, S. (Eds.). (2009). *Safeguarding children living with trauma and family violence: Evidence-based assessment, analysis, and planning interventions.* London: Jessica Kingsley.

Compton, B. R., Galaway, B., & Cournoyer, B. R. (2005). *Social work processes* (7th ed.). Pacific Grove, CA: Brooks/Cole.

Congress, E., & Gonzales, M. (Eds.). (2013). *Multicultural perspectives in working with families* (3rd ed.). New York: Springer.

Constable, R., & Lee, D. (2004). *Social work with families: Content and process.* Chicago: Lyceum.

Cooper, M., & Lesser, J. (2011). *Clinical social work practice: An integrated approach.* Boston: Allyn & Bacon.

Corcoran, J. (2000). *Evidence-based social work practice with families: A lifespan approach.* New York: Springer.

Cournoyer, B. (2013). *The social work skills workbook* (7th ed.). Belmont, CA: Cengage.

Dolgoff, R., Lowenberg, F., & Harrington, D. (2011). *Ethical decisions for social work practice* (9th ed.). Belmont, CA: Brooks Cole.

Garvin, C., Gutierrez, L., & Galinsky, M. (2006). *Handbook of social work with groups.* New York: Guilford Press.

Greif, G., & Ephross, P. (Eds.). (2010). *Group work with populations at risk* (3rd ed.). New York: Oxford University Press.

Malekoff, A. (2014). *Group work with adolescents: Principles and practice* (3rd ed.). New York: Guilford Press.

Van Hook, P. (2013). *Social work practice with families: A resiliency approach* (2nd ed.). Chicago: Lyceum.

CHAPTER 6

Social Work Practice with Agencies and the Community

Vanessa Bernal is an administrator for a large county social services agency located in the northeastern part of the United States. A licensed social worker with her master's degree, she worked her way up through the agency ranks from a child protective services investigator to her current position as Deputy Director of the Children's Services Division. Although she no longer works directly with clients, Vanessa's role as an agency administrator has a major impact on children and families in the community. Daily, she is faced with a variety of critical issues that affect the lives of children throughout the county. Despite the recent launching of a number of primary prevention programs and special initiatives to strengthen families in need of parenting education and supportive services, the rates of child maltreatment continue to rise at an alarming rate. Staff caseloads are increasing, and the turnover rate is approaching 50%.

Vanessa has been asked by the County Board of Supervisors to convene a task force to develop strategies that will address these issues before they result in the tragic deaths of children. Taking a "clean sheet" approach, the task force will propose recommendations for changes in agency administration, including staffing patterns and agency structure, as well as identify policy initiatives that will garner more resources for the agency. There will be no "sacred cows" spared in this exercise; everything is on the table for consideration. As Vanessa thinks about the problems, she realizes that a first step is to determine what research has been conducted and what best practices have been developed that can help her and the task force members gain a better understanding of the issues.

This chapter addresses the roles of social workers in generalist macro practice at the exo- (community) and macro- (societal) levels of the environment, including agency administration, community organizing, policy advocacy and development, and research. Assistance to individuals and families is mediated (for good or bad) by conditions in the community. Such assistance is enhanced in communities with strong social supports and diminished in communities in which such supports are limited or nonexistent. Assistance to individuals and families is also mediated by the actions (or inactions) of policymakers at all levels of government. That is why it is important to remember that social work practice is neither "micro" nor "macro," but the intersection of both.

Social welfare issues are complex and often difficult to comprehend by elected officials tasked with making decisions about the direction and funding of critical programs and services. Consequently, agency administrators should always have good data to support their requests to community, state, and federal leaders for resources. Vanessa, for example, is aware of the substantial body of research that has shown the importance of preventive programs in reducing the incidence of child maltreatment and strengthening families. She is acutely aware of the inadequate funding that is available to help alleviate social welfare–related problems, and in particular, child maltreatment.

Another dilemma faced by social agency administrators such as Vanessa is how best to develop collaborative working relationships with key policymakers to support programs that will result in positive change for the individuals and families that their agencies serve. Ironically, state and federal laws that affect the welfare of individuals and families often are made without input from the very people that provide services to members of this population.

Social workers in direct micro practice (delivering social services in direct interactions with clients) hear firsthand what clients think about these laws and the related policies put in place to comply with them. The flow of information from client to policymaker and the sensitivity of policymakers to clients' circumstances are best accomplished when social workers appreciate and understand both the opportunities and the limitations of the American policymaking process.

Social Work with Communities

EP 2.1.8b

Social work with communities is a generalist practice method that enables individuals and groups to achieve greater life satisfaction, as well as more effective levels of adaptation. Community social work may take a variety of forms (see Box 6.1 for an example).

Successful social work intervention, as in the case of Mary, often requires the social worker to involve community agencies and organizations in the process. Without Tiffany's knowledge and skill, Mary probably could not have made the arrangements that resulted in a positive solution to her need to complete her high school education. Clients frequently are unaware of available resources or the process through which successful solutions can be achieved. In some instances, clients do not have the self-confidence to pursue alternatives that would result in goal attainment. Also, critical resources may not be available in their communities. Sooner or later, social workers in direct practice find that work with the community (i.e., macro social work) is essential to the problem-solving process.

Community: Definition and Social Work Roles

Community is a descriptive term with many meanings. Communities are said to be groups of people who live within certain incorporated limits, such as Philadelphia, Pennsylvania; Boise, Idaho; or Dime Box, Texas. Others speak of a "religious community," which refers to a group of people who share common religious values. A community also may be a subunit of a larger metropolitan area, such as the Watts area in Los Angeles or the Lower East Side in New York City. Members of an ethnic group who live in a specific geographic area, too, are often referred to as a community. The illustrations are

Box 6.1   Making a Difference at the Community Level

Tiffany Williams, a BSW social worker, has been working with Mary Whitecloud for several months. Mary, age 16, is a single parent who lives on a small Native American reservation at the outskirts of town, aspires to complete her high-school education with the hope that she can find a good job and provide a decent life for herself and her child. She has experienced difficulty concentrating on her schoolwork because she often has to miss school to care for her baby. She has also missed school to participate in tribal rites that are central to maintaining her cultural identity as a Native American. On several occasions, officials at the off-reservation school Mary is attending have suspended her for absences, and she has become more discouraged every day about her future.

With Mary's consent, Tiffany visited with the school officials to engage them in working out an educational program for Mary so she would be successful in her studies. Tiffany contacted a local child-care center in the community and helped Mary arrange for child care for her daughter while she attended class. Also, Tiffany helped Mary secure free bus passes so she would have a reliable means of getting to and from school as well as to her child's child-care center.

Working with Mary and other teen parents, Tiffany soon realized that the community had no formal resources for working specifically with teen parents. She helped organize a network of interested social workers and school officials who worked together to secure accessible and affordable child-care and transportation services for all teen parents in the community so they could attend school regularly while fulfilling their parenting responsibilities. Under Tiffany's leadership, network members secured funding to establish a comprehensive program to work exclusively with pregnant and parenting teens.

Social workers who practice at the community level use a number of approaches to improve the well-being of community members.

CIRO CESAR/LA OPINION/Newscom

endless, and the purpose here is to call attention to the broad nature of the concept.

As a workable definition, **communities** may be defined as spaces, interactions, and identifications that people share with others in place-specific and non-place-specific locations. Of the many types of communities, those in which social work professionals engaged in macro practice are most likely to be involved are classified as geographical or territorial communities, communities of identification and interest, traditional communities, and communities of diversity.

- **Geographic or territorial communities** (sometimes referred to as modern communities) include neighborhoods, cities, towns, villages, and boroughs that have clearly defined geopolitical boundaries.
- **Communities of identification and interest** (also referred to as functional communities, relational/associational communities, communities of affiliation or affinity, or communities of the mind) are formed around shared concerns and deeply held beliefs and values that often bring community members into conflict with other communities. Examples are communities based on ethnicity, race, religion, lifestyle, sexual orientation, or profession.
- **Traditional communities** exist side by side with communities that are more heterogeneous. For the

most part, members of traditional communities attempt to maintain their separateness, uniqueness, cultural integrity, and historical identity. Traditional communities are characterized by their emphasis on mutual relationships, commonality, tradition, ritual, and social bonds. Examples of traditional communities are the Amish, Native Americans, Hasidic Jews, and aborigines.
- **Communities of diversity** constitute a subset of modern communities whose community members often engage in a struggle to navigate a hostile world. Examples of these communities are barrios, ghettos, and Native American reservations.

Roles of Social Workers in Communities

EP 2.1.1a
EP 2.1.1c

The same basic (micro) skills necessary to work effectively with people are used in macro practice in communities. Generalist social work practitioners engaged in community practice play many of the same professional roles as those who work with individuals, families, and groups (see Box 2.3). Social work with the community may encompass a wide range of problems and issues; the case illustration with which we initiated this chapter is only one example.

A social worker may serve as a **broker** (linking clients with resources and services) with several agencies to obtain resources necessary to achieve intervention goals. In the broker role, the social worker helps clients navigate the often bewildering maze of agencies that offer programs and services that are most appropriate to problem resolution. In addition to the active role of **negotiator** (an intermediary to resolve conflicts) with agencies, the social worker gathers and transmits information between client systems and the broader environment (Kirst-Ashman & Hull, 2011).

Sometimes the social worker in community practice serves as an **enabler** in helping people identify and clarify their problems (assessment) and in supporting and stimulating the group to unite in its efforts to secure change. For example, a group of tenants in a rat-infested apartment might be encouraged to unite and confront the owners or landlords and seek redress for those conditions.

At other times the social worker in community practice functions in the role of **advocate** (promoting fair and equitable treatment of clients and working to obtain needed resources) for a client system in confronting unresponsive representatives of community institutions. In the advocate role, the social worker clearly is aligned with the client system in urging unresponsive institutions to take action. A social worker may, for example, represent the client system in trying to increase police protection in high-crime neighborhoods.

Social workers engaged in community macro practice also might serve in the **educator** role (providing information/ teaching skills to facilitate change), for example, by organizing an effort to educate non-English-speaking women in the community about the importance of obtaining mammograms. Other roles that social workers in the community typically take on, according to Kirst-Ashman and Hull (2015, pp. 21–26), are

- **analyst/evaluator** (determining the effectiveness of programs or agencies),
- **facilitator** (bringing participants together to promote change through improved communication),
- **general manager** (assuming administrative responsibility for an agency at some level),
- **initiator/coordinator** (bringing people together and helping organize for change),
- **mediator** (helping factions work out their differences), and
- **mobilizer** (identifying and convening resources to address unmet community needs).

As indicated, generalist social work practitioners are constantly engaged in community practice as they work with various organizations to address specific needs of their clients or the population in general. In Mary's case, the social worker had to engage the school system, a child-care center, and the local transportation company to establish an effective solution for the challenges Mary and other teen parents faced.

Community Practice Models and Approaches

EP 2.1.3b

Social workers engage in a variety of **community practice** approaches (Netting, Kettner, & McMurtry, 2011):

- neighborhood and community organizing;
- organizing functional communities;
- community, social, and economic development;
- social planning;
- program development and community liaison;
- political and social action;
- coalition building; and
- social movements

The desired outcome of **neighborhood and community organizing** is to develop the capacity of community members to organize around quality-of-life issues in the community (e.g., air quality, noise pollution, activities for children to participate in after school, planning for controlled neighborhood development, affordable housing). Systems targeted for change include municipal government, developers, and community members. Social justice directed to advocacy and changing behaviors is the desired outcome of **organizing functional communities.** The system targeted for change is the general public and government institutions. The scope of concern is advocacy for a specific issue or population (e.g., marriage rights for lesbians and gays, a living wage, resources for the homeless, and legal rights of unaccompanied minors who enter the country without required documentation.

The desired outcome of **community social and economic development** is to prepare citizens to make use of social and economic investments (e.g., Earned Income Tax Credit, child-care tax credit, low-interest housing loans, and weatherizing programs). The systems targeted for change include banks, foundations, developers, and the general public. The scope of concern is income, resources, and social support development.

The desired outcomes of **social planning** are proposals for action by elected bodies or human services planning councils. The system targeted for change consists of community and human services leaders. The scope of concern is the integration of social needs into planning in the public arena. Social planning strategies include working behind the scenes with others to bring to the table a specific proposal for action, direct participation in the planning, and influencing people who participate in the planning.

The desired outcome of **program development and community liaison** is expansion or redirection of agency programs (e.g., school-based services for pregnant or parenting teens, or after-school programs that offer safe passage from school to home for children who live in neighborhoods with high crime rates). The system targeted for change consists of agency funding sources and beneficiaries of agency services.

The desired outcome of **political and social action** is social justice focusing on changing policy or policymakers. The system targeted for change includes the voting public, elected officials, and potential participants. The scope of concern is to build political power and institutional change (get the message to those who can do something about the issue or problem).

The desired outcome of **coalition building** is to create a multiorganizational power base large enough to influence program direction or draw resources. The system targeted for change consists of elected officials, foundations, and government entities. The scope of concern is a specified issue related to a social need or concern (e.g., eliminating open-air drug markets or creating a safe place in which community members can live).

The desired outcome of **social movements** is action for social justice (social reform) that provides a new paradigm for an identified population or issue. The system targeted for change is the general public or political systems. The scope of concern is social justice within society. Historical examples of social movements include the settlement house movement, welfare rights movement, civil rights movement, anti–Vietnam war movement, gay rights movement, immigrant rights movement, and feminist movement.

Profile of an Effective Community Organizer

EP 2.1.1c

Using their knowledge of the ecological/systems framework, social workers can be effective community organizers. The profile of an effective community organizer includes the following elements:

- familiarity with community customs and traditions, social networks, and values (sometimes referred to as "settling in")
- leadership capability

- knowledge of political systems with their access and leverage points
- knowledge of past organizing strategies, their strengths, and their limitations
- skill in developing critical consciousness and empowerment
- skill in evaluative and participatory research
- skill in program planning and development
- awareness of self and personal strengths and limitations
- an understanding of power
- a sense of curiosity
- the ability to imagine and dream

Social workers engaged in macro community practice are obligated to seek opportunities to develop or expand skills in these areas, work with others who have these skills, and learn by example (and, conversely, to reach out and help others gain these skills after mastering them), put the skills into practice once gained, and embrace a "lifetime learning" approach to skills development.

Policy Practice

EP 2.1.8a

DiNitto and Johnson (2012) define **social welfare policy** as "anything a government chooses to do, or not to do, that affects the quality of life of its people" (p. 2). Social welfare policies are influenced by the prevailing social values.

The Development of Social Welfare Policy

Day and Schiele (2012, pp. 5–12) identify the following social values that have the potential for influencing the development of social welfare policies:

- *Judeo-Christian charity values:* Those requiring assistance have a right to help, and society has an obligation to respond.
- *Democratic egalitarianism:* No one has privileges based on class, heritage, wealth, or other factors not related to basic citizenship.
- *Individualism* (also referred to as the "bootstrap mentality" or "frontier mentality"): Failure to achieve is the fault of the individual, not society.
- *Protestant work ethic and capitalism:* The emphases are on work as a means of achieving religious salvation; individualism; personal achievement; and the morality of wealth.
- *Social Darwinism:* The lives of the "economically unfit" should not be saved by giving them public assistance; the poor are morally degenerate and

should perish; any society aiding the poor will be destroyed by its immorality.

- *Patriarchy:* Power and authority are vested in men.
- *New Puritanism:* Society must return to patriarchy and the Puritan values of the past—chastity, particularly for women; honesty in dealing with others; abstinence from things defined by religion and custom as immoral; and behavior that will not offend others.
- *Marriage and the nuclear family:* The traditional marriage system—husband, wife, and one or more children—should be preserved.
- *"American Ideal":* The "ideal" consists of looking and acting a certain way, coupled with race and gender stereotypes.

Taken alone or in combination, these values can have a powerful influence on the social welfare policies that guide the work of the social work profession.

Gilbert and Terrell (2012) view social welfare policy as an explicit course of action, stressing decisions and choices that help determine the outcomes of that course of action. They believe that social welfare policies can be interpreted as choices among principles determining what benefits are offered and to whom, how the benefits are provided, and how they are financed. They express these dimensions of choice in the following four questions.

1. What are the bases of social allocations? (the "who" of social welfare policy—recipients or beneficiaries)
2. What are the types of social provisions to be allocated? (the "what" of social welfare policy—financial support or goods and services)
3. How will these provisions be delivered? (the organizational arrangements made for delivering benefits to clients)
4. What are the ways these provisions will be financed? (identifying the necessary funds to deliver the agreed-upon services to the agreed-upon clients or beneficiaries). (p. 61)

According to Gilbert and Terrell, the choices that are made in determining who gets what, how services are delivered, and how services are financed are influenced by the range of available alternatives, the social values that support the alternatives, and the theories or assumptions that underlie them (p. 61). Each choice is subject to tradeoffs between what is desirable, what the circumstances necessitate, and what the public will support.

Models of Policy Analysis

Haynes and Mickelson (2009, pp. 77–82) argue that understanding policy models (patterns of something to be made) is central to simplifying and clarifying our understanding of social welfare policy. They offer the following models as a framework for determining how social welfare policy is developed and implemented:

1. *Institutional model:* The focus is on social welfare policy as the output of governmental institutions such as Congress, state legislatures, the courts, and political parties.
2. *Process model:* The focus is on gaining an appreciation for and an understanding of how social welfare policy decisions are made.
3. *Group theory model:* The focus is on the interaction between political interest groups such as advocacy groups, policy institutes or "think tanks," political action committees (PACs), or lobbying organizations.
4. *Elite theory model:* The focus is on the preferences, values, and behaviors of a "governing elite," usually at the expense of other members of society.
5. *Rational model:* The focus is on efficiency, positive outcomes, costs–benefits, long-term results, and the common good (rational policymaking is comprehensive, objective, and free from the influence of special-interest groups).
6. *Incremental model:* The focus is on using existing policies as a baseline for change; attention is concentrated on how new or proposed policies affect (increase, decrease, or modify) that base (this approach typically involves limited change, political expediency, or fine-tuning rather than dramatic change, resulting in something for everyone and minimal conflict).

Understanding the framework from which social welfare policy is developed enables social workers to be more effective in influencing the policy-development process.

The Practitioner's Role in Social Welfare Policy

EP 2.1.1a
EP 2.1.8b

As noted above, social welfare policy provides the basis for determining who (clients or beneficiaries) is eligible for services, the extent of services provided, the manner in which those services are delivered, and the funding that undergirds the provision of those services. Social welfare policy is the blueprint upon which social welfare programs are planned, designed, and operated. Social work professionals of all kinds—direct service workers, planners, administrators, advocates, and researchers—are all affected by and have the potential for affecting social welfare policy.

Social welfare program administrators are obligated to follow the rules and regulations that have been established to translate social welfare policy into action. *Direct service workers* have first-hand knowledge of the impact of social welfare policies on their clients—what works, what doesn't work, and what needs to be changed. *Program planners* are knowledgeable about which policies lead to trouble-free, straightforward implementation and which do not. *Social welfare researchers* develop the evidence base for deciding which policies are best suited for which clients or client systems and under what conditions.

Social welfare advocates provide important information to policymakers about the needs and concerns of the client groups they represent. They also monitor policy development and implementation to ensure that those needs and concerns are not neglected. An effective social welfare advocate can be characterized as someone who has the following attributes: knowledgeable about the issues, passionate, determined, a visionary, an excellent communicator, a critical thinker, a good problem solver, curious, able to dream and imagine, risk-positive, honest, reliable, dependable, authentic, ethical, and a good negotiator. Many of these attributes can be traced to one's personality; others are gained through hard work, experience, and the guidance of a helpful mentor.

Social welfare advocates face many challenges in applying their knowledge and skills. They are forced to work in a crowded field characterized by multiple groups with different (an often competing) agendas vying for the attention of the same policymaker. Many times, social welfare advocates have difficulty choosing the right group or groups to which they should target their actions. Because of the nature of their business, they are almost always required to work with stakeholders who have divergent and/or conflicting values and ideologies. Regardless of the issue, social welfare advocates are almost always required to accommodate different (and often controversial) opinions about what works best and why (Jansson, 2014, p. 17).

Research plays a number of key roles in the practice of policy advocacy. Perhaps most importantly, it lends credibility to the process. Equally important, it provides an empirical basis for appreciating differing (and sometimes conflicting) points of view regarding the social nature, scope, and etiology of welfare problems. Research can provide important information about what works and why, but the policy advocate has to be aware of the specific conditions under which the research was generated. Finally, properly conceptualized and carried out, research can serve as the basis for evaluating the efficacy of policy advocacy efforts (Jansson, 2014).

It is an inescapable conclusion that good social welfare policy simply cannot be developed without the input and involvement of the social work profession.

Administration and Delivery of Social Welfare Services

EP 2.1.9b

Most social welfare services are delivered by some type of agency. Today, there are almost as many types of agencies as the problems they address. These agencies can be public or private, nonprofit of for profit, faith-based, or in some combination. The social welfare agency is many things to many people. It is a place where people go for help when problems arise and a place that society holds responsible for addressing specific problems. It also is a place of employment for some and a setting for voluntary action by others. With the multiple motives of multiple actors, the social welfare agency serves a myriad of purposes.

Meeting the Challenge

Above all, the primary task of the social welfare agency's administrator is to bring resources, opportunities, and goals together to accomplish a variety of social missions. Contrary to popular belief, management activities are not the sole purview of agency administrators. All staff members of the agency, members of the board of directors or other governance oversight body, and, in some cases, the agency's clients play vital roles in the administrative process.

The administrator of any social welfare agency is faced with the following key tasks:

- Creating the structure of the agency;
- Determining who should be hired and the best way to organize and support staff;
- Determining what role(s) volunteers can play in the work of the agency, and the best way to recruit, train, and support them as well as evaluating their efforts;

- Identifying which programs should be offered, and the manner in which they should be delivered;
- Creating systems for tracking client-related and other information;
- Developing financial and other controls that ensure transparency and accountability;
- Securing the necessary funding to provide services and enable the agency to thrive; and
- Determining whether agency programs and services are achieving their intended outcomes.

The social work literature offers a wide variety of tools and techniques aimed at supporting agency administrators in accomplishing these tasks (see, for example, Netting, Kettner, & McMurtry, 2011; Renz & Herman, 2010).

Weighing the Client's Best Interests

Social service agencies that represent clients with little or no political power face unique dilemmas. Too much concern with the needs and desires of clients served can erode the economic and political support necessary for the agency's very existence; too little concern can result in exploitation of the clients the agency purports to serve.

Another dilemma faced by social service administrators is determining who makes what choices. Children, individuals with mental illness, those with developmental disabilities, and others may not be in a position to know what is in their best interest; often, the agency is left to make such decisions. As noted above, the complexity of the situation, the number of available options, and the acceptability or support of those options influence these decisions.

The professional social worker in the social service agency has to steer between two dangers. Rigid adherence to the rules that govern the agency or the wishes of those who fund the agency can result in a subtle but debilitating form of tyranny. On the other hand, while voices of clients served need to heard and their suggestions seriously considered, over-involvement of clients in decisions that affect the structure of the agency or the nature of the services being offered also can result in a limited agency perspective or intractable stalemates that can derail the work of the agency, or worse yet, jeopardize the future of the agency. Conventional wisdom holds that the best course of action is to engage governing bodies, funders, and clients in a meaningful way while maintaining the integrity of the agency's overall decision-making process.

Social Welfare Agencies

Social welfare has its roots in the 1700s, as detailed in Chapter 1. Today's structures, while maintaining the integrity of those their roots, have evolved to meet today's conditions.

A Historical Perspective

EP 2.1.9a Organized social welfare in colonial America was essentially nonexistent. Times were tough and resources were scarce. All able-bodied adults were expected to work to support themselves and their families. Movement between cities and towns was restricted. Families were accountable for taking care of their own. Children from families who could not support them were apprenticed out to others, where they earned their keep through forced labor.

Adults who could were unable to support themselves through no fault of their own (those with disabilities and the elderly) were cared for in the homes of others or were relegated to almshouses or poorhouses, where they received minimal care. Able-bodied individuals who refused to work or were unable to find work were placed in workhouses, where they lived in squalid conditions in return for forced work. Some charitable associations existed, but their resources were limited and the number of people they were able to serve was small in comparison to the need.

In the 1700s, the **private voluntary sector** evolved in response to the public disgrace surrounding the living conditions in the almshouses, where children often lived with the adults in the same quarters. Limited government involvement in providing social welfare services continued throughout the 18th century and well into the 19th century. Care for the poor and for others in need was relegated almost exclusively to religious institutions and private charitable organizations.

Successive waves of immigration throughout the 1800s, coupled with the aftermath of the Civil War, brought about a rapid expansion of private voluntary agencies (charity organization societies and **settlement houses**), particularly in urban areas along the Eastern Seaboard and in large Midwest cities such as Chicago. Advocacy efforts of early social workers during the so-called Progressive Era (1875–1925) forced the federal government to at least take notice of the problems, as well as to begin developing policies and programs addressing the plight of the poor and the needy.

It was not until the stock market crash of 1929 and the ensuing Great Depression that the federal government assumed a central role in the American social welfare system. Local governments, religious institutions, and private voluntary organizations were unable to meet the demand for services created by the Great Depression. Like it or not, the federal government had no choice but to get involved. Passage of the Social Security Act in 1935 marked the formal entry of the federal government into the public social service arena. The age of large-scale, public social services had begun.

Growth of federal government involvement in public social welfare programs continued through the first half of the 20th century. This growth peaked in the mid-1960s with the War on Poverty and the Great Society programs of the Johnson administration and has been on the decline (devolved) since that time. Republican presidential administrations since the 1970s have emphasized a "new federalism" (actually, a throw-back to colonial times) characterized by limited government involvement, transfer of responsibility for social welfare programs to the states through block grants, renewed emphasis on personal and family responsibility, privatization of public social services, reliance on religious institutions and faith-based organizations and the private voluntary sector to pick up the slack, and strict accountability requirements. Although some Democratic administrations and members of Congress of both parties have worked to expand social welfare programs (the most notable being reform of the country's ailing health-care system), the role of the federal government in providing social welfare and related services continues to be more limited than in the past. As noted above the contemporary social welfare system in the United States is similar in many ways to the one found in colonial America. For a detailed discussion of the evolution and subsequent devolution of the American social welfare system, see Stern and Axinn (2011) and Day and Schiele (2012).

Contemporary Structures

Today, organized social service activities are provided by local, state, and federal governments (or for-profit entities operating under contract to them), by sectarian or faith-based organizations, and by private nonprofit agencies. **Private nonprofit agencies** provide a host of services to individuals, groups, neighborhoods, and communities. They also serve as an organizing entity and conduit for charitable funds and voluntary efforts.

Three interdependent parts make up the social service portion of private nonprofit agencies, of which a specific agency can represent one or all three:

1. agencies that serve public and charitable purposes principally for fund-raising and planning, such as United Way agencies;
2. advocacy organizations, which bring together a group of like-minded people who seek to generate government funding or promote public understanding of and support for a specific social problem or a specific class of individuals;
3. direct-service agencies that deal with clients who have specific or multiple problems of social functioning.

Voluntary agencies are bounded on one side by the private, profit-oriented approach of the free market and on the other side by a politically driven public sector. They are free to be creative and innovative but, at the same time, can be vulnerable to being too non-mainstream. Thus, any agency may exist only briefly. Few private voluntary agencies have existed for a hundred years or more. The majority of such agencies have been in existence for 25 years or less. There is a plethora of agencies less than 10 years old.

Will private voluntary agencies survive as a significant provider of social welfare services? Probably so, but they will look quite different in the future. Recent shifts in private charitable giving have forced private voluntary agencies to look at the benefits of social entrepreneurship, to engage in strategic alliances and partnerships with the business sector, and to entertain the thought of merging with one another to secure their future. Increasingly, the distinction between public and private social service agencies is blurring as public agencies, under pressure to consolidate or downsize, are entering into purchase of service and other arrangements to fulfill their statutory mandates (some have referred to these arrangements as the "mixed marketplace" of the social welfare delivery system) (see, for example, Gilbert & Terrell, 2012).

Research Practice

EP 2.1.6a
EP 2.1.6b

Research is playing an ever-increasing role in determining how resources are allocated in the social welfare arena. Social work as a profession is committed to **evidence-based practice**, or a process in which social work practitioners use research-based interventions to inform the delivery of services. This approach ensures that interventions, when used as intended, result in the most effective outcomes (Social Work Policy Institute, 2010).

Social workers incorporate three types of research in assessing their interventions at all levels of the environment: disciplinary research, policy research, and evaluative research. All three types are *scientific* (they depend on the scientific method), *objective* (the investigator is required to conform to established canons of logical reasoning and formal rules of evidence), and *ethically neutral* (the investigator does not take sides on issues of moral or ethical significance). Although the three types are similar in their demand for objectivity, each type has its own specific purposes.

Disciplinary Research

Disciplinary research is the term that denotes investigations to expand the body of knowledge of a discipline. The intent is explanation for its own sake. Disciplinary research begins with a **paradigm** or perspective that structures the research, the research goals, and the research methods. The paradigm directs the investigator to where and how to seek evidence.

Paradigms allow researchers within a discipline to build on the work of others in their field. Social workers also must make use of these paradigms to identify pragmatic methods of intervention with individuals, families, groups, and communities. The social investigator is primarily interested in providing an explanation of why something happened.

The first step in this inquiry is to identify a *dependent* or *outcome* variable (the phenomenon we wish to explain) and show how it is related to one or more *independent* variables (factors that produce changes in the dependent variable). For example, with changes in economic and social circumstances (independent variables), observable changes in employment opportunities (dependent variable) follow. Careful selection of independent and dependent variables, use of both inductive and deductive reasoning, and precise application of the established rules of evidence are required to produce correct inferences about relationships.

The "glue" that holds together any disciplinary investigation is theory. A **theory** is a set of logically related, empirically verifiable generalizations that intend to explain relationships clearly. A theory is derived from a set of generalizations. No one theory is right or wrong, but some are more useful than others in informing practice. Theory can be used to generate one or more **hypotheses**, which can direct attention to certain observations, which in turn can be used to formulate certain empirical generalizations. Because of the cyclical nature of the research process, the process can begin at any one of the four points (theory, hypothesis, observation, and generalizations).

Policy Research

Policy research is a specialized form of inquiry whose purpose is to provide reliable, valid, and relevant knowledge for public officials, agency managers, and others to support the decision-making processes of government. Although it is used (or misused) at all levels of government, scientific research does not always guide or control policy choices. History is replete with examples of public officials' rejecting the advice of the research community. Deciding on the contribution to, and limits of, research findings to public decision making is a complex undertaking (Majchrzak & Markus, 2013). There may be general agreement about what the consequences are, but the value placed on that information can be enormously different.

Reducing the uncertainty surrounding policy formulation and evaluating the consequences of policy implementation are central tasks of policy research. How a society uses the products or outcomes of policy research is a political issue (Committee on the Use of Social Science Knowledge in Public Policy, 2012). Politicians often select the research finding that best fits the ends or goals they seek. Just as expert medical testimony is used (or misused) by both prosecution and defense attorneys in the same case, so, too, the results of policy research can be used (or misused) for political purposes.

Problems arise in the design, execution, and interpretation of research for specific policy choices that are not encountered in disciplinary research. Policy analysis frequently is expected to produce specific kinds of information in a short time within a limited budget. Both policy research and disciplinary research are governed by the canons of scientific methodology. They differ in that disciplinary research is structured to develop theoretically relevant explanations of social phenomena, while policy research is structured to identify, assess, and evaluate public strategies used to produce public ends (Committee on the Use of Social Science Knowledge in Public Policy, 2012).

The importance of policy research cannot be underestimated. All too often, social policies are formulated with no empirical basis. These policies are doomed to fail at some point because they do not reflect the realities of the situation(s) they address.

Evaluative Research

Evaluative research is used to assess the efficacy of a given policy or set of policies or to measure the impact of a specific intervention method. The typical starting point of evaluative research is to conduct a review of relevant literature. This task is made easier today because of search tools available through the Internet. Once the literature search has been conducted, the researcher can examine the information for trends and unique differences.

In evaluative research, the scientific method is the basic analytic tool used to determine the impact of the program. Because social work research rarely takes place under controlled laboratory conditions, specific research designs have been developed to accommodate such research in the field (Martens & Wilson, 2012; Rubin & Babbie, 2013). The principal task of the policy evaluator is not just to show success or failure but also to indicate the range of certainty with which that judgment is made.

In addition to evaluating the effectiveness of social work programs, social workers evaluate the effectiveness of their direct work with clients. **Single-subject designs** or **single-case designs** (DiNoia & Tripodi, 2008; Kazdin, 2010) are used to evaluate the impact of interventions on a single client or case. These designs typically are used by social workers and other professionals in clinical settings.

Demonstrating a Causal Connection

To report that a favorable outcome occurred while a program was in place is not sufficient. The evaluator must demonstrate that the outcome reasonably can be attributed to the policy action or program and not to some other explanation. For example, if an intervention is developed to help children adjust to their parents' divorce, we have to be able to demonstrate that the children were better adjusted because of the intervention, not because of some other factor such as time spent with sympathetic teachers or relatives or merely because the children grew older or more mature.

In the classical research design, the evaluator uses both theory and probability to increase the likelihood that the observed relationship is truly a causal one. Because theory is used to select the observations to be made, theories guide observations and bring investigators closer to a realistic understanding of the relationship between observed outcome and the program or policy action. The real understanding depends on adequacy of the theory (Rubin & Babbie, 2012).

Social work researchers have to be keenly aware of chance as an alternative explanation for observed results. Statistical tools are available that allow the researcher to calculate the probability that the observation would occur by chance versus the specific intervention under study (see, for example, Weinbach & Grinnell, 2014).

Regardless of the researcher's level of sophistication or the statistical tools available to analyze results, researchers cannot *prove* that "A" caused "B." The best they can do is to conclude that there is a strong relationship between the two. Thus, social science evaluation can be used to help decision makers reject bad policy, but it cannot help them select with certainty the "best policy" (Committee on the Use of Social Science Knowledge in Public Policy, 2012).

The Status of Macro Social Work Practice

EP 2.1.1c

In shaping communities and social welfare agencies, the social work profession shares key roles with a number of other groups, including politicians, economists, psychologists, educators, attorneys, and, increasingly, lobbyists for various constituent groups. Social work researchers have played a key role in shaping practice and policies at local, state, and federal levels. To strengthen its relationship with these other entities and its role as a key shaper of social welfare policies and programs, the profession has continued to seek new ways to maintain credibility in an increasingly technological and politicized society. One way the profession has increased its status is through state and national licensing and certification programs. Certification as a professional by the state protects the public from unwarranted claims by individual purveyors of a service and also protects the intellectual property rights of a person who is trained and educated to perform the service (Bibus & Boutté-Queen, 2010).

Whether the real purpose behind the certification of a professional group is to protect an unsuspecting public or to protect the practice rights of a politically powerful professional group is often difficult to discern. Through certification, each professional group seeks to enlarge its own domain of practice, make more restrictive the rights to operate within that domain, and justify its expansive and protective stance with the ethic of client interest. Social work professionals are not exempt from this generalization (Bibus & Boutté-Queen, 2010).

Another way that the social work profession has attempted to strengthen its relationship with other entities is through the Social Work Reinvestment Initiative, a collaborative effort of leading social work organizations and other stakeholders committed to securing federal and state investments related to recruitment, training, retention, and research that strengthens the social work profession (National Association of Social Workers, 2014). Federal endorsement of these goals is being pursued through the Dorothy I. Height and Whitney M. Young, Jr. Social Work Reinvestment Act. Originally introduced in the 110th Congress in 2008, this bill never gained traction, despite considerable support by members of both parties. It was reintroduced in Congress in May 2013 and was referred to the Subcommittee on Higher Education and Workforce Training. No action has been taken on the legislation since that time.

Increasingly, social workers are saying that their practice wisdom is highly relevant to policy development. To date, however, this policy–practice perspective has not been highly developed. A clear challenge for the future is to find ways to make the practice knowledge—the local-level knowledge about effective interventions—a central part of policy development.

Signs of a new professional commitment to the development of policy perspectives are emerging across national lines (see, for example, Alcock & Craig, 2009). Sometimes referred to as **comparative social research**, this approach enables one nation to build on the policy design initiatives of others, thereby avoiding the need to start afresh.

Making social welfare policy is the result of a political process. In the main, the social work literature has neglected a methodology for intervention in that process, relying instead on teaching policy development from a case or historical perspective. Traditionally, policy analysis has used frames of reference to answer questions about who is covered by the policy, what benefits are provided, the form of delivery, and the financial source (see, for example, Gilbert & Terrell,

2012). This is changing. Analyses of the dynamics of policy—legislative, judicial, and administrative processes—are finding their way increasingly into social work writings (Blau & Abramovitz, 2010).

During the coming decade, hard choices have to be made. Should state or national governments play the leading role in the delivery and funding of social welfare programs? Should everyone be required to maintain health insurance, and if so, who should be responsible for implementing and monitoring compliance with that requirement? Should immigrants who are not citizens receive health-care and social and educational services? To what extent, if at all, should abortion be restricted? To what extent can a cultural group move away from the general standards of child welfare? These are tough questions, and they involve technical, political, and value considerations. Regardless of the auspices of the social agencies in which they work, social workers must maintain a strong professional presence in both the policy and practice arenas at community, state, and national levels.

Career Opportunities in Macro Social Work Practice

There are many career opportunities available for social workers interested in agency administration, community social work, policy, and research. The baccalaureate (BSW) social worker develops beginning competency in working within agencies and the community as part of the BSW educational program. Accredited BSW programs require coursework in both theory and practice in working within the community, and many opportunities are available for work with communities at the BSW level.

Family service agencies, state departments of human services, hospitals, correctional centers, mental health agencies, programs for individuals with disabilities, school social services, youth organizations, and related service delivery organizations all use community practice methods. Social workers with master of social work degrees are often employed as community organization workers, sometimes specializing in that area as a field of practice. At this level, they may serve as administrators of state or federal programs, department heads in a city's human services division, or directors of agencies.

Many state and local government agencies, including those that oversee programs providing public assistance, services to abused and neglected children and their families, services for individuals who have problems with substance abuse and their families, and services that address the myriad other social welfare problems discussed in this text, employ social workers as policy analysts in some capacity. Policy analysts work with state and federal legislators to initiate legislation, provide interpretations regarding the impact of proposed legislation, and oversee the implementation of legislation once it is passed. These individuals play a key role in interpreting policy to direct service practitioners in their agencies. Policy analysts, too, are employed by social action agencies such as the Child Welfare League of America and the Children's Defense Fund, and think tanks such as the Center for Budget and Policy Priorities, the Center for Law and Social Policy, and the Brookings Institution, which provide their constituents and allies with information about the impact of existing and proposed policies.

Social workers also are employed as policy advocates, working for activist organizations such as the National Alliance on Mental Illness and Amnesty International. And many social workers are employed in policy-related jobs in the offices of state and federal elected officials, as well as congressional and state legislative committees. A social worker in this role might work with attorneys to draft bills, meet with client advocates (and sometimes, with actual clients), and attend hearings relating to bills on topics such as homelessness, child care, welfare reform, hate crimes, health care, child abuse and neglect, domestic violence, long-term care and nursing homes, criminal justice, and unaccompanied minors who have entered the country without required documentation and have been apprehended by immigration authorities.

More and more social workers are being elected to local, state, and national office where they are playing important roles in strengthening our social welfare system and protecting the rights of disenfranchised and marginalized citizens. Other social workers serve as agency administrators for public, private nonprofit, and private for-profit organizations that address the wide range of issues discussed in this text.

Social workers serve as senior administrators and commissioners for large state agencies, heads of local government agencies, and heads of private agencies of all sizes. Some social workers, frustrated with the lack of services available in an area in which they work or have an interest, have successfully started their own agencies. One enterprising social worker, for example,

had difficulty getting existing agencies that served persons with AIDS to address the needs of the Mexican American women with AIDS with whom she worked. She began a small outreach program to several women, and it has grown into a nationally recognized program serving Latino women and their families.

Other social workers are engaged in research-related jobs. State social welfare agencies; federal, state, and local governments; United Way and other agencies that distribute funds for human services programs; and local agencies, both public and private, employ social workers in research roles to determine the needs of the clients they serve and evaluate the success of their programs. The emphasis on outcome measures for social services provided at all levels of society has increased the demand for social work researchers. Social workers' knowledge about the bio-psycho-social relationships between individual social problems and the broader environment (an application of the ecological/systems framework), coupled with the profession's emphasis on an interdisciplinary approach, make them excellent candidates for research positions.

Summary

Social work in the community, in policy, in agency administration, and in research is a key component of generalist or macro social work practice. To be effective, social workers involved in generalist practice with individuals, families, and groups must rely heavily on, and collaborate with, their colleagues at exo-levels and macro-levels of the environment.

Social work within the community (community practice) enhances the capacity of that community to better serve the needs of its diverse members. Community change efforts are facilitated through social action, social planning, and community development approaches. In all of these, members of the community establish goals and objectives and a social worker serving as a facilitator helps the members achieve their goals. Democratic decision making is important to the process. Monitoring and evaluation are major activities that help the community achieve its goals and enrich practice methods.

Social welfare policy determines who gets what servicers, how the services are organized and delivered, and the amount of funding for these services. Who becomes a client with need, how clients are served, and the likelihood that they will get their needs addressed are directly or indirectly the result of social welfare policies. How and which social service agencies are funded and what roles the staff, including social workers, play in those agencies are also determined largely by social welfare policy. Social workers play critical roles in developing and shaping policy at all government levels. Increasingly, social workers are being elected to political office. Social work as a profession is gaining credibility in policy arenas at local, state, national, and international levels.

Policy has shaped the historical development and current status of social welfare agencies. The first social welfare agencies were primarily nonprofit agencies. The Depression gave rise to large bureaucratic public agencies that provided a variety of social services, including public assistance, unemployment benefits and cash assistance for unwed mothers with dependent children. Since the 1980s, under Republican presidential administrations, the public social service system in the United States has devolved to one that relies heavily on the private nonprofit sector, volunteerism, and the faith community. The traditional distinction between public agencies, private nonprofit agencies, and the for-profit sector has resulted in a mixed marketplace for the delivery of social services. Clear lines between these three entities are no longer discernable. Public, private nonprofit, and even profit-oriented agencies are becoming more similar to one another, with administrators facing similar issues regardless of the type of agency they oversee. Social workers in administrative roles bring critical profession-based knowledge, values, and skills that are needed to be effective in dealing with increasingly complex funding, political, and service delivery situations.

The wide range of activities that constitute social work research is paramount to effective social welfare policy and agency administration. Social workers are committed to empirical research to generate new knowledge and evaluate practice methods. Three types of research are commonly used: (1) disciplinary research, which is designed to expand the body of knowledge of a particular discipline and to test theory with a set of hypotheses; (2) policy research, used to provide knowledge for public officials and others to support the decision-making processes of government; and (3) evaluative research, used to assess the efficacy of a particular policy or to measure the impact of a specific intervention. Single-subject designs are used to evaluate the impact of policy changes or interventions on a single client or case.

If this chapter has one message, it is that policy, administration, research, and practice at individual, family, group and community levels are not separate spheres but, rather, are interrelated domains, each fundamentally dependent on the other. All social workers should be actively involved in evaluating their efforts and continuing to generate new knowledge that will strengthen social welfare policies and services.

Competency Notes

EP 2.1.1a: Advocate for client access to the services of social work (pp. 147, 150). Social workers engaged in organizational and community practice advocate for client access to social services.

EP 2.1.1c: Attend to professional roles and boundaries (pp. 147, 149, 155). Social workers engaged in organizational and community practice maintain professional boundaries and assume a number of roles in their efforts to enhance the well-being of clients and communities.

EP 2.1.3b: Analyze models of assessment, prevention, intervention, and evaluation (p. 148). Social workers engaged in organizational and community practice analyze models of assessment, prevention, intervention, and evaluation to determine which are most appropriate in meeting the needs of clients and the communities in which they live and work.

EP 2.1.6a: Use practice experience to inform scientific inquiry (p. 153). Social workers engaged in organizational and community practice use practice experience to inform scientific inquiry.

EP 2.1.6b: Use research evidence to inform practice (p. 153). Social workers use research evidence to inform and evaluate their practice at all levels of the environment.

EP 2.1.8a: Analyze, formulate, and advocate for policies that advance social well-being (p. 149). Social workers analyze, formulate, and advocate for policies at all levels of the environment to advance the social well-being of individuals and communities.

EP 2.1.8b: Collaborate with colleagues and clients for effective policy action (pp. 146, 150). Social workers who work with organizations and communities collaborate with colleagues and clients for effective policy action and changes in service delivery at all levels of the environment.

EP 2.1.9a: Continuously discover, appraise, and attend to changing locales, populations, scientific and technological developments, and emerging societal trends to provide relevant services (p. 152).

Social workers who work with organizations and communities continuously discover, appraise, and attend to changing locales, populations, scientific and technological developments, and emerging societal trends to provide relevant services, advocate for policy change, or engage in research efforts.

EP 2.1.9b: Provide leadership in promoting sustainable changes in service delivery and practice to improve the quality of social services (p. 151). Social workers act as leaders in the profession, organizations, and communities to promote sustainable changes in service delivery.

Key Terms

The terms below are defined in the Glossary.

advocate	mediator
analyst/evaluator	mobilizer
broker	negotiator
coalition building	neighborhood and
communities	community
communities of diversity	organizing
communities of	organizing functional
identification and	communities
interest	paradigm
community practice	policy research
community social and	political and social action
economic	private nonprofit
development	agencies
comparative social	private voluntary sector
research	program development
disciplinary research	and community
educator	liaison
enabler	settlement houses
evaluative research	single-case designs
evidence-based practice	single-subject designs
facilitator	social movements
general manager	social planning
geographic or territorial	social welfare policy
communities	theory
hypotheses	traditional communities
initiator/coordinator	

Discussion Questions

1. Review the definition of communities, and discuss the characteristics identified in the definition in terms of their importance for community social work practice. How might a social worker's role differ when working with the following types of communities?
   a. a geographically defined neighborhood comprised of recent immigrants;
   b. the deaf (persons with hearing impairments) community in a large city;
   c. a group of first-generation Italians living within a neighborhood with many other ethnic groups;
   d. a small, rural community of fewer than 1,000 residents.

2. Identify and discuss the community practice approaches discussed in this chapter. Compare and contrast those approaches. Identify three issues of concern in your community. Which community practice approach or approaches described in this chapter would work best to address each of these issues?

3. Identify *three* factors that an agency should always take into consideration when developing and implementing new programs.

4. How many social services agencies in your community are public? How many are voluntary? Are there ones about which you are unsure? Discuss the differences between voluntary and public social service agencies in your community.

5. Do you think that the private for-profit sector should be involved in the provision of social services? Why?

6. What principle of separation into public and voluntary would you use as an ideal for social services agencies in the United States? What principle of separation seems to operate in practice?

7. What roles should the social work profession play in developing and administering social welfare programs? Why do you think so?

8. To what extent do you think the practice of social work research helps efforts to assist a client? Give examples.

9. Can you think of an example in which the research process and the practice process actually reinforce one another?

10. Select a social work–related topic of interest to you. What are some research questions you might address at each of the three levels of research discussed in this chapter?

On the Internet

http://cbpp.org
http://www.brookings.edu

http://www.clasp.org
http://www.kff.org
http://www.independentsector.org
http://www.mdrc.org
http://naswdc.org
http://www.rand.org
http://www.urban.org

References

Alcock, P., & Craig, G. (2009). *International social policy: Welfare regimes in the developed world.* New York: Palgrave Macmillan.

Bibus, A., & Boutté-Queen, N. (2010). *Regulating social work: A primer on licensing practice.* Chicago: Lyceum Books.

Blau, J., & Abramovitz, M. (2010). *The dynamics of social welfare policy* (3rd ed.). New York: Oxford University Press.

Committee on the Use of Social Science Knowledge in Public Policy. (2012). *Using science as evidence in public policy.* Washington, DC: National Academies Press.

Day, P. J., & Schiele, J. (2012). *A new history of social welfare* (7th ed.). Boston: Pearson.

DiNitto, D. M., & Johnson, D. D. (2012). *Essentials of social welfare: Politics and public policy.* Boston: Pearson.

DiNoia, J., & Tripodi, T. (2008). *A primer on single-case design for clinical social workers* (2nd ed.). Washington, DC: NASW Press.

Gilbert, N., & Terrell, P. (2012). *Dimensions of social welfare policy* (8th ed.). Boston: Pearson.

Haynes, K. S., & Mickelson, J. S. (2009). *Affecting change: Social workers in the political arena* (7th ed.). Upper Saddle River, NJ: Prentice-Hall.

Jansson, B. S. (2011). *The reluctant welfare state* (7th ed.). Boston, MA: Cengage Learning.

Kazdin, A. (2010). *Single-case research designs: Methods for clinical and applied settings* (2nd ed.). New York: Oxford University Press.

Kirst-Ashman, K. K., & Hull, G. (2015). *Generalist practice with organizations and communities* (6th ed.). Boston, MA: Cengage Learning.

Majchrzak, A., & Markus, M. (2013). *Methods for policy research: Taking socially responsible action* (2nd ed.). Thousand Oaks, CA: Sage.

Martrens, D., & Wilson, A. (2012). *Program evaluation theory and practice: A comprehensive guide.* New York: Guilford Press.

Netting, F. E., Kettner, P., & McMurtry, S. (2011). *Social work macro practice* (5th ed.). Boston: Pearson.

Renz, D., & Herman, R. (2010). *The Jossey-Bass handbook of nonprofit leadership and management (3rd ed.).* Hoboken, NJ: Jossey-Bass.

Rubin, A., & Babbie, E. (2013). *Research methods for social work* (8th ed.). Stamford, CT: Cengage Learning.

Social Work Policy Institute. (2010). *Evidence-based practice.* Washington, DC: Author. Retrieved January 10, 2010, from www.socialworkpolicy.org

Stern, M. J., & Axinn, J. (2011). *Social welfare: A history of the American response to need* (8th ed.). Boston: Pearson.

Weinbach, R.W., & Grinnell, R. M. (2014). *Statistics for social workers* (9th ed.). Boston: Pearson.

Suggested Readings

Gardella, L. G., & Haynes, K. S. (2004). *A dream and a plan: A woman's path to leadership in human services.* Washington, DC: NASW Press.

Janssen, B. (2013). *Becoming an effective policy advocate: From policy practice to social justice* (7th ed.). Boston, MA: Cengage Learning.

Kettner, P. (2013). *Excellence in human service organization management* (2nd ed.). Boston: Pearson.

Kraft, M. E., & Furlong, S. R. (2012). *Public policy: Politics, analysis, and alternatives* (4th ed.). Thousand Oaks, CA: CQ Press.

Leon-Guerrero, A. (2013). *Social problems: Community, policy and social action* (4th ed.). Thousand Oaks, CA: Sage.

Lewis, J. A., Packard, T. R., & Lewis, M. D. (2011). *Management of human service programs* (5th ed.). Stamford, CT: Cengage Learning.

Moran, M., Rein, M., & Goodin, R. E. (Eds.). (2008). *The Oxford handbook of public policy.* New York: Oxford University Press.

Sandburg, S. (2013). *Lean in: Women, work, and the will to lead.* New York: Knopf.

PART 3

Fields of Practice and Populations Served by Social Workers

Elizabeth Crews/PhotoEdit

Part 3 explores many of the settings in which social workers practice and the special populations served. Each chapter presents, from an ecological/systems perspective, the issues that social work practitioners face in their work with specific populations. This information will help you make career decisions based on what social work jobs are available in the various fields of practice and what each job entails.

This section emphasizes competencies needed to be an effective social work practitioner that focus on understanding the multiple sources of knowledge about different social issues generated by diverse groups, as well as the contexts, both past and present, that shape policy and practice with diverse populations. As you read these chapters, it is expected that you will begin to develop an understanding of the social work profession's commitment to advocacy for client access to services within the social welfare system and the many roles that social workers play in meeting client needs.

Chapter 7, Poverty, Income Assistance, and Homelessness, defines poverty and explores why people are poor, who is poor in the United States, and what types of policies and programs are available to help reduce poverty in the United States. The chapter concludes with a discussion of the roles social workers play in the fight to eradicate poverty.

Chapter 8, Health Care, offers an explanation of the current health-care system in the United States, the problems it faces, and the types of health-care policies and programs that guide and shape the health-care delivery system in the country. Health issues include, increased costs of care, ethical decisions when balancing available technology with costs and needs, and how best to prevent and treat chronic medical conditions such as diabetes, cancer, and HIV/AIDS. Health care is the fastest-growing area of employment for social workers today, and we describe career opportunities for social workers in health-care settings.

Chapter 9, Mental Health, Substance Use, and Disabilities, covers definitional issues as well as a discussion of the historical and contemporary events that have shaped the way mental health problems are viewed and the types of mental health services available. Among the critical current mental health issues discussed are substance use and suicide, along with the roles of social workers in alleviating these social problems.

Chapter 10, The Needs of Children, Youth, and Families, presents an overview of the diverse types of families today and the many issues that even the healthiest families face in contemporary society. The chapter explores factors that contribute to healthy families, as well as factors that place families at risk for social problems, including divorce, alcoholism and other forms of substance use, child abuse and neglect, and interpersonal violence. Issues that are more likely to be associated with at-risk adolescents include teenage pregnancy, gang membership, youth crime, and gun-related violence.

Chapter 11, Services to Children, Youth, and Families, addresses current policies and programs that attempt to prevent or alleviate the problems discussed in Chapter 10. The present child welfare service-delivery system focuses on family preservation and other programs and policies, with the goal of keeping families together. The chapter concludes with a discussion of the wide variety of activities that social workers provide in serving children, youth, and families, including child protective services and school social work.

Chapter 12, Older Adults: Needs and Services, highlights a special population that increasingly is requiring attention from the social welfare system and social work practitioners—older adults. This chapter describes physical and social support systems to meet their specific needs. As more people are fitting this age category and as the field of social work is growing rapidly to respond to their needs, so, too, are activities and roles of social workers who assist this population.

Chapter 13, Criminal Justice, focuses on youth and adults who become involved in some aspect of the criminal justice system. The chapter covers the nature of crime and the criminal justice system, including the roles of law enforcement, the courts, and the prison system. A special section explains the juvenile justice system and differences in treatment of adult and juvenile offenders. Again, the roles of social workers in providing services are described.

Chapter 14, Social Work Contexts: Rural and Urban Settings and Environmentalism speaks about an important segment of social work that often is neglected—rural America. The chapter differentiates rural and urban life and the unique issues facing rural and urban populations. The chapter also includes a discussion about environmental concerns that impact social workers and their clients, including environmental risks such as hazardous waste disposal. Career choices for social workers who choose to work in rural or urban settings or as environmentalists are also explored.

Chapter 15, Social Work in the Workplace, investigates a field of social work that is increasingly important because of changes in workplace demographics. Interaction between the family setting and the work setting is important in understanding how the individual functions at work and what social workers can do to promote better functioning in the workplace and beyond.

Chapter 16, The Globalization of Social Work, focuses on global issues that relate to economic development and social injustice and the many roles that social workers can play in international settings.

What lies ahead for the social work profession and social welfare as they are influenced by future changes at the global level? The "Postscript" to this book offers opportunities to reflect on what you have learned about our social welfare system, the profession of social work, the diversity of our society, and the many challenging issues we face at all levels of our environment.

CHAPTER 7

Poverty, Income Assistance, and Homelessness

EP 2.1.1a
EP 2.1.8a

William and Nancy White, both age 68, have just retired from satisfying jobs. Their three grown children are well established, with their own families. By any standard, the Whites are financially well off. They planned their retirement around their employers' pension plans and social insurance, commonly known as Social Security. Their annual retirement income amounts to nearly $120,000. Along with the income derived from their savings, their retirement income is actually larger than their income during their working years.

Neither William nor Nancy thinks of these benefits or their government health-care benefits (Medicare) as a form of welfare because, in their view, they paid for them through taxes while they were employed. William has been a vocal critic of the Affordable Care Act, landmark national health-care legislation enacted by Congress in 2010, because he and his wife already are covered by a private plan, and both believe that the changes brought about by the legislation hurt them. In their working years, Unemployment Insurance provided the Whites with much-needed cash during brief periods of unemployment. Now Social Security is contributing to their income security. Although they are pleased with their income, both worry about the future of Medicare funding, on which they also are dependent. Their children worry about the future of the Social Security program, but the senior Whites do not.

Audrey Bennett, a 75-year-old widow, is another recipient of social insurance. Her $1,254-a-month Social Security check provides 80% of her income. The remaining amount is from the income she invested from the sale of her house 5 years ago. Now she lives in a pleasant apartment and is covered by Medicare for major illness and hospitalization. She is not covered for the more immediate threat of a long stay in an assisted living facility. Her investment income and Social Security payments would not be sufficient to cover the costs of living in those facilities.

Sophia and Ricardo Maldonado live in a two-bedroom apartment in a rapidly deteriorating part of a large city. Both in their early 30s, they have five children, ranging in age from 2 to 14. Joe works on construction projects and has received three promotions in the past 3 months. Sophia was employed in the housekeeping department at a local hotel when she could find child care for her younger children. When Ricardo's work picked up, she quit working to be a stay-at-home mom. Sophia and Ricardo have a combined annual income of $37,000—just above the federal poverty level for a family of seven. The rent for their two-bedroom house is $575 a month. Money spent for bus fare, utilities, and other necessities often leaves the Maldanados short on cash at the end of the month.

Neither of the Maldanados works at a job that provides health insurance, which means that the family usually goes without medical care when someone is sick. Both grew up in poverty, and both quit school before graduation to earn money to help their parents provide for their brothers and sisters. Although they have a strong value system and are hard workers, only recently is their hard work paying off. Before Ricardo found his construction job, he was unemployed for more than a year when the local economy took a downturn and he was laid off. He and his family had to rely on public benefits (Temporary Assistance for Needy Families [TANF], the Supplemental Nutrition Assistance Program (SNAP, benefits for food purchases, formerly known as food stamps), and Medicaid). However, benefits were extremely limited since Joe is an able-bodied male. To continue to receive the much-needed benefits, Sophia had to show due diligence that she was looking for a job. When she returned to work at the hotel housekeeping job she had held previously, the family's already-meager TANF benefits as well as their food benefits were reduced. In addition, the child care needed for three young children cost more than she was earning. Because of their situation, Sophia and Ricardo were forced to rely on local charities for food and other necessities. In desperation, it was decided that the Maldanado's 14-year-old daughter would drop out of school to care for the younger children since the family could not pay for child care and still make ends meet.

Now that Joe is reemployed in a construction job, things are somewhat better for the Maldanado family. Sophia has received a promotion at her hotel job, and between both jobs the Maldanados are now able to pay for child care for their younger children, which has enabled their daughter to return to school. Neither Ricardo nor Sophia has health insurance, but the children are covered by the state's Children's Health Insurance Program (CHIP). In spite of the precariousness of their economic situation, both Sophia and Ricardo think their income future is the best it has ever been, though they are fearful that if they have another job setback they will lose what they have.

Sophia' sister, Elisa, is not so well off. She is a single mother of three children and has not seen their father since 6 months before her youngest child was born. For a while, with TANF, SNAP, Medicaid, and subsidized public housing, Elisa was better off than Sophia. However, because of recent changes in state and federal eligibility requirements, her cash and food benefits have declined by more than 25% and 15%, respectively, which for a family with limited financial resources represents a significant challenge. Now Elisa hears that her public housing assistance also may be threatened because of recent cuts in that program. She is nearing the 5-year lifetime limit of TANF benefits, unless her caseworker extends her benefits, which is highly unlikely.

Although Elisa wants to work and has dreams of becoming a nurse, she quit school at age 15 to help support her younger siblings. Because of her limited skills, finding a job that allows her to meet her financial needs, including affordable child care, is almost impossible.

From the preceding stories, it seems as if the better off people are, the more that the country's social welfare system helps them. Our social welfare system provides temporary help when income from work is disrupted; however, the system provides a tenuous safety net, as it is structured to encourage quick reentry into the labor force, except for those who are no longer able to work or have left the labor force to retire. The way current welfare reform theory goes, gainful employment is supposed to keep people from a life of poverty and welfare dependence. In practice, it does not always work that way.

In this chapter we look at the poverty debate from colonial times to the present. As a society, we have been uncertain about the relative importance to place on explanations of poverty linked to the person and explanations of poverty linked to the social and economic system. Even when we agree that individual responsibility should be enhanced, we vacillate between a strategy of deterrence and a strategy of compassion. The fundamental purpose of antipoverty programs is at the heart of the debate.

To some people, the primary goal of the social welfare system is to help the truly needy, but in a way that discourages dependency. To other people, the social welfare system should provide real opportunity to all citizens. Ideally, we would like to have a society with a guarantee against poverty but with the caveat that the family must do all it can to help itself.

Views on Poverty and How to Help

EP 2.1.1a
EP 2.1.8a

Before you were born, suppose you were given the following "opportunities":

- You are endowed with a native intelligence (whatever that is) above the normal range.

- Your parents are married, and they love both you and each other.

- At least one of your parents has a marketable job skill and is gainfully employed.

To be born with these three opportunities is to be born with economic advantage. If one, two, or all three of these opportunities is absent, you are at risk of being poor for part or all of your life. Antipoverty programs are designed to compensate for people who do not have these opportunities. In our society, intellectual endowment, family support, and employment opportunities influence most fundamentally our efforts to avoid poverty and also the stigma of being on welfare. In reality, social welfare policy can do little with respect to any of these three variables.

We do not know how much of a person's intellectual endowment is genetic and how much is influenced by the environment. Furthermore, we do not know how much is immutable and how much is changeable. Few people doubt, however, that skills in science, technology, math, and verbal and written communication are the strongest individual antipoverty weapons. Poverty is concentrated among those who lack these skills.

Intellectual endowment by itself, however, is not enough. Having hopes and dreams about the future, coupled with a strong sense of self and an unwavering determination to succeed, are necessary to avoid a life of poverty. All of these characteristics must be nurtured. In our society, nurturing traditionally has been the primary role of the family. If a child from birth to age 18 lives in a family in which the parent(s) enjoy(s) continuous employment that pays enough for food, housing, and other necessities, chances are that the child will not experience poverty at any time in his or her life. Assuming that one is paid at least a living wage, employment seems to be a strong deterrent to poverty at any time during one's life (Troxell, 2010).

Discussions about how to promote factors that are most likely to result in gainful employment, what type of safety net should be available for those who are not gainfully employed, and who should be supported by that net have become increasingly emotional in recent years. Virtually no one is indifferent to poverty in the United States, but very different ideas prevail about how to help the poorest in our society.

The average citizen wants successful and efficient antipoverty programs, even if he or she is against "welfare." Some believe that public social welfare programs should be the responsibility of state governments, and others believe that the federal government should bear this responsibility. Some prefer giving cash to the poor; others want to provide aid as in-kind goods. Still others want to offer service and job training. Most people believe that a proper policy includes some mix of cash, in-kind benefits, service, and training.

Some people want to limit the duration of federal assistance; others disparage that approach. Some are concerned about the increases in nonmarital births. Some prefer a "tough love" approach that would limit assistance to very young single mothers. Others think this idea is out of touch with the *real* causes of poverty, dependency, and the rise in number of births to unmarried women.

Poverty and dependency are linked in the public mind. One thing is clear: resolving the poverty problem in a democratic society requires a healthy respect for those who have distinct and different ideas about how best to conceptualize the problem.

Conceptualizations of Poverty

DiNitto (2010) has defined five different approaches to the conceptualization of poverty in the United States: poverty as deprivation, poverty as inequality, poverty as culture, poverty as exploitation, and poverty as structure.

Poverty as Deprivation   Those who view poverty as deprivation conceptualize poverty as having insufficient food, housing, clothing, medical care, and other items required to sustain a decent standard of living. This definition assumes a standard of living (poverty level) below which individuals and families can be considered "deprived." Each year, the federal government computes the amount of income—**Federal Poverty Income Limit (FPIL)**—required for individuals and families to satisfy their minimum living needs. These figures are published every January in the *Federal Register,* a government document that includes a wide range of information about the legislative and policy-development activities of the federal government.

The 2014 FPIL for the 48 contiguous states and the District of Columbia was $11,670 annually for one person and $23,850 for a family of four (U.S. Department of Health and Human Services, 2014a). Separate figures are given for Alaska and Hawaii because the cost of living in these states is higher than that of the remaining states and the District of Columbia. FPIL figures are adjusted annually to reflect changes in the **Consumer Price Index (CPI)**, which adjusts the prices of goods and services for inflation.

Poverty as Inequality in the Distribution of Income   In this view, some people perceive that they have less income than most Americans (relative deprivation) and believe they are entitled to more. One way to look at poverty as inequality in the United States is to measure the distribution of total personal income across various classes or groups of families.

The most common method of achieving this is to divide American families into five groups, from the lowest one-fifth in personal income to the highest one-fifth. If each fifth of U.S. families were to receive 20% of all family personal income, income equality would be achieved. This is not the case (U.S. Census Bureau, 2013a). Rather, the Census indicates that the poorest fifth of U.S. families received just 3.2% of all family income. Conversely, the wealthiest fifth of U.S. families received nearly 51% of all family income. The top 5% of families received 22.3% of all family income.

Poverty as Culture   In viewing poverty as culture, poverty is seen as a way of life passed on from generation to generation. This conceptualization encompasses more than low income to also include attitudes of hopelessness, indifference, alienation, apathy, lack of incentives, and self-respect. Proponents of this view argue the futility of providing opportunities for upward mobility for the poor, as they would be unlikely to take advantage of them. This view of poverty is perhaps the most controversial—and the position that has generated the most debate among scholars and policymakers.

Poverty as Exploitation by the Ruling Class   In the view of poverty as exploitation, more government assistance is seen as going to the middle and upper classes than to the poor. For example, the middle classes receive government assistance in the form of home mortgage loans and associated tax deductions. The wealthy receive government assistance through various income tax deductions, government contracts, and subsidies to business. Whatever this assistance, the middle class and the wealthy receive more than their poor and near-poor counterparts. If this view of poverty were to prevail, the only way to resolve the issue would be to radically restructure society to eliminate class differences.

Poverty as Structure   Those who view poverty as structure see the continuation of poverty as being fostered by institutional and structural discrimination. For example, poorer school districts typically receive fewer resources than schools in wealthier districts to purchase the latest technologies in support of their educational programs. This results in deepening of what has come to be known as the **digital divide**— the economic and social gaps between those with computer skills and access to technology and those without these skills and access.

Definitions of Poverty

Regardless of how poverty is conceptualized, the definition of poverty is elusive. **Poverty** generally means that household income is inadequate as judged by a specific standard. Translating this concept into practical terms produces ideological debate as well as technical problems. Even defining the term *household* for

a census count is not simple. Is the unit to be composed of only the nuclear family, or do we count elders, boarders, roommates, foster children, and others who share the dwelling? Similarly, *income* is elusive. Should income include gifts or in-kind benefits provided by the employer or the government? What about goods and services traded in barter? What should the time frame be? How do we address wealth as opposed to income? Does choice enter into the notion? Should a Jesuit priest or Carmelite nun be considered poor? After all, they have vowed to be poor.

What should the standard be? As each question is confronted, the challenge of definition becomes more complex. As each question is given a specific answer, the numbers of persons who are considered poor changes. Several methods to define poverty are used today.

The Standard   When the federal government began measuring poverty in the early 1960s, the continued existence of poor people in an affluent society was considered an anomaly. One way to explain this anomaly is to look at the distribution of income and make adjustments in terms of **relative poverty.** By this definition, after adjusting for family size, the lowest one-third, one-fourth, or one-fifth would be considered poor. One problem with this definition is that the proportion of the population of poor would remain constant, regardless of whether the economy were to worsen or improve or antipoverty programs were to help large numbers of individuals improve their standard of living.

Another way to measure poverty is to consider the relative income of the lowest income class. Measured in this way, our progress against poverty is not good. After adjusting for family size, the lowest fifth's share continues to decrease, while the share of income to the richest fifth continues to increase.

A third way—the one used in the United States—is to measure poverty by the number of households with incomes below some fixed official standard. How the fixed standard is determined is one reason that different poverty rates are reported by various sources.

The Market Basket   To counter the problem of standards, public officials use a definition of poverty based on a **market basket concept**. Mollie Orshansky (1965) developed this concept based on some relatively simple calculations. She used a survey that determined the cost of a minimum adequate nutritional diet for families of different sizes. She used another survey to determine that families generally spend one-third of their income on food. Orshansky then multiplied the diet figure for a household of a given size by 3 so a family could purchase the minimum diet and still have twice that amount left over for housing and all other purchases.

Since 1969, poverty thresholds based on this definition have been adjusted by taking into account the changes in the CPI. Poverty guidelines represent a simplification of poverty thresholds.

The federal government uses these for administrative purposes to determine who is eligible for federal poverty programs. The poverty guidelines for various sized families for 2010–2014 are shown in Table 7.1.

The "official" measures of poverty based on Orshansky's model and used by the federal government count income from wages, salaries, and self-employment income plus interest, dividends, and cash grants from the government. The measures do not estimate or consider the value of SNAP benefits, Medicaid, or public housing subsidies. To include these benefits would lower the numbers of those who are considered poor. The poverty line is calculated before taxes are paid or tax credits are calculated. The wealth available to the household is counted for the real interest it produces, not for its purchasing potential. A *household* is defined as a group of individuals who are not necessarily related but share a domicile and share income and responsibilities for those in that domicile.

No economist's line in the sand could account for the real dynamics of family incomes. Nonetheless, this line and the proportion of the population under this line are used in calculating the proportion of the United States that is poor. Regardless of how poverty is measured, the important issues to address are who is poor and why they are poor so antipoverty programs relevant to these groups and their need can be developed.

Who Are America's Poor?

Many factors interact to determine who is poor in the United States. Four factors, however, predominate in affecting poverty

EP 2.1.3a demographics:
EP 2.1.7b

1. the state of the economy,
2. the composition of households and their access to the economic system,
3. the levels of expenditure for social programs, and
4. the types of programs implemented and the effectiveness of those programs.

The first factor significantly influences the others. If the free-market economy cannot provide jobs that keep everyone above the poverty line, certain groups of individuals will be locked out of the opportunity structure that enables them to be self-reliant.

Although the stereotype of a poor family in the United States is an African American single mother on welfare with three or more children living in an

TABLE 7.1 FEDERAL POVERTY GUIDELINES FOR DIFFERING FAMILY SIZES, 2010–2014

SIZE OF FAMILY	2010	2011	2012	2013	2014
1	$10,830	$10,890	$11,170	$11,490	$11,670
2	$14,750	$14,710	$15,130	$15,510	$15,730
3	$18,310	$18,530	$19,090	$19,350	$19,790
4	$22,050	$22,350	$23,050	$23,550	$25,580
5	$25,790	$26,170	$27,010	$27,570	$27,910
6	$29,530	$29,990	$30,970	$31,590	$31,970
7	$33,270	$33,810	$34,930	$35,610	$36,030
8	$37,010	$37,630	$38,890	$39,630	$40,080

NOTE: Figures are for the 48 contiguous states and the District of Columbia. Separate figures are available for Alaska and Hawaii.
SOURCE: U.S. Department of Health and Human Services (2014). *Prior HHS poverty guidelines and Federal Register references.* Washington, DC: Author. Retrieved August 3, 2014, from http://aspe.hhs.gov/poverty/figures-fed-reg.cfm.

inner-city ghetto, the poor actually comprise a diverse group. Most individuals on "welfare" in the United States are children, and many people who are poor live in two-parent families in which one or both parents work full-time, often with a second job. Table 7.1 shows, for example, that a single parent with two children who is employed in a minimum-wage job at $7.25 per hour ($15,080 annually) would be living in poverty regardless of gender, ethnicity, or place of residence. See Box 7.1 for a description of one poor person's experience.

Table 7.2 reveals a great deal about who is poor in the United States. According to the latest statistics available from the U.S. Census Bureau (2013b), some 15% of the general population is living in poverty. About 1 in 10 adults 65 years or older lives in poverty. More women than men live in poverty (13.6% vs. 16.3%, respectively). This difference is particularly pronounced for heads of households who are women (11.9% vs. 18.9%, respectively). The poverty rates for blacks (27.2%) and Latinos (25.6%) are more than twice the rate for whites (12.7%).

A similar pattern is revealed when comparing the poverty rate of the nation's children under 18 years of age. Many individuals are surprised to learn that more than one in five children in the United States (21.9%) lives in poverty when the country is portrayed as being so wealthy. When comparing child poverty rates by race, the rates for children who are black or Latino (39.6% and 33.7%, respectively) are more than double the rate for their white counterparts (13.9%). The poverty rate for non-naturalized citizens (24.9%) is nearly twice that for native-born individuals (14.3%).

Interestingly, the poverty rate for naturalized citizens (12.4%) is lower than that of native-born persons (14.3%). Poverty rates also vary considerably depending on where one lives. For example, the percentage of people who live in poverty in central cities of large metropolitan areas (19.7%) is nearly double that for persons who live outside such areas (presumably in suburban neighborhoods).

Finally, many people assume that all poor people are on welfare. With increasingly limited access to education and the subsequent inability of those who are not well educated to obtain well-paying jobs, many individuals in the United States who fall below the poverty line work at least one, and often two, full-time jobs. Nearly one in three families in the United

TABLE 7.2 U.S. POVERTY RATES FOR SELECTED POPULATION GROUPS, 2012

POPULATION GROUP	PERCENTAGE (100%) BELOW POVERTY LINE
All persons	15.0
Children under 18 years of age	21.8
Persons 65 years of age or older	9.1
Female householder, no husband present	42.5
Ethnicity (all persons)	
White	12.7
Black	27.2
Latino	25.6
Ethnicity (children under 18)	
White	18.5
Black	37.9
Latino	33.8
Nativity	
Native	14.3
Foreign-born	19.2
Naturalized citizen	12.4
Not a citizen	24.9
Residence	
Inside metropolitan areas, inside central cities	19.7
Inside metropolitan areas, outside central cities	11.2
Outside metropolitan areas	17.7

SOURCE: U.S. Census Bureau (2013b, c). Current Population Survey, 2013 Annual Social and Economic Supplements. Washington, DC: Author.

States can be characterized as "working poor" (i.e., those living at or below 200% of poverty) (U.S. Census Bureau, 2013a, b).

Box 7.1   Jamie's Story

It is 5:30 in the morning and Jamie's alarm clock is beckoning her to get up. She is bone tired from working long hours as a domestic in one of the downtown hotels. She would give anything to sleep a little longer, but that is not in the cards. She has to get up, get dressed, get her two-year-old daughter up, and then dress and feed her and drop her off at her mother's house before going to work. It takes nearly an hour to get to her mother's house by bus (sometimes longer if there is a traffic accident or the weather is bad) and then take another bus downtown to her job. Jamie has to retrace these steps at the end of the workday, and sometimes she and her daughter do not get back to her cramped one-bedroom apartment in a deteriorating part of town until 7:00 o'clock in the evening. She feels badly that she has to rely on her mother to provide child care for her daughter, but her only other choice is to leave her daughter with a neighbor or a friend, which she is hesitant to do because of the horror stories she has heard about such arrangements.

Jamie worries that the local child protective services agency will take her daughter away if she places her with a neighbor or friend because of the potential of her daughter being in harm's way. To make matters worse, Jamie must stay at home when her daughter is sick, as her mother has health problems of her own that prevent her from being around a sick child. Jamie risks losing her job every time she has to stay at home to care for her sick daughter, as jobs for which she qualifies are limited and others are eager to replace her.

To make ends meet, Jamie holds down a second job on the weekends at a nearby convenience store where she works as a clerk. She relies on her boyfriend to care for her daughter on those days, but she recently has become worried about her daughter's safety because he threatened to harm the child when he and Jamie argued last weekend about the fact that she is always too busy and too tired to spend time with him. Jamie loves her daughter, and wants to be a good mother to her. She hopes to move into a supervisory position at the hotel at some point so she can make more money and hopefully not have to work on weekends any more, leaving time to perhaps complete her GED and spend more time with her daughter. She also worries about her daughter, who has become harder to handle when she and Jamie are together because she is not used to her mother's rules and ways of doing things. Jamie worries about how she will manage if her mother's health continues to deteriorate or if she and her boyfriend break up.

Jamie is 19 years old. She dropped out of school soon after learning that she was pregnant. She would like to finish school through a credit recovery program, or if that is not possible, obtain a high school equivalency diploma, so she can study at the local community college to become a vocational nurse. The father of her child is chronically unemployed and lives in another state. She has not heard from him since their baby was born. He does not provide any financial or other support for his daughter, and the likelihood of his doing so in the future is slim to none.

The stress that Jamie experiences on a daily basis often results in her becoming overwhelmed and wanting to give up on improving her life and that of her daughter. Jamie has been diagnosed with depression and anxiety disorder. However, she does not take the medication the doctor prescribed because she has heard that it will make her sleepy and that would jeopardize the jobs that she currently holds.

Jamie's story is typical of thousands of young people across the United States forced to work in low-paying, dead-end jobs, with few (if any) benefits and little promise for advancement. Such individuals are destined to a life of poverty or near-poverty, with limited chances for improving their situation. The opportunity structure in the U.S. is not designed to meet the needs of individuals such as Jamie, and the prevailing social values of the country hold out little chance for that to change.

Although significant sums have been spent on anti-poverty programs in the United States, these expenditures have not been targeted at specific groups of the poor and increasingly are meeting only a small fraction of the total need. Therefore, the number of poor people in this country has continued to rise, particularly for vulnerable populations such as people of color and female-headed households with children. Tracing how the needs of the poor have been addressed historically will help us see how we have arrived at the current provision of services and why these services are not working.

Welfare Reform—An End to Welfare as We Knew It

EP 2.1.3
EP 2.1.8a

Structures and systems of aid for the needy are derived from the dominant social values of the historical period in which they are formulated. Prevailing social values have a significant impact on the attitudes toward, and delivery of, economic assistance to the poor. Chapter 1 provides a detailed discussion of the history of assistance to the needy in the United States. As pointed out there, decisions about who should receive assistance, the type and amount of assistance to be provided, and the mechanism for providing that assistance are all affected by dominant social values of the time.

Relevant Legislation

The Social Security Act of 1935 established a "right to welfare" (entitlement) under conditions established by federal law. That act instituted the Aid to Dependent Children program, later retitled **Aid to Families with Dependent Children (AFDC)**. This program—a broader version of mothers' pension programs established earlier for war widows—was intended to support children of single, and most often widowed, mothers.

The Personal Responsibility and Work Opportunity Reconciliation Act (Public Law 104–93, also known as PRWORA), signed into law by President Bill Clinton in 1996, is considered to be the most significant social welfare legislation since the Social Security Act. This law ended the AFDC entitlement program and featured deep cuts in basic programs for low-income children, families, the elderly, and persons with disabilities, as well as fundamental structural changes in the AFDC program.

The act converted the AFDC program to **Temporary Assistance to Needy Families (TANF)**, a block grant program. Under this arrangement, states received a fixed level of resources for income support and work programs based on what they spent on these programs in 1994, without regard to subsequent changes in the level of need in the state. Ironically, by using 1994 as the base funding year for the TANF grant, the federal government actually created the opportunity for large state surpluses in unexpended TANF block grant funds, as welfare rolls were substantially higher in 1994 than they were in 1996 and subsequent years. These unexpended funds found their way into state (general revenue) "rainy day" fund accounts where they were often used for purposes only tangential to those established by the TANF legislation.

The Personal Responsibility Act of 1996 also created supplemental grants for 17 states with high population growth or low block grant allocations relative to their needy population. Congress continued these supplemental grants each year until 2011, when it only partially funded them; in 2012 Congress provided no supplemental grant funding. In 2009, Congress created a temporary Emergency Fund to assist states that face increases in caseloads or certain program costs during the economic downturn. Congress appropriated $5 billion to the Emergency Fund for 2009 and 2010, which states fully used by the time the fund expired in September 2010.

The 1996 TANF legislation also allowed states to withdraw or divert substantial amounts of state resources from basic income support and work programs for poor families with children from federal TANF block grant funds to other uses (a process called "supplementation") without affecting the level of federal block grant funds they receive. For example, in one large southwestern state, nearly 25% of the state's child protective services program is funded through TANF block grant dollars.

This legislation also allows states to deny aid to any poor family or category of poor families. In addition, with some exceptions, the legislation prohibits states from using block grant funding to provide aid to families that have received assistance for more than 5 years (the so-called federal lifetime limit), with a 20% "hardship" exemption (20% of the state's clients can be exempted from the lifetime limit if they live in economically depressed areas where opportunities for employment are minimal or nonexistent). The act also included an almost 20% reduction in SNAP program expenditures. These reductions affect all SNAP recipients, including the working poor, the elderly, and people with disabilities (Urban Institute, 2006a).

The legislation includes a particularly harsh SNAP provision that affects poor, unemployed individuals between the ages of 18 and 50 who are not raising children. Under the act, these individuals are generally limited to 3 months of SNAP benefits while being unemployed in any 3-year period. Many of these individuals qualify for no government benefits other than food benefits, leaving them with an extremely limited safety net.

The legislation made most poor legal immigrants ineligible for almost all forms of assistance. Of the net savings in the act, 40% was achieved by denying a wide range of benefits to immigrants, including poor immigrant children and poor immigrants who are very old or who have incurred disabilities after entering the United States and are no longer able to work. Immigrants in the United States illegally already were ineligible for most major means-tested entitlement benefits at the time the law was passed.

Many states, in anticipation of the federal **welfare reform** legislation, applied for and were granted "welfare waivers" that allowed them to implement their own, and often more punitive, version of welfare reform. These waivers, which typically have a 5-year life cycle, allowed states even more flexibility in using federal funds for welfare reform.

Revisions to the Law

Some of the initial provisions of the federal welfare reform law have been relaxed, as the provisions were recognized as actually creating the reverse of the intended effect. For example, in 1998, as part of reenactment of the federal food stamp legislation, SNAP benefits were restored to the elderly, people with disabilities, and children of legal immigrants. Although welfare caseloads throughout the country have dropped dramatically since Public Law 104-93 was enacted, the decrease in the percentage of people who are poor has lagged far behind those declines.

Over time, the country's primary public assistance program has shifted from concern with cash benefits (1935–1961), to providing a number of services to those who wanted help to become self-sufficient (1962–1981), to requiring behavioral changes as a condition of future assistance (1982–present). An examination of state welfare reform initiatives reveals that states with the greatest decline in caseload also have implemented the most aggressive or punitive welfare reform initiatives. One can't help but wonder about the fate of all the women, children, and families who once populated the U.S. welfare caseload.

Without question, the "work first" (emphasis on clients taking any job, regardless of wages and benefits) initiatives throughout the country have resulted in many clients becoming employed. With some notable exceptions, however, most of these clients have been able to find jobs that pay at best the minimum wage ($7.25 per hour or $15,080 per year), with little opportunity for advancement, and well below the living wage needed to get off government benefits. These jobs typically do not include employee benefits,

particularly benefits related to health care. These jobs also are less likely to have flexible work arrangements that support the child care needs of former recipients (e.g., schedules that include evening and weekend work, and schedules that allow for time off when children are sick or need heath checkups or for parent–teacher conferences).

Welfare reform initiatives have drastically reduced the welfare rolls in the United States, but to consider this a victory would be shortsighted. While some of the families that left the TANF rolls went to work, many others left because they were terminated since they exceeded the 5-year lifetime limit or were sanctioned for failing to comply with program requirements. Research has shown that these families often have barriers to employment that impede their ability to meet state expectations (e.g., mental and physical impairments, substance use, interpersonal violence, low literacy or skill levels, learning disabilities, having a child with a disability, or problems with housing, child care, or transportation). Many such families have become disconnected from both work and welfare, leaving them with neither a reliable safety net nor assistance that adequately addresses their employment barriers (Center on Budget and Policy Priorities, 2012, p. 6).

The PRWORA was scheduled for reauthorization a third time in 2010; however, Congress turned its attention to other domestic priorities such as health-care reform and a flagging economy, and the reauthorization never took place. Instead, the act has been renewed annually through a series of continuing resolutions, the latest expiration for which is September 30, 2014, enabling the legislation to remain in effect. As of the time of this writing, it appears that the legislation will be extended yet again, as Congress seems to be in no hurry to enact TANF reauthorization in the current congressional session.

Advocates for the poor argue that the overarching goals of reauthorization of the 1996 welfare reform legislation (as amended) should be to alleviate poverty and prevent material hardship among children and families and to create effective pathways to economic opportunity (CLASP, 2013). Although many advocates for the poor agree that the previous welfare system created dependency for many recipients, they also believe that the 1996 legislation, as amended, will not reduce poverty in the long term because, like previous efforts, it fails to come to grips with the root causes of poverty (Abramsky, 2013; Corbet & Fikkert, 2014; Edelman, 2013; Iceland, 2013; Katz, 2013).

In contrast, welfare reform advocates argue that local resources such as faith-based organizations, food banks, voluntary agencies, and the like should take up the slack in addressing the unmet needs of former welfare recipients. This private or voluntary infrastructure, however, may not be robust enough to accomplish the job. As a result, increasing numbers of former welfare recipients are becoming mired more deeply in poverty (Abramsky, 2013; Collins & Mayer, 2010; Iceland, 2013; Morgan & Weigt, 2009).

Although the White House and Congress herald their accomplishments in "ending welfare as we knew it," welfare rolls would not have decreased as significantly without the strong economy of the late 1990s. Employment rates improved significantly among single mothers in TANF's early years; however, they started declining in the early 2000s and have continued to decline ever since. The share of never-married mothers with a high school education or less who were employed jumped from 51% in 1992 to a high of 76% in 2000, but by 2011, it had fallen back to 54%, the same level as in 1997 (Center on Budget and Policy Priorities, 2012). The rush to dismantle America's public welfare infrastructure marks the disappearance of a safety net for those who need temporary assistance in difficult times (Abramsky, 2013; Iceland, 2013).

Current Strategies for Addressing Poverty

Current strategies for addressing poverty include a strong market and family system, social insurance programs (Social Security), public assistance programs, and in-kind benefits and tax credits, among others.

EP 2.1.1a
EP 2.1.8a
EP 2.1.8b

A Strong Market and Family System

The first defense against poverty is a market and family system structured to provide full employment at wages sufficient to bring workers and their families out of poverty. Within the family, work and child care are to be integrated in a way that children are cared for and jobs are done.

It is increasingly difficult for families to earn enough to pay for housing, food, and other necessities needed to maintain a decent standard of living. Even though regulations require workplaces to pay a minimum wage, this amount in many geographic areas falls far short of a **living wage**, defined as three times the amount of money needed in a given location for fair market rent, established by the U.S. Department of Housing and Urban Development (Universal Living Wage Campaign, 2014). Affordable housing has become increasingly difficult to obtain in the United States, and costs for child care, health care, and other basic necessities have become a luxury for many families.

Social Insurance Programs

The second line of defense against poverty is a social insurance system that provides retirement income to supplement private pensions and savings of the elderly and persons with disabilities and their survivors. The social insurance system is structured to provide income security for all income classes, not just the poor. The most extensive social insurance program in the United States is **Old Age and Survivors Disability Insurance (OASDI)**, commonly referred to as **Social Security**. This program operates much like a private insurance program; employees and their employers contribute funding to federally operated trust funds. When retirement, disability, or death ends continuous employment, members or their dependents draw income from the trust funds. Greater numbers of senior citizens and higher costs of living have raised questions about whether Social Security trust funds will be able to continue to provide adequately for those who are now paying into the system when they need to draw income from the funds. In addition, because Social Security provides a fixed income that is limited, even though there are provisions for periodic cost-of-living increases, many retired persons cannot afford to live on just this income, particularly because increased costs of housing and health care are not covered by Medicare, the health-care program for the elderly.

Another type of social insurance is **unemployment compensation**, a program that operates much like OASDI. The federal government requires employers to contribute to state-operated unemployment trust funds. These monies are used to provide assistance to employees who have been laid off involuntarily. Unemployment compensation has some problems: Benefits are not paid to persons who are fired, and employers sometimes fire rather than lay off employees so they will not qualify for benefits. Other employees do not meet guidelines to qualify or they live in economically depressed areas and are unable to locate other jobs before the benefit time period runs out.

Workers' compensation, another type of social insurance program, provides medical assistance and cash benefits to employees who are injured on the job and those who develop job-related illnesses. This program is not mandatory in all states, nor are all employers required to participate, although most employers do provide some sort of workers' compensation program.

Public Assistance Programs

The third line of defense against poverty is a system of public assistance to those whose family system has fallen apart and to those who have limited or no income from wages. Simply put, these people do not have enough money to maintain an adequate standard of living. They are helped by cash assistance programs (cash grants determined by category of need) such as Temporary Assistance for Needy Families (TANF), general assistance, and Supplemental Security Income (SSI).

These benefits are funded from general tax revenues (local, state, and federal) and are provided on the basis of applicants' ability to prove need and their eligibility for assistance. The benefit amount is not enough to bring a person above the poverty line, only up to a standard that is established for the specific benefit program and the level of funds that a state is willing to put up to match federal funds for this purpose.

The real purchasing power of government cash assistance benefits has declined over the years because of inflation. Although TANF allocations vary by state, the average monthly amount of assistance for TANF recipient families across the United States in FY 2010 was $392. Monthly cash payments to TANF families averaged $327 for one child, $412 for two children, $497 for three children, and $594 for four or more children. Some TANF families who were not employed received other forms of assistance such as child care, transportation, and other supportive services to help them locate jobs. The majority of TANF recipients also received SNAP benefits, which averaged $378 per family, and 97% also received medical assistance (Office of Family Assistance, 2012). Since the majority of TANF recipients report TANF and SNAP as their only sources of funding, this means that on average, a family with one child has an average monthly income of $705; a family with two children, of $790; a family with three children, of $875; and a family with four or more children, of $972.

Many individuals living in poverty receive SNAP benefits that allow them to purchase food items. Almost 50% of SNAP households in 2010 included children, 16% were 60 and older, 20% were younger than 60 but had a disability; and 24% were individuals younger than 60 with no children or disability, either unemployed and looking for jobs or employed with a limited income. Only 8% of these households were also receiving TANF (Congressional Budget Office, 2012). The average SNAP grant per household was $287, or $4.30 per person per day (see Table 7.3).

General assistance is a state and local public assistance initiative. No federal funds are used to support general assistance programs. This aid may be furnished to needy people and to those with disabilities who are ineligible for federal categorical programs. Eligibility criteria and benefit levels vary by state and often within states. Payments generally are limited and for a short duration. Benefits range from cash payments to groceries and shelter.

As part of the Social Security Act, federal–state programs were enacted for old-age assistance and aid to the blind. Aid to individuals with permanent and total disabilities was added in 1950. In 1974, the means-tested, federally administered **Supplemental Security Income (SSI)** replaced these state-administered programs. SSI provides minimum national monthly cash payments indexed to the CPI with uniform, nationwide eligibility requirements to needy persons who are aged, blind, or disabled. People with disabilities have become the primary recipients of SSI, viewed as the "deserving poor." In June 2014, disability benefits totaling $56 billion were paid to 8.4 million eligible recipients. The average monthly SSI benefit paid to these recipients was $535.88 (U.S. Social Security Administration, 2014).

In-Kind Benefits and Tax Credits

The final line of defense against poverty is a complex system of in-kind benefits and tax credits, the most significant of which is the **Earned Income Tax Credit (EITC)** program. From its passage in 1975 until its dramatic expansion in 1996, EITC has grown from a small program to one that provides more Americans with more cash than any other public welfare program. EITC has become the largest public assistance program in the United States (Karger & Stoesz, 2013).

TABLE 7.3 CHARACTERISTICS OF SNAP HOUSEHOLDS, FISCAL YEAR, 2010

HOUSEHOLD—TYPE OF PEOPLE	# OF PARTICI-PATING HOUSEHOLDS (MILLIONS)	PERCENTAGE	AVERAGE GROSS MONTHLY INCOME	AVERAGE MONTHLY SNAP BENEFIT
With children	8.9	49	$923	$419
With people 60 and older	2.9	16	$813	$144
With person disabled under 60	3.6	20	$946	$219
Without children, person disabled, or person 60+	4.3	24	$268	$194
Household—Income				
Earned income	5.5	30	$1,174	$343
Household no earned income	12.9	70	$542	$263
Unearned income	11.1	60	$858	$265
Social security	3.9	21	$948	$164
SSI	3.9	21	$863	$212
TANF	1.5	8	$719	$428
No income	3.6	20	0	$297
All households	18.4	100	$731	$287 (an average of $4.30/person/day)

SOURCE: Congressional Budget Office (2012). *The Supplemental Nutrition Assistance Program*. Washington, DC: Author.

Basically, EITC supplements the income of the working poor that do not exceed the following income requirements:

For tax year 2013, the maximum EITC credit was $6,044 with three or more qualifying children, $5,372 with two qualifying children, $3,250 with one qualifying child, and $487 with no qualifying children. Because it is an earned income tax credit, poor people outside the labor force receive no benefit. The idea is to encourage work and to reduce the regressive impact of the Social Security tax.

Other types of in-kind benefits designed to assist the poor include the **Supplemental Nutrition Assistance Program** (**SNAP**, formerly known as food stamps) subsidized housing, and Medicaid. Administered and funded by the U.S. Department of Agriculture and states, SNAP benefits can only be used for food items, primarily at retail food stores. Diapers, paper products such as toilet tissue, soap and shampoo, light bulbs, and other household necessities cannot be purchased

2013 EARNED INCOME TAX CREDITS (EITCS)

FILING STATUS	NUMBER OF QUALIFYING CHILDREN	AMOUNT
Single	3 or more	$46,227
Married, filing jointly	3 or more	$51,567
Single	2	$43,038
Married, filing jointly	2	$48,378
Single	1	$37,870
Married, filing jointly	1	$43,210
Single	0	$14,340
Married, filing jointly	0	$19,680

SOURCE: *2013 tax year fast facts: Earned income tax credit*. Washington, DC, downloaded July 20, 2014 from http://www.eitc.irs.gov/EITCCentral/FASTFACTgrnlogbo2.pdf.

with SNAP benefits because of the historical connection of the SNAP program to the agricultural industry, which still has a strong influence on the program. Most states have replaced paper food stamps with an online debit card or an offline "smart card" (card with an embedded computer chip). For this reason, the federal food stamp program was renamed the Supplemental Nutrition Assistance Program (SNAP) as part of the Food Conservation and Energy Act of 2008. Other in-kind benefits, including subsidized housing and **Medicaid** (health care for the poor), are discussed elsewhere in this text.

Other forms of in-kind benefits include health-care benefits through the workplace, vouchers given by some employers for child care, and employee retirement plans. Most employers, however, do not offer these benefits to individuals who are employed in lower-level jobs, or they require that the employees share a substantial part of the cost of these benefits, thereby making them inaccessible to a large portion of the nation's working poor.

Other Antipoverty Programs

Five types of programs exist to combat poverty:

1. cash support;
2. direct provision of basic necessities such as food, shelter, and medical care;
3. efforts to help the poor learn new behaviors that will empower them to feel more in control of their own lives;
4. job training and job-searching help; and
5. restructuring of existing institutions to produce a better quality of economic opportunity.

Basic Political Perspectives

EP 2.1.1a
EP 2.1.8a

Considerable efforts have been expended on behalf of the poor over the years. Billions of state and federal dollars have been spent since the Social Security Act was passed to eradicate poverty in the United States and to ameliorate the negative effects of a market (capitalist) economy on those who were unable to reap its benefits.

Gilbert and Terrell (2012) propose two basic political perspectives on American social welfare policy: the individualist perspective and the collectivist perspective. The market economy favors the **individualist perspective**, which holds that individual problems are the result of bad choices, personal dysfunction, and a culture of poverty. In essence, this perspective "blames the victims" for the situation they are in, even though they may have had no choice in the matter, such as when children are born into poverty. The individualist perspective also supports markets with few or no government controls. The primary social policy agenda of the individualist perspective is to minimize government intervention and provide a minimum safety net for the poor.

The alternative to the individualist perspective, the **collectivist perspective**, holds that social problems reflect fundamental socioeconomic circumstances, barriers to access, and lack of opportunity. In a collectivist's view, unregulated markets create dangerous swings in the economy, resulting in widespread business failures and periods of persistent unemployment, expand the ranks of the poor, and produce distortions in the distribution of wealth. The primary social policy agenda of the collectivist perspective is to ensure full opportunity and economic security; the market economy is antithetical to that perspective.

Looking back to the passage of the Social Security Act of 1935, one might ask what went wrong. Given the expenditure of billions of state and federal dollars, why hasn't the problem of poverty been resolved in the United States? Where did all that money go? Why didn't the expenditures have the intended effects?

The question has many possible answers. One is that money itself rarely solves a problem; it must be accompanied by a carefully crafted and well-implemented plan as to how the money will be spent and accounted for. It takes time to solve serious problems that have deep roots and a long history. To help solve the problem, the United States must invest in human capital and pay less attention to the immediate functioning of the marketplace. Although many individuals may be able to survive at some minimum level in a healthy economy, ignoring human capital places those in poverty at considerable risk and also makes it increasingly difficult for the country to successfully compete in a global economy. Society must embrace the notion of social and economic justice, and that belief should be reflected in all of the social welfare programs provided to its citizens (Barusch, 2011; Jimenez & Pasztor, 2014; Reisch, 2013).

The United States has the necessary tools to solve contemporary social welfare problems. There is no "silver bullet" here; on the contrary, the solution is well within our reach if we are willing to embrace diversity, opportunity, and prosperity for all citizens.

The concepts of social justice and economic justice are easy to comprehend but difficult to achieve unless members of society are committed to spreading the wealth and power held by so few. Creating a just world is not about taking something away from one person or group and giving it to another. It is about sharing the wealth of society with *all* members of society rather than a select few.

You might ask yourself how, then, do we reach consensus or agreement on these issues? Most social welfare professionals agree that all five strategies noted earlier have their place in a comprehensive program to combat poverty in the United States. Most also acknowledge that all five strategies can be, and have been, misused, which results in making things worse for the individual, for society, or for both.

The poverty debate in this country is not about the appropriate mix of strategies to address the problem. When all the rhetoric is cast aside, the debate is really about equality of opportunity and sharing the wealth. One thing is painfully clear: despite a long history of efforts to eradicate poverty in this country, poverty is still one of the most significant social problems and is at the core of a host of other social problems in the United States today.

2014 and Beyond

State and federal governments continue to hold the line with regard to the size of public assistance rolls throughout the United States, despite the challenges of an economy that has not fully recovered from the financial downturn that began in 2007. This "success," however, presents a distorted picture of reality. As noted previously, while there was a mass exodus from the welfare rolls in the years following passage of the landmark welfare reform legislation of 1996, many individuals who exited the system did so because they exceeded the 5-year lifetime limit on benefits or were pushed off the rolls because of sanctions incurred for violating program requirements. They work at low-wage, dead-end jobs with little prospects for improving their status in life. Some have given up altogether, barely surviving on the margins of society. One could argue that the groundswell of welfare reform that began with passage of the PRWORA of 1996 and has continued with the political leadership in the country has been negligent in caring for members of society who are unable to cope with the demands of a market economy through no fault of their own. For many of those

in decision-making power in the United States, the population of deserving poor in America is all but extinct. While many social welfare policy advocates argue that the American dream no longer exists even for middle-class individuals and families, for those who are poor, even if they are working, the so-called American dream has turned into a nightmare.

One thing is clear: The latest efforts to reform welfare have swelled the ranks of the American underclass. Karger and Stoesz (2013) define the **underclass** as "the lowest socioeconomic group in society, characterized by chronic poverty; that is, its members are poor regardless of the economic circumstances of the society at large" (p. 519). Thus, these individuals are unable to rise above their situation even if the society in which they live enjoys a sustained level of prosperity.

Consider, for example, the plight of children who live in poverty in the United States. About 16 million children are living at or below the official poverty level. Child poverty is most prevalent among the very young (those under age 6) and among populations at risk, such as African American and Latino youth. About 1 in 10 children living in the United States in 2012 were without health insurance coverage of any kind. Children of color were more likely to be uninsured than their white counterparts (14.3%, 9.1%, and 6.7% for Hispanic, black, and white children, respectively) (Children's Defense Fund, 2014). According to UNICEF (2012) the United States has the second worst record among industrialized nations in reducing the poverty of children.

Researchers agree that the following factors related to poverty have a detrimental effect on children (see, for example, Alderman, 2011; Fieldler & Kuester, 2010; Jones & Sumner, 2011; Maholmes & King, 2012; National Center for Children in Poverty, 2014; Rawlinson, 2011):

- Stress and conflict related to low income can undermine the strength of the family.
- Learning opportunities at home are limited.
- Child care is of lower quality.
- Nutrition is poor.
- Housing is inadequate.
- There is increased homelessness.
- Transportation options are fewer.
- The family is more isolated.
- Elevated levels of stress may interfere with early brain development in some children.

Children who grow up in poverty often have limited opportunities for health care, education, and other programs that promote success in later life, resulting in long-term poverty that persists across generations.

David H. Wells/Historical/Corbis

The myths about people who are poor in the United States continue to drive many of the policy decisions that could have the potential to help the poor move out of poverty. Those whose limited income makes them eligible for food benefits such as SNAP include two parent families with both adults employed full-time, the elderly, those with disabilities, and low ranking members of the military. Most adults who are poor want a better life for themselves and their families. Many are working two and even three jobs to try to achieve the elusive American dream, if not for themselves, for their children. Most adults who are not working want to work. We have yet to achieve the right mix of economic gains, programs, and policies that can improve the quality of life for the many individuals and families struggling to make ends meet.

Homelessness

EP 2.1.1a
EP 2.1.3a
EP 2.1.8a

Increases in the poverty rate in the United States, coupled with marked increases in the costs of housing and the precipitous decline in availability of public assistance benefits, have resulted in large numbers of homeless individuals and families (National Coalition for the Homeless, 2014). Demographic groups that are more likely to experience poverty also are more likely to be homeless. According to the Stewart B. McKinney

Act (42 U.S.C. Section 11301, et seq., 1994), a person who is considered **homeless**

> *lacks a fixed, regular, and adequate night-time residence; and . . . has a primary night-time residency that is: (A) a supervised publicly or privately operated shelter designed to provide temporary living accommodations . . . (B) an institution that provides a temporary residence for individuals intended to be institutionalized, or (C) a public or private place not designed for, or ordinarily used as, a regular sleeping accommodation for human beings.*

This definition does not include any individual imprisoned or otherwise detained because of an act of Congress or a state law.

Homelessness is not a recent phenomenon in the United States (Day & Schiele, 2012; Goetz, 2013; Howard, 2013; Stern & Axinn, 2012; Vale, 2013). During colonial times, individuals who were poor and had nowhere to live were housed in poorhouses (also called "almshouses") and orphanages. The conditions within these institutions were, at best, dismal. Following the tradition of the English Poor Laws of 1601, colonial America had little tolerance for ablebodied men and women who were not gainfully employed (Stern & Axinn, 2012). Thus, the most meager of accommodations were provided for them. This early tradition of treating individuals experiencing homelessness as second-class citizens carried forward through the growth and development of this country to present times.

During the Great Depression, a nationwide census conducted by the National Committee on Care of Transient and Homeless suggested that some 1.2 million persons, about 1% of the country's population, were homeless. (Ironically, this percentage is about the same today.) (Day & Schiele, 2012; Stern & Axinn, 2012) These people were not vagrants and vagabonds, tramps, or thieves but, instead, were responsible members of society who had lost their jobs and their homes as a result of economic chaos in the country.

The classic stereotype of the homeless individual in America is a white male alcoholic who has lost his job and his family to his addiction and is forced to live on the streets. Another stereotype is that experiencing homelessness people have chosen homelessness as a lifestyle and have an aversion to working and following the rules of society. Although some among the homeless might fit these stereotypes, for the most part they have been forced to live on the streets because of a wide array of problems and issues, many of which are not of their doing or are beyond their control.

Composition of the Homeless Population

The homeless population is composed of a broad cross section of society including youth, elderly people, families with children, survivors of interpersonal violence, veterans, people with mental illness, those with addiction disorders, the unemployed and underemployed, individuals in ill health (including those with HIV/AIDS), and people living in rural areas. Compounding the situation, isolation tends to accompany homelessness.

Youth   Youth experiencing homelessness (sometimes referred to as "unaccompanied minors" or "unaccompanied youth") are individuals under the age of 18 who lack parental, foster, or institutional care. The homeless youth population has been estimated at between 500,000 and 1.3 million young people each year (National Coalition for the Homeless, 2014). According to the National Coalition for the Homeless (2014), unaccompanied minors comprise some 1% of the urban homeless population.

Causes of homelessness in youth fall into three interrelated categories: family problems, economic problems, and residential instability (National Coalition for the Homeless, 2014). Many experiencing homelessness youth leave home after years of physical and sexual abuse, strained relationships, addiction of a family member, and parental neglect. Disruptive family conditions (their parents told

them to leave or knew they were leaving and did not care) represent the main reasons for young people leaving home (U.S. Conference of Mayors, 2013).

Some youth become homeless when their families experience financial crises resulting from lack of affordable housing, limited employment opportunities, insufficient wages, no medical insurance, or inadequate welfare benefits. These youth become homeless as part of their families but later are separated from them by shelter, transitional housing, or child welfare policies.

Residential instability also contributes to homelessness among youth. A history of foster care has been shown to be correlated with becoming homeless at an earlier age and remaining homeless for a longer time. Some youth living in residential or institutional placements become homeless upon discharge (National Coalition for the Homeless, 2014; Zlotnick, 2014). Youth experiencing homelessness face many challenges on the streets. Because of their age, they have few legal means by which to earn enough money to meet their basic needs. Adolescents experiencing homelessness often suffer from severe anxiety and depression, poor health and nutrition, and low self-esteem. They face difficulties attending school because of legal guardianship requirements, residency requirements, lack of proper records, and lack of transportation.

Elderly   About 30% of persons experiencing homelessness are older than 45 years of age. While the proportion of older persons in the homeless population has declined over the past two decades, their absolute number has grown (National Coalition for the Homeless, 2014).

Increased homelessness among the elderly is largely the result of the declining availability of affordable housing and poverty in certain segments of the elderly population (Joint Center for Housing Studies, 2014; National Low Income Housing Coalition, 2012). Although people 65 years of age or older have a lower poverty rate than the general population (about 9%, as compared with 15% for all people), they are more likely than the nonelderly to have incomes just above the poverty-level threshold (U.S. Census Bureau, 2013b). With less income for other necessities such as food, medicine, and health care, the elderly population is particularly vulnerable to homelessness (National Coalition for the Homeless, 2014; National Low Income Housing Coalition, 2012). In addition, overall economic growth will not alleviate the income and housing needs of elderly poor people, as they are unlikely to continue or return to work or to gain income through marriage.

Once on the street, elderly persons experiencing homelessness often have difficulty getting around and, distrusting the crowds at shelters and clinics, they are more likely to sleep on the streets. Some studies indicate that elderly persons experiencing homelessness are prone to victimization and more likely to be ignored by law enforcement. Elderly people experiencing homelessness also are more likely than other people to have a variety of health problems, including chronic disease, functional disabilities, and high blood pressure (National Low Income Housing Coalition, 2012).

To prevent older Americans from becoming homeless, they must be able to sustain independent living through access to low-income housing, income supports, and health-care services. For those who have lost their homes already, comprehensive outreach health and social services must be made available, as well as special assistance to access existing public assistance programs (National Coalition for the Homeless, 2014; National Low Income Housing Coalition, 2012).

Families with Children   Families with children represent the fastest-growing segment of the homeless population; nearly 25% of people who become homeless today represent this group (National Coalition for the Homeless, 2014). Families, single mothers, and children constitute the largest group of people who

are homeless in rural areas (Duncan & Blackwell, 2014; Housing Assistance Council, 2012).

Stagnating wages and changes in welfare programs account for increasing poverty in families (National Low Income Housing Coalition, 2012). Housing rarely is affordable for families leaving welfare for low wages, yet subsidized housing is so limited that fewer than one in four TANF families nationwide lives in public housing or receives a housing voucher to help rent a private unit (National Coalition for the Homeless, 2014).

According to the National Low Income Housing Coalition (2012), some 80% of American renter families live in counties where a two-bedroom apartment at the Fair Market Rent is unaffordable to a family with two full-time minimum-wage earners. In 2012, the *housing wage*—the hourly wage necessary to pay the Fair Market Rent for a two-bedroom home while spending no more than 30% of income on housing costs—was $25 nationally, equivalent to an annual income of $52,000 (National Low Income Housing Coalition, 2012).

For most families leaving the welfare rolls, housing subsidies are not an option (Homelessness Research Institute, 2014; National Alliance to End Homelessness, 2014). Extensive waiting lists for public housing mean that families must remain in shelters or inadequate housing arrangements longer. Families experiencing homelessness that live in shelters are not allowed to

Families experiencing homelessness represent the fastest-growing segment of the homeless population. Here a mother and her daughter, both homeless, share time together.

live there indefinitely. Living with friends or family members is almost always short-lived as well. Thus, many families experiencing homelessness are forced to live in abandoned buildings or in their cars, and when that fails, they have no choice but to live on the streets.

Homelessness impacts the health and well-being of all family members, particularly children. Compared to housed poor children, children experiencing homelessness have worse health; more developmental delays; more anxiety, depression, and behavioral problems; and lower educational achievement. Moreover, many children experiencing homelessness do not receive their proper immunizations, and they have asthma and middle-ear infections at rates much higher than the national average (National Coalition for the Homeless, 2014).

Persons of Color

The homeless population is made up of about 45% African Americans, 35% Caucasians, 12% Latinos, 5% Native Americans, and 3% Asians (National Law Center on Homelessness and Poverty, 2014). Those experiencing homelessness in rural areas are more likely to be white, and homelessness among Native Americans and migrant workers is largely a rural phenomenon (National Coalition for the Homeless, 2014). Oppression and subsequent lack of access to quality education, good jobs, and other opportunities account for the large numbers of people of color living in poverty, compounded by the lack of networks, both formal and informal, that can help provide affordable housing.

Survivors of Interpersonal Violence

The homeless population in the United States includes survivors of interpersonal violence (National Coalition for the Homeless, 2014; National Law Center on Homelessness and Poverty, 2014; National Network to End Domestic Violence, 2013). Of the cities surveyed by the U.S. Conference of Mayors (2013), 16% of respondents identified domestic or interpersonal violence as a cause of family homelessness. National Alliance to End Homelessness (2014) reported that survivors of interpersonal violence make up about 12% of homeless population. There is no accurate way to estimate the number of individuals whose homelessness can be directly tied to their escape from a violent partner. A substantial number of welfare recipients have been subjected to violence from a current or former partner (Davies & Lyon, 2013).

When a woman leaves an abusive relationship, she often has no place to go. Lack of affordable housing and long waiting lists for assisted housing force many women to choose between abuse and homelessness. Shelters provide immediate safety to survivors of interpersonal violence and their children and help them gain control over their lives. The provision of safe emergency shelter, therefore, is a necessary first step in meeting the needs of women who are fleeing interpersonal violence (Davies & Lyon, 2013).

Veterans

It has been estimated that nearly 60,000 veterans are homeless on any given night. Over 1 million veterans are considered at risk of homelessness because of poverty, lack of support networks, and dismal living conditions in overcrowded or substandard housing (National Coalition for Homeless Veterans, 2014). The National Coalition for Homeless Veterans (2014) indicates that:

- most homeless veterans are single males (only 8% are female) from poor, disadvantaged communities;
- nearly half suffer from some type of mental illness;
- and 47% served in the Vietnam War;
- nearly two-thirds served in the military for at least 3 years; and
- a third of veterans experiencing homelessness were stationed in a war zone.

A large number of displaced veterans or veterans at risk of homelessness live with the lingering effects of posttraumatic stress disorder (PTSD) and substance use, both of which are exacerbated by a lack of family and social support. It is estimated that upward of 28% of veterans returning from Operation Iraqi Freedom and Operation Enduring Freedom are likely to suffer from a mental health disorder such as PTSD and/or severe depression (Brookshire & Tecoanta, 2011; Hoge, 2010; McLay, 2012; Moore & Penk, 2012). The existing mental health services system does not have the resources needed to address the needs of this burgeoning population, placing a substantial portion of these individuals at risk of homelessness.

The U.S. Department of Veterans Affairs administers two special programs for veterans experiencing homelessness: the Domiciliary Care for Homeless Veterans program and the Health Care for Homeless Veterans program. Both provide outreach, psychosocial assessments, referrals, residential treatment, and follow-up case management to veterans experiencing homelessness. The U.S. Department of Veterans Affairs has initiated several programs for veterans experiencing homelessness and has expanded partnerships with public, private, and nonprofit organizations to increase the range of services for this group (National Coalition for the Homeless, 2014).

People with Mental Illness One-third of the homeless population has an untreated mental illness (Mental Illness Policy Org, 2014). Their diagnoses include severe, chronic depression; bipolar disorder; schizoaffective disorders; and severe personality disorder (National Resource and Training Center on Homelessness and Mental Illness [NRTCHM], 2014). Although many people become homeless because their mental illness impairs their ability to function, some individuals experience severe emotional problems *after* becoming homeless (see Chapter 8).

People with serious mental illness have more difficulty than other people in exiting homelessness. They are homeless more frequently and for longer than other homeless subgroups. Many have been on the streets for years (NRTCHM, 2014). Almost half of those experiencing homelessness with severe mental illness have both mental health disorders and substance use disorders. Their symptoms often are active and untreated, making it difficult for them to negotiate basic needs for food, shelter, and safety. Many are not receiving benefits for which they may be eligible (NRTCHM, 2014).

The majority of individuals experiencing homelessness with severe mental illness have had prior contact with the mental health system. They may have been hospitalized involuntarily or received treatment and medications of little or no benefit to them. The symptoms exhibited by persons experiencing homelessness with severe mental illness, often accompanied by poor hygiene, tend to result in many untreated physical health problems such as respiratory infections, dermatologic problems, as well as risk of exposure to HIV and tuberculosis (see Box 7.2).

Box 7.2 Street Crazy—America's Mental Health Tragedy

The bus doors whooshed open, and the driver finally spoke. 'Ask for Big John,' he said, without turning. 'And God help you.'

I don't recall thanking him because the instant I stepped off the bus I was surrounded. 'Spare change?' said a man with a 'ZZ Top' beard and shoulder-to-shoulder tattoos, gruffly thrusting a hand toward me.

'Nice shirt,' an even stragglier fellow lisped, fingering the cloth of my left sleeve. He had no teeth.

'Got money for food?' demanded a third person, reeking of gin. He was swaying two inches from my face.

It was time to scream and run. Turning to hail the bus, its exhaust trail was just fading around the corner. Certain the three men were going to stab me, I almost wet my pants. Then, like Daniel in the lion's den, I was saved. The front doors of the mission exploded open and Goliath himself stood in the maw. 'Dinner!' he shouted, and with that, my tormentors were gone, scrambling to join an instantly assembled line of people forming at the entrance.

They came from alleyways, behind dumpsters, and out of rusting, tireless cars slumped at the curb. They sprang, it seemed, from the very refuse that lay rotting in the gutter. Watching this, I was filled with the strangest sense of nauseating familiarity. There were men in that queue so filthy their skin was no longer visible and women so rank with accumulated secretions even the dirt-stained men turned away. Children were gaunt from malnutrition. Nearly everyone had open sores, poorly healed fractures or caked blood. I could see the lice and vermin. They were a symphony of coughs and wheezes" (Saeger, 2000, p. 87).

So went the first (and possibly the last) visit by Dr. Stephen Saeger to the Safe Haven Rescue Mission located in the skid row area of downtown Los Angeles. Saeger was looking for someone who could tell him about the next of kin of one of his patients, "John Doe," who was found dead, face down in the pool spa at the apartment complex where Saeger and his wife lived.

Saeger spent the first nine years of his medical career as an emergency room physician at a level-one trauma center in a large southwestern city. The defining event that signaled his departure from emergency medical work was the night that the ER team had to resuscitate four shooting victims, all bleeding to death at the same time. There were only three breathing tubes available to use, so one of the victims had to go. The man died quietly, alone.

After considerable soul searching, Saeger decided that he would become a psychiatrist, as this would afford him a quiet respite from the constant chaos of the ER —or so he thought. He applied for and was

(continued)

Box 7.2 Street Crazy—America's Mental Health Tragedy
(continued)

accepted into a psychiatric residency training program at a Southern California county hospital, which he completed four years later. After completing his residency Saeger became employed as a psychiatrist at another large county hospital in Los Angeles, the Benjamin H. Miller Medical Center (referred to on the street as the "Mill"). The Mill is a collection of outpatient clinics, research buildings, and machinery that supplies heating and cooling to the complex. It is also home to numerous cafeterias, laboratories, a helicopter landing pad, waiting rooms, parking lots, and gift shops—overall, it encompassed four city blocks. Saeger had two jobs at the Mill—he was one of the doctors responsible for what happened to patients who were hospitalized and he also ran the psych ER on specified days where he saw people as they came in off the street.

John Doe was a young white male with 84 admissions to the Mill in four years. No one knew much about him. He was found by the police wandering down the 91 freeway covered in excrement and surrounded by flies and other insects. In an agitated state when he was admitted, John Doe was required to be placed in restraints twice—once for threatening to punch the night nurse and the other for calling another patient a "Nazi faggot." He was administered Haldol, one of a powerful group of antipsychotic drugs. He was characterized by the staff as "still crazy but doing better." John Doe suffered from untreated severe chronic schizophrenia.

Many persons who are homeless and mentally ill have severe chronic schizophrenia. As Saeger points out in his book *Street Crazy*, they are usually relegated to a miserable life and an early death. *Street Crazy* is about how the mental health system fails people like John Doe. Saeger asserts that physicians (including psychiatrists) fail to see the connection between mental illness and homelessness because it is not something taught in medical school. He argues further that few judges, lawyers, politicians, and policymakers who deal with persons who are both homeless and mentally ill are conversant with the facts either. Often, the only help that those who are both mentally ill and homeless receive is a three-day emergency stay at a facility like the Mill, where they are cleaned up, detoxified, and fed a few decent meals before being released back into the streets.

What can you do as an aspiring social worker to help address the problems experienced by persons who are both mentally ill and homeless? You can become aware and involved. Many of you have brain-diseased relatives or friends, some of them living on the streets. Inform others about the problem. Provide them literature about the problem and available services. Find ways to use the media to help make everyone aware of the problem. Finally, help make treatment for the chronically brain diseased a national priority.

SOURCE: Saeger, S. (2000). *Street Crazy: America's Mental Health Tragedy*. Redondo Beach, CA: Westcom Press.

People experiencing homelessness typically are citizens of the communities in which they are homeless; however, their social support and family networks usually are nonexistent (family members often have lost regular contact with relatives who are homeless or are no longer equipped to be the primary caregivers). Those who are homeless with severe mental illness are twice as likely as other people who are homeless to be arrested or jailed, primarily for misdemeanor offenses (NRTCHM, 2014).

Addiction Disorders Untreated addictive disorders contribute to homelessness. The onset or exacerbation of an addictive disorder for individuals with below-living-wage incomes and just one step away from homelessness can plunge them into residential instability. Many people experiencing homelessness with addictive disorders desire to overcome their addiction, but the combination of being homeless and a service system that is ill-equipped to respond to these circumstances essentially prevents their access to treatment services and recovery supports.

The prevalence of addiction disorders among adults who are homeless is difficult to determine. The destruction of single-room occupancy housing is a major factor in the growth of homelessness, particularly among people with addiction disorders (National Coalition for the Homeless, 2014).

Unemployed and Underemployed Homeless

Inadequate income and lack of affordable rental housing leave many people homeless (Joint Center for Housing Studies, 2014). The U.S. Conference of Mayors (2014) survey of 25 major U.S. cities found that 20% of the urban homeless population was employed. About 19% of people experiencing homelessness have jobs, yet they are unable to escape homelessness because those with limited skills or experience have difficulty finding jobs that pay a living wage (National Coalition for the Homeless, 2014; U.S. Conference of Mayors, 2014). The declining value of wages as a result of increases in cost of living has put housing out of reach for an ever-growing number of people in society, including those experiencing homelessness. The homeless often are employed in nonstandard jobs (contracting, working for a temporary help agency, day labor, and regular part-time work). These kinds of work arrangements typically offer lower wages, fewer benefits, and less job security (National Coalition for the Homeless, 2014). Individuals experiencing homelessness who do work tend to be underemployed. They may want to work full-time but are able to secure only part-time work (Economic Policy Institute, 2014).

People in Ill Health

Poor health is closely associated with being homeless. The rates of both chronic and acute health problems are extremely high in the homeless population. Conditions requiring regular, uninterrupted treatment, such as tuberculosis, HIV/AIDS, diabetes, hypertension, addictive disorders, and mental disorders, are difficult to treat or control in those who do not have adequate housing (National Coalition for the Homeless, 2014; National Health Care for the Homeless Council [NHCHC], 2011).

Many people experiencing homelessness people have multiple health problems and also are at greater risk of trauma resulting from muggings, beatings, and rapes. Homelessness precludes good nutrition, personal hygiene, and basic first aid. Some people experiencing homelessness with mental disorders use drugs or alcohol to self-medicate, and those with addictive disorders are more at risk of contracting HIV and other communicable diseases.

People who are homeless are overwhelmingly uninsured and often lack access to the most basic health-care services for their health-care needs (NHCHC, 2011). Access to affordable, high-quality, comprehensive health care is essential in the fight to end homelessness. A universal health-care system could reduce the current homeless population as well as prevent future episodes of homelessness. It also could prevent unnecessary deaths on the streets and reduce the fiscal impact and social cost of communicable diseases and other illnesses.

One resource that is available to provide heathcare to the homeless is the Health Care for the Homeless (HCH) program included as part of the Stewart B. McKinney Homeless Assistance Act of 1987 (as amended) and operated by the Health Resources and Services Administration (HRSA), a division of the U.S. Department of Health and Human Services. HCH is a competitive grant program that provides funds for primary health-care and addiction services to people experiencing homelessness. HCH programs are initiated and managed at the community level. Any local public or private nonprofit entity—freestanding nonprofit organizations, community health centers, local health departments, homeless shelters, and homeless coalitions—is eligible to apply for HCH funds.

HRSA currently funds HCH projects in all 50 states, the District of Columbia, and Puerto Rico. In 2009, the latest date for which data were available, HCH projects served approximately 1 million persons experiencing homelessness.

The prevalence of HIV among those experiencing homelessness is between 3% and 20% (National Coalition for the Homeless, 2014). Adolescents experiencing homelessness are particularly vulnerable to contracting HIV because they may find that exchanging sex for food, clothing, and shelter is their only chance for survival on the streets. HIV-infected persons experiencing homlessness are believed to be sicker than their housed counterparts. For example, they tend to have higher rates and more advanced forms of tuberculosis and higher incidences of other opportunistic diseases. People experiencing homelessness with HIV face many barriers to optimal care. Injection-drug use and lack of insurance have been shown to negatively affect utilization of health care, level of medical care, and health status.

Persons experiencing homelessness with HIV/AIDS need safe, affordable housing and supportive, appropriate health care. Those who are about to lose their homes would benefit greatly from emergency housing grants, and those who are already on the streets would welcome housing assistance. The federal government could play a key role by providing adequate funding for targeted housing and health programs for homeless people with health problems.

People in Rural Areas Although homelessness often is assumed to be an urban phenomenon, small towns and rural areas have many individuals experiencing homelessness (Duncan & Blackwell, 2014). Because rural areas have far fewer shelters, those experiencing homelessness in these areas are more likely to live in a car or camper or with relatives in overcrowded or substandard housing. People experiencing homelessness in rural areas are likely to be white, female, married, currently working, homeless for the first time, and homeless for a shorter time. Families, single mothers, and children make up the largest group of people who are homeless in rural areas (Duncan & Blackwell, 2014).

Rural homelessness, like urban homelessness, is the result of poverty and lack of affordable housing. It is most prevalent in regions that are primarily agricultural; regions whose economies are based on declining extractive industries such as mining, timber, and fishing; and regions with economic problems.

Housing costs are lower in rural areas than in urban areas, but so are rural incomes. Homelessness in rural areas is often precipitated by a structural or physical housing problem that jeopardizes safety. When families have to relocate to safer housing, housing is less available, which leads to higher rents. If the rent is often too much to handle, they become homeless again.

Efforts to end rural homelessness are often hampered by isolation, lack of awareness, and insufficient resources. Ending homelessness in rural areas requires jobs that pay a living wage, adequate income supports for those who cannot work, affordable housing, access to health care, and transportation.

People Who Are Isolated People experiencing homelessness increasingly detach from traditional social roles, such as being a family member or an employee. They reaffiliate with new groups of people in the same situation. In doing so, they become more comfortable with this new group because of the shared stigma and discrimination. As time goes on, the homeless become more isolated from others, more entrenched with others experiencing homelessness, and they lose touch with social support systems that might alleviate their situation, such as locating employment or housing.

Policies and Programs That Address Homelessness

EP 2.1.6b
EP 2.1.8b
EP 2.1.9b

In the early 1980s, the initial responses to homelessness were primarily local. In the years that followed, advocates from around the country demanded that the federal government acknowledge homelessness as a national problem requiring a national response.

The Stewart B. McKinney Homeless Assistance Act In late 1986, legislation containing emergency relief provisions for shelter, food, mobile health care, and transitional housing for persons experiencing homelessness was introduced as the Urgent Relief for the Homeless Act. After the death of its chief sponsor, Representative Stewart B. McKinney of Connecticut, the act was renamed the Stewart B. McKinney–Vento Homeless Assistance Act and was signed into law by President Ronald Reagan in 1987.

The McKinney Act originally consisted of 15 programs that provided a range of services to people experiencing homelessness, including emergency shelter, transitional housing, job training, primary health care, education, and some permanent housing. Since then, the act has been amended several times, and, for the most part, these amendments have expanded the scope and strengthened the provisions of the original legislation.

Federal funding for programs designed to prevent and end homelessness in America has fluctuated dramatically since passage of the landmark McKinney Act. However, the federal government adopted a strategic plan ("Opening Doors") in 2010 to prevent and end homelessness that promises to change the federal response to homelessness across the country (United States Interagency Council on Homelessness, 2014). President Obama's FY 2015 budget of nearly $5.7 billion for homeless programs focused on the strategic targeting of resources aimed at effective implementation focused on evidence-based solutions and demonstrable outcomes (U.S. Interagency Council on Homelessness, 2014, p. 1). Current federally funded programs designed to prevent and end homelessness are shown in Table 7.4.

There is no question that we have come a long way in addressing the problem of homelessness in America, but only by addressing the **root causes** of homelessness—lack of jobs that pay a living wage, inadequate benefits for those who cannot work, lack of affordable housing, and lack of access to health care—will homelessness be ended.

Besides affordable housing, individuals and families experiencing homelessness need increased employment, education, and job-training opportunities, allowing them to accumulate assets; comprehensive physical and mental health services and treatment

TABLE 7.4 FEDERAL PROGRAMS DESIGNED TO PREVENT AND END HOMELESSNESS IN AMERICA	
DEPARTMENT	PROGRAMS COVERED
Health and Human Services	*Health Care for the Homeless*—Provides primary health care, substance use treatment, emergency care with referrals to hospitals for in-patient care services and/or other needed services, outreach services to assist difficult-to-reach people experiencing homelessness in accessing care, and assistance in establishing eligibility for entitlement programs and housing. *Projects for Assistance in Transition from Homelessness*—Provides financial assistance to states to support services for individuals who are experiencing homelessness and who have serious mental illness or co-occurring mental illness and substance abuse disorders. *Grants for the Benefit of Homeless Individuals*—Enables communities to expand and strengthen treatment services for individuals experiencing homelessness with substance use disorders, mental illness, or co-occurring substance use disorders and mental illness. *Services in Supportive Housing Grants*—Addresses the need for treatment and support service provision to individuals and families experiencing homelessness while living with severe mental illness or co-occurring mental and substance disorders. *Runaway and Homeless Youth Act*—Funds more than 740 public, community, and faith-based organizations through three grant programs that serve the runaway and homeless youth population.
Housing and Urban Development	*Continuum of Care (CoC) Program*—Funds evidence-based programs and approaches like permanent supportive housing, rapid re-housing, and Housing First; provides the infrastructure for the implementation of a comprehensive planning approach, data collection and analysis, and performance measurement. *Emergency Solutions Grant (ESG) Program*—Funds a variety of life-saving activities in addition to newer interventions that have proven successful in many communities at preventing and ending homelessness. *Emergency Food and Shelter Program*—Allocates funds for the provision of food, shelter as well as homelessness prevention through the administration of rent, utilities, and mortgage assistance.
Education	Provides assistance to states to establish or designate an Office of Coordinator of Education of Homeless Children and Youths, develop and carry out a state plan for the education of children who are homeless, and make sub-grants to local educational agencies to support the education of children experiencing homelessness.
Justice	*Transitional Housing Assistance Grants for the Victims of Sexual Assault, Domestic Violence, Dating Violence, and/or Stalking Program*—Funds support programs that provide assistance to survivors of sexual assault, domestic violence, dating violence, and/or stalking who are in need of transitional housing, short-term housing assistance, and related support services (transitional housing programs may offer individualized services such as counseling, support groups, safety planning, and advocacy services as well as practical services such as licensed child care, employment services, transportation vouchers, telephones, and referrals to other agencies).
Labor	*Homeless Veterans' Reintegration Program*—Provides services to help veterans experiencing homelessness obtain meaningful employment and to stimulate the development of effective service delivery systems to address the complex problems facing these veterans. The program also includes funds specifically for grantees providing specialized services to female veterans and veterans with families experiencing homelessness.

(*Continued*)

TABLE 7.4 FEDERAL PROGRAMS DESIGNED TO PREVENT AND END HOMELESSNESS IN AMERICA (CONTINUED)

DEPARTMENT	PROGRAMS COVERED
Veterans' Affairs	*Supportive Services for Veteran Families*—Provides supportive services to very low-income veteran families in or transitioning to permanent housing. Funds are provided through grants to private non-profit organizations and consumer cooperatives that provide a range of supportive services designed to promote housing stability. The program aims to prevent veterans from falling into homelessness whenever possible and to rapidly re-house veterans' families who become homeless. *Homeless Providers Grant and Per Diem Program*—Funds community agencies that provide services to veterans experiencing homelessness (the purpose of these services is to promote the development and provision of transitional housing and services with the goal of helping homeless veterans achieve residential stability, increase their skill levels and/or income, and obtain greater self-determination). *The Domiciliary Care for Homeless Veterans Program*—Provides 24 × 7 structured and supportive residential rehabilitation and treatment services for economically disadvantaged veterans and veterans experiencing homelessness who have health problems. *Healthcare for Homeless Veterans Program*—Funds outreach to identify veterans experiencing homelessness who are eligible for VA services and assist these veterans in accessing appropriate health care and benefits. The program also provides residential treatment through contracts with community providers. *The Justice Outreach, Homelessness Prevention: Healthcare for Reentry Veterans and Veteran's Justice Outreach*—Justice Outreach addresses the justice involvement continuum from first contact with law enforcement through release from prison or jail. Veteran's Justice Outreach is designed to help justice-involved veterans avoid the unnecessary criminalization of mental illness and extended incarceration by ensuring that eligible veterans have timely access to Veterans Health Administration mental health and substance abuse services when clinically indicated, and other VA services and benefits as appropriate. Health Care for Reentry Veterans assists veterans released from prison to readjust to community life through access to community reintegration, health, and social services provided through the VA and community services.
United States Interagency Council on Homelessness	Ensures interagency collaboration and local engagement, helping to guide homelessness funds into evidence-based solutions that are measurably reducing homelessness in America. The Council performs this work through support to federal council members and partners in the field.

for substance disorders and trauma; discharge planning for individuals from institutions; child care and education for children experiencing homelessness; and attention to public laws prohibiting the criminalization of sleeping and panhandling in public places.

A number of innovative programs to address problems of homelessness have been developed throughout the United States. Examples of evidence-based practices being used by state-of-the-art homeless programs through the country include the following (Substance Abuse and Mental Health Services Administration [SAMHSA], 2014):

- *Illness, Management and Recovery (IMR).* This intervention focuses on teaching individuals experiencing severe mental illness techniques for understanding and overcoming their mental illness, while also helping to develop goals to enrich their lives.

- *Housing First.* This intervention operates under the principle that housing is not a privilege, but a right and also an important tool in the process of recovery. When individuals move out of homelessness and into a home, they are given a new opportunity to examine issues of substance abuse and mental illness and become empowered to determine their own process of recovery.

- *Critical Time Intervention (CTI).* This intervention focuses on the prevention of homelessness for individuals in highly-vulnerable situations such as prisoner re-entry and discharge from a mental institution. CTI involves a time-limited, intensive case management during critical phases of transition.

- *Assertive Community Treatment (ACT).* This intervention is a team-oriented model that involves providing services to consumers in the communities in which they live. The ACT model stresses the importance of providing services in a coordinated, targeted fashion.

- *Motivational Interviewing and Enhancement Therapies.* Motivational interviewing is a collaborative, person-centered approach designed to elicit and strengthen motivation to change. This technique is rooted in an understanding of how hard it is to change learned behaviors, many of which have been essential to survival on the streets.
- *Integrated Dual-Disorders Treatment (IDDT).* This intervention provides treatment for the entire constellation of existing conditions simultaneously in a single setting.
- *Permanent Supportive Housing.* This intervention provides case management and wrap around care to individuals who are homeless to assist them with their transition from homelessness and progression through the different stages of recovery.
- *Recovery and Wellness.* This intervention focuses on providing services designed to address the adverse effects of life on the streets such as prolonged and unprotected exposure to the elements, harassment, incarceration, food insecurity, and fear for personal safety.
- *Trauma-Informed Care.* Trauma histories create significant barriers to therapeutic intervention for homeless individuals. Trauma-informed care is more than just an intervention, but rather an ideology of how to approach treatment.
- *Supported Employment.* Through the efforts of supportive employment programs individuals experiencing homelessness are capable of re-engaging with the work force or entering into educational programs. These programs help to bolster self-worth and connectedness with society.

The common theme among these programs is an emphasis on community-based initiatives that include both those who are homeless and homeless service providers in program design and development and empowerment. These efforts capitalize on the strengths perspective of social work by recognizing that people experiencing homelessness have the desire, motivation, and skills to better their situation.

Finally, a number of child welfare service programs offer special transition programs to help youth in the foster care system make the transition to independent living (see for example, Youth Transition Funders Group, 2014). Economic development and small-business programs for the homeless involve clients who are homeless in business efforts such as producing and selling artwork, newspapers, and other printed media; contracting services such as housekeeping and home repair; and furniture refinishing and repair. One innovative program builds low-income housing and trains youth who are homeless and disenfranchised for jobs in the construction industry (Youthbuild USA, 2014).

The Roles of Social Workers in the Fight against Poverty

EP 2.1.1a
EP 2.1.8b

Social work, more than any other profession, maintains a strong commitment to fighting poverty at all levels. Social workers provide direct services to individuals and families living in poverty; advocate for programs and policies that improve the lives of the poor and reduce poverty at the community, state, and federal levels; and develop and administer policies and programs that serve America's poor.

Some BSW graduates become public-assistance workers in state and local human services agencies. They help individuals apply for TANF, SNAP, Medicaid, and general assistance benefits. They also help individuals apply for social insurance programs such as Social Security and Medicare and oversee public assistance and social insurance benefit programs.

Many public assistance programs have furthered the roles of social workers in the fight against poverty by mandating that all TANF clients receiving employment services be assigned a case manager to help them become self-sufficient. Applying a generalist practice approach, these social workers assess client strengths and needs; work with clients to develop appropriate goals to achieve self-sufficiency; create appropriate service plans; assist clients in accessing needed resources; and terminate with their clients when the plans have been completed. Case managers also assist clients in developing skills in areas such as interviewing, assertiveness, and handling stress on the job; help them enroll in job-training and education programs; and assist them in locating appropriate resources such as transportation, housing, child care, health care, and family counseling.

In an effort to serve adults, children, youth, and families who live in poverty, social workers also are employed by faith-based organizations such as the Salvation Army, housing programs, child-development programs such as Head Start, teen pregnancy and parenting programs, school dropout-prevention programs, settlement houses, and health clinics and hospitals. In addition, social workers work with federal, state, and local agencies and governments; state legislatures and the U.S. Congress; and advocacy organizations in developing, lobbying for, and administering antipoverty programs.

Urban housing authorities employ social workers to work with individuals and families living in public housing to help break the cycle of poverty and homelessness. Because many individuals have difficulty making the transition from public housing to paying for housing themselves when they become employed and no longer meet income guidelines for public housing, social workers link families with resources that can help them make this transition.

Social workers also are outreach workers that serve the homeless in many areas. In a number of cities, roving workers provide services to youth who are homeless, helping them access health care, safe shelter, counseling, education, and employment. In some areas, programs for women who have experienced interpersonal violence have worked with programs serving the homeless, such as the Salvation Army, to establish transitional living programs for women and their families until they can locate employment and save enough money to locate housing independently.

In advocacy and administrative roles, social workers are employed in programs that aim to alleviate homelessness, such as Habitat for Humanity, an international program in which volunteers and future homeowners work together to build low-income housing. In one city, a dropout-recovery agency for young adults operates a highly successful construction program that trains individuals in a variety of construction jobs while building affordable housing. In another program, a social worker is the director of a private foundation that leverages funding from corporate and private donors to create affordable housing.

The values base of the social work profession mandates that social workers treat all clients, including those living in poverty, with dignity and respect and work to empower them to be in charge of their own lives. Much of the debate in the years ahead will be about the place of faith-based organizations in supplementing publicly funded efforts to combat poverty and dependency.

Summary

Poverty in America has a long history that begins with the austere times of colonial America. Although numerous public programs to eradicate poverty have been implemented over time, none have been successful in eliminating the problem. Why these programs have failed to reach their mark is a matter of speculation tempered by one's personal and political ideology, as well as the prevailing social values of the time. The one reality is of the growing underclass in America composed of a diverse mix of people who are not likely to fight their way out of poverty despite their desire and efforts to do so.

Lack of affordable housing, low-wage jobs, and the impact of welfare reform have contributed to a growing homeless population—the fastest-growing segment of which consists of women with children. Poverty is a complex problem with no easy solutions, and efforts continue to solve the myriad issues involved.

Competency Notes

EP 2.1.1a: Advocate for client access to the services of social work (pp. 164, 166, 174, 177, 179, 189). Social workers advocate on behalf of the poor, the homeless, and others in need of income assistance or social services.

EP 2.1.3a: Distinguish, appraise, and integrate multiple sources of knowledge, including research-based knowledge and practice wisdom (pp. 169, 179). Social workers draw on multiple sources of knowledge, including current research, in their work with individuals and families who are poor, homeless, and/or in need of public assistance and the communities in which they work and live.

EP 2.1.6b: Use practice experience to inform scientific inquiry (p. 186). Social workers use research evidence to inform practice with individuals and families who are poor, homeless, and/or in need of public assistance and the communities in which they work and live.

EP 2.1.7b: Critique and apply knowledge to understand person and environment (p. 169). Social workers critique and apply knowledge to how being poor, homeless, and/or in need of public assistance impacts individuals and families and their interactions with the broader environment.

EP 2.1.8a: Analyze, formulate, and advocate for policies that advance social well-being (pp. 164, 166, 172, 174, 177, 179). Social workers analyze, formulate, and advocate for policies that advance the social well-being of those who are poor, homeless, and/or in need of public assistance, as well as the communities in which they work and live.

EP 2.1.8b: Collaborate with colleagues and clients for effective policy action (pp. 174, 186, 189). Social workers collaborate with colleagues and clients for effective policy action at all levels of the environment to enhance the well-being of those who are poor, homeless, and/or in need of public assistance and the communities in which they work and live.

EP 2.1.9b: Provide leadership in promoting sustainable changes in service delivery and practice to improve the quality of social services (p. 186). Social workers act as leaders in promoting sustainable changes in service delivery and practice to improve the quality of social services for those who are poor, homeless, and/or in need of public assistance.

Key Terms

The terms below are defined in the Glossary.

Aid to Families with Dependent Children (AFDC)
collectivist perspective
Consumer Price Index (CPI)
digital divide
Earned Income Tax Credit (EITC)
Federal Poverty Income Limit (FPIL)
general assistance
homeless
individualist perspective
living wage
market basket concept
Medicaid
Old Age and Survivors Disability Insurance (OASDI)
poverty
relative poverty
root causes
Social Security
Supplemental Nutrition Assistance Program (SNAP)
Supplemental Security Income (SSI)
Temporary Assistance to Needy Families (TANF)
underclass
unemployment compensation
welfare reform
workers' compensation

Discussion Questions

1. Historically, we have tended to categorize those who are poor into two groups: the "deserving poor" and the "undeserving poor." Which groups do you think the majority of persons in the United States would consider the today's "deserving poor?" Today's "undeserving poor?" How would your own personal list differ?
2. Do you believe that a preference for living on welfare keeps TANF recipients out of the workforce?
3. How does the changing shape of the American economy change the shape of poverty in America?
4. To what extent is the number (or percentage) of poor people a good measure of a society's commitment to the well-being of its citizens?
5. Compare social welfare benefits available to corporations and those who are wealthy with benefits available to those who are poor.
6. Which level of government—local, state, or national—do you think is best equipped to deal with poverty? Why?
7. What strategies do you think would be most effective in reducing poverty in the United States?
8. Imagine that you are a single parent with two children receiving TANF and SNAP benefits, your only sources of income. Develop a monthly budget showing how you would cover expenses for you and your children.
9. Identify at least *five* factors associated with homelessness, and identify at least one possible intervention strategy for each.

On the Internet

http://www.urban.org
http://www.nlihc.org
http://www.nrchmi.samhsa.gov
http://www.aspe.hhs.gov
http://www.nlchp.org
http://www.rand.org
http://www.huduser.org
http://www.universallivingwage.org
http://www.bls.gov
http://www.census.gov
http://www.nccp.org
http://www.cbpp.org
http:/www.aclu.org
http://www.nami.org
http://www.mentalhealth.gov
http://samhsa.gov
http://www.naswdc.org
http://www.nationalhomeless.org

References

Abramsky, S. (2013). *The American way of poverty: How the other half still lives.* Washington, DC: Nation Books.

Barusch, A. (2011). *Foundations of social policy: Social justice in human perspective* (4th ed.). Stanford, CT: Cengage Publishing.

Congressional Budget Office. (2012). *The supplemental nutrition assistance program.* Washington, DC: Author.

Davies, J., & Lyon, E. (2013). *Domestic violence advocacy: Complex lives/difficult choices.* Thousand Oaks, CA: Sage.

Day, P., & Schiele, J. (2012). *A new history of social welfare* (7th ed.). Boston: Pearson.

DiNitto, D. M. (2010). *Social welfare: Politics and public policy* (7th ed.). Boston: Pearson.

Duncan, C., & Blackwell, B. (2014). *Worlds apart: Poverty and politics in rural America* (2nd ed.). New Haven, CT: Yale University Press.

Economic Policy Institute. (2014). *The state of working America* (12th ed.). Villanova, PA: Author. Retrieved August 2, 2014, from http://library.villanova.edu/research/reource/4814

Edelman, P. (2013). *So rich, so poor: Why it's so hard to end poverty in America.* New York: The New Press.

Fieldler, A., & Kuester, I. (Eds.). (2010). *Child development and child poverty.* Hauppauge, NY: Nova Science Publishers.

Gilbert, N., & Terrell, P. (2012). *Dimensions of social welfare policy* (8th ed.). Boston: Allyn & Bacon.

Hoge, C. (2010). *Once a warrior—always a warrior: Navigating combat stress, PTSD, and MTBI.* Guilford, CT: Globe Pequot Press.

Homelessness Research Institute. (2014). *A research agenda for ending homelessness.* Washington, DC: Author.

Housing Assistance Council. (2012). *Poverty in rural America.* Washington, DC: Author.

Iceland, J. (2013). *Poverty in America: A handbook* (3rd ed.). Berkeley: University of California Press.

Internal Revenue Service. (2014). *2013 tax year fast facts: Earned income tax credit.* Washington, DC: Author. Retrieved July 20, 2014, from http://www.eitc.irs.gov/EITCCentral/FASTFACTgrnlogbo2.pdf

Jimenez, J., & Pasztor, E. (2014). *Social policy and social change: Toward the creation of social and economic justice.* Thousand Oaks, CA: Sage.

Joint Center for Housing Studies. (2014). *The state of the nation's housing 2014.* Cambridge, MA: Author.

Karger, J., & Stoesz, D. (2013). *American social welfare policy: A pluralistic approach* (7th ed.). New York: Longman.

Katz, M. (2013). *The undeserving poor: America's confrontation with poverty* (2nd ed.). New York: Oxford University Press.

McLay, R. (2012). *At war with PTSD: Battling PTSD and virtual reality.* Baltimore, MD: Johns Hopkins University Press.

Mental Illness Policy Org. (2014). *People with untreated mental illness comprise 33% of the homeless population.* New York: Author. Retrieved August 2, 2014, from http://www.mentalillnesspolicy.org

Moore, B., & Penk, W. (Eds.). (2011). *Treating PTSD in military personnel: A clinical handbook.* New York: Guilford Press.

Morgan, S., & Weigt, J. (2009). *Stretched thin: Poor families, welfare work, and welfare reform.* Ithaca, NY: Cornell University Press.

National Alliance to End Homelessness. (2014). *A research agenda for ending homelessness.* Washington, DC: Author.

National Coalition for the Homeless. (2014). *Homeless in America.* Washington, DC: Author. Retrieved August 2, 2014, from http://www.nationalhomeless.org/about-homelessness/

National Health Care for the Homeless Council. (2014). *NHCHC infographics.* Nashville, TN: Author. Retrieved August 2, 2014, from http://www.nhchc.org/wp-content/uploads/2011/09/nhchc-inforgrsphic.pdf

National Law Center on Homelessness and Poverty. (2014). *Key data concerning homeless persons in America.* Washington, DC: Author.

National Low Income Housing Coalition. (2012). *Out of reach 2012: America's forgotten housing crisis.* Washington, DC: Author.

National Low Income Housing Coalition. (2014). *Housing wage calculator.* Washington, DC: Author. Retrieved August 2, 2014, from http://www.nlihc.org/library/wagecalc

National Network to End Domestic Violence. (2013). *Domestic violence counts 2013.* Washington, DC: Author.

National Resource and Training Center on Homelessness and Mental Illness. (2014). *Get the facts.* Washington, DC: Author.

Orshansky, M. (1965, January). Counting the poor. *Social Security Bulletin,* 3–29.

Reisch, M. (Ed.) (2013). *Social policy and social justice.* Thousand Oaks, CA: Sage.

Seccombe, K. (2010). *So you think I drive a Cadillac? Welfare recipients' perspectives on the system and its reform* (3rd ed.). Upper Saddle River, NJ: Prentice-Hall.

Substance Abuse and Mental Health Services Administration (SAMHSA). (2014). *Evidence-based practices and innovations.* Washington, DC: Author. Retrieved on August 3, 2014, from http://homeless.samhsa.gov/channel/S

Troxell, R. (2010). *Looking up at the bottom line: The struggle for the living wage.* Austin, TX: Plainview Press.

United Nations Children's Fund. (2012). *Child poverty in rich countries 2012.* Florence, Italy: UNICEF Innocenti Research Centre. Retrieved July 19, 2012, from www.unicef-irc.org

Universal Living Wage Campaign. (2014). *Universal living wage formula.* Retrieved July 19, 2014, from http://www.universallivingwage.org

U.S. Census Bureau, Income Statistics Branch. (2013a). *2013 social and economic supplement: Percent distribution by household, by selected characteristics within income quintile and top 5%.* Washington, DC: Author.

U.S. Census Bureau, Income Statistics Branch. (2013b). *Age and sex of all people, family members and unrelated individuals iterated by income-to-poverty ratio and race: 2012.* Washington, DC: Author.

U.S. Census Bureau, Income Statistics Branch. (2013c). *People in families with related children under 18 by family structure, age, and sex, iterated by income-to-poverty ratio and race: 2012.* Washington, DC: Author.

U.S. Conference of Mayors. (2013). *Hunger and homelessness survey: A status report on hunger and homelessness in America's cities.* Washington, DC: Author.

U.S. Department of Health and Human Services. (2014a). *2009 HHS poverty guidelines.* Washington, DC: Author. Retrieved July 19, 2010, from http://aspe.hhs.gov/poverty/07poverty.htm

U.S. Department of Health and Human Services. (2014b). *Prior HHS poverty guidelines and Federal Register references.* Washington, DC: Author. Retrieved August 3, 2014, from http://aspe.hhs.gov/poverty/figures-fed-reg.cfm

U.S. Interagency Council on Homelessness. (2014). *Proposed FY 2015 fact sheet.* Washington, DC: Author. Retrieved August 3, 2014, from http://www.ich.gov

U.S. Social Security Administration. (2014). *Annual statistical report on the social security disability insurance program, 2014.* Washington, DC: Author. Retrieved July 19, 2014, from http://www.ssa.gov/policy/docs/statcomps/di_asr/2004/index.htm

Vale, L. (2013). *Purging the poorest: Public housing and the design politics of twice-cleared communities.* Chicago: University of Chicago Press.

Youth Transition Funders Group. (2014). *Youth in transition publications.* Scarsdale, NY: Author. Retrieved August 2, 2014, from http://www.ytfg.org/knowledge/publications

Youthbuild USA. (2014). *Youthbuild programs.* Somerville, MA: Author. Retrieved August 2, 2014, from http://www.youthbuild.org/youthbuild-programs

Zlotnick, C. (2014). *Children living in transition: Helping homeless and foster children and families.* New York: Columbia University Press.

Suggested Readings

Boland, D., & Waddan, A. (2012). *The politics of policy change: Welfare, medicare, and social security reform in the United States.* Washington, DC: Georgetown University Press.

Brodkin, E., & Marston, G. (Eds.). (2013). *Work and the welfare state: Street-level organizations and welfare politics.* Washington, DC: Georgetown University Press.

Bullock, H. (2013). *Women and poverty: Psychology, public policy, and social justice.* Hoboken, NJ: Wiley-Blackwell.

Buzawa, E., & Buzawa, C. (2011). *Responding to domestic violence: The integration of criminal justice and human services.* Thousand Oaks, CA: Sage.

Culp, A. (Ed.). (2014). *Bridging the gaps between research, practice, and policy.* New York: Springer.

Dolgoff, R., & Feldstein, D. (2012). *Understanding social welfare* (9th ed.). Boston: Pearson.

Goetz, E. (2013). *New deal reins: Race, economic justice, and public housing policy.* Ithaca, NY: Cornell University Press.

Howard, E. (2013). *Homeless: Poverty and place in urban America.* Philadelphia: University of Pennsylvania Press.

Johnston, D. (Ed.). (2014). *Divided: The perils of our growing inequality.* New York: The New Press.

Marotz, L. (2011). *Health, safety, and nutrition for the young child* (8th ed.). Stanford, CT: Cengage Learning.

Page-Reeves, J. (Ed.). (2014). *Women redefining the experience of food insecurity: Life off the edge of the table.* Lanham, MD: Lexington Books.

Pickering, K., & Harvey, M. (2011). *Welfare reform in persistent rural poverty: Dreams, disenchantments, and diversity.* University Park, PA: Penn State Press.

Poole, R., & Higgo, R. (2013). *Mental health and poverty.* New York: Cambridge University Press.

Pringle, P. (2013) (Ed.). *A place at the table: The crisis of 49 million hungry Americans and how to solve it.* New York: Public Affairs.

Raz, M. (2013). *What's wrong with the poor? Psychiatry, race, and the war on poverty.* Durham, NC: University of North Carolina Press.

Rich, M. (2014). *Federal policymaking and the poor: National goals, local choices, distributional outcomes.* Princeton, NJ: Princeton University Press.

Taibbi, M., & Crabapple, M. (2014). *The divide: American injustice in the age of the wealth gap.* New York: Spiegel & Grau Publishers.

CHAPTER 8

Health Care

Romero and Estella Ramirez and their 2-year-old daughter Araceli live in an economically depressed area of a large city in the Southwest. Until 2 years ago, Romero and Estella owned a small food catering company. Because of a downturn in the economy, however, business dropped off sharply. Unable to pay their bills and with no financial reserves, they were forced into bankruptcy. Romero took a job as a contract laborer at a construction site located some 15 miles from home. A big chunk of the money Romero made at this job went to pay for transportation costs to and from home and the construction site. Still unable to make ends meet, Estella got a job as a housekeeper in a local motel. Neither job provided health-care benefits.

Not long after, Estella became pregnant. Because she and Romero did not have health insurance, Estella did not see a doctor for pre-natal health-care check-ups until she experienced serious medical complications when she was 6 months pregnant. Soon thereafter, Estella gave birth prematurely to Araceli, who spent the first three months of her life in the neonatal care unit of the city's public hospital battling severe respiratory and cardiac problems that required multiple surgeries to correct as well as an extended period of post-surgical care.

When Araceli finally was allowed to go home from the hospital, she required extensive rehabilitative care, making it impossible for Estella to return to work. Financially strapped and without any monetary reserves, the Ramirez family now faced medical bills in excess of $100,000 for Araceli's delivery and care. At this point, Romero and Estella had no choice but to turn to the local social services department for help. Even though Estella and Romero's combined income was low, they were only able to qualify for limited medical assistance. Friends and family members were able to raise $5,000 to help pay for Araceli's medical expenses, but this was still woefully short of what was needed.

At this point, Alicia and Arturo are overwhelmed with medical bills and unsure they will be able to pay for them. Doctors say that Araceli has developmental delays and is likely to require extensive physical therapy and possibly more surgery down the road. Romero and Estella had hoped to have a large family, but that appears to be a faded dream now. Over the past 6 months, Romero has developed back problems and has missed 5 days of work already, but he can't bring himself to see a doctor, considering the already extensive medical bills. He hopes that whatever is wrong will get better with time.

In this chapter we give an overview of our country's current health-care system, the problems it faces, and the types of health-care policies and programs available. We trace the relevant legislation and discuss the roles that social workers play in making those policies and programs possible.

The State of Health in the United States

EP 2.1.1a
EP 2.1.3a
EP 2.1.8a

Currently, **health care**—care provided to individuals to prevent or promote recovery from illness or disease—can best be characterized as in a state of flux. The health-care landscape in the United States was changed dramatically with the passage of the landmark Patient Protection and Affordable Care Act of 2009 (Affordable Care Act or ACA), which was signed into law by President Obama on March 23, 2010. The requirements of the act will be implemented over the 10-year period from 2010 to 2019; however, most of the requirements were implemented between 2010 and 2014. The act called for sweeping reforms of the U.S. health-care system in the following areas (Urban Institute, 2014a):

- regulation of private health insurance, particularly in the small group and nongroup markets;
- provision of tax credits to small low-wage employers for the purchase of health insurance;
- reductions in cost-sharing associated with recommended preventive care;
- establishment of health insurance exchanges for the purchase of private coverage plus subsidies for the individual purchase of exchange-based coverage and cost-sharing by those with modest income;
- expansion of eligibility for the Medicaid program to all nonelderly with incomes up to 133% of the federal poverty level;
- phasing out of the Medicare prescription drug benefit "doughnut hole";
- a requirement for nonelderly individuals to enroll in qualified health insurance coverage with tax penalties imposed on many of those that do not comply;
- imposition of financial penalties on large- and medium-sized employers in cases where an employer's full-time workers obtain subsidized coverage through a health insurance exchange;
- establishment of a national, voluntary insurance program for purchasing community living assistance services and supports (CLASS program);
- implementation of an array of initiatives for reducing costs in the Medicare program;
- creation of incentives to establish cost-efficient health-care systems, such as accountable care organizations and quality improvement initiatives; and

- tax changes that will generate revenue to help finance the new programs.

The Urban Institute (2014b) is undertaking a comprehensive monitoring and tracking project to examine the implementation and effects of the Affordable Care Act across the country. This initiative has produced the following findings as of September 2014:

- Competition has led to lower insurance premiums in certain markets;
- Participation of small employers has gotten off to a slow start;
- States have made very different design choices in implementing the law;
- States will benefit from the establishment of marketplaces and income-related subsidies;
- Employer coverage is not expected to change significantly;
- States that are expanding Medicaid will witness large reductions in the number of uninsured;
- Medicaid expansion will offset cuts to Medicare provider payment rates and Medicaid and Medicare disproportionate share hospital payments;
- State health insurance marketplaces must have a robust technology platform that supports eligibility determination and facilitates enrollment into health coverage;
- Meeting enrollment goals hinges on the effectiveness of marketing campaigns to raise public awareness and application assistance programs that help consumers enroll;
- Access to care is essential to the success of the ACA; and
- Medicaid plays a critical role in the law's effort to expand coverage and reform the nation's health-care system.

Initial enrollment in the program, which began in November 2013 and ended in March 2014, got off to a slow start because glitches in the web-based enrollment system caused the system to crash. These problems were resolved and the initial enrollment period eventually resulted in about 8 million individuals signing up for health care under the new provisions of the act. Fully implemented, the ACA is expected to cut the number of uninsured persons in the country by 60%, leaving an estimated 19 million people without any form of health insurance. Those left without any insurance includes those without affordable coverage options available to them (the largest among this group); those choosing to pay tax penalties instead of enrolling in coverage; undocumented immigrants; and those eligible for subsidized coverage but who do not enroll in it for reasons such as language barriers, lack of awareness that such subsidies exist, and distrust of the government (Urban Institute, 2014b). In the end, success of health-care reform in reducing the number of uninsured individuals in the country will depend on the effectiveness of outreach efforts and strategies designed to make enrollment and retention in subsidized public and private insurance options both simple and affordable, as well as significant progress in containing health-care costs, which currently comprise some 18% of the U.S. gross national product (GNP) (discussed later in this chapter).

Not having health insurance coverage has serious consequences for individuals and families (Kaiser Commission on Medicaid and the Uninsured, 2013):

- Individuals who are uninsured receive less preventive care, are diagnosed at more advanced stages of disease, and, once diagnosed, tend to receive less therapeutic care and have higher mortality rates than insured individuals;
- Uninsured adults often are unable to fill a drug prescription or to go forward with a recommended treatment because of the cost;
- Patients who are unable to pay up front in cash for the full medical bill may be turned away from receiving care;
- Individuals without health insurance coverage sometimes turn to the emergency room to get their health-care needs met, which is one of the costliest options;
- Uninsured individuals frequently have problems paying medical bills, and many are forced to change their life significantly to pay them; and

- Uninsured individuals at times require hospitalization for problems that could have been prevented had they received appropriate and timely outpatient care.

Having insurance ameliorates some of these problems and results in improved health overall. It has also been estimated that mortality rates among the uninsured could be lowered by some 10–15% if they had health insurance. Additionally, having health insurance lowers the debt incurred by individuals and families due to medical bills for which they lack the resources to pay and the stress in coping with this debt. Such debt also has a negative impact on a person's credit history.

As noted earlier, the success of health-care reform in reducing the number of uninsured individuals in the country will depend in large part on the ability to contain the nation's burgeoning health-care costs. National expenses for health care have increased exponentially over the past 30 years—from $73.2 billion in 1970 to an estimated $4.8 trillion in 2021 (Centers for Medicare and Medicaid Services, 2012a). Health spending in 2014 is projected to account for about 18% of the U.S. GNP, or a cost per person of $9,807 (Centers for Medicare and Medicaid Services, 2012a). The United States spends billions of dollars annually to provide health services to uninsured persons for preventable diseases and to those who could be treated more efficiently and at considerably less expense with earlier diagnosis. Health-care expenditures in the country are expected to increase to nearly $5 trillion by 2021 (see Figure 8.1 and Table 8.1). The Obama administration has implemented a number of cost containment measures as part of the reforms brought about by the ACA. The administration has also introduced financial incentives for health-care providers who deliver services that result in a high level of satisfaction in the eyes of the

FIG 8.1 **National Health Expenditures— Projections From 2011 to 2021**
SOURCE: Centers for Medicare and Medicaid Services (2012a).

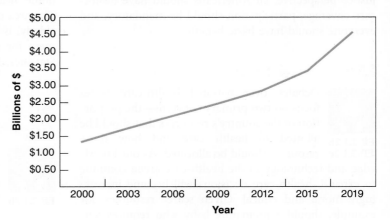

TABLE 8.1 NATIONAL HEALTH EXPENDITURES—2011–2013 AND PROJECTIONS TO 2021	
YEAR	PROJECTED EXPENDITURES (IN TRILLIONS OF DOLLARS)
2011	$2.70
2012	$2.81
2013	$2.92
2014	$3.13
2015	$3.31
2016	$3.51
2017	$3.72
2018	$3.95
2019	$4.21
2020	$4.49
2021	$4.78

SOURCE: Centers for Medicare and Medicaid Services (2012a). *National health expenditure projections: 2011–2021*. Baltimore, MD: Author.

individuals who receive these services. Consumers will also need to live healthier lifestyles as well as change the way in which they use health-care services. Additionally, the medical profession will have curb its use of expensive technology in situations in which it is not really needed. Notwithstanding these efforts, cost containment remains a significant challenge to the future of the country's health-care system.

Not having health insurance is a significant impediment to achieving one's full potential. From a social justice perspective, all Americans should have health-care coverage, participation should be mandatory, and everyone should have basic benefits.

Moral and Ethical Issues

EP 2.1.2b
EP 2.1.2c

Debates over national health-care issues focus on two primary concerns—the proportion of the country's resources that should be allotted to health care and how those resources should be allocated. As our knowledge and technology in the health-care arena continue to expand, health-care decisions will become increasingly moral and ethical. Given scarce resources, for example, should a premature baby who requires tens of thousands of dollars to be kept alive be given maximum treatment to save his or her life, particularly when the child may live a life continually fraught with health problems? And what about organ transplants? Should this costly procedure be available to everyone? If not, who should receive transplants and under what conditions?

Given the growing numbers of persons with life-threatening diseases such as diabetes, HIV/AIDS, and cancer, how many dollars should be allocated to research, education, and treatment, and who should pay what costs? Does the government have the right to mandate good health practices for women drug users who are pregnant or to impose penalties on individuals with HIV/AIDS who do not practice safe sex? With more U.S. citizens living longer, to what extent should resources be allocated toward health care for older persons? And to what extent should attention be given to threats to the ecosystem posed by the quest to reduce the nation's dependence on foreign oil assets through questionable drilling practices (both on- and offshore), poor sanitation associated with urban decay, and air and water pollution, and their impacts on personal health? Finally, given the high costs of health care, who should pay for health care for those who are unable to afford it—the federal government, states, local communities, or individuals and their families themselves? If individuals cannot afford health care, should it be denied to them?

Increasingly, social workers are playing a central role in helping policymakers, medical practitioners, and family members struggle with these critical decisions. Social workers are providing services in health-related settings ranging from basic care and specialty hospitals to family-planning clinics, rape crisis centers, home health-care programs, and hospice programs. The area of health care, particularly as it relates to the elderly, is one of the fastest-growing areas of employment for social workers today (U.S. Bureau of Labor Statistics, 2014).

An Ecological/Systems Approach to Health Care

EP 2.1.3b

Because the ecological/systems perspective was first introduced as a mechanism to explain the functioning of the human body, this perspective has a longer history within the health-care arena than other arenas in which social workers function. As early as the Greek and Roman eras of civilization, many health problems were observed to be precipitated by changes in the environment. An ancient Greek medical text titled *Airs, Waters, and Places,* said to be authored by Hippocrates, explained health problems in terms of person–environment relationships. This work attributed human functioning to four body fluids: blood, phlegm, and black and yellow bile. As long as these body fluids were in equilibrium, the individual was considered to be healthy. But Hippocrates attributed changes in the balance of these fluids to ecological variations in temperature, ventilation, and an individual's lifestyle in relation to eating, drinking, and working. Negative influences in the environment caused these fluids to become unbalanced, which in turn resulted in illness (DiClemente, Crosby, & Kegler, 2009).

Other early works subscribed to germ theory, based on the premise that illness is a function of the interactions among an organism's adaptive capacities in an environment full of infectious agents, toxins, and safety hazards. The Greeks and Romans also were cognizant of the relationship between sanitation and illness. Early Roman writings suggested that people could predict and control their health through the environment and prevent epidemic diseases by avoiding marshes, standing water, winds, and high temperatures. Public baths, sewers, and free medical care were ways by which early civilizations promoted health and reduced disease (DiClemente, Crosby, & Kegler, 2009).

The focus on the relationship between individual health and the environment continued during later centuries. Johann Peter Frank's medical treatise, *System of a Complete Medical Policy* (written in 1774–1821), advocated education of midwives and new mothers, a healthy school environment, personal hygiene, nutrition, sewers and sanitation, accident prevention, collection of vital statistics such as births and deaths, and efficient administration of hospitals to care for the sick.

Numerous studies throughout the years have attributed the incidence of infant mortality, heart disease, and cancer to environmental influences. A number of early studies (see, for example, Dohrenwend & Dohrenwend, 1974) show strong relationships between stressful life events and the subsequent development of physical disorders, supporting Hippocrates' earlier theories of the ways that a negative lifestyle can affect health. Brenner (1973) demonstrated the

relationships between health problems—heart disease, infant and adult mortality rates, and other health indicators—and national employment rates between 1915 and 1967. When employment rates were high, health problems were low, and low employment rates were associated with higher incidences of health problems.

Interactions between environmental factors, such as unemployment, and mental health significantly affect individual health (Falvo, 2013). The relationship between health problems and mental health problems began to receive more attention in the late 1970s with the release of the U.S. Surgeon General's national health report, *Healthy People,* which emphasized the link between physical and mental health and noted the significance of strong family ties, supportive friends, and informal and formal support systems in promoting healthy individuals.

Israel, Eng, Schulz, and Parker (2012) take a somewhat different systems perspective. They present research showing that people who perceive their environments as stressful, such as those living in highly urban or highly rural areas, place their psychological systems in jeopardy and develop ways to cope that are tied to their perception of the situation. For example, an elderly man living in a rural area who perceives himself as being extremely isolated and without the resources to get him to a hospital quickly if he becomes ill is more likely to incur health problems than an elderly man who perceives that he is living in an area where health care is more readily available.

Factors Affecting Health

EP 2.1.3a

Studies show that the leading factors affecting health are related to income, ethnicity, gender, age, disability, and where one lives (National Center for Health Statistics, 2013). Note that all of these factors interact with environmental and lifestyle factors to either increase or decrease the likelihood of good health. These factors are explained later in this chapter.

Income   The higher a person's income, the more likely that person is to be in good health. This is because people with higher incomes are more likely to have health insurance, seek medical care earlier and more often, buy and eat more nutritious foods, and have less mental stress than people who are poor.

Those who are poor also are more likely to live in environmentally unhealthy places, such as areas close to hazardous waste disposal sites or manufacturing sites that use toxic substances with a known history of causing serious health problems or even death (Fitzpatrick, 2013).

Even families in which all adult members are employed have difficulty affording health insurance. Approximately one in six nonpoor working adults 18–64 years of age had no health coverage in 2012 (U.S. Census Bureau, 2013). Poor working adults fared even worse. Among this group, about one in three had no health coverage in 2012 (Kaiser Commission on Medicaid and the Uninsured, 2013). According to the Centers for Disease Control and Prevention (2013a), adults with low incomes reported feeling unhealthy more days a month than those with higher incomes. Studies show that the impact of low income on health is especially damaging to infants and children. The chances of death or serious illness at birth can be linked directly to whether the mother has health insurance. Uninsured babies are more likely than insured babies to die or to have serious medical problems at birth, and the infant mortality rate of births to women living in poverty is higher than for women above the poverty line who are giving birth (Annie E. Casey Foundation, 2014).

Nationwide, nearly 13% of children living in families at or below the poverty line had no health insurance in 2012. This figure is considerably higher for pockets of deep poverty in the country, such as the area along the Texas–Mexico Border, where the rates of uninsured children range from 30% to nearly 50% (Texas Medical Association, 2014).

Ethnicity   Whites as a group enjoy better health than people of color. Native Americans report the highest number of unhealthy days, and nearly twice as many African Americans as whites report that they are in fair or poor health (Centers for Disease Control and Prevention, 2013a). Chronic disease has a devastating impact on minority populations. For example, the prevalence of diabetes among African Americans and Latinos is nearly twice that among whites (National Center for Health Statistics, 2013).

Although life expectancy is increasing for all groups, the expectancy rates for groups of color are still lower than for whites. The **infant mortality rate**—the

number of infant deaths compared to total infant births during a given time period—is twice as high for people of color as for whites. Infants born to uninsured African American mothers are twice as likely as babies born to insured mothers to die or to have serious medical problems (National Center for Health Statistics, 2013).

Further, people of color are less likely to seek health care for themselves and their children. Although special outreach programs and mandatory vaccination programs associated with preschool programs have increased the number of all preschoolers receiving immunizations, fewer African American, Latino, and Native American children than white children are fully immunized. African American preschoolers, for example, are apt not to be fully immunized, and twice as many African American women as white women do not receive any prenatal care during their first trimester of pregnancy (Health Resources and Services Administration, 2013).

People of color also are at higher risk to develop heart disease, diabetes, and cancer. High blood pressure—a major cause of kidney failure, strokes, and heart disease—affects African Americans one-half more often than whites. Research indicates that low socioeconomic status is the link between high blood pressure and ethnicity. The high blood pressure could be attributed to environmental stress caused by oppression and limited access to social and economic resources (National Center for Health Statistics, 2013). And African Americans are twice as likely as whites to have a disability, often because of high blood pressure and related problems.

Health practitioners are concerned about the growing number of individuals in the United States who are diagnosed with diabetes as a result of poor diets and lack of regular exercise. Many states and local communities are conducting special outreach efforts to reduce diabetes among people of color. Serious concern also has been raised about the increased numbers of African American children developing asthma associated with unsafe environmental living conditions, including excessive rodent and insect debris, which has serious life-threatening implications if not properly addressed (Children's Defense Fund, 2014).

Health conditions that should not be major problems in a wealthy industrialized country such as the United States are increasing among all groups, but particularly in people of color. Studies of health care along the U.S.–Mexico border, for example, show high rates of tuberculosis, hepatitis, and malaria (U.S.–Mexico Border Health Commission, 2013). Life expectancies for people of color, especially African Americans males, also are shorter than for whites (76.5 years versus 71.1 years, respectively) (National Center for Health Statistics, 2013). Common causes of death also differ by ethnicity (see Table 8.2).

Latino immigrants are less likely than members of other groups of color to be insured. Many immigrants who are eligible for coverage are afraid to apply because they think it will jeopardize their citizenship status. Many also are unaware that their children may be eligible for benefits if they are born in the United States (Fernandez-Kelly & Portes, 2012).

Gender   The average life expectancy continues to increase for men and women alike. In 2010, the latest year for which national data are available, life expectancy was 76.2 years for men and 81.0 years for women (National Center for Health Statistics, 2013). Although the longer average life expectancy for women might be viewed as an advantage for women, it also is a disadvantage for them. Because of the difference in life expectancy and because women have less built

up in Social Security as a result of staying home and rearing children, more elderly women who become widowed have little or no health insurance coverage and limited Social Security benefits. Thus, these women are more likely to spend their last years in poverty, which in turn places them at more risk for poor health.

Age   Our country's oldest and youngest citizens are at the highest risk for poor health. The elderly are at risk as a result of aging and because many live in poverty. One-third of today's elderly are poor and do not seek health care as needed because the high costs are prohibitive. One group of at-risk elderly is the more than 5.2 million persons in the United States with Alzheimer's disease. The number of people in the United States with Alzheimer's disease is projected to reach 15 million by 2050 (Alzheimer's Association, 2013). Alzheimer's disease now is the sixth leading cause of death among white males (National Center for Health Statistics, 2013).

The aging factor will be of even greater significance as the U.S. population continues to age. About 14% of the population is over age 65, and by 2060, nearly one

TABLE 8.2 AGE-ADJUSTED DEATH RATES FOR SELECTED CAUSES OF DEATH BY RACE/ETHNICITY, 2010 (PER 100,000)

CAUSE	WHITE	BLACK	HISPANIC	INDIAN	ASIAN/PACIFIC ISLANDER
Heart disease	176.9	224.9	132.8	128.6	100.9
Cancer	172.4	203.8	119.7	122.4	108.9
Strokes	37.7	53.0	32.1	28.1	33.2
Accidents	40.3	31.3	25.7	46.9	15.0
Diabetes	19.0	38.7	27.1	36.4	15.5
Respiratory diseases	44.6	29.0	19.6	33.8	13.9
Liver diseases	9.9	6.7	13.7	22.8	3.2
Homicide	3.3	17.7	5.3	5.7	1.8
Suicide	13.6	5.2	5.9	10.8	6.2
HIV	1.4	11.6	2.8	1.6	0.4

Source: National Center for Health Statistics (2012, January). *Age-adjusted death rates for selected causes of death, by sex, race, and Hispanic origin: United States, selected years, 1950–2010* (Table 26). Washington, DC: Author.

in every five persons in the United States will be over age 65 (U.S. Census Bureau, 2013). The nursing-home population is expected to at least double by 2030 for persons ages 65, and perhaps triple for those ages 85 or older (Administration on Aging, 2012).

One of the wealthiest countries in the world, the United States nevertheless continues to have a higher infant mortality rate (6.1 deaths per 1,000 live births) than any other Western country (National Center for Health Statistics, 2013). As the number of children growing up in poverty continues to increase and health-care options for them are reduced because of funding, U.S. children will be at more risk for serious health problems.

The major causes of death vary significantly by age. Although tremendous gains have been made in preventing some major causes of death, many deaths are not related to major physical illness, particularly in youth. Unintentional injuries (accidents) are still the leading cause of death for individuals under 25 years of age. Homicide is one of the three leading causes of death for persons ages 15–25. Although HIV/AIDS is no longer one of the 15 leading causes of death for the general population, it is seventh for individuals 25–44 years of age (National Center for Health Statistics, 2013).

Disability   People with both permanent and temporary disabilities are much more at risk than people without disabilities to have serious health problems. People with a severe disability are more likely to have Medicaid or Medicare coverage, to live below the poverty level, to report their health status as "fair or poor," and to receive public assistance (Disabilitystatistics.org, 2014). Their lesser resilience as a result of their disability often is compounded by the lack of affordable, accessible, appropriate health care that would allow them to maintain good preventive health practices. According to the U.S. Census Bureau (2012), there are 56.7 million people in the United States (18.7% of all people) who have some level of disability; 38.3 million (12.6% of all people) reported having a severe disability.

Rural and Urban Areas   People who live in either rural or highly populated urban areas are more at risk to have health problems. In a highly populated urban area, this can be attributed to more environmental hazards, such as pollution and increased stress. In sparsely populated rural areas, poorer health can be attributed to a lack of medical facilities for prevention and early medical care. More than half of all people at the poverty level live in rural areas, and they also are more likely than persons in urban areas to have emotional disorders (see Chapter 14).

Applying an Ecological/Systems Perspective

EP 2.1.8a
EP 2.1.9b

An ecological/systems perspective focuses on the interaction and interdependence between person and environment in understanding **health risk factors**—the factors that affect individuals' health and place them at risk for serious health problems and health conditions (e.g., lifestyle, environment, inadequacy of health-care services and genetic/heredity factors).

The current emphasis on **holistic health care** stems from a systems/ecological approach. This perspective views all aspects of an individual's health in relation to how that individual interacts with family members, the workplace, and the community, and also to how the environment, including community quality of life, as well as legislation and funding available to support quality of life, affects a person's health.

This perspective gradually is replacing the more traditional medical model used by health practitioners, which is concerned with symptoms and malfunctions of only one part of the body to the exclusion of other body systems or the environment within which the individual interacts. The World Health Organization (2003) has defined **health** as "a state of complete physical, mental, and social well-being and not merely the absence of disease or infirmity." This definition reflects the systems/ecological perspective in viewing health as clearly dependent on a combination of environmental, physiological, sociological, and psychological factors.

U.S. health experts are directing more attention to indicators of health. The U.S. Department of Health and Human Services established indicators to measure the health of Americans, with anticipated gains targeted to be met by 2010 (see Table 8.3). The 28 focus areas shown in the table represented a total of 969 objectives; tracking data were available for about 75% of these objectives. A summary of progress toward attainment of these objectives revealed that 48% moved toward the target; 24% moved away from the target; 23% met or exceeded the target; and 5% demonstrated no change (National Center for Health Statistics, 2012).

TABLE 8.3 HEALTHY PEOPLE 2010 LEADING HEALTH INDICATORS

LEADING INDICATOR

- Increase the proportion of persons with health insurance.
- Increase the proportion of persons of all ages who have a specific source of ongoing care.
- Reduce the proportion of persons exposed to air that does not meet the U.S. Environmental Protection Agency's health-based standards for ozone.
- Increase the proportion of sexually active females 18 to 44 years of age whose partners use condoms.
- Increase the proportion of sexually active males 18 to 44 years of age who use condoms.
- Increase the proportion of children 19 to 35 months of age who receive all vaccines that have been recommended for universal administration for at least 5 years.
- Increase the proportion of adolescents 13 to 15 years of age who receive all the vaccines that have been recommended for universal administration for at least 5 years.
- Increase the proportion of noninstitutionalized adults 65 years of age or older who are vaccinated annually against influenza.
- Increase the proportion of noninstitutionalized adults 65 years of age or older who were ever vaccinated against pneumococcal disease.
- Reduce the number of deaths per 100,000 population caused by motor vehicle crashes.
- Reduce homicides.
- Increase the proportion of pregnant women who receive early and adequate prenatal care beginning in the first trimester of pregnancy.
- Increase the proportion of adults 18 years of age or older with recognized depression who receive treatment.
- Reduce the proportion of adults who are obese.
- Reduce the proportion of children and adolescents 6 to 19 years of age who are obese.
- Increase the proportion of adults who engage regularly, preferably daily, in moderate physical activity for at least 30 minutes per day, 5 or more days per week, or vigorous physical activity for at least 20 minutes per day, 3 or more days per week.
- Increase the proportion of adolescents who engage in vigorous physical activity that promotes cardiorespiratory fitness, 3 or more days per week for 20 or more minutes per occasion.
- Increase the proportion of currently sexually active adolescents who used a condom the last time they had sexual intercourse.
- Increase the proportion of adolescents not using alcohol or any illicit drugs during the past 30 days.
- Reduce the proportion of adults using any illicit drug during the past 30 days.
- Reduce the proportion of adults 18 years of age or older engaging in binge drinking.
- Reduce cigarette smoking by adults.
- Reduce cigarette smoking by adolescents (past month).
- Reduce the proportion of nonsmokers exposed to environmental tobacco smoke.

SOURCE: Centers for Disease Control and Prevention (2010). *Healthy People 2010: Leading health indicators, Appendix E. Health, United States, 2009.* Washington, DC: Author.

The Evolution of Health Care in America

EP 2.1.9a

The early emphasis for health care in the United States was on keeping people alive. Those born in the United States 200 years ago had only a 50% chance of surviving long enough to celebrate their 21st birthday. One-third of all deaths were of children younger than 5 years old. Even then, people of color had higher death rates. In the late 18th century, the death rate was 30 per 1,000 lives for whites and 70 per 1,000 lives for slaves (U.S. Public Health Service, 1977). Health practitioners at that time were limited in number and training, and they faced great difficulty in keeping their patients alive because of environmental constraints such as poor sanitation and extreme poverty.

Many illnesses resulted in catastrophic epidemics, which claimed the lives of entire families. In 1793, during a yellow fever epidemic in Philadelphia, three physicians were available to care for 6,000 patients stricken with the disease. Thus, early attempts to improve health care in the United States included national and state legislation relating to control of communicable diseases, sanitation measures such as pasteurization of milk, and education for midwives, physicians, and young mothers (U.S. Public Health Service, 1977).

Although more recent legislation and programs have been directed to controlling chronic, degenerative diseases such as heart disease and cancer, self-inflicted illnesses such as cirrhosis of the liver, and other health problems such as accidents and violence, most efforts are still directed to restoring health *after* illness has occurred. The health-care system in the United States still allows many U.S. citizens to remain unserved or underserved, and mortality rates remain higher than in many other developed countries (U.S. Census Bureau, 2013).

Critical Issues in Current Health-Care Delivery

Many domestic-policy professionals believe that the United States is in the midst of a crisis in health care. While health-care costs are increasing significantly, more and more Americans are finding that health care is inaccessible to them. More infants are dying at birth, and other people are developing serious health problems that go untreated.

Funding and Costs of Health Care

EP 2.1.1a
EP 2.1.8a
EP 2.1.9b

The rapidly increasing cost of health care at all levels in the United States—for consumers, local health-care practitioners, community hospitals, local governments, and state and federal programs—is considered to be one of the most critical issues facing our country today. The United States is projected to spend over $4.5 trillion on health care by 2019, about 20% of the U.S. GNP (Centers for Medicare and Medicaid Services, 2014). The major sources of health-care spending in 2010, the latest date for which such data are available, include hospital care (37.2%); physician/clinical services (23.6%); prescription drugs

(11.8%); nursing home facilities and continuing care retirement communities (6.5%); government administration and net cost of health insurance (8.1%); and other personal health care or medical services (12.8%) (Centers for Disease Control and Prevention, 2013a) (see Figure 8.2A).

One of the major issues being debated at all government levels is who should pay for what. In 2010, the latest date for which such data are available, include out-of-pocket payments (13.7%), Medicare (22.6%), Medicaid and CHIP (17.5%), other third-party payers and programs (8.4%), private health insurance (34.1%), and all other sources (3.7%) (Centers for Medicare and Medicaid Services, 2013a) (see Figure 8.2B). Governments at all levels are trying to find ways to reduce health-care costs at the same time that more and more individuals and families currently paying health costs themselves are struggling to afford rapidly rising costs.

Individuals like Romero and Estella Ramirez, introduced at the beginning of this chapter, are not the only ones facing financial bankruptcy because of health-care costs. Physicians are leaving independently owned practices or have stopped taking reimbursements from third parties such as Medicaid, Medicare, and private health insurance, particularly in rural and poverty-stricken areas; hospitals are closing; insurance companies are consolidating or going out of business; communities and states are in the red because of increased costs of indigent health care; and the federal government's Medicaid and Medicare systems are in need of increasingly large sums of money to meet the needs of eligible clients.

The emphasis during the 1950s and 1960s was on providing the best possible health care to all Americans

FIG 8.2A The Nation's Health Dollar, Calendar Year 2010: Where It Went
NOTE: Other spending includes dentist services, other professional services, home health, durable medical products, over-the-counter medicines and sundries, public health, other personal health care, research and structures and equipment.
SOURCE: Centers for Medicare and Medicaid Services (2012b).

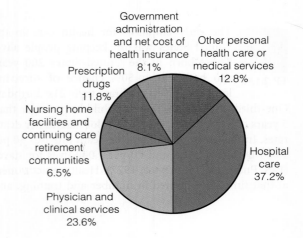

FIG 8.2B **The Nation's Health Dollar, Calendar Year 2010: Where It Came From**

[1]Other third-party payers and programs include programs such as workers' compensation, public health activity, Department of Defense, Department of Veterans Affairs, Indian Health Service, state and local hospital subsidies, and school health.

[2]All other sources include industrial in-plant, privately funded construction, and nonpatient revenues, including philanthropy.

[3]Out-of-pocket includes copays, deductibles, and treatments not covered by Private Health Insurance.

NOTE: Numbers shown may not add to 100.0 because of rounding.

SCHIP = State Children's Health Insurance Program.

SOURCE: Centers for Medicare and Medicaid Services (2012c).

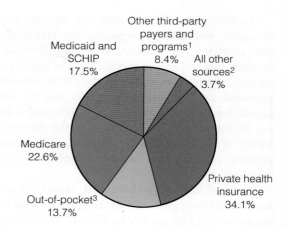

and improving health personnel, services, and research. As costs for health care have skyrocketed, though, attention has shifted to ways to control costs and to determine who should pay for what expenditures.

Health Insurance Plans and Managed Care

EP 2.1.1a
EP 2.1.8a
EP 2.1.9b

In 2007, almost 70% of the U.S. population under 65 years of age had some form of **private health insurance** (purchased by individuals or employers from companies such as Blue Cross/Blue Shield or United Health Care). The major source of insurance coverage for this group is private employer-sponsored group health insurance obtained through a current or former employer or union. Historically, the standard practice among employers was to provide health insurance coverage (employer-sponsored insurance) at no cost to their employees.

As health-care costs skyrocketed, employers began to charge employees for a portion of the premiums for health-care insurance (a practice called "premium sharing"), restricted coverage to only the employee and not the employee's spouse or children, or stopped providing coverage at all. Between 2003 and 2013, employer-sponsored health insurance premiums rose by 80% for premiums for family coverage ($9,068 and $16,351, respectively). The average share of a family premium that employees were required to pay rose from $2,412 a year in 2003 to $4,565 a year in 2013 (Kaiser Family Foundation, 2013).

Here, we point out that employees' earnings grew more slowly than the increase in health-care premiums, making health care even less affordable. As a result, employees are either dropping coverage or, if their coverage is provided, not paying for the far more expensive coverage for their families. The intersecting issues of who should get employee- or government-sponsored health-care benefits, the extent of those benefits, and what types of illness are covered are increasingly becoming issues of social justice as large segments of society (predominantly low-wage workers) are being relegated to a life of low income or even poverty, for which there is no way out.

One factor that has contributed to the higher costs for private and public health care alike has been the shift from retrospective to prospective payment systems. In the past, with the exception of insurance for hospitalization, most health care was paid for *after* it was used. People went to the doctor and paid the full amount after the visit. Today, most health care is paid in advance through premiums to private insurance companies or federal programs such as Medicaid, because the health-care industry is trying to contain costs and promote preventive health care.

Most current health-care plans are based on a **managed-care system**, in which health-care delivery limits the use and cost of services and measures performance through a program of careful monitoring and control. Under managed care, "health-care professionals" hired by health insurance companies and large employers systematically review specific health-care needs and determine the most cost-effective ways to provide for them. After review, limited options are presented to consumers. For example, some plans include preferred provider organizations, which offer health care through a network of specific providers. An individual who chooses providers other than those in the preapproved network usually must get specific permission from the health-care plan to do so, pay additional costs to use other providers, or not have those health-care costs covered by the plan at all.

Another group in the health-care industry consists of **health maintenance organizations (HMOs)**, prepaid medical group practices to which individuals pay monthly fees and receive specific types of health care at no cost or minimum costs per visit. HMO enrollment increased steadily during the 1990s, but the rate of growth has declined since that time, reflecting a shake-out in the industry, a reduction in the number and variety of plans available for selection, and consumers' growing dissatisfaction with the quality of services delivered.

Managed-care plans have had mixed success in meeting the twin goals of cost containment and ensuring accessible, high-quality health care. If anything, the pendulum has swung to the cost-containment side at the expense of ensuring accessible, high-quality health-care services.

Because the health-care system is part of the free-market system in the United States, there always will be tensions between those who wish to maximize profit and return on investment and those who demand accessible, high-quality health care for all Americans. Thus, social work professionals must advocate for a health-care system that is accessible to everyone, regardless of their ability to pay for services.

In short, attempts have been made to promote early preventive health care to create a nation that is physically healthier and to reduce costs. Neither task has been successful. Administrative costs alone to manage such a complex system have escalated over the years. Health-care costs continue to rise rapidly in spite of efforts at cost containment. Increases can be seen at every level, and the average cost of health care per person per year in the United States ($8,508 in 2013) is the highest of that of any industrialized country (Commonwealth Fund, 2014).

Comparing Health-Care Costs to Outcomes

Although the United States spends more on health care than any other country (estimated to be nearly 18% of the **gross domestic product (GDP)** in 2014), its health-care system does not produce superior outcomes in comparison to other countries. For example, in 2011, the United States ranked 26th in life expectancy among the 36 member countries of the Organisation for Economic Cooperation and Development (OECD, 2014) (see Table 8.4). When comparing

EP 2.1.1a
EP 2.1.8a
EP 2.1.9b

significant health-care indicators, the U.S. investment in health care has failed to achieve its intended outcomes.

Reasons for Rising Health-Care Costs

Although costs of health care, like costs in other areas, have risen because of inflation, other reasons for rising health expenditures must be considered, too. Some attribute the increased costs to more extensive use of medical resources by a more educated population interested in preventive health care. They argue that accessibility to group insurance plans through the workplace and the increase in HMOs and other health programs aimed at reducing health costs actually increase costs because of more extensive use. Statistics show, however, that many Americans, particularly poor people—people of color, single-parent females, and the elderly—work for employers that do not offer health insurance or are paid such low wages that they cannot afford the health insurance offered. Thus, they are less apt to use health-care resources, and when they do, they are more likely to need more costly services because they have not sought preventive care.

EP 2.1.1a
EP 2.1.8a
EP 2.1.9b

Even with today's emphasis on wellness and public awareness about the potential damages of smoking, use of alcohol and other drugs, and lack of exercise, private citizens and all levels of U.S. government spend relatively few dollars. This trend continues even though studies show that dollars spent for prevention more than pay for themselves in the long run (The Prevention Institute, 2010).

An Increasing Elderly Population Because of greater access to health care, improved knowledge and technology, and a better quality of life, life expectancy is on the rise, resulting in greater needs for medical care for people age 65 or older. Comprising approximately 12% of the population and more likely to be poor and unable to pay for health care than other groups, people over age 65 have three times more health problems and needs than people in younger age groups. Between 2015 and 2060, the population over age 65 is projected to nearly double and the population over age 85 is projected to nearly triple in the United States (U.S. Census Bureau, 2013).

As this population continues to grow, the accompanying costs will increase. Few insurance premiums

TABLE 8.4 COMPARISONS OF HEALTH-CARE COSTS, LIFE EXPECTANCY, AND INFANT MORTALITY RATES FOR 20 INDUSTRIALIZED COUNTRIES

COUNTRY	% GDP ALLOCATED TO HEALTH CARE/RANK	INFANT MORTALITY RATE PER 1,000 LIVE BIRTHS/RANK	LIFE EXPECTANCY AT BIRTH
Australia	8.5/9	3.3/5	84.3/7
Belgium	11.8/2	3.8/9	83.1/11
Canada	10.9/4	4.8/11	83.6/8
Chile	8.2/10	7.7/16	81.4/14
Czech Republic	7.9/12	2.6/2	81.2/15
France	3.5/18	3.5/6	85.4/3
Germany	8.1/11	3.3/5	83.3/10
Greece	7.4/13	2.9/3	83.4/9
Hungary	8.2/10	4.9/13	78.8/17
Italy	5.1/12	2.9/3	84.8/5
Japan	9.3/8	2.2/1	86.4/1
Netherlands	10.8/5	3.7/8	83.0/12
Poland	7.1/14	4.6/11	81.1/16
South Korea	6.5/16	2.9/3	84.6/6
Spain	9.7/9	3.1/4	85.5/2
Sweden	9.9/6	2.6/2	83.6/8
Switzerland	11.3/3	3.6/7	84.9/4
Turkey	6.7/15	7.4/15	77.2/18
United Kingdom	9.3/8	4.1/10	82.8/13
United States	16.2/1	6.1/14	81.1/16

SOURCE: Organisation for Economic Cooperation and Development (2012). *OECD StatExtracts*. Paris, France: Author.

cover the costs of long-term care (assisted living), and those that do are rapidly raising the premiums for this coverage. The insurance system, particularly care for the elderly, also is fragmented, with separate systems paying for home health care, medical equipment, nursing home care, and medical transportation to and from health-care facilities. By 2040, people age 65 or older are expected to account for more than half of the total personal health-care expenditures in the United States.

Increased Knowledge and Availability of Technology A second explanation for the increased costs of health care is the wider availability of knowledge and technology for saving lives—neonatal procedures for infants born prematurely; heart, lung, and other organ transplants; heart surgery to restore circulation and reduce the incidence of heart attacks and other cardiac problems; and sophisticated combinations of medications for a variety of conditions that would have resulted in death in earlier years.

Currently, the extent of and knowledge about technology exceed the dollars necessary to support such sophisticated systems and make them available to everyone in need. In many instances, heroic procedures are covered by health-care policies, but preventive care—such as long-term care, rehabilitative services, and health education—are not. Recognizing that value issues are inherent when discussing health care, our current health technologies have become cost prohibitive. Current studies suggest, for example, that individuals who receive heart transplants live an average of 4 years longer than persons who do not receive transplants, at a cost of $271,000 for the surgery and first year of care and $21,000 per year for medical tests and medications thereafter, or $83,500 for every additional year of life.

In addition, with more private hospitals and the difficulties faced by public medical facilities in remaining solvent, health care has become increasingly competitive. Many private hospitals are now owned by large corporations with real estate subsidiaries and their own insurance divisions. In many instances, the heightened competition has resulted in the duplication of expensive technology by hospitals in close proximity.

While hospitals struggle to compete with each other for paying clients, the number of people who are unable to pay hospital bills continues to increase. The limits on **public health insurance** (Medicare and Medicaid) reimbursements to hospitals also have resulted in serious financial problems for hospitals that are unable to provide services at reimbursement levels. The number of hospitals in the United States has been declining steadily in recent years, from 6,965 in 1980 to 5,723 in 2012 (American Hospital Association, 2014). In addition, hospitals are losing large sums of money as a result of uncompensated care. Today, about 1 in 10 patients is indigent and unable to pay for medical costs.

Emphasis on Third-Party Payments   A third reason suggested for escalated health-care costs is the use of third-party billing by many medical practitioners (billing an insurance company directly rather than billing the patient). Many physicians and hospitals charge the maximum amount allowable under an insurance system, whereas they might be reluctant to charge individual clients the same amount if they knew the clients would be paying for the services directly.

Faced with rapidly increasing costs, private insurance companies in the United States, which cover about half of the population, are minimizing their risks by reducing the benefits covered, requiring second opinions in many instances, increasing copayments from consumers, and excluding individuals with chronic health conditions. At the same time, insurance premiums continue to rise, with high costs to employers who pay a portion of employees' premiums, as well as to employees themselves. As a result, many employers, particularly smaller ones, no longer cover employees or their families, or they cover a smaller percentage of premiums, which means that employees are paying much larger shares. More and more people who carry health insurance on an individual basis rather than an employee policy are being forced to cancel their policies because they cannot afford them, requiring local communities to pick up the rising costs of their health care if these individuals become ill and cannot pay their bills. The reforms to the country's health-care system brought about by the Affordable Care Act are intended to ameliorate these problems, but it is too early to tell how successful they will be in achieving this purpose.

Increased Costs of Health Care for the Poor   A fourth reason for the higher costs of health care is the number of poor people who need health care and cannot afford to pay for it. As this number continues to increase, federal and state governments struggle with the high costs of health care. But efforts to reduce Medicaid and Medicare expenditures by setting ceilings for reimbursable costs have led some physicians and nursing homes to refuse to accept clients under these health-care assistance plans, claiming that they lose too much money because the actual costs are much higher than the payments allowed. For physicians who do continue to see Medicare and Medicaid clients, low reimbursement rates have led some to inflate their billings so they can be paid the prevailing market rate for their services. Ironically, if this practice goes undetected (which, in many cases, it does), the government's desire to drive down the cost of health care is actually reversed.

One of our country's highest priorities is how to pay for health care while addressing the needs of those who cannot afford it. **Medicaid**, the federal–state partnership program that assists states in providing medical services to eligible low-income individuals, is the single largest source of funding for health services for low-income people. In 2012, Medicaid and Medicare spending in the United States amounted to $421.2 billion and $ billion, respectively (nearly 40% of total national health expenditures). During the period from 2010 to 2019, Medicare and Medicaid spending are expected to grow an average of 6.9% and 7.9% per year, respectively (Centers for Medicare and Medicaid Services, 2013a).

Though eligibility requirements vary by state, all states must provide coverage for children under age 6 and pregnant women in families with incomes at or below 133% of the poverty level ($31,720 for a family of four). Many states cover children under age 1 and pregnant women whose family income is at or below 185% of the poverty level ($44,122 for a family of four). States are required to provide early and periodic screening, diagnosis, and treatment services to children, as well as physicians' services and inpatient and outpatient hospital care. States are reimbursed a certain portion of funds they spend for Medicaid, depending on what they cover and whom they serve. The Medicaid program uses the Federal Medical Assistance Percentage (FMAP) to determine the federal government's share of the cost of covered services in state Medicaid programs. On average, since the time the Medicaid program was implemented in 1965, the FMAP has been 57%. Beginning in 2014, the Affordable Care Act (ACA) establishes highly enhanced FMAPs for the cost of services to low-income adults with incomes up to 138% of the FPIL who are not currently covered. The federal government will pick up 100% of these costs in 2014 through 2016, phasing down to 90% in 2020 and beyond (Centers for Disease Control and Prevention, 2013b). States would be foolish not to take advantage of these highly favorable matching rates in an effort to provide health-care coverage for the state's poor. Such action would help the state meet the needs of its citizens who cannot afford health-care coverage, while reducing costs paid by states and local governments associated with receiving primary care in an emergency room as well as those related to increased morbidity among this population resulting from the lack of preventive care and serious health problems that have gone untreated. In colloquial terms, it's a case of "pay me now or pay me a lot more later." As the U.S. population continues to age, costs of **Medicare**—the medical care coverage program for older adults established as one of the pillars of the War on Poverty programs of the mid-1960s—continue to

increase. One major source of concern among senior adults and their families has been the high cost of prescription drugs (see discussion later in this chapter). Compounding the situation, health-care services are fragmented, inaccessible, and unattainable for many U.S. residents, and when they are provided, they are not well matched to the needs of those receiving them. The health-care system in the United States is an unfortunate example of how market forces and the lack of political will have created an ineffective, narrowly focused, fragmented, and expensive approach to a major social welfare problem. The reforms to the country's health-care system introduced by the Affordable Care Act are designed to address these problems; however, it is too early to tell how successful the reforms will be in achieving this purpose.

Even though the Medicaid system of health care for the poor and group insurance programs have their problems, of greater concern are the many persons who have no health coverage at all. A significant portion of the poor in the United States either are not covered by Medicaid or do not use the system. Those who have neither Medicaid nor other health insurance coverage can become destitute immediately when they or members of their family incur catastrophic health problems. Poor families simply cannot afford the costs of health care associated with serious health problems, especially those that require hospitalization. When individuals have no way to pay for their health care, local communities are left to pick up the costs. For many poor people, the emergency room—one of the most expensive forms of health care—is the only choice they have to receive primary health-care services. And by the time they do seek care, their problems are more advanced, further escalating the cost of their care.

Many local public hospitals that are obligated to accept medically indigent patients (referred to by the federal government as "disproportionate share hospitals") are operating at a deficit.

Many state legislators do not understand the complicated reimbursement system for government programs such as Medicare and Medicaid, or they are ideologically opposed to providing government services to needy persons who they believe are capable of findings jobs and supporting themselves with their earnings. Although the proportion of reimbursement to states varies by category of service, for every dollar of Medicaid money spent, the state contribution is currently between 65 and 81 cents. Some state legislatures limit dollars allocated for state health care, not always understanding that limiting state costs reduces the number of federal dollars available to the state (sometimes referred to as "leaving money on the table") and ultimately results in more money, not less, paid by that state's citizens as a result of nonreimbursed costs that are passed on to consumers who are able to pay for services.

An example is provided by one large state that consistently limits its legislative authorization of state dollars for health-care coverage for the poor. As a result, less federal matching money comes into that state and more goes to other states. This means that many of the dollars paid by citizens and businesses of that state in federal taxes go to other states. In one recent year, for example, for every $3.00 that a citizen of the state paid in federal income taxes, only $1.89 was returned to the state. The other $1.11 went to other states for their programs. Most recently, the state leadership refused to expand the state's Medicaid program, leaving nearly $8 billion in match-free federal funds on the table and some 350,000 women and children without any health-care coverage at all. When they became ill, they went to public hospitals, funded by local tax dollars, while the hospitals and the communities in which they were located had to absorb the costs of their unpaid care. As noted, these nonreimbursed costs ultimately are borne by those who can afford to pay for their health services, creating a vicious cycle with no apparent end in sight.

Increasing Malpractice Suits   The propensity to instigate lawsuits is another cost-raising factor in the United States. Medical practitioners fear the increasing number of malpractice suits being filed. It is estimated that all medical practitioners face at least one lawsuit during their careers, regardless of their level of competence (National Center for Policy Analysis, 2007). This development has resulted in extremely high costs for malpractice insurance and practitioners' feeling compelled to order numerous tests, exploratory surgery, and other medical procedures when they are not sure what is wrong with an individual, to eliminate the risk of a lawsuit for a wrong decision (National Center for Policy Analysis, 2007). Although legislation has been introduced in many states to limit malpractice suits and the amount of settlements allowable under the

broad category of tort reform, these efforts have met with mixed success (National Center for Policy Analysis, 2007).

Current Major Health Problems

Many health problems that faced Americans in the past have been all but eliminated, but new ones have arisen to take their place. Current major health problems facing the United States and its citizens include heart disease, cancer, stroke, pulmonary disease, diabetes, kidney disease, and liver disease.

The three leading causes of death in the United States in 2012 were heart disease, cancer, and chronic lower respiratory diseases (Centers for Disease Control and Prevention, 2013a). Nearly half of these deaths were a result of diseases of the heart and cancer. Cancer rates continue to rise and are increasingly associated with environmental factors. Cancer is projected to be the cause of death for one in five persons in the United States. Though new technology and medications have made treatment of these diseases more effective, they remain major causes of death.

HIV and AIDS

 Acquired immunodeficiency syndrome (AIDS) has affected all of the social institutions and most communities in the United States. With recently discovered medication regimens, the life spans of many persons diagnosed with HIV (human immunodeficiency virus) infection have been extended considerably. Over time, however, the majority of individuals with HIV develop AIDS, which has a high fatality rate associated with the opportunistic diseases that result from a weakened immune system. HIV continues to spread to all segments of the population. Because the method of transmission of the virus is tied to culturally sensitive topics, including illegal drugs, sex, and sexual orientation, HIV and AIDS often are viewed in political, cultural, and moral contexts rather than as a serious public health issue.

EP 2.1.3a
EP 2.1.7b
EP 2.1.9a

AIDS first came to the attention of health authorities in the early 1980s. More than 1 million people in the United States are living with HIV infection (Kaiser Family Foundation, 2014). Additionally, more than 16,000 AIDS-related deaths occurred in the United States in 2010, the latest year for which such data are available. The Joint United Nations Programme on

HIV/AIDS (UN AIDS, 2013) estimates that worldwide, 35 million people were living with HIV/AIDS in 2013. About 2.4 million people became newly infected, and 1.5 million lost their lives to the disease during that same year.

Women are becoming increasingly affected by HIV. Approximately half of adults living with HIV or AIDS worldwide are women. About 70% of all HIV-infected people now live in least-developed parts of the world (UN AIDS, 2013).

Definitions   In 2014, the Centers for Disease Control and Prevention updated previous HIV/AIDS surveillance case definitions to accommodate recent changes in diagnostic criteria. The revision was also prompted by recognition of early HIV infection and several technical classification issues (Centers for Disease Control and Prevention, 2014d). A person referred to as being **HIV-positive** has tested positively for the human immunodeficiency virus, is infected with the virus, and has HIV antibodies present in his or her blood. HIV is an intracellular parasite that binds to molecules in the body. Unless the spread of HIV is interrupted by treatment, the infection spreads throughout the body, causing the destruction of cells that help maintain the immune system and leading to a gradual but progressive destruction of the entire immune system (Weeks & Shors, 2013).

During the primary HIV-infection period, 50–90% of individuals develop a mononucleosis-like infection that begins 1–3 weeks after infection and continues for 1–2 weeks. Most individuals do not recognize HIV-related symptoms at this point, and many of them do not receive HIV testing until much later, when their health is more at risk and they are more likely to have infected others. An estimated third of those infected with the virus are unaware that they have it (Weeks & Shors, 2013). Many persons with HIV are living longer, healthier lives because of the development of antiviral and other effective medications that can slow the rate at which HIV weakens the immune system.

If the immune system becomes seriously damaged, AIDS is more likely to develop. As medications have improved the health of persons with HIV, definitions of what constitutes AIDS have changed. Currently, certain markers—including the number and ratio of T-helper cells to other cells, and the presence of opportunistic diseases—determine a diagnosis of AIDS. Opportunistic diseases common among persons diagnosed with AIDS include PCP (*Pneumocystis carinii* pneumonia, a lung infection), KS (Kaposi's sarcoma, a skin cancer), CMV (cytomegalovirus, an infection that usually affects the eyes), and Candida, a fungal infection. Other AIDS-related illnesses include brain tumors and serious weight loss (aids.org, 2014). As more women are diagnosed with HIV and AIDS, cervical cancer and chronic yeast infections have been added to the list of conditions associated with these conditions.

More and more is becoming known about how the disease can be treated, and with new medications and medical treatment, the death rate from AIDS-related diseases has declined. Many individuals infected with HIV are living 10 years or longer before being diagnosed with AIDS. Still, research efforts have yet to find a cure or a vaccine to prevent its spread.

Prevalence and Populations Affected   In 2011, 75% and 25% of new HIV/AIDS cases involved males and females, respectively. About half of all new cases were men who reported having sex with other men. The rates for newly infected individuals also are high among women as a result of high-risk sexual contact or injection-drug use (Centers for Disease Control and Prevention, 2011). AIDS specialists have suggested that because AIDS symptoms do not show up for several years, we should look at the numbers of individuals who have HIV in their blood instead of data relating to the numbers of persons with AIDS.

Results of blood testing of persons with AIDS reported to the Centers for Disease Control and Prevention (2011) confirm that whereas rates among homosexual and bisexual men have stabilized, rates in the heterosexual population, particularly intravenous-drug users, women, and children, are increasing. According to the Centers for Disease Control and Prevention (2011), the distribution of new cases of HIV/AIDS in the United States in 2011 according to race/ethnicity was as follows: black (49.8%), white (25.9%), Hispanic (19.8%). The remaining cases involved Asian/Pacific Islander (0.1%), American Indian/Alaska Native (0.5%), Asian (1.5%), and multiple races (2.3%) (percent figures do not add to 100% because of rounding). Of the HIV/AIDS cases reported, 69.7% were acquired through male-to-male sexual contact, 9.8% through injection-drug use, 5.8% through male-to-male sexual contact coupled with injection-drug use, and 14.7%

Box 8.1   Humane Treatment for Persons with AIDS: National Association of Social Workers Policy Statement on AIDS

Social workers provide a range of services to clients who are at risk of becoming or are HIV-positive and their families. It is important that the social work profession play an active role in HIV prevention and education, as well as reducing the stigma for this population and ensuring their access to health and mental health services. NASW has developed a policy statement that delineates what is needed to ensure the humane treatment of persons with HIV/AIDS and their families (2014):

Prevention and Education

- collaboration with organizations that provide HIV and AIDS research, education, and treatment to develop and implement culturally sensitive education and prevention strategies that meet the needs of diverse groups and incorporate "the language, culture, ethnicity, sexual orientation, gender and gender identity, religion, and age of the target population" (p. 174)
- "evidence-based prevention efforts that target children and adolescents in both public and private school systems and comprehensive sexuality education programs for youths and adults" (p. 174)
- development and implementation of programs that reduce the incidence of HIV among IV drug users, including needle exchange programs and increased access to drug treatment

Social Work Education

- education of social workers about strategies that prevent the transmission of HIV, including the use of appropriate assessment tools to assess risk and educate clients about safer sex and harm reduction
- greater awareness among social workers about the need to continuously update their knowledge about all aspects of HIV
- social work education programs that include content on HIV/AIDS incorporating social work values, the health and mental health needs of persons living with HIV/AIDS and their families, and the importance of HIV/AIDS prevention and intervention at the community and societal levels

Testing

- education of practitioners about the availability and accessibility of HIV antibody testing and resources for persons living with HIV and AIDS and their families
- availability of "voluntary and confidential testing on an anonymous basis and includes prior informed consent" (p. 174)
- availability of rapid testing that is provided only when consent is granted by the person being tested and conducted only by certified and trained personnel
- availability of counseling programs provided by trained personnel to clients prior to and after HIV testing
- access to free counseling by trained personnel by telephone or other methods to those individuals who use home-testing kits, as well as referrals to resources that provide formal HIV testing
- ensuring that informed consent is obtained from women who are pregnant or have given birth prior to mandatory HIV testing of either themselves or their newborn children
- obtaining prior consent before releasing HIV test results of clients
- using clinical social work skills to encourage clients who are HIV-positive and have not informed needle-sharing or sexual partners about their sero status to do so

Service Delivery, Care, and Treatment

- ensuring the right of individuals living with HIV/AIDS, including those residing in correctional institutions, to receive the highest-quality care
- "a comprehensive services delivery system ... that includes access to suitable and affordable housing, mental and health care services, adult and child foster care, legal services, and transportation" (p. 175)
- accessible client-centered support for people with HIV/AIDS and those affected that incorporates their biological, psychosocial, spiritual, linguistic, and cultural needs
- elimination of barriers that limit access to affordable medication, clinical trials, and providers of

(continued)

Box 8.1   Humane Treatment for Persons with AIDS: National Association of Social Workers Policy Statement on AIDS (continued)

HIV services "that ensure psychological, social, cultural, and economic well-being" (p. 175)

- "policies that facilitate access to affordable pharmaceuticals worldwide. Clients should have sufficient supports to help them maintain difficult medication regimens" (p. 175)
- "the right to confidentiality relating to HIV/AIDS status. Clients should be informed of the limits of confidentiality, including the existence of partner notification and record keeping. Social workers should be familiar with applicable state laws, regulations, and federal guidelines" (p. 175)

Political Action and Advocacy

- continued funding of HIV/AIDS prevention and intervention programs at the local, state, national, and international levels
- development and support of efforts that address structural factors that increase the risk of HIV/AIDS, including poverty, interpersonal violence, and community disengagement
- leadership at local, state, and federal levels to "improve the quality of life of all persons living with HIV/AIDS and their families and to protect their civil liberties, including maximum access to confidential testing, diagnosis, and treatment" (p. 175)
- "advocacy for funding of research on all aspects of HIV/AIDS, including prevention, clinical interventions, and vaccine development" (p. 175)

Research

- federally funded research that incorporates epidemiological, clinical, and comprehensive biopsycho-social-spiritual perspectives
- culturally sensitive research protocols that "address the unique needs of women, children and adolescents, and the psycho-social-spiritual needs of all people living with and affected by HIV/AIDS" (p. 175)
- "funding for research to accurately assess the effectiveness of primary and secondary prevention and educational strategies, service delivery models, and the effect of related policies" (p. 175)

SOURCE: Copyrighted material reprinted with permission from the National Association of Social Workers, Inc.

---

through heterosexual contact (Centers for Disease Control and Prevention, 2011).

AIDS, which first appeared in the United States among urban middle-class adults, has now spread to rural communities and to poorer and younger population groups (Centers for Disease Control and Prevention, 2011). The brunt of the epidemic is being felt most by groups whose access to services and information is limited by low income.

Treatment   About half of persons with HIV are not receiving any treatment. The costs of medications to delay onset of AIDS and treat AIDS once it occurs are exorbitant, and coverage of prescriptions is becoming a problem for affected individuals, as well as the insurance companies that cover the costs of their care. Although the issues faced by those with AIDS and their families are similar to those of others with life-threatening illnesses, persons with AIDS and their families also face discrimination in communities where they live and the places they work. They also have difficulty obtaining health insurance, a place to live, housing, employment, needed social services, and emotional support. The Americans With Disabilities Act (see Chapter 9) specifically mentions persons with AIDS in its listing of disabilities covered under the act, but oppression and discrimination remain major issues for individuals with AIDS and their families (see Box 8.1 for the National Association of Social Workers [NASW] policy statement on AIDS).

To complicate matters further, more than 100,000 children in the United States have lost one or both of their parents to AIDS. Developing permanent plans for their children is a difficult issue that confronts persons with AIDS who are parents. Many of these children go to live with relatives, but increasing numbers are placed in foster care or become candidates for adoption.

Other Illnesses and Health Problems

EP 2.1.3a
EP 2.1.7b
EP 2.1.9a

Other illnesses receiving more attention are diabetes, musculoskeletal diseases such as arthritis and osteoporosis, and respiratory diseases. These conditions are much more prevalent among the poor, people of color, and the elderly, who are unable to afford either preventive or rehabilitative health care. Some life-threatening diseases, such as Huntington's disease and cystic fibrosis, are genetically linked. Prenatal genetic screening currently is available to detect the presence of Down syndrome, Tay–Sachs disease, cystic fibrosis, and sickle-cell anemia. Researchers believe that it is just a matter of time before prenatal genetic testing will be able to identify those who are predisposed to hypertension, dyslexia, cancer, manic depression, schizophrenia, type 1 diabetes, familial Alzheimer's disease, multiple sclerosis, myotonic muscular dystrophy, and alcohol and other drug abuse.

These discoveries have raised the level of debate regarding moral and ethical choices in relation to birth, fetal and parental rights, abortion, and the associated emotional and financial costs to individuals and society. If it is known that a child will be born with multiple sclerosis, HIV antibodies, or cancer, who should decide the outcome of the pregnancy? If the child is born with one of these diseases, who should pay the costs for the child's care?

Present pregnancy-termination rates for women who have undergone genetic screening are nearly 100% for muscular dystrophy and cystic fibrosis, 60% for hemophilia, and 50% for sickle-cell anemia. But what if the disease is one that occurs much later in life, such as Huntington's disease; is not fatal, such as Down syndrome; or reveals a predisposition to a disease, such as cancer, heart disease, or schizophrenia? And how do these issues relate to decision making to terminate a pregnancy? **Bioethics**, the moral and ethical implications of biomedical advances for individuals, their families, and the broader society, is a fast-growing field in which social workers can play a major role.

Another health concern is the increasing numbers of persons with serious head or spinal injuries who have permanent brain injuries or multiple disabilities. Many require years of rehabilitation, and some require institutional care for the remainder of their lives. As technology enables many more people with such injuries to remain alive more often than in the past, costs for their care also increase. Because many individuals have received head and spinal injuries from motorcycle accidents when they were not wearing helmets or had alcohol-or drug-related accidents or car accidents when they were not wearing seat belts, additional concerns are raised about who should pay for health costs and how much should be paid.

A growing number of individuals with these injuries involves those in the military who have seen combat in recent conflicts such as the war in Iraq. Advances in field medicine in war zones have made it possible to save the lives of many soldiers who receive traumatic injuries and would have died in previous wars. Accurate statistics regarding the number of these individuals have been difficult to obtain, but they are projected to be in the thousands. The American public bears the cost of caring for these soldiers, which for many extends for their entire lifetime (RAND, 2008).

Catastrophic Illness

EP 2.1.3a
EP 2.1.7b
EP 2.1.9a

National attention also is being directed to the problems of catastrophic illness. A **catastrophic illness** is a chronic and severely debilitating condition that results in long-term dependence on the health-care system. Although many families can provide health care for themselves during typical, less serious bouts of illness, a catastrophic illness can wipe out family savings and force some to declare personal bankruptcy or relinquish their care to the already overloaded public health-care system.

To date, no legislation has been passed to address this serious issue. The debate centers on who should be covered, how much care should be provided and at what cost, and how long the care should be provided. These questions have no ready answers. One bill passed by Congress in 1988, the Catastrophic Health Care Act, provided coverage for families and the elderly who experienced catastrophic illness or disability. This law was repealed in 1989 after a strong lobbying effort by well-to-do elderly persons who protested against increased Medicare premiums resulting from the legislation. The law also did not cover long-term nursing home care.

The Affordable Health Care Act of 2009 signed into law by President Barak Obama in March 2010, does not contain a specific provision for catastrophic health care; however, it does provide for some type of health care for everyone in the United States (see "Health-Care Reform").

Teen Pregnancy

In recent years, one of the most publicized at-risk groups has been teenage parents. The United States has the highest adolescent pregnancy rate of industrialized countries. The birth rate of teens 15–19 years of age in 2012 was 29.4 per 1,000 women in this age group. Teen pregnancy and childbearing result in substantial social and economic costs. In 2011, teen pregnancy and childbirth accounted for upward of $9 billion in costs to U.S. taxpayers for increased health care and foster care, increased incarceration rates among children of teen parents, and lost tax revenue because of lower educational attainment and income among teen mothers. Pregnancy and birth are significant contributors to dropping out of high school among girls. Only about half of teen mothers receive a high school diploma. The children of teenage mothers are more likely to have lower school achievement and drop out of high school, have more health problems, be incarcerated at some time during adolescence, give birth as a teenager, and face unemployment as a young adult (Centers for Disease Control and Prevention, 2014a).

EP 2.1.3a
EP 2.1.7b
EP 2.1.9a

Pregnant teens receive little or no prenatal care, poor nutrition during pregnancy, and limited services (Findyouthinfo.gov, 2014). As a result, they are at more risk of having miscarriages and of giving birth to premature and low-birth-weight infants, and infants with congenital problems.

Prenatal services and nutritional assistance such as the Supplemental Nutrition Program for Women, Infants, and Children (WIC) are cost-effective and result in healthy infants who are better able to grow up to become healthy adults. Premature births declined and birth weight of infants increased among low-income pregnant women who participated in a food and nutrition education program (U.S. Department of Agriculture, 2014).

Environmental Factors

In recent years, increasing attention has been directed to environmental factors and their impact on people. These factors include hazardous household substances and other poisons, as well as household building materials, such as lead-based paints and formaldehyde in insulation. Workplaces also present risks to health, resulting in environmental protections for employees from dangerous chemicals, pollutants in the air, and hazardous jobs. In 2012, 7% of fatal work injuries were caused by exposure to harmful substances or environments (U.S. Department of Labor, 2012). An estimated one-fifth of all deaths from cancer are associated with occupational hazards.

EP 2.1.3a
EP 2.1.7b
EP 2.1.9a

One of the environmental hazards associated with an increased incidence of cancer and respiratory diseases is the discovery of harmful asbestos in many older buildings. In spite of the known health risk, workers hired to remove asbestos in many instances have not received the needed information and protection to avoid being exposed to the substance. Of those with long-term exposure to asbestos, half die and the remainder suffer long-term debilitation from respiratory complications such as asbestosis (National Institute for Occupational Safety and Health, 2011).

For everyone living in the United States, regardless of occupation, the environment is an increasing health hazard. Increasing pollutants in the air and in food products are associated with significant increases in heart disease, cancer, and respiratory diseases in the United States in comparison to other countries. Other environmental risks include:

- road and traffic safety;
- unsafe housing;
- contaminated food;
- pest and animal control;
- biomedical and consumer product safety;
- inappropriate disposal of chemical and human wastes;
- storage and treatment of potable water; and
- control of nuclear energy plants.

According to the Centers for Disease Control and Prevention (2012), chronic diseases, including heart disease and stroke, cancer, and diabetes are among the most costly and preventable of all health problems.

Seven of every 10 Americans who die each year die of a chronic disease. Chronic, disabling conditions cause major limitations in activity for more than 1 of every 10 Americans. Tobacco use greatly increases the risk of developing the leading chronic diseases. Upward of 300 billion cigarettes were purchased in the United States in 2011, the latest year for such figures are available. Each year, more than 480,000 Americans die from smoking or other tobacco use. An estimated 42,000 of tobacco-related deaths are the result of secondhand smoke exposure. The direct and indirect costs associated with smoking are estimated to be $289 billion annually (Centers for Disease Control and Prevention, 2014b,c).

Concern has risen because of the increasing number of young people who smoke. Each day in the United States, more than 3,200 people younger than 18 years of age smoke their first cigarette, and an estimated 2,100 youth and young adults who have been occasional smokers become daily cigarette smokers. From 2011 to 2012, electronic cigarette use doubled among middle and high school students, and hookah use increased among high school students (Centers for Disease Control and Prevention, 2014c). Federal and state legislation, local community ordinances, and workplace policies are limiting smoking to designated areas or prohibiting it completely in public areas. Smoking has not been allowed on airline flights for some time. Numerous other initiatives have been undertaken at the national level to promote smoking cessation (American Lung Association, 2014).

Prevention and Wellness Programs

EP 2.1.3a
EP 2.1.7b
EP 2.1.9a

The preventive aspects of health care are receiving more attention, although prevention is still secondary to taking action after a health problem has developed. Some businesses have established wellness programs— exercise and fitness programs, nutrition and weight-control programs, smoking-cessation workshops, and other health and prevention efforts. A number of employers are working with insurance companies to offer incentives, such as salary bonuses or reduced insurance rates, to employees who are considered low risk. Problems in the workplace and the

broader society from substance abuse have led employers and insurance companies to establish substance-abuse prevention programs in the workplace.

Most recently, obesity in youth and its relation to major health problems such as diabetes have become a concern. Many public schools have removed unhealthy snacks and sodas from school buildings altogether or limited access to these, and at the same time, have introduced fitness and physical education programs.

Ethical Issues

EP 2.1.2a
EP 2.1.2c

As health-care costs continue to escalate, more people need health care, and new technology and knowledge make it possible to keep people alive who previously could not have been helped. These changes have given rise to ethical dilemmas in the area of health care, and many of these issues are before our courts. Examples of these pressing questions are:

- When infants require extensive neonatal care to survive, should such care be made available even if the parents cannot afford the costs?
- Should the circumstances change if it is decided that the infant can survive, but with serious mental and/or physical disabilities?
- If technology for heart and lung transplantations is available, who should have access to these procedures?
- If genetics testing reveals that a fetus has a serious illness or disability, what choices should be considered, and who should be involved?
- If individuals can survive with medical care or special procedures, should they have a right to decide whether to receive the care or to be allowed to die?
- Do people have the right to choose unsafe behaviors, such as riding motorcycles without helmets, not using seat belts, or using drugs or alcohol, when injuries or other health problems may result in high costs to taxpayers, state and local governments, and other individuals in the same insurance group?
- Does a pregnant woman have the right to drink alcoholic beverages, use other drugs, or smoke if it is known that these substances compromise the survival or health of her child?

Related questions are:

- Who should make such decisions?

Preventive health care is far more cost-effective than medical problems that arise when preventive services are not provided. This father was able to access early medical care for his daughter, who was born with a serious medical condition, that will allow her to live a full life; doctors told him she would have died before age three if her medical problems had not been identified and addressed.

What are the rights of the individual?
- … of the parents if the person is a child?
- … of the state or local governments faced with paying for the care?
- … of our society at large?

There is no neutral ground from which to make these decisions, as they all involve values based on cultural, social, and religious beliefs (Beauchamp, Walters, Ka, & Mastroianni, 2013).

Baby Doe Cases

EP 2.1.2b
EP 2.1.2c

A number of court cases have attempted to address some of the issues listed earlier. In the early 1980s, the so-called Baby Doe case received national attention. This case involved an infant born with major health problems who would have been seriously disabled—physically and mentally—with surgery and who would have died immediately without surgery. The parents did not want the child to have surgery or to suffer but, instead, to die a peaceful death. Some members of the hospital staff wanted the child to have the surgery; others wanted to allow the child to die. In 1986, the U.S. Supreme Court invalidated government regulations ("Baby Doe" rules) based on Section 504 of the Rehabilitation Act of 1973 that required life-prolonging medical treatment for newborn infants with severe disabilities, citing that there was no basis for federal intervention in such sensitive decisions. This action resulted in new amendments to the rules that govern the Child Abuse Prevention and Treatment Act (CAPTA), signed into law in 1974. Concern has been raised in similar situations throughout the country. In some instances, infants were reported to have been starved to death or had experienced great pain when life supports were removed.

Federal legislation was introduced requiring local child welfare agencies to handle this type of situation as child protective services cases and to conduct investigations before reaching medical decisions in order to ensure that children are being protected. The legislation was changed before it passed, but it did mandate that hospitals establish special review boards to deal with such cases.

Some states, too, have enacted legislation to address serious ethical issues.. Many states have set limits on what the state will pay for organ transplantations. Citizens groups are being formed throughout the United States to address ethical decisions like these.

Right-to-Die Cases

EP 2.1.2b
EP 2.1.2c

Another major ethical issue relates to decisions surrounding what is called "the right to die." Cases involving people who are kept alive by life-support systems, but are in what the medical community refers to as a "vegetative state," have generated much debate. Other situations involving persons who have serious health problems and decide themselves that they wish to die are receiving attention, too.

Ethical issues also are raised regarding the role of others in aiding those who decide they want to die. For example, the state of Oregon passed the Death With Dignity Act in 1994, which allows dying patients to control their own end-of-life care (a copy of the statute, as revised, can be found at http://public.health.oregon.gov). **Physician-assisted suicide** is legal in four other states—Washington, Vermont, New Mexico, and Montana. There are relatively substantial restrictions attached to each of these provisions. The Death With Dignity Act allows terminally ill Oregon residents to obtain and use prescriptions from their physicians for self-administered, lethal medications. Under this law, ending one's life in accordance with the law does not constitute suicide. The law allows for physician-assisted suicide, but specifically prohibits euthanasia, in which a physician or other person directly administers a medication to end one's life. The term *physician-assisted suicide* is used in the medical literature to describe ending one's life through the voluntary self-administration of lethal medications prescribed by a physician for that purpose.

To request a prescription for lethal medications, the Death With Dignity Act requires that a patient be 18 years of age or older, a resident of Oregon, able to make and communicate health-care decisions, and diagnosed with a terminal illness that will lead to death within 6 months. Patients meeting these criteria then are eligible to request a prescription for lethal medication from a physician licensed by the state of Oregon. The following procedures are required to receive a prescription for lethal medication:

- The patient must make two oral requests to his or her physician, separated by at least 15 days.
- The patient must provide a written request to his or her physician, signed in the presence of two witnesses.
- The prescribing physician and a consulting physician must confirm the diagnosis and prognosis.

- The prescribing physician and a consulting physician must determine whether the patient is capable of making the decision to end his or her life. If either physician believes that the patient's judgment is impaired by a psychiatric or psychological disorder, the patient must be referred for a psychological evaluation.
- The prescribing physician must inform the patient of feasible alternatives to assisted suicide, including comfort care, hospice care, and pain control.
- The prescribing physician must request, but may not require, the patient to notify his or her next-of-kin of the prescription request. Physicians are required to report to the Oregon Department of Human Services, within 7 working days of prescribing the medication, all prescriptions for lethal injection. The Oregon Legislature added a requirement in 1999 that pharmacists must be informed of the ultimate use for the prescribed medication. Physicians and patients who adhere to requirements of the law are protected from criminal prosecution, and the choice of legal physician-assisted suicide cannot affect the status of a patient's health or life insurance policies.

Since the law was passed in 1997, a total of 1,173 people have had DWDA prescriptions written and 752 patients have died from ingesting medications prescribed under the DWDA. There was about an equal split between males and females requesting lethal medication. Nearly all of the 752 patients were white. More than half were widowed, divorced, or never married. About half (45.6%) had earned a baccalaureate degree or higher. The major underlying illness was malignant neoplasms (Oregon Department of Human Services, 2014).

Opponents of physician-assisted suicide object that physicians' assisting people to die violates the basic moral obligations of physicians to do no harm. The debate about legalizing euthanasia (painless termination of life to end a terminally ill patient's suffering) raises ethical and legal questions such as: How does one assess the competency of those requesting death? Is the involvement of a physician or nurse necessary and, if so, to what extent, for those seeking to end their lives?

The American Medical Association has estimated that 70% of the 6,000 U.S. deaths that occur each day involve some sort of negotiation regarding life or death.

In many instances, ethical dilemmas can be avoided, and dollars saved, by providing accessible and affordable health care before the problem arises.

Bioethics

New genetic technologies promise to make medical ethics an even more central part of social decision making. For example, completed in 2000, the Human Genome Project, a federally funded $3 billion effort to code the entire human genetic map, has resulted in the discovery of a number of genes that lead to specific diseases or traits. Results of the project will enable individuals to receive more information about their own genetic makeup, with the potential to enhance individual health. Medical ethicists are debating whether such information is the exclusive property of patients or should be shared with insurers, employers, and society at large.

EP 2.1.2b
EP 2.1.2c

New computational tools will allow knowledge that can impact specific populations. For example, researchers have learned that one reason African Americans die from heart attacks more than members of other ethnic groups is that a drug commonly given to heart-attack patients is less effective in people of African ancestry. Because much of the current biological research focuses on DNA, it is expected that in the years to come, unique medication regimens will be developed that are tailored to a specific individual, not just to an age or ethnic group.

Further, gene therapies are being developed using genetically engineered viruses to manipulate patients' cells. Some people wonder about whether the manipulation of human cells through genetic engineering is contrary to the laws of nature or religion. Others have proposed that it will lead to the manipulation of human sperm or eggs for purposes of improving the hereditary qualities of a race. Still others applaud the therapies and see them as a way to improve the quality and longevity of life.

Cloning—the production of organisms genetically identical to a parent—has become another controversial topic in medical ethics. In 1997, Scottish scientist Ian Wilmut and his colleagues announced the birth of a sheep named Dolly that was produced from a cell of an adult female sheep. This event and other attempts at cloning mammals have led many people to believe that cloning humans may be possible one day. This possibility has touched off a vigorous debate about the ethics of creating human clones, the circumstances under which human cloning might be used, and the possibility of using the technique to manipulate the traits of children. This issue remains unresolved and will continue to challenge medical ethicists well into the 21st century.

Another major issue being debated by state legislatures, Congress, and ethicists relates to the use of stem-cell tissue. Adult stem cells have effectively saved the lives of individuals who would have died otherwise. Issues that will be addressed in state and federal courts in the coming years include what kind of tissue can be used to obtain stem cells, and under what conditions.

Some of these issues may become less controversial. Knowledge is shifting to computer-generated therapies based on individual DNA profiles, making drug development faster, cheaper, and better and tissue, organ, and stem-cell therapies obsolete (U.S. Department of Energy, 2010a,b).

Alternative Medicine

Finally, bioethicists are debating the rights of patients to insurance reimbursement for alternative therapies and the need for standards for their use. Examples of research include the potential use of psychoactive alternative medicines, including St. John's wort and gingko biloba, to treat depression, memory loss, and Alzheimer's disease. The lack of standards for their use has prompted concern that healthy Americans will engage in unsafe experiments with life-enhancing drugs. Several other alternative therapies, including acupuncture and crystal healing, have been formally included in managed-care plans around the United States.

EP 2.1.2b
EP 2.1.2c

Health Planning

Several important pieces of legislation have been enacted to reduce the duplication of health care in some areas and close gaps in others. A brief review of this legislation is presented later in this chapter.

Hill–Burton Act

Passed in 1946, the Hill–Burton Act was funded for the purpose of constructing rural hospitals. Amendments in 1964 authorized the development of areawide hospital planning councils and the concept of areawide hospital planning. The law also specified that hospitals receiving funding through this legislation

EP 2.1.8b
EP 2.1.9b

cannot refuse to serve clients who are unable to pay for services. Later legislation authorized hospitals that provide more than their fair share of health care to medically indigent patients (disproportionate-share hospitals) to receive additional funding from Medicare and Medicaid to cover costs (Centers for Medicare and Medicaid Services, 2014).

Medicare and Medicaid

 National legislation enacted in 1965 amended the Social Security Act by adding the Medicaid and Medicare programs (Titles 19 and 20, respectively) which provide the majority of federal financing for health care in the United States. Both programs have undergone major changes over the years in terms of the people who are eligible for services, the kinds of services covered, and the financing needed to support the programs.

EP 2.1.8b
EP 2.1.9b

Medicaid   Under the Medicaid program, the federal government provides matching funds to states to enable them to provide medical assistance to residents who meet certain eligibility requirements. The objective is to help states provide medical assistance to residents with insufficient income and resources to meet the costs of necessary medical services. Medicaid serves as the nation's primary source of health insurance coverage for low-income populations. States are not required to participate in the Medicaid program; however, those that do must comply with federal regulations under which each participating state administers its own program, establishes eligibility standards, determines the scope and types of services it will cover, and sets payment rates. Benefits vary from state to state. The Centers for Medicare and Medicaid Services (CMS) monitors the state-run programs and establishes requirements for service delivery, quality, funding, and eligibility standards. Medicaid expenditures in 2012 amounted to $421.2 billion, or 15% of national health expenditures.

The Affordable Care Act signed into law by President Obama in 2010 contains provisions to expand Medicaid eligibility starting in 2014. States that wish to participate in the Expanded Medicaid program are required to provide health-care coverage for people with incomes up to 133% of the poverty line,

including adults without dependent children. In return, the federal government pays 100% of the cost of expansion in 2014–2016; 95% in 2017, 94% in 2018, 93% in 2019, and 90% in 2020 and beyond (Centers for Medicare and Medicaid Services, 2013b).

However, the Supreme Court ruled in *NFIB v. Sebelius* that the Medicaid expansion provision of the ACA was coercive, and that the Federal government must allow states to continue at pre-ACA levels of funding and eligibility if they choose to do so. As of January 2014, twenty-three states (Alabama, Alaska, Florida, Georgia, Idaho, Kansas, Louisiana, Maine, Mississippi, Missouri, Montana, Nebraska, New Hampshire, North Carolina, Oklahoma, South Carolina, South Dakota, Tennessee, Texas, Utah, Virginia, Wisconsin, and Wyoming) have chosen not to expand Medicaid coverage under the ACA. This is a substantial loss to individuals who are poor because over half of the nation's uninsured live in those states.

Medicare   Under this program, health insurance is provided to people age 65 and older, regardless of income or medical history, who have worked for at least forty quarters (10 years) and paid into the system, as well as younger people with disabilities, people with end stage renal disease, and persons with amyotrophic lateral sclerosis (Medicare.gov, 2014). On average, Medicare covers about half (48%) of the health-care charges approved for coverage by the program. Medicare enrollees must then cover the remaining approved charges, either with supplemental insurance or with another form of out-of-pocket coverage. Out-of-pocket costs can vary depending on the amount of health care needed.

Medicare includes Part A (Hospital Insurance), Part B (Medical Insurance), and Part D (Prescription Drugs). Medicare beneficiaries can receive Part A, B, and D benefits through Part C health plans, the most popular of which are branded "Medicare Advantage." No part of Medicare pays for all of a beneficiary's covered medical costs and many costs are not covered at all. The program contains premiums, deductibles and coinsurance, for which the covered individual must pay out-of-pocket. All Medicare benefits are subject to medical necessity.

The Centers for Medicare and Medicaid Services (CMS) is the federal agency that administers the Medicare program. The Social Security Administration (SSA) is the federal agency responsible for determining Medicare eligibility, eligibility for and payment of Extra

Help/Low Income Subsidy payments related to Part D Medicare, and collecting some premium payments for the Medicare program. CMS has contracts with private insurance companies to operate as intermediaries between the government and medical providers. Contracted processes include claims and payment processing, call center services, clinician enrollment, and fraud investigation. The Medicare program is subject to the reforms brought about by the Affordable Care Act related to reductions in waste, fraud and abuse, and cost containment, the savings for which are used to help fund the Expanded Medicaid program as well as help states offset reductions in disproportionate share hospital allotments. Savings will also be realized in terms of reduced insurance premiums and coinsurance payments shouldered by covered individuals. Medicare spending in 2012 amounted to $572.5 billion, or 21% of national health expenditures.

Maternal and Child Health Act

EP 2.1.8b
EP 2.1.9b

Title V of the Social Security Act (as amended), through the Supplemental Food Program for Women, Infants, and Children (WIC), provides screening, counseling, and food supplements for pregnant women and children up to 5 years of age who are at nutritional risk because of low income. Because states have the option of offering the program; only half of eligible women and children in the country receive WIC services. Studies show that WIC reduces infant deaths, low birth weight, and premature births and increases good health and cognitive development in preschoolers (see, for example, Center on Budget and Policy Priorities, 2010).

Healthy Steps for Young Children Program

EP 2.1.8b
EP 2.1.9b

Healthy Steps is a holistic approach to pediatric health care for all children from birth to age 3, encompassing their physical, psychological, emotional, and intellectual growth and development. This program encourages strong relationships between pediatric practices and parents. By focusing on families with very young children, the Healthy Steps approach helps ensure that children are nurtured at a critical time in their development, with the expected outcomes that they will grow and develop into well-adapted, healthy children who are confident young learners.

Among the several agencies and organizations involved in the Healthy Steps initiative are the Commonwealth Fund; community and regional foundations and local health-care providers; the American Academy of Pediatrics; Boston University School of Medicine, Department of Population and Family Health Sciences; and the Johns Hopkins University School of Public Health (promisingpractices.net, 2014).

EP 2.1.8b
EP 2.1.9b

In August 1997, Congress enacted legislation that created the **Children's Health Insurance Program** (CHIP) to expand health insurance coverage for low-income children up to age 19. CHIP is administered by the states, but is jointly funded by the federal government and states. The Federal matching rate for state CHIP programs is typically about 15 percentage points higher than the Medicaid matching rate (FMAP) for that state. States administer the CHIP program with broad guidance from the Centers for Medicare and Medicaid Services (CMS). Total federal outlays for services provided through the CHP program in Federal Fiscal Year 2013 equaled about $9.5 billion. Expenditure projections for FFY 2014 and FFY 2015 amount to $10.3 billion and $10.6 billion, respectively.

The Balanced Budget Act of 1997 provides states with three options for increasing coverage under CHIP: (a) expand Medicaid, (b) establish a new insurance program separate from Medicaid, or (c) implement a combination of both. States receive federal block-grant payments on a matching basis, up to a limit established for each state based on the allocation formula in the law. The law limits the extent to which states can impose premiums or cost-sharing (deductibles, co-insurance, and copayments) for health care provided to children who are enrolled in separate state programs financed with child health block-grant funds.

In general, states cannot adopt cost-sharing or premium policies that favor higher-income families over lower-income families. States also are prohibited from imposing cost-sharing for well-baby and well-child care, including immunizations. Finally, states cannot count money raised through premiums or cost-sharing as state dollars for purposes of meeting the block grant's matching requirements.

As noted, the CHIP program requires state matching funds as a requirement to draw down federal funds to operate the state's CHIP program. These matching rates are lower than those of any other federal program having a matching requirement and are designed to maximize state participation in the program. Despite this incentive, some states have elected to restrict their investment in the state's CHIP program. As a result, many eligible children are prevented from receiving benefits from the program.

On average, 8.5 million children received services under the CHIP program nationwide in 2013. The Affordable Care Act (ACA) extended funding for CHIP by providing $19.1 billion for FY 2014 CHIP allotments and $21.1 billion for FY 2015 CHIP allotments. Also, the ACA increased funding for grants and a national campaign to improve outreach and enrollment and extended its availability through FFY 2015 (U.S. Department of Health and Human Services, 2014).

Other Child Health Provisions Under the Balanced Budget Act of 1997

EP 2.1.8b
EP 2.1.9b

In addition to the child health block grant, the Balanced Budget Act of 1997 included a number of provisions designed to increase children's health-care coverage through the Medicaid program. These provisions are largely independent of the child health block grant and apply regardless of whether a state elects to use its block grant funds to expand Medicaid or establish a separate state program.

Comprehensive Health Planning Act

Passed in 1966, the Comprehensive Health Planning Act expanded on the concept of local health-planning districts to coordinate services and requires review of other factors affecting the health of area residents, such as lifestyle and environmental conditions. The National Health Planning and Resources Development Act of 1974 further mandated the establishment of health systems agencies and statewide health-coordinating councils to prevent the overbuilding of medical facilities such as obstetric and neonatal special care units and to monitor the availability of pediatric beds, open-heart surgery, and expensive technological equipment such as megavoltage radiation equipment. The intent of this legislation was to increase the availability of services in rural and other underserved areas and to eliminate duplication in other areas, as well as to provide high-quality care at reduced costs by requiring rate review panels and professional standards of care.

Health Maintenance Organization Legislation

The Health Maintenance Organization Act of 1972 enabled the development of health maintenance organizations (HMOs) to reduce health-care costs for individuals. Most HMOs require a monthly fee, which allows free or low-cost visits to a special facility or group of facilities for health care. HMOs are intended to reduce health costs and encourage preventive health care. Nevertheless, because of increased concerns raised by HMO clients and physicians about limited access to needed health care, a number of states have passed legislation specifying the rights of clients served by HMOs. (The student is also referred to the discussion on HMOs found earlier in this chapter.)

CARE Act

The Ryan White Comprehensive AIDS Resources Emergency (CARE) Act of 1989, named in honor of 18-year-old Ryan White (who died of AIDS in 1989) authorizes emergency funds to metropolitan areas hardest hit by AIDS, grants to states for comprehensive planning and service delivery, early intervention with HIV-infected infants, and the development of individual pilot projects to serve children with AIDS and to provide AIDS services in rural areas. The act has five titles:

Title I: provides grants to eligible metropolitan areas based on case rates

Title II: provides grants to states for health care and support services for persons with HIV/AIDS

Title III: provides support to primary care providers through local health departments' homeless programs, community and migrant health centers, hemophilia centers, and family-planning centers

Title IV: provides health and support services for children, adolescents, and women and families using comprehensive, community-based services

Title V: provides funding for the education and training of service providers

Part F of the law provides funding for Special Projects of National Significance, awarded on a competitive procurement basis to support the development of innovative models of HIV/AIDS care with special emphasis on hard-to-reach populations, including Native Americans and other minorities. Areas targeted for this funding include managed care, infrastructure development, training, comprehensive primary care, and access to care.

The law also provides funding to support the provision of dental and oral health services for HIV-positive individuals (the Dental Reimbursement Program and the Community-Based Dental Partnership Program). Signed into law in 1990, the act has been amended and reauthorized five times: in 1996, 2000, 2006, 2009, and most recently in 2013. The federal fiscal year 2014 budget includes $2.4 billion for the Ryan White HIV/AIDS CARE Act to continue its critical role in support of patients across the HIV/AIDS continuum. Included in this total is $943 million for the AIDS Drug Assistance Program, an increase of $10 million to provide life-saving and extending medications to 218,900 individuals, an additional 1,600 people living with HIV/AIDS (HHS.gov, 2014).

Health-Care Reform

EP 2.1.8b
EP 2.1.9b

Because of the reasons for high health-care costs discussed earlier in this chapter and the many groups concerned about health care in the United States, tackling health-care reform has been difficult. President Bill Clinton made health-care reform the single most important issue when he first took office, but his administration's efforts to oversee the overhaul of the health-care system met with resistance from a wide range of sources. Efforts by the Bush administration to tackle health-care reform likewise were largely stymied (with the exceptions mentioned earlier). Although most individuals and constituency groups agreed that reform was needed, a great deal of controversy persisted regarding the types of reforms that should be adopted.

Many advocates of a **universal health-care system** in the United States called for a national health insurance program for all types of health care, not just catastrophic illness. Those in favor of such a program based their support on the following arguments:

- Costs for health insurance are too high for large numbers of individuals to afford.
- Many local hospitals are going into debt or even going out of business because they are faced with paying health-care costs for rapidly increasing numbers of indigent persons.
- Health costs are higher because people are not seeking preventive health care, which would be more likely if there were a national health insurance program with such an emphasis.

Those who oppose such a program counter with the following arguments:

- Such a program would mean going to a system of socialized medicine.
- The costs would be too high.
- Individuals would lose their freedom of choice regarding which health-care provider they wanted.
- People would clog the health-care delivery system with trivial health problems that did not require medical attention.

Proponents of government-funded health-care programs advanced a variety of alternatives. Many called for a universal-access, single-payer system with national standards. They wanted to eliminate the relationship between health care and employment so those who are jobless, or employed by employers without available or affordable health care, or not covered because of prior health conditions could still receive health coverage. Some plans called for the federal government to collect funds for a national health-care program from various taxes, with the program administered by private insurance companies instead of by a single government system.

Others advocated for a "pay-or-play" proposal, in which employers would provide health care to their employees, contributing to a public fund to pay for those without insurance or who are underinsured. Critics of this plan argued that such a system was punitive, did not guarantee universal coverage, and still created a dual health-care system. Still other proposals called for having people claim a tax credit on their income tax form if they used health care and provided health coverage for only catastrophic illnesses.

On February 26, 2009, President Obama outlined eight principles for health-care reform in his fiscal year 2010 Budget overview that incorporated some of the ideas discussed earlier:

- Reduce long-term growth of health-care costs for businesses and government.
- Protect families from bankruptcy or debt because of health-care costs.
- Guarantee choice of doctors and health plans.
- Invest in prevention and wellness.
- Improve patient safety and quality care.
- Ensure affordable, high-quality health coverage for all Americans.
- Maintain coverage when you change or lose your job.
- End barriers to coverage for people with preexisting medical conditions.

After months of contentious debate, Congress enacted the Patient Protection and Affordable Care Act of 2009 (Affordable Care Act), which was signed into law by President Obama on March 23, 2010. Passage of the act resulted from months of intense negotiations between the White House, members of Congress, reform advocates, the insurance industry, the pharmaceutical industry, taxing authorities, local and state officials, health-care providers, regulatory agencies, and the community at large. As can be seen from the discussion that follows, the act was successful in achieving all of president's principles for health-care reform noted earlier, and more.

The act comprises nine titles as shown in the following table.

Title	Caption
I	Quality, Affordable Health Care for All Americans
II	Role of Public Programs
III	Improving the Quality and Efficiency of Health Care
IV	Prevention of Chronic Disease and Improving Public Health
V	Health Care Workforce
VI	Transparency and Program Integrity
VII	Improving Access to Innovative Medical Therapies
VIII	Community Assistance Services and Supports
IX	Revenue Provisions

The Kaiser Family Foundation (2010, pp. 1–13) has categorized the key requirements or provisions of the law according to the themes shown in the following table.

Category	Requirements
Individual mandate	Requirement to have coverage.
Employer requirements	Requirement to offer coverage.
Expansion of public programs	Expansion of the Medicaid program and the Children's Health Insurance Program (CHIP).
Premium and cost-sharing subsidies to individuals	Eligibility for premium credits and cost-sharing subsidies, verification of income and citizenship status, premium credits and cost-sharing subsidy schedules, and limitations on use of premium credits and cost-sharing subsidies to purchase coverage for abortion.
Premium subsidies to employers	Small business tax credits and reinsurance program.
Tax changes related to health insurance and financing health reform	Tax changes related to health insurance and financing health reform.
Health insurance exchanges	Creation and structure of health insurance changes, eligibility to purchase in the exchanges, public plan option, creation of the Consumer Operated and Oriented Plan (CO-OP), benefit tiers, insurance market and rating rules, qualifications of participating health plans, requirements of the exchanges, basic health plan, and state option to include abortion coverage in the exchanges.
Benefit design	Essential benefits package and specifications for abortion coverage.
Changes to private insurance	Temporary national high-risk pool to provide health coverage

Category	Requirements
	to individuals with preexisting medical conditions, reporting by health plans of medical loss ratios and reviewing increases in health-plan premiums, administrative simplification, dependent coverage, insurance market rules, consumer protections, health-care choice compacts and national plans, and health insurance administration
State role	State role in health reform and requirements for administrative simplification, the Medicare and Medicaid program, prescription drugs, and waste, fraud, and abuse.
Improving quality/ health systems performance	Comparative effectiveness research, medical malpractice, changes to the Medicare and Medicaid programs, primary care, national quality strategy, disclosure of financial relationships between health entities and manufacturers and distributors of covered drugs, devices, and medical supplies, and elimination of health disparities.
Prevention/wellness	Development of national prevention/wellness strategy as coordinated by the National Prevention, Health Promotion and Public Health Council, expanded coverage of preventive services and elimination of cost sharing for preventive services in Medicaid and Medicare, employer-sponsored wellness programs, and nutritional information of food products sold by chain restaurants and dispensed by vending machines.
Long-term care	Guidelines for the Community Living Assistance and Services Supports (CLASS) program,

Category	Requirements
	improvements to the Medicare program, enhancements to the Medicaid programs, skilled-nursing facilities, health-care workforce training and development, community health centers and school-based health centers, trauma care, public health and disaster preparedness, nonprofit hospitals, and impact of health reform on American Indians.
Financing	Requirements for coverage and financing.

The requirements of the Affordable Care Act will be implemented in their entirety over the 10-year period from 2010 to 2019; however, most of the requirements will be implemented between 2010 and 2014. Refer to the work of a number of organizations to learn more about specific provisions of the law, including projected costs and savings, and a timeline for implementing the law's various provisions (see, for example, Congressional Budget Office, 2010; Families USA, 2010; Kaiser Family Foundation, 2010; National Association of Insurance Commissioners, 2010; and Rural Policy Research Institute, 2010).

The Congressional Budget Office (CBO, 2010) estimates that the new health reform law will provide coverage to an additional 32 million persons when fully implemented in 2019. CBO estimates the cost of the coverage components of the new law to be $938 billion over the 10-year implementation period (2010–2019). These costs will be financed through a combination of savings from Medicare and Medicaid, new taxes and fees, including an excise tax on high-cost insurance, and savings accrued from reductions in fraud and abuse and other cost containments measures already in force. The CBO (2010) also estimates that the health reform law will reduce the federal deficit by $124 billion over the law's 10-year implementation period.

Key benefits of the ACA to the health-care consumer include the following (Whitehouse.gov, 2014):

- Creates the Health Insurance Marketplace, a new way for individuals, families, and small businesses to get health coverage.

- Requires insurance companies to cover people with pre-existing health conditions.
- Makes it illegal for health insurance companies to arbitrarily cancel health insurance.
- Gives consumers the right to choose the doctor they want from their health plan's provider network.
- Covers young adults under 26.
- Provides free preventive health screenings.
- Ends lifetime and yearly dollar limits on coverage of essential health benefits.
- Gives consumers the right to appeal a decision by their insurer to refuse to pay a claim or end coverage and to have the appeal reviewed by a third party.
- Requires plans in the Health Insurance Marketplace to cover contraceptive methods and counseling for all women, as prescribed by a health-care provider without charging a copayment, coinsurance, or deductible when they are provided by an in-network provider.
- Requires most health insurance plans to provide breastfeeding equipment and counseling for pregnant and nursing women.
- Requires health insurance plans available in the Marketplace to cover mental health and substance use disorder services.
- Requires Marketplace plans to provide certain "parity" protections between mental health and substance use disorder benefits on the one hand, and medical and surgical benefits on the other (financial, treatment, and case management limits applied to mental health and substance use disorder services can't be more restrictive than limits applied to medical and surgical services).
- Requires insurance companies to publicly justify any rate increase of 10% or more before raising premiums.
- Requires insurance companies to spend at least 80% of the money they take in on health-care premiums and quality improvement activities.
- Makes Medicare stronger by adding new benefits, fighting fraud, cutting costs, and improving care.

Supreme Court Ruling on Constitutionality of the ACA   On June 28, 2012, the U.S. Supreme Court upheld the constitutionality of the Affordable Care Act, saying its requirement that most Americans obtain insurance or pay a penalty was authorized by Congress's power to levy taxes. The vote was 5 to 4, with Chief Justice John G. Roberts Jr. joining the court's four more liberal members. This decision paved the way for moving forward with implementation of the act, which has been the subject of much dissention and debate since the time the law was enacted in 2010. At the same time, the court rejected the argument that the administration had pressed most vigorously in support of the law, that its individual mandate was justified by Congress's power to regulate interstate commerce. The vote was again 5 to 4.

The court also substantially limited the law's expansion of Medicaid, the joint federal-state program that provides health care to poor and disabled people. Seven justices agreed that Congress had exceeded its constitutional authority by coercing states into participating in the expansion by threatening them with the loss of existing federal payments. The latter decision has had the ripple effect of denying some 6 million low-income individuals insurance coverage in the 26 states that have opted out of the Expanded Medicaid program. One can only conclude that the states choosing not to participate in the Expanded Medicaid program did so for political reasons, given the unprecedented federal matching rate associated with the program (100% in 2014–2016, tapering down to 90% in 2020 and thereafter).

Passage of the Affordable Care Act represents a stunning accomplishment, considering the sheer magnitude of the task, the complexity of the issues addressed, the goal that the legislation be cost-neutral to the government, the need for transparency and accountability, the fact that the prevailing method of policy change in this country is incremental, and the need to achieve consensus among a long list of entities that have a significant stake in the outcome.

Other critical health-care issues for the coming decades include reducing the fragmentation of care, developing private and/or government insurance for long-term health care for the elderly, and increasing the availability of funding for home health and respite care. More resources will be devoted to outpatient community-based care and case management. And more attention also will be directed to prevention, including teen pregnancy as well as AIDS education, and to the promotion of lifestyle changes such as improved diet and the elimination of substance abuse and smoking.

Social Work Roles in the Delivery of Health Services

EP 2.1.1a
EP 2.1.1c
EP 2.1.8b
EP 2.1.9b

Today, social workers have many roles in providing health care in a variety of settings. Social work in health care, particularly in working with the elderly, is one of the fastest-growing occupational areas today. Overall, health care is the third largest field of social work practice.

Federal legislation relating to nursing homes requires that all nursing homes in the United States with 120 or more beds must have a social worker with a bachelor's of social work (BSW) or a master's of social work (MSW) degree. Changes in legislation relating to Medicare now mandate that social workers with an MSW degree who also have professional social work certification be reimbursed for providing outpatient mental health services to the elderly. (Previously, only psychiatrists or psychologists could be reimbursed under Medicare for these services.)

As the number of home health-care agencies increases, the role of social workers in assessing mental health needs and providing intervention and case-management services will expand as well. Social workers will have to direct more attention to fostering the strengths of family members as they face greater demands as caregivers of family members with health needs (Dziegielewski, 2013; Gehlert & Browne, 2011). Too, as individuals with serious physical and mental injuries continue to live longer because of technological advances, the role of social workers in rehabilitation hospitals will become more important. Federal legislation provides training monies for those who are interested in health care, including social workers along with nurses and physicians.

Historical Background

Roles and settings have changed significantly since social workers first became involved in health care. As early as 1888, social workers were advocating for some sort of insurance coverage for all U.S. citizens. Jane Addams and other social workers advocated prevention of illness and community action relating to concerns such as poor sanitation, malnutrition, unsafe housing, and poverty, among others (Stern & Axinn, 2012).

The first known hospital social worker was employed at Massachusetts General Hospital in Boston in 1905. At that time, hospitals and general physicians were the major sources of health care. The social worker worked with the physician, other hospital staff members, and the patient's family to ensure that high-quality care and attention would continue after the patient returned home.

Contemporary Roles in Health-Care Settings

EP 2.1.1a
EP 2.1.1c
EP 2.1.8b
EP 2.1.9b

Although responsibility for care after a patient leaves the hospital is still a major focus for many social workers in health-care settings, social workers in these settings today provide a variety of other services as well. Social workers often serve as a liaison between the patient's family and health-care staff. They assist the staff in understanding family concerns and how family constraints and other environmental factors may affect a patient's ability to recover. They explain to patients and their families the implications of illness and issues relating to recovery and care. In many instances, the social worker provides support to the family in cases of death or if a patient's condition worsens.

Among the functions of social workers in health-care settings, they:

- conduct screening and assessments to determine health risk factors, particularly those involving the family and the broader environment;
- offer social services to patients and their families, such as individual counseling to help a patient deal with a major illness or loss of previous capabilities following an accident or illness, support family members who are grieving for a dying individual, or reinforce a teenage mother's decision to place her child for adoption;
- provide case-management services, including working with other social and health-services agencies regarding patient needs, such as helping to arrange for financial assistance to pay hospital bills, nursing home or home health care for patients when they leave the hospital, or emergency child care for a single parent who is hospitalized;
- serve as a member of a health-care team and help others understand a patient's emotional needs and home or family situation;
- advocate for the patient's needs at all levels of the environment, including the patient's family,

hospital and other health-care settings, social-services agencies, school, workplace, and community;

• represent the hospital and provide consultation to other community agencies, such as child protective services agencies in child abuse cases;

• provide preventive education and counseling to individuals, including family planning, nutrition, prenatal care, and human growth and development; and

• make health planning and policy recommendations to local communities, states, and the federal government in areas such as hospital care, community health care, environmental protection, and control of contagious diseases.

Many social workers function in agencies administered by and hiring primarily social workers, called **primary settings**. In comparison, health-care settings are considered **secondary settings** because they are administered and staffed largely by health-care professionals who are not social workers. Social workers in health-care settings must be comfortable with their roles and able to articulate their roles and functions clearly to other health-care professionals.

A strong professional identity is important for **medical social workers**. In addition, social workers in health-care settings must be able to work comfortably within a medical model. Knowledge and understanding of the medical profession and health care are important for these social workers, as is the ability to function as a team member with representatives from a variety of disciplines. Social workers in health-care settings, particularly hospital settings, must be able to handle crisis intervention, and they typically prefer short-term social work services rather than long-term client relationships. They must be able to work well under pressure and high stress and be comfortable with death and dying.

Hospital Settings

EP 2.1.1a
EP 2.1.1c
EP 2.1.8b
EP 2.1.9b

The American Hospital Association requires that a hospital maintain a social services department as a condition of accreditation. Social workers in hospitals may provide services to all patients who need them, or they may provide specialized services. Larger hospitals employ emergency-room social workers, pediatric social workers, intensive-care social

workers, and social workers who work primarily on cardiac, cancer, or other specialized wards.

Some hospitals have added social workers who provide social services primarily to HIV/AIDS patients. Other hospitals employ social workers in preventive efforts, providing outreach services, including home visits to mothers identified during their hospital stay as potentially at risk to abuse or neglect their children. Still other hospitals employ social workers to coordinate rehabilitative services, serving as case managers to ensure that occupational, physical, recreational, speech, and vocational therapy services are provided.

Social workers work in public and private hospitals alike, providing both inpatient and outpatient care. Many are employed by Veterans Administration (VA) hospitals, which have a long-standing tradition of using social workers to work with persons who have served in the armed forces. Many VA social workers provide specialized counseling relating to physical disabilities and alcohol and drug misuse. A number of VA social workers now specialize in posttraumatic stress disorder and traumatic brain injury, providing services to military veterans and their families.

Because of accreditation standards, most medical social workers must have an MSW degree. Many graduate schools of social work offer specializations in medical or health care.

Long-Term Care Facilities and Nursing Homes

EP 2.1.1a
EP 2.1.1c
EP 2.1.8b
EP 2.1.9b

Many people with illness or disability do not need the intensive services of a hospital, but they cannot care for themselves in their own homes without assistance. Particularly for the frail elderly, **long-term care facilities**, such as assisted-living facilities (often referred to as "nursing homes"), are most appropriate. These facilities provide medical care and other services to individuals including the elderly and people with disabilities.

Licensing and accreditation requirements vary depending on the levels and types of care facilities. From 1965 to 1972, social work services were mandated for all nursing homes that cared for residents covered by Medicare. Beginning in 1990, all nursing homes with 120 or more beds must employ a social worker. Social workers in these settings help residents adjust to the nursing home environment, help families deal with their guilt and feelings of loss after such placements, serve as liaisons to other social services and health-care agencies, provide individual and group counseling and other social services for nursing home residents and their families, network with others who are involved with and interested in services for the elderly at local and state levels, and advocate for improved services for the clients they serve.

Provision of social work services to the elderly in health-care settings is probably the fastest-growing area of social work. Many schools of social work are offering specializations at the MSW level in health and gerontology and special courses at the BSW level in these areas to meet the demand. NASW has also developed certifications in health care.

Community-Based Health-Care Programs

EP 2.1.1a
EP 2.1.1c
EP 2.1.8b
EP 2.1.9b

Many social workers at both the BSW and MSW levels are employed in local community-based health-care programs. Most state health departments operate local health clinics, which offer a variety of health services to low-income residents, as well as community-education programs for all residents. The topics of these programs include immunizations, family planning services, prenatal care, well-baby and pediatric services, nutrition and other types of education programs, and basic health care.

Health clinics frequently employ social workers to work with patients and their families in the context of other health-care services. For example, some clinics operate high-risk infant programs, which include social services for parents of infants at risk for abuse, neglect, or other serious health problems and children who already have serious health problems and whose parents need monitoring and support. Social workers also work with local community groups and schools, providing outreach programs to publicize and prevent problems such as sexually transmitted diseases and teen pregnancy.

Social workers are employed, too, in family-planning clinics such as Planned Parenthood, providing counseling and help in reaching decisions regarding pregnancy prevention or intervention, such as planning for adoptive services in the case of an unwanted pregnancy. With new technology that can diagnose problems in embryos in the uterus, many health providers are employing social workers to offer genetic counseling that will help clients understand the possibility of giving birth to infants with potential problems and make appropriate decisions regarding whether to become pregnant or to terminate a pregnancy.

Many social workers are employed in community health-care settings that provide services to persons with AIDS and their families. Social workers perform individual, family, and group counseling; serve as case managers assisting clients and their families in accessing community resources; advocate for clients and their families; and offer community-education programs.

Increasingly, health-care settings are recognizing the impact of environmental factors, such as unemployment, on mental and physical health. To help address this concern, traditional health-care settings increasingly are employing social workers. For example, local physicians' clinics—usually operated by a small group of physicians who share a practice—are hiring social workers to provide counseling to patients in an effort to improve their mental health and reduce stress. HMOs are hiring social workers to perform similar functions.

Home Health Care

EP 2.1.1a
EP 2.1.1c
EP 2.1.8b
EP 2.1.9b

Many states and communities are recognizing the need for **home health care**—services that enable persons with health problems to remain in their own homes. Home health-care services strive to preserve self-esteem and longevity for the individual and are far less costly than hospital or nursing home care. Trained nurses and home health aides, as well as social workers, make visits to perform health care in a person's home. Social workers provide counseling to the client and family, help clients cope emotionally, and serve as case managers, ensuring that appropriate resources are accessed to deal with client needs.

Home health care allows the elderly, persons with AIDS, and other people who do not have to be hospitalized to have greater control over their lives. Home care affords them dignity and the emotional support they might not receive in a hospital or other institutional setting. Because home health-care programs are more cost-effective than hospitalization or other institutional care, these programs will be expanded during the next several decades, and more social workers will be needed to work in them.

State Department of Health and Health-Planning Agencies

EP 2.1.1a
EP 2.1.1c
EP 2.1.8b
EP 2.1.9b

Many social workers at both the BSW and MSW levels are employed in health-care policy and planning jobs. They have input into critical decisions regarding funding, policies, and programs for state legislatures, federal officials, and state and local health departments and planning agencies. A social worker might determine, for example, how many more elderly persons could be served if Medicaid income eligibility requirements were to change from 130% to 150% above the poverty line. Or a social worker might develop plans to implement a community-wide HIV/AIDS education program, or suggest ways that a local hospital can be more responsive to the needs of the primarily African American and Latino population it serves.

In one state, for example, planners in the state health department recommended that the agency solicit bids for infant formula for infants served by the WIC program instead of contracting with the same company the agency had used over the years. The bids received were much lower than the amount the department had been paying for the formula, which enabled the department to serve many more clients while saving money.

Other programs in which social workers become involved include those related to the impact of environmental changes on individuals, disease prevention and control, monitoring of solid waste and water facilities, and emergency and disaster planning. State health departments provide services involving dental health, family planning, nutrition, and teenage pregnancy; nutrition programs for pregnant women and young children; periodic health screening of infants and young children; substance-abuse programs; and teen-parent services. Health departments and other federal, state, and local agencies also develop policies and implement plans for the provision of emergency and disaster services. Social workers from a number of federal, state, and local public and private agencies from around the United States were involved in planning and overseeing emergency services after the September 11, 2001, terrorist attack, and many others provided assistance after Hurricanes Katrina and Rita in 2005 and Hurricane Ike in 2008.

The U.S. Public Health Service (USPHS) provides health and health-related services to indigent populations in areas with few medical practitioners, such as American Indian reservations and migrant areas. The USPHS also monitors communicable diseases and provides research in a variety of health areas. Many students who receive federal funds to attend college or professional schools in health-related areas, including social work, are required to devote a set number of years of service to the USPHS after graduation.

Other federal programs, such as the National Institutes of Health (NIH), also provide research and policy alternatives. Both the USPHS and the NIH employ social workers at the BSW and MSW levels. The NIH, for example, employs social workers in direct-care settings established to develop new techniques in health care, such as its pediatric AIDS program in Washington, DC.

Other Health-Care Settings

EP 2.1.1a
EP 2.1.1c
EP 2.1.8b
EP 2.1.9b

Among the numerous other health-related programs in which social workers are involved is the American Red Cross, which provides emergency services to families when disaster strikes. Social workers also are employed in women's clinics that provide reproductive, gynecological, and primary care using a holistic health approach; genetic counseling centers; and rape crisis centers. Many emergency medical service programs in large cities are employing social workers to assist in crisis intervention as a result of family violence, child maltreatment, rape, and homicide.

Increasingly, social workers are being employed in military hospitals and at military installations around the world to help individuals and families cope with the medical and mental health casualties of wars in which the United States is involved around the globe. State-of-the-art mobile medical care units have saved the lives of military personnel in combat situations. Many injuries involve the amputation of limbs, severe damage to the brain and central nervous system, spinal-cord injuries, and loss of hearing and/or sight. Helping military members with disabilities and their families deal with the realities of these injuries is a natural role for social work professionals, and military social work represents a growing field of endeavor for social workers worldwide.

Hospices are multiplying throughout the country. Since their inception in England, hospice programs have allowed terminally ill persons to die at home or in a homelike setting surrounded by family members rather than in an often-alien hospital environment. Applying the stages of grief described by Elizabeth Kübler-Ross (1969/1997) as a framework, many hospices employ social workers to work with families and the dying person or to supervise a cadre of volunteers who provide similar services. As more elderly individuals and persons with HIV/AIDS continue to live longer, the need for hospice programs will increase. Similarly, as critical issues in health care continue to be identified, the functions of social workers in health-care settings will continue to expand.

Summary

Social work in health-care settings is one of the fastest-growing areas of social work today. Issues relating to health care continue to be controversial and complex. Along with new technical and medical discoveries, health-care costs continue to rise. This reality brings up ethical issues in health care—who should receive services at what cost, who should be allowed to make decisions about the right to refuse medical care, and who should be held accountable when a person's health is jeopardized by that person or another individual.

Because cultures shape one's views about health, wellness, and illness, understanding and addressing issues of diversity in health care are essential. Social workers must be able to convey individuals' own roles in preventing and dealing with health-related concerns and to communicate this understanding to others involved in their care.

Recent legislation in the health-care arena, while aimed at streamlining and reducing the costs of the health-care services in the United States through cost controls and privatization, has failed to accomplish the intended effect. On the contrary, such legislation has left millions of low-income Americans or those on fixed incomes with a limited health-care safety net, forcing them to forgo preventive health care and to use more expensive forms of health care such as hospital-based emergency services. Social workers can play a key role in working with members of federal and state legislative bodies to educate them about the long-term effects of current efforts to cut health-care costs through managed care, increased deductibles and copay costs, and a host of privatization schemes.

With people living longer, concerns about health care will become increasingly evident. The relationships between environmental factors and health require additional exploration. Finally, the large numbers of Americans, particularly children and the poor, who receive inadequate health care, if any, and the long-term implications for these individuals in all areas of their lives and for our country as a whole must be addressed. Whatever is in store, social workers will play an ever-increasing role in both the planning and the delivery of health-care services.

Competency Notes

EP 2.1.1a: Advocate for client access to the services of social work (pp. 196, 204–206, 227–230). Social workers advocate for client access to affordable health-care services, including preventive services.

EP 2.1.1c: Attend to professional roles and boundaries (pp. 227–230). Social workers in the field of health care must maintain professional roles and boundaries and also respect the roles and boundaries of other professionals with whom they collaborate.

EP 2.1.2b: Make ethical decisions by applying standards of the National Association of Social Workers Code of Ethics and, as applicable, of the International Federation of Social Workers/International Association of Schools of Social Work Ethics in Social Work, Statement of Principles (pp. 198, 217–219). Social workers in the health-care arena must apply standards within codes of ethics of the profession when making ethical decisions.

EP 2.1.2c: Tolerate ambiguity in resolving ethical conflicts (pp. 198, 216–219). Social workers advocating for and providing health-care services must be comfortable with ambiguity in resolving ethical conflicts.

EP 2.1.3a: Distinguish, appraise, and integrate multiple sources of knowledge, including research-based knowledge and practice wisdom (pp. 196, 199, 210, 214–216). Social workers advocating for and providing health-care services distinguish, appraise, and integrate multiple sources of knowledge, including research-based knowledge and practice wisdom, in their work with clients/client systems.

EP 2.1.3b: Analyze models of assessment, prevention, intervention, and evaluation (p. 198). Social workers engaged in the delivery of health-care services analyze models of assessment, prevention, intervention, and evaluation.

EP 2.1.7b: Critique and apply knowledge to understand person and environment (pp. 210, 214–216). Social workers engaged in health-care delivery critique and apply knowledge about the ways that health impacts human behavior and a person's or group's interactions with their environment.

EP 2.1.8a: Engage in policy practice to advance social and economic well-being and to deliver effective social services (pp. 196, 202, 204–206). Social workers analyze, formulate, and advocate for health-care policies that advance social well-being.

EP 2.1.8b: Analyze, formulate, and advocate for policies that advance social well-being (pp. 219, 220–223, 227–230). Social workers collaborate with colleagues and clients for effective health-care policy action.

EP 2.1.9a: Continuously discover, appraise, and attend to changing locales, populations, scientific and technological developments, and emerging societal trends to provide relevant services (pp. 203, 210, 214–216). Social workers engaged in the health-care arena must understand the contexts of populations served, changes in the health-care field, and the impact of broader societal priorities and trends.

EP 2.1.9b: Provide leadership in promoting sustainable changes in service delivery and practice to improve the quality of social services (pp. 202, 204–206, 219–223, 227–230). Social workers provide leadership in promoting sustainable changes in health-care service delivery and practice to improve the quality of social and health-care services.

Key Terms

The terms below are defined in the Glossary.

acquired immunodeficiency syndrome (AIDS)
bioethics
catastrophic illness
Children's Health Insurance Program
gross domestic product (GDP)
health
health care
health maintenance organizations (HMOs)
health risk factors
Health Savings Accounts (HSAs)
HIV-positive
holistic health care
home health care
hospices
infant mortality rate
long-term care facilities
managed-care system
Medicaid
medical social workers
Medicare
physician-assisted suicide
primary settings
private health insurance
public health insurance
secondary settings
universal health-care system

Discussion Questions

1. Identify *five* significant changes in health care that have taken place in the United States since colonial times. What are the reasons for these changes?
2. Identify *three* reasons that health-care costs have increased over the past decade.
3. Which groups of persons in the United States are most at risk for problems with their health? Why?
4. Identify *three* ethical issues faced by health-care providers and policymakers. Whom do you think should receive priority in access to health care if costs prevent it being available to everyone? Why?
5. Select one of the components of the Patient Protection and Affordable Health Care Act of 2010. Who will benefit from this component and in what ways?
6. Identify *three* preventive programs that social workers can implement to reduce the need for health-care services in the United States.
7. Identify *three* roles social workers might play at various levels of the environment in dealing with pollution and other external conditions that compromise health.
8. What are *five* roles that social workers can play in the delivery of health-care services? How do careers for social workers in health care compare to careers in other areas in terms of availability and opportunity? Why?

On the Internet

http://www.cms.hhs.gov
http://www.cdc.gov
http://www.nga.org
http://www.kff.org
http://www.aids.org

http://www.urban.org
http://rand.org
http://cbpp.org

References

Administration on Aging. (2012). *A profile of older Americans: 2011.* Washington, DC: Author.

Aids.org. (2014). *What is AIDS?* Los Angeles, CA: Author. Retrieved from http://www.aids.org/factsheets

Alzheimer's Association. (2014). *2014 Alzheimer's disease facts and figures.* Chicago: Author.

American Hospital Association. (2014). *Fast facts on U.S. hospitals.* Chicago, IL: Author. Retrieved from http://www.aha.org/research/rc/stat-studies/fast-facts.shtml

American Lung Association. (2014). *Stop smoking: Helping smokers quit with our smoking cessation programs.* Washington, DC: Author. Retrieved from http://www.lungusa.org/stop-smoking

Annie E. Casey Foundation. (2014). *KIDS COUNT data book.* Washington, DC: Author.

Beauchamp, T., Walters, L., Kahn, J., & Mastroianni, A. (2013). *Contemporary issues in bioethics* (8th ed.). Stanford, CT: Cengage Learning.

Brenner, M. H. (1973). Fetal, infant and maternal mortality during periods of economic stress. *International Journal of Health Sciences, 3,* 145–159.

Centers for Disease Control and Prevention. (2010). *Healthy people 2010: Leading health indicators, Appendix E. Health, United States, 2009.* Washington, DC: Author.

Centers for Disease Control and Prevention. (2011). *Rates of diagnoses of HIV infection among adults and adolescents by area of residence, 2011—United States and 6 dependent areas.* Atlanta, GA: Author.

Centers for Disease Control and Prevention. (2012). *Healthy people 2010: Final review.* Atlanta, GA: Author.

Centers for Disease Control and Prevention. (2013a). *Health, United States, 2012.* Washington, DC: Author.

Centers for Disease Control and Prevention. (2013b). *Increased federal medical assistance percentage change under the Affordable Care Act of 1010: Final rule.* Atlanta, GA: Author. Retrieved from http://www.cms.gov/Medicare/Medicare-Fee-for-Service-Payment/AcuteInpatientPPS/dsh.html

Centers for Disease Control and Prevention. (2014a). *Teen pregnancy in the United States.* Retrieved from http:www.cdc.gov/TeenPregnancy/About_Teen_Prog.html

Centers for Disease Control and Prevention. (2014b). *Economic facts about U.S. tobacco production and use.* Atlanta, GA: Author. Retrieved, from http://www.cdc.gov/tobacco/data-statistics/fact_sheets/economics/econ_facts/index.html

Centers for Disease Control and Prevention. (2014c). *Tobacco-related mortality.* Atlanta, GA: Author. Retrieved from http://www.cdc.gov/tobacco/data-statistics/fact_sheets/health_effects/tobacco-related-mortality/index.html

Centers for Disease Control and Prevention. (2014d). *Revised surveillance case definitions for HIV infection—United States, 2014.* Atlanta, GA: Author.

Centers for Medicare and Medicaid Services. (2012a). *National health expenditure projections: 2011–2021.* Baltimore, MD: Author. Retrieved from http://www.cms.gov/Research-Statistics-Data-and-Systems/Statistics-Trends-and-Reports/NationalHealthExpendData/Downloads/Proj2011PDF.pdf

Centers for Medicare and Medicaid Services. (2012b). *The nation's health care dollar: Where it went.* Washington, DC: Author. Retrieved from http://www.cms.gov/Research-Statistics-Data-and-Systems/Statistics-Trends-and-Reports/NationalHealthExpendData/Downloads/PieChartSourcesExpenditures2010.pdf

Centers for Medicare and Medicaid Services. (2012c). *The nation's health care dollar: Where it came from.* Washington, DC: Author. Retrieved from http://www.cms.gov/Research-Statistics-Data-and-Systems/Statistics-Trends-and-Reports/NationalHealthExpendData/Downloads/PieChartSourcesExpenditures2010.pdf

Centers for Medicare and Medicaid. (2013a). *National health expenditures: Levels and annual percent change by source of funds: Selected calendar years 1960–2012.* Baltimore, MD: Author.

Centers for Medicare and Medicaid. (2013b). *Fact Sheets: Increased federal medical assistance percentage through the Affordable Care Act of 2010.* Atlanta, GA: Author. Retrieved from http://www.cms.gov/Newsroom/MediaReleaseDatabase/Fact-Sheets/2013-Fact-Sheets-Items/2013-03-29.html

Centers for Medicare and Medicaid Services. (2014). *Medicare disproportionate share hospital.* Washington, DC: Author. Retrieved from http://www.cms.gov/Medicare/Medicare-Fee-for-Service-Payment/AcuteInpatientPPS/dsh.html

Center on Budget and Policy Priorities. (2010). *WIC food package should be based on science: Foods with new functional ingredients should be provided only if they deliver health and nutritional benefits.* Washington, DC: Author.

Children's Defense Fund. (2014). *The state of America's children yearbook, 2014.* Washington, DC: Author.

Commonwealth Fund. (2014). *Mirror, mirror on the wall 2014 update: How the U.S. health care system compares internationally.* New York: Author.

Congressional Budget Office. (2010). *Selected CBO publications related to health care legislation, 2009–2010.* Washington, DC: Author. Retrieved from http://www.cbo.gov/ftpdocs/120xx/doc12033/12-23-Selected HealthcarePublications.pdf

DiClemente, R. J., Crosby, R. A., & Kegler, M. (Eds.). (2009). *Emerging theories in health promotion practice and research* (2nd ed.). San Francisco: Jossey-Bass.

Disabilitystatistics.org. (2014). *Disability statistics.* Ithaca, NY: Cornell University.

Dohrenwend, B. S., & Dohrenwend, B. P. (Eds.). (1974). *Stressful life events: Their nature and effects.* New York: Wiley.

Dziegielewski, S. (2013). *The changing face of health care social work* (3rd ed.). New York: Springer.

Falvo, D. (2013). *Medical and psychosocial illness and disability.* Burlington, MA: Jones & Bartlett Learning.

Families USA. (2010). *A summary of the health reform law.* Washington, DC: Author.

Fernandez-Kelly, P., & Portes, A. (2012). *Health care and immigration: Understanding the connection.* Florence, KY: Routledge.

Findyouthinfo.gov. (2014). *Teen pregnancy prevention.* Washington, DC: Author. Retrieved from http://www.findyouthinfo.gov/youth-topics/teen-pregnancy-prevention.

itzpatrick, K. (2013). *Poverty and health: A crisis among America's most vulnerable.* Santa Barbara, CA: Praeger.

Gehlert, S., & Browne, T. (Eds.). (2011). *Handbook of health social work.* Hoboken, NJ: Wiley.

Health Resources and Services Administration. (2013). *Child health USA, 2013.* Baltimore: Author.

HHS.gov. (2014). *The President's fiscal year 2014 budget.* Washington, DC: Author. Retrieved from http://www.hhs.gov/as/testify/2013/04/t20130418a.html

Israel, B., Eng, E., Schulz, A., & Parker, E. (2012). *Methods in community-based participatory research for health* (2nd ed.). San Francisco, CA: Jossey-Bass.

Kaiser Commission on Medicaid and the Uninsured. (2013). *The uninsured: A primer—Key facts about health insurance on the eve of health care reform.* Menlo Park, CA: Author.

Kaiser Family Foundation. (2010). *Summary of new health reform law.* Menlo Park, CA: Author.

Kaiser Family Foundation. (2013). *Employer health benefits: 2013 summary of findings.* Menlo Park, CA: Author.

Kaiser Family Foundation. (2014). *AIDS 2014: What happened and what's next?* Retrieved from http://kff.org/hivaids/event/august-7-event-aids-2014-what-happened-and-whats-next/

Medicare.gov. (2014). *What Medicare covers.* Retrieved from http://medicare.gov/what-medicare-covers/index.html

National Association of Insurance Commissioners. (2010). *Patient protection and affordable care act of 2009 section-by-section analysis.* Washington, DC: Author. Retrieved from http://naic.org/documents/index_health_reform_general_ppaca_section_by_section_chart.pdf

National Association of Social Workers. (2014). *NASW policy statements, 2012–2014* (9th ed.). Washington, DC: Author.

National Center for Health Statistics. (2012). *Healthy people 2010 final review.* Hyattsville, MD: Author.

National Center for Health Statistics. (2013). *Health, United States, 2012.* Hyattsville, MD: Author.

National Center for Policy Analysis. (2007). *Medical malpractice reform.* Washington, DC: Author.

National Institute for Occupational Safety and Health. (2011). *Asbestos fibers and other elongate mineral particles: State of the science and roadmap for research* (Revised ed.). Atlanta, GA: Author.

Oregon Department of Human Services. (2014). *Annual report on Oregon's Death with Dignity Act—2013.* Salem, OR: Author.

Organisation for Economic Cooperation and Development. (2012). *OECD StatExtracts.* Paris, France: Author. Retrieved from http://stats.oecd.org/Index.aspx?DatasetCode=HEALTH_STAT

Organisation for Economic Cooperation and Development. (2014). *Society at a glance 2014.* Paris, France: OECD Publishing.

The Prevention Institute. (2010). *Prevention is primary: Strategies for community well-being.* Oakland: Author.

Promisingpractices.net. (2014). *Healthy steps for young children.* Retrieved from http://www.promisingpractices.net/program.asp?progeamid=273#participants

RAND. (2008). *Invisible wounds of war: Psychological and cognitive injuries, their consequences, and services to assist recovery.* Santa Monica, CA: Author.

Rural Policy Research Institute. (2010). *The patient protection and affordable care act: A summary of provisions important to rural health care delivery.* Ames, IA: University of Iowa. from http://www.unmc.edu/ruprihealth

Stern, M., & Axinn, J. (2011). *Social welfare: A history of the American response to need* (8th ed.). Boston, MA: Pearson.

Texas Medical Association. (2014). *The uninsured in Texas.* Austin, TX: Author. Retrieved from http://www.texasmed.org/Unisured_in_Texas

UNAIDS. (2013). *Global report: UNAIDS report on the global AIDS epidemic 2013.* Geneva: Author.

Urban Institute. (2014a). *Health care reform.* Washington, DC: Author. Retrieved from http://www.urban.org/health_policy/health_care_reform

Urban Institute. (2014b). *The launch of the Affordable Care Act in selected states* (8-part series). Washington, DC: Author.

U.S. Bureau of Labor Statistics. (2014). *Occupational Outlook Handbook (OOH), 2014–2015 Edition.* Washington, DC: Author.

U.S. Census Bureau. (2012). *Americans with disabilities: 2010.* Washington, DC: Author.

U.S. Census Bureau. (2013). *Statistical abstract of the United States: 2013.* Washington, DC: Author.

U.S. Department of Agriculture. (2014). *How WIC helps.* Washington, DC: Author. Retrieved from http://Wicworks.nal.usda.gov/nutrition-education/how-wic-helps

U.S. Department of Health and Human Services. (2014). *HHS FY 2015 budget brief.* Washington, DC: Author. Retrieved from http://www.hss.gov/budget/FY2015-hhs-budget-in-brief-cms-chip.html

U.S. Department of Energy. (2010a). *Gene therapy.* Washington, DC: Author.

U.S. Department of Energy. (2010b). *Genomics and its impact on society.* Washington, DC: Author.

U.S. Department of Labor. (2012). *Fatal occupational injuries by event or exposure, 2011–2012.* Washington, DC: Author.

U.S.–Mexico Border Health Commission. (2013). *Prevention and health promotion among vulnerable populations on the U.S.–Mexico border 2013.* El Paso, TX: Author. Retrieved September 8, 2014, from http://www.borderhealth.org/files/res_2654.pdf

U.S. Public Health Service. (1977). 200 years of child health. In E. Grotberg (Ed.), *200 years of children.* Washington, DC: U.S. Department of Health, Education and Welfare.

Weeks, B., & Shors, J. (2013). *AIDS: The biological basis.* Burlington, MA: Jones & Bartlett.

Whitehouse.gov. (2014). *Health care that works for Americans.* Washington, DC: Author. Retrieved September 13, 2014, from http://www.whitehouse.gov/healthreform/healthcare-overview

World Health Organization. (2003). *WHO definition of health: Preamble to the Constitution of the World Health Organization as adopted by the International Health Conference, New York, 19–22 June, 1946.* Geneva, Switzerland: Author. from http://www.who.int/about/definition/en

Suggested Readings

Barr, D. (2014). *Health disparities in the United States: Social class, race, ethnicity, and health.* Baltimore, MD: Johns Hopkins University Press.

Burton, L., Kemp, S., Leung, M., Matthews, S., & Takeuchi, D. (Eds.). (2011). *Communities, neighborhoods, and health: Expanding the boundaries of place.* New York: Springer.

Daschle, T., & Nather, D. (2010). *Getting it done: How Obama and Congress finally broke the stalemate to make way for health care reform.* New York: Dunne.

Fasano, P. (2013). *Transforming health care: The financial impact of technology, electronic tools, and data mining.* Hoboken, NJ: Wiley.

Harvey, U., Housel, T., & Kreps, G. (Eds.). (2014). *Health care disparities and the LGBT population.* Lanham, MD: Lexington Books.

McCree, D., Jones, K., & O'Leary (Eds.). (2014). *African Americans and HIV/AIDS: Understanding and addressing the epidemic.* New York: Springer.

McIntosh, E., Clarke, P., Frew, E., & Louviere, J. (2010). *Applied methods of cost-benefit analysis in health care.* New York: Oxford.

Strarr, P. (2013). *Remedy and reaction: The peculiar American struggle over health care reform.* New Haven, CT: Yale University Press.

CHAPTER 9

Mental Health, Substance Use, and Disability

Caitlyn Counihan

EP 2.1.1a
EP 2.1.7a
EP 2.1.9b

For 3 months, 24-year-old Lindsey Andrews has been living in a half-way house in the inner-city area of a large northern city. This living arrangement came on the heels of her 14th stay at a state mental hospital since the age of 16. Lindsey and her roommates earn money for food and part of the rent by working for an industrial cleaning company. They are supervised by a social worker from the local mental health outreach center that meets with them as a group twice a week and is available on call whenever they need support. With her social worker's help, Lindsey is planning to enroll in a job-training program next month and to move into her own apartment with one of the other residents of the halfway house within the next 6 months. She is excited at the prospect of living on her own.

Lindsey enjoyed a relatively stable childhood, growing up in a rural area of the South with her middle-class parents and four brothers. During middle school, she began to experience severe headaches and what she terms *anxiety attacks*. Her parents took her to several doctors, who could find no physical reasons for these problems. At about age 15, Lindsey's behavior changed from being calm and stable to becoming erratic—ranging from screaming rages to long periods of crying to fun-loving, carefree behavior.

She began to experiment with drugs, ran away from home a number of times, and got into several physical altercations with other girls at school. Her family had difficulty coping with her behavior. After one serious incident when Lindsey threatened her mother and her younger brother with a knife, she was hospitalized in a local private psychiatric hospital for 30 days. She was placed on medication to help stabilize her erratic behavior, and she and her family received therapy.

After her release from the hospital, Lindsey functioned better for several months. But she soon reported feeling overwhelmed and pressured and told her family that "I can't stop the frightening thoughts that keep running through my head." Her psychiatrist wanted to rehospitalize her, but her family's insurance benefits had been exhausted during her first hospitalization, and Lindsey did not want to admit herself to the state mental hospital nearby.

After continual arguments with her family and school personnel and several minor run-ins with the law, Lindsey quit school and moved with a boyfriend to

California, where she held a series of temporary jobs. When the boyfriend left her because of her mood swings, her behavior became even more erratic. Finally, after she was found asleep in a dumpster and unable to remember who or where she was, the police picked her up and took her to the state hospital.

For the next 6 years, Lindsey repeated a pattern of holding a menial job for a short time, losing the job, living on the streets, entering the state hospital, and being released in a more stable condition. When Lindsey was released from her last hospital stay, the local mental health center in Lindsey's area finally had space available at the halfway house where she is living now. She has developed a real bond with her social worker and hopes to be living independently in the near future. Lindsey is quick to say that without her social worker, she would not be ready to make this move toward independence.

Because of increased individual stresses, financial pressures, interpersonal conflicts including divorce, and work-related pressures, most individuals are expected to experience emotional problems at some point in their lives. Others experience them because of biological factors, such as an imbalance of chemicals needed for optimal mental health. These same factors can lead to misuse of alcohol and other drugs, including addiction. While problems with mental health and substance use can be classified as disabilities depending on their nature and extent, other individuals have physical or intellectual disabilities. These three major topics—mental health, substance use, and disability—are presented in one chapter, not because one condition leads to or causes another, but because they all can result in stigmatization and marginalization when they occur.

Emotional problems are often correlated with substance use and addiction, a related field of practice in which large numbers of social workers are employed. The ecological/systems framework discussed in Chapter 3 can be used to understand the relationships among environmental factors that contribute to emotional problems and substance use. Problems in one area, such as mental illness, are not automatically accompanied by substance use. But researchers find that about one in four individuals with severe mental disorders also misuse alcohol and/or other drugs (Substance Abuse and Mental Health Services Administration, 2010). In addition, many people in the United States have some type of disability, with mental disorders the most common. Sometimes individuals with disabilities misuse alcohol or other drugs as a way to cope with their disabilities. Some types of developmental disabilities are a result of drug use by mothers during pregnancy. The relationship between disabilities and substance use is supported by legislation prohibiting discrimination against individuals with disabilities in which the definition of disability includes both substance users and persons with emotional problems.

As you can see, the topics of mental illness, substance use, and disability are interconnected. However, one cannot assume that a person who has a physical disability is an alcoholic and is mentally ill; in other words, these issues are sometimes, but not always, associated with each other. Regardless of whether a person has some type of disability, has a mental illness, is a substance user, or has some combination of all these, he or she is often misunderstood, judged, and marginalized by society.

In this chapter, we provide definitions and characteristics related to mental health and mental illness, substance use and addiction, and disabilities. As you read, you will see that different histories, policies, and issues surround each. Nevertheless, they have many similarities, particularly in the stigma, oppression, and discrimination experienced by persons with mental illness, substance use disorders, and disabilities. The later part of the chapter focuses on policies, services and programs, current breakthroughs that are likely to change how these issues are addressed, and roles that social workers play in addressing these issues.

Social workers play many important roles at all levels of the environment in working with individuals, families, and communities to address relevant needs. Key roles include recognizing the strengths of individuals, families, cultural groups, and communities and empowering them to draw on those strengths to develop a healthier environment in which to live.

Mental Health and Mental Illness

Like Lindsey Andrews, about one-fourth of the adult population in the United States is estimated to be affected by some type of diagnosable mental disorder in any given year (National Alliance on Mental Illness, 2013). Nearly two-thirds of all people with mental illness do not seek treatment, although about half of all adults with some type of mental illness report that it impairs their ability to function (National Institute of Mental Health [NIMH], 2010b).

Direct costs associated with mental disorders such as medication, clinic visits, and hospitalization represent only a small portion of the economic burden these illnesses place on society. Other costs associated with mental disorders include lost productivity at work for people with mental illness as well as family members who care for them; cost of work-related and other accidents; direct and indirect financial costs for families caring for mentally ill persons; unemployment, alienation, and crime in young people with mental disabilities; poor cognitive development in children whose parents are mentally ill; and the emotional burden and diminished quality of life for family members. Mental health services in the United States are available to only one in every eight individuals who need them, and they are available to far fewer individuals worldwide. Barriers to the effective treatment of mental illness include a lack of available and affordable treatment resources; the stigma associated with mental illness; social isolation of those with mental health

problems; noncompliance with prescribed medicines; lack of political will required to address the problems that stem from mental illness; and a lack of community support for mental health services.

Mental Health

EP 2.1.7b
EP 2.1.8a
EP 2.1.9b

How do we determine what mental health is and who should receive mental health services? The stigma placed on individuals with mental health problems and the stereotypes about the services offered to them cause many individuals with mental health problems to avoid seeking services. People think of mental health services and those who receive them as portrayed in popular movies and books, such as the classic novel *One Flew Over the Cuckoo's Nest* (Kesey, 1962) and the films *A Beautiful Mind, Girl Interrupted, Rain Man, Monster, I Am Sam, The Silence of the Lambs, Black Swan, American Hustle,* and *Silver Linings Playbook.* For this reason, many communities are passing zoning or other ordinances to disallow individuals with mental health problems from moving into their neighborhoods, a form of "not in my backyard," or NIMBY, experienced by such groups as the homeless, persons recovering from addiction to alcohol and other drugs, immigrants, and refugees.

The rights of people with mental health problems also are receiving more attention. Should they be forced to be hospitalized, receive electric shock treatments, or get drug therapy against their wishes? Or, like Lindsey, when they desperately need treatment that is not available because of scarce resources, do they or their advocates have a right to demand services, especially if it means that they will be less likely to need more intensive services, such as institutionalization, in the future? Does someone who currently is in an institution but could function in a less restrictive environment have the right to demand such a placement?

From another perspective, what about protections for those in our society who may encounter individuals with serious mental health problems? What should happen if those individuals become dangerous to themselves or others?

This issue was exemplified by court cases involving Andrea Yates, a mother from Texas who drowned her five young children in a bathtub in 2001. At her initial trial in 2002, her attorneys argued that she should be found not guilty by reason of insanity. A number of mental health professionals testified that she had post-partum depression and other mental illness, which raised the issue of whether she knew right from wrong at the time of the deaths. Jurors found Yates guilty and sentenced her to life in prison. Because of a procedural error, however, the case was retried 4 years later and a second jury found her not guilty by reason of insanity. She was committed to a high-security mental health facility, where she will be held until she is deemed to no longer be a threat to herself or to others.

In a contrasting case, a young adult who killed a number of women over several years, and was diagnosed by several psychiatrists as having severe psychological problems, was sentenced to death in a Florida court and executed. And a young adult with mental retardation who aided in a murder at the age of 17—when his mental age was about 6—was put to death.

Individuals who have been found guilty in courts of killing their children, killing their partners, committing serial murders across the country, or killing large numbers of people at one site have received disparate sentences. The mental health status of all of those charged has been introduced in these cases. Are these individuals less accountable to society for their actions because of their diminished mental capacity? Who is responsible for looking after them to ensure that they do not harm themselves or others? What legal protections should be guaranteed?

Studies also show a strong relationship between mental health problems and physical health problems. When people do not get help for their mental health problems, they are much more likely to become physically ill. For example, researchers found that half of those going to company physicians with health-related problems had mental health problems (Loeppke et al., 2009). A number of studies have found that those who receive mental health services for a specific psychological problem experience a significant drop in subsequent medical costs (National Alliance on Mental Illness, 2009a). Because these studies show that the high costs of health care could be reduced if more attention were directed to people's mental health needs, it is hoped that the **Affordable Care Act**, which mandates treatment coverage for mental health and substance use, will result in reduced health-care costs for many individuals.

If left untreated, mental health problems increase the financial costs to taxpayers and decrease productivity in the workplace. Disruptions to the individual with the problem and family members take financial and emotional tolls, although it is difficult to obtain accurate data on actual expenditures for mental health services and other related costs to individuals with mental health problems, as well as the costs to their families, workplaces, and communities.

The areas of mental health and addiction offer many vital roles for social workers. According to the Bureau of Labor Statistics (2014), 114,200, or about 20% of social workers in the United States in 2012, were classified as mental health and substance-abuse social workers. They worked in state mental hospitals, private psychiatric treatment facilities, community outreach facilities, child guidance clinics and family service agencies, emergency hotlines, crisis centers, and private offices. It is estimated that between 2012 and 2022, this number is projected to increase by 23%.

Mental Health and Mental Illness: Definitions

EP 2.1.3a

Societies throughout history have developed their own systems for labeling acceptable and unacceptable behavior. What is tolerated in one society may be unacceptable in another. For each society there is a continuum, with certain definitely unacceptable behaviors at one end and definitely acceptable and appropriate behaviors at the other end. Members of a society agree almost uniformly on the behaviors at either end of the continuum, while the behaviors in the middle of the continuum are often the subject of extensive disagreement and debate. For example, most would consider murder as a definitely unacceptable behavior, but where on the continuum would they place continually talking aloud to oneself?

Some societies tolerate little deviance from acceptable behavior. For a brief period during colonial times in Salem, Massachusetts, for example, some individuals whose behaviors were considered "deviant" were labeled as witches and were tortured and burned at the stake. Other individuals with mental illness in colonial times were locked in attics or cellars or warehoused in "lunatic" asylums. Later research (Mechanic, 2007) suggested that many of these individuals had severe psychological problems, and others were women in nontraditional roles who refused to give them up.

By contrast, in certain other societies, those whose behavior deviates from the norm are given special roles and, in some instances, elevated to high-status positions. For example, in many Native American tribes, nonconforming individuals often became shamans, or medicine men, assuming high-status positions within the tribes.

More often, historically, those labeled as mentally ill or "retarded" have been isolated or punished. Although society has advanced, there is carryover ambivalence about how they should be regarded and treated. Attempts at integrating individuals with emotional disturbance and mental illness into classrooms and communities are often met with much resistance. David Mechanic (2007), a prominent social policy analyst in the mental health field, has argued that the stigma attached to the labels "mentally ill" and "disabled" further damages those already stigmatized and increases their problems. Some advances have been made in the current preference for referring to the condition instead of the individual, as in "individuals with mental illness" rather than "the mentally ill," for example.

Informal definitions have their genesis in groups within which the person operates, usually family members or coworkers. The definitions depend on the norms of the specific group and what is tolerated, as well as the position the person occupies within the group. A boss's behavior, for example, may be defined as outside the group norms much less quickly than a file clerk's behavior. Informal definitions also depend on whether the other members of the group can empathize. Can they fit that behavior into their own frame of reference? In an example by Mechanic (2007), a person who continually carries on an imaginary conversation with his mother while on the job is more likely to be tolerated if the group is aware that the mother recently died and the son is still grieving her death. But if there is no apparent context for the behavior or if the behavior persists, the individual is likely to be labeled as strange or odd.

Definitions of so-called abnormal behaviors typically are based on visible symptoms—such as talking to people who are not present—rather than on the severity of the actual problems. Attempting to define a condition based on invisible factors, such as what is going on inside an individual's mind, is difficult. Only those who in some way enter the mental health system are likely to be defined specifically as having some type of emotional or mental problem. This results in overestimates of the number of individuals defined as having emotional problems.

Categorizing Mental Illness

EP 2.1.3b
EP 2.1.7a
EP 2.1.7b

Formal definitions of mental illness traditionally have followed the **medical model,** which considers those with emotional problems to be sick. This model also assumes that sick people are entitled to be helped, and that help or treatment should be guided by medical experts in medical settings or settings such as psychiatric facilities directed by medical professionals. The medical model conceptualizes **mental illness** as severe emotional problems caused by brain dysfunction or intrapsychic causes, with little attention to systems or environmental influences. (See Chapter 3 for a comparison of the medical model and the ecological/systems perspective.) Traditionally, mental illness also has been viewed from a genetic or physiological perspective as a disease of the mind or a disturbance in the individual's functioning.

DSM Classification System The American Psychiatric Association has attempted to monitor the categorization and definition of various types of emotional disorders through a classification system termed the **Diagnostic and Statistical Manual of Mental Disorders (DSM).** This classification system, currently in its fifth revision, is referred to informally as the DSM-5. It uses a multidimensional system for evaluation, which focuses on the psychological, biological, and social aspects of an individual's functioning. The system was revised in 2013 to better reflect interrelationships and shared symptoms between diagnoses as well as greater attention to contributing cultural and contextual factors. The DSM-5 also incorporates definitions that are consistent with the World Health Organization, thus taking a more global approach (Coleman, 2013).

Some social work professionals believe that the DSM classification system is consistent with an ecological/systems perspective in assessing an individual, allowing a focus on organic factors or environmental factors, or both, that affect an individual's condition. They believe when completing an assessment that the DSM allows for incorporating the individual's strengths as well as problems. They are supportive of the revised DSM-5, particularly the fact that it focuses more on an individual's life experiences and allows for incorporating cultural factors such as ethnicity and religion (Franklin, 2014; Reardon, 2014). Of equal importance is the fact that this classification system is used as the basis for third-party insurance reimbursement when mental health services are provided.

Other social workers argue the opposite perspective. They say that the new DSM still focuses way too much on disorders and deficits, assigning labels through diagnosis that can stigmatize individuals and is more consistent with the medical model than the tenets of the social work profession. These critics argue that a diagnostic process of this nature actually may be more detrimental to clients, because labels such as "schizophrenia" and "conduct disorder" can negatively affect clients and the way others treat them, particularly if the label included in a client's records is obtained and misused. They also raise concerns because the DSM-5 is not evidence based, which can result in mis- and overdiagnosis of mental health disorders, leading to unneeded treatment and medication, an argument that the National Institute of Mental Health also has raised (Reardon, 2014). These critics say that the increased knowledge gained from brain-based research calls for a system that focuses on causes of mental illness rather than symptoms and that while some of this knowledge resulted in changes in the DSM-5, they haven't gone far enough (Miller, 2010). This group of social workers would prefer a system that incorporates not only more evidence-based context but also the ecological/systems perspective and social work values, including the strengths perspective. Regardless of feelings about the DSM, social workers are locked into using the system if they or the agencies they work for submit third-party reimbursement claims to insurance companies. Only one person with social work education was a member of the more than 100-person DSM task force that oversaw the recent revisions. Increasing advocacy efforts and involving more social workers in the dialogue about DSM revisions may lead to a more balanced document in the future (Reardon, 2014).

PIE Classification System The National Association of Social Workers (Karls & O'Keefe, 2008; Karls & Wandrei, 1994) published an alternative classification system, the person-in-environment (PIE) system, which offers a more holistic approach based on the ecological/systems framework. Like the DSM, this system can be used to describe, classify, and code the emotional, mental, and social problems of adults. The PIE system assesses clients according to four major factors:

1. *social functioning* (the social role in which each problem is identified: type of problem, severity of problem, duration of problem, and client's ability to cope with the problem);

2. *environmental problems* (the social system in which each problem is identified, specific type of problem within each social system, severity of the problem, duration of the problem);
3. *mental health problems* (clinical syndrome and personality and developmental disorders); and
4. *physical health problems* (diseases diagnosed by a physician and other health problems reported by the client and others).

A major difference between the PIE and the DSM is that the PIE system emphasizes the interrelationship of the person and the environment (Corcoran & Walsh, 2010). A significant limitation of the PIE system is that it cannot be used as a basis for securing third-party payment, as the DSM can. Thus, in spite of its advantages, the system has been downplayed in comparison to the DSM.

National Survey on Drug Use and Health The National Survey on Drug Use and Health, administered by SAMHSA, collects data on types and prevalence of mental illness in the United States. The Survey defines any mental illness (AMI) as "a mental, behavioral, or emotional disorder (excluding developmental and substance use disorders); diagnosable currently or within the past year; and of sufficient duration to meet diagnostic criteria specified within the DSM" (NIMH, 2014, p. 1). In 2012, 18.6% of all U.S. adults were estimated to have AMI.

About 4% of U.S. adults have a serious mental illness (SMI). This group meets the same criteria as those with AMI, but their illness results in serious impairment in their ability, which significantly interferes with or limits one or more primary life activities (NIMH, 2014, p. 1). (See Table 9.1 for a demographic comparison of those with AMI and those with SMI.)

Mental Health: A Matter of Viewpoint

EP 2.1.7a
EP 2.1.7b

The traditional view of mental health and mental illness is that they are found at opposite ends of a continuum. Other viewpoints, like that of psychiatrist Thomas Szasz (2008, 2009, 2010), suggest that mental health and emotional problems defy specific boundaries. Szasz objects to labeling the mentally ill, arguing that there is no such thing as mental illness. He agrees that some mental illnesses are the result of neurological impairment, but he believes that these illnesses are "brain diseases" rather than mental illnesses. Although he acknowledges the existence of emotional problems,

TABLE 9.1 PREVALENCE OF ANY MENTAL ILLNESS AND SERIOUS MENTAL ILLNESS AMONG U.S. ADULTS (2012)

DEMOGRAPHIC	ANY MENTAL ILLNESS	SERIOUS MENTAL ILLNESS
Females	22%	4.9%
Males	14.9%	3.2%
Age 18–25	19.6%	4.1%
Age 26–49	21.2%	5.2%
Age 50+	15.8%	3.0%
Hispanic	16.3%	4.4%
White	19.3%	4.2%
Black	18.6%	3.4%
Asian	13.9%	2.0%
Native Hawaiian/Other Pacific Islander	No data	1.8%
American Indian/Alaska Native	28.3%	8.5%
2 or More Ethnic Groups	20.7%	8.5%
OVERALL	18.6%	4.1%

Source: National Institute of Mental Health (2014a) *Any mental illness (AMI) among adults.* Rockville, MD: Author and National Institute of Mental Health (2014e). *Serious mental illness (SMI) among adults.* Rockville, MD: Author.

Szasz contends that labeling nonorganic emotional problems implies a deviation from some clearly specified norm. Szasz thinks such labeling not only stigmatizes individuals but also may actually cause them to assume those behaviors.

Szasz argues that instead of talking about definitions of mental illness, we should talk about problems of living—the individual's struggle with how to live in our world. He and others believe that positive **mental health** is promoted by our competence in dealing with our environment and our confidence of being able, when necessary, to cause desired effects. He advocates an ecological/systems perspective for viewing mental health. Within his framework, problems in living can be viewed as stemming from biological/physiological, economic, political, psychological, or sociological constraints. Promoting positive

interactions between individuals and their environments is viewed as congruent with promoting optimal mental health and social functioning for individuals. A longtime activist in the mental health arena, Szasz (1998) pioneered a classification system with three categories of mental health problems:

1. *personal disabilities,* such as depression, fears, inadequacy, and excessive anxiety;
2. *antisocial acts,* such as violent and criminal behaviors; and
3. *deterioration of the brain,* such as Alzheimer's disease, alcoholism, and brain damage.

Many mental health experts prefer this system and its emphasis on healthy functioning rather than a system that emphasizes mental illness. Szasz's system assumes that at some point all individuals have difficulties in negotiating their complex environments. It assumes that mental health services are available to and needed by all individuals at some time during their lives instead of something to be avoided. This perspective is much more consistent with the ecological/systems perspective and the PIE classification system than the medical model and the DSM-5.

The Development of Mental Health Problems

Considerable debate surrounds the question of how mental health problems arise. To say that one specific factor causes a mental health problem is difficult, if not impossible. More likely, mental health problems are the result of a variety of factors. Research suggests a number of possible explanations.

Heredity, Biological, and Genetic Factors Modern brain-imaging technologies have contributed significantly to understanding and treating mental health and mental disorders (NIMH, 2014). For example, researchers indicate that in depression, neural circuits responsible for regulating moods, thinking, sleep, appetite, and behavior do not function properly and critical neurotransmitters (chemicals used by nerve cells to communicate) are imbalanced.

Researchers also have identified genes and their interactions that seem to impact other conditions such as Alzheimer's disease and alcoholism and drug addiction. Imaging techniques that allow "real-time" viewing of the tiniest components of a cell make it possible to determine the impact of various stressors in the environment on a living organism, as well as to introduce various drugs into an organism and determine not only the impact of a drug, but also the reasons why the organism reacts as it does. Scientists indicate that before long a scan of an individual can be conducted, followed by computer-generated determinations tailored specifically to that individual, identifying appropriate medication or other interventions to address identified problems.

Many researchers, however, caution that the impact of the environment cannot be disregarded. Genetics research indicates that vulnerability to mental disorders such as depression results from the influence of multiple genes acting together with environmental factors (NIMH, 2009). A number of studies have found that individuals who were more likely to experience depression after life stressors had a different serotonin transporter gene variant than others (Brummett et al., 2008; Willhelm, Niven, Finch, & Wedgwood, 2006). One study, for example, found that reactions to stress resulted in small chemical changes to DNA in teenagers' brains, which could put them at greater risk for developing depression later in life (Nikolova et al., 2014).

Research also suggests that schizophrenia, like heart disease and diabetes, results from the complex interaction of genetic, biological, developmental, and environmental factors. Mental illnesses are viewed increasingly as chemical imbalances in the brain. "Just as diabetes is a disorder of the pancreas, mental illnesses are brain disorders that often result in a diminished capacity for coping with the ordinary demands of life" (National Alliance on Mental Illness, 2009, p. 1).

Research exemplified by genetic studies on depression and life stressors suggests that genetic factors alone do not cause mental health disorders. Many research findings indicate that individuals are predisposed to certain problems through heredity, and certain environmental conditions trigger this predisposition, resulting in the emotional problem. A variation of this position is that, because of genetic traits or physiological characteristics, some individuals are biologically less capable of coping with environmental stress (Flint, Greenspan, & Kendler, 2010; Jacobs et al., 2006; Keller, Neale, & Kendler, 2007; Licinio & Wong, 2005).

Psychosocial Developmental Factors Based on the work of developmental theorist Erik Erikson and others, the psychosocial developmental perspective suggests that mental health problems result from environmental experiences during childhood. Research shows that individuals who experience severe trauma during childhood—such as physical or sexual abuse, separation from a close family member, or alcoholism or drug misuse by family members—are much more likely to develop mental health problems later in life. Posttraumatic stress disorder, common in combat veterans, also is often experienced by survivors of child sexual and physical abuse and individuals who have witnessed violent attacks on others, particularly family members. Research indicates that exposure to such trauma also changes a person's brain chemistry, suggesting an interactive effect between physiological and developmental factors (see Figure 9.1) (Barth et al., 2008; Child Welfare Information Gateway, 2009b).

FIG 9.1 Rates of depression by persons experiencing stressful life events according to gene type
NOTE: Among people who had inherited two copies of the stress-sensitive short version of the serotonin transporter gene (s/s), 45% developed depression following four stressful life events in their early 20s, compared to 17% among people with two copies of the stress-protective long version (l/l). About 17% of the 847 subjects carried two copies of the short version, 31% two copies of the long version, and 51% one copy of each version.
SOURCE: Avshalom Caspi, University of Wisconsin, from National Institute of Mental Health, *Gene More Than Doubles Risk of Depression Following Life Stresses*, July 2003.

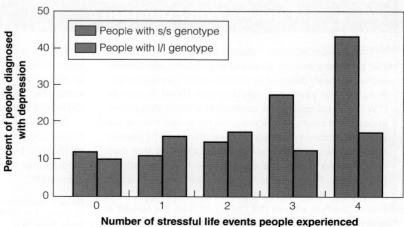

Social Learning   The social learning perspective proposes that mental health problems are the result of learned behaviors. The behaviors may be learned by observing parents or other role models, or used as survival mechanisms to cope with difficult life experiences.

Social Stress   The social stress perspective, based on the work of Szasz (1998), emphasizes the relationship between environmental stress and mental health. This perspective suggests that individuals who are under duress—including the poor, people of color, and women—are more likely to develop mental health problems (El-Mallakh, 2007; Kuruvilla & Jacob, 2007).

Societal Reactions and Labeling   This perspective suggests that society creates individuals with mental health problems through a societal reaction process. By establishing social norms and treating as deviant those who do not subscribe to the norms, a society identifies individuals with mental health problems. In addition, individuals who are identified or labeled as somehow different will assume the role prescribed to them; that is, individuals labeled as having mental health problems will behave as they would be expected to if they had the problem. Individuals labeled as having mental health problems, even though they do not behave any differently from those without problems, also may also be perceived as behaving differently because of how they are labeled (see Box 9.1).

Collective Mobilization   The collective mobilization perspective emphasizes the importance of social expectations, social stigma, and exclusion from opportunities in understanding mental health problems (Mechanic, 2008). Organizations representing persons with mental disabilities have mobilized to advocate for their inclusion in educational opportunities, employment, and access to social participation. These collective mobilization efforts have changed social definitions and viewpoints toward these groups, which in turn have changed individual behavior (Mechanic, 2008).

The Ecological/Systems Perspective on Mental Health Issues   The ecological/systems perspective

EP 2.1.7a

suggests that mental health problems are the result of a variety of factors that interact in a complex fashion and vary according to the uniqueness of the individual and the environment within which he or she interacts. Research on brain chemistry elevates the importance of physiological factors but also lends support to the ecological/systems perspective.

Although the environment cannot completely control whether a person develops an emotional disorder, it can exacerbate the problem or, in some instances, facilitate an individual's ability to cope more effectively. Within the ecological/systems framework, many factors that shape a person's self-concept, competence, and behaviors can be addressed. These factors include the person's biological characteristics; ethnicity; gender; place within the

Box 9.1   Does Labeling Shape Our Expectations of How People Will Function?

The identification of individuals with mental health problems and the ways those problems are defined are issues hotly debated by mental health professionals. A number of years ago, psychologist David Rosenhan (1973) and his associates conducted a study that exemplifies this concern. Rosenhan and his seven colleagues went separately to the admissions offices of 12 psychiatric hospitals in 5 different states, all claiming that they were hearing voices. In every instance, they were admitted to the hospitals as patients. Immediately upon admission, they all assumed normal behavior. At least one of the researchers did not try to hide his role as a researcher. He sat on the ward and took copious notes on legal pads of all of the events going on around him.

Even though the researchers all behaved normally while hospitalized, hospital professionals were unable to distinguish them from other patients. In a number of instances, however, the other patients were able to determine that they were not mentally ill.

Rosenhan and his associates remained at the hospitals as patients from 7 to 52 days, with an average stay of 19 days, before they were discharged. The diagnosis at discharge for each of them was "schizophrenia in remission."

Source: David Rosenhan, "On Being Sane in Insane Places," *Science, 179* (1973), 250–257. Reprinted with permission from Rosenhan, *Science* 179: 240–248. Copyright 1973 by AAAS.

broader environment, including family, peer groups, and the neighborhood and community in which the person functions; and cultural and societal expectations.

In addressing mental health problems, the ecological/systems perspective allows us to consider all of the factors within an individual's past and present environment, as well as the individual's physiological characteristics. For example, a person may be predisposed biologically toward mental health problems, may have suffered from sexual abuse as a child, may have had a parent who had mental health problems, and currently may be in an extremely stressful living situation (e.g., an unhappy long-term relationship, a stressful job, or financial problems). If we know which factors are most important, we are better able to intervene successfully to alleviate the problems.

This emphasis on both the individual and the individual's environment allows the social worker and the client to "map out" the factors that are most likely to account for the problems and then to develop an intervention plan to specifically address those factors. How and when an individual's emotional problems are identified and defined depend on a number of factors (Mechanic, 1999, p. 114):

1. the visibility, recognizability, or persistence of inappropriate/deviant behaviors and symptoms;
2. the extent to which the person perceives the symptoms as serious;
3. the extent to which the symptoms disrupt family, work, and other activities;
4. the frequency of the appearance of the signs and symptoms, or their persistence;
5. the tolerance threshold of those who are exposed to and evaluate the signs and symptoms;
6. the information available to, the knowledge of, and the cultural assumptions and understandings of the evaluator;
7. the degree to which processes that distort reality are present;
8. the presence of needs within the family/environment that conflict with the recognition of problems or the assumption of the sick role;
9. the possibility that competing interpretations can be assigned to the behaviors/signs once they are recognized; and
10. the availability of treatment/intervention resources, their physical proximity, and psychological and monetary costs of taking action, including money, time, and effort as well as costs of stigmatization and humiliation.

Types of Mental Health Problems

EP 2.1.3a Although people with mental disorders are still stigmatized, increasing openness by many individuals with various diagnoses has resulted in more public awareness about them. Depression is the leading cause of mental disability in the United States for adults, afflicting almost 10% of the population (Centers for Disease Control and Prevention, 2013). Other common types of mental disorders are bipolar disorder, schizophrenia, anxiety and panic disorders, attention-deficit/hyperactivity disorder, posttraumatic stress disorder, and autism (see Table 9.2). The following data are from the NIMH (2010), unless indicated otherwise. (Attention-deficit/hyperactivity disorder and autism are discussed later in the chapter.) Unfortunately, persons with these mental disorders are more at risk to make suicide attempts than others. Thus, we have included discussion on suicide in this section as well.

Mood Disorders

Mental illnesses classified as mood disorders affect a person's persistent emotional state, or their mood. Types include major depression and bipolar disorder. A chemical imbalance in the brain causes moods to become either elevated (mania) or lowered (depression) (National Institute of Mental Health, 2014c).

Bipolar Disorder

According to the National Institute of Mental Health (2010b), about 2.6 million people in the United States have bipolar disorder, characterized as mood cycles alternating between depression and mania. Those with mild disorder have rapid swings between depression and anxiety, and sometimes panic disorder as a result of the constant abrupt recycling of their moods that they cannot control. Those with more serious bipolar disorder alternate between episodes of major depression and mania. In the manic condition, the individual has periods of abnormally and persistently elevated mood or irritability, often accompanied by overly inflated self-esteem, less need for sleep, talkativeness, racing thoughts, distractibility, increased goal directed activity or physical agitation, and excessive involvement in pleasurable activities that have a highpotential for painful consequences. A combination of medications and holistic approaches has been successful in treating many individuals with bipolar disorder.

TABLE 9.2 ESTIMATED PERSONS WITH MENTAL DISORDERS IN THE UNITED STATES IN A GIVEN YEAR

Mood disorders	20.9 million (9.5% of adult population)
Major depressive disorder	14.8 million (6.7% of adult population)
Dysthymic disorders (chronic, mild depression)	3.3 million (1.5% of adult population)
Bipolar disorder	5.7 million (2.6% of adult population)
Anxiety disorders	40 million (18.1% of adult population)
Panic disorder	6 million (2.7% of adult population)
Obsessive-compulsive disorder (OCD)	2.2 million (1% of adult population)
Posttraumatic stress disorder (PTSD)*	7.7 million (3.5% of adult population)
Generalized anxiety disorder	6.8 million (3.1% of adult population)
Social phobia	15 million (6.8% of adult population)
Agoraphobia	1.8 million (0.8% of adult population)
Specific phobia	19.2 million (8.7% of adult population)
Eating disorders	0.6%, 1.0%, and 2.8% of the adult population for anorexia, bulimia, and binge-eating disorders, respectively
Attention-deficit disorder	4.1% of adults 18–44
Autism	3.4 cases per 1,000 children ages 3–10
Alzheimer's disease	4.5 million (1 in 10 over age 65 and nearly half over age 85 are affected)
Schizophrenia	2.4 million (1.1% of adult population)
Suicide	39,518 in 2011; more than 90% had a diagnosable mental disorder

*The number of individuals in the United States suffering from PTSD is expected to increase significantly as more cases among soldiers returning from military operations in Iraq and Afghanistan are diagnosed (RAND, 2008).

SOURCES: American Foundation for Suicide Prevention (2014); National Institute of Mental Health (2010a, 2010b).

Depression is the leading cause of disability worldwide, with many individuals incapacitated for weeks or months if untreated. Breakthroughs in effective medication have allowed many persons with depression to lead typical lives. Still, people in general often do not realize how debilitating depression can be, and even make fun of those who cannot function without medication. Depression is more than having a few bad days or sad moments. It is an overwhelming feeling of incapacitation that, in the extreme, may result in a person not being able to get out of bed, go to work or school, or otherwise function.

Nearly twice as many women as men are affected by depression each year, leading some researchers to suggest a relationship between hormonal imbalance and neurotransmitters in the brain. This argument is bolstered in that most women diagnosed with depression are of childbearing age. Many women develop depression after the birth of a child. This depression has been linked to the abrupt postchildbirth hormonal changes (National Alliance on Mental Illness, 2009).

With improved clinical skills and increasing attention directed to mental health issues in children and adolescents, more young people also are being diagnosed with depression. Estimates by the NIMH (2014) indicate that about 11% of adolescents experience depression, and children can be diagnosed well before they reach their teens. Although depression is brain-based, it is often directly related to environmental stressors. Because stress causes changes in levels and use of serotonin and other chemicals that impact a person's moods, major depression can also become debilitating because of a major life event, such as the death of a partner or child or loss of a job.

Depressive disorders often occur concurrently with anxiety disorders and substance use. Approximately 80% of individuals with depression respond positively to treatment, which often combines medication, counseling, exercise, and diet (National Alliance on Mental Illness, 2013).

Anxiety Disorders

While major depression is the most common debilitating type of mental illness, the most common types experienced in the United States are anxiety disorders. Almost 20% of the adult population experiences an anxiety disorder in a given year (NIMH, 2010).

Anxiety disorders include panic disorder, obsessive–compulsive disorder, posttraumatic stress disorder (PTSD), phobias, and generalized anxiety disorder. Symptoms of each are as follows:

- *panic disorder:* feelings of extreme fear and anxiety that strike for no apparent reason, resulting in an overpowering shortness of breath, feelings of being out of control, and other intense physical symptoms.
- *obsessive–compulsive disorder:* repetitive, intrusive thoughts or behaviors, such as washing the hands excessively or checking to see whether lights are turned off when leaving a room.
- *posttraumatic stress disorder (PTSD):* a reaction to previously experienced terrifying trauma, such as war-related incidents or sexual abuse, that results in frightening memories or intense body reactions.
- *phobia:* the fear of specific or generalized objects or events.
- *anxiety disorder:* excessive worry over everyday events and decisions.

Women are more likely than men to have anxiety disorders, which often occur concurrently with depression, eating disorders, and substance use.

Anxiety disorders may occur because of a chemical imbalance in the brain, an emotional trauma, or a learned response to specific situations. Anxiety disorders are increasingly treatable with medication and therapy, and cognitive behavioral and desensitization therapies have been found to be especially effective in treating anxiety disorders.

Schizophrenia

More than 2 million adults in the United States are affected by schizophrenia—the most chronic and disabling of the mental disorders (National Alliance on Mental Illness, 2014). Increasingly thought to be a chemical disorder, schizophrenia usually first appears in women in their 20s or early 30s and in men in their late teens or early 20s. It is manifested by impaired ability to manage emotions, interact with others, and think clearly. Symptoms include hallucinations, delusions, disordered thinking, and social withdrawal.

Although medication has helped many individuals with schizophrenia, this disease is particularly debilitating and often results in periodic hospitalizations. More than half of individuals with schizophrenia receive inadequate care. They may spend time in a mental hospital, where they are put on medication and then released. Without appropriate community mental health facilities and outreach, many of them run out of medication or have undesirable side effects and stop taking their medication.

Impacts of Mental Health Status on At-Risk Populations

EP 2.1.3b

A number of studies have shown that women; people of color; the elderly; the poor; individuals who are gay, lesbian, bisexual, or transgender; and individuals living in rural areas are at high risk of having mental health problems (National Rural Health Alliance, 2009; Nicklett & Burgard, 2008). Members of marginalized groups who are isolated from mainstream society do not have ready access to basic resources such as food, clothing, shelter, and employment and are more at risk to have their mental health impacted by their circumstances than those in more positive circumstances. In addition, when members of marginalized groups begin to experience symptoms of mental health problems, they are much less likely to have access to needed services than are those in society who are not marginalized.

Children   It has been estimated that one in five U.S. children ages 0–18 has a diagnosable mental disorder, and one in ten has a disorder so serious that it interferes with the ability to learn and relationships with families and peers. The onset of mental illness can occur as early as seven, with roughly half of all lifetime mental health disorders surfacing by mid-teens. Risk factors associated with the likelihood of a mental disorder during childhood or adolescence include being in the foster care system, poverty, having unemployed or teen parents, receiving public assistance, using illegal drugs and alcohol, being from a military family, and involvement with the juvenile justice system (Stagman & Cooper, 2010). Diagnosing children with mental disorders is controversial, as some mental health professionals believe that many children are diagnosed too early, misdiagnosed, and/ or prescribed inappropriate or unnecessary medications. Others point out the benefits of early intervention, including medication, therapy and other services to help children develop coping strategies. For many children, early intervention facilitates greater success in school and in relationships with peers and family members.

Survivors of Disaster and Trauma
Other populations at-risk for mental health problems include survivors of disaster and trauma. Among these are individuals who experience or observe trauma, such as rape, serious injury or death of another person, combat, or a natural disaster such as a hurricane or earthquake. Although strong reactions to trauma are expected, some individuals have long-term impacts and are diagnosed with posttraumatic stress disorder (PTSD). This condition is characterized by signs of intense fear, nightmares and flashbacks to the event; problems with sleeping, concentrating, eating, and focusing on common tasks; increased use of alcohol and other drugs; and physiological symptoms.

Although most people who go through trauma do not get PTSD, individuals are more at risk to develop it if they were directly exposed to trauma either as a survivor or a witness; were seriously injured as a result; believed they were in danger; believed a family member was in danger; felt helpless during the trauma; were exposed to extremely severe or long-lasting trauma; had a severe reaction during the traumatic event (feeling separated from surroundings, crying, shaking, vomiting); have experienced previous trauma (i.e., child abuse); have another mental health diagnosis; have family members with a mental health diagnosis; have little or no support from family or friends; have experienced a previous loss of someone important in their lives, especially if the loss was unexpected; have

experienced recent life stressors; drink a lot of alcohol or use other drugs; are female; have a limited education; are African American or Hispanic; and are young (National Center for PTSD, 2014, p. 1).

Although survivors of sexual abuse and other traumas are at risk to develop PTSD, the experiences of military personnel have increased awareness about its symptoms as well as research on how to best treat survivors. As many as 11–20% of veterans of the Afghanistan and Iraq Wars, 10% of Gulf War veterans, and 30% of Vietnam veterans are estimated to have PTSD. Another military-related cause of PTSD is military sexual trauma (MST). MST can include any sexual harassment or sexual assault that takes place during military service. Almost one-fourth (23%) of women veterans reported sexual assault when they were in the military while 55% of women and 35% of men experienced sexual harassment (National Center for PTSD, 2014). Those who work with individuals who have experienced trauma—emergency-room personnel, rescue squad workers, police officers, firefighters, and emergency medical service personnel—also can experience PTSD (National Center for PTSD, 2014). Reports from many soldiers who had been in Vietnam, their families, and those who provided care for them observed serious mental health issues upon their return, but not until much later did the U.S. Departments of Defense and Veterans Affairs acknowledge and give serious attention to their concerns. Soldiers and veterans who experience PTSD create problems for their families and the communities to which they return. Many returning soldiers do not seek treatment for PTSD-related problems, and few among those that have sought services have received adequate care. The Department of Veterans Affairs hosts a National Center for Post-Traumatic Stress Disorder (see http://www.ncpsd.va.gov), which provides information and training for military personnel and their families and also for those who work with survivors of natural disasters such as hurricanes and earthquakes. Reports after devastating hurricanes indicate that many survivors have PTSD and that suicide rates also are higher than national averages for this group (Substance Abuse and Mental Health Services Administration, 2008a).

Increased attention is also being given to the likelihood that children and adolescents have experienced PTSD. For example, many children in foster care who have experienced trauma due to abuse have been diagnosed with, and are taking medication, to address attention-deficit disorder (ADD). Many of the symptoms for both PTSD and ADD are the same, leading children's mental health professionals to advocate for more careful diagnosis (Ruiz, 2014).

Many social workers are trained to deal specifically with PTSD and are members of emergency-response teams that work with survivors after traumatic experiences. New breakthroughs in treatment based on brain chemistry and an individual's ability to reframe the trauma with specific interventions have the potential to help the many individuals and families impacted by this disorder. Despite increased attention to PTSD, there are still major gaps in awareness of the problem, acknowledgment of its extent and impact, and availability of services among both providers and consumers.

Persons Who Are Homeless Homelessness was discussed in Chapter 7, but we note here the relationship between homelessness and mental health and substance-use problems. Homelessness is both a cause and a result of mental illness, alcoholism, and other drug misuse (National Alliance to End Homelessness, 2014). The release of individuals with mental illness, intellectual disabilities, and chemical dependency from institutional care and the lack of community services have resulted in a significant risk of their becoming mentally ill or chemically dependent.

Approximately one-third of persons experiencing homelessness meet the criteria for having serious mental illness (National Alliance to End Homelessness, 2014). Almost half of persons who are homeless, and 70% of veterans who are homeless, have substance use disorders. A majority of those with substance use disorders also experience moderate to severe mental illness (United States Interagency Council on Homelessness, 2014).

The characteristics of mental illness make it difficult for persons who are homeless to negotiate street life and meet basic needs for food, safety, and shelter. They also are at greater risk for developing serious health problems such as tuberculosis, HIV, and severe upper respiratory infections. Because they lack a permanent address and often are unaware of or unable to apply for benefits, many do not receive funds and services for which they might be eligible (National Resource and Training Center on Homelessness and Mental Illness, 2014). Other people who are homeless develop mental health problems *after* becoming homeless, as a result of the stress of survival and the associated stigma. Their problems often are serious enough to require hospitalization (National Coalition for the Homeless, 2014).

Many people who are homeless and mentally ill have serious cognitive disturbances, like Lindsey (in the vignette at the beginning of this chapter), and are out of touch with reality, unaware of where they are going or where they have been. Their most frequent contacts with community resources are with the police and emergency psychiatric facilities. Typically, they remain on the streets, extremely vulnerable, until they are unable to function and are rehospitalized. For many, their lives become a pattern of homelessness and hospitalization (National Coalition for the Homeless, 2014; Pfeiffer, 2007; Seager, 2000).

Suicide

According to the World Health Organization (WHO, 2014), someone in the world commits **suicide** every 40 seconds, and 800,000 people were reported to have lost their lives in 2013, the first time that WHO collected data on suicides (many countries did not participate in the reporting process, so this is an under-represented figure). Suicide is a serious mental health problem in the United States, which has a higher suicide rate than many other Western countries. In 2011, the latest year for which nationwide data are available, 39,518 people committed suicide in the United States, an average of 105 deaths a day. In that year, suicide was the 10th leading cause of all deaths in the United States. Suicide impacts all age groups: it was the third leading cause of death for children ages 10–14, the third for young adults ages 15–24, the second for persons ages 25–34, and the fourth for persons ages 35–54 in 2011. The highest rate when comparing age groups was among people ages 45–64, with the second highest rate for those ages 85 and older. That same year, 3.7% of adults in the United States contemplated suicide, 1% had specific plans regarding how to carry it out, and .5% attempted it (Centers for Disease Control and Prevention, 2014b).

Determining which groups are most at risk to commit suicide is difficult, as risk factors associated with suicide vary by ethnicity, gender, and age and often occur in combination. In 2011, the suicide rate was highest for whites, with the second highest rate for Native Americans and Alaska Natives. Native Americans and Alaska Natives 15–24 years of age had a rate two and a half times the national average. When combining ethnicity and gender, in 2011 it was highest for white males and lowest for black females (Centers for Disease Control and Prevention, 2014b). The suicide rate for children and adolescents has increased significantly in recent years, which emphasizes the need to pay more attention to mental health issues at an earlier age.

Gender differences can also be seen when comparing suicides and suicide attempts. Men choose more lethal methods and are more than four times as likely as women to commit suicide, while women are two to three times more likely as men to attempt suicide (American Foundation for Suicide Prevention, 2014). In general, attempts at suicide are increasing. While no complete data are kept on suicide attempts, the CDC gathers data from hospitals annually. In 2012, the latest year for which data are available, 483,596 persons in the United States were treated for suicide, suggesting that for every reported death by suicide, twelve people make attempts (American Foundation for Suicide Prevention, 2014; Centers for Disease Control and Prevention, 2014b).

Interactions between individual, relational, community, and societal factors contribute to the risk of suicide. Risk factors associated with suicide (they may not be direct causes) include a family history of suicide and/or child maltreatment; previous suicide attempts; a history of mental disorders, particularly depression; a history of alcohol and misuse of other drugs; impulsive or aggressive characteristics; feeling hopeless; isolation/feeling cut off from others; cultural and religious beliefs (e.g., that suicide is a noble way to resolve a personal problem or will avoid bringing shame to a family; local epidemics of suicide; loss, often more than one, for example, a relationship, job, financial, one's health; easy access to lethal methods; and an inability to seek help either because of feelings of being overwhelmed or stigma (Centers for Disease Control and Prevention, 2014b, p. 1). Research by the NIMH (2010a) indicates that 90% of people who commit suicide have some type of diagnosable mental or substance-use disorder. Alterations in neurotransmitters such as serotonin are not only associated with depression, impulsive disorders, and substance abuse but also with suicide (NIMH, 2009b).

In contrast to risk factors, protective factors at the individual, relational, community, and societal levels reduce the risk of suicide. Protective factors include a stable support system; accessible, affordable and effective care for mental, physical, and substance use disorders; continued support from medical and mental health providers; skills in problem solving and conflict resolution; and cultural and religious beliefs that encourage self-preservation and discourage suicide (Centers for Disease Control and Prevention, 2014b, p. 2). Suicide

is a tragedy not only for the person who dies, but also for family members and others who have a hard time understanding why individuals want to end their lives and often blame themselves for not being able to prevent the death. Persons who commit suicide most often are in severe emotional pain and see no hope that their pain will improve. They are completely focused on ending their pain and typically are unable to focus on the impact their death will have on others.

Clues that a person may have decided to die by suicide include a sudden change from a depressed state and a hopeless perspective to seeming to improve and giving away possessions. Most suicide threats are not just attempts to get attention but are cries for help. Therefore, suicide threats should be taken seriously. In such situations, individuals should not be left alone, and immediate mental health intervention should be sought. All firearms and other weapons should also be removed. According to the American Association of Suicidology (2009), about half of all suicides are committed with firearms, and firearms are used to commit suicide far more often than to commit homicide.

Because the reasons for attempting suicide are so complex and varied, multiple prevention efforts are needed. Community- and school-based prevention programs, therefore, should be directed to reducing stress, instilling coping skills, preventing and reducing substance abuse, and working toward early identification and treatment of emotional problems, as well as limiting access to firearms. Public schools, universities, and some communities have developed suicide prevention programs and been able to successfully reduce the number of attempts made.

Alcoholism and Substance Use

EP 2.1.7b

In addition to the relationship between alcohol/chemical dependency and mental illness, problems of alcoholism and misuse of other drugs can be related to developmental disabilities, child and family issues, poverty, criminal justice, and the workplace. And vulnerable populations, including women, the elderly, people of color, and gays and lesbians, are at higher risk than other groups for serious problems with alcoholism and chemical dependency.

Until recently, excessive use of alcohol and other drugs were considered to be moral issues. The general societal perception was that people drank too much or used other drugs because they were weak and they could stop drinking or using drugs if they wanted to. Although many people still hold this view, attention began to be directed during the 1940s and 1950s to the concept that alcoholism is a disease and that people with this disorder must be treated in the same way as a person with diabetes or another chronic illness is treated. Although there is more stigma about misuse of other drugs, particularly those that are illegal, the prevalent contemporary view considers alcoholism and misuse of other drugs to be a chronic condition (is treatable but incurable), progressive (becomes worse if the drinking or drug use does not stop), and fatal (can result in death if untreated). Current research also shows that alcoholism and misuse of other drugs are more biologically-based than previously thought. The American Society of Addiction Medicine views alcoholism and other addictions as chronic brain disorders rather than behavioral problems, maintaining that the behaviors are manifestations of the brain disease (American Society of Addiction Medicine, 2011). Specialists in addiction also advocate against using the term *substance abuse*, and preferring to use the term *substance misuse* or the medical term *substance use disorder*, which is included in the DSM-5. Their rationale is that the term *abuse* implies stigma and the belief that people can cause and control their drinking and drug use, when addiction is genetically as well as environmentally based (CommonHealth, 2013).

Although the debate continues on whether alcoholism should be considered as an individual disease, a family or societal disease, or an individual, family, or societal problem, the disease model of alcoholism offers the advantages that

1. individuals and their families are more likely to accept the alcoholism and become involved in an intervention program if they view the alcoholism as a disease rather than as a moral weakness or a social problem.
2. conceptualizing alcoholism as a disease allows for insurance coverage for treatment and hospitalization and coverage for public health-care programs.

The laws in many states also allow the serious misuse of other drugs to be treated as a disease, but because use of drugs other than alcohol more often involves illegal and/or counterculture activities, there has been much more reluctance to consider as a disease the misuse of drugs other than alcohol.

Many substance users and their families deny that alcoholism and the misuse of other drugs is a problem that affects them. To absolve themselves, they define someone who misuses substances in many ways—as someone who takes one more drink or drug than they or their family member takes; as someone who drinks excessive amounts of only hard liquor and not beer or wine as they do; as someone who uses more dangerous drugs and not marijuana, which they use; or as someone who drinks and uses the substance every morning or every day, not just evenings or weekends as they do.

Contemporary definitions of alcoholism emphasize the personal implications of drinking rather than the amount or frequency. The National Institute on Alcohol Abuse and Alcoholism (2010) has defined **alcoholism** as a disease with four symptoms:

1. craving, or a strong need or urge to drink;
2. loss of control, or not being able to stop once drinking has begun;
3. physical dependence, or withdrawal symptoms that occur when one has stopped drinking, such as nausea, sweating, shakiness, and anxiety; and
4. tolerance, or the need to drink greater amounts of alcohol to get "high."

Alcoholism also has been defined as any use of alcohol that results or interferes with personal life—including school, jobs, family, friends, health, or the law—or spiritual life (Alcoholism and Drug Addiction Help, 2013).

Definitions of **substance use disorder** are similar. Although the misuse of alcohol is considered more socially acceptable than the misuse of other drugs, it is increasingly difficult to separate the two. Alcohol is still the most widely misused drug, with serious individual and societal costs, but many individuals misuse more than one substance (SAMSHA, 2014).

Research on addiction reveals further that many individuals treated for one type of substance misuse stop using that substance and "cross-addict" to another drug. Thus, some professionals in the field refer to the substance a person has used as his or her "drug of choice" and those who use more than one drug as "polyaddicts." Other professionals view substance use and chemical dependency as a problem of **addiction**, a primary chronic disease of brain reward, motivation, memory, and related circuitry, with genetic factors accounting for about half of the likelihood that an individual will develop an addiction with environmental factors, including exposure to trauma and stressors, also playing a role. Addiction is characterized by an inability to abstain from substance use; impairment in control of behavior, craving for drugs or rewarding experiences, diminished recognition of significant problems and interpersonal relationships, and dysfunctional emotional responses to situations (American Society of Addiction Medicine, 2011). Addiction can be viewed as physical and/or psychological dependence on mood-altering substances or experiences including, but not limited to, alcohol, drugs, pills, food, sex, pornography, gambling, shopping/spending, or exercise. This conceptualization supports an intervention focus on eliminating addictive behaviors in all areas of a person's life, including food, work, and relationships, as well as drugs.

Commonly Misused Substances

EP 2.1.3a

Alcohol, the oldest and most commonly misused substance in the world, is most often viewed as a depressant, although it also can be a stimulant and, for some individuals, a hallucinogen. According to the Substance Abuse and Mental Health Services Administration (2014a), slightly more than half of people over age 12 in the United States use alcohol, and about 23% report being binge drinkers. Of the 16.5 million persons (6.3% of the population) in the United States who are considered heavy drinkers, an estimated 1.6 million (6.2%) are adolescents (see Table 9.3).

The leading cause of death for U.S. teens is alcohol-related auto accidents. In 2012, alcohol impaired driving was involved in 31% of motor vehicle traffic motor vehicle traffic accidents (National Highway Traffic Safety Administration, 2014). Medical problems stemming from alcohol misuse include neurological, cardiological, and respiratory problems; liver disease; damage to the gastrointestinal system, pancreas, and kidneys; malnutrition; suppression of the immune system; and psychological problems.

An estimated 24.6 million individuals, 9.4% of the U.S. population, reported using illicit drugs in a 2013

national survey conducted by SAMHSA (2014; see Table 9.4).

As can be seen from Table 9.4, marijuana and hashish are used most often by all age groups, followed by nonmedical use of prescription drugs, including pain relievers, and cocaine. Teens were more likely than other groups to use inhalants and hallucinogens and less likely to use cocaine. Women and those who have experienced chronic pain, including veterans, are more at risk to misuse **depressants**, including sedatives, such as sleeping pills, tranquilizers, and pain killers. **Narcotics** such as opium and its derivatives (morphine and heroin) are also highly addictive. Legally, cocaine is considered a narcotic, but it often acts more like a stimulant than a depressant. Cocaine is the most powerful central nervous system stimulant known. The use of crack—the smokable, rapidly reacting form of cocaine—has become popular in recent years because of its lower cost, easy availability, and highly addictive nature. Use of crack and cocaine often results in high rates of addiction and also can produce delusional and paranoid behavior, acute toxic psychosis, cardiovascular problems including strokes and heart attacks, depression, neurological problems, lung problems including respiratory failure, increased injury from accidents, aggressive and violent behavior, and risks of hepatitis, HIV infection, and endocarditis (heart inflammation) (Phoenix House, 2010). Crack use also has been associated with increases in crime, overdoses, prostitution, AIDS, and homelessness. Publicity also has been drawn to "crack babies," who are born addicted and are at risk to die during their first year or to survive with serious physical and emotional problems. Because non-crack cocaine is most often used by individuals from higher income brackets who are more likely to be white than persons of color, its use receives less attention, including prosecution for drug use, than use of crack.

TABLE 9.3 ALCOHOL USE IN THE PAST MONTH AMONG INDIVIDUALS 12 OR OLDER, 2013

AGE	CURRENT		BINGE		HEAVY	
12 or older	52.2%	136.9 million	22.9%	60.1 million	6.3%	16.5 million
12–17	11.6%	2.9 million	6/2%	1.6 million	1.2%	293,000
18 or older	56.4%	134.0 million	24.6%	58.5 million	6.8%	16.2 million

Source: SAMHSA (2014a). Substance use and mental health estimates from the 2013 *National Survey on Drug Use and Health: Overview of Findings*. Washington, DC: Author. Available at www.samhsa.gov/data/2k14/DSDUH200/sr200-findings-overview-2014htm.

TABLE 9.4 ILLICIT DRUG USE IN THE PAST MONTH AMONG INDIVIDUALS AGED 12 OR OLDER: 2013

SUBSTANCE	AGE 12+		AGE 12–17		AGE 18+	
	NUMBER (IN 1,000S)	PERCENT	NUMBER (IN 1,000S)	PERCENT	NUMBER (IN 1,000S)	PERCENT
Illicit drug use, total	24,573	9.4	2,197	8.8	22,376	9.4
Marijuana and hashish	19,810	7.5	1,762	7.1	18,048	7.6
Cocaine	1,549	0.6	43	0.2	1,505	0.6
Inhalants	496	0.2	121	0.5	375	0.2
Hallucinogens	1,333	0.5	154	0.6	1,179	0.5
Heroin	289	0.1	13	0.1	277	0.1
Nonmedical use of prescription-type drugs	6,484	2.5	549	2.2	5,935	2.5
Pain relievers	4,521	1.7	425	1.7	4,096	1.7

Source: SAMHSA (2014). Substance use and mental health estimates from the 2013 *National Survey on Drug Use and Health: Overview of findings*. Washington, DC: Author. Available at www.samhsa.gov/data/2k14/DSDUH200/sr200-findings-overview-2014htm.

Heroin, which in the past was more likely to be used by people living in poverty in inner-city areas, more recently has become a drug of choice by middle-class youth and currently is the most commonly misused of all narcotics. Use of heroin, a morphine derivative, affects the autonomic nervous system and often causes euphoria, which results in dangerous and often violent behaviors, life-threatening cardiorespiratory problems, hepatitis, AIDS and other infections, and addiction. Most habitual users are incapable of clear thought, holding a job, or maintaining relationships (Phoenix House, 2010).

Stimulants are drugs that work on the central nervous system, creating a sense of heightened euphoria. Common stimulants include caffeine, amphetamines such as speed, ecstasy, and methylphenidate and other similar often-misused legal drugs prescribed to individuals with attention-deficit disorder. Amphetamines are highly addictive, particularly because users often plunge into extreme depression when they are coming down from the euphoric high as the drug begins to wear off.

Use of the stimulant methamphetamine—commonly called "meth"—has increased at an alarming rate. This highly addictive drug produces a strong reaction even when taken in small doses, and it has serious side effects. Use of meth increases the risks of contracting HIV/AIDS and hepatitis because of impaired decision making when on the drug. Methamphetamines are especially dangerous to children born to pregnant women who use the drug. Prolonged use of high doses leads to psychotic behavior, delusions, paranoid episodes, seizures, and permanent brain damage. Meth-amphetamine use has had significant impacts in many areas of the United States, including rural areas, where meth labs are more easily located to avoid arrest. Entire families can become addicted to methamphetamines, resulting in loss of jobs (and thus family income), child abuse and neglect, domestic violence, and criminal behavior. In efforts to reduce manufacturing of methamphetamine, many businesses are restricting the purchase of common cold medications, which contain a key ingredient in meth, and possession of common laboratory equipment outside of a lab is now a felony.

Illicit drugs also include the **hallucinogens** such as LSD as well as marijuana, the most commonly used. One group of substances that is misused and often overlooked consists of **inhalants**. Use of inhalants is especially prevalent among Latino youth and often results in intellectual disability or death. The wide variety of inhalants includes, among others, petroleum products such as gasoline, chlorofluorocarbons (Freon), aerosol products, paint, and glue. Amyl nitrate and butyl nitrate, commonly called "poppers," are also inhalants. Use of inhalants can result in irresponsible, dangerous behavior, permanent brain damage, cardiorespiratory problems, and sudden death (Phoenix House, 2010).

A drug that has received recent attention is Rohypnol (flunitrazepam), commonly called the "date rape" drug. Prescribed as a sleeping pill outside of the United States, Rohypnol is a sedative hypnotic drug that is 10 times more potent than Valium (diazepam). When Rohypnol is dissolved in a drink, it is undetectable. Teens often use it in combination with alcohol or other drugs to create a dramatic high, or to incapacitate a victim of intended rape. Rohypnol induces blackouts and memory loss, but it is addictive and also can result in death, especially when combined with other drugs.

In 2013, marijuana was used by 80.6% of current illicit drug users and was the only drug used by the majority of them (SAMHSA, 2014). Many individuals have called for the legalization of marijuana, indicating that it is "safer" than alcohol when used judiciously. Two states, Washington and Colorado, have legalized marijuana for both recreational and medicinal purposes, 23 states and the District of Columbia allow some degree of use of marijuana for medicinal purposes, and 14 states have decriminalized its use. Like alcohol, marijuana use has its drawbacks, though its use may be less dangerous than use of alcohol and other drugs. A recent study of teens found that frequent drinkers were over 13 times more likely to report that their alcohol use led to unsafe driving than non-drinkers, while marijuana users were three times more likely to report unsafe driving than non-users. Alcohol use was also more commonly used to compromise relationships, including sexual behavior, while marijuana was more often reported to compromise relationships with teachers or supervisors and also result in less energy and interest in school and job performance. Frequent marijuana users also were 23 times more likely to report problems with law enforcement officers than users of alcohol (Nauert, 2014). Although many do not consider marijuana use to be dangerous, the effects last for several days after its use. The drug can inhibit the ability to learn and retain information and can also produce respiratory and hormonal problems. Further, like alcohol use, impairment of judgment and perception can result in accidents and casual sex, linked to sexually transmitted diseases and pregnancy.

In addition to its addictive nature, marijuana is considered to be a "gateway drug." The majority of individuals who use other illegal drugs report using marijuana initially. In one report, teens who used marijuana were 85 times more likely to use cocaine than those who did not use the drug, and of those who used marijuana before the age of 15 years, 60% later went on to use cocaine (Phoenix House, 2010).

Increased concern is being raised about the use of synthetic marijuana, readily available in most communities for little cost. Synthetic marijuana, commonly called "spice," is the second-most often used drug by teens. Many users believe that it is made of natural plant material and is thus safe, and also point out that it is largely undetectable during drug screens. The Drug Enforcement Administration has delineated five active chemicals typically found in synthetic marijuana as controlled substances; however, manufacturers often substitute different and dangerous chemical additives to avoid detection. Although experiences using this drug can be similar to marijuana use, some of the compounds used in synthetic marijuana have a more powerful and unpredictable impact on the brain, resulting in psychotic effects including extreme anxiety, hallucinations, and paranoia. Other side effects can include rapid heart rate, increased blood pressure, and heart attacks (National Institute on Drug Abuse, 2012). A number of teens have died or suffered permanent brain damage from its use.

Social and Economic Costs of Substance Misuse

EP 2.1.9a

Substance misuse is said to be the most serious public health problem in the United States, resulting in more deaths and disabilities each year than any other cause. Highly correlated with substance misuse are child abuse and neglect, interpersonal violence, homicide and other violent crimes, and serious traffic accidents. Most of the media attention highlights the use of drugs other than alcohol—cocaine/crack, heroin, and methamphetamines. Yet, alcohol remains the drug of choice for most individuals who misuse substances in the United States.

The number of individuals affected in some way by alcoholism is staggering. Upward of 18 million alcoholics reside in the United States. Seventy-six million Americans (about 43% of the U.S. adult population) have been exposed to alcoholism in their families. There are nearly 27 million adult children of alcoholics in the United States (National Association for Children of Alcoholics, 2010).

The typical image of an alcoholic is an older male, unkempt, unemployed, and living on the streets. In reality, only 3% of alcoholics can be characterized this way. Stereotypes about those who misuse other drugs also are misleading. Occupations that have high percentages of employees who misuse alcohol and other drugs include food service and food preparation workers (17.4%); construction workers (15.1%); and entertainment, sports, design, and the arts (12.4%) (SAMSHA, 2014). Lawyers and law enforcement officers have higher rates than the general public, while physicians have higher rates of misuse of prescription drugs. About 45% of alcoholics hold professional or managerial positions, 25% are white-collar workers, and 30% are manual laborers (Heather & Stockwell, 2003).

Children who grow up in families where addiction is a problem are at risk for becoming addicts. Studies have found that 25% of males and 10% of females who grow up in families in which their parents misuse either alcohol or other drugs become addicts themselves. Even those who do not develop substance-misuse problems themselves often develop other addictive behaviors or emotional problems. Fewer women than men repeat the pattern of substance misuse, but they are much more likely to select a mate who misuses substances.

Parents who misuse alcohol and other drugs are more likely than parents who do not misuse them to abuse or neglect their children. Between one and two thirds of all child protective services cases involve parental substance misuse (Child Welfare Information Gateway, 2009a). Three-fourths of survivors of intimate partner violence reported that the perpetrator had been drinking (National Coalition Against Domestic Violence, 2009); and alcohol was a major contributing factor in 32% of all homicide cases, 31% of all deaths from unintentional injury, 23% of all suicides, and 32% of all fatal accidents involving an intoxicated driver or pedestrian. Alcohol is also reported to be a factor in the majority of sexual assaults.

As substance misuse becomes more widespread, the implications are becoming more obvious, more costly, and of greater concern. Costs go beyond intervention for the addict to also include lost productivity, motor-vehicle losses from accidents, and property losses from violent crimes. And cost estimates typically do not include personal costs such as physical and emotional injury and loss of life. The economic costs of alcoholism and alcohol and other drug misuse were estimated to in the United States in 2006 were estimated to be $416.5 billion (Centers for Disease Control and Prevention, 2014a).

At-Risk Populations and Substance Misuse

EP 2.1.7b

Even though substance misuse and addiction can affect anyone, some groups of people are more at risk than others. These groups include adolescents, the elderly, people of color, women, and children.

Adolescents   Although data on use of alcohol and other drugs by teens were given earlier in this chapter, their use of alcohol and other drugs is cause for concern. Because their brains are still developing, they are unable to fully ascertain the risks from impulsive behavior, which are exacerbated by drug misuse. Use of alcohol and other drugs by adolescents often is viewed as a way to be an adult—a "rite of passage" from childhood to adulthood—and is part of the risk-taking behavior common among adolescents. Heavy substance use and addiction among adolescents are more often found among those who are faced with other problems, such as survivors of childhood sexual abuse, gay and lesbian teens subjected to discrimination and oppression, and individuals with depression. These adolescents turn to alcohol and other drugs to deaden their pain, as a form of self-medication so they will feel better, or as a way to relate to peers more comfortably (see Box 9.2). Alcohol consumption in childhood or early adolescence is a strong predictor of later problems, including substance misuse.

The Elderly   Substance misuse, particularly alcoholism, is a problem in the elderly population (Lichtenberg, 2010). This age group, like adolescents and young adults, has a high death rate from alcoholism. Among the elderly, primary contributors to death are chronic alcohol-related diseases such as cirrhosis of the liver, digestive diseases, and hepatitis. Factors associated with substance misuse by this group include loneliness and isolation, for which older adults use substances as a coping mechanism to deaden the emotional or physical pain, present or past.

People of Color   Some ethnic groups are more at risk to misuse alcohol and drugs and to experience serious problems as a result. African Americans, for example, are three times more likely to die as a result

Box 9.2   A Young Adult's Story

Years of drinking and substance experimentation pushed a seemingly put-together, outgoing, successful student to the depths of depression and self-hate. This is her story:

I guess my use truly started in high school, but the signs it would happen were always there. I sought out a particular group of friends very early on, in middle school, that I knew would participate in what I thought was normal teen fun. I was always the type of person who was very independent, and I excelled at almost everything I set my mind to: good grades, sports teams, extracurricular activities, popular friends. I think because of how good I was at multitasking all the things going on in my life, my parents never really tried to regulate my behavior or check up on me. I believe they assumed I was always doing what I said I was because I never really failed.

I drank for the first time in the ninth grade when I was 14, and I didn't just drink—I got drunk. It was at a sleep over with my soccer team. Some tried it and didn't like it, some had done it before. It was casual and seemed thrilling, doing something you weren't supposed to. Looking back, there really wasn't an experimentation phase for me; after that first time I always drank to get out of control drunk.

From there my drinking escalated. I was part of the popular group, there was always a party to go to, a social event to be seen at, and I participated in all of them when I wasn't traveling with my soccer team. Mostly I drank to forget all the stress I put on myself by involving myself with so many things at one time and feeling the pressure to be perfect in all of them.

I continued drinking socially until the beginning of 11th grade. I had run myself ragged being involved in so many things. I quit playing soccer because it was where I experienced the most pressure to be perfect. I now realize that it was after I freed that significant amount of time that I developed a serious substance use problem. I began dating a guy who was older than I was. He was on the football team, he was in the same group of friends I was, and he liked being with the girl who was the life of every party. So I gave him what he wanted. I became known as the girl who had all the alcohol hookups, was fun and outgoing, and threw parties at her house when her parents were gone. People were always asking me for alcohol and I could deliver it. During this time people started asking for things I had no experience with: cocaine, ecstasy, and marijuana. As I didn't want to lose my title of being the "it" girl, the life of the party, I developed new connections for drugs as well as liquor.

My boyfriend never approved of doing drugs even though he drank. He didn't have a problem with my connecting my friends to where they could get drugs, but he absolutely forbid me from doing them, so I didn't. In the 12th grade after he graduated and went away to college, I rationalized trying them because he would never find out. I tried coke for the first time at my 17th birthday party. My friends threw a surprise party at a beautiful house. Everyone was drinking and well on their way to being drunk when a friend pulled out a baggie of cocaine. She offered it to me as a birthday gift. I was already drunk and my inhibitions were low. So I tried it and I can't explain the feeling adequately in words to this day. It was like all at once the world righted itself.

My parents never suspected me of drinking or using. I always came home sober, I always hid my drugs in my car where they never would have looked, and I continued to be successful in everything I was involved in. I broke up with my longtime boyfriend the March before my high school graduation. From then until the time I graduated from high school I was snorting coke and drinking every Thursday, Friday, and Saturday night, as well as any time a friend would call looking to buy from my dealer. I almost always got coke for free because I referred so many people to my dealer, and since my best friend was over 21, I could always buy liquor with no problem.

Once I graduated I moved in with one of my closest friends. We began going to clubs. I had many friends who worked at 21 and up clubs that could get us in and get us free drinks. My ex started calling me all the time and we began an extremely unhealthy on and off thing. I constantly felt emotionally drained or stressed, but particularly unsure of myself. I had never felt unsure of myself before. I thought if I could just get back to who I was in high school, the last time I felt like I knew myself, I would be fine. So I partied constantly, thinking it would make me feel more like me, but really I just lost myself further. I started dating really sketchy guys I knew would drive my ex crazy, I always had drugs on my person or in my car, I drove home from clubs so drunk I don't remember driving, and I started pushing the good influences in my life further and further away. I was getting out of control. It all culminated when on New Year's Eve of my freshman year of college I got so drunk and high on coke I don't remember the entire night. I was supposed to work the next morning—I was a manager at a retail store making good money, and I didn't wake up until 2 pm, 5 hours after I was supposed to open my store. I remember waking up and bursting into tears upon realizing how badly I

(continued)

Box 9.2   A Young Adult's Story *(continued)*

had messed up. I had never failed at anything before. I somehow managed to lie myself out of getting fired and I came to terms with the fact that my life was spinning out of control and that continuing to use into oblivion wasn't going to help me take back control. This was the first time I consciously stopped drinking and using. I never looked at it as getting sober—I just was too busy to continue with it. I was clean for a year.

After a year, I quit my full-time job so I could go to school full time and finish my degree. I met amazing new friends, and I got really close to them. We spent every day together, had every class together, and always worked together on group projects. So when they started a weekly happy hour, of course I went. I rationalized beginning to drink again because it was only a happy hour. It was casual, I wasn't in clubs, I wasn't throwing parties at my house, and I wasn't snorting coke. I was just being an adult, I thought.

I wasn't like my friends though, I couldn't be casual. I couldn't have one drink at a happy hour. It was like the more I tried to control my drinking, the more impossible it seemed. I always ordered five or six drinks within two hours and I always drove home afterward. I thought I was fine. It wasn't like before. I wasn't failing in my responsibilities. I got comfortable in my use again and that's when it all really fell apart. I went to happy hour, I drank way too much to be casual, and I drove home, except I never made it home. I never thought I would be the drunk driver you saw in all the terrible PSAs, but in a split second I was.

I cannot describe how badly it hurts to hurt another person so severely. That feeling alone is worse than getting arrested, paying fines, and paying legal fees. Damaging another human being is absolutely life altering in the worst possible way. I spent the night in jail. I remember calling my mother, and her being literally so surprised I was in jail, she burst into tears. I was always the good kid in our family. She just kept saying she never would have expected this from me.

When I got out of jail, I immediately went to the counseling center on my college campus and sought extensive help. I started the 12 steps that night and found an outpatient program the next day. I cried constantly, it seems like for months straight, because I couldn't believe what I had done, and how much guilt I was feeling. In those first few months of sobriety, I honestly believed it might be better if I wasn't around. I was, in my mind, the worst kind of person, I deserved every bad thing that happened to me for the rest of my life, and I never deserved to be happy. I was tired, I was

overwhelmed, and I began feeling hopeless. I was incredibly vulnerable to relapse, and sometimes I thought maybe it would be better to just give up altogether. Then something amazing happened. My sponsor said to me, "You are allowed to live again. In fact, the only way you can make up for what has happened is to effect everything you touch for the rest of your life as positively as you possibly can. You deserve to be happy. Those 10 seconds when you were at your worst cannot define your whole life. Those 10 seconds cannot ever adequately describe who you are and you need to remember that." I still remember what she said to me word for word.

In that second I think I truly surrendered myself to the 12 steps. Even though I had been working them before, I never felt like I deserved to finish them. I committed myself to something in that moment. I committed myself to being the best version of myself from that day on so that I could effect change. I wanted to say those words to someone else one day. I wanted them to realize they were worth it. They deserved to be happy. They deserved to be someone other than the worst 10 seconds of their life. I threw myself into AA, I went to as many meetings as I could, I volunteered for every service opportunity I could, I went to strictly sober parties, I surrounded myself with the most supportive community possible, and I started feeling like myself again. In fact I started feeling like I was who I was always supposed to be. I felt peace and looking back, even in high school, I never felt peace.

I have been sober for two years; I will graduate from college this semester, and finding sobriety is by far the best thing I have ever done and my greatest accomplishment. I am in an extremely loving relationship with someone who wants nothing but for me to be who I want to be. I plan on attending graduate school. I have worked in the community on as many recovery-related issues I could, including helping to set up a program for teens going through the same experiences I had with alcohol and other drugs in high school. Some days it is still hard. I have a passing thought about celebrating New Year's Eve with champagne or drinking red wine on the beach, but then I remember I deserve to be more than the worst 10 seconds of my life, and it is my responsibility to effect positive change, not move backward. I can honestly say today I am myself, and I can never express the gratitude I feel for being shown the way back to myself.

SOURCE: Journal entry written by a college student.

of alcoholism than are whites, even though their actual rates of alcohol use are less than for whites, because of the interactive effects of oppression on access to healthy food and health care (National Institute on Alcohol Abuse and Alcoholism, 2009). The situation is similar for Latinos. Native Americans have the highest incidence of alcoholism of any ethnic group in the United States. Overall, this group has high rates of alcohol-related homicide, suicide, and serious car accidents. An estimated half of Native American children are born with either fetal alcohol syndrome or fetal alcohol effect—medical conditions at birth usually resulting in serious developmental disabilities—caused by the mother's consumption of alcohol during pregnancy (Centers for Disease Control and Prevention, 2009).

Members of marginalized groups outside the mainstream of society also are more at risk to misuse substances because they are more likely to be unemployed and living in poverty. Many of them turn to alcohol and other drugs as coping mechanisms to overcome feelings of despair and hopelessness and the added burden of discrimination. In addition, in some communities drug pushers easily tempt children, often from impoverished families, to become drug runners so they can make a lot of money quickly. Still too young to realize the consequences of using drugs, they begin experimenting with the drugs they are delivering and become addicted themselves. The heightened risk of some ethnic groups for suffering the personal, emotional, and economic consequences of substance misuse and addiction raises a number of issues, as nonmembers of these groups are most often those who oversee large-scale production and sale of drugs and reap the economic profits.

To be effective, interventions for people of color must be culturally relevant and sensitive (Stuart, van Wormer, & Thyer, 2009). For example, participation in Alcoholics Anonymous groups may be highly effective for some, but if group membership consists largely of whites, people of color may not feel comfortable participating. In addition, some cultures are reluctant to divulge any personal information outside of their families. Many Asians, for example, have been socialized to believe that their personal problems, such as substance misuse, bring shame to their families and should not be discussed with people outside the family. From a macro perspective, opportunity and access to economic success are important ways to reduce substance misuse.

Women   The National Institute on Alcohol Abuse and Alcoholism (2009) estimates that one-third of all alcoholics in the United States are women and that 6 million women are addicted to substances other than alcohol; the largest increases are among younger women. Women who misuse substances have different issues than men do (Hien, Litt, Cohen, Miele, & Campbell, 2008). They are more likely than male drug addicts to misuse legal drugs such as tranquilizers, sedatives, and pain killers. Also, they are more likely to become addicted to multiple drugs and to use drugs in isolation rather than in combination with other drugs. They also are more likely to be in a family in which another member is an addict, and to have experienced rape, incest, or other sexual assault.

Women also are much less likely than men to seek treatment, even though they develop more health problems related to their substance misuse and their lives often are more disrupted. Females who misuse substances, too, are subjected to greater stigma than males. Many women receive opposition from friends and family when they enter treatment programs for substance use disorder.

Women also are less likely than men to have support from family members during treatment. In families in which alcoholism is a problem for male spouses, women remain in the relationship in 90% of situations; in families in which alcoholism is a problem for female spouses, however, men remain in the relationship only 10% of the time (Heather & Stockwell, 2003). Substance misuse has been accompanied by increases in AIDS, prostitution, and homelessness among women (Meschede, 2009).

Few intervention programs have been designed specifically for women with substance use disorder, who face different issues than men. Women are more likely to experience depression and to misuse substances as a way to cope with it. They, too, are more likely to have been sexually abused, and repressed memories of sexual abuse sometimes surface after they have been sober for a period of time. Recovery programs for women must include recognition of clients' strengths and encouragement to set healthy boundaries and establish positive and healthy relationships, with a focus on increasing self-esteem. As they recover from substance misuse, women often need assistance with child care, transportation, parenting, housing, education, and employment (Institute on Women and Substance Abuse, 2003).

Children   Alcoholism and chemical dependency have serious effects on children (see Chapters 10 and 11). The number of abused and neglected children in the United States has more than doubled over the past decade as a result of substance misuse, and increased use of methamphetamine has escalated these numbers in some areas of the United States. In one survey, 85% of states reported that substance misuse was one of the two major problems in families in which child abuse or neglect was suspected (Child Welfare Information Gateway, 2009a).

More attention is being directed to infants born addicted or impaired because of their mothers' addiction or misuse of alcohol or other drugs during pregnancy. Because infant brain development occurs early in pregnancy, no amount of alcohol is considered safe (Berk, 2014). Fetal alcohol syndrome, one of the three leading causes of developmental disabilities and birth defects, is the most serious of fetal alcohol spectrum disorders, prenatal alcohol-related conditions experienced by infants born to mothers who drank alcohol during pregnancy (Centers for Disease Control and Prevention, 2009). Child welfare advocates suggest that the United States has not yet begun to see the long-term effects of so many children being born to women who used alcohol or other drugs during pregnancy.

Other Factors Associated with Substance Misuse and Addiction   Research suggests that genetic/hereditary factors may be associated with substance use (Erickson, 2007; Jacobs et al., 2006). Some researchers believe that substances are metabolized or broken down differently for certain individuals, resulting in an inability of the body to eliminate some chemicals, which then build up in the body and also serve as stimulants for even greater use when the addictive substance is used again. Studies linking differences in serotonin levels in the brain to both substance misuse and depression support the idea that some individuals may "self-medicate" with alcohol or other drugs to try to deal with the chemical imbalance impacted by the serotonin.

EP 2.1.3a

Other researchers suggest that for some individuals, substance misuse is a form of self-medication to attempt to regulate their emotions or dampen their emotional pain (Khantzian & Albanese, 2008; Ostrowsky, 2008). These include, among others, individuals who have been sexually abused, have had a

significant personal loss or series of losses, or are depressed. Other experts on substance misuse suggest that people use drugs for excitement, to fit in with peers, to alleviate pressure, or to improve their performance along one or more dimensions. Still other experts propose that it is behavior learned from family members.

Persons with Disabilities

EP 2.1.7b

Persons with disabilities comprise the largest minority group in the world, comprising about 10% of the population. The types of disabilities are as varied as the people who have them. Some disabilities are relatively minor and don't change a person's lifestyle, while others have a significant impact on a person's ability to complete typical daily activities. Some are visible, while others are hidden and known only to the people who have them and those they choose to tell. Advocates for persons with disabilities point out that we should refer to ourselves as "temporarily able-bodied" because we have no idea when we might become disabled because of illness, war, an accident, or just the process of growing older (Castaneda, Hopkins, & Peters, 2013).

Disability is socially constructed, with perceptions about various types of disability varying across cultures. Availability of basic resources such as food, safe drinking water, and health-care and environmental constraints such as violence and exposure to dangerous chemicals also contribute to a person's ability or disability. In addition, cultural factors that include stereotypes and stigma about disability and societies that are organized around individuals who are able-bodied result in exclusion of individuals and failure to recognize the significant contributions they make to society (Wendell, 2013).

The Americans With Disabilities Act, passed in 1990 and amended in 2008, covers a broad range of physical and mental conditions considered disabilities, including physical disabilities, such as those that impact mobility, hearing, and vision or those that are health-related, such as HIV/AIDS and diabetes; intellectual disabilities, such as those that impact cognitive ability; emotional disabilities, such as depression and schizophrenia; and learning disabilities, such as dyslexia. Rather than focus on the diagnosis, however, the ADA focuses on how the condition interferes with major life activities, such as "walking, seeing, hearing, learning, speaking, breathing, standing, lifting, or caring for oneself" (Castaneda, Hopkins, & Peters, 2013, p. 461). Some individuals experience *developmental disabilities*, which, as the term suggests, refer to problems, such as intellectual disability and cerebral palsy, that become apparent before adulthood. In the past, terms often used were *mentally retarded* or *handicapped*. Now the preferred terminology emphasizes the person, not the disability—for example, "individuals with developmental disabilities." Because individuals with disabilities may have preferences about which term to use for their specific condition, it is best to ask them how they would like to be addressed.

In 1984, Congress passed the Developmental Disabilities Assistance and Bill of Rights Act (PL 98-527), which defined **developmental disability** as follows:

A severe, chronic disability of a person 5 years of age or older which

a. is attributable to a mental or physical impairment or combination of mental and physical impairments;
b. is manifested before the person attains age 22;
c. is likely to continue indefinitely;
d. results in substantial functional limitations in three or more of the following areas of major life activity: (i) self-care, (ii) receptive and expressive language, (iii) learning, (iv) mobility, (v) self-direction, (vi) capacity, for independent living, and (vii) economic self-sufficiency; and
e. reflects the person's need for a combination and sequence of special, interdisciplinary, or generic services, supports, or other assistance that is of lifelong or extended duration and is individually planned and coordinated, except that such term, when applied to infants and young children means individuals from birth to age 5, inclusive, who have substantial developmental delay or specific congenital or acquired conditions with a high probability of resulting in developmental disabilities if services are not provided. (PL 98527, Title V, 1984)

This definition was expanded in the **Americans With Disabilities Act (ADA)**, to include persons with HIV/AIDS, substance use disorder, and individuals with mental disorders as well as physical problems that occur later in life.

More than three-fourths of those classified as having a developmental disability have a mental impairment. Others may be classified as having cerebral palsy; epilepsy; autism; spina bifida; or speech, hearing, vision, or orthopedic disabilities. Still others have learning disabilities such as dyslexia (a reading disability in which symbols are perceived differently than they are) or attention-deficit disorder (an inability to pay attention for a reasonable amount of time [which may also include hyperactivity], so as to impede learning).

Intellectual disability classification is based on the results of an IQ test, with a score of 100 typically considered "average." Someone scoring between 71 and 85 is considered to have borderline intellectual functioning and someone with a score below 70 to have an intellectual disability. Persons with an IQ between 50 or 55 and 70 (about 80% of those with intellectual disabilities)can be educated to function fairly independently or with some supervision. About 10% are in the "moderate" classification, with IQs generally between 35 and 50; persons with this classification usually progress to about a second-grade level academically but can take care of themselves as adults with supervision and can perform unskilled or semi-skilled work. Only 3–4% of persons classified as having an intellectual disability have "profound" disabilities that necessitate constant care and supervision (Odom, Horner, Snell, & Blacher, 2009). However, it is important to note that there is extensive controversy about the use of IQ tests, as results can be skewed depending on the type of test administered, the person administering the test, and the mental and physical condition of the person who takes the test at the time it is administered. Individuals tested more than once usually score within a range rather than achieving the exact same score each time, which makes an arbitrary cut off score when making decisions about a person's educational, social service, financial, or legal options questionable.

Attention is turning to early identification of children with developmental delays, to try to prevent more serious disabilities in later life. **Developmental delay** occurs when children have not reached changes in skill development during predictable periods. Risk factors for developmental problems include (Howkidsdevelop, 2010):

• genetic or chromosomal abnormality associated with intellectual disability;
• metabolic disorders;
• poor maternal nutrition;
• exposure to toxins;
• exposure to infections that are passed to the baby by the mother during pregnancy;
• premature birth; and
• harsh life experiences such as living in severe/persistent poverty, poor nutrition, or lack of care).

Factors Associated with Developmental Disabilities

EP 2.1.7a

The types of disabilities vary as much as the factors associated with them, and researchers still are uncertain why some types of disabilities occur. Among the factors associated with developmental disabilities, based on current knowledge and research, are the following (Arc, 2009):

- *Hereditary and fetal development factors:* Metabolic disorders, brain malfunctions, or chromosomal abnormalities can result in disabilities such as Tay–Sachs disease and Down syndrome. Fragile X syndrome, a genetic disorder, is the leading cause of intellectual disability.
- *Prenatal factors:* Chemical and alcohol addiction, radiation, infections such as rubella (a form of measles), syphilis, and HIV, or exposure to environmental contaminants during pregnancy can result in disabilities, as can fetal malnutrition if mothers do not receive adequate prenatal care. Smoking also increases the risk of developmental delays, including intellectual disability.
- *Perinatal factors:* Premature birth, trauma at birth, and infections transmitted during birth, such as herpes, can result in developmental disabilities.
- *Postnatal factors:* Infections after birth, such as meningitis, trauma from accidents or child abuse, lack of oxygen during illness or an accident, and nutritional deficiencies can result in developmental disabilities.

Environmental factors, such as lead poisoning, parents with severe emotional problems, or parental deprivation, are additional factors that can precipitate developmental disabilities. Children who do not receive proper nurturing, especially during their early years, often show developmental delay, and if intervention does not come soon enough, intellectual disability, learning disabilities, or other problems can result and may be permanent.

Specific causes of developmental disabilities often cannot be identified. Many parents who have children with these problems spend a great deal of time—sometimes their entire lives—blaming themselves for their children's disabilities. Research has enabled the early identification of many types of disabilities, such as phenylketonuria (PKU), which causes intellectual disability. A simple test at birth can allow for immediate treatment, and this has virtually eliminated the condition in most Western countries.

Many persons develop disabilities later in life. They often must adjust to changes in lifestyle, how they view themselves, and how society views them. Many individuals are uncomfortable with disability because unlike other conditions, any of us can develop a disability at any point in our lives and being around someone with a disability confronts us with that possibility. However, increased visibility of persons with a wide range of disabilities and new technologies and treatment approaches have led to greater awareness and acceptance of this group, particularly since the passage of the ADA.

Regardless of when and how a person developed a disability, those who have them are typically resilient and often point out that their disability is an important part of who they are, but not their entire identity. Many persons with disabilities, for example, are considered "twice exceptional," exceptional because they have one or more disabilities, but exceptional because they are also highly gifted and talented in other areas. Nobel Prize–winning physicist Stephen Hawkins and Albert Einstein are two examples of individuals who are "twice exceptional."

Changing Views Toward Individuals with Mental Health Problems, Substance Use, and Disabilities

EP 2.1.1a
EP 2.1.8b
EP 2.1.9a

Interventions for individuals with mental health and substance-use problems and disabilities have undergone considerable change (Brooker & Repper, 2008; Frank & Glied, 2006; Gould, 2009; Grob, 2006). Historically, the fate of substance users and individuals with mental illness or other disability depended on their families. In most cases they remained at home. In some cases they were treated humanely, but many people with mental illness and disabilities, particularly intellectual disabilities, were chained in attics and cellars, and sometimes they were killed. When no family members could provide for them, they often were transported to the next town and abandoned.

Later, almshouses were established (see Chapter 1). Individuals with mental illness or disabilities sometimes were jailed if they were deemed too dangerous for the almshouse. Alcoholics also were jailed, and their remaining family members, unable to care for themselves, were sent to almshouses.

The Pennsylvania Hospital, established in 1751 for the sick poor and "the reception and care of lunatics" was the first hospital in the United States that provided care for individuals with mental illness, although treatment of these patients was little better than it had been in jails and almshouses. Individuals who were deemed "mentally ill" were assigned to hospital cellars and were placed in bolted cells, where they were watched over by attendants carrying whips, which they used freely. Sightseers paid admission fees to watch the cellar activities.

The First Revolution: From Inhumane to Moral Treatment

During the late 1700s, people throughout the world began to seek better approaches to address the needs of those with mental illness. The first revolution in caring for those with mental illness began in France rather than the United States, with a shift from inhumane to moral treatment. Philippe Pinel, director of two hospitals in Paris, ordered "striking off the chains" of the patients in 1793, first at the Bicêtre Hospital for the Insane in Paris. He espoused a philosophy of **moral treatment**, which meant offering patients hope, guidance, support, and treatment with respect in small, family-like institutions.

The moral-treatment movement soon spread to America. Benjamin Rush, a signer of the Declaration of Independence, wrote the first American text on psychiatry, advocating that people with mental illness have a moral right to humane treatment. But not until the 1840s, through the efforts of Dorothea Dix, a schoolteacher, did people with mental illness in the United States actually begin to receive more humane treatment (see Chapter 1). As a Sunday school teacher for a group of patients in a Massachusetts hospital, Dix became aware of the plight of individuals with mental illness. Appalled by what she saw, she gave speeches, wrote newspaper articles, and met with government officials to bring attention to the inhumane and abusive treatment she observed in the many facilities she visited.

As a result of her efforts, a bill was introduced in Congress to use the proceeds from the sale of Western land to purchase land for use in caring for people with mental illness. This bill, vetoed by President Franklin Pierce, set a precedent for the federal government's refusal to be involved in state social services programs, which remained unchanged until the New Deal era (see Chapter 7).

Refusing to give up, Dix turned her efforts to the individual states, and by 1900, a total of 32 states had established state mental hospitals. But Dix and other advocates for the humane treatment of persons with mental illness soon had additional cause for concern. What had begun in many hospitals as humane treatment changed as hospitals became overused and overcrowded, admitting all who could not be cared for elsewhere. State insane asylums became warehouses, called "snake pits."

Dix and her group of reformers demanded that strict guidelines be established for the treatment of patients in mental hospitals. Again the states responded, by expanding facilities and adopting detailed but often burdensome operating procedures. While abuse and neglect of patients decreased dramatically, the guidelines left little room for innovation, and until the 1960s, patients in state mental hospitals received little more than custodial care.

In the years immediately following the Dix reform, nearly half of patients who had been admitted were released, often for the sole reason of making room for new admissions and alleviating overcrowding. Once the overcrowding stabilized somewhat, however, long stays in mental hospitals became the norm and discharge rates fell to as low as 5% annually. Although these state institutions had been intended to house a transitory patient population, the absence of effective treatment technologies forced the retention of many patients until their death. The desire for single state facilities to house large populations of patients with mental illness resulted in their being located in rural areas, where land was less expensive, expansion of facilities was possible, and the safety of the community was protected. Thus, the state mental hospitals became—and, in many instances, still are—the principal industries in the areas where they are located.

Although much less attention was given to the population with disabilities, institutionalization became prevalent for this group as well, particularly those with intellectual disabilities. During the 1850s, many states established state training schools for individuals with what was then called mental retardation, which housed persons ranging from those with profound retardation to those with mild retardation. Many individuals with retardation were mistakenly labeled as having mental illness and placed in state hospitals for the mentally ill.

In spite of the efforts of Dorothea Dix and others, overcrowded conditions and neglect of residents with mental illness and disabilities continued in many state facilities, which also housed many immigrants. Staff members who provided moral support, love, and respect to certain residents had difficulty transferring this attitude to those they didn't consider Americans. Also, it was increasingly difficult to find competent medical personnel who were willing to work in state mental institutions. Graduates from medical schools often were repelled by the alcoholics, severely disturbed individuals, and recent immigrants who populated the institutions.

A second effort to reform conditions in state mental hospitals was undertaken in the early 1900s by Clifford Beers, a Yale graduate from a wealthy family who had been hospitalized in a Connecticut mental hospital for 3 years. After his release, Beers almost immediately suffered a relapse and was hospitalized for a second time. During this stay, he began to formulate plans for more effective treatment of those deemed to be mentally ill. He kept careful notes of the maltreatment he received from physicians and the well-intended but ineffective care he received from caregivers.

After his release in 1908, Beers wrote a book, *A Mind That Found Itself,* which exposed the horrendous conditions in mental hospitals. This book led to the formation of state mental health advocacy organizations, such as the Connecticut Society for Mental Health. Later, state organizations formed the National Association for Mental Hygiene, which became a lobbying force for the continual reform of state hospitals and the development of alternative systems of care.

The Second Revolution: The Introduction of Psychoanalysis

What has been described as the second revolution in the mental health field occurred in the early 1900s with the writings of Sigmund Freud and the introduction of **psychoanalysis** in the United States. Professional mental health workers who were trained in Freud's techniques attempted to gain cooperation and insight through verbal or nonverbal communication with patients, seeing them at regular intervals over long periods of time.

The first social workers employed in state mental hospitals actually were hired before Freud's teachings were introduced into the United States. Their primary role was to provide therapy to clients, but it was based on limited knowledge about what the therapy should entail. As psychoanalysis gained popularity in the United States, psychiatric social workers, like others working with individuals with mental illness, quickly adopted a system of therapy that reportedly was much more effective than the often haphazard treatment they had been using.

In 1905, Massachusetts General Hospital in Boston and Bellevue Hospital in New York City hired psychiatric social workers to provide therapy to patients. Because of staff shortages and the large numbers of patients, however, few patients actually received psychotherapy—which requires highly trained therapists, fairly verbal patients who speak the same language as the therapist, and long hours of treatment. Psychotherapy as a treatment approach for dealing with mental health problems was more likely to be used in outpatient facilities—either private practices established by psychiatrists or child guidance centers—which were established in the United States in the 1920s primarily to promote healthy relationships between middle-class children and their parents.

The Third Revolution: A Shift to Community Mental Health Programs

The third revolution in mental health, a shift in the care of individuals with mental health problems, substance use disorder, and developmental disabilities from institutions to local communities, began in the 1940s and continues today. Public interest in mental health issues and treatment of those with mental illness was stimulated by the onset of World War II.

The military draft brought mental health problems to the attention of Congress. Military statistics showed that 12% of all men drafted into the Armed Forces were rejected for psychiatric reasons. Of the total number rejected for any reason, 40% were rejected for psychiatric reasons (Felix, 1967). Serious questions began to be raised about the magnitude of mental health problems within the entire U.S. population.

Initial Post-War Developments After the war ended, mental health concerns, which had been neglected during the war, began to receive attention again. In 1946, Congress passed the National Mental Health Act, which enabled states to establish **community mental health programs** aimed at preventing and treating mental health problems. The act also provided for research and educational programs and mandated that each state establish a single state entity to receive and allocate federal funds provided for by the act.

Attention also began to turn toward state facilities for the mentally ill. Albert Deutsch (1949) wrote a series of exposés on state mental hospitals, later published as *Shame of the States*. This stimulated a series of similar books, one of which was made into a film, *The Snake Pit*. All of this attention resulted in widespread public outcry and furthered the climate for reform.

In 1949, Congress created the **National Institute of Mental Health (NIMH)**, the first federal entity to address mental health concerns. In 1955, with impetus from a working coalition of leadership from the National Institute of Mental Health and the **National Association of Mental Health (NAMH)**, university medical schools and schools of social work, and organizations of former mental patients and their families, the National Mental Health Study Act was passed. This act verified the belief among mental health professionals and government officials alike that large custodial institutions could not deal with mental illness effectively. The act authorized an appropriation to the Joint Commission on Mental Illness and Health to study and make recommendations for mental health policy.

In the late 1950s and early 1960s, the commission published a series of documents calling for major reform. The commission sought a substantial increase in mental health expenditures to be used for comprehensive community mental health facilities, increased recruitment and training programs for staff, and long-term mental health research. The commission also called for an expansion of treatment programs for the acutely mentally ill in all facilities while limiting the numbers of patients at each hospital to no more than a thousand inpatients.

The commission further recommended a major emphasis on community programs, including preventive outpatient treatment and after-care services that could reduce the numbers of institutionalized patients and allow for their successful treatment within their local communities. The group recommended that the states play a smaller role in providing services and that the federal role be increased in addressing mental health needs. At this time, President John Kennedy made mental health issues a high priority and strongly supported the commission's efforts, becoming the first U.S. president to address mental health concerns publicly. Furthermore, the public was beginning to see the effectiveness of **psychotropic drugs** in treating individuals with mental illness, and consequently became more receptive to the idea of community care.

Community Mental Health Initiatives Congress passed the Mentally Retarded Facilities and Community Mental Health Center Construction Act in 1963. This act provided major funding to build community mental health centers and community facilities for people with developmental disabilities. The act mandated that centers built with federal funds be located in areas accessible to the populations they serve and that they provide the basic service components: inpatient services, outpatient services, partial hospitalization (day, night, or weekend care), emergency services, consultation, and educational services. By 1980, more than 700 community mental health centers had been established in the United States, partially funded with federal funds.

The intent of the community mental healthcare legislation was to replace the custodial care provided in large-scale institutions with therapeutic care in the community. The emphasis was to be on **deinstitutionalization**—keeping individuals from being placed in hospitals whenever possible—and on the **least restrictive environment**—a setting as much like one for individuals without disabilities as possible. The Presidential Commission on Mental Health (1978) defined the purpose of providing a least restrictive environment as

> *maintaining the greatest degree of freedom, self-determination, autonomy, dignity, and integrity of body, mind, and spirit for the individual while he or she participates in treatment or receives services.* (p. 44)

These programs were deemed cost-effective because many individuals could work at paid jobs and live in situations that were less expensive than in an institution, and they also were seen as encouraging individuals' self-esteem and feelings by their contributing to society. (A discussion of the impact of deinstitutionalization on current services is included later in this chapter.)

The community health center legislation, coupled with the use of psychotropic drugs, significantly reduced the numbers of individuals housed in mental institutions. In 1955, of all patients, 77.4% received inpatient services and 22.6% outpatient services. By 1980, the numbers had virtually reversed themselves, with only 28% receiving inpatient services and 72% receiving outpatient services (Mechanic, 1999). The treatment emphases had shifted from custodial care, shock treatment, and long-term psychotherapy to short-term treatment, group therapy, helping individuals cope with their environments, and drug treatment. The number of outpatient clients visiting community mental health centers continues to increase.

The Fourth Revolution: Legal Rights of Clients and Consumer Advocacy

Mental health and developmental disabilities professionals have identified clients' rights as the fourth revolution in the mental health/disabilities arena. The legal advocacy movement, which began in the 1960s, was part of the Civil Rights Movement of the 1960s. It received further impetus in 1971 in the landmark case *Wyatt v. Stickney,* in which a federal judge restricted "extraordinary or potentially hazardous modes of treatment" (Lin, 1995, p. 1706) with patients in state mental hospitals in Alabama. In a landmark 1975 decision, the U.S. Supreme Court ruled that being mentally ill and in need of treatment did not constitute sufficient grounds for involuntary confinement.

The increasing options available to individuals with developmental disabilities and mental health problems, including placement in less restrictive facilities, new counseling techniques, and drug treatment, have spawned a number of legal issues that merit serious deliberation. On the one hand, do individuals have the right to refuse treatment? On the other hand, if treatment technology or knowledge about more appropriate types of treatment exists but such treatment is not available, do individuals have the right to demand treatment? In some states, class-action lawsuits have been brought on behalf of persons in institutions demanding that they be placed in less restrictive settings where they can receive treatment that is unavailable to them in the institutions.

The NAMH and other advocacy organizations have forced the court system to establish a series of patients'/clients' rights, including the right to treatment, the rights to privacy and dignity, and the right to the least restrictive condition necessary to achieve the purpose of commitment (see Box 9.3 for the National Association of Social Workers' Mental Health Bill of Rights). The courts also have determined that individuals cannot be deemed incompetent to manage their affairs; to hold professional, occupational, or vehicular licenses; to marry and obtain divorces; to register to vote; or to make wills solely because of their admission or commitment to a hospital.

Patients in mental institutions have the same rights to visitation and telephone communication as do patients in other hospitals, along with the right to send sealed mail. They also have the right to freedom from excessive medication or physical restraint and experiments and the rights to wear their own clothes and worship within the dictates of their own religion. And patients have the right to receive needed treatment outside a hospital environment (Mechanic, 2008).

Most states make it difficult to commit a person to an institution involuntarily. In many states, however, law-enforcement agencies can order that persons be detained in state institutions for a limited time without a court hearing. At the end of that time, a court hearing must be held, and involuntary commitments can be ordered only if persons are found to be dangerous to themselves or others (Mental Health America, 2010; Slobogin, 2007).

Often, individuals who are not really capable of functioning on their own but who are not found to be dangerous to themselves or others are released to be on their own. As a result, many individuals receive what some mental health professionals have termed "the revolving door approach to treatment." Individuals who are too incapacitated to function on their own are picked up on the streets, admitted to the hospital, given medication, food, and rest, then released quickly because they legally cannot be held against their wishes any longer.

An issue that has received even less attention is the right of children to refuse or to demand mental health treatment. In many instances, parents commit children to institutions because they do not want or are unable to care for them. Some parents have exhausted all of their resources and are desperately seeking some type of help for children they no longer have the ability to care for. In other instances, the child's problems stem from family problems that the parents do not want to deal with. The rights of individuals to avoid treatment and to receive treatment are unclear and await clarification by the U.S. Supreme Court (Slobogin, 2007).

Consumers of services and their families, like social work professionals, are becoming more concerned about these issues. Advocacy groups for people with mental health problems have stepped up their efforts to include individuals with mental health problems and their family members in treatment planning, and in many instances also have involved them as employees, board members, and spokespersons for their organizations. The consumer movement emphasizes empowerment

Box 9.3   Bill of Rights for Persons Who Need Mental Health and Substance Use Treatment

The National Association of Social Workers collaborated with a number of organizations to develop a bill of rights that promotes culturally sensitive quality services to persons in need of mental health and substance use treatment. The bill incorporates the following areas:

Our commitment is to provide quality mental health and substance abuse services to all individuals without regard to race, color, religion, national origin, gender, age, sexual orientation, or disabilities (NASW, 2003).

Right to Know

Individuals have the right to:

Benefits—clear written information from insurance providers and those from whom they have purchased insurance about their benefits for mental health and substance use treatment, including appeal procedures, in understandable language.

Professional expertise—information from potential treatment providers about their credentials, including education, skills, and experience, and available treatment options and their effectiveness.

Contractual limitations—be informed by treatment providers about any agreements between third-party payers (insurance companies) and the provider that could potentially interfere with or influence treatment options and outcomes, as well as the type of information disclosed to third-party payers about their treatment.

Appeals and grievances—information about ways they can appeal decisions about their care to employers, third-party payers, and regulatory organizations and file complaints and grievances about their care to the provider's professional association and regulatory board.

Confidentiality—be guaranteed that the confidentiality of their treatment and relationship with the service provider is protected, "except when laws or ethics dictate otherwise" (NASW, 2003) and that any disclosure to an outside entity be made with written informed consent of clients, be time-limited, and be limited to information about diagnosis, type of treatment, time and length, cost, and expected outcome. Those entities that receive information to determine benefits, community health-care needs, or other legitimate reasons must ensure that information provided is confidential, and

they will be subject to the same penalties as treatment providers if confidentiality is violated.

Entities receiving information for the purposes of benefits determination, public agencies receiving information for health-care planning, or any other organization with legitimate right to information will maintain clinical information in confidence with the same rigor and be subject to the same penalties for violation as is the direct provider of care.

Information technology will be used for transmission, storage, or data management only with methodologies that remove individual identifying information and assure the protection of the individual's privacy. Information should not be transferred, sold, or otherwise utilized.

Choice

Individuals have the right to choose any duly licensed/certified professional for mental health and substance abuse services. Individuals have the right to receive full information regarding the education and training of professionals, treatment options (including risks and benefits), and cost implications to make an informed choice regarding the selection of care deemed appropriate by the individual and professional.

Determination of Treatment

Recommendations regarding mental health and substance abuse treatment will be made only by a duly licensed/certified professional in conjunction with the individual and his or her family as appropriate. Treatment decisions should not be made by third-party payers. The individual has the right to make final decisions regarding treatment.

Parity

Individuals have the right to receive benefits for mental health and substance abuse treatment on the same basis as they do for any other illnesses, with the same provisions, co-payments, lifetime benefits, and catastrophic coverage in both insurance and self-funded/self-insured health plans.

Discrimination

Individuals who use mental health and substance abuse benefits will not be penalized when seeking other health

(continued)

Box 9.3   Bill of Rights for Persons Who Need Mental Health and Substance Use Treatment *(continued)*

insurance or disability, life, or any other insurance benefit.

Benefit Usage

The individual is entitled to the entire scope of the benefits within the benefit plan that will address his or her clinical needs.

Benefit Design

Whenever both federal and state law and/or regulations are applicable, the professional and all payers will use whichever affords the individual the greatest level of protection and access.

Treatment Review

To assure that treatment review processes are fair and valid, individuals have the right to be guaranteed that any review of their mental health and substance abuse treatment will involve a professional having the training, credentials, and licensure required to provide the treatment in the jurisdiction in which it will be provided. The reviewer should have no financial interest in the decision and is subject to the section on confidentiality.

Accountability

Treating professionals may be held accountable and liable to individuals for any injury caused by gross incompetence or negligence on the part of the professional. The treating professional has the obligation to advocate for and document necessity of care and to advise the individual of options if payment authorization is denied.

Payers and other third parties may be held accountable and liable to individuals for any injury caused by gross incompetence or negligence or by their clinically unjustified decisions.

Participating Groups

*   American Association for Marriage and Family Therapy (membership: 25,000)
*   American Counseling Association (membership: 56,000)
*   American Family Therapy Academy (membership: 1,000)
*   American Nurses Association (membership: 180,000)
*   American Psychological Association (membership: 142,000)
*   American Psychiatric Association (membership: 42,000)
*   American Psychiatric Nurses Association (membership: 3,000)
*   National Association of Social Workers (membership: 155,000)
*   National Federation of Societies for Clinical Social Work (membership: 11,000)

Supporting Groups

*   National Mental Health Association
*   American Group Psychotherapy Association
*   American Psychoanalytic Association
*   National Association of Alcoholism and Drug Abuse Counselors

SOURCE: Copyrighted material reprinted with permission from the National Association of Social Workers, Inc.

and self-sufficiency. Many social workers work closely with consumer groups and have become strong allies of the consumer movement and the changes they advocate.

Neurobiology and Implications for Mental Health, Addiction, and Disabilities

EP 2.1.6b

The wave of the future in mental health, substance misuse, and disabilities is being driven by discoveries in neurobiology and related technology (Bear & Conners, 2006; Charney & Nestler, 2008; Flint, Greenspan, & Kendler, 2010; Meyers, 2008). Genetic and genome research, computer modeling, and other technologies offer tremendous hope for individuals with mental-health and substance-misuse problems and disabilities, as well as for their families.

Specific genes have been identified, for example, that cause diseases associated with developmental disabilities, such as cystic fibrosis, and identify those who are at more risk for depression. Although schizophrenia previously was thought to be more environmentally than biologically related, research now is showing that factors associated with this serious illness are more likely related to genetic makeup or chemical functioning within the brain. Research suggests that similar factors are associated with Alzheimer's and other forms of dementia and neurodegenerative diseases.

Understanding the genetic and biochemical abnormalities associated with these diseases, possibly related to complex involvement with how the body uses proteins, will likely lead to early detection of such diseases as well as possible gene therapy treatment. Research relating to regenerative medicine suggests possible breakthroughs in combating many brain and spinal cord injuries, as well as diseases such as Parkinson's and Alzheimer's.

These discoveries represent tremendous advances, because they pave the way for interventions such as gene therapy and medication to change the course of, or even prevent, these illnesses. Drugs such as naltrexone and buprenorphine have been approved by the Food and Drug Administration to treat addiction to opiates such as cocaine and heroin. These drugs act as opiate blockers in the brain, thereby eliminating the rush or euphoria associated with the use of opiates. They are also intended to reduce the feelings of craving that accompany opiate dependence. Newer drugs such as ibogaine are being used outside the United States to treat opiate addiction; however, their use in the United States has not yet been approved (National Institute on Drug Abuse, 2009).

The National Institutes of Health and the National Institute of Mental Health have funded a number of research efforts on mapping human genomes and studying the impact of various illnesses, addictions, and trauma on brain development and brain chemistry. Researchers can observe features of neuron ensembles and signaling mechanisms that help to determine how the brain responds to addictive substances. For example, they can document cellular and molecular adaptations during the use of addictive drugs, as well the depressive state that follows the use of many substances. These adaptations in the brain's system indicate why individuals increase the use of a drug to maintain brain stability (Erickson, 2007; Koob & Le Moal, 2006; National Institute of Mental Health, 2014b).

Innovations in social neuroscience through neuroimaging of how the brain interacts with the social world show that the brain is activated differently when making judgments about people versus judgments about inanimate objects (Bernston, & Cacioppo, 2009; de Haan & Gunnar, 2009; Harmon-Jones & Beer, 2009). Functioning of the brain and discoveries about the role it plays in moral reasoning, too, have implications in understanding some types of deviant behavior.

Neuroscience discoveries coupled with advances in other types of technology have also resulted in significant changes in adaptive technology available to persons with physical as well as other types of disabilities. Personal emergency response systems; robotic devices that assist in daily life skills or are part of prostheses that replace ankles and other body parts; assisted computer technology for persons with visual, auditory, or other types of needs; automated home systems; devices that help with memory and recognition of emotions; technology-driven wheelchairs and walkers; and neurotransmitters that help regulate pain and motor functioning are examples of some of the technology available. The U.S. military and Veterans Administration are conducting extensive research on ways to use technology to assist soldiers and have shared their innovations with the nonmilitary community (Veterans Administration, n.d.).

Although these are exciting advances, they raise new issues for social workers (Plows, 2010; Sensen, 2005; Valverde, 2010). First, what are the ethical implications of such knowledge relating to the detection and prevention of mental illness, substance misuse, and disabilities? If early detection is possible—for example, before birth—what are the choices, and who should make them? No matter when problems are identified in individuals, should all individuals have affordable access to these interventions, even if they are expensive? Who should pay for the interventions? What if an individual decides not to take advantage of the interventions? The issues of right to treatment and client empowerment will surface in new areas that have important implications for social workers.

Availability of Resources and Responsibility for Care

EP 2.1.1a
EP 2.1.9a
EP 2.1.9b

Perhaps the most overriding issue in working with persons with mental illnesses, substance misuse, or disabilities is how to manage limited resources to best address the needs of those who require services. More than 10% of national health-care resources are spent on public and private mental health care. Medicaid is the largest funding source of seriously ill people, and mental health costs continue to increase. Mental health delivery systems also are changing with the trend toward community-based programs and the implementation of the Affordable Care Act. Many state mental hospitals have either closed or offer nonhospital care as part of their services.

The 1970s and 1980s witnessed a dramatic growth in private psychiatric hospitals and residential treatment centers for children and youth with emotional disturbances. This trend was curtailed by the emergence of managed care, an overriding theme in the delivery of mental health services today. When patients are hospitalized, the stays are much shorter than in the past. The predominant pattern of mental health care today consists of brief hospital stays to stabilize symptoms, and often initial monitoring of prescribed medication, followed by outpatient care at a community facility (Frank & Glied, 2006; Mechanic, 2007). Many individuals, like Lindsey in the opening vignette, are caught in a lifelong cycle of numerous short-term hospitalizations, discharge to the community, escalation of symptoms, and rehospitalizations.

Individuals with mental illness and developmental disabilities, often unable to advocate for themselves, do not always receive their just share of funding. Public attitudes that persist in viewing alcoholism and substance misuse as moral issues have an influence on, and can limit funding for, substance-disorder programs. Many of the gains in mental health and developmental disabilities programs established in the 1960s have been eroded as governments battle over who should have the responsibility for individuals with mental illness or developmental disabilities and what constitutes appropriate levels of service for these groups. Although attitudes have changed significantly since colonial times, ongoing change is required to achieve normalization of these populations. We will explore a number of issues relating to current resources.

Deinstitutionalization

The field of mental health has been subjected to considerable shock since the movement toward deinstitutionalization. Some have argued that deinstitutionalization has resulted in the "ghettoization" of those with mental illness and other disabilities. In many instances, communities have neither the funding nor the commitment to provide care for individuals released from institutions, forcing them to subsist in subhuman conditions in poverty areas (Rosenberg & Rosenberg, 2012).

In 1976, two social workers from the Mental Health Law Project visited Mr. Dixon, who had won his right to freedom in a class-action lawsuit several months after being transferred from the hospital to a boarding care facility. The workers described their observations in testimony before a Senate subcommittee:

> The conditions in which we found Mr. Dixon were unconscionable. Mr. Dixon's sleeping room was about halfway below ground level. The only windows in the room were closed and a plate in front of them made it impossible for Mr. Dixon to open them. There was no fan or air conditioner in the room. The room had no phone or buzzer. There would be no capacity for Mr. Dixon to contact someone in case of fire or emergency and this is significant in the face of the fact that Mr. Dixon is physically incapacitated. Mr. Dixon had not been served breakfast by 10 a.m. He stated that meals were highly irregular and he would sometimes get so hungry waiting for lunch that he would ask a roomer to buy him sandwiches. He can remember having only one glass of milk during his entire stay at his new home. (U.S. Senate Subcommittee on Long-Term Care, 1976, p. 715)

Shortly after this testimony, Mr. Dixon returned to St. Elizabeth Hospital and was placed in a more suitable home. More than 35 years later, in 2013, in a large southwestern state, men with mental and physical disabilities were found living in similar or worse conditions. In one location, many men were found living in unheated, un-air-conditioned metal buildings with no indoor plumbing. They were malnourished and stayed indoors most of the time. In another location, several men died when the unregulated boarding home in which they were living caught on fire. Investigations in other states also have found persons with physical and mental disabilities in unsafe living situations. Although states have begun to establish regulations, including licensing or certification systems for group and boarding homes for clients of the mental health system and requiring sprinkler and other fire safety systems, monitoring and sanctioning are difficult. Even if facilities are forced to close, often no other facilities are available to house the displaced residents (Gostin, McHale, Fennell, MacKay, & Bartlett, 2010; Klein, 2009).

Many states and local communities have successfully reduced the number of individuals with developmental or other disabilities or mental illness who are living in institutions. However, some are reluctant to do so because of inadequate local resources and the economic disruption caused by shutting down institutions in areas where they are a major source of employment.

Deinstitutionalization also has resulted in some unintended consequences (Erickson & Erickson, 2008; Traustadottir & Johnson, 2008). Many people who could function well within an institutional setting do not do as well in a community setting, particularly if they have little day-to-day supervision. And deinstitutionalization carries with it the potential for failure to meet established standards of care as well as failure to provide follow-up services to clients. Decentralization of care requires a case-management system in which social workers or other mental health professionals are responsible for a specific number of clients, ensuring that their living conditions are appropriate, that they are maintaining health care and taking medication, and that their other needs are being met.

Some community-based mental health programs have been extremely successful. For example, George Fairweather, a noted mental-health professional, has established a series of community programs for individuals who were institutionalized previously. Called Fairweather Lodges, these facilities provide supervised living for individuals in small groups, and residents share housekeeping chores. Residents also work in the community, and a lodge coordinator ensures that residents are successful in the workplace. The coordinator facilitates support group meetings for residents' families as well as for lodge members. The rate of reinstitutionalization for this program has been extremely low. Some communities that initially were reluctant to establish lodge programs now view the lodges and their residents as important to the community.

Much remains to be done to develop adequate community-based mental health programs for people of all ages. Many previously deinstitutionalized individuals have difficulty adjusting to community living, particularly when adequate support programs are not available (Traustadottir & Johnson, 2008). To date, the most significant problem with deinstitutionalization has been the inability of communities to develop the necessary infrastructure to support these individuals (Rosenberg & Rosenberg, 2012).

Wide-Ranging Program Alternatives

Although similar characteristics have been identified for programs that serve persons with mental illness, substance use disorder, and developmental and other types of

EP 2.1.9b

disabilities, there are also some quality programs based on needs specific to each population.

Intervention for Persons with Mental Illness

Consumer groups and experts in mental health care suggest that quality mental health programs should have the following characteristics (National Alliance on Mental Illness, 2009b):

- comprehensive services and supports; an integrated service delivery system; sufficient funding;
- consumer and family-driven systems; safe and respectful treatment environments; accessible information for consumers and family members;
- access to acute care and long-term treatment; cultural competence;
- an emphasis on health promotion and morality reduction; and
- an adequate mental health workforce.

Beneficial community programs that have been established for people with mental illness include:

- partial hospitalization, through which individuals attend hospital day programs and receive treatment, leave the hospital to sometimes work in the community and to return to their homes at night, returning to the hospital for treatment and monitoring the next day;
- day programs that provide education, supervision, and in some instances employment opportunities (also available for persons with developmental disabilities in many communities); and
- halfway houses and refurbished apartment complexes, with resident supervisors who oversee and lend support to residents with mental illness (also for persons with and disabilities and recovering substance users in many communities).

Many former residents have been able to return to their own homes. Some go to adult or special children's day-care centers during the day while their family members work and return home at night. Respite-care programs established in some communities, using trained volunteers, make it possible for family members to find substitute caregivers so they can have some time away from the person on occasion to regain their energies.

Community-based alternatives for the elderly also have received increased attention as the general population continues to age. Prior to deinstitutionalization, many residents of state mental hospitals (and state schools for people with developmental and other types of disabilities) were elderly people who could function in a less restrictive environment if someone helped to care for them. A number of elderly individuals have been successfully placed in assisted living facilities (nursing homes), often in integrated facilities that accept residents with and without mental illness or disability. But with our increasingly aging population, mental health advocates are concerned about the availability of mental health services for the elderly. It has been estimated that about 20% of individuals over age 55 suffer from a mental disorder that is not a typical part of aging, such as depression, substance misuse, Alzheimer's disease, anxiety disorders, and late-onset schizophrenia (American Psychological Association, 2010).

Specialized Interventions for Persons with Substance Use Disorder and Their Families

EP 2.1.3b
EP 2.1.8b

Early efforts to eliminate problems of alcoholism and substance misuse were aimed at moral rehabilitation, prohibition, and temperance. The most significant breakthrough in the area of alcohol misuse came in 1935 with the founding of **Alcoholics Anonymous (AA)**, a self-help group for alcoholics. AA was established by Bill W., a New York stockbroker, and Dr. Bob, a physician, who discovered that they could maintain sobriety by supporting one another and following a formal program of gradual recovery, which since has been incorporated into the 12 steps for which AA is known. AA continued to grow in numbers and in popularity, and, over time, intervention efforts shifted from the moral concept of alcoholism to the disease concept. Education and advocacy groups such as the National Council on Alcoholism, founded in 1944, drew further attention to alcoholics' problems.

Federal attention to the problem of alcoholism did not come about until 1970, when Senator Harold Hughes of Iowa (a recovering alcoholic at the time of his election) advocated for passage of the Comprehensive Alcohol Abuse and Alcoholism Prevention, Treatment, and Rehabilitation Act. This act provided financial assistance to states and communities to embark on treatment, education, research, and training programs and established the National Institute on Alcohol Abuse and Alcoholism. The act also provided for withdrawing federal funding from any hospital that refused to treat alcoholics.

Programs have expanded significantly since that act was passed. Early intervention models were based on inpatient hospitalization and participation in Alcoholics Anonymous; however, research has shown that these programs are not effective with all substance users. Different types of clients require different intervention approaches. Some clients are so entrenched in their addiction that they require hospitalization, and they often must undergo detoxification before they can effectively begin treatment. Most hospitalization programs range in duration from 30 to 60 days.

Many addiction professionals argue that 30 days is not sufficient for those receiving treatment to recover enough to stay sober after being released from the hospital. Prior to passage of the Affordable Care Act of 2010, some insurance companies refused to pay for even short-term inpatient treatment. However, the ACA requires parity for health and mental health services, making inpatient treatment available to more individuals. Proponents of outpatient and partial hospitalization programs argue that clients should be made to deal with the pressures of day-to-day living while receiving support from the program, rather than being placed in a sheltered therapeutic environment away from the previous pressures and individuals with whom they misused substances.

Whether treatment is inpatient or outpatient, treatment programs usually incorporate community-based self-help groups such as Alcoholics Anonymous or Narcotics Anonymous (NA). Individuals released from treatment programs typically are encouraged to continue attending NA or AA meetings as well as aftercare programs, usually held on evenings and weekends, for up to a year after leaving the more intensive intervention program.

Many addiction specialists view a family systems model as the most effective approach to treat substance use disorder, because family members reinforce, often unconsciously, the user's addiction and learn individual patterns of coping that frequently result in intergenerational substance use disorder in families (Fisher & Roget, 2008; Juhnke & Hagedorn, 2006; Straussner & Fewell, 2006). Therefore, many chemical-dependence programs in which social workers are employed incorporate a family systems model and provide psychoeducational experiences for family members in addition to the client. These experiences involve educational and therapy sessions with other clients and their families, as well as individual, group, and family therapy.

Some chemical-dependence programs take a more cognitive/behavioral approach, particularly with adolescents and individuals in the criminal-justice system. These programs emphasize consequences for misusing substances and other inappropriate behaviors and reinforcers for appropriate actions. Some juvenile and adult corrections programs, including jails and prisons, incorporate addiction treatment. But services often are limited in both duration and numbers served, in spite of the large numbers of inmates who are incarcerated for crimes involving substance misuse. Without treatment, these individuals are likely to be incarcerated again, often for more serious crimes.

The use of alternative peer groups (APG) is another model that has been shown to be effective with youth with substance use disorder. Studies show that between 65 and 89 percent of teens relapse within thirty days of leaving a substance use disorder treatment program if they return to their previous high schools and sets of friends. The APG model takes into account the importance of peers for teens, and helps those in recovery develop new groups of friends that support recovery instead of their previous using friends. Some communities have created sober high schools that incorporate the APG model, and many universities have also developed programs for students in recovery to create a continuum of care for teens and young adults (Holleran-Steiker & Counihan, 2014).

Agencies that serve clients with a wide range of problems are incorporating special programs that target substance misuse. Child protective services agencies that work with abusive and neglectful parents are reporting that the bulk of the increased reports are related to substance misuse (Cleaver, Nicholson, Tarr, & Cleaver, 2007; Straussner & Fewell, 2006). In response, these agencies have developed substance-use disorder treatment programs for their clients. The programs not only deal with the substance misuse but also provide parenting programs that address the impacts of substance misuse on children.

Of the inpatient or residential programs available for women with children, few provide care for the children. Those that do provide this care emphasize modeling of parenting skills, working through communication problems and other family dynamics, and providing a safe, supportive environment for the mothers and their children with others who are in similar circumstances so they do not have to face the added stress of reuniting with their children when the treatment is concluded. Increasingly, addiction programs also are addressing the needs of clients who have emotional problems in addition to substance use disorder, called **dual diagnosis** or co-occurring disorders. Frequently, an individual will go through treatment for chemical dependence and, after maintaining sobriety for a long time, return to the mental-health system for help in dealing with other emotional problems such as depression or family-of-origin issues, including sexual abuse (Phillips, McKeown, & Sandford, 2009).

Specialized Interventions for Persons with Disabilities and Their Families

Block (2009) suggests that there are a number of ways of viewing disability that have framed society's response (or lack thereof) to improving the conditions of people with disabilities, including developmental disabilities:

- People with disabilities are partial or limited people in an "other" and lesser category than others.
- The successful "handicapped" person has triumphed over adversity and is an exemplar for others to emulate.
- The burden of disability is unending.
- The able-bodied are obligated to help those with disabilities.
- A disability is an abnormality, something to be fixed, corrected, or cured.
- People with mental disabilities are a menace to themselves, to others, and to society; they lack the moral sense that would restrain them from hurting themselves or others.
- People with disabilities are consumed by rage and anger at their loss and at those who are not disabled.
- People with cognitive impairments are holy innocents endowed with the function of inspiring others to value life.
- The person with a disability will be compensated for his/her lack by greater abilities and strengths in other areas.

It should come as no surprise, then, that early efforts to improve conditions for people with developmental disabilities focused primarily on segregating them in large public institutions, out of sight of mainstream society. As is discussed elsewhere in this chapter, the condition of people with developmental disabilities did not change significantly until the advent of the community mental health center movement in the 1960s and the deinstitutionalization movement of the 1970s. President John Kennedy was a strong advocate since his sister Rosemary had a developmental disability. The Community Mental Health Centers Act, passed during the Kennedy administration, included funding for research and facilities for those with developmental disabilities. For a time, it appeared that the needs of people with developmental disabilities would be met in a humane way and in the least restrictive setting. This period of improved treatment was short-lived, however, as adequate funding for community-based mental health care never materialized and people with developmental disabilities and their families were left largely to fend for themselves.

EP 2.1.1a
EP 2.1.9b

This twist of fate spawned a developmental disabilities advocacy movement that remains strong today. One of the most successful developmental disabilities advocacy organizations was founded in 1950 as the Association for Retarded Children. This group later became the Association for Retarded Citizens and, now, simply the Arc. Today, the Arc is a national organization with chapters or affiliates throughout the country. This group has been instrumental for over six decades in advocating for improved conditions for those with developmental disabilities.

While significant improvements have been made over the years regarding the condition of people with disabilities, much remains to be done to ensure that they are treated fairly, receive the legal protections to which they are entitled, and are able to live their lives in the least restrictive environment.

The Arc joined United Cerebral Palsy to form the Disability Policy Collaboration in partnership with the American Association on Intellectual and Developmental Disabilities, the American Network of Community Options and Resources, the Association of University Centers on Disabilities, and the National Association of Councils on Developmental Disabilities, to advocate for significant changes in the way the federal government provides supports for people with mental disabilities (Arc, 2009). Key areas of advocacy include:

- expanding Social Security benefits and streamlining their administration;
- ensuring that the needs of people with mental disabilities are considered in emergency preparedness and response initiatives;
- overhauling tax policies to enable families of people with mental disabilities to stay together;
- increasing the availability of affordable and accessible housing for people with mental disabilities;
- improving the quality of services for people with disabilities and their families;
- ensuring that recently enacted health-care reform legislation addresses the needs of persons with disabilities;
- expanding workforce development, supported employment and vocational rehabilitation programs for people with disabilities;
- providing accessible and affordable transportation systems for people with disabilities;
- ensuring that people with disabilities have access to affordable, usable technology to support and enhance their lives;
- expanding funding of basic and applied research and prevention initiatives aimed at improving the lives of people with disabilities;
- providing for the appropriate training and adequate reimbursement of workers (including family members) who provide direct supports to people with disabilities;
- ensuring that the educational needs of children with disabilities are met; and
- preserving the civil rights of people with disabilities and their families.

This ambitious agenda requires the collective efforts of many to accomplish. It also serves as stark testimony to just how far we need to go to achieve parity for people with disabilities in our society.

The Americans with Disabilities Act

EP 2.1.8a
EP 2.1.18b
EP 2.1.9b

In 1986, the National Council on the Handicapped published its report, *Toward Independence,* which provided a comprehensive national approach for addressing problems of individuals with disabilities. The Americans With Disabilities Act (ADA) (PL 101-336) passed both the House and Senate with little opposition and was signed into law on July 26, 1990. Although referenced earlier in this chapter when discussing legal determination of disability, the ADA is the most significant piece of federal disability legislation passed because, for the first time, persons with disabilities are considered a protected class like other minority groups. Prior to passage of ADA, people with disabilities could readily be discriminated against. A major problem for many persons with mental illness or developmental disability has been the denial of basic rights that others take for granted.

ADA bans discrimination based on disabilities by private employers with a workforce of more than 15, mandating public accommodations, public services, transportation, and telecommunications. This act also extends protections provided by the 1964 Civil Rights Act to millions of individuals with physical and mental disabilities including heart disease, diabetes, emotional illnesses, drug addiction, alcoholism, and persons with AIDS. The act requires public places—including nongovernmental entities such as restaurants, hotels and motels, business places, and other facilities used by the general public—to provide "reasonable accommodations" to persons with disabilities, in terms of both service and employment. In short, the act mandates the elimination of discrimination and establishes standards and mechanisms for enforcement.

This law significantly changed the way that individuals with disabilities historically have been treated. Ever since the Elizabethan Poor Laws, people with disabilities have been considered to need public assistance,

and definitions of who has a disability have been used primarily for determining eligibility for public assistance. The intent of ADA is to reduce the stigma toward individuals with disabilities and remove barriers that resulted in their forced isolation. The law has empowered many persons with disabilities to take charge of their lives and has helped to reduce the stigmatization. Under ADA, individuals with disabilities and their family members can insist on reasonable accommodations. For example, a person with a disability who can perform a job with reasonable accommodations cannot be passed over for that job, nor can the primary caregiver of a child with a disability. States and local communities now have to establish special transportation systems, place elevators and ramps in buildings, and install special telephones for individuals with hearing impairments, as well as for those in wheelchairs.

ADA also advocated for supported employment of individuals with disabilities, including employment for wages and benefits in workplaces that integrate persons with and without disabilities, and continuous on-the-job training to reinforce job skills. Community-based programs in many areas have obtained employment for clients with disabilities in recycling centers, mail centers, offices, food-service settings, grocery stores, and landscaping and park programs. Some programs have placed clients as aides in schools and centers that mainstream children with disabilities, giving them a

Although changes are still needed to better address their needs, The Americans with Disabilities Act and advocates have paved the way to provide opportunities not available to persons with disabilities in the past.

Tony Freeman/PhotoEdit

chance to work—and to be successful role models for the children.

The 20th anniversary of ADA was celebrated in 2010. Despite the ADA mandates, stereotypes still raise significant barriers for individuals with disabilities. The Special Olympics commissioned an international study, conducted in 10 countries. It found that while 46% of the respondents believed that persons with intellectual disabilities could play on a team with others with similar disabilities, only 14% believed they would be capable of playing on a team with players without intellectual disabilities. In addition, 79% believed that children with intellectual disabilities should be educated in segregated settings, either at home or in special schools, and 54% thought that including people with intellectual disabilities in the workplace would increase the risk of accidents (Special Olympics, 2003). While these attitudes are changing, change has been slow and much remains to be done before parity for the developmentally disabled population is achieved.

Individuals with physical disabilities face similar discrimination (see Box 9.4). A student at the university where one of the authors teaches arrived on campus wheelchair-bound and connected to a breathing tube so he could receive oxygen. Modest and quiet, the student did not disclose that he had received a perfect SAT score. At first, peers and faculty treated him as if he were both physically and intellectually challenged. Three years later, however, with a straight-A average in computer science, he had changed many attitudes about persons with disabilities.

In spite of the passage of the ADA, gaps in services that impact the well-being of persons with disabilities still exist. In 2005, the U.S. Surgeon General, in collaboration with the federal government's Health and Human Services Office on Disability, released a call to action to improve the health and wellness of individuals with disabilities (U.S. Department of Health and Human Services, 2005). This report, issued on the 15th Anniversary of the Americans With Disabilities Act, included four priorities (see www.surgeongeneral.gov):

1. increasing understanding that people with disabilities can lead long, healthy, and productive lives;
2. increasing knowledge among health-care professionals and providing them with tools to screen, diagnose, and treat the whole person with a disability with dignity;
3. increasing awareness by people with disabilities of the steps they can take to develop and maintain a healthy lifestyle; and
4. increasing accessible health-care and support services to promote independence for people with disabilities.

A review 5 years after the report was released found that while disparities still exist for persons with disabilities, the federal government has worked with businesses and other entities to focus on health rights and greater attention to health and wellness for this population (Carmona, Giannini, Bergmark, & Cabe, 2010). The implementation of the Affordable Care Act, which prohibits insurance companies from refusing to cover preexisting conditions, also has had a significant positive aspect on individuals with disabilities and their families.

Among the many implications of ADA for social service providers and social workers, services must be accessible and individuals cannot be denied participation in a program because of their disability, nor can they be required to participate. Clients with disabilities who participate in social service programs report that many social services providers play a significant role in disempowering rather than empowering them to meet their own needs (Linhorst, 2005). Social workers should ensure that clients have access to people who can meet their needs. For example, clients with hearing problems may need social workers who can sign or interpreters to help them communicate. Further, social service agencies must be able to lead persons with disabilities to employment opportunities (and not just in agencies that work with individuals with disabilities). Jobs can be structured with special equipment and accommodations such as part-time work and job sharing. Successful programs for individuals with disabilities require consistent advocacy and community support if they are to receive the services they need.

Other Disabilities Legislation

EP 2.1.8a
EP 2.1.9b

Prior to 1970, federal funding of programs for persons with disabilities focused primarily on rehabilitation for medical conditions. The first major federal legislation that focused on this population was the Rehabilitation Act of 1973, which prohibits discrimination of persons with disabilities by entities receiving federal assistance. Section 504 of this act sets guidelines for public education programs, including universities. This act and the ADA

Box 9.4 Looking Back on 20 Years of Disability Rights

Ben Mattlin lives in Los Angeles, where he's working on a memoir. He blogs at benmattlin.blogspot.com.

When I was younger, it was legal to discriminate against people like me. I was born with spinal muscular atrophy. I've always used a wheelchair, and my hands are too weak to scratch an itch. My parents said I could be anything I wanted when I grew up. It wasn't quite true.

Back in the 1960s and '70s, my parents struggled to find a decent school willing to take a handicapped kid. I assumed the problem was I wasn't smart enough. In 1980, I entered Harvard. It was the year Harvard had to become accessible, under a forerunner of the Americans With Disabilities Act, the Rehabilitation Act of 1973. The ancient cobblestone campus proved challenging. But what really bothered me was the administration's refusal to grant me roommates. I might impair their experience, one dean explained. Never mind how this segregation would impact mine.

The sting of discrimination worsened after graduation. No one would hire me. Once, an editor invited me to interview for a staff opening, but upon seeing me, she asked, "How would you make photocopies? I mean you'd be here to help us, not for us to help you."

Then, on July 26, 1990, when I was 27, the ADA became law. It didn't get me a job. But it addressed the differences between essential and nonessential job tasks. It identified a "reasonable accommodation" from an "undue hardship"—a critical distinction for employers and public places alike. If I encountered a restaurant or store with a 6-inch threshold and no ramp, I had constructive language to use, beyond cursing or crying. Most of all, by recognizing the injustices millions of us were confronting, it provided not just legal recourse, but validation and hope.

Now, the ADA's impact is everywhere: wheelchair lifts on city buses, signs in Braille, sign-language interpreters. Many young disabled people are growing up with a marvelous sense of belonging, entitlement, and pride I never had.

Yes, there is still a long way to go. Yet in defining the terms of disability, the ADA made us impossible to ignore. So now people should understand we're just part of the human landscape, and we're here to stay.

SOURCE: Mattlin, B. (2010). *Looking back on 20 years of disability rights.* NPR, July 26, 2010. Retrieved July 26, 2010, from http://www.npr.org/templates/story/story.php?storyId=128697147.

work in tandem to provide protections to persons with disability.

Individuals with Disabilities Education Act and the No Child Left Behind Act

The **Individuals With Disabilities Education Act (IDEA)**, enacted in 1990, replaced previous legislation providing special education resources for children and youth with disabilities and included funding for early intervention programs for infants and toddlers with disabilities and their families. The legislation emphasizes the development of comprehensive, coordinated, multidisciplinary, interagency programs that include public school systems, health agencies, and social services agencies.

This law mandates that public school systems provide educational and social services for children with a range of disabilities, including emotional disturbance, mental retardation, and speech, vision, hearing, and learning disabilities. Parents and educators are required to develop jointly an individualized educational plan

(IEP) for each child. The law also requires that each child be placed in the least restrictive setting possible, with the intent of including as many children with disabilities and emotional problems as possible in general classrooms; special education classes are to be a last alternative.

Preschool early intervention programs are required to develop an individualized family intervention plan to ensure that families of these children receive the services they need. Services usually include counseling, as parents often believe there is a "cure" somewhere for their child's disability and may succumb to denial, self-blame, anger, and grief and loss. Parents also need help in navigating the myriad of available services that often are confusing and difficult to access, as well as respite care so they can take time for themselves and their other children.

Many communities have preschool programs, funded with state and federal monies to assist children with disabilities, that combine early childhood education with physical and speech therapy and other needed services. Working and nonworking parents alike can bring their children to the centers, where trained staff members work with the children individually and in small groups to help them progress developmentally. Some preschool programs include children both with and without disabilities so both groups can learn to value each other and discover and grow together.

While IDEA has gained a fairly positive reputation among disability advocates because of its policies and programs, concerns have been raised about another recently-passed piece of education legislation, the No Child Left Behind Act, a centerpiece of the George W. Bush administration. Passed in 2001, this act is intended to increase accountability in public schools to ensure that all students have an opportunity to master expected educational content. However, its heavy emphasis on testing has led to criticism from special education advocates, concerned that children with special needs may not be treated appropriately in testing and assessment as well as placement. Although accommodations can be made for children with special needs under the act, procedures are heavily regulated with some advocates worried that the needs of some children are being ignored at the expense of accountability.

Advocates for individuals with disabilities are calling for additional resources for children with special needs. Those diagnosed with autism, attention-deficit disorder, and other disabilities can make significant gains with early intervention. Some children have disabilities that prohibit them from remaining in their own homes and attending neighborhood schools, and still others have parents who are overwhelmed by their own needs and the added stress from having a child with a disability and being unable to provide adequate care. Advances in technology have enabled children with serious disabilities, who formerly would not have lived, to remain alive. How best can these children be cared for? The costs to keep such children in hospitals are prohibitive, and a hospital setting does not provide the nurturing that a child needs to develop to his or her maximum potential.

Many state schools for individuals with intellectual and developmental disabilities have closed, and attention is turning to how to care for the children who previously were housed there. In some instances, they have been placed in nursing homes with elderly residents, and these facilities are not likely to be equipped to meet the special needs of children. The United States has the capacity to support children and adults with

mental health problems and developmental disabilities in community-based settings. With adaptive equipment and facilities, and in some instances a personal-care attendant, many individuals with disabilities can function well in their own homes or in a residential, apartment-like facility with some assistance. Many can drive themselves to and from a workplace or use public transportation if it is disability-accessible, allowing them to attend public schools, hold jobs, and make a living. Significant advances in assistive technology have been made as a result of the military's response to the thousands of soldiers returning from the wars in Iraq and Afghanistan with severe physical injuries, brain damage, or both. One can only hope that the benefits of these technologies will be extended to the civilian sector as well.

Prevention Versus Treatment

 EP 2.1.8a EP 2.1.9b It is evident that many types of mental illness, addiction, and disability can be prevented from occurring at all, or with early intervention, eliminated completely or managed so a person can experience a high quality of life. A major policy issue continuously debated is what the balance should be between prevention and intervention, particularly when there are not enough resources for both.

Mental health professionals address prevention issues at three levels (National Center on Education, Disability and Juvenile Justice, 2010):

1. **primary prevention**—prevention targeted at an entire population (e.g., prenatal care for all women to avoid developmental disabilities in their infants; parenting classes for all parents to decrease mental health problems among children);
2. **secondary prevention**—prevention for at-risk populations, for example, groups more likely to develop the identified problem than others (e.g., individual and group counseling for families with members having schizophrenia or alcoholism); and
3. **tertiary prevention**—prevention targeted at individuals who already have problems, to prevent the problems from recurring (e.g., treatment groups for alcoholics or mental health programs for individuals who have attempted suicide).

Numerous studies show that prevention programs are cost-effective in reducing substance use disorder, mental illness, and many types of disabilities. Still, policymakers often develop only short-term solutions to these problems. For example, although substance-misuse prevention programs can be expensive, the costs are greater for residential or other more extensive treatment programs later or for imprisonment if substance misuse leads to involvement with the criminal justice system.

Other problems involving mental health, such as homelessness and family and youth violence, while not new, are having significant negative impacts on the individuals with these problems and on the entire family. The emphasis on intergenerational, cyclical problems has refocused attention on the need to provide resources not just to the children and families experiencing these problems but also to adults who grew up in such families (see Chapters 10 and 11).

Cultural and gender differences must also be taken into account when discussing mental health, mental illness, substance misuse, and developmental and other types of disabilities. The importance of these differences, including the impact of oppression and social injustice, must be considered in relation to theories used to understand human behavior and to identify "normal" and pathological behavior. These differences, too, must be considered when using diagnostic classification systems such as the DSM-5, identifying the ways that practitioners view and relate to individuals with whom they interact, and determining the ways by which mental health, substance use disorder, and services to persons with disabilities are organized and delivered (Dziegielewski, 2010).

Trends in Services and Treatment

Funding

EP 2.1.3b
EP 2.1.9a
EP 2.1.9b

Since the pattern of categorical funding to states by the federal government to programs tied to specific client groups has been replaced largely by block grants, each state has considerable latitude in how it spends its funds. The Deficit Reduction Act, passed in 2006 under the George W. Bush administration, has raised additional concerns about funding services for persons with a mental health issue, addiction, or disability. This Act gives states more control over federal funding they receive, allowing them to offer packages of benefits to Medicaid recipients that actually can be less than what states were offering prior to the legislation. These changes mean that advocacy groups have to ensure

that resources are allocated to these groups directly, rather than to supplement state funding deficits or other programs. Thus, advocates and program administrators that serve persons with mental illness, addiction, and disabilities often find themselves competing with each other for limited funds.

It is expected that as the Affordable Care Act is implemented, access to affordable health and mental health care for members of these populations will improve. However, advocates are concerned that failure of states to expand Medicaid and proposed cuts in Medicare (see Chapter 8) will negatively impact availability and quality of needed services.

Funding constraints also have limited community-based programs that provide the kinds of supports that are most effective in helping children with serious mental illnesses and disabilities and their families. In many instances, children are hospitalized only briefly, then released to communities with only minimal follow-up services, resulting in a revolving door of inconsistent treatment that often exacerbates conditions as children grow older. Community-based programs that include parental support and training, respite care services, social workers and other staff members who can provide crisis intervention and prevent hospitalization, transportation, and adaptive equipment also would likely reduce fragmentation as schools, juvenile justice programs, social service providers, and hospitals collaborate to provide referrals and coordinated "wrap-around" services to meet individual needs.

Because of deinstitutionalization and the closing of state schools for persons with disabilities and state hospitals for persons with mental illness, the only available care for many individuals requiring intensive services has been nursing homes. Young adults, and in some instances children, have been housed in facilities with primarily elderly adults, which are poorly equipped to meet their specific needs.

Managed Care

One major effort to contain costs has been **managed care**, which is at the core of the current debate surrounding mental health services (Mechanic, 2007). Many of the pros and cons are similar to those discussed in Chapter 8, addressing health care. Managed health care has raised a number of ethical dilemmas for social workers and other mental health professionals. With insurance company personnel rather than mental health treatment providers increasingly making treatment decisions, concern has been raised about whether adequate services are being provided. Managed care emphasizes accountability and ensuring that services are provided only if they are needed. Many mental health services are paid for by third-party insurers or, if the client meets eligibility requirements, by Medicaid (see Chapter 8).

Third-party insurers also restrict the choice of service providers available, often to a list of professionals and specific hospitals who have agreed to the managed-care terms and conditions for that insurance company. Hospital stays, particularly for substance use disorder, have been limited, and more insurance providers are mandating outpatient treatment first to determine whether that approach is successful.

Managed-care initiatives, too, have changed the types of outpatient services provided. More agencies are seeing clients in groups and limiting the number of group and individual counseling sessions in which a client can participate. The trend is toward case management, with a case manager, sometimes from the insurance company, sometimes from the agency, monitoring the services received to ensure that they are appropriate.

Legislation Promoting Access to Health Care

EP 2.1.9b

Until the passage of recent legislation, including the Affordable Care Act, insurance coverage for mental health and substance use disorder was generally much more restricted than for other types of health care. Arguably one of the most significant pieces of legislation ever passed that affects insurance coverage for individuals with mental health or substance misuse problems is the Paul Wellstone and Pete Domenici Mental Health Parity and Addiction Act of 2008 (PL 110-460). The act requires that group health plans provide both medical and surgical benefits and mental health or substance-use disorder benefits to ensure that:

- deductibles and copayments applicable to such mental health or substance use disorder benefits are no more restrictive than those applied to medical and surgical benefits covered by the plan;
- there are no separate cost-sharing requirements that are applicable only with respect to mental health or substance-use disorder benefits;
- the treatment limitations applicable to mental health or substance-use disorder benefits are no

more restrictive than the predominant treatment limitations applied to medical and surgical benefits covered by the plan; and
- there are no separate treatment limitations that are applicable only with respect to mental health or substance-use disorder benefits. In response to the high costs of medication for a number of mental health problems, such as schizophrenia, legislation passed in 2003 provides senior adults and persons with disabilities covered by Medicare with prescription drug benefits. However, mandatory copayment and refill policies vary by state, making it difficult for some individuals to maintain the medications needed to keep them healthy.

Patient Protection and Affordable Care Act (Affordable Care Act)

EP 2.1.1a
EP 2.1.8a

The Affordable Care Act, which is the single most important piece of legislation passed relating to insurance coverage for health and mental health care, incorporates principles from the Wellstone and Domenici legislation. This landmark legislation includes a number of provisions that are expected to improve care for people living with mental illness, addiction, and disability and their families (National Alliance on Mental Illness, 2010):

- Parity for mental health and substance abuse services—under this provision, insurance companies will be required to reimburse mental health providers at the same rate they reimburse other health-care providers for similar services. Ending the practice of reimbursing mental health providers at a lower rate than other health-care providers is intended to ensure that patients with mental illness receive the care they need without breaks in service or the added expense of higher copayments. This provision of the law also makes it possible for patients who need medication to see a specialist in mental health care rather than a general practitioner. One of the hoped-for long-term benefits of the parity provision of the law is that it will encourage more health-care practitioners to enter the field of mental health, a specialty for which credentialed providers are currently in short supply.
- No discrimination based on preexisting conditions—this provision will end the practice by insurance

companies of refusing coverage for people with pre-existing conditions such as mental illness.

- No rate changes based on health status—this provision prevents insurance companies from raising rates for patients who develop a chronic or expensive condition.
- Greater availability of insurance, at lower cost—this provision will result in a greater availability of insurance plans to those who can't currently afford them.
- Expansion of Medicaid—the law expands coverage of the government-run health-care program for the poor by changing the definition of the poor to include more working-class, low-income families (i.e., those living at or below 200% of the federal poverty level).

The various provisions of the law will be rolled over the 6-year period, 2010 to 2014. The reader is referred to Chapter 8 for a more detailed discussion of the Affordable Care Act.

Evolving Therapies

EP 2.1.7a
EP 2.1.7b

The Commission on Mental Health, established by President Jimmy Carter in 1978, found that people of color, children, adolescents, and the elderly were underserved, as were residents of rural and poor urban areas. The commission also found that many of the services provided were inappropriate, particularly for those with differing cultural backgrounds and lifestyles. In many instances when mental health centers were first established, they were directed by psychiatrists trained in psychotherapy or influenced by educational psychologists who were accustomed to testing and working with students. As a result, the staff members often were inexperienced at dealing with involuntary clients, who did not want to be seen, failed to keep appointments, and were unfamiliar with the concept of 1-hour therapy sessions. Staff members often were also unequipped to deal with problems such as family violence, child abuse, and sexual abuse.

As programs developed, many centers became skilled at reaching special populations and developing more effective ways of addressing client needs. In the 1970s, centers were required to establish special children's mental health programs. Currently, many centers provide programs that address special populations such as abused children, individuals with substance use disorder, and veterans. Social workers also assist in establishing self-help groups, such as Alcoholics Anonymous, Adult Children of Alcoholics, Alateen, Parents Without Partners, and Parents Anonymous (a child-abuse self-help and mutual assistance program).

Today, social workers in mental health settings provide crisis intervention, operate telephone hotlines, conduct suicide-prevention programs, and provide treatment for alcoholism and misuse of other drugs. Mental health services increasingly are provided in settings other than mental health centers—churches, assisted living facilities/nursing homes, police departments, schools, child-care centers, the workplace, and health and medical settings. Problems addressed by mental health professionals have expanded to include loneliness and isolation, finances, intimate partner violence and child abuse, male–female relationships, housing, and use of alcohol and other drugs. Mental health staff members have become more multidisciplinary, using teams of professionals as well as volunteers.

Short-Term Therapy Intervention approaches based on "brief" or "short-term" therapy, often taking a cognitive-behavioral approach, are being used to stabilize clients and help them cope more quickly. One short-term intervention approach is solution-focused therapy (Elliott & Metcalf, 2009; Macdonald, 2007), which emphasizes the strengths of clients and empowers them to come up with effective solutions. Questions such as "What worked for you before?" and comments such as "How have you managed to do as well as you have with all this going on?" take clients' own ideas and affirm their abilities to cope.

Psychoeducational Approaches Research and current thinking support a systems/ecological approach for dealing with issues of mental health, substance abuse, and developmental disabilities and, in particular, a family systems perspective. Treatment interventions that involve the entire family are more likely to reduce recidivism (recurrence of the problem) or prevent the problem from getting worse.

A psychoeducational approach is highly successful in many situations. Individuals and their families receive education that helps them understand the problem their family member is experiencing, the roles they have played in trying to cope with the problem, and possibly more effective ways of coping, as well as family therapy to address the dynamics within their own families.

Emphasis on Trauma-Informed Care Social workers and other service providers have become increasingly aware of the fact that many persons with mental health and substance use disorders as well as those with disabilities have experienced trauma in their lives, including physical abuse and sexual and other types of violence, that may have either resulted in or exacerbated their disorder. Clinicians are giving increased attention to specific interventions which address the consequences of the trauma and facilitate healing. These approaches recognize signs and symptoms of trauma that include substance misuse, eating disorders, depression, and anxiety; integrate knowledge about trauma in policies and practices; incorporate addressing the trauma as part of the therapy process; and work to avoid re-traumatizing clients and their families. Interventions that build on evidence-based practice focus on "safety; trustworthiness and transparency; peer support; collaboration and mutuality; empowerment, voice and choice; and cultural, historical and gender issues" (Substance Abuse and Mental Health Services Administration, 2014b, p. 1).

Community Emphasis Community-level services are expected to continue to expand, with local communities determining the level and type of services needed. Pressure from the federal government for community mental health centers to become financially independent continue. Although some individuals with mental health or substance-misuse problems still require hospitalization in state or private psychiatric facilities, more and more individuals are being treated in community-based programs. Numerous studies have found that the vast majority of people in psychiatric hospitals can be treated successfully in local communities at significantly reduced costs, and with more effective outcomes than hospitalization.

In the future, community-based treatment models will include more "one-stop mental health centers" that incorporate individual and group counseling services, expanded-day and partial-day treatment programs, social skills training, and recreation programs, as well as assistance with housing and employment. More social workers in therapist or case-management positions will be sent into clients' homes to provide services there, further reducing the need for outpatient and inpatient care. Intensive case management and therapy services provided in the home on a short-term basis often can stabilize situations and get the entire family to work together with the client before problems escalate, requiring hospitalization or other out-of-home services.

NIMH Report In late 2004, the National Institute of

EP 2.1.6b

Mental Health convened a panel of mental health consumers, providers, researchers and academicians, advocates, and government officials at all levels to determine how mental health care should be strengthened to better meet client and family needs. The report, *Transforming Mental Health Care in America, Action Agenda: First Steps* (Substance Abuse and Mental Health Services Administration, 2006), cited recovery as the single, most important goal, noting that "mental health recovery is a journey of healing and transformation enabling a person with a mental health problem to live a meaningful life in a community of his or her choice while striving to achieve his or her full potential."

The report called for

- sending a message that mental illnesses are treatable and recovery is possible;
- reducing suicides by developing a national strategy for suicide prevention;
- helping the mental health workforce become more culturally competent;
- increasing employment of persons with psychiatric disabilities;
- enhancing technology to protect privacy and confidentiality of consumer health information;
- expanding services that are based on evidence-based practice;
- improving coordination between health and mental health services; and
- increasing the focus on the mental health needs of children and early intervention to meet their needs.

The report indicated that recovery should be a primary first goal and advocated the following 10 components of recovery:

1. self-direction;
2. individualized and person-centered;
3. empowerment;
4. holistic;
5. nonlinear (based on growth, setbacks, and learning);

6. strengths-based;
7. peer support;
8. respect;
9. responsibility; and
10. hope.

These components overlap with social work values and the focus on the client. NASW is partnering with other advocacy groups to promote the concept that mental health is a national priority for the public and private sectors alike. Social workers are involved in political action efforts at national, state, and local levels to increase funding for prevention, treatment, and research in mental health and for passing legislation that requires adequate mental health benefits for all citizens as part of any health reform. They also are working to ensure that social workers are included as providers of mental health services under such legislation. Finally, they advocate for policies that clients be placed in least restrictive environments and for a mental health service delivery system that allows for a continuum of care, including community-based prevention programs.

Other Trends

Other trends include additional emphasis on web-based treatment interventions used either concurrently or alone with clients so that they don't have to leave their homes to receive help; greater focus on nutrition and a holistic approach to wellness; emphasis on mindfulness programs, which include meditation, yoga, and other strategies that keep individuals centered in the present and the healing process; and support groups (Battisa, 2013).

A negative trend that advocates and consumers are concerned about is the increased criminalization of persons with mental health, substance misuse, and disabilities. Since the occurrence of deinstitutionalization, many communities lack resources, including skilled personnel in law enforcement, health care, and social services trained to work effectively with these populations. As a result, rather than coming in contact with the social services delivery system, persons who have mental and other disabilities and addicts end up in the court system and ultimately our country's jails and prisons. It is estimated that between one-third and one-half of all prisoners in

the United States have mental disorders, and that ten times as many persons with mental illness are in prisons and jails than in institutions for the mentally ill. The prison environment is not conducive to recovery and rehabilitation, and, in fact, often leads to serious declines in physical and mental health, including suicide attempts as well as successful suicides. If released, individuals have difficulty finding jobs, re-establishing relationships with families and others, and have the stigma of mental illness, addiction, or disability and now incarceration. Recidivism rates are high for members of these groups because of limited community support and failure to provide more appropriate resources (Pfeiffer, 2007).

Roles and Opportunities for Social Workers

EP 2.1.1a
EP 2.1.8b
EP 2.1.9b

Social workers today are involved in the total continuum of mental health and developmental disabilities services. They provide these services in a variety of settings, including traditional social services agencies—such as community mental health centers, child guidance centers, and public social services departments—as well as nontraditional settings—the courts, public schools and colleges and universities, hospitals and health clinics, child-care centers, workplaces, and the military. While they fulfill a variety of roles, social workers currently form the largest group of psychotherapists in the United States.

Historical Background

The first social workers credited with providing mental health services were the psychiatric social workers hired in New York and Boston mental hospitals in the early 1900s. They were responsible primarily for providing individual therapy to hospitalized mental patients and overseeing the care of discharged patients in foster homes. The mental health field expanded during the 1920s with the establishment of child guidance centers.

With the influence of psychoanalysis and the child-guidance movement, social workers in mental health moved increasingly into the role of psychotherapist, in which the individual is the unit of attention. The unique perspective of social work on the person-in-environment and intervention at levels of the environment beyond the individual waned during the 1930s, 1940s, and 1950s. But the Civil Rights Movement and Vietnam War in the 1960s prompted activism in the social work profession as a whole, redirected again to community organization, advocacy, and a return to the roots of the profession.

Emphasis on the ecological/systems perspective since the late 1960s has broadened the roles of social workers in all fields, including mental health. While psychiatrists traditionally have played a more technical role in the mental health system, stressing medication and biopsychological perspectives, social workers have tried to maintain leadership in the mental health arena (Dumont & St-Onge, 2007; Gould, 2009; Thyer & Wodarski, 2007).

For instance, social workers might consider the following questions:

- Why do some communities and geographic areas have higher incidences than others of mental illness, substance misuse, people with disabilities, and homelessness?
- What can be done to reduce disparities between groups based on race and ethnicity, gender, class, and sexual orientation in areas such as mental illness, substance misuse, and disability?
- What factors constitute a healthy community—or society—that promotes mental health and values diversity?

Quality of life for individuals and families can be improved by eliminating environmental racism, oppression, and discrimination; creating adequate housing and employment; and maintaining an environment that values diversity and difference, children and families, and the elderly. Regardless of their field or the environment in which they practice, social workers have important roles to play.

Career Opportunities in Mental Health, Substance Use, and Disability Services

Clinical Social Workers   Many social workers in

EP 2.1.1a
EP 2.1.8a
EP 2.1.9b

mental health settings provide individual counseling, including psychotherapy, to clients. Instead of being referred to as psychiatric social workers, though, most are called **clinical social workers**. Most agencies that hire clinical social workers require that they

meet the qualifications of the National Association of Social Workers Academy of Certified Social Workers (ACSW) certification or obtain appropriate state certification or licensing.

ACSW certification requires a master of social work (MSW) degree from an accredited graduate school of social work, 2 years of social work experience under the direct supervision of an ACSW social worker, and a satisfactory score on a competency examination administered by the NASW. State licensing and certification programs have similar requirements, but they vary by state.

Crisis Intervention and Child and Family Services   Many social work jobs are available in the fields of mental health, addiction/substance use disorder, and disabilities for social workers with a bachelor of social work (BSW) degree. BSW social workers provide services such as crisis intervention for women and their children at battered women's centers, and they operate suicide, runaway youth, child abuse, and other types of crisis hotlines (see Chapter 2).

They also counsel adolescents and their families at youth-serving agencies and are employed as social workers in state hospitals and community living programs for individuals with mental illness and state schools and community programs for individuals with developmental disabilities. In these settings, they counsel residents and serve as the primary professional involved with the individual's family.

School-Based Services and Drug Treatment Programs   Social workers work in schools with troubled students and their families, providing individual counseling, family counseling, and family outreach, and they lead groups for children and their families on topics such as divorce, child maltreatment, anger management, techniques for getting along with adults, and substance use. Legislation establishing services for children with disabilities requires social workers among the professionals who are authorized to provide services.

Public Mental Health Services   Social workers currently comprise the largest professional group in public mental health services. More than half of the labor force employed in mental health–related jobs are social workers, and in more than a third of the federally funded community mental health centers, a social worker is the executive director.

Social Workers in Multidisciplinary Teams
Many mental health programs take a multidisciplinary team approach, in which social workers, psychiatrists, physicians, psychologists, psychiatric nurses, child development specialists, and community aides work together to provide a multitude of services. Although social workers on multidisciplinary teams are involved in all aspects of treatment, most often they are given the responsibility of working with the client's family and the community in which the client resides.

Because of their training from an ecological/systems perspective, social workers help other team members understand the many competing factors that can support or impede a client intervention plan. If resources from another agency are needed, the social worker usually is the one who obtains them and ensures that they are provided.

Social Workers as Case Managers Even if they are not employed in agencies that use multidisciplinary teams, social workers in mental health settings often provide case-management services. Case managers are responsible for monitoring cases to ensure that clients receive the needed services. A case manager does not necessarily provide all services directly but manages the case, coordinating others who provide the services.

BSW social workers who work with people who have mental illnesses, disabilities, or addictions often serve as case managers. Assigned a group of clients, they ensure that their clients are following intervention plans and are functioning adequately. Case managers empower clients to become as self-sufficient as possible by promoting their strengths and providing support and affirmation. They also serve as the liaison with the client and other service providers, monitoring the provision of services and advocating for changes in services, including additional services when necessary. Individuals frequently can function fairly well with a case manager to lend support, ensure that they are taking medication if needed, advocate with an employer if there is a problem, help them access health care if they get sick, and keep them from becoming isolated from their environment.

Many states are employing case managers at community mental health centers to oversee clients who are living in the local community, including those previously in institutions, who can function independently with supervision and support. Case managers assist the client in problem-solving about job and family-related conflicts, managing finances, following health regimens that often include taking medication, and establishing supportive relationships with appropriate community resources. The case manager meets regularly with the client and contacts family members, employers, and other appropriate individuals to ensure that the client is functioning adequately.

Social Workers as Advocates Still other social workers involved in the mental health field serve as advocates. Organizations such as The Arc advocate for persons with disabilities on an individual basis, ensuring that they receive needed services. For example, a 14-year-old girl with intellectual disabilities in a junior high school in an urban area was not receiving special education services and had been suspended several times for behavior problems. An advocate assigned to her arranged for the school district to provide the needed testing, saw that she was placed in a special education program that reduced her anxiety level and allowed her to function in a setting where she felt better about herself, and arranged for her to receive counseling.

Advocates also work to ensure that groups of citizens are provided for, such as being involved in a community to ensure that housing is available to individuals with mental health problems and developmental disabilities. Advocates work within an empowerment framework, urging the targeted population to advocate for themselves for individual and social change.

Social Workers as Policymakers Social workers function in the mental health, addiction/substance use, and disability arenas as administrators and policymakers. Many direct social service programs, and others work for government bodies at local, state, and federal levels. They develop and advocate for legislation, develop policies and procedures to meet the needs of individuals with mental health and addiction problems and disabilities, and oversee governing bodies that monitor programs. Increasingly, social workers are being elected to local, state, and national office. Social workers at all governmental levels have played key roles in getting legislation passed to improve services for individuals who have mental illness, chemical dependencies, and/or disabilities.

Summary

Services for individuals with mental health and addiction challenges and disabilities have changed significantly since colonial times. Mental health services have seen major revolutions since that time: the shift from inhumane to moral treatment, the introduction of psychoanalytic therapy, the move from institutions to community programs and the development of psychotropic drugs to effectively treat many types of mental health problems, a new emphasis on the rights of clients and patients, and increased knowledge about biological implications and technology in developing effective prevention and intervention strategies.

Current issues in the mental health, addiction, and disability fields encompass the legal rights of clients and whether they should be able to refuse or demand treatment; scarce resources and conflict over the roles of federal, state, and local governments in providing services; attention to substance use disorder and the expansion of treatment facilities; and the need for more effective services for women, people of color, those who are homeless, and individuals in rural settings.

Social workers play a critical role in providing mental health, addiction, and disability services, serving as therapists, advocates, case managers, administrators, and policymakers. Rapid changes in society brought about by technology and globalization are expected to further expand the roles of social workers in meeting needs for these populations.

Competency Notes

EP 2.1.1a: Advocate for client access to the services of social work (pp. 236, 261, 268, 273, 279, 282–283). Social workers advocate for access to appropriate mental health, substance misuse, and disability services for clients and their families.

EP 2.1.3a: Distinguish, appraise, and integrate multiple sources of knowledge, including research-based knowledge and practice wisdom, when making and communicating professional judgments (pp. 239, 245, 252, 259). Social workers draw on multiple sources of knowledge, incorporating research-based knowledge and practice wisdom, when making and communicating professional judgments about policies and services that impact those who are mentally ill, homeless, disabled, or substance users.

EP 2.1.3b: Analyze models of assessment, prevention, intervention, and evaluation (pp. 240, 247, 271, 278). Social workers analyze models of assessment, prevention, and evaluation and adapt them accordingly to ensure that they are appropriate for persons who need assistance in dealing with mental health problems, addiction problems, and/or disabilities.

EP 2.1.6b: Engage in research-informed practice and practice-informed research (pp. 267, 281). Social workers use research to inform their practice and draw on practice experience to inform their research when working with persons who are mentally ill, homeless, disabled, or addicts.

EP 2.1.7a: Use conceptual frameworks to guide the process of assessment, intervention, and evaluation (pp. 236, 240–241, 244, 261, 280). Social workers use the ecological/systems and other conceptual frameworks in working with persons who need assistance in dealing with mental health problems, substance misuse, and/or disabilities.

EP 2.1.7b: Critique and apply knowledge to understand person and environment (pp. 238, 240–241, 250, 255, 259, 280). Social workers critique and apply knowledge to understand factors associated with mental health, substance misuse/addiction, and disabilities and how those factors impact individual development and an individual's ability to function within the broader social environment.

EP 2.1.8a: Analyze, formulate, and advocate for policies that advance social well-being (pp. 238, 273, 275, 277, 279, 283). Social workers analyze, formulate, and advocate for policies across all levels of the environment that advance the social well-being of individuals with mental health problems, addiction, and disabilities.

EP 2.1.8b: Collaborate with colleagues and clients for effective policy action (pp. 261, 271, 282). Social workers collaborate with colleagues across disciplines and clients and their families to advocate for effective policies for those with mental health problems, addiction, and disabilities.

EP 2.1.9a: Continuously discover, appraise, and attend to changing locales, populations, scientific and technological developments, and emerging

trends to provide relevant services (pp. 254, 261, 268, 278). Social workers incorporate changing contexts when developing and implementing policies and services for persons with mental health problems, addiction, and disabilities.

EP 2.1.9b: Provide leadership in promoting sustainable changes in service delivery and practice to improve the quality of social services (pp. 236, 238, 268, 270, 273, 275, 277, 278, 279, 282, 283). Social workers provide leadership in promoting sustainable changes in service delivery and practice to improve the quality of social services for persons with mental health problems, addiction, and disabilities.

Key Terms

The terms below are defined in the Glossary.

addiction
Affordable Care Act
alcohol
Alcoholics Anonymous
   (AA)
alcoholism
Americans With
   Disabilities Act
   (ADA)
clinical social workers
community mental
   health programs
deinstitutionalization
depressants
depression
developmental delay
developmental disability
*Diagnostic and Statistical
   Manual of Mental
   Disorders (DSM 5)*
dual diagnosis
hallucinogens
Individuals With
   Disabilities Education
   Act (IDEA)

inhalants
least restrictive
   environment
managed care
medical model
mental health
mental illness
moral treatment
narcotics
National Association
   of Mental Health
   (NAMH)
National Institute of
   Mental Health
   (NIMH)
primary prevention
psychoanalysis
psychotropic drugs
secondary prevention
stimulants
substance use disorder
suicide
tertiary prevention

Discussion Questions

1. Discuss the problems in defining mental illness. Give a recent example from the media that exemplifies the complexity of how mental illness is defined.

2. Do you agree with Szasz's concept of mental health? Discuss your rationale for either agreeing or disagreeing.

3. Identify the major revolutions in the field of mental health. What do you predict will be the next revolution?

4. What is your definition of someone who misuses alcohol or other drugs? Identify at least three factors at each level of the environment that can place an individual at risk to become an alcoholic or a drug addict.

5. What are some of the diverse types of disability that people experience today? How does the use of the term *disability* contrast with previously used terminology to identify those within this category?

6. Discuss the advantages and disadvantages of deinstitutionalization. What are your thoughts about hospitalization versus community-based care?

7. How have the media portrayed people with emotional problems, addictions, and intellectual and other types of disabilities? Compare the portrayals in two popular films. What messages do these portrayals send to individuals with similar characteristics? To the general public about individuals with these characteristics?

8. Identify some of the roles that social workers who work with persons who are mentally ill, persons recovering from using alcohol and/or other drugs, or persons with a disability might play. Which of these career opportunities interests you the most, and why?

9. Identify at least three provisions of the Patient Protection and Affordable Care Act that are of particular interest to people living with a mental disability, a physical or intellectual disability, or an addiction, and their families. Give at least two examples of how each of these provisions provides consumer protections for people from this population.

10. How do you think scientific breakthroughs will shape the future of services for persons with mental illness, disabilities, and addictions? How do you think the roles of social workers might change as a result?

On the Internet

http://www.nami.org
http://www.cms.gov
http://www.apa.org
http://www.mentalhealth.gov
http://samhsa.gov
http://www.naswdc.org
http://www.ddrcco.com
http://www.nrchmi.samhsa.gov

References

Alcoholism and Drug Addiction Help. (2013). *Definition of alcoholism.* Retrieved from http://www.alcoholism-and-drug-addiction-help.com/definition-of-alcoholism.html

American Association of Suicidology. (2009). *Suicide statistics.* Washington, DC: Author. Retrieved July 19, 2010, from www. suicidology.org

American Foundation for Suicide Prevention. (2014). *Facts and figures.* Retrieved from http://www.afsp.org/understanding-suicide/facts-and-figures

American Psychological Association. (2010). *Alzheimer's.* Washington, DC: Author. Retrieved July 19, 2010, from http://www.apa.org/topics/alzheimers/index.aspx

American Society of Addiction Medicine. (2011). *The definition of addiction.* Chevy Chase, MD: Author.

Arc. (2009). *Developmental disabilities.* Silver Spring, MD: Author. Retrieved July 19, 2010, from www.thearc.org

Barth, R., Lloyd, E., Casanueva, C., Scarborough, A., Losby, J., & Mann, T. (2008). *Developmental status and early intervention service needs of maltreated children.* Washington, DC: Institute for Social and Economic Development.

Battisa, S. (2014). *New trends in mental health treatment.* Arlington, VA: National Alliance on Mental Illness. Retrieved from http://www.nami.org/Template.cfm?Section=Top_Story&template=/contentmanagement/contentdisplay.cfm&ContentID=158934

Bear, M., & Conners, B. (2006). *Neuroscience: Exploring the brain* (3rd ed.). Philadelphia: Lippincott, Williams & Wilkins.

Beers, C. W. (2004). *A mind that found itself.* Whitefish, MT: Kessinger.

Berk, L. (2014). *Development through the lifespan* (6th ed.). Boston: Pearson.

Bernston, G., & Cacioppo, J. (2009). *Handbook of neuroscience.* New York: Wiley.

Block, L. (2009). *Stereotypes about people with disabilities.* Retrieved July 19, 2010, from http://facsimile-magazine.com\2009\04\index.html

Brooker, C., & Repper, J. (Eds.). (2008). *Mental health: From policy to practice.* Bel Air, CA: Churchill-Livingstone.

Brummett, B. H., Boyle, S. H., Siegler, I. C., et al., (2008). Effects of environmental stress and gender on associations among symptoms of depression and the serotonin transporter gene linked polymorphic region (5-HTTlPR). *Behavioral Genetics, 38,* 34–43.

Bureau of Labor Statistics. (2014). *Occupational outlook handbook: Social workers.* Retrieved from http://www.bls.gov/ooh/community-and-social-service/social-workers.htm

Carmona, R., Giannini, M., Bergmark, B., & Cabe, J. (2010). The Surgeon General's call to action to improve the health and welfare of persons with disabilities: History, research, rationale, and implications 5 years after publication. *Disability and Health Journal, 3*(4), 229–232.

Caspi, A. (2003). *Gene more than doubles risk of depression following life stresses.* Bethesda, MD: National Institute of Mental Health.

Castaneda, C., Hopkins, L., & Peters, M. (2013). *Ableism: Introduction.* In M. Adams, W. Blumenfeld, C. Castaneda, H. Hackman, M. Peters, & X. Zuniga (Eds.), *Readings for diversity and social justice* (3rd ed., pp. 461–468). New York: Routledge.

Centers for Disease Control and Prevention. (2009). *Fetal alcohol spectrum disorders.* Washington, DC: Author. Retrieved from cdc.gov/ncbddd/fas/faqs.htm

Centers for Disease Control and Prevention. (2013). *Mental health basics.* Retrieved from www.cdc.gov/mentalhealth/basics/htm

Centers for Disease Control and Prevention. (2014a). *Substance abuse and mental disorders: Early diagnosis, prevention, and treatment: Healthy People 2020 update.* Retrieved from http://www.cdc.gov/nchs/ppt/hp2020/hp2020_MH_MD_and_SA_progress_review_presentation.pdf

Centers for Disease Control and Prevention. (2014b). *Suicide prevention.* Retrieved from http://www.cdc.gov/ViolencePrevention/suicide/

Charney, D., & Nestler, E. (2008). *Neurobiology of mental illness* (3rd ed.). New York: Oxford University Press.

Child Welfare Information Gateway. (2009a). *Parental substance use and the child welfare system*. Retrieved from http://www.childwelfare.gov/pubs/factsheets/parentalabuse.cfm

Child Welfare Information Gateway. (2009b). *Understanding the effects of maltreatment on brain development*. Retrieved from https://www.childwelfare.gov/pubs/issue_briefs/brain_development/

Cleaver, H., Nicholson, D., Tarr, S., & Cleaver, D. (2007). *Child protection, domestic violence and parental substance misuse: Family experiences and effective practice*. London: Kingsley.

Coleman, M. (2013). *DSM-5 is coming*. Washington, DC: NASW. Retrieved from http://socialworkers.org/practice/clinical/2013/051013.asp

CommonHealth. (2013). *At the White House, learning how not to talk about addiction*. Retrieved from commonhealth/wbur.org/2013/language-substance-abuse-addiction

Corcoran, J., & Walsh, J. (2012). *Mental health in social work: A casebook on diagnosis and strengths-based assessment*. Upper Saddle River, NJ: Pearson.

de Haan, M., & Gunnar, M. (2009). *Handbook of developmental social neuroscience*. New York: Guilford.

Deutsch, A. (1949). *Shame of the states*. New York: Columbia University Press.

Developmental Disabilities Assistance and Bill of Rights Act, Pub. L No. 98527, Title V (1984).

Dumont, S., & St-Onge, M. (Eds.). (2007). *Social work and global mental health: Research and practice perspectives*. New York: Haworth.

Dziegielewski, S. (2010). *DSM-IV-TR in action*. Hoboken, NJ: Wiley.

Elliott, C., & Metcalf, L. (Eds.). (2009). *The art of solution focused therapy*. New York: Springer.

El-Mallakh, P. (2007). Doing my best: Poverty and self care among individuals with schizophrenia and diabetes mellitus. *Archives of Psychiatric Nursing, 21*, 49–60.

Erickson, C. (2007). *The science of addiction: From neurobiology to treatment*. New York: Norton.

Erickson, P., & Erickson, S. (Eds.). (2008). *Crime, punishment, and mental illness: Law and the behavioral sciences in conflict*. New Brunswick, NJ: Rutgers University Press.

Felix, R. (1967). *Mental illness: Progress and prospects*. New York: Columbia University Press.

Fisher, G., & Roget, N. (Eds.). (2008). *Encyclopedia of substance abuse prevention, treatment, and recovery*. Thousand Oaks, CA: Sage.

Flint, J., Greenspan, R., & Kendler, K. (2010). *How genes influence behavior*. New York: Oxford University Press.

Frank, R., & Glied, S. (2006). *Better, but not well: Mental health policy in the United States*. Baltimore: Johns Hopkins University Press.

Franklin, C. (2014). *Changes in the DSM-5: What social workers need to know*. Encyclopedia of Social Work Online. Oxford University Press. Retrieved from http://blog.oup.com/2014/03/changes-in-the-dsm-5-what-social-workers-need-to-know/

Gostin, L., McHale, J., Fennell, P., Mackey, R., & Bartlett, P. (2010). *Principles of mental health law*. New York: Oxford University Press.

Gould, N. (2009). *Mental health social work in context*. London: Routledge.

Grob, G., & Goldman, H. (2006). *The dilemma of federal mental health policy: Radical reform or incremental change?* New Brunswick, NJ: Rutgers University Press.

Harmon-Jones, E., & Beer, J. (2009). *Methods in social neuroscience*. New York: Guilford.

Heather, N., & Stockwell, T. (Eds.). (2003). *The essential handbook of treatment and prevention of alcohol problems*. Hoboken, NJ: Wiley.

Hien, D., Litt, L., Cohen, L., Miele, G., & Campbell, A. (2008). *Trauma services for women in substance abuse treatment: An integrated approach*. Washington, DC: American Psychological Association.

Holleran-Steiker, L. & Counihan, C. (2014). *Implementing a sober high school: A case study*. Austin: University of Texas at Austin.

Howkidsdevelop. (2010). *What are the risk factors for developmental delay?* San Diego, CA: Author. Retrieved July 19, 2010, from http://www.howkidsdevelop.com/developDevDelay.html#riskFactors

Institute on Women and Substance Abuse. (2003). *Women and substance abuse*. Lexington: University of Kentucky Center on Drug and Alcohol Research. Retrieved from http://www.uky.edu/RGS/CDAR/IOWASA/abuse

Jacobs, N., Kenis, G., Peeters, F., Derom, C., Vlietnick, R., & van Os, J. (2006). Stress-related negative affectivity and genetically altered serotonin transporter function. *Archives of General Psychiatry, 63*, 989–996.

Juhnke, G., & Hagedorn, B. (2006). *Counseling addicted families: An integrated assessment and treatment model.* London: Routledge.

Karls, J. M., & O'Keefe, M. (2008). *Person-in-environment system manual* (2nd ed.). Washington, DC: NASW Press.

Karls, J. M., & Wandrei, K. E. (1994). *Person-in-environment system: The PIE classification system for social functioning problems.* Washington, DC: NASW Press.

Keller, M., Neale, M., & Kendler, K. (2007). Association of different adverse life events with distinct patterns of depressive symptoms. *American Journal of Psychiatry, 164,* 1521–1529.

Kesey, K. (1962). *One flew over the cuckoo's nest.* New York: New American Library.

Khantzian, E., & Albanese, M. (2008). *Understanding addiction as self medication: Finding hope behind the pain.* Lanham, MD: Rowman & Littlefield.

Klein, G. (2009). *Law and the disordered: An explanation in mental health, law, and practice.* Lanham, MD: University Press of America.

Koob, G., & Le Moal, M. (2006). *Neurobiology of addiction.* London: Academic Press.

Kuruvilla, A., & Jacob, K. (2007). Poverty, social stress, and mental health. *Indian Journal of Medical Research, 126,* 273–278.

Lichtenberg, P. (2010). *Handbook of assessment in clinical gerontology* (2nd ed.). Maryland Heights, MO: Academic Press.

Licinio, J., & Wong, M. (2005). *Biology of depression: From novel insights to therapeutic strategies.* Hoboken, NJ: Wiley.

Lin, A. (1995). Mental health overview. In *Encyclopedia of social work* (19th ed., Vol. 2, pp. 1705–1711). Silver Spring, MD: NASW Press.

Linhorst, D. (2005). *Empowering people with severe mental illness: A practical guide.* New York: Oxford University Press.

Loeppke, R., Taitel, M., Haufle, V., Parry, T., Kessler, R. C., & Jinnett, K. (2009). Health and productivity as a business strategy: A multiemployer study. *Journal of Occupational and Environmental Medicine, 51*(4), 411–428.

Macdonald, A. (2007). *Solution-focused therapy: Theory, research & practice.* Thousand Oaks, CA: Sage.

Mattlin, B. (2010, July 26). Looking back on 20 years of disability rights. *NPR.* Retrieved July 19, 2010, from http://www.npr.org/templates/story/story.php?storyId=128697147

Mechanic, D. (1999). *Mental health and social policy: The emergence of managed care* (4th ed.). Boston: Allyn & Bacon.

Mechanic, D. (2007). *Mental health and social policy: Beyond managed care* (5th ed.). Boston: Allyn & Bacon.

Mechanic, D. (2008). *The truth about health care: Why reform is not working in America.* New Brunswick, NJ: Rutgers University Press.

Mental Health America. (2010). *Position statement 22: Involuntary mental health treatment.* Alexandria, VA: Author. Retrieved July 19, 2010, from http://www.mha.org/go/position-statements/p-36

Meschede, T. (2009). *Bridges and barriers to housing for homeless street dwellers: The impact of health and substance abuse services on housing.* Saarbruken, Germany: VDM Verlag.

Meyers, R. (Ed.). (2008). *Neurobiology: From molecular basis to disease.* Hoboken, NJ: Wiley.

Miller, G. (2010). Beyond DSM: Seeking a brain-based classification of mental illness. *Science, 327*(5972), 1437.

National Alliance on Mental Illness. (2009a). *Grading the states: A report on America's health care system for serious mental illness.* Arlington, VA: Author.

National Alliance on Mental Illness. (2009b). *What is mental illness? Mental illness facts.* Arlington, VA: Author. Retrieved from http://www.nami.org/Content/NavigationMenu/Inform_Your-self/About_Mental_Illness/About_Mental_Illness.htm

National Alliance on Mental Illness. (2010). *The new health care reform law: What it means for people living with mental illness.* Arlington, VA: Author. Retrieved July 19, 2010, from http://www.nami.org/Content/Groups/Policy/Issues/T

National Alliance on Mental Illness. (2013). *Mental illness: Facts and numbers.* Arlington, VA: Author.

National Alliance on Mental Illness. (2014). *Schizophrenia.* Arlington, VA: Author. Retrieved from http://www.nami.org/Template.cfm?Section=schizophrenia9

National Alliance to End Homelessness. (2014). *About homelessness.* Washington, DC: Author. Retrieved from http://www.endhomelessness.org/pages/about_homelessness

National Association of Children of Alcoholics. (2010). *Children of alcoholics: Important facts.* Rockville, MD: Author. Retrieved from www.ncacoa.net/impfacts.htm

National Association of Social Workers. (2003). *Joint initiative of mental health professional organizations—mental health bill of rights project: Principles for the provision of mental health and substance abuse treatment services.* Washington, DC: Author. Retrieved from http://www.social workers.org/practice/behavioral_health/mental .asp

National Center for Post Traumatic Stress Disorder. (2014). *How common is PTSD?* Washington, DC: U.S. Department of Veterans Affairs. Retrieved from http://www.ptsd.va.gov/public/PTSD-over view/basics/how-common-is-ptsd.asp

National Center on Education, Disability and Juvenile Justice. (2010). *Levels of prevention.* Retrieved July 19, 2010, from http://www.edjj.org/focus/preven -tion/LevelsPrevention.html

National Coalition Against Domestic Violence. (2014). *Domestic violence and substance abuse.* Retrieved from http://www.ncadv.org/files/SubstanceAbuse .pdf

National Coalition for the Homeless. (2014). *Homelessness in America.* Washington, DC: Author. Retrieved from http://nationalhomeless.org/about -homelessness/

National Highway Traffic Safety Administration. (2014). *Traffic safety facts: 2012 data.* Washington, DC: Author.

National Institute on Alcohol Abuse and Alcoholism. (2009). *The scope of the problem.* Bethesda, MD: Author. Retrieved from http://www.pubs.niaa.nih .gov/publications/arh283/111-120.htm

National Institute on Alcohol Abuse and Alcoholism. (2010). *What is alcoholism?* Bethesda, MD: Author. Retrieved from http://www.niaa.nih.gov/FAQs /General-English/FAQ1.htm

National Institute on Drug Abuse. (2009). *Drug treatment facts.* Bethesda, MD: Author.

National Institute on Drug Abuse. (2012). *Drug Facts: Spice (Synthetic marijuana).* Bethesda, MD: Author. Retrieved from www.drugabuse.gov/publications /drugfacts/spice-synthetic-marijuana

National Institute of Mental Health. (2009a). *Depression.* Washington, DC: Author. Available from http://www.nimh.nih.gov

National Institute of Mental Health. (2009b). *Suicide in the U.S.: Statistics and prevention.* Washington, DC: Author. Retrieved from http://www.nimh.gov /publicat/harmsway.cfm

National Institute of Mental Health. (2010a). *Suicide in America: Frequently asked questions.* Rockville, MD: Author. Retrieved from http://www.nimh.nih.gov /health/publications/suicide-in-america/index.shtml

National Institute of Mental Health. (2010b). *The numbers count.* Washington, DC: Author. Retrieved from http://www.nimh.nih.gov/healthin-formation /statisticsmenu.fcm

National Institute of Mental Health. (2014a). *Any mental illness (AMI) among adults.* Rockville, MD: Author.

National Institute of Mental Health. (2014b). *Brain basics.* Retrieved from http://www.nimh.nih.gov /health/educational-resources/brain-basics/brain-basics .shtml

National Institute of Mental Health. (2014c). *Depression.* Washington, DC: Author. Retrieved from http://www.nimh.nih.gov/health/topics/depression /index.shtml

National Institute of Mental Health. (2014d). *Depression in children and adolescents (fact sheet).* Washington, DC: Author. Retrieved from www.nimh.nih.gov /health/publications/depression-in-children-and-adole scents/index.shtml

National Institute of Mental Health. (2014e). *Serious mental illness (SMI) among adults.* Rockville, MD: Author.

National Resource and Training Center on Homelessness and Mental Illness. (2014). *Current statistics on the prevalence and characteristics of people experiencing homelessness in the United States.* Washington, DC: Author. Retrieved from http:// homeless.samhsa.gov/Channel/HRC-Facts-Character istics-and-Prevalence-of-Homelessness-556.aspx

National Rural Health Alliance. (2009). *Fact sheet #9: The state of rural health.* Retrieved from http://www .ruralhealth.org.au.

Nauert, R. (2014). Comparing adverse effects of marijuana, alcohol. *PsychCentral.* Retrieved from psychcentral.com/news/2014/09/03/comparing-adverse -effects-of-marijuana-alcohol/74450.html

Nicklett, E., & Burgard, S. (2008). Downward social mobility and major depressive episodes among Latino and Asian-American immigrants to the United States. *American Journal of Epidemiology, 170,* 793–801.

Niklova, Y. S., Koenen, K., Galea, S., Wang, C.-M., Seney, M., Sibille, E., et al. (2014). Beyond genotype: serotonin transporter epigenetic modification predicts human brain function. *Nature Neuroscience*. Retrieved from www.nature.com/neuro/journal/vaop/ncurrent/full/nn.3778.html

Odom, S., Horner, R., Snell, M., & Blacher, J. (Eds.). (2009). *Handbook of developmental disabilities*. New York: Guilford.

Ostrowsky, M. (2008). *Self-medication and violent behavior*. El Paso, TX: LFB Scholarly Publishing.

Pfeiffer, M. B. (2007). *Crazy in America*. New York: Basic Books.

Phillips, P., McKeown, O., & Sandford, T. (Eds.). (2009). *Dual diagnosis: Practice in context*. Hoboken, NJ: Wiley.

Phoenix House. (2010). *Drug facts*. New York: Author. Retrieved from http://www.phoenix-house.org/National/DrugFacts/drugfacts

Plows, A. (2010). *Debating human genetics: Contemporary issues in public policy and ethics*. London: Routledge.

Presidential Commission on Mental Health. (1978). *Report of the Presidential Commission on Mental Health*. Washington, DC: Government Printing Office.

Reardon, C. (2014). DSM-5—deviate, soul searching, changes. *Social Work Today*, 3(10), 10. Retrieved from www.socialworktoday.com/archie/051214p.10.shtml

Rosenberg, J., & Rosenberg, S. (Eds.). (2006). *Community mental health: Challenges for the 21st century*. London: Routledge.

Rosenhan, D. (1973). On being sane in insane places. *Science*, *179*, 240–248.

Ruiz, R. (2014). How childhood trauma could be mistaken for ADHD. *The Atlantic*. Retrieved from http://www.theatlantic.com/health/archive/2014/07/how-childhood-trauma-could-be-mistaken-for-adhd/373328/

Seager, S. (2000). *Street crazy*. La Quinta, CA: Westcom.

Sensen, C. (Ed.). (2005). *Handbook of genome research, two volume set: Genomics, proteomics, metabolomics, bioinformatics, ethical and legal issues*. New York: Wiley-VCH.

Slobogin, C. (2007). The Supreme Court's recent criminal mental health cases. *Criminal Justice*, *22*(3), 1–8.

Special Olympics. (2003). *Multinational study of attitudes: Groundbreaking international study reveals stereotypical views greatest barriers to better quality of life for individuals with intellectual disabilities*. Washington, DC: Author. Retrieved July 19, 2010, from http://www.specialolympics.org/Special+Olympics+Public+Website/English/Press

Stagman, S., & Cooper, J. (2010). *Children's mental health: What every policy maker should know*. New York: National Center for Children in Poverty, Columbia University.

Straussner, S., & Fewell, C. (Eds.). (2006). *Impact of substance abuse on children and families: Research and practice implications*. London: Routledge.

Substance Abuse and Mental Health Services Administration. (2006). *Transforming mental health care in America*. Rockville, MD: Author. Retrieved from http://www.samhsa.gov/Federalactiona-genda/NFC_execsum.sapx

Substance Abuse and Mental Health Services Administration. (2008a). *Impact of hurricanes Katrina and Rita on substance use and mental health*. Rockville, MD: Author.

Substance Abuse and Mental Health Services Administration. (2008b). *Quantity and frequency of alcohol use among underage drinkers*. Rockville, MD: Author.

Substance Abuse and Mental Health Services Administration. (2010). *National survey reveals 45.1 million adults in the U.S. experienced mental illness in the past year*. Retrieved from www.samhsa.gov/newsroom/advisories/1011180411.aspx

Substance Abuse and Mental Health Services Administration. (2011). *Current statistics on the prevalence and characteristics of people experiencing homelessness in the United States*. Washington, DC: Author.

Substance Abuse and Mental Health Services Administration. (2014a). *Substance use and mental health estimates from the 2013 National Survey on Drug Use and Health: Overview of findings*. Washington, DC: Author. Retrieved from www.samhsa.gov/data/2k14/DSDUH200/sr200-findings-overview-2014htm

Substance Abuse and Mental Health Services Administration. (2014b). *Trauma and "trauma informed" care*. Rockville, MD: Author. Retrieved from http://beta.samhsa.gov/samhsaNewsLetter/Volume_22_Number_2/trauma_tip/

Szasz, T. (1998). Myth of mental illness. In H. Friedman, R. Schwarzer, R. Cohen Silver, D. Spiegel, N. Adler, R. Parke, & C. Peterson (Eds.), *Encyclopedia of mental health* (Vol. 2, pp. 743–752). New York: Academic Press.

Szasz, T. (2008). *Psychiatry: The science of lies.* Syracuse, NY: Syracuse University Press.

Szasz, T. (2009). *Antipsychiatry: Quackery squared. (2009).* Syracuse, NY: Syracuse University Press.

Szasz, T. (2010). *The myth of mental illness: Foundations of a theory of personal conduct.* New York: Harper Perennial.

Thyer, B., & Wodarski, J. (Eds.). (2007). *Social work in mental health: An evidence-based approach.* Hoboken, NJ: Wiley.

Traustadottir, R., & Johnson, K. (Eds.). (2008). *Deinstitutionalization and people with intellectual disabilities: In and out of institutions.* London: Kingsley.

U.S. Department of Health and Human Services. (2005). *U.S. Surgeon General issues first call to action on disability.* Washington, DC: U.S. Government Printing Office. Retrieved from Substance Abuse and Mental Health Services Administration Website: http://www.surgeon-general.gov

U.S. Interagency Council on Homelessness. (2014). *Substance abuse.* Washington, DC: Author. Retrieved from http://usich.gov/issue/substance_abuse/

U.S. Senate Subcommittee on Long-Term Care. (1976). *Hearings on long-term care.* Washington, DC: U.S. Department of Health, Education, and Welfare.

Valverde, C. (Ed.). (2010). *Genetic screening of newborns: An ethical inquiry.* Hauppauge, NY: Nova Science.

van Wormer, K. S., & Thyer, B. (2009). *Evidence-based practice in the field of substance abuse: A book of readings.* Thousand Oaks, CA: Sage.

Veterans Administration. (n.d.). *Prosthetics and related technology.* Washington, DC: Veterans Administration Research and Development Program. Retrieved from http://www.research.va.gov/resources/pubs/docs/prosthetics-brochure.pdf

Wendell, S. (2013). The social construction of disability. In M. Adams, W. Blumenfeld, C. Castaneda, H. Hackman, M. Peters, & X. Zuniga (Eds.), *Readings for diversity and social justice* (3rd ed., pp. 481–485). New York: Routledge.

Willhelm, K., Niven, H., Finch, A., & Wedgwood, L. (2006). Life events, first depression onset and the serotonin transporter gene. *British Journal of Psychiatry, 188,* 210–215.

World Health Organization (WHO). (2014). *First WHO world suicide report—preventing suicide: A global imperative.* Geneva, Switzerland: Author.

Suggested Readings

Abbott, A. (Ed.). (2010). *Alcohol, tobacco, and other drugs: Challenging myths, assessing theories, individualizing interventions* (2nd ed.). Washington, DC: NASW Press.

Applegate, J., & Shapiro, J. (2005). *Neurobiology for clinical social work: theory and practice.* New York: Norton.

Barsky, A. (2005). *Alcohol, other drugs, and addictions: A professional development manual for social workers and the human services.* Belmont, CA: Cengage.

Bentley, K., & Walsh, J. (2013). *The social worker and psychotropic medication: Toward effective collaboration with clients, families, and providers.* Belmont, CA: Cengage.

Bigby, C., & Frawley, P. (2011). *Social work practice and intellectual disability: Working to support change.* New York: Palgrave Macmillan.

Cohen, D., & Cichetti, D. (Eds.). (2006). *Developmental neuroscience.* Hoboken, NJ: Wiley.

Eshun, S., & Genung, R. (Eds.). (2009). *Culture and mental health: Sociocultural influences on theory and practice.* Hoboken, NJ: Wiley-Blackwell.

Fisher, G., & Harrison, T. (2012). *Substance abuse: Information for school counselors, social workers, therapists, and counselors* (5th ed.). Boston: Pearson.

Garland, E. (2013). *Mindfulness-oriented recovery enhancement for addiction, stress, and pain.* Washington, DC: NASW Press.

Gould, N. (2009). *Mental health social work in context.* Florence, KY: Routledge.

Johnson, W. (Ed.). (2010). *Social work with African American males: health, mental health, and social policy.* New York: Oxford University Press.

Karban, K. (2011). *Social work and mental health.* Boston: Polity.

Luby, J. L. (2006). *Handbook of preschool mental health development, disorders, and treatment.* New York: Guilford Press.

National Institute on Alcohol and Alcohol Abuse. (2006). *The cool spot.* Bethesda, MD: Author. Retrieved from http://www.thecoolspot.gov

Rothman, J. (2002). *Social work practice across disability.* Boston: Pearson.

Rovinelli Heller, N., & Gitterman, A. (2010). *Mental health and social problems: A social work perspective.* New York: Routledge.

Sands, R., & Gelliz, Z. (2011). *Clinical social work practice in behavioral mental health: Toward evidence-based practice* (3rd ed.). Boston: Pearson.

Siegel, A., & Zakman, S. (2008). *The neuroimmunological basis of behavior and mental disorders.* New York: Springer.

Springer, D., & Robert, A. (2007). *Handbook of forensic mental health with victims and offenders: Assessment, treatment, and research.* New York: Springer.

Strausser, S. (2013). *Clinical work with substance abusing clients* (3rd ed.). New York: Guilford.

Vaughn, M., & Perron, B. (2013). *Social practice in addictions.* New York: Springer.

CHAPTER 10

The Needs of Children, Youth, and Families

Divorced for 2 years, Ernestine Moore is struggling to survive. Her five children are in a foster home while she tries to stabilize her life. Ernestine is looking forward to the day when she and her children can live together as a family again.

Ernestine comes from a large family. Her father drinks often and beats her mother, her siblings, and Ernestine herself. Pregnant at age 16 and afraid of her father, she eloped with the father of her child, a 19-year-old high school drop-out, James Moore, who worked at a fast-food restaurant. The first year was fairly peaceful for the new family, although lack of financial resources was a continual problem. Both James and Ernestine were excited about the baby, and Ernestine worked hard to provide a good home for her husband and baby. She wanted desperately to have the kind of home and family she had not had as a child.

During the next 6 years, Ernestine and James had three more children. One of the children had developmental disabilities, which added to the financial pressures, and life became increasingly stressful. James began to drink heavily and started to beat Ernestine. He also physically and verbally abused the children. When Ernestine became pregnant with their fifth child, James left her. Since that time, he has paid child support for only 6 months.

After James left, Ernestine moved in with a sister, who has three children of her own. To support her children and contribute to the rent her sister was paying, Ernestine got two jobs—one during the day at a fast-food restaurant and one at night, cleaning a bank. Shortly after her new baby was born, this arrangement ended because of continual arguments between the two sisters over money, space, and child rearing.

At that point Ernestine moved into a low-rent apartment of her own. She also applied for low-income housing and, although she was eligible, she was told there was a 2-year waiting list. Ernestine hired a teenage girl to care for her children while she worked. Tired and overwhelmed, Ernestine had little time or energy left to devote to her children and became increasingly abusive toward them. The older children fell behind in school and fought continually. Then they began to steal and vandalize. Neighbors in the apartment complex saw the younger children outside at all hours, unsupervised, often wearing only diapers. The neighbors heard screaming and the baby crying throughout the night.

The babysitter quit because Ernestine fell behind in paying her. After Ernestine missed 2 days of work while she tried desperately to find another sitter, she was fired from her fast-food job. Afraid that she also would lose her cleaning job, she began to put the younger children to bed at 6 o'clock and leave the oldest child (age 9) in charge until she returned home.

Ernestine and her children were evicted from the apartment because of failure to pay the rent, and for 2 weeks the entire family slept in a friend's van. Finally, when the oldest child came to school with bruises, complaining of a sore arm, she revealed the family's living situation to her teacher when asked about the bruises. The school called the local child protective services agency. When the social worker arrived, she observed the bruises and obvious malnourishment of the children. When the social worker talked with Ernestine, it was apparent that Ernestine was overwhelmed and angry and that she felt extremely guilty about what had happened to her children.

The children were placed in foster care with an older, nurturing couple. With more structure and a stable living situation, the children began doing better in school and were able to develop some positive relationships with others. Ernestine visited the children often and began to see the foster parents as caring people who almost seemed like parents to her.

Ernestine enrolled in a job-training program and was hired as a health-care aide for a local nursing home. She enjoys her job and is talking about getting her high school equivalency certificate and going to nursing school. Her social worker encouraged her to join Parents Anonymous, a support group for abusive parents. For the first time, Ernestine has developed positive, trusting relationships with others. She has located affordable housing, and she and her social worker are making plans to have the children return home permanently.

The family is considered to be the most significant social system within which all individuals function. Traditionally, the family has been looked upon as a safe, protective haven where its members can receive nurturing, love, and support. In today's complex and rapidly changing world, however, families are encountering more difficulties. Increasingly, children are affected by the family's financial pressures, the need for one or both parents to work long hours, or the physical or mental illness of a family member.

Unable to cope with the pressures, family members often turn to alcohol or other drugs, resort to violence, or withdraw from other family members. Sometimes, because they did not grow up in a loving, nurturing environment, they are unable to provide a healthy environment for their own children. Sometimes parents do not know how to provide for their children because they have not learned what children need or what to expect

from them at various ages. Many parents are emotionally unable to meet the needs of other family members during a crisis, such as a serious illness or death.

How well a family is able to meet the needs of its members also depends on other systems with which the family interacts—the neighborhood, community, and broader society. The quality and consistency of these interactions have a tremendous impact on the family's well-being. Many experts who work with children and families suggest that attention to these broader systems is essential to effective intervention with families (Bronfenbrenner, 1979, 2005; Duncan & Goddard, 2005; Garbarino, 1992, 2009; Maynard & Martini, 2005; McKenry & Price, 2005; Powell & Cassidy, 2005; Yuen, Skibinski, & Pardeck, 2003).

A family that functions within an unsupportive environment is much more susceptible to family problems than one that functions within a supportive environment.

If the family lives in a community that provides few family supports, that also may threaten the family's well-being. Consider Ernestine's situation. Abused as a child, her emotional needs were not met and she learned to distrust others. This left her feeling worthless and inadequate. Individuals with low self-esteem are more likely to become pregnant at an early age. They also are more likely than other parents to abuse their children. Ernestine also learned from her own parents to deal with anger by hitting. And life with an alcoholic father taught Ernestine many dysfunctional behavior patterns that she carried into her own life.

In this chapter we consider general issues and trends involving the needs of children, youth, and families; the types and extent of problems that influence children and adolescents and their families; and factors that place families at risk for encountering problems. Chapter 11 builds on this chapter, detailing services and policies that prevent or alleviate problems of children, youth, and families, as well as the roles of social workers in providing these services and developing and implementing these policies. While all of the issues covered in this book are important to understand as social workers, we have included two chapters on children and families because many issues, if not addressed during childhood, result in intergenerational problems for families as children grow up and have their own families.

What Is a Family?

EP 2.1.7a

All families have strengths as well as different ways of coping. No matter how many strengths a family has, however, the impact (past and present) of the broader environment may make it difficult, if not impossible, for the family to cope with crisis without additional support. Actually, all families need support beyond the family to survive and to reinforce their internal strengths. The African saying, "It takes a village to raise a child" is perhaps more true today than ever before.

The typical American family in the 1950s, 1960s, and 1970s consisted of a husband, a wife, and two or more children. Today's families are much more diverse. In 2012, almost one-fourth of children 17 and under were living with their mothers in single parent households, while almost ten percent lived in a household with that included a step-parent (Federal Interagency Forum on Child and Family Statistics, 2013).

Many family households today include extended family members—grandparents, aunts, uncles, or cousins. Some families include lesbian, gay, bisexual, or transgender parents, while some include adopted or foster children. A growing number of individuals not related by blood or marriage are living together. Some families are headed by one or more grandparents who assume parenting responsibilities because one of their own children is unable or unwilling to do so—a practice referred to as *second-time parenting* (DiSciullo & Dunifon, 2012). In 2012, More than 1.5 million children in the United States were living in households in which grandparents were responsible for their care; of the 4% of children not living with parents, about 55% were living with their grandparents (Federal Interagency Forum on Child and Family Statistics, 2013).

Two popular television shows portray the diversity of today's families. *Modern Family* portrays three diverse interrelated families: a white husband and wife and their three teenage children in a more traditional family constellation; the wife's brother and his male partner and their adopted Vietnamese daughter; and the father of the two now-adult siblings, his much younger wife who is Latina, her middle-school age son, and the couple's new baby. *The Fosters* is about a lesbian couple and their family that includes one of the woman's teenage birth son, two Latino teenagers who are adopted, two foster children middle and high school age they are trying to adopt, and a baby, the result of a male sperm donor, on the way. Positive reaction to these acclaimed programs from the public has been more about the authenticity of typical situations experienced by any family rather than the personal categorizations of the family members.

As you can see from the examples above, families today are diverse. In fact, some would argue that it is not possible to come up with a standard definition of a **family**. Others provide a broad definition of a family, exemplified by Crosson-Tower (2014) as "any group of individuals who live together (or at least have regular contact) and who are expected to perform specific functions, especially in reference to the children involved" (p. 25).

When discussing the needs of children and families, a *family* is referred to within the context of a parent figure or figures and at least one child. Perhaps the most important issue in relation to what constitutes a family is that no two families are alike. Each family may be viewed as its own unique system.

How Are Families of Today Viewed?

EP 2.1.7a

Two of the most relevant frameworks for considering the family in the context of the social welfare system are the *ecological/systems framework* and the *life-span development framework*. The ecological/systems framework emphasizes the interactions between family members and other levels of the environment, including extended family members, the neighborhood, the school, places of worship, the workplace, the community, the state, and other larger systems such as the economic system and the political system. (This framework and the life-span development framework are discussed in Chapter 3.)

The family as a social system has more impact on the individual than any other system throughout the life cycle. Even before birth, the physical and emotional health of the family in which the child will be born and the environment in which the family functions affect the child's future significantly. How well individuals learn to trust others, develop autonomy, take initiative, be industrious, have a positive identity, be intimate with others, give something of themselves back to others, and face death with integrity all are shaped extensively by relationships within the family.

Families, too, go through distinct stages of development (Crosson-Tower, 2014). McGoldrick, Carter, and Garcia-Preto (2011) discuss the following stages in the life cycle of a family that includes children:

1. unattached young adult,
2. courtship and early marriage/long-term relationship,
3. transition to parenthood and care of young children,
4. raising adolescents,
5. launching the children and moving on, and
6. later life, including involvement in the next generation of marriage/long-term relationship and parenting.

Although the stages delineated above are typical of many families across the globe, the life cycle of a family is not a fixed progression. Divorces or death of a parent and remarriage; children moving back home, sometimes with their own children; and parents raising their grandchildren all change the life cycle of a family.

In fact, McGoldrick, Carter, and Garcia-Preto (2011) have identified specific changes characteristic of divorced families and families involving the remarriage of a parent. Additionally, some individuals choose not to be in long-term relationships or do not have children. Regardless of its constellation, every family undergoes changes as its members grow and change, and the family's needs and interactions with the social welfare system will differ according to the family's stage of development at the time.

What Is a Healthy Family?

EP 2.1.7a

All families go through some sort of problem at some point during the family life cycle, but some families are better able to cope with family problems because of the availability of financial resources and social support systems and the strong physical and mental health of family members. In any case, though, a major crisis—no matter how healthy the family is—will have a serious impact on the family and is likely to result in at least a temporary need for some kind of assistance from the social welfare system.

Among the factors associated with healthy families are the opportunity to express ideas and feelings, the absence of family secrets, valuing of everyone's opinions and feelings, rules that are flexible yet enforced with consistency, positive energy, and regular opportunities for growth and change. Children are more likely to grow up to be successful adults if, as a child, they have a positive, nurturing relationship with at least one caregiver; consistent parenting, particularly during their first year of life; well-balanced discipline; at least a 2-year separation in age between siblings; and access to others who can provide emotional support if their immediate families cannot do so (Newman & Newman, 2012).

How Are Family Problems Defined?

EP 2.1.7a
EP 2.1.7b

What constitutes a family problem depends on the perspective of the individual defining the problem. It also depends on factors such as the cultural context within which the problem takes place, community norms and values, attitudes and professional values of the person defining the problem, legal definitions of the problem, and the availability of resources to address the problem.

Cultural Context   Cultural attitudes, values, and practices shape how family problems are defined. In cultures in which women become sexually active as soon as they reach menses, teenage pregnancy is not likely to be considered a problem. Some cultures think it is abusive to make young children sit in a dental chair and force them to open their mouths and have a tooth pulled out. Some family policy experts suggest that our country's fascination with violence, as exemplified through the media and sports events, strongly influences the high incidence of violence within families, and that the emphasis on sex in the media contributes to the high incidence of teenage pregnancy.

Community Norms and Values   The norms and values of the community also shape the way in which family problems are defined. For example, if all employable community members are unemployed and, as a consequence, their children live in substandard housing and are poorly fed and clothed, the families in that community living under those circumstances are not likely to be seen as neglecting their children. But children in such a family in a wealthy community most likely would be considered neglected.

Attitudes and Values   The attitudes, values, personal life experiences, and professional background of the person defining the problem also influence problem definition. For example, a person who grew up in a family in which any drinking of alcohol was taboo might define alcoholism differently than a person who grew up in a family in which wine was part of evening meals. A physician may be more likely to define child abuse only in terms of physical characteristics, whereas a social worker may be more likely to take a more holistic approach to defining child maltreatment.

Legal Definitions   Legal statutes also provide a basis for defining family problems. These definitions vary by country and state and often leave a great deal of room for interpretation. For example, the landmark **Child Abuse Prevention and Treatment Act** (CAPTA), amended during the CAPTA Reauthorization Act of 2010, defines child abuse and neglect as:

> *Any recent act or failure to act on the part of a parent or caretaker which results in death, serious physical or emotional harm, sexual abuse or exploitation;*
> *or an act or failure to act which presents an imminent risk of serious harm.* (42 U.S.C.A. §5106g, Child Welfare Information Gateway, 2011)

Terms such as *emotional harm, exploitation,* and *imminent risk* often are difficult to interpret. At the same time, they allow leeway for the protection of children. For example, a child who is constantly threatened with a knife or gun, even though never actually hurt physically, can be viewed as experiencing emotional harm and is likely to have serious emotional problems.

Availability of Resources   Availability of resources may be the most important factor in how a problem is defined. That is, the broader the definition, the more children and families will be identified as having the problem and needing assistance; and the narrower the definition, the fewer children and families will be identified as having the problem and needing assistance. The legal definition just given, for example, allows for the inclusion of neglected and emotionally maltreated children.

Resources are stretched so thin in most states today that they are using narrower definitions of child maltreatment. Also, the debate over the proper role of government in intervening with families has resulted in conflicting child welfare policies, which leaves many children vulnerable to child maltreatment in all its forms. As the debate continues, children in the United States, particularly children of color, continue to fare poorly when looking at key indicators of child well-being (see Boxes 10.1 and 10.2).

What Causes Families to Have Problems?

EP 2.1.7a
EP 2.1.7b

Families have problems for many reasons, and some families have similar problems but for different reasons. A given problem has no single cause, which makes an ecological/systems perspective important in addressing family problems. Also, saying that certain factors are *associated* with specific family problems is more appropriate than saying that those factors *cause* those problems. This means that a family with a problem may have other problems as well, but determining which problem caused the other is difficult.

We know that problems often go together. For example, child abuse, partner abuse, alcoholism, and teenage pregnancy are likely to be found within the same family. Individuals with these problems are more often under stress and are worried about financial

Box 10.1   Overview of the State of America's Children 2014

- The U.S. is reaching a tipping point in racial and ethnic diversity. For the first time, the majority of children under 2 were nonwhite.
- Child poverty has reached record levels: One in 5 children—16.1 million—was poor in 2012. Over 40% of children, and almost half of children under 5, lived in extreme poverty.
- Children of color are disproportionately poor. Children in single-parent families and Southern families are at greatest risk of poverty.
- The average wealth of white households in 2011 ($110,500) was 14 times greater than that of Hispanic households and 17 times that of Black households.
- Employment does not guarantee an above-poverty income. More than 2/3 of poor children live in households were one or more family member works.
- Neatly 1.2 million public school students were homeless in 2011–2012, 73% more than before the recession, while more than 1 in 9 children did not receive adequate food.
- More than 7.2 million children were uninsured in 2012 in spite of increased access to health care benefits.

- 40% of children who needed mental health services did not receive them in 2011–2012.
- A child is abused or neglected every 47 seconds; nearly 40% of abused and neglected children receive no services after investigation and many more receive far fewer services than they need.
- 4,028 children are arrested every day and 1,790 are serving sentences in adult prisons.
- Guns kill or injure a child or teen every half hour; in 2010 2,694 were killed by guns and 15,576 were injured. US children and teens are 17 times more likely to die from gun violence than their peers in 25 other high-income countries. Since 1963, three times as many children and teens have died from guns on American soil than US soldiers killed in action in the Vietnam, Afghanistan, and Iraq wars.
- Black children and teens were nearly 5 times more likely, and Hispanic children and teens nearly 3 times more likely to be killed by guns than white children and teens.

Source: Children's Defense Fund. *Overview of the State of America's Children 2014*. Washington, DC: Author.

---

pressures, have low self-esteem, and come from families in which similar problems existed than are individuals in families without these problems.

Meanwhile, services for children and families often are provided by the "problem area"—for example, alcoholism, child abuse and neglect, spouse abuse—rather than as services for the family as a system. This is largely because of the categorical basis on which state and federal funding generally is allocated. This categorical funding system has resulted in fragmented and duplicated services, as well as gaps in services in which client groups "fall through the cracks."

Increasingly, our nation's children are at risk. The Children's Defense Fund, a national advocacy organization, publishes an annual report, *The State of America's Children*, that gives statistics on child well-being. The 2014 report indicates that child poverty has increased to record levels, with nonwhite children disproportionately poor. See Box 10.1 for a summary of the report.

How Do Cultural and Gender Differences Affect Family Problems?

EP 2.1.7b

In 2012, slightly over half of the children in the United States were white, 24% were Hispanic/Latinos, 14% were African American, 3.4% were Asian American, 2% were Native Hawaiian or other Pacific Islander, 1% were Native Americans, and 2% were members of more than one racial/ethnic group. The nonwhite child population in the United States is growing faster than the white child population; in fact, in 2012 for the first time, there were more nonwhite children under 2 years of age than white children. It is projected that by 2019, the majority of children in the United States will be nonwhite (Children's Defense Fund, 2014).

However, it is important to consider not only simple raw numerical counts, but also *rates*—the number of individuals of a certain group who are doing well or are experiencing problems—compared with the total population of that group. These comparisons show that some groups are more vulnerable, or at risk, than other groups to have certain problems. Because of the historical and continuing impact of structural and cultural oppression on many nonwhite populations in the United States, children of color are often more at risk to experience problems than white children. As discussed in Chapter 4, children of color experience **disproportionality**, or the overrepresentation of a particular group of people in a particular category (e.g., child abuse or poverty), because of the impact of historical and current oppression. See Box 10.2 for a better understanding of disproportionality.

In the United States, single women and people of color with children are more at risk than men and whites to have family problems. Several reasons have been offered for their vulnerability. In 2012, almost one of every three children of color was growing up in poverty. Black children were the poorest: 39.6% lived below the federal poverty level, nearly two and a half times the rate for whites. The percentage of Native American/Native Alaskan children who were

Box 10.2 Indicators of Child Well-Being by Race/Ethnicity

Millions of children thrive in America, but a profile of U.S. children developed by KIDS COUNT, a project of the Annie E. Casey Foundation (2014), reveals a nation with children of color more likely to be at greater risk than their white counterparts. In its Race for Results Project, the Foundation developed 12 indicators of well-being, and then compared data state-by-state and nationally by racial/ethnic group. Although no group met all of the indicators, whites and Asian and Pacific Islanders generally rated higher than other groups.

Indicator	National Average of All Groups	African Americans	American Indians	Asian and Pacific Islanders	Latinos	Whites	Two or More Races
Babies born at normal birth weight (2011)	92%	87%	92%	92%	93%	93%	NA
Children 3–5 enrolled in preschool or kindergarten (2011–2012)	60%	63%	56%	65%	54%	62%	60%
4th graders who scored at or above proficiency in reading (2013)	34%	17%	22%	51%	19%	45%	39%
8th graders who scored at or above proficiency in math (2013)	34%	14%	21%	60%	21%	44%	37%
Females 15–19 who delay childbearing until adulthood (2010)	93%	89%	87%	98%	88%	96%	NA
High school students graduating on time (2009–2010)	78%	66%	69%	94%	71%	83%	NA
Young adults 19–26 in school or working (2010–2012)	83%	72%	65%	93%	77%	86%	82%
Young adults 25–29 who have an associate's degree or higher (2010–2012)	39%	26%	19%	66%	19%	47%	40%
Children who live with a householder who has at least a high school diploma (2010–2012)	85%	85%	83%	88%	63%	93%	92%
Children who live in two-parent families (2010–2012)	68%	37%	53%	84%	65%	77%	64%
Children who live in families with income at or above 200% of poverty (2010–2012)	55%	35%	36%	68%	36%	69%	56%
Children who live in low poverty areas (poverty <20%)	74%	50%	51%	84%	57%	86%	75%
Total ratings using indicator system 0–1000 with 0 worst and 1000 best	NA	345	387	776	404	704	NA

SOURCE: National Race for Results Indicators (2014). Baltimore, MD: Annie E. Casey Foundation. Available at www.aect.org

poor was 36.6%, followed by 34% of Latino/Hispanic children. Although a child is most at risk to be poor if she or he is black, more Latino/Hispanic children are poor than any other group (5.8 million). Slightly over 5 million white children and slightly over 4 million black children are poor (Children's Defense Fund, 2014).

Gender also plays a role in child poverty. Children in single parent families were four times more likely to be poor in 2012 than those in two-parent families. Seventy per cent of single parent families are headed by women, with more than half of black children and almost one-third of Latino/Hispanic children living in single parent households, compared to one in five white children (Children's Defense Fund, 2014).

Because people living in poverty conditions are far more likely to undergo stress, they are far more at risk to have other family problems as well. Thus, women and people of color, by the very nature of their positions within the socioeconomic hierarchy, are more likely to develop family problems. In addition, these groups traditionally have had less power than other groups, so they are more vulnerable to being ignored or blamed for causing their problems and also are unable to advocate for solutions and resources to address their problems. Women, for example, are paid less overall than men, and are hired into lower-level jobs. Those who have not been employed while parenting children and then reenter the workplace (often labeled "displaced homemakers") are at a disadvantage in getting jobs that allow them to support their families adequately, even though most likely have a strong skill set from managing a household and parenting. When they do find jobs, they are most often forced to bear the brunt of child care and other child-related needs. Traditional attitudes about women and people of color are changing, but because resources available to address their needs are scarce, they continue to be at the bottom of the social structure in our country.

Children growing up in families in which positive social support is not available are more likely to have problems in development, have low self-esteem, drop out of school, become pregnant at an early age, and have difficulty finding adequate employment. Because they often lack appropriate role models and have grown up in an environment of isolation, hopelessness, and despair, having children is often the only way they may feel competent. With few skills and even fewer

resources and opportunities, they frequently repeat the cycle of the at-risk family with their own children.

Although some attention is being directed to the special needs of women and people of color and their families, it does not always address the problems from a broad context. For example, with the growing divorce rate and people having children outside of marriage, women are much more likely to be poor than men, who often earn more than their female counterparts and do not always pay required child support. Thus, the term the **feminization of poverty** was coined in the 1980s to call attention to the link between poverty and gender, although women have always been much more poor as a group than men (DiNitto & Johnson, 2012). In addition to providing more social supports to women and their families, however, the problem has to be addressed from an ecological/systems perspective. Women alone are not responsible for pregnancy or divorce. Men's responsibility in these situations also must be addressed.

When considering the relationship between family problems and people of color and women, additional factors must be taken into account. At the same time as these families are more likely to experience poverty and stress, and thus are more likely to experience alcoholism or intimate partner violence or child abuse or be too overwhelmed by these pressures to parent their children adequately, they also are more likely to be *labeled* as having such problems. An African American or Latino parent who abuses a child, for example, is much more likely to take the child to a public hospital or clinic for treatment, where the case is likely to be reported to authorities. A white parent, in comparison, is much more likely to take the child to a private physician and perhaps to a different private physician if the child is abused again.

Families of color and single-parent women also are more likely to seek help for family problems at public agencies, such as local community mental health centers, than at private psychological counseling programs. White parents having problems with children are far more likely to be able to afford to send them to private residential treatment facilities for therapy, whereas children of color are much more likely to be sent to juvenile detention centers, where such treatment usually is not available.

Individuals who study social welfare systems must be aware that children who grow up in families headed by people of color and women are more vulnerable than children who grow up in other families. Family problems must be considered within the context of the broader environment, including the impacts of oppression and discrimination, and these considerations are important in shaping the environment to make it more supportive for children and their families.

Changing Family Situations

Issues of diversity have to be taken into account when working with children and their families. Many families today are undergoing changes in composition as a result of separation and divorce, and those transitions are difficult for all family members. More children are growing up in female-headed, single-parent families. Because single parents can't share the responsibilities of providing income, parenting, and household maintenance, additional effort is required to provide for their children. Many single parents who marry or remarry already have children, creating additional transitions and the development of new relationships for children and adults alike. Increasingly, children are being reared by gay and lesbian parents, often in the face of oppression from the community and society in which they live.

Divorce and Separation

EP 2.1.7a
EP 2.1.7b
EP 2.1.8a

Couples do not get married with the expectation that they will divorce, but if trends noted in 2014 continue, it is estimated that 40–50% of all marriages will end in divorce or legal separation (Casey & Maldonado, 2012). Divorce rates had been increasing; however, when the Great Recession occurred in 2009, both marriages and divorces hit a 40-year low (Centers for Disease Control and Prevention, 2013). The likelihood of divorce occurring is even higher for a second marriage and still higher for a third (Elliott & Simmons, 2011). Although couples with children are somewhat less likely to divorce than those who are childless, current projections suggest that more than half of today's children will spend at least some time in a single-parent household (Casey & Maldonado, 2012).

Divorce and separation frequently result in crises for family members. For adults, the separation or divorce signifies the loss of an intimate relationship that brought security and support. Separation or divorce also represents a loss of hopes and dreams, as well as feelings of failure. Although the divorce may bring relief, being alone brings fear, anxiety, loneliness, and guilt as well, especially if children are

involved. Initially, parents are apt to be so caught up in dealing with their own emotions that they have little energy left to help their children cope with their feelings. Thus, at a time when their children need them most, the parents find themselves unable to reach out and help them.

For children, the divorce almost always is traumatic. If the family fought a great deal, children may feel a sense of relief, but at the same time they feel anger, guilt, fear, and sadness. Typically, children blame themselves for their parents' divorce. They frequently change their behavior, acting either overly good or overly bad, in the hope that this will bring their parents back together. Moreover, parents often fail to say anything to their children about an impending divorce, because of their own grieving and the belief that their children will cope better if they are not burdened with adult problems. Studies suggest that the most important factor that helps children get through a divorce is having someone who will listen to them and give them support. Parents need to explain that they are divorcing each other and not the child and that both of them will continue to love and spend time with the child. Some children do not react visibly when they are informed that their parents are separating or divorcing. If children do not react immediately after the divorce, however, they probably are holding their feelings inside and will express them at a later age (Marquardt, 2006; Wolfinger, 2005).

Talking about the divorce and giving children a chance to express their feelings are important in helping them cope with divorce. Children experiencing a divorce in their family may regress at the time of the divorce. They may have nightmares and exhibit bedwetting, thumb sucking, behavioral problems at school and at home, a drop in academic performance at school, listlessness and daydreaming, changes in eating habits, and more frequent illnesses. If they are preadolescents or adolescents, they may express anger at one or both parents, and engage in experimentation with alcohol and other drugs, sexual activity, and other risk-taking behaviors. If one parent has much less contact than in the past, children may develop extreme fear that the other parent will abandon them or worry about what will happen to them if the parent they are living with dies (Marquardt, 2006).

Although children are likely to cope better with divorce if the adults cope well, children usually take longer to recover, primarily because they have no control over the situation. Various studies show that children require at least 3.5 years to process their parents' divorce (Marquardt, 2006; Wolfinger, 2005). Some individuals still struggle with the situation two or three decades later. Children fare better after a divorce if they maintain a positive relationship with both parents and if the parents do not speak negatively about each other or use the children to fight their battles with each other.

Custody and visitation problems often have a negative impact on a child following a divorce (see Figure 10.1). Although the situation is changing, mothers are more likely to obtain custody in a divorce. In the past, courts have emphasized a long-held doctrine that, in a child's "tender years," the mother is more important in the child's life, and unless she is totally unfit, she should

receive custody of children in a divorce. Courts now are more likely to take a gender neutral stance, making a decision on the basis of what is the least detrimental alternative for the child. If **joint custody**, or custody shared by both parents, is not an option, the court is likely to focus on which parent will be not only a good parent, but also most likely to facilitate contact between the child and the other parent. Instead of gender in divorce situations, income equality has become an often defining factor, as men who can afford attorneys and court costs to fight for custody are more likely to gain custody than men with more limited incomes.

Because most divorces don't involve a custody battle and women are still viewed as the primary caregivers, they are still more likely to be awarded sole custody than men, and, even if the custody is joint, the children most often live with the mother. Because the average

FIG 10.1 Depiction by a 9-Year-Old Girl Whose Parents Are Involved in a Custody Battle

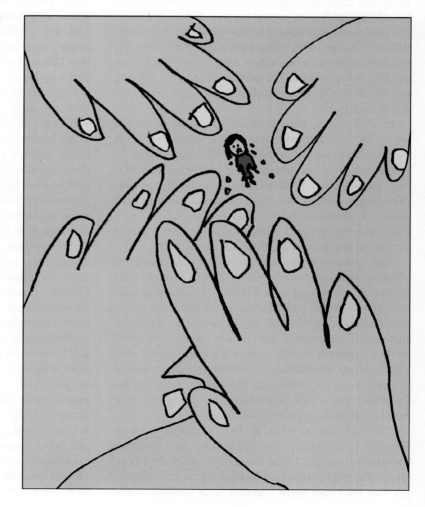

woman's income decreases significantly following a divorce and the average man's income increases, children of divorce frequently view their fathers as "Santa Clauses" or "Disney dads." Their fathers may buy them presents and take them special places, let them stay up later, and impose fewer rules than their mothers, who are buying the necessities and maintaining the daily routine, which usually requires more discipline. Mothers may resent not being able to give their children the same fun aspects of life, whereas fathers often find visitation time with their children artificial and awkward.

Increasingly, parents are opting for joint custody, in which both parents share not only custody, but often the amount of time the child lives with each parent. While often the child lives with one parent the majority of the time and visits the other, in some cases, the child alternates more equally between parents, living with each parent for 3 or 4 days at a time. In other cases, one parent has the child for 6 months, followed by the child living with the other parent for the next 6 months. In a few instances, to maintain stability for the child, the parents take turns moving in with the child, who remains in the same home, for a specified time.

In some cases, parents expect the child to decide where to live and where to spend holidays, which puts undue pressure on the child, who knows that he or she will hurt one parent no matter what the decision. Child welfare professionals recommend that children be given input into these decisions, but that final decisions should be made either by the parents or, if they cannot agree, by a trained mediator who is skilled in divorce conflicts or by the court (Virk, 2009).

The research is inconclusive as to the benefits of different types of custody. Many experts suggest joint custody if the parents have a positive relationship with each other, as this provides the child with two strong role models who love and pay attention to the child; this communicates that the child is wanted and loved by both parents equally. Other experts suggest that joint custody, particularly if it involves a great deal of moving back and forth on the child's part, creates instability and a lack of permanence, giving the child no place to truly call her or his own.

The need for support to families going through divorce, particularly for children, is receiving increased attention. Many cities have established **family mediation centers**, in which a team of social workers and attorneys work together with families in the divorce process. The aim is to help parents maintain positive relationships with each other in an adult way and to resolve conflicts together rather than take adversarial roles, as is often the case when the parents have separate attorneys and pursue the divorce through court action. Public schools and family service agencies also have established special programs and support groups for children who are involved in divorce and their parents.

Single Parenting

EP 2.1.7a
EP 2.1.7b
EP 2.1.8a

Nearly 30% of families in the United States are headed by a single parent, either because of divorce or separation or, increasingly, because of unmarried women giving birth (Federal Interagency Forum on Child and Family Statistics, 2013). Eighty percent of single parent households are headed by mothers. Of those, 44% have never married, 18% are separated, 33% are divorced, and 4% are widowed. Half of all single parent mothers have one child, while 30% have two. About two-fifths are white, one-third are black, and one-fourth are Latino/Hispanic. One-sixth have not graduated from high school, while one-fourth have a college degree (Casey & Maldonado, 2013). While no evidence suggests that growing up in a single-parent family is inherently positive or negative, single parents, particularly mothers, are often viewed from a pathological perspective, which only serves to marginalize both the mothers and their children. Researchers have found that when socioeconomic status is controlled for, children in single-parent families fare as well as those in two-parent families.

Factors that have a significant influence on how children fare include poverty and conflict between parents (Broadhurst, 2009; Casey & Maldonado, 2013; Cleaver, Cawson, Gorin, & Walker, 2009). Single-parent families, like other families, should be viewed from a strengths perspective, with attempts to eliminate environmental barriers that place these families at risk and to build on family strengths. The major barrier for most is income. A female single-parent is more likely to be poor and, if not within the poverty definition of poor, under financial duress than a male single-parent. Table 10.1 shows the income differences between single-parent households headed by women and other households. As can be seen from the table, households headed by single-parent mothers are worse off economically than other households. Although 84% of single-parent mothers are in the workforce, 40% are

TABLE 10.1 COMPARISON OF INCOME OF HEADS OF HOUSEHOLDS

HOUSEHOLD	NO HIGH SCHOOL DIPLOMA	HIGH SCHOOL DIPLOMA, NO COLLEGE	COLLEGE DEGREE
Single-parent households headed by mothers	$20,000	$25,000	$53,000
Single-parent households headed by fathers	$26,000	$38,000	$62,000
Income from head of two-parent household	$30,000	$42,000	$80,000

SOURCE: T. Casey and L. Maldonado (2012). Worst off—Single-parent families in the United States: A cross-national comparison of single parenthood in the U.S. and sixteen other high-income countries. New York, NY: Legal Momentum.

employed in jobs that pay low wages. If single-parent mothers earned as much as males with a comparable education, their earnings would increase by 17% and the percentage living below the poverty level would fall by half (Casey & Maldonado, 2013).

In addition to financial pressure, single parents have sole responsibility for overseeing the household and child rearing. As a result, children growing up in single-parent families often have different lifestyles than others. A paradox of children growing up in single-parent families is that, on one hand, they are likely to have more freedom than other children and, on the other hand, they must take on much more responsibility.

Children of single parents tend to have more freedom because they must spend more time by themselves while the parent is working. Because child care is so expensive, many children of single parents, especially school-age children, become "latch-key" children, responsible for themselves until their parent gets home from work. Others are responsible for younger siblings while the parent is at work. It is not unusual for a child of a single parent to come home from school alone, do homework and household chores, and prepare the evening meal. And single-parent children must assume more responsibility for themselves because of the absence of supervision.

Single-parent children who are the same gender as the parent who has left the home also may assume many of the roles of the absent parent—for example, mowing the lawn and doing household repairs if the father is gone. And they may serve as companions to their parents, who may be lonely or too busy or hurt to establish adult relationships. Parents may confide in children about money, relationships with the ex-spouse, and other adult matters, and expect children to accompany them on shopping trips, to meetings, and to social events. They may place children in a situation of role reversal (parentification), expecting their

children to comfort them. Or they may become overly protective, worrying that because they have lost a significant relationship with an ex-spouse, they may lose the relationship with the child as well. Further, discipline of children in single-parent families may be inconsistent. A parent may be too tired or too stressed to discipline at some times and may over-discipline at other times. Parents' dating and development of opposite-sex relationships also can be stressful to children in single-parent families.

Some children, particularly if they feel abandoned by the absent parent or do not have a positive relationship with that parent, may be anxious for the parent with whom they reside to remarry. Conversely, older children who have been in a single-parent family for a longer time may consider any dating by their parent as a threat to their own relationship with the parent and do everything possible to destroy competing relationships. Of concern to single parents and their families are issues such as how much to tell children about dating, how involved they should be in decision making about serious relationships or remarriage, whether the parent should have "overnight guests" and live-in partners, and how to help children handle a relationship that has ended.

Children growing up in single-parent families, too, generally have fewer options regarding long-range plans for their future. Income and time limitations of these families may preclude college or other post–high school education. Additional issues affecting some children are a fear of being kidnapped by the noncustodial parent, one or more forms of child abuse by the parent or parent's friends, alcoholism or other drug abuse by one or both parents, and concerns about the child's own sexuality and ability to establish long-term, opposite-sex relationships.

Increasingly, schools, child-guidance centers, and community mental-health centers offer programs for children in single-parent families. These programs provide individual and group counseling, family counseling, and self-help groups for children. Big Brother/Big Sister programs, which match adult role models in one-to-one relationships with children, help children in single-parent families develop healthy relationships with adults of the opposite gender from the custodial parent figure to ensure that children have positive relationships with both male and female adults.

Gay and Lesbian Parenting

EP 2.1.7a
EP 2.1.7b
EP 2.1.8a

Many individuals who are lesbian, gay, bisexual, or transgender have children. They have become parents through fostering, adoption, donor insemination, surrogacy, or having children in a heterosexual relationship before coming out (American Civil Liberties Union, 2014). In recent years, men and women alike have had difficulty gaining custody through U.S. courts if they are LGBTQ, in spite of research indicating few differences between parenting of same-sex couples and opposite-sex couples (Patterson, 2008).

The American Psychological Association (Patterson, 2008) has conducted an extensive meta-analysis of research findings on lesbian and gay parenting. Although LGBTQ parents are as diverse as heterosexual parents, they are more likely to be subject to prejudice because of their sexual orientation. Most often the prejudice is not based on personal experience with LGBTQ parents, but cultural transmission of common stereotypes. However, research does not support any of the stereotypes. Studies show that there are no differences in mental health of parents or approaches to parenting, and that being LGBTQ does not detract from one's ability to care for children. Household tasks are divided among parents just as they are in households with opposite-sex parents, and parent and child satisfaction with family relationships is also similar.

There are also no differences among children raised in same-sex partner families when compared to opposite-sex partner families in gender identity, gender role behavior, or type of activities and toys preferred. Studies have shown that children born and/or reared in families in which one or more parents is lesbian or gay are no more likely to be lesbian or gay themselves than children born and/or reared in families in which both parents are heterosexual. Studies also have found that lesbian and gay parents do not influence their children to become lesbian or gay and that children reared by lesbian or gay parents are not emotionally impaired.

Another common stereotype is that gay parents are likely to sexually abuse their male children. Researchers have found that a child is more at risk to be molested in a heterosexual household than in a home with LGBTQ parents. In short, children raised in families with same-sex parents are much like those of children raised in families with opposite-sex parents (Patterson, 2008; American Academy of Pediatrics, 2002; Goldberg, 2009).

Families with parents who are LGBTQ must address some specific issues, however. For example, lesbian or gay parents may not want their employers to know that their sexual orientation because they fear being fired. Thus, children may have to keep their parents' sexual orientation a secret from others. Research suggests that LGBTQ parents actually have more open communication with their children, perhaps because they are transparent about their sexual orientation, which opens the door for discussion about other personal issues commonly experienced by children and families. Many LGBTQ parents have been open with their children about their sexual orientation since their child's birth, just as many adoptive parents don't have a specific moment when they inform a child that she or he is adopted, and most heterosexual parents don't engage their children in a "we're in a heterosexual relationship" conversation. However, studies suggest that if children are not aware that a parent is an LGBTQ or is in an LGBTQ relationship, they should be given this information prior to early adolescence if possible, as children of this age are forming their own identities (Patterson, 2008).

Many lesbian and gay parents worry about how their children's friends and their parents will react to their sexual orientation, and children may fear this as well, particularly as they become older and more aware. LGBTQ parents may be afraid that their children will be ridiculed or discriminated against. Research has found that children with LGBTQ parents are no more likely to be targets of bullying or taunting from other children than children with heterosexual parents (Patterson, 2008).

The greatest challenge for LGBTQ-headed families with children is the limited legal protections afforded to them. Most states do not have laws or formal policies prohibiting adoption by LGBTQ parents, but there are significant barriers regardless. In many states, a single parent can adopt a child, but there are no avenues for the other parent in an LBGTQ relationship to adopt in states where same-sex marriage is prohibited. Some parents try to obtain a "second parent" adoption, but in many states this is either not possible or up to the presiding judge. This denies children legal relationships with both parents, and also results in problems with

custody if the couple decides to divorce, as one parent may have no legal rights to the child. A 2014 Texas case exemplifies the legal issues. Two gay parents had children by the same surrogate mother. The two males asked the court to include both fathers' names on the birth certificate. When told this was not possible, they asked the court to remove the surrogate mother and list only the male birth parent on the birth certificate, planning to then petition the court for a second parent adoption by the other parent. The judge denied the petition, refusing to list the male parent on each birth certificate, even though DNA testing showed that he

Studies show that there are no differences in children raised by gay and lesbian parents when compared to children raised by parents who are heterosexual.

Bart Geerligs/The Image Bank/Getty Images

clearly had fathered the child. The judge's rationale was that the fathers are gay, and Texas, like 17 other states, does not recognize same-sex marriage. Prior to the judge's decision, a federal judge ruled that the Texas ban on same-sex marriage is unconstitutional (see Chapter 4), but the ruling remains pending an appeal. Decisions on child custody like the Texas case ultimately will be shaped by appeals court rulings on same-sex marriage (Edwards, 2014). Who has custody of a child incorporates major decision-making about a child's life and future, including living arrangements, health and mental health care, education, and inheritance. As this discussion indicates, in many instances children in families with LGBTQ parents are not afforded the same protections that are afforded to children with heterosexual parents.

Stepparenting and Blended Families

EP 2.1.7a
EP 2.1.7b
EP 2.1.8a

Along with increasing numbers of single-parent families, second marriages are on the rise. Of divorced adults, 75% remarry, and 65% of these remarriages involve at least one child. About one-third of all marriages in the United States today create step families, and about 40% of all married couples with children are stepcouples. Almost half of all adults in the United States have some type of steprelationship, either to a stepparent, a stepsibling, and/or a stepchild. By the time a child reaches age 15, about one-third will experience two or more mother partnerships (Deal, 2014; Pew Research Center, 2011). The most common **stepfamilies** with children are stepfather-families or combined stepfather–stepmother families. These families often are referred to as **blended families** or re-coupled families (Marsolini, 2006; Wooding, 2008). It is estimated that by 2020, stepfamilies will be the predominant family form in the United States (Stepfamily Foundation, 2014).

Because remarriage typically generates a number of strong feelings in the children and adults involved that are challenging to resolve, more than 70% of second marriages that involve children fail (Partridge, 2006). At first, adults and children alike may feel a sense of joy and security. However, children also are likely to have a sense of loss of relationship to the parent, whom they now must share with the parent's new partner, as well as anxiety over what the addition of another adult will mean to their own well-being. Children may be concerned about balancing the stepparent

relationship with that of the birth parent, who is absent from the home. If the new marriage brings other children into the family, relationships between stepsiblings may incite competition and jealousy.

Because developing stepfamily relationships can be difficult, time and effort are required by all family members to make the new family constellation work. The children frequently feel distant from their new stepparent and may see that parent as a replacement for their absent parent. Even if they like the stepparent, conflicts over loyalty to their birth parent may prevent them from establishing a positive relationship with the stepparent. If, prior to the new marriage, the child functioned as more of a "partner" than a child in the family, she or he may feel displaced and jealous of the stepparent.

Further, many children, no matter how old, retain fantasies of their birth parents reuniting, and the remarriage represents a threat to these fantasies. And stepsiblings may mean less attention to birth children, as well as possible competition outside the family boundaries regarding friends, sports, and school.

In addition to developing emotional bonds among family members, children have to adjust to changing family roles, responsibilities, and family identity. Rules often are readjusted, and many times are stricter than they were in the single-parent household. If children are still in regular contact with their birth parent, they now are essentially members of two households, each with its own distinct culture and rules. Problems regarding multiple role models and parental figures can be confusing to children.

Some experts in stepparent family relationships suggest that the stepparent should not in any way undermine the relationship between the child and the absent birth parent but should establish himself or herself as a parental figure in the family and take an active role in immediate family issues such as rules and discipline. Other experts say that the parenting should be left completely to the child's birth parents, while the stepparent should work to establish a positive bond with the child, but as an adult friend rather than a parental figure, staying out of decisions regarding rules and discipline.

Positive steps that can be taken to create stable blended families, include waiting several years or more after a divorce to remarry and not creating too many changes for family members all at once; taking time for relationships and trust to develop by getting to know each other; experiencing "real day-to-day life" together as opposed to "theme park" experiences; insisting that family members treat each other with respect; creating clear, safe boundaries; acknowledging and showing compassion for age and developmental differences in needs; limiting expectations and allowing room for growth; keeping all parents involved; communicating often and openly; establishing routines and rituals that create bonding; and demonstrating love, appreciation, and encouragement (Kemp, Segal, and Robinson, 2014, pp. 1–6).

Although remarriage can increase stability, security, and financial resources for children, working through the implications of the changes takes a great deal of time before acceptance. In many communities, special parent-education classes for stepparents, support groups for stepparents, spouses, and children in stepparent families, and family counseling programs are available to capitalize on the strengths of the families and provide support in working through problem areas. In the long-run, however, it appears that there is little difference in overall life satisfaction if a person is raised in a family with at least one step-relative. A study conducted by the Pew Research Center found that 70% of adults surveyed who have had at least one step-relative indicated they were very satisfied with their family life, compared to 78% of adults with no step-relatives (2011).

Family Problems Affecting Children

Families today face increasing pressures from the broader environment. They often live in communities that have limited support available to families. Because today's families are more diverse, the issues to consider when addressing their needs are more complex than in the past. More and more children and families need social support beyond the family because of problems such as substance misuse, interpersonal violence, and child maltreatment.

In addition, as increasing numbers of children are growing up in communities rife with poverty and violence and do not receive the nurturing and guidance they need for healthy development, they are more likely to enter adolescence angry, depressed, and searching for attention and acceptance wherever they can find it. The consequences of family conflict can be linked directly to problems associated with youth crime, membership in gangs, violence, and teen pregnancy and parenthood (Federal Interagency Forum on Child and Family Statistics, 2013). These behaviors are also on the rise among younger children.

Addiction and Substance Misuse

EP 2.1.7a
EP 2.1.7b
EP 2.1.8a

Addiction and misuse of alcohol and other drugs have significant impacts on children and families in the United States. Latest estimates indicate that about 43% of U.S. children were living in households with one or more adults who were **alcoholics** or alcohol abusers at some point in life (National Institute on Drug Abuse, 2014). Approximately 15% of these children lived in households with an adult misusing alcohol during the preceding year. Until recently, dependence on or abuse of alcohol or other drugs was viewed as an individual disease rather than a family problem, but new studies have found that individuals growing up in these families are four times as likely to become drug dependent themselves. Of juvenile delinquents and children seen in child guidance and mental health clinics, 20% come from families in which alcohol misuse is a problem. Other studies show a strong relationship between substance use and family violence (see Chapter 8 for additional information on substance misuse and addiction).

The U.S. Children's Bureau (2013b) estimated that approximately 8.3 million children in the country were being reared by at least one parent with substance use disorder. Parents who regularly misuse substances are less likely to be able to carry out their parental role effectively. Statistics vary, but between 40% and 80% of child maltreatment cases are said to involve substance use (Child Welfare League of America, 2009). Maltreated children of substance-using parents are more likely to have poorer physical, intellectual, social, and emotional outcomes and are at higher risk for substance-abuse problems themselves. Abused or neglected children from families with a parent misusing alcohol or other drugs are more likely to be placed in foster care and more likely to remain there longer than maltreated children from families where parental use of alcohol or other drugs is not a problem (U.S. Children's Bureau, 2013a). Of infants abandoned in hospitals, 70% have parents who are drug addicts, and many of these children are born addicted to drugs.

Children who manage to survive in families that misuse alcohol or other drugs seldom escape unscathed (National Institute on Alcoholism and Drug Dependency, 2014). **Adult children of alcoholics** manifest coping characteristics that they developed as children within their own families, including a compulsion to control, a need to overachieve, and a need to please others (Black, 2002, 2006). They also have many fears—about abandonment, emotional harm, and personal violence to themselves or other family members. They also feel lonely, guilty, angry, shamed, and sad.

Because of messages they receive in their families and the resulting feelings of guilt and shame, they maintain as secrets what is going on in the family and their own feelings as well. In looking at a family with one or more parents that misuse alcohol or other drugs from an ecological/systems perspective, one can see how the family has developed a way of functioning with the abuser as the central family member that, although dysfunctional to outsiders, is functional within the family and facilitates the survival of its members (Childwelfare Information Gateway, 2009).

Roles and Codependence   Family members and others who facilitate continuation of substance misuse are called **enablers**. For example, an adult partner may make excuses for the substance user's behavior to other family members, friends, or employers. An older child may take on a "hero" role, believing that by being a "perfect" child, the substance misuse will stop or be less likely to disrupt the family. This child is likely to get excellent grades in school, take care of younger children, nurture both parents, and strive to keep family members happy no matter what the costs are to the child.

Another child in the family may take on a "scapegoat" role, subconsciously believing that negative attention directed at him or her will take the attention away from the parent who is misusing alcohol or other drugs. Conflict between the parents over the substance misuse may instead be directed at the child, who continually gets in trouble at home, at school, and in the neighborhood.

Yet another child may assume the role of the "lost child," believing that the family is better able to cope if he or she is out of sight. These children seem to be always in their room or at friends' homes. They seek little attention and actually go out of their way not to call any attention to themselves.

A final role that a child in families where substance misuse is a problem may assume is that of "mascot." These children, often the youngest, become the pets or clowns of the family, always available to be cuddled when cuddling is demanded or to entertain when entertainment can alleviate some of the family's pain (Black, 2006).

Some experts in the chemical dependence field take issue with the term *enabler*. They prefer the term **codependent**, a person who relies extensively on others for self-worth and self-definition, focusing more on pleasing or controlling others than creating a healthy sense of self (Black, 2006). The term *codependence,* they propose, defines the problem more clearly as belonging to the codependent person and indicates a need for individual recovery for that person separate from the person misusing alcohol or other drugs (Beattie, 2008; Casey, 2008; Sipp & Gallup, 2007; Weinhold & Weinhold, 2008). All definitions and models of codependence focus on the impact of the behavior on the codependent individual and the long-term consequences, regardless of whether the person remains in a relationship with the person misusing substances.

The costs of these roles to the individual family members throughout their lives, as well as the total family, are enormous. These roles actually promote the substance misuse, with family members unknowingly encouraging it. This is why current substance misuse intervention strategies view the abuse as a family systems problem. If communication patterns and roles within families are not changed concurrently with treatment for the person abusing substances, the substance misuse behavior is likely to return quickly, reinforced by the behaviors of other family members.

Phases of Coping   The ways in which families typically cope with substance misuse can be divided into four phases.

1. *Reactive phase.* Family members deny that the misuse of alcohol or other drugs exists and develop their own coping strategies around the substance-misusing parent, usually—sometimes intentionally—enabling the misuse to continue. These strategies range from nagging to making excuses or covering up the misuse, to staying at home and trying to prevent the substance misuse, to denying emotional feelings.

    Children in these families may have birth defects as a result of the mother using alcohol or other drugs during pregnancy (see Chapter 9 for additional information on the relationships between substance misuse, mental health, and developmental disabilities). They may be torn between parents who demonstrate conflicting and often confusing behavior. They may avoid activities with peers because of fear and shame. They may distrust others, or they may learn destructive and negative ways to get attention (Conyers, 2003).

2. *Active phase.* Family members become aware that there is a substance-misuse problem, they do not live in a normally functioning family, and help is available. Family members begin to realize that the person misusing the substances does not control the family, that they have the power to make changes in their own behaviors, and that they cannot assume responsibility for the substance misuser. At this point, members may join self-help groups such as Al-Anon or Alateen, in which others going through similar experiences within their own families can lend support.

3. *Disequilibrium phase.* While painful and difficult, all family members must go through this phase if the problem is to be alleviated. It follows family members' awareness that a problem exists and all efforts to change the abuser or the family dynamics have been unsuccessful. During this phase, family members consider openly whether disruption is the only alternative. This may cause polarization of family members and frequently ends in divorce, with subsequent separation of family members if the abuser still will not seek help. Although the family usually fares better in the long run, this outcome is often doubly traumatic for children, who then have to cope with the problems of both alcoholism or other drug misuse and divorce.

   Approximately 40% of family situations that reach this phase end up in divorce (Lawson & Lawson, 2004; Rubin, 2009). In families that do not choose separation, the traditional family communication patterns may be shaken enough that the family begins to change actively. Whether it is disrupted or the family member who is misusing substances agrees to make a concerted effort to change, the family is forced to reorganize. This entails new and different roles for family members (Black, 2006; Conyers, 2003).

4. *Family unity phase.* Many families with substance misuse problems do not reach this phase. Being free of misuse of substances is central to this phase, but it is not enough. Accepting the family member

as a non-substance user and lasting changes in family communication patterns must take place if the family is to remain free of recurring substance-misuse problems.

The ecological/systems framework can help understand factors associated with addiction and misuse of alcohol and other drugs. Scientists indicate that genetic factors account for 40–60% of a person's risk for addiction, including environmental impact on gene functioning. Environmental factors also play a key role, including the kinds of interactions children experience within their families as well as peer and school relationships and the availability of community and social support.

Addiction typically begins during childhood or adolescence: In 2012, 3.5% of teens aged 12–13, 8.2% of teens aged 14–15, and 16.6% of teens aged 16–17 reported using an illegal drug in the past month; the figure is much higher (24.3%) for underage use of alcohol. Use of cigarettes among teens, however, has declined in recent years, from 13% in 2002 to 6.6% in 2012 (National Institute on Drug Abuse, 2014). Use of alcohol and other drugs is associated with a wide range of health and social problems that impact children and teens, including injury and death from motor vehicle and other accidents such as drowning; interpersonal violence, including assaults, rapes, and homicides; risky sexual behavior; alcohol and other drug poisoning; and brain impairment. Use of alcohol and other drugs by children and adolescents can alter the structure and functioning of various parts of the still-developing brain, further impairing decision-making and creating long-term consequences (SAMSHA, 2013).

Family and Intimate Partner Violence

EP 2.1.7a
EP 2.1.7b

Although definitions of **family violence** differ from state to state, a general definition often used is that it is an act carried out by one family member against another family member that causes or is intended to cause physical or emotional pain or injury to that person. Family violence typically has been separated into three major categories: intimate partner violence (also called "domestic violence," "battering," or "relationship abuse"), child abuse, and elder abuse (Centers for Disease Control and Prevention, 2014).

Intimate partner violence (IPV) includes the "physical, sexual, or psychological harm by a current or former partner or spouse" (Centers for Disease Control and Prevention, 2014a, p. 1). These acts of violence can range from threatening to harm someone to chronic, severe beatings that can result in death, and can occur among both heterosexual and same sex couples.

Before IPV received national attention during cases such as the well-publicized O.J. Simpson trial, most of the attention focused on the abuse of children, with legislative roots going back to the 1960s. As a result, federal dollars have been appropriated for child abuse, with more limited funds for IPV.

Limited funding for IPV in states is often housed under women's programs, implying that it is a woman's problem rather than a family problem of concern to everyone. Some child abuse programs have funded IPV programs only by suggesting that children growing up in a home in which spouse or partner abuse is present are emotionally abused.

Although men are abused in partner relationships, the majority of IPV is perpetrated by men and although women can also be violent in relationships, they are more likely to be seriously injured or killed when an IPV incident occurs than a man (Centers for Disease Control and Prevention, 2014). Attention to IPV was late in developing because of the ways that our society views men and women. Men are regarded in power positions both inside and outside the home, and some still subscribe to the myth that women who are beaten somehow deserve it or that they must enjoy it or they would not put up with it. Additionally, because many men subscribe to the stereotype that they must be tough and are not masculine if they allow someone to be violent against them, they are less likely to report violence perpetrated against them by either a female or a male partner.

Estimates vary, but more than one in three women and one in four men in the United States have been raped, experienced physical violence, or been stalked by a current or former intimate partner in their lifetime. One in three women and three in ten men reported lasting repercussions, such as being concerned about their safety, needing medical care, needing housing or legal services, missing work or school, and/or experiencing symptoms of post-traumatic stress disorder. More than half of female survivors of rape report being raped by a current or former intimate partner (Black, Basile, Breiding, Smith, Walters, Merrick, Chen & Stevens, 2011). While interpersonal violence impacts all ethnic and racial groups, reports of rape, physical violence, and stalking by current or former

intimate partners are higher for African Americans, Hispanics, American Indians, and Alaskan Natives than for other groups. The majority of women reported that their intimate partner perpetrators were male across all types of violence, while male survivors reported the perpetrators more likely to be male if the violence was rape or other unwanted sexual contact, male in nearly half the stalking incidents, but female in other types of violence (Black et al., 2011).

The risk of injury increases for survivors of female rape and physical assault when their assailant is a current or former intimate. Only an estimated third of injured female rape or assault victims receive medical treatment. Moreover, there is a relationship between victimization as a minor and subsequent victimization as an adult. More than 22% of female and 15% of male adult survivors of IPV reported experiencing some form of IPV for the first time when they were between 11 and 17 years of age (Black et al., 2011). Women who reported being raped before age 18 were twice as likely to report being raped as an adult. Women who reported that they were stalked before age 18 were seven times more likely to report being stalked as an adult (U.S. Bureau of Justice Statistics, 2009).

Forms of IPV

EP 2.1.3a

Although physical violence has received the majority of attention in the media, other types of IPV include:

- *verbal abuse*—yelling, screaming, name-calling; embarrassing, making fun of, or mocking the partner, either alone in the household, in public, or in front of family or friends; criticizing or diminishing the person's accomplishments or goals; telling partners that they are worthless.
- *nonverbal abuse*—destruction of the partner's personal property and possessions; excessive possessiveness and isolation from friends and family; excessive checking up on partners to make sure they are where they said they would be; making partners remain on the premises after a fight, or leaving them somewhere after a fight, just to "teach them a lesson."
- *sexual abuse*—sexual assault (forcing partners to participate in unwanted, unsafe, or degrading sexual activity); sexual harassment, including ridiculing partners to try to limit their sexuality or reproductive choices; sexual exploitation (e.g., forcing someone to look at pornography, or

forcing someone to participate in pornographic film-making).

- *stalking and cyber-stalking*—harassment of or threatening another person, especially in a way that haunts the person physically or emotionally in a repetitive and devious manner. Stalking an intimate partner can take place during the relationship or after a partner or spouse has left the relationship. The stalker may be motivated to get the partner back or wish to harm the partner as punishment for the departure. Stalking can take place at or near the partner's home, near or in the workplace, on the way to the store or another destination, or on the Internet (cyber-stalking). Stalkers may never show their face, or they may be everywhere. **Cyber-stalking** is defined as the use of telecommunication technologies such as the Internet or e-mail to stalk another person. Cyber-stalking is deliberate, persistent, and personal (U.S. Bureau of Justice Statistics, 2009).
- *economic or financial abuse*—withholding economic resources; stealing from or defrauding a partner of money or assets; exploiting the intimate partner's resources for personal gain; withholding resources such as food, clothes, necessary medications, or shelter from a partner; or preventing the spouse or partner from working or choosing an occupation.
- *spiritual abuse*—using spouses' or intimate partners' religious or spiritual beliefs to manipulate them; preventing partners from practicing their religious or spiritual beliefs; ridiculing the other person's religious or spiritual beliefs; or forcing the children to be reared in a faith with which the partner does not agree.

Two additional forms of intimate partner abuse often cited by experts are (a) "crazy-making" or placing responsibility for the abuse on the person who is being abused, changing interpretations of the person's reality, and other erratic behavior that leads the abused person to begin to believe that she is crazy, and (b) suicidal and homicidal threats (Helpguide, 2009).

Characteristics of Abusers and Those Who Are Abused

EP 2.1.3a

A number of factors are associated with IPV (see Box 10.3). Men who assault their partners generally have low self-esteem and feel inferior. Feeling powerless outside the family, they exert their power within the domain of their homes. Male perpetrators of IPV are likely to be young and abuse alcohol or drugs (National Council on Child Abuse and Family Violence, 2009).

Factors associated with women who are abused are more difficult to interpret. Lenore Walker (2000) identified "learned helplessness" as a trait common in abused women: They become passive and helpless as a way to cope with their violent spouses. In some cases, they blame themselves for their abuse, or they may redefine the event, rationalizing that it was not that serious or that it was a rare occurrence. Others (see, for example, Wilson, 2005) have compared the symptoms of battered women to posttraumatic stress disorder, a diagnosis of some individuals who have been exposed to severe trauma.

Many times, abused women are reluctant to leave violent situations because they have no employable skills and are concerned about being able to survive, particularly if they have children. But other studies show that battered women are not always passive. Some seek help in dealing with the abuse, but they love their partners in spite of the violence and stay with them, believing they will reform.

In many violent situations between partners, the period following the violence is almost like a honeymoon. The abusive partners are extremely loving and supportive. They often cry and say they are extremely sorry for the episode, even threatening suicide if the partner leaves. They promise never to be violent again. At least initially, it is difficult for a person who loves her or his partner not to be taken in by this repentant behavior.

Other studies show that women with low self-esteem, particularly those who were physically or sexually abused as children, feel so worthless that they believe they deserve the violent treatment. These women are more at risk than other women to be abused.

It should be noted that in most situations, the woman is passive and the man is abusive, but in some situations both partners are violent, with the same differences seen in same-sex relationships. Because of the typical difference in size and strength between men and women, however, the woman most often is the one who is physically hurt in an IPV encounter. Finally, factors that place couples more at risk for IPV include substance use, financial stress and poverty, and unemployment or underemployment.

Box 10.3   Environmental Risk Factors for Intimate Partner Violence

Individual Risk Factors

Low self esteem	Anger and hostility	Desire for power and control in relationships
Low income	Depression	Perpetrating psychological aggression
Low academic achievement	Prior history of being physically abusive	Being a victim of physical or psychological abuse
Young age	Having few friends and being isolated from other people	History of experiencing poor parenting as a child
Aggressive or delinquent behavior as a youth	Unemployment	History of experiencing physical discipline as a child
Heavy use of alcohol and/or other drugs	Emotional dependence and insecurity	Belief in strict gender roles

Relationship Factors

Conflict in relationship—fights, tension, other struggles	Relationship instability—divorces, separations, breakups	Dominance and control of relationship by one partner over the other
Economic stress	Unhealthy family relationships and interactions	

Community Factors

Poverty and associated factors (overcrowding)	Low social capital, lack of institutions and norms that provide positive social supports	Weak community sanctions against IPV (unwillingness of neighbors and family members to intervene, limited involvement of law enforcement and other community agencies)

Societal Factors

Traditional gender norms	Culture that supports violence through media, sports, etc.	Limited policies and funding that support violence prevention and intervention

SOURCE: Adapted from Centers for Disease Control and Prevention, National Center for Injury Prevention and Control (2013). *Risk factors for intimate partner violence. Atlanta*, GA: Author.

IPV not only impacts the couple engaged in the conflict, but it has a significant impact on children. They often feel helpless when the adults argue, responsible for protecting siblings, responsible for the conflict, and they may try to, or be expected to, intervene and break up the argument or protect one of the adults involved. Children may end up being abused physically in the process, and in some instances, state definitions for child maltreatment include exposure to IPV. In fact, 23 states have enacted legislation specifically addressing the protection and care of children who witness episodes of IPV, and some states include harsher penalties for perpetrators if children were present.

Children exposed to IPV often suffer long-term consequences without intervention, including posttraumatic stress disorder, low self-esteem, problems relating to peers and adults, problems dealing with anger and expressing other feelings, and problems in their own relationships as they grow up. They are more likely to recreate patterns of interpersonal violence in their own relationships, allowing violence to be perpetrated against them or becoming a perpetrator themselves.

Relevant Legislation

EP 2.1.3b

Several laws have been passed to support efforts relating to the prevention of and intervention in IPV situations. The first of note was the Family Violence Prevention and Services Act of 1984, which provided funding for shelters for abused persons. The Victims of Crime Act, also passed in 1984, gave priority to abused spouses in receiving compensation for crime-related costs.

The landmark Violence Against Women Act (VAWA), passed in 1994, makes it a crime to cross state lines to abuse a partner, prohibits individuals who have restraining orders filed against them for intimate partner from possessing firearms, imposes tougher penalties for sex offenders, requires sex offenders to pay restitution to their victims, requires states to pay for rape examinations, and creates protections for survivors of rape from inappropriate inquiries about their personal lives. The act committed more than $1.6 billion over a 6-year period for domestic violence programs, including hiring police, prosecutors, and victim-witness counselors and establishing prevention programs.

The VAWA of 2000 (PL 106-386) improved legal tools and programs addressing domestic violence, sexual assault, and stalking. VAWA 2000 reauthorized critical grant programs created by the original Violence Against Women Act and subsequent legislation, established new programs, and strengthened federal laws. The Act was renewed again in 2005 almost unanimously with a bipartisan vote, adding additional protections with an emphasis on providing more culturally competent services. The VAWA of 2013, however, stalled in Congress for some time because Republicans did not want to adopt the Senate version that added protections relating to sexual orientation and gender identity. Finally passed after extensive advocacy by a coalition of diverse organizations, the 2013 VAWA adds protections for women who are undocumented immigrants, Native Americans, LGBT, and students on college campuses; improves legal tools; and adds additional programs for intimate partner violence, sexual assault, and stalking.

Since its original passage in 1994, female homicides that are the result of IPV have decreased by 35%, male homicides have decreased by 46%, law enforcement reports of IPV as well as arrests have increased, and all states now have stalking laws. The Act also provides funding for the National Domestic Violence Hotline, which has answered over 3 million calls since its inception and receives an average of 22,000 calls each month. Ninety two percent of callers report that this is their first call for help (Fact Sheet, 2013).

Many states and communities have laws relating to IPV; require training for law enforcement, court, health care, and other service providers likely to work with survivors of IPV and have established safe houses and shelters where partners who are victims of intimate partner violence and their children can seek refuge as well as counseling for partners and children, assistance with legal issues, locating housing and employment, and developing support networks. But many individuals seeking shelter at these places are turned away because of lack of space and other resources. Also, while community outreach programs have been established to provide counseling and other services to survivors and perpetrators of IPV, most of these programs begin to treat the violence after it has reached an intolerable point and any change, particularly for the abuser, is difficult.

Child Maltreatment

 Although many children in the United States grow up in loving, supportive families, far too many experience child abuse and neglect. As reported cases continue to increase, existing resources are unable to serve the many abused and neglected children and their families who come to the attention of available programs.

EP 2.1.7a
EP 2.1.7b

Although the 50 states and the District of Columbia have laws that define child maltreatment somewhat differently, the federal Child Abuse Prevention and Treatment Act (CAPTA), amended in 2010, defines child maltreatment as "any recent act or failure to act on the part of a parent or caretaker which results in death, serious physical or emotional harm, sexual abuse or exploitation; or an act or failure to act, which presents and imminent risk of serious harm" (Child Welfare Information Gateway, 2013). In federal fiscal year 2012, child protective services (CPS) agencies in the United States accepted an estimated 3.4 million reports alleging maltreatment involving approximately 6.3 million children (U.S. Children's Bureau, 2013a). Of those reports, 62% (2.1 million reports) were investigated, while 32% were screened out, with cases sometimes referred to other agencies. These figures are lower than the true scope of the problem (see Figure 10.2) because most maltreatment happens within the confines of family privacy, and even when cases are known to others, they often are not reported to the appropriate authorities (Sedlak, Mettenburg, Basena, Petta, McPherson, Greene, & Li, 2010).

Categories of Child Maltreatment

Child maltreatment falls into four main categories: physical abuse, sexual abuse, child neglect, and psychological maltreatment (see Figure 10.3). Neglect is the

FIG 10.2 Knowledge About Maltreated Children: The Tip of the Iceberg

This figure depicts the incidence of cases of child maltreatment and who in the community knows about them. The known cases of child maltreatment are only the "tip of the iceberg."

SOURCE: Sedlak, A.J., Mettenburg, J., Basena, M., Petta, I., McPherson, K., Greene, A., and Li, S. (2010). *Fourth National Incidence Study of Child Abuse and Neglect (NIS–4): Report to Congress.* Washington, DC: U.S. Department of Health and Human Services, Administration for Children and Families.

most frequently reported type of maltreatment; more than three-fourths of all reports are of this type. Almost one-fifth of reports involve physical abuse, and another ten percent involve sexual abuse. Some reports involve more than one type. Reports of sexual abuse have increased in recent years, possibly because of greater awareness of sexual abuse, which has eliminated some of the secrecy that previously surrounded the problem (U.S. Children's Bureau, 2013a).

Children of all ages are maltreated. The highest rates in 2012 occurred among infants and toddlers under a year old, who are the most vulnerable both because of their size and their inability to escape from or report the abuse or neglect to anyone. Preschoolers, school age children, and teenagers, however, are also maltreated, with rates in 2012 declining with the victim's age. Girls were slightly more likely to be victimized than boys. Forty four percent of victims were white, 21.8%

Latino/Hispanic, and 21% were African American (U.S. Children's Bureau, 2013a).

The most tragic outcomes of child maltreatment are fatalities. In 2012, 1,592 children in the United States were reported to have died from abuse or neglect. Again, these figures are underreported, as some child deaths due to maltreatment are unsubstantiated. Almost three-fourths of all child fatalities due to abuse or neglect were children under three years of age, with higher rates for boys than girls. Almost 40% of children were white, about 30% were African American, and about 15% were Hispanic/Latino. Four-fifths (80%) of fatalities were determined to have been caused by one or both parents (U.S. Children's Bureau, 2012a).

The number and rate of children confirmed as maltreated can vary considerably from year to year. The numbers vary not only because there may be an actual increase or decrease in cases but also because of factors

FIG 10.3 Sometimes parents can't provide the right care because they are in trouble themselves, experiencing problems such as depression, drugs, or alcohol. If an adult in your family is in this kind of trouble, the kids may not be safe. Protect your family by finding help.
SOURCE: Courtesy of the Texas Department of Family and Protective Services. Public awareness campaigns have been developed by national, state, and local organizations to focus attention on positive parenting and child abuse prevention.

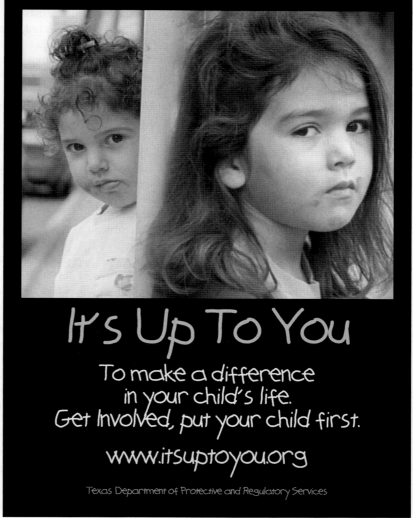

It's Up To You
To make a difference
in your child's life.
Get Involved, put your child first.
www.itsuptoyou.org

Texas Department of Protective and Regulatory Services

Courtesy of the Texas Department of Family and Protective Services

such as the availability of resources to address the problem (if resources are not available to respond, people are more likely to report only the most serious cases); public awareness about the problem and how to make a report; and economic conditions. For example, although reports have remained about the same in number in recent years, rates are actually higher because the child population has declined.

Most perpetrators, or persons responsible for the abuse or neglect, are parents (80%), with slightly more than half women (53.5%), which is consistent with the fact that women are more likely to be caregivers of children, particularly young children.

Physical Abuse   Most children who are victims of

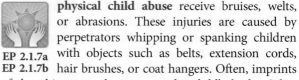

EP 2.1.7a
EP 2.1.7b

physical child abuse receive bruises, welts, or abrasions. These injuries are caused by perpetrators whipping or spanking children with objects such as belts, extension cords, hair brushes, or coat hangers. Often, imprints of the objects can be seen on the child's body. Other physical abuse is caused by kicking; biting; punching; throwing; stabbing, or choking a child. When these types of injuries appear on the face, head, or more than one plane of a child's body (such as the back and arms) and are in various stages of healing (e.g., bruises in varying colors), child abuse is suspected.

Children also receive broken bones and burns, as well as internal injuries, as a result of physical child abuse. Physicians can use x-rays to determine the types of breaks and when they occurred. In spiral fractures, for example, the bone may have been broken when a caregiver became angry and twisted one of the child's limbs. Often, children who are physically abused with one suspected broken bone or other serious injury have fractures or other injuries in various stages of healing in several areas of the body. This condition, termed **battered child syndrome** by C. Henry Kempe, a physician instrumental in advocating for child abuse legislation, is a diagnosis that now is recognized by medical professionals.

One of the most serious types of child maltreatment is an internal injury to the head, which can result in internal bleeding, brain damage, and death. Shaking a child severely also can cause serious injury, including blindness (resulting from detached retinas), brain injury, and death. Children may be burned on their hands, feet, and other parts of their bodies with cigarettes or lighters. And parents with unrealistic expectations about toilet training have burned children by placing them in extremely hot water when they have soiled themselves.

The types of injuries discussed here are considered physical abuse regardless of whether the perpetrator intended to hurt the child. While many child development specialists advocate against spanking, physical discipline is not considered physical abuse as long as it is reasonable and does not cause any bodily injury to a child.

Among the many factors associated with families who physically abuse children are financial problems such as unemployment and poverty, isolation, unrealistic parental expectations about child development or children's abilities to meet parental needs for love and attention, alcoholism and other drug use, abuse or maltreatment of the parent himself or herself during childhood, lack of education about nonphysical alternatives to discipline, low impulse control, and inability to cope well with stress. Only about 10% of parents who maltreat their children have a serious psychological disturbance (Crosson-Tower, 2014).

Some children are more at risk than others for physical abuse. These include children who are born prematurely or with congenital problems, children who do not meet parental expectations or whose parents perceive them as different, and children who are the result of unwanted pregnancies. Many parents who abuse children begin with role reversal in the family system, expecting the child, even as an infant

or toddler, to meet their emotional needs. When the child resists or is unable to do so, the parent may feel rejected, become angry and frustrated, and abuse the child.

Children who grow up in communities with few economic resources and few support systems available to families also are more at risk to be abused (U.S. Children's Bureau, 2013a, b) (see Box 10.4). Cultural conditions also have an impact on physical abuse. Child abuse is less prevalent in cultures that value children and share parenting with others beyond the nuclear family (Crosson-Tower, 2014).

Sexual Abuse   Sexual abuse is receiving more attention in recent years because of: (a) increased public awareness of the problem, and (b) exposure of children to more adults than in the past, including child-care providers, stepparents, and other adults, which increases the likelihood of sexual abuse. Child **sexual abuse** has been defined by CAPTA as:

EP 2.1.7a
EP 2.1.7b

> The employment, use, persuasion, inducement, enticement, or coercion of any child to engage in, or assist any other person to engage in, any sexually explicit conduct or simulation of such conduct for the purpose of producing a visual depiction of such conduct; or the rape, and in cases of caretaker or inter-familial relationships, statutory rape, molestation, prostitution, or other form of sexual exploitation of children, or incest with children. (cited in Child Welfare Information Gateway, 2013)

Thus, child sexual abuse can include, in addition to sexual intercourse, acts such as fondling, sodomy, and indecent exposure. Federal legislation mandates, too, that state child abuse laws include child pornography and sexual exploitation through prostitution. This expands the definition to acts such as taking pictures or other visual images of children in sexual poses or for purposes of sexual gratification.

Many individuals are unaware until later in life that they have been sexually abused. They repressed their childhood sexual abuse until they became adults or assumed that all children had the same treatment, not realizing what constitutes healthy adult–child interactions. Others have been reluctant to report the abuse because they are ashamed or embarrassed, have been threatened, or are worried about possible repercussions to themselves and their families. Some studies suggest that one in four women and one in five men have been

Box 10.4 Factors That Contribute to Child Abuse and Neglect

1. **Child has been reported previously:** There have been previous founded or unfounded reports of abuse or neglect of the child or his or her siblings in the family system.
2. **Parent abused as a child:** Children who are maltreated may learn violent behavior and how to justify that behavior.
3. **Age of the parent:** Some studies of physical abuse, in particular, have found that teenage mothers have higher rates of child abuse than older mothers.
4. **Age of the child:** Infants and young children are more at risk of maltreatment than older children and adolescents.
5. **Family composition:** Most at risk are single parents rearing children alone, including a never-married, separated, or divorced parent and children living in an extended family household.
6. **Child-rearing approaches:** Negative attitudes about a child's behavior and inaccurate knowledge about child development may play a contributing role in child maltreatment. Maltreating parents are more likely to use harsh discipline and less likely to use positive parenting practices.
7. **Domestic violence in the home:** Children who witness violence between their parents or caregivers may learn violent behavior as well as how to justify that behavior.
8. **Separation of a parent or child for a long period:** The child may have been reared by a grandmother or other family member or have been in foster care.
9. **Parent's or caretaker's substance use:** Substance use is suspected to be a contributing factor for between one-third and two-thirds of maltreated children in the child welfare system.
10. **Physical, mental, or emotional impairment of the child:** The child has been diagnosed or observed to have cognitive physical or emotional limitations, or chronic illness.
11. **Physical, mental, or emotional impairment of the parent:** The parent or other caretaker has low self-esteem, a belief that events are determined by chance or outside forces beyond one's personal control, poor impulse control, depression, anxiety, and antisocial behavior.
12. **Low socioeconomic status:** Lower economic status, lack of social support, and high stress levels may contribute to the incidence of child maltreatment, especially for adolescent mothers and young parents.

SOURCES: Crosson-Tower, C. (2014). *Understanding child abuse and neglect.* Boston: Pearson; and U.S. Children's Bureau (2013b). *Factors that contribute to child abuse and neglect.* Washington, DC: Author.

---

sexually abused before reaching the age of 18 (Whealin & Barnett, 2014) but that only a very small percentage of cases are reported to law enforcement agencies at the time they occur.

Although individuals tend to think of sexual abusers as strangers who accost children in the park, the majority are known and trusted by the children they abuse. There are four categories of sex abusers:

1. *Parents.* Most professionals agree that sexual abuse by birth parents, **incest**, has the most serious personal and social consequences (Crosson-Tower, 2014). Abusers also may be other parental figures such as stepparents.
2. *Family members other than parental figures.* This category includes siblings, grandparents, and uncles or aunts. Of these, sexual relationships between siblings are reported to be the most prevalent. The broadest definition of incest includes sexual relationships between any family members. About 30% of perpetrators are either parents or other family members (American Psychological Association, 2014).
3. *Trusted adults.* Among others, they can be teachers, child care providers, neighbors, coaches, leaders of children's groups, or other adults. About 60% of perpetrators fall into this category (American Psychological Association, 2014).
4. *Strangers and remote acquaintances.* This is the least frequent category of sexual abusers. An estimated 10% of the cases of child maltreatment involve perpetration by someone outside the child's family are strangers to the child (American Psychological Association, 2014).

Although all children are at risk to be sexually abused, perpetrators often single out those whom they perceive as most vulnerable. Children who are more likely to be sexually abused are those living without their birth fathers, living in stepparent families, having mothers employed outside the home, having a mother who is ill, observing violence between parents, or having a poor relationship with their parents (Crosson-Tower, 2014). Boys are most likely to be abused by non–family members, and girls by family members. Both girls and boys are more likely to report being sexually abused by males than females. Not all perpetrators are adults; almost one in four reported cases involve perpetrators under age 18 (American Psychological Association, 2014).

Characteristics of perpetrators of sexual abuse include poor impulse control, low tolerance for frustration, low self-esteem, denial, manipulation, social and emotional immaturity, use of alcohol and other drugs, and isolation (Crosson-Tower, 2014). About one-fourth of male offenders report having been sexually abused as children, and about half began sexually abusing others during adolescence.

Most abusers engage in a seductive power role with children with whom they become involved. Children, wanting affection and too young to know how to draw boundaries between positive affection and sexual abuse, initially may become involved—and then be too afraid to tell anyone what is going on. Although the sexual abuse acts themselves may not involve physical force on the adult's part, the child is trapped in the situation because adults are in a power position with children. Some abusers within the family tell the children they abuse that the relationship is the only thing that is keeping the family together or that the abuser is the only one in the family who really loves and understands them. Other abusers threaten physical harm to the child or to other family members if the child refuses to cooperate or tells anyone what is going on. For example, they may say that their mother will "go crazy," that the child will be taken out of the home, or that the adult will sexually abuse a younger sibling.

Studies on the effects of sexual abuse on children agree that it is extremely harmful emotionally and that individuals who have been sexually abused suffer long-term effects. The impact of sexual abuse on children depends on factors such as the following (Crosson-Tower, 2014):

- the child's age when the abuse occurred;
- the form of sexual abuse;
- the relationship of the abuser to the child;
- the duration, over time, when the abuse occurred;
- the length of time between when the abuse occurred and when someone found out that it was going on;
- other characteristics of the child's family and available positive support to the child; and
- reactions from family members and professionals when the sexual abuse is discovered.

Issues faced by survivors of sexual abuse include lack of trust and feelings of betrayal, powerlessness, isolation, blame, and a sense of loss. Others have problems such as depression, anxiety or panic disorder, eating disorders, chronic pain, and posttraumatic stress disorder. Many individuals who have been sexually abused see themselves as victims because of the trauma of the abuse and have extremely low self-esteem and difficulty establishing and maintaining intimate, trusting relationships with others (Crosson-Tower, 2014; American Psychological Association, 2014).

Without intervention, those who have been sexually abused are more at risk than others to turn to alcohol, other drugs, or suicide to ease their pain. Many communities have established programs that promote public awareness of sexual abuse, early intervention with families once cases are reported, and evidence-based interventions that are effective in working with survivors to address the long-term effects.

Child Neglect   Neglect is characterized by acts of omission, which usually means that something that should have been done to or for a child was not done (Crosson-Tower, 2014). **EP 2.1.7a** **Child neglect** has been defined as the failure of a parent or other caregiver responsible for a child "to provide needed food, clothing, shelter, medical care, or supervision to the degree that the child's health, safety, and well-being are threatened with harm" (Child Welfare Information Gateway, 2013).

Many states include specific categories in their definitions of child neglect:

- failing to provide adequate food, clothing, or shelter for a child (physical neglect);
- leaving a child unattended for inappropriate periods of time (lack of supervision);
- leaving a child alone or not returning when expected to care for a child (abandonment);

- not providing medical or mental health treatment for a child (medical neglect);
- failing to provide an education for a child, including attending to a child's special education needs (educational neglect); and
- not tending to a child's emotional needs, such as failing to provide mental health treatment or allowing a child to use alcohol or other drugs (emotional neglect) (Child Welfare Information Gateway, 2014).

More children die each year from neglect than from abuse (Child Welfare Information Gateway, 2014). Many are burned in fires or drown in bathtubs while left alone or with inadequate supervision. Others die because their parents did not obtain medical care for them soon enough when they became ill. Adults who did not have their physical or emotional needs met as children are much more likely than others to have problems finding and maintaining jobs, developing positive relationships with other individuals, remaining in marriages, and parenting their own children adequately.

One type of neglect that is receiving more attention is **nonorganic failure to thrive**, a form of parental deprivation. Failure to thrive is medically described as a child who is 3 percentiles or more below the normal weight for his or her age. The child seems to be fed regularly by his or her caregivers, and nothing organically wrong can be found, yet the child does not gain weight and literally fails to thrive.

When placed in a hospital and given nothing more than regular feedings of the child's normal diet, coupled with love and attention (e.g., holding and cuddling), the child begins to gain weight immediately. Bowlby's (1951) classic studies of maternal deprivation and children raised in orphanages in Europe without love and attention found a high death rate and significant differences in intelligence quotient (IQ) and physical and emotional development as compared with children in environments where they received love and attention. Similar findings are evident in children diagnosed with failure-to-thrive syndrome.

Although there is a strong relationship between poverty and neglect, not all parents who are poor neglect their children. Typical neglectful parents, as compared with non-neglectful parents who also are living in poverty, are more isolated, have fewer relationships with others, are less able to plan and to control impulses, are less confident about the future, and are more plagued with physical and psychological problems.

Neglectful parents also are more likely to say that they did not receive love from, and were unwanted by, their parents. Many were raised by relatives or were in foster care. Neglectful parents often began life lonely, and they continue to live in isolation. The U.S. Children's Bureau (2013b) reported that neglectful parents had difficulty identifying neighbors or friends with whom they could leave their children if they needed emergency child care or from whom they could borrow $5 in an emergency. They are extremely isolated from both formal and informal support networks. Many neglecting parents describe their social workers as being their best or only friends.

Early research by Polansky, Chalmers, Buttenweiser, & Williams (1983) identified the following five types of inadequate or neglectful parents:

1. *Apathy–futility syndrome:* These neglecting parents have all but given up on life. They see little hope for the future and view all efforts to try to relate to either their children or others as futile. They convey an attitude of hopelessness and despair. Usually neglected themselves as children, and in many instances beaten down whenever they tried to make a go of life, they lack the physical or emotional energy to relate to their children. A neglectful parent with apathy–futility syndrome is likely to be found lying on the couch in a chaotic household that hasn't been cleaned or cared for, with children unkempt and uncared for, left largely to fend for themselves. Children of this type of neglectful parent suffer from physical, medical, educational, and/or emotional neglect, as well as lack of supervision.

2. *Impulse-ridden behavior:* This type of parent may be loving and caring and provide adequate food, clothing, and medical care most of the time. But these parents have trouble making appropriate decisions and often behave impulsively. They may decide suddenly to go to a party and leave the children alone, or answer the phone and become so engrossed in the conversation that they forget that their child is unattended in the bathtub. They often get in trouble with employers over impulsive behavior at work, with creditors because of impulsive spending habits, and with friends because they make commitments and then

impulsively change their mind and go off with others instead.

Neglectful parents with impulse-ridden behavior are restless, intolerant of stress, and inconsistent. Their children never know exactly what to expect and may be abandoned for long periods by them. Children of neglecting parents of this type are likely to suffer the effects of abandonment, lack of supervision, and emotional neglect. In addition, because of the inconsistency of the parent, these children may have difficulty trusting others, developing positive relationships, and being consistent themselves.

3. *Cognitive disabilities:* Although only a small percentage of neglectful parents have cognitive disabilities that limit their caretaking abilities, they may neglect their children if they do not receive, or cannot comprehend, parenting information or have adequate supervision to help them care for the child.

4. *Reactive–depressive behavior:* These parents are so depressed that they cannot parent adequately. The depression may be a result of the death or loss of a significant person in their lives or the end of a love relationship, among other possibilities.

5. *Psychotic behavior:* These parents may be in such a delusional state that they cannot parent the child adequately.

Neglectful parents often are more resistant than abusive parents to be helped, particularly those who are apathetic and feel hopeless. Unlike abusive parents, who still have enough spirit to be angry, neglectful parents generally have feelings of despair and futility, which can be much more difficult to change. Social workers can make a start in helping these parents develop trust in other individuals and increasing their self-esteem, particularly through links with supportive individuals. This, in turn, will enable them to care for their children more adequately (Crosson-Tower, 2014).

Neglect is affected more by environmental factors than are the other forms of maltreatment. Because of its relationship to poverty, it may be more appropriate to consider the unmet needs of the child and the community and social response to meeting those needs rather than the inappropriate actions of the parents (Crosson-Tower, 2014; DePonflis, 2006). Most of the attention and resources in the area of child maltreatment have been directed to physical and sexual abuse at the expense of neglect, which merits much more concern.

Psychological Maltreatment Psychological mal-treatment, also called **emotional maltreatment**, is the most difficult form to define, the most difficult to substantiate, and the most difficult for which to obtain resources. Nevertheless, it is the most prevalent form of child maltreatment and, like other types of child maltreatment, it can result in serious long-term consequences for the child (Crosson-Tower, 2014; U.S. Children's Bureau, 2013b). Almost all states include emotional maltreatment in their definitions of child maltreatment. A typical definition includes content such as "injury to the psychological capacity or emotional stability of the child as evidenced by an observable or substantial change in behavior, emotional response, or cognition" and "injury as evidenced by anxiety, depression, or aggressive behavior" (Child Welfare Information Gateway, 2011).

EP 2.1.7a
EP 2.1.7b

One conceptualization is of two types of emotional maltreatment: emotional abuse and emotional neglect.

Emotional abuse refers to acts of commission, or emotional acts against a child. Emotional abuse often is verbal. It includes constant criticism and threats, such as telling the child how bad he or she is, perhaps saying that the parents wish the child had never been born, and blaming the child for all the parents' and family's problems.

Almost all parents emotionally abuse their children at one time or another (Crosson-Tower, 2014), but continual emotional abuse can lower self-esteem and undermine a child's feelings of competence. Parents emotionally abuse their children in other ways, too. Some parents, for example, give a child's prized possession to "another child who will appreciate it," telling the child that "you don't deserve special things, because you're bad." Parents have also psychologically abused children by shaving their head or doing other humiliating things as forms of punishment.

Children who are exposed to parents or others in the family being beaten or otherwise abused also experience psychological abuse. And children who are sexually abused are also psychologically/emotionally abused by that experience. Some experts suggest that the psychological abuse has just as severe, if not more severe, consequences for the sexually abused child than the sexual abuse itself (U.S. Children's Bureau, 2013b).

The other form of emotional abuse, *emotional neglect,* refers to acts of omission, or failure to meet the child's emotional needs. Parents who psychologically neglect their children may provide for their physical needs but interact very little with their children. They do not interact by cuddling or holding the child or engage in activities such as reading, singing, going places together, or just talking together. Children who do not have their emotional needs met are likely, as adults, to be unable to give emotionally to their own children. These adults may psychologically neglect their own children and also subject them to other types of maltreatment.

Garbarino, Guttman, and Seeley (1986, as cited in Crosson-Tower, 2014) provide a broader conceptualization of psychological maltreatment, which they define as "a concerted attack by an adult on a child's development and social competence, a pattern of psychically destructive behavior." They suggest that psychological maltreatment takes five forms:

1. *rejecting,* in which the adult refuses to acknowledge the child's worth and the legitimacy of the child's needs;
2. *isolating,* in which the adult cuts the child off from normal social experiences;
3. *terrorizing,* in which the adult verbally assaults the child, creating an environment of fear and terror;
4. *ignoring,* in which the adult deprives the child of essential stimulation and responsiveness; and
5. *corrupting,* in which the adult stimulates the child to engage in destructive antisocial behavior and reinforces deviance (p. 216).

The conceptualization offered by Garbarino and colleagues is based on an ecological/systems perspective, which suggests that emotional deprivation or emotional trauma in one domain of children's lives increases their vulnerability to similar experiences in other domains.

Problems Associated with Adolescents

Until recently, the literature about children and family problems has paid scant attention to the special needs of adolescents. However, youth violence, particularly the mass murders that have occurred in school settings, has drawn extensive media attention. Other problems associated with adolescents include gangs, teenage pregnancy, human sex trafficking and prostitution, and suicide. Many family-development specialists are

quick to point out that prevention and early intervention efforts aimed at young children and families would likely have eliminated many of these adolescent problems. They note that adolescents who enter the juvenile justice system as delinquents, gang members, runaways, victims of sex trafficking who have engaged in prostitution, or who are pregnant often come from families with many of the problems discussed in this chapter who have not received appropriate services and support. In other instances, families have attempted to seek services for their now-adolescent children for years without success because of issues of affordability, accessibility, and lack of knowledge among professionals about how to address serious mental illness in children and adolescents.

The Juvenile Justice System

EP 2.1.7b

Although delinquent adolescents are required by law to be treated differently than adults, the present juvenile justice system does not have the resources to address the numerous family problems and provide the extensive treatment that many juveniles need. Those who are released from the juvenile justice system more often than not quickly enter the adult criminal justice system. As juveniles are committing more severe crimes at younger ages, the issue of how to address their needs effectively and protect them, as well as those they harm, is becoming more pressing. Many states are responding by making the laws relating to juveniles tougher, such as certifying juveniles as adults and sending them to the adult criminal justice system to be prosecuted (see Chapter 13 for additional discussion).

Runaways

EP 2.1.7b

Most children who run away from home do so to escape serious family problems, such as physical and sexual abuse, alcoholism or other drug use, divorce, IPV, or oppression because they are LGBTQ. Because of the limited resources available to them while they are on the run, the majority of runaway youth engage in prostitution within 48 hours of being on the streets. They also are prone to become victims of crime, assault, robbery, sex trafficking, rape, and participation in the development of pornographic materials, and they are susceptible to acquiring sexually transmitted infections, including HIV/AIDS.

The needs of adolescents are often difficult to get help for because of scarce resources usually targeted at younger children. Many adolescents receive help for the first time after they come to the attention of the juvenile justice system.

Ben Molyneux People/Alamy

Resources for families are largely targeted toward younger children and don't allow teens to stay at their facilities. Youth shelters and services are a possible resource, but these are limited. One youth advocate suggested that some adolescents get arrested so they could gain shelter, food, and services by being booked into the juvenile detention center. In some cases, adolescents labeled as delinquent can be considered more appropriately as "throwaways" or "push-outs," when families fail to provide for their children's needs and now cannot cope with the problems of their emotionally damaged adolescents (Colby, 2011; Lopez, 2012).

An estimated 1.9 million youth in the United States experience homelessness each year because they have either run away or been forced out of their homes. Of those, half a million will be homeless more than a week, including teen parents with children, teens with mental health issues, and teens forced out of their homes because they are lesbian, gay, bisexual, or transgender. More than half of runaway youths are aged 15 or 16. Almost two-thirds of these youth seek assistance from youth shelters because of problems with parental relationships (National Network for Youth, 2014). However, there are limited services to assist runaway and homeless youth in many communities, particularly

those who need shelter. The U.S. Department of Housing and Urban Development reports that there are fewer than 4,200 beds nationally for this population (cited in National Network for Youth).

The Runaway and Homeless Youth Act of 1974 was passed in response to concern about runaway youth, who were exposed to exploitation and the dangers of street life. That act since has been expanded to assist homeless youth in making the transition to independent living and to provide drug education and prevention services to runaway and homeless youth. Advocates for youth have worked with the federal government to develop a plan to end youth homelessness by 2020. The plan calls for additional resources for safety net programs such as shelter, street outreach and transitional housing; increased coordination between mental health, juvenile justice, and child welfare institutions; better access to housing and health and mental health care; increased attention to youth who have been underserved historically: those who have been in foster care or received other child welfare services; those who have been part of the criminal justice system, and those are sexually exploited, LGBTQ, pregnant or parenting, nonwhite, or have mental health needs; greater focus on re-engaging youth in education programs that meet their needs; assistance with child care and parent education for those pregnant or with children; and increased opportunities for affordable housing (National Network for Youth, 2014).

Academic and Employment Problems

EP 2.1.7b

Many adolescents with problems suffer academically, and some have learning disabilities and other learning problems that undermine their confidence. In short, young people who do not feel good about themselves and are faced with daily problems at home, rather than support and encouragement, are not likely to do well in school. Dropout rates are of increasing concern, as are the consequent high illiteracy rates. The 2011–2012 high school completion rate was 93% for Asian Americans/Pacific Islanders, 85% for whites, 76% for Hispanics/Latinos, and 68% for American Indians/Alaskan Natives and blacks/African Americans (U.S. Department of Education, 2014). Adolescents who do not complete high school encounter difficulty in locating suitable employment and are more likely to end up in the criminal justice system, pregnant, homeless, and living in poverty.

Teen Pregnancy

EP 2.1.7b

Another problem facing our country today is teen pregnancy. Teenage childbearing can have long-term negative effects on both the adolescent mother and the newborn. Babies born to teen mothers are at higher risk of being low birth weight and preterm. They also are far more likely to be born into families with limited educational and economic resources. A child born to an unmarried, teenage high school dropout is 10 times more likely to be living in poverty as a child born to a mother with none of these characteristics. Most teenage mothers are unmarried and have not completed high school. They are not settled in a job or career, and many young fathers are not in a position to provide financial help. Finally, children born to teenage mothers are less likely to receive the emotional and financial resources that support their development into independent, productive, and well-adjusted adults (Annie E. Casey Foundation, 2010, p. 26). In addition, becoming a teenage parent interrupts, sometimes permanently, the teen's successful transition into adulthood.

Teens today are faced with a great deal of pressure from many sources—peers, the media, advertising—to view their primary self-worth in terms of their sexuality. With limited opportunities to be successful in other arenas—family, school, and the workplace—some teens think that producing a baby is the only way they can feel good about themselves and have someone to love them.

Among the many factors associated with teen pregnancy are poverty, low self-esteem, lack of information about reproduction, failure in school, lack of appropriate health care and other services, and poor family relationships. The emphasis on pregnancy prevention and intervention, however, has been primarily on teenage females, to the exclusion of prevention and intervention with teenage males.

One-third of 16-year-olds and nearly half of 17-year-olds report having had sex. The majority of sexually active teens use some form of contraception, most often condoms. Use of contraception among teens aged 15–19 during first time and later sex has increased, from 48% in 1982 to 78% in 2006–2010. However, the 16% of teens that report having sex when they were 14 or younger are less likely to have used contraception the first time and also take longer to begin using contraceptives than older teens (Guttmacher Institute, 2014). Although attention to pregnancy prevention often begins only when teens (females) reach age 13, developing positive self-esteem, effective decision-making skills, a strong value system, and a sense of responsibility for oneself and others—all major deterrents to teen pregnancy—are shaped from birth on.

In the past, most teens who became pregnant relinquished their babies for adoption, either formally through agencies or informally through relatives. Today, the majority of teens are choosing to keep their babies. Because infants born to teenagers are much more likely to have low birth weight or be premature, they are also more likely to have congenital or other health problems as those born to older mothers. The mothers are more likely to drop out of school, remain unemployed or underemployed, and bring up their children in poverty. The cycle often repeats itself. Teen pregnancy is both a cause and a result of poverty.

Youth Crime and Violence

EP 2.1.7b

While the increased number of multiple murders committed by youth, particularly in school settings, has received extensive media attention, violent youth crime in the United States actually is at a 32-year low

(Butts, 2013). Between 2003 and 2012, the estimated number of arrests of youth for murder declined 37%; for forcible rape, 36%; for robbery, 20%; and for aggravated assault, almost 43% (Travis & Waul, 2002). Analysts speculate that the reasons for this decline are complex. First, the youth population has declined, although it is now on the upswing again. The crack cocaine epidemic that took place toward the end of the 21st century has also waned. New policing strategies and stricter gun control policies are also cited as factors for the decline. Analysts who follow crime data believe that this period of decline is ending.

In addition to a growth in the youth population, increases in youth crime are likely to be seen because of a weakened economy and the return of large numbers of persons currently incarcerated to their communities. Identifying predictors of youth violence can help shape violence prevention strategies. Hawkins, Herrenkohl, Farrington, Brewer, Catalano, Harachi, and Couthern (2000) spent 2 years analyzing research on risk and protective factors for serious violent offenses committed by youth. Using a framework similar to the ecological/systems framework, they identified predictors in five domains:

- *Individual factors*—pregnancy and delivery complications, hyperactivity, aggressiveness, early initiation of violent behavior, participation in other forms of antisocial behavior, beliefs and attitudes favorable to deviant social behavior internalizing disorders
- *Family factors*—parent criminality, child abuse and/or neglect, poor family management, limited parental involvement, poor family bonding, family conflict, parent-child separation, parental attitudes favorable to substance use and violence
- *Peer-related factors*—delinquent siblings and peers, gang membership
- *Community and neighborhood factors*—poverty, community disorganization, access to drugs and guns, adults in neighborhood involved in criminal activity, exposure to violence and racial prejudice (p. 2).

Analysts suggest that the following strategies can be implemented to try to keep youth violence from increasing:

- Capitalize on the strengths of youth
- Collect better data to be better able to anticipate trends

- Revitalize community correction programs
- Improve policing and increase and strengthen police-community relationships (Travis and Waul, 2002).

Even though teen homicides have declined in recent years, the horror of school-based murders has received extensive attention in the media. Homicide is the third leading cause of death among teens 15–19, and firearms were the source of death in 85% of teen homicides and 42% of teen suicides. The homicide rate for Black male teens was more than 18 times higher than the rate for white male teens, and three times higher than the rate for Hispanic male teens (rates are 2.7 per 100,000 for white males 15–19, 48.5 for black male teens, 15.4 for Hispanic males, 7.6 for American Indian males, and 3.0 for Asian and Pacific Islanders. Black and American Indian females aged 15–19 had the highest rates in 2011 (Child Trends Data Bank, 2014).

Guns were the primary weapon used in the majority of violent deaths experienced by youth. Guns kill or injure a child or teen every half hour; in 2010, 2,694 children and teens were killed by guns and additional 15,576 were injured. In 2010, guns were used as weapons to kill "more infants, toddlers, and preschoolers than law enforcement officers in the line of duty, and … since 1963, three times as many children and teens have died from gun-related violence than U.S. soldiers killed in the Vietnam, Afghanistan, and Iraq Wars" (Children's Defense Fund, 2013, p. 6). Children and teens of color are much more likely to be killed by guns than white children and teens. Rates for firearm deaths were highest for black teens and lowest for Asians (Child Trends Data Bank, 2014). In 2010, black children and teens were almost times more likely to be killed by guns than whites, while Hispanic youth were more than three times more likely (Children's Defense Fund).

In contrast, white males have been the perpetrators of almost all school-based murders. Although fewer than 1% of student homicides and suicides occur at school, at a school event, or on the way to school, they create considerable distress for a large number of students, families, and entire communities. Some child advocates have raised concern about the fact that large numbers of black youth are dying by gunfire in urban areas like Chicago with little publicity, while school shootings in primarily middle- and upper-class white areas with mostly white victims have garnered national and international attention. Although there is no clear profile for someone who shoots students at a school, studies suggest that many youth tell at least one peer prior to the incident, have reported feeling bullied, are isolated with few friends and often limited interaction with family members, have a history of mental health problems, and have often made suicide threats prior to the incident (Brock, Nickerson, & Serwacki, 2014). It should be noted here that youth with mental health problems are much more likely to be victims rather than perpetrators of crime, and few of them even have access to guns, making it difficult to profile those more likely to commit violent crimes with firearms.

Youth advocates point out that 25% of youth in the United States report having easy access to a gun in the home, most indicate that they know how to access them, and many report handling them without their parents' knowledge (Baxley & Miller, 2006, cited in Brock, Nickerson, & Serwacki, 2014). Studies show that problem-oriented community-based police initiatives rather than indiscriminant crack downs are associated with decreases in gun-related violence. Another strategy cited by policy advocates and researchers is "pulling levers," an approach that reduces recidivism rates among offenders by varying responses that include repeated communication stressing crime avoidance as well as greater access and coordination with social service and other community resources. Finally, advocates call for eliminating loopholes in gun safety laws that make access to guns easy for children and youth, as well as those who may be likely to harm them (Brock, Nickerson & Serwacki, 2014).

Gangs

EP 2.1.7b

Many youth join gangs, which also contribute to youth violence. Although the number of gangs has remained stable in recent years, gang activity continues to raise concern in many communities across the United States. In 2011, almost 30,000 gangs with an estimated 782,200 gang members were active in 3,300 jurisdictions (Egley & Howell, 2013). Although many rural areas have gangs, gang activity is more prevalent in urban areas, particularly larger cities. Although gang related homicides declined nationally, they decreased only slightly in urban areas. Factors that contribute to homicides and other gang violence include inter-gang conflict, gang members returning from prison, and drug trafficking (Egley & Howell, 2013).

Many youth join gangs to "belong," indicating that gangs are "like families to me." Gangs replace the nurturing, support, and sense of belonging that youth lack in their own families. Using an ecological/systems perspective, the following risk factors contribute to the likelihood that a youth will join a gang:

- *Micro level* (individual risk factors)—Exposure to gun violence, limited social ties, high substance use, extensive drug dealing, illegally owning and carrying a gun, physical violence/aggression, being the victim of a violent crime
- *Meso level* (family, peer, and school factors)—
Family: delinquent and or gang-involved siblings; family history of criminal activity and other problematic behaviors; poverty/low socioeconomic status; family violence (child abuse, intimate partner violence); living in a small house or apartment; lack of parental supervision
Peers: Gang membership, association with peers who are delinquent, antisocial or aggressive; association with peers or relatives involved in gangs; peer substance use
School: Frequent truancy and absences, suspensions and expulsions; school drop out; limited connection to school; not motivated or committed to attending school; poor school performance; poorly functioning school, negative school environment, negative singling out and labeling by teachers
- *Exo level* (community factors)—Availability of guns; disorganized community; availability of/use of drugs in neighborhood; economic deprivation/ poverty; exposure to violence and racism; living in unsafe neighborhood with high crime rates; neighborhood youth in trouble (National Gang Center, 2014).

Gang members often commit crimes or violent acts as part of initiation rites or other gang-related activities. Peer pressure is considerable for youth who join gangs, and gang members have difficulty saying no to their peers when they become involved in inappropriate and/or illegal activities or to leaving gangs once they join them (Short, 2006). Law enforcement agencies in many communities have gang units that specialize in working with gangs. They collect and maintain information about local gang activities, sharing it with other local law enforcement agencies. Strategies to reduce gang activity include community policing by law enforcement officers who engage personally with gang members and outreach workers who work with youth in gangs to meet their medical and mental health needs and also try to influence them to leave the gang (Spergel, 2007).

Children's Mental Health and Suicide

EP 2.1.7b

Children are too often the victims of divorce, family and community violence, substance use, and other family, community, and societal dysfunctions. Still others are born or develop chemical imbalances or other biological conditions that impact their mental health. One in five children 18 and under has a diagnosable mental health disorder; one in ten has a mental health problem serious enough to affect functioning at home, at school, and in the community. In the past, it was believed that major mental illnesses did not occur until young adulthood or adulthood; today, we know that the onset may occur as early as seven and that roughly half of all lifetime disorders develop by adolescence. Youth also engage in use of alcohol and illicit drugs, often to self-medicate but exacerbating their mental health condition when they do so (Stagman and Cooper, 2010).

Children and teens with mental health problems struggle to succeed in school academically and with their peers. They are often bullied and have trouble making and keeping friends. Children and youth in the juvenile justice and foster care systems are much more at risk to have mental health problems than others their age. Those who have experienced or witnessed violence such as child abuse may have post traumatic stress disorder, which may impact their brain development and their ability to process information and make healthy decisions. Often, children are misdiagnosed. For example, children in foster care are often diagnosed with attention deficit disorder and put on medication. However, symptoms are similar to those of individuals with post traumatic stress disorder, which children who have experienced abuse may well have developed (Ruiz, 2014).

Many children are diagnosed with illnesses such as bipolar disorder as early as three. They may be put on strong psychotropic medications at very early ages, sometimes on medications that have not been tested adequately for children their age. Many children do not receive the therapy that they need to learn effective coping strategies, which medication alone cannot resolve.

The two greatest sources of treatment/counseling for children are mental health practitioners (including social workers) and school-based personnel such as counselors and psychologists. Treatment or counseling for children and teens is sought when they have thoughts about suicide or actual suicide attempts, depression, feelings of panic, eating problems, inappropriate behavior, problems at home, problems with friends, and problems with school. Many children and adolescents get involved in substance use and become alcoholics or addicts, often at young ages, and may also suffer serious physical and emotional injuries as a result.

In 2011, unintentional injury or accidents were the number-one cause of death for adolescents. Suicide was the third leading cause of death for adolescents 15–19 years of age and the sixth leading cause of death for children 5–14 years old (Centers for Disease Control and Prevention, 2014). Substance use, accidents, and suicide attempts often are interrelated. Depressed youth are more likely to abuse alcohol and other drugs and when they do, more likely to take unhealthy risks that can result in accidents, and also to attempt suicide. Other mood disorders, stressful life events, and limited communication with parents are also risk factors (Child Trends Data Bank, 2014).

Male youth are more than four times more likely than females to die from suicide, but females are more likely than males to attempt suicide (Child Trends Data Bank, 2014). Each suicide is estimated to intimately affect at least six other people. Suicidal individuals often try other ways to stop their pain first, frequently with drugs and alcohol, as indicated earlier. Children and adolescents who attempt suicide feel helpless, hopeless, and powerless, often in connection with a series of losses in their lives. When they are in an environment over which they feel they have no control, they ultimately may seek suicide as an escape.

Professionals who work with youth at risk for mental health problems, including suicide, believe that *mattering*—the extent to which a person believes he or she is important to others—has a significant influence in preventing such problems. Joiner (2006) has identified the following three significant aspects of mattering:

1. feeling that you command attention from others,
2. feeling that you are important to others, and
3. feeling that others depend on you.

Summary

Children, youth, and families in the United States develop problems for many reasons. From an ecological/systems perspective, factors associated with family problems are complex and interactive. Societal and cultural factors, as well as the level of support available to families from the communities in which they reside, have an impact on the nature and extent of family problems.

All families have strengths they can draw upon when they do have problems. Effective intervention and prevention programs can capitalize on these strengths when working with children, youth, and families. Still, effective intervention and prevention efforts must be undertaken within the broader context of understanding the complexities of the family problems discussed in this chapter.

Problems that result from changing family situations, substance use, interpersonal violence, child maltreatment, teen pregnancy, homelessness, and involvement with the juvenile justice system can have a dramatic impact on the well-being of families. Left unchecked, such problems often are passed on from generation to generation and thus are more resistant to family-strengthening interventions. In Chapter 12, we address programs and policies that help families in need and the roles that social workers play in providing these policies and programs.

Competency Notes

EP 2.1.3a: Distinguish, appraise, and integrate multiple sources of knowledge, including research-based knowledge and practice wisdom (pp. 312–313). Social workers use multiple sources of knowledge, including information gathered from clients, research-based knowledge, and practice wisdom, in making informed professional judgments about family dynamics and their impact on children.

EP 2.1.3b: Analyze models of assessment, prevention, intervention, and evaluation (p. 314). Social workers need to understand the diverse needs of children, youth, and families and then analyze models of assessment, prevention, intervention, and evaluation to determine which are most appropriate for the client(s) they are serving.

EP 2.1.7a: Use conceptual frameworks to guide the process of assessment, intervention, and evaluation (pp. 296–298, 302, 304, 306, 308–309, 311, 315, 317–318, 320, 322). Social workers use the ecological/systems and other conceptual frameworks to guide the processes of assessment, intervention, and evaluation to understand the needs of children and their families.

EP 2.1.7b: Critique and apply knowledge to understand person and environment (pp. 297–299, 302, 304, 306, 308–309, 311, 315, 317, 318, 322–323, 325, 327–328). To provide effective services to children and their families, social workers need to understand their developmental needs and the many ways that the environment impacts those needs.

EP 2.1.8a: Analyze, formulate, and advocate for policies that advance social well-being (pp. 302, 304, 306, 308–309). Social workers must understand the diverse needs and problems of children, youth, and families in order to analyze, formulate, and advocate for policies that advance their well-being.

Key Terms

The terms below are defined in the Glossary.

adult children of alcoholics	family mediation centers
alcoholics	family violence
battered child syndrome	feminization of poverty
blended families	incest
Child Abuse Prevention and Treatment Act	intimate partner violence (IPV)
child neglect	joint custody
codependent	nonorganic failure to thrive
custody	physical child abuse
cyber-stalking	psychological maltreatment
disproportionality	sexual abuse
emotional maltreatment	stepfamilies
enablers	
family	

Discussion Questions

1. What are three issues that must be considered when defining a family problem? How can the ecological/systems framework contribute to this process?
2. Name the four roles that family members play when substance use is a problem. How do family dynamics help shape these roles?

3. Describe the dynamics of a violent spousal/partner relationship.

4. Define four types of child maltreatment. What are their characteristics?

5. What are five factors that are likely to be associated with families who abuse or neglect their children?

6. Discuss the reasons that teenagers today are likely to become parents.

7. Why are children from unstable families more likely to become involved with juvenile delinquency and criminal behavior than those who come from stable families?

8. The chapter discusses disproportionality and points out the fact that children and teens of color are more likely to experience some of the problems discussed than white children and teens. Choose one of the topics covered in this chapter and discuss reasons why you think this might be the case.

9. What are some of the reasons why so many incidents of violence are committed against (and by) children and youth using firearms? What do you think can be done to curb these incidents?

On the Internet

http://www.acf.hhs.gov
http://www.americanhumane.org
http://child.cornell.edu
https://www.childwelfare.gov/
http://childhelpusa.org
http://www.childrensdefense.org
http://www.cwla.org
http://www.preventchildabuse.org

References

American Academy of Pediatrics. (2002). Co-parent or second-parent adoptions by same-sex parents (Technical report). *Pediatrics, 109*(2), 341–344.

American Civil Liberties Union. (2014). *LGBT parenting*. New York: Author. Retrieved from https://www.aclu.org/lgbt-rights/lgbt-parenting

Annie E. Casey Foundation. (2014a). *Kids count data book*. Baltimore, MD: Author. Retrieved from http://www.aecf.org

Annie E. Casey Foundation. (2014b). *National race for results indicators*. Baltimore, MD: Author. Retrieved from http://www.aecf.org/

Beattie, M. (2008). *The new codependency: Help and guidance for today's generation*. New York: Simon & Shuster.

Black, C. (2002). *Changing course: Healing from loss, abandonment, and fear*. Center City, MN: Hazelden.

Black, C. (2006). *Family strategies: Practical tools for professionals treating families impacted by addiction*. Bainbridge Island, WA: MAC.

Black, M. C., Basile, K. C., Breiding, M. J., Smith, S. G., Walters, M. L., Merrick, M. T., et al. (2011). *The National Intimate Partner and Sexual Violence Survey (NISVS): 2010 summary report*. Atlanta, GA: National Center for Injury Prevention and Control, Centers for Disease Control and Prevention.

Bowlby, J. (1951). Maternal care and mental health. *Bulletin of the World Health Organization, 3*, 355–534.

Broadhurst, K. (2009). *Critical perspectives on safeguarding children*. Hoboken, NJ: Wiley-Blackwell.

Brock, S., Nickerson, A., & Serwacki, M. (2013). *Youth gun violence fact sheet*. Bethesda: MD: National Association of School Psychologists.

Bronfenbrenner, U. (1979). *The ecology of human development*. Cambridge, MA: Harvard University Press.

Bronfenbrenner, U. (2005). *Making human beings human: Bioecological perspectives on human development*. Thousand Oaks, CA: Sage.

Butts, J. (2013). *Violent youth crime in U.S. falls to new 32-year low*. New York: Research and Evaluation Center, John Jay College of Criminal Justice.

Canfield, J., Hansen, M., Hartman, L., & Vogl, N. (2005). *Chicken soup for the single parent's soul: Stories of hope, healing, and humor*. Deerfield Beach, FL: HCI.

Casey, K. (2008). *Codependence and the power of detachment*. Berkeley, CA: Conari.

Casey, T., & Maldonado, L. (2012). *Worst off—single parent families in the United States: A cross-national comparison of single parenthood in the U.S. and sixteen other high-income countries*. New York: Legal Momentum. Retrieved from www.legalmomentum.org

Centers for Disease Control and Prevention. (2013). *National marriage and divorce rate trends*. Atlanta, GA: Author.

Centers for Disease Control and Prevention, National Center for Injury Prevention and Control. (2013). *Risk factors for intimate partner violence*. Atlanta, GA: Author.

Centers for Disease Control and Prevention. (2014a). *Intimate partner violence: Definitions*. Atlanta, GA:

Author. Retrieved from www.cdc.gov/violence prevention/intimate partnerviolence/definitions.html

Centers for Disease Control and Prevention. (2014b). *Suicide prevention.* Retrieved from http://www.cdc .gov/violenceprevention

Child Trends Data Bank. (2014). *Teen homicide, suicide, and firearm deaths.* Retrieved from www.child trends.org/?indicators=teen-homicide-suicide-and-firearm-deaths

Child Welfare Information Gateway. (2009). *Protecting children in families affected by substance use disorders.* Retrieved from https:www.childwelfare.gov/ pubs/usermanuals/substance use

Child Welfare Information Gateway. (2011). *About CAPTA: A legislative history.* Washington, DC: U.S. Department of Health and Human Services, Children's Bureau.

Child Welfare Information Gateway. (2013). *What is child abuse and neglect? Recognizing the signs and symptoms.* Washington, DC: U.S. Department of Health and Human Services, Children's Bureau.

Child Welfare Information Gateway (2014). *Child abuse and neglect fatalities 2012: Statistics and intervention.* Washington, DC: Department of Health and Human Services, Children's Bureau.

Child Welfare League of America. (2009). *Children of substance abusers fact sheet.* Washington, DC: Author.

Children's Defense Fund. (2013). *The state of America's children: 2014.* Washington, DC: Author.

Cleaver, H., Cawson, P., Gorin, S., & Walker, S. (Eds.). (2009). *Safeguarding children: A shared responsibility.* Hoboken, NJ: Wiley.

Colby, I. (2011). Runaway and throwaway youth: Time for policy changes and public responsibility. *Journal of Applied Research on Children: Informing Policy for Children at Risk, 2*(1). Retrieved from http://digitalcommons.library.tmc.edu/childrenatrisk /vol2/iss1/4

Conyers, B. (2003). *Addict in the family: Stories of loss, hope, and recovery.* Center City, MN: Hazelden.

Crosson-Tower, C. (2014). *Understanding child abuse and neglect* (9th ed.). Upper Saddle River, NJ: Prentice Hall.

Deal, R. (2014). *Marriage, family, & stepfamily statistics.* Retrieved from http://www.smartstepfamilies .com/view/statistics

DePonflis, D. (2006). *Child neglect: A guide for prevention, assessment, and intervention.* Washington, DC: U.S. Children's Bureau, Office on Child Abuse and Neglect.

DiNitto, D., & Johnson, D. (2012). *Essentials of social welfare: Politics and public policy.* Saddle River, NJ: Pearson.

DiSciullo, E., & Dunifon, R. (2012). *The benefits of parenting a second time around.* Ithaca, NY: Cornell University College of Human Ecology.

Duncan, S. F., & Goddard, H. W. (2005). *Family life education: Principles for effective outreach.* Thousand Oaks, CA: Sage.

Edwards, D. (2014). Texas judge ignores DNA tests, refuses parental rights because gay dads are married. *Raw Story.* Retrieved from http://www.rawstory.com/ rs/2014/06/19/texas-judge-ignores-dna-tests-refuses-parental-rights-because-gay-dads-are-married/

Egley, A., & Howell, J. C. (2013). *Highlights of the 2011 National Youth Gang Survey.* Washington, DC: US Department of Justice, Office of Juvenile Justice and Delinquency Prevention. Retrieved from www.ojjdp .gov/pubs/237542.pdf

Elliott, D., & Simmons, T. (2011). *Marital events of Americans: 2009 American Community Survey Reports.* Washington, DC: U.S. Census Bureau.

Fact sheet: The Violence Against Women Act. (2013). Washington, DC: The White House. Retrieved from http://www.whitehouse.gov/sites/default/files/ docs/vawa_factsheet.pdf

Federal Interagency Forum on Child and Family Statistics. (2013). *America's children–key natural indicators of well-being, 2013.* Washington, DC: Author. Retrieved from http://www.childstats.gov/americas children/famsoc1.asp

Frisbie, D., & Frisbie, L. (2007). *Raising great kids on your own: A guide and companion for every single parent.* Eugene, OR: Harvest House Publishers.

Garbarino, J. (1992). *Children and families in the social environment* (2nd ed.). New York: Aldine de Gruyter.

Garbarino, J. (2009). *Children and the dark side of human experience: Confronting global realities and rethinking child development.* New York: Springer.

Garbarino, J., Guttman, L., & Seeley, J. (1986). *The psychologically battered child.* Lexington, MA: Lexington.

Garner, A. (2005). *Families like mine: Children of gay parents tell it like it is.* New York: Harper.

Goldberg, A. E. (2009). *Lesbian and gay parents and their children: Research on the family life cycle.* Washington, DC: American Psychological Association.

Guttmacher Institute. (2014). *American teens' sexual and reproductive health.* New York: Author. Retrieved from www.guttmacher.org

Hawkins, J. D., Herrenkohl, T., Farrington, D., Brewer, D., Catalano, R., Harachi, T., et al. (2000). *Predictors of youth violence.* Washington, DC: Office of Juvenile Justice and Delinquency Programs.

Helpguide. (2009). *Domestic violence and abuse: Types, signs, symptoms, and effects.* Santa Monica, CA: Author.

Joiner, T. (2006). *Why people die by suicide.* Cambridge, MA: Harvard University Press.

Kemp, G., Segal, J., & Robinson, L. (2014). *Guide to step-parenting and blended families.* Retrieved from http://www.helpguide.org/mental/blended_families _stepfamilies.htm

Lawson, A., & Lawson, G. (2004). *Alcoholism and the family: A guide to treatment and prevention* (2nd ed.). Austin, TX: Pro-Ed.

Lopez, V. (2012). Thrown away children: An American epidemic. New York: *The Huffington Post.* Retrieved from http://www.huffingtonpost.com/victor-lopez -homeless-children-covenant-house

Marquardt, E. (2006). *Between two worlds: The inner lives of children of divorce.* New York: Crown.

Marsolini, M. (2006). *Raising children in blended families: Helpful insights, expert opinions, and true stories.* Grand Rapids, MI: Kregel.

Maynard, A., & Martini, M. (2005). *Learning in cultural context: Family, peers, and school.* New York: Springer.

McGoldrick, M., Carter, E., & Garcia-Preto, N. (2011). *The extended family life cycle: Individual, family, and social perspectives.* Boston: Pearson Allyn & Bacon.

McKenry, P. C., & Price, S. J. (2005). *Families and change: Coping with stressful events and transitions.* Thousand Oaks, CA: Sage.

Morrisette, M. (2008). *Choosing single motherhood: The thinking woman's guide.* Boston: Education Media and Publishing.

National Council on Child Abuse and Family Violence. (2009). *Spouse/partner abuse information.* Retrieved from http://www.nsvrc.org/organizations/73

National Gang Center. (2014). *National Youth Gang Survey Analysis.* Retrieved from http://www.national gangcenter.gov/Survey-Analysis

National Institute on Drug Abuse. (2014). *DrugFacts: Nationwide trends.* Washington, DC: Author.

National Network for Youth. (2014). *Youth homelessness in America: The current status and the way forward.* Washington, DC: Author.

Newman, B., & Newman, P. (2012). *Development through life: A psychosocial approach* (11th ed.). Belmont, CA: Cengage.

Partridge, D. (2006). *Blended families can work.* Pleasanton, CA: Author. Retrieved from http:// www.blendingfamily.com/article1.html

Patterson, C. (2008). *Lesbian and gay parenting.* Washington, DC: American Psychological Association.

PEW Research Center. (2011). *A portrait of step-families.* Washington, DC: Author.

Polansky, N. A., Chalmers, M. A., Buttenweiser, E. W., & Williams, D. P. (1983). *Damaged parents: An anatomy of child neglect.* Chicago: University of Chicago Press.

Powell, L. H., & Cassidy, D. (2006). *Family life education: Working with families across the life span.* Long Grove, IL: Waveland.

Ruiz, R. (2014, July 7). How childhood trauma could be mistaken for ADHD. *The Atlantic.* Retrieved from http://www.theatlantic.com/health/archive/2014/07/ how-childhood-trauma-could-be-mistaken-for-adhd/ 373328/.

Sedlak, A.J., Mettenburg, J., Basena, M., Petta, I., McPherson, K., Greene, A., and Li, S. (2010). *Fourth National Incidence Study of Child Abuse and Neglect (NIS–4): Report to Congress.* Washington, DC: U.S. Department of Health and Human Services, Administration for Children and Families.

Short, J. (2006). *Studying youth gangs (violence prevention and policy).* Lanham, MD: Alta Mira.

Sidel, R. (2006). *Unsung heroines: Single mothers and the American dream.* Berkeley: University of California Press.

Sipp, C., & Gallup, G. H. (2007). *The turn-around mom: How an abuse and addiction survivor stopped the toxic cycle for her family—and how you can, too.* Deerfield Beach, FL: HCI.

Spergel, I. A. (2007). *Reducing youth gang violence.* Lanham, MD: AltaMira Press.

Stagman, S., & Cooper, J. L. (2010). *Children's mental health: What every policy maker should know.* New York: National Center for Children in Poverty, Columbia University Mailman School of Public Health. Retrieved from www.nccp.org/publications/ pub_929.html

Stepfamily Foundation. (2014). *Stepfamily statistics.* New York: Author.

Substance Abuse and Mental Health Services Administration. (2013). *Facts on underage drinking.* Washington, DC: Author.

Travis, J., & Waul, M. (2002). *Reflections on the crime decline: Lessons for the future?* Washington, DC: Urban Institute Justice Policy Center.

U.S. Census Bureau. (2009). *Living arrangements of children under 18 years.* Washington, DC: Author.

U.S. Bureau of Justice Statistics. (2009). *Stalking victimization in the U.S.* Washington, DC: Author.

U.S. Children's Bureau. (2013a). *Child maltreatment: 2012.* Washington, DC: Author.

U.S. Children's Bureau. (2013b). *Factors that contribute to child abuse and neglect.* Washington, DC: Author.

U.S. Department of Education, National Center for Education Statistics. (2014). *The Condition of Education 2014* (NCES 2014–083), Educational Attainment. Washington, DC: Author.

Virk, R. L. (2009). *The four ways of divorce: A concise guide to what you need to know about divorce using litigation, negotiation, collaboration, and mediation.* Karachi, Pakistan: Vanguard.

Walker, L. (2000). *The battered woman syndrome* (2nd ed.). New York: Springer.

Weinhold, J. B., & Weinhold, B. K. (2009). *Breaking free of the co-dependency trap* (2nd ed.). Novato, CA: New World Library.

Whealin, J., & Barnett, E. (2014). *Child sexual abuse.* Washington, DC: National Center for PTSD, U.S. Department of Veterans Affairs.

Wilson, K. J. (2005). *When violence begins at home: A comprehensive guide to understanding and ending domestic abuse.* Alameda, CA: Hunter House.

Wolfinger, N. H. (2005). *Understanding the divorce cycle: The children of divorce and their own marriages.* New York: Cambridge University Press.

Wooding, S. (2008). *Step parenting and the blended family: Recognizing the problems and overcoming the obstacles.* Markham, ON, Canada: Fitzhenry and Whiteside.

Yuen, F. K., Skibinski, G. J., & Pardeck, J. T. (2003). *Family health social work practice: A knowledge and skills casebook.* Binghamton, NY: Haworth.

Suggested Readings

Aronson-Fontes, L. (2008). *Child abuse and culture: Working with diverse families.* New York: Guilford Press.

Bent-Goodley, T. (2011). *The ultimate betrayal: A renewed look at interpersonal violence.* Washington, DC: NASW.

Danzer, G. (2011). *My girls: A story of survival and togetherness in the inner city.* Washington, DC: NASW Press.

Fraser, M. (Ed.). (2004). *Risk and resilience in childhood: An ecological perspective.* Washington, DC: NASW Press.

Pipher, M. (2005). *Reviving Ophelia: Saving the selves of adolescent girls.* New York: Penguin.

Roche, P. (2008). *Unloved: The true story of a stolen childhood.* New York: Penguin Global.

Steiner, L. (2009). *Crazy love.* New York: St. Marten's Press.

Walsh, F. (2006). *Strengthening family resilience* (2nd ed.) New York: Guilford Press.

White, S. (Ed.). (2006). *Handbook of youth and justice.* New York: Springer.

CHAPTER 11

Services to Children, Youth, and Families

As a social worker with the local family services agency, Juanita Kingbird is involved in a number of activities to prevent families from becoming dysfunctional, as well as activities that help families when they have special needs. Her agency provides a variety of programs, including parenting programs that teach child care to teenage parents, an outreach program that seeks out parents who are under stress or need help with parenting, and individual, family, and group counseling for children and family members of all ages. Recently, the agency opened a shelter for adolescents who cannot remain in their own homes and a respite-care program for families of children with developmental disabilities. The agency also provides child care, classes in managing household finances, and employment services to help families stay together and remain economically self-sufficient.

At the start of a typical day, Juanita returns a crisis call from a mother whose son ran away from home the night before following a family argument. She calls the school social worker and asks her to check to see if the boy is in school and, if so, to talk with him. Then she holds two counseling sessions with adolescents who are staying in the shelter, exploring their feelings about becoming independent and separating from their families.

Juanita then leaves her agency for the high school, where she leads a support group for teen parents. Afterward, she meets individually with several of the parents and helps one of them make an appointment with a specialist for her infant with developmental delays. She has a quick lunch with the school social worker to coordinate services that the two of them are providing to some of her clients and then meets with the boy who ran away—who did go to school. He agrees to meet with her and his mother later in the day. On the way back to her office, Juanita stops to make a home visit with a client who has been emotionally abusing her two young children. Juanita interacts with the mother and her children, role-modeling good communication patterns and ways to give feedback and set limits positively.

She returns to the office in time to attend a meeting, with social workers from the five other agencies involved, regarding another family. Although the family has many serious problems, the coordinated intervention plan developed by the agencies seems to be effective, as everyone reports that the family is making progress. Juanita then meets with the boy who had run away and his mother. They negotiate family rules and boundaries, and mother and son agree to try to live together without major conflicts, and to return in a week for another counseling session. After a long and eventful day, Juanita leaves the agency for home, glad that she has a supportive family waiting for her so she does not burn out from getting too emotionally involved with her clients.

Juanita enjoys her job very much. Although she finds it difficult to deal with the many needs of the families with whom she is assigned to work, especially when children are suffering, she appreciates even small successes. "If I can make things better in some small way each day for one child or one parent, my job is more than worthwhile," she stated in a recent newspaper interview.

Programs and policies that address the needs of children, youth, and families are as diverse as the types of needs encountered. Traditionally, the system that has provided programs and policies that address child and family concerns has been called the **child welfare service delivery system**, "a group of services designed to promote the well-being of children by ensuring safety, achieving permanency, and strengthening families to successfully care for their children" (U.S. Children's Bureau, 2008, p. 1).

In this chapter we focus on services that address the children, youth, and family-related needs discussed in Chapter 10. We also discuss the roles that social workers play in providing services to children, youth, and families.

Current Philosophical Issues

All policies and programs that address the needs of children, youth, and their families must consider a number of philosophical issues and assumptions in addition to the social and cultural context of the child's family, the community, and the broader environment discussed in the preceding chapters. These are detailed, beginning with the child's right to a permanent, nurturing home life.

The Right to a Permanent, Nurturing Family

EP 2.1.7b

Every child has a right to grow up in a permanent, nurturing home, and every attempt must be made to provide such a home. The underlying assumption is that the child's own home is the best option for that child whenever possible. This philosophical position dictates that services should be provided first to the child's family and that every attempt should be made to keep the

child and the family together. This position has led to the development of **family preservation programs**, or services provided to a child and his or her family while they remain together, rather than placing the child in a foster home or other substitute care. Increasingly, emphasis is placed on services that will keep families together rather than removing children from their family settings.

In the past, many children receiving services in an overloaded service delivery system became lost in the system, with no chance to return home, be adopted, or become emancipated. There was no way to determine exactly how many children were in substitute care, and in some instances children were sent to other states because care was less expensive and the responsibility for their care could be shifted elsewhere. Although foster care was, and still is, supposed to be temporary, many children placed in foster care "aged out" of the system when they reached age 18 because no other options or alternatives were available to them. Children often lived in five or more foster homes and had as many or more social workers. Some children moved around so much that they didn't go to the same school for an entire school year.

Concern among many individuals and advocacy organizations led to legislation at both state and federal levels that mandates **permanency planning**. This concept ensures that when a child and family first receive services, a specific plan is developed to help keep that family together if possible and, if not, what will be done to provide a permanent, nurturing home for the child. Specific actions are identified to take place within certain time limits, and these actions are monitored for compliance by the court or a citizen review panel, or both.

If a family receives services without making enough progress to provide for a child's most basic needs, parents' rights can be terminated and the child can be placed in an adoptive home rather than the child remaining in limbo in the foster-care system. This planning allows agencies to make more realistic decisions about helping children and their families and ensures that families know specifically what they need to do to be allowed to continue to parent their children.

Best Interests of the Child

EP 2.1.7b

Decisions about the needs of children and families should be based on what is in the **best interests of the child**. Sometimes, even with the most appropriate intervention, it is questionable whether children's best interests are served by their remaining with their own families. In these circumstances, should decisions regarding where a child is placed (remain with his or her own family or be placed elsewhere) center on the child's best interests, the parents' best interests, or the family's best interests? Although experts agree that the rights of both the parents and their children have to be considered, attention first must go to the child's best interests. This means that before any decision is made, careful attention has to be given to the most beneficial outcome for that child.

The landmark book, *The Best Interests of the Child: The Least Detrimental Alternative* (Goldstein, Solnit, Goldstein, & Freud, 1996), carefully considers this issue. The authors argue that determining what is *best* for a child often places decision makers in a position of rendering a decision for which they have no experience or training. As a result, the interests of a child are best served by choosing the **least detrimental alternative** from a number of available alternatives. Other researchers have come to a similar conclusion. There are many issues to consider, and states have various definitions and processes that must be followed when considering child placement (Child Welfare Information Gateway, 2013a).

Federal legislation now requires that courts appoint a guardian *ad litem* (one who advocates for the minor on a limited and special basis) in certain child welfare situations, such as hearings when a parent's rights are being terminated. The sole purpose of the guardian *ad litem* is to represent the best interests of the child and to make a recommendation to the court with those interests in mind. This is especially important in situations in which the parents and the state child welfare agency disagree about what is in the best interest of a child.

Goldstein and colleagues (1996) also consider *who* should be involved in planning changes in a child's life.

Until recently, decisions regarding where a child should be reared usually favored the child's biological mother, and then the father. But often the early child rearing is by a relative or a foster parent, not one or both biological parents. More recent thinking considers the child's **psychological parent**, or person the child views as her or his parent from a psychological or emotional standpoint, who is not always the child's biological parent.

Considerations Before State Intervention

EP 2.1.7b
EP 2.1.9b

Under what circumstances should the community or state intervene in family matters? In the past, the family was considered sacred, and intervention in family matters was rare. When allowed, it was based on the doctrine of *parens patriae*—that the state is a parent to all of its children and has the obligation, through regulatory and legislative powers, to protect them and, when necessary, provide them with resources needed to keep them safe.

Many children grow up in unsafe and nonnurturing environments. Some family advocates argue that early intervention is necessary to keep a family together, as well as to protect the child from growing up with severe emotional damage. Others suggest that intervention in families should take place less often because in too many instances the intervention—especially when limited resources do not allow for the family to be rehabilitated—is more harmful than no intervention at all. These advocates suggest that intervention in families should take place only when requested by a parent, such as in child-custody disputes; when a parent chooses to relinquish parental rights and place that child for adoption; or when a parent is seriously maltreating a child.

The issue of when a government entity has the right or the obligation to intervene is increasingly before the courts. Many child advocacy groups have filed class-action suits against state child protective services agencies, charging failure to provide needed services to protect children from serious maltreatment (Children's Rights, 2014; American Prosecutors Research Institute, 2003; Hirschy & Wilkinson, 2009; Martell, 2005; Vieth, Bottoms, & Perona, 2005).

Preventing Family Disruption and Dysfunction

EP 2.1.7a

Another major issue is whether scarce resources should be targeted toward preventing family problems. And if prevention is chosen, should it be universal (or primary), secondary, or tertiary? All three are important in strengthening families. Most intervention with families today occurs *after* problems have occurred, and even then, services are not always available to the families that need them (see Box 11.1).

Because resources are scarce, little attention is given to any type of prevention. Of the few prevention programs available, the focus is tertiary in nature, well after the problems began. In many instances, this means that children must be severely abused or

Box 11.1   Lottie Wants the Best for Her Children

Lottie loves her children and wants the best for them. Putting their needs first has always been her priority. Her two youngest children, two year old Aaron and three year old Lucy, crawl into her lap and smother her with kisses, laughing as she gives them each hugs. Her two oldest children, eight year old twins Davis and Marcella, sit nearby at a table in the shelter common area, doing homework.

"I was 14 when I had the twins," Lottie says. I didn't know a thing about raising babies, and they were both premature." Lottie and her children have been at the shelter for a month. While cafeteria staff and residents prepare the evening meal nearby, a new family arrives, a mother with a baby and a boy about the age of the twins, looking lost and scared. After watching carefully, the twins go to greet the new family. "It's ok here," Davis tells them. "The people are nice, there are kids to play with, and we go to school right here. I got a hundred on my spelling test today," he adds proudly.

The younger children are now curled up around Lottie, almost asleep, their innocent faces full of possibility. Lottie worries that because of her choices, their options may be limited. She answers questions asked by the young social worker who is trying to help her so that she can expand options not only for herself, but for her children.

My dad left my mom before I was born, so I never knew him. For as long as I can remember, my mom was always drunk or drugged up and was usually passed out. I took care of her and my younger brothers the best I could. My brothers were put in a foster home when I was ten, but I loved my mom so I got to stay with her. She died of a drug overdose when I was 14. I moved in with a guy in the neighborhood who said he would take care of me. I was too innocent to know that 'taking care of me' meant becoming a prostitute.

When I was 16 I escaped from him and ran off with a guy I thought I was in love with. I got pregnant with the twins. They were born premature and stayed for a month in the hospital. The twins' father tried to hang in there with me, but he was overwhelmed and took off before they got out of the hospital. There I was, 16, and clueless about how to take care of my poor babies. Luckily, my great auntie took me and the babies in for a while. She had no money but she did have love, and she took care of the babies while I worked two different jobs cleaning hotel rooms and serving up burgers.

I saw hope for us all and was starting to feel good about life again. Then my poor auntie all of a sudden died of a heart attack. I was destroyed and got majorly depressed. I got started drinking and found myself on the streets with my kids. I got pregnant again. The father of my baby took us all in and for a while things were good. But when I got pregnant again with Aaron, I found out that my boyfriend was doing and selling drugs behind my back. He was really violent to me when I got on his case about the drugs, and also hit Davis when he tried to stop the fighting. I realized I wanted more for my kids and came here.

Lottie looks at her kids and her eyes fill with tears. "I'm going to do whatever I can to make sure their lives are better no matter how hard it is." "What do I need?" I need a job that pays me enough to live on my own and feed my kids and pay the rent, but I need child care 'cuz I don't want to leave my kids alone. I really had a close relationship with my auntie. I loved her so much. So I was thinking maybe I could do home health care or work at some kind of nursing home. I dropped out of school early, so I'd like to get a GED. My kids are really smart and I've been making them go to school and do their homework, so I'd like them to get in any programs you have and be able to learn more myself so I can help them. I want them to be educated, not like me. I started drinking again after Aaron was born and my drinking got pretty bad. I've been going to AA since I got here. I don't want to end up like my mom and have my kids have to take care of me."

The twins have finished their homework and are playing a board game with other kids, their laughter and their smiles filling the room with happiness and hope while Lottie's younger children continue to snooze cuddled up with her on the couch.

The social worker wants life to be better for Lottie and her kids. She knows there are many obstacles ahead, and that many women even as determined as Lottie are unable to achieve their dreams, or even be self-sufficient enough to provide for their kids. But the social worker is also determined, and she is hopeful that if she and Lottie work together, not only will Lottie have a better chance at life, but so will Davis, Lucy, Marcella, and Aaron.

families must be going through a serious crisis before services are available, and by that time, preserving the family is not as likely to be a realistic option.

How Accountable Are Parents?

EP 2.1.7b

A final issue receiving attention today is the extent to which parents should be held accountable for providing adequate care for their children and what should be done to parents who fail do so. Some specialists in family dynamics say that punishment is more likely to make parents angry and less likely to teach them how to be better parents. These specialists hold that effective intervention programs should be directed toward meeting the needs of the child, with an emphasis on keeping the child in the home. Others suggest that parents whose family problems pose severe consequences for their children be brought before the court and ordered to receive help, with punishment ordered if they refuse the help.

The relationships between parents' problems and consequences for a child are also coming before the courts. For example, should a woman who fears for her own life if she were to intervene to protect her child be held accountable if the father injures the child? In two high-profile child-abuse fatalities, a battered woman was charged with failing to protect her child from her violent husband. In one case, the mother was found not guilty. In the other case, the woman received a prison sentence that was longer than the sentence her husband received because she was tried separately by a different jury. The court also terminated her parental rights.

Recent cases of parents who have killed their children for seemingly unexplained reasons have also precipitated extensive debate. Should parents who have experienced severe maltreatment themselves as children and/or who have serious emotional or mental health problems be held accountable for their actions? If so, should those experiences be considered when assessing penalties for their actions? When the South Carolina woman was a young child, her mother committed suicide, as a young teenager she was molested by her stepfather, and she had a history of psychiatric problems. The prosecuting attorney asked that the woman receive the death penalty, but the jury recommended that she receive a life sentence. Tragic situations like these are likely to be repeated without stronger efforts to prevent problems such as domestic violence and child maltreatment and to intervene quickly and effectively when they come to light.

Defining Services to Children, Youth, and Families

EP 2.1.3a

Traditionally, services to children, youth, and families have been defined as **child welfare services**. Early definitions of child welfare focused on *residual* services—services provided *after* family breakdown. In his seminal child welfare book, Kadushin (1980) proposed, as the goals of child welfare services:

> to reinforce, supplement or substitute the functions that parents have difficulty in performing; and to improve conditions for children and their families by modifying existing social institutions or organizing new ones (p. 5).

The Social Security Act of 1935—the cornerstone of American social welfare policy—has a specific section (Title IV-B) that mandates states to provide a full range of child welfare services, defined as follows (Section 425):

> [P]ublic social services which supplement, or substitute for parental care and supervision for the purpose of:
>
> 1. preventing or remedying, or assisting in the solution of problems which may result in the neglect, abuse, exploitation or delinquency of children,
> 2. protecting and caring for homeless, dependent, or neglected children,
> 3. protecting and promoting the welfare of children of working mothers, and
> 4. otherwise protecting and promoting the welfare of children, including the strengthening of their own homes where possible or, where needed, the provision of adequate care of children away from their homes in foster family homes or day care or other child care facilities.

Because of negative connotations associated with the term *welfare* and the current emphasis on strengthening the family to support the child, child welfare services today more often are referred to as services to children, youth, and families (or as child and family services). They also are viewed more broadly, encompassing the traditional child welfare services of child protection, foster care, and adoption, as well as family preservation and supportive services such as child care and parenting programs.

The History of Services to Children, Youth, and Families

EP 2.1.3a

Some historians argue that societal attitudes toward children and families have improved significantly since the United States was settled, as have policies and programs supportive of children and families. Others disagree, saying that little has really changed. They suggest that the debate about the needs of children and families in the late 1800s and early 1900s is not much different from contemporary debate about the same issues. Regardless of whether today's children and families are better off or worse off than in the past, a review of the history of services to children, youth, and families shows clearly the historical base of our present child welfare service delivery system.

Colonial Times

In colonial times, children were considered to be the responsibility of their families, and little attention was directed to children whose families were available to provide for them, no matter how well the family actually met their needs. Children usually came to the attention of authorities only if they were orphaned and relatives were not available to provide for them. Churches and a few private orphanages cared for some dependent children. Prior to 1800, however, most orphans were placed in almshouses (poorhouses) or given to families to work as servants. The emphasis during this period was on survival. Fewer than half of all children born in this country prior to the 1800s lived to the age of 18.

The 19th Century

During the 1800s, more attention was aimed at the negative effects of placing young children in almshouses with adults, particularly adults who were criminals. In 1853, Charles Loring Brace founded the Children's Aid Society of New York, which established orphanages and other programs for children. Brace and others believed that these programs were the most appropriate way to "save" children from the negative influences of urban life (Stern & Axinn, 2012). Brace viewed rural Protestant families as ideal for these children, and he recruited many foster families from the rural Midwest to serve as foster parents.

"Orphan trains" carrying hundreds of children from New York City traveled throughout the Midwest, delivering children who had been selected by foster families. By 1880, the Children's Aid Society of New York had sent 40,000 children to live with rural farm families (Stern & Axinn, 2012). This was not a universally accepted practice. A number of prominent individuals called attention to the negative effects of separating children from their parents, even if the parents were deemed "unfit," but most of the criticism involved religious conflicts. The majority of children placed in foster homes were from Irish immigrant families who were predominantly Catholic, whereas their foster families were primarily German and Scandinavian Protestants. The outcry led to the development of more Catholic orphanages and foster homes.

Still, the needs of abused and neglected children and their families were not addressed. This changed in the 1870s as the result of a now-famous case involving a young girl in New York named Mary Ellen. Abandoned by her parents at birth, Mary Ellen was living with relatives who beat her severely, tied her to her bed, and fed her meager amounts of food from a bowl—like a dog. A visitor to Mary Ellen's neighborhood was appalled at the girl's abusive treatment and reported the situation to a number of agencies in New York City. When none would intervene, the visitor—reasoning that Mary Ellen fell under the broad rubric of "animal"—finally convinced the New York Society for the Prevention of Cruelty to Animals to take the case to court and request that the child be removed from the family immediately.

As a result of the Mary Ellen case, New York established the Society for the Prevention of Cruelty to Children, and other cities in the Northeast followed suit. The primary aim of these organizations, however, was on prosecuting parents rather than providing services to children or their families. Charity Organization Societies (COS) and settlement houses established in the late 1800s directed more attention to children and families, as well as to the environments in which they lived.

Other efforts in the late 1800s and early 1900s were aimed at children's health needs. Deaths of children were common during this period. Well-off families saw prevention of disease as a way to keep the diseases of immigrants from spreading to their own children (Stern & Axinn, 2012). During this time, various public health laws were passed. Other relevant legislation dealt with preventing child labor as well as mandating compulsory school attendance. More attention was given to the responsibilities of government to provide for children and families, and many states passed legislation establishing monitoring systems for out of home care and separating facilities for dependent, neglected, and delinquent children from those for adults.

The Early 20th Century

The most significant effort toward establishing a true service-delivery system for children, youth, and families was the inception of the **U.S. Children's Bureau** in 1912. This was a direct result of the first White House Conference on Children, held in 1910, and the activities of a coalition of child advocates from the settlement houses, COS groups, and state boards of charities and corrections.

The legislation establishing the U.S. Children's Bureau was significant, because it was the first law that recognized the federal government's responsibility for the welfare of the country's children. Julia Lathrop, a prominent member of society and a resident of Hull House in Chicago, was appointed the first chief of the bureau. The bureau's earliest efforts were aimed at birth registration and maternal and child health programs, in an attempt to reduce the high infant mortality rate and improve children's health.

One of the bureau's first publications, *Infant Care,* a booklet for parents, underwent more than 20 revisions and was the most popular document available from the U.S. Government Printing Office for many years. In its current form, the Children's Bureau is responsible for a number of federal programs for children, youth, and families and is under the umbrella of the U.S. Department of Health and Human Services.

During the first three decades of the 1900s, state governments continued to become more involved in services to children, youth, and families, particularly in the South and West, where strong private agencies did not exist. Many states established public departments of welfare that also were responsible for child and family services, including protecting children from abuse and neglect, providing foster homes, and overseeing orphanages and other children's institutions. Establishment of the American Association for Organizing Family Social Work (which later became the Family Service Association of America) in 1919 and the **Child Welfare League of America** in 1920 gave further impetus to the child and family services movement. Both of these organizations stressed the importance of the social work profession and established recommended standards for the provision of services.

During the 1920s, attention turned to facilitating the development of healthy parent–child relationships. Child guidance centers were established, and the

emphasis on psychoanalysis led to increased attention to child therapy. During this period, adoption was included as a formal child welfare service, and adoption legislation followed.

Services to children, youth, and families became more formalized when the **Social Security Act** was passed in 1935. This act established mothers' pensions, which later became the Aid to Families with Dependent Children (AFDC) program, and also mandated states to establish, expand, and strengthen statewide child welfare services, especially in rural areas. Child welfare programs incorporated the following trends:

- recognition that poverty is a major factor associated with other child and family problems;
- a shift from rescuing children from poor families and placing them in substitute care to keeping children in their own homes and providing supportive services to prevent family breakup;
- state intervention in family life to protect children;
- increased professionalization and bureaucratization of child welfare services; and
- an emphasis on the federal government's responsibility to oversee delivery of child welfare services within states to ensure that all children and families in the United States have access to needed services.

Notwithstanding the Social Security Act, problems persisted in the delivery of services to children, youth, and families. Access to services remained unequal, and many children continued to grow up in poverty. Some child welfare services, such as adoption, were provided primarily to white, middle-class families, and few child welfare services addressed the needs adequately. Many children, particularly children of color, spent their entire childhood in some form of substitute care.

The 1960s and 1970s

In the 1960s, the Kennedy and Johnson administrations took a strong interest in children, youth, and families. Services during these administrations were broader and were targeted at preventing and eliminating poverty. Many of these programs were based on the emerging belief that children's lives are influenced by their environment and that heredity plays only a minimal role in individual outcomes. The goal became to "maximize the potential of all individuals" and to help them become productive adults.

One result was the establishment of infant care centers and **Head Start**, a preschool program incorporating physical, social, emotional, and cognitive development. Other emphases were on education, as well as job training and employment programs for youth and their parents. With this broad base, traditional child welfare services received less attention in favor of strengthening families and preventive services.

When President Nixon took office, child and family services shifted from providing maximum resources to meeting minimum standards. Available services to children, youth, and families were narrowed greatly. Funding, programs, and policies reverted to more traditional child welfare services, including child protection, foster care, and adoption.

Because of increased concern about the high costs of child care and the number of children left alone because their parents could not afford child care, Congress attempted to pass legislation that would give states funds for child care subsidies for low-income working parents. The reasoning was that this approach would keep more children safe and also would reduce the number of women on AFDC and the number of families living in poverty. Not until 1990 was child care legislation—called the Act for Better Child Care (ABC)—introduced in Congress with a wide base of support.

Significant legislation enacted in the 1970s includes the Juvenile Justice and Delinquency Prevention Act (1974), which established limited funding for runaway youth programs; the Indian Child Welfare Act (1976), to prevent disruption of Native American families; and the Education for All Handicapped Children Act (1975), mandating, through public school systems, the provision of educational and social services to children with disabilities.

CAPTA The most significant piece of child welfare legislation in the 1970s was the Child Abuse Prevention and Treatment Act, or CAPTA (PL 93-247). This act established the National Center on Child Abuse and Neglect (now called the Office of Child Abuse and Neglect and under the Department of Health and Human Services). It required that states receiving federal funds strengthen child maltreatment programs in the areas of state definitions and reporting laws. It established research and technical-assistance programs to help states in developing child maltreatment prevention and intervention programs. And it established special demonstration programs that could be replicated later by other states. When the act was renewed

3 years later, a new section was added to strengthen adoption services for children with special needs (children who were waiting to be adopted and considered difficult to find homes for because of ethnicity, age, or developmental disabilities).

Adoption Assistance and Related Child Welfare Legislation A number of studies (see, Maas & Engler, 1959; Vasaly, 1976) indicated that the child welfare services delivery system perhaps was doing more harm than good. Researchers in one study (Shyne & Schroeder, 1978) found that although foster care philosophically was (and is) intended to be short term (6 months or less) while parents were preparing for family reunification through counseling and other types of assistance, this was not the experience of many children. A national study found that of the 1.8 million children served by public child welfare agencies, 38% were nonwhite, almost 40% were in out-of home placements with an average length of stay in foster care of 2.5 years, and approximately 200,000 children in out-of-home-care were waiting for permanent homes with half already available for adoption, but of that group, only half were receiving adoption services (U.S Department of Health and Human Services, 1977, pp. 4–5).

The Adoption Assistance and Child Welfare Act (PL 96-272), passed in 1980, changed the thrust of services to children, youth, and families. By placing ceilings on the amounts that states could receive for foster care, the act encouraged establishment of **own-home services** and reductions in the number of children in foster care. It also required the development of comprehensive case plans and 6-month reviews for all children receiving child welfare services, so they would not languish in foster care, and provided federal funding to subsidize the adoption of children with special needs.

Although PL 96-272 authorized more funding for services to children and families in their own homes, as is often the case with federal legislation, not enough funding was provided to overcome the imbalance that continued between foster care and child welfare services designed to prevent placement.

The 1980s and 1990s

Between 1980 and 1994, the number of children receiving child welfare services declined dramatically, from an estimated 1.8 million to 1 million. This decrease reflected a child welfare system that had evolved from a more broad-based child and family services system into a system serving primarily abused and neglected children and their families. The intent of PL 96-272 and other federal policies to shift child welfare from a foster care system to an in-home, family-based system was not realized. The number of children in foster care changed little in spite of the earlier legislation, and between 1980 and 1994 the number of children receiving in-home services declined by about 60%. Despite provisions in PL 96-272 for conducting an inventory of children in foster care for more than 6 months and for holding administrative and dispositional hearings, foster care drift remained a problem. Although the average length of stay in foster care declined overall, more than one-third of children placed in foster care remained there for more than 18 months.

Children of color, particularly African American children, were more likely than white children to be placed in foster care, even when they shared the same problems and characteristics, and to remain in foster care longer than white children.

Because so many children were growing up in foster care, many were leaving the system not knowing any other way of life. Many lacked skills to survive independently once they aged out of foster care. In 1986, PL 99-272 established the Independent Living Program, which provided funding for states to develop or strengthen services for youth age 16 or older who either were in, or had been in, the foster care system. The Abandoned Infants Assistance Act (AIAA), passed in 1988, provided grants to support demonstration programs to prevent the abandonment of children and identify the needs of infants and young children, particularly those born with HIV/AIDS and addicted to drugs. Other legislation passed during the mid-1980s focused on runaway and homeless youth, provisions for one-time payments to adoptive parents for adoption-related costs such as legal fees, grant programs for family preservation and support services, and the Children's Justice Act.

One of the most significant pieces of child welfare legislation in the 1990s was the Omnibus Budget Reconciliation Act of 1993 (OBRA, 1993), which established a new family preservation and family support services program. This act provided an important piece that had been missing from the earlier 1980 Adoption Assistance and Child Welfare Act by providing $1 billion in new funding over a 5-year period for states to prevent foster-care placement. Creating a separate funding source for family preservation and family support programs was intended to ensure that

funds be used to strengthen families, and not for child abuse and neglect investigations and foster-care placements (U.S. Department of Health and Human Services, 1994, p. 7).

This legislation highlighted family services and prevention as national priorities and provided opportunities for states to implement child welfare reforms.

During the 1980s and 1990s, the debate also was related to the extent to which race and ethnicity should be factors in foster care and adoptive placement. In 1994, Congress passed the Multiethnic Placement Act (PL 103-382) to promote the placement of children of color, who remained in foster care much longer than white children and were less likely to be adopted. This act prevents children from being denied placement with a foster or adoptive parent solely on the basis of the race, color, or national origin of either the prospective parent or the child. The act also requires states to "recruit and retain foster and adoptive families that reflect the racial and ethnic diversity of the children for whom homes are needed" (U.S. Children's Bureau, 1997, p. 3). Congress amended the Multiethnic Placement Act in 1996, repealing some of the language in the earlier legislation that could have been used to circumvent the intent of the law, and providing strict penalties for agencies receiving federal funding if they violate the act.

Although child welfare advocates heralded the greater emphasis on supportive services to families and decreasing foster care placements, new concern began to emerge about the balance between foster care and in-home services. In many geographic areas, the foster care numbers decreased and children and families remained together and improved their functioning. In other areas, however, large numbers of children continued to remain in foster care even when assessments showed that they most likely would have done well in their own homes with appropriate supportive services. In still other areas, the increased funding received for fewer children in foster care was coupled with an increase in severe injuries and deaths of children remaining in their own homes.

To address the concerns regarding the balance between safety and permanency, Congress passed the Adoption and Safe Families Act (ASFA) of 1997 (PL 105-89) as an amendment to the child welfare section of the Social Security Act. Funding and services provided under this act are based on the principles that 1) child safety must guide all child welfare services, 2) foster care is temporary 3) permanency-planning efforts should begin as soon as a child enters care, 4) the child welfare system must focus on results and accountability, and 5) innovative approaches are needed to achieve goals of safety, permanency, and well-being (U.S. Children's Bureau, 1997, pp. 4–5).

The Foster Care Independence Act (John H. Chafee Foster Care Independence Program) was passed in 1999. This act attempted to address the fact that, even with the recent improvements in state foster care programs mandated by Congress, many children still were leaving foster care only because they had "aged out" (turned 17 or 18 depending on the state) and were no longer eligible for services. This act was intended to ensure that young people who leave foster care get the tools they need to make the most of their lives: better educational opportunities, access to health care, life skills and other training, housing assistance, and counseling.

During the late 1980s and early 1990s, Congress also passed legislation in other areas of health and human services that had the potential to affect the child welfare system: PL 99-457 (Special Education for Infants and Toddlers), which provides services, including case-management services, to children from birth to age 2; the Omnibus Budget Reconciliation Act of 1984, which made limited funding available to states to develop services for children with emotional disturbances; the Developmentally Disabled Assistance and Bill of Rights Act (1990), requiring states to establish services in the least restrictive settings possible; and the Adolescent Family Life demonstration program, which provides support for pregnancy prevention as well as services to pregnant and parenting teens.

Despite the demands of serving a child welfare population of increasing size and complexity, states made significant inroads, particularly in reducing foster care and providing family-centered services during the 1980s and 1990s. Important components of a strong child welfare service-delivery system are the development of family preservation programs, efforts to reduce the length of stay in foster care, emphasis on culturally appropriate casework practice, and expansion of **kinship care** (Farmer, 2008; Iwaniec, 2006; Wilson & Crewe, 2007).

Support to Get Families off Welfare   The federal legislation that had the potential to be the most significant for children and families since the Social Security Act of 1935 was the Family Support Act of 1988 (see Chapter 7). Proponents of this legislation argued that this comprehensive package of services would reduce some of the problems with previously fragmented services created by categorical legislation. But funding to provide such services was limited from the beginning. Moreover, implementation of the act at the state and local levels required extensive coordination and services among human services agencies, school districts, community colleges and universities, employment- and job-training programs, child-care programs, health-care providers, transportation programs, and employers in the private and public sectors.

Because of the costs involved in initiating or strengthening welfare reform programs, many states were unable to provide sufficient resources to address the needs of AFDC recipients who wanted to get off welfare. Often-disappointed and otherwise motivated clients were placed on waiting lists for education, job training, and child care programs. Other clients were placed in jobs that paid the minimum wage so states could meet federal requirements to maintain funding for their programs, but these jobs did not pay enough or provide benefits that would allow clients to become self-sufficient.

In the mid-1990s, the mood of Congress and the rest of the country took a dramatic turn with regard to public welfare programs. Hailing the legislation as "the end of welfare as we know it," President Clinton signed into law the Personal Responsibility and Work Opportunity Budget Reconciliation Act of 1996 (HR 3734). This law, which eliminated AFDC as an entitlement program and replaced it with the Temporary Assistance to Needy Families (TANF) block grant, has serious implications for children. Under TANF, rigid time limits were imposed as to how long and under what conditions clients can continue to receive assistance for themselves and their children.

The legislation also consolidated separate child-care programs created during the 1980s. In addition, it mandated changes in the Supplement Nutrition Assistance Program (SNAP, formerly the Food Stamp Program), SSI for children, benefits for legal immigrants, the Child Support and Enforcement Program, and child nutrition programs (U.S. Department of Health and Human Services, 1994).

Moving into the 21st Century

In an executive memorandum dated December 14, 1996, President Clinton said:

> *I am committed to giving the children waiting in our Nation's foster care system what every child in America deserves—loving parents and a healthy, stable*

home. The goal for every child in our Nation's public welfare system is permanence in a safe and stable home, whether it be returning home, adoption, legal guardianship, or another permanent placement.

While the great majority of children in foster care will return home, for about one in five, returning home is not an option, and they will need another home, one that is caring and safe. These children wait far too long, typically over 3 years, but many children wait much longer to be placed in permanent homes. Each year state child welfare agencies secure homes for less than one-third of the children whose goal is adoption or an alternate permanent plan. I know we can do better. (U.S. Children's Bureau, 1997, p. 1)

This was the first time in history that a U.S. President had specifically made adoption and permanency planning a priority. President Clinton directed the Secretary of Health and Human Services to recommend strategies to move children more quickly into permanent homes and to double the number of children adopted or permanently placed during the next 5 years. The report called for the development of model state legislation to advance the goal of giving every child in the U.S. child welfare system a safe,

permanent home. The report urged that child welfare reform be broad-based and interdisciplinary.

Changes Under the George W. Bush Administration

The 1996 welfare reform legislation was reauthorized by the **Deficit Reduction Act of 2005**, signed into law by President George W. Bush in February 2006. The reauthorization maintained the original law's requirement that 50% of states' welfare caseloads fulfill statutory work requirements. It also updated incentives for states to reduce welfare caseloads, expanded the pool of families subject to work requirements, and created a new penalty for failing to comply with work-verification procedures (U.S. Department of Health and Human Services, 2006).

Overall, the reauthorization of the Personal Responsibility and Work Opportunity Budget Reconciliation Act of 1996 tightened the focus on work requirements for recipients and strengthened state accountability. This reauthorization was even more restrictive than the original 1996 legislation. Early studies on the negative effects of the 1996 welfare reform law on former welfare clients have failed to convince most politicians and the general public that the United States is pursuing a social welfare policy that has disastrous consequences for millions of children and families (see Figure 11.1).

FIG 11.1 Who's watching those kids?
SOURCE: Reprinted with permission from the *Austin* (Texas) *American Statesman.*
NOTE: Ben Sargent, an editorial cartoonist with the *Austin American Statesman,* captures the essence of the systems/ecological framework and the need for giving attention to children at all levels of the environment.

Ben Sargent/Universal Press Syndicate

2000–2010

A number of other activities at the federal level designed to have a positive impact on children and families have taken place during the first decade of the 21st century.

- The Child and Family Services Improvement Act of 2006 reauthorized the Promoting Safe and Stable Families program for a 5-year period.
- The U.S. Children's Bureau awarded the Adoption Exchange Association in Denver $22 million over a 5-year period to operate the National Adoption Internet Photo-listing Service (AdoptUSKids).
- Kinship foster care was promoted as a viable foster-care placement alternative. The Kinship Caregiver bill called for establishing a Kinship Guardianship Assistance program to provide federal assistance for subsidized guardianship programs. The bill also required states to notify grandparents and other relatives when children enter the foster-care system. The bill died in committee and did not become law.
- The U.S. Department of Health and Human Services published a final rule to establish a new approach to monitoring state child welfare programs. Under the rule, states were to be assessed for substantial conformity with the following federal requirements for child protective, foster care, adoption, family preservation and family support, and independent services.
- Using funds from the Department of Justice's Victims of Crime Fund, the Children's Justice Act helps states develop, establish, and operate programs designed to improve the investigation and prosecution of child abuse and neglect cases.
- The Children's Health Act of 2000 reauthorized programs within the jurisdiction of the Substance Abuse and Mental Health Services Administration to improve mental health and substance-abuse services for children and adolescents and implement proposals giving states more flexibility in the use of block-grant funds with accountability based on performance. The act also consolidated discretionary grant authorities to provide more flexibility to respond to those who need mental health and substance-abuse services.
- State child welfare legislation was also enacted, addressing critical issues such as parent and child involvement in case planning, education of children in foster care, kinship care and guardianship, children's exposure to drug manufacturing, and tribal affairs.

- The Safe and Timely Interstate Placement of Foster Children Act of 2006 (PL 109-239) was passed to improve protections for foster children and to hold states accountable for the safe and timely placement of children across state lines. Under the legislation, each state must complete home studies requested by another state within 60 days (this time may be extended to 75 days under certain conditions). The law also calls for an increase in the frequency of state caseworker visits for children in out-of-state foster-care placements as well as requires each state to include in its plan for child welfare services the assurance that the state will eliminate legal barriers to facilitate timely adoptive or permanent placements for children.
- The Adam Walsh Child Protection and Safety Act of 2006 (PL 109-248) established a comprehensive national system for sex offender registration and community notification. Under this legislation, states are required to conduct national fingerprint-based criminal records checks and checks of state child abuse and neglect registries for all prospective foster or adoptive parent placements.
- The Federal Consent Decree Fairness Act legislation was introduced in both the House and the Senate in 2005. This proposed legislation would have introduced time limits and other restrictions for Federal Court consent decrees that place state or local government agencies under court control. The goal of the legislation was to place control of programs and funding back into the hands of lawmakers once the issue that prompted the lawsuit has been resolved. The bill died in committee and never became law.
- In September 2007, the U.S. Children's Bureau awarded multi-year funding to 53 grantees representing 29 states and 6 tribes designed, among other things, to expand family drug courts, improve systemwide collaboration, expand access to comprehensive family-centered treatment, and promote the use of evidence-based practice approaches.
- The Fostering Connections to Success and Increasing Adoptions Act of 2008 (PL 110-351) amended titles IV-B and IV-E of the Social Security Act to provide support to some relatives who are caregivers, provide for Tribal foster care and adoption access, and improve incentives to promote adoption.
- The National Center for Housing and Child Welfare launched a new website to promote

collaborations at the local, regional, and state levels in order to better assist families when the primary barrier to reunification with their children in foster care is the lack of affordable, safe, decent, and permanent housing.

• Finally, the U.S. Children's Bureau launched a website for grandparents and other relatives raising children ("grandfamilies"). Users of the website gain access to a searchable database of state laws and pending legislation that may impact their circumstances. The database has also served as a valuable resource for policymakers, attorneys, advocates, and others interested in child welfare policy and law.

One of the most ambitious proposed child welfare undertakings of the new millennium was the Leave No Child Behind Act (S 448/HR 936). This omnibus legislation was aimed at achieving a healthy start (health coverage for all of the more than 9 million uninsured children in the United States), a head start (increased funding for child care for 3- and 4-year-olds in the Head Start program), a fair start (support for working parents to remain employed and help lift themselves and their children out of poverty), and a safe start (assurance that more children are in safe, nurturing, and permanent families by extending support to families before they incur family breakdown). This bill was among a plethora of domestic legislation that fell by the wayside when federal priorities shifted after the terrorist attacks of September 11, 2001.

The most significant piece of legislation impacting children since the passage of the Social Security Act in 1935 was the Patient Protection and Affordable Care Act of 2010 (see Chapter 8 for detailed discussion). Estimates show that this act will extend insurance coverage to 94.7% of U.S. children, moving some from other programs for low income children such as CHIP and Medicaid. Increased access to care is expected to include early prevention and intervention of both health and mental health needs that can reduce long-term consequences for children as well as greater access to reproductive and prenatal care for women (Kenney, 2012).

Child Welfare After 2010: Mixed Results

The second decade of the 21st century has seen mixed results for children. The historic passage of the Affordable Care Act 2010 was heralded as a milestone in improving health and mental health care for children and families. However, continuous pressure to repeal the Affordable Care Act and the reluctance of some states to expand Medicaid eligibility still leave many children in limbo who need health and mental health services.

International as well as national events have made children and their needs a lower priority during the second decade of the 21st century. The wars in Iraq and Afghanistan, the economic recession that began in 2007, and the increasing polarization of the federal and many state governments have resulted in a reduction in the availability of services to children at the same time that their needs are increasing. Congressional gridlock in particular has resulted in failure to reauthorize critical child welfare legislation. New bills, even on topics that in the past would have passed with extensive bipartisan support, languish indefinitely.

In addition to the limited funding authorized to implement the requirements of each act, one of the drawbacks to these legislative efforts has been the continued categorization of legislation. Such categorization leads to the establishment of programs limited to narrow populations and reinforces the fragmentation of services. More recent sessions of Congress have placed additional ceilings on amounts available for child and family services. Thus, even attention to a newly publicized area deemed important, such as legislation establishing programs targeted at gangs and youth crime, usually has not resulted in increased funding.

Policies and funding that provide services for children and families today typically fall into two categories: those that provide economic security, such as Medicaid, CHIP, and SNAP, and programs that focus on protecting children, such as CAPTA. Before the recent conflict over the federal budget, federal cuts had left protection programs alone. They are relatively small in comparison to other programs, and it is hard to argue that vulnerable populations should not be protected. Economic security programs have continuously been slated for cuts, with the House passing bills repeatedly that cut programs entirely or severely limited them. In some instances, such as the Farm Bill of 2013, the major cuts to SNAP did not occur, while in other instances, bills are still pending with limited hope for compromise. However, even without the recent budget logjam, funding of both kinds of programs has not kept up with inflation in spite of a growing need for them (CWLA, 2013).

Threats to children and families, particularly those who are low income, remain at both state and federal levels. Advocacy groups such as the Child Welfare League of America and the Children's Defense Fund are promoting the following principles as funding and programmatic decisions are made, with evidence-based practices to support their efforts:

- make budget cuts carefully, with careful attention to their long-and short-term impact on children and families,
- reduce racial disparities in economic and social supports available to children and families,
- invest in education through early childhood programs and improved graduation rates,
- invest in health coverage and nutrition for children,
- invest in work supports such as child care and job training,
- reform immigration policies,
- extend the age to remain in foster care to 21 and increase programs that promote self-sufficiency, including higher education participation, for youth in care,
- expand programs for fathers, particularly teen parents,
- revise federal legislation to cover preventive and post-placement services for families,
- focus services more heavily on the impact of trauma on children and families,
- keep the Earned Income Tax Credit, and
- ensure that the wealthiest individuals and corporations pay their fair share of taxes (CWLA, 2013; Children's Defense Fund, 2012).

Preventive Services for Children

Although preventive services receive less attention than other types of services, many programs strengthen families and reduce the chances for family dysfunction. These include natural support systems; home-based services; parent education; child development and child care programs; recreational, religious, and social programs; health and family-planning programs; and educational opportunities. In recent years, many states have curtailed or eliminated these services because of economic constraints.

Such actions tend to save funds in the short term but raise the possibility of having to spend even more in the long term to address problems that might have otherwise been prevented.

Natural Support Systems

EP 2.1.7a
EP 2.1.7b
EP 2.1.9b

Given the scarcity of formal resources, more and more attention is being directed to strengthening **natural support systems**. Many families develop social networks of friends, relatives, neighbors, or co-workers who provide emotional support; share child care, transportation, clothing, toys, and other resources; offer the opportunity to observe other children, parents, and family constellations and how they interact; and provide education about child rearing and other family life situations. But studies show that many families with problems lack such support systems. Much could be learned about informal family supports, for example, by studying the child-rearing practices of indigenous groups such as those that can be found in communities with significant refugee populations.

A key role of social services agencies, religious groups, and other community organizations is to provide support systems for new families and other families who lack natural support systems. For example, some communities have established telephone support programs for various groups, through which individuals can receive information about appropriate resources, while others have implemented home visitor programs where a volunteer serves as a mentor and coach to new or struggling parents.

In-Home Services

EP 2.1.7a
EP 2.1.7b
EP 2.1.9b

A relatively recent focus has been on **in-home family-centered services**—services delivered to children and families in their own homes, with a goal of preserving the family system by strengthening the family to bring about needed change. Comprehensive services, usually overseen by a single case manager assigned to the family, include homemaker services, respite care, child care, crisis intervention, financial assistance, substance-abuse treatment, vocational counseling, and help in locating housing and transportation. Those providing services serve as coaches, mentors, and help build skills relating to parenting, child safety, and coping with stressful situations.

Most home-based service programs include the following features (Crosson-Tower, 2012):

- a primary worker or case manager who establishes and maintains a supportive, nurturing relationship with the family;
- small caseloads with a variety of service options used with each family;
- a team approach, in which team members provide some services and serve as a backup to the primary worker/case manager;
- a support system available 24 hours a day for crisis calls and emergencies;
- the home as the natural setting, with maximum use of natural support systems, including the family, extended family, neighborhood, and community;
- parents remaining in charge of and responsible for their families as educators, nurturers, and primary caregivers; and
- willingness to invest at least as much in providing home-based services to a family as society is willing to pay for out-of-home care for our children.

Most families receiving home-based, family-centered services are those with multiple needs. Because of the chronic, severe problems and repeated crises in these families, past efforts have been largely ineffective. Although federal and state funds are much more likely to be used for foster care, studies show that children who receive in-home services have lower rates of post traumatic stress symptoms (Kolko et al., 2010, cited in Child Welfare Information Gateway, 2014c).

Home-based family-centered services are based on an ecological/systems approach to family intervention, viewing the *entire family* as the unit of help. Intervention is short-term and goal-oriented, aimed at specific behavioral change. Intensive services usually are provided to families over a period of 60 to 90 days.

Providing intensive services to a limited number of families at home has significant benefits. First, it gives workers a chance to stabilize the family so it can function either independently or with fewer services while allowing the children to remain in the home. Second, it allows workers to determine more quickly and with more documentation if the family cannot be stabilized. This enables children to be placed in adoptive homes, if

indicated, rather than remain in limbo in either a dysfunctional, life-threatening family situation or the instability of foster care.

Research has shown that, for the most part, short-term gains achieved by in-home service programs do not persist over time. Many programs are now targeting more specific services to families with a greater focus on strengthening family functioning, coupled with other services such as therapy and substance abuse treatment, rather than a "last resort" to keep children from going into foster care in a family with a wide range of serious problems (Child Welfare Information Gateway, 2014c). Studies also suggest different durations of service and intensity that address the unique needs of each family are critical if in-home services are to be successful (U.S. Children's Bureau, 2003; WESTAT & James Bell Associates, 2002).

Parent Education

EP 2.1.7a
EP 2.1.7b
EP 2.1.9b

While math and English are school staples, little attention is given to one of the most important roles that children are likely to play as adults: being a parent. Many communities offer parenting classes aimed at a wide range of parents: prenatal classes for parents before the birth or adoption of their first infant, classes for parents of toddlers and preschoolers, classes for parents of school-age children, and classes for parents of adolescents. These programs offer education about basic developmental stages of children and adolescents and alternative methods of child rearing and discipline. They also encourage the development of mutual support systems among participants.

A number of organizations certify parenting programs based on evidence that they are effective after conducting research with participants. One example of a successful evidence-based parent education program is the Nurturing Parenting Program. This program helps parents learn nurturing parenting skills and reduce incidents of abusive and neglectful parenting practices. The curriculum has been adapted to be culturally sensitive to various populations. Children also participate, meeting in separate groups (Child Welfare Information Gateway, 2013b).

Education about the various types of family problems—and, if they occur, about resources available—is a significant form of prevention. And many communities offer programs specifically about sexual abuse of children and how to avoid it by teaching children about types of touch and what to do when they find themselves in an uncomfortable situation with an adult or older child. Finally, some communities offer education in the form of alcohol and drug awareness programs.

Child Development and Child Care Programs

EP 2.1.7a
EP 2.1.7b
EP 2.1.9b

Accessible, high-quality child care programs that are affordable for working parents, particularly single parents, can help to prevent family breakdown. These programs provide a safe, comfortable, nurturing environment for children while their parents work, thereby reducing parental stress. Many child care programs offer additional opportunities for parents, including parenting education classes, babysitting cooperatives, and social programs, as well as the opportunity to develop support systems with other parents and children. But affordable, high-quality, child care programs often are unavailable to working parents, particularly in inner-city and rural areas. Child care for infants, children with disabilities or other special needs, school-age children during vacations and holidays, and children who are ill also is not widely available in the United States or if it is, the cost is prohibitive for most families. An additional gap in services relates to evening and night child care for parents who must work two jobs or late shifts.

Although special programs are available for low-income parents, they often are limited in the hours and in the number of children they can serve. Head Start—perhaps the most successful federal program established under the Office of Economic Opportunity in the 1960s—provides a developmental learning program for preschool children, as well as health care, social services, and parent education. Also available to some parents on a limited basis are infant–parent centers that allow parents an opportunity to learn how to interact and play with their children and stimulate their development.

Recreational, Religious, and Social Programs

EP 2.1.7a
EP 2.1.7b
EP 2.1.9b

When discussing programs that strengthen the welfare of children and their families, the broader social, recreational, and religious programs must be included. Faith-based organizations such as churches, synagogues, and mosques meet the spiritual, emotional, social, and recreational needs of many children, youth, and families. They can play a major role in establishing special preventive services, such as child care programs, outreach centers, and parent-education programs.

Federal faith-based initiatives have come under criticism from groups claiming that these programs violate the separation of church and state provisions of the U.S. Constitution. Other concerns revolve around whether faith-based organizations have the resources required to deliver services effectively and efficiently and that are culturally sensitive to the needs of diverse groups.

Increasingly, the business community is providing preventive services through the workplace, including informational programs during the lunch hour for working parents, recreational facilities and programs for employees and their families, and the facilitation of coworker support systems. Many communities offer substantial recreation and family entertainment programs for families without charge. Coalitions involving schools, social service agencies, recreational programs, and religious groups have formed in many areas to provide activities that are both educational and recreational. A number have targeted reduction in obesity, diabetes, heart disease, and other health issues, engaging children and families through health fairs, sports events, leadership retreats, and media campaigns. Most communities, however, seem to lack programs geared to adolescents. Some experts attribute increases in adolescent problems, including teen pregnancy and delinquency to the lack of available programs for this age group.

Health and Family-Planning Programs

EP 2.1.7a
EP 2.1.7b
EP 2.1.9b

Early health screening can reduce child and family problems (Children's Defense Fund, 2014; Federal Interagency Forum on Child and Family Statistics, 2014). Health problems place increased stress on families, and access to affordable health care from prenatal care to adult care is vital in helping to prevent family breakdown. In addition, programs can assist families in deciding whether to become parents and in exploring options when pregnancy occurs.

About 1 in 12 babies born in the United States is low birth weight (weighing less than 2,500 grams, or about 5.5 pounds). These babies are at high risk for developmental problems and infant mortality (Children's Defense Fund, 2014), but potential problems can be reduced substantially through comprehensive prenatal care (National Committee for Quality Assurance, 2008; U.S. Department of Health and Human Services, 2009).

Educational Opportunities

EP 2.1.7a
EP 2.1.7b
EP 2.1.9b

Many studies identify the strong relationship between difficulties in school and individual and family problems (Becvar, 2006; Berrick & Gilbert, 2008; Garbarino, 2008; Liebenberg & Ungar, 2008; McElwee, 2007). Programs that offer children an opportunity to learn in ways that help them feel good about themselves and develop a sense of competence help to prevent family and child-related problems. As a result, these children are less likely to have children themselves while they are in school, to drop out of school, or to live their lives in poverty. School-based social services allow for close cooperation among children and adolescents, teachers and school administrators, parents, and community members.

Many communities have focused attention on early childhood education programs for children 3–5 so that they are better prepared socially, emotionally, and academically when they enter kindergarten and more likely to continue to do well in later years. Voters in San Antonio, Texas, for example, approved a 1/8 cent sales tax increase in 2012, with funds allocated to establish early childhood centers throughout the city. Civic leaders and government officials are promoting greater attention to education, including high school graduation and college participation, to help reduce risks as children grow, but also to help ensure a stable, well-trained workforce that will be globally competitive in the future.

Services to Children and Families at Risk

EP 2.1.7a
EP 2.1.7b
EP 2.1.9b

A lack of coordination is a problem identified by service providers and recipients alike. Some communities have made special efforts to increase coordination, avoid duplication, and reduce gaps in services available to at-risk children and families. These include:

- "first-stop" resource centers where families can receive thorough assessments so they can be referred to appropriate agencies rather than going from agency to agency only to learn that services are not available to them or do not meet their needs;
- computerized databases that contain critical information about the services available to the target population;
- centralized information and referral systems;
- co-location of offices and programs;
- coordinated multi-agency service networks; and
- systems of care, multiple agencies that provide "wrap-around services" to families who are receiving or need services from child welfare, mental health, health care, and/or juvenile justice agencies.

Through such efforts, at-risk families—often reluctant to trust service providers and without transportation to access services—can receive individual and family counseling, complete forms to receive public assistance, get help in finding employment and housing, and attend parenting classes and parent support groups—all at the same location. In many settings, if they complete services they have been receiving but still need other types of help, a continuum of care model moves them to the next level of services, often with the same case manager to ensure that services build on what has already been provided. For example, a teen may receive an assessment for substance use, spend time in an in-patient treatment facility, then move to a halfway house or day treatment program, then to outpatient care and a school with special programs for teens in recovery and twelve step meetings.

A lack of coordination can also be seen in services to military families and veterans. Tours of duty in Afghanistan and Iraq are extremely challenging to military personnel and their families, who have to shift roles and responsibilities while worried about the safety of the absent parent. Many personnel return from duty with Post Traumatic Stress Disorder and other mental health and health conditions, creating adjustments in couple and parent–child relationships as well. For many military families, their limited income is also a hardship, with an increasing number receiving SNAP benefits. Schools, veteran's programs, and family support programs on military installations have developed special programs for military personnel and their families, but participation in these programs can be an issue for military members who are concerned about risking their military careers.

Health and Hospital Outreach Programs

EP 2.1.9b

Many health clinics and hospitals have established special programs to address the needs of children and families who are at risk of family disruption or dysfunction. (These and other services to families at risk are shown in Box 11.2.) Some clinics have high-risk infant programs, for example, that provide intensive services to teenage parents, parents of low-birth-weight or premature infants or infants with disabilities, parents with substance-abuse problems, and parents who have not established appropriate relationships with their children. Clinics offer a variety of services, such as weekly outreach programs conducted by a public health nurse, home visits from a social worker or parent educator, individual counseling, play groups for children and support groups for parents, role-modeling of appropriate child care, and assistance in obtaining other resources as needed.

Hospitals offer similar programs. In some hospitals, specially trained nurses identify at-risk mothers in the delivery room and work with hospital social workers to give those mothers intensive care and support during their hospitalization, in addition to outreach services for both parents after the hospital stay. These programs, in some instances, help parents realize that they do not wish to be parents and assist them in relinquishing the children for adoption or placing them in foster care.

Often, programs in health settings are developed to prevent child abuse and neglect and help parents achieve positive relationships with their children. In response to an identified need, pediatric AIDS programs have been established in many major

---

Box 11.2   Support Service Options for Families at Risk

Informal Support to Participants: Opportunities for informal nurturing and interaction among participants and between participants and staff members to facilitate acceptance and support.

Parent Education: Formal and informal instruction, self-development programming, and modeling of healthy parent–child interaction for program participants.

Peer Support Groups and Peer Counseling: Opportunities for parents to share experiences, successes, and frustrations, as well as gain insights into other parents' methods of carrying out their child-rearing responsibilities.

Recreation Services: Opportunities to develop new interests, learn new skills, and have fun.

Early Developmental Screening: Early and continuing developmental screening of infants and children to reinforce healthy child development and to identify potential developmental problems or delays.

Enhancement of Child Development: Developmentally appropriate activities that enhance child development, as well as model appropriate adult–child interaction.

Child (Day) Care Services: Developmentally appropriate child care for children during the day.

Home Visits: Visits to the home designed to assist parents in structuring a safe, caring, stimulating home environment for their children.

Referral and Linkage to Appropriate Resources: Assistance to families in obtaining health, mental health, social service, education, employment, and other services they may need, and follow-up to ensure that those services have been received.

Outreach: Outreach in communities to ensure that isolated parents are aware of, and have full opportunities to participate in, available programs.

Education and Job Skill Development: Assistance in completing education, obtaining employment, and upgrading job skills.

Specialized Services for Adolescent Parents: Education and discussion groups on sexuality and sexual responsibilities, referral for reproductive health care, assistance in returning to school or obtaining a GED certificate, life-skills education, tutoring or homework assistance, involvement of extended family members and significant others, job orientation and training, parent–child interaction groups, groups for adolescent males and adolescent fathers, and discussion groups on personal growth and development.

Source: Adapted and reproduced by permission of the Child Welfare League of America. From Child Welfare League of America (2003). *Child Welfare League of America standards for services to strengthen and preserve families with children* (pp. 18–26). Washington, DC: Author.

metropolitan-area hospitals, to attempt to stabilize the health of children infected with HIV.

In some areas, special health clinics provide services for adolescents. Clinics offer basic health care; information on adolescent development and puberty and sexually transmitted infections and diseases; and, in some instances, pregnancy tests, contraceptive information, and prenatal care. Some clinics of this type are located in public high schools. Although this has caused some controversy, the results reveal that physical and emotional problems, sexually transmitted infections and diseases, and pregnancies have decreased significantly in these schools.

Child Care

EP 2.1.9b

Although most child care programs are targeted at working parents, child care also is a service for nonworking parents. Some parents need respite from their children and from attending to their needs 24 hours a day. Child care for these parents can be either in the home or elsewhere. In any case, it gives parents time to meet their own needs while offering children emotional support that their parents may not be able to provide. This service is less costly than foster care and less traumatic for the child.

Child care providers in many states receive special training to enable them to work more effectively with at-risk parents and children. In some instances, child care providers develop surrogate parent or positive role relationships with parents, giving them and their children much needed emotional support.

Parents under extreme stress may lack natural support systems to help them during a crisis and can reach a point at which they maltreat their children. For example, families with children who have severe developmental disabilities often need extra support. Many communities have established crisis or respite care programs for such families. Some agencies have respite care programs for parents of children with developmental disabilities, in which specially trained adults care for children evenings or weekends so parents can have time to themselves. Other communities have established crisis shelters, where parents under severe stress or in a serious emergency can leave their children for a limited time. Some programs even provide emergency transportation for the children to get out of the home. Most crisis programs require counseling for parents while their children are in crisis care.

Adolescents often can benefit from specialized services, and some communities offer respite care for adolescents who need time away from their parents. Most emergency-shelter facilities for teens also provide crisis and family counseling to help stabilize the situation so the teen can return home. In many areas, however, special services for teens are lacking. In some communities the only resource available for children as young as 12 or 13 who need time away from their parents is an emergency shelter facility for adults who are homeless.

One group that is receiving more attention lately consists of working parents, particularly the working poor, whose inability to find affordable child care can be the last straw before a crisis. These families are more likely to be at risk and under severe stress, and some single parents lose their jobs because of the lack of child care. Out of desperation, parents who need jobs and want to keep their children with them leave them locked in apartment bedrooms at night, have them play at a nearby park with a cell phone in case of emergency, or leave them in parked cars while they work. These circumstances usually result in a child protective services case and sometimes removal of the child from the home when a better alternative that would impact larger numbers of children would be the establishment of safe and affordable child care programs.

Home Management Services

EP 2.1.9b

Many agencies provide home management services to families who are at risk or have neglected or abused their children. Home management service providers are specially trained individuals, often indigenous to the community, who have been parents themselves and can serve as a nurturing, supportive role model for other parents. Providers serve as coaches and role models, offering practical suggestions and education about child care, nutrition and cooking, health and safety, household maintenance, shopping, budgeting, family team-building, the assignment of age-appropriate responsibilities to children, and access to community resources. In addition, they often serve as surrogate parents, developing positive, trusting relationships with family members who have been isolated. Home management services are far more cost-effective than out-of-home care and may prevent separation of children from their parents.

Crisis Intervention Programs

EP 2.1.9b

Various community agencies provide **crisis intervention** services to families. This intervention frequently results in a subsequent referral for additional help, such as counseling. Law-enforcement agencies in many communities have crisis intervention teams that handle family disputes, including interpersonal violence and child abuse. Some youth shelters include crisis intervention for adolescents and their parents. Hospitals, too, provide crisis intervention services in emergency rooms, dealing with child maltreatment, interpersonal violence, substance use, and other serious family problems.

Studies show that families are more receptive to change and more readily agree to services such as counseling during times of crisis because their usual defenses and the family balance are no longer intact.

Counseling

EP 2.1.7a
EP 2.1.7b
EP 2.1.9b

In many communities, individual, couples, and family counseling services are available for families with problems. Mental health centers, social service agencies, child and family service agencies, child guidance clinics, employee assistance programs, religious institutions, schools, youth services programs, and hospital outreach programs are various types of counseling services (see Box 11.3 for a young woman's experience with her school district's teen parent program). These services often are available on a limited basis, because of scarce resources in relation to the large number of persons needing services, or available only on a fee basis. Specialized counseling to address problems such as interpersonal violence or sexual abuse is unavailable in many communities.

For many problems, group counseling has been shown to be more effective than individual counseling, and a combination of the two may be more effective than individual counseling alone. For example, children and adults who have been sexually abused need to hear from others that they are not the only ones who have had that experience. Sexual and physical abusers, as well as others with family problems, typically deny their problem, and group therapy sessions with others in similar situations are apt to break down their defenses more quickly than individual counseling.

Family counseling is garnering more attention as an effective means of strengthening individual functioning and addressing needs. Family counseling has been shown to be effective in helping families understand behavior and coping patterns, establish more productive communication patterns, identify needs and resolve problems, and support each other as family members. In almost all situations in which a family member has a problem or is undergoing a stressful change, family counseling can help the entire family reinforce positive changes, address negative patterns appropriately, and serve as a source of support to each other.

Some agencies have initiated multifamily groups—groups of families that receive therapy jointly. Individuals frequently can see their own issues and family dynamics more clearly while watching other families interact, because they are too involved when these interactions occur within their own families. Teenagers, for example, are more likely to listen to another parent who offers feedback than to their own parents, and parents, too, may be more likely to listen to other teens or parents than to family members.

Social workers have played an important role in this shift from individual to family counseling. In particular, social workers emphasize the strengths of family members and of the family as a total system, building on those strengths to make the system more supportive of its individual members.

Support and Self-Help Groups

EP 2.1.7a
EP 2.1.9b

Support groups and **self-help groups** are effective ways of helping children, youth, and families cope with family problems. These groups help individuals realize that they are not the only ones coping with a given problem. They also assist members in developing new ways to cope as they learn from and support each other, help develop leadership skills, and learn to be accountable for their actions (Pion-Berlin, Williams, Polinsky, & Pickens, 2013). Perhaps most important, persons who see themselves as being inadequate have a chance to reach out and give something to someone else. Examples of self-help groups are:

- 12-step programs such as Alcoholics Anonymous for alcoholics, Al-Anon for family members of alcoholics, Alateen for teen family members of alcoholics, Narcotics Anonymous, and Adult Children of Alcoholics;

Box 11.3 Impact of Social Work Intervention

Elena Vasquez grew up in an inner-city area with her mother and five brothers and sisters. Her father left the family when Elena was a toddler, and her mother worked long hours to try to keep the family fed and clothed until her diabetic condition prevented her from keeping a job. Forced to go on welfare, Elena's mother became depressed and was in and out of the hospital constantly as her diabetes created additional health problems.

As the oldest girl living at home, Elena took care of her brothers and sisters and tried to maintain the household. Increasingly behind in school and lacking attention from adults and peers her own age, she fell in love with a neighbor boy at age 13 and became pregnant at 14. Although she tried to stay in school, after the baby was born she found it increasingly difficult to care for her infant, her siblings, and her mother.

Leaving her baby with her boyfriend's mother in the afternoons, Elena got a part-time job at a fast-food restaurant so her family could have some additional income. Overwhelmed with life, Elena's boyfriend and his family provided her with emotional support, and 6 months after the birth of her first baby, Elena found herself pregnant again. A short time later, however, her boyfriend found another girlfriend, leaving Elena alone and discouraged.

Desperate, Elena went to her junior high school counselor, who sent her to the school district's special program for teen parents. There she was assigned to meet regularly with a social work intern from a neighboring university. The intern referred Elena's mother to a nearby health clinic that was better able to meet her health care needs and got her siblings involved with the school social workers at their schools.

Seeing an incredible resiliency in Elena, the intern slowly gained Elena's trust and helped her realize the potential she had to create a viable life for herself, her baby, and her soon-to-be-born child. Elena met with the intern weekly for the remainder of the year. Her attendance was almost perfect, and she soon was getting excellent grades. Then, when Elena was 15, she vowed to become a social worker just like the intern and work with teenagers who become pregnant.

Although life wasn't easy for her, Elena graduated from high school and, because of her experiences with her mother's health, got a job at a local health clinic. A hard worker who was highly motivated, Elena moved up through the support staff ranks quickly and became a clinic supervisor. When her children started school, Elena began taking classes at the local community college. Slowly she progressed through school while working full-time, volunteering at the local family violence shelter and a nursing home, and providing exceptional care for her children, attending their sports events and prodding them to do well academically.

When her children were in junior high school, and her oldest child the same age Elena had been when she first became pregnant, Elena transferred to the social work program at the state university. In her senior year she asked to do her internship at the same agency where she had been a client 15 years ago. After determining that Elena was mature enough to work with pregnant teens without her own personal experiences influencing her work with clients, the university placed Elena in one of the agency's teen parent programs.

While Elena was an intern, the funding for the agency was being reviewed by the state legislature, and she asked to testify on behalf of the program and share with legislators the impact the program had had on her life. As you can imagine, Elena's testimony was powerful and well received. At this point, Elena has graduated and is working with teen parents as a case manager at the agency. Her children are doing well in school and making plans for their own careers.

- Parents Anonymous and Circle of Parents for abusive or potentially abusive parents;
- Parents without Partners for single parents.

Many communities have established support groups for adults, children, or teens dealing with divorce, stepparenting, the death of a loved one or other type of loss, or those living with a family member with a physical or emotional disability. Schools have established support groups for students who have difficulty functioning within the school setting, coping with family problems such as divorce or abuse, and recovering from substance abuse, as well as for students who are teen parents. With constrained resources, social service agencies are realizing that in many instances more individuals and families can be served effectively through support and self-help groups.

Volunteer and Outreach Programs

EP 2.1.7a
EP 2.1.9b

Most traditional social service agencies are overloaded and can provide only limited services—and those services only to the families with the most severe problems. A number of these agencies have established volunteer components; others use volunteers exclusively to perform the work of the agency. Because they are able to spend more time with families, volunteers can be highly successful in preventing family disruption. Most volunteer programs have effective screening mechanisms for recruiting volunteers who can relate well to clients. Many have been parents themselves, some are grandparents, and others are students or are involved in human services already. Volunteers usually receive extensive training and are supervised by a social work case manager.

An example of a successful community-based volunteer program is the Court Appointed Special Advocates for Children (CASA) program. This program uses highly trained volunteers to serve as advocates for abused and neglected children in the courts and communities. Operating in almost one thousand communities nationwide, CASA volunteers advocate for what is in the child's best interest, developing a relationship with the child and often the entire family and providing feedback to the court and others who are working with the family on how best to meet the child's needs.

Other volunteer programs work with parents, mentoring and supporting them, assisting in problem solving, helping gain access to community resources, and serving as a surrogate parent/role model/friend to parents and family members. Similar programs have been developed in which volunteers work with teenage parents and children from at risk families. In the national Big Brothers/Big Sisters program, for example, volunteers are paired with children from single-parent families as friends and role models. Volunteer programs like the ones mentioned here can help families stay together (Center for Urban Policy and the Environment, 2003). Given the continuing increase in the number of families needing services and the declining resources available to help them, volunteer programs are likely to expand significantly in the future (U.S. Department of Labor, 2014).

Programs for at-risk families are funded by federal, state, and local governments, as well as the private sector, of which the United Way is a prominent example, providing assistance to families at risk in many communities throughout the nation. Faith-based organizations, foundations, and private contributions fund other programs. Increasingly, public–private partnerships are being developed with funding from a variety of sources. State and local governments are contracting with private agencies to provide services, and many private agencies receive funding from multiple sources, both public and private.

Which entity should pay for what type of services? This is a complex issue at all levels in the United States as the number of at-risk families continues to expand while federal and state funding programs decline. Local governments, employers, and private contributors are not always able or willing to provide the needed assistance. New ways of providing services, along with new and more effective ways of cost sharing, are being explored in more depth during these first years of the 21st century.

School Social Work

EP 2.1.1a
EP 2.1.7a
EP 2.1.7b

A specialized field involving services to children, youth, and families is school social work. **School social work**—social services offered in a school-based setting—provides the opportunity to identify needs of children and their families early and to facilitate early intervention before problems become more serious. Social workers in school settings offer parenting education and facilitate positive mental health for children through special outreach programs in the school.

School social work includes individual, family, and group counseling, as well as case management, crisis intervention services, and the implementation of schoolwide programs relating to topics such as bullying. School social workers deal with suicidal students; students and their families and friends in the aftermath of serious injury or death; and students in conflict with family members, peers, or school authorities (see Box 11.4 for an account of a school social worker in an inner-city elementary school).

School social workers are members of intervention teams that work with children who have developmental disabilities and other special needs, often as liaison to parents and the community when special services are needed. The Education for All Handicapped Children Act has been updated to specify that schools may hire

School-based social services help many children and youth address emotional needs and become successful academically. Here, two social work interns develop plans for a group session they are co-facilitating with fifth graders to help them better manage feelings of frustration and anger.

Hinkle/Index Stock

Box 11.4   A Day in the Life of a School Social Worker

7:30 a.m.: A teacher meets me in the parking lot as I arrive at school. She is concerned about one of her students, a second grader who told the teacher yesterday that her mother's boyfriend is coming into her bedroom at night and "hurting her privates."

8:00 a.m.: I attend our campus leadership meeting with our principal, assistant principal, and school counselor. We talk about a number of students we are concerned about, including the second grader who made the sexual abuse outcry yesterday. We agree that a report needs to be made to child protective services (CPS). We also talk about a kindergartener and a third grader whose mother made a suicide attempt last night and is in the hospital. The children are staying with their grandmother but are expected at school tomorrow. The grandmother has asked for support, so I agree to make a home visit later in the day to give her some help in identifying resources and to talk with the children.

9:30 a.m.: I call CPS and then call the grandmother to set up a time to meet with her. I make calls to some of our business partners I am trying to get to help several refugee families who have recently enrolled their children in our school. The families need furniture, clothing, food, and help in finding employment for the adults.

10:00 a.m.: The assistant principal calls. She has a first grader in her office sent there because he became angry in the classroom and threw a chair at another child. The child has many emotional outbursts at school and we are concerned about him. I've met with his parents once, but they are reluctant to schedule an assessment to find out what may be causing the outbursts because they don't want him labeled unnecessarily. The father thinks his son just needs more discipline. I talk with the child and then call his parents to schedule a staffing with his parents, teacher, and a behavior specialist from the school district who can help us develop an intervention plan for the child. I hope we can convince the parents to get their child an assessment before he moves into higher grades. If his aggressive behavior continues, it is likely that he will be avoided by peers even more than he is now, and he will become even farther behind academically because his energy, and his teacher's, will continue to be directed at his behavior rather than his learning.

10:30 a.m.: I meet with the third- fourth- and fifth-grade grief and loss group that I facilitate. We meet weekly and, through activities and discussion, try to address their feelings about the losses they have experienced in their families. Of the eight group members,

(continued)

Box 11.4   A Day in the Life of a School Social Worker
(continued)

three have lost siblings because of gang-related violence, two have lost parents or siblings because of cancer or other serious illnesses, two have parents or older siblings who have committed suicide, and one has lost a sibling in a car accident. After the group session ends, I prepare for the kindergarten, first- and second-grade grief and loss group that meets tomorrow and the boys' group focusing on anger management that meets later in the week.

12:00 p.m.: I eat lunch in the cafeteria with a group of fifth-grade girls who are having trouble getting along with each other, which is spilling over into the classroom. I'm trying to help them recognize each other's strengths and learn to give feedback to each other appropriately when they are upset with each other, rather than reacting like the "Mean Girls" they seem to want to emulate.

12:45 p.m.: I've just walked in the door to my office when I receive another call from the assistant principal. A third grader came to school this morning and told her teacher that last night her father beat her mother up, and she has spent the morning crying because she is worried about her mom. I walk down to the classroom, talk briefly with the teacher, and then bring the child to my office so we can talk. We agree that I will call her mom and set up a time to talk with her about her own safety and her daughter's concerns. I plan to give the mom some resources that work with survivors of interpersonal violence and determine ways that we can work together to help her daughter and her other children feel safe.

1:30 p.m.: I talk with the child who made the sexual abuse outcry and let her know that CPS is coming this afternoon to meet with her. I reassure her that she did the right thing in telling her teacher and wait with her

until the CPS worker arrives to talk with the child. When the CPS worker arrives, I introduce them to each other and let them use my office to talk, as space for private meetings in our school is at a premium. While they meet, I meet with several teachers during their planning time to talk about students and families they are concerned about.

2:30 p.m.: I follow up with the CPS worker before she leaves to meet with the child's mother and then talk briefly with the child. We come up with a plan she can follow if she needs someone to talk to. She says she is close to her grandmother and an aunt who live a block from her home, and she can contact one of them and stay with them if she needs to.

3:00 p.m.: I head to a meeting with a teacher and a parent about a kindergartner who is refusing to come to school. The parents are going through a divorce, and the child is worried that her mom will abandon her just as her father has. We make a plan to help the child feel more secure in the classroom and come up with some suggestions the mom can do at home to reinforce the fact that she is not abandoning her child. I also give her some referrals for individual and family counseling as well as a support group for parents going through a divorce.

4:00 p.m.: I go to my office to catch up on never-ending paper work and plan for the rest of the week. I love my job, our school, and the students and their families. I am glad that our principal and school district value the important roles that social workers play in helping children remove barriers that get in the way of their ability to succeed academically.

SOURCE: Based on an interview with a school social worker in an urban school district in Texas.

---

social workers to provide social services to special-needs children and schools have also hired social workers to assist in implementation of the No Child Left Behind Legislation. Although NASW noted the number of school social workers across the country providing school-based services and advocated for including the hiring of social workers in the legislation when the bill was being considered for reauthorization this specific language was not included.

Dropout-prevention legislation in some states also includes a mandate to hire school social workers. School-

based social-work services are advantageous for many reasons, including:

- The social worker sees the child or adolescent in a natural setting, interacting with peers, teachers, and school administrators, which gives the social worker a different perspective than seeing a client in an office or agency.
- The social worker has access to a large number of children and families in need of services.
- The social worker can help parents and school personnel apply an ecological/systems approach to

better address the child's needs, encompassing the child, home, school, and broader community.

- The social worker can help school personnel understand the importance of family and community variables in relation to the child's capacity to function in the school setting.

NASW has developed a specialized certification program in school social work as well as recommended standards for school-based social work.

Child Protective Services

EP 2.1.9b

Although a number of federal and state laws govern how child abuse and neglect services are delivered across the United States, the most comprehensive is the federal Child Abuse and Neglect Prevention and Treatment Act (CAPTA, as amended). This law mandates that all states designate a single agency to oversee services to abused and neglected children and their families. These services usually come under the rubric of **child protective services (CPS)**. This agency receives reports about possible cases of child maltreatment from a variety of sources and makes a determination about the risk to the children involved based on the report. Although anyone who has reason to believe a child is being abused or neglected is expected to make a report to either CPS or law enforcement, all states also have mandatory reporting requirements. Although mandatory reporters and requirements vary from state to state, they include professionals such as social workers, medical and mental health professionals, teachers, and child care providers. It is not up to the reporter to determine whether the case is an actual situation of abuse or neglect, and if a reporter makes a report in good faith (for example, not reporting someone just because the person is involved in a custody situation and wants to make the other parent look like a poor parent to the judge), the reporter is immune from prosecution for making an unwarranted report. Many children's lives are saved because someone took the time to make a report, and children's lives are lost because individuals who knew or suspected a child was being mistreated failed to make a report.

If the report indicates that there are risk factors to the child being reported that fall within the agency guidelines, individuals and families reported to that agency as being abusive or neglectful must be investigated by the agency to ascertain whether the maltreatment report can be substantiated. All states have statutes establishing a minimum standard of care that caregivers are expected to provide to their children. If the worker investigating the case determines that parents are not meeting this standard, a safety plan may be developed delineating specific actions parents must follow, referrals may be made to other agencies for services, or the family may be slated to receive protective services, depending on the risk to the child. In some instances, the child may be removed from the home and placed with a relative judged to be a safe caregiver for the child or in foster care. Child Protective Services is an involuntary program—that is, the parents involved did not request or volunteer to receive the services.

Investigations of Child Maltreatment

In implementing the mandated services, CPS workers cooperate closely with other professionals, including law enforcement officers, attorneys, health care providers, and educators. Child protective services workers assume a variety of roles in cooperation or jointly with other agencies. They may offer intake services, in which they screen reports of child maltreatment and interview persons who report cases by phone and in person to obtain the information necessary to make a preliminary determination about how serious the report is and whether it requires immediate investigation. Most states require that life-threatening situations be investigated immediately or within 24 to 48 hours, and that less serious cases be investigated within 10 days.

CPS workers, by themselves or jointly with law-enforcement officers, conduct investigations of child maltreatment, interviewing children, parents, other family members, and collateral contacts such as teachers and neighbors, to determine the nature and extent of the reported maltreatment. Investigations involve examining and interviewing the child, attending to the child's immediate emotional needs during the investigation, and making a preliminary assessment about whether maltreatment is occurring. If maltreatment is confirmed, investigators determine whether it is causing or could cause permanent damage to the child's body or mind, how severe it has been, and whether the situation is life-threatening and warrants immediately removing the child to a safer environment.

In some instances, other resources, such as physicians, are asked to assist in gathering the needed information. Investigations of child maltreatment require knowledge and skill in identifying various types of maltreatment, as well as interviewing techniques appropriate with children and adults who may be apprehensive and reluctant to cooperate. Achieving a balance between authority and compassion, or between the ability to confront and the ability to be empathic, is one of the challenges of being a child protective services worker (Brittain & Hunt, 2004; Brown, 2002; Crosson-Tower, 2012; Child Welfare Information Gateway, 2014d).

Determination of Intervention

Following the investigation of child maltreatment, the situation is assessed to determine the most appropriate actions to take. CPS workers are not expected to prove that the maltreatment is a criminal offense or to determine who perpetrated the maltreatment. Those actions are within the domain of the courts. Rather, the role of CPS workers is to determine whether the child has to be protected and what is needed to provide that protection. When assessing a possible situation of child maltreatment, workers have four options:

1. Determine that the child is not being maltreated and withdraw from the case.
2. Offer help to the family.
3. Determine that the child is at serious risk and/or that the parents are uncooperative, and make arrangements to take the family to court.
4. With the court's permission, remove the child from the home immediately and place the child in emergency care (and, later, usually foster care).

Usually CPS workers determine that, although services are required, leaving a child in the home is safe while the services are being provided. When children are removed from the home, this is done most often for the following reasons:

- The child or a sibling has been seriously injured or abandoned.
- The parent/caregiver states that he or she is going to injure or kill the child.
- Evidence suggests that the child has been sexually abused and the perpetrator is still in the home or has easy access to the child.
- A current crisis exists, such as a psychotic parent or a parent in jail because of a crime connected with substance abuse.
- The parents are not cooperative, and the child is at serious risk for substantial harm.

Most child protective service agencies use some type of risk assessment instrument to help guide through the decision-making process regarding which options are best to protect a child. If removal is warranted, approval from a CPS supervisor and a judge are required.

Like other helping professionals, CPS workers are most effective if they identify strengths in their clients and the clients' environment and work to empower clients to make choices that will keep the children safe. But if, after trying to provide mandated services to a family with the children still at home, a protective services worker believe that the family is resisting services and is making choices that fail to keep the child(ren) safe, CPS may take the case to court and request that the court order services. In so doing, if the family does not comply, the worker can bring the case back into court and request more serious options, such as placing the child in foster care. Some states mandate court involvement with all families receiving child protective services.

The issue of when to involve the court in CPS cases does not have universal agreement. Advocates for early involvement argue that it gives workers leverage in dealing with families because the authority of the courts is present immediately. Advocates for limited involvement believe that most families are more receptive to services without court action because families feel empowered and thus can maintain a less adversarial relationship with their social worker.

A number of states are developing two-track CPS programs: (a) clients who can be charged with criminal acts under the auspices of an investigative unit, and (b) the majority of other clients under the auspices of an assessment/intervention unit. Those cases referred to an investigative unit, usually the most serious and potentially criminal cases, are investigated by CPS workers or law enforcement officers who gather forensic evidence as part of the investigation. Cases that are not as serious are referred to a different unit that follows a more traditional social work approach, conducting an assessment that focuses on the family's strengths, needs, and capacity for change. Proponents of this approach believe it will remove the adversarial relationship that arises when a law-enforcement investigation is done for families that need family preservation or other supportive services. Still other states have law enforcement officers conduct all investigations, with CPS staff stepping in depending on the results of the investigation. Proponents of this approach argue that law enforcement officers are more likely to be objective when conducting investigations, and that if the CPS workers get involved with the family after the investigation they are more likely to be seen by the family as neutral and thus able to develop a more positive relationship with the family. Both approaches focus on the safety and well-being of the children in the family, keeping the family together if at all possible, seeking community resources other than CPS if appropriate, and recognizing that CPS is the agency authorized to make decisions whether to involve the court and/or remove children from the home. Approaches that allow for differential responses based on the needs and circumstances of the child and family can result in better decisions and outcomes (Child Welfare Information Gateway, 2014a; Brayne & Carr, 2008; Davis, 2007; Maschi, Bradley, & Ward, 2009; Roberts, 2008; Williams, 2008).

Typical Services Provided

CPS workers provide a variety of services to the families with whom they work, including

EP 2.1.7a
EP 2.1.7b

- making every effort to ensure that children can be safe in their own homes;
- serving as case managers—arranging for community resources such as housing, employment, transportation, counseling, health services, child care, home management services, or financial assistance;
- providing counseling, parent education, and support;
- helping clients get involved in a parent support group or be assigned a volunteer; and
- developing a contract with a parent that delineates specific goals the family must accomplish to be removed from the CPS caseload.

Being a CPS worker is challenging because of the emotional aspects of working with abused and neglected children and the multiple roles that CPS workers must play. A number of national organizations, including the Child Welfare League of America, the American Association for Protecting Children, and the American Public Human Services Association, have established specialized training for staff, and have explored with states new ways to provide protective services. Many states have adopted a computerized risk-management system that helps workers assess family situations and needs and the safety of children involved.

CPS agencies also are expanding their efforts to collaborate with other systems that come in contact with abused and neglected children, and promoting collaboration between child welfare and domestic violence programs. Interpersonal violence and child abuse often appear within the same families, and programs targeted at them serve overlapping populations. Collaborative training, shared use of resources, and coordinated

case-management efforts can remove many barriers that prevent women from being harmed when their children are under protection, or vice versa. These programs strengthen the concept of family preservation. In some shelters for those who have experienced interpersonal violence, for example, a social worker is assigned to the shelter to work onsite with the program's clients and their children (Humphreys & Stanley, 2006; National Association of Social Workers, 2012).

As reports of child maltreatment continue to increase and involve children who are injured more severely than in the past, the role of CPS as part of the child and family service delivery system is undergoing extensive debate. Because of the scarcity of resources, CPS is the dominant child welfare service in many communities. Although CPS agencies once publicized their role as providing services to children and families to prevent child maltreatment from occurring or recurring, their overriding message at present is that they protect children.

However, because of staff shortages, many agencies can barely respond to all the reports they receive and are unable to investigate all except the most serious reports. With increases in child maltreatment, attributed in part to more extensive use of drugs such as cocaine and meth, poverty, and homelessness, the emphasis of child protective services is more often one of "damage control" rather than intensive services. Whenever a death of a child occurs in a community because of abuse or neglect, even though most child deaths occur to children not known to CPS, the agency undergoes extensive criticism and scrutiny. Sometimes funding is increased and more workers are hired, but more often, procedures are tightened, more paper work and documentation are required, and CPS staff say that they are even less able to be involved with the families assigned to them than before. The shift in philosophy to one of protection places other community organizations in the role of preventing child maltreatment, as well as providing the extensive services needed to keep it from recurring.

Family Preservation Services

Today the emphasis is on keeping together families that would have been separated in the past. These families have complex needs, often involving some form of child maltreatment, substance abuse, or children exhibiting

EP 2.1.7a
EP 2.1.7b

oppositional behavior or delinquency in the home, school, and community (Crosson-Tower, 2012, 2013). The goals of family preservation programs are to:

- allow children to remain safely in their own homes,
- maintain and strengthen family bonds,
- stabilize the crisis situation that precipitated any need for outside placement,
- increase the family's coping skills and competencies, and
- facilitate the family's use of appropriate and informal helping resources.

Efforts in family preservation have built on the permanency-planning emphasis of the late 1970s, after several studies found that many children were remaining in foster care with little attention to alternatives.

In reaction to more children—particularly children of color and those living in poverty—being removed from their own homes and placed in foster care, attention turned to finding ways to keep families together or to reunite children with their biological families rather than leaving the children to languish in foster care. In most instances, because of insufficient resources, efforts to work with families were limited and families generally were viewed as a large part of the problem rather than the solution.

The Adoption Assistance and Child Welfare Act of 1980 (PL 96-272) required that efforts be made to avoid family disruption, reunify families after separation, and place children in permanent settings if they could not be reunited. The number of family preservation programs grew rapidly in the 1980s and 1990s, supported by the passage of P.L. 96-272, the Adoption Assistance and Child Welfare Act of 1980, which required that agencies prevent foster care placement whenever possible, and P.L. 103-66, the Family Preservation and Support Program, passed in 1993, which provided funds to states to enable children to remain in their own homes (Popple & Leighninger, 2011).

Based on traditional social work practice, family preservation programs emphasize home visits and intensive approaches with high-risk families. Currently there are more than 400 family preservation programs in the United States. Horchak-Andino (2003) delineated the following three types of family preservation programs:

1. *family support programs,* which usually are community-based and provide support and education services;

2. *family-centered preventive programs,* which provide case management; counseling, and education for families with problems that threaten their stability; and

3. *intensive family preservation services,* designed for families in crisis when removal of the child is imminent or reunification with the family is under way when a child is being returned home after placement.

Although the programs vary, they offer crisis intervention, staff members available to provide around-the-clock services if needed, low caseloads, and highly intensive, time-limited services similar to other in-home services described previously.

In working with families, family preservation programs incorporate a family systems perspective. Thus, they view families that need services as being in disequilibrium or out of balance because the needs of various family members are unmet. The emphasis in family preservation programs is on empowering family members to get their needs met and develop new skills in problem solving and communication to stabilize the family system.

Family preservation social workers do not blame families for failure (Loveless & Holman, 2006; Sousa, 2008; Walsh, 2006). The model is based on the assumption that the family has a significant influence on children and that separation has detrimental effects on parents and children alike. Through role-modeling, counseling, and interactions with family members, the program stresses values, respect, listening rather than giving advice, and help with goal setting, coping, and problem-solving skills.

Social workers try to connect with and get to know all family members in a nonjudgmental way. At the first stage of services, concrete needs, such as housing and food, are addressed. As the social worker develops a relationship with the family, the emphasis is consistent with good social work practice—not on diagnosis and labeling but, instead, on understanding the day-to-day reality of the family and how it functions. Interventions often involve contracting, encouraging, and reframing of issues (Crosson-Tower, 2012; Horchak-Andino, 2003).

Evaluation of family preservation programs is difficult because families' needs and how they are addressed vary, as do the interventions used. Workers in these programs are finding that, although the original program goal was to prevent out-of-home placement, the program may not be able to prevent such a placement and that sometimes out-of-home placements are necessary. Findings indicate that family preservation is more effective in preventing placement of children in multi-problem families where serious abuse has not yet occurred and that in many instances, long-term intervention is needed as some families need constant ongoing support. Still, family preservation programs can keep families together in situations where the parent has the ability or the potential to be a positive parent figure in the child's life (Child Welfare Information Gateway, 2014b). Other outcome measures, such as an increase in positive communication among family members, have yet to be studied (WESTAT & James Bell Associates, 2002).

Substitute Care

Sometimes the best solution is to remove children from their own homes. Parents may have too many unmet needs of their **EP 2.1.7a** own, or be too uninterested in parenting to **EP 2.1.7b** care for their children adequately. In such situations, **substitute care** is located for the children involved. Unless the situation is an emergency—which many state laws define as a life-threatening situation—a CPS worker cannot remove a child from a family without a court order. Even with emergency removals, court orders must be obtained, usually within 24 hours, and hearings held with parents present.

Substitute care is of different types. In many communities, crisis shelters are available to take in children 24 hours a day until a family situation can be stabilized or other care that best meets a child's needs can be located. Attempts are made to place children with relatives or neighbors so that they can remain in their immediate environment, but this is not always possible. Other types of substitute care include foster homes, group homes, residential treatment facilities, and psychiatric treatment facilities.

Once a child is placed in substitute care, the social worker (in collaboration with the family, if possible, and the child, depending on the child's age) must develop a plan either to return the child to the home or to terminate parental rights and place the child in an adoptive family. Under federal law, the court must review the case every 6 months to ensure that the child is not in limbo in the child welfare system.

If a child does require placement in substitute care, every effort should be made to ensure that the placement is the least restrictive option. After first considering relatives, neighbors, and others with whom the child is familiar and if those individuals fail to meet the criteria to be positive substitute parents for the child, consideration is given to finding care that is consistent with the child's cultural background, preferably in the same neighborhood or school area. Usually it is deemed important that the birth parents visit the child (if this is in the best interests of the child), so attention must be given to accessibility for the parents.

Foster Care

In 2012, children were removed from their homes and placed in foster care in 37.1% of substantiated cases of child abuse or neglect. **EP 2.1.7a** If appropriate relative or kinship placements **EP 2.1.7b** or other suitable arrangements are not possible, children removed from their families because of abuse or neglect most often are placed in foster care. **Foster care** means that children live in homes with families other than their birth parents until they are returned to their birth parents or are adopted. Foster parents are recruited and trained to relate to children and their birth parents. They are often parents already and may take in more than one foster child. Many foster parents keep in touch with their foster children after they leave, and some adopt the children if they become available for adoption.

All states have strict standards regarding foster care, including training that individuals must complete before becoming and continuing as foster parents, the number of children foster parents can take, appropriate discipline and treatment of the children, and supervision of foster parents. A number of states train foster parents to parent certain types of children—for example, adolescents, children with AIDS, or children who have been sexually abused. Foster parents also develop support systems, and many belong to local and national foster parent organizations. Foster parents are paid monthly to care for each child, but they often spend more than they receive, in addition to giving the children love and attention (CWLA, 2006; Johnson & Grant, 2004; Rowell, 2008).

Currently, almost all children who require foster care have been abused or neglected. Because more children whose safety is threatened are being removed from their homes, the need for additional foster parents is acute nationwide. Many localities are having difficulty finding foster parents who are willing to parent adolescents or younger children with serious emotional problems that often have resulted from child maltreatment (Kerman, Freundlich, & Maluccio, 2009).

Some children have trouble handling the intimacy of a foster family, particularly if they have been seriously neglected or abused. In other instances, a foster family may not be found for a given child. Adolescents are the foremost example. As an alternative to foster care, group homes have a set of house parents to care for 5 to 10 children or adolescents. These homes attempt to maintain a homelike atmosphere and provide rules and structure for children and adolescents. They also may include regular group counseling sessions for residents (Guishard-Pine, McCall, & Hamilton, 2007).

As noted, a major problem with the foster care system is the dearth of adequate foster homes. As a result, children often remain in emergency shelters and institutions for a long time and many foster homes have more children than they can adequately handle. The shortage of foster homes results in children frequently being moved from home to home (National Coalition for Child Protection Reform, 2006; Pew Charitable Trusts, 2004).

In 2012, 399,546 children were in foster care in the United States. Because of federal and state legislation in recent years, which has emphasized keeping children and families together and providing in-home services as opposed to out-of-home care, the number of children in foster care declined by almost 25% between 2002 and 2012. Of this number, 38% were 5 or younger, 44% were 6–15, and 20% were 16 and older. Most were nonwhite: 42% were white, 26% were black; 21% were Hispanic/Latino, 2% were American Indian/Alaskan Native, 7% were of other races and ethnicities or multiethnic, and 2% were undetermined. While numbers of children declined for all ethnic groups from 2002–2012, the decline was most dramatic for Black children: 47% fewer Black children were in foster care in FY 2012 than in FY 2002 (U.S. Department of Health and Human Services, 2013).

About 25% of children in foster care were waiting to be adopted that year. During that same year, 245,260 children left foster care. The average length of stay of those who left was two years (Foster Care Resource Center, 2014). A little over half (51%) were reunited with family or went to live with other relatives, about 6% went to live with guardians, about 20% were adopted, and the remaining 23% left care without a permanent family. The number of children adopted through a public child welfare agency decreased almost 6% from the previous year (Child Welfare League, 2013).

The federal government is spending more than $9 billion each year to maintain children in foster care, including costs for medical care, SNAP, and reimbursements to states for a portion of child care payments to foster families and other expenses (Fixen, 2011). The federal government reimburses states for 50% of eligible administrative costs, with no limit.

Most are loving and caring foster parents who nurture and support children who often have mental and physical health challenges because of the abuse and neglect they may have received. Many eventually adopt the children they take into care. However, some are not prepared to take on the role of fostering and may actually place the children in their care in greater danger than they were in their own homes. As states continue to experience budget shortfalls, many look for ways to cut costs, including costs for child welfare services. Some state legislators and child welfare administrators have determined that one way to save costs and reduce state-funded staff is to contract out child welfare services. Thus, a number of states have contracted out foster care placement and oversight to private for-profit and nonprofit agencies. While it has the potential to reduce costs, this approach shifts the primary role of the state agency to contract management, with oversight of foster families and children in their care falling to contractors. In Texas in 2014, several deaths and serious injuries to children in contracted foster care settings raised concern among child welfare advocates and some elected officials. At the same time, one of the large contractors cancelled the contract, indicating that it was more expensive than anticipated to provide quality services to the population they were expected to serve. The debate about whether to contract out child welfare services and which services to contract out remains an important one for children and families in need of services.

Residential Treatment

Children and adolescents who need more structure than foster care or group homes can provide may be placed in **residential treatment** programs. More expensive to maintain than foster care and group homes, these programs provide consistent structure for children and adolescents, as well as intensive individual and group counseling. Most residential treatment programs help the child establish boundaries that were missing from home, work to build self-esteem and competence, and help the child resolve anger and other issues from his or her family experience.

EP 2.1.7a
EP 2.1.7b

The goal of residential treatment is for the child to develop enough coping skills to be able to deal with the family situation after returning home. Ideally, the family also undergoes counseling so the parents and other family members do not revert to old roles that may force the child back into previous behaviors. Family counseling does not always take place, however, and the child has to cope with the former problems on returning to the family and community. In situations in which returning home or living with a nonparent relative is not possible, a child exiting residential treatment may be placed in a less restrictive setting, such as a group home or foster care.

Children and adolescents with more serious problems may be hospitalized. In hospital settings, the child typically has more restrictions, more intensive therapy, and possibly, prescription medication. In other instances, children or adolescents, primarily delinquent adolescents, are placed in juvenile detention facilities. Studies suggest that white, middle-class children are more likely to be placed in residential treatment or hospital programs, while poor children and children of color are more likely to be placed in juvenile detention facilities (see, for example, Crosson-Tower, 2012).

Although attempts have been made to strengthen the substitute care system, problems remain. Perhaps the biggest problem is the lack of resources to enable birth parents to reunite with their children. Overloaded service delivery systems often thwart social workers from providing needed services to parents. As a result, social workers may be reluctant to terminate parental rights and free children for adoption. Or, conversely, because they cannot provide the needed services, they may be reluctant to return children to unsafe homes. Thus, children languish in the foster care system. When intensive services are provided to parents, however, even children who have multiple problems and have been separated from their parents for long periods can be reunited successfully with their birth family (National Coalition for Child Protection Reform, 2006).

Because many children are unable to reunite with their birth parents and are not adopted, they are growing up in foster care and leaving the system only because they "age out" when they reach 17 or 18, depending on the state in which they live. Each year, and estimated 20,000 youth leave foster care for this reason. Youth who age out of foster care often lack skills in daily living. Without a support system once they are on their own, they are much more likely to

misuse alcohol and other drugs, become pregnant at an early age, become involved in the criminal justice system, become homeless, and experience mental health and health problems than youth not raised in foster care. States have made a concerted effort to focus on helping youth in foster care ease the transition to independence through skill building programs that focus on making choices, money management, and relationships. Most states have policies that allow youth who have resided in foster care to attend state universities tuition-free, but few foster care youth have role models who can help them navigate often complex university systems. Even the fact that residence halls close over holidays and semester breaks can be traumatic for a former foster child who has no home. As a result, efforts to help former foster care youth attend and graduate from college have increased in recent years. Some become social workers in foster care programs and other child welfare agencies.

Child welfare advocates want to get the age that youth leave foster care increased from 17 or 18 depending on the state to age 21 to give youth additional support for a longer period of time. They say that in the long run, the increase in age would be cost effective, as it would reduce the problems often experienced by youth when they do leave care that are not only costly to the individuals, but to society as well.

Adoption

EP 2.1.7a
EP 2.1.7b
EP 2.1.8a

When parents choose not to or cannot provide for their children, the court terminates their parental rights and the child becomes legally free for **adoption**. But many children in the United States, particularly African American children, are adopted informally by relatives without a formal court hearing ever taking place. The whole concept of adoption has changed significantly in recent years. In the past, the aim was to match an adoptive child as closely as possible, according to physical features such as hair and eye color, with parents who could not have children biologically. Today, the emphasis has been redirected to finding a parent who can best meet the child's needs.

Adoption Issues

The forms of adoption in the United States have changed, too. Until the 1970s, most formal adoptions in the United States involved couples adopting healthy infants. Most adoptions today are by stepparents—a result of the higher rates of divorce and remarriage. Also, there are fewer infant adoptions today because many young women of all ethnic groups are choosing to keep their babies rather than place them for adoption. Still, some traditional maternity homes/adoption agencies remain, providing residential and health care and counseling services before birth and, in some instances, post-adoption counseling as well.

A major issue relating to adoption is the length of time to move children through the child welfare services system once they have been removed from their homes. Because of the priority given to family preservation, efforts are made first to ensure that parents are given the opportunities and resources to provide safe, supportive homes for their children. If children are in substitute care, the initial plan, whenever possible, is to return them to their birth parents.

Reaching a decision to terminate parental rights and sever the parent–child relationship is one of the most difficult decisions anyone has to make. Even when parents are not able to provide for their children's needs, most children who are not reared by their birth parents find themselves dealing with separation and loss issues throughout their lives. The extent to which they address these issues depends on many factors, but no matter how superb their adoptive and foster parents are, these children still question why they did not remain with their birth parents.

Most children who become legally free for adoption because their parents' rights have been terminated spend a number of years in foster care, and many have been in multiple foster homes. Social workers in child-placing agencies work with children before placement, preparing them for what adoption is like and helping them address grief and loss issues surrounding their birth parents so they can begin to attach more readily to their adoptive parents. Many children in foster care have parents whose legal rights have not been terminated and have to wait for that legal process to play out. Increasingly, foster parents are adopting children they have fostered; in 2011, 54% of youth leaving foster care were adopted by their foster parents. Recent efforts have also been made to focus more on kinship care, locating relatives of the children who may be willing to adopt. Thirty one percent of children adopted in FY 2011 were adopted by a relative, including a stepparent (Foster Care Resource Center, 2011).

Adoption of Children with Special Needs

EP 2.1.1a

The majority of children who are legally free and available for adoption in the United States are termed **children with special needs**. These children, formerly considered unadoptable in many cases, have been placed successfully in a variety of family settings. Children with special needs are those who are children of color, are older, have physical or emotional disabilities, or are members of sibling groups. In 2009, public child welfare agencies reported that of the 56,011 children adopted, 85% had one or more special needs (U.S. Children's Bureau, 2013).

Adoption agencies, too, are looking at potential parents they had not considered before. During the 1960s and 1970s, the emphasis was on trans-racial adoption. Currently, most agencies are seeking parents of the same ethnic or cultural background as the child, if possible. Advocacy by groups such as the Association of Black Social Workers has given impetus to ethnicity in placing children for adoption. A number of agencies have established special outreach programs to African American and Latino communities to recruit adoptive parents.

In the 1980s, Father George Clements, an African American priest in Chicago, worked on the "One Church, One Child" campaign. This effort was based on the premise that if each church in the United States, particularly churches with primarily minority congregations, could work to have one child adopted by a member of its congregation, the adoption of children with special needs would no longer be such a critical problem. This campaign spread throughout the United States as one of many successful efforts to place these children in adoptive families.

Concern about children of color awaiting adoption has raised a number of issues about how and when ethnicity should be considered in child placement. The Howard M. Metzenbaum Multiethnic Placement Act (MEPA I), enacted by Congress in 1994, prohibits any federally funded program from denying the opportunity to become a foster or adoptive parent based solely on the ethnicity, race, or national origin of the foster parent or the adoptive parent or the child involved. The act also prohibits any federally funded program from engaging in discrimination in a placement decision on the basis of ethnicity. Race, ethnicity, or national heritage can be used as one of a number of factors in making placement decisions, but not as the only factor (Mizrahi & Davis, 2008). The act was amended in 1996 (MEPA II), repealing some of the language in the earlier legislation that could have been used to circumvent the intent of the law and providing strict penalties for agencies receiving federal funding if they violated the act.

Many children have become caught in the middle of arguments about the role of ethnicity in placement—and this is psychologically damaging to the child no matter what the decision. In several situations that have received national attention, children of color have been placed with white foster parents, and remained with them for a long time. Later, when the foster parents have tried to adopt these children, the children have been placed in adoptive homes with parents of the same heritage as the child. Any young child, regardless of ethnicity, goes through separation trauma after being removed from a psychological parent who has been the child's primary caregiver. Conflicts can be mitigated by carefully assessing the child's background and current situation, as well as other demographic variables such as age and ethnicity, when placing children in temporary settings prior to placing them in permanent homes (Fineman & Worthington, 2009; Marre & Briggs, 2009; Rothman, 2006; Trenka, Oparah, & Shin, 2006).

In addition to trying to recruit more families of color, adoption agencies are recruiting single parents, working parents, foster parents, and parents who already have large families. Experience is showing that all of these individuals can be successful adoptive parents. Also, attempts are being made to place siblings together in the same adoptive family rather than separating them, as was done often in the past.

The Adoption Assistance Act, previously noted, allows monthly living allowances and medical expenses for families who otherwise could not afford to adopt children with special needs. More assertive and creative outreach efforts have resulted in children being adopted who previously were considered unadoptable, including many who would have been relegated to a life in a state institution.

Other adoption trends include international adoptions and open adoptions (U.S. State Department, 2014; Child Welfare Information Gateway, 2013c). Over the past decade, the number of intercountry adoptions to the United States more than doubled. In 2013, U.S. parents adopted 7,094 children internationally.

The countries from which most of the adoptive children came in 2013 were, first, China (2,306), followed by Ethiopia (993), the Ukraine (438), Haiti (388), the Congo (313), Uganda (276), Russia (250), Nigeria (183), the Philippines (178), Ghana (170), Columbia (159), and Bulgaria (159) (U.S. State Department, 2014).

From the time the practice began in the early 1970s, members of the international child welfare community have raised concerns about the wisdom of international adoptions. These concerns culminated in 1993, when 66 countries reached an agreement on the Hague Convention on Protection of Children and Cooperation in Respect to Inter-country Adoption (Hague Convention, 1993). The Hague Convention sets minimum standards and procedures for adoptions between countries that are parties to the Convention (U.S. Children's Bureau, 2006) that:

- seek to prevent abuses such as the abduction or sale of children;
- ensure proper counseling and consent(s) before an adoption placement may proceed;
- require that the prospective adoptive parents be eligible and suitable to adopt and that the child may enter and reside permanently in the receiving country;
- require the accreditation/approval of adoption service providers for Convention adoptions; and
- require the recognition of Convention adoptions by all countries party to the Convention (p. 16).

In the United States, federal legislation was required to implement the provisions of the Hague Convention fully and uniformly. The Intercountry Adoption Act of 2000 (PL 106-279) was enacted by Congress to fulfill this requirement. The United States signed the Hague Convention in 1994. All intercountry adoptions between the United States and parties to the Convention must comply with the Convention, the Intercountry Adoption Act of 2000, and applicable regulations. Currently, 89 countries are parties to the Hague Convention (U.S. State Department, 2014).

Another recent trend, open adoptions, allows the birth parent(s) to be involved in selecting the adoptive parents. In some instances, depending on agreements made through the adoption agency with adoptive parents, birth parents also are able to keep in touch with adoptive parents through the exchange of pictures and letters and, in some instances, maintain contact with the child as the child grows up (Crosson-Tower, 2012; Lears & Farnsworth, 2005; Waters, 2005; Child Welfare Information Gateway, 2013). Research shows that birth mothers and adoptees who participate in open adoption fare better than those who participate in closed adoption with no contact with each other (Child Welfare Information Gateway, 2013c).

Even though adoption services have been strengthened, barriers to successful placements remain, particularly for children with special needs. Agencies and individuals still consider some children unadoptable, and some agencies are reluctant to try to place children across state lines, even when parents (or children) in other states can be located.

As the number of adoptions of children with special needs has increased, agencies and adoptive parents have recognized the need for post-adoption services for children and their adoptive families. Children who have lost their birth parents and have suffered extensive child maltreatment have special needs that often continue or do not surface until long after the adoption is final. Adoptive parent groups have been instrumental in advocating for legislation establishing adoption programs, and support groups for adoptive parents. Currently these groups offer the primary support after placement in many communities. Adoption advocates are pushing to get language added to one of the child welfare bills slated for reauthorization that allows Title IV-E child welfare funds to be used for pre and post-placement services, including counseling.

An additional issue relating to adoption that has gained attention is what should be decided when birth parents want to reclaim their children after the children have been adopted. These incidents are traumatic for everyone involved but, like the conflicts with ethnic placements, usually can be avoided by following sound child welfare practice and using licensed adoption agencies. If the system does fail in some way, however, the courts are required to decide who obtains custody of the child. In many instances, however, despite the work of Goldstein et al. (1996) in developing the concept of the psychological parent and the extensive research on attachment and the impact of separation on children have not been considered and children have been moved into new settings with total strangers.

Among the adoption-related issues that will continue to be raised in the next decade are the following:

- Who has priority in gaining custody of children in an adoption dispute after an adoption has taken place?
- What impact will privately arranged adoptions and intercountry adoptions have on the number of children and youth awaiting adoption in the United States?

- How important is ethnicity in determining child placement, and at what point should ethnicity be considered?
- To what extent should adopted children have contact with birth parents and siblings?
- What ethical issues should be considered in paying young pregnant girls for their unborn children without going through an agency?
- What rights should surrogate parents have?

Child Welfare and Cultural Diversity

EP 2.1.4a

Whatever the child welfare services provide, they must be responsive to the day-to-day realities of diverse populations. Ideally, this means that the child welfare services system should be culturally competent throughout. That is, federal, state, and local entities, as well as individual social workers who provide child welfare services, must:

- understand the impact of culture on individuals, families, and communities;
- recognize that, although some factors may be more typical of one ethnic group than another, in general, there is vast diversity within groups, and specific factors should not be assumed just because someone is from a given group;
- value the diversity of individuals and cultural groups, and view the diversity as a strength rather than a deviation; and
- recognize the impact of oppression and social and economic injustice on at-risk populations.

Child welfare workers should learn as much as possible about the cultures of the diverse populations with which they work, including history, family structure, family dynamics, religion, language, music and art, traditions, communication patterns, views about seeking help, and about social work and social welfare (Crosson-Tower, 2012; Fontes, 2008; Procter, Thoburn, & Chand, 2004; Samantrai, 2003; Green, Belanger, McRoy, & Bullard, 2011). For example, strengths of African American families identified by various researchers include strong kinship bonds that go beyond the nuclear family, flexibility of family roles, and a strong religious orientation. These strengths are seen from a child welfare perspective in the informal kinship system regarding children's living situations, in which many African American children live with relatives other than their birth parents or nonrelatives who are considered kin without going through a formal foster care or adoption process (Everett, Chipungu, & Leashore, 2004).

Until recently, child placement agencies did not consider the possibility of placing a child with a relative or kin, which meant that African American children often were placed with nonrelatives when family members were available who could serve in parental roles for them. Child welfare agencies also often overlooked the church as a resource in keeping African American families together or helping children when families could not care for them. In one southern city, a church was awarded custody of a sibling group.

Many Asians, particularly first-generation immigrants, hold traditional Asian values, which place the needs of the family above the needs of the individual and emphasize the importance of bringing honor to a family. Thus, outsiders who make Asian family problems known can be viewed as bringing shame to the family. Similarly, Asian family members may be reluctant to divulge information to social workers about how their children are being cared for or what is needed to help them. They also may hesitate to openly disagree with individuals they view as authority figures, including social workers. This cultural pattern may be seen when an Asian client seems to agree with a social worker but then does not follow through on what was agreed (Coalition for Asian American Children and Families, 2006).

Latino cultures value the family as a means of socializing family members about their culture, as well as sources of social support and coping. Many Latinos have left their jobs and immediate family members and traveled long distances to help other family members in need. In most Latino cultures, males play important roles as protectors, and they consider supporting their families as crucial. The role of mothers in Latino families, too, is defined and respected. Social support systems in many Latino families include not only parents and extended family members but also godparents, who frequently are looked to as a resource. The church, too, is a viable resource for many Latino families (Congress & Gonzales, 2005; Fontes, 2008; Torres & Rivera, 2002; Lum, 2011).

Native American cultures show vast diversity. Some tribes are matrilineal (the mother's family is looked to first when legal issues such as adoption are addressed, as well as for other types of social support), while other

tribes are patrilineal. Native Americans as a whole value the family, with particular emphasis on cooperation and respect for the elderly. Therefore, they may seek advice from elderly members of the family or the tribe in matters of child welfare issues and may defer to them (Fixico, 2008; Mihesauh, 2009; Lum, 2011; Washburn, 2006).

These are just a few examples of how culture can shape interactions with social workers and child welfare agencies and must be placed in the context of the rich heritage of each cultural group. Most important is to view the client from his or her day-to-day reality and from the way that person's culture shapes that reality, rather than to overlook culture completely, misunderstand it, or assume an "expert" role and assign stereotypes at the expense of the uniqueness of each individual. To be culturally competent when dealing with children, youth, and families, social workers first must be self-aware and in touch with their own culture and the ways their culture shapes their beliefs about and interactions with others. Social workers, too, must also become knowledgeable about other cultures and willing to learn from clients, seeing them as knowledgeable in regard to their own lives and needs.

Child Welfare and the Future

EP 2.1.8a
EP 2.1.9b

A major debate in the child welfare field relates to what direction to take in providing services to children, youth, and families in the future. Some child welfare leaders caution that much more knowledge is needed before we can make significant changes for the better. Others claim that we already have the answers and that the real challenge is to mobilize the political will to implement them. Still others indicate that to be effective, wide-scale change will be required (Daley, 2006; Dominelli, 2009; Morris & Hopps, 2007).

This debate reflects a fundamental flaw in U.S. child welfare policy. Put simply, the country has not yet developed a cogent, consistent, and comprehensive system for addressing the needs of children and their families. The American people remain ambivalent about the role of government in the private lives of its citizens. The market economy and the individualist perspective have resulted in the primarily residual focus of contemporary social welfare programs. We seem to be content with letting families spiral out of control and break down before offering services, and even then, the services provided are often too little, too late.

Patriarchy and puritanism have played a strong role in the development of child welfare policy in the United States. The latest attempts at welfare reform have brought us back to the era of personal and family responsibility valued during colonial times (Stern & Axinn, 2012). The middle class has all but disappeared in the United States. In its place, two classes of people have emerged—the "haves" and the "have nots" (sometimes called the "underclass"). Millions of children are living in families at or below the poverty level. A large portion of those families are living in *extreme* poverty, defined as having an income below half of the official poverty level (Lindsey, 2008).

The development of social welfare policy, of which child welfare policy is a subset, tends to reflect the prevailing social values of the country. Although most people would agree that "children are the future of the world," we seem reluctant, if not immobilized, as a nation to act on that conviction. And so we study the problem a little more or, through incremental policy making, tinker with the existing system, with the hope that things will improve. Or we blame the victims of poor policy or decision making for things that largely are not of their doing and are beyond their control (Day & Schiele, 2013).

If, indeed, "it takes a village" to raise a child—and most serious-minded child welfare professionals would agree that it does—it is time to act with regard to the future of children and families in the United States. And that action must be both deliberate and decisive. We must work together as a nation to develop a child welfare system that is comprehensive, strengths-based, flexible, culturally competent, based on the premise that all children truly are created equal and should have equal opportunities in life, and invests in children as human capital. Social workers at all levels of the environment—agency, community, state, nation, and world—are in a unique position to advocate for improving services to children, youth, and families.

The Role of Social Workers in Providing Services to Children, Youth, and Families

EP 2.1.1c

Social workers play many roles in providing services to children, youth, and families. In fact, this is the most traditional area of social work practice. The "child welfare worker," first a volunteer during the 1800s and then a trained

social worker in the 1900s, is most often the stereotype of social workers. But the roles of social workers in this area have expanded significantly, and social workers at the bachelor's of social work (BSW), master's of social work (MSW), and doctorate (PhD) levels are actively involved in providing services to children, youth, and families. At the BSW level, social workers are involved as:

- child-care workers in group homes and residential treatment centers;
- adult and children's counselors at shelters for individuals and families who have experienced intimate partner violence;
- counselors at youth shelters;
- crisis counselors in law enforcement agencies; and
- child protective services and foster care workers in public social services agencies.

An entry-level position in the area of child and family services usually offers broad-based experience that gives social workers a great deal of flexibility to move to other jobs in working with children and families (in either direct services or supervisory positions) or other areas of social work. Some states require a minimum of a BSW degree for certain child and family positions, such as child protective services and foster care staff.

A growing number of social workers are specializing in child protective services, investigating reported cases of abuse and neglect and intervening when necessary. They work closely with the courts, law-enforcement agencies, and community-based family intervention, self-help, and volunteer programs. Foster care staffs recruit foster families and oversee their training, and they often work with the child and foster family while the child is in foster care, helping the child adjust (see Box 11.5).

Many BSW graduates are employed as child-care workers in residential treatment and psychiatric care facilities, serving as members of treatment teams and working directly with children and adolescents to implement the team's plan. This experience is valuable in learning the skills necessary for working with children who have emotional disturbance and their families. Other social workers are employed in agencies such as Big Brothers and Big Sisters of America, assessing children and potential volunteers and monitoring the matches afterward.

Increasingly, BSW graduates are being hired as social workers in family preservation programs, family support programs that assist families in getting off public assistance, and programs that provide services to

Box 11.5 Do You Have the Characteristics to Be a Competent Social Worker?

A number of researchers have studied what constitutes an effective client–worker relationship.* According to the research, child welfare clients want social workers who are:

- Willing to listen and help
- Accurately empathic
- Genuine and warm
- Respectful and nonjudgmental
- Fair
- Accessible
- Supportive and practical
- Experienced and competent

Many of these characteristics relate to social work values and skills learned in BSW and MSW social work programs.

*See, for example, Morales, A., Sheafor, B., & Scott, M. (2011). *Social work: A profession of many faces* (12th ed.). Boston: Allyn & Bacon; Grobman, L. M. (2004). *Days in the lives of social workers: 54 professionals tell "real-life" stories from social work practice* (3rd ed.). Harrisburg, PA: White Hat; and Grobman, L. M. (2005). *More days in the lives of social workers: 35 "real-life" stories of advocacy, outreach, and other intriguing roles in social work practice.* Harrisburg, PA: White Hat.

children with developmental disabilities and their families. Social workers at the BSW level also are hired as addiction counselors in inpatient and community-based adult and adolescent treatment programs. Special certification in the area of substance use often is required for these jobs.

School social workers often require special state certification, which varies from state to state. In some states, BSW graduates can be hired as school social workers, whereas other states require teaching experience and graduate-level courses or an MSW degree. With more attention to school dropouts and increases in problems such as school violence and teen pregnancy, school social work is a rapidly growing area. School social workers:

- provide individual, parent, and family counseling;
- lead groups of students who are teen parents, are on probation, are recovering from substance abuse, are experiencing family problems such as divorce or abuse, or are having problems relating to teachers and peers;
- provide crisis-intervention services such as suicide intervention;
- organize parent-education and parent-support groups;
- advocate for the needs of children and families within the school system and the community; and
- network with other social services agencies in the community to assist parents and their children in accessing appropriate services.

The National Association of Social Workers has a school social work division, a certifcation in school social work, and two school social work journals are published nationally.

Other BSW graduates become employed in advocacy or policy-related positions as legislative assistants or staff members of state or federal child and family services organizations or agencies, such as the Children's Defense Fund. An MSW degree may be required for some of these positions, particularly those related to policy analysis.

A number of other social work jobs in the child and family services arena require an MSW degree, partly because of the standards established by the CWLA, which many agencies follow, and partly because some child and family services are highly specialized. In almost all instances, an MSW is required of an adoption worker. Most child guidance centers and child and family service agencies also require an MSW degree. Many social work or therapist positions in residential treatment centers require an MSW, as do clinical social work positions in adolescent and child mental health and psychiatric treatment programs. Most schools of social work have child and family or child welfare concentrations at the graduate level, which provide special coursework in this area, as well as field placements in child and family services settings.

With implementation of the PhD degree in social work, some child guidance or child and family services agencies are attempting to hire agency directors at this level. In addition, persons who want more highly specialized clinical experience are earning the PhD degree, enabling them to undertake more intensive therapy with children, youth, and families.

If students are interested in a social work career in the area of child and family services, a number of child welfare and child and family journals, as well as numerous books on all areas discussed in this chapter, are readily available. In addition, many child and family services programs have volunteer programs. Volunteer experience is highly recommended, as it helps students determine whether they are interested in this area and also provides sound social work experience. Box 11.5 asks, "Do you have the characteristics to be a competent social worker?"

Summary

Policies and programs directed to the needs of children, youth, and families are developed and implemented within the context of society, as well as community attitudes and values, awareness about the needs, and the availability of resources. The preferred emphases at present are prevention and early intervention, keeping families together, and making decisions based on the least harm to the children. Nevertheless, the lack of prevention and early intervention resources, as well as a focus on the most serious situations, places large numbers of families with children at risk of family breakdown, often leading to placement of children in foster care and adoption. Many of these placements could have been avoided if the family had received comprehensive family preservation services designed to help the family function in ways that do not place their children at risk of child maltreatment, failure in school, juvenile delinquency, and criminal behavior.

The needs of families with children are complex and diverse. Available programs designed to address these needs are limited in both number and the scope of services offered. Thus, plenty of employment opportunities are available in both the public and private sectors for social workers who are interested in children, youth, and family services.

Competency Notes

EP 2.1.1a: Advocate for client access to the services of social work (pp. 355, 365). Social workers advocate for access to social work services for children, youth, and families.

EP 2.1.1c: Attend to professional roles and boundaries (p. 369). Social workers attend to professional roles and responsibilities when working with children, youth, and families, with particular attention given to the vulnerability of children.

EP 2.1.3a: Distinguish, appraise, and integrate multiple sources of knowledge, including research-based knowledge and practice wisdom (pp. 338–339). Social workers distinguish, appraise, and integrate sources of knowledge, including knowledge gained from clients, research-based knowledge, and practice wisdom in their work with children, youth, and families.

EP 2.1.4a: Recognize the extent to which a culture's structures and values may oppress, marginalize, alienate, or create or enhance privilege and power (p. 367). Social workers recognize the extent to which a culture's structures and values may oppress, marginalize, alienate, or create or enhance privilege and power and the resulting impacts on children, youth, and families and the services provided to them.

EP 2.1.7a: Use conceptual frameworks to guide the process of assessment, intervention, and evaluation (pp. 336–350, 353, 355, 360, 362–364). Social workers use the ecological/systems and other conceptual frameworks to guide the processes of assessment, intervention, and evaluation when working with children, youth, and families.

EP 2.1.7b: Critique and apply knowledge to understand person and environment (pp. 335–336, 338, 347–350, 353, 355, 360, 362–364). Social workers critique and apply knowledge about the developmental needs of children, youth and families within the context of the social environment to understand and address the needs of clients and their families.

EP 2.1.8a: Analyze, formulate, and advocate for policies that advance social well-being (pp. 364, 368). Social workers analyze, formulate, and advocate for policies that advance the social well-being of children, youth, and families.

EP 2.1.9b: Provide leadership in promoting sustainable changes in service delivery and practice to improve the quality of social services (pp. 336, 347–353, 355, 358, 368). Social workers act as leaders in promoting sustainable changes in service delivery and practice to improve the quality of social services for children, youth, and families.

Key Terms

The terms below are defined in the Glossary.

adoption
best interests of the child
child protective services (CPS)
Child Welfare League of America
child welfare service delivery system
child welfare services
children with special needs
crisis intervention
Deficit Reduction Act of 2005
family preservation programs
foster care
Head Start
home-based family-centered services
in-home family-centered services
kinship care
least detrimental alternative
natural support systems
own-home services
permanency planning
psychological parent
residential treatment
school social work
self-help groups
Social Security Act
substitute care
U.S. Children's Bureau

Discussion Questions

1. What is meant by the concepts "best interests of the child," "least detrimental alternative," and "psychological parent"?
2. Based on the discussion about the least detrimental alternative when intervening in family matters, compare the advantages and disadvantages of early intervention with a family who is at risk for abuse versus waiting until abuse has already taken place.
3. Describe briefly at least three prevention programs used with children and their families.
4. Find out what the reporting laws are for child abuse and neglect in your state. Who is required to make a report according to state law? Do you think other groups should be added as mandatory reporters?
5. Compare home-based family-centered services with substitute care and adoption. What are the advantages and disadvantages of each?
6. What is meant by *special-needs adoption*?
7. What are two areas in which social workers at the BSW and MSW levels might be employed in a child and family services position?
8. Select one of the "family problem areas" discussed in this chapter. Identify one prevention program and one intervention program that you would suggest to address that problem area.
9. Identify three problems with the current children, youth, and families service delivery system. What are some possible solutions?
10. Debate the following arguments, giving a rationale for both pro and con positions:
    a. Child abuse is a "red herring" that has directed attention away from the more critical child welfare issue of poverty.
    b. The knowledge to make things better for children and families is within our reach; we just have to begin to put the tools in place to do so.

On the Internet

http://www.childwelfare.gov
http://www.cwla.org
http://www.childrensdefense.org
http://www.nicwa.org

References

Becvar, D. S. (2006). *Families that flourish: Facilitating resilience in clinical practice.* New York: Norton.

Berrick, J., & Gilbert, N. (Eds.). (2008). *Raising children: Emerging needs, modern risks and social responses.* New York: Oxford University Press.

Brayne, H., & Carr, H. (2008). *Law for social workers* (10th ed.). New York: Oxford University Press.

Brittain, C., & Hunt, E. (Eds.). (2004). *Helping in child protective services: A competency-based casework handbook.* New York: Oxford University Press.

Brown, V. A. (2002). *Child welfare: Case studies.* Boston: Allyn & Bacon.

Center for Urban Policy and the Environment. (2003). *Family volunteering: An exploratory study of the impact of families.* Indianapolis: Indiana University–Purdue University.

Children's Defense Fund. (2012). *Children's budget watch.* Washington, DC: Author.

Children's Defense Fund. (2014). *The state of America's children, 2014.* Washington, DC: Author.

Child Welfare Information Gateway. (2013a). *Determining the best interests of the child.* Washington, DC: U.S. Department of Health and Human Services, Children's Bureau.

Child Welfare Information Gateway. (2013b). *Parent education to strengthen families and reduce the risk of maltreatment.* Washington, DC: U.S.

Department of Health and Human Services, Children's Bureau.

Child Welfare Information Gateway. (2013c). *Working with birth and adoptive families to support open adoption.* Washington, DC: U.S. Department of Health and Human Services, Children's Bureau.

Child Welfare Information Gateway. (2014a). *Differential response to child abuse and neglect.* Washington, DC: U.S. Department of Health and Human Services, Children's Bureau.

Child Welfare Information Gateway. (2014b). *Family preservation services.* Washington, DC: U.S. Department of Health and Human Services, Children's Bureau.

Child Welfare Information Gateway. (2014c). *In-home services in child welfare.* Washington, DC: U.S. Department of Health and Human Services, Children's Bureau.

Child Welfare Information Gateway. (2014d). *Responding to child abuse and neglect.* Washington, DC: U.S. Department of Health and Human Services, Children's Bureau.

Child Welfare Information Gateway. (2014e). *Volunteer programs.* Washington, DC: U.S. Department of Health and Human Services, Children's Bureau.

Child Welfare League of America (CWLA). (2003). *Standards for services to strengthen and preserve families with children.* Washington, DC: Author.

Child Welfare League of America (CWLA). (2006). *CWLA standards of excellence for family foster care services.* Washington, DC: Author. Retrieved September 9, 2010, from http://www.cwla.org

Child Welfare League of America (CWLA). (2013). *Adequately funding child welfare supports and services: 2013 CWLA legislative agenda for children and families.* Washington, DC: Author.

Children's Rights. (2014). *Class actions.* New York: Author. Retrieved from http://www.childrensrights.org/reform-campaigns/legal-cases/

Coalition for Asian American Children and Families. (2006). *Understanding the issues of abuse and neglect and Asian American families.* New York: Author.

Congress, E., & Gonzales, M. (Eds.). (2005). *Multicultural perspectives in working with families* (2nd ed.). New York: Springer.

Crosson-Tower, C. (2012). *Exploring child welfare: A practice perspective* (6th ed.). Boston: Allyn & Bacon.

Crosson-Tower, C. (2013). *Understanding child abuse and neglect* (8th ed.). Boston: Allyn & Bacon.

Daley, J. G. (Ed.). (2006). *Advances in social work: Special issue on the futures of social work.* Victoria, BC, Canada: Trafford.

Davis, L. (2007). *See you in court: A social worker's guide to presenting evidence in care proceedings.* London: Kingsley.

Day, P. J., & Schiele, J. (2013). *New history of social welfare* (7th ed.) Boston: Allyn & Bacon.

Dominelli, L. (2009). *Social work: Theory and practice for a changing world.* Williston, VT: Polity.

Everett, J., Chipungu, S., & Leashore, B. (Eds.). (2004). *Child welfare revisited: An Africentric perspective.* Piscataway, NJ: Rutgers University Press.

Farmer, E. (2008). *Kinship care: Fostering effective family and friends placements.* London: Kingsley.

Federal Interagency Forum on Child and Family Statistics. (2014). *America's children: Key national indicators of well-being.* Washington, DC: Author.

Fineman, M. A., & Worthington, K. (2009). *What is right for children?* United Kingdom: Ashgate.

Fixen, A. (2011). *Children in foster care: Societal and financial costs.* Eugene, OR: A Family for Every Child.

Fixico, D. (2003). *The American Indian mind in a linear world.* Oxford, England: Routledge.

Fontes, L. A. (2008). *Child abuse and culture: Working with diverse families.* New York: Guilford Press.

Foster Care Resource Center. (2014). *Foster care facts.* San Francisco, CA: Children's Action Network/Tides Center.

Friedman, L. M. (2005). *Private lives: Families, individuals, and the law.* Cambridge, MA: Harvard University Press.

Garbarino, J. (2008). *Children and the dark side of human experience: Confronting global realities and rethinking child development.* New York: Springer.

Goldstein, J., Solnit, A., Goldstein, S., & Freud, A. (1996). *The best interests of the child: The least detrimental alternative.* New York: Free Press.

Green, D., Belanger, K., McRoy, R., & Bullard, L. (2011). *Challenging racial disproportionality in child welfare.* Washington, DC: Child Welfare League of America.

Grobman, L. M. (Ed.). (2004). *Days in the lives of social workers: 54 professionals tell "real-life" stories from social work practice* (3rd ed.). Harrisburg, PA: White Hat.

Grobman, L. M. (Ed.) (2005). *More days in the lives of social workers: 35 "real-life" stories of advocacy, outreach, and other intriguing roles in social work practice,* Harrisburg, PA: White Hat, 2005.

Guishard-Pine, J., McCall, S., & Hamilton, L. (2007). *Understanding looked after children: An introduction to psychology for foster care.* London: Kingsley.

Hague Convention. (1993). *The Hague Convention on the protection of children and cooperation in respect to intercountry adoption.* Geneva, Switzerland: Author.

Hirschy, S., & Wilkinson, E. (2009). *Protecting our children: Understanding and preventing abuse and neglect in early childhood.* Florence, KY: Delmar-Cengage Learning.

Horchak-Andino, K. (2003). *Family preservation and preventive programs—alternatives to foster care placement.* New York: National Resource Center for Foster Care and Permanency Planning.

Humphreys, C., & Stanley, N. (Eds.). (2006). *Domestic violence and child protection: Directions for good practice.* London: Kingsley.

Iwaniec, I. (Ed.). (2006). *The child's journey through care: Placement stability, case planning, and achieving permanency.* New York: Wiley.

Johnson, J. L., & Grant, G. (2004). *Casebook: Foster care.* Boston: Allyn & Bacon.

Kadushin, A. (1980). *Child welfare services* (3rd ed.). New York: Macmillan.

Kenney, G. (2012). *Maximizing benefits for children under the Affordable Care Act and beyond.* Washington, DC: Urban Institute.

Kerman, B., Freundlich, M., & Maluccio, A. (Eds.). (2009). *Achieving permanence for older children and youth in foster care.* New York: Columbia University Press.

Lears, L., & Farnsworth, B. (2005). *Megan's birthday: A story about open adoption.* Morton Grove, IL: Whitman.

Liebenberg, L., & Ungar, M. (Eds.). (2008). *Resilience action: Working with youth across cultures and contexts.* Toronto: University of Toronto Press.

Lindsey, D. (Ed.). (2008). *The child poverty and inequality: Securing a better future for America's children.* New York: Oxford University Press.

Loveless, A., & Holman, T. (Eds.). (2006). *The family in the new millennium: World voices supporting the natural clan.* Santa Barbara, CA: Praeger.

Lum, D. (2011). *Culturally competent practice: A framework for understanding diverse groups and justice issues.* Belmont, CA: Brooks/Cole Cengage.

Maas, H., & Engler, R. (1959). *Children in need of parents.* New York: Columbia University Press.

Marre, D., & Briggs, L. (2009). *International adoption: Global inequalities and the circulation of children.* New York: New York University Press.

Martell, D. R. (2005). *Criminal justice and the placement of abused children.* New York: LFB Scholarly Publishing.

Maschi, T., Bradley, C., & Ward, K. (Eds.). (2009). *Forensic social work: Psychosocial and legal issues in diverse practice settings.* New York: Springer.

McElwee, N. (2007). *At-risk children & youth: Resiliency explored.* New York: Haworth.

Mizrahi, T., & Davis, L. (2008). *The encyclopedia of social work.* New York: Oxford University Press.

Morales, A., Sheafor, B., & Scott, M. (2011). *Social work: A profession of many faces* (12th ed.). Boston: Allyn & Bacon.

Morris, R., & Hopps, J. (Eds.). (2007). *Social work at the millennium: Critical reflections on the future of the profession.* Northampton, MA: Free Press.

National Association of Social Workers. (2012). *Social work speaks: NASW policy statements, 2012–2014.* Washington, DC: Author.

National Coalition for Child Protection Reform. (2006). *Foster care vs. family preservation: The track record on safety.* Alexandria, VA: Author.

National Committee for Quality Assurance. (2008). *The state of health care quality 2006.* Washington, DC: Author.

Pew Charitable Trusts. (2004). *Home at last: Moving in foster care to safe, permanent families.* Philadelphia: Author.

Pion-Berlin, L., Williams, S., Polinsky, M., & Pickens, D. (2013). *Parents anonymous groups address protective factors—the evidence.* Clarement, CA: Parents Anonymous.

Popple, P., & Leighninger, L. (2011). *The policy-based profession: An introduction to social welfare policy analysis for social workers* (5th ed.). Boston: Allyn & Bacon.

Procter, J., Thoburn, J., & Chand, A. (2004). *Child welfare services for minority ethnic families: The research reviewed.* London: Kingsley.

Roberts, A. R. (2008). *Social workers' desk reference.* New York: Oxford University Press.

Rothman, B. K. (2006). *Weaving a family: Untangling race and adoption.* Boston: Beacon Press.

Rowell, V. (2008). *The women who raised me: A memoir.* New York: Amistad.

Samantrai, K. (2003). *Culturally competent public child welfare practice.* Belmont, CA: Wadsworth.

Sanders, M. G. (2005). *Building school-community partnerships: Collaboration for student success.* New York: Corwin Press.

Selbin, D. (n.d.). *A day in the life of a school social worker*. Austin, TX: Communities in Schools Central Texas.

Shyne, A., & Schroeder, A. (1978). *National study of services to children and their families*. Washington, DC: U.S. Children's Bureau, Department of Health, Education, and Welfare.

Sousa, L. (Ed.). (2008). *Strengthening vulnerable families*. Hauppauge, NY: Nova Science.

Stein, T. J. (2007). *Child welfare and the law*. New York: CWLA.

Stern, M., & Axinn, J. (2012). *Social welfare: A history of the American response to need* (8th ed.). Saddle River, NJ: Pearson.

Stoltzfus, E. (2012). *Child welfare funding for children and family services authorization under Title IV-B of the Social Security Act*. Washington, DC: Congressional Research Service.

Torres, J. B., & Rivera, F. G. (2002). *Latino/Hispanic liaisons and visions for human behavior in the social environment*. Binghamton, NY: Haworth Social Work.

Trenka, J., Oparah, J., & Shin, S. Y. (Eds.). (2006). *Outsiders within: Writing on transracial adoption*. Cambridge, MA: South End Press.

U.S. Children's Bureau. (1997). *Adoption 2002: A response to the Presidential Executive Memorandum on adoption*. Washington, DC: Author.

U.S. Children's Bureau. (2003). Evaluation of family preservation and reunification. *Children's Bureau Express, 4*(6). Retrieved from https://cbexpress.acf.hhs.gov/index.cfm?event=website.viewArticles&issueid=44&articleID=689&keywords=Evaluation%20of%20family%20preservation%20and%20reunification%20programs.

U.S. Children's Bureau. (2006). *Major federal legislation concerned with child protection, child welfare, and adoption*. Washington, DC: Author.

U.S. Children's Bureau. (2008). *How does the child welfare system work?* Washington, DC: Author.

U.S. Children's Bureau. (2013a). *Child is identified as a special needs adoption: October 1, 2008–September 30, 2009 (FY 2009)*. Washington, DC: Author.

U.S. Children's Bureau. (2013b). *Trends in foster care and adoption (FFY 2002-FFY 2012)*. Washington, DC. Author.

U.S. Department of Health and Human Services. (1994). *National study of protective, preventive and reunification services delivered to children and their families*. Washington, DC: Author.

U.S. Department of Health and Human Services. (2006). *Welfare reform: Interim final regulations*. Washington, DC: Author. Retrieved from http://www.act.hhs.gov/programs/ofa/regfact.htm

U.S. Department of Health and Human Services. (2009). *Prenatal care*. Washington, DC: Author. Retrieved from http://www.4woman.gov/Pregnancy/pg.cfm?page=264

U.S. Department of Health and Human Services. (2013). *Recent demographic trends in foster care*. Washington, DC: Author.

U.S. Department of Labor. (2014). *Volunteering in the United States, 2013*. Washington, DC: Author.

U.S. State Department. (2014). *International adoption*. Washington, DC: Author.

Vasaly, S. (1976). *Foster care in five states*. Washington, DC: Department of Health, Education, and Welfare.

Vieth, V., Bottoms, B., & Perona, A. (Eds.). (2005). *Ending child abuse: New efforts in prevention, investigation, and training*. Binghamton, NY: Haworth Press.

Walsh, F. (2006). *Strengthening family resilience* (2nd ed.). New York: Guilford Press.

Washburn, F. A. (2006). *Elsie's business (Native stories: A series of American narratives)*. Lincoln, NE: Bison.

Waters, J. (2005). *Arms open wide: An insight into open adoption*. Bloomington, IN: Authorhouse.

WESTAT & James Bell Associates. (2002). *Evaluation of family preservation and reunification programs: Final report*. Washington, DC: Author.

Williams, J. (2008). *Child law for social work*. Thousand Oaks, CA: Sage.

Wilson, R. G., & Crewe, S. E. (Eds.). (2007). *Tradition and policy perspectives in kinship care*. New York: Haworth Press.

Suggested Readings

Child Welfare. A bimonthly journal published by the Child Welfare League of America, New York: New York.Information about this journal can be found at http://www.cwla.org/child-welfare-journal/.

Cox-Petersen, A. (2010). *Educational partnerships: Connecting schools, families, and the community*. Thousand Oaks, CA: Sage.

Douglas, E. (2010). *Innovations in child and family policy: Multidisciplinary research and perspectives on strengthening families and their children*. Lenham, MD: Lexington.

Epstein, J. L., Sanders, M. G., Sheldon, S., Simon, B. S., Salinas, K. C., Jansorn, N. R., et al. (2008). *School,* family, and community partnerships: Your handbook for action. Thousand Oaks, CA: Corwin.

Fong, R. (2006). *Intersecting child welfare, substance abuse, and family violence.* Washington: Council on Social Work Education.

Freymond, N., & Cameron, G. (Eds.). (2006). *Towards positive systems of child welfare: International comparisons of child protection, family service, and community caring.* Toronto, ON, Canada: University of Toronto Press.

Goldstein, S., & Brooks, R. (Eds.). (2005). *Handbook of resilience in children.* New York: Springer.

Krebs, B. (2006). *Beyond the foster care system: The future of teens.* Piscataway, NJ: Rutgers University Press.

Lerner, R. M., Sparks, E. E., & McCubbin, L. D. (2010). *Family diversity and family policy: Strengthening families for America's children.* New York: Springer.

Nowinski, J. (2010). *The divorced child: Strengthening your family through the first three years of separation.* New York: Palgrave-Macmillan.

Shirk, M., & Stangler, G. (2006). *On their own: What happens to kids when they age out of the foster care system?* New York: Perseus.

Weiss, H. B., Kreider, H. M., Lopez, M. E., & Chatman, C. M. (Eds.). (2005). *Preparing educators to involve families: From theory to practice.* Thousand Oaks, CA: Sage.

CHAPTER 12
Older Adults: Needs and Services

Samantha Parker is an 88-year-old widow who lives alone in a northern state. She is unable to care for herself, and her home lacks an adequate heating system. Samantha lives on a limited income derived from her husband's social security benefits plus a small Supplemental Security Income benefit. She has been the object of concern to many in the community for quite some time, and she has frustrated all those who have attempted to assist her. Her personal appearance and home are cause for serious concern. Besides being unkempt, Samantha has many large sores on her hands, face and legs. Communication is difficult because she is unable to hear. She also has difficulty seeing without glasses. Her conversation often consists of delusional and paranoid comments about her neighbor, whom Samantha claims is responsible for the condition of her home.

Samantha has two daughters who live several hundred miles away, making it difficult for them to look after their mother on a regular basis. Both daughters think their mother should be in some type of protective environment such as an assisted living facility, but they have been unwilling to force her to enter such a living environment. Efforts by community agencies have been rebuffed, and the dilemma over whether to intervene forcibly and provide Samantha with adequate health care in a protective environment continues.

Recently, an adult protective services social worker has been assigned to the case and is working with Samantha and her daughters to find a solution that will best meet Samantha's needs. The social worker is slowly gaining Samantha's trust, and Samantha has agreed to go with the social worker to the local health clinic. The social worker and the daughters hope that Samantha finally will agree to obtain the services and living situation that can provide the care she needs.

Samantha's experience is not typical of most older adults, although far too many share similar experiences. In general, older adults experience life satisfaction, purpose in life, good health, and contentment. For those with problems similar to those of Samantha's, however, the struggle to survive often limits their ability to enjoy life. Unfortunately, the myth that all older persons are alike obscures the reality that there is as much variation among the elderly as there is between the young and the old. In this chapter we examine the more salient issues and problems of older people, review their problems of adaptation, and identify physical and social support systems and resources designed to meet their needs.

An Increasingly Aging Population with Many Implications

EP 2.1.3a
EP 2.1.7b

The number and percentage of people reaching old age are greater than they have been throughout recorded history. This is in part because life expectancy has been extended dramatically since 1900. That year, for example, the life expectancy for individuals was approximately 47 years; by 2012, females reaching age 65 had an average life expectancy of 85.4, while males had an average life expectancy of 82.8 years (Administration on Aging, 2014). The percentage of persons living in the United States age 65 or older is projected to grow to nearly 20% by 2030 and to almost 40% by 2050 (Federal Interagency Forum on Aging-related Statistics, 2014). See Figure 12.1 for a visual portrayal of how much the older adult population is growing compared to other age groups.

Today, persons who are 65 are not considered to be at the end of the life cycle. In fact, one consequence of extended longevity is that many adults in their 60s are caring for their parents who are in their 80s and 90s. In 2012, 37.2 million persons living in the United States were between the ages of 65 and 84, compared to 3 million in 1900. An additional 5.9 million were 85 or older, compared to only 100,000 in 1900 (Administration on Aging, 2014). To many experts this increase in

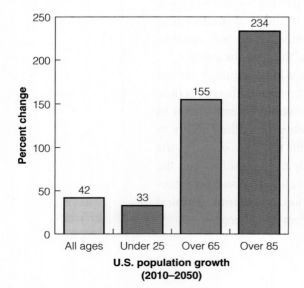

FIG 12.1 U.S. aging population
SOURCE: U.S. Census Bureau, 2010.

individuals 85 and older suggests that there are really two groups of older adults—the "old" (in their mid-60s and 70s) and the "oldest old" (age 80 or older).

Aging viewed from an international perspective is instructive. Statistics released by the United Nations (2014, pp. 1–14) reveal the following trends in the global elderly population:

- The increase in the elderly population is a global phenomenon that is unprecedented in history. The rapid growth in numbers of elderly people worldwide is attributable primarily to historical declines in fertility coupled with the general aging of the population. At the same time that there has been an increase in elderly worldwide, there has been a decline in persons age 15 and under, resulting in a median age in 2010 of 26. Projections show that by 2050, the percentage of older adults word wide will exceed the percentage of younger adults. This will move the median age of world citizens to 36. In developed countries as a whole, the number of persons aged 60 or over has already surpassed the number of children (persons under age 15).
- In 2013, the 841 million persons aged 60 and older comprised 11.7% of the world's population. This number is projected to grow to more than 2 billion, or 21.1% of the population by 2050.
- The older population itself is aging. In 2013, persons 80 and older comprised 14% of the population of older adults. This figure is expected to increase to 20%, or 392 million persons 80 and older, by 2050.
- By 2050, women will continue to outnumber men throughout the world. The ratio of men to women 60 and older will be 85:100, while for those 80 and older it will be 61:100.
- By 2050, 8 in 10 older adults will live in developing countries.

The consequences to society of a larger older population have significant impact on the economy, health care, family composition and living arrangements, housing and migration. Ensuring that essential resources are available to meet the health, social, and economic needs of the older population places a heavy burden on government and private resources, including families. Middle-aged Americans are being referred to as the "sandwich generation," as they are providing for their children while they also are providing for their aging parents. But many families cannot offer such support, especially when major health problems occur, and many older people do not have families available to give even emotional support. Thus, there is an increasing reliance on federal and state governments to provide for such needs.

Physiological Aging

Theories About Why We Age

EP 2.1.7b

Scientists have yet to determine why we age. A number of theories have been proposed to explain the aging process though there is no consensus on any one. Current biological theories of aging fall into two categories. *Programmed theories* are based on the premise that aging follows a timetable that begins at birth. These theories suggest that aging results in programmed factors as we age, such as deficits in the ways that various genes switch on and off, diminishing endocrine and hormonal production over time, or a decline in our immune system resulting in increased risk of infectious disease. Another set of theories of aging is based on *damage and error*. These theories suggest that our cells and tissues wear and tear as we age for a variety of reasons. This wear and tear can be due to cross-linked proteins that damage cells and tissues, free radicals in the environment that damage cell structure and organs, and DNA damage that occurs continuously in cells as they replicate, but that over time multiplies and thus can no longer be eliminated or repaired (Kunlin, 2010).

Physiological Characteristics of Aging

Physiological changes, through growth and physical maturation, continue throughout the life cycle. During midlife (around age 45), we go through a stage of physical change termed "senescence," defined as the onset of the degenerative process. At this stage, individuals begin to undergo significant bodily changes—graying or loss of hair, wrinkling of the skin, and changes in vision and hearing. It is at this time that many become aware that old age eventually will be a reality. Most persons are physically healthy and able to live independently when they reach age 65; however, as they reach their mid-70s assistance is more likely to be needed. About 9% of persons age 75 and older living in the United States find it challenging to carry out daily living activities such as eating, bathing, getting dressed, and getting in and out of bed on their own, while 17% cannot carry out essential activities that require both physical and cognitive ability, such as paying bills, shopping, cooking, and housekeeping (Berk, 2014).

Typically, aging is accompanied by sensory losses. Changes in vision and hearing take place, and in very late life, tactile (touch) and olfactory (taste) senses are much less acute. These changes do not happen at any specific age, nor do they affect all individuals to the same extent. In some, the losses are minor and hardly detectable, and in others, the losses represent major barriers. Unless sensory losses are profound, they usually do not limit the older person's social interactions and ability to live a typical and fulfilling life. Even when older people experience more serious sensory changes, the proper prosthetic supports often allow them to maintain productive lives.

More significant changes occur internally. Changes in the cardiovascular system often are reflected in elevated blood pressure and loss of elasticity in the lungs. Renal (kidney) capacity is reduced, and the bladder loses approximately a third of its capacity. There is a loss of brain weight as well as of muscular strength. Estrogen and testosterone levels are lowered, and other hormonal changes occur. For most, these factors can be mitigated by adjustments in lifestyle—a change in diet, a program of regular exercise, surgical procedures, a therapeutic drug regimen, or some combination of these.

Many of the symbolic definitions assigned to old age are buttressed by scientific data. Physiological changes, including the loss of muscular strength, sensory losses, and reduced lung elasticity, are but a few of the measurable differences between younger and older adults. But many of the presumed losses associated with cognitive functioning have been shown to have little substance in fact. Intelligence and intellectual functioning, once thought to decline appreciably in old age, are not measurably reduced.

However, the ability to "age well" and adapt to biological changes is related to access to a nutritious diet and affordable and effective health care. For example, the cost of prescription drugs has risen dramatically in recent years. Further, the proliferation of managed-care health plans and significant changes in the Medicare program has made it difficult for older Americans to reap the benefits that modern medicine can offer. It is anticipated that the Affordable Care Act will provide some relief, but costs of health care for seniors as they age remains a formidable problem for them as well as the United States.

Emotional and Psychological Adaptation to Old Age

Behavior in old age is an individual matter and not attributable to aging alone. Any accurate assessment of adaptation in late life must consider the effects of the

EP 2.1.7b

environment on behavior, as well as the ways that physiological and cognitive characteristics contribute to behavior. Students who plan to work with older adults should familiarize themselves with these perspectives, and social workers who specialize in working with older adults should be sensitive to the both the physiological changes that reflect typical aging processes and the ways that they impact psychological and emotional functioning. When placed in the proper perspective, these changes should not be viewed negatively but, rather, as part of the life continuum.

Social workers should be aware that aging is not a fixed dimension of the life cycle. Young children are aging, as are older adults. All societies attach significance to various stages of the life cycle. **Aging** is not just a chronological process; it has symbolic meaning as well. Cultures determine, for example, the age at which their members should enter school, marry, begin careers, enter the military, have children, become grandparents, and retire. Norms for behavior are prescribed at various developmental stages of the life cycle. Too often, old age has been viewed as a period of dramatic decline. Thus, older adults often are expected to be less active, require fewer resources, contribute less to society, and become more content and serene.

Psychosocial Theories of Aging

EP 2.1.7a

Several psychosocial theories of aging have emerged to explain or describe adaptation in late life. Among the more prominent ones are continuity theory, activity theory, developmental theory, social emotional selectivity theory, and exchange theory (Berk, 2014; Baudisch, 2008; Bengston, Gans, Putney, & Silverstein, 2008; Blackburn & Dulmus, 2007; Finch, 2007; Lee, 2008).

Continuity Theory

Continuity theory emphasizes that a person's personality, formed early in life, changes little over the life span. How a person adjusts to old age is largely a product (or extension) of adaptive patterns developed in earlier years (Moody, 2009). Continuity theory stresses the maintenance and integrity of one's personality and social experiences over the life span as generally effective in adjusting to old age. This theory suggests that individuals continue engaging in roles and activities that fit with their identities, interests, and skills.

Activity Theory

Activity theory stresses the importance of maintaining adequate levels of activity, including social activity, as people grow older (Moody, 2009). Presumably, more active older adults will achieve greater satisfaction and thus age more adaptively. Activity theory has provided the basis for a number of programs developed for older adults, such as the Retired Seniors Volunteer program, mentoring programs in public schools, Senior Luncheon programs, Foster Grandparents programs, Green Thumb programs, and activity programs in assisted-living facilities. While some have applied this theory to "keeping seniors busy" with activities they are thought to enjoy, such as bingo and crafts, expanded applications suggest that people who are learning new things or making contributions to others are likely to enjoy their older age more than those who do not feel this way. Thus, participation in courses on college campus; political groups; book clubs; senior activism efforts; and returning to the workplace, including nonprofit agencies, to share wisdom and experience are examples of many of the ways that seniors stay actively engaged in their environment.

Developmental Theory

Developmental theory emphasizes positive adaptation and life satisfaction based on mastering new tasks as the individual moves through the life cycle, including old age. Life-span development is viewed as a typical process that encompasses new challenges, new tasks, and flexibility in incorporating changes into the repertoire of behaviors. Older adults must accept the physiological changes, reconstruct their physical and psychological life accordingly, and integrate values that validate their worth as older adults (Newman & Newman, 2012).

This theory postulates that the psychological crises of late life are "ego integrity versus despair" and "immortality versus extinction" (Newman & Newman, 2012). *Integrity,* according to Newman and Newman, is "not so much a quality of honesty and trustworthiness ... as it is an ability to integrate one's sense of past history with one's present circumstances and to feel content with the outcome" (p. 551). *Despair* suggests the opposite of integrity—the inability to integrate past history with the present or to achieve contentment with the outcome.

Confrontation with the psychosocial crisis of immortality versus extinction occurs in very late life. Joan Erikson, developmental psychologist Erik Erikson's widow, refers to this psychosocial stage as gerotranscendence, "a cosmic and transcendent perspective directed forward and outward, beyond the self" (Berk, 2014, p. 605). *Immortality* refers to the extension of one's life through one's children, contributions to social institutions, spirituality, and positive influences that one has had on others. *Extinction* suggests a lack of connectedness and attachment and the fear that death brings nothingness (Newman & Newman, 2012).

Social Emotional Selectivity Theory

Social emotional selectivity theory focuses on an individual's social networks, suggesting that as individuals age, their social networks narrow to fewer, but closer, relationships, with more emphasis on harmonious relationships that are supportive of their changing needs (Berk, 2014).

Exchange Theory

Exchange theory attributes social withdrawal of the aged to a loss of power. Having once exchanged their expertise for wages, the aged must comply with mandatory retirement in exchange for pensions, Social Security payments, and Medicare. Thus, the power advantage has shifted from them as individuals to society. The effect of this loss of power results in withdrawal from meaningful social interaction and more dependence on those who hold power over them (Rook, 1990).

Mental Health and Adaptation to Old Age

EP 2.1.7b
EP 2.1.9b

The role of society in creating the behavioral and value context for older adults must be examined to gain insights into the problems and issues implicit in understanding adaptation in later life. Our society, for example, stresses productivity and distributes rewards and power in relation to it. Retirement disengages older adults from socially recognized productive efforts. Instead of being consumers of products from their own currently productive efforts, those who are elderly are forced to be consumers of products from others' efforts. Social work with older adults who are marginalized because of their age does not address the causes of the marginalization. Changing the social systems that produce the marginalization and resulting negative impact on the elderly is a more tenable, albeit more difficult, solution.

Problems of old age may be analyzed using the ecological/systems perspective, discussed in Chapter 3. The way in which an individual interacts within the environment strongly influences the quality of that person's mental health. Many problematic mental health symptoms that appear in old age are attributable to environmental factors. Social isolation and loneliness, in particular, are often related to mental health challenges. And overmedication can result in loss of appetite, loss of vigor, memory loss, or disorientation. Research shows that being active and having a future orientation are associated with good mental health for older adults. Maintaining enthusiasm and working toward goals are deterrents to declines in one's mental health. Other factors that support positive mental health include feeling in control of one's life rather than dependent on others and having a strong social support system that offers a sense of belonging, affection, and reinforcement of self-worth (Berk, 2014).

While the state of mental health in older adults is not appreciably different from that of the general population, myths regarding inherent disorientation, memory loss, excessive dependency, and senility in older people are pervasive. Certainly, some older adults have problems of a mental nature that impact their quality of life, but, as with younger people, these problems generally are responsive to treatment. Late in life, mental health problems may be a result of interpersonal loss, organic deterioration, or some traumatic event. These problems are often overlooked by family members and even mental health professionals not skilled in working with the elderly. Depression, for example, which can be treated readily with medication for many, may be interpreted as inactivity due to ageing and thus disregarded.

Depression—one of the more common mental health problems in late life—may be the result of bereavement, anxiety related to income, a limited social friendship network, health concerns, relocation, and similar factors. Ageism and lack of attention to problems of the elderly have led to increased concern about this group's high suicide rate. In 2012, the suicide rate for the population in general was 11.1 per 100,000 people. By comparison, the rate per 100,000 for those who are 75 and older was 16.3, and the rate for males 75 and older was higher than any other age group: 36 per 100,000 (Centers for Disease Control and Prevention, 2012).

Alzheimer's disease, the sixth leading cause of death in the United States and the fifth leading cause for persons 65 and older, has emerged as one of the more challenging mental/brain conditions in later life, afflicting an estimated 5.3 million Americans. Approximately 200,000 of those are younger than 65 and have early onset of the disease. Two-thirds of those with Alzheimer's disease are women. Projections indicate that while one in 8 women will develop breast cancer during their lifetime, one in six will develop Alzheimer's disease. This is due in part to the fact that women live longer than men and that Alzheimer's often occurs when people are in their 80s. By 2050, the number of individuals with Alzheimer's disease in the United States is expected to reach 16 million without medical breakthroughs. Alzheimer's disease is one of the few illnesses for which there is no known cure; while deaths for other major health conditions have declined in recent years, deaths from Alzheimer's disease increased 68% between 2000 and 2010. Half a million lives annually would be saved without this disease (Alzheimer's Association, 2014).

Alzheimer's is an insidious, progressive disease that results in increasing inability to function independently. Symptoms include memory loss that disrupts life; challenges in planning and solving problems; difficulty completing familiar tasks; confusion with time or place; difficulty understanding visual images and spatial relationships; problems with words when speaking or writing; misplacing things and being unable to retrace steps; poor judgment; withdrawal from activities; and changes in mood and personality, including apathy and depression. In the later stages, the person requires total care, including feeding, bathing, and all routine maintenance activities. Alzheimer's disease imposes heavy demands on family members, who are the primary caregivers in the initial stages. There are nearly 15.5 million unpaid caregivers in the United States who contribute 17.7 billion hours and $220 billion in unpaid care for persons with this disease (Alzheimer's Association, 2014).

Alzheimer's disease has also increased health care costs; it is the most expensive condition a person can incur. Health-care costs in 2013 just for Alzheimer's disease totaled $214 billion, with $150 billion of that amount expended by Medicare and Medicaid (Alzheimer's Association, 2014).

Scientific advances in neuroimaging and DNA research offer hope for early diagnosis, prevention, and treatment of the disease (Alzheimer's Association, 2014). A study conducted by the Lewin Group for the Alzheimer's Association concluded that an annual investment of $1 billion in Alzheimer's research could yield results that would significantly reduce Medicare and Medicaid costs, achieving annual Medicare savings of $51 billion by 2015, $126 billion by 2025, and $444 billion by 2050. The same investment is projected to result in annual savings in Medicaid spending on nursing-home care for Alzheimer's patients of $10 billion by 2015, $23 billion by 2025, and $70 billion by 2050 (Alzheimer's Association, 2014).

The physical and emotional demands related to caring for a loved one with Alzheimer's disease increase as the disease progresses. Social workers can play a significant role in establishing community-based Alzheimer's support groups to provide emotional support for caregivers, as well as an opportunity to share effective techniques in caring for the person. Social workers also can work side by side with Alzheimer's advocates to implement public information campaigns about the disease, as well as to promote state and federal legislation providing assistance to family caregivers of those with Alzheimer's disease. Also, they can engage in political advocacy, encouraging Congress to appropriate funding aimed at early diagnosis, prevention, and treatment of the disease.

Changes in mental health are not always as devastating as Alzheimer's disease. Individuals who have well-integrated personalities, who prepare themselves for changes related to retirement, who develop leisure-time interests, and who plan for the future are less vulnerable than others to many other age-related stress factors and conditions.

Attitudes Toward Growing Old

EP 2.1.7b

Among the many harsh realities that older adults in the United States face are negative attitudes toward the elderly. Despite a positive turn in recent years, these attitudes persist. Although one's chronological age is biological, views about age our socially constructed. In many cultures, persons who are old are considered to be respected elders and are revered and cared for by those who are younger when they can no longer care for themselves. However, the United States has been characterized by an emphasis on youth and productivity, stressing independence that is enabled by financial support gained through employment. Retirement often drastically reduces a person's available income and may contribute to dependency. As a result, older adults often are considered to be of less value.

Negative attitudes also are expressed through exclusion. The U.S. media, for example, have avoided using older adults in television commercials altogether or have cast them in stereotypical roles as doting, kind and benevolent, irascible, or dependent. Advertisements in newspapers and magazines rarely use older persons to convey messages because they do not resonate with the younger population to which the ads are directed. The media, however, do seem to be changing their stance, as one of the most populous generations of Americans—those born in the years immediately following World War II (the so-called baby boomers)—is about to enter retirement. This has given rise to an explosion in marketing a wide array of highly profitable products and services to a population that is willing and able to afford them.

Collectively, societal practices have reinforced negativism toward old age. Many of these practices, such as mandatory retirement, have supported the idea that older adults are less capable of making contributions through work and to society. Even if they cannot afford or choose not to fully retire, various rules and regulations governing employment limit the opportunities for them to make such contributions. Discrimination or differential treatment based on age alone is called **ageism**. Like other forms of discrimination, ageism is institutionalized and, as a result, often subtle (DeJong & Love, 2013). Individuals frequently are unaware that they reinforce ageism through their attitudes and practices. Negative attitudes toward older adults sometimes are expressed by professional practitioners as well as the general public. In a classic study, Riley (1968) identified nurses, medical doctors, attorneys, the clergy, and social workers, among others, as giving preference to younger individuals as clientele. Little evidence indicates that this situation has changed. The elderly, particularly those who are more likely to be more reclusive, are also often invisible to others around them. After the terrorist attack on the World Trade Center in New York City, animal activists rescued dogs and cats within twenty four hours, while persons who were elderly and disabled waited as long as seven days to be rescued. Similar situations were reported after Hurricane Katrina (Butler, 2013).

Negative attitudes toward older adults often result in their loss of social status, with accompanying diminished self-concept. And real-life issues compound the problem. For example, as adults grow older, they invariably lose significant others through death, and they must deal with their own physical decline, which may limit their activities and opportunities for mobility. Although the majority of older adults are independent and find life satisfying, these changes (or losses) invariably affect their quality of life (Berk, 2014).

As we review other challenges faced by older adults, we must keep in mind that attitudes, although not always linked directly with behavior, tend to shape our priorities and practices. Viewing the older population as "excess baggage" is not the bedrock on which positive responses to the needs of older adults will be achieved.

Needs of Older Adults

Older adults need to be part of a supportive environment, surrounded by family and friends, just like all individuals, regardless of age. However, there are a number of needs that are more critical for people in this age group than others. Because older adults face retirement and then living on a fixed income at the same time that they are likely to have added expenses for health care, income security is a high priority. Other needs include affordable and accessible health care, safe and affordable housing, reliable transportation, long-term care when needed, and protection from abuse and neglect.

Income, Work, and Retirement

EP 2.1.1a
EP 2.1.3a
EP 2.1.7b

In the past, individuals were expected to retire on or about age 65 and live primarily on Social Security benefits. However, the cost of living, particularly for health care, has increased. At the same time, many workplaces have increased the age when retirement is possible and/or have reduced retirement benefits. Thus, many older adults find themselves unable to retire when they had planned, while still others find themselves without work or enough income to provide economically.

Income Security and Employment

EP 2.1.1a
EP 2.1.9b

One of the more persistent anxieties for older adults is income security. Because wages and employee benefits for American workers have slowly eroded over time, many workers are being forced to work well into their 70s and extend the age at which they could officially retire.

FIG 12.2 More people are working longer: 35% of men and 28% of women age 65-74 are projected to be working in 2020.
SOURCE: *The Aging US Workforce* (2013). Palo Alto, CA: Stanford Center on Longevity, Stanford University, p. 12.

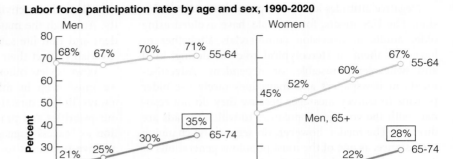

Labor force participation rates by age and sex, 1990-2020

Figure 12.2 shows percentages of adults 55–64, 65–74, and 75 and older in the workforce. Projections show that labor force participation for older adults is expected to increase, with both men and women working longer, even after reaching age 75 (Stanford Center on Longevity, 2013).

As a person grows older, the ability to secure income through employment declines while reliance on pensions, savings, investments, and Social Security increases. For the majority of older adults, income available after retirement is below what they received while working full-time. For some, income is less than half of what it was before retirement. Few present-day older adults earned sufficient income to be able to reserve money for retirement. Also, retirement-incentive plans such as IRAs, tax-deferred annuities, and Keogh plans did not exist during the time of their employment. As a result, most older adults (75%) are forced to live on Social Security payments alone (National Council on Aging, 2013b). Table 12.1 details the sources of income for persons 65 and older in 2012. Major sources of income are Social Security, assets, private and government employee pensions, and earnings. As Table 12.1 shows, the percentage of elderly persons in the United States receiving income from pensions and retirement plans ranges from a low of 15.3% for Hispanics to a high of 32.5% for whites (Wu, 2013). Thus, many older Americans are not covered by any kind of pension plan. This, coupled with the fact that Social Security was not designed to be a "complete" retirement

system, creates a financial dilemma for the vast majority of retirees.

There are also disparities in income for those over 65 by ethnic group. As can be seen in Table 12.2, in 2012 the median household income for whites was significantly higher than for Hispanics/Latinos and African Americans, with Asians having the highest median income.

There are also significant differences in income by gender: the median income in 2012 for a single person 65 and older was $27,612 for males and $16,040 for females.

The income threshold for being below the poverty level in 2012 was $11,490 for a single elder. Over 3.9 million elderly persons in the United States, or 9.1% of all persons 65 and older, were below the poverty level that year. Rates differ by both ethnic group and gender. As Table 12.3 clearly shows, elderly Latinos, blacks, and Asian Americans are much more likely than whites to be poor.

Statistics on individuals 65 and older living in poverty show that older men were less likely to be living in poverty (6.6%) than older women (11%). Those living alone were also much more likely to be living in poverty (16.8%) than those living with families (5.4%) (Administration on Aging, 2014).

Increasingly, older adults find it challenging to make ends meet as they are faced with increased costs for food, housing, and transportation and reduced, if any, savings. One health crisis can send them into poverty. Many older adults are too proud to request government assistance and go without food, health care, and other

TABLE 12.1 RETIREMENT INCOME SOURCES, 2012 (PERCENTAGE RECEIVING INCOME FROM MAJOR SOURCES BY ETHNICITY)

SOME INCOME SOURCES	TOTAL PERCENTAGE			
	WHITE	AFRICAN AMERICAN	HISPANIC	ASIAN
Social Security	86.5	78.6	73.4	66.1
Interest	52.2	23.4	21.0	34.7
Pensions and Retirement Savings	32.5	28.4	15.3	16.0
Dividends	23.0	5.2	5.3	15.3
Earnings	22.2	18.8	19.2	21.8
Supplemental Security Income	1.5	5.2	7.8	10.2

SOURCE: K. B. Wu (2013). *Sources of income for older Americans, 2012.* Author tabulation of U.S. Census Bureau March 2013 *Current Population Survey, Annual Social and Economic Supplement.* Washington, DC AARP Public Policy Institute.

TABLE 12.2 MEDIAN INCOME OF FAMILY HOUSEHOLDS HEADED BY PERSONS 65 YEARS OF AGE AND OLDER, 2012, BY ETHNIC GROUP

ETHNICITY	MEDIAN INCOME
White (Non-Hispanic)	$50,701
African American	$40,348
Hispanic/Latino	$33,913
Asian	$56,378
All groups	$48,957

SOURCE: Administration on Aging (2013). *Profile of older Americans 2012: Income.* Washington, DC: Author.

TABLE 12.3 PERCENTAGE OF PERSONS OVER 65 LIVING IN POVERTY IN 2012

ETHNICITY	PERCENTAGE (%)
White	6.8
African American	18.2
Hispanic/Latino	20.6
Asian	12.3
All groups	9.1

SOURCE: Administration on Aging (2013). *Profile of older Americans: 2012.* Washington, DC: Author.

necessities instead. Only one-third of seniors eligible for benefits from the Supplemental Nutrition Assistance Program (SNAP) actually receive them (National Council on Aging, 2014b).

Table 12.4 shows tax rates, earnings limits, and Social Security and Medicare benefits allowable in 2014. Although some benefits have remained the same since 2000, many costs have increased substantially (Social Security Administration, 2000, 2014). For example, the cost of Medicare Part B monthly premiums increased from $45.50/month to $104.90 for

the majority of individuals, though those in higher income brackets pay more (approximately 5% of Medicare recipients). These increases add to the financial burden that elderly persons already face while trying to make ends meet on a limited, fixed income.

The Social Security Act serves as a clear disincentive to work for individuals between the ages of 65 and 67 (those considered to be below normal retirement age [NRA]) (Michaud & van Soest, 2007). These recipients find that earnings over $15,480 are taxed at the rate of $1 for every $2 earned above the limit—a 50% tax rate (applies in 3 years before attaining NRA). The taxation rate is 33% (or $1 for every $3 earned over $41,400) for

TABLE 12.4 SOCIAL SECURITY AND MEDICARE 2014

BENEFIT CATEGORY	2014
2000 cost-of-living adjustment for SS and SSI recipients (COLA)	1.50%
Tax rate for employees	7.65%
Maximum tax rate if self-employed	15.3%
Maximum Taxable Earnings	
Social Security portion	6.2% up to $117,000 of income
Medicare portion	1.45%, increases to 1.54% for those with incomes over $200,000 ($250,000 for married couples filing jointly)
Maximum taxable payroll earnings	
Social Security	$117,000
Medicare	No limit
Retirement earnings tax exemption	
Under full retirement age	$15,480/year
Year individual reaches full retirement age	$41,400/year
Maximum Social Security monthly benefit for worker retiring at full retirement age	$2,642
Estimated average monthly Social Security benefits	
All retired workers (after COLA)	$1,294
Older couple, both receiving benefits	$2,111
Older widow(er) living alone	$1,243
Maximum SSI monthly payments	
Individual	$721
Couple	$1,082
Medicare	
Part B monthly premium	$104.90/month; increases for persons in higher income brackets
Part B deductible	$147/year
Part A deductible for hospital stay—first 60 days (also for inpatient mental health)	$1,216 deductible for each benefit period
Copayment for days 61–90	$304/day
Copayment for lifetime reserve days	$608/day
Copayment for skilled nursing facility—days 21–100	$152/day; all costs beyond 100 days

SOURCE: Social Security Administration (2014). *2014 Social security changes.* Washington, DC: Author and Centers for Medicare and Medicaid Services (2014). *Medicare 2014 costs at a glance.* Washington, DC: Medicare.gov.

recipients who have reached NRA (applies in the year of attaining NRA, for months prior to such attainment) (Social Security Administration, 2014).

Many concerns have been raised about the future of Social Security. The Social Security "trust fund" has long been tapped by Congress to offset shortages in national general revenue expenditures. Older adults fear that their benefits will be reduced. Younger adults fear that as the population ages and there are more retired adults living in the United States than younger working adults, they will be unable to sustain the current system. Proposals and discussions about privatizing some part of Social Security, raising the age at which an individual would become eligible for Social Security benefits, and means-testing eligibility for benefits have caused skepticism as to if, or in what form, Social Security will be available in the future.

Although money does not equate to happiness, money is related to satisfaction in later life. The notion that older adults need less income to meet their living needs has little basis in fact. The needs for food, clothing, shelter, recreation, transportation, and the ability to engage in discretionary spending, such as buying gifts for family members, does not decline with age, while the cost of health care usually increases, often significantly. Lowered standards of living, unmet needs, and the inability to meet those needs adequately may result in feelings of inadequacy, despair, loss of self-esteem, and poor health. Income is an enabling resource that affects the options available in life. As income declines, so do those options, with a resulting loss of independence.

Many of the supports and social services designed to assist older adults with their unmet needs might not be necessary if retirement incomes were sufficient to enable the nonworking aged to meet those needs. The United States continues to lag behind other industrialized nations in replacement (retirement) income for its aged, ranking eleventh in payments (pensions, social security, and other sources of income) received by older adults after retirement (Ebeling, 2013).

Retirement

The relationship between retirement and old age has swung like a pendulum over the years. Traditionally, retirement and aging were viewed as one and the same: People retired from work to enter into the "golden age" of life. A combination of private retirement and Social Security benefits made it possible for most retired persons to live comfortably.

This view of **retirement**, or the point where a person stops working for pay, changed dramatically beginning in the 1980s and continues to the present. It costs more now for basic needs such as food, housing, and health care than in the past, particularly as one grows older. At the same time, as people live longer, also resulting in increased health-care needs, retirement benefits and social security often are not sufficient sources of income. Additionally, many people value working and are not ready to retire at age 65 when they are likely to live 15 or 20 years longer. The changing workplace in the United States has also shaped how retirement is viewed.

The Information Age, which emerged in the late 1970s and early 1980s, forever changed the landscape of American industrial dominance. Blue-collar workers in heavy industries such as steel-making suddenly were displaced as American companies were unable to compete with low-cost labor from abroad, given the high labor costs and associated benefits that labor unions had negotiated since the time they were introduced in the United States in the 1930s. This economic shift affected entire generations of families. Workers no longer were able to depend on the retirement benefits to which they were entitled, forcing them to postpone retirement and try to find employment elsewhere. The recession that began in 2007 (that some would argue continues today) resulted in changes in policy that have significantly impacted retirement decisions for many living in the United States. Many businesses changed their retirement plans, reducing or cancelling the amount contributed by the business, changing policies about when benefits could be received and the amounts, or cancelling plans altogether. Many state and local government entities, for example, increased the age of retirement with full benefits to 70.

Another phenomenon that began in the late 1980s that has had a significant impact on older workers is the increasing use of contract workers in a wide variety of businesses throughout the country, especially those engaged in computer-related industries. In an attempt to reduce costs to stay even with low-cost competition from abroad, American companies began to outsource work to independent consultants who did not receive any employee benefits, including retirement benefits. These workers were expected to self-fund health care and retirement benefits from the monies they earned as contractors. Because of the high cost of self-funding benefits such as health care and private retirement plans, many of these contract workers simply did not invest in these benefits, thereby disrupting the traditional retirement paradigm once again.

During the decade of the 1990s, the "dot-coms" spawned a large cadre of young people who worked for and invested heavily in penny stocks of nascent computer hardware and software companies, only to become millionaires in their 30s. Many of these newly minted millionaires chose to retire from work early to pursue personal, nonwork interests. Once again, the traditional retirement paradigm shifted, even after the crash of the dot-coms. A historical event that also has changed the traditional retirement paradigm in the United States is the globalization of the economic marketplace, which has forced American business and industry to cut operating costs substantially and look elsewhere across the globe for low-cost alternatives to support their business interests. Increasingly, American companies are relocating to countries in India, Mexico, China, and Southeast Asia to take advantage of the favorable business climate, as well as skilled workers who are willing to work at substantially lower wages than their American counterparts. Many American workers today are happy just to have a job, let alone worry about their retirement benefits.

An additional concern for older workers is job stability. As businesses have closed, older workers with significant work experience have struggled to find new employment, often taking jobs for which they are over-qualified if they are able to find employment at all. While some workplaces are trying to retain older employers because of the expertise that they bring, others are eliminating their positions or offering retirement incentives, then hiring younger workers at lower salaries with fewer benefits. Older workers displaced in the years following the recession that began in 2007 were half as likely to have regained employment as the nationwide average (National Council on Aging, 2014c).

EP 2.1.1a
EP 2.1.3a
EP 2.1.7b

The traditional retirement paradigm in the United States has been altered forever. There is no guarantee that a lifetime of work will result in adequate retirement benefits that will allow older Americans to live out their lives in some measure of comfort. One of the primary functions of retirement in the past was to clear out workers from one generation to make way for workers from the next. If this is no longer possible—as appears to be the case—will older workers

be forced out of the workplace regardless of their need or desire to continue working? What will happen to these workers? What changes in federal and state laws would be required to ensure a decent quality of life for older Americans after leaving the workforce? Who should bear the costs of these changes? Is the concept of retirement in the United States so out of kilter that it is no longer operative? If so, what role does society have in changing this picture?

As the pendulum swings, some employers are beginning to see older persons who have retired from the workforce as valuable assets to their organizations. For one thing, employers do not have to pay for expensive employee benefits such as health care because health-care benefits are often covered by the employee's retirement benefits. In addition, older persons are recognized as being agreeable, dependable, and knowledgeable. Many also are part of the institutional history of the organization that is at the heart of the organization's culture (Lipkin & Perrymore, 2009; Nazareth, 2007; Salkowitz, 2008).

Further, many companies are concerned about the "brain drain" that is expected to occur when millions of highly skilled and experienced workers (baby boomers) retire in large numbers a few years from now. Although this has been postponed somewhat due to the economy, employers are concerned about finding new workers to replace the seniors exiting the workforce (Munnell, 2014).

At the same time as there is a growing interest in retaining older workers in the workforce, there are many economic, legal, and institutional barriers to achieving more flexible work arrangements for them. Chief among these obstacles are out-of-date employee compensation systems, rigid employee benefit plans, and legal restrictions on phased-retirement plans (Vickerstaff, White, & Loretto, 2007). These problems are not insurmountable, but existing laws will have to be changed and new ones introduced to implement those solutions. This may be easier said than done, as considerable political will is necessary to bring about reform in this area. Which political leaders, if any, will be willing to champion this cause? What role does the social work community have in advocating for such changes? How can social workers learn more about this situation to be more effective advocates?

Primarily because of the definitional problems just described, it is difficult to ascertain how many individuals are added to the retirement pool each year, but it certainly must be large. Persons age 65 or older comprised about 5% of the total workforce in 2012, a 2% increase since 2002 (Kromer & Howard, 2013). For many retirees, income resources often are reduced drastically when they retire. Few would disagree that quality of life is related to disposable income. The luxurious lifestyles and world cruises that appear in magazines targeted for the retired "over-50" population and sponsored by organizations such as the American Association of Retired Persons (AARP) are within reach of only a relatively small percentage of retirees. Understandably, many retirees remain concerned about the stability of the Social Security system, the government-sponsored retirement system in the United States.

The need for research on retirement continues to be pressing. Although social scientists have made great strides over the past several decades, the potential value of retirement-related research becomes more manifest as the number of retirees rises. The emerging body of knowledge and understanding of the effects of retirement on individuals is helpful, but much remains to be learned. Appropriate and valid social policies must be guided by a sound knowledge base.

Over the past decade, considerable emphasis has been given to preparation for retirement. Called **pre-retirement planning**, it is based on the notion that people who prepare adequately for retirement adjust better to the lifestyle changes that accompany retirement. Many major corporations, as well as public agencies, have developed pre-retirement training programs for their employees. These programs usually emphasize estate planning; forecasting of income; identifying federal, state, and private resources for older adults; and strategies for dealing with issues such as relocating, living alone, and planning for leisure-time activities. Although no compelling evidence indicates that pre-retirement planning affects adaptation to retirement positively, a mounting consensus indicates that it does. Logic alone suggests that life changes can be managed more successfully with adequate preparation.

Health and Health Care

Income is not the only factor affecting positive adjustment to aging. Health is a matter of great importance and concern. In 2010–2012, 42% of persons 65 and older not living in institutions assessed their health as excellent or very good, compared to 55% for persons age 45–64. Although there were few differences between males and females, persons of color were less likely to rate their health as excellent or very good than whites The most often reported conditions were arthritis (50%), heart disease (30%), cancer (24%), diabetes (20%), and hypertension/high blood pressure (72%) (Administration on Aging, 2014). Older adults also are more prone than the general population to develop illnesses such as pneumonia, influenza, and gastrointestinal complications as well as emphysema, osteoporosis, and visual impairments (Hillier & Barrow, 2010). Hospitalization rates for persons 65 and older are about three times higher than for those under 65. Table 12.5 shows the leading causes of death for older adults.

Only 5% of the older adult population is affected by health problems so severe that their mobility is limited. Most are able to remain mobile and continue prior daily activities even though they have one or more diseases. For others with more severe conditions, the role of patient eclipses preferred retirement activities. Concerns about meeting medical expenses, or anticipated expenses, may curtail spending patterns and, in turn, reduce options and activities.

Some medical practitioners dismiss concerns expressed by older patients as due to the typical process of aging and difficulty adjusting to physiological and behavioral changes, overlooking conditions that require medical care, even those often experienced by older adults. They may also believe that persons who are in "old old" age are at the end of the life cycle and extensive assessment and intervention is not warranted. Others stereotype older adults and also misdiagnose as a result. One example is sexually transmitted infections (STIs), including HIV and AIDS. The number of older adults with STIs has more than doubled in the last decade, with similar rates for HIV and AIDS. This increase is attributed to the fact that 80% of adults 50–90 are sexually active and remaining sexually active longer than in the past, increased use of medication such as Viagra to sustain one's ability to be sexually active, and a decrease in use of condoms by older adults who no longer fear pregnancy so believe they are not needed (Boyles, 2012). By the time many older adults are diagnosed, particularly with HIV, they are in the later stages of the disease as most health care providers do not screen older adults for STIs. Even those diagnosed earlier with HIV face challenges as they age. Although 40% of persons in the United States with HIV are 50 and older, there is limited knowledge about how

TABLE 12.5   TEN LEADING CAUSES OF DEATH FOR PERSONS AGED 65 OR OLDER (% OF DEATHS WITHIN EACH AGE GROUP)

CAUSE OF DEATH	65–74 YR	75–84 YR	≥ 85 YR
Malignancies/cancer	35.5%/1	25.1%/1	12.4%/2
Heart diseases	21.8%/2	24.5%/2	30.8%/1
Pulmonary diseases	7.8%/3	7.7%/3	5%/5
Cerebrovascular diseases	4.4%/4	6%/4	7.1%/3
Diabetes	3.6%/5	3%/6	2%/9
Alzheimer's disease	—	3.9%/5	7.1%/3
Accidents	2.3%/6	2.2%/8	2.4%/7
Nephritis/kidney diseases	2.1%/7	2.4%/7	2.4%/7
Septicemia	1.6%/8	1.6%/10	—
Influenza/pneumonia	1.5%/9	2.1%/9	3.1%/6
Liver diseases	1.4%/10	—	—
Hypertension/renal disease			1.5%/10
All other	18%	21.5%	26.3%

Source: M. Heron (2013). *Deaths: Leading causes for 2010.* Hyattsville, MD: National Center for Health Statistics.

HIV will impact them as they age (Auldridge & Espinoza, 2013).

EP 2.1.1a
EP 2.1.3a
EP 2.1.7b

Health-care resources for the elderly are provided primarily through Medicare and Medicaid. Most older adults rely primarily on **Medicare**, the country's oldest and largest public health-care program for individuals age 65 or older and persons with disabilities. Medicare provides health insurance coverage for physicians' visits, hospital care, and other related medical expenses, for 43.6 million elderly people and 8.8 million nonelderly people with permanent disabilities. Persons enrolled in the Medicare program increased from 19.1 million in 1966 to 52.4 million in 2013. The number of beneficiaries is expected to grow to nearly 70 million persons by 2025.

Because of the high costs of health care, benefits paid by Medicare have decreased to cover approximately half (48% in 2012) of the total cost of care, with individuals expecting to cover the remainder. Older Americans spend about almost 13% of their income on health, almost twice the amount others spend. Average health-care costs for older persons in 2012 were $5,118: $3,186 for insurance (62%), $935 for medical services (18%),

$798 for medications (16%), and $200 for medical supplies (4%) (Administration on Aging, 2014).

Although some individuals have private or employment-based health-care plans to supplement Medicare or have "Medigap insurance," not everyone can afford them. The inability of older adults to pay the portion of fees not covered by Medicare has resulted in large number of the elderly not seeking taking prescribed medication, not seeking necessary medical attention, or delaying treatment until their health conditions become severe and often life-threatening. It is hoped that the Affordable Care Act and changes in reimbursement of health-care expenses to providers will contain Medicare costs even as the baby-boom generation enters retirement.

Health-care costs as people age are a growing concern to consumers and their families as well as governments at the federal, state, and local levels. In 2012, public expenditures for health care in the United States amounted to $2.8 trillion, an average of $8,915 per person. The average per person expenditure for someone 65 and older was $18,424, more than five times the average amount for a child and more than three times the average amount for a working adult

(Sherman, Greenstein, & Ruffing, 2012). The cost of health-care services provided through Medicare represented the largest single component of public health-care expenditures, $572.5 billion, or 20% of the total amount. Many older persons in the United States cannot afford out-of-home care as they age, and these costs are not covered by Medicare (Centers for Medicare and Medicaid Services, 2014a). Medicaid expenditures in 2012 were almost as high as those for Medicare, at $421.2 billion. Although **Medicaid** is a health-care program for those who are low income, in 2012 30% of Medicaid expenditures were used to cover nursing home and other long-term care for persons who were elderly and/or disabled. Sixty percent of all residents in long-term care facilities are covered by Medicaid, which covers 40% of all long-term care costs in the United States (National Council on Aging, 2014a).

In 2012 persons 65 and older received 53% of federal government entitlement spending (Medicaid, Medicare, and Supplemental Security Income, and other government benefit programs) (Sherman, Greenstein, & Ruffing, 2012). With continually increasing numbers of older adults in our society (see Figure 12.1), even larger government allocations will be necessary in the future. Various solutions have been implemented or are under consideration. These include changes in Medicare coverage of prescription drugs, reduction of benefits, higher copayments for care, more stringent eligibility requirements, and an expansion of government coverage for catastrophic cases. It is anticipated that implementation of the Affordable Care Act will result in reduced health-care expenditures to seniors, particularly in regard to Medicare payments and prescription drugs (see Chapter 8 for further discussion). However, we must find creative solutions to financing and providing health care services for elderly persons in the United States to meet the increasing health needs of this population.

Housing

EP 2.1.7b
EP 2.1.9b

About 80% of older adults are homeowners (Administration on Aging, 2014). Most homes owned by persons age 65 or older are 20 years old or older. Older homes are attractive to low-income homeowners because they generally are more affordable to purchase, but older homes typically have higher utility and maintenance costs. As a result, many of these homes become dilapidated over the years, and in later life the ability of their owners to maintain or repair them becomes more and more difficult, so the homes deteriorate further. In addition, older adults have difficulty securing home-repair loans. Thus, they are faced with living in homes that provide inadequate protection from the elements, as well as a host of other problems, and they become safety hazards. Many older adults pay more than the suggested 30% of their income on either rent or mortgage payments: 59% pay more for rent, and 33% pay more for mortgages (National Council on Aging, 2014b). Even if those who are homeowners decide to sell their homes, many older adults don't stand to gain much financially if at all; 16% of older adults owed more on their homes than they were worth in 2012 (National Council on Aging, 2014b).

Another factor that makes it more difficult for older persons to stay in their homes, even if they own them outright, is **gentrification**—the restoration and upgrading of deteriorated urban property by middle-class or affluent people, which often results in displacement of low-income people. At the beginning of the gentrification process, property values and property taxes are generally low. As the process unfolds, property values skyrocket and the taxing authorities impose a sharp rise in property taxes. Low-income homeowners who reside in areas undergoing gentrification find that they no longer can afford to pay their property taxes and are forced to sell their houses at well below market value and move out of their neighborhoods, where sometimes generations of their family have lived.

To make matters worse, the displaced persons do not have enough money to purchase a new home outright and do not qualify for a home mortgage, so they may have to move in with a family member, live in an undesirable part of town, or move to a rural area where the cost of living is affordable. Disruption and displacement may cause older people to become confused, develop stress-related medical problems, or withdraw and become isolated—all of which are antithetical to a healthy lifestyle.

Government housing for older people typically is difficult to secure because of the high demand for low-cost housing by younger persons, especially those with children. Even when available, low-cost housing may be unattractive, impersonal, and lacking in privacy; often in areas with a high crime rates; and too noisy. Without question, more affordable housing options are needed for older adults, but this is not likely to happen because of other government spending priorities, as well as the lack of government incentives to homebuilders to construct more affordable housing units.

Meanwhile, housing alternatives for more economically secure elderly people have expanded. Self-contained apartment complexes have been developed through the auspices of religious organizations and private sponsorship. These facilities typically are attractive, provide all the amenities for comfortable living, and ensure peer interactions and essential social supports. Many of these facilities, as discussed, also provide medical care, nursing services, and meals, if individuals become unable to care for themselves in their own apartments. These facilities, however, are much more costly, and many require a substantial down payment before an individual is accepted as a resident.

Although housing communes are not abundant, this option is growing in popularity and provides a family-type living experience for older participants. This is a housing arrangement in which several older adults pool their resources to rent or purchase a dwelling and share in its upkeep. Basic living costs for things such as food and utilities are shared, enabling participants to spend less on basic living needs.

Transportation

EP 2.1.7b
EP 2.1.9b

Transportation is essential for grocery shopping, attending religious services, keeping appointments with doctors and dentists, visiting friends, and maintaining contact with families. Most older adults must travel some distance to procure the necessities for daily living, and this likely is difficult for them. Many who once drove are no longer able to do so, and even if they can drive, the costs of maintaining a vehicle and buying insurance often are beyond their means. Consequently, they depend on alternative sources of travel. Public means of transit—buses and trains—have been geared primarily to ambulatory individuals who typically use these forms of transportation to get to and from work during the week. For older people, navigating the public transportation system can be problematic, as the nearest bus stop may be some distance from their home, riding times may be long, and transfers may be needed from one line to another. Further, older adults may have trouble getting grocery bags and other items on and off a bus or a train and then carrying them several blocks or more from the stop to their residence.

Some transit systems have developed specialized services for the elderly and people with disabilities, operating on a door-to-door basis by appointment.

Few, however, are available to provide on-call service to the elderly. Users must anticipate their needs (often as long as 2 weeks in advance), make the appointment, and hope they are not forgotten.

On the positive side, volunteers have been engaged in providing transportation services for the elderly in some communities, and public transportation has taken into account the needs of many older adults to secure needed goods and services. Nutrition programs have provided transportation to lunch programs, and some have extended their transportation services to include shopping and social visits. These transportation alternatives, however, are available to only a comparatively few older adults in need. The absence of transportation has resulted in many older adults' becoming homebound. Frequently, the result is social isolation, which leads to a loss of incentive, less activity, self-deprecation, and eventually psychological and physical deterioration.

Long-Term Care

EP 2.1.1a
EP 2.1.7b
EP 2.1.9b

Most older Americans enjoy reasonably good health, with only 5% experiencing health problems so debilitating that they require long-term care (often thought of as nursing-home care). The contemporary long-term care industry has emerged primarily as a result of Medicare and Medicaid legislation, which allows third-party payments to the providers of health-care services.

Nursing homes (now called assisted living facilities) and other **long-term care facilities** typically are licensed by state health departments, which have the responsibility of reviewing these facilities periodically to ensure minimal standards of care. In addition, all states require that administrators of long-term care facilities be licensed, although administrator-licensing requirements vary considerably among the states.

The media quite often portray long-term care facilities as dehumanizing warehouses where residents are neglected and abuse is common. Staff members of these facilities often are characterized as incompetent, uncaring, and uninterested in providing high-quality care for the residents. For some assisted living and other long-term care facilities, these allegations are valid. Even though most of these facilities make every effort to provide high-quality care, caring for debilitated, aging residents is both physically and emotionally demanding. High rates of staff turnover are common, which places further stress on long-term care facilities in the selection and training of nursing staff.

In recent years, more stringent state standards and skillful investigation and evaluation techniques by state regulatory agencies have resulted in a higher level and quality of services. The Nursing Home Reform Act, part of the **Omnibus Budget Reconciliation Act (OBRA) of 1987**, introduced major nursing home reforms, including strengthening residents' rights, establishing written care plans, providing staff training, and requiring the employment of certified social workers if a facility has over 120 beds. This landmark legislation was designed to create a safe and secure environment for residents, with appropriate medical and nursing care administered by a caring staff.

The Nursing Home Reform Act also established the following rights for nursing-home residents:

- the right to freedom from abuse, mistreatment, and neglect;
- the right to freedom from physical restraints;
- the right to privacy;
- the right to accommodation of their medical, physical, psychological, and social needs;
- the right to participate in resident and family groups;
- the right to be treated with dignity;
- the right to exercise self-determination;
- the right to communicate freely;
- the right to participate in the review of one's care plan and to be fully informed in advance about any changes in care, treatment, or status in the facility; and
- the right to voice grievances without discrimination or reprisal (Klauber & Wright, 2001).

Most long-term care facilities in the United States are private, profit-making businesses. Some facilities are non-profit, usually operated through the auspices of religious organizations or units of state or local governments. The quality of care of private profit-making facilities and non-profit ones seems to be about the same. Although privately owned facilities are more vulnerable to "shaving" services to maximize profit, strict enforcement of standards minimizes any significant differences in the services provided to residents.

Without question, long-term care has improved since the Nursing Home Reform Act was passed in 1987. For example, the number of citations for deficiencies issued by official monitors who survey long-term care facilities dropped by nearly 50% in the 10 years following passage

of the act, despite the increasing population of those with disabilities and cognitive impairments, who require more rigorous care, in assisted living facilities. After passage of the act, assisted living facilities were allowed time to correct deficiencies before civil penalties were imposed, and the term *widespread problems* was redefined to apply only when a violation affects every resident of the facility. The federal government has been encouraging states to limit circumstances that would lead to the imposition of civil penalties, while the nursing-home/ assisted-living industry has undertaken efforts to weaken enforcement (American Society on Aging, 2009). Thus, concern remains for the future. Too many long-term care facilities are out of compliance with the law, limiting visiting hours, restraining residents because of limited caregiver training on other approaches, and cutting corners when it comes to required care (Carlson, 2013).

Long-term care facilities will continue to be the most viable resource for the severely incapacitated elderly. However, many elderly no longer feel comfortable or unable to function completely on their own, and prefer to live in settings that offer some type of support. Many facilities, particularly those that wealthier elderly people can afford, offer a wide range of living options. An individual or couple can move into an independent living facility, residing in a private apartment that is part of the facility, and maintain independence if desired, although meals in a central dining area, educational and recreational activities, and some health care may be available to them, often at an increased cost.

As health deteriorates and their independence diminishes, nursing care, meals, and other services are readily available without the individual having to move. If the person's health deteriorates to the point at which she or he cannot be alone in an apartment, an assisted living facility more like the traditional nursing home is often located on the same property. This option is preferable to many individuals who are elderly because they can remain in the same familiar location with a minimum of disruption if their health deteriorates.

One practice becoming more common at a number of facilities, including some that accept Medicaid clients, is termed **aging in place**. This practice allows individuals to remain in their own apartments, bringing needed services to them rather than moving them to another location as their health deteriorates. Individuals can live in apartment-style units with their own furnishings and other items important to them, even after assistance in daily living, including nursing care, is needed, rather than moving to another portion of the facility or a completely different facility. Because this practice is much less disruptive, individuals often remain healthier longer.

Because it enhances quality of life and is also cost effective, Medicare and other health insurance programs are increasingly funding in-home services. Alternatives such as home health care, visiting nurses, and respite care services enable older adults to reside in the community longer, but they tend to defer, not replace, the need for long-term care. In 2012, approximately 1.5 million older adults lived in long-term care facilities, either community-care facilities (usually small facilities whose residents have disabilities or other challenges that require supervision but do not require extensive health care) or nursing homes. Almost half of residents were 85 and older (Administration on Aging, 2014). It is estimated that 70% of people 65 and older will need long-term care at some point in their lives. An increasing number of individuals have long-term care insurance that will cover costs of long-term care, up to a certain daily dollar amount depending on the plan (U.S. Department of Health and Human Services, 2014).

As the need for additional assisted living/long-term care beds increases, financing will become more critical. More cost-effective plans must be developed to ensure that the debilitated elderly receive essential health care services. In a number of communities, faith-based organizations, unions, and private profit-making organizations are establishing residential facilities for the elderly.

Protection from Abuse and Neglect

EP 2.1.7b

As is the case with children, the vulnerable elderly population has been subjected to abuse and neglect—antithetical to our social morality. "Any knowing, intentional, or negligent act by a caregiver or any other person that causes harm or a serious risk of harm to a vulnerable adult" can be considered **elder abuse** (National Center on Elder Abuse 2014, p. 1). Precise estimates of the number of older persons living in the United States who are being abused, neglected, or exploited are difficult to obtain because definitions of elder abuse differ, state statistics vary widely, there is no uniform reporting system, and comprehensive national

data are not collected. Because the perpetrators of elderly persons who are being abused and neglected are most likely to be their adult children or other family members, elder abuse is significantly under-reported. It is estimated that one in ten elders have experienced some type of abuse or neglect, other than financial exploitation (National Center on Elder Abuse, 2014).

Although elder abuse and neglect occur most often in domestic situations, where the elder is abused by a family member or caregiver, elder maltreatment also occurs in institutional settings (National Center on Elder Abuse, 2014). Although state statutes vary, elder abuse can be considered to fall into one or more of the following categories:

- *Physical abuse:* inflicting or threatening to inflict physical pain or injury on a vulnerable elder, or depriving him or her of a basic need
- *Emotional abuse:* inflicting mental pain, anguish, or distress on an elder person through verbal or nonverbal acts
- *Sexual abuse:* nonconsensual sexual contact of any kind
- *Exploitation:* illegal taking, misuse, or concealing of funds, property, or assets of a vulnerable elder
- *Neglect:* refusal or failure by those responsible to provide food, shelter, health care, or protection for a vulnerable elder
- *Abandonment:* desertion of a vulnerable elder by anyone who has assumed the responsibility for care or custody of that person

The most common type of neglect investigated by state agencies responsible for the protection of the elderly is self-neglect (hoarding, failing to take essential medications or refusing to seek medical treatment for serious illness, leaving a burning stove untended, poor hygiene, not wearing suitable clothing for the weather, confusion, inability to attend to housekeeping, and/or dehydration) followed by caregiver neglect and financial exploitation.

Those at risk for abuse and neglect are more likely to be female, age 80 or older, isolated, living in a family with a history of interpersonal violence, or experiencing Alzheimer's disease or another form of dementia (National Center on Elder Abuse, 2014). Warning signs of elder abuse include bruises, pressure marks, broken bones, abrasions, and burns; unexplained withdrawal from normal activities; sudden change in alertness; unusual depression; bruises around the breasts or genital area; sudden changes in one's financial situation; bedsores, unattended medical needs, poor hygiene, and unusual weight loss; belittling, threats, and other uses of power and control by spouses; and strained and tense relationships and frequent arguments between the caregiver and the elderly person (National Center on Elder Abuse, 2014).

Many states have enacted legislation to protect older adults from abuse and neglect. Family violence is an unfortunate and dehumanizing product of our society that generally is directed toward those who are dependent on others for some aspect of their care. Adult protective services are designed to shield older adults from further harm. As the number of elderly persons being cared for by adult family members and in long-term care facilities has increased, more attention has been given to mistreatment of the elderly. Perhaps one of the most ambitious legislative undertakings designed to address the problem of elder abuse in the United States is The Elder Justice Act (S. 795), part of the Affordable Care Act, which was signed into law in 2010. The Act provides funding to state and local adult protective services programs and law enforcement agencies to strengthen domestic and institutional investigation and intervention in suspected cases of elder abuse as well as competitive grants to long-term care facilities for staff training and the development of certification programs. Although this critical legislation was passed in 2010, funding to authorize implementation has yet to be authorized by Congress in the federal budget (Elder Justice Coalition, 2014).

Understanding Death and Dying

EP 2.1.7b
EP 2.1.8a
As a society, the United States has paid little attention to the process of dying. Although a person can die at any point in the life cycle, death rates rise dramatically in individuals aged 50 or older. Unlike deaths in younger people, deaths in later life are more often the product of disease than accidents. Every culture shapes its attitudes toward death as well as life. Our society tends to over-emphasize a rational view of death as being a natural, yet highly individualized event. Because most of us are not engaged with the dying process, we have little experience to prepare us for coping with either the death of others or our own death. Consequently, too many people are uncomfortable when confronted with dying individuals and apprehensive about their own death.

In a classic work, Elisabeth Kübler-Ross (1975/1997) laid the groundwork for helping dying persons come to grips with the remaining part of their lives. Her contribution, along with others, created a framework for social workers and other professionals to provide assistance for the dying as well as their families, often through the aid of a **hospice**, a program or facility designed to help individuals who are in the process of dying remain in comfortable environments that allow for dignity and support their physical and emotional needs. The hospice movement originated in England, and the first United States hospice was established in Connecticut in the 1970s. This movement has grown rapidly since that time, and now hospices are found in major cities as well as some rural areas. Many terminally ill persons and their families receive hospice services, both in their own homes as well as assisted living facilities. Medicare covers in-home hospice services, and increasingly health insurance programs are also providing coverage for hospice care.

Controversy has been introduced into the dying process in the form of "voluntary" or "involuntary" euthanasia (see Chapter 9 for a discussion of this topic). The medical community has long embraced the philosophical tenet that life should be preserved as long as medically possible, including the use of artificial means such as respirators. Taking a contrary position, supporters of the "right-to-die" movement believe that the individual should have the right of choice in governing the time and circumstance under which his or her death should occur. Proponents of the right-to-die position promote the **living will**, a legal device in which the individual delineates the conditions under which he or she would refuse artificial means to maintain life. Organizations such as the Hemlock Society support the concept of the living will and also the right of individuals to induce their own death under circumstances in which they are in great pain and suffering without hope of recovery.

Social workers who work with older adults invariably will work with those who are dying and their loved ones. Applying their clinical skills, social workers can assist individuals and families in handling interpersonal losses and protect the dying person's dignity, integrity, and right to choices. Social workers also can act as advocates alone or in conjunction with an established advocacy group such as the National Family Caregivers Association, to promote state and federal legislation that will provide assistance to family caregivers. They also might work with insurance companies to be sure that hospice care is covered in their health-care policies. Finally, social workers can assist in the design and implementation of public information campaigns aimed at increasing the public's knowledge and understanding of end-of-life issues.

The Families of Older Adults

 Family members are the primary source of emotional support and, in times of illness, care for their elderly members. The following **EP 2.1.7b** is a snapshot of family caregivers in the **EP 2.1.9b** United States (National Family Caregivers Association, 2014):

- More than 65 million people are participating in **family caregiving** during any given year, 31% of all U.S. households; 70% care for someone over age 50.
- Women make up about 66% of the caregiving population in the United States.
- The typical family caregiver is a 48-year-old woman who is both married and employed, caring for her widowed mother who lives on her own.
- About one-third of family caregivers of elderly persons are 65 years of age or older.
- The estimated value of services that family caregivers provide is $306 billion a year.

Economics of caregiving:

- The median incomes of caregiving families are lower than those of non-caregiving families.
- Women who are family caregivers are significantly more likely than their non-caregiving counterparts to live in poverty.
- Nonreimbursable medical expenses for caregiving families are significantly higher than for non-caregiving families.
- In 2000, family caregivers who provided full-time care at home lost $109 per day in wages and health benefits.

Family impacts of caregiving:

- The stress of family caregivers has been shown to have a negative impact on the caregiver's immune system (and, thus, susceptibility to chronic illness), especially when caring for a member with dementia.
- Depression is fairly common in family care-givers who provide care for 36 hours or more a week.

- Extreme stress by family caregivers has been shown to lead to the caregivers' premature aging.

Caregiving and work:

- About 13% of the American workforce is engaged in some form of family caregiving.
- Two in five human resource directors expressed concern that their organizations were not doing an adequate job of informing employees about help they could get in managing work and family responsibilities.
- On average, women who spend time out of the paid labor force to care for an elderly member or one with disabilities forgo about $400,000 in earnings and health benefits.
- American businesses lose more than $30 billion in productivity and absenteeism annually because of family caregiving.
- Caregiving responsibilities require that the caregivers make significant adjustments to their work schedules, such as coming to work late, leaving work during the day, or leaving work early.

Caregiving and health care:

- Most of the long-term care services in the United States are provided by family caregivers.
- One in five family caregivers has difficulty communicating with physicians.
- More than 40% of family caregivers give medications, change bandages, manage equipment, and monitor vital signs—tasks normally assigned to a professional nurse.
- Often, family caregivers who change dressings or manage equipment have received no formal instructions on how to do so.

The recession that began in 2007 has had a dramatic impact on family caregiving in the United States. Many working caregivers are concerned about their employment status and are less comfortable taking time off from work to provide care. They also are often working more hours or have had to get an additional job in order to maintain the same level of caregiving. Caregivers report that because they have to pay more to cover costs of those they assist, they are cutting back on their own health care and other basic necessities, saving less for their own retirement, increasing credit card debt and depleting their savings. Some families have consolidated households to further cut costs, moving into the same household as the person for whom they are caring. In spite of the stresses, almost all caregivers reported that the quality of care had not decreased (National Family Caregivers Association, 2014; National Alliance for Caregiving, 2009).

The Lifespan Respite Care Act of 2006 (PL 109-442) provided nearly $300 million to support competitive grants to state agencies, other public or private non-profit entities capable of operating on a statewide basis, political subdivisions of states with a population of more than 3 million, or already recognized state respite-care coordinating authorities to implement programs and services that have a high likelihood of enhancing life-span respite care services statewide (National Respite Coalition for Lifespan Respite Task Force, 2006). Under separate authority, the act also established the ARCH National Respite Network and Resource Center. Additional information on respite care can be found in http://archrespite.org/home.

The family caregiver statistics summarized above have enormous policy and practice implications for the social work profession. In the future, social workers will have more career opportunities to work with older Americans in the areas of direct service to elderly individuals and their families, family education and support, educating the public about the nature and extent of the issues surrounding family caregiving, advocating for additional resources for caregiving families, and helping state and federal lawmakers understand the importance of enacting legislation that provides support to caregiving families. The future of the family caregiving movement will depend in large part on the contributions of social work professionals and the organizations to which they belong, such as the National Association of Social Workers and the National Council on Social Work Education. NASW has developed standards for social work practice with family caregivers of older adults.

Families continue to be a viable resource for older adults, giving them comfort and self-identity. The research on family caregiving continues to provide inconclusive findings about the overall quality of inter-generational relationships, but it does suggest that, for the most part, older people maintain regular contact with their family members, who are the primary source of assistance when needed.

Many older adults are caregivers themselves, either caring for other older adults or persons with disabilities, or, increasingly, grandchildren. In 2010, 3.1 million older adults lived with a grandchild under the age of 18. Although some lived in multi-generation

households, 43% were living in skipped-generation households; in other words, the parents of the children they were caring for did not live in the household, and the grandparents were primarily responsible for the children's food, clothing, shelter, and other needs (Scommegna, 2012). Grandparents raising their grand-children were more likely to be female, African American, and living below the poverty line. While studies show that many grandparents raising their grandchildren were in poorer health and experiencing more stress than other older adults, it is unclear whether it was due to the added stress of raising a grandchild or risk factors associated with being poor or African American. Studies have found that grandparents often become more vulnerable when they *stop* raising a grandchild, becoming depressed because of the strong bond they formed with the child (Scommegna & Mossaad, 2011). Increased attention needs to be given to this group of older adults to ensure that they receive the support needed to benefit both themselves and the children they are raising.

Diversity of Older Adults: Resilience and Oppression

EP 2.1.4a

The challenges of aging discussed in this chapter are applicable to older people of color; women; those who are lesbian, gay, bisexual, or transgender; and those with disabilities, but to a much greater extent. The resilience that members of these groups have demonstrated throughout their lives serves them well as they face even greater oppression in old age. However, they are often overlooked even more so than elderly members of dominant social groups.

Older Adults of Color

In 2010, 8.1 million (20%) persons 65 and older living in the United States were nonwhite: 8.4% were African American/black, 6.9% were of Latino/Hispanic origin, 3.5% were Asian or Pacific Islander, fewer than 1% were Native American or Native Alaskan, and almost 1% identified as being from more than one group. The population of older nonwhites grew 15% between 2000 and 2010 and is projected to grow to 55 million by 2020, a 36% increase (Administration on Aging, 2014). Life expectancy for most groups of color is appreciably less than for whites for persons 65 or older, particularly African Americans (see Table 12.6). Persons of color 65 and older account for only 7.7% of

TABLE 12.6 LIFE EXPECTANCY* IN 2010 AT BIRTH, AGE 65, AND AGE 75 BY GENDER AND RACE/ETHNICITY FOR WHITES, BLACKS, AND HISPANICS

LIFE EXPECTANCY	WHITE			BLACK			HISPANIC		
	Both Males and Females	Male	Females	Both Males and Females	Males	Females	Both Males and Females	Males	Females
At birth	78.8	76.4	81.1	74.7	71.4	77.7	81.2	78.5	83.8
At age 65	19.1	17.1	20.3	17.7	15.8	19.1	20.6	18.8	22.0
At age 75	12.0	11.0	12.8	11.6	10.1	12.5	13.2	11.7	14.1

*Average number of additional years persons will live by age.

Source: National Center for Health Statistics (2014). *Life expectancy at birth, at age 65, at age 75, by sex, race, and Hispanic origin: United States, selected years 1900–2010.* Washington, DC: Author.

nonwhites living in the United States, while their white counterparts account for 17.3% of the total U.S. white population (Administration on Aging, 2014). Because neither genetics nor heredity has been a factor contributing to a shorter life expectancy for these groups, social and cultural factors are more likely to account for this differential in longevity.

As a result of social discrimination, a large proportion of nonwhite populations have lower incomes, more physically demanding work, and fewer opportunities to achieve essential life-support services. This has led to more severe and unattended health problems, inadequate nutrition, fewer opportunities for social advancement, below-market wages, and an oppressive cultural environment for many people of color. Growing old under these adverse conditions is stressful, accelerating the aging process for these individuals.

Resilience is a key factor in life longevity. This can be seen particularly among Hispanics/Latinos, who face significant barriers regarding income and other forms of discrimination, yet tend to live longer than other groups, including whites. Researchers are not sure why this is the case. Some suggest it is cultural factors, including family ties and social support in Hispanic community, while others suggest it has to do with the fact that far fewer Hispanics smoke than members of other groups (Scommegna, 2013).

As discussed earlier in this chapter, the percentage of elderly people in the United States who are living below the poverty level is still high, especially for persons of color. Latina/Hispanic women living alone had the highest poverty rates (41.6%), with the rates

for African American/black women living alone also high (33%) (Administration on Aging, 2014). Living arrangements of older adults also vary by racial and ethnic group. In 2012, older black, Asian, and Latina/Hispanic women and older Latino/Hispanic men were more likely than whites to live with relatives other than a partner/spouse (Administration on Aging, 2014).

Many of the necessary support services are not available to older people of color because of discrimination, language differences, complex or confusing eligibility requirements, limited entitlement, and limited outreach efforts, as well as their own pride, which prevents them from seeking services. About half of nonwhite older adults live in cities, while two-thirds of white older adults live in suburbs, where they report better health, higher income, and less concern about crime and safety than their urban counterparts. However, older adults in suburbs are more likely to face problems with transportation and access to needed services (Berk, 2014). Language is another barrier that many older adults of color experience. For example, 60% of Asian Pacific Islanders 65 and older have limited English proficiency; this population is expected to grow from 1.6 million to 7.6 million by 2050. Many Latinos also experience language barriers; this population is projected to comprise 20% of the population of persons 65 and older by 2050. Language barriers can result in misdiagnosis of medical conditions by health-care professionals, problems in accessing health care, and misunderstandings in how to take medication and meet other health needs by older consumers. For example, an older woman who only spoke Lebanese had to go by herself to a medical appointment because her family members were working and could not take her. The driver of the medical van they had arranged for asked her if she was going to her appointment at a specific medical facility. Not understanding what he said, she nodded her head and ended up being dropped off for her appointment at the wrong location, miles from where she was supposed to be with no one who spoke her language to help her. Language barriers can also result in exploitation of the elderly and their families, who are more vulnerable to sales pitches from unscrupulous persons about home repairs and purchase of medical equipment and other items.

Older adults of color have significant disparities in health when compared to their white counterparts. African American and Latino/Hispanic older adults are more likely to experience and die from heart disease, strokes, cancer, asthma, influenza, pneumonia, complications from obesity including diabetes, and HIV/AIDS because of limited access to health care, poor nutrition, and the toll that marginalization has taken on them over time (Administration on Aging, 2014; Rastogi, Johnson, Hoefel, & Drewery, 2011).

In spite of the challenges, older adults of color demonstrate resilience in many ways. They often enjoy strong support from extended family members as well as each other and are resourceful in using informal support systems to get needs met when they are overlooked by or cannot access formal support systems because of income and geographic accessibility. However, poverty, limited options, and discrimination mean that many elderly people of color cannot attain the security, contentment, and life satisfaction of most other elderly Americans.

Older Adults Who Are Lesbian, Gay, Bisexual, or Transgender

Only limited attention has been given to the needs of older adults who are lesbian, gay, bisexual, or transgender. They are marginalized in many ways, and if they are of color, even more so (Auldridge & Espinoza, 2013). The LGBT population in 2013 was estimated to be almost 1.5 million, and is expected to reach 3 million by 2050. It is estimated that about 40% of persons over 65 who are LGBT are also persons of color. Both groups face disparities in many areas, and if an older adult is both LGBT and of color, she or he is further marginalized. Because of employment discrimination, lower wages, and fewer protections as they

aged, members of this group often have limited health and savings plans when they reach old age.

Though a common stereotype is that persons who are LGBT move from one short-term relationship to another, many have been in long-term relationships with partners much longer than heterosexual couples and enjoy the stability of each other's support as they age. However, due to federal, state, and local policies, it is unlikely that they have been able to be afforded the benefits of their partners, such as being listed as beneficiaries in retirement plans or dependents on health-care plans. Many also are ineligible to receive social security benefits if they have not been workforce attached but their partners have, as same sex couples are not eligible to receive benefits afforded to heterosexual married couples. Because of the stresses of being LGBT throughout the years, members of this group are more likely to have heart disease, high blood pressure, high cholesterol, or diabetes. Some face additional health-care challenges if they are living with HIV/AIDS. One study found that more than half had been diagnosed at some point with depression, 39% had had serious thoughts about suicide, and 59% felt isolated. Unlike members of other vulnerable groups, persons who are LGBT are not included as a protected group in the Older Americans Act. They face challenges finding safe and affordable housing, are often discriminated against when buying homes or renting apartments and may be evicted after they more in. Few programs funded by OAA are awarded to LGBT groups, and only one-third of providers of services to older adults have received any training about the needs of persons who are LGBT. Policies in long-term care facilities often prohibit same sex couples from living together, and members of this group often face additional insensitivity and discrimination from staff as well as other residents and their families (Auldridge & Espinoza, 2013).

Older Adults and Gender

Women over 65 experience greater challenges than men. This is due somewhat to the fact that they live longer (women make up 59% of the population of persons over 65), and thus are more likely to end their lives in assisted living facilities and/or poverty. However, the marginalization they have experienced throughout their lifetime also takes a toll. They are less likely to have their own retirement plans and pensions, receive less than spouses from the spouses' plans, and receive less in social security benefits as well. As discussed earlier in this chapter, women 65 and over are much more likely to be living in poverty than men (Administration on Aging, 2014). Health needs of women are also significantly greater than they are for men in this age group, but women have far fewer economic resources. Thus, they are less likely to seek medical care, often waiting until their health needs are far more serious. Because women outlive men, they also are more likely to be living alone and are extremely vulnerable to exploitation and violence (Administration on Aging, 2014).

Gender differences in socialization also play a role in how aging is experienced. Many women are used to taking care of others, and, in fact, often are caring for grandchildren and their own elderly parents well into their own senior years. They may be less likely to put their own financial and health needs first and thus more reluctant to ask others for help. More attention needs to be devoted to the needs of women over 65, as the projections of older adults through 2050 show that these increases will be greater for women than for men (Administration on Aging, 2014).

Older Adults with Disabilities

Older adults with disabilities also face added challenges. In 2012 36% of persons over 65 living in the United States reported having some type of disability vision (6.5%), managing self-care (8.7%), cognition (9.3%), hearing (14.7%), living independently (15.8%), and mobility (23.1%). In 2010, 28% of Medicare recipients who did not live in institutions reported difficulty in performing one or more tasks in daily living (bathing, eating, dressing, moving around one's home to get needs met), compared to 92% of persons who were residing in institutions. About 1.3 million elderly live in long-term care facilities because of disability; more than half are 85 and older (Administration on Aging, 2014).

Although some older individuals had a disability prior to turning 65, many did not become disabled until 65 or older. Both groups face challenges: strategies that were effective for coping with disability most likely have to be adapted as aging takes place, and having a prior disability can place someone at risk for additional health problems in later life. For those who don't face a life with disability until they have already reached old age, adjustment to two types of oppression and its related treatment by others can mean grieving loss of both health and age at the same time. Making public facilities, transportation, and living spaces ADA-compliant makes things more accessible for all older adults regardless of ability

and reduces some of the loneliness and isolation this group experiences when they have limited mobility and other related declines in ability.

Services for Older Adults

EP 2.1.1a
EP 2.1.9b

A wide array of social, health, and related support services has been developed or extended to provide for the needs of older people in the United States. At the federal level, these programs are based largely in the Social Security Act—social insurance and SSI—and health services through Medicare or Medicaid. And the Older Americans Act provides supplementary services through funding of nutrition programs, transportation, social services, and coordination of services for older people.

Through both government-sponsored and private sources, older-citizen participation programs have been developed. The Corporation for National and Community Service, a federal agency that oversees Americorps and other volunteer programs, operates Senior Corps, volunteer programs targeted for adults 55 and over. Senior Corps members organize neighborhood watch programs, tutor and mentor at risk youth, renovate homes, teach English to immigrants, and assist survivors of natural disasters. Others serve as companions to other older adults, assisting with their needs. Older adults in the Foster Grandparents program are work with children in state schools, hospitals, and child-care centers, as well as with pregnant teenagers and abusive and neglectful parents. Some organizations focus on matching retired seniors with expertise in areas such as fund-raising, administration, and budgeting with non-profit organizations that need assistance. Many communities offer special educational programs for seniors interested in volunteering and then match participants with organizations based on interests. A number of universities across the United States offer seminars and other educational programs for seniors, and many libraries offer reading materials for senior book clubs. Senior centers in many communities offer a place where older adults can interact, eat nutritious meals, participate in educational and recreational activities, and pursue hobbies or crafts. Many also offer counseling, help completing income tax forms, and other services.

Under the auspices of the Older Americans Act, areawide agencies on aging (AAAs) have been established throughout the country to coordinate services to older people. Among their many functions are activities such as assessing the needs of the older population, providing or contracting for congregate meals programs, developing transportation services, serving as information and referral resources, and acting as advocates to ensure that communities will be attentive to the needs of older people. Meals-on-Wheels programs provide hot meals for the homebound elderly and essential social contact for older adults who have difficulty leaving their homes because of limited mobility. The reauthorization of the Supplemental Nutrition Assistance Program (SNAP) in 2014 allows SNAP benefits to be used to cover meals through Meals-on-Wheels programs for the first time, enabling more seniors nationwide to receive already-prepared nutritious meals (Bolen, Rosenbaum, & Dean, 2014).

Adult day care centers also enable older adults to avoid long-term care. Often, older people with a working son or daughter cannot be monitored during the day, so day care centers assume caregiving responsibilities at those times. These centers also allow seniors to develop relationships with peers, reducing loneliness and isolation. Programs usually offer a variety of activities and provide health checkups and supervision for participants. Mental health services are provided through mental health outreach centers, and counseling services usually are available to older people and their families through local social services agencies. In rural areas, all of these services may not be readily available, although nutrition and transportation resources usually are offered.

Technology has enabled many more services to be accessible to older adults. Some programs enable seniors to be monitored through electronic devices that can be worn like a necklace so that they can call for assistance if they have an emergency and checked on if they don't contact the provider by a certain time each day. Electronic scales also monitor blood pressure and other health data, providing information to healthcare providers who can intervene as needed. Medical professionals and social workers can hold sessions with seniors via the Internet who may not otherwise be able to access services. One program that worked with older adults with depression was skeptical that seniors would participate. After supplying them with a laptop and providing training to some seniors, mental health providers provided counseling via the Internet to them and face-to-face counseling to another group. To their surprise, the seniors with the laptops not only reduced their symptoms of depression, but used social media and other Internet resources to stay engaged

after the study ended. A second study focused on Internet use in general by seniors, finding that those that used the Internet had a 33% lower probability of depression than those who did not (Cotten, Ford, Ford, & Hale, 2014). Older adults are one of the fastest-growing groups of individuals using social media, and as those already skilled at using the Internet and other sources of technology age, there are almost limitless possibilities that can be linked to enhanced services for this population.

Although community services are helpful in meeting many needs of older adults, even with technology these are not widely available in proportion to the numbers in the community who potentially could benefit from them. Outreach efforts have been reasonably successful in securing participation; however, funding levels of available resources limit the number who can be served. Often, agencies exclude the participation of many older adults because they aren't viewed as culturally relevant, are not affordable, or have eligibility requirements that restrict access. Services would be more effective if older adults were employed by agencies who serve this population, which also is often not the case. Seniors, particularly those whose characteristics and experiences are similar to those served, can serve as "cultural guides" for other employees to help them understand client needs and appropriate ways to address them (Leigh, 2002).

Federal, state, and local policies have an impact on older adults, their caregivers, and helping professionals who provide assistance to them regardless of the type of services needed. Key federal legislation that impacts older adults stands to be jeopardized by the stalemates that have occurred in Congress in recent years. As of summer of 2014, Congress has yet to reauthorize the Older Americans Act (OAA), which expired in 2011. If reauthorization does not occur by 2015, a new act will be required. OAA provides funding for critical services that allows older adults to remain healthy and independent, such as meals, transportation, job training, senior centers, caregiver support, health education and assistance with enrollment in benefits such as Social Security and Medicare. Senior adults also stand to lose when the 2015 federal budget is approved. Proposals include cutting funds for Medicare, Medicaid, Social Security, SNAP, and SSI (SSI cuts alone would affect over 2 billion seniors), eliminating the Senior Corps; reducing funding for caregiver training and other assistance. The Elder Justice Act, passed in 2010 as part of the Affordable Care Act to focus on abuse and neglect of older adults, has yet to be funded (National Council on Aging, 2014).

Advocates for older adults are also collaborating with organizations that support persons with disabilities to make it easier for individuals to remain in their own homes and receive help with daily living skills. The Affordable Care Act includes provisions to expand these services through Medicaid and other programs, but efforts to dismantle this legislation place older adults who need these services in jeopardy. Funding and regulation of long-term out-of-home care are other critical policy issues impacting older adults (National Council on Aging, 2014a). Social workers and other advocates are also promoting legislation that improves access to evidence-based care for older adults.

In addition to advocacy efforts by NASW and CSWE, a number of state and national advocacy and special interest organizations focus specifically on older adults. Perhaps the best known is AARP, formerly the American Association of Retired Persons. Founded in 1958 with membership open to anyone age 50 and older, this organization now had over 37 million members and is one of the largest membership organizations in the U.S. AARP offers Medicare gap and other health insurance as well as other benefits for members, has an online newsletter and magazine, offers extensive information of interest to older adults through its website, and advocates on behalf of its members on topics that are of importance to them (AARP, 2014).

Other key advocacy organizations that focus specifically on the needs of older adults include the National Council on Aging, the American Society on Aging, the Gray Panthers, and the Center for Advocacy on the Rights and Interests of the Elderly (CARIE). Like NASW and CSWE, many national organizations such as the American Bar Association and the American Medical Association have special programs that focus on issues that impact older adults. Most states and many communities also have advocacy groups that focus on this population.

Social Work with Older Adults

EP 2.1.1a
EP 2.1.1c

Many schools of social work have expanded degree programs and course offerings in **gerontology**—the scientific study of aging, the aging process, and the aged—and related fields. They also have increased the extent to which they work with community-based agencies that provide assistance to family caregivers, with the goal of developing meaningful field experiences for social work

students who are interested in this area. About 5% of today's social workers are employed as gerontology social workers, although 75% work in some capacity with older adults. (NASW, 2014a). The U.S. Bureau of Labor Statistics (2014a) projects an overall increase of 19% for social work jobs between 2012 and 2022. That figure increases to 27% for social workers in health care, largely because of the influx of baby boomers entering old age. A bachelor's degree in social work is the minimum requirement, and a master's degree in social work or a related field has become the standard for many positions in social work with older adults. Because of the increased demand for social workers in the field of gerontology, NASW has worked with other organizations to advocate for student loan forgiveness for those social workers who work with older adults.

Increasingly government entities and health-care organizations are mandating the hiring of social workers as team members to work with older adults. The 1987 Omnibus Budget Reconciliation Act requires that nursing homes with more than 120 beds hire social workers. A study on long-term care services conducted by the National Center for Health Statistics found that 42.8% of adult day care, 44.9% of home health care, 75.9% of nursing homes, and 98.9% of hospice programs surveyed employed social workers (Harris-Kojetin, Sengupta, Park-Lee, & Valverde, 2013). NASW has developed standards for social workers in a number of jobs with older adults, as well as special publications on social work in hospice and palliative care (NASW, 2014b).

Many schools of social work have developed specializations in gerontology, and social work research has focused on problems of adaptation and life satisfaction in old age. The Council on Social Work Education has collaborated with the Hartford Project to create a GeroCenter which focuses on social work education in gerontology. The Center's website has a wealth of research and literature on this topic. Other professions interested in gerontology are also conducting research, the knowledge base for assessment and intervention with older adults expanding rapidly. Older adults, we now recognize, have many of the same needs and challenges that are evident at other stages in the life cycle: adjusting to life changes, relationships, relocation, family conflict, separation and loneliness, anxiety about limited income, mental illness, and interpersonal loss, among others. Along with this recognition is the acknowledgment that the aged are responsive to social work change efforts. Social workers, like others who interact with older adults, need to avoid ageist perspectives that older adults are debilitated, rigid and set in their ways, can't make decisions regarding what is best for them, and need to be told what to do. Most adults 65 and older are resilient, open to personal growth and change, and have strengths and wisdom that can benefit others around them, including social workers.

The most common form of social work intervention with older adults is generalist practice at the micro-level. This includes working with older adults and their families on specific problems, such as enhancing personal adjustment, securing resources to meet their needs, providing emotional support in decision making, dealing with death and dying, and managing family conflict. Intervention often involves counseling and guidance approach, stresses problem clarification and the development of options and priorities from strengths and empowerment perspectives, and provides an opportunity for the client to express anxiety and emotion.

Community-based practice is directed to exo-level community systems as targets for creating a more responsive opportunity structure for older adults. In an advocacy approach, social workers identify issues such as inadequate housing and lack of transportation and health care, and they mobilize community resources to bring about change by developing resources to meet these needs. Advocates for older adults support the concept of community aging in place, which places emphasis on the role of the community in supporting the needs of this population to enable them to remain as active members of their communities rather than being isolated in their homes or in long-term care facilities (Administration on Aging, 2014).

CSWE's GeroCenter has developed a list of skills needed by social workers to be effective in working with older adults and their families. They include skills in applying values and ethics, such as being able to "assess and address biases regarding aging" and "applying ethical principles to decisions on behalf of older clients"; skills in assessment, such as "adapting interviewing techniques to potential sensory, language, and cognitive limitations of older adults"; skills in intervention, such as "enhancing the coping capacities and mental health of older persons through a variety of modalities"; skills in programs, policies, and services, such as "advocating and organizing with service providers, community organizations, policy makers and the public to meet the needs and issues of a growing aging population"; and skills in leadership, such as "building

collaborations across disciplines to assess access, continuity, and reduce gaps in services to older adults" (2014, p. 1–6).

Social workers working with older adults must recognize the strengths as well as the challenges that this population encounters. Most older people have been self-sustaining members of society and have extensive wisdom and life experience to share with social workers throughout the helping process. Many developed problems of adaptation only at an older age. Without support, accumulated interpersonal losses (such as the loss of a spouse, friends, familiar environment, job, income, physical health) threaten the fulfillment of daily living needs and life satisfaction.

Social workers are employed in a variety of agencies that older adults, including mental health centers, family service agencies, long-term care facilities, nutrition programs, recreational centers, hospitals, health and nutrition centers, volunteer programs, transportation and housing programs, protective services programs, and community planning agencies. As the theoretical knowledge base expands, social work services for older adults will continue to be intensified and intervention techniques refined, resulting in more effective services to the ever-increasing older population.

Summary

A dramatic increase in the number of Americans age 65 or older is expected in years to come as millions of baby boomers enter retirement and advances in medicine and medical technology allow individuals to live longer. The projected growth will strain our contemporary health and welfare delivery systems and require additional resources. This growth will create expanded job opportunities for employment in health and human services organizations. In turn, this will create a need for additional educational opportunities for those who are interested in becoming employed in one of the health or social services fields. A cadre of trained and knowledgeable social work profession will have to be developed to maintain a high quality of life for older adults as they continue to increase in numbers.

To formulate effective interventions, social workers who work with older adults must be aware of the physiological, psychological, and social changes that accompany aging. Of particular concern are problems related to income inadequacies, health-care costs, housing and transportation, abuse and neglect, family support, and the availability and efficiency of various community programs that assist older adults with their living needs and are culturally sensitive, recognizing the diversity among the elderly.

Far too many older adults, particularly those from marginalized groups, suffer from deprivation related to limited resources and unattended health problems. Social workers can assist by developing knowledge, skill, and understanding when working with older individuals. Social workers also must work within the community in developing and using resources that will enrich the quality of life for vulnerable older adults and at the societal level to ensure that their just treatment.

Competency Notes

EP 2.1.1a: Advocate for client access to the services of social work (pp. 383, 388, 390, 392, 400, 402). Social workers demonstrate an understanding of the importance of employment and workplace policies and practices when advocating for client access to social work services.

EP 2.1.1c: Attend to professional roles and boundaries (p. 402). Social workers attend to professional roles and responsibilities when working with older adults, their families, the communities in which they live

EP 2.1.3a: Distinguish, appraise, and integrate multiple sources of knowledge, including research-based knowledge and practice wisdom (pp. 378, 383, 388, 390). Social workers distinguish, appraise, and integrate multiple sources of knowledge, including research-based knowledge and practice wisdom, to inform services with older adults and their families.

EP 2.1.4a: Recognize the extent to which a culture's structures and values may oppress, marginalize, alienate, or create or enhance privilege and power (p. 397). Social workers recognize the impact a culture's structures and values can have on older adults and the resulting impacts of oppression, marginalization, alienation, or creation or enhancement of privilege and power.

EP 2.1.7a: Use conceptual frameworks to guide the process of assessment, intervention, and evaluation (p. 380). Social workers use the systems/ecological and other conceptual frameworks to guide the processes of assessment, intervention, and evaluation when working with older adults, their families, and the communities in which they live.

EP 2.1.7b: Critique and apply knowledge to understand person and environment (pp. 378, 379, 381, 382, 383, 388, 390, 391, 392, 394, 395, 396). Social workers who work with older adults critique and apply knowledge of their developmental needs and the ways in which those needs are shaped by the broader environment.

EP 2.1.8a: Analyze, formulate, and advocate for policies that advance social well-being (p. 395). Social workers analyze, formulate, and advocate for policies that advance the social well-being of older adults.

EP 2.1.9b: Provide leadership in promoting sustainable changes in service delivery and practice to improve the quality of social services (pp. 381, 383, 391, 392, 396, 400). Social workers act as leaders in promoting sustainable change in service delivery and practice to improve the quality of social services for older adults.

Key Terms

The terms below are defined in the Glossary.

activity theory	hospice
ageism	living will
aging	long-term care facilities
aging in place	Medicaid
Alzheimer's disease	Medicare
continuity theory	Omnibus Budget
developmental theory	Reconciliation Act
elder abuse	(OBRA) of 1987
exchange theory	pre-retirement planning
family caregiving	retirement
gentrification	social emotional
gerontology	selectivity theory

Discussion Questions

1. In what ways does physiological aging affect adaptation in late life?
2. Compare the social theories of aging discussed in this chapter. What are the strengths and limitations of each theory? How does each fit with the ecological/systems framework?
3. What are some of the major challenges with which adults must cope as they grow older?
4. What is the role of a generalist social work practitioner in identifying needs and resources for older adults?

5. How could a generalist social work practitioner contribute to a better quality of life for residents in a long-term care facility?

6. Choose one of the diverse populations of older adults discussed in this chapter (women, a non-white racial or ethnic group, persons who are LGBT, or persons with a disability). Identify strengths and challenges members of this group might experience when they reach age 65 and beyond.

7. Identify a policy that you think should be created or changed to better meet the needs of older adults and explain why you are advocating for this needed policy.

8. Discuss some of the ways that our increasingly aging population is impacting health care. What strategies do you suggest to lessen the impact?

9. As the population continues to grow older, what effect do you think this will have on our society? On social work practice?

On the Internet

http://www.aoa.gov
http://www.aarp.org
http://www.cdc.gov/aging/data/index.htm
http://www.ssa.gov
http://www.cswe.org/CentersInitiatives/GeroEdCenter.aspx
http://www.alz.org
http://www.nia.nih.gov/
http://www.caregiving.org/
http://www.elderweb.com

References

AARP Public Policy Institute. (2014). *About PPI*. Washington, DC: Author. Retrieved from http://www.aarp.org/research/ppi/about_ppi/

Administration on Aging. (2014). *Profile of older Americans, 2013*. Retrieved from http://www.aoa.gov/AoARoot/Aging_Statistics/Profile/2013/docs/2013_Profile.pdf

Alzheimer's Association. (2014). *Alzheimer's facts and figures*. Chicago: Author.

American Society on Aging. (2009). *Problems beset nursing home reform*. San Francisco: CA: Author.

Auldridge, A., & Espinoza, R. (2013). *Health equity and LBGT elders of color: Recommendations for policy and practice*. New York: SAGE (Services and Advocacy for GLBT Elders).

Baudisch, A. (2008). *Inevitable aging? Contributions to evolutionary-demographic theory*. New York: Springer.

Bengston, V. L., Gans, D., Putney, N., & Silverstein, M. (Eds.). (2008). *Handbook of theories of aging* (2nd ed.). New York: Springer.

Berk, L. (2014). *Development through the lifespan* (6th ed.). Boston: Pearson.

Blackburn, J. A., & Dulmus, C. N. (Eds.). (2007). *Handbook of gerontology: Evidence-based approaches to theory, practice, and policy*. Upper Saddle River, NJ: Wiley.

Bolen, E., Rosenbaum, D., & Dean, S. (2014). *Summary of the 2014 farm bill nutrition title*. Washington, DC: Center on Budget and Policy Priorities. Retrieved from http://www.cbpp.org/files/1-28-14fa.pdf

Boyles, S. (2012). Sex and the elderly: STD risk often ignored. *WebMD*. Retrieved from http://www.webmd.com/healthy-aging/news/20120202/sex-and-elderly-std-risk-often-ignored

Butler, R. (2013). Ageism: Another form of bigotry. In M. Adams, W. Blumenfeld, C. Castaneda, H. Hackman, M. Peters, & X. Zuniga (Eds.), *Readings for diversity and social justice* (3rd ed.). New York: Routledge, pp. 559–565.

Carlson, E. (2013). The nursing home reform law: A partially realized vision. *Aging Today*. Retrieved from http://www.asaging.org/blog/nursing-home-reform-law-partially-realized-vision

Centers for Disease Control and Prevention. (2012). *Suicide: Facts at a glance: 2012*. Atlanta, GA: Author. Retrieved from http://www.cdc.gov/violenceprevention/pdf/suicide_datasheet-a.pdf

Centers for Medicare and Medicaid Services. (2014a). *Medicare 2014 costs at a glance*. Washington, DC: Medicare.gov. Retrieved from http://www.medicare.gov/your-medicare-costs/costs-at-a-glance/costs-at-glance.html

Centers for Medicare and Medicaid Services. (2014b). *Nursing homes: Paying for care*. Washington, DC: Medicare.gov. Retrieved from http://medicare.gov

Cotten, S., Ford, G., Ford, S. & Hale, T. (2014). Internet use and depression among retired older adults in the United States: A longitudinal analysis. *Journal of Gerontololgy*. doi:10.1093/geronb/gbu018

Cubanski, J., Neuman, T., Jacobson, G., & Smith, K. (2014). *Raising Medicare premiums for higher income beneficiaries: Assessing the implications*. Menlo Park, CA: Kaiser Family Foundation.

Retrieved from http://kff.org/medicare/issue-brief/income-relating-medicare-part-b-and-part/

DeJong, K., & Love, B. (2013). Ageism and adultism: Introduction. In M. Adams, W. Blumenfeld, C. Castaneda, H. Hackman, M. Peters, X. Zuniga (Eds.), *Readings for diversity and social justice* (3rd ed.). New York: Routledge, pp. 535–549.

Ebeling, A. (2013). *As U.S. retirement crisis builds, 10 other countries get better marks*. Jersey City, NJ: Forbes. Retrieved from http://www.forbes.com/sites/ashleaebeling/2013/10/07/as-u-s-retirement-crisis-builds-10-other-countries-get-better-marks/

Elder Justice Coalition. (2014). *Update on the Elder Justice Act*. Washington, DC: Author.

Federal Interagency Forum on Aging-related Statistics. (2014). *Population*. Retrieved from http://www.agingstats.gov/agingstatsdotnet/Main_Site/Data/2012_Documents/Population.aspx

Finch, C. E. (2007). *The biology of human longevity: Inflammation, nutrition, and aging in the evolution of lifespans*. Maryland Heights, MO: Academic Press.

Gero-Ed Center. (2014). *Geriatric social work competency scale II with life-long leadership skills: Social work practice behaviors in the field of aging*. Alexandria, VA: Council on Social Work Education.

Harris-Kojetin, L., Sengupta, M., Park-Lee, E., & Valverde, R. (2013). *Long-term care services in the United States: 2013 overview*. Hyattsville, MD: National Center for Health Statistics.

Heron, M. (2013). *Deaths: Leading causes for 2010*. Hyattsville, MD: National Center for Health Care Statistics.

Hillier, S. M., & Barrow, G. M. (2010). *Aging, the individual, and society* (9th ed.). Belmont, CA: Wadsworth.

Klauber, M., & Wright, B. (2001). *The 1987 nursing home reform act*. Washington, DC: AARP Public Policy Institute.

Kromer, B., & Howard, D. (2013). *Labor force participation and work status of people 65 years and older: American Community Survey Briefs*. Washington, DC: U.S. Census Bureau. Retrieved from http://www.census.gov/prod/2013pubs/acsbr11-09.pdf

Kübler-Ross, E. (1997). *Death: The final stage of growth*. Upper Saddle River, NJ: Prentice-Hall. (Originally published 1975.)

Kunlin, J. (2010). Modern biological theories of aging. *Aging and Disease, 1*(12), 72–74.

Lee, J. (2008). *The force in biology: Understanding and measuring the role of cell mechanics in cancer and aging*. Saarbrukin, Germany: VDM.

Leigh, J. (2002) *Communicating for cultural competence*. Long Grove, IL: Waveland Press.

Lipkin, N., & Perrymore, A. (2009). *Y in the workplace: Managing the "me first" generation*. Franklin Lakes, NJ: Career Press.

Michaud, P., & van Soest, A. (2007). *How did the elimination of the earnings test above the normal retirement age affect retirement expectations?* Ann Arbor: University of Michigan Retirement Research Center.

Moody, H. R. (2009). *Aging: Concepts and controversies* (6th ed.). Boston: Pine Forge Press.

Munnell, A. (2014). *The impact of aging baby boomers on labor force participation*. Boston: Boston College Center for Retirement Research.

National Alliance for Caregiving. (2009). *The Evercare survey of the economic downturn and its impact on family caregiving*. Washington, DC: Author.

National Association of Social Workers. (2014a). *Social work career center*. Washington, DC: Author. Retrieved from http://careers.socialworkers.org/explore/default.asp

National Association of Social Workers. (2014b). *Social work in hospice and palliative care*. Washington, DC: Author.

National Center for Health Statistics. (2014). *Life expectancy at birth, at age 65, at age 75, by sex, race, and Hispanic origin: United States, selected years 1900–2010*. Washington, DC: Author.

National Center on Elder Abuse. (2014). *Frequently asked questions*. Washington, DC: Author.

National Council on Aging. (2014a). *Benefits access*. Washington, DC: Author. Retrieved from http://www.ncoa.org/press-room/fact-sheets/

National Council on Aging. (2014b). *Economic security for seniors*. Washington, DC: Author. Retrieved from http://www.ncoa.org/press-room/fact-sheets/

National Council on Aging. (2014c). *Mature workers*. Washington, DC: Author. Retrieved from http://www.ncoa.org/press-room/fact-sheets/

National Family Caregivers Association. (2014). *Caregiving statistics*. Kensington, MD: Author.

National Respite Coalition for Lifespan Respite Task Force. (2006). *Summary of Lifespan Respite Care Act of 2005, S. 1283*. Annandale, VA: Author.

Nazareth, L. (2007). *The leisure economy: How changing demographics, economics, and generational attitudes will shape our lives and our industries.* Upper Saddle River, NJ: Wiley.

Newman, B. M., & Newman, P. R. (2012). *Development through life: A psychosocial approach* (11th ed.). Belmont, CA: Wadsworth.

Rastogi, S., Johnson, T., Hoefel, M., & Drewery, M. (2011). *The Black population: 2010.* Washington, DC: U.S. Census Bureau.

Riley, M. W. (1968). *Aging and society.* New York: Russell Sage Foundation.

Rook, K. (1990). Stressful aspects of older adults' social relationships: Current theory and research. In M. Stephens, J. Crowther, S. Hoball, & D. Tennenbaum (Eds.), *Stress and coping in later life families.* New York: Routledge, pp. 173–192.

Salkowitz, R. (2008). *Generation blend: Managing across the technology age gap.* Upper Saddle River, NJ: Wiley.

Scommegna, P. (2012). *More US children raised by grandparents.* Washington, DC: Population Reference Bureau.

Scommegna, P. (2013). *Exploring the paradox of U.S. Hispanics' longer life expectancy.* Washington, DC: Population Reference Bureau.

Scommegna, P. & Mossaad, N. (2011). The health and well-being of grandparents caring for grandchildren. *Today's Research on Aging.* Washington, DC: Population Reference Bureau.

Sherman, A., Greenstein, R., & Ruffing, K. (2012). *Contrary to "Entitlement Society" rhetoric, over nine-tenths of entitlement benefits go to elderly, disabled, or working households.* Washington, DC: Center on Budget and Policy Priorities. Retrieved from http://www.cbpp.org/cms/index.cfm?fa=view&id=3677

Social Security Administration. (2000). *2000 Social security changes.* Washington, DC: Author.

Social Security Administration. (2014). *2014 Social security changes.* Washington, DC: Author.

Stanford Center on Longevity. (2013). *The aging US workforce.* Palo Alto, CA: Author.

United Nations. (2014). *World population ageing: 2013.* New York: Author. Retrieved from http://www.un.org/en/development/desa/population/publications/pdf/ageing/WorldPopulationAgeing2013.pdf

U.S. Bureau of Labor Statistics (2014). *Occupational outlook handbook: Social work.* Washington, DC: Author. Retrieved from http://www.bls.gov/ooh/communityand-social-service/social-workers.htm

U.S. Department of Health and Human Services. (2014). *Costs of care.* Washington, DC: Author. Retrieved from http://longtermcare.gov/costs-how-to-pay/costs-of-care/

Vickerstaff, S., White, P., & Loretto, W. (2007). *The future of older workers: New perspectives.* Bristol, UK: Policy Press.

Wu, K. B. (2013). *Sources of income for older Americans, 2012.* Washington, DC: AARP Public Policy Institute.

Suggested Readings

Baars, J., Dannefer, D., Phillipson, C., & Walker, A. (Eds.). (2006). *Aging, globalization and inequality: The new critical gerontology.* New York: Springer.

Berkman, B. (Ed.). (2006). *Handbook of social work in health and aging.* Amityville, NY: Baywood.

Berkman, B., & Harootyan, L. (Eds.). (2006). *Social work and health care in an aging society: Education, policy, and research.* New York: Oxford University Press.

Birren, J. E., & Schaie, K. W. (Eds.). (2005). *Handbook of the psychology of aging* (6th ed.). New York: Springer.

Connidis, I. (2009). *Family ties and aging.* Thousand Oaks, CA: Sage.

Greene, B., Cohen, H., Galambos, C., & Knopf, N. (2007). *Foundations of social work practice in the field of aging: A competency-based approach.* Washington, DC: NASW Press.

Hunter, S. (2005). *Midlife and older GLBT adults: Knowledge and affirmative practice for the social services.* Binghamton, NY: Haworth.

Innes, A. (2009). *Dementia studies: A social science approach.* Thousand Oaks, CA: Sage.

Kaye, L. (Ed). (2005). *Perspectives on productive aging: Social work with the new aged.* Washington, DC: NASW Press.

Magnus, G. (2008). *The age of aging: How demographics are changing the global economy and our world.* Upper Saddle River, NJ: Wiley.

McInnis-Dittrich, K. (2013). *Social work with older adults.* Boston: Pearson.

Mehrotra, C. M., & Wagner, L. S. (2008). *Aging and diversity: An active learning experience* (2nd ed.). London: Routledge.

Moody, H., & Sasser, J. (2014). *Aging: Concepts and controversies.* Thousand Oaks, CA: Sage.

Morgan, L., & Kunkel, S. (2001). *Aging: The social context.* Thousand Oaks, CA: Sage.

National Association of Social Workers. (2012). *Social work speaks: NASW policy statements, 2012–2014.* Washington, DC: Author.

Phillips, J., Ajourch, K., & Hillcoat-Nalletamby, S. (2010). *Key concepts in social gerontology.* Thousand Oaks, CA: Sage.

Quadagno, J. (2010). *Aging and the life course: An introduction to social gerontology.* New York: McGraw-Hill.

Qualls, S. H., & Zarit, S. H. (Eds.). (2009). *Aging families and caregiving.* Upper Saddle River, NJ: Wiley.

Soniat, B., & Micklos, M. (2010). *Empowering social workers for practice with vulnerable older adults.* Washington, DC: NASW Press.

Turner, F. J. (2010). *Adult psychopathology: A social work perspective.* New York: Free Press.

Wilmoth, J. M. (Ed.). (2005). *Gerontology: Perspectives and issues.* Binghamton, NY: Haworth.

CHAPTER 13

Criminal Justice

Ray Jasperson is a 32-year-old man whose current address is Huntsville State Prison. He is serving a 20-year sentence for armed robbery and will be eligible for parole next year. This is not Ray's first prison term, but he hopes that it will be his last.

Ray first came to the attention of the justice system at age 14, when he was arrested for stealing a car. The third child in a family with six children, he grew up living with his mother and siblings in a poverty-stricken area of a large Midwestern city. He was physically and emotionally abused by his mother during his childhood and received little positive attention from her. From first grade on, Ray had difficulty in school. He had a short attention span, disrupted the classroom regularly, rarely completed his schoolwork, and did poorly on those assignments that he did manage to complete.

At the time of his first arrest, Ray was repeating seventh grade. As a first-time offender, he was placed on deferred adjudication, and he and his family were referred for a variety of services, including anger management for Ray, parenting education for Ray's mother, and counseling for the entire family, the successful completion of which would result in the removal of charges against Ray by the juvenile authorities and the closing of his case. Because Ray's mother worked long hours, however, she was not able to attend either the parenting education or the counseling sessions. Without reliable transportation, Ray failed to complete the anger management program as well. His problems unaddressed, Ray's behavior in school worsened and he became a chronic truant. He began to hang out with older friends from his neighborhood who were engaged in a number of criminal activities in which he was encouraged to participate. It was at this time that Ray began experimenting with drugs. By now, Ray's mother could no longer get him to respond to the limits she set for him.

When Ray was 16 he spent 3 months in a juvenile detention facility where he responded well to the required activities in which he participated and the structure provided by the program. When he left the program, he was assigned a probation officer and returned to live with his family. The conditions of his probation stipulated that he attend school regularly, maintain a strict curfew, and report to his probation officer monthly. Ray followed these conditions for several months but continued to have difficulty in school and dropped out 4 months after returning home.

He worked at several fast-food restaurants but had difficulty getting to work on time or at all and soon became frustrated because he was not earning much money. Increasingly, he gravitated toward young adults who hung out on the street and seemed to have the freedom and the money for which he yearned. Ray's new friends liked him and he felt accepted and enjoyed being with them. Ray soon became involved with them in selling drugs and committing a string of burglaries.

Over the next few years, Ray had a series of arrests for drug dealing, burglary, and assault, which eventually resulted in his current stay in Huntsville State Prison. Shortly before his last arrest and subsequent prison sentence, Ray married a 19-year-old girl from his former neighborhood. He is anxious to get out of prison and begin a family. He has enrolled in a prison program to earn his high school equivalency certificate. He hopes to be released to a community halfway house and enroll in a job-training program, knowing that he will need a job with decent pay to maintain a successful marriage and stay out of prison.

In this chapter we look at the four components of the criminal justice system: legislative, law enforcement, judicial, and corrections. Although social workers play some role in all of these, our attention will be directed to the corrections component and social work roles involved in rehabilitation. Consistent with the overall focus of this text, we will look at rehabilitation strategies in light of the competing views of criminal behavior and the role the environment plays in shaping behaviors that lead to both crime and rehabilitation.

The Criminal Justice System

EP 2.1.7a
EP 2.1.7b

In its broadest sense, the **criminal justice system** refers to the means used to enforce the standards of conduct required to protect individuals and property and to maintain a sense of justice in the community. A system of criminal justice creates the laws governing social behavior, attempts to prevent violations of these laws, and apprehends, judges, punishes, and makes efforts to rehabilitate those who violate the laws. **Crime** is a legal concept with political origins. Crimes are acts that are considered to be a threat to individual or community well-being—and some acts are more serious than others. The reader can learn about the various types or categories of crimes by accessing one or both of the two official crime tracking systems used in the United States—the Uniform Crime Reports (UCR) and the National Incident-based Reporting System (NIBRS) (National Institute of Justice, 2014). The NIBRS is the more robust tracking system of the two; therefore, the types of crimes tracked by this system are highlighted here (see Table 13.1).

As can be seen from the table, there is no shortage of criminal activities in which an individual can engage.

Criminal behavior is restrained by *morality,* as enforced by an individual's social conscience; and *law,* as enforced by the police and the courts. A decline in morality is usually matched by an increase in law. When traditional restraints on behavior are eroded (e.g., disapproval of family, friends, and others we love and respect; informal discipline within social institutions such as schools and places of employment; and private lawsuits), legal restraints must be brought to bear on that behavior (Abadinsky, 2014; Schmalleger, 2013).

The criminal justice system consists of four components:

1. *Legislative,* which defines certain acts to be criminal;
2. *Law enforcement,* which seeks to deter crime and to apprehend and prosecute lawbreakers;
3. *Judicial,* which determines if the laws are valid under our Constitution as well as prescribes penalties for illegal behavior; and

TABLE 13.1 TYPES OF CRIME TRACKED BY THE NATIONAL INCIDENT-BASED REPORTING SYSTEM (NIBRS)

Below is a listing of the types of crime tracked by the National Incident-Based Reporting System (NIBRS).

- Arson, Assault Offenses (aggravated assault, simple assault, intimidation)
- Bad Checks
- Bribery (except sports bribery)
- Burglary/Breaking and Entering
- Counterfeiting/Forgery, Curfew/Loitering/Vagrancy Violations
- Destruction/Damage/Vandalism of Property
- Disorderly Conduct
- Driving Under the Influence (DUI)
- Drug/Narcotic Offenses (drug/narcotic violations, drug equipment violations)
- Drunkenness—except DUI
- Embezzlement, Extortion/Blackmail, Family Offenses—Non-violent
- Fraud Offenses (false pretenses/swindle/confidence game, credit card/automated teller machine fraud, impersonation, welfare fraud, wire fraud)
- Gambling Offenses (betting/wagering, operating/promoting/assisting gambling, gambling equipment violations, sports tampering)
- Homicide Offenses (murder and non-negligent manslaughter, negligent manslaughter, justifiable homicide)
- Kidnapping/Abduction
- Larceny/Theft Offenses (pocket-picking, purse snatching, shoplifting, theft from building, theft from coin-operated machine or device, theft from motor vehicle except vehicle parts or accessories, theft of motor vehicle parts or accessories, all other larceny)
- Liquor Law Violations
- Motor Vehicle Theft
- Peeping Tom
- Pornography/Obscene Material
- Prostitution Offenses (prostitution, assisting or promoting prostitution)
- Robbery
- Runaway
- Sex Offenses—Forcible (forcible rape except statutory rape, forcible sodomy, sexual assault with an object, forcible fondling)
- Sex Offenses—Non-forcible (incest, statutory rape)
- Stolen Property Offenses
- Trespass of Real Property
- Weapon Law Violations
- All Other Offenses

SOURCE: *National Incident-based Reporting System (NIBRS)*. (2014). Washington, DC: National Institute of Justice.

4. *Corrections,* which administers penalties and performs the rehabilitative functions.

Each of these components is discussed below.

Legislative Component

EP 2.1.7a

Criminal codes define conduct that is considered to constitute crimes and establish a range of penalties for such behavior. Three basic kinds of crime are measured by the major criminal statistics in the United States (Samaha, 2005, p. 28):

1. actions that hurt or threaten to hurt people;
2. actions that take, damage, or destroy or threaten to take, damage, or destroy people's property; and
3. other behaviors such as disorderly conduct, public drunkenness, drug use, and prostitution.

In the United States, each state is allowed to enact its own criminal laws or statutes, as long as they conform to the dictates of the U.S. Constitution. The U.S. Congress, state legislatures, and local bodies such as city councils are constantly defining or redefining criminal behavior to reflect social and political change.

Social workers may be involved in political action to persuade legislative bodies to classify certain behaviors as criminal, such as abusing or neglecting a child; or to declassify certain prohibited behaviors as noncriminal, such as homeless people sleeping on the streets. Social workers who engage in such actions should be prepared for opposition by those who discount their commitment to social justice. The ideal legislative system attempts to define and enact a criminal code that forbids, or extracts penalties for, behavior that most of us find threatening to the community while protecting the rights of the minority to express their own lifestyles.

Law Enforcement Component

EP 2.1.7a

Law enforcement encompasses the functions of preventing crime, investigating crime, apprehending criminal suspects, and assisting in criminal prosecution (Schmalleger, 2013). Law enforcement officers are bound to enforce all criminal statutes with equal emphasis (a practice called **full enforcement**). Rarely, however, do they attempt to enforce every criminal statute all of the time. Instead, they use their discretion, enforcing some laws some of the time and against some people (a practice called **selective enforcement**). The amount of discretion is inversely related to the severity of the crime; the less the severity, the more discretion that is applied, and vice versa. Little discretion typically is associated with behaviors such as public drunkenness, threatening behavior and harassment, and street prostitution.

Law enforcement officers can legally make an arrest when they have probable cause to believe that an individual has violated a law. Arrested persons are either released without prosecution or taken into custody until a preliminary hearing is held, at which time the charges are either dropped or dismissed, bail is set, or the person is jailed. If the charges are not dropped or dismissed, an arraignment takes place, at which time the charge is either dismissed, a guilty plea is entered, or a trial date is set. As shown in Figure 13.1, the law enforcement process has many "stops," from suspicion that a person has committed a crime to sentencing and correction (Schmalleger & Smykla, 2012).

Social workers can have a significant influence on the law enforcement process, particularly as it relates to selective enforcement. For example, what discretion, if any, should law enforcement officers have in dealing with domestic-disturbance cases? Most law enforcement officers agree that intervention in domestic

cases is the most dangerous part of their job. How might this belief influence law enforcement's handling of these situations? Are more women harmed or killed as a result?

Law enforcement officers also have a responsibility to identify people with mental illness who are a threat to themselves or others. How much discretion, if any, should law enforcement officers exercise when dealing with people with mental illness? Who makes that decision? How do we ensure that law enforcement officers are trained adequately to deal with these decisions? What options do they have when apprehending people with mental illness? These examples constitute important areas for social workers in law enforcement.

Judicial Component

EP 2.1.7a

Following arrest, individuals charged with a crime become defendants, and decision making regarding their future shifts from law enforcement to the criminal courts. Most decision making takes place behind closed doors and in the corridors of the courthouse. **Courts** are political and social institutions as much as they are legal institutions; they are sensitive and respond to the needs and demands of the public, special-interest groups, and individuals. They use discretionary decision making to balance the law and extralegal, professional, organizational, and societal goals. Formal court proceedings simply ratify what lawyers and other criminal justice personnel already have decided informally (Abadinsky, 2014; Schmalleger & Smykla, 2012).

There are three levels or tiers of criminal courts (Berman & Saliba, 2009):

1. **lower criminal courts** (also referred to as superior, municipal, county, justice of the peace, and magistrate courts): courts with the power to decide minor cases and to conduct pretrial proceedings;
2. **trial courts:** courts with the power to conduct pretrial and trial proceedings in all criminal cases; and
3. **appellate courts:** courts with the authority to review the decision of trial courts and lower criminal courts.

Lower Courts   The lower courts decide the majority of criminal cases involving minor crimes such as traffic offenses, drunk and disorderly conduct, shoplifting, and prostitution. These are the only contacts that

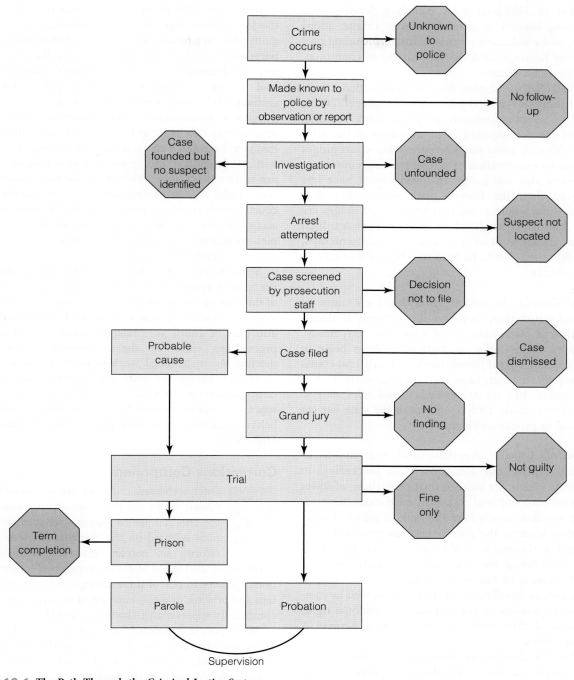

FIG 13.1 The Path Through the Criminal Justice System
NOTE: The stop signs show how a crime drops out of the system. Rectangles represent stages in the system.

most people have with the criminal courts. Lower courts are courts of limited jurisdiction; their authority is limited to trying misdemeanor cases and conducting preliminary proceedings in felony cases.

Defendants in lower courts have the same rights as defendants in trial courts; however, lower-court judges try most cases less formally than trial courts and they try them without juries. Lower courts perform a number of additional tasks, including deciding bail; assigning lawyers to defendants who cannot afford them; and conducting pretrial hearings, including preliminary hearings, to decide the legality of confession, searches, and seizures.

The U.S. Constitution does not require that lower-court judges have legal training (Schmalleger, 2013). And in about two-thirds of lower-court systems, judges are not required to be members of the state bar. Although some states require lower-court judges to pass an examination or attend training courses, as a general rule the judges in lower courts have less training than the lawyers with whom they deal daily. Some would argue that lower-court judges are only minimally qualified to rule on complex legal issues, decide guilt or innocence, or pass sentences, and that they should be held to a higher standard of competence.

Trial Courts   In contrast, trial courts are courts of general jurisdiction; they have the authority to decide all criminal cases, from capital felonies to petty misdemeanors. Adjudication or court proceedings begin in trial courts (original jurisdiction), and only trial courts can adjudicate felony cases (exclusive jurisdiction). Not surprisingly, trial courts adhere to formal rules more so than lower courts. Only members of the state bar are allowed to preside as judges.

Appellate Courts   Appellate courts hear and decide appeals of trial court decisions. Thus, proceedings in appellate courts are more formal than those of lower criminal courts or trial courts. In most states, intermediate appellate courts hear the bulk of initial appeals, deciding whether the government has proved its case beyond a reasonable doubt and whether defendants have established their defenses adequately. Supreme courts (courts of last resort) review the decisions of intermediate appellate court decisions, as well as complicated questions of law and the constitutional rights of criminal defendants (Abadinsky, 2014; Berman & Saliba, 2009).

The U.S. Constitution does not guarantee the right to a review of a lower-court decision; however, all jurisdictions by law allow defendants to have the decisions of lower courts reviewed by courts of appeals. Overturning a decision of a lower court does not close a case automatically. In many cases in which a lower-court decision is overturned by an appellate court, the government proceeds with retrying the defendant.

More than 90% of all criminal cases do not reach the formal trial stage; they are adjudicated by way of guilty pleas in a process known as plea bargaining. **Plea bargaining** involves negotiations among the prosecutor, the defendant, and the defendant's counsel that lead to the defendant's entering a guilty plea in exchange for a reduction in charges or the prosecutor's promise to recommend a more lenient sentence. The process may take place at the arraignment, at the preliminary hearing (if there is one), or during the trial itself. A defendant who agrees to a plea bargain may not receive the trial to which he or she has a constitutional right. Plea bargaining does, however, relieve the courts, which could not possibly handle the trials of all accused persons. Prosecutors often are willing to accept plea bargaining when they believe that a trial could otherwise result in an acquittal.

Social workers must have a working knowledge of the judicial system in the United States because many of their clients are involved with or at risk of becoming involved with that system at some level. Social workers also may be called as special witnesses in trial-court proceedings, either for the prosecution or for the defense. As such, social workers must clearly understand their obligations under the National Association of Social Workers (NASW) *Social Work Code of Ethics* when it comes to criminal behavior or alleged criminal behavior on the part of their clients (Kirst-Ashman & Hull, 2013).

Corrections Component

EP 2.1.7a

Once convicted, criminals are sentenced and passed on to the corrections component of the criminal justice system. The term *corrections* is based on the idea that the state can reform, or correct, criminals. Convicted criminals in the United States are supervised by corrections agencies in one of three settings: the community; jails and prisons; or a combination of incarceration and community supervision (Abadinsky, 2014).

Most people convicted of crimes in the United States are not in prison. According to the Bureau of Justice Statistics (2013), about 4.1 million men and women moved onto or off probation in this country during 2012, a slight decrease from the previous year.

Probation   **Probation** is not the same as parole. Probation replaces incarceration, and parole follows incarceration. Another difference between probation and parole is that counties typically administer probation, whereas states are responsible for administering parole. Probation is a criminal sentence that substitutes community supervision for incarceration. Those who receive probated sentences are in the custody of the state and have limited freedom and privacy.

About half of those on probation in 2012 had committed minor offenses such as driving while intoxicated (DWI) (Bureau of Justice Statistics, 2013). The rest were felons who had committed violent and serious property offenses. Most minor offenders receive probation because they are not considered to be a high risk to public safety. Probation was not set up for, nor is it intended to deal with, repeat felony offenders.

Individuals on probation typically are required to obey the law, work, go to school or get vocational training, pay child support, and refrain from using or selling drugs. They also must obtain written permission from their probation officer to change residence, change employment, or travel outside the community. Further, they are required to notify their probation officer of any arrests or criminal investigations. The requirements for felony probationers typically are more stringent: submit to regular drug testing, participate in drug or alcohol treatment, perform community service work, obtain mental health counseling, and reside in a community facility or be under house arrest. They also are required to help pay the cost of probation (Smalleger, 2013).

Probation ends when the probationer completes the term of probation successfully or the court cancels or revokes the probation. Probation can be revoked when the probationer is either arrested for or convicted of a new crime, called **recidivism,** or in cases of a technical violation of probation such as failing to notify the probation officer of a change of address or a change in employment status. The total exit rate (ratio of the number of probationers exiting supervision during the year to the average daily probation population) for probationers in 2012 was 53%. Of this percentage, 36% completed their probation successfully, 8% were re-incarcerated, 1% absconded, 5% failed to meet all conditions of their probation but were not re-incarcerated, and 2% were either discharged from probation through a legislative mandate because they were deported or transferred to the jurisdiction of Immigration and Customs Enforcement; transferred to another state through an interstate compact agreement; had their sentence dismissed or overturned by the court through an appeal; had their sentence closed administratively, deferred or terminated by the court;

were awaiting a hearing; or were released on bond (Bureau of Justice Statistics, 2013).

Intermediate Punishments and Community Corrections **Intermediate punishments,** in which

offenders remain in the community under strict supervision (community corrections), are increasingly replacing both probation
EP 2.1.3b and parole in response to a rapidly expanding prison population, reduction in state and federal funding to construct new jails and prisons, a shift in criminal justice policy from rehabilitation to retribution, and the desire to have a middle ground between either/or choices of probation or parole. Community corrections are gaining in popularity because they allow for better protection of community members, reduce the costs of incarceration, and increase the likelihood of successful reintegration of offenders into the community.

Community corrections are facilitated through **problem-solving courts** or community justice partnerships that include public agencies and nonprofit or for-profit social service providers. Participants in a problem-solving court are required to attend all judicial status hearings and court sessions and agree to frequent monitoring. They are given access to a broad array of treatment services and are subject to sanctions for noncompliance with the provisions of such services or incentives for positive outcomes. Core elements of problem-solving courts include the coupling of behavioral modification principles with recurring courtroom experiences that include the interaction between the judge and the participant, the public aspect of being sanctioned or complimented, and a collaborative approach among key stakeholders (Urban Institute, 2012, pp. 9–10).

Problem-solving courts are fundamentally different from conventional courts in the following ways:

- voluntary participation;
- an nonadversarial, problem-solving focus;
- integration of a continuum of outpatient and residential treatment with informal support groups;
- intensive supervision of the treatment process by judges and case managers;
- direct conversational interaction between defendants and the judge;
- graduated sanctions are used to monitor compliance and respond to problems;
- routine and random drug testing;

- team approach to decision making; and
- incentives to motivate and acknowledge accomplishments.

The procedural court model was used as the basis for developing mental health courts, adult and juvenile drug courts, and veterans' courts (Office of Justice Programs, 2014).

- **Mental health courts** are designed to combat the criminalization of persons who are mentally ill by separating those with mental illness from a criminal population. These courts are comprised of specific dockets dedicated to individuals with mental illnesses. The purpose of mental health courts is to divert persons with mental illnesses away from jail or prison in lieu of community-based treatment services. Defendants are closely monitored by an appointed judge and community mental health staff, often social workers, assigned to their cases.
- **Drug courts** are specialized court docket programs that target criminal defendants and offenders, juvenile offenders, and parents with pending child welfare cases who have alcohol and other drug dependency problems. Programs are generally managed by a multidisciplinary team including judges, prosecutors, defense attorneys, community corrections, social workers and treatment service professionals. Support from stakeholders representing law enforcement, the family and the community is encouraged through participation in hearings, programming and events like graduation.

There are three types of drug courts:

- *Adult drug courts* involve programs that are designed to reduce drug use relapse and criminal recidivism among defendants and offenders through risk and needs assessment, judicial interaction, monitoring and supervision, graduated sanctions and incentives, treatment and various rehabilitation services.
- *Veteran's courts*—a type of adult drug court that helps veterans involved with the criminal justice system tackle their substance use disorder so that they can safely return to their communities. Drawing heavily from the adult drug court model, these courts integrate substance abuse treatment, mandatory drug testing, sanctions and incentives, and transitional services in a supervised court setting. In addition, participants are connected with Veterans Justice Outreach specialists for help with obtaining veterans' benefits and services to address

their substance abuse treatment and other recovery support needs.

- *Juvenile drug courts* use a program model similar to that of the adult drug court that is tailored to the needs of juvenile offenders. These programs provide youth and their families with counseling, education and other services to promote immediate intervention, treatment and structure; improve the youths' levels of functioning; address problems that may contribute to drug use; build skills that increase the ability of the youth to lead drug- and crime-free lives; strengthen families' capacities to offer structure and guidance; and promote accountability for all involved.
- *Family drug courts* use programs that are designed to aid in the reunification and stabilization of families affected by parental drug use. These programs apply the adult drug court model to cases entering the child welfare system that include allegations of child abuse or neglect in which substance abuse is identified as a contributing factor. Program goals include helping the parent to become emotionally, financially and personally self-sufficient and promoting the development of positive parenting and coping skills. Family drug court programs also provide an array of services to the children for whom allegations of child abuse or neglect have been confirmed.

All drug courts have high initial costs, especially those associated with treatment; however, savings associated with criminal justice system costs outweigh up-front investment costs due to fewer crimes, rearrests and incarceration (Office of Justice Programs, 2014).

A notable example of the gaining popularity of the community corrections movement is the passage of historic legislation by the California Legislature in 2011 (Public Safety Realignment Act of 2011) aimed at closing the revolving door of low-level inmates cycling in and out of state prisons. The law, which went into effect on October 1, 2011, mandates that individuals sentenced to nonserious, nonviolent, or nonsex offenses serve their sentences in county jails instead of state prisons.

The California legislation also changed the state's system of community corrections. Prior to the passage of the Realignment Act, every inmate released from prison was supervised by state parole agents, and parole violators could be sent back to state prison for up to one year. Under Realignment, county probation departments administer a system of post-release community supervision (PRCS) to complement state parole. State parole agents continue to supervise high-risk sex offenders, offenders with life sentences, and any other offenders who have been released from prison after having been incarcerated for a current serious or violent crime. All other inmates released from prison are placed under PCRS. Offenders who violate the terms of PCRS or state parole supervision face a range of sanctions, including a revocation term in county jail for up to 90 days. Repeat violators are eligible for revocation to state prison.

In November, 2012, California voters approved Proposition 30, which created a constitutional amendment aimed at protecting ongoing funding to counties for Realignment by prohibiting the state legislature from reducing or removing funding to counties for implementing the provisions of Realignment.

The California Department of Corrections and Rehabilitation released a report in December 2013 documenting statewide outcomes for offenders released from prison during the first year after implementation of Realignment (California Department of Corrections and Rehabilitation, 2013). Overall, the report shows that there is very little difference between the one-year arrest and conviction rates of offenders released pre- and post-alignment. The reader of the report is cautioned, however, when interpreting the findings of the report, as the data upon which the report are based are limited to only one year of releases.

The community corrections movement is compatible with a philosophy of restorative justice, which works to heal victims, communities, and offenders who have been physically, psychologically, and/or emotionally injured by crime (Alarid, 2014; Hanser, 2013; Van Wormer & Walker, 2012). Examples of intermediate sanctions programs include fines, intensive supervision, restitution (i.e., financial or community service), substance abuse treatment, electronic monitoring, boot camps, and half-way houses. Different punishments can be customized to the crime and the person who committed it by some combination of sanctions (e.g., restitution with intensive supervision) or using them in a specified sequence (e.g., boot camp followed by intensive supervision) (Center for Community Corrections, 2014).

Incarceration   The U.S. state and federal prison population has been on a slow but steady decline over the past several years. That figure stood at about 1.6 million inmates at the end of 2012, about a 2% decline from the previous

EP 2.1.3b

year. While the number of inmates in state and federal prisons declined for both males and females from the previous year, the number of female prisoners dropped to its lowest level since 2005. California had the greatest decline in state prison inmates due in large part to the state's recently enacted Realignment policy described above (Bureau of Justice Statistics, 2013a). One thing that hasn't changed in the state and federal prison population is the disparity in the number of inmates who represent racial and ethnic minorities and the growing number of women who have been incarcerated for low-level drug crimes. More than 60% of the current prison population is comprised of racial and ethnic minorities. Racial disparities are most pronounced for blacks; nationwide (across all states and the District of Columbia), the ratio of incarcerated blacks to whites is 5.6:1. The ratio of incarcerated blacks to whites is the highest in the District of Columbia (19:1), followed by Iowa (13:6), Vermont (12:5), New Jersey (12:4), and Connecticut (12:0). The ratio of incarcerated blacks to whites is the lowest in Georgia (3:3). It is sobering that nearly one in three black males is at risk of becoming incarcerated at some point in his life. The ratio of incarcerated Hispanics is also sobering—the ratio of incarcerated Latinos/Hispanics to whites nationwide is nearly 2:1. Despite the fact that the number of females in prison is at its lowest since 2005, the number of women in prison is increasing at nearly double the rate for men. A third of these women have been incarcerated for low-level drug offenses (The Sentencing Project, 2014).

California, Texas, and the federal system hold about one-third of all prisoners in the nation; however, the growth in the prison population for large states in the country has leveled off and is actually dropping. This finding reflects an emerging trend for states to trim their prison populations and consider alternatives to prison as they continue to recover from the near financial collapse of the country in 2007 and the resulting period of financial uncertainty that has continued to the present time (Bureau of Justice Statistics, 2013b).

In federal fiscal year 2010, the latest year for which state-level expenditure data are available, total taxpayer costs of prisons exceeded $1 billion in 12 states, led by California ($7.9 billion) and Texas ($3.3 billion) (Vera Institute of Justice, 2012). The average per person cost to support the state prison system in these states was $34,405, a figure that exceeds the annual cost of in-state tuition and fees to attend one of the component institutions in either state's university system.

Many social work graduates become probation or parole officers. Here, a probation officer counsels his young client about employment opportunities.

Heinle/Index Stock

Longer sentences and more frequent **incarceration** have been seen by proponents of incarceration as a powerful solution to reducing crime and curbing recidivism. Research has not confirmed this to be the case (Alarid, 2014; Hebenton & Jou, 2014; Wilson & Petersillia, 2011). Violence in crime often is linked to participation in other criminal activities, such as drug use. Thus, the incarcerated offenders are replaced quickly on the streets by other offenders. Incapacitation of the one offender does not necessarily reduce the propensity of others to commit the same offense. Many prisoners, particularly those whose are members of prison gangs, continue criminal behavior of one form or another while in prison. Prison time seems to have been used as an expression of public outrage with little thought to its deterrent or incapacitation effect on other criminals (Alarid, 2014; Brooks, 2014).

Mental Health Issues in Adult Correctional Facilities

As discussed in Chapter 9 of this textbook, the community mental health-care movement in the United States can be traced back to passage of the landmark Community Mental Health Care Act of 1963. This act held great promise for better and more humane treatment of individuals with serious mental health problems in community-based settings rather than the mental health hospitals or other institutions in which they had previously been placed. The decade following passage of the act, sometimes referred to as "the decade of deinstitutionalization," was marked by a mass exodus of individuals with serious mental health problems from secure hospital-based settings into far less restrictive settings in communities across the country. The era of large-scale commitment of individuals with serious mental health problems to state mental hospitals came to an abrupt end.

The promise of community-based mental health care was short-lived. First and foremost, the federal government failed to provide the funds required to build and operate a sufficient number of community health centers to meet the needs of the burgeoning population of persons with serious mental health problems now living in the community. In addition, members of many communities did not readily embrace the idea of having people they often labeled as "crazy" living among them. There was fear generated by ignorance that these individuals would make communities an unsafe place to live. As a consequence, thousands of people suffering from serious mental illness found themselves on the streets and, as their mental health deteriorated without needed supports, eventually in jails and prisons. The country's correctional system became the de facto mental health system for these individuals. The correctional system was then, as it is now, ill-equipped to take on this new role. To make matters more complex, a large proportion of the members of this new prison population also had a co-occurring substance use disorder.

Obtaining current statistics on the prevalence of mental health disorders among prison and jail inmates can be a daunting task. The U.S. Bureau of Justice Statistics tracks trends in this area through the National Inmate Survey (NIS), the latest results which cover the period 2008–2009. Results for the 2011–2012 survey have not yet been released, and the 2013–2014 survey is still underway. With these caveats in mind, results of the most recent survey reveal some startling statistics:

- 56.2%, 44.8%, and 64.2% of state, federal, and local jail inmates, respectively, reported having a major depressive disorder (persistent sadness, loss of interest in activities, or insomnia or hypersomnia), a major mania disorder (psychomotor agitation or persistent anger or irritability), or a major psychotic disorder (any signs of delusions or hallucinations during the previous twelve months);
- Female inmates had much higher rates of mental health problems than male inmates across all three facility types;
- No discernible patterns of mental health problems were observed by racial or ethnic group or by age of the inmates;
- State prisoners and local jail inmates with a mental health problem were twice as likely as their counterparts without a mental health problem to have been homeless in the year before their incarceration;
- State prisoners who had a mental health problem were over two times more likely than those without a mental health problem to report being physically or sexually abused in the past (this finding was even more pronounced for local jail inmates);
- Inmates who had a mental health problem were more likely than inmates without a mental health problem to have family members who abused drugs or alcohol or both;
- Over half of prison and jail inmates who had a mental health problem reported that they had a family member who had been incarcerated in the past;
- Three out of four state prison and local jail inmates and three out of five federal prison inmates with mental health problems reported alcohol or drug dependence (over a third of these

inmates had used drugs at the time of their offense);
- Inmates who had a mental health problem had served more prior sentences than inmates without a mental problem; and
- Rule violations and injuries from a fight (some of which were severe in nature), were more common among inmates who had a mental health problem.

Statistics for female inmates with mental health problems who were incarcerated in state prisons deserve special attention here because of the dramatic nature of the findings for this group:

- Nearly three out of four met the criteria for substance dependence;
- Two out of five had a current or past violent offense;
- About one in five had been homeless in the year before their arrest;
- Three out of five had experienced past physical or sexual abuse; and
- Almost one out of two reported they had parents who abused alcohol or drugs or both (U.S. Bureau of Justice Statistics, 2009).

However one looks at it, the high prevalence of mental health problems among inmates in state and federal prisons and local jails in this country is a reality that cannot be ignored. The mental health problems of these individuals are exacerbated by prolonged exposure to often inhumane treatment at the hands of prison staff or by other inmates, fear for their personal safety, witnessing violence of many kinds, solitary confinement and other forms of isolation, taking medications that have debilitating side effects or, in some instances, going without needed medication to stabilize their mental health.

Women prisoners suffer especially high rates of mental illness. In many jurisdictions, rates of mental illness among women prisoners range from one quarter to one half of the population, roughly two to three times the rate seen in male prisoners. Estimates of the rate of PTSD among women prisoners due to sexual or physical abuse suffered prior to incarceration range from 48% to 88%.

Despite the soaring rates of women's incarceration and women inmate's mental health needs, most prisons lack adequate facilities, services, and programming for women prisoners. Therapeutic counseling is rarely available. As a consequence, women attempting to access mental health services are often denied care, or administered psychotropic medication without being offered psychotherapeutic treatment. Studies across custodial settings have found that detainees and inmates with mental health problems are held for longer periods of time than others, despite the fact that providing mental health treatment services in a custodial setting is the most costly and the least effective form of mental health care.

Controversy Over the Death Penalty

The death penalty has been a controversial issue since it was first introduced. Over two-thirds of countries worldwide have abolished the death penalty. In 2010 the vast majority of executions took place in five countries: China, Iran, North Korea, Yemen, and the United States (Amnesty International, 2012). In 2014, 32 states had legislation authorizing the death penalty. Eighteen states have repealed it: Wisconsin repealed it in 1853, while the most recent state, Maryland, repealed it in 2013 (Death Penalty Information Center, 2014). While many in the United States support the death penalty when someone commits an especially reprehensible crime, opponents raise the following concerns:

- The death penalty is racially biased: since 1977, 77% of those executed had murdered white victims, even though about half of homicide victims are African American. A number of studies have concluded that a defendant is several times more likely to be sentenced to death if the murder victim was white. A report released by the American Bar Association concluded that one-third of African American inmates on death row in Philadelphia would have received life sentences if they had been white (Amnesty International, 2012).
- Convictions are not always accurate: since 1973, 140 people have been removed from death row because of evidence that they were wrongly convicted, and a number have been determined to be innocent after their execution had already taken place. For example, Daniel Wade Moore of Alabama, who was sentenced to death in 2002 for murder and sexual assault, was acquitted in 2009 when it was revealed that 256 pages of evidence had been withheld (Amnesty International, 2012). Michael Morton, who lived in a suburb of Austin, Texas, was convicted of murdering his wife in

1986, even though he was at work at the time, his three year old son described a different man he saw commit the murder, neighbors described a stranger parking a van and walking into a nearby wooded area, near the Morton home that day, and a blood-stained bandana was found nearby. None of that evidence was included in Morton's trial. After the involvement of the Innocence Project, a legal clinic associated with the law school at Yeshiva University, the court agreed to conduct DNA testing on the bandana. Not only was the testing a match for someone other than Morton, the convicted felon it matched had killed another woman in the Austin area two years after the murder of Morton's wife. After 25 years, Morton was released from prison and proceedings of criminal contempt of court were filed against the prosecutor in the case (Levs, 2013).

The death penalty does not deter people from committing serious crimes: FBI data shows that the 14 states without the death penalty actually had homicide rates at or below the national rate (Amnesty International, 2012).

The death penalty is expensive and diverts resources from crime prevention and other forms of crime control, with the greatest costs occurring prior to and during trial, not because of appeals that take place after conviction. For example, in Maryland, the cost of a death penalty case is three times the cost of a non-death penalty case (Amnesty International, 2012).

The death penalty disregards mental illness in the United States; constitutional protections for persons who are mentally ill or intellectually disabled are minimal (Amnesty International, 2012).

Public support for the death penalty in the United States is waning; the majority of persons in the United States prefer alternatives other than execution (Amnesty International, 2012). Support for the death penalty has waned most recently over concerns about the methods of lethal injection used by states (Denno, 2014). The growing number of legal challenges to the practice that resulted in split decisions at the circuit court level prompted the U.S. Supreme Court to weigh in on the matter. The court chose a Kentucky case (*Baze v. Rees*) to determine the future direction of lethal injection. In a 7–2 plurality opinion in 2008, the Court upheld the constitutionality of Kentucky's lethal injection protocol under the Eighth Amendment's Cruel and Unusual Punishments Clause. The Court found that the defendants had failed to show that Kentucky's three-drug combination posed a substantial risk of serious harm compared to known and available alternatives. As the number of legal challenges to the use of lethal drugs in executions has increased, many states have changed protocols and drugs used, resulting in problems in drug administration in several instances. A shortage of drugs used by most states has exacerbated concerns. As public opinion about the death penalty shifts, legal challenges continue, and five states have recently abolished the practice: New Jersey in 2007, New Mexico in 2009, Illinois in 2011, Connecticut in 2012, and Maryland in 2012 (Death Penalty Information Center, 2014).

The Juvenile Justice System

EP 2.1.7a

Whether juvenile offenders should be treated differently from adult offenders remains a topic of extensive debate. State definitions of juveniles vary considerably. Most exclude children under age 8 from juvenile justice jurisdiction, but the states differ in the upper age, with some using 16 and others 18 for determining juvenile or criminal justice jurisdiction (Champion, Merlo, & Benekos, 2012; Elrod & Ryder, 2014). **Juvenile delinquency** can refer to a youth who has committed a crime, a status offense (e.g., truancy, underage drinking, curfew violation, running away, incorrigibility), or both.

Several facts stand out regarding juvenile delinquency (Agnew & Brezina, 2011; Champion, Merlo, & Benekos, 2012; Siegel & Welsh, 2013, 2014):

- Youths are substantially more crime-prone than adults.
- The juvenile arrest rate for serious property crimes and violent crimes is significantly higher than for adults.
- Most youth arrests are for property crimes such as theft and burglary and status offenses such as truancy and curfew violations.
- Younger offenders commit crimes in groups more often than adults.
- Serious juvenile crime is concentrated in urban areas, with the highest arrest and conviction rates among youths of color.

- Youths are frequently armed when committing crimes.

How to handle youthful offenders has been debated throughout the history of the United States. Until the late 1800s, youthful offenders were treated in the same way as adult offenders—for example, imprisoned with adults and even sentenced to death. **Juvenile courts** in the United States were first established in Cook County, Illinois, in 1899 (Stern & Axinn, 2012; Elrod & Ryder, 2014). The philosophy of juvenile courts has been that they should act in the child's best interest. Juvenile courts, thus, have had a treatment-and-rehabilitation orientation instead of a focus on a specific crime, as in adult criminal proceedings. Historically, the focus of juvenile courts has been on the child's psychological, physical, emotional, and educational needs rather than on the child's guilt. But an increase in serious and violent crimes committed by very young offenders in the mid-2000s put pressure on the juvenile justice system to rethink the efficacy of the treatment-and-rehabilitation emphasis that had been the hallmark of that system for so long (Chambliss, 2011).

The Gault Decision

In the 1960s, Gerald Gault, age 15, was tried in the

EP 2.1.3b

Arizona juvenile court for allegedly making an obscene phone call to a neighbor. Neither the accused nor his parents were given advance notice of the charges against him. He was not informed of his legal rights and, if found guilty, could have been held within the criminal justice system until he reached the age of majority. The procedures used by the Arizona officials in the Gault proceeding were not unreasonable. They were in accord with the thinking of the times—namely, that advance notice and formal trial are likely to stigmatize a child and violate confidentiality. The concern was with the state as a parent rather than the state as the embodiment of a social conscience. Thus, Gault was brought before the juvenile court and tried without proper safeguards.

In 1967, the case went to the U.S. Supreme Court. The majority opinion, written by Justice Abe Fortas, vehemently criticized the juvenile correctional establishment and made it clear that regardless of intent, juveniles should not be deprived of their liberty without the full set of due-process rights available to an adult. This case restored to juvenile procedures safeguards that often had been ignored, including notification of charges, protection from self-incrimination, confrontation, and cross-examination (Tannenhaus, 2011).

The wisdom of the *Gault* decision is still disputed today. It undoubtedly gives minors the same basic constitutional rights enjoyed by adults, but the return to a focus on whether a young person has or has not committed a crime often masks the need for help by youth caught up in the court processes. The *Gault* case has brought about a critical reassessment of juvenile procedures and has suggested that the treatment and rehabilitative role of the juvenile correctional system must be secondary to protecting the rights of the juvenile before the criminal justice system (Tannenhaus, 2011).

Juvenile Justice Agencies

Many entities deal with juvenile delinquency: lawmaking bodies, police departments, prosecutors, defense attorneys, correctional facilities, treatment centers, halfway houses, and social service agencies. Lawmaking bodies define the scope of legal authority of these entities. They also determine when older juveniles can be transferred to the adult criminal justice system in a process called "certification." Finally, lawmaking bodies determine the budgets needed to support agencies administering juvenile justice programs and services (Champion, Merlo, & Benekos, 2012).

Juvenile Courts

EP 2.1.3b

Juvenile courts in the United States have several, often competing goals: helping children in need, treating and/or punishing juveniles who commit crimes, and protecting society from juvenile crime. The juvenile court process typically involves intake, adjudication, and disposition (Champion, Merlo, & Benekos, 2012; Whitehead & Lab, 2012).

Intake   Intake takes place after police referrals to juvenile court and usually involves detaining juveniles during case investigation, filing a petition for a formal court hearing, and dismissing cases altogether. The offense profile of juvenile delinquency cases in 2010, the latest year for which such data are available, shows that status and property offenses accounted for three-fourths of referrals to juvenile court. The remaining referrals involved crimes against persons, two-thirds of which were minor assaults (Puzzanchera & Hockenberry, 2013).

Adjudication   Adjudication, which takes place after intake, is the legal process that judges conduct in juvenile court with assistance from probation officers. If the judge determines that the allegations in a petition are proved, the juvenile for whom the petition was filed is considered to be formally delinquent (Champion, Merlos, & Benekos, 2012).

Disposition   Disposition follows adjudication and is the legal process by which judges decide how best to resolve delinquency cases. Juvenile court judges choose from a wide array of dispositions, from dismissing the case to committing the juvenile to a secure juvenile correctional facility (Champion, Merlo, & Benekos, 2012).

Juvenile Corrections

Juvenile corrections can be divided into community corrections and institutional corrections. **Community corrections** can be defined as all correctional activities in the community. Probation is the most widely used form of community juvenile corrections. Juvenile probation is administered by county juvenile probation departments. Under this type of probation, juveniles are assigned a probation officer with whom they are required to meet on a regular basis to review their case and ensure that they are following all of the conditions in the probation agreement. (Siegel & Welsh, 2014).

EP 2.1.3b

Juvenile correctional institutions range from short-term, nonsecure facilities serving a limited geographic area to long-term, highly secure facilities serving large geographic areas. (Siegel & Welsh, 2014):

- *Foster homes* are used at all stages in the juvenile justice process.
- *Shelters* (nonsecure residential facilities) hold juveniles who are temporarily assigned to them, usually in lieu of detention or returning home following arrest, or after adjudication while awaiting more permanent placement.
- *Group homes* (nonsecure, relatively open, community-based facilities) hold primarily juveniles who have been adjudicated as delinquent. Larger and less family-like than foster homes, group homes allow more independent living in a more permanent setting. Residents of group homes usually attend school—in the home or in the community—or work. Group homes provide

support and structure in unrestrictive settings that facilitate reintegration into the community.

- *Halfway houses* (large, nonsecure residential centers) provide both a place to live and a range of personal and social services that emphasize normal group living, attending school, securing employment, working with parents to resolve problems, and participating in community events.
- *Ranches and camps* (nonsecure facilities, almost always located in rural and remote areas) emphasize outside activity, self-discipline, and the development of vocational and interpersonal skills. Juveniles adjudicated as delinquent usually are placed in camps and ranches as an alternative to more secure facilities such as training schools.
- *Detention centers* (temporary custodial facilities) are secure institutions that hold juveniles both before and after adjudication.
- *Training schools* house the most serious delinquents—those who are security risks, those who have substantial prior records, and those who have exhausted other juvenile court dispositions.

Dual System of Justice

Every jurisdiction in the United States operates separate systems for responding to juvenile and adult criminal behavior. Each system is governed by a different set of laws and procedures. Juvenile courts typically handle cases for individuals under age 18 and adult criminal courts handle the others. This **dual system of justice** received considerable scrutiny in the mid-2000s as a result of an increase in serious youthful offenders, with calls for certifying such offenders as adults and remanding them to adult prisons (Agnew & Brezina, 2011; Chambliss, 2011). The controversy over the certification of juvenile offenders as adults has subsided somewhat, as the proportion of serious and violent crimes committed by youth has steadily declined over the past several years as well as strides made by juvenile justice advocates to abolish the practice (Puzzanchera & Hockenberry, 2013). The current emphasis in the juvenile justice system is on how to prevent crimes committed by youth in the first place or to intervene early with first-time offenders (see section on alternatives to get-tough policies later in this chapter).

Get-Tough Policies   Various get-tough policies aimed at changing the manner in which serious youthful

offenders were treated appeared on the horizon in the late-1990s and early-2000s, in response to what was considered to be an epidemic in serious juvenile crime and violence (Champion, Merlo, & Benekos, 2012; Zimring & Tannenhaus, 2014):

- reducing the juvenile court's maximum age limit from 18 to 16;
- increasing the use of juvenile records, particularly in adult courts, to help identify high-risk offenders and treat them accordingly;
- replacing the juvenile court's rehabilitation philosophy with a policy in which the sentencing objective becomes punishment that fits the crime;
- making mandatory the sentencing of juveniles charged with specific, violent crimes;
- prosecuting juvenile career criminals in adult criminal courts;
- meting out life sentence without the possibility of parole and
- replacing the dual system of justice with a three-track system: a family court for neglected and dependent youths under 14 years of age; a juvenile court for 14- to 18-year-olds whose crimes are not particularly serious; and a criminal court to handle offenders age 18 or older and juveniles whose crimes are serious.

The U.S. Supreme Court ruled in 2012 that mandatory life sentences for offenders under 18 constitute cruel and unusual punishment and are therefore unconstitutional. At the time this text went to press in 2014, 15 states had not yet eliminated this practice because of confusion over the decision, which struck down mandatory life without parole sentences for juveniles, but not all life sentences for these offenders.

Trying and Sentencing Youths as Adults   Since the beginning of the juvenile court system more than 100 years ago, juvenile court judges have had the option to transfer a chronic, violent teen offender to adult criminal court.

EP 2.1.1a

Many states have expanded this practice with broad-based laws that require automatic transfer of juvenile offenders into adult court based on the type of offense or age of the offender, without the benefit of individualized assessment. Box 13.1 provides a synopsis on how a youth ends up in the adult justice system.

Box 13.1 How a Youth Ends Up in the Adult Justice System

Age of Juvenile Court Jurisdiction	These laws determine the age of adulthood for criminal justice purposes. They effectively remove certain age groups from the juvenile court control for all infractions, whether violent or non-violent, and place them within the adult court jurisdiction.
Transfer and Waiver Provisions	These laws allow young people to be prosecuted in adult courts if they are accused of committing certain crimes. A variety of mechanisms exist by which a youth can be transferred to adult court. Most states have transfer provisions, but they vary in how much authority they allow judges and prosecutors to exercise.
Judicial Waiver	This is the most traditional and common transfer and waiver provision. Under judicial waiver laws, the case originates in juvenile court. Under certain circumstances, the juvenile court judge has the authority to waive juvenile court jurisdiction and transfer the case to criminal court. Some states call the process "certification," "remand," or "bind over for criminal prosecution." Others "transfer" or "decline jurisdiction" rather than waiver. State statutes vary in how much guidance they provide judges on the criteria used in determining if a youth's case should be transferred.
Prosecutorial Waiver	These laws grant prosecutors discretion to file cases against young people in either juvenile or adult court. Such provisions are also known as "concurrent jurisdiction," "prosecutorial discretion," or "direct file."
Reverse Waiver	This is a mechanism to allow youth whose cases are being prosecuted in adult court to be transferred back down to the juvenile court system under certain circumstances.
Statutory or Legislative Exclusion	These laws exclude certain youth from juvenile court jurisdiction entirely by requiring particular types of cases to originate in criminal rather than juvenile court.
"Once an Adult, Always an Adult"	These laws require youth who have been tried as adults to be prosecuted automatically in adult courts for any subsequent offenses.
Blended Sentencing	These laws allow juvenile or adult courts to choose between juvenile and adult correctional sanctions in sentencing certain youth. Courts often will combine a juvenile sentence with a suspended adult sentence, which allows the youth to remain in the juvenile justice system as long as he or she is well-behaved.

SOURCE: Campaign for Social Justice (2012). *Snapshot of national organization's policy statements on youth in the adult criminal justice system.* Washington, DC: Author.

In some states, prosecutors are *required* to file certain juvenile cases in adult courts, at times against their better judgment (Griffin, Addie, Adams, & Firestone, 2011).

The Texas 40-Year Rule

Texas is one of the 15 states that has not yet eliminated the practice of transferring youthful offenders to the adult correctional system. "Determinate sentencing" for juvenile offenders was approved by the Texas legislature in 1987 as an alternative approach to lowering the age at which a juvenile may be certified to stand trial as an adult.

The original law provided that juveniles adjudicated for certain serious, violent offenses could receive a determinate sentence of as long as 30 years. As the law originally was written, the first portion of the sentence was to be served in a Texas Juvenile Justice Department (TJJD) facility. Prior to the youth's 18th birthday, a hearing was to be held before the committing court to determine what would happen next for the youth. There were three outcomes of this hearing:

- Release on parole and continue under TJJD's custody until age 21;
- Discharge from TJJD's jurisdiction; and
- Transfer to the Institutional Division of the Texas Department of Criminal Justice (TDCJ) for the balance of the sentence.

In 1995, the Texas Legislature amended the original law to allow sentences to range from a maximum of 10 years for third-degree felonies to a maximum of 40 years for capital and first-degree felonies. This means that if a juvenile is 15 and is tried as an adult and receives a mandatory 40 year sentence, she or he will be 55 when released from prison. Advocates to change the system suggest that making decisions about sentencing on a case-by-case basis is more humane, as a 40 year sentence is almost like life without parole for a juvenile.

Another concern about placing juveniles in adult prisons is that the services available in the adult criminal justice system are not geared to meet teens' educational, emotional, physical, and social needs. Many youths who end up in the adult criminal justice system come into the system with undiagnosed and untreated mental health disorders that are exacerbated by the stress of being confined, especially with adults (Grigorenko, 2012; Lambie & Randell, 2013; Pfeiffer, 2007; Rosner & Schwartz, 2013). Teenagers in adult institutions are at high risk of being sexually assaulted or beaten by prison staff and are more likely to commit suicide than youths held in a juvenile facility. Box 13.2 contains selected quotes juveniles transferred to adult correctional facilities and the parents of these youths. They were taken from testimony provided before the House Committee on Education and Labor Healthy Families and Communities Subcommittee in 2012 (Campaign for Youth Justice Policy, 2014).

Box 13.2   Quotes Taken from Testimony Provided by Youth and Relatives Before the House Committee on Education and Labor Healthy Families and Communities Subcommittee in 2012

- At the age of sixteen, I got into an argument with my grandma. As she was disciplining me, I attempted to get her off me. I left the house and later on that day she died of a heart attack. I was charged as an adult with causing her death and spent eleven months in the Baltimore City Detention Center. I was forced to shower with a woman twice my age and shamelessly exposed to a squat and cough in front of everyone while menstruating. I was neglected and did not receive the psychological and health care help I needed throughout my stay.
- To get to school we had to walk through a tunnel that went through the adult men's prison. One day the facility went on lock down. We were told to turn our backs and close our eyes. But, in jail you learn to never turn your back or close your eyes. That day, we saw a man get stabbed to death.
- Words can't explain what I went through in the adult system. Tears hardly express the pain and discomfort of being judged as a criminal.
- Some of the cell doors are broken so you are never safe and you can be attacked by other inmates at night.
- People get sick a lot because of spider bites, boils, or breakouts from unsanitary conditions like dirty covers. Things that require medical attention are ignored or left unattended.
- Even now that I am out of adult jail, I feel like I am serving a second sentence. With an adult record, I can't vote and it's hard to get a job. I still have a piece of jail that is going to be part of me for the rest of my life. Every once and awhile I wake up and think I'm still there. There's so much in adult jail that can mess kids up physically and emotionally.
- As Jonathan approached his side of the glass, my husband and I were shocked by what we saw. Jonathan had cuts and bruises all over his face, ears, and head. His hair was shaved off and he had a tattoo under his eye. He was told by the other inmates in the facility he needed the tattoo to survive. I immediately broke down and wept because I was utterly powerless to keep him safe.
- My grandson, whom I will call "D," was sentenced to juvenile life without the possibility of parole, a sentence of six years in a maximum secure-care prison. D had always been physically and emotionally fragile. He was a sensitive child who required protection. Needless to say, maximum security incarceration was not the place for this child.

SOURCE: Youth and relative testimony regarding a child transferred to the adult correctional system. Washington, DC: Campaign for Youth Justice Policy.

Advances in brain research show that the area of the brain that permits anticipation of consequences, consideration of alternatives, planning, setting of long-range goals, and organization of sequential behavior does not fully mature until *well past the age of 18* (National Institute of Mental Health, 2011) Research on the impact on community safety of trying and sentencing youths in adult criminal court reveals that prosecuting juveniles in the adult criminal system actually increases the likelihood that they will re-offend and, upon re-offense, will commit more serious crimes than their counterparts in the juvenile system (Mulvey & Schubert, 2012). Also, the majority of youth who are under age 18 when admitted to the criminal justice system are released to probation before the age of 22. Without age-appropriate services and supports to help them become productive citizens, they return to their communities hardened and angry, with an increased number of criminal skills (Mulvey & Schubert, 2012).

EP 2.1.9b

In *Childhood on Trial: The Failure of Trying and Sentencing Youth in Adult Criminal Court,* the Coalition for Juvenile Justice (2005, p. 4) the following recommendations are given regarding transferring juveniles to the adult criminal system:

- All organizations and individuals invested in child and family health, and community well-being, should adopt a formal position calling on policymakers to revisit and reform state laws that inappropriately send far too many youths under the age of 18 (including first-time and nonviolent offenders) into the adult criminal justice system.
- States must reexamine their practices related to youths sent into the adult criminal court to gain a clear picture of the circumstances and characteristics of youths who are treated like adults.
- Policymakers, law enforcement officers, and justice officials need to take a hard look at whether "adult-time" policies in their jurisdictions truly fulfill the public safety mandate.
- Policymakers and justice administrators cannot continue to use cost savings as the principal rationale for continuing to try and sentence youths in adult criminal court rather than juvenile court.
- Policymakers and juvenile justice professionals should call for changes in state and federal laws to restore the authority of juvenile court judges

to assess a juvenile's fitness for adult court and hold the boundary between childhood and adulthood at age 18.

In a powerful show of unity, 40 national organizations that represent and serve millions of children, youth, and families throughout the United States have made a clear statement of their support for ending the trying and sentencing of minor offenders in adult criminal court by signing the *National Resolution Regarding Trying and Sentencing Youth Offenders in Adult Criminal Court* (see Box 13.3). It will take the collective and sustained effort of organizations such as these to end this unnecessary and harmful practice.

Differential Treatment of Nonwhite Youth in the Justice System

EP 2.1.3b

Several authors have addressed the issue of differential treatment of nonwhite youth in the juvenile system, indicating that their over-representation often reflects questionable actions made at critical points throughout the juvenile justice system (see, for example, Gabbidon & Greene, 2012; Puzzanchera & Hockenberry, 2013; The Sentencing Project, 2014). In what is often referred to as the "cumulative disadvantage," the overrepresentation of nonwhite youth in the juvenile justice system tends to accumulate as youth are processed through the system (Siegel & Welsh, 2014). According to the Campaign for Youth Justice, African American youth receive harsher treatment than white youth at most stages of case processing. Stunningly, African American youth represent over 60% of the youth prosecuted in the adult criminal system and are nine times more likely than white youth to receive an adult prison sentence. Latino youth are 43% more likely than white youth to be transferred to the adult criminal system and 40% more likely than white youth to be admitted to adult prison. Native American youth are 1.5 times more likely than white youth to be transferred to the adult criminal system (Campaign for Youth Justice, 2012). As noted above, these disparities did not appear overnight; they are the result of decades of institutional racism and benign neglect, a "get tough" perspective, poor leadership, and an entrenched bureaucracy with little incentive to change.

The mandate for federal and state governments is resoundingly clear—to do something to eliminate the causes of the differential treatment of nonwhite youth brought about by a broad range of current policies and

Box 13.3   National Resolution Regarding Trying and Sentencing Youth Offenders in Adult Criminal Court

WHEREAS, policies and practices providing "adult time for adult crime" are often harmful—rather than helpful—to community safety, as evidenced by research demonstrating that prosecuting juveniles in the adult criminal system increases rather than decreases the likelihood that they will re-offend, as compared with handling them in the juvenile justice system;

WHEREAS, 75% of youth under age 18 sent to adult facilities will be released by the age of 22 and most will have been denied adequate education, mental health, drug treatment and employment skills training;

WHEREAS, trying and sentencing youth in adult court is not reserved for the most serious, chronic and violent juvenile offenders, but inappropriately includes more than half of the cases involving only nonviolent drug and property crimes.

WHEREAS, there exists serious human rights, as well as physical and emotional health concerns when youth held in adult facilities are sexually assaulted five times more often, commit suicide eight times more often, and are assaulted with a weapon 50% more often than youth held in juvenile facilities;

WHEREAS, there exists serious civil rights concerns given that youth of color are disproportionately represented in cases sent to adult court—as shown in 18 of the largest court jurisdictions where 82% of juvenile cases filed in adult court involved youth of color;

WHEREAS, research continues to establish and reaffirm that the adolescent brain—particularly the part

that makes judgments, reins in impulsive behavior and engages in moral reasoning—is not fully developed until age 19 or 20, laying the foundation for laws that prohibit youth under age 18 from taking on major adult responsibilities such as voting, jury duty, and military service;

WHEREAS, the use of statutes or procedures that automatically exclude youth from the juvenile court without assessment of individual circumstances deny them basic fairness;

WHEREAS, more than 250,000 offenders under the age of 18 are sent each year to adult criminal courts across the United States, including an estimated 218,000 excluded from juvenile court jurisdiction, not because of the severity of their crimes, nor because they are habitual offenders, but because states have lowered the age of adulthood in the criminal code;

BE IT RESOLVED that the national organizations listed herein will work to build broad acceptance for reform, as well as to create reform, in state policies and practices, so as to significantly reduce the number of youth sent to adult criminal court and to ensure that young offenders are appropriately adjudicated in ways that enhance community safety and vitality.

Source: Coalition for Juvenile Justice. (2003). *Unlocking the future: Detention reform in the juvenile justice system*. Washington, DC: Author.

---

practices, or the criminal justice system will continue to have a negative and disproportionate impact on non-white youth (Walker, Spohn, & DeLone, 2011).

Reform of the Juvenile Justice System

EP 2.1.9b

The seeds of reform of the juvenile justice system were sewn in the late-1990s with implementation of the Juvenile Detention Alternatives Initiative (JDAI), funded through the Annie E. Casey Foundation. This multi-year demonstration project represents a significant step in reducing the negative consequences of involvement with the country's juvenile justice system. The JDAI provides an unprecedented opportunity for jurisdictions across the country to re-shape their youth-detention

policies and practices by eliminating the inappropriate or unnecessary use of secure detention, reducing the incidence of delinquent behavior, redirecting public finances from building new facility capacity to responsible alternative strategies, and improving conditions in secure detention facilities. Currently, JDAI is helping to reform juvenile detention practices in 40 states and 250 jurisdictions across the United States through structured planning, an emphasis on leadership and collaboration, revising ineffective admissions policies and practices, planning and implementing detention alternatives, reducing unnecessary delays in processing of cases, creating strategies for handling difficult populations, and changing roles and relationships among key stakeholders in the juvenile justice system (Annie E. Casey Foundation, 2014).

Several reports on reforming the juvenile justice system in the United States were published by the JDAI, including a report titled *Reducing Racial Disparities in Juvenile Detention* (Annie E. Casey Foundation, 2006). This report includes a synthesis of the experiences (successes as well as failures) of the various sites that participated in the JDAI initiative. These experiences are captured in the following set of 10 "lessons learned:"

1. Without a commitment to juvenile detention reform in general, reducing racial disparities is unlikely.
2. An explicit focus on reducing racial disparities is essential.
3. Reducing racial disparities requires authoritative leadership.
4. Define the problem in terms that can be changed.
5. Emphasize action, not just discussion or training.
6. Broad, diverse coalitions can facilitate disproportionate minority contact reduction.
7. Individual agencies can make a difference.
8. Keep the police in the work.
9. Data really helps.
10. It *is* possible to reduce racial disparities in juvenile detention (pp. 65–70).

It is hoped that efforts such as the JDAI will encourage others to make significant investments to reduce racial disparities in the country's juvenile justice system and build a brighter future for youths who come into contact with that system.

The Role of the Federal Government in Juvenile Justice Reform

Needed Changes in Policy Outlook

A 2012 report by the Federal Advisory Committee on Juvenile Justice addresses the role of the federal government in reforming the juvenile justice system. Swings in federal policy outlook include (p. 2):

- An emphasis on rehabilitation vs. punishment;
- Service supports and interventions vs. criminalizing criminal behavior;
- Family- and community-connected care vs. institutional care; and
- National policy that builds on state and local innovations vs. national policy that takes the lead and spurs states forward.

Policy Innovations Recent policy innovations in juvenile justice system reform include prohibiting of transfer of juveniles to adult criminal court; reclassifying status offense cases as nonoffenses; prohibiting isolation, seclusion, and constraint in schools; expanding federal support for detention reform; creating a hotline for families and others to report dangerous or counterproductive conditions in detention and corrections facilities; and prohibiting life without parole sentences for youth under federal jurisdiction (p. 8).

Challenges to Continued Reform Federal agencies responsible for juvenile justice reform face a number of challenges that have the potential for sidetracking or even derailing recent reform gains. These challenges include a seeming lack of political will in Congress to reauthorize the Juvenile Justice and Delinquency Prevention Act of 1974, the single most important piece of federal legislation affecting youth involved with juvenile justice system across the country (reauthorization is currently more than 6 years overdue); the Congressional practice of enacting unfunded mandates; waning support for developing and vetting evidence-based practices; significantly reduced funding for maintaining current programs; and declining interest in eliminating racial and ethnic disparities in the juvenile justice system.

The Role of State and Local Governments in Juvenile Justice Reform

State Governments Increasingly, states have implemented or are in the process of implementing comprehensive juvenile justice reforms in the following areas:

- Improving public safety;
- Eliminating racial and ethnic disparities at all stages of the system;
- Holding offenders accountable for the consequences of their crimes;
- Reallocating spending for expensive facility costs to early intervention, diversion, and community-based programs;
- Enhancing standards for out-of-home placement;
- Implementation of evidence-based programs and services;
- Reducing burdens on taxpayers associated with out-of-home placement; and
- Developing innovative re-entry/aftercare initiatives (Federal Advisory Committee on Juvenile Justice, 2012).

Local Governments   Local governments are focusing their efforts on juvenile justice reform in three areas: alternatives to arrest and detention by holding youth accountable and avoiding the consequences of detention and confinement; supports for youth returning to the community after arrest and detention by enhancing opportunities for work, school, community engagement, and other pro-social activities; and implementation of evidence-based practices that reduce racial and ethnic disparities (National League of Cities, 2014)

Alternatives to Get-Tough Policies

Significant Investments Needed   Several alternatives to get-tough policies aimed at reducing youth crime have been identified. A landmark study spearheaded by the American Youth Policy Forum in collaboration with the Child Welfare League of America, Coalition for Juvenile Justice, National Collaboration for Youth, National Crime Prevention Council, National League of Cities, and National Urban League, which is as relevant today as it was some 15 years ago, identified four areas for which significant investments must be made to effectively reduce juvenile crime in America (Mendel, 2000, pp. 65–69):

EP 2.1.9b

1. *Prevention in early childhood:* home-based visitation services for high-risk families
2. *School-based prevention:* nationally recognized school-based violence and substance-abuse prevention programs that are evidence-based and are implemented with strong training and technical support
3. *Effective child welfare:* increased funding, worker training, and family support services
4. *Intervening with behaviorally troubled children:* family-focused intervention strategies for families with troubled youth.

The study identified a number of strategic action areas considered to offer the most promise for reducing juvenile crime and violence in the United States (see Box 13.4).

Emerging Practices   Below is a list of emerging practices designed to divert youth from detention and incarceration (ACT4 Juvenile Justice, 2014).

- *Evening reporting centers* that are open immediately after school until 9:00 PM or 10:00 PM that allow youth to complete homework, learn life skills, participate in community service, receive meals, and have recreation time. Center staff monitor school attendance and performance, stay in contact with parents, and provide transportation to and from the center;
- *Home detention programs* that require youth to live at home under curfews. Agency staff members visit youth in their homes, in school, and other settings (sometimes several times a day) to ensure they are complying with release requirements, including school attendance and behavior, curfew, abstinence from drugs, and other expectations. Some home detention programs include electronic monitoring;
- *Short-term shelter care* for youth who are not a danger to the community but cannot return home because it is unsafe or adequate supervision will not be provided. These cases are best handled through the child welfare system;
- *Community-based alternatives to secure placement* allow youth to stay close to home and allow families to be more involved in their rehabilitation such as Multisystemic Therapy (MST) for serious youth offenders and Functional Family Therapy (FFT). MST has been shown to reduce recidivism by upward of 70% as well as achieving other positive outcomes. FFT has been shown to reduce recidivism by between 25% and 60%;
- *Pre-trial alternatives to secure placement* ensure that youth comply with conditions of release, do not commit new crimes, and show up for all court dates.

These and similar practices offer great potential for reducing or avoiding the harmful outcomes often associated with detention and incarceration.

Strategies for Preventing Juvenile Crime and Violence or Its Re-Occurrence

Juvenile justice reform advocates from a broad representation of organizations recommend the following strategies for preventing juvenile crime and violence or its re-occurrence. Note the emphasis on connection to community and importance of taking a "wraparound" or "systems of care" approach.

- increased accountability and improved quality assurance in public and private agencies mandated to provide essential resources for infants, toddlers, and school-age children;

Box 13.4   Strategic Action Areas for Reducing Juvenile Crime and Violence in the United States

Action Area	Recommended Actions
End overreliance on corrections and other out-of -home placements	States are encouraged to revise their funding formulas to reward localities for serving youths in their homes and communities whenever possible.
Invest in research-based interventions for juvenile offenders, as well as research-based prevention.	The federal government should invest heavily in the replication and further refinement of proven strategies, as well as in continuing research efforts to develop even better strategies for reducing delinquent conduct by troubled youths. This investment should include funds for training and technical assistance and matching funds for implementation. Both process and outcome evaluations should be required for all funded projects.
Measure results, fund what works, and cut funds to what doesn't work.	Developing new knowledge must be a core goal for all federal spending to reduce juvenile crime and violence. States must provide the leadership necessary to support ongoing data collection and program evaluation, and this should be a national effort.
Engage community partners.	Youths should be reconnected to their communities through innovative, restorative justice initiatives such as family-group conferencing, teen courts, drug courts, and youth aid panels. State and local juvenile justice authorities should increase their efforts in these areas. Juvenile courts and probation agencies should be encouraged or even required to strengthen partnerships with community residents and organizations. Local courts and probation departments should consider funding set aside for contracts with community-based service providers. States should support "systems of care" reforms that reward and support multi-agency partnerships to provide case management and intervention treatment services for delinquent youth. The federal government should expand funding for community mental health services to children with severe emotional problems.
Mobilize whole communities to study, plan, and implement comprehensive strategies for combating youth crime.	Congress should continue to expand funding for comprehensive, community analysis; planning; and mobilization. States should require local jurisdictions to create local policy boards and to develop and submit community plans as a condition for receiving state funds and federal pass-through funds for juvenile justice and delinquency prevention programming.

SOURCE: Mendel, R.A. (2000). *Less hype, more help: Reduce juvenile crime, what works—and what doesn't.* Washington, DC: American Youth Policy Forum (pp. 71–76).

- knowledgeable advocates who are able to help caregivers and adolescents circumvent bureaucratic barriers in agencies mandated to provide essential resources;
- neighborhood-based organizations that provide sustained and comprehensive support and opportunities needed for wholesome youth development from early childhood through the teen years;
- hands-on parenting classes for offenders with babies and young children;
- perinatal care for pregnant offenders;
- comprehensive services for children with incarcerated parents and their caregivers using a "wraparound" or "systems of care" approach;

- referral and advocacy for health, nutrition, and related services for children of parents under juvenile/criminal justice system supervision or conditional release;
- accessible educational services and employment-skills training for young mothers, especially in tandem with developmentally appropriate child care for their infants, toddlers, and preschool-age children;
- recruitment of stable extended family members to care for the children of offenders—especially in cultural groups in which the extended family traditionally has played a key role in child rearing;
- neighborhood-based programs that emphasize provision of basic needs for infants and preschool

children and positive youth development services for older children during non–school hours;

- referrals of 10-, 11-, and 12-year-olds detained by the police to neighborhood organizations that provide sustained activities during non–school hours—the types of support and opportunities from which young adolescents and their families can benefit and that they can enjoy;

- for older teens who have persistently been engaging in delinquent behavior, placement in communal detention settings where they gradually earn status and privileges through vocational achievement and through contributions to the welfare of all in the community— followed by supervised participation in similar activities after they earn their way out of detention.

EP 2.1.9b

Social workers can play a significant role in advancing these strategies, by engaging in a variety of individual roles—as educator, advocate, mediator, researcher, teacher, community organizer, mobilizer, and policy analyst (Kirst-Ashman & Hull, 2013). Solutions also will require a sustained commitment by society at large to ensure that each child born in this country has the opportunity to grow and thrive.

Gang Peace is a youth organization in Massachusetts that works with teens active in gangs or at risk of becoming gang members. The organization helps empower youth to identify positive goals and develop the skills to realize them.

Rehabilitation

EP 2.1.7a

Rehabilitation programs for criminal offenders serve three broad purposes. They:

- replace criminal behaviors with non-criminal behaviors;

- raise awareness of the impact of their behavior on the victims of their crimes and the community in which the crimes were committed; and

- help guard against further criminal activity.

Programs aimed at the rehabilitation of offenders include a wide array of options from which a customized rehabilitation plan can be developed to fit the unique needs of the offender (Day, Casey, Ward, Howells, & Vess, 2010; Gideon & Sung, 2010; Goodman, 2012; Polizzi, Braswell, & Draper, 2013; Van Wormer & Walker, 2012). These options can be organized around the following themes:

- *personal development* (spirituality, cognitive restructuring, anger management, therapeutic counseling, substance abuse education and treatment, mentoring, parenting education, domestic violence awareness);

Kristin Finnegan/Getty Images

- *community re-integration* (basic living/life skills, assistance with finding a job and a place to live, referrals to critical services, victim-offender mediation, re-connecting with children/other family members);
- *education-related* (basic adult education, obtaining a GED, enrolling in community college/trade school); and
- *work-related* (prison industries, work release, vocational training).

Box 13.5 lists the conditions that offender rehabilitation programs must meet to be considered the most successful.

Issues in Rehabilitation

EP 2.1.7a
EP 2.1.8a
EP 2.1.9a

Prison rehabilitation programs have been controversial from their inception. Two primary questions are at the heart of this controversy: *Should* we rehabilitate prisoners? and *Can* we rehabilitate prisoners? Results of studies evaluating the efficacy of offender rehabilitation programs are mixed—if one considers whether the programs actually rehabilitate the offender. However, rehabilitation programs serve purposes other than preparing offenders to work hard and play by the rules when they leave prison. Rehabilitation programs

also keep prisoners busy, and keeping them busy keeps them out of trouble. Finally, rehabilitation programs are viewed as consistent with orderly, safe, and humane confinement (Bottoms, Rex, & Robinson, 2013).

Crime Prevention

In what has become a landmark study, the National Institute of Justice (1998) conducted a systematic review of more than 500 scientific evaluations of crime-prevention practices in the United States. The study revealed that most crime-prevention programs have not yet been evaluated with enough scientific evidence to draw defensible conclusions. The study concluded, however, that enough evidence is available to create provisional lists of what works, what doesn't, and what's promising. Key promising prevention initiatives included the following (pp. 6–12):

In Communities:

- gang offender monitoring by community and probation and police officers
- community-based mentoring by Big Brothers/Big Sisters of America
- community-based after-school recreation programs
- dispersing inner-city public housing residents to scattered-site suburban public housing

---

Box 13.5 Characteristics of Successful Offender Rehabilitation Programs

- The programs use an evidence-based approach;
- The programs address criminogenic needs (factors identified by research as predictors of crime and/or related recidivism such as antisocial personality, family dysfunction, poor self-control, poor problem-solving skills, substance abuse, and lack of employment and employment skills);
- The programs are delivered at the highest level of intensity;
- The programs use positive incentives as well as appropriate sanctions;
- Program staff possess the appropriate education and training;
- Funding for program development and implementation is adequate and consistent;
- The programs are delivered both in the community as well as in the prison setting;
- There is a high level of commitment by staff and administrators to program quality and integrity;
- The programs are routinely evaluated and changes are made to enhance the programs' effectiveness;
- An effective case-management system is used;
- The programs take into consideration any special needs of participants, such as those who are intellectually and mentally challenged; and
- A comprehensive, holistic approach to program planning, implementation, and evaluation is taken.

Source: Center for Evidence-based Corrections. (2006). *Evidence-based practices in corrections: A training manual for California program assessment process (CPAP)*. Irvine, CA: Author.

In Schools:

- schools-within-schools that group students into smaller units
- training or coaching in thinking skills for high-risk youths
- teaching social-competency skills
- communicating and reinforcing clear, consistent norms
- building school capacity to initiate and sustain innovation through organizational-development strategies
- improving classroom management and instructional techniques

In Families:

- battered women's shelters aimed at reducing the rate of repeat victimization for women who take steps to seek help beyond staying in the shelter

In Labor Markets:

- Job Corps (intensive residential training programs for at-risk youth)
- prison-based vocational programs for adult inmates
- enterprise zones with tax-break incentives in areas of extremely high unemployment

By Criminal Justice Agencies After Arrest:

- drug courts that order and monitor a combination of rehabilitation and drug treatment
- intensive supervision and after-care of minor and serious juvenile offenders
- fines for criminal acts in combination with other penalties
- drug treatment in jails followed by urine testing in the community

In Places:

- adding a second clerk to potentially reduce robberies in already-robbed convenience stores
- redesigning the layout of retail stores to reduce shoplifting
- improving training and management of bar and tavern staffs
- metal detectors to reduce weapon carrying in schools
- street closures, barricades, and rerouting

By Police:

- proactive arrests for carrying concealed weapons
- proactive drunk-driving arrests
- **community policing** with meetings to set priorities
- policing with more respect for offenders

- field interrogations of suspicious persons
- mailing arrest warrants to domestic-violence suspects who leave the scene before police arrive
- more police officers in cities.

A number of authors have identified building blocks for successful community **crime prevention** initiatives (see, for example, Cromwell & Birzer, 2013; Kleiman, 2010; Tilley, 2011):

EP 2.1.9b

- community-based partnerships that draw upon the knowledge and experience of all stakeholders;
- programs that build community capacity to address local problems;
- integrated programs that nurture families and communities;
- comprehensive efforts that support parenting, prevention of child abuse and domestic violence, victim assistance, child-support enforcement, truancy, conflict resolution, youth mentoring, teen-pregnancy prevention, and other child-development and supervision programs;
- knowledge base of best practices to share across disciplines and communities; and
- process and outcome evaluations of community-based crime-prevention efforts.

The U.S. criminal justice system is evaluated not only by its capacity to prevent and contain crime but also by the justice meted out by the system. Its dual responsibility to protect the citizenship rights of criminals as well as those of their victims constitutes the core of the criminal justice system. Law-abiding citizens want to be protected from criminal behavior but also want protection from unwarranted intrusion of the criminal justice system into their private lives. The duality of these demands imposes costs and constraints on police, court officers, and prison and parole officials. In the final analysis, then, law-and-order proponents and civil libertarians want the same things. So the policy problem lies in emphasis and balance, and the latter seldom seems to exist.

Views of Criminal Behavior

A number of views of criminal behavior have been set forth to explain why people commit crimes (see, for example, Barkan, 2011; Conklin, 2012; Hickey, 2012; Siegel, 2012). The **etiology of crime** can be viewed as

EP 2.1.3a

psychologically aberrant behavior, or socially induced behavior, or a consequence of rational thought in which criminals see crime as just another way to make a living, or as a complex interactive process of an individual's personal characteristics and the many factors that constitute his or her environment.

Psychological Views of the Criminal Personality

EP 2.1.7a

One school of psychological thought suggests that criminals differ from noncriminals in some fundamental way—other than the obvious one of having been convicted. Over the years the distinguishing trait has been proposed to reside in the body or head shape, skull size, chromosome structure, specific patterns of response to projective tests, or the complex labeling process of psychiatric diagnosis. All of the psychological/physiological attempts to establish a criminal type demonstrate a circular reasoning process. The notion of a criminal type brings a kind of satisfaction because crime policy then becomes, simply, segregating criminals from the rest of society.

A second psychological interpretation of the etiology of crime is only slightly more sophisticated. Crime is seen simply as a manifestation of a compulsion derived from unresolved conflicts between the superego (Freud's personality component that serves as one's conscience), and the id (Freud's personality component that serves as one's free spirit). Someone with a criminal personality—by definition a defective ego—is unable to overcome the desire to defy social taboos, yet the conflict is reflected in an unconscious desire to be caught.

Anecdotal evidence suggests that some criminals do operate this way. They may deliberately, albeit unconsciously, leave the clues that lead to their arrests. Were it not for the seriousness of the incidents, this behavior often would be truly comic. One young criminal brought a pair of slacks to the cleaners and, after being presented with the claim check, pulled a gun and robbed the attendant. He returned 3 days later with the stub of the claim check to pick up his slacks and was patient enough to wait when the same attendant went to retrieve them. The young man waited calmly until the police came and arrested him. Another pair of criminals left the motor running in the getaway car, but because they had failed to check the fuel gauge before the robbery, their car ran out of gas while they were holding up the bank.

A more sophisticated psychosocial theory also contains in its assumptions the prescription for a proper anticrime policy. As the theory goes, criminal behavior is learned. The type of criminal behavior that individuals learn is related to their socioeconomic status in society. That is, certain classes of persons learn different criminal ways. The processes involved in learning criminal behavior are the same as those in learning other behavior that entail learning a technique as well as values.

This psychological view of criminality is less encompassing than the simpler etiological–psychological views of crime. It does not attempt to explain which people will commit crimes—an impossible task—but, rather, why and how those who have committed crimes are systematically different from those who do not.

Social Views of Criminal Behavior

EP 2.1.1a

Another perspective suggests that crime is not caused by individual physical or mental deficiencies but, instead, by societal breakdown. Proponents of this perspective identify industrialization, racism, poverty, and family breakdown as major factors in creating social disorganization, and, in turn, increases in crime. Sociological inquiries into crime frequently are based on statistical correlates, such as the analysis of traditional family or variations in unemployment and crime rates. The more sophisticated inquiries fall short of establishing a direct path of causation. Crime is seen as a result of many factors within the context of the offender's society. Street crime and white-collar crime are viewed as very different expressions of social maladjustment. Regardless of specifics, the essence of the sociological perspective is that general **deterrence factors** (things that are likely to stop people from committing crimes), rehabilitation, and reeducation of offenders constitute the best safeguards against repeated crimes.

The social view of crime advocates a criminal justice system that offers a variety of social intervention strategies. One of these—of particular importance to social work practitioners—is collaboration between social workers and police officers at the earliest intervention point. When the suspected offender is in police custody initially, social workers and police officers are expected to concur on the case disposition. The argument is made that, despite their disparate professional orientations, social workers and police officers alike are experienced in dealing with troubled people at crisis points in their lives. Individualization of response is considered essential. No one sociological perspective is seen as dominant. Consider, for example, the following typology of crime:

- violent personal crimes (e.g., murder);
- sexual offenses;
- occupational/white-collar crimes;
- political crimes;
- organized crimes;
- professional crimes; and
- crimes without victims.

Each of these types of crime has its own sociological pattern, and each places a unique set of demands on the criminal justice system.

Economic Rationale of Crime

EP 2.1.7a

A final perspective is that crime is simply another form of entrepreneurship that happens to be illegal. Proponents of this view see the criminal as an amoral person who calculates the costs and benefits of a crime, much as a businessperson calculates the costs and benefits of opening a new store. In the economic formulation, potential criminals assess the costs of getting caught and sentenced against the probable benefits of completing the crime successfully. Depending on the outcomes of their calculations, they decide to be criminal or not. People who are not poor commit fewer crimes because the costs of going to prison (in lost wages, deprivation of status, amenities of life, and so forth) are too high. If we subscribe to this theoretical perspective, all we need to do to contain crime is to increase the probability of being caught, sentenced, and sent to jail. This theory has little or no empirical evidence as a valid basis to support it.

Each of these views of crime—and we have described only three—provides a policy paradigm for the criminal justice system, from the role of the arresting officer to the responsibilities of the parole and probation workers. One's beliefs about *why* some people commit crimes are the obvious source of ideas about how to contain crime.

Social workers would probably not agree completely with any of these three views. However, the ecological/systems framework incorporates pieces of each. This framework can be used to help understand why some people may be more at risk to commit crimes than others. Physiological and psychological factors, family structure and support, and social factors such as poverty, racism, and the availability of needed community

resources must all be considered. Effective prevention and intervention programs must take all of these factors into account.

Program Alternatives

EP 2.1.9b

For every 36 crimes committed, one person is sentenced to prison. Only one crime in every four that are reported results in an arrest of a suspected offender. There is roughly one arraignment for every three arrests, and although nearly 95% of all criminal arraignments result in criminal conviction or guilty pleas, only one in three ends up in a prison term (Schmalleger & Smykla, 2012). These numbers mislead as much as they reveal, because tracking a given crime (acknowledging that crimes are greatly underreported) to a specific sentence is a Herculean statistical task. One thing that is unambiguous in these numbers is the enormous amount of discretion operating within the criminal justice system. Figure 13.1, presented earlier, portrays the complex pathways in the criminal justice system. Each new stage (represented by the rectangles) signifies an opportunity for dropping out of the criminal justice system. Only a small percentage of all crimes results in criminal convictions.

The U.S. criminal justice system has largely British roots, but it includes some innovations that are unique to the United States. These innovations are those in which social work is involved most explicitly: probation, parole, and juvenile procedures. The U.S. system perhaps is more fragmented than the criminal justice system in most countries. The criminal justice system can be seen first as composed of three parts—police, courts, and correctional arrangements. With federal, state, and local involvement at each level and separation into adult and juvenile divisions, a multipartite system emerges. More dramatically, no subsystem views the criminal problem from a total perspective. Each is busily resolving its own problems. The result is a highly fractured system that is difficult to describe, evaluate, or control.

Despite the lack of cohesion and the internal tensions, actions within one system component clearly reverberate throughout the entire system. "Success" or "failure" in one part may generate significant problems for another part. If state and local police, by virtue of more personnel or better investigation, were to apprehend 25% more offenders, both the courts and the correctional system would have to absorb more defendants and prisoners. If the prison system were to release a higher proportion of recidivists, police and the courts would have to deal with a larger population of criminals. But overcrowded prisons generate backups in local jails. All elements of the criminal justice system must respond to the factors in the larger society that accelerate criminal behavior. Because the criminal justice system is not examined or funded as an entity, each component accepts and adopts its own strategies. The fundamental adaptation for one part often produces problems for another entity within the system.

The Role of Social Work in the Criminal Justice System

EP 2.1.1a
EP 2.1.9b

The role of the social work community in the criminal justice system has been relegated almost exclusively to the correctional components of the system. Only recently have police agencies begun to use social workers (see below). These social work functions have low priority in law enforcement budgets and often fall quickly to budget cuts. Adult courts have made relatively little use of professional social workers, with the notable exception of adult drug courts, in which social workers play a key role in assessing individuals referred to the program. Therefore, social workers most frequently work in the criminal justice system in juvenile courts, rehabilitation centers, prisons, and parole programs. These uses of social workers, however, should be assessed in a system wide context.

Some law enforcement officials suggest that the most police calls are family- or crisis-oriented rather than crime-related. When crimes occur, they frequently are the result of family problems. Many homicides, for example, are perpetrated by family members rather than by someone outside the family. Increasingly, crime is associated with other social problems, such as alcohol or drug abuse.

Social workers play various roles in law enforcement agencies. Many departments have crisis intervention teams, consisting of police officers as well as social workers who respond to domestic-violence calls or calls to assist victims of rape or other violent crimes. Some law enforcement agencies have established special victim-assistance programs. Often staffed by social workers, these programs provide follow-up services to victims of crime, such as child and family counseling, support groups, information and referral, and case management.

They also help victims locate emergency funding, shelter, employment, counseling, and other needed services.

Many police departments have special child-abuse or sex-crimes units, which sometimes include social workers on their staffs. The social workers assist in investigating reported cases, interviewing children and other individuals involved, contacting child welfare departments and hospitals, and arranging for emergency services when needed. A number of police departments also hire social workers to work in youth programs in a variety of roles such as operating inner-city recreation programs and managing dropout-prevention programs in the public schools in which the social workers provide counseling and drug and alcohol education, and serve as positive law enforcement role models to youths at risk for becoming involved in crime.

The role of the social worker in prison and prison life is peripheral. The social worker most likely is involved only when convicts enter or leave prison. The classification and assignment process at the entry point is influenced heavily by social work practice. The pardon and parole recommendation also is influenced by social workers. Probation or parole officers often have a bachelor's of social work (BSW) degree, and they help youth and adults learn new skills and behaviors that will deter them from committing additional crimes and recommending stricter penalties to the court if they violate probation or parole. Others work in youth correction facilities, including halfway houses and community-based programs. Although social services in prisons for problems such as substance abuse are limited, some BSW graduates work within prisons as well.

Summary

In the history of crime and punishment, reform has always been just beyond the horizon. This chapter paints a dreary picture of practice and current procedures. Police practices do not deter crime, the courts do not dispense justice, the corrections system does not correct, and the parole system does not facilitate ex-prisoners' reentry into society as law-abiding citizens. Part of the problem is that while large sums of money are spent, the emphasis has historically been on building more prisons and jails to house criminals rather than spending that money on crime-prevention efforts. As pointed out in this chapter, things have started to change in this regard as states face severe crowding in existing prisons, coupled with budget shortfalls that prevent them from expanding existing prisons or building new ones.

Funds alone are not the problem. Despite a considerable and growing body of knowledge of what works and what does not work in police, court, and correctional settings, insufficient attention is directed to integration within the system. Each unit of the system seeks to improve its operation and to clarify its mission, but at the expense of other components within the system. More effective integration of police, court, and prison practices is required.

Failure of the criminal justice system also stems from uncertainty about what it is expected to deliver: Is it safe streets, a just system, effective rehabilitation, or simple containment? Effective policies require clarity, choice, commitment, and closure. The segmented structure of the criminal justice system precludes all of these. As a consequence, during some periods, society throws money at aspects of the overall problem; during other periods it funds other aspects (Messner & Rosenfeld, 2012). Clearly, careful diagnosis and prescription are needed.

Competency Notes

EP 2.1.1a: Advocate for client access to the services of social work (pp. 423, 434, 436). Social workers in the juvenile and criminal justice systems advocate for access to services for clients and their families.

EP 2.1.3a: Distinguish, appraise, and integrate multiple sources of knowledge, including research-based knowledge and practice wisdom (p. 433). Social workers in the juvenile and criminal justice systems distinguish, appraise, and integrate multiple sources of knowledge, including research-based knowledge, and practice wisdom in their work with clients/client systems.

EP 2.1.3b: Analyze models of assessment, prevention, intervention, and evaluation (pp. 415–417, 421–422, 426). Social workers in the juvenile and criminal justice systems analyze and adapt models of assessment, prevention, intervention, and evaluation in their work with clients and their families.

EP 2.1.7a: Use conceptual frameworks to guide the process of assessment, intervention, and evaluation (pp. 410–414, 421, 431–432, 434–435). Social workers in the juvenile and criminal justice systems use the ecological/systems and other conceptual frameworks to guide the processes of assessment, intervention, and evaluation in their work with clients/client systems.

EP 2.1.7b: Critique and apply knowledge to understand person and environment (p. 410). Social workers in the juvenile and criminal justice systems use knowledge gathered from clients and the social systems within which their clients interact to provide them with appropriate services and programs.

EP 2.1.8a: Analyze, formulate, and advocate for policies that advance social well-being (p. 432). Social workers in the criminal and juvenile justice systems analyze, formulate, and advocate for justice policies that advance social well-being.

EP 2.1.9a: Continuously discover, appraise, and attend to changing locales, populations, scientific and technological developments, and emerging social trends to provide relevant services (p. 432). Social workers in the juvenile and criminal justice systems pay careful attention to contexts that impact their clients and the delivery of social services.

EP 2.1.9b: Provide leadership in promoting sustainable changes in service delivery and practice to improve the quality of social services (pp. 426–427, 429, 431, 433, 435–436). Social workers provide leadership in promoting sustainable changes in service delivery and practice within the juvenile and criminal justice systems to improve the quality of social services provided to clients and their families.

Key Terms

The terms below are defined in the Glossary.

adjudication	intake
appellate courts	intermediate
community corrections	punishments
community policing	juvenile correctional
courts	institutions
crime	juvenile courts
crime prevention	juvenile delinquency
criminal codes	lower criminal courts
criminal justice system	mental health courts
deterrence factors	plea bargaining
disposition	probation
drug courts	problem-solving courts
dual system of justice	recidivism
etiology of crime	rehabilitation
full enforcement	selective enforcement
incarceration	trial courts

Discussion Questions

1. Compare policy issues between the criminal justice system and the juvenile justice system. What are some of the policy dilemmas unique to the juvenile justice system?
2. Which of the three views of crime, if any, is most consistent with social work perspectives?
3. Discuss the relationships between crime and other social problems.
4. Compare differences in treatment in the criminal and juveniles justice systems between persons who are white and persons who are not white. What are some of the reasons for the racial/ethnic disparities?
5. If systems integration is the central problem of the criminal justice system, how can the contemporary social worker further integration?
6. It has been said that prisons have become today's mental health institutions. Discuss some of the reasons why this is the case and identify solutions to address this problem.
7. Identify possible differences in worldviews of social workers and others working in the criminal justice field, and discuss strengths and problems that might arise in work settings or collaborative efforts because of those differences.

On the Internet

http://www.aecf.org
http://www.nij.gov
http://www.vera.org
http://www.sentencingproject.org
http://www.ojp.usdoj.gov/bjs
http://www.fbi.gov/ucr/ucr.htm
http://ojjdp.ncjrs.gov

References

Abadinsky, H. (2014). *Law and justice: An introduction to the American legal system* (7th ed.). Upper Saddle River, NJ: Prentice-Hall.

ACT4 Juvenile Justice. (2014). *Fact sheet: Community-based and home-based alternatives to incarceration.* Washington, DC: Author. Retrieved on June 22, 2014, from http://www.cclp.org/documents/JJDPA/Community_Based_Alternatives_Fact_Sheet.pdf

Agnew, R., & Brezina, T. (2011). *Juvenile delinquency: Causes and control* (4th ed.). New York: Oxford University Press.

Alarid, L. F. (2014). *Community-based corrections* (10th ed.). Stamford, CT: Cengage Learning.

Amnesty International. (2012). *Death penalty facts.* Washington, DC: Author.

Annie E. Casey Foundation. (2006). *Reducing racial disparities in juvenile detention.* Baltimore, MD: Author. Retrieved September 6, 2010, from http://www.aecf.org/initiatives/jdai

Annie E. Casey Foundation. (2014). *The JDAI story: Building a better juvenile detention system.* Baltimore, MD: Author. Retrieved on June 22, 2014, from http://www.aecf.org/m/resourcedoc/AECF-TheJDAYIStoryOverview-1999.pdf

Barkan, S. E. (2011). *Criminology: A sociological understanding* (5th ed.). Upper Saddle River, NJ: Prentice-Hall.

Berman, H. J., & Saliba, S. N. (2009). *The nature and functions of law* (7th ed.). Eagan, MN: West.

Bottoms, A., Rex, S., & Robinson, G. (Eds.). (2013). *Alternatives to prison.* New York: Willan/Routledge.

Brooks, T. (Ed.). (2014). *Crime and punishment: Critical essays in legal philosophy.* Burlington, VT: Ashgate.

Bureau of Justice Statistics. (2013a). *Correctional populations in the United States, 2013.* Washington, DC: Author. Retrieved June 19, 2014 from http://bjs.ojp.usdoj.gov/content/pub/pdf/cpus12.pdf

Bureau of Justice Statistics. (2013b). *Probation and parole in the United States, 2012.* Washington, DC: Author. Retrieved June 19, 2014 from http://bjs.ojp.usdoj.gov/content/pub/pdf/ppus11.pdf

California Department of Corrections and Rehabilitation. (2013). *An examination of offenders released from state prison in the first-year of Public Safety Realignment.* Sacramento, CA: Author. Retrieved June 19, 2014 from http://www.cdcr.ca.gov/Adult_Research_Branch/Research_Documents/Realignment_1_Year_Report_12-23-13.pdf

Campaign for Youth Justice. (2012). *Key facts: Youth in the justice system.* Washington, DC: Author.

Center for Community Corrections. (2014). *What is an intermediate punishment?* Washington, DC: Author. Retrieved June 19, 2014 from http://centerforcommunitycorrections.org/?page_id=35

Center for Evidence-based Corrections. (2006). *Evidence-based practices in corrections: A training manual for California program assessment process (CPAP).* Irvine, CA: Author.

Chambliss, W. (Ed.). (2011). *Juvenile crime and justice.* Thousand Oaks, CA: Sage.

Champion, D., Merlo, A., & Benekos, P. (2012). *The juvenile justice system: Delinquency, processing, and the law* (7th ed.). Upper Saddle River, NJ: Prentice-Hall.

Coalition for Juvenile Justice. (2003). *Unlocking the future: Detention reform in the juvenile justice system*. Pittsburgh: Author.

Coalition for Juvenile Justice. (2005). *Childhood on trial: The failure of trying and sentencing youth in adult criminal court*. Pittsburgh: Author.

Coalition for Juvenile Justice. (2010). *Trying and sentencing youth in adult criminal court*. Washington, DC: Author.

Conklin, J. E. (2012). *Criminology* (11th ed.). Upper Saddle River, NJ: Prentice-Hall.

Cromwell, P., & Birzer, M. (Eds.). (2013). *In their own words: Criminals on crime* (6th ed.). New York: Oxford University Press.

Day, A., Casey, S., Ward, T., Howells, K., & Vess, J. (2010). *Transitions to better lives: Offender readiness and rehabilitation*. New York: Willan/Routledge.

Death Penalty Information Center. (2014a). *Race of death row inmates executed since 1976*. Retrieved from http://www.deathpenaltyinfo.org/race-death-row-inmates-executed-1976

Death Penalty Information Center. (2014b). *States with and without the death penalty*. Retrieved from http://www.deathpenaltyinfo.org/states-and-without-death-penalty/

Denno, D. (forthcoming). Lethal Injection Secrecy Post-*Baze*. *The Georgetown Law Journal*, 102.

Elrod, P., & Ryder, R. S. (2014). *Juvenile justice: A social, historical and legal perspective* (4th ed.). Sudbury, MA: Jones & Bartlett.

Federal Advisory Committee on Juvenile Justice. (2012). *Federal policy trends in juvenile justice reform*. Washington, DC: Coalition for Juvenile Justice.

Gabbidon, S. L., & Greene, H. T. (2012). *Race and crime* (3rd ed.). Thousand Oaks, CA: Sage.

Gideon, L., & Sung, H. (2010). *Rethinking corrections: Rehabilitation, reentry, and reintegration*. Thousand Oaks, CA: Sage.

Goodman, A. (2012). *Rehabilitating and resettling offenders in the community*. New York: Wiley-Blackwell.

Griffin, P., Addie, S., Adams, B., & Firestone, K. (2011). *Trying juveniles as adults: An analysis of state transfer laws and reporting*. Washington, DC: U.S. Department of Justice Office of Justice Programs.

Grigorenko, E. (Ed.). (2012). *Handbook of juvenile forensic psychology and psychiatry*. New York: Springer.

Hammond, S. (2007). *Mental health needs of juvenile offenders*. Washington, DC: National Conference of State Legislatures.

Hanser, R. D. (2013). *Community corrections* (2nd ed.). Thousand Oaks, CA: Sage.

Hebenton, B., & Jou, S. (2014). *Comparative research in crime and punishment*. New York: Palgrave Macmillan.

Hickey, T. (2012). *Taking sides: Clashing views in crime and criminology* (10th ed.). New York: McGraw-Hill/Dushkin.

Juvenile Law Center. (2014). *Youth in the adult system*. Philadelphia, PA: Author. Retrieved June 21, 2014 from http://www.jlc.org/current-initiatives/promoting=fairness-courts/youth-adult-system

Kirst-Ashman, K., & Hull, G. H. (2013). *Understanding generalist practice* (4th ed.).Stanford, CVT: Cengage Learning.

Kleiman, M. A. (2010). *When brute force fails: How to have less crime and less punishment*. Princeton, NJ: Princeton University Press.

Lambie, I., & Randell, I. (2013). The impact of incarceration on juvenile offenders. *Clinical Psychology Review*, 33(2013), 448–459.

Levs, J. (2013). *Innocent man: How inmate Michael Morton lost 25 years of his life*. Atlanta, GA: CNN. Retrieved from http://www.cnn.com/2013/12/04/justice/exonerated-prisoner-update-michael-morton/

Mendel, R. A. (2000). *Less hype, more help: Reduce juvenile crime, what works—and what doesn't*. Washington, DC: American Youth Policy Forum.

Messner, S., & Rosenfeld, R. (2012). *Crime and the American dream* (5th ed.). Stanford, CT: Cengage Learning.

Mulvey, E., & Schubert, C. (2012). *Transfer of juveniles to adult court: Effects on broad policy in one court* (Juvenile Justice Bulletin NCJ 232932). Washington, DC: Office of Juvenile Justice and Delinquency Prevention.

National Institute of Justice. (1998). *Preventing crime: What works, what doesn't, what's promising*. Washington, DC: Author. Retrieved September 6, 2010, from http://www.ojp.usdoj.gov/nij

National Institute of Mental Health. (2011). *The teen brain: Still under construction* (Publication No. 11-4829). Bethesda, MD: Author.

National League of Cities. (2014). *Juvenile justice reform.* Washington, DC: Author. Retrieved from June 22, 2014 from http://www.nlc.org/find-city-solutions/institute-for-youth-educationandfamilioes/at-risk-youth/jjr

Office of Justice Programs. (2014). *Drug courts.* Downloaded on June 25, 2014 from http://www.ncjrs.gov/pdffiles1/nij/238527.pdf

Office of Juvenile Justice and Delinquency Prevention. (2014, June 17). Smart on juvenile justice: A comprehensive strategy to juvenile justice reform. *Youth Today.* Washington, DC: Author.

Pfeiffer, M. B. (2007). *Crazy in America: The hidden tragedy of our criminalized mentally ill.* New York: Basic Books.

Polizzi, D., Braswell, M., & Draper, M. (Eds.). (2013). *Transforming corrections: Humanistic approaches to corrections and offender treatment.* Durham, NC: Carolina Academic Press.

Puzzanchera, C., & Hockenberry, S. (2013). *Juvenile court statistics 2010.* Washington, DC: Author. Retrieved June 21, 2014 from http://www.ojjdp.gov/ojstatbb/ncjda/pdf/jcs2010.pdf

Rosner, R., & Schwartz, H. (Eds.). (2013). *Juvenile psychiatry and the law.* New York: Springer.

Samaha, J. (2005). *Criminal justice* (7th ed.). Belmont, CA: Wadsworth/Thomson.

Schmalleger, F. (2013). *Criminal justice: A brief introduction* (10th ed.). Upper Saddle River, NJ: Prentice-Hall.

Schmalleger, F., & Smykla, J. O. (2010). *Corrections in the 21st century* (6th ed.). New York: McGraw-Hill.

The Sentencing Project. (2014). *Disproportionate minority contact in the juvenile justice system.* Washington, DC: Author. Retrieved June 21, 2014 from http://www.sentencingproject.org/doc/publications/jj_disproportionate%20minority20contact.pdf

Siegel, L. J. (2012). *Criminology: Theories, patterns, and typologies* (11th ed.). Stanford, CT: Cengage Learning.

Siegel, L. J., & Welsh, B. C. (2013). *Juvenile delinquency: The core.* Stanford, CT: Cengage Learning.

Siegel, L. J., & Welsh, B.C. (2014). *Juvenile delinquency: Theory, practice and law* (12th ed.). Stanford, CT: Cengage Learning.

Stern, M., & Axinn, J. (2012). *Social welfare: A history of the American response to need* (8th ed.). Boston: Pearson.

Tannenhaus, D. (2011). *The constitutional rights of children: In re Gault and juvenile justice.* Lawrence, KS: University Press of Kansas.

Texas Juvenile Justice Department. (2014). *Sentenced offenders.* Retrieved June 25, 2014 from http://www.tjjd.texas.gov/a/sentenced_offenders.aspx

Tilley, N. (Ed.). (2011). *Handbook of crime prevention and community safety.* New York: Willan/Routledge.

Urban Institute. (2012). *Criminal justice interventions for offenders with mental illness: Evaluation of mental health courts in Bronx and Brooklyn, New York (Final Report).* Washington, DC: Author.

Van Wormer, K., & Walker, L. (2012). *Restorative justice today: practical applications.* Thousand Oaks, CA: Sage.

Vera Institute of Justice. (2012). *The price of prisons: What incarceration costs taxpayers.* New York: Author. Retrieved June 20, 2014 from http://www.vera.org/sites/default/files/resources/downloads/the-price-of-prisons-40-facty-sheets-updated-72012.pdf

Walker, S., Spohn, C., & DeLone, M. (2011). *The color of justice: Race, ethnicity, and crime in America* (5th ed.). Stanford, CT: Cengage Learning.

Whitehead, J., & Lab, S. (2012). *Juvenile justice: An introduction* (7th ed.). New York: Anderson/Reed-Elsevier.

Wilson, J., & Petersillia, J. (Eds.). (2011). *Crime and public policy.* New York: Oxford University Press.

Zimring, F., & Tannenhaus, D. (Eds.). (2014). *Choosing the future on American juvenile justice.* New York: New York University Press.

Suggested Readings

Bartollas, C., & Miller, S. (2010). *Juvenile justice in America* (6th ed.). Upper Saddle River, NJ: Prentice-Hall.

Beckett, K., & Herbert, S. (2011). *Banished: The new social control in America.* New York: Oxford University Press.

Cole, G. F., & Gertz, M. G. (2012). *The criminal justice system: Politics and policies* (10th ed.). Stanford, CT: Cengage Learning.

Cole, G. F., Smith, C. E., & DeJong, C. (2013). *Criminal justice in America* (7th ed.). Stanford, CT: Cengage Learning.

Hunter, R. D., & Barker, T. D. (2010). Police community nity relations and the administration of justice (8th ed.). Upper Saddle River, NJ: Prentice-Hill.

Johnstone, G. (Ed.). (2013). *A restorative justice reader* (2nd ed.). New York: Willan/Routledge.

Pollock, J. M. (2013). *Ethical dilemmas and decisions in criminal justice* (8th ed.). Stanford, CT: Cengage Learning.

Samaha, J. (2011). *Criminal procedure* (8th ed.). Belmont, CA: Wadsworth.

Samaha, J. (2013). *Criminal law* (11th ed.). Stanford, CT: Cengage Learning.

Scott, E. S., & Steinberg, L. (2010). *Rethinking juvenile justice*. Cambridge, MA: Harvard University Press.

Taylor, R., & Fritsch, E. (2014). *Juvenile justice: Policies, programs, and practices* (4th ed.). Columbus, OH: McGraw Hill.

Umbreit, M., & Peterson, M. (2010). *Restorative justice dialogue: An essential guide for research and practice.* New York: Springer.

Van Ness, D. W. (2014). *Restoring justice: An introduction to restorative justice* (5th ed.). Southington, CT: Anderson.

CHAPTER 14

Social Work Contexts: Rural and Urban Settings and Environmentalism

Joe and Linda McDowell live on a 160-acre farm in southern Missouri. Joe inherited this farm from his father. His grandfather originally obtained the farm in the early 1900s, and three generations of McDowells have eked out their living on this farm and raised their families there. Joe and Linda both dropped out of high school in the 10th grade and were married on Linda's 18th birthday. They now have four children: Tommy, 9; Grace, 7; Sue, 6; and Jimmy, 4.

Over the past few years, the McDowells have had increasing difficulty producing farm products sufficient to meet the family's basic needs. They are heavily in debt for farm equipment loans and owe back taxes on the farm. They find themselves unable to compete with large commercial farming operations.

The children are attending school sporadically, and they do not wear clothing appropriate to the weather (a luxury the McDowells cannot afford). Tommy has severe dental problems. Linda's health problems have limited her ability to help with the crops. Living 85 miles from a small city has not allowed Joe to try to supplement the family's income through gainful employment, and, even if he could locate a job, he would be able to earn only minimum wages because of his limited skills.

Joe and Linda are deeply invested emotionally in their farm, its family traditions, and the rural way of life. Considering their indebtedness, the back taxes they owe, and limited opportunity to make their farming operations productive, they likely will lose the farm through foreclosure. Joe and Linda worry about their future and that of their children.

Joe's sister Melanie left the farm as soon as she graduated from high school, seeking a more adventurous life, and moved to urban St. Louis, Missouri. There she met her husband, Will Lindstrom, and has lived in St. Louis, with a metropolitan-area population of almost 3 million, ever since. Although their living environment is a stark contrast to the rural environment in which Joe and his family live, Melanie, Will, and their three children face similar challenges of poverty and uncertainty. They live in a rented duplex in an inner-city area that is undergoing gentrification. Recently their landlord notified them that they need to move in the next two months because she is selling the property to make way for condominiums. Will works on the loading docks at a rail yard, and Melanie works as a home health aide for a local health-care company. Between the two of them, they make well below the living wage for the area and cannot afford to pay the rapidly increasing rents and required deposits in the areas of urban St. Louis that Melanie thinks provide an adequate education for their children. The Lindstrom's oldest son has attention deficit disorder, and Melanie has already spent countless hours with his teachers in the children's current school working to try to meet his educational needs. Melanie also worries about Will, who has had back problems and is unsure how much longer he will be able to withstand the physical labor his job loading cargo requires.

Wherever social workers practice, they have to work within the context of the broader environment and the unique aspects of the community and geographic location. Although social work as a profession has some general values, a common body of knowledge, and a common skills set, certain aspects of the profession vary by the location in which social workers practice. Social workers in rural settings face issues different from those who practice in urban settings and have other social workers nearby.

In its most recent update, the federal government indicated that nearly 15% of the nation's population lives in nonmetropolitan or rural areas, although it is spread out across 72% of the land area of the country. By contrast, 85% of the nation's population lives in metropolitan or urban areas, concentrated in 27% of the country's land area (U.S. Department of Agriculture, 2013). As the population in the United States continues to grow, urban/metropolitan areas are absorbing more of the growth than rural areas. Between 2000 and 2010, growth in metropolitan areas increased by an average of about 10%, while the average growth in rural areas was less than 2% (U.S. Census Bureau, 2012).

The context in which social workers provide services shapes the lives of their clients, their needs, and the strategies social workers must take to address those needs. In this chapter we will review some of the more salient characteristics of rural and urban life in America, identify social welfare and social work resources available in rural and urban communities, and discuss unique aspects of social work in the two settings. We will also focus on other environmental issues that social workers face in their work with clients.

Operational Definitions

EP 2.1.3a

What is considered rural and what is considered urban is often debated, with official definitions changing over time to accommodate current geopolitical considerations. For statistical purposes, the U.S. Census Bureau classifies densely developed residential, commercial, and other nonresidential areas of the country as **urban**. Two types of

urban areas are included in this definition—urbanized areas of 50,000 or more people and urban clusters of at least 2,500 and no more than 50,000 people. According to this definition, there are some 500 urbanized areas and 3,000 urban clusters nationwide. The top three most populous urban areas in the country are New York-Newark, Los Angeles-Long Beach-Anaheim, and Chicago, with a combined population of about 39.0 million residents. The order of the top three most populated urban areas has not changed since 1960. Among urbanized areas with populations of 1 million or more, Las Vegas-Paradise, Nevada, grew at the fastest rate between 2000 and 2010, followed by Raleigh-Cary, North Carolina and Austin-Round Rock-San Macros, Texas (see Table 14.1

for data on metropolitan population growth for the period 2000 to 2010). Taken together, urban areas account for about 81% of the U.S. population; all other areas of the country are classified by the U.S. Census Bureau as **rural**. (U.S. Census Bureau, 2012; U.S. Office of Management and Budget [OMB], 2010).

TABLE 14.1 POPULATION CHANGE FOR THE 10 MOST POPULOUS AND 10 FASTEST-GROWING METROPOLITAN STATISTICAL AREAS: 2000 TO 2010

	2000 POPULATION	2010 POPULATION	CHANGE	PERCENTAGE
MOST POPULOUS				
New York-Northern New Jersey-Long Island, NY-NJ-PA	18,323,002	18,897,109	574,107	3.1
Los Angeles-Long Beach-Santa Ana, CA	12,365,627	12,828,837	463,210	3.7
Chicago-Joliet-Naperville, IL-IN-WI	9,098,316	9,461,105	362,789	4.0
Dallas-Fort Worth-Arlington, TX	5,161,544	6,371,773	1,210,229	23.4
Philadelphia-Camden-Wilmington, PA-NJ-DE-MD	5,687,147	5,965,343	278,196	4.9
Houston-Sugar Land-Baytown, TX	4,715,407	5,946,800	1,231,393	26.1
Washington-Arlington-Alexandria, DC-VA-MD-WV	4,796,183	5,582,170	785,987	16.4
Miami-Fort Lauderdale-Pompano Beach, FL	5,007,564	5,564,635	557,071	11.1
Atlanta-Sandy Springs-Marietta, GA	4,247,981	5,268,860	1,020,879	24.0
Boston-Cambridge-Quincy, MA-NH	4,391,344	4,552,402	161,058	3.7
FASTEST GROWING				
Palm Coast, FL	49,832	95,696	45,864	92.0
St. George, UT	90,354	138,115	47,761	52.9
Las Vegas-Paradise, NV	1,375,765	1,951,269	575,504	41.8
Raleigh-Cary, NC	797,071	1,130,490	333,419	41.8
Cape Coral-Fort Myers, FL	440,888	618,754	177,866	40.3
Provo-Orem, UT	376,774	526,810	150,036	39.8
Greeley, CO	180,926	252,825	71,899	39.7
Austin-Round Rock-San Marcos, TX	1,249,763	1,716,289	466,526	37.3
Myrtle Beach-North Myrtle Beach-Conway, SC	196,629	269,291	72,662	37.0
Bend, OR	115,367	157,733	42,366	36.7

SOURCE: Mackun, P. & Wilson, S. (2011). *Population distribution and change: 2000–2010. 2010 Census Briefs.* Washington, DC: Census Bureau. Retrieved from http://www.census.gov/prod/cen2010/briefs/c2010br-01.pdf.

Limitations of Rural and Urban Classification Systems

The Census Bureau's classification system has limited utility in that it enables us only to separate communities statistically identified as rural or urban from those that are not. For example, a small isolated community in southwestern Kansas can have the same population as an incorporated "bedroom community" located 30 miles from Chicago, but can they really be considered to be the same? What criteria would you use to compare them? One thing we know to be true is that the advantage of so-called bedroom communities lies in their proximity to larger cities within commuting distance for employment, health services, shopping alternatives, and related resources that are not available to the more isolated rural towns and villages. However, as we will see below, there are characteristics of small rural communities that often cannot be found in similarly sized communities located near urbanized areas and help to offset a lack of such resources.

Defining What Is Rural

Small towns have been struggling to maintain their "persona" and traditions. With the advent of regional shopping and discount centers moving into remote rural areas, many rural communities have become virtual ghost towns as shops that were once the economic mainstay of the community have closed. The social discourse that once was prevalent on Main Street has all but disappeared, as have the informal social networks of which they were a part. Government grants designed to restore once bustling downtown areas have met with limited success. Although federal monies have provided subsidies for electric cooperatives and rural water systems and, thus, provided incentives for people to remain in rural areas, much remains to be accomplished to reconfigure downtown areas in rural communities into viable resource opportunities.

In addition, millions of Americans live on farms and ranches some distance from villages, towns, or cities. In many of these areas, small farms are close together, and in others, miles may separate families from each other. Rural inhabitants often are identified as rural-farm or rural nonfarm to further clarify the nature of rural residency. The daily living requirements and patterns of farm dwellers are vastly different from those of small-town residents.

To identify rural life as a primarily statistical anomaly is to miss the essence of rural existence. One can gain a better understanding of rural life experiences by reviewing the cultural ethos, environmental characteristics, and the means through which the people are able to provide

Migrant workers and their families often face extreme hardship and discrimination, including low wages, substandard housing, and limited access to education, health care, and other needed services.

Jonathan Blair/Historical/Corbis

sustenance for themselves and their families. These characteristics, reflected in the discussion that follows, are contrasted with urban issues. The reader must keep in mind that the life of a small farmer in Missouri is likely to be appreciably different from that of a cattle rancher in Montana, and the Missouri farmer may have more in common with a St. Louis urbanite than the cattle rancher would.

Finally, definitions of *urban* or *rural* are not subject to the behavioral attributes of population groups but, instead, to population size; such definitions do not take into account the complexity of life in either place.

Characteristics of Rural and Urban Populations

EP 2.1.3a

Approximately 46 million Americans (about 15% of the total population) live in rural areas in the United States (U.S. Department of Agriculture, 2013). The population of nonmetro counties has been on a gradual decline over recent years, as population growth from natural change (births minus deaths) is no longer sufficient to counter net migration losses when they occur. This pattern of population loss has reversed (in some cases dramatically) in areas of the country where large-scale investments are being made in the unconventional extraction of gas and oil from deep rock formations that are plentiful in these areas. However, these situations are the exception and not the norm, and the population influx is because of people moving in from outside areas to run these operations. Much of this increase in population is expected to disappear once the extraction operations are complete and the oil and gas captured have been capped for sale on the commercial market (U.S. Department of Agriculture, 2013).

Agriculture no longer dominates rural America; today, the economy in rural areas is dominated by industries involving agricultural inputs, processing and marketing of agricultural goods, wholesale and retail trade of agricultural products, and agribusiness. Manufacturing, which is particularly important in rural areas that are not favored by natural resources such as mountains, lakes, and climates attractive for recreation and retirement, now accounts for more than 25% of private-sector earnings in rural areas. Much of this manufacturing is occurring in so-called footloose activities that are unrelated to natural resources, such as computing, biotechnology, and assembly operations that often require significant

investments by the community in infrastructure development (e.g., land improvement and improvements in water and wastewater, communication, and transportation systems), as a condition of attracting the industry to locate in the community. Many of these industries require workers with specialized training who must be recruited from outside the community. In addition, because of the footloose nature of the activities in which these industries are engaged, it is not uncommon for them to pull up stakes on short notice, leaving the community with buildings that are difficult to re-lease and a significant decrease in tax revenues typically that were used to support municipal and other operations (U.S. Department of Agriculture, 2013). To be sure, economic development in rural areas through the introduction of manufacturing-based industries is not without its risks.

Rural areas, with their characteristic small towns, farms, and ranches of varying sizes, offer an appreciably different environment and lifestyle than metropolitan areas. Although some rural residents are able to access the resources of major cities, isolation and the need to travel long distances to use them pose problems for others. As a whole, people living in rural areas have more limited resources than urban residents. The most recent indicators of social and economic conditions in rural and urban areas in the United States are summarized in Table 14.2.

Other, less measurable characteristics of rural areas of the country that can be said to set them apart from urban areas include relationships based on trust, friendly atmosphere, isolation, resistance to change, suspicion toward newcomers or outsiders, strong sense of patriotism, independence of spirit, presence of informal and/or natural helping systems, social and political conservatism, and political values (Daley, 2015; Ginsberg, 2011; Scales, Streeter & Cooper, 2013). The strength and intensity of any (or all) of these characteristics vary, depending on the social organization and density of the rural population in question; nonetheless, these characteristics still make life in rural areas of the country considerably different from that in their urban counterparts.

Life in Rural Communities

EP 2.1.7a

Social networks in rural communities are more personalized and informal than those typically found in urban communities. Many prominent and powerful community leaders are descendants of early settlers, often large landowners, and leaders in community affairs.

TABLE 14.2 RECENT INDICATORS OF SOCIAL AND ECONOMIC CONDITIONS IN RURAL AND URBAN AREAS OF THE UNITED STATES

INDICATOR	DESCRIPTION
Race and Ethnicity	• Racial and ethnic minorities comprise nearly 20% of nonmetro residents and are geographically disbursed throughout the country. • Hispanics/Latinos account for the largest percentage of the nonmetro population growth in recent years.
Age	• Nonmetro areas have a larger share of older people when compared to the country as a whole. • Nonmetro older Americans generally have less income, lower educational attainment, and a higher dependence on medical, social, and financial assistance when compared to the country as a whole.
Poverty	• Poverty rates for the general population are higher in nonmetro areas (17.7%) than in metropolitan areas (14.5%). • Child poverty rates are higher in nonmetro areas (26.7%) than in metropolitan areas (20.9%). • *Deep poverty* (defined as households with incomes less than 50% of the federal poverty level) among children is more acute in rural areas (12.2%) than in urban areas (9.2%).
Food insecurity	• Food insecurity (defined as households in which there is uncertainty of having, or the inability to acquire, enough food to meet the needs of all members of the household) in nonmetro areas historically exceeds that of metropolitan households, especially in the South.
Employment	• Average earnings are substantially lower among workers in nonmetro areas compared to workers in metro areas. Lower rural earnings reflect lower shares of highly skilled jobs and lower returns to college degrees in rural labor markets. • Nonmetro Hispanics/Latinos without a high school degree occupy the highest proportion of low-skill, low-paying jobs. • After several years of steady growth, nonmetro employment began to decline in the latter part of 2006, with the sharpest declines taking place in southeastern states, industrial areas of the Midwest, and several western states.
Home Ownership	• Nonmetro area homeownership has been steadily declining since 2008; foreclosure or abandonment rates in nonmetro areas are some 1.5 times those in metro areas of the country.

SOURCE: Race and ethnicity in rural America (2012). Washington, DC: Housing Assistance Council. Retrieved 2014 from http://slideshare.net/ruralhome/race-and-ethnicity-in-rural-america.

Residents, affluent and poor alike, tend to be known by many people in the community. Residents seldom achieve privacy and anonymity. News, both good and bad, travels through the informal community network with amazing speed. Residents gain reputations that are changed only with great effort. Newcomers often find themselves in an out-group category and, regardless of their interest or endeavor, have difficulty being accepted fully into the inner circles of community life. Judgments concerning the character, ability, and competency of individuals tend to be based on subjective assessments.

The success or failure of community residents in rural areas usually is attributed to personal effort and motivation. Hence, the poor, unemployed, and downtrodden are viewed as lacking initiative or the determination to achieve. Divorce and poverty typically are thought to be a reflection of personal failure, and strong negative sanctions serve as constant reminders that deviation from the norm is accompanied by increasing social distance and exclusion from free and full participation in community life.

Relatively speaking, rural areas are more politically conservative than urban areas; rural communities are typically characterized by resistance to innovation and skepticism concerning modern technological innovations. Outsiders, particularly those from urban areas, are met with suspicion and often disdain; many times they are considered to be interlopers or opportunists with little interest in the well-being of the community in which they have moved or the needs of its residents and as such, are not to be trusted.

Community responses to people in need in rural areas are often quick and personal. A death in the family or a farm failure stimulates neighbors to respond with goods and services to assist those in need through the crisis. Droughts, floods, tornadoes, and other natural disasters create a bond among farmers and ranchers, engendering a unity of purpose with shared concern. People often show reciprocity by sharing labor for the harvesting of crops, helping others in times of need, and organizing to counteract threats to community life. Honesty and strong character are valued traits.

The action hub of rural communities is composed of the church (church is used here because most rural communities are Christian, though other religious entities can also be found in rural areas), the local bank, the county extension office, small businesses, the feed store, and the local school system. As a consequence, the local bankers, ministers, county agricultural agents, store owners, and school administrators usually have a powerful influence on community life. County government typically is relegated to the county judge and county commissioner, who wield considerable power and authority. The sheriff's office often handles law enforcement, although many small towns also have a police force whose members have strong community ties. While violations of the law are considered to be a personal offense against the community, tension between law enforcement and certain membership groups within the community often found in urban areas occurs less often in rural communities. The social organization of rural communities is as varied as their locations. Although a community in any setting has common threads of roles and relationships that knit it together, each locale has its own character (Daley, 2015; Ginsberg, 2011; Scales, Streeter & Cooper, 2013).

Life in Urban Communities

In contrast to rural communities the social organization of urban communities is highly influenced by population size, extent of urban sprawl, existence of urban blight, amount of urban sprawl, degree of gentrification taking place, patterns of in-migration, and the diversity of community members (Hurley, 2010; Macionis & Parillo, 2012; Zukin, 2011). Thus, life in urban communities is fundamentally different than that found in rural areas of the country. In general

terms, the pace of life is much faster, population density is greater, the sense of neighborliness is not as pronounced, and the involvement of community members in the affairs of the community is often mixed. On the positive side, urban communities typically contain more public venues for arts and entertainment, sports, and leisure activities, a community college system that provides a wide range of vocational and higher education opportunities, an abundant supply of hospitals that offer state-of-the art medical care, and a robust public transit system. Urban communities across the country are increasingly facing a variety of challenges. For one, the availability of affordable housing stock is often quite limited, especially in those areas of the community in which **gentrification** (renewal accompanied by the influx of affluent people into deteriorating areas that often displaces poorer residents) is taking place. Homelessness is on the rise. Urban decay continues to be a problem, particularly in areas of the country that were once proud manufacturing centers like Detroit. The poverty rate in inner city core areas exceeds that of noncore areas and surrounding suburbs. Racial tension often exists between law enforcement and areas of the community inhabited by racial and ethnic minorities. Disparities exist in access to quality public education and health care. Employment opportunities are limited, especially for those without a high school degree or its equivalency, and even for those with some college education.

Notwithstanding the challenges noted above, urban areas also offer exciting opportunities for community engagement, whereby community members "take back" what once belonged to them. Many such communities are using the principles of asset-based community development (Green & Goetting, 2013; McKnight & Block, 2012) to mobilize the talents and gifts of *all* community members to develop solutions to problems such as those noted above. Examples include the development of community gardens, microenterprise zones that serve as incubators for local economic development, community land trusts, and neighborhoods that embrace the principles of **new urbanism** (walkability, connectivity, mixed-use and diversity, mixed housing, quality architecture and urban design, traditional neighborhood structure, increased density, green transportation, sustainability, and quality of life) (Davis, 2010; DeFillippis & Saegert, 2012; Jurik, 2005; Munoz, 2010; Newurbanism.org).

Support Services in Rural and Urban Communities

EP 2.1.1a
EP 2.1.8a

Support services in rural areas are often scarce or even nonexistent. Doctors, nurses, social workers, dentists, and attorneys typically are lacking in small rural towns. Adequately staffed hospitals with state-of-the-art equipment often are not found in small communities because of the lack of resources to finance their development and ongoing maintenance. As a consequence, many health-related problems go unattended, or people rely on nontraditional cures or folk medicine. Resources for treating mental illness are particularly lacking, but individuals who exhibit "peculiar" behavior often find acceptance in rural areas, and their families may benefit from considerable understanding and social support from neighbors. Because of the community's mores or limited financial support, social work and social services tend to be distributed sparsely in rural areas. By contrast, support services in urban areas are typically more robust (sometimes even redundant), although access to those services varies depending on their location, the ability of people to pay for them, and the degree to which their doors are open to all membership groups of the community (Dear & Wolch, 2014; Porter, 2012; Small & Allard, 2013). Health disparities exist in both rural and urban areas, but they are more visible in urban areas because of the sheer number of people affected. Urban areas typically have at least one public hospital where the financially indigent receive care. The emergency departments of these hospitals are almost always overwhelmed by the volume of individuals needing to be seen. It is not uncommon in some of these settings for a person with a condition that is not determined to be life threatening to wait upward of one or more days to see a doctor. Often, the doctors who work in urban public hospitals are medical graduates from schools outside the United States who have limited practice privileges. Many of these doctors have difficulties with the English language, which presents yet another barrier to receiving health care services for those who are unable to afford it.

Additionally, the greater diversity of clients in urban areas requires knowledge and acceptance of cultural differences from many groups. Clients often face barriers because of language, dietary preferences, child rearing practices, and living situations that are often not taken into account by service providers, who are less likely than their rural counterparts to be well acquainted with their clients and aware of their needs.

As noted, religious institutions play significant roles in both rural and urban communities. Congregations respond quickly to those in need and set the pace for community action in times of crisis. In urban areas, faith-based organizations provide shelter to homeless individuals and families, operate food pantries, serve as a sanctuary for undocumented immigrants, provide resettlement service for recently arrived refugees, and operate health clinics for the medically indigent. In rural areas and some urban neighborhoods, particularly those populated largely by one ethnic group, faith-based organizations also are the center of community activities, sponsoring social gatherings and recreational opportunities. Religion plays a vital role in setting the moral tone and in meeting the spiritual needs of residents of both rural and urban areas. Leaders or faith-based organizations are viewed as more than spiritual advisers; they are considered community leaders as well (Bovee, 2010; Fuder & Castellanos, 2013; Lupton, 2011; Moore, 2012). When a crisis occurs, religious leaders are looked to for commentary and support, and they often quell unrest and facilitate dialogue to address concerns. They also rally their members to provide assistance to those in need.

In agricultural areas, the county extension office, funded by the **U.S. Department of Agriculture (USDA)**, provides many services that the farm community values, and the county liaison office provides a variety of community and family services. Technical assistance is made available for crop planting and harvesting, ranch management, disease control, care of livestock, food preparation, home canning, and other activities related to farm, ranch, and home management.

Informally, the **county agent** often becomes aware of personal problems and serves as counselor, case manager, and resource finder. He or she also often functions as an advocate or a broker (with the local banker or other lending agencies) for farmers undergoing financial disaster. The USDA also provides vital funding for rural community initiatives such as creating affordable housing opportunities and community service centers where residents can obtain information or critical services. County agents and Agricultural Extension Services have also moved into urban areas on a more limited basis, organizing programs on obesity and nutrition, forming urban 4-H clubs that focus on the urban environment, and providing family-based outreach.

The public health nurse could be considered to be the equivalent of the county agent in urban areas. The public health nurse works at the local level to promote healthy lifestyles, encourage parents to get their children immunized against common childhood diseases, provide referrals to critical health resources, help ensure that young parents and vulnerable families understand the importance of healthy child development and effective parenting, and connect community members to important health care resources (Nies & McEwen, 2014; Truglia-Londrigan & Lewenson, 2012).

Promotion of positive health practices is often facilitated in low-income immigrant communities by a *promotora*, an indigenous member of the community who is viewed by the community as one of their own and a trusted and credible source of information. A *promotora* will often conduct an information session or engage in a focus group with concerned residents in a community park, on a porch, or even under a tree in the neighborhood. Because they are a trusted member of the community, *promotoras* are many times able to gain access to community members that would not be possible by public health or other workers from outside the community (Anderson & Olson, 2014; Lujan, 2009).

An important link to obtaining information in rural areas has been the introduction of computer technology. Virtually all small businesses, service agencies, and school systems are computer equipped, with access to the Internet. Most small, rural school systems provide instruction in technology, and many are linked to statewide networks that help residents access information. This technology has enabled a closer link with urban areas in acquiring essential information, along with its potential use as a problem-solving resource. Many residents of rural areas are increasingly knowledgeable about health issues, for example, because of their access to the Internet. In some rural areas, access to such technology is not yet available, or the technology that is available is limited or out-of-date, which furthers the **digital divide** and adds to the employment and educational barriers. The digital divide exists in urban communities as well, particularly in low-income areas of the community where the acquisition of state-of-the art technology is cost prohibitive. This too, places residents of these areas at a distinct disadvantage in terms of employment and educational opportunities. Some would argue that this creates a cumulative disadvantage

for these individuals, as many of them are likely to be beyond the technology power curve throughout their lives if they continue to live in poverty (Ragnedda & Muschert, 2013; Rank, Hirschl, & Foster, 2014).

Recreational activities, too, may be limited in rural areas. The absence of a local movie theater, skating rink, park, library, and other outlets for children and teenagers severely restricts opportunities for leisure-time activities. Many small communities "roll up the sidewalks" at dark. As a consequence, the local school has become a prominent source for recreational get-togethers, dances, and music and other fine arts programs. Athletic events usually are well attended and serve as a central focus for young people and adults to meet and socialize. In addition to religious organizations, the school is a primary institution for social organization in the rural community.

The importance of **natural helping networks** should not be minimized in either **rural social work** or social work in urban settings. Historically, networks of friends, relatives, congregations, clubs, civic groups, and related entities have constituted the backbone of assistance to those in need. These networks can be readily seen in many communities that are largely African American or Latino, accompanied by a strong sense of collective identity. In many African American and Latino communities, the church is the center of the community and the priest or pastor is an important leader. Avant (2013) talks about informal kinship care in rural African American communities as contrasted with formal foster care or adoption and notes that individuals rally around community members and support each other by sharing resources, including food, shelter, and transportation. Lusk, Staudt, & Moya (2012) describe life in rural *colonias* (Spanish for "neighborhoods" or "communities") or communities of primarily Mexican immigrants who share many of the same struggles as underdeveloped countries and may lack running water, an adequate sewer system, electricity, and paved roads.

In spite of these conditions, residents support each other, often bringing a network of extended family members who live together until they can afford to live in their own residences. They also share food, electricity, child and elder care, and they help each other bridge the barrier to the broader, primarily English-speaking community in making necessary transactions. Celebrations, especially those involving children and youth, are important traditions in many African American and Latino rural communities (Esparza & Donelson, 2010).

Social Problems and Needs in Rural and Urban Areas

EP 2.1.7a

Many people have a romantic view of rural areas as peaceful, serene, and devoid of the problems in large cities and metropolitan areas. These views fail to portray the reality of rural life. To the contrary, rural areas are not devoid of social problems, and the impacts on rural residents are likely to be greater than on those living in cities because of the lack of services to address them. A few of the more prominent problems in both rural and urban areas are discussed next.

Mental Health

EP 2.1.7b

People living in rural areas have the same kinds of mental health problems and needs for services as individuals who live in urban and suburban areas, yet rural areas have unique characteristics that present barriers to mental health care. Access to and availability of mental health specialists is extremely limited. Poverty, geographic isolation and cultural differences, lack of transportation, staff shortages, inadequate facilities, few treatment alternatives, and the high cost of medications further limit the amount and quality of mental health care available to people in rural areas (Smalley, Warren, & Rainer, 2012). Rural areas, for example, have far fewer psychiatrists than urban areas to serve the population, and even if residents can obtain an appointment, they may have to wait weeks or even months to get an appointment and sometimes drive hundreds of miles, which can be a problem, especially for ill and elderly people who do not have access to reliable transportation.

Overall, residents of rural areas are more likely than urban residents to have mental health–related problems. Rates of suicide, child maltreatment, and mental illness are higher in rural areas. In addition to these more severe problems, the psychological and emotional anguish associated with marital discord and parent–child conflicts has intensified in many rural areas as increasing numbers of farm owners are unable to pay for the loans they took out to finance their farming operations and face the likelihood that the bank from which the loans were secured will foreclose on property that may have been in the family for generations. Many farmers faced with this reality feel that they have no way out of their situation and commit suicide. Suicide rates among farmers have been reported to be the highest of any occupation (Kutner, 2014).

Child maltreatment, once thought to be a primarily urban problem, is found in rural areas with increasing

Rural life often involves having to travel long distances for services, education, and jobs.

Jim Craigmyle/Flirt/Corbis

frequency. Incidents of child abuse and neglect in rural areas mirror incidents found in urban areas; over half of cases are neglect, associated with the poverty and isolation seen in many rural areas, coupled with increased incidents of drug abuse. However, rural areas see more maltreatment in families headed by single parents and those who endure economic and family stress (Mattingly & Walsh, 2010).

As well, many have considered drug misuse to be primarily an urban problem. However, methamphetamine ("meth") production and use have become a concern in many rural communities. Initially produced in rural areas because of the availability of abandoned barns and farmhouses in remote locations, as well as a key ingredient used in producing the illegal drug also used as a fertilizer, methamphetamine has devastated thousands of individuals and families in rural communities. Its addictive nature and the resulting debilitation often leads to unemployment, neglect of parental responsibilities such as feeding and clothing one's children, and serious health problems. Rural areas with meth labs also have had to deal with problems of toxic waste from the labs' contaminating fields and household drains (Garriott, 2011).

The federal government and a number of states have established special programs to deal with this growing problem in rural areas, as treatment for methamphetamine addiction is much more difficult to access in rural locations than in urban areas. Crack cocaine and heroin are more likely to be the drug of choice among urban drug users because of their low price and abundance. In many impoverished urban neighborhoods, drug dealers make more money in one day selling drugs than can be made in a year for someone with a minimum wage job. Drug dealers are looked upon as someone to emulate by many urban youth who live in poverty and who have limited opportunities for escaping the conditions in which they live. In some urban communities, virtually the entire community is engaged in some way in the use and/or distribution of drugs. In many of these communities, gangs have become a common way of life among youth and adults alike.

The pathway to success for most community members is strewn with challenges that seem almost insurmountable, yet many succeed in spite of the conditions in which they live through hard work, diligence, and staying focused on positive life goals (Kozol, 2012a, 2012b, 2013). Depression and anxiety are common

mental health conditions found in urban areas that result from crowded living conditions in crime-infested neighborhoods with limited municipal services, police protection or social supports (formal or otherwise). It is not uncommon for parents in urban areas to work at two jobs just to make ends meet, forcing them to leave their children at home alone or with a friend or relative, possibly placing the children in harm's way. The disappearance of the public assistance safety net resulting from continuous waves of welfare reform over the past two decades has taken away what little hope large numbers of urban dwellers (especially single mothers with children) had for rising out of poverty and creating some measure of opportunity for themselves and their children (Jansson, 2011; Seccombe, 2010). Children and adults alike suffer from posttraumatic stress disorder (PTSD) resulting from the constant threat of or occurrence of community violence (Ladicola & Shupe, 2012; Rosenfeld, Edberg, Fang, & Florence, 2013).

Depression and other mental illnesses are also found in rural areas in high numbers, but they are less likely to be diagnosed and thus treated than in urban areas. Family members and others in rural areas may be less likely to label a behavior as a mental illness, and instead either adapt family and community settings to accommodate those with mental illnesses or ignore their needs altogether. The fact that there is often more stigma about having a mental illness in rural areas is also a barrier to seeking services, as is the limited availability of services even if help is sought.

As indicated earlier, persons in need of formal services are more likely to find them in urban areas. Even when services do exist, hiring professionally trained social workers, physicians, and other service providers in rural areas can be challenging. The National Institute of Mental Health and other national and state programs have called for internships and training programs directed specifically to mental health service delivery in rural areas— hiring more staff in rural areas and ensuring that they are trained to work effectively with rural populations, offering "wrap-around services" that provide holistic care for rural families, developing networks of multidisciplinary teams that can work collaboratively to address needs in rural areas, and using technology as a tool for assessment, intervention, and coordination (Scales, Streeter, & Cooper, 2013).

Health Care

EP 2.1.7b

Health care is of great concern to people who live in both rural and urban America. Rates of infant mortality and chronic disease are higher in rural areas than in urban areas.

The rural elderly suffer from chronic illness and poor health in far greater numbers than their urban counterparts. One example is diabetes, which is more likely to be untreated in rural areas than in urban areas, resulting in more serious problems when it does come to the attention of health care providers.

Rural hospitals are funded on the same per-service basis as urban hospitals, but, because of the smaller capacity of rural hospitals, the costs to deliver services are higher. Many rural hospitals also do not have the ability to purchase the expensive equipment that larger urban hospitals do. Thus, rural residents may go to more distant urban hospitals to receive more extensive care. These factors lead to inadequate financial capability to continue operations—a factor that all too often results in the hospital's having to close.

By way of contrast, most urban cities have several hospitals, often competing for the same population of users; however, the hospital that is most likely to be accessed by members of the community who are poor is the public hospital operated by the city, county, or a public hospital district. These hospitals are often designated as disproportionate share hospitals because of the high numbers of medically indigent that they serve. While many of these hospitals have been classified as Level 1 trauma centers and have some of the best medical practitioners in the community on hand 7 days a week and 24 hours a day, they are often shunned by those who can afford to pay for their medical care on their own or through some third-party insurance arrangement. Service in these hospitals is often slow, especially in the emergency department, because of the sheer numbers of people who are poor using the facility for primary care because they are uninsured and have no other place to receive such care. Ironically, the cost of providing primary care in an emergency department setting is among the most expensive medical care available (Morganti, Bauhoff, Blanchard, & Iyer, 2013). Many Level 1 trauma centers across the country are closing down because of the costs to maintain high level staff and equipment. Even urban trauma hospitals have difficulty hiring medical specialists such as neurosurgeons, who can work fewer hours, work in a less stressful

environment, and earn more money if they work in a private practice or other non-ER setting. Although most rural areas do have emergency medical services, these services typically are not prepared to handle life-threatening diseases or severe traumatic injuries. In addition, recruiting doctors, nurses, and other health care professionals for rural areas is more challenging when compared with urban and suburban areas.

Although solutions to rural health problems are not easy to come by, the health needs of rural residents must become a priority for policymakers (Klugman & Dalinis, 2012). The shortage of medical doctors and specialists imposes limited choices from which to select treatment options for disease and illness in many rural areas. Patients who require kidney dialysis or have other complicated health problems often must travel long distances for treatment or, in some cases, must even move to a location where treatment facilities are easily accessed. Further, turnover rates among medical practitioners tend to be higher in rural areas, and attracting and retaining qualified medical personnel are difficult (Health Resources and Services Administration, 2014).

Our high-tech society has resulted in the development of innovative approaches to improving the quality of care for rural residents. Mobile vans equipped with state-of-the-art equipment and health practitioners are making health care more accessible in many rural areas. And, through **telecommunications**, rural medical practitioners have immediate access to large medical centers, where consultation is available for both diagnostic and treatment regimens. Technology also enables rural patients to have electronic equipment in their homes, to transmit data such as blood pressure and blood sugar levels to health practitioners for monitoring. The use of technology to deliver mental health services is gaining traction in rural areas as increasing numbers of combat veterans from Operation Iraqi Freedom (OIF) and Operation Enduring Freedom (OEF) with mental health issues such as posttraumatic stress disorder, severe depression, and anxiety disorder are returning home to rural areas of the country (Department of Veterans Affairs, 2012). Clients in rural areas can access service providers who will conduct assessments as well as therapy. Many individuals also participate in online support groups. **Telemedicine** has rapidly expanded throughout rural areas of the United States, with the capacity to enhance the quality of care for clients who lack the capacity to receive care in a major medical or mental health center (Mehrotra, 2014; Mehrotra, Paone, Martich, & Albert, 2013; Uscher-Pines & Mehrotra, 2014).

Poverty

EP 2.1.7b

In 2012, nearly 18% of the population living in nonmetropolitan areas of the United States lived in poverty. Residents in some parts of the country, such as Appalachia and the 1,200 mile border between Texas and Mexico, experience poverty rates of 30% to 50%. Poverty rates for rural areas are higher than those for urban areas, and income is approximately 30% lower for rural residents than for their urban counterparts (U.S. Department of Agriculture, 2013).

People of color living in both rural and urban areas are more likely to be poor than their white counterparts (U.S. Census Bureau, 2013). The rural poor tend to have primarily low-wage jobs; and their ability to attain higher-paying jobs is limited because they generally are less well educated than their urban counterparts. Their income-earning capacity is affected further by seasonal employment, illness, and injury.

Most of the rural poor are involved with crop harvesting, which is characteristically unpredictable, pays poor wages, and frequently requires that families move from place to place to secure employment. Although many of these families no longer travel long distances to harvest crops, they retain the terminology of *migrant workers* (Holmes & Bourgois, 2013).

The children of these workers have less education than their counterparts in urban areas. Higher rates of disease and infant mortality reflect the substandard conditions under which many live. Small-town school systems often are not diligent in enforcing mandatory school-attendance laws. Many children are not encouraged to pursue an education and, instead, work alongside their parents to help the family earn enough money to survive. Consequently, a vicious cycle is set in motion, perpetuating intergenerational patterns of farm laborers who are poor and lack the necessary education and skills to break out of poverty.

Older Adults

EP 2.1.3a
EP 2.1.7b

Another group that receives less attention in rural areas than in comparison to urban areas is older adults. The aging population accounted for 19% of the total population in 2012. Older adults residing in rural America tend to age in place (not change geographic location as they age); between 2012 and 2013, only 4% of older adults living in rural areas moved. Rural elderly face several unique challenges that vary in intensity depending on where they live and the family and other supports available to them: the need to migrate to urban centers as a result of loss of profitability of family holdings; environmental challenges such as lack of safe drinking water, lack of proper sanitary facilities for disposal of sewage and garbage, low quality housing, lack of electricity, poor and badly maintained roads, and extreme climatic conditions for parts of the year; living in isolated areas with limited or no access to health care, lack of educational opportunities, and difficulties in communication; and health issues such as obesity and illnesses such as diabetes, Alzheimer's, and depression (Rural Assistance Center, 2014). The median age is 40 in rural areas, as compared with 36 in urban areas, reflecting the higher proportion of elderly (Center for Rural Affairs, 2010).

Ethnic Composition

Racial segregation, limited political participation, and impoverishment continue to characterize the plight of people of color in rural communities. Attempts to organize farm labor and implement civil rights legislation have met with only limited success, primarily because of the resistance of large landowners and commercial farmers who seek to maintain the status quo and exert sufficient influence to foil reform efforts.

Immigrants have increased the population in many rural areas that had been declining. Immigrants are employed not only on farms and ranches in rural areas but also in food-processing plants and other jobs where English proficiency is not vital and low wages prevail. This helps to keep plants open that had been having difficulty finding employees who were willing to remain in the area (Holmes & Bourgois, 2013; Singer, 2012).

Many people view undocumented persons negatively, believing that they compound problems in the farm labor market through their willingness to work for lower wages. Experience has shown, however, that they take jobs that otherwise would not be filled. Because most undocumented persons are concerned with being detected by federal immigration officials (and being returned to Mexico), they are vulnerable to exploitation by landowners who seek cheap labor.

Nearly 75% of agricultural workers do not have health insurance, and the fact that agricultural workers are at greater risk for chronic diseases, including stroke, diabetes, asthma, high blood pressure, and heart disease, as well as respiratory ailments brought on by constant exposure to various chemicals and pesticides applied to the fruits and vegetables they harvest, makes this even more problematic (National Center for Farmworker Health, 2014). Poor white farm workers have many of the same problems as farm workers of color. Typically less educated than urban whites, they are viewed stereotypically as people with less incentive and motivation to succeed. Limited resources and skill levels keep them on the farm. Illiteracy rates are higher and poverty is more pervasive among rural whites than urban whites. When rural whites do migrate to cities, they often are relegated to low-paying jobs and have considerable difficulty assimilating into the urban environment.

Perhaps the conditions of the rural poor are best described in an article by Colby (1987), who cites an anonymous poor rural resident:

Poverty is dirt. You say in your clean clothes coming from a clean house, "Anybody can be clean." Let me explain housekeeping with no money. For breakfast I give my children grits with oleo, or cornbread with no eggs or oleo. What dishes there are, I wash in cold water with no soap.... Look at my hands, so cracked and red.... Why not hot water? Hot water is a luxury. Fuel costs money.... Poverty is ... remembering quitting school in junior high because "nice" children had been so cruel about my clothes and my smell.... Poverty is a chisel that chips on honor until honor is worn away. (pp. 9–10)

By contrast, the urban poor can be said to have the following characteristics (Butra, 2013):

- The urban poor are a diverse group with diverse needs.
- Urban poverty can be episodic or persistent.
- Urban areas can include wide extremes of wealth and poverty.
- Conflict and security in urban areas are significantly different than in rural communities.
- In recently settled urban areas such as those created by displacement because of gentrification, networks of mutual exchange, if they exist at all, are likely to be more fragile than those found in rural communities.

- Access to services may appear enhanced in urban areas, but often the quality of those services is uneven and the competition for them can be intense.
- Poor urban dwellers are subject to high levels of environmental hazards such as toxic waste and airborne pollutants.
- The urban poor buy most, if not all, of their food and thus are more likely than their rural counterparts to experience food insecurity.
- Information communication technologies such as the Internet and cell phones have a higher penetration rate in urban areas than in rural areas (p. 1).

The Rural Family

EP 2.1.3a
EP 2.1.7b

The notion that rural families are harmonious, problem free, and enjoy life to its fullest is more myth than fact. This idyllic view is an illusion that filters out the reality of existing conditions. Just as in urban areas, the negatives related to strained relationships, illegal use of drugs, divorce, child abuse and neglect, sexual exploitation, and related problems are found in rural areas, but are often easier to hide because of the isolation that is frequently found in rural settings. Solutions to such problems can be elusive for rural families. Formal programs are limited in number, nature, and scope, often resulting in problems going unreported or becoming worse by the time they are identified.

In contrast, most urban areas have a robust social service system, with many options for families in crisis; however, these services may not be located in inner city core areas and can only be accessed by traveling (sometimes long distances) to other parts of the community. Often, the services provided are not culturally appropriate. Asset mapping (mapping the availability of current resources, both formal and informal, to identify gaps) often is required to redistribute existing resources or create new ones where none exist (Delgado & Humm-Delgado, 2013; Green & Goetting, 2013).

Even where limited support services are available, rural families tend to be hesitant to call upon them. Strong values tied to a propensity for self-management of problems and a reluctance to share problems with others deter residents from using available assistance. Often, mental health and other service providers are forced to come up with innovative approaches to packaging and encouraging the use of their services, and even then, there is no guarantee that those most in need of services will actually seek them (Crosby, Wendel, Vanderpool, & Casey, 2012).

The Crisis of the Small Farmer

Like the McDowells at the start of the chapter, many small farmers are strruggling to survive. The convergence of low farm prices, high production costs, imports, and related factors have created a crisis for the small farmer. Reemerging in the 1990s, farm and ranch foreclosures again have skyrocketed, which has resulted in the displacement of large numbers of farmers and ranchers who depended on agricultural production for their livelihood.

EP 2.1.3a
EP 2.1.7b

Like the McDowells, intergenerational farms and ranches are being lost through foreclosure. Displaced farmers and ranchers often lack the skills required to become absorbed readily into other parts of the labor market, particularly in the instance of older farmers and ranchers. Major commercial farm operations (sometimes called "mega farming" or "precision farming") have contributed to the demise of small farm operations through volume production, which lowers the unit prices for products. The small operator, even under optimal conditions, has great difficulty competing (Pritchard, 2014).

Currently, few resources are available to assist small farmers and ranchers in maintaining their property and purchasing the equipment essential to compete successfully. The federal government priority of reducing deficit spending has taken its toll on farm supports. Along with these problems, the stress and tension associated with the loss or probable loss of one's farm or ranch create havoc for these families. Problems such as increased family conflict—including spouse and child abuse—alcoholism, and depression are common in rural areas populated by ranchers and farmers operating as single-family businesses.

The increase in stress and the accompanying problems serve as disincentives for prospective new farmers to engage in agricultural operations. Some individuals who once were productive and self-sustaining must turn to public assistance as a means of survival. Urbanites must be reminded that their survival depends on a healthy agricultural industry.

Social Welfare in Rural and Urban Communities

The United States has many small communities and towns that vary in size and in their proximity to major metropolitan areas. For example, Tilden, Texas, a county-seat town of approximately 350 residents, is situated in a county that covers approximately 1,400 square miles. It is the largest town in the county. What social welfare programs might be needed in this community? To what extent could the community support the delivery of such services?

EP 2.1.1a
EP 2.1.8b
EP 2.1.9b

Generalizations about the nature and extent of organized social welfare programs in rural and urban areas should be avoided, because they vary greatly in size and ability to finance needed services. Many rural areas have few services, and those tend to be basic. Typically, public welfare services, mental health and developmental disabilities outreach centers, and public health services are available, although they usually have minimal staffs, offer limited assistance. Rural counties sometimes offer a limited welfare assistance program with a few county workers to determine eligibility for and administer benefits.

A few rural communities have Community Action Agencies (first developed during the 1960s as part of the War on Poverty programs), although attempts to organize rural areas through community action efforts have been mostly unsuccessful. The opposite is true for Community Action Agencies in urban areas, many of which have been successful in mobilizing residents to confront city and county officials to expand available services or create new ones where none exist. Programs for seniors in rural areas may be provided by a local branch of an area-wide agency on aging, or more likely a group of volunteers from a local church. Employment agencies, family-planning services, and family counseling agencies and related services are rarely found in rural areas.

A number of authors have suggested some innovative changes that would increase the service capacity to meet the needs of rural populations (see for example, Scales, Streeter, & Cooper, 2013). They include the following.

- Integrate services into a single, seamless service delivery system in recognition of the transportation problems that residents of rural communities frequently encounter.

- Capitalize on informal networks of exchange to supplement limited formal services.
- Draw upon the spirit of cooperation, neighborliness, and helping to enhance available services.
- Be sensitive to cultural issues that might prevent people in need from accessing services.
- Use organizations such as the county agricultural extension service to promote social programs for individuals and families in need.

By forming a Community Action Agency or Community Development Corporation, all of these strategies could be used to increase needed services in low-income inner city areas where few such services exist (DeFillippis & Saegert, 2012; Ledwith, 2011).

More attention is being directed at the state and federal levels to sustainability in rural areas. The U.S. Department of Agriculture's rural development programs assist rural areas in financing local water and wastewater systems, alternative energy systems, access to technology, housing, community facilities, electricity generation and distribution, conservation of natural resources, and research into new uses for agricultural products (USDA, 2014a). Other federal agencies such as the Small Business Administration, Environmental Protection Agency, U.S. Health and Human Services Department, U.S. Department of Labor, and the U.S. Department of Commerce have rural development programs. After a two year delay, the Agricultural Act of 2014 (commonly referred to as the Farm Bill) was reauthorized by Congress and signed in February, 2014. This act, which will remain in place through 2018, established funding and guidelines for the Supplemental Nutrition Assistance Program (SNAP), food commodities, and other supports for farmers and others in the agricultural industry. Note that many farmers benefit from SNAP and food commodities not only because their products are used in these programs but also because their families qualify for and are beneficiaries of these programs. The Farm Act benefits the agricultural industry in many ways, including support for horticulture, livestock and dairy programs; crop insurance options; conservation programs; agricultural research; new emphasis on specialty crops such as organic farming; bioenergy; programs for new farmers and ranchers; and rural development (USDA, 2014b).

Social Work, the Natural Environment, and Environmental Justice

Whether working in a rural or an urban setting, social workers must be aware of the impact that the natural environment has on clients and the communities in which they live. Social workers have a long history of focusing on the interactions between the person and the environment and the role the environment plays in individual, family, and community well-being, beginning with the efforts of Mary Richmond and Jane Addams. However, the emphasis has been primarily on the *social* rather than the *natural* environment. But as the world population continues to grow, with the emphasis on production of food, shelter, and other consumer goods, it is becoming increasingly clear the earth cannot continue to sustain its ever-growing population unless immediate actions are taken.

Scientists point to the increased production of carbon dioxide that the earth is unable to absorb, resulting in a widening gap in the ozone layer and global warming. Increased use of land for crops, often singular crops, has resulted in destruction of rain forests and other natural habitats, which has in turn led to the destruction of both plant and animal life. Our dependency on fuel and water has also led to shortages across the globe of these important resources, even in the United States. Additionally, the use of toxic chemicals and hormones in food production, land use, and war has also created health and other problems for individuals across the globe (van Wormer, Besthorn, & Keefe, 2007). What some consider progress others question as damaging to the environment. Concerns about the impact of shale extraction, commonly known as "fracking," to gain additional access to oil and gas in various parts of the United States include pollution and depletion of ground water, seismic disturbances, laying of miles of potentially dangerous pipelines, and creation of a landscape with drilling wells and pumping stations that may not be sustainable for the quickly growing communities established at the sites.

As noted earlier in this text, the population across the world continues to increase as people have access to better nutrition and health care and live longer lives. At the same time, hurricanes, floods, tsunamis and other natural disasters, land erosion, water and air pollution, genetic engineering of plants and animals used as sources of food, overfishing, use of dangerous chemicals in fertilizers and pesticides, and global pandemics such as ebola have drawn increased attention to the need to do more to manage our natural environment. Van Wormer, Besthorn, and O'Keefe (2007) note that in the next few years, as many as 50 million people will become environmental refugees, moving elsewhere to escape their deteriorating environment because of the aftermath of intense weather, global warming, or scarcity of water and other resources needed to survive. The aftermaths of Hurricane Katrina in the United States, the earthquake in Haiti, and the tsunamis in Sri Lanka and Japan called attention to not only the displaced hundreds of thousands individuals, but the fact that many of them were living in poverty and did not have resources to relocate without assistance.

Current focus on the natural environment also promotes **environmental racism**. Persons of color and their families are much more likely to be exposed to environmental hazards than others because of where they live and work. They are more likely to live in older homes with exposure to lead paint and asbestos. Incinerators, toxic waste dumps, landfills, and factories that use and often spew toxic chemicals into the air are disproportionately located in neighborhoods populated by Blacks/African Americans, Hispanics/Latinos, and recent immigrants and on Native American reservations. Increased cancer among residents in a largely Black/African American low income neighborhood in Alabama occurred when Monsanto, a large chemical company, located there. It was discovered that dangerous chemicals released by the plant polluted soil and water in the community. Environmental justice advocates filed a class action suit against Monsanto, resulting in a $42.8 million settlement for residents (van Wormer, Besthorn, & Keefe, 2007).

Attention has also been given to increased consumerism across the world as it becomes more industrialized. Not only does this result in overuse of natural resources and products difficult to recycle (cell phones, computers, automobiles) but also stigmatization of those who cannot afford to be part of the consumer movement and increased pressure to compete—and pay the bills—for those who do participate.

Human problems that social workers help clients address often stem from their natural environment. Research shows that mismanagement of the natural environment can have devastating impacts on individuals, families, and entire communities that result in

infertility, still born births, birth defects, developmental and intellectual disabilities, respiratory problems including asthma and lung disease, multiple types of cancer, and lead and radiation poisoning. Workers in coal mines, chemical plants, oil fields, and agriculture are more likely to develop cancer, lung disease, and other illnesses and to die earlier than those employed in other settings. Smoking, even exposure to secondary smoke, also negatively impacts health. Exposure to dangerous toxins can even impact prenatal development. Many teratogens (any environmental agent that causes damage during the prenatal period) result in both immediate and long-term effects. Because the foundations for all body parts are being established during the first eight weeks of pregnancy, teratogens can have the most significant impact during this time period, when a woman may not even be aware that she is pregnant. Exposure to radiation, pollutants such as mercury or lead, dioxins resulting from incineration, and smoke, even secondary smoke, can result in miscarriage, physical defects, brain damage and other developmental disabilities, and various types of cancer (Berk, 2014).

A question for all of us who live on this planet is how to redirect resources so that they don't just balance the needs of people equitably, but also the needs of the rest of the biological world (van Wormer, Besthorn, & Keefe, 2007). For social workers, an additional question is, What is our role in helping individuals, families, communities, and the broader society in advocating for these changes? One concept that social workers can support is **deep ecology**. This concept goes beyond shallow ecology, which is concerned with the impact of changes in the natural environment on humans, and most often those with privilege. Deep ecology is "concerned with issues of equality and ecojustice in humanity's relationship with nature ... giving all people and all beings equal respect and consideration" (van Wormer, Besthorn, & Keefe, 2007, p. 243). Social workers must understand the impact of both the natural and the social environment on clients from an individual and a global perspective, as well as their impact on the environment. The NASW is doing more to engage members of the profession in discussion about the natural environment. Social workers have a vested interest both personally and professionally in protecting the earth so it can support the well-being and survival of its citizens (Dewane, 2011). They can organize grass roots participation, collaborate with other groups in environmental justice efforts, educate others about the issues, and vote to support elected officials who support environmental justice and preserving the natural environment. Working to promote environmental justice and to eradicate environmental racism should be a priority for all social workers.

Social Work in Rural and Urban Settings and Environmentalism

EP 2.1.1a
EP 2.1.7b
EP 2.1.8a

The practice of social work in rural communities is both similar to and different from that practiced in urban areas. The core of knowledge, methods, and skills of social work practice is the foundation for practice efforts in both environments (Hepworth, Rooney, Rooney, & Strom-Gottfried, 2012). The nature of rural and urban settings, the problems experienced, and the lack of resources create a unique set of challenges. Creativity, innovation, and the ability to influence community members to mobilize in meeting their needs are crucial skills for successful practice in both rural and urban settings. Social workers must be involved at the individual client level and also in the revitalization of rural and urban areas, through asset building to create healthy communities that use everyone's capabilities (Green & Goetting, 2013). Social work in both settings requires intervening within the total environment.

Although many of the skills needed to practice social work are the same as those that urban social workers use, an important difference is the emphasis on informal and personal relationships in rural settings. Social workers Michael Daley and Freddie Avant present a model for rural social work that is a modified type of the generalist method. Their model incorporates the elements of generalist practice, social exchange, and the strengths perspective and views social problems within the context of a wider community, taking into account the effects of living in a rural community on a person's behavior. The model focuses not just on the strengths of individuals and families, as with generalist practice, but also ensure that rural communities are also viewed as strengths with opportunities, as opposed to deficits (Daley, 2015, pp. 202–203). Their model also incorporates the concepts of Gemeinschaft and Gesellschaft, which you might have studied in a sociology course. Rural social work is more consistent with Gemeinschaft, with its emphasis on family, geographic place, friendship, and the dynamics of informal relationships and social status. In contrast, urban social work is more consistent with Gesellschaft, which emphasizes more impersonal, formal transactions.

Rural social workers often must provide rural dwellers with services, support, and hope while helping simultaneously to change the environment to provide better transportation, improved medical care, and a more responsive community. Unlike urban social workers, the social worker in a rural area may feel frustrated by the absence of the company and support of fellow social work professionals, as well as the absence of a formal social service network. Opportunities for consultation and feedback on one's work are limited, so rural social workers may be left to make critical decisions on their own.

Social workers who both live and practice in rural areas find themselves as neighbors as well as professional practitioners. Almost everyone in the community knows who they are, and they may be called at home as well as the office to provide a wide range of services. Their service constituency may consist of children, adults, those with mental illness, the incarcerated, the bedridden, the distressed, and the abandoned. At any one time, a social worker may be helping a family locate a nursing-home placement for an older parent, securing resources for a child with a disability, counseling with a pregnant teenager and her family, collaborating with local ministers in developing leisure-time activities for youth, assisting school personnel in developing management techniques for a hyperactive child, or working with the court to secure rehabilitation resources for a delinquent child. These varied demands require that the social worker be flexible, have good communication skills, engage both private and public resources, and have a basic understanding of community values and practices.

Practicing social work at the ground level in both rural settings subjects the social worker to "life in a fish bowl." Everyone seems to know the social worker both professionally and personally. His or her private life is closely scrutinized. Because social workers, like everyone else, have problems, the way these problems are managed becomes a matter of community concern. Like ministers, their work is expected to meet high personal and moral standards, and any deviation may lower the esteem in which they are held in the community. In rural communities, the ability to separate personal life from professional competence is difficult.

Box 14.1   NASW Professional Policy Statement in Rural Social Work

This statement was approved by NASW's Delegate Assembly in 2002. Excerpts from the policy statement are presented below:

Social work practice in rural communities challenges the social worker to embrace and effectively use an impressive range of professional intervention and community skills. It is critical that the social worker have practice expertise in multiple areas. Like all subcultures, rural populations must be understood to be effectively engaged. The difficulties associated with experiencing social problems are magnified in rural areas because close social and personal relationships coexist with a low population base. This and other unique features require the social worker to apply professional ethical constructs more consistently to protect confidentiality, analyze relationship issues, and otherwise behave in the best interests of clients.

Rural areas suffer disproportionately when urban-based policies are forced upon them. Corporate mergers, centralization, managed care, globalization, and similar cost-saving strategies based solely on urban models are disadvantageous to rural areas, where distance and time are the enemies of efficiency and of access to social services, health care delivery, and health maintenance....

Public and social policy must take into account the unique nature of rural areas and residents. Equitable policy formation should be the goal, so that urban and rural populations and jurisdictions are not pitted against each other over issues of livelihood, lifestyle, economy, or ecology....

The skills of professional social workers are uniquely suited to helping rural people organize their lives, families, communities, and organizations to overcome adversity, identify and develop resources, and change lives for the better....

SOURCE: NASW Professional Policy Statement in Rural Social Work. (2013). T.L. Scales & C. L. Avant (Eds.). *Rural social work: Building and sustaining community assets* (2nd edition). (pp. 317–322). Hoboken, NJ: Wiley.

Often, the social worker's credibility is at stake if a personal problem goes unresolved.

Maintaining the client's confidentiality when practicing in rural settings can be difficult. Residents typically know when anyone in the community is having problems and when someone is seeking professional assistance. A casual encounter at the grocery store may prompt a resident to inquire about a client whom they know through the grapevine is receiving services.

Similar experiences are typical of social workers in urban areas if they work in a designated neighborhood. School social workers and those who work in settlement houses in urban areas, for example, report similar experiences. A social worker who works in either a rural or an urban area but does not live there may encounter other problems. Typically, they are regarded as outsiders. In some instances, they have not had the opportunity to become aware of community priorities and values. Often, they are viewed as having little vested interest in the community and, as a result, may respond to client problems out of context.

An old social work axiom suggests that "change comes slowly." Social workers in both rural and urban areas must learn to stifle their frustration and impatience while maintaining their persistent efforts in the helping process. As their credibility and competence become better established, community resistance will turn into support, and social workers' contribution to the community will be enhanced.

Interpersonal relationships with community leaders are essential in gaining support for change efforts in both rural and urban areas. Small communities and neighborhoods within larger communities are varied in culture and values. Ethnic settlements often cling to traditional values and practices—an important factor in getting to know the community. Values and traditions often are identified as the driving dynamic of community life. Understanding this phenomenon enhances the social worker's ability to communicate effectively with community leaders.

The social work profession has long been concerned about the needs in rural areas and how best to address them. In the mid-1970s, the Rural Social Work Caucus was created to direct attention to practice and research issues related to rural communities and social work practice (Hickman, 2014). The caucus meets regularly and has been instrumental in developing policy statements on rural social work adopted by both the National Association of Social Workers (NASW) and the Council on Social Work Education (CSWE).

Caucus members submitted a new policy statement to NASW in 2002, which was adopted by the organization (see Box 14.1 for a summary of this statement).

By now you should be aware of some of the more salient differences between social work practice in rural and urban areas. As noted above, the models of intervention used in rural communities provide important lessons for working in urban neighborhoods.

While many social workers have been environmental activists for some time, they are increasingly becoming involved in efforts to sustain our environment and fight against environmental injustice. Some social workers are employed by grassroots organizations that focus on environmental injustice, while others represent their agencies or are personally involved in efforts at local, state, and national levels. The Global Alliance for a Deep Ecological Social Work (www.ecosocialwork.org) promotes social work efforts to support environmental sustainability. The University of Denver Graduate School of Social Work also has courses and an emphasis on environmental conservation, with field placements in China at the Chengdu Research Base of Giant Panda Breeding and in Kenya working with an African network for Animal Welfare. The program has developed competencies for students interested in social work conservation that incorporate knowledge about conservation and models of practice that support the natural environment (conservationsocialwork.org).

Rural, Urban, and Environmental Social Work as Generalist Practice

EP 2.1.1a
EP 2.1.7b
EP 2.1.8b

The variety and diversity of the tasks inherent in rural work practice can best be accomplished by the generalist practitioner. Haulotte and Oliver (2004) identified six steps critical for a social worker who is entering a rural community. As you read, note the parallel with the concepts of generalist practice discussed earlier in the text and also ask yourself whether these skills also apply to a social worker in an urban community, and under what conditions.

Social workers in both rural and urban settings are called upon to work with individuals, families, and groups and in community organizations. Administrative and management skills are essential in rendering needed services in both settings (see Box 14.2). The abilities to define problems operationally, collect and analyze data, and translate findings into practical solutions are requisites for enriched practice. The social work practitioner in these settings is a multi-method worker who appropriately facilitates the problem-solving process. Knowledge of resources, resource development, methods of linking clients with resources, and case management is required of the social worker in both settings. However, knowledge and skills may be used differently. In both settings, collaboration is key to effectiveness. However, in a rural area or an urban neighborhood, collaborations may be more informal and more likely to involve community participants in all kinds of roles. Additionally, social workers may be more likely to be involved in a multitude of tasks, including transportation, setup and clean up, purchasing of supplies, and they may function more autonomously from their agencies. In urban areas where a social worker may provide more specialized services, most collaborations may be with other professionals rather than community members, and tasks may also be more specialized and connected more closely to agency functions. Social workers in urban areas often also struggle with the depersonalization and lack of identity that their clients might feel when they come to them for services. Clients may have received services from a multitude of agencies with limited success and may believe that the social worker is not going to be able to understand their needs or relate positively to them based on past experiences. Clients may also have difficulty understanding the specialization and criteria for receiving services, and as a result may come to an agency that is unable to meet their needs, resulting in further frustration.

Social workers working to promote environmental justice and in conservation efforts also use generalist practice knowledge and skills, though they are more likely to work at the macro level in education, policy, community organizing, and research efforts. Generalist practice skills that focus on strengths, empowerment, and collaboration are critical as well. Like rural social workers, environmental social workers must be comfortable with autonomy, paving new ground for a field of social work practice not yet well developed, and collaborating with people and groups at all levels who are not likely to be social work practitioners. Like urban social workers, they must be comfortable with working in a complex environment and relating to diverse groups of people who often have competing worldviews.

Box 14.2   Some Characteristics of Effective Rural Social Workers

- They embody the generalist perspective of social work practice and link people with resources, both traditional and nontraditional, to address client needs.
- They are skillful at networking with a variety of traditional and nontraditional resources to address client and community needs.
- They are quick to understand the nuances of the rural communities in which they work, including traditions, values, culture, and formal and informal sources of support, and adapt their practice methods accordingly and with sensitivity to best meet client needs.
- They are able to establish informal mechanisms of communication with clients and other community members, yet maintain appropriate professional boundaries.
- They are creative in determining effective strategies to address client and community needs.
- They are comfortable with the use of technology to link the communities they serve with the broader environment.
- They are able to work independently and make critical decisions about client and community

needs within the boundaries of agency guidelines without ready access to immediate supervision.
- They have a strong sense of identity with the social work profession and are able to exemplify the values and methods of the profession without constant reinforcement from other social workers.
- They are able to gather and use feedback effectively to evaluate their professional work.
- They are strong advocates for the needs of rural areas.
- They are comfortable working across all levels of the environment and at becoming actively involved at the community level and beyond to create needed change.
- They understand the value of evidence-based practice and share what they learn about best practice in rural areas.

SOURCE: Haulotte, S. & Oliver, S. (2004). A strategy for uncovering, accessing, and maximizing assets and strengths in rural area social services. In T.L. Scales and C.L. Streeter (Eds.), *Rural social work: Building and sustaining community assets*. Belmont, CA: Brooks/Cole.

Social work in rural and urban communities and as an environmentalist is both challenging and rewarding. To function effectively, social workers in these arenas must be self-reliant and confident in their ability to effect positive change. Often, they are required to work apart from social work support systems. Many social work programs are located in small cities or large towns adjacent to rural areas. Field placements typically call upon rural agencies to familiarize students with the skills essential for practicing in those settings. Students and social workers, once they obtain their BSW or MSW degrees, are likely to be called upon to work autonomously and demonstrate knowledge and skill in clinical work, administration, and community building.

In contrast, social work students in urban settings may work in a bureaucratic organization with an extensive chain of command or an organization that collaborates extensively with a multitude of other agencies. Field placements in urban areas typically call for students to learn about the extensive resources available to

clients, but may find that their clients are not eligible to receive them or that there is a waiting list if they are. BSW graduates are often hired as case managers to assist clients in identifying needs and navigating the resources that they need, while MSW graduates may provide clinical services or become involved in macro social work in urban planning, research, or policy advocacy.

Social workers focusing on the environment can be employed with either BSW or MSW degrees and in either rural or urban environments. Thus, a blend of skills needed for both rural and urban settings is needed.

The generalist practice perspective of the social worker will prove invaluable in working with both rural and urban populations and in focusing on the natural environment. The opportunity to engage existing formal and informal organizations in extending or developing resources to meet community needs is a continuing challenge that the social workers can address competently. Also, knowledge and expertise in problem identification, outreach, linking of target systems with resources, resource development, education, and problem solving enrich the lives of rural and urban inhabitants, strengthen community support systems, and help to sustain the natural environment and eliminate dangerous aspects that impact vulnerable clients. The abilities to understand community value systems and to experiment with innovative techniques in working with community residents are essential assets for productive practice.

Specialization at the graduate level also is invaluable in both urban and rural settings and when working to sustain the natural environment. A number of graduate programs focus on rural or urban social work, and many offer courses that emphasize work with these populations. Some also promote environmental sustainability. Other programs offer joint specializations in urban and regional planning or public health. Although many rural social work jobs draw on generalist practice skills, clinicians and macro practitioners are also in demand. Sometimes salaries are higher in rural areas if they have trouble recruiting social workers; in other areas there are limited opportunities because the few social workers who are there like their jobs and their communities and have no desire to leave.

Although there are differences in how their clients may access services and their expectations, social workers in both urban and rural environments draw on similar knowledge, skills and values, as do social workers focusing on the natural environment. The successful social worker in either setting is authentic, flexible, and client-centered, letting the client's or client system's story and setting guide assessment and intervention.

Summary

Approximately 20% of the nation's population lives in nonmetropolitan or rural areas on 80% of the country's land. Rural areas differ from urban areas in social organization, lifestyle, informal and formal helping networks, and the types of problems that are more likely to be experienced. Rural areas are becoming increasingly Latino, with most of the growth in rural areas in the West. Household incomes in rural areas are below those of household incomes in urban areas. Communities in rural areas are characterized by trust, independence of spirit, and basic friendliness; isolation, resistance to change, and traditional values; informal social networks, and a personal response to human need.

Unique issues related to diversity and availability of resources to meet human needs are present in both rural and urban settings. Because the scarcity of organized social services rural dwellers depend on local faith-based organizations, as well as natural helping networks of friends, relatives, and civic groups.

The impact of social problems is often greater on rural residents than on their urban counterparts. These problems include mental health disorders, child abuse and neglect, family violence, and poverty. Generalist practice is well suited to addressing rural and urban social issues, and an ideal fit for the BSW, with emphases on linking clients with informal resources, the need to be innovative and creative, and working with individuals and families while influencing community members to meet identified needs. There is a demand for MSWs in both rural and urban areas as well, as clients experience similar problems that need to be addressed at both the micro and macro levels in either setting.

Although social workers have been addressing problems that are the result of the natural environment for years, increased attention is being given to the roles that they can play in eradicating environmental racism and injustice as well as working to create an environment that focuses on deep ecology, supporting a sustainable earth for both humans and other biological entities. There are opportunities for both BSW and MSW social workers, often in nontraditional settings, that will help pave the way for other social workers interested in this area.

Competency Notes

EP 2.1.1a: Advocate for client access to the services of social work (pp. 449, 456, 459, 461). Because clients in rural areas often do not have the same access to services that clients in other areas have, an important role for rural social workers is advocating for increased services. In contrast, urban social workers may need to help clients access a complex array of services. All social workers need to advocate for a sustainable earth that promotes environmental justice.

EP 2.1.3a: Distinguish, appraise, and integrate multiple sources of knowledge, including research-based knowledge and practice wisdom (pp. 443, 446, 454, 455, 456). Social workers in both rural and urban areas and those working to sustain the natural environment must distinguish, appraise, and integrate multiple sources of knowledge, including clients and community members, research, and practice wisdom.

EP 2.1.7a: Apply knowledge of human behavior and the social environment (pp. 446, 451, 454). Social workers in rural and urban areas use the ecological/systems framework and other conceptual frameworks to guide the processes of assessment, intervention, and evaluation, with particular attention to the informal relationships often established in rural areas and collaboration with multiple formal organizations in urban areas. Both settings need to incorporate the impact of the natural environment on their clients and promote efforts that will sustain natural resources.

EP 2.1.7b: Use conceptual frameworks to guide the process of assessment, intervention, and evaluation (pp. 451, 453, 455, 456, 459, 461). Rural social workers critique and apply knowledge of human behavior and development, with emphasis on the impact of living in a rural environment, to understand the needs of their clients. Urban social workers need to incorporate the impact of living in an urban area when working with their clients. Those working in both rural and urban settings need to incorporate the natural environment when using conceptual frameworks with clients and client systems.

EP 2.1.8a: Analyze, formulate, and advocate for policies that advance social well-being (pp. 449, 459). Social workers in rural areas analyze, formulate, and advocate for policies that advance social well-being, with attention to the needs of their rural clients, to ensure that policies and programs are not targeted toward those primarily in non-rural areas. Social workers in urban areas need to navigate often complex policies at organizational, city, state, and federal levels to ensure that they meet the needs of their diverse clients. Environmental social workers need to work to ensure that polices related to the natural environment are applied justly and do not marginalize certain groups and that they also promote a sustainable balance between humanity and other biological entities.

EP 2.1.8b: Collaborate with colleagues and clients for effective policy action (pp. 456, 461). Because access to professional colleagues is often more limited in rural areas, rural social workers must emphasize collaboration with colleagues and clients for effective policy action. In contrast, urban social workers must collaborate with multiple colleagues, often focusing on the same services, to meet their clients' needs. Both must work to ensure that clients are not exposed to natural environmental hazards or are targets of environmental racism.

EP 2.1.9b: Provide leadership in promoting sustainable changes in service delivery and practice to improve the quality of social services (p. 456). Leadership in both rural and urban communities is critical to help ensure that the appropriate services exist for individuals and families. Leadership is also needed to ensure that the natural environment is preserved in a just way that sustains the lives of all people as well as other living things.

Key Terms

The terms below are defined in the Glossary.

county agent	rural social work
deep ecology	support services
digital divide	telecommunications
environmental racism	telemedicine
gentrification	urban
natural helping networks	U.S. Department of
new urbanism	Agriculture (USDA)
rural	

Discussion Questions

1. Review the case study at the beginning of this chapter. How might a generalist social worker help the McDowell family? The Lindstrom family? How would geographic location shape the social work skills these families' needs?

2. Identify at least three examples of how a social problems in rural areas different from those in urban areas.

3. To what extent is generalist social work practice viable in working with individuals and families in rural communities? In urban areas? Why?

4. With fewer formal social welfare programs available in rural areas, how are natural helping networks useful to the social worker in providing services in these areas?

5. Why is it important to understand the culture, traditions, and values of rural communities, and how would you learn about them as a social worker in a rural area? How does this

understanding enable social workers to be more effective?

6. How are the problems facing rural Americans today different from those facing urban Americans? How are they similar?

7. What kind of plan would you develop in a rural community to move toward sustainability? Who would you involve in the plan? In an urban area? Who would you involve in the plan?

8. Give three examples of ways that the natural environment impacts social workers and their clients.

9. Give two examples of environmental racism. What can social workers do to reduce environmental racism?

On the Internet

www.cirsinc.org
www.cardi.cornell.edu
www.conservationsocialwork.org
www.ecosocialwork.org
www.ncfh.org
www.ruralinstitute.umt.edu
www.rupri.org
www.uncp.edu/home/marson/rural
www.rwhc.com
www.worh.org
www.wfan.org
www.ers.usda.gov
www.kumc.edu/instruction/medicine/NRPC

References

Anderson, K., & Olson, S. (2014). *Leveraging culture to address health inequalities: Examples from native communities.* Washington, DC: National Academies Press.

Avant, F. (2014). African Americans in rural areas: Building on assets from an Afrocentric perspective. In T. Scales, C. Streeter, & S. Cooper (Eds.), *Rural social work: Building and sustaining community assets* (2nd ed.) (pp. 75–86). Hoboken, NJ: Wiley.

Berk, L. (2014). *Development through the lifespan.* Boston: Pearson.

Bovee, D. (2010). *The church and the land: The national Catholic rural life conference and American society.* Washington, DC: Catholic University of America Press.

Butra, N. (2013). *Urban poverty: Its challenges and characteristics.* Retrieved September 4, 2014, from http://terraurban.wordpress.com/2013/04/09/urban-poverty-its-challenges-and-characteristics

Center for Rural Affairs. (2010). *2010 annual report.* Lyons, NE: Author.

Colby, I. (1987). The bottom line: A personal account of poverty (anonymous author). *Human Services in the Rural Environment, 11*(1), 9–11.

Crosby, R., Wendel, M., Vanderpool, R., & Casey, B. (2012). *Rural populations and health: Determinants, disparities, and solutions.* San Francisco, CA: Jossey-Bass.

Daley, M., & Avant, F. (2014). Down-home social work: A strengths-based model for rural social work. In T. Scales, C. Streeter, & H. Cooper (Eds.), *Rural social work: Building and sustaining community assets* (2nd ed.) (pp. 5–18). Hoboken, NJ: Wiley.

Davis, J. (Eds.). (2010). *The community land trust reader.* Cambridge, MA: Lincoln Institute for Land Policy.

Dear, M., & Wolch, J. (2014). *Landscapes of despair: From deinstitutionalization to homelessness.* Princeton, NJ: Princeton University Press.

DeFillippis, J., & Saegert, S. (2012). *The community development reader* (2nd ed.). New York: Routledge.

Delgado, M., & Humm-Delgado, B. (2013). *Asset assessments and community social work practice.* New York: Oxford University Press.

Department of Veterans Affairs. (2012). *VA to increase mental health care access through 200,000 telemental health consultations in 2012.* Washington, DC: Author. Retrieved September 26, 2014, from http://www.va.gov/opa/pressrel/pressrelease.cfm?id=2325

Dewane, C. (2011). Environmentalism and social work: The ultimate social justice issue. *Social Work Today, 11*(5), 4.

Esparza, A. X., & Donelson, A. J. (2010). *The colonias reader: Economy, housing, and public health in U.S.—Mexico border colonias.* Tucson: University of Arizona.

Fuder, J., & Castellanos, N. (2013). *A heart for the community: New models for urban and suburban ministry.* Chicago, IL: Moody Publishers.

Garriott, W. (2011). *Policing methamphetamine: Narcopolitics in rural America.* New York: NYU Press.

Ginsberg, L. (2011). *Social work in rural communities* (5th ed.). Washington, DC: Council on Social Work Education.

Green, G., & Goetting, A. (Eds.). (2013). *Mobilizing communities: Asset building as a community development strategy.* Philadelphia, PA: Temple University Press.

Health Resources and Services Administration. (2014). *Health professional shortage areas (HRSAs)*. Washington, DC: Author. Retrieved September 26, 2014, from http://www.bhpr.hrsa.gov/shortage/hpsas/designationcriteria/index.html

Hepworth, D., Rooney, R., Rooney, G., & Strom-Gottfried, K. (2012). *Direct social work practice: Theory and skills* (9th ed.). Independence, KY: Cengage Learning.

Hickman, S. (2014). Rural is real: Supporting professional practice through the rural social work caucus and the NASW professional policy statement for rural social work. In T. Scales, C. Streeter, & S. Cooper (Eds.), *Rural social work: Building and sustaining community assets* (2nd ed.) (pp. 19–28). Hoboken, NJ: Wiley.

Holmes, S., & Bourgois, P. (2013). *Fresh fruit, broken bodies: Migrant farmworkers in the United States*. Oakland, CA: University of California Press.

Housing Assistance Council. (2012). *Race and ethnicity in rural America*. Washington, DC: Author. Retrieved September 24, 2014, from http://slideshare.net/Ruralone/Race-and-ethnicity-in-rural-America

Hurley, A. (2010). *Beyond preservation: Using public history to revitalize inner cities*. Philadelphia, PA: Temple University Press.

Jansson, B. (2011). *The reluctant welfare state: Engaging history to advance social work practice in contemporary society* (7th ed.). Stanford, CT: Cengage Learning.

Jurik, N. (2005). *Bootstrap dreams: U.S. microenterprise development in an era of welfare reform*. Ithaca, NY: ILR Press.

Klugman, C., & Dalinis, P. (Eds.). (2012). *Ethical issues in rural health care*. Baltimore, MD: Johns Hopkins University Press.

Kozol, J. (2012a). *Amazing grace: The lives of children and the conscience of a nation*. New York: Broadway Books.

Kozol, J. (2012b). *Ordinary resurrections: Children in the years of hope*. New York: Broadway Books.

Kozol, J. (2013). *Fire in the ashes: Twenty-five years among the poorest children in Americas*. New York: Broadway Books.

Kutner, M. (2014, April 18). Death on the farm. *Newsweek, 162*(15).

Ladicola, P., & Shupe, A. (2012). *Violence, inequality, and human freedom* (3rd ed.). Lanham, MD: Rowen & Littlefield.

Ledwith, M. (2011). *Community development; A critical approach*. Bristol United Kingdom: Policy Press.

Lujan, J. (2009, July). Got Hispanic clients: Get a promotora. *Journal of Allied Health Sciences and Practice, 7*(3).

Lupton, R. (2011). *Theirs is the Kingdom: Celebrating the gospel in urban America*. New York: HarperCollins.

Lusk, M., Staudt, K., & Moya, E. (Eds.). (2012). *Social justice in the U.S.-Mexico border region*. New York: Springer.

Macionis, J., & Parillo, V. (2012). *Cities and urban life* (2nd ed.). Boston, MA: Pearson.

Mackun, P., & Wilson, S. (2011). *Population distribution and change: 2000–2010*. 2010 Census Briefs. Washington, DC: Census Bureau. Retrieved from http://www.census.gov/prod/cen2010/briefs/c2010br-01.pdf

Mattingly, M., & Walsh, W. (2010). *Rural families with a child abuse report are more likely headed by a single parent and endure economic and family stress*. Durham, NH: Carsey Institute, University of New Hampshire.

McKnight, J., & Block, P. (2012). *The abundant community: Awakening the power of families and neighborhoods*. San Francisco: Berrett-Koehler.

Mehrotra, A. (2014). *Expanding the use of telehealth: Promise and potential pitfalls*. Santa Monica, CA: Rand. Retrieved September 26, 2014, from http://www.rand.org/pubs/testimonies/ct409.html

Mehrotra, A., Paone, S., Martich, D., Albert, S., & Shevchik, G. (2013, July). Characteristics of patients who seek care via e-visits instead of office visits. *Telemedicine and e-Health, 19*(17), 515–519.

Moore, W. (2012). *Rural revival: Churches in shrinking communities*. Rogersville, AL: Eleos Press.

Morganti, K., Bauhoff, S., Blanchard, J., & Iyer, N. (2013). *The evolving role of emergency departments in the United States*. Santa Monica, CA: Rand.

Munoz, J. (Ed.). (2010). *Contemporary microenterprise: Concepts and cases*. Northampton, MA: Edward Elgar.

National Center for Farmworker Health. (2014). *Migrant health 2014*. Buda, Texas: Author.

Nies, M., & McEwen, M. (2014). *Community/public health nursing: Promoting the health* (5th ed.). Philadelphia, PA: Elsevier.

Porter, D. (2012). *Breaking the development log jam: New strategies for building community support*. Lincoln, NE: Urban Land Institute.

Pritchard, F. (2014). *Gaining ground: A story of farmer's markets, local food, and saving the family farm*. Guilford, CT: Lyons Press.

Ragnedda, M., & Muschert, G. (2013). *The digital divide: The Internet and social inequality in international perspective*. New York: Routledge.

Rank, M., & Hirschl, T., & Foster, K. (2014). *Chasing the American dream: Understanding what shapes our fortunes.* New York: Oxford University Press.

Rosenfeld, R., Edberg, M., Fang, X., & Florence, C. (Eds.). (2013). *Economics and youth violence: Crime, disadvantage, and community.* New York: NYU Press.

Rural Assistance Center. (2014). *What significant issues face the rural aging population today.* Grand Forks, ND: Author. Retrieved September 26, 2014, from http://www.raconline.org/topics/aging/faqs#issues

Scales, T., Streeter, C., & Cooper, S. (Eds.). (2014). *Rural social work: Building and sustaining community assets* (2nd ed.). Hoboken, NJ: Wiley.

Seccombe, K. (2010). *So you think I drive a Cadillac?* (3rd ed.). Boston, MA: Pearson.

Singer, A. (2012). *Immigrant workers in the U.S. labor force.* Washington, DC: Brookings.

Small, M., & Allard, S. (2013). *Reconsidering the urban disadvantaged: The role of systems, institutions, and organizations.* Thousand Oaks, CA: Sage.

Smalley, K., Warren, J., & Rainer, J. (2012). *Rural mental health: Issues, policies, and best practices* [The New York: Springer. The Economist (2010). *Field of tears 2010.* San Francisco, CA: Author].

Truglia-Londrigan, M., & Lewenson, S. (2012). *Public health nursing: Population-based care* (2nd ed.). Burlington, MA: Jones & Bartlett.

Uscher-Pines, L., & Mehrotra, A. (2014, February). Analysis of teledoc use seems to indicate expanded access to care for patients without prior connection to a provider. *Health Affairs, 33*(2), 258–264.

U.S. Census Bureau. (2012). *Growth in urban population outpaces rest of nation.* Washington, DC: Author.

U.S. Census Bureau. (2013). *Income and poverty in the United States: 2013.* Washington, DC: Author.

U.S. Census Bureau. (2014). *Type of health insurance coverage by selected demographic characteristics.* Washington, DC: Author.

U.S. Department of Agriculture. (2013). *Rural America at a glance: 2013 edition.* Washington, DC: Economic Research Service.

U.S. Department of Agriculture. (2014a). *About rural development.* Washington, DC: Author. Retrieved September 27, 2014, from http://www.rurdev.usda.gov/Home.html

U.S. Department of Agriculture. (2014b). *2014 Farm bill highlights.* Washington, DC: Author. Retrieved from http://www.usda.gov/documents/usda-2014-farm-bill-highlights.pdf

U.S. Office of Management and Budget. (2010). 2010 Standards for delineating metropolitan and micropolitan statistical areas. *Federal Register.* Retrieved November 15, 2010, from http://edocket.access.gpo.gov/2010/pdf/2010–15605.pdf

van Wormer, K., Besthorn, F., & Keefe, T. (2007). *Human behavior and the social environment: Macro level.* New York, New York: Oxford.

Zukin, S. (2011). *Naked city: The death and life of authentic urban places.* New York: Oxford University Press.

Suggested Readings

Alexander, K., Entwisle, D., & Olson, L. (2014). *The long shadow: Family background, disadvantaged urban youth, and the transition to adulthood.* New York: Russell Sage Foundation.

Carr, P. J., & Kefalas, M. J. (2010). *Hollowing out the middle: The rural brain drain and what it means for America.* Boston: Beacon.

Harvey, P. (2014). *The farmer in all of us: An American portrait.* Washington, DC: National Geographic.

Pugh, R., & Cheers, B. (2010). *Rural social work: International perspectives.* Bristol, UK: Policy Press.

Sugrue, T. (2014). *The origins of the urban crisis: Race and inequality in postwar Detroit.* Princeton, NJ: Princeton University Press.

CHAPTER 15

Social Work in the Workplace

Bill and Meredith Hunt, both 32 years old, live in a small house in a rapidly deteriorating part of the city with their three children, ages 2, 4, and 8. Bill is one of several workers who monitor a mostly automated assembly line at a large manufacturing plant. Meredith is a computer programmer for a large company. The Hunts' two youngest children attend a child-care center, and their oldest child attends public school.

Until recently, Bill's job has been the most important aspect of his life. He is well liked as an employee, but he is finding that his job is a lot less meaningful to him than in the past. His raises are less frequent and are insufficient to cover cost-of-living increases. Last year, Bill and the other assembly-line workers were laid off for 2 months because of a production slowdown. Most manufacturing companies in the area are buying their parts from abroad, and Bill's company increasingly is automating its operations, which reduces the need for employees. There is even talk of shutting down the plant and moving it offshore. Bill is frustrated about the recent layoff and the lack of pay and is concerned about how long his job will last. Although he knows that his wife has to work to make ends meet, Bill is resentful that she has less time for him and he feels badly that he can't provide for his family on his own.

Recently Bill has begun drinking heavily. During these drinking bouts, he has hit Meredith several times, and he yells at the children and spanks them. Bill's supervisor has noticed a change in his job performance and is ready to give him formal notification that his performance has to improve or he risks being fired. Bill feels constantly tired, financially pressured, and emotionally defeated.

Meredith also feels emotionally drained. In addition to her job, she maintains primary responsibility for the house and the children. She gets up at 5:30 a.m., and finally, after midnight, everything is done and she collapses into bed. Because the child care for the Hunts' two children costs more than half of Meredith's take-home pay, they can't afford child care for their oldest son before and after school. Meredith worries about him being at home alone and calls him several times each afternoon.

Neither of the companies the Hunts work for allows employees to take leave when the children are sick, and all three children have been sick a lot lately. Meredith has missed 6 days of work in the last 2 months to stay home and care for her sick children. On three other occasions she has kept her oldest son home from school to take care of the younger children.

Meredith's mother, who lives in a neighboring city, recently was diagnosed with Stage 3 cancer and is in need of major surgery with a lengthy recovery period. Meredith would like to spend several days with her mother during and after the surgery, as her siblings live out of state. But she has used all of her vacation days for her children's illnesses, and her company doesn't have any policies that provide for leave in situations like this.

Recently, Meredith has been having trouble sleeping and has developed stomach problems. Her doctor prescribed tranquilizers, which she takes more often than she should. Meredith's coworkers are worried about her, but at the same time they resent having to do extra work when she is absent or not as productive as usual. Her boss has commented on the decline in her job performance. Meredith likes her job very much but is worried about her husband, her children, and her mother. She feels guilty because her working places extra pressures on her family. Her oldest son is not doing well in school, and Meredith is too tired to help him. All three children vie constantly for her attention. Both Meredith and Bill feel caught between the pressures of work and their family, and they are becoming increasingly overwhelmed by the demands on them.

Most individuals who are older than 18 have two major domains in which they interact: the family and the workplace. Attention to social problems and individual needs usually centers on the family and rarely considers the relationship between the individual and the workplace. This omission has resulted in social workers not helping individuals and their families as effectively as they could.

Consider again the ecological/systems perspective to understanding problems discussed in Chapter 3, particularly the way in which the systems overlap and interact with each other and the individuals who function within those systems. Think about this perspective in relation to the Hunt family. Though until recently the Hunts have been a close-knit family, work has become the focal point in their lives. Work produces the economic resources needed to provide food, clothing, shelter, and the recreational activities that are affordable to them.

When we meet someone, our first question frequently is not, "What about your family?" but, rather, "Where do you work?" In U.S. society, a person's status in life is defined largely by occupation. The type of work we do defines much of our self-respect, self-fulfillment, identity, and status. Until recently, both Bill and Meredith had received positive fulfillment in their workplaces. They got along well with coworkers and received raises and recognition for jobs well done.

At first their two jobs allowed the Hunts to support their family adequately. The positive aspects of work spilled over into the family, allowing them to maintain positive support within the family. But the overlap between the two domains began to create additional pressures for both Bill and Meredith. Conflicts arose about which has to come first—home or work—when they are drained of energy for both. What should be done when a child or relative gets sick? How much money should be spent on child care? Who is going to prepare the meals when both parents are tired? What jobs and career paths should be pursued in the rapidly changing workplace? All of these issues have an impact on Bill and Meredith's relationships and ability to function, both at home and at work.

For Bill and Meredith, work currently has many negative implications. Ideally, they will seek help from some social service program before either their family or their jobs become jeopardized further. A social worker or other helping professional who becomes involved with the Hunts' problems must consider work issues in the total intervention.

In this chapter, we explore current and projected workforce demographics, the changing nature and meaning of work, problems created by work and family tensions, and the roles the workplace and social workers can play in attempting to prevent these problems from occurring or recurring.

A Historical Perspective on Work and Family Relationships

EP 2.1.3a

In most Western countries, particularly in the United States, the roots of society can be traced to the Protestant work ethic, which stems from the Protestant Reformation of the 17th century. This ethic suggests that work is an expectation of God and that laziness is sinful. Attitudes toward paupers during the early colonization of the United States and toward welfare recipients today are derived from the impact of this belief. For women, however, the emphasis was different: The primary role of women was to maintain the family and to support the ability of men in the family to work outside the home.

Until the 1970s, this pattern changed only during wartime, when women were needed in the factories while men were away at war. But as soon as peace was restored, the women returned to the home and men to the workplace. The women who did work outside the home—because of necessity, interest, or both—often were considered to be outside their appropriate role. Until the 1970s, most studies regarding work concentrated on the negative impact of the *unemployed* male on his family or on the negative impact of the *employed* female on her family (Major & Burke, 2014).

In recent years, much has changed in regard to the relationship between the individual and the workplace. Probably the biggest change has come from the large number of women who are working, including women with children. Other changes include a more diverse workplace, not only in gender but also in ethnicity. African Americans, Latinos, and other people of color are entering the workplace in historically large numbers.

Between 2012 and 2022, the U.S. civilian labor force is expected to change in three significant ways (U.S. Bureau of Labor Statistics, 2013a):

- Older age cohorts (65 or older for men and 55 or older for women) will make up a larger share of the labor force.
- A significant increase in the share of the workforce held by minorities will occur.
- There will be a slowdown in the overall growth of the labor force.

These changes will have a dramatic impact on employee recruitment, hiring and retention, the nature and scope of employee benefits, and how to manage a multigenerational workforce with very different views on the meaning and importance of work (Gratton, 2011; Maitland & Thomson, 2014; Morgan, 2014).

Employees today expect more from the workplace than just a paycheck. They seek recognition, a voice in decision making, a wide range of benefits, and flexible working hours. Numerous studies have found that many workers today have placed other priorities, such as leisure time and personal pursuits, ahead of their jobs (see for example, Lancaster & Stillman, 2010; Meister & Willyerd, 2010).

A growing number of experts view the relationship between work and family life as one of the most critical policy issues to be addressed during this decade (Kunin, 2012; Liss & Shiffrin, 2014; Sweet, 2013). In many instances, special social services and other programs have been established in the workplace to help employees and their families maintain or increase productivity (Kelloway & Hurrell, 2014).

Occupational social work (sometimes called "industrial social work") has emerged as a growing field for social workers. Occupational social workers usually work in the human resources department or health unit of a company. Occupational social workers are also employed as contract staff by third-party employee assistance programs or provide employee assistance services as part of private practice. They help employees cope with job-related pressures and personal problems that affect the quality of their work. They provide counseling to employees whose performance on the job is hindered by personal or family problems or substance abuse. They also develop educational programs on a variety of quality-of-life issues and refer workers to community programs for assistance (U.S. Bureau of Labor Statistics, 2014a). By applying a systems/ecological perspective, occupational social workers have the potential to play a major role in strengthening relationships among individuals, families, the community, and the workplace.

The Current Workforce

EP 2.1.3a

The single most defining characteristic of today's workforce is that it is diverse. A disproportionate share of women, people of color, and recently arrived immigrants are employed in often low-paying, dead-end jobs with little opportunity for advancement (Clements, 2012; Massengill, 2013).

In addition, as a result of technological and economic changes, the globalization of the marketplace, and the lingering effects of the 2007–2008 recession, many workplaces have closed, **downsized** their operations, or redefined the nature of their work and the type of resources needed, especially personnel (Vance & Paik, 2010). Workplace longevity has been redefined; hard work and loyalty to one's employer no longer guarantee anything (Delcampo, Haggerty, Haney, & Knippel, 2011). Increasingly, the vertical career ladder is giving way to so-called horizontal advancement. That is, employees who are able to add value *across* the organization are viewed as being a greater asset by employers than those who focus only on vertical advancement (Castellano, 2013).

More Women in the Workforce

In 2013, nearly 71% of all mothers with children less than 18 years of age were employed in full-time or part-time jobs (U.S. Department of Labor, 2014b). The rate of workforce participation by female heads of household exceeds that of two-parent families regardless of the ages of children in the household. The increase in the number of women employed outside the family has been fairly sudden, leaving employers and families alike unprepared to deal adequately with the resulting implications. Many argue that the reason for this phenomenon has been primarily economic—that the majority of women work as an economic necessity rather than by choice. Others argue that the women's movement and the realization that women have choices other than remaining at home created this influx. Still others believe that the women's movement took hold because women were forced by economics to enter the workforce and, once there, they faced unfair conditions and began lobbying for improvements and more options. Still others counter that more women are working because of the greater emphasis on self-fulfillment and consumption in both genders (Shriver, 2009; Shriver, Morgan, & Skelton, 2014).

Welfare reform measures that emphasize work first also have had the result of increasing the numbers of women in the workplace. Though the *economic* status of these women has improved, many would argue that, because of their primarily low-wage, dead-end jobs, the overall quality of their lives has not (Bartlett & Steele, 2012; Chappell, 2011; Gautie & Schmitt, 2010; Neumark & Wascher, 2010; Campbell, 2014; Seccombe, 2010).

The fact that more women are in the labor force has drawn renewed attention to the relationship between work and family. When only one family member worked outside the home for pay, there was less overlap between the work and family life and it was fairly easy to keep them separate. But when two family members become involved in employment outside the home, the overlap between the work domain and the family domain is inescapable (Sweet, 2013).

Single-Parent Families   In 2013, the percentage of family households in the United States maintained by a female was 19.1%. The percentage of family households maintained by a female within the African American and Hispanic population was considerably higher (43.7% and 25.9%, respectively). In 2013, nearly 71% of all female-headed households had incomes below 200% of the federal poverty level (low-income families). That figure jumped to 77.6% and 78.9% for female households headed by African Americans and Hispanics, respectively (U.S. Census Bureau, 2013).

EP 2.1.1a
EP 2.1.8a

The percentages of female-headed households living below the poverty line in 2013 could be best described as bleak, ranging from 37.2% for white families, 49.8% for African American families, and 47.0% for Hispanic families (U.S. Census Bureau, 2013). The poverty status of children in family households of all types in 2013 ranged from 15.9% for white families to 38.0% for African American families and 30.0% for Hispanic families (U.S. Census Bureau, 2013).

The level of financial insecurity among single-parent families, especially those headed by women, is exacerbated by the historical wage gap between men and women in the United States. Nationally, in 2013 the wage gap between men and women was 18%, a slight improvement from the year before (Catalyst, 2014). Progress in achieving pay equity for women in the United States has been slow (an 8.7% improvement from the year 2000, despite women representing more and more of the total workforce). It is estimated that the current wage gap of 18% amounts to a loss in lifetime wages of $547,826 for a high school graduate and $1.6 million for a professional school graduate (National Committee on Pay Equity, 2013).

The issue of pay equity is particularly salient for social workers, as the profession is dominated by women and thus considered to be "women's work." Therefore, it would be in the best interest of a social worker to advocate for the passage of two key pieces of legislation currently before the U.S. Congress: the Social Work Reinvestment Act and the Paycheck Fairness Act. The reader is referred to the National Committee on Pay Equity website at http://www.pay-equity.org to learn more about current initiatives that are aimed at closing the wage gap as well as how to get involved in these initiatives.

Low wages with limited or no benefits make survival extremely difficult, particularly for those with families. The annualized value of the current federal minimum wage of $7.25 per hour is $15,080 (before deductions). According to the 2014 federal poverty guidelines, a mother with two children, who works at a job paying the federal minimum wage, would be classified as living in poverty. That said, it should come as no surprise that a minimum wage is not equivalent to a "living wage." Proponents for a living wage recommend that no more than 30% of take-home pay be spent on housing, yet many poor families have to spend upward of 70% on housing, thereby cutting into the money they have left for food, clothing, and other essential items. Advocating for a living wage is a critical area of involvement for social workers, as the federal minimum wage is always lower than a living wage because the minimum wage does not take into consideration the actual cost of living in a particular geographic area. Detailed information about a universal living wage can be found at http://www.universallivingwage.org.

Emerging Issues   For women and their families, crucial issues, in addition to salary, benefits, and pensions, include patterns of child rearing and availability and accessibility of affordable child care, flexible working hours, access to reliable transportation to and from work, and job training. For their employers, critical factors are absenteeism and tardiness, sick leave, and employee stress. As more and more women enter the workforce, the following changes are expected:

EP 2.1.1a
EP 2.1.3a
EP 2.1.8a

- expanded child-care options;
- elimination of the cap on child-care deductions on federal income tax returns;
- two-career families becoming less willing to relocate;
- achievement of pay equity between men and women;
- more family-friendly policies at work such as more job flexibility (e.g., part-time, flexible, and stay-at-home jobs) and fewer total work hours per employee;
- restructuring of private benefit policies to reflect the needs of two-income families and single-parent workers; and
- standardization of health care and other benefits available to low-income earners and the unemployed.

An Older Workforce

The civilian labor force for individuals age 55 or older is projected to increase by nearly 30% between 2012 and 2022. The median age of the labor force is projected to continue to rise, especially since the youth labor force (ages 16 to 24) is projected to decline by over this same period (U.S. Bureau of Labor Statistics, 2013a). The aging of the workforce and of society in general is likely to have the following impacts:

- The workforce will be more experienced, stable, and reliable.
- The average age of retirement is likely to rise to accommodate the financial strain on the Social Security system as well as the need to remain financially solvent.
- Older workers will be at risk of being displaced by younger workers as companies seek to reduce costs to remain competitive. Ironically, even younger workers may face the same risk, as American companies continue to move their operations offshore to save money and compete in the global marketplace.
- Workers who leave or lose jobs will have a difficult time finding new jobs at their previous salary and benefit levels.

Greater Ethnic Diversity within the Workforce

The demographic composition of the labor force is projected to change over this decade because of changes in the demographic composition of the population as well as in the rates of workforce participation across demographic groups. The share of the labor force held by ethnic groups is projected to rise, with the most rapid growth by Asians and Hispanics (U.S. Bureau of Labor Statistics, 2013b).

The number of immigrants entering the United States also is expected to increase. The Hispanic-origin population is expected to more than double between 2015 and 2060. The Asian and Pacific Islander population is expected to increase twofold during that same period (U.S. Census Bureau, 2012). This shift in population will be most significant in the South and the West, particularly Texas, Arizona, and California. The increased ethnic diversity in the workforce has the following implications:

- People of color will continue to be discriminated against, work in lower-paying jobs, and be promoted to management positions less often than whites.
- People of color will continue to earn less than whites, and unemployment rates and earnings may actually worsen for them.
- Unemployment rates will continue to be higher for people of color in comparison with whites.
- Blacks and Hispanics will continue to be overrepresented in low-wage, dead-end jobs and in declining occupations.
- Blacks and Hispanics will continue to live in innercity core areas with severe financial and infrastructure problems that place them more at risk for unemployment.
- Immigrants will represent the largest increase in both the population and the workforce since World War I and also will face barriers related to language and lack of education.

These issues indicate that the changing nature of the workforce will have significant implications for employers and employees alike, particularly for companies that historically have employed white males of all ages.

Types of Jobs Available

The types of jobs in which workers are employed have changed, too. Through the 1960s, most workers were employed in blue-collar manufacturing jobs. But as the United States has changed from a manufacturing-based economy to a service-based economy (all activities not involved with producing something physical, or "goods"), fewer and fewer workers are employed in blue-collar positions. In 2014, the service sector accounted for approximately 75% of the nonagricultural civilian workforce (U.S. Census Bureau, 2014). Given the current domestic financial outlook and the continued decline in the manufacturing industry, the trend toward a service-based economy is expected to continue.

EP 2.1.3a

The *service industry* is a subset of the service sector. Examples of jobs in the service industry include health services, legal services, engineering and architectural services, and computer and data-processing services.

New jobs created by an ever-expanding services industry will require higher levels of education. Most of the new jobs will require at least an associate's degree, and many will require at least a bachelor's or Master's degree (U.S. Bureau of Labor Statistics, 2013c). Labor force groups with less than average educational attainment, including Latinos and African Americans, will continue to have difficulty obtaining a share of the high-paying jobs unless they attain a better education.

The types of jobs available are likely to lead to increased segregation of the workforce, with people of color, immigrants, and women relegated to the less-skilled, lower-paying jobs.

The service industry is a major source of **contingent employment** in the United States. Contingent work arrangements include temporary and part-time employees, consultants, leased employees, subcontractors, and short-term, life-of-the-project employees (U.S. Bureau of Labor Statistics, 2014b). Contingent work arrangements typically offer less economic security than fulltime, core, or permanent-wage jobs, as they do not provide health, pension, and other benefits such as paid vacation and sick leave.

The shift in jobs away from major industrial centers in the North and East to the Sunbelt and West Coast, as well as the shrinking small-farm agricultural production, has had a significant impact on workers and their families. Many individuals and families who remained in industrial centers or farm areas have been forced to move or to take lower-paying jobs or seek financial assistance for the first time in their lives. They often have lost their homes, farms, and businesses and face an unpredictable future.

The Changing Nature of Work and the Workplace

During the 1990s, workplaces of all kinds continued to change to remain competitive in the expanding global marketplace by streamlining their operations, reducing the size of their workforce, or both. As a result, many workers have lost jobs, have had to take new roles within the organization, or have become contract workers for the organization by which they were once

EP 2.1.1a
EP 2.1.8a

employed. Organizations are seeking to be leaner and more agile to take advantage of changing market opportunities.

Cross-functional work teams, or teams formed to meet a specific organizational goal, are becoming more common in today's workplace. In some organizations, salaries and raises are based on the performance of the entire team rather than on individual performance.

All of these changes have significantly affected employees in all sectors of business and commerce. The key to being a successful employee today is to be flexible and willing to work at multiple tasks and to be able to switch to new tasks quickly. Interpersonal skills are more important than in the past, as is knowledge of new technology. Today's workers have to find new ways to measure their job performance, as salary increases often are less frequent because organizations have to remain economically competitive. Promotions now are based on how well an employee can add value across his or her organization as well as to its customers.

In addition, because the costs of employee benefits have grown so rapidly, many workplaces are eliminating benefits or requiring workers to pay a larger share of the cost of these benefits. The trend to add new benefits to keep employees on the job also has ended in most workplaces. These changes have created additional stress for employees at all levels of work organizations.

These issues have important implications when addressing employee concerns and the roles that social workers and others can play in dealing with them. Because of the many changes in the workplace and the nature of work, it is difficult to predict accurately the future needs of employees and their families, how those needs will surface in the workplace, and which strategies are most likely to meet them (see Box 15.1).

Unemployment and Underemployment

EP 2.1.1a

Although being employed presents challenges for employees with families, and vice versa, the ramifications of unemployment are far more serious. Layoffs and unemployment are expected to increase along with changes in the nature of work. Since the beginning of the recession in 2007, millions of workers have been displaced from their jobs (U.S. Bureau of Labor Statistics, 2012). **Displaced workers** are defined as persons age 20 and older who have lost or left jobs because their plant or company closed or moved, the work was insufficient, or their position or shift was eliminated.

Because work provides economic support to families and also defines an individual's self-worth, increased unemployment is a double-edged issue of national concern (Cusworth, 2012). Unemployment and low economic status are associated with weak family cohesion and family deterioration (Campbell, 2014; Seccombe, 2010).

Underemployment—placement in jobs that are at a lower level than the person is qualified for—is another growing problem (Mishel, Bivens, Gould, & Shierholz, 2012). When faced with unemployment or underemployment, many individuals and their families relocate to what they believe is a more opportune area. These areas, however, may be largely unprepared to address the many needs created by a rapidly expanding population, including housing, education, social services, health care, transportation, and utilities. Those relocating to new areas are also required to establish new support systems in an unfamiliar and sometimes hostile environment.

For employees and their families who remain in unproductive areas, as well as those who relocate to new areas, stress levels rise significantly (Mishel, Bivens, Gould, & Shierholz, 2012; Moretti, 2013). Social services agencies in these areas report significant increases in family financial problems, suicides, family violence, substance abuse, marital problems, juvenile delinquency, and other mental health–related problems.

Changing Attitudes and Values Toward Work

EP 2.1.3a

Demographic changes in the workforce have had a considerable impact on attitudes and values with regard to work. Although most employees continue to be fairly satisfied with their jobs, discontent is growing in certain segments of the labor force concerning the nature and meaning of work. Employers today see a new type of worker, first described by policy analyst Daniel Yankelovich (1979) as the "new breed worker."

Yankelovich contrasted today's worker with the "organization man" of the 1950s (Whyte, 1956). This term would be considered sexist today, but it was appropriate at that time because the workforce was primarily male. Whyte's organization man was one who put the needs of the organization for which he worked above all else. He came to the company intending to remain there for his entire career, worked long hours, willingly traveled and relocated for the company, and viewed his paycheck as his primary reward for his loyalty and hard work.

Box 15.1 The Changing Work Paradigm

What It Used to Be (Pre-1970s)

- The workforce is predominantly white and male—with few women and people of color.
- Companies are paternalistic, yet they don't always act in the best interests of employees.
- Companies meet the most basic needs of employees.
- Employees have little say in the workings of the organization.
- Benefit programs are traditional and limited.
- Most employees work for the same organization for their entire work lives.
- In many instances, generations of families work for the same organization.
- Employees do what they are told to get ahead—the company comes first.
- Organizations are highly structured with a rigid chain of command.
- The only talk about families is to ensure that top executives have one (marriage is assumed to be a virtue).
- Big is definitely better.
- The only economy is the U.S. economy.

What It Became (1970s, 1980s, 1990s, and Early-2000s)

- The "new-breed worker" replaces the "organization man"; quality of work life becomes more important than simply getting ahead.
- Women and people of color enter the workforce in increasing numbers.
- Employees begin to demand more say in what happens at work.
- The dual wage—earning family is common.
- Employee loyalty to the company is no longer unquestioned.
- The global economy emerges—companies can no longer be concerned only with what goes on at home.
- New "perks" are created to retain highly sought-after employees.
- Leveraged buyouts become popular.
- Average employee tenure drops significantly.
- Many companies falter because they do not adapt to the global economy or cannot change quickly enough to meet new and different markets.
- The information age explodes.
- Increasingly, companies merge, downsize, or do both to become more competitive
- The service industry grows by leaps and bounds.
- Workers with limited skills and little education are increasingly displaced.
- Companies start to realize that past success guarantees nothing.

What It Is Now (2014 and Beyond)

- Women and people of color constitute more than half of the workforce, but their presence in executive and management positions is still disproportionate.
- Successful organizations are flexible and able to change their focus quickly.
- Advances in information technology are making the global marketplace the only marketplace.
- Traditional employee benefits are replaced with a menu of benefits, many of which require significant employee contributions.
- Organizations are flatter and leaner.
- Current success guarantees nothing.
- Only those organizations that can adapt to constantly changing market conditions are able to survive.
- Having satisfied customers is not enough; organizations must provide additional value to retain their customers.
- Increased use of contract labor and outsourcing is displacing many traditional employees.
- Strategic planning is redefined.
- Outside of legal protections, employee entitlements are a thing of the past.
- There are no job guarantees.
- Employees are asked to "give at the office" in new ways.
- Faster is better.
- Product development cycles decline significantly.
- What makes sense today may have no relevance tomorrow.

Source: Ambrosino, R.J. (2014). *The changing work paradigm.* San Antonio, TX: University of Texas at San Antonio.

Today's worker is much different. Concerns about quality of life and willingness to express these concerns to employers have forced employers to offer incentives beyond the paycheck. Insistence on individual accomplishment and self-fulfillment, priorities given to interests outside the workplace, and personal recognition on the job suggest that employees expect work to have meaning beyond the intrinsic rewards of a paycheck.

In addition, a growing number of younger, more educated workers, especially in high-tech fields, expect rapid promotions and challenging jobs; when this doesn't happen they leave their current job with little concern about readily securing one in which these demands can be met. Another phenomenon in the contemporary workplace is the employment of mixed generations under the same roof. Researchers have identified four generational types in today's workplace (see for example, Castellano, 2013; Delcampo, Heggerty, Haney, & Knippel, 2011; Zemke, Raines, & Fillpczak, 2013):

1. *World War II Generation*—born 1945 and before;
2. *Baby Boom Generation*—born between 1946 and 1964;
3. *Generation X*—born between 1965 and 1980; and
4. *Millennial Generation* (also referred to as Generation Y or Echo Boomers)—born between 1980 and 2000.

The values and perceptions of each of these groups are quite different and sometimes conflicting: (Society for Human Resource Management, 2010). Members of the *World War II Generation* are reported to understand well-defined boundaries, to be dependable and reliable, and to have a good work ethic. They are said to be more tolerant of "marginal" working conditions and to be highly committed to the organization.

- *Baby Boomers* are reported to have somewhat rigid work habits, to be "workaholics" (work is their life), and to be rather formal (they like agendas, meetings, schedules, lists, and being on time). Also, they often are taking on the burden of caring for their parents, which in turn affects their work and retirement decisions.
- *Generation Xers* are said to be bold, savvy, confident, and often demanding. They are less understanding of the concept of teamwork, defend the right to a full life outside of work, and are unafraid to ask for something they want. They are willing to switch careers to accommodate their personal

needs but unwilling to change their personal lives to satisfy work demands.
- *Millennials, Generation Y, the millennium generation,* or *echo boomers* are said to be radically diverse (one in five is not Caucasian, one in four lives with a single parent, and three in four have working mothers), to have grown up in a media-saturated, brand-conscious world (and thus to respond to the world differently); and to be more likely to respond to humor, irony, and the unvarnished truth. They are confident beyond their years and have access to an almost unlimited array of material goods.

These characteristics can best be summed up in Table 15.1.

Notwithstanding the differences between the needs and preferences of a multigenerational workforce highlighted in Table 15.1, there are similarities across generations and recognizing and capitalizing on these similarities is in the best interest of any organization employing a multigenerational workforce (Castellano, 2013; Zemke, Raines, & Fillpczak, 2013):

1. Most people, regardless of age, consider work to be a source of personal fulfillment and satisfaction.
2. Employee productivity and job satisfaction are enhanced by a positive workplace culture.
3. Almost all employees seek a work environment where they are recognized and appreciated.
4. Flexibility in work hours is critical.

Generally speaking, the following strategies have been identified for managing generations successfully:

1. Encourage conversations about generational differences;
2. Solicit information about personal needs and preferences;
3. Offer an array of choices;
4. Be flexible;
5. Seek strengths; and
6. Embrace differences.

Today's employers need to understand and embrace the needs and preferences of a multigenerational workforce to recruit and retain top talent, maintain high levels of productivity, and remain competitive in the marketplace they serve. Social workers too, must understand the workforce changes discussed above when confronting their own workplaces as well as when working with clients with workplace-related

TABLE 15.1 CHALLENGES OF MANAGING A MULTIGENERATIONAL WORKFORCE				
	WORLD WAR II	**BABY BOOMERS**	**GENERATION X**	**MILLENNIALS**
Outlook	Practical	Optimistic	Skeptical	Hopeful
Work Ethic	Dedicated	Driven	Balanced	Ambitious
View of Authority	Respectful	Love/Hate	Unimpressed	Relaxed, polite
Preferred Leadership Style	Hierarchy	Consensus	Competence	Achievement, pulling together
Relationships	Self-sacrifice	Personal gratification	Reluctance to commit	Loyal, inclusive
Perspective	Civic-minded	Team-oriented	Self-reliant	Civic-minded
Turn-offs	Vulgarity	Political incorrectness	Clichés, hype	Cynicism, condescension

Source: Claire Raines Associates (2006). Challenges for managers, as cited in American Association of Retired Persons (2007). *Leading a multigenerational workforce* (p. 18). Washington, DC: Author.

issues. This includes private enterprise, the nonprofit sector, and the public sector.

The Impact of Changes on Employees and Their Families

EP 2.1.1a
EP 2.1.3a
EP 2.1.8a

Most of the recent attention relating to changes in the types of individuals now in the workplace has been directed more toward the impact of the changes on the workplace rather than on the family. As noted earlier, when work and family domains overlap, this overlapping can result in the following conflicts:

- individuals' lack of time for themselves and family members;
- stress caused by balancing work and family schedules and priorities;
- problems in obtaining adequate child care and other parenting issues;
- feelings of isolation because of lack of time and energy to develop friendships and support systems; and
- financial difficulties.

Balancing Work and Family Life

Several studies addressing the impact of work on family life have stemmed from Wilensky's (1960) early work in this area suggesting that people undergo a **spillover effect**, in which feelings, attitudes, and behaviors from

the workplace enter their leisure life, and vice versa. The spillover effect is one of five possible work–family relationships that emerged from these studies:

1. *spillover effect,* in which one domain affects the other in either a positive or a negative way; for example, if you really like your job, this will add satisfaction to your family life;
2. *independent,* in which work and family life exist side by side but are independent from each other, allowing you to be satisfied and successful with your job but not your family, for example;
3. *conflict,* in which work and family are in opposition to each other and cannot be reconciled; in a conflict relationship, sacrifices are required in one area to be satisfied and successful in the other—for example, spending less time at home with family members to be successful at one's job;
4. *instrumental,* in which one domain is primarily a means to obtain something for the other; for example, a job is seen only as a way to earn money to maintain a satisfying family life; and
5. *compensation,* in which one domain is a way of making up for what is missing in another; for example, a recently divorced man puts all of his energies into his job, works long hours, and socializes only with coworkers.

In helping employees and their family members understand how they can better balance work and family life, social workers and other helping professionals have to get them to look at how they view their work–family relationships. Several authors have noted that the quality of employees' jobs and the supportiveness of their workplaces are strongly related to job satisfaction, commitment, performance, and retention (see, for example, Friedman, 2014; Kelloway & Hurrell, 2014; Major & Burke, 2014; Meister & Willyerd, 2010; Sweet, 2013). In this context:

- *job quality* includes attributes such as the ability to manage one's work, the availability of personal and professional learning opportunities, meaningful work, opportunities for advancement, and a semblance of job security.
- *workplace support* incorporates attributes such as flexible work schedules, support from supervisors, a workplace culture that acknowledges the dynamics of work–family relationships, the absence of discrimination of any kind, an atmosphere of mutual respect among employees and between management and employees, and a commitment to equal opportunity for all workers, regardless of their backgrounds.

Based on the preceding discussion, one could conclude that if employers want to maximize satisfaction, commitment, performance, and retention, they must provide high-quality jobs in a supportive environment, regardless of the industry involved.

When examining the impact of work on the individual and family, one additional perspective that deserves attention is the importance of life events. Newman & Newman (2014) advocate use of a **life-span model**, in which the meaning of work and family changes as individuals move through childhood, adolescence, youth, adulthood, midlife, and old age. Individuals often are pressured to give full attention to both work and family life at the same period of life—for example, learning and beginning a successful career at the same time that they have married recently and are beginning to have children. Some policy analysts suggest that companies should not emphasize promotions and climbing the career ladder for their employees until they have already dealt with the childrearing years. The importance of looking at life-span stages also can be seen when considering the many individuals who make midlife career changes, not because they are necessarily unhappy with their jobs but, rather, because they are dealing with personal, developmental issues that are age-related.

Most of the attention given to the impact of work on the family has been directed to working wives and mothers. For all families in which mothers work, the impact on the family, particularly the children, is a well-researched issue. Taken by itself, though, a mother's employment outside the home has not been found to have any negative effects on the child. Factors that may affect children of working mothers include (Cassano, 2010; Lerner, 2010; Working Mother Institute, 2010):

- the quality of care the child receives while the mother is working;
- the overall stability of the family itself;
- the type of employment;
- the family's socioeconomic status; and
- the quality and quantity of time that either parent spends with the child.

Increased Stress

EP 2.1.1a
EP 2.1.8a

The issue identified most often in studies focusing on work and family issues is the increased stress on the family unit. Some mental health professionals suggest that the growth in the number of individuals seeking mental health services can be attributed to the heightened pressures they face trying to balance the demands of job and family.

Recent studies have also focused on **dual-career families**—in which both spouses are pursuing their own careers—particularly in relation to the changes in family roles and responsibilities when both parents work (see, for example, Schein & Maanen, 2014). Although both parents in dual-career families experience stress and have less time for themselves and family members, most studies find that the wives and mothers feel these pressures the most. In many dual-career families, the husbands are sharing more in child-rearing responsibilities, but most of the child-rearing responsibility still falls on the wife. Even if husbands are taking on more of the parenting tasks, the housekeeping responsibilities fall almost totally on the wives, even in families in which both husbands and wives view themselves as being less traditional than other couples in the division of household tasks.

Men and women from dual-career families list, among advantages, additional income, more opportunities for meaningful communication and growth because both individuals are stimulated by jobs, and more sharing in parenting roles. But women in these families face numerous role conflicts, citing lack of time to accomplish tasks both at home and at work, lack of time for self, lack of time for spouse, and lack of time for children (Cusworth, 2012; Mischel, Bivens, Gould, & Shierholz, 2012; Schein & Maanen, 2014).

Relocation

Increases in the number of dual-career families also have resulted in problems when one spouse has a job opportunity in another geographic location. Determining which spouse's job should prevail, and under what conditions, presents conflicts in many marriages when such opportunities arise. These dilemmas have resulted in more employers providing relocation services that include help in finding employment for spouses, as well as an increase in the number of **commuter families**—families in which spouses are employed in different locations, often in different parts of the country. Many more workers also are refusing promotions that require relocation.

Financial Problems

In many families, even though both parents are employed outside the home, their incomes still are below or barely above the poverty level. Financial pressures are especially severe for women, people of color, and other workers who are less likely to be well educated or well trained, and as a result, they are more likely to be employed in low-paying jobs. Single parents (also most likely to be women and people of color) are particularly vulnerable to financial pressures.

Working poor is becoming one of the largest categories of poor people in the United States. In 2010, of poor people (those who were living at or below the federal poverty level) 16 years of age or older, 25.5% worked full-time year-round. In contrast, of all people 16 years and older, 67.0% worked full-time year-round (U.S. Census Bureau, 2014). Even those who work full-time at the federal minimum wage ($7.25 per hour in 2014, or $15,080 per year), experience severe difficulties in supporting themselves and their families (Campbell, 2014; Chappell, 2011).

Advocates for the working poor and those moving from welfare assistance to employment argue that continuing to ignore this population will result in substantial costs to families as well as to the U.S. economy. The following are strategies for promoting job retention and advancement among the working poor (including welfare clients) (MDRC, 2013):

- Provide intensive, team-based case-management services to help clients secure employment and retain employment.

- Develop effective postemployment services such as financial assistance in emergency situations, mentoring and community-support programs, reemployment assistance, and career-advancement initiatives.
- Integrate job retention and advancement with job-placement efforts.
- Use intermediaries who have established relationships with employers to deliver postemployment services aimed at job retention and advancement.
- Provide wage supplements and work incentives to reward behaviors and outcomes associated with steady employment.
- Improve access to support services such as child care, transportation, health care, and housing.
- Provide intensive, family-based support services.
- Provide preemployment services that prepare clients for the world of work, help them find a job, and expose them to possible career choices.
- Focus on job placement aimed at getting good jobs, not just any job.
- Promote the use of federal and state earned income tax credits.
- Improve access to education and training in the workplace as well as outside work.
- Help individuals achieve growth in earnings, and access career ladders/pathways.

About 40% of the U.S. workforce is not covered by employee health insurance (Kaiser Family Foundation, 2013a). Among those who are covered, only about half actually participate in one of the plans that are offered. The medical care plans that most employers make available to employees require employee contributions for both single and family coverage—an average across all plans of $999 per year for single coverage and $4,565 per year for family coverage (Kaiser Family Foundation, 2013a).

Most employees with families who are engaged in full-time, low-wage work (most often women and people of color) cannot afford to pay these costs and, thus, go without health coverage for themselves and their families. When these families do have health crises, they are likely to face severe financial problems in paying the full cost for the care they receive.

In the same study cited above, employer premiums for medical care plans in 2009 ranged from $490 per month ($5,584 per year) per participant for single coverage to $1,363 per month ($16,351 per year) per participant for family coverage. In attempting to avoid these costs, many employers continue to hire workers as temporary, part-time, or contract workers (Kaiser Family Foundation, 2013a).

In accordance with the Affordable Care Act, beginning in 2014 employers with at least 50 full-time employees (or equivalent full- and part-time workers) will be required to provide "qualified" health insurance coverage to their full-time employees and their dependents. Qualified coverage means that plans are both comprehensive (pay at least 60% of health care expenses) and affordable (cost less than 9.5% of employees' household incomes). Employers that fail to provide qualified coverage are subject to financial penalties beginning in 2015 of up to $2,000 per full-time employee beyond the first 30 employees. The amount of the penalty will be indexed to the growth in national insurance premium costs (Physicians for a National Health Program, 2011). For tax years 2014 and later, eligible small businesses that purchase health coverage for their employees through the state Exchange will receive a tax credit of up to 50% of the employer's contribution toward the employee's health insurance premium if the employer contributes at least 50% of the total premium cost. The credit will be available for 2 years (Kaiser Family Foundation, 2013b).

Family and Medical Leave Act

EP 2.1.1a
EP 2.1.3a

One of the most significant pieces of legislation in regard to work and family issues, the **Family and Medical Leave Act**, was passed by Congress in 1993 after several previously unsuccessful attempts. The act requires employers with more than 50 employees to provide up to 12 weeks of unpaid leave to eligible employees for the following reasons (U.S. Department of Labor, 2014a):

- for the birth and care of an employee's newborn child;
- for placement with the employee of a son or daughter for adoption or foster care;
- to care for an immediate family member (spouse, child, or parent) with a serious health condition; or
- to take medical leave when the employee is unable to work because of a serious health condition.

The act also specifies that most employees must be able to return to their original jobs or equivalent positions with equivalent pay, benefits, and other conditions of employment.

Accidents and Other Occupational Hazards

Accidents and other on-the-job health hazards create additional problems for employees and their families. Coal miners who come into contact daily with coal dust can contract black lung disease; workers in chemical plants can contract cancer and miscarry or produce children born with congenital deformities; and construction workers may be hurt by heavy equipment—placing themselves and their families in jeopardy. A number of individuals have successfully sued employers for mental anguish that they or their family members experienced as a result of situations like these.

The United States has a high rate of industrial health and safety accidents (U.S. Bureau of Labor Statistics, 2013d, 2014c). In 1970 the federal Occupational Safety and Health Act was passed to address this problem. The act sets health and safety standards in industrial workplaces through on-site inspections and citations for violations. The regulatory function is housed in the U.S. Department of Labor, and research and technology are addressed through the **National Institute of Occupational Safety and Health (NIOSH)** within the Department of Health and Human Services. NIOSH also sets standards related to hazardous materials.

Approximately 12 deaths each workday result from industrial accidents, according to the **Occupational Safety and Health Administration (OSHA)** (U.S. Department of Labor, 2014c). African Americans and Latinos are likely to be employed in the most dangerous jobs and occupations and are most at risk to incur accidental injury or death while on the job (U.S. Bureau of Labor Statistics, 2013d, 2014c). Although occupational hazards such as exposure to asbestos and other dangerous chemicals have received more publicity of late, efforts to deal effectively with these concerns have been limited at both state and federal levels.

Violence in the Workplace

EP 2.1.8a

Employers and employees are increasingly identifying **workplace violence (WPV)** as a problem. Some employees are bringing their family problems to work or are harassed by others, often family members, while at work. Nearly 2 million American workers report having been victims of workplace violence each year (Occupational Safety & Health Administration [OSHA], 2014). Factors that place workers at risk for violence in the workplace include interacting with the public, exchanging money, delivering services or goods, working during late night or early morning hours, working alone, guarding valuable goods or property, and dealing with violent people or volatile situations (OSHA, 2014).

In what has now become a classic in the area of workplace violence, the University of Iowa Injury Prevention Research Center (2001, p. 4) identified four categories of workplace violence:

- Type I—*Criminal intent:* The perpetrator has no legitimate relationship to the business or its employees and usually is committing a crime in conjunction with the violence. Typical crimes in this category are robbery, shoplifting, and trespassing.
- Type II—*Customer/Client:* The perpetrator has a legitimate relationship with the business and becomes violent while being served by the business. This category includes customers, clients, patients, students, inmates, and any other group for which the business provides services.
- Type III—*Worker-on-Worker:* The perpetrator is an employee or past employee of the business who attacks or threatens another employee(s) or past employee(s) in the workplace.
- Type IV—*Personal Relationship:* The perpetrator usually does not have a relationship with the business but has a personal relationship with the intended victim. This category includes victims of domestic violence assaulted or threatened while at work.

The Crime Prevention Institute (2014) provides the following tips for preventing workplace violence:

- Critically examine all areas of your work environment, including parking lots, entryways, reception areas, work areas, and offices to ensure that there is adequate lighting, a convenient escape route, and a method for summoning assistance.
- Report threats from customers, coworkers, or third parties immediately.
- Foster a day-to-day attitude of respect and consideration in your work environment.
- Take a mental inventory of objects available in your immediate work area that could be potential weapons and remove or secure objects that could be thrown.
- Develop violence response procedures and include a plan to summon assistance and move people to a safe area.

- Don't ignore your internal warning system; if you sense impending danger, react accordingly.
- Use the "buddy system" in a situation in which hostility could occur.

Social workers at all levels can play a number of roles to assist the partners referenced above in promoting workplace violence (WPV) prevention. For example, a social worker could serve as an advocate for victims of WPV in either a public or a private setting. A social worker could act as a convener of community-based stakeholders who currently are involved or could provide valuable assistance to WPV prevention. A social worker could serve as a teacher by providing information to a variety of audiences about WPV and its effects on individuals, workplaces, and the community. Finally, a social worker could be a mediator between parties who have different views about WPV and how it can be prevented.

Sexual Harassment

EP 2.1.1a
EP 2.1.8a

Sexual harassment is another concern in the workplace. The costs of sexual harassment can be extremely damaging to employees, both emotionally and from a cost perspective, and employers are legally responsible to ensure that sexual harassment does not occur (Reeves, 2010; Shaw & Lee, 2014; Shuy, 2012). Obtaining accurate figures about the actual incidence of sexual harassment in the workplace is difficult because it is thought that about half of those who are harassed do not report it. They may fear that they will lose their jobs or be subjected to other retribution, that they will not be taken seriously, or that they somehow have contributed to the harassment.

Title VII of the Civil Rights Act of 1964 specifies that discrimination that violates individual rights occurs when (Conte, 2010):

- individuals are offered rewards in return for sexual favors, or threatened with punishment if they do not provide them;
- a hostile environment is created that interferes with employees' ability to concentrate on their job tasks because of behaviors such as making lewd comments and telling inappropriate sexual jokes, displaying inappropriate artwork and other materials, and touching or threatening to touch individuals in inappropriate ways; and

- an employee's job or job opportunities are jeopardized because of another person who is responding positively to requests for sexual favors.

Social workers in the workplace often provide employee training regarding what constitutes sexual harassment and how to handle it if it does occur, assessment and conflict resolution if incidents are reported, and counseling to those who have been sexually harassed. Social workers also advocate and encourage employee empowerment to ensure that the workplace culture does not support such behavior.

Child Care for Working Parents

EP 2.1.1a
EP 2.1.8a

Of the 80.4 million families in the United States in 2012, about 21% had one relative child under age 18, about 18% had two relative children under 18, and about 7% had three or more relative children under 18 (U.S. Census Bureau, 2013). Nearly 28 million married couple families with both wife and husband in the labor force and 6.4 million female-headed families with the woman in the labor force can be considered likely to have work-related child care requirements. In 2013, about 57% of women ages 15–50 who have infants were in the labor force (U.S. Bureau of Labor Statistics, 2014d).

In a report titled *Parents and the High Price of Child Care: 2013 Update,* the National Association of Child Care Resource and Referral Agencies (NACCRRA, 2013) revealed the following rather sobering findings about child care in the United States:

- Families are paying a significant part of their earnings for child care.
- Child care is one of the highest budget items for families.
- Safety, health, and school readiness come at a cost that many parents cannot afford.
- High costs make child care unaffordable for many low-income families.
- Families in urban areas pay dramatically more for child care than families in rural areas.
- The high costs of child care affects families' ability to choose the child care arrangement and the quality of care they want for their children.
- Some families can afford to pay the full cost of care at a child care center or family child care home, but many cannot—these families end up choosing child care based on how much they can afford, usually from a relative or friends or neighbors.

- Although child care in informal situations may be an affordable arrangement in the short run, there may be hidden costs that are paid later.
- Some families put together several different child care options;
- Finding and affording child care are especially difficult for single parents, families of children with special needs, families of children who are dual-language learners, immigrant parents, parents who work nontraditional hours (evenings, nights, and weekends), and low-income families.
- Depending on the funding source, child care and early education programs offer vastly different quality of care and charge parents vastly different fees.
- Some programs make compromises to balance what they think parents can afford with financial considerations about the quality of care they provide.

The implications of this report are far-reaching for today's families. Although most families agree that they want the best child care available for their children, they simply cannot afford to pay for that care. In short, their children do not have access to the benefits of developmentally appropriate care that nationally certified child-care agencies provide. To be able to work, most low-income families are faced with placing their children in substandard and potentially dangerous child-care arrangements. Women who have exited the welfare system to enter the low-paid workforce have even fewer choices (Campbell, 2012; Chappell, 2011; Seccombe, 2010). Being aware that the child care arrangement they have chosen for their child is marginally beneficial and perhaps even dangerous for their child is stressful for low-income parents, which saps their strength to face other challenges in their lives.

Finally, children who are able to benefit from high-quality child care have an advantage over children who do not have access to this care as it relates to school achievement. Access to high-quality child care is important for *all* families, not just those that can afford it.

Family Caregiving

EP 2.1.1a
EP 2.1.8a

Family caregiving is another problem that increasingly affects employees.

A study of caregiving costs to working caregivers conducted by the Metropolitan Life Insurance Company in collaboration with the National Alliance for Caregiving, and the Center for Long-Term Care Research and Policy at

New York Medical College (MetLife, 2011) revealed the following key findings:

- The percentage of adult children providing personal care and/or financial assistance to a parent has more than tripled over the past 15 years.
- Currently, a quarter of adult children, mainly Baby Boomers, provide these types of care to a parent.
- The total estimated aggregate lost wages, pension, and Social Security benefits of the parents of these caregivers is nearly $3 trillion.
- For women, the total individual amount of lost wages, Social Security benefits, and pension due to leaving the labor force early because of caregiving responsibilities was computed to be $324,044; for men, that same figure equaled $283,716.
- Working and non-working adult children are almost equally as likely to provide care to parents in need.
- Overall, daughters are more likely to provide basic care and sons are more likely to provide financial assistance.
- Adult children 50+ who work and provide care to a parent are more likely to be in fair or poor health than those who do not provide care for their parents.

The study concludes that assessing the long-term financial impact of caregiving for aging parents on caregivers themselves, especially those who must curtail their working careers to do so, is especially important, since it can jeopardize their future financial security. Because caregivers experience considerable health issues as a result of their focus on caring for others, there is a need for increased flexibility in the workplace and in policies that would benefit working caregivers, as more working caregivers approach their own retirement.

Formal elder care services vary tremendously. Types of elder care include the following (Capezuti, Malone, & Katz, 2013; Malone, Capezuti, & Palmer, 2014; Weiner, Ronch, & Lunt, 2013):

- *adult day care programs,* which make it possible for elders to participate in structured social and personal activities, receive basic and therapy services, or participate in educational programs;
- *home health care,* which allows elders to remain in a familiar environment and to maintain a certain level of independence with the assistance of housekeepers and chore workers, homemakers, and/or health aides;

- *independent living facilities* allow elders the opportunity to live independently while being part of a community of others in similar circumstances by renting or purchasing an apartment or condominium within a complex or campus offering recreational or social activities, and sometimes transportation services;
- *assisted living facilities (sometimes referred to as board and care, residential care, community-based retirement care, personal care or adult foster care facilities)* offer elders comprehensive help with activities of daily living, but also feature an independent living arrangement;
- *nursing homes* provide care by licensed health professionals (registered nurses, licensed practical nurses, and nurses' aides) for elders requiring "round the clock" basic care, skilled care, or subacute care;
- *continuum of care facilities* offer elder residents the widest range of care options in an "a la carte" fashion (services are added to assist residents as necessary);
- *dementia or memory care (Alzheimer's) facilities* provide elders with Alzheimer's or other forms of dementia with comprehensive assistance with activities of daily living.

Changing Expectations About Work and Family Life

EP 2.1.1a
EP 2.1.8a

Changing expectations regarding what is important in life have implications both for families and for the workplace. More individuals are reassessing tradeoffs between work and family life. Assuming that no financial hardship exists, many people today are willing to reduce their salaries to have more personal or family time. Others are willing to turn down a promotion if it seriously jeopardizes the amount of time they could spend with their families or pursuing personal interests. The term **downshifting** refers to voluntary limitation of job demands so employees can devote more time to their families or to themselves.

Implications for the Mental Health of Employees and Their Families

Increasingly, employees and their families who lack a robust support system and are unable to cope with life's pressures experience divorce, family violence, substance abuse, suicide, or other health or emotional problems. For workers and their families facing such pressures, however, the options often are limited. Many individuals work because they must support their families, often as the sole source of support. For those who earn low wages and cannot rely on other family members to offer emotional support or assistance in family needs such as child care, the toll on them and their families can be extensive (refer to the Hunts, the family described at the beginning of the chapter). Even for those who have more options, such as being able to rely on relatives for child care, balancing work and family pressures is difficult.

Implications for the Workplace

The problems that have an impact on the individual employee and his or her family also have a significant impact on the workplace. Job turnover, absenteeism, and other costs created by employee and family problems are expensive to the workplace as well as consumers, who ultimately are forced to absorb these costs.

Costs of Substance Misuse   The total overall cost of drug misuse in the United States, including health- and crime-related costs as well as losses in productivity, is estimated to be in excess of $600 billion annually (National Institute on Drug Abuse, 2014). Of that figure, an estimated $193 billion is associated with illicit-drug misuse, $172 billion is associated with tobacco use, and $235 billion is associated with alcohol use. Substance use disorder among employees can result in lost productivity, absenteeism, injuries, fatalities, theft and low employee morale, and an increase in health care, legal liabilities, and workers' compensation costs. In financial terms, alcoholism and misuse of other drugs cost employers $81 billion annually (National Council on Alcoholism and Drug Dependence, 2014). In the workplace, employees reporting drug use or heavy alcohol use are more likely to have worked for more than three employers in the past year, to have skipped work more than 2 days in the past month, and to have missed more than 2 days of work because of illness or injury.

Other Problems That Cost Employers   Other health and mental health problems also are expensive, particularly if they are not addressed early. National health care expenditures in the United States in 2014 are projected to reach $3.3 trillion (Centers for Medicare and Medicaid Services, 2014). Mental illness and workplace stress result in billions of dollars in absenteeism and lost productivity each year and also can lead to higher rates of worker illness and injury (Biron, Karanika, & Cooper, 2012; Gatchel & Schultz, 2012; Naswall, Hellgren, & Sverke, 2010; Race & Furnham, 2014).

According to CIGNA Behavioral Health Care (2010), depression exacts a significant health and productivity cost in the workplace:

- People diagnosed with depression have nearly twice the annual health care costs of those who are not depressed.
- The burden of depression on employers has been estimated to be $6,000 per depressed worker per year.
- Depressed workers have a 1/4-day more per month occurrence of absence than nondepressed workers.
- Depressed workers experienced 1.09 more days per month of "work cutback" than workers with no psychiatric problems.
- Workers suffering from depression experienced as many as 2.3 more short-term disability days per month than workers not suffering from depression.
- This translates into a salary-equivalent productivity loss of as much as $395 per depressed employee during a 30-day period.

Increased Demands on Employers

Many studies suggest that emotionally based individual and family problems exact a heavy toll on both the individual and the workplace in relation to health care costs. In June 2014, employer costs for employee compensation for civilian workers (private industry and state and local government) in the United States averaged $30.11 per hour worked (U.S. Bureau of Labor Statistics, 2014c). Wages and salaries accounted for about 70% of these costs, and benefits accounted for the remaining 30%.

In 2013, labor unions covered 11.3% of the U.S. workforce (U.S. Bureau of Labor Statistics, 2014e). Historically, labor unions have wielded significant collective bargaining powers on behalf of union members, including efforts to keep employee costs for benefits low and the extent of benefits available high. However, their presence in the U.S. workplace today is hardly a factor in negotiations between labor and management. The high cost of employee health care benefits is a major issue facing employers today. In response, many employers are increasing the employee-paid costs of health care and also reducing the extent of benefits available.

Affiliation Needs

As more and more workers are looking to the workplace to meet their need for affiliation, additional concerns arise on the job. Coworkers and supervisors find themselves spending work time listening to employees' problems ranging from marital disputes to more serious problems such as substance abuse and family violence. A supervisor who oversees 15 employees noted that in one day she had helped find temporary shelter for a female employee who had suffered spouse abuse, listened to another employee whose son was in jail for cocaine abuse and theft and referred him to a counseling center, confronted an employee regarding a job error and learned that he was in the midst of a divorce after a 25-year marriage, and covered for another worker who had to leave early because she had a sick child.

Addressing Work and Family Problems

EP 2.1.8a
EP 2.1.9b

Given the serious costs to workers of employee- and family-related problems, their families, and the workplace, strategies are being developed to address these challenges. When working with individuals and family members, social services counselors today are much more likely to address job-related factors than they have in the past. Many communities have initiated task forces and programs to provide affordable child care and transportation for employees. A number of public schools have established before-school and after-school child care programs, and some schools schedule parent–teacher conferences and other events during evening hours, when most working parents can attend. Social services agencies in some communities have come into the workplace to provide noontime seminars and other programs relating to topics such as coping with divorce, substance abuse, and parenting.

A growing number of employers have recognized their social responsibility to address these problems. Today, personnel departments have been replaced largely with human resources departments, which have expanded roles, including a more holistic approach to employee needs. Human resources departments oversee personnel, social services, and health and wellness, along with other employee-related programs. Some employers have called upon social workers as consultants to assist managers in determining how they can better meet their employees' needs. In an ecological/systems approach, appropriate interventions can be directed to all levels of the workplace, from the individual employee to the total corporate environment.

Some companies have established employee assistance programs (EAPs, discussed in detail in the next section), which provide counseling and other social services to employees, and often to their families, through the company. Others have expanded health coverage to include treatment for substance abuse, mental health counseling, and dental care.

A number of public and private employers have established flexible working hours for their employees, called **flex time**, which allows employees to work hours that vary from the traditional 8 a.m. to 5 p.m. workday. For example, an employee might work four 10-hour days each week, or work hours different from those of other employees, perhaps 6 a.m. to 3 p.m.

Other employers offer **job sharing**, a system that allows two people to share one job; usually, each person works half-time. Another alternative for employers is to create permanent part-time positions. Some employers also allow employees to work in their homes. Particularly, some workers with disabilities and workers with children can access employers' computer networks to complete word-processing and other tasks without leaving their homes. This practice is sometimes called **flexi-place**.

Still other employers have stress-reduction and health-promotion programs, including on-site fitness centers where employees and their families can exercise. Some employers also provide on-site child care for employees or other child care programs; and companies even have established special programs that provide care for school-age children during the summer or when the children are sick (Kelloway & Hurrell, 2014). The Affordable Care Act creates new incentives and builds on existing wellness program policies to promote employer wellness programs and encourage opportunities to support healthier workplaces.

Employee Assistance Programs

A number of organizations have established formal **employee assistance programs (EAPs)** to provide counseling to their employees.

EAPs are mandated in federal government agencies, including the military, and in most state, county, and city governments as well. A related group of programs known as **membership assistance programs (MAPS)** provided under the auspices of labor unions, offer similar employee support services to union members (Kelloway & Hurrell, 2014).

Originally, EAPs were established to provide counseling and treatment for employees with alcohol problems, and a recovering alcoholic—often one of the company's own employees—was the program coordinator. Today, a wide variety of EAPs are available. Although many are still primarily alcohol-related, others are "broad-brush" programs, addressing a wide range of employee issues, including divorce, child rearing, family violence, and financial problems. Many innovative programs have been developed for employees and their families through EAPs. More EAPs now are offering services relating to the care of elderly parents. EAPs also are called upon when workers are relocated or laid off and when companies close.

Social workers employed in EAPs become involved in a wide range of situations involving employees—discrimination, including unfair treatment of people of color, women, new immigrants, and persons with AIDS; the needs of workers with disabilities; the effects of toxic chemicals and pollutants on employees; and the effects of the physical and emotional demands of the workplace on employees.

EAPs have a proven track record in reducing employee absenteeism, decreasing health care costs, and increasing employee productivity (Gatchel & Schultz, 2012). Examples of successful interventions include reduction of absenteeism stemming from alcoholism; programs that improve family relations, resulting in improved employee productivity; and the introduction of site-based fitness programs that result in substantial savings in health insurance–related claims (Corcoran & Roberts, 2015).

Also, EAPs oversee managed health care and mental health care for employees, in an attempt to reduce inadequate and ineffective services (Kongstvedt, 2012). In this role, EAP staffs conduct assessments of employee needs, determine the most appropriate type of care needed, and refer the employee or family member to the most appropriate resource. EAP personnel also often serve as case managers in these situations, ensuring that the services are received and monitoring the case until it is terminated. Employees receive an incentive in reduced copayments for using these services. This role has raised ethical issues for social workers in some instances if the emphasis is on saving costs for the employer at the expense of providing the most appropriate services for the client.

Dependent-Care Programs

Companies and organizations are responding to the needs of employees by establishing a variety of child care programs with the following options:

- access to information about where to find child care in the community;
- child care at or within close proximity to the work site;
- payment for child care with vouchers or other subsidies paid for by the company;
- dependent-care plans which allow employees to pay for child care with pretax dollars;
- reimbursement of child care costs when employees are required to work after regular hours ;
- reimbursement of business travel-related child care costs ;
- child care for school-age children home from school for a variety of reasons;
- backup or emergency care for children of employees; and
- care for sick children of employees.

EP 2.1.3a

A growing number of corporations have responded. The following are examples from the "100 Best Companies for Working Mothers" (2014):

- Abbott Health Care offers abundant child care resources via a child care center at HQ (serving 800 kids annually). The company also provides employee discounts at 2,800 U.S. day care facilities. Mothers can also access six internal networks with which to share information about child care options, utilize a robust employee assistance program and engage in self-care through health coaching, fitness challenges and stress-management workshops. In some offices, they can arrange for up to six free, confidential counseling. Alternative work options have been used at the company since 1992.

There are a plethora of opportunities for women at AOL, a web services company, which offers them four leadership development programs, a nationwide women's network with mentoring circles and workshops, and unlimited tuition aid. Employees who maintain a healthy lifestyle can earn up to $1,100 in rewards annually, facilitated by on-site nutrition counseling, fitness classes, and smoking-cessation and weight-management sessions. Mothers-to-be may schedule consultations with nurses and lactation experts, take free childbirth classes and parenting courses, and join new-mom, breastfeeding and parenting groups.

At AstraZeneca, a biopharmaceutical company, employees with children about to attend college have access to free coaching services that focus on selecting institutions, completing essays and interviews, and applying for financial aid. Employees with younger children can use the company's on-site child care center, summer camps, day care discounts or backup dependent care.

Capital One Financial Services recently increased its adoption aid to $10,000 per child from $5,000 and removed its annual limit on coverage for infertility treatments. Expectant moms are offered a financial incentive when they join a maternity management program, and they get 8 fully paid weeks off to give birth. Additionally, anyone who becomes a parent by birth, adoption, or foster care (including same-sex spouses and partners) receives 2 to 6 paid weeks off. Employees can also request priority access at day care facilities nationwide or use a backup dependent-care program.

Deloitte, a large professional services firm, offers competitive salaries, a 401(k) with match, a defined-benefit pension plan, $10,000 in annual tuition aid, mortgage assistance and pretax health, dependent care, and transportation accounts. Employees receive on average 40 paid days of leave annually; after 2 years with the company, they earn sabbaticals lasting 3 to 6 months (at 40% salary). A new initiative permits some executive and senior administrative assistants to work remotely up to 3 days a week.

Other companies have worked with communities in establishing child care referral services, helping employees locate child care that best meets their needs, or they offer flexible spending packages in which employee benefits can be designed for the care of elderly dependents.

Some companies provide vouchers for child care, which permit parents to contribute a portion of their employee benefits for child care of their choice. Others offer a variety of after-school and summer child care programs and programs for sick children. Recognizing the amount of money lost every time a child is sick, some companies provide nurses to go to parents' homes and care for children, paying a portion of the cost for this service ("100 Best Companies for Working Mothers," 2014).

The National Child Care Information Center (http://www.nccic.acf.hhs.gov) provides a list of organizations and publications that have information about the costs and benefits of employee-sponsored child care. Although few companies actually have conducted formal cost–benefit analyses, businesses have posited the following reasons as to why child care can have a significant impact on their bottom line:

- Lack of access to affordable, quality child care may make it difficult for businesses to hire qualified employees.
- Productive and valued employees may leave their jobs because of child care problems, which increases hiring and training costs.
- Employees may be forced to take time off because of child care problems or spend time at work handling child care concerns.
- Companies with employer-supported child care services have reported improved employee morale, reduced absenteeism, increased productivity, and lower turnover.

Because so many employers were finding that their employees had problems with dependent care for their elderly parents as well as children, a number have expanded their efforts to include this population. For example, IBM, a founding member of the American Business Collaboration for Quality Dependent Care, has provided funding to improve the quality and availability of dependent care for the elderly since the early 1990s.

Some firms have implemented programs to increase productivity, including flexible work schedules, health and wellness programs, transportation systems, recreation teams, and employee work groups, that together attempt to improve the workplace environment.

Many employers offer on-site child care programs or other types of child care benefits to support working parents.

Lawrence Migdale/Getty Images

Coworkers, too, are turning to their fellow employees for support—helping with child care and transportation and offering advice about coping with teenagers, among many examples. Coworkers are increasingly assuming this role, which traditionally has been the province of neighbors, friends, or relatives.

The need for affordable, accessible child care for working parents has been identified as the most critical need for families. In the United States, 32.7 million children currently need child care, but many parents—particularly those at or near the poverty level—cannot afford the costs of good care. Child care costs are less than 10% of total expenditures for the average family but often more than a third of total expenditures for the working poor (Luce, Luff, McCartin, & Milkman, 2014).

Social Work in the Workplace

EP 2.1.1a
EP 2.1.9b

Social work is expanding its provision of social services in the workplace, known as industrial or occupational social work. Although many view this specialization as relatively new, this is not the case. Actually, the profession of social work owes its name to industry. The term *social work*, introduced in the United States in the early 1890s (apparently a direct translation of the German phrase *Arbeiten sozial*), referred to housing, canteens, health care, and other resources provided to employees by Krupp munitions plants to support the industrial workforce (Carter, 1977).

Industrial Social Work

In many other countries, industry is the largest field for social work practice. In the United States, industrial social work developed and was practiced between 1890 and 1920, and then was largely dormant until it reemerged in the 1970s.

The development of welfare and social work programs in industry began with the mutual aid societies and volunteer programs accompanying many of the progressive reform movements during the late 1800s and early 1900s. Positions of "social secretary," "welfare manager," and "welfare secretary" were found in many American industries, including textile mills in the South, as well as Kimberly Clark and International Harvester. Welfare secretaries had backgrounds primarily in religious or humanitarian work, with little previous experience in either social work or industry. In general, they were responsible for overseeing the physical welfare (safety, health, sanitation, and housing), cultural welfare (recreation, libraries, and education programs), economic welfare (loans, pensions, rehabilitation, hiring, and firing), and personal welfare, which included social work (then called "case work"), of employees and their families (Carter, 1977).

According to a U.S. Bureau of Labor Statistics survey, by the mid-1920s, most of the largest companies in the United States had at least one type of welfare program and about half had comprehensive programs (Stern & Axinn, 2012). Sociologist Teresa Haveren (1982) reviewed old records and conducted a historical study of work and family relationships at the Amoskeag Textile Mill in New Hampshire in the late 1800s and early 1900s. Like many other industries during that time, this company provided the following for employees:

- corporate housing close to the mill for working parents;
- boarding houses for young, single employees;
- English, sewing, cooking, and gardening classes;
- nurses who provided instruction in housekeeping, health care, and medical aid and visited the sick and elderly regularly to provide food and assistance;
- a charity department to provide needy families with clothing, food, and coal, and assistance to widows with large families if their husbands died or were injured on the job or were former employees;
- a hospital ward for employees injured on the job;
- a dentist for employees' families;
- a child care program and kindergarten;
- a children's playground with attendants to supervise the children;
- a swimming pool and ice-skating rink;
- an Americanization program;
- an athletic field and showers;
- lectures, concerts, and fairs; and
- a Boy Scouts program.

Although many companies were generous with assistance, services were denied if an individual refused to work. Thus, the system was designed to encourage loyalty to the organization, not simply to provide benefits to employees. Because many industries employed entire families, often in the same work unit, it can be argued that this system made it easier for workers to make the transition from family to factory, with many family members seeing little difference between work life and family life.

During the late 1920s, opposition to these programs came from a number of fronts, including employees themselves. Many employees, including women, were immigrants. As they became more acculturated within the United States, they saw the welfare programs as paternalistic. The rise of the labor movement also increased opposition to corporate welfare programs. Labor leaders considered the programs antiunion, believing that the welfare secretary diffused employee unrest without bringing about changes that would improve working conditions for employees.

The emergence of scientific management of the workplace redirected attention to improving workers' efficiency. Later, scientific management and welfare work merged into a new field—personnel management. At the same time, public and private social services agencies became more prevalent, lessening the need for businesses to offer many of their previous services. Thus, corporate welfare programs declined.

During World War II, the National Maritime Union and United Seaman's Service operated an extensive industrial social work program, providing assistance to the families of the more than 5,000 union members who had been killed during the war. Because unions feared that social workers hired by companies would not be sympathetic to unions, other unions initiated industrial social work programs. Until recently, unions were responsible for most of the social work programs in the United States (Carter, 1977).

Occupational Social Work

With the decline in manufacturing and other heavy industries and the shift to a service economy, the term *industrial social work* has been replaced by *occupational social work*. Historically, occupational social work has served a variety of functions in business and industry. Profit often has been a major motivation of employers who provide social work services, with the hope that these services would increase productivity and morale. But social workers have affected the workplace in ways other than providing social services to employees and their families. Social workers also have played a role in:

- integrating new groups of inexperienced workers (such as women, people of color, and immigrants) into the work world;
- consulting with businesses on how to increase diversity in the workplace and to be sensitive to the needs of diverse groups; and
- strengthening relationships between the corporate world and the community; and in organizational development through redesign of work to make the workplace more humane for employees.

In addition to expertise in working with troubled individuals and families, social workers are trained in effective communication and negotiation—skills that lend themselves well to advocating for employee needs or working to improve conditions within a workplace and increase understanding between employees and employers.

It seems logical that social workers should become more actively involved in the workplace. Occupational social work lends itself to providing services within a natural setting. After all, the majority of adults are employed. The opportunity for a universal service-delivery system that goes beyond services to the poor, the elderly, and the sick also is ideal for providing preventive services—an area that is almost negligible from the broader perspective of total services provided.

Social work as a profession is strengthening its interests and capabilities in the area of occupational social work (see Box 15.2). The two major professional bodies that guide the profession—the National Association of Social Workers and the Council on Social Work Education—have established task forces, developed publications, and held conferences dealing with occupational social work.

In some instances, university social work programs offer courses in occupational social work and related areas, sometimes in collaboration with other departments such as business administration. All programs provide future occupational social workers with knowledge and skill in dealing with substance abuse, marriage and family problems, and other individual and family problems. They also offer courses relevant to working in organizations and the corporate world.

To be successful in the workplace, social workers need additional knowledge and skill in business principles, planning and management, marketing, financial management, human resources administration, family counseling, and organizational behavior. And students in occupational social work programs also are placed in field internships in corporations and unions, where they work directly with troubled employees and their families or are involved in administration and planning activities.

Although social work as a profession must recognize the importance of work within the individual's life, the emphasis of occupational social work has been primarily at the individual casework level through EAPs and other forms of one-to-one counseling or information and referral services. The focal point seems to be the relationship of work to emotional problems. Social workers also have played a role in addressing work-related social policy issues such as the appropriate division between corporate and social welfare sectors in providing services; the relationships between work and family roles for men and women; the impact of affirmative action programs on women, people of color, and individuals with disabilities; and unemployment. But little attention has been given to the role that social work might play from an organizational-change perspective.

Box 15.2 The Occupational Social Worker

A job description for an occupational social worker might include the following:

- linking individuals and family members to entitlements and other public and private resources;
- conducting short-term counseling involving a full range of job-related and non-job-related psychosocial and health/disability concerns;
- providing specialized emergency services in areas such as substance abuse, disability management, and mental health;
- identifying and addressing the needs of special populations within the workplace, such as older workers and retirees, workers with disabilities, chemically dependent workers, relocated workers, unemployed individuals, dislocated and underemployed workers, ethnic and racial

groups, workers exposed to hazardous conditions, and workers with mental health problems;
- addressing issues such as violence in the workplace;
- collaborating with others to identify and address issues of workplace health and safety;
- working with management to minimize problems encountered by part-time and temporary employees;
- assisting workers in accessing vocational and educational opportunities.

SOURCE: Social Work in the 21st Century, by M. Reisch and E. Gambrill (Thousand Oaks, CA: Pine Forge Press), 1997, pp. 226–238.

Social Work in the Changing Workplace

EP 2.1.1a
EP 2.1.9b

Since the 1990s, many workplaces are making changes that are not new to social workers. The emphasis on empowering employees to take responsibility for initiative and product design and completion, for example, is consistent with the social work focus of client empowerment. The use of task groups to make decisions and complete projects also is not new to social workers. Social workers are skilled at understanding group dynamics, leadership styles, and the use of a systems/ecological perspective in achieving synergy among systems, including groups. The need for occupational social work continues to be supported by legislation relating to civil rights and equal opportunities for employees, safe work conditions, and the financial and legal protection of at-risk populations through programs such as workers' compensation, unemployment insurance, and income support programs (Mizrahi & Davis, 2010).

Social workers can play key roles at all levels of the workplace. They can incorporate these new directions into the workplace culture from both employer and employee perspectives and balance individual and organizational interests.

Applying an Ecological/Systems Perspective

EP 2.1.8a

Because social workers focus on the interactions between the individual and his or her environment, they are well equipped to develop strategies of intervention at various levels of the systems within which the individual functions (see Box 15.3) (Akabas & Kurzman, 2007). Consider again the Hunt family, discussed at the beginning of this chapter. Social work intervention could consist of individual counseling for Bill and Meredith relating to their respective jobs. Because the problems the Hunts face, however, are associated with their relationship to each other, a social worker might propose marital counseling for the couple, seeing both of them together. Remember, though, that the Hunt children, too, were having difficulties in the family. Therefore, the social worker should provide counseling for the entire Hunt family.

Other individuals within the systems in which the Hunts function may have to be involved, too. Coworkers and supervisors with whom they interact may be exacerbating their problems. The oldest son's teacher might offer insight into the boy's problems, and the social worker might work with other individuals who interact with the Hunts to be more supportive of the family's needs. The social worker might tap into

Box 15.3　Client Assessment Incorporating Work and Family Domains

I. Employee Perceptions

a. Employment history, including education and training

b. Current employment situation—culture of organization, hours worked, responsibilities, relationships with supervisors and coworkers, stresses of job, strengths of job and workplace

c. Performance expectations and how well employee is meeting them

d. Adequacy of income and benefits

e. What employee values regarding workplace (autonomy, relationships, pay) and how well organization is meeting expectations

f. Career goals of employee

g. Value employee places on job and workplace in comparison to other life domains

h. Opportunities within the workplace that help employer better understand family needs and demands

II. Workplace Expectations and Perceptions

a. Culture of organization and expectations of its employees

b. Demographics of organization—size, geographic location, structure, setting

c. Policies and practices and fit with employee needs and concerns (e.g., health insurance and other benefits, child care, flex time)

d. Opportunities available to employee for upward mobility or horizontal growth

e. Specific concerns about employee, including job performance, employee relationships, inappropriate use of alcohol or other drugs, potential for workplace violence/harm to self or others

III. Workplace/Family Interaction

a. Expectations of employee regarding work and family

b. Expectations of other family members regarding employee's job and family

c. Fit between workplace support, i.e., salary, benefits, time on job, and family needs

d. Ways that job stresses and job satisfaction of employee impact employee within family and other family members (partner, children, other relatives)

e. Negative impacts of employment on employee and family members, including inappropriate use of alcohol or other drugs, potential for workplace or family violence/harm to self or others

f. Other benefits of work/employment to employee and family

g. Opportunities for employee and family members to participate in workplace activities or leisure activities that help family members better understand workplace and its demands

Source: Content from Akabas, S.H., & Kurzman, P.A. (2007). *Work and the workplace: A resource for innovation practice and policy.* New York: Columbia University Press; and Cohen, J., and McGowan, B. (1982). What do you do? An inquiry into the potential of work-related research. In: Akabas, S., & Kurzman, P. (2007). *Work, workers, and work organizations: A view from social work.* Upper Saddle River, NJ: Prentice-Hall.

---

resources within the community such as low-cost afterschool child care, a recreational program for the son, parenting classes, Alcoholics Anonymous, or a family violence program.

Thus, the role of a social worker can go beyond individual and family interventions. The social worker might recognize that many individuals in the workplace have the same kinds of problems as the Hunts. Therefore, he or she might establish support groups for employees with similar concerns and needs. An additional role could be to advocate with management for company policies that better support the needs of employees like the Hunts.

Social workers might work with others within the workplace to implement child-care programs, flexible work hours, and adequate sick-leave policies. Finally, they might stretch beyond the workplace in developing state and federal legislation to mandate policies that are more supportive of employees and their families, such as expanding family-leave and sick-leave policies that allow leave for family-related issues beyond the employee's illness to include all workplaces.

Service Models

The following three models of service have been identified for occupational social workers, incorporating a variety of roles inherent to the profession of social work (Mizrahi & Davis, 2010):

1. *Employee service model*: focuses primarily on the micro-level of the systems within which employees and their families function. In this model, social work functions include counseling employees and their families, providing educational programs to employees, referring employees to other agencies, implementing recreational programs, consulting with management regarding individual employee problems, and training supervisors to recognize and deal appropriately with employee problems.

2. *Consumer service model*: emphasizes intervention at a broader level within the same systems. This model views employees as consumers and assists them in identifying needs and advocating to get those needs met. Social workers work with consumers/employees in assessing their needs, developing strategies to best meet the needs identified, locating and providing community resources to meet the needs, serving as a liaison between consumer/employee groups and social services agencies, and developing outreach programs to meet employee needs.

3. *Corporate social responsibility model*: intervenes at the exo-level and macro-level within the various systems in which employees and their families function. Within the realm of this model, social workers are found in the workplace, community, and society in general, developing and strengthening programs that support individual employees and their families. They consult about human resources, policy, and donations to tax-exempt activities within the workplace and to community organizations such as the United Way; analyze relevant legislation and recommend additional legislation; administer health and welfare benefits; conduct research to document needs and evaluate programs and policies; and serve as community developers, providing a link among social service, social policy, and corporate interests.

These models often overlap, with social workers in workplace settings providing tasks that fall within more than one model. Most of the social work activity in the workplace to date has followed the employee service model. It is anticipated that as a growing number of social workers practice in occupational settings, more of their activity will reside within the other two models.

Summary

An ecological/systems approach to social needs and problems focuses on the interactions between individuals and their environments. Until recently, little attention has been given to the interactions among the individual, the individual's place of employment, and the individual's family. But as more women, both with and without children, enter the workforce, and as rapid social change continues to affect many individuals negatively, the relationship between the workplace and the family cannot be ignored. Individuals with workplace stresses invariably bring those stresses home, and vice versa. The costs of employee and family substance abuse, marital discord, parenting problems, and other mental health problems are extensive to the family and the workplace alike.

A number of communities and workplaces have developed programs that assist individual employees and their families to better balance work and family pressures. These include employee assistance programs (EAPs), as well as child care, transportation, and health and wellness programs. Studies show that these programs are effective in preventing family and workplace dysfunction.

The field of occupational social work is an emerging area that can have some impact through intervention in the workplace to improve family functioning, as well as to increase profitability and productivity for the work organization. Social work as a profession will play a major role in developing programs within the workplace, as well as advocating for appropriate policies and legislation to support employees and their families.

Competency Notes

EP 2.1.1a: Advocate for client access to the services of social work (pp. 471, 472, 473, 474, 477, 478, 480, 481, 482, 483, 489, 491). Social workers demonstrate an understanding of the importance of employment and workplace policies and practices when advocating for client access to social services.

EP 2.1.3a: Distinguish, appraise, and integrate multiple sources of knowledge, including research-based knowledge and practice wisdom (pp. 470, 472, 473, 474, 477, 480, 486). Social workers distinguish, appraise, and integrate multiple sources of knowledge about employment and workplace-related issues, including research-based knowledge, and practice wisdom, to inform services with individuals, families, groups, organizations, and communities.

EP 2.1.8a: Analyze, formulate, and advocate for policies that advance social well-being (pp. 471, 472, 473, 477, 478, 480, 481, 482, 483, 485, 491). Social workers analyze, formulate, and advocate for policies that advance social well-being, including those that promote positive employment opportunities and social and economic justice in the workplace.

EP 2.1.9b: Provide leadership in promoting sustainable changes in service delivery and practice to improve the quality of social services (pp. 485, 489, 491). Social workers act as leaders in promoting sustainable changes in service delivery and practice to improve the quality of social services, including changes that relate to employment policies and practices.

Key Terms

The terms below are defined in the Glossary.

commuter families	membership assistance
contingent employment	programs (MAPS)
cross-functional work	National Institute of
teams	Occupational Safety
displaced workers	and Health (NIOSH)
downshifting	Occupational Safety
downsized	and Health
dual-career families	Administration
employee assistance	(OSHA)
programs (EAPs)	occupational social work
Family and Medical	spillover effect
Leave Act	underemployment
flexi-place	working poor
flex time	workplace violence
job sharing	(WPV)
life-span model	

Discussion Questions

1. Identify at least *three* ways the composition of the workplace has changed over the past three decades. What effect have these changes had on the workplace?
2. From a systems/ecological perspective, what are the relationships among individuals, their workplaces, and their families?

3. What are *three* types of employee- and family-related problems, and how do these problems affect the workplace?
4. What are *three* types of work-related problems for an employee? How might these problems affect an employee's family?
5. What are *five* types of programs that employers have established to address employee and family needs?
6. Describe the three models on which an industrial social work program might be based. List at least *three* of the roles an industrial social worker employed in a workplace setting might play.

On the Internet

http://www.stats.bls.gov
http://www.dol.gov/wb
http://www.osha.gov
http://www.naswdc.org

References

100 best companies for working mothers. (2014). Retrieved September 21, 2014, from http://www.workingmother.com

Akabas, S. H., & Kurzman, P. A. (2007). *Work and the workplace: A resource for innovative practice and policy*. New York: Columbia University Press.

Ambrosino, R. J. (2014). *The changing work paradigm*. San Antonio: University of Texas at San Antonio.

American Association of Retired Persons (AARP). (2007). *Leading a multigenerational workforce*. Washington, DC: Author.

Bartlett, D., & Steele, J. (2012). *The betrayal of the American dream*. New York: Public Affairs.

Biron, C., Karanika-Murray, M., & Cooper, C. (Eds.). (2012). *Improving organizational interventions for stress and well-being: Addressing process and context*. New York: Routledge.

Campbell, A. (2014). *Trapped in America's safety net: One family's struggle*. Chicago, IL: University of Chicago Press.

Capezuti, E., Malone, M., & Katz, P. (Eds.). (2013). *The encyclopedia of elder care: The comprehensive resource on geriatric health and social care*. New York: Springer.

Carter, L. (1977). Social work in industry: A history and a viewpoint. *Social Thought, 3,* 7–17.

Cassano, G. (2010). *Class struggle on the homefront: Work, conflict, and exploitation in the household.* New York: Palgrave MacMillan.

Castellano, W. (2013). *Practices for engaging the 21st century workforce: Challenges of talent management in a changing workplace.* Boston: Pearson.

Catalyst. (2014). *Women's earning and income.* New York: Author.

Centers for Medicare and Medicaid Services. (2014). *National health expenditures and selected economic indicators, levels and annual percent change: Calendar years 2007–2023.* Washington, DC: Author.

Chappell, M. (2011). *The war on welfare: Family, poverty, and politics in modern America.* Philadelphia, PA: University of Pennsylvania Press.

CIGNA Behavioral Health Care. (2010). *What is the health and productivity cost burden of depression in the workplace?* Retrieved December 15, 2010, from http://cignabehavioral.com/web/basicsite/broker/misc/workplaceDepression.jsp

Clements, J. (2012). *Corporations are not people: Why they have more rights than you do and what you can do about it.* San Francisco, CA: Berrett-Koehler.

Conte, A. (2010). *Sexual harassment in the workplace: Law and practice* (4th ed.). New York: Aspen.

Corcoran, K., & Roberts, A. (Eds.). (2015). *Social workers' desk reference* (3rd ed.). New York: Oxford University Press.

Crime Prevention Institute. (2014). *Seven tips for preventing workplace violence.* Milwaukee, WI: Author. Retrieved September 19, 2014, from http://crisisprevention.com/resources/knowledge-base/general/workplace-violence

Cusworth, L. (2012). *The impact of parental employment.* Surrey, United Kingdom: Ashgate.

Delcampo, R., Haggerty, L., Haney, J., & Knippel, L. (2011). *Managing the multi-generational workforce: From the GI generation to the millennials.* Burlington, VT: Gower.

Edelman, P. (2013). *So rich, so poor: Why it's so hard to end poverty in America.* New York: New Press.

Friedman, S. (2014). *Leading the life you want: Skills for integrating work and life.* Cambridge, MA: Harvard Business Review.

Gatchel, R., & Schultz, I. (2012). *Handbook of occupational health and wellness.* New York: Springer.

Gautie, J., & Schmitt, J. (Eds.). (2010). *Low-wage work in the wealthy world.* New York: Russell Sage Foundation Publications.

Gratton, L. (2011). *The shift: The future of work is already here.* New York: HarperCollins.

Haveren, T. (1982). *Family time and industrial time.* Cambridge, MA: Harvard University Press.

Kaiser Family Foundation. (2013a). *Employer health benefits survey summary of findings.* Menlo Park, CA: Author. Retrieved September 19, 2014, from http://www.kff.org/report-section/2013-summary-of-findings

Kaiser Family Foundation. (2013b). *Summary of the affordable care act.* Menlo Park, CA: Author. Retrieved September 19, 2014, from http://www.kff.org/health-reform/fact-sheeyt/summary-of-the-affordable-caree-act/

Kelloway, K., & Hurrell, J. (2014). *Workplace well-being: How to build psychologically healthy workplaces.* Hoboken, NJ: Wiley-Blackwell.

Kongstvedt, P. (2012). *Managed care: What it is and how it works* (6th ed.). Sudbury, MA: Jones & Bartlett.

Kunin, M. (2012). *The feminist agenda: Defining the next revolution for women, work, and family.* White River Junction, VT: Chelsea Green Publishers.

Lancaster, L., & Stillman, D. (2010). *The M-factor: How the millennial generation is rocking the workplace.* New York: HarperBusiness.

Lerner, S. (2010). *The war on moms: On life in a family-unfriendly nation.* New York: Wiley.

Liss, M., & Schiffrin, H. (2014). *Balancing the big stuff: Finding happiness in work, family, and life.* Lanham, MD: Rowan & Littlefield.

Luce, S., Luff, J., McCartin, J., & Milkman, R. (Eds.). (2014). *What works for workers? Public policies and innovative strategies for low-wage workers.* New York: Russell Foundation Publications.

Maitland, A., & Thomson, P. (2014). *Future work: Changing organizational culture for the new world of work.* New York: Palgrave Macmillan.

Major, D., & Burke, R. (Eds.). (2014). *Handbook of work-life integration among professionals: Challenges and opportunities.* Northampton, MA: Edgar Elgar Publishers.

Malone, M., Capezuti, E., & Palmer, R. (Eds.). (2014). *Acute care for elders: A model of interdisciplinary care.* Valley Stream, NY: Humana Press.

Martin, E. (2011). *Stopping the train: The landmark victory over same-sex sexual harassment in the workplace.* Mustang, OK: Author.

Massengill, R. (2013). *Wal-mart wars: Moral populism in the twenty-first century.* New York: New York University Press.

MDRC. (2013). *Promoting employment stability and advancement among low-income adults.* New York: Author.

Meister, J., & Willyerd, K. (2010). *The 2020 workplace: How innovative companies attract, develop, and keep tomorrow's employees today.* Hoboken, NJ: Wiley.

MetLife. (2011). *The MetLife study of caregiving costs to working caregivers: Double jeopardy for Baby Boomers taking care of their parents.* New York: Author.

Mishel, A., Bivens, J., Gould, E., & Shierholz, H. (2012). *The state of working America.* Ithaca, NY: ILR Press.

Mizrahi, T., & Davis, L. (2010). *The encyclopedia of social work* (20th ed.). New York: Oxford University Press.

Moretti, E. (2013). *The new geography of jobs.* New York: Mariner Books.

Morgan, J. (2014). *The future of work: Attract new talent, build better leaders, and create a competitive organization.* Hoboken, NJ: Wiley.

Naswell, K., Hellgren, J., & Sverke, M. (Eds.). (2010). *The individual in the changing working life.* New York: Cambridge University Press.

National Association of Child Care Resource and Referral Agencies (NACCRRA). (2013). *Parents and the high price of child care: 2013 update.* Arlington, VA: Author.

National Committee on Pay Equity. (2013). *The wage gap over time: In real dollars, women see a continuing gap.* Washington, DC: Author.

National Council on Alcoholism and Drug Dependence. (2014). *Drugs and the workplace.* New York: Author.

National Institute on Drug Abuse. (2014). *Costs of substance abuse.* Bethesda, MD: Author. Retrieved September 20, 2014, from http://www.drugabuse.gov/related-topics/trends-statistics

Neumark, D., & Wascher, W. (2010). *Minimum wages.* Cambridge, MA: MIT Press.

Newman, B. M., & Newman, P. R. (2014). *Development through life: A psychosocial approach* (12th ed.). Belmont, CA: Cengage Learning.

Occupational Safety & Health Administration. (2014). *Workplace violence.* Washington, DC: Author. Retrieved September 19, 2014, from http://www.osha.gov/SLTC/workplaceviolence/

Physicians for a National Health Program. (2011). *Employer-sponsored health plans under the Affordable Care Act.* Chicago: Author. Retrieved September 19, 2014, from http://pnhp.org/blog/2011/03/15/employer-sponsored-health-plan-under-the-affordable-care-act

Race, M., & Furnham, A. (2014). *Mental illness at work: A manager's guide to identifying, managing, and preventing psychological problems in the workplace.* New York: Palgrave Macmillan.

Reeves, M. (2010). *Women in business: Theory, case studies, and legal challenges.* New York: Routledge.

Reisch, M., & Gambrill, E. (Eds.). (1997). *Social work in the 21st century.* Thousand Oaks, CA: Pine Forge Press.

Schein, E., & Maanen, J. (2014). *Career anchors: The changing nature of work and careers* (4th ed.). Hoboken, NJ: Wiley-Pfeiffer.

Seccombe, K. (2010). *So you think I drive a Cadillac? Welfare recipients' perspectives on the system and its reform* (3rd ed.). Upper Saddle River, NJ: Prentice-Hall.

Shaw, S., & Lee, J. (2014). *Women's voices, feminist visions: Classic and contemporary readings.* Columbus, OH: McGraw-Hill.

Shriver, M. (2009). *The Shriver report: A woman's nation changes everything.* Mankato, MN: The Free Press.

Shriver, M., Morgan, O., & Skelton, K. (2014). *The Shriver report: A woman's nation pushes back from the brink.* New York: Rossetta Books.

Shuy, R. (2012). *The language of sexual misconduct cases.* New York: Oxford University Press.

Society for Human Resource Management. (2010). *The multigenerational workforce: Opportunity for competitive success.* Alexandria, VA: Author.

Stern, M., & Axinn, J. (2012). *Social welfare: A history of the American response to need* (8th ed.). Boston: Pearson.

Sweet, S. (2013). *The work-family interface: An introduction.* Thousand Oaks, CA: Sage.

University of Iowa Injury Prevention Research Center. (2001). *Workplace violence: A report to the nation.* Iowa City: University of Iowa.

U.S. Bureau of Labor Statistics. (2012). *Industry employment and output projections.* Washington, DC: Author. Retrieved September 18, 2014, from http://www.bls.gov/opub/mlr/2012/01/art4fulll.pdf

U.S. Bureau of Labor Statistics. (2013a). *Employment projections—2012–2022.* Washington, DC: Author. Retrieved September 19, 2014, from http://www.bls.gov/news.release/pdf/ecopro.pdf

U.S. Bureau of Labor Statistics. (2013b). *Labor force projections to 2022: The labor force participation rate continues to fall.* Washington, DC: Author.

U.S. Bureau of Labor Statistics. (2013c). *Workplace injuries and illnesses—2012.* Washington, DC:

Author. Retrieved September 19, 2014, from http://www.bls.gov/news.release/oslu.nr0.htm

U.S. Bureau of Labor Statistics. (2014a). *Census of fatal occupational injuries summary, 2013*. Washington, DC: Author. Retrieved September 19, 2014, from http://www.bls.gov/news.release/cfoi.nr0.htm

U.S. Bureau of Labor Statistics. (2014b). *Employees on non-farm payrolls by industry sector and selected industry detail*. Washington, DC: Author.

U.S. Bureau of Labor Statistics. (2014c). *Employer costs for employee compensation—June 2014*. Washington, DC: Author. Retrieved September 21, 2014, from http://www.bls.gov/news.release/pdf/ecec.nr0.htm

U.S. Bureau of Labor Statistics. (2014d). *Employment characteristics of families—2013*. Washington, DC: Author. Retrieved September 20, 2014, from http://www.bls.gov/news.releases/pdf/famee.pdf

U.S. Bureau of Labor Statistics. (2014e). *Union members—2013*. Washington, DC: Author. Retrieved September 21, 2014, from http://www.bls.gov/news.release/union2.nr0.htm

U.S. Census Bureau. (2012). *Projections of the population by sex, race, and Hispanic origin for the United States: 2015 to 2060*. Washington, DC: Author.

U.S. Census Bureau. (2013). *America's families and living arrangements 2013: Family households*. Washington, DC: Author.

U.S. Census Bureau. (2014). *Work experience during year by age, sex, household relationship and poverty status for people 16 years old and over: 2013*. Washington, DC: Author.

U.S. Department of Labor. (2014a). *Family and Medical Leave Act*. Washington, DC: Author. Retrieved September 19, 2014, from http://www.dol.gov/who/fmla/

U.S. Department of Labor. (2014b). *Women in the labor force: Databook*. Washington, DC: Author.

Vance, C., & Paik, Y. (2010). *Managing a global workforce: Challenges and opportunities in international human resource management*. Armonk, NY: Sharpe.

Weiner, A., Ronch, J., & Lunt, E. (2014). *Models and pathways for person-centered elder care*. Towson, MD: Health Professions Press.

Whyte, W. (1956). *The organization man*. New York: Doubleday.

Wilensky, H. (1960). Work, careers and social integration. *International Social Science Journal, 7*(4), 543–560.

Working Mother Institute. (2010). *The working mother report: What moms think—Career vs. paycheck*. New York: Working Mother Media.

Yankelovich, D. (1979). Work, values, and the new breed. In C. Kerr & J. Rosow (Eds.), *Work in America: The decade ahead* (pp. 3–26). New York: Van Nostrand Reinhold.

Zemke, R., Raines, C., & Fillpczak, B. (2013). *Generations at Work: Managing the clash of boomers, Gen Xers, and Gen Yers in the workplace*. Chicago, IL: AMACOM.

Suggested Readings

Benedict, H. (2009). *The lonely soldier: The private war of women serving in Iraq*. Boston: Beacon.

Gerson, K. (2009). *The unfinished revolution: How a new generation is reshaping family, work, and gender in America*. New York: Oxford.

Lawhorne-Scott, C., Philipott, D., & Scott, J. (2014). *Sexual assault in the military: A guide for victims and families*. Lanham, MD: Rowan & Littlefield.

Melnick, S. (2013). *Success under stress: Powerful tools for staying calm, confident, and productive when the pressure's on*. Chicago: AMACOM.

Williams, J. (2010). *Reshaping the work-family debate: Why men and class matter*. Cambridge, MA: Harvard University Press.

Yarbrough, C., & Blankston, T. (2013). *Pay equity: Gender differences and legislation*. Happauge, NY: Nova Science Publishers.

CHAPTER 16
The Globalization of Social Work

Sonia Rosales is a social worker working in a refugee resettlement camp located in East-Central Africa. The camp, under the control of the United Nations High Command on Refugees (UNHCR), has recently swollen to 28,000 individuals, some 5,000 more than the camp's capacity. Sonia's tasks are many and demanding, and she is forced to work with limited resources in an environment characterized by dilapidated housing; chronic health problems; widespread infectious diseases such as hepatitis B, tuberculosis, and typhoid fever; poor sanitary conditions; shortage of medical supplies for use by the camp's only hospital; contaminated drinking water; lack of schools; dearth of recreational programs for children and youth; pervasive and serious mental health problems among camp members of all ages, including severe depression, posttraumatic stress disorder (PTSD), and anxiety disorder; the emergence of human trafficking; and the constant threat of violence, both from within and outside the camp. She has been working with a network of social workers from the region and across the world to connect children separated from their families by the widespread displacement of households resulting from civil wars and sectarian violence in the region. This task is compounded by the fact that the children and families she seeks to reunite speak many different languages or dialects, communications in and out of the camp are highly controlled and limited, and few people are available to assist her in her work. Many of the children Sonia is working with will never see their parents again. The parents either are dead or have been forced to settle in another region or country, with little chance of returning to their homes. Other children may be reunited with their families but will suffer the emotional scars of the war and violence to which they have been exposed for the rest of their lives.

Sonia also works closely with representatives of a number of international humanitarian agencies such as the International Red Cross, Oxfam International, and Catholic Relief Services as well as large pharmaceutical companies to ensure that the basic health needs of the refugees are met. Together, they are trying desperately to stem the outbreaks of contagious and sometimes deadly diseases in the camp before they reach crisis levels. Even though the refugee camp is located in a so-called neutral country, Sonia and her colleagues are exposed constantly to the dangers of war.

Shawn Brennan, a social worker and Peace Corps volunteer from Ireland, is hard at work in an ill-equipped medical clinic in the heart of a small African country. He works side by side with representatives from a variety of international relief organizations to clothe and feed thousands of people suffering from malnutrition. Many face imminent death from starvation. Shawn's compassion for his fellow human beings is tested daily in the decisions he must make. Some are so weak or sick by the time they reach the clinic that they die shortly thereafter, leaving families and loved ones behind. He is helpless to do anything for them except perhaps to console them or their loved ones who accompanied them on their journey to the clinic.

The resources available to Shawn and his colleagues are meager in comparison to the need. He also must wrangle daily with local authorities who sometimes prevent relief cargo from being unloaded, divert that cargo for some other purpose, or demand bribes in exchange for access to the cargo. If he pushes too hard for what he believes to be the right thing to do for his clients, Shawn faces time in jail where he could be subjected to torture, or even summary execution.

Kristin and Mario Diaz, recently married and both social workers from the United States, are working at a rural outpost high in the mountains of the Oaxaca region of Mexico. They are part of a multidisciplinary team of medical personnel and other volunteers who have come to the region to provide basic medical care, including immunizations, for the local peasant population. The team also promotes preventive health-care practices among members of this population, which is difficult to accomplish because of the severe poverty conditions in which its residents live. Many of the people Kristin and Mario treat have spent days traveling to the outpost, walking over terrain that is barely passable and exposing themselves to the growing lawlessness in the region, to seek help for themselves and their loved ones.

In trying hard to establish positive relationships with members of the community, Kristin and Mario are working with a group of women to develop a cooperative to make crafts and clothing from specially dyed and handwoven cloth. They also are helping to establish a school and a child development program for preschoolers. No money changes hands for these services; the local residents are so poor that such an exchange would be out of the question. The payment that Kristin and Mario receive is in the knowledge that they have helped preserve the life of a child, reduced the pain and suffering of a person who would have died without the medical care provided, and helped the residents of the area become better able to support themselves through education and enterprise.

Sonia, Shawn, Kristin, and Mario exemplify the many different roles in international social work, with the common aim of achieving social, economic, and political justice throughout the world. Working side by side with other professionals, government representatives, and volunteers from humanitarian organizations, social workers play a key role in improving the quality of life for persons who are victims of persecution, war, famine, dislocation, and political strife, as well as protecting and preserving the rights of marginalized populations throughout the world. They often work in highly volatile political environments, and their physical well-being frequently is in danger. They often work in isolated, out-of-the-way places that have little communication with the outside world. They have come together to ensure that basic human rights are honored and to do what they can to normalize the lives of individuals who, through no fault of their own, have been forced to live a life not of their choosing. Despite language barriers, cultural differences, exposure to violence of many forms, and the threat of being jailed, tortured, and even executed, these individuals work tirelessly to advance the cause of social work across the globe.

In this chapter, we discuss international social work and global issues currently addressed by social workers throughout the world.

A Changed World

EP 2.1.1a
EP 2.1.1e
EP 2.1.9a

The future of the world has changed significantly from what it was before the terrorist attacks on the United States on September 11, 2001: the subsequent global war on terrorism waged by the United States and its allies; the social, political, and economic aftermath of the extended military conflicts in Iraq and Afghanistan for the United States and the world; and the instability of countries that have been besieged by the actions of religious extremists. We have witnessed the loss of lives of thousands of soldiers and civilians, including innocent children; other tragic human rights violations; and the displacement of millions of civilians throughout the world. Ethnic and racial bias as well as religious and economic differences divide hemispheres, nations, communities, and neighborhoods.

The role of the United States as a world power has changed at the same time. The country faces a number of daunting issues at home: A significant and sustained downturn in the economy that has resulted in millions of people being unemployed with a dim prospect of being reemployed; a growing homeless population, fueled by the return of an estimated 230,000 soldiers who served one or more tours of duty in Iraq and/or Afghanistan, many suffering from the so-called "invisible wounds of war" (severe depression, PTSD, and/or pervasive anxiety) (RAND, 2008); a public school system that is increasingly challenged in achieving its primary goal of educating students; the lingering effects of welfare reform and its impact on the country's underclass; the large-scale exporting of jobs to

countries such as India; the escalating costs of going to college, making access to the higher education system by traditionally undeserved populations increasingly difficult to achieve; recently-enacted health-care reform legislation that is being assailed by a growing number of individuals and groups opposed to the requirements of the legislation; and the continued debate about what to do with the millions of undocumented immigrants entering the country each year that has been recently intensified by the influx of thousands of unaccompanied minors from Central and South America who are seeking to be reunited with family members already in the country, protection as an asylee, or both.

Our international, national, local, and personal priorities are being debated vigorously by religious, government, and civic leaders, as well as individual citizens. The resources available to us as social workers, the prevailing attitudes and values of society, and the level of civic engagement and sense of community are major factors in making a difference in the clients we serve, as well as how we define the role of social work in achieving a just and a fair world.

As more attention is directed nationally and internationally to social welfare and social and economic justice issues—and the roles that various segments of society should play in meeting unmet human needs—the social work profession is receiving increased importance. The future of social work holds numerous challenges and opportunities for the profession across the globe.

International Social Welfare and Globalization

EP 2.1.1a
EP 2.1.9a
EP 2.1.9b

International social welfare is the field of practice concerned with promoting basic human well-being in a context in which cross-national efforts are involved (Cox & Pawar, 2012; Healy & Link, 2011). A number of authors have discussed reasons why social workers should have knowledge of international social work practice, as well as skill in working in other countries or with international populations within the United States (see, for example, Cox & Pawar, 2012; Healy & Link, 2011; Mapp, 2014). They argue that such knowledge and skills expand one's perspectives about political, economic, and social systems across the globe; increase awareness of and sensitivity to diverse cultures; provide an opportunity to assess one's personal values and cultural preferences; allow one to view social policy and services using a comparative lens; and stimulate cross-national collaboration between social workers and other professionals. This international perspective will allow social workers to practice more effectively in a world that is increasingly interdependent along economic, political, and social lines, as well as to contribute in meaningful ways to reduce conflict and exploitation throughout the world.

EP 2.1.5b
EP 2.1.5c

Social welfare practice in an international context focuses on the study of social problems between and among nations. Such problems include, but are not limited to, the following (Amnesty International, 2013; UNICEF, 2014):

- deaths from war;
- global governance that deals with problems that affect all peoples;
- social justice;
- the rights of women and children;
- religious, economic, and political oppression;
- the rights of immigrants and those seeking asylum from political persecution;
- displacement of persons because of war, ethnic cleansing, political strife, and natural disasters;
- marginalization of people through marketplace globalization;
- the distribution of wealth;
- poverty; and
- human and environmental exploitation.

Global governance that has clearly defined and limited authority and deals with global problems that affect all peoples is also central to achieving a **global village** of social and economic justice, lasting peace, and a sustainable environment (Muller, 2013). The time must come when people will accept international law to settle global disputes as they now accept their national government in settling disputes between states and provinces, as evidenced by the *Universal Declaration of Human Rights,* adopted by the United Nations in 1948 (see Box 16.1).

Achieving a global village is seriously hindered by the inequitable distribution of power and wealth throughout the world (Goldin, 2013). Today, while they comprise only a little more than 10% of the world's population, wealthy countries and their multinational corporations make virtually all of the world's

economic decisions, and most of the military ones, without any consultation from the world community. For example, the global arms trade involves billions of dollars of weapons sales every year (Feinstein, 2011). The United States leads this business, with more than half of such sales.

World peace cannot be accomplished unless every country is allowed only enough military capability to defend its borders and never enough to wage aggression against its neighbors. Along with this fulfillment of international law is the complete elimination of nuclear, chemical, and other weapons of mass destruction that serve no valid purpose in maintaining a world community in which social and economic justice exist (Djelic & Quack, 2012; Human Rights Watch, 2010; Ife, 2012).

EP 2.1.5c

The social work profession has long embraced the notion that justice, particularly social justice, is a critical component in creating the global village. The global village cannot be achieved without overcoming the many historic prejudices and fears that divide the peoples of the world. Nor can there be peace and lasting stability in the world without achieving a reasonable degree of economic justice. Today, less than 20% of the world's people hold 80% of the world's wealth, while more than 80% hold the rest (Global Issues, 2010; Payne, 2012; Seitz & Hite, 2012). The same relationship exists when it comes to consumption of the world's resources. The richest 50 million people in Europe and North America have the same income as 2.7 billion people. The gap between the rich and the poor continues to widen every year. Nearly 3 *billion* people in the world live on less than $2.50 a day (Milanovic, 2012).

The Gross Domestic Product (GDP) of the 41 heavily indebted poor countries with a population of 567 million people is less than the wealth of the world's seven richest people combined. Nearly a billion people entered the 21st century without being able to read a book or sign their names. Less than 1% of what the world spent every year on weapons was needed to put every child in school by the year 2000 and yet it did not happen. One billion children live in poverty (one in two children in the world), 640 million live without adequate shelter, 400 million have no access to safe water, 270 million have no access to health services, and 11 million children under 5 years of age die each year as a consequence of poverty. The wealthiest nation on earth, the United States, has the widest gap between

Box 16.1   Universal Declaration of Human Rights

Preamble

Whereas recognition of the inherent dignity and of the equal and inalienable rights of all members of the human family is the foundation of freedom, justice and peace in the world,

Whereas disregard and contempt for human rights have resulted in barbarous acts which have outraged the conscience of mankind, and the advent of a world in which human beings shall enjoy freedom of speech and belief and freedom from fear and want has been proclaimed as the highest aspiration of the common people,

Whereas it is essential, if man is not to be compelled to have recourse, as a last resort, to rebellion against tyranny and oppression, that human rights should be protected by the rule of law,

Whereas it is essential to promote the development of friendly relations between nations,

Whereas the peoples of the United Nations have in the Charter reaffirmed their faith in fundamental human rights, in the dignity and worth of the human person and in the equal rights of men and women and have determined to promote social progress and better standards of life in larger freedom,

Whereas Member States have pledged themselves to achieve, in cooperation with the United Nations, the promotion of universal respect for and observance of human rights and fundamental freedoms,

Whereas a common understanding of these rights and freedoms is of the greatest importance for the full realization of this pledge,

Now, therefore, The General Assembly, Proclaims this Universal Declaration of Human Rights as a common standard of achievement for all peoples and all nations, to the end that every individual and every organ of society, keeping this Declaration constantly in mind, shall strive by teaching and education to promote respect for these rights and freedoms and by progressive measures, national and international, to secure their universal and effective recognition and observance, both among the peoples of Member States themselves and among the peoples of territories under their jurisdiction.

Article 1

All human beings are born free and equal in dignity and rights. They are endowed with reason and conscience and should act towards one another in a spirit of brotherhood.

Article 2

Everyone is entitled to all the rights and freedoms set forth in this Declaration, without distinction of any kind, such as race, colour, sex, language, religion, political or other opinion, national or social origin, property, birth or other status. Furthermore, no distinction shall be made on the basis of the political, jurisdictional or international status of the country or territory to which a person belongs, whether it be independent, trust, non-self governing or under any other limitation of sovereignty.

Article 3

Everyone has the right to life, liberty, and security of person.

Article 4

No one shall be held in slavery or servitude; slavery and the slave trade shall be prohibited in all their forms.

Article 5

No one shall be subjected to torture or to cruel, inhuman or degrading treatment or punishment.

Article 6

Everyone has the right to recognition everywhere as a person before the law.

Article 7

All are equal before the law and are entitled without any discrimination to equal protection of the law. All are entitled to equal protection against any discrimination in violation of this Declaration and against any incitement to such discrimination.

Article 8

Everyone has the right to an effective remedy by the competent national tribunals for acts violating the fundamental rights granted him by the constitution or by law.

Article 9

No one shall be subjected to arbitrary arrest, detention or exile.

Article 10

Everyone is entitled in full equality to a fair and public hearing by an independent and impartial tribunal, in the determination of his rights and obligations and of any criminal charge against him.

(continued)

Box 16.1   Universal Declaration of Human Rights *(continued)*

Article 11

1. Everyone charged with a penal offence has the right to be presumed innocent until proved guilty according to law in a public trial at which he has had all the guarantees necessary for his defence.
2. No one shall be held guilty of any penal offence on account of any act or omission which did not constitute a penal offence, under national or international law, at the time when it was committed. Nor shall a heavier penalty be imposed than the one that was applicable at the time the penal offence was committed.

Article 12

No one shall be subjected to arbitrary interference with his privacy, family, home or correspondence, nor to attacks upon his honour and reputation. Everyone has the right to the protection of the law against such interference or attacks.

Article 13

1. Everyone has the right to freedom of movement and residence within the borders of each State.
2. Everyone has the right to leave any country, including his own, and to return to his country.

Article 14

1. Everyone has the right to seek and to enjoy in other countries asylum from persecution.
2. This right may not be invoked in the case of prosecutions genuinely arising from non-political crimes or from acts contrary to the purposes and principles of the United Nations.

Article 15

1. Everyone has the right to a nationality.
2. No one shall be arbitrarily deprived of his nationality nor denied the right to change his nationality.

Article 16

1. Men and women of full age, without any limitation due to race, nationality or religion, have the right to marry and to found a family. They are entitled to equal rights as to marriage, during marriage and at its dissolution.
2. Marriage shall be entered into only with the free and full consent of the intending spouses.
3. The family is the natural and fundamental group unit of society and is entitled to protection by society and the State.

Article 17

1. Everyone has the right to own property alone as well as in association with others.
2. No one shall be arbitrarily deprived of his property.

Article 18

Everyone has the right to freedom of thought, conscience and religion; this right includes freedom to change his religion or belief, and freedom, either alone or in community with others and in public or private, to manifest his religion or belief in teaching, practice, worship and observance.

Article 19

Everyone has the right to freedom of opinion and expression; this right includes freedom to hold opinions without interference and to seek, receive and impart information and ideas through any media and regardless of frontiers.

Article 20

1. Everyone has the right to freedom of peaceful assembly and association.
2. No one may be compelled to belong to an association.

Article 21

1. Everyone has the right to take part in the government of his country, directly or through freely chosen representatives.
2. Everyone has the right to equal access to public service in his country.
3. The will of the people shall be the basis of the authority of government; this will shall be expressed in periodic and genuine elections which shall be by universal and equal suffrage and shall be held by secret vote or by equivalent free voting procedures.

(continued)

Box 16.1 Universal Declaration of Human Rights *(continued)*

Article 22

Everyone, as a member of society, has the right to social security and is entitled to realization, through national effort and international cooperation and in accordance with the organization and resources of each State, of the economic, social and cultural rights indispensable for his dignity and the free development of his personality.

Article 23

1. Everyone has the right to work, to free choice of employment, to just and favourable conditions of work and to protection against unemployment.
2. Everyone, without any discrimination, has the right to equal pay for equal work.
3. Everyone who works has the right to just and favourable remuneration ensuring for himself and his family an existence worthy of human dignity, and supplemented, if necessary, by other means of social protection.
4. Everyone has the right to form and to join trade unions for the protection of his interests.

Article 24

Everyone has the right to rest and leisure, including reasonable limitation of working hours and periodic holidays with pay.

Article 25

1. Everyone has the right to a standard of living adequate for the health and well-being of himself and of his family, including food, clothing, housing and medical care and necessary social services, and the right to security in the event of unemployment, sickness, disability, widowhood, old age or other lack of livelihood in circumstances beyond his control.
2. Motherhood and childhood are entitled to special care and assistance. All children, whether born in or out of wedlock, shall enjoy the same social protection.

Article 26

1. Everyone has the right to education. Education shall be free, at least in the elementary and fundamental stages. Elementary education shall be compulsory. Technical and professional education shall be made generally available and higher education shall be equally accessible to all on the basis of merit.

2. Education shall be directed to the full development of the human personality and to the strengthening of respect for human rights and fundamental freedoms. It shall promote understanding, tolerance and friendship among all nations, racial or religious groups, and shall further the activities of the United Nations for the maintenance of peace.
3. Parents have a prior right to choose the kind of education that shall be given to their children.

Article 27

1. Everyone has the right to participate freely in the cultural life of the community, to enjoy the arts and to share in scientific advancement and its benefits.
2. Everyone has the right to the protection of the moral and material interests resulting from any scientific, literary or artistic production of which he is the author.

Article 28

Everyone is entitled to a social and international order in which the rights and freedoms set forth in this Declaration can be fully realized.

Article 29

1. Everyone has duties to the community in which alone the free and full development of his personality is possible.
2. In the exercise of his rights and freedoms, everyone shall be subject only to such limitations as are determined by law solely for the purpose of securing due recognition and respect for the rights and freedoms of others and of meeting the just requirements of morality, public order and the general welfare in a democratic society.
3. These rights and freedoms may in no case be exercised contrary to the purposes and principles of the United Nations.

Article 30

Nothing in this Declaration may be interpreted as implying for any State, group or person any right to engage in any activity or to perform any act aimed at the destruction of any of the rights and freedoms set forth herein.

SOURCE: United Nations, 1948.

the rich and the poor of any industrialized nation (Global Issues, 2010). These facts are staggering—even to those who are the most cynical about world poverty. They also point out how much work is needed to close the income gap between the rich and the poor and between wealthy countries and poor countries across the globe.

EP 2.1.8b

The concept of **world citizenship** is also central to achieving the global village. Technologically, we have achieved a world community, as evidenced by modern communications, travel, and international trade. But the world remains a place that is dramatically divided into political, social, religious, and ethnic tribes. Although a number of proposals have been advanced to overcome the divisions, the only concept that comes close to conquering them is the idea of world citizenship, or people accepting their responsibility in this interdependent world by thinking and acting as citizens of that world (Abraham, Chow, Maratou-Alipranti, & Tastsoglou, 2010; Altinay, 2011; Cabrera, 2010; Nikolpopoulou, Abraham, & Mirbagheri, 2010).

Responding to the Challenge of Globalization

Is the social work profession prepared to respond to the challenges and opportunities of globalization? The answer to this question is: not entirely, but things are improving. The International Federation of Social Workers (IFSW, 2012) has developed global standards for the education and training of social work professionals that address specific actions that colleges and universities with social work education programs across the globe can take to respond to the challenges and opportunities of globalization in the following areas:

* core purpose and mission statement;
* program objectives and outcomes;
* program curricula, including field education;
* core curriculum;
* faculty and staff;
* students;
* structure, administration, governance, and resources;
* cultural and ethnic diversity and inclusiveness;
* ethical codes of conduct.

Colleges and universities that provide social work education around the world are encouraged to apply these standards in both their undergraduate and graduate programs. Despite these recent advances, significant work remains to be done in the following areas: increase the level of participation of social workers in the activities and programs of international agencies; expand the international influence of professional social work organizations; and promote the international exchange of ideas, staff, and other resources.

A number of social work advocates and authors have stepped forward to address concerns about a more global focus of the social work profession (see, for example, Fitzpatrick, Kwon, Manning, Midgley, & Pascall, 2010; Holton & Sonnert, 2010; Lyons, Hokenstad, Pawar, Huelger, & Hall, 2012; Valtonen, 2012). The *Educational Policy and Accreditation Standards* (EPAS) developed by the Council on Social Work Education (CSWE), establish guidelines for the accreditation of both undergraduate and graduate social work programs across the United States. These standards include a mandate that international content be integrated across the curriculum (CSWE, 2008). Social work educators across the globe are working together on a number of projects to globalize the social work curriculum by increasing international research on social welfare practice and policy issues and arranging student and faculty exchanges and linkage projects.

Children and Human Rights

EP 2.1.5b
EP 2.1.9a

Millions of children make their way through life impoverished, abandoned, uneducated, malnourished, discriminated against, neglected, and vulnerable to exploitation (UNICEF, 2014). According to UNICEF,

all children have rights, regardless of race, color, sex, language, religion, political or other opinion, ethnic, national, or social origin, property, disability, or other status. (p. 8)

Dependent and vulnerable children throughout the world experience many of the same human rights abuses as adults (Amnesty International, 2013; UNICEF, 2014):

* torture by state officials;
* unlawful or arbitrary detainment, often in appalling conditions;
* death, maiming, or being forced to flee their homes because of armed conflicts;
* death or abuse in the name of social or ethnic cleansing;
* work at exploitative and/or hazardous jobs;

- conscription as combatants by armed forces and armed opposition groups;
- sex trafficking; and
- observing family members (including their parents) being beaten, mutilated, taken away in the middle of the night never to be seen again, or murdered.

Children often suffer abuse, neglect, and violence in the administration of juvenile justice. They frequently are beaten and humiliated, their legal rights are ignored, and their parents are not informed of their whereabouts. They are held in degrading conditions and often are incarcerated with adults. Some are denied their right to fair trial and are given sentences typically reserved for adults. According to UNICEF (2014), poverty, armed conflict, and HIV/AIDS are among the greatest threats to childhood throughout the world, but in particular in least developed countries (LDCs).

Poverty

Children in LDCs are most at risk of becoming excluded and invisible. They are represented disproportionately among the poor, are more likely to be engaged in labor, to experience extreme deprivation, and to die before the age of 5 (UNICEF, 2014).

Armed Conflict

For millions of children, living in the midst of war is the only existence they have ever known (United Nations, 2010a). Others are forced to flee and end up as refugees or displaced persons, often separated from their families. Numerous international laws or protocols apply to the rights and protection of children in armed conflict (United Nations, 2010a):

- Geneva Conventions of 1949 and additional protocols;
- Convention on the Rights of the Child of 1989;
- United Nations Child Soldiers Protocol;
- Convention on Prohibitions or Restriction on the Use of Certain Conventional Weapons Which May Be Deemed to Be Excessively Injurious or to Have Indiscriminate Effects;
- International Labour Organization Convention No. 182 concerning the Prohibition and Immediate Action for the Elimination of the Worst Forms of Child Labour;
- 1997 Convention on the Prohibition of the Use, Stockpiling, Production and Transfer of Antipersonnel Mines and on Their Destruction; and
- Convention on Cluster Munitions.

These laws address grave violations committed against children such as recruiting and using them as soldiers, killing and maiming them, committing rape and other acts of sexual violence against them, abducting them, denying them access to humanitarian aid, attacks on schools and hospitals, and the denial of humanitarian aid (United Nations, 2010a, p. 1).

HIV/AIDS

HIV/AIDS undermines adults' ability to protect and provide for their families, increasing the risk to all members and restricting access to essential services. Worldwide, nearly 18 million children have lost one or both of their parents to AIDS (UNICEF, 2014). Millions more children have become vulnerable, as the disease presents challenges to the health and development of families as well as the maintenance of viable communities and provinces, and in the worst areas, entire nations.

> The protracted illness and eventual death of parents and other caregivers exert enormous pressure on children, who often have to assume adult roles in treatment, care, and support. Surviving siblings can suffer stigma and discrimination in their communities and societies, experience greater exposure to violence, abuse and exploitation, and drop out of school for a variety of reasons. (UNICEF, 2009, p. 16)

Other Risks Faced by Children

Children throughout the world are forced to work in fields, sweatshop factories, mines, and brothels, and other such dangerous and unhealthy environments, where they are accorded few or no rights. Many are sold, forced into labor, or trafficked for sex. In some countries, children are forced by the government into dangerous or inappropriate work. Most of the estimated 250 million child workers are engaged in domestic labor. Child domestics often are forced to work long hours for little or no salary, endure permanent or long-term isolation from their families and friends, and rarely have the chance to attend school (Amnesty International, 2013).

The illegal transport and sale of human beings for their labor are serious violations of human rights. Every year, thousands of women and girls around the world are lured, abducted, or sold into forced labor, prostitution, domestic service, and other forms of involuntary servitude. Trafficked children are often rounded up by the police and face an uncertain future. Sometimes, the police are bribed to hand over the children to the very traffickers from whom they were "rescued." Other times, they are handed over to the juvenile authorities, where a decision is made to either detain them further, transfer them to the child protection system, or make arrangements for them to return home, often to the very environment that led them to be trafficked in the first place (Amnesty International, 2013). It is not uncommon for children placed in out-of-home care by the child protection system or those who are returned home to run away and rejoin their trafficker, with whom they have formed a strong bond, despite the horrific conditions under which they have been forced to live. Child sex trafficking experts would explain children's desire to reunite with their trafficker as "trauma bonding." Trauma bonds involve chains of trust that result in a strong connection to someone who is exploitive, abusive, and/or toxic (in this case, the trafficker). A person who has developed a trauma bond with another individual feels very confused about the relationship, but is unable to break free from it. Trauma bonding often makes it difficult for the authorities to prosecute traffickers because the individuals being trafficked are unwilling to identify them or testify in court against them (Shared Hope International, 2014).

It is estimated that upward of 100 million children live and work on the streets throughout the world—begging; peddling fruit, cigarettes, or trinkets; shining shoes; or engaging in petty theft or prostitution. Many have been abandoned, rejected, orphaned, or have run away from home to escape intolerable conditions, including physical and sexual abuse. Many are addicted to drugs. Street children are often victims of "social cleansing" campaigns, in which local business owners pay to have them chased away or even killed (Amnesty International, 2013).

International Efforts to Alleviate the Plight of Children

EP 2.1.1a
EP 2.1.5b
EP 2.1.5c
EP 2.1.8a
EP 2.1.9b

In 2000, the *Millennium Declaration* was adopted by 189 countries (see Box 16.2 for a list of the *Millennium Declaration*'s values and principles), which resulted in the development of a set of Millennium Development Goals (MDGs) that established specific targets to reduce or eliminate by the year 2015

extreme poverty and hunger, child and maternal mortality, and HIV/AIDS and other diseases, while promoting universal primary education, gender equality, environmental sustainability, and a global partnership for development (UNICEF, 2009, p. vii). Each of the MDGs is related directly to the well-being of children. Failure to achieve them would have a dramatic effect on the well-being of children throughout the world and for the adults they will become if they make it through childhood.

The MDGs are a catalyst for improved access to essential services, protection, and participation for children, but they are not an end in themselves. Children around the globe deserve our commitment and dedication to helping provide them with a better world in which to live. (UNICEF, 2009, p. vii)

The most recent report on the status of the MDGS (United Nations, 2013) acknowledges that while significant progress (albeit uneven) has been made toward achievement of the MDGs, full achievement of the goals by 2015 is unlikely. According to the report, accelerated progress and bolder action are needed in the following areas:

- improvements in environmental sustainability;
- prevalence of maternal and child deaths;
- availability of antiretroviral therapy and knowledge about HIV prevention;
- number of children out-of-school;
- improved sanitation;
- decline in humanitarian aid;
- closing of rural-urban gaps in progress;
- continued reduction of poverty rates; and
- elimination of gender-based inequalities in decision-making power (pp. 4–5).

Experience has shown that progress toward achievement of the MDGs is shaped by three key factors: policy choices that govern how a country participates in the global economy, an enabling environment needed for securing progress, and the ability to make the public investments necessary for MDG outcomes.

The report concludes that the continuation of efforts to achieve a world of prosperity, equity, freedom, dignity, and peace will be required well beyond 2015. The United Nations is working with governments, civic groups throughout the world, and other partners to build on the momentum generated by the MDGs, by crafting an ambitious, yet realistic post–2015 development agenda (United Nations, 2013, p. 5).

Box 16.2   Values and Principles of the United Nations Millennium Declaration

We consider certain fundamental values to be essential to international relations in the twenty-first century. These include:

- **Freedom.** Men and women have the right to live their lives and raise their children in dignity, free from hunger and from the fear of violence, oppression or injustice. Democratic and participatory governance based on the will of the people best assures these rights.
- **Equality.** No individual and no nation must be denied the opportunity to benefit from development. The equal rights and opportunities of women and men must be assured.
- **Solidarity.** Global challenges must be managed in a way that distributes the costs and burdens fairly in accordance with basic principles of equity and social justice. Those who suffer or who benefit least deserve help from those who benefit most.
- **Tolerance.** Human beings must respect one another, in all their diversity of belief, culture, and language. Differences within and between societies should be neither feared nor repressed, but

cherished as a precious asset of humanity. A culture of peace and dialogue among all civilizations should be actively promoted.

- **Respect for nature.** Prudence must be shown in the management of all living species and natural resources, in accordance with the precepts of sustainable development. Only in this way can the immeasurable riches provided to us by nature be preserved and passed on to our descendents. The current unsustainable patterns of production and consumption must be changed in the interest of our future welfare and that of our descendants.
- **Shared responsibility.** Responsibility for managing worldwide economic and social development, as well as threats to international peace and security, must be shared among the nations of the world and should be exercised multilaterally. As the most universal and most representative organization in the world, the United Nations must play the central role.

SOURCE: United Nations (2000). *Millennium declaration* (p. 2). New York: Author.

The Plight of World Refugees

EP 2.1.5b
EP 2.1.8b
EP 2.1.9a

In common terms, a refugee is any person in flight from dire circumstances in search of a safe haven. In a strict sense, according to the 1951 United Nations Convention on the Status of Refugees, a **refugee** is a person who,

owing to well-founded fear of being persecuted for reason of race, religion, nationality, or membership in a particular social group or political opinion, is outside the country of his [her] nationality and is unable or, owing to such fear, unwilling to avail himself/herself of the protection of that country. (United Nations, 1951)

Any person without the protection of at least one nation is a concern to the international community. Social workers who work with refugees assist nations and volunteer organizations to provide early warning, protection, maintenance, rehabilitation, and guided reestablishment of a protective relationship via safe

return to one's original country (repatriation), integration in the country of refuge, or, in some instances, relocation and resettlement in a third country including, but not limited to, the United States. Refugee movements and the presence of displaced persons anywhere in the world generate humanitarian and often political responses from the international community.

In many instances, despite humanitarian intervention, there are tragic consequences for refugees including:

- deliberate persecution and/or lack of protection within the national borders of refugee-producing nations;
- the inability or unwillingness of governments of countries receiving refugees to fulfill their treaty responsibilities of ensuring protection of the legitimate asylum-seekers who come within their territory;
- the inability or unwillingness of countries receiving refugees to accept the financial responsibility of providing assistance to the United Nations and its

volunteer agency partners and those countries willing to take in refugees; and

- the inability or unwillingness of the international community to press for sanctions against those entities that produce refugees as a result of persecution and violence.

The most recent report from the United Nations High Command on Refugees (UNHCR) shows that the plight of refugees across the globe continues. The statistics below are based on data for calendar 2012, the latest period for which such information is available.

- An estimated 7.6 million people were newly displaced *outside* the borders of their country (another 6.5 million people were displaced *within* the borders of their country);
- Almost 36 million persons (refugees, asylum seekers, internally displaced persons served by UNHCR, returned refugees and internally displaced persons, and stateless persons) were of concern to UNHCR;
- Developing countries hosted 8 out of 10 of the refugees;
- Pakistan was host to the largest number of refugees worldwide, followed by Islamic Republic of Iran, Germany, and Kenya;
- One in two refugees under UNHCR's mandate lived in countries where the gross domestic product (GDP) per capita was less than $5,000 USD;
- One in two refugees worldwide came from Afghanistan, Somalia, Iraq, the Syrian Arab Republic, and Sudan;
- With regard to age, 46% of the refugees were children under 18, 49% were between 18 and 59, and 5% were 60 and over;
- Twenty-two countries admitted 86,000 refugees (with or without UNHCR assistance), with the United States admitting about 75% of this number; and
- Refugee women and girls accounted for about half of the refugee population.

Many refugees live their entire lives in make-shift camps while waiting for resettlement elsewhere. The world's largest refugee camp is actually a complex of five camps located in Dadaab in northeastern Kenya. The camps were originally intended to host 90,000 individuals; today, they are home to some 500 million refugees and asylum seekers (UNHCR, 2013).

One of the policy issues that countries like the United States struggle with is the humanitarian role it

should play in global strife that results in extreme risk, including death, to large numbers of individuals. On one hand, the social welfare needs of many individuals in the United States are not being met and resources are limited in providing needed support to help them achieve self-sufficiency. On the other hand, needs can be considered relative when considering the plight of refugees in other parts of the world. The expectation that countries will come together and create sanctions against those countries that are violating human rights is precarious at best given the shifting balance in world power. Even if sanctions are imposed, leaders of the countries sanctioned may still not change their treatment of those being persecuted. The United States, like a number of other countries, has continued to reach out to refugees, including opportunities for resettlement for some in the United States. However, the number of refugees for whom resettlement is achieved is paltry in comparison to the need.

Myths and facts about refugees resettled in the United States are shown in Box 16.3. As you can see, there are many misconceptions about this population.

Challenges faced by refugees resettled in the United States are many and varied: separation from family members still awaiting resettlement; stress brought about by the expectation to become "self-sufficient" within 4–6 months after arrival in the United States; loneliness and isolation; mental health conditions, including severe depression, PTSD, and pervasive anxiety; issues with alcoholism and substance use; differences in child rearing practices; maintaining one's cultural identity while being pressured to "fit in"; navigating a multitude of complex (and sometimes conflicting) systems; obtaining quality, affordable housing; securing quality, affordable, and culturally appropriate child care; tensions over intergenerational differences between children and their parents (and sometimes grandparents); stress associated with having to pay back the cost of passage to the United States; "parentification" of children; involvement with the child welfare and juvenile justice systems; domestic violence; gang involvement; children dropping out of school to help support the family; eviction; food insecurity; restricted family time because of pressure to work; and the lack of personal transportation.

Social workers at both the BSW and MSW levels can play a number of roles helping refugees address these issues:

- setting and managing priorities;
- securing free or low-cost and reliable personal transportation;

Box 16.3   Myths and Facts About the Refugee Population in the United States

Myth	Fact
• Refugees come here for economic reasons	• Refugees would rather live and work in their native country
• The U.S. is the only country to resettle refugees	• There are over a dozen countries involved in refugee resettlement
• Refugees automatically receive special monies from the U.S. government	• Refugees must apply for benefits and meet an income and resource test to qualify for any assistance
• Refugees do not pay taxes	• Refugees pay taxes the same as any citizen living in the U.S.
• Refugees take jobs from Americans	• Refugees must apply and compete for jobs the same as any citizen or resident alien; in many cases, they take jobs no one else wants to fill
• The U.S. spends millions of dollars every month supporting refugees	• Statistics have shown that the tax contribution of refugees is considerably greater than the cost of services they use
• Refugees do not contribute or participate in this society	• Refugees contribute a great wealth to this country through their culture and customs
• Refugees do not want to learn English	• Most refugees want to learn English to better navigate the world around them
• Refugees are all on welfare	• There is no "welfare" in the U.S.
• The taxpayer pays the way for refugees to come to the U.S.	• The old welfare entitlement programs no longer exist
• Refugees bring diseases into the country	• Refugees borrow money to pay for their trip to the U.S. They sign a promissory note to repay the loan within 5 years or forego any federal services and benefits to which they are entitled
	• Refugees receive strict health screenings for contagious diseases as a condition for entering the country; if they don't pass these tests, they are not allowed to enter the country
• Churches bring refugees into local communities	• Refugee resettlement is a program operated by the U.S. government.

Source: Office of Refugee Resettlement, 2014.

- helping to resolve domestic issues;
- facilitating parent education and support groups;
- making referrals to community resources;
- providing individual and group counseling;
- helping to find jobs that pay a decent salary with benefits; and
- serving as a case manager.

If the doors are closed to refugees, millions of displaced persons throughout the world will be prevented from reaching safety outside their homelands or will require protection in safe havens within their homelands. Only federally-approved agencies/organizations are allowed to resettle refugees.

EP 2.1.1a
EP 2.1.5b
EP 2.1.7b
EP 2.1.9b

Immigration in the United States

Immigration policy has become a lightning rod for heated discussion across the United States. While many are sympathetic to the plight of refugees, immigration is often viewed differently. Working with recent immigrants and

Social work transcends geographic boundaries and political ideologies. Social work professionals play many critical roles in helping make the world a better place so today's children can enjoy a successful future.

Paula Bronstein/Getty Images News/Getty Images

addressing immigration-related policy and practice issues have long been within the domain of social workers. The influx of immigrants to the United States, coupled with concerns by citizens about who should have access to resources already perceived as scarce, has escalated discussions about the ease of entry of immigrants who want to come to the United States; whether they should be allowed to enter at all; and if they do come, what services they should receive and who should pay for them. Immigration policy in the United States serves the following fundamental purposes (U.S. Congressional Budget Office [CBO], 2010, p. vii):

- reuniting families by admitting immigrants who already have family members living in the United States (439,460 in 2013);
- admitting workers with specific skills to fill jobs that have labor shortages;
- providing a refuge for persons who face political, racial, or religious persecution in their country of origin (i.e., asylees); and
- ensuring diversity of the immigrant population by admitting people from countries with historically low rates of immigration.

Lawful Entry

Noncitizens (or *aliens,* as the federal government refers to them) may achieve lawful entry into the United States by being accorded the status of "lawful permanent resident" (LPR) by U.S. immigration authorities. Those admitted in this manner are classified formally as "immigrants" and are given a permanent resident card, called a *green card.* They are eligible to work and apply for U.S. citizenship. In 2013, LPR status was granted to 459,751 new immigrants, as well as to 530,802 noncitizens already in the country (Office of Immigration Statistics, 2014).

Noncitizens also may achieve lawful entry into the United States by being granted temporary admission. These individuals are allowed to enter the country for a specific purpose on a time-limited basis (e.g., tourism, diplomatic missions, education, or temporary work). By law, these individuals are classified as *nonimmigrants.* As such, they may be permitted to visit, study, or work for a limited time, but they must apply for LPR status if they wish to remain in the country permanently (Congressional Budget Office, 2010).

In 2012, the U.S. State Department authorized temporary admission to the United States for some 3.0 million noncitizens. Another 16.4 million noncitizens were allowed to remain in the country for no more than 90 days (Office of Immigration Statistics, 2013). These figures do not reflect the flow of noncitizens *out* of the United States, estimated to be about 200,000 in number annually (presumably to reenter their country of origin) (Office of Immigration Statistics, 2013).

Unlawful Entry

An estimated 11.4 million unauthorized persons were living in the United States as of January 2013 (Office of Immigration Statistics, 2013). Unauthorized persons who have violated U.S. immigration laws may be removed from the country through a process that can include fines, incarceration, or prohibition against future entry, or they may be offered the chance to depart voluntarily (CBO, 2010). In 2013, 388,644 unauthorized persons were removed from the country formally, and some 1 million others left the country voluntarily (U.S. Immigration and Customs Enforcement [ICE], 2014). Table 16.1 shows the current requirements for naturalization in the United States.

A Brief History of U.S. Immigration Policy and Legislation

EP 2.1.3b
EP 2.1.7b
EP 2.1.8a

Immigration policy first emerged in the United States in 1790 when Congress established a process for enabling people born abroad to become U.S. citizens (Zohlberg, 2008). The first federal law limiting immigration—The Page Act of 1875—prohibited the admission of criminals and prostitutes. The U.S. Immigration Service was established in 1891 in response to the millions of immigrants who came into the country throughout the 19th century to fuel the Industrial Revolution (CBO, 2010; Zinn & Arnove, 2011).

Concerned about how to support the social and economic needs of the millions of immigrants entering the country, Congress established a national-origins quota system as part of the Quota Law of 1921. This law was revised in 1924 to restrict immigration by assigning each nationality a quota based on its representation in past U.S. census figures. The Quota Law of 1921 as revised favored family reunification, in which immediate relatives of U.S. citizens and other family members either were exempted from numerical restrictions or were granted preference within the restrictions (CBO, 2010; Zinn & Arnove, 2011).

The Immigration and Nationality Act Amendments of 1965 (Nationality Act) replaced the national-origins quota system with a categorical preference system. That provided preferences for relatives of U.S. citizens with job skills considered to be useful to the country. Neither the preference categories nor country-specific caps applied to immigrants from the Western Hemisphere. Amendments to the Nationality Act in 1976 and 1978 extended the categorical preference system to applicants from the Western Hemisphere and combined Eastern and Western Hemisphere restrictions into a single annual worldwide ceiling of 190,000 (CBO, 2010).

The Refugee Act of 1980 created a comprehensive refugee policy in which the President, in consultation with Congress, had the authority to determine the number of refugees who would be allowed to enter the United States yearly. This act adopted the internationally accepted definition of "refugee" contained in the U.N. Convention and Protocol Relating to the Status of Refugees (CBO, 2010).

The Immigration and Control Act of 1986 addressed the issue of unauthorized immigration and sought to strengthen enforcement of unauthorized immigration as well as create new opportunities for legal immigration. For the first time, employers who knowingly hired or recruited unauthorized persons were subject to financial and other penalties. The act also provided for two amnesty programs for unauthorized immigrants—the Seasonal Agricultural Worker program and the Legally Authorized Workers program—and created a new classification for seasonal agricultural workers.

The Seasonal Agricultural Worker amnesty program allowed individuals who had worked for at least 90 days in certain agricultural jobs to apply for permanent resident status. The Legally Authorized Workers amnesty program allowed current unauthorized immigrants who had lived in the United States since at least 1982 to legalize their status. Under the two programs, some 2.7 million undocumented persons living in the United States became lawful permanent residents (CBO, 2010).

The Immigration Act of 1990 added a new category of admission based on diversity and raised the worldwide immigration ceiling to the current "flexible" cap of 675,000 per year. That cap allows for transferring unused immigration visas from one year to the next. Concerns about continued unauthorized immigration led to passage of the Illegal Immigration Reform and Immigrant Responsibility Act of 1996, which increased the number of border patrol agents, broadened border-control measures, reduced government benefits available to immigrants, and established a pilot program whereby employers and social service agencies could check by telephone or electronically to verify the eligibility of immigrants applying for work or social service benefits (CBO, 2010).

EP 2.1.5b

The Homeland Security Act of 2002 restructured the Immigration and Naturalization Service (INS), transferring immigration services, border enforcement, and border inspection to a newly created Department of Homeland Security (DHS). The immigrant services and

TABLE 16.1 REQUIREMENTS FOR NATURALIZATION IN THE UNITED STATES

CHARACTERISTICS OF APPLICANT	PRECONDITIONS			
	TIME AS LAWFUL PERMANENT RESIDENT (LPR)	CONTINUOUS RESIDENCE IN THE U.S.[a]	PHYSICAL PRESENCE IN THE U.S.	TIME IN DISTRICT OR STATE[b]
LPR with no special circumstances	5 years	5 years	30 months	3 months
Married to and living with a U.S. citizen for the past 3 years	3 years	3 years	18 months	3 months
In Armed Forces for at least 1 year	Must be an LPR at the time of interview	Not required	Not required	Not required
In Armed Forces less than 1 year, or in Armed Forces less than 1 year and discharged more than 6 months earlier	5 years	5 years	30 months	3 months
Performed active military duty during WWI, WWII, Korea, Vietnam, Persian Gulf, on or before 9/11/01	Not required	Not required	Not required	Not required
Widow or widower of a U.S. citizen who died during active duty	Must be an LPR at the time of interview	Not required	Not required	Not required
Employee of or under contract to U.S. government	5 years	5 years	30 months	3 months
Performing ministerial or priestly functions for a religious organization with a valid U.S. presence	5 years	5 years	30 months	3 months
Employed by certain U.S. research institutions, a U.S.-owned firm involved with development of U.S. or foreign trade or commerce, or public international organization of which the U.S. is a member	5 years	5 years	30 months	3 months
Employed at least 5 years by a U.S. nonprofit organization supporting U.S. interests abroad through communications media	5 years	Not required	Not required	Not required
Spouse of a U.S. citizen who is a member of the Armed Forces, or in one of the four previous categories, and who is working abroad under an employment contract with a qualifying employer for at least 1 year[c]	Must be an LPR at the time of interview	Not Required	Not required	Not required

[a]Trips outside of the United States for 6 months or longer are considered a break in continuous U.S. residency. Exceptions are made for members of the Armed Forces whose service takes them out of the country.

[b]Most applicants must be a resident of the district or state in which they are applying.

[c]Spouse must have been a citizen for the past 3 years.

SOURCE: Department of Homeland Security, U.S. Citizenship and Immigration Services (February 2010). *A guide to naturalization,* as cited in CBO, 2010.

enforcement functions were combined under the INS, but these functions have been split up among different bureaus of DHS. Some immigration officials have challenged the wisdom of these changes, citing concerns about the new organizational structure, as well as the leadership at DHS, which had little knowledge or experience in dealing with immigration issues (CBO, 2010).

The REAL ID Act of 2005 was enacted into law in May 2005 in response to continued concerns in Congress about homeland security. Key provisions of the law include changing visa limits for temporary workers, nurses, and Australian citizens; establishing new national standards for state-issued driver's licenses and nondriver identification cards used for "official purposes" (boarding commercially operated airline flights and entering federal buildings and nuclear power plants); funding pilot projects related to border security; introducing rules covering "delivery bonds" for aliens who have been released pending hearings; updating and tightening the laws on application for asylum and deportation of aliens for terrorist activity; and waiving laws that interfere with the construction of physical barriers at the borders. Several attempts have been made to repeal the law, but to date, none of them has been successful.

The Secure Fence Act of 2006 became law in October 2006. The law calls for the construction of over 700 miles of secure fence to be built along the U.S.–Mexico border in California, Arizona, New Mexico, and Texas, particularly in areas that have experienced a high concentration of illegal drug trafficking and illegal immigration. The law also authorizes the installation of more lighting, vehicle barriers, and border checkpoints, as well as more advanced equipment like sensors, cameras, satellites and unmanned aerial vehicles in an attempt to control illegal immigration into the United States. While public sentiment about this law has been positive overall, mayors from some border towns on either side of the border have expressed strong opposition to construction of the fence on the grounds that it will make things worse, not better.

The Development, Relief and Education for Alien Minors Act (DREAM Act) was introduced in Congress in March 2009. This bill would provide certain undocumented students who graduate from U.S. high schools the opportunity to earn conditional permanent residency for a 6-year period, during which the student must obtain a degree from a U.S. institution of higher education, complete at least 2 years in good

standing in a program for a bachelor's (or higher) degree, or serve in the uniformed services for at least 2 years and be in good standing or have received an honorable discharge (National Immigration Law Center, 2011).

Recent efforts to address immigration reform have fallen victim to the Congressional gridlock that has plagued President Obama's second term in office. In 2013, the U.S. Senate passed a bipartisan reform bill (The Border Security Economic Opportunity and Immigration Modernization Act) that would create a "pathway to citizenship" (albeit long and arduous) for the estimated 11 million undocumented immigrants living in the country through the creation of a Registered Provisional Immigrant (RPI) status. RPI status would be available to individuals who demonstrated continuous physical presence in the United States on or before December 31, 2011, were not convicted of any serious crime, and did not have a federal tax liability. They also have to pay an application fee as well as a penalty for being in the country illegally, and submit a completed application.

Initial registration for RPI status would be valid for 6 years, at which time those holding this status must apply for renewal. Renewal requirements include undergoing a criminal background check, payment of additional fees and a fine, and proof of employment. After 10 years, RPIs can apply for an adjustment in status, like Lawful Permanent Resident (LPR). After a period of another 3 years, RPIs can apply for naturalization, for which additional requirements apply (National Council of State Legislatures, 2014). One year later, the House has failed to take action on this bill, and it appears that no such action will be taken by the time the current Congress is declared over.

There has been no such shortage of action, however, on the passage of immigration reform-related legislation by states across the country. A search of the NCSL Immigration Enactments Database revealed the following immigration reform-related bill enactment activity during the 5-year period 2009–2013 (figures include both bills and resolutions that addressed such topics as budgets, education, employment, health, law enforcement, human trafficking, and identification):

- 2009: 212 bills in 44 states;
- 2010: 356 bills in 47 states;

- 2011: 321 bills in 44 states;
- 2012: 262 bills in 45 states; and
- 2013: 436 bills in 46 states.

EP 2.1.7b
EP 2.1.9b

One of the most polarizing pieces of state-initiated immigration-related legislation is Senate Bill 1070, which became law in the state of Arizona in April 2010. This law authorizes local police to check the immigration status of anyone they reasonably suspect of being in the country illegally. Proponents of the law argue that it is necessary to combat illegal immigration. Those who oppose the law argue that it is an infringement on civil liberties and promotes racial/ethnic profiling of Hispanics by the police. The law has sparked sharp debate across the country about how best to address illegal entry into the United States. Some would say that it is not surprising that such a law was passed, given the prolonged economic woes of the country and the perceived threat that undocumented individuals present to destabilizing the employment, health care, and social services systems in the United States (Hessick & Chin, 2014; Varsanyi, 2010). On June 25, 2012, The U.S. Supreme Court handed down a split decision on the Arizona law. The court sustained the best known and most hotly disputed part of the law, which requires police to determine the immigration status of someone arrested or detained when there is "reasonable suspicion" they are not in the United States legally, but it blocked implementation of other provisions of the law. The debate over the "show me your papers" provision of the Arizona law continues to this day, fueled by the failure of Congress to enact omnibus immigration reform legislation and concerns over the recent influx of unaccompanied minors entering the country illegally (see below for a brief discussion of this issue).

Myths and Facts About Immigrants

As with refugees, there are many myths about immigrants, both documented and undocumented. As you can see from Box 16.4, immigrants actually have higher graduation rates, have lower levels of poverty, are less likely to be receiving government benefits, and contribute billions of dollars each year to the U.S. economy in businesses, taxes, and purchases.

A recent nationwide survey conducted by the Pew Research Center (2013) revealed overall support among respondents of allowing people illegally in the United States to remain, but mixed responses when it comes to

what to allow if they do remain in the country. Key findings from this study are summarized below.

- Seventy-one percent of those surveyed said that there should be some way for people illegally in the United States to remain in the country if they meet certain requirements;
- Of the 71% who indicated that the people illegally in the country should stay, less than half (43%) indicated that they should be eligible for citizenship, 24% indicated that they should only be eligible for permanent residency, and 4% indicated that they were uncertain or did not know;
- When asked about immigration today, about one in two respondents (49%) indicated that immigrants in the United States strengthened the country because of their hard work and talents, 41% indicated that they were a burden to society, and 10% indicated that they were uncertain or didn't know;
- When asked about the increase in newcomers from other countries, just over half of the respondents (52%) indicated that such an increase strengthens American society, 43% indicated that such an increase threatens traditional American customs and values, and 5% were uncertain or didn't know;
- Eight out of ten blacks and Hispanics (combined) and two out of three whites indicated that people illegally in the country should be allowed to stay;
- Sixty-four, seventy-four, and seventy percent of those who declared themselves as Republicans, Democrats, and Independents, respectfully, indicated that people illegally in the country should stay;
- Thirty-three, fifty-eight, and fifty-one percent of those who declared themselves as Republicans, Democrats, and Independents, respectively, indicated that the growing number of newcomers from other countries strengthens the country; and
- Thirty-four, sixty-one, and fifty-five percent of those who declared themselves as Republicans, Democrats, and Independents, respectively, indicated that the growing number of newcomers from other countries strengthens society.

The general public is deeply divided about how to effectively curtail the flow of undocumented immigrants in the future. The two main approaches to reducing the flow of undocumented immigrants are:

1. greater enforcement along the border between Arizona, California, New Mexico, Texas, and

Box 16.4 How Immigrants Contribute to the U.S. Economy

1. They start businesses. Immigrants are 30% more likely to start a business in the U.S. than non-immigrants, and almost 20% all small business owners in the U.S. are immigrants.
2. The businesses they own create jobs for U.S. workers. Immigrant-owned businesses employed about 4.7 million people in 2007 and generated an estimated $776 billion annually.
3. They are more likely to be self-employed than non-immigrants.
4. They develop cutting-edge technologies and companies, including Google, eBay, Yahoo!, Sun Microsystems, and Intel. About one-fourth of public U.S. companies backed by venture capital investors were started by immigrants
5. They are scientists, engineers, and innovators. Although only 16% of those with a bachelor's degree are immigrants, 33% of engineers, 27% of mathematicians and computer scientists, and 24% of physical scientists are immigrants.
6. They increase earnings for American workers. More immigrants in the U.S. means increased demand for goods and services and correlates with an increase in wages for U.S. workers.
7. They boost demand for local consumer goods with purchasing power that contributes billions of dollars to the U.S. economy.
8. They can help reduce the federal deficit. Immigration reform legislation like the Dream Act can reduce the federal deficit by over $2 billion over ten years because of increased tax revenues. Since Dreamers would contribute to the economy in other ways, estimates show they would add $329 billion to the economy by 2030.
9. They will fill needed jobs. Between 2010 and 2030, an estimated 58.6 million baby boomers will leave the workforce. Economic growth will also create a demand for jobs, with a projection of 83 million new jobs needed by 2030. Grown children of native born parents can fill 51.3 million of those jobs. Comprehensive immigration reform could help fill the remaining jobs. Projections show that 18.6 million first generation immigrants and 12.9 million grown children of immigrants will be needed to fill them.
10. They pay taxes each year and contribute to the Social Security System. In 2010, undocumented immigrants paid $11.2 billion in state and local taxes. These taxes support many social service benefits that they are ineligible to receive. Projections show that immigrants will add a net of $611 billion to the Social Security System over the next 75 years, but that cutting off immigration would increase the Social Security deficit by 31% over 50 years.

Source: J. Furman and D. Gray (2012). *Ten ways immigrants help build and strengthen our economy.* Washington, DC: The White House; M. Fritz, P. Wolgin, and P. Oakford (2013). *Immigrants are makers, not takers.* Washington, D.C.: Center for American Progress; A. Kugler and P. Oakford (2013). *Immigration helps American workers' wages and job opportunities.* Washington, D.C.: Center for American Progress.

Mexico, bolstered by a large increase in the number of U.S. Border Patrol agents and the use of high-tech devices to prevent individuals from entering the country illegally or tracking their whereabouts should they attempt to do so, and

2. greater enforcement of the 1986 law that prohibits the employment of undocumented persons.

Surge in Unaccompanied Minors Coming into the United States

The most recent immigration crisis facing the United States is the recent surge in unaccompanied minors coming into the country (projected to be 90,000 in 2014) from the Central American states of Honduras, El Salvador, and Guatemala. Several factors have been attributed to this surge: severe and persistent poverty and organized criminal violence in the sending countries; the belief by those who care for the children in the sending countries that the risks of the journey to the United States are worth the gains achieved; willingness by family members in the United States to pay traffickers thousands of dollars to transport the child to the United States (estimated to be between $540 million and $630 million in 2014); and the emergence of trafficking rings in the sending countries that offer door-to-door service (Negroponte, 2014).

The Trafficking Victims Protection Reauthorization Act (TVPRA) requires that unaccompanied minors from non-contiguous states be transferred to the Office of Refugee Resettlement (ORR) within 72 hours and simultaneously placed in removal proceedings with the Executive Office for Immigration Review, located within the U.S. Department of Justice. ORR is responsible for sheltering and feeding unaccompanied minors from the time they are apprehended by the U.S. Border Patrol until their case is processed in the Immigration Courts.

Two events have conspired to make the recent surge in unaccompanied minors coming into the United States a humanitarian crisis—insufficient capacity to shelter and feed the children and a growing backlog of preliminary hearings by the Immigration Courts (currently pegged at nearly 20 months).

The federal government has determined that the most humane and expeditious way to deal with the crisis is to place the unaccompanied minor child with a parent or family member who must vouch that the child will appear in Immigration Court on the appointed date. Those children for whom a family placement is not possible are placed in foster care. Ironically, the practice of placing the children with parents or other family member or in temporary foster care creates an additional burden on the Immigration Courts for those cases in which the child fails to appear and/or those who age out of the foster care system by that time. The children are allowed to attend school and receive medical care while they are awaiting their court hearing.

Two grounds exist for an unaccompanied minor to remain in the United States (Negroponte, 2014): *refugee asylum* (granted to those individuals who fear persecution for reasons of race, religion, nationality, and membership in a particular social group or political opinion); and *Special Immigrant Juvenile Status* (granted to children who can establish that they were abused, neglected, or abandoned by one or both parents). It is estimated that some 40% of unaccompanied minors will have humanitarian claims recognized by U.S. Immigrations Courts; the remaining 60% will be returned to their home country, often after a period of several years living with their parents or other family members in the United States (Vera Institute of Justice, 2012).

The humanitarian crisis brought about by the surge in unaccompanied minors entering the United States will worsen unless a concerted effort is made by the United States (and in some cases, sending countries) to

- vigorously prosecute criminal organizations that profit from trafficking of unaccompanied minors;
- expedite the screening of apprehended children to determine the validity of their claims;
- make it clear to sending countries that their unaccompanied children will not be able to join their parents or other family members while they wait for their case to be processed by the Immigration Courts;
- increase the number of asylum officers and Immigration Court judges as well as provide training for prosecutors and defense attorneys, in order to achieve a swift resolution of *refugee asylum* and *Special Immigration Juvenile Status* cases;
- send a strong disincentive message to the adults who both send and receive unaccompanied minors (this could include the assessment of fines and even criminal penalties against those who receive unaccompanied minors);
- consider handling unaccompanied minors from non-contiguous countries and Canada and Mexico in the same manner (nearly all unaccompanied Mexican children are quickly returned to Mexico); and
- provide financial and other assistance to sending countries to improve the standard of living and safety in these countries to persuade those who care for the children that the risks associated with sending children to the United States are not worth the gains (Negroponte, 2014).

One thing is clear from the preceding discussion: the immigration debate in the United States is not likely to be resolved soon because of the magnitude and complexity of the problem and the deep divisions among the people it affects. All social workers should become familiar with this issue because of the accompanying social, economic, and political justice implications.

The International Federation of Social Workers

EP 2.1.8b

Problems such as those described in this chapter demand the attention and active collaboration of all nations if they are to be resolved satisfactorily. This is the focus of the **International Federation of Social Workers (IFSW)**, founded in 1956. The aims of the IFSW (2014a) are to:

- promote social work as a profession through international cooperation, especially regarding professional values, standards, ethics, human rights, recognition, training, and working conditions;
- promote the establishment of national organizations of social workers or professional unions for social workers and, when needed, national coordinating bodies (collectively "social work organizations") where they do not exist; and
- support social work organizations in promoting the participation of social workers in social planning, and the formulation of social policies, nationally and internationally, recognition of social work, enhancement of social work training, and the values and professional standards of social work.

To achieve these aims, the Federation (IFSW, 2014b, p. 1) engages in the following activities:

- encourages cooperation among social workers of all countries;
- facilitates opportunities for discussion and the exchange of ideas and experiences through meetings, study visits, research projects, and publications; and
- establishes and maintains relationships with, and presents and promotes the views of, social work organizations and their members to international organizations relevant to social development and welfare.

The IFSW is divided into five geographic regions: (1) Africa; (2) Asia and the Pacific; (3) Europe; (4) Latin America and the Caribbean; and (5) North America (IFSW, 2014b). Regions arrange their own meetings and conferences and elect representatives to regional organizations and the IFSW Human Rights Commission and Permanent Committee on Ethical Issues. Only one national professional organization in each country may become a member of the Federation. This organization may be a national association or a coordinating body that represents two or more national associations. Each member association or coordinating body must observe the IFSW Constitution.

Member organizations require their membership to engage in regular professional training that reflects an organized sequence of social work education and incorporates ethical standards of practice and a body of knowledge compatible with social work principles. Member organizations also are prohibited from discriminating against groups of social workers or individual social workers on grounds of race, color, ethnic origin, gender, language, religion, political opinion, age, or sexual orientation. Admission is decided by the general meeting and is based on information required by the Federation (p. 1).

EP 2.1.8b

IFSW partnerships include the following organizations (IFSW, 2014c):

- *Amnesty International,* a worldwide organization working to support human rights globally, both in general and for individuals;
- *CONGO,* the Conference of Nongovernmental Organizations (NGOs) in Consultative Relations with the United States—an independent international organization that facilitates the participation of NGOs in UN debates and decisions;
- *Council of Europe* with 46 member states, set up to defend human rights, parliamentary democracy, and the rule of law; to develop continent-wide agreements to standardize social and legal practices; and to promote awareness of a European identity;
- *ENSACT,* a European network of professional associations, faculties of social work and national councils of social welfare;
- *UN Department of Economic and Social Affairs, NGO Section,* an organization that works to strengthen and enhance dialogue between NGOs and the United Nations to enable NGOs to participate in the economic and social development activities of the organization.
- *World Health Organization (WHO),* an organization that provides leadership on global health matters, shaping the health research agenda, setting norms and standards, articulating evidence-based policy options, providing technical support to countries and monitoring and assessing health trends.
- *European Union,* an organization focusing on political, social, and economic cooperation among its 15 European member states;
- *International Association of Schools of Social Work (IASSW),* an international community of schools and educators in social work promoting quality education, training, and research for the theory

and practice of social work, administration of social services, and formulation of social policies;

- *International Council on Social Welfare (ICSW),* an international NGO operating throughout the world for the causes of social welfare, social justice, and social development;
- *United Nations Children's Fund (UNICEF),* an organization dedicated to assisting—particularly the developing countries of the world—in the development of permanent child health and welfare services; and
- *United Nations,* an international organization formed to promote peace, security, and cooperation throughout the world.

One purpose of the IFSW is to provide social workers throughout the world with practical as well as philosophical guidelines on many issues central to the profession of social work. The IFSW has developed a series of policy papers that represent a consensus of professionals from different geographic and professional backgrounds. Topics covered include health, HIV/AIDS, human rights, migration, older persons, protection of personal information, refugees, conditions in rural communities, women, youth, peace and social justice, displaced persons, globalization and the environment, and indigenous peoples.

Today, the IFSW represents nearly half-a-million social workers in 116 different countries. Its affiliate in the United States is the National Association of Social Workers (NASW).

EP 2.1.8a
EP 2.1.9b

International Social Work Organizations and Agencies

International social work encompasses refugee programs, relief efforts, community development, intercountry and international adoption, education, family planning, substance use disorders, posttraumatic stress, and mental health care. Numerous opportunities also are available to work with national government organizations, international government organizations, and volunteer organizations to provide technical assistance in implementing new programs and strengthening existing efforts and developing and enhancing social welfare policy (National Association of Social Workers, 2014). The following categories of organizations and agencies employ social workers in an international social work capacity (Cox & Pawar, 2012):

- *International intergovernmental organizations (IGOs).* The best-known IGO is the United Nations, with its 12 specialized agencies (e.g., UN Development Program, World Health Organization, UN High Commissioner for Refugees, and International Labour Office). Often, employees of these organizations come from the ranks of senior members of national governments. Positions in these organizations require extensive experience, linguistic abilities, and political contacts. Entry-level positions are available, but they are difficult to obtain and often require a 2-year application period.
- *International nongovernmental organizations (INGOs).* Like their IGO counterparts, NGOs are international in membership and scope; however, they tend to be relatively free of governmental restrictions and bureaucracy. NGOs are more likely than IGOs to focus on specialized issues or take specific political or philosophical stances. Examples of NGOs are Amnesty International, International Planned Parenthood Federation, International Red Cross, International Salvation Army, and the Women's International League for Peace and Freedom. NGOs are a good place for less experienced social workers to look for international positions. NGOs strongly prefer prior experience living abroad and having relevant language skills. Prospective applicants may want to consider serving in an international volunteer capacity to build their credibility and increase their chances of securing a paid position with this type of organization.
- *U.S. government agencies.* These agencies perform services to Americans visiting abroad, as well as to the local populace. Obtaining positions in these agencies requires careful planning, as well as the optimal combination of skills and experience. Persons assuming these positions also must be comfortable with being an official representative of U.S. government's foreign and domestic policies. Examples of agencies in this category of international social work employment include the U.S. Agency for International Development, U.S. Information Agency, Peace Corps, and U.S. State Department.
- *U.S.-based nongovernmental organizations (NGOs).* These organizations may offer some of the most fruitful opportunities for international careers in social work, either as volunteers or in

entry-level positions, with little or no prior experience. Examples of agencies in this category of international social work are the American Friends Service Committee, Direct Relief International, Save the Children, and World Vision.

- *Professional organizations and associations with major international commitments.* These organizations usually are located in the United States but have a substantial commitment to international problems and issues. Positions at all levels are available within these entities, and often individuals will begin their careers in these organizations and work their way up within them over time. Examples of organizations and associations in this category of international social work are the Council for the International Exchange of Scholars, the National Association of Social Workers, and the Society for International Development.

- *University-based programs.* Universities in many countries have active research and service connections with their surrounding communities, especially if they offer social work degrees. Social workers who are considering pursuing doctoral studies, and those who already hold doctoral degrees, may wish to consider applying for either short- or long-term faculty or research positions in universities and research centers in other countries.

- *Foundation programs.* Foundations engaged in international projects of a human services nature employ social workers as consultants, field representatives, and country directors for programs that the foundation supports. The best way to obtain an entry-level position in a major international grant-giving foundation is to work as part of a project-implementation team or as a member of the core professional staff. Examples of large foundations in this category of international social work employment are the Carnegie Foundation, the Ford Foundation, and the Rockefeller Foundation.

- *Religious groups and organizations.* Religious groups and organizations sponsor thousands of human service programs around the world. Most of these programs are located in the developing countries of Africa, Asia, and Latin America, and most are targeted toward the poor, women, and children. Rarely is the religious preference of the professional considering working for a religious organization's human service program considered in employment.

- *Social work in international corporate settings.* Social work positions within corporate contexts are numerous, especially for social workers with the sought-after mix of qualifications and interests. As a general rule, these positions involve providing support services to local personnel or to a company's national personnel assigned abroad. Most multinational corporations prefer to base their personnel in their home country for extended time periods before considering them for international assignments. Work experience, language skills, and good interpersonal skills are important qualifications for these jobs.

Finally, social workers are increasingly speaking out about violations of human rights and acting to ensure that rights of individuals throughout the world are protected (Cox & Pawar, 2012; Healy & Link, 2011; Mapp, 2014).

Summary

Global issues affect social work clients, individually and collectively, on a daily basis. The basic mission and role of social workers are being challenged as never before. Two primary questions face the social work community in the first decade of the 21st century: What role will the social work profession play in this new world? What should social work do to promote equitable societies? The social work profession is in a pivotal position to articulate and develop alternatives to the new social order.

Social workers around the world are actively engaged in a wide variety of community-development activities and national movements and organizations as people everywhere struggle to survive. Social workers come together internationally to develop a world community that supports the right of all individuals to grow and develop to their fullest potential. If social workers are committed to promoting equitable societies, we must promote inclusion and the empowerment of people. We must strengthen links among education, technology, and the environment, and promote progressive change in a global economy. We must strive to maintain individual cultures and cultural identity in the face of global pressures to become homogeneous. We must actively exchange information and experiences about innovative projects. We must be willing to share lessons learned so that successful ideas and programs can be applied across communities. Finally, we must build on the promise of information technology that made the global village a reality.

Competency Notes

EP 2.1.1a: Advocate for client access to the services of social work (pp. 507, 510). Social workers throughout the world advocate for client access to social services across all levels of the environment.

EP 2.1.1e: Engage in career-long learning (p. 500). Social workers across the globe engage in career-long learning to enhance their own growth and the growth of the profession.

EP 2.1.3a: Distinguish, appraise, and integrate multiple sources of knowledge, including research-based knowledge and practice wisdom (p. 519). Social workers use the ecological systems framework to distinguish, appraise, and integrate multiple sources of knowledge, including research-based knowledge and practice wisdom, as they work with clients across the globe, keeping in mind that knowledge must be applied within a cultural context.

EP 2.1.3b: Analyze models of assessment, prevention, intervention, and evaluation (p. 512). Social workers across the globe analyze models of assessment, prevention, intervention, and evaluation, applying models that are culturally appropriate to the population served.

EP 2.1.5b: Advocate for human rights and social and economic justice (pp. 501, 505, 507, 508, 510, 512). Social workers across the globe advocate for human rights and social and economic justice on behalf of their clients and citizens of the world.

EP 2.1.5c: Engage in practices that advance social and economic justice (pp. 501, 507). Social workers throughout the world engage in practices that advance social and economic justice across all levels of the environment.

EP 2.1.7b: Critique and apply knowledge to understand person and environment (pp. 510, 512, 515). Social workers across the globe use the ecological/systems framework to organize, critique, and apply knowledge to understand the diverse clients they serve and the ways that the environment shapes their development and functioning.

EP 2.1.8a: Analyze, formulate, and advocate for policies that advance social well-being (pp. 507, 512, 519). Social workers across the globe analyze, formulate, and advocate for policies that advance social and economic well-being.

EP 2.1.8b: Collaborate with colleagues and clients for effective policy action (pp. 505, 508, 517, 518). Social workers across the world collaborate with colleagues and clients for effective policy action.

EP 2.1.9a: Continuously discover, appraise, and attend to changing locales, populations, scientific and technological developments, and emerging societal trends to provide relevant services (pp. 500, 505, 508). Social workers across the globe continuously discover, appraise, and attend to changing locales, populations, scientific and technological developments, and emerging societal trends to provide relevant services.

EP 2.1.9b: Provide leadership in promoting sustainable changes in service delivery and practice to improve the quality of social services (pp. 500, 507, 510, 515, 519). Social workers provide leadership in promoting sustainable changes in service delivery and practice to improve the quality of social services throughout the world.

Key Terms

The terms below are defined in the Glossary.

global village
International Federation
    of Social Workers
    (IFSW)

international social
    welfare
refugee
world citizenship

Discussion Questions

1. Choose one of the problems or social issues discussed in an earlier chapter in the text. How might this problem/issue be addressed differently if you were a social worker in another country?

2. What are some ways an international social worker might intervene from a generalist practice standpoint: working with individuals, with families, with groups, with organizations, with communities, as an administrator, as a social policy expert, as a researcher?

3. If you were a social worker in a country operating under a values base different from your own, what

perspective would you take in working with clients from that country? Where, if anywhere, would you draw the line between respecting cultural differences and advocating for basic human rights?

4. Compare differences between refugees and immigrants. What policy approaches do you think the United States should take regarding each group and why?

5. Choose one of the following articles in the Universal Declaration of Human Rights: Article 7, Article 9, or Article 10. How do you think the United States measures up in meeting this declaration?

6. What do you see as the three major social welfare issues the world is facing during the first decade of the 21st century and why? What major issues do you think will have the greatest impact on the social work profession?

7. What should the role of the United States be as a global citizen? What can social workers to help the United States in fulfilling this role?

8. How do you think our increasingly global society impacts social work as a profession and your life? What should the role of social work be from a global perspective?

On the Internet

http://ncsl.org
http://vera.org
http://amnesty.org
http://www.unhcr.org
http://www.brookings.edu
http://www.rand.org
http://www.cswe.org
http://www.sharedhope.org
http://www.polarisproject.org

References

Abraham, M., Chow, E. N., Maratou-Alidranti, L., & Tastoglou, E. (Eds.). (2010). *Contours of citizenship: Gender in a global/local world*. London, England: Ashgate.

Altinay, H. (Ed.). (2011). *Responsibilities and rights in an independent world*. Washington, DC: Brookings Institution.

Amnesty International. (2013). *Amnesty International report 2013: The state of the world's human rights*. New York: Author. Retrieved July 1, 2014, from http://www.files.amnesty.org/air13/AmnestyInternational_AnnualReport2013_complete_en.pdf

Cabrera, L. (2010). *The practice of global citizenship*. New York: Cambridge University Press.

Congressional Budget Office. (2010). *Immigration policy in the United States*. Washington, DC: Author.

Council on Social Work Education (CSWE). (2008, revised 2010). *Educational policy and accreditation standards*. Washington, DC: Author.

Cox, D., & Pawar, M. (2012). *International social work: Issues, strategies, and programs*. Thousand Oaks, CA: Sage.

Djelic, M., & Quack, S. (2012). *Transnational communities: Shaping global economic governance*. New York: Cambridge University Press.

Feinstein, A. (2011). *The shadow world: Inside the global arms trade*. New York: Farrar, Strauss, and Giroux Publishers.

Fitzpatrick, T., Kwon, H., Manning, N., Midgley, J., & Pascall, G. (Eds.). (2010). *International encyclopedia of social policy*. London: Routledge.

Fritz, M., Wolgin, P., and Oakford, P. (2013). *Immigrants are makers, not takers*. Washington, DC: Center for American Progress.

Furman, J., and Gray, D. (2012). *Ten ways immigrants help build and strengthen our economy*. Washington, DC: The White House.

Global Issues. (2010). *Causes of poverty*. Retrieved December 14, 2010, from http://www.globalissues.org/2/causes_of_poverty

Goldin, I. (2013). *Divided nations: Why global governance is failing and what we can do about it*. New York: Oxford University Press.

Healy, L., & Link, R. (Eds.). (2011). *Handbook of international social work: Human rights, development, and the global profession*. New York: Oxford University Press.

Hessick, C., & Chin, C. (Eds.). (2014). *The role of states in immigration policy*. New York: New York University Press.

Holton, G., & Sonnert, G. (Eds.). (2010). *Helping young refugees and immigrants succeed: Public policy, aid, and education*. New York: Palgrave-Macmillan.

Human Rights Watch. (2010). *World report 2010*. New York: Author.

ICE. (2014). *ICE immigration removals*. Washington, DC: Author.

Ife, J. (2012). *Human rights and social work: Towards rights-based practice* (3rd ed.). New York: Cambridge University Press.

International Federation of Social Workers. (2012). *Global standards.* Berne, Switzerland: Author. Retrieved June 28, 2014, from http://www.ifsw.org/policies /global-standards/

International Federation of Social Workers. (2014a). *Aims of the IFSW.* Berne, Switzerland: Author. Retrieved July 14, 2014, from http://www.ifsw.org

International Federation of Social Workers. (2014b). *IFSW Membership.* Berne, Switzerland: Author. Retrieved July 14, 2014, from http://www.ifsw.org/

International Federation of Social Workers. (2014c). *IFSW Partnerships.* Berne, Switzerland: Author. Retrieved July 14, 2014, from http://www.ifsw.org/

Kugler, A., and Oakford, P. (2013). *Immigration helps American workers' wages and job opportunities.* Washington, D.C.: Center for American Progress.

Lyons, K., Hokenstad, T., Pawar, M., Huelger, N., & Hall, N. (Eds.). (2012). *The SAGE handbook of international social work.* Thousand Oaks, CA: Sage.

Mapp, S. (2014). *Human rights and social justice in a global perspective: An introduction to international social work* (2nd ed.). New York: Oxford University Press.

Milanovic, B. (2012). *The haves and have-nots: A brief and idiosyncratic history of global inequality.* New York: Basic Books.

Muller, G. (2013). *The new world reader: Thinking and writing about the global community* (4th ed.). Stanford, CT: Cengage Learning.

National Association of Social Workers (NASW). (2014). *Careers in social work: Part II.* Washington, DC: Author.

National Council of State Legislatures. (2014). *The border security economic opportunity and immigration modernization act.* Washington, DC: Author.

National Immigration Law Center. (2011). *DREAM Act: Summary.* Washington, DC: Author.

Negroponte, D. (2014). *The surge in accompanied children from Central America: A humanitarian crisis at our border.* Washington, DC: Brookings Institution.

Nikopopoulou, A., Abraham, T., & Mirbagheri, F. (Eds.). (2010). *Education for sustainable development: Challenges, strategies, and practices.* Thousand Oaks, CA: Sage.

Office of Immigration Statistics. (2013). *Estimates of the unauthorized immigrant population living in the U.S.: January 2012.* Washington, DC: Author.

Office of Immigration Statistics. (2014). *Estimates of legal permanent population residing in 2012.* Washington, DC: Author.

Office of Refugee Resettlement. (2014). *Report to Congress FY 2012.* Washington, DC: Author. Retrieved June 28, 2014 from http://www.acf.hhs.gov/sites /default/files/orr/fy_2012_orr_report_to_congress _final_041014.pdf

Payne, R. (2012). *Global issues.* Boston: Pearson.

Pew Research Center. (2013). *Most say illegal immigrants should be allowed to stay, but citizenship more divisive.* Washington, DC: Author.

RAND. (2008). *Invisible wounds of war: Psychological and cognitive injuries, their consequences, and services to assist recovery.* Santa Monica, CA: Author.

Seitz, J., & Hite, K. (2012). *Global issues: An Introduction.* Hoboken, NJ: Wiley-Blackwell.

Shared Hope International. (2014). *Why so young? Why the average age a child is first exploited through prostitution is 13.* Vancouver, Washington: Author. Retrieved June 28, 2014, from http://sharedhope .org//?s=trauma+bonding

UNICEF. (2009). *The state of the world's children 2009: Maternal and newborn health.* New York: Author.

UNICEF. (2014). *The state of the world's children in numbers 2014: Every child counts.* New York: Author.

United Nations. (1948). *Universal declaration of human rights (General assembly resolution 217A (III)).* New York: Author. Retrieved December 14, 2010, from http://www.um.org/overview/rights .html. Reprinted by permission.

United Nations. (1951). Convention relating to the status of refugees. *UN Treaty Series, 189,* #2545. Geneva, Switzerland: Author.

United Nations. (2000). *Millennium declaration* (p. 2). New York: Author.

United Nations. (2010a). *Children and armed conflict: Report to the Secretary General.* New York: Author.

United Nations. (2010b). *The midpoint: Achieving the millennium development goal.* New York: Author.

United Nations. (2013). *Millennium development goals report.* Geneva, Switzerland: Author.

United Nations High Command on Refugees (UNHCR). (2013). *UNHCR global trends 2012:* Geneva, Switzerland: Author.

Valtonen, K. (2012). *Social work and migration.* Burlington, VT: Ashgate.

Varsanyi, M. (Ed.). (2010). *Taking local control: Immigration policy activism in U.S. cities and states.* Redwood City, CA: Stanford University Press.

Vera Institute of Justice. (2012). *The flow of unaccompanied children through the immigration system:*

A resource for practitioners, policy makers, and researchers. Washington, DC: Author.

Zinn, H., & Arnove, A. (2011). *Voices of people's history of the United States* (2nd ed.). St. Paul, MN: Seven Stories Press.

Zohlberg, A. R. (2008). *A nation by design: Immigration policy in the fashioning of America.* Cambridge, MA: Harvard University Press.

Suggested Readings

American Immigration Council. (2014). *Basics of the U.S. immigration system.* Washington, DC: Author.

Audretsch,D. B. (2010). *Local heroess in the global village: Globalization and the new entrepreneurship policies.* New York: Springer.

Bywaters, P., McLeod, E., & Napier, L. (Eds.). (2009). *Social work and global health inequalities: Practice and policy developments.* Bristol, UK: Policy Press.

Call, W. (2011). *No word for welcome: The Mexican village faces the global economy.* Lincoln, NE: University of Nebraska Press.

Carens, J. (2013). *The ethics of immigration.* New York: Oxford University Press.

Diehl, P., & Frederking, B. (2010). *The politics of global governance: International organizations in an interdependent world.* Boulder, CO: Lynne Rienner Publishers.

Harrison, G., & Melville, R. (2010). *Rethinking social work in a global world.* New York: Palgrave-Macmillan.

Motomura, H. (2014). *Immigration outside the law.* New York: Oxford University Press.

Ramalingam, B. (2014). *Aid on the edge of chaos: Rethinking international cooperation in as complex world.* New York: Oxford University Press.

Sinclair, T. (2012). *Global governance.* Hoboken, NJ: Polity Press.

Stern, M., & Axinn, J. 2012. *Social welfare: A history of the American response to need* (8th ed.). Boston: Pearson.

Riddell, R. C. (2008). *Does foreign aid really work?* New York: Oxford.

APPENDIX

A Look to the Future

EP 2.1.1a
EP 2.1.3a
EP 2.1.8a
EP 2.1.9a

Social work has a historical commitment to helping people cope with change, and if the past 10 to 15 years are any indication, change—both positive and negative—will become a way of life in the 21st century. The ambiguity and strain that have existed in the United States since its founding regarding how to address the unmet needs in our society have intensified during recent years. Many Americans are dissatisfied with the way things are but do not relish the thought of change. At a time when the world is an uncertain place for all of us, many want to focus on their families and their own needs and are either too overwhelmed or fearful of taking risks to do more than reach out to those they know and trust (Loeb, 2014; Olds & Schwartz, 2010; Song, 2009).

As a nation, we tend to be generous and compassionate when it comes to helping one or two individuals in need but limiting and suspicious in helping large groups of individuals. How our country balances individual freedom versus collective responsibility is a theme that has been present since colonial times and continues into the 21st century. Recent economic and world events have jeopardized the trust and commitment of many people to assume collective responsibility, especially in the face of moral and political confusion about what and whom we should be responsible for collectively—others in our neighborhood, only in certain parts of the world, or groups that represent some values but not others. Who are we, and what do we stand for? What does the future hold, and how will it be shaped by the actions we take, as individuals, as a nation, as a world, as a profession?

Any attempt to forecast future trends must be tentative at best. History has shown us that change does not progress at an even rate, nor is its direction predictable. The events of September 11, 2001, were testament to that. Nevertheless, we can identify certain trends that suggest factors that will have an impact on the profession of social work and the social welfare system, at least in the near future. And regardless of the future, the profession of social work and its core values can play a major role and make a significant difference at all levels of society.

The Past as Prologue

EP 2.1.1e
EP 2.1.3a

To comprehend the difficulty of predicting the effects of social change on social work and social welfare, it is helpful to review the earlier chapters of this book. The history of the social work profession is related integrally to the unpredictable nature of the world in which we live. The social work profession is called on to respond as social change alters the economic base and values of society, as well as other basic social institutions, including the family, education, religion, and political and social organizations. The rapid growth of the social work profession in the latter part of the 19th century was related directly to the emergence of large urban communities and the problems associated with them. During those times, common problems included displaced persons, high rates of unemployment, large-scale migration from rural areas into the cities, slums, a rise in poverty, and increasing health-related problems.

To reduce or eliminate the sources of these problems and to provide support for the displaced people and their families, educated helpers had to become an integral part of the solution. The social work profession emerged in response to the need for a cadre of professionals with an understanding of human behavior, awareness of how social organizations function, and sensitivity to the effects of the environment on individual growth and development.

When the American Industrial Revolution erupted, the stability inherent in a primarily agrarian society began to disintegrate rapidly. Change intensified as new ways of manufacturing gave way to new ways of thinking, leading to what has been termed the Information Age. Moreover, the structure and function of the family, once stable and secure, have been affected by the stresses and tensions produced by the economic marketplace, which calls for greater mobility, division of labor outside the home, and consequent restructuring of family priorities. As a result, families have become less stable, the divorce rate has increased dramatically, multiple marriages are more common, and child abuse, spouse abuse, and various forms of neglect at all levels of society have emerged as more visible problems.

As the nature of work has become more unpredictable, the long-sought goal of financial security has become more difficult to achieve for many people. The poor have continued to be victimized by the lack of opportunity and increasingly blamed for their condition. With recent fiscal crises, hundreds of government workers at state and local levels, as well as employees of high-tech firms and other businesses, are losing their jobs to outsourcing or international competition, which limits the scarce resources and cannot help those who already were the poorest of the poor.

EP 2.1.1a
EP 2.1.5b

Increasingly, individuals' health and mental health needs have been neglected. The residual effects of the terrorist attacks of September 11, 2001, the wars in Iraq and Afghanistan, global strife in Syria and other areas, the continuing spread of HIV and AIDS-related deaths, and threats of new pandemics such as ebola throughout the world have had far-reaching effects on the health and mental health of society. On the domestic front, the U.S. population has grown older and more individuals have become detached from meaningful production, resulting in a lack of sufficient supports to provide for their needs. Violence, crime, delinquency, substance misuse, homelessness, and a variety of related problems have become sources of constant societal concern.

The Challenges of Today

EP 2.1.1e
EP 2.1.7b
EP 2.1.8a
EP 2.1.8b

The organization of social welfare services is far different today from that during colonial times. Gone are the almshouses, the poorhouses, and "indoor" relief. Since passage of the Social Security Act of 1935, the social welfare system in the United States has expanded to meet the proliferation and magnitude of new needs, and then contracted in response to welfare devolution and current welfare reform efforts; it now requires substantial societal resources to maintain.

Social workers have done their best to step up to this challenge, actively assisting a wide variety of individuals whose personal resources cannot provide an adequate level of social functioning and life satisfaction. Today, social workers are skilled in working with persons who are homeless, poor, addicts, single parents, and juvenile and criminal offenders. They also are actively involved with helping those beset by relationship conflicts with partners, child maltreatment, mental illness, and problems associated with later life, as well as many other personal and social problems.

In addition, the roles of social workers as promoters of social and economic justice and as advocates for disenfranchised populations—the poor; women; people of color; gays, lesbians, and transgender individuals; people with disabilities—have become increasingly important as society tends more and more to marginalize or reject these groups. As new problems have emerged, the capacity of the social work profession to incorporate the knowledge and skills essential to providing assistance has been forthcoming. Our profession's emphasis on empowerment, collaboration and problem solving, and open discussion about issues from multiple points of view challenges us to use these skills and model our values as we work in our many roles as social workers, and as individuals, family members, and citizens.

The positions that members of society take toward social problems and the resolution of those problems invariably relate to the availability of resources. Not all members of society, however, take an unequivocally progressive stance on this issue. For example, federal government indebtedness and reluctance to raise taxes have resulted in reductions in funding to address social problems. Monies for social welfare services have been cut significantly, and populations at risk have not received the assistance they need to become or remain productive citizens. This problem has been exacerbated, first after the terrorist attacks of September 11, 2001, when billions of dollars shifted to defense and security programs while many public and private social welfare agencies are either downsizing their operations or closing, and then with the economic downturn from 2007–2009.

The reduction of public monies for social welfare services has resulted in a cry for the private sector to "take up the slack." However noble they may be, private efforts have fallen far short of their intended goals because of the magnitude of the need and the drastic reduction of available resources. The line in the sand has been drawn: Unless we do something to overturn this chain of events—and soon—it may be too late to make much of a difference in the lives of millions of people in need of critical services.

In a materialistically oriented society like that of the United States, the definition of need paradoxically is related to the amount of resources that society is willing to allocate (Gilbert & Terrell, 2013). Thus, in times of monetary scarcity or when demands are made on individuals to share more of their earned incomes (through the taxing process), the tendency to redefine need levels is inevitable. In this manner, the true need becomes relative need and everyone seems to feel better. Today we stand at a crossroads. Do we continue to advance a global military policy of "preemptive democracy," or do we reorganize our priorities to ensure that the basic needs of all members of society are met?

EP 2.1.8a
EP 2.1.9a
EP 2.1.9b

A related challenge is to determine which of the many societal and individual problems properly fall within the domain of the social welfare system. We know that the social welfare system cannot be all things to all people—a panacea that addresses all needs not being met by other systems. There is a need to define and limit the boundaries that encompass the social welfare system so its services can be effective and sustained by available resources. Regardless of this argument, social workers constantly face value conflicts over if and when to address human needs when no one else is meeting them.

How does one deny benefits, for example, to a woman with four young children with no housing, no food, and a temporary part-time job, who makes $5 more each month than the income eligibility guidelines allow for receiving cash assistance under the Temporary Assistance to Needy Families (TANF) program? If the federal government or states refuse to provide for certain groups (e.g., teen parents, mothers whose public assistance time limits have run out but who are still not

self-sufficient), who should provide for them, and in what ways? Should children be removed from parents who cannot afford to care for them and placed in other settings? And, if this is the case, who should pay for that care? How does one determine whether limited funding should be allocated to the elderly, children, or individuals with disabilities? How does one decide who should have first priority for heart and other organ transplants, whether limited dollars should be spent on neonatal care for premature infants whose prognosis is poor, or at what point resources no longer should be provided to families with little potential to be rehabilitated?

If limited resources do not allow for a full range of preventive and remedial/rehabilitative services, which should be chosen? Should the goal be to try to prevent problems such as child maltreatment, knowing that in the short run this may limit the resources for those already abused but in the long run may prevent more abuse? We seem to be stuck with a classic "pay now or pay later" dilemma. That is, if we pay now to implement a wide range of preventive social welfare programs, the expectation is that we will not have to pay later to address the remedial or rehabilitative needs of those who did not benefit from such preventive programs. But one might ask: Is this simply a political issue, or does it reflect mainstream thinking about the value of prevention?

Metaphorically, there is an increasing trend in the United States to lease things rather than buy them outright. The terms of the leases are fixed, and when they expire, most people return the product to the leasing agent and renew the cycle. In doing so, the lessee is absolved of any preventive maintenance on the product being leased.

EP 2.1.9a

Rapidly changing technology, too, has affected the ways that members of society think about product longevity. The technological gadget you buy today has practically no shelf life at all, even though it was marketed as "state of the art" or "cutting edge." In actuality, that product became obsolete the day after it was invented. Thus, a person's political ideology, sense of social consciousness, and perspective on technology and change all have an impact on whether she or he supports social welfare programs with a preventive focus. The main difference for social workers is that we are talking about people or human capital, not some resource that can be readily renewed when it becomes used.

Also, as technology continues to generate new knowledge, the social work profession increasingly will have to grapple with emerging ethical issues. Issues including genetic engineering, cloning, assisted death, destruction of the environment, and technological measures to prolong life—all are matters of growing concern for social workers in the 21st century.

Leaders in the social work profession point to a number of critical issues that the profession faces in the decades ahead. First, the profession must value the diversity within the profession while not abandoning its roots. Two social work educators, Harry Specht and Michael Courtney, wrote a thought-provoking book shortly before Specht's untimely death. In *Unfaithful Angels: How Social Work Has Abandoned Its Mission* (1994), the authors chastise the profession for its attention to clinical issues at the micro-level of the environment. Even though this book was written more than a decade ago, the message continues to resonate with social workers worldwide (Adams & Dominelli, 2005; Jimenez, 2009; Mapp, 2010; Payne & Askeland, 2008).

Specht and Courtney (1994) argued that social work as a profession has to work at all levels of the environment in an overall commitment to promoting social and economic justice and eliminating oppression and discrimination. According to these authors, social work has abandoned this commitment by ignoring the poor, abused and neglected children, the homeless, and other vulnerable populations. Further, they wrote that the profession has not directed enough attention to empowering individuals, families, groups, and communities to improve their own lives. They advocated for the profession to pay more attention to community-based programs that educate individuals about how to solve problems so they are empowered to address their own needs. In this manner, the community's problem-solving capacity can be increased.

Others, too, while perhaps not as dire in their statements as Specht and Courtney, project that social work will lose ground as a profession if it abandons its previous perspective and its uniqueness. Morris and Hopps (2007) have raised similar questions and have suggested that because social workers will function in an even more diverse and complex environment in the coming years, more attention must be paid to interventions at community and societal levels.

Many leaders of the social work profession caution that social workers will have to play a more significant role in providing health and mental health services and in shaping the changes needed to make managed care more responsive to client needs. They point out that, just as the profession values diversity in its clients, it must value diversity within its own group. They further argue that while debating the future of the profession is healthy, the debate diverts attention from the necessity to view social needs along a continuum in which social workers play critical policy, research, and service roles at all levels. Social work educator June Hopps (as cited in Morris & Hopps, 2007) provides an excellent perspective on the profession of social work in the 21st century:

> It has had a long history of concerns (for example, child welfare, poverty, and family relations) but it has not developed sufficient theoretical and empirical foundations and skills to address social ills comprehensively in an effort to impact and ameliorate problems. The profession must be attuned to its context of time, place and public awareness if it is to be effective. Precisely because of this contextual immediacy, we cannot simply invoke history for solutions to contemporary problems. (p. 43)

The social work profession and the issues facing us are challenging—whether the work is with individuals, families, groups, or organizations, at the community, state, national, or international level. Social work practitioners must increase their advocacy on behalf of the clients they serve and their involvement at the legislative and policy levels, becoming more involved in the political arena, where key social welfare decisions are made. As society becomes ever more complex, the number of social workers will continue to grow, with broadened roles at all levels of practice.

Trends in Social Work Careers

EP 2.1.1e
EP 2.1.3a
EP 2.1.9b

As we indicated in earlier chapters, social workers today function in a variety of job settings and fields of practice and hold degrees at the undergraduate (BSW), master's (MSW), and doctoral (PhD or DSW) levels. As of 2014, the Council on Social Work Education (CSWE) accredited 500 BSW programs and 233 MSW programs (CSWE, 2014). The Group for the Advancement of Doctoral Education (GADE, 2014) listed over 80 doctoral programs for PhDs in social work or DSWs (Doctor of Social Work), including 8 in Canada and 1 in Israel. Since the late 1980s, enrollment in schools of social work at both the undergraduate and the graduate levels has

MEDIAN ANNUAL WAGES AND PROJECTED GROWTH FOR SOCIAL WORKERS BY SETTING/FIELD OF PRACTICE

SOCIAL WORK SETTING/FIELD OF PRACTICE	MEDIAN ANNUAL WAGE IN 2012	PROJECTED GROWTH BY 2022
Child, Family, and School Social Workers	**$41,530**	15%
Educational services—state, local, and private	$54,590	
State and local government, excluding education and hospitals	$44,370	
Health care and social assistance	$36,130	
Religious, grant making, civic, professional, and similar organizations	$35,910	
Health Care Social Workers	**$49,830**	27%
Hospitals—state, local, and private	$56,290	
Ambulatory health-care services	$51,580	
Nursing and residential care facilities	$43,330	
Social assistance	$38,920	
Mental Health and Addiction/Substance Misuse Social Workers	**$39,980**	23%
Hospitals—state, local, and private	$47,880	
Ambulatory health care services	$39,840	
Social assistance	$37,170	
Nursing and residential care facilities	$34,950	
All Other Social Workers	**$54,560**	19%

Source: Bureau of Labor Statistics. (2014). Social work. *Occupational outlook handbook, 2014–2015 edition*. Washington, DC: U.S. Department of Labor. Retrieved from http://www.bls.gov/ooh/community-and-social-service/social-workers.htm.

increased substantially as more young people commit themselves to joining the profession.

Social workers held approximately 607,300 jobs in 2012. Of these jobs, 47% involved work as a child, family, or school social worker; another 24% involved work as a medical or public health social worker; and 19% involved mental health or substance-misuse/addiction social work; the remaining 10% represented social workers in all other types of jobs (U.S. Bureau of Labor Statistics, 2014). About 90% of jobs held by social workers in 2012 were in health care and social assistance industries, as well as state and local government agencies, primarily in departments of health and human services (Bureau of Labor Statistics, 2014).

Median annual earnings in the industries employing the most social workers are shown in the table below, as is the projected growth in those areas through the year 2022. According to the U.S. Bureau of Labor

Statistics (2014), employment of social workers is expected to increase faster than the average for all occupations through 2022, an average of 19%. Gerontology social workers, in particular, will be in high demand to address the social service needs of the rapidly expanding elderly population in the United States. Social workers also will be needed to address the mental health concerns of the Baby Boom generation as they deal with concerns stemming from midlife, career, and other personal and professional difficulties. Social workers also will be needed to address issues related to crime and juvenile justice; and assist individuals with mental illness, persons with intellectual and other disabilities; persons with HIV/AIDS, diabetes, and other serious health conditions; and individuals and families in crisis.

The number of social workers in hospitals and long-term care facilities is expected to increase in response to the discharge needs of these individuals and to provide follow-up services for them in the community. The employment of social workers in the home health-care industry is also growing, as hospitals are releasing clients earlier than in the past, and, as mentioned, the elderly population is continuing to increase.

Employment of social workers in state and local government is expected to grow only marginally as many of the services provided by government agencies will be contracted to private agencies. More social workers will be employed in child protective services as more and more families crumble under the pressures of poverty, unemployment, and welfare reform. Steady employment in child protective services is almost guaranteed because of the high staff turnover experienced in that field.

Social workers also will be required to address the needs of more families for which one or more family members is incarcerated, as well as individuals who are being released from prison with the hope of reuniting with their families. Social workers, too, will be in demand to address the needs of those who misuse alcohol and other substances who are placed in community treatment programs rather than being sentenced to prison.

Employment of social workers in school settings also is expected to grow as school administrators recognize the connection between family life and academic performance. Social workers are well suited for programs that deal with truancy, school dropouts, juvenile delinquency, adolescent pregnancy, and involvement with gangs. The Education for All Handicapped Children Act provides for hiring social workers in school settings to work with children with disabilities. The actual growth of jobs for social workers in school settings will depend in large part on the availability of state and local funding.

Finally, opportunities for social workers in private practice are expected to expand, but this growth will be tempered by funding cutbacks and the restrictions that managed-care organizations place on services. Some demand for private practitioners will be created by the growing popularity of employee assistance programs in business and industry, services that are contracted out to individual providers or groups of providers in the community.

EP 2.1.5b
EP 2.1.5c
EP 2.1.7b

The commitment of the social work profession to social and economic justice provides opportunities for social workers at all levels of society to become more culturally competent and to empower diverse groups to advocate for their share of resources. This challenge means that social workers, individually and collectively,

must continue to educate themselves about the various cultural groups and to advocate for hiring more social workers who reflect the diversity of the populations that the profession serves.

The social work profession is becoming younger and less experienced as many long-term social workers enter retirement (Morris & Hopps, 2007). Currently, schools of social work and social work employers are attempting to recruit more diverse student bodies and workforces. Whatever the field of practice or the setting, social workers today and in the future face many challenges—as well as many opportunities for professional and personal growth.

Global issues affect social work clients, individually and collectively, on a daily basis. The basic mission and role of social workers are being challenged as never before. Two primary questions face the social work community in the first decade of the 21st century: What role will the social work profession play in this new world? What should social work do to promote equitable societies? The social work profession is in a pivotal position to articulate and develop alternatives to the new social order.

Social workers around the world are actively engaged in a wide variety of community-development activities and national movements and organizations as people everywhere struggle to survive. Social workers come together internationally to develop a global village or world community that supports the right of all individuals to grow and develop to their fullest potential. If social workers are committed to promoting equitable societies, we must promote inclusion and the empowerment of people. We must strengthen links among education, technology, the environment, and progressive change in a global economy. We must strive to maintain individual cultures and cultural identity in the face of global pressures to become homogeneous. We must actively exchange information and experiences about innovative projects. We must be willing to share lessons learned so that successful ideas and programs can be applied across communities. Finally, we must build on the promise of information technology that made the global village a reality that touches everyone and make the world a truly better place to live for everyone.

In this book we have addressed the current state of the art in social work and social welfare. Throughout each chapter, the effects of social problems on various segments of the population have been identified and the societal responses through the social welfare system described. We also have explored the many roles that social workers play in addressing social welfare problems. The significant and dramatic modifications in both the social welfare system and the social work profession since the early days of organized helping efforts are apparent. Armed with knowledge and understanding of human behavior and complex organizations, and bringing an ecological/systems perspective to bear, the contemporary professional social worker is uniquely capable of skillful intervention in the resolution of problems. The social worker of the future will have many challenging opportunities to make major contributions to society. We hope that you will consider joining us as members of the social work profession.

References

Adams, R., & Dominelli, L. (Eds.). (2005). *Social work futures: Crossing boundaries, transforming practice.* New York: Palgrave Macmillan.

Bureau of Labor Statistics. (2014). Social workers. *Occupational Outlook Handbook, 2014–15 Edition.* Washington, DC: U.S. Department of Labor. Retrieved from http://www.bls.gov/ooh/community-and-social-service/social-workers.htm

Council on Social Work Education (CSWE). (2014). *Directory of accredited social work degree programs.* Alexandria, VA: Author.

Gilbert, N., & Terrell, P. (2013). *Dimension of social welfare policy* (7th ed.). Boston: Allyn & Bacon.

Group for the Advancement of Doctoral Education (GADE). (2014). *Membership directory.* Retrieved from http://www.gadephd.org/mbrstate.asp

Jimenez, J. (2009). *Social policy and social change: Toward the creation of social and economic justice.* Thousand Oaks, CA: Sage.

Loeb, P. R. (2014). *Soul of a citizen: Living with conviction in challenging times* (3rd ed.). New York: St. Martin's Griffin.

Mapp, S. (2010). *Global child welfare and well-being.* New York: Oxford University Press.

Morris, R., & Hopps, J. G. (Eds.). (2007). *Social work at the millennium: Critical reflections on the future of the profession.* New York: Free Press.

Olds, J., & Schwartz, R. (2010). *The lonely American: Drifting apart in the twenty-first century.* Boston: Beacon Press.

Payne, M., & Askeland, G. (2008). *Globalization and social work.* Surrey, UK: Ashgate.

Song, F. (2009). *Virtual communities: Online together.* New York: Lang.

Specht, H., & Courtney, M. (1994). *Unfaithful angels: How social work has abandoned its mission.* New York: Free Press.

Glossary

AA *See* Alcoholics Anonymous.

Ableism Unfair advantage afforded to persons who are able-bodied, with a tendency to either blame or ignore those who are not able to keep up physically, cognitively, or emotionally with cultural expectations.

Acquired immunodeficiency syndrome (AIDS) Disease spectrum of the human immune system caused by infection with human immunodeficiency virus (HIV).

Activist An individual who believes strongly in social change and works to try to create it; important social work role.

Activity theory A theory relating to aging based on the premise that social activity is the essence of life for all ages and that all people must maintain adequate levels of activity if they are to age successfully.

Addams, Jane Social worker in the late 19th century who was instrumental in creating the settlement house movement as a resource for preparing immigrants to live in a new society.

ADA *See* Americans with Disabilities Act.

Addiction A physical or psychological dependence on mood-altering substances or activities, including but not limited to alcohol, other drugs, pills, food, sex, and gambling.

Adjudication The legal process used by judges in juvenile court to review information and make decisions, with assistance from probation officers, about juveniles who come before them.

Adoption A process by which a child whose birth parents choose not to or cannot care for him or her is provided with a permanent home and parents who are able to provide for the child; legal adoptions can take place only when the court terminates the parental rights of the birth parents, but many adoptions, particularly in nonwhite communities, are informal and do not involve the court.

Adult children of alcoholics Adults who as children lived in a family in which one or both parents was an alcoholic.

Adult protective services Protects the physical and emotional well-being of vulnerable adults who may be abused, neglected, or financially exploited.

Advocate Individual who intercedes or acts on behalf of another person or group; important social work role.

Adultism Discrimination or differential treatment based on a person's youth; a form of ageism.

Affirmative action program A legally mandated program established within education, business, and industry to improve opportunities for people of color and for women.

Affordable Care Act Term often used as short-hand for the Patient Protection and Affordable Care Act, a U.S. federal statute signed into law by President Barack Obama on March 23, 2010. The act represents the most significant regulatory overhaul of the U.S. health-care system since the passage of Medicare and Medicaid in 1965.

Ageism Discrimination or differential treatment based on age.

Aging The process of growing old.

Aging in place Practice that allows individuals to remain in their own residences, bringing needed services to them rather than moving them to another location as their health deteriorates.

Aid to Families with Dependent Children (AFDC) A public assistance program that provides cash assistance to families with children in need because of the loss of financial support as a result of death, disability, or the continued absence of a parent from the home (changed to Temporary Assistance to Needy Families [TANF] in 1996).

AIDS *See* Acquired immunodeficiency syndrome.

Alcohol Oldest and most commonly abused substance in the world, usually functions as a depressant but for some persons it can serve as a stimulant or hallucinogen.

Alcoholics Anonymous (AA) Self-help group for alcoholics based on abstinence and a 12-step philosophy of living; similar programs exist for family members of alcoholics and addicts and for persons with other types of addictions.

Alcoholism Use of alcohol that interferes with personal life, including family and friends, school, job, health, spiritual life, or the law.

Alzheimer's disease Degenerative disease of the central nervous system characterized by premature mental deterioration.

Americans with Disabilities Act (ADA) Federal legislation that provides protections for persons with disabilities, including employment and accessibility of accommodations.

Amnesty international International nongovernmental organization that promotes social justice and human rights throughout the world.

Analyst/evaluator Individual who determines the effectiveness of programs or agencies; important social work role.

Apathy futility syndrome Term used to describe a set of behaviors exhibited by a neglectful parent who is severely depressed and apathetic toward her or his immediate environment, including her or his children.

Appellate courts Courts with the authority to review the decisions of trial, lower, and criminal courts.

Assessment The process of making tentative judgments about how the information derived from a client system affects the system.

Assimilation The expectation that members of nondominant groups in society will adopt the values and behaviors of the dominant group.

Association A relationship between two or more factors that occur together but are not necessarily causative (such as alcoholism and child abuse).

Battered child syndrome A medical term used to describe a child with physical injuries in various stages of healing, indicating that the child has been physically abused on a number of occasions.

Behavior modification An action intervention, based on the assumption that all behaviors are learned and can be changed, that focuses on reinforcing present positive behaviors to eliminate inappropriate behaviors.

Best interests of the child A standard of decision making used by courts and child welfare agencies that emphasizes what is best for a specific child as opposed to what is best for other family members or persons.

Bioethics Moral and ethical decisions associated with advanced technology in the health-care field.

Blended family A family formed by marriage or long-term relationship between partners in which at least one partner brings children from a previous relationship into the new family system.

Boundary The limit or extent of a system; the point at which one system ends and another begins.

Brain-based economy An economy that is driven primarily by the intellectual capabilities of its workers.

Broker A social worker who assists clients in locating appropriate resources.

Case management Actions taken by social workers to manage the various aspects of cases they are working on.

Casework Services provided to individuals, families, groups, organizations, and the community to strengthen social functioning, based on assessing the client situation, identifying client needs, determining appropriate interventions to address identified needs, and monitoring and evaluating the process to ensure that outcomes address the needs identified.

Catastrophic illness A chronic and severely debilitating illness that results in high medical costs and long-term dependence on the health-care system.

Categorical assistance Cash assistance programs given to individuals and families under the provision of the Social Security Act, which established specific categories of persons in need of cash assistance including the aged, blind and permanently disabled (Supplemental Security Income), and children (Aid to Families with Dependent Children, now Temporary Assistance to Needy Families).

Cause-and-effect relationship A relationship between factors in which one or more factors can be shown to directly cause a change in an additional factor or set of factors.

Charity Organization Society (COS) The first relief organization in the United States that developed a systematic program to help the needy; promoted "scientific philanthropy," which incorporated individual assessment and development of coordinated service plans before providing services.

Child abuse legislation The enactment by a federal or state legislative body of laws that affect the physical and emotional well-being of children.

Child Abuse Prevention and Treatment Act Federal legislation first enacted in 1974 and re-authorized by Congress several times since then aimed at increasing identification, reporting, investigation, prevention, and treatment of child abuse and neglect.

Children's Health Insurance Program Federal program that expands health insurance coverage for low-income children financed jointly by federal and state governments and administered by states.

Child neglect A condition in which a caretaker responsible for a child either deliberately or by extraordinary inattentiveness fails to meet a child's basic needs, including failing to provide adequate food, clothing, shelter, medical assistance, or education and/or to supervise a child appropriately.

Child protective services (CPS) Mandated services provided by state social services agencies to families who abuse or neglect their children, for the purpose of protecting children whose safety is seriously endangered by the actions or inactions of their caretaker.

Child Welfare League of America A national organization consisting of agencies, professionals, and citizens interested in the well-being of children and families; CWLA promotes standards for services, advocates for child welfare policies and programs, conducts research, and provides publications related to child welfare issues.

Child welfare service delivery system A network of agencies and programs that provides social services to children, youth, and families.

Child welfare services Social services that supplement or substitute for parental care and supervision when parents are unable to fulfill parental responsibilities and that improve conditions for children and their families.

Children with special needs Children of color, who are older, who have physical or emotional disabilities, or who are members of sibling groups; term used in reference to adoption.

Chronosystem Dimension of the ecological/systems framework that focuses on changes, or ecological transitions that take place over time.

Civil Rights Act Landmark federal legislation passed in 1964 that prohibits discrimination based on race, gender, religion, color, or ethnicity in public facilities, government programs or those operated or funded by the federal government, and employment.

Civil rights movement Far-reaching struggle that sought the full and equal participation of people of color, women, and other marginalized groups in the social and economic arenas of our society.

Class The stratification of individuals and groups according to their social and economic assets.

Classism Discrimination toward members of a group because of their economic status.

Client system Individuals, families, groups, organizations, or communities at whom intervention is directed to enhance social functioning.

Client-centered therapy Intervention based on the perspective that clients know the most about their problems and needs; the therapist seeks to provide an acceptable emotional climate in which the client can work out solutions with support and reflection from the therapist.

Clinical social workers Persons whose major focus is to provide clinical social work services, usually individual, group, or family counseling; often in a psychiatric, hospital, residential treatment, or mental health facility; usually requires a master's of social work (MSW) degree (also called *psychiatric social worker* in some settings).

Closed system A system with a boundary that is difficult to permeate; such systems are usually unreceptive to outsiders.

Coalition building Process of creating a multi-organizational power base large enough to influence program direction or draw down resources.

Codependent An individual who places lower priority on her or his own needs, while being excessively preoccupied with the needs of others.

Collectivist perspective Holds that social problems reflect fundamental socioeconomic circumstances, barriers to access, and lack of opportunity.

Communities of diversity Communities usually made up of members of marginalized groups who often struggle to navigate within a depressive, discriminatory environment.

Communities of identification and interests Communities that are formed around shared concerns and deeply held beliefs and values that sometimes bring them into conflict with other communities.

Community A group of individuals who usually live near each other; share a common environment, including public and private resources, and identify themselves with that community.

Community corrections Practice of supervising convicted criminals in a community setting rather than in jails or prisons.

Community development A social work approach to working with communities that considers and respects the diversity of a community's population and uses those differences to achieve positive outcomes for all of its citizens.

Community mental health programs Mental health services provided in the community, usually through a community mental health center.

Community organization A method of social work practice that involves the development of community resources to meet human needs.

Community policing A philosophy of personalized policing in which assigned officers patrol and provide outreach in a geographic area on a permanent basis, working in a proactive partnership with area residents to identify and solve problems.

Community practice Activities engaged in by social workers designed to improve conditions in the community.

Community social and economic development Community intervention designed to assist in the development of community programs and to prepare citizens to make use of social and economic investments (e.g., Earned Income Tax Credit, low-interest housing loans, and weatherization programs).

Commuter families Families with spouses employed in different locations, often in different parts of the country.

Comparable worth The concept that persons should receive measurably equal pay for the same type of work, regardless of their gender.

Comparative social research Approach that enables one nation to build on the policy design initiatives of others, thereby avoiding the need to start afresh.

Comparative social work The comparison of what social workers do in nations other than one's own.

Compassionate conservatism Term used by President George W. Bush to promote the philosophy that people and communities should help themselves and one another rather than relying government to meet their needs, arguing that this approach could be conservative and insist on responsibility and results.

Competencies Skills that are essential to perform certain functions; social workers must have competencies in a number of areas to be effective professionals.

Consumer Price Index (CPI) A measure of the average change in prices over time for a fixed "market basket" of goods and services purchased by a specified group of consumers.

Contingent employment Work arrangements that include temporary and part-time employees, consultants, leased employees, subcontractors, and short-term, life-of-the-project employees.

Continuity theory Theory of aging that emphasizes how a person adjusts to old age is largely a product or extension of adaptive patterns developed in earlier years.

Contracting A process of formulating a verbal or written agreement with a client system of established goals based on identified needs, usually including the steps that will be taken to meet those goals, the entities involved, and target dates for completion.

COS *See* Charity Organization Society.

Council on Social Work Education (CSWE) The national organization of schools of social work that focuses on social work education and serves as the accrediting body for professional social work undergraduate (BSW) and master's (MSW) programs.

County agent An employee of a county extension office funded by the U.S. Department of Agriculture; provides technical assistance to persons living primarily in rural areas, including agricultural and home management, as well as community and family services.

Courts Legal institutions in which lawyers play the leading roles and make most of the decisions.

CPS *See* Child Protective Services.

Crime An act that is considered to be a threat to individual or community well-being; a violation of a law.

Crime prevention Any effort designed to reduce the incidence of criminal behavior.

Criminal codes Define the types of conduct that are criminal and establish a range of penalties for such behaviors.

Criminal justice system The means used to enforce those standards of conduct required to protect individuals and property and to maintain a sense of justice in the community.

Crisis intervention Intervention provided when a crisis exists to the extent that one's usual coping resources threaten individual or family functioning.

Cross-functional work teams Work teams comprised of members from multiple functions within the organization.

Cultural competence Cultural sensitivity emphasizing the need to work with clients and client systems within the context of their culture and to recognize the interplay between one's own cultural perspectives and those of the client.

Cultural diversity The coexistence of various groups whose cultural differences are respected as equally valid. Group membership can be based on ethnicity, race, gender, class, religion, ability or disability, or sexual orientation.

Cultural divide The "distance" between different cultural belief systems.

Cultural pluralism The existence of two or more diverse cultures within a given society in which each maintains its own traditions and special interests within the confines of the total society.

Culture shock Feelings that may occur when moving to an unfamiliar cultural environment; often results in temporary or long-lasting effects such as anxiety or depression.

Custody A legal charge given to a person requiring her or him to provide certain types of care and to exercise certain control in regards to another individual, as in parental child custody.

CWLA *See* Child Welfare League of America.

Cyber-stalking Stalking that takes place using the Internet.

Deficit Reduction Act of 2005 Signed into law by President George Bush in 2006, legislation designed to restrain federal spending and leave more money in the hands of the American people (also reauthorized the Personal Responsibility and Work Opportunity Budget Reconciliation Act of 1996 for an additional 5 years).

Deinstitutionalization A philosophy that advocates for care of individuals with mental health problems and developmental disabilities in local community outpatient programs whenever appropriate to the client's needs, as opposed to institutionalization.

Delinquency Behavior of juveniles that would be criminal in adults.

Depressant An agent that reduces a bodily functional activity such as staying awake or an instinctive desire such as eating.

Depression Overwhelming feeling of incapacitation that, in the extreme, may result in a person not being able to function.

Deterrence factors Things that are likely to stop people from committing crimes.

Developmental delay Delay in communication, self-help, social-emotional skills, motor skills, sensory development, or cognition in comparison to skills typically observed in other individuals within the same age range.

Developmental disability A severe, chronic disability resulting from physical or mental impairment, usually prior to age 21, which results in substantial limitations of the individual's social, emotional, intellectual, and/or physical functioning.

Developmental niche Concept borrowed from biology that incorporates the idea that everyone has a unique cultural world that differs from all others, even other family members living in the same household.

Developmental theory A theory of human development that emphasizes psychological adjustment to the demands from the environment; these demands change as the individual moves through the life cycle.

Devolution The transfer of responsibility for social welfare programs from the federal government to state and local governments.

Diagnostic and Statistical Manual of Mental Disorders (DSM) A classification system of types of mental disorders that incorporates both organic and environmental factors, developed by the American Psychiatric Association for assessment and intervention purposes (now in its fifth edition, it is referred to as the *DSM-5*).

Digital divide The economic and social inequality of persons in their access to, use of, or knowledge of information and communication technologies.

Direct practice A method of social work involving face-to-face contact with individuals, families, groups, and organizations and actual provision of services by the social worker for the purpose of addressing unmet needs; also referred to as *casework* or *social casework*.

Disability insurance A government fund established by the U.S. government in 1957 that provides cash benefits to workers who become totally and permanently disabled; note that some employers also now offer private disability insurance.

Disciplinary research Studies designed to expand the body of knowledge of a particular discipline; also called *pure* or *basic research*.

Discrimination Action that maintains and supports prejudice.

Disengagement theory A theory related to aging based on the premise that as adults decline physically, they have less need and desire for social interaction and progressively become disengaged from social roles.

Displaced workers Persons 20 years of age or older who have lost or left jobs because their place of employment closed, there wasn't sufficient work for them to do, or their position or shift was eliminated.

Disposition The legal process by which judges decide how best to resolve delinquency cases.

Disproportionality Overrepresentation of a particular group of people in a particular category (e.g., people of color and diabetes).

Diversion A process by which persons coming to the attention of the criminal justice system are diverted to other programs such as social services, community services, or educational (defensive driving) programs, rather than going through the court process.

Dorothea Dix A philanthropist and social reformer who observed the care given the "insane" in the United States and sought to convince President Franklin Pierce to allocate federal and land grant monies for establishing federal institutions to care for the mentally ill. Dix's work was successful in raising public awareness about the problems of the mentally ill and set the tone for an era of significant reform during the mid- to late-1800s.

Downshifting The voluntary limiting of job demands so employees can devote increased time to their families and to themselves.

Downsizing Reduction in workforce and/or scope of goods and services produced or delivered to remain economically competitive and/or manage decreasing resources.

Drug courts   Specialized court docket programs that target criminal defendants and offenders, juvenile defenders, and parents with pending child welfare cases who have alcohol and other drug dependency problems.

DSM   *See* Diagnostic and Statistical Manual of Mental Disorders.

Dual-career family   A family in which both partners/ spouses have careers outside the family.

Dual diagnosis   A determination that an individual has other diagnosable emotional problems in addition to substance use disorder.

Dual system of justice   Separate systems of justice for juveniles and adults.

Dysfunctional   Impaired or abnormal functioning.

Earned Income Tax Credit (EITC)   A provision of the federal income tax system to give a cash supplement to working parents with low incomes; parents file a tax statement, and if their taxable earnings are below a specific amount, they receive a check for a percentage of their earnings regardless of whether they paid that amount or less in taxes.

Ecological/systems framework   A major framework used to understand individual, family, community, organizational, and societal events and behaviors that emphasizes the interactions and interdependence between individuals and their environments.

Economic justice   Fair allocation of resources.

Educational group   A group formed for the purpose of transmitting knowledge and enabling participants to acquire more complex skills, such as parenting.

Educator   Person who provides information and/or teaching skills to facilitate change.

Egalitarianism   A belief in human equality, especially with respect to social, political, and economic rights and privileges.

Ego psychology   A theoretical perspective that emphasizes ego growth and development.

EITC   *See* Earned Income Tax Credit.

Elder abuse   Term referring to any intentional or negligent act by a caregiver or any other person that causes harm or poses a serious risk of harm to a vulnerable older adult.

Elizabethan Poor Law   Legislation passed in England in 1601 that established categories of the poor, including the deserving poor (orphans, widows, and others) and the non-deserving poor (able-bodied males), and the treatment they were to receive from national and local governments; this law established precedents for policies toward the poor in the United States.

Emotional maltreatment   *See* Psychological maltreatment.

Employee assistance program (EAP)   A work-place sponsored program providing mental health and social services to employees and their families; services may be provided directly at the workplace or through a contractual arrangement by a social service agency.

Empowerment   A process to help others increase their personal, interpersonal, or political power so they can take action themselves to improve their lives.

Enabler   A person whose behavior facilitates another person's behavior to continue; used most often to describe situations in families in which substance abuse is a problem and other family members enable the substance use to continue by their reinforcing behaviors.

Encounter group   A group oriented toward assisting individuals in developing more self-awareness and interpersonal skills through in-depth experiential activities and extensive group sharing.

Entitlement   A social welfare program to which any individual is entitled if certain eligibility requirements are met; such programs are based on numbers of individuals in need of the services rather than other limitations, such as resources available or caps put on funding by government bodies.

Entropy   Unavailable energy in a closed system that creates dysfunction within that system and eventually results in the system's inability to function.

Equal Rights Amendment (ERA)   A proposed amendment to the U.S. Constitution to assure the complete and equal rights of all citizens without regard to race, color, creed, or gender; the amendment was not ratified by the number of states necessary for its adoption.

Equifinality   The idea that the final state of a system can be achieved in many different ways.

Ethics   A framework for determining what is right and wrong and how specific situations should be handled; the National Association of Social Workers Code of Ethics relates to the moral principles of social work practice.

Etiology of crime   Theories relating to the origins or causes of crime, including physiological, psychological, and sociological perspectives.

Evaluation   A method of showing how a client system or a program has achieved or failed to achieve established goals.

Evaluative research   Research undertaken to show how a program achieves (or fails to achieve) its goals.

Evidence-based practice   A process in which practitioners make practice decisions in light of the best research evidence available (also referred to as evidence-informed practice).

Exchange theory   Theory based on the premise that relationships are exchanges of goods and services, with those in power having the goods and services; in relation to aging, this theory attributes the social withdrawal of the elderly to a loss of power as they lose their income and move to pensions and Medicare.

Exosystem level   The level of social environment that incorporates community factors in which an individual does not participate directly but that affects the individual's functioning, such as actions by school boards and city councils.

Facilitator   Person who brings participants together to promote change through improved communication.

Family   A group of individuals bonded together through marriage, kinship, adoption, or mutual agreement.

Family and Medical Leave Act (FMLA)   Requires employers with more than 50 employees to provide up to 12 weeks of unpaid leave to eligible employees for certain medical or family reasons such as the birth of a child or the serious illness of a child, spouse, or parent.

Family caregiving   Emotional, physical, and/or financial support provided by family members to a family member in need, such as a child with severe disabilities or an elderly parent.

Family preservation programs   Family intervention programs whose goal is to keep families together by increasing the coping skills and competencies of family members.

Family roles   Roles taken on by family members as a way to cope with the behaviors of other family members and maintain the family system's patterns of functioning.

Family Support Act   Mandated that states provide job opportunities and basic skills (JOBS) programs for most recipients of Aid to Families with Dependent Children (AFDC). The act also provided up to 12 months of Medicaid (health care) and child care after recipients found jobs to ease the transition from welfare to work without loss of income; mandated that states provide AFDC benefits for a limited time to families with previously employed men who were unable to find employment; and required stronger enforcement of child support payments by absent parents.

Family violence   The use of force by one family member against another, usually by a family member who is more powerful against a member who is less powerful.

Federal Poverty Income Limit (FPIL)   The amount of money required for individuals and families to satisfy their minimal living needs, published by the federal government each year.

Feminism   Theory based on the economic, political and social equality of all people, regardless of their gender.

Feminist therapy   Intervention that empowers individuals who may be members of an oppressed group to find their own voice and view themselves as equals as they make decisions about their lives.

Feminization of poverty   A term used to describe the result of the increasing numbers of single-parent women being classified as poor.

Flexiplace   A system that allows employees to work at alternative work sites as opposed to a standard workplace (e.g., working in their own homes).

Flextime   A system that allows employees to have varied work hours as opposed to standard work hours (e.g., working from 6 a.m. to 3 p.m. rather than from 8 a.m. to 5 p.m.).

Food stamps   *See* Supplemental Nutrition Assistance Program (SNAP).

Foster care   A form of temporary substitute care in which children live with a family other than their birth family until they are able to be returned to their birth family, adopted, or placed in a more permanent setting that best meets their needs.

FPIL   *See* Federal Poverty Income Limit.

Full enforcement   The principle that law enforcement officers enforce all criminal statutes with equal emphasis.

Gender equity/equality   Social, political, and economic equality between men and women.

Gender gap   A reference to gender inequality in society.

General assistance   Public assistance programs that provide financial aid to persons who are in need but do not qualify for federally authorized programs; usually administered by county and local government; also referred to as *relief programs.*

General manager   Person who assumes administrative responsibility for an agency at some level.

Generalist   A social worker who operates from a systems/ecological perspective, using multiple interventions in working with client systems at the individual, family, group, organizational, community, or societal level and using the strengths of those systems to empower them to change their environment.

Generalist practice   Orderly sequence of progressive stages in engaging a client (or client system such as a family, organization, or community) in activities and actions that promote agreed-on goals.

Generalizable   The ability of a theory to use what happens in one situation to explain what happens in other situations.

Gentrification   Restoration and upgrading of deteriorated urban property by middle class or affluent people, which often results in displacement of low-income people.

Geographic or territorial communities   Places that have clearly-defined geopolitical boundaries.

Gerontology   The study of aging and the aging process.

Global village   A place where social and economic justice, lasting peace, and a sustainable environment are achieved.

Goal setting   A process used by social workers and other helping professionals with client systems to identify ways to meet their needs; usually includes the identification of specific goals, steps to be taken in meeting those goals, resources needed, and a time frame for completion.

Great Depression   The stock market crash of 1929 resulted in a drastic economic downturn that led to the Great Depression. Businesses closed, banks declared bankruptcy, and millions of individuals lost jobs and savings, creating economic disaster and chaos.

Great Society   A social reform program proposed by the Johnson administration in the 1960s to improve the quality of life for all Americans, with emphasis on the poor and disenfranchised; the War on Poverty was one of the major Great Society programs.

Gross Domestic Product (GDP)   The total monetary value of a nation's annual output of goods and services.

Group   A social unit consisting of individuals who define status and role relationships to one another; it possesses its own set of values and norms and regulates the behavior of its members.

Group work   A process that seeks to stimulate and support more adaptive personal functioning and social skills of individuals through structured group interaction.

Hallucinogen   A substance that induces hallucinations.

Hate crimes   Crimes (such as assault or defacement of property) motivated by hostility against individuals because they are members of a social group, such as one based on race, ethnicity, religion, gender, or sexual orientation.

Hague Convention on the Protection of Children and Cooperation in Respect to Intercountry Adoption   International effort to set minimum standards and procedures for adoptions between countries that are parties to the convention.

Head Start   A comprehensive early childhood education program, initially established as a Great Society program, which provides developmental learning for preschool children; it has health care, social services, and parent education components.

Health   A state of complete physical, mental, and social well-being that is not merely the absence of disease or infirmity.

Health and welfare services   Programs providing services that facilitate individual health and welfare, such as maternal health and child care, public health, family planning, and child welfare services.

Health care Services provided to individuals to prevent or to promote recovery from illness or disease.

Health-care system reforms Measures taken to address problems associated with the health-care delivery system, usually legislative in nature.

Health insurance exchange A single market for all kinds of health insurance plans (e.g., traditional insurance plans, health maintenance organizations, and health savings accounts) and other new coverage options that might emerge in response to consumer demand.

Health maintenance organization (HMO) Prepaid medical group practice for which individuals pay monthly fees and receive specific types of health at no cost or a minimum cost per visit.

Health risk factors Factors that affect a person's health and place her or him at risk for serious health problems (e.g., smoking).

Health savings accounts (HSAs) A type of savings account not subject to federal income tax available to U.S. taxpayers enrolled in high-deductible health plans. Funds can be used for many out-of-pocket medical expenses such as doctors' office visits, prescriptions, and vision and dental care.

Heterosexism Bias that favors individuals who are heterosexual, such as school personnel who assume that all students and their parents are heterosexual, parents who assume that their children will marry a person of the opposite sex, and workplace policies that provide benefits only to those partners in a legal marriage.

HIV-positive The first stage of acquired immunodeficiency syndrome (AIDS), also called the *seropositive state,* which occurs when a person has tested positive for AIDS and has HIV (human immunodeficiency virus) antibodies in his or her blood.

Holistic health care Views all aspects of an individual's health in relation to how that individual interacts with family members, the workplace, and the community.

Home health care Health care provided in a person's home as opposed to a hospital or other institutional health-care setting; made available through outreach visits by social workers, nurses, physicians, and other health practitioners.

Home-based family-centered services Services delivered to children and families in their own homes, with a focus on preserving the family system and strengthening the family to bring about needed change in an effort to prevent family breakup.

Homeless Having no fixed, adequate, and regular nighttime residence.

Homophobia A fear of homosexuals and homosexuality.

Hospices Programs for terminally ill individuals and their families that enable them to die with dignity and support, often away from a hospital.

Hull House Patterned after Toynbee Hall in London, Jane Addams established Hull House in 1869 in one of the worst slum neighborhoods of Chicago. By addressing the problems of poor housing, low wages, child labor, juvenile delinquency, and disease, Hull House and other settlement houses became major social action agencies.

Humanitarianism Promotion of human welfare and social reform.

Hypothesis A tentative assumption, derived from theory, that is capable of empirical verification.

IDEA *See* Individuals with Disabilities Education Act.

IFSW *See* International Federation of Social Workers.

Implementation strategy A plan for carrying out steps required to put a program or plan into practice.

Impulse-ridden behavior Behavior exhibited by neglectful parents with low impulse control, including acting inconsistently, leaving a child alone or in an unsafe situation without realizing the consequences to the child, or giving higher priority to a new activity.

Incarceration The placing of someone in prison.

Incest Sexual abuse between family members.

Inclusive The ability of a theory to consistently explain events in the same way each time they occur.

Individualist perspective Belief that individual problems are the result of bad choices, personal dysfunction, or a culture of poverty.

Individuals with Disabilities Education Act (IDEA) Federal legislation that mandates that school systems provide educational and social services for children with a range of disabilities, including emotional disturbance, mental retardation, and speech, vision, hearing, and learning disabilities.

Indoor relief Assistance given to the poor and the needy through placement in institutions, such as poorhouses, orphanages, and prisons.

Infant mortality rate The number of infants who die at birth or before they reach a certain age compared to the total number of infants, both living and not living, within that age range, within a specified geographic location and a specified time frame.

Inhalants Class of toxic chemicals whose vapors are inhaled as a form of "getting high" (e.g., gasoline, Freon, aerosol products, paint, and glue).

In-home family-centered services Services delivered to children and families in their own homes with a goal of preserving the family system by strengthening the family to bring about needed change.

Initiator/coordinator Person that brings people together to help them organize for change.

Institutional discrimination Discrimination that occurs as the result of accepted beliefs and behaviors and is codified in societal roles and policies.

Intake The process that follows police referrals to juvenile court.

Intellectual disability A disability that originates before age 18 and is characterized by significant limitations in intellectual functioning and often results in an inability to perform many routine social and self-care skills. Previously referred to as "mental retardation."

International nongovernmental organizations (NGOs) Organizations that are international in membership and scope that focus on specialized issues or take specific political or philosophical stances. Examples of international NGOs are Amnesty International, International Planned Parenthood Federation, International Red Cross, International Salvation Army, and the Women's International League for Peace and Freedom.

Intermediate punishments A middle ground between either/or choices of probation or parole.

International Federation of Social Workers (IFSW)   An organization founded in 1956 to promote social work as a profession through cooperation and action on an international basis and to work toward social and economic justice throughout the world.

International social welfare   The field of practice concerned with promoting basic human well-being in a context involving cross-national efforts.

International social work   The practice of social work to meet social welfare needs from an international perspective.

Intervention   Planned activities designed to improve the social functioning of a client or client system.

Intrapsychic aspects   Being or occurring within the mind, psyche, or personality.

Intimate partner violence (IPV)   The inflicting of physical, sexual, or psychological harm by a current or former partner or spouse. These acts of violence can range from threatening to harm someone to chronic, severe beatings that can result in death and can occur among heterosexual and same sex couples.

Invisible wounds of war   Term coined during the U.S. War with Iraq (Operation Iraqi Freedom or OIF) and global war on terrorism (Operation Enduring Freedom or OEF) to describe combat-related injuries such as traumatic brain injury (TBI), post-traumatic stress disorder (PTSD), and severe depression.

Job sharing   The sharing of one full-time job by two or more individuals; this practice is increasingly being allowed by employers and is advantageous to women with young children and persons with disabilities who do not want to work outside the home on a full-time basis.

Joint custody   Divorce arrangement in which parents share child custody equally.

Juvenile correctional institutions   Secure and non-secure facilities used to detain juveniles who have committed status or other offenses.

Juvenile courts   Courts structured to act in a child's best interest.

Juvenile delinquency   Refers to youth who have committed a crime, a status offense (e.g., truancy, underage drinking, curfew violation, or running away), or both.

Kinship care   The full-time parenting of children by kin.

Laissez-faire   An economic theory developed by Adam Smith that emphasizes persons taking care of themselves with limited government intervention.

Least detrimental alternative   A decision-making premise that places priority on making decisions regarding children based on which decision will be least damaging or upsetting to the child.

Least developed country (LDC)   The name given to a country that, according to the United Nations, exhibits the lowest indicators of socioeconomic development, with the lowest Human Development Index ratings of all countries in the world.

Least restrictive environment   A living environment for an individual that maintains the greatest degree of freedom, self-determination, autonomy, dignity, and integrity for the individual, often while he or she participates in treatment or receives services.

Life span model   A framework that focuses on relationships between individuals and their environments, with major emphasis on where persons are developmentally and what transitional life processes they are experiencing (for example, teenagers exploring their identities as they move into adulthood).

Living wage   Three times the amount of money needed in a given location to rent an apartment of a given size; rental costs (fair market rents) are established by the U.S. Department of Housing and Urban Development (HUD).

Living will   A formal written statement made by an individual specifying the individual's wishes about her or his death should be handled, including delineation of which medical procedures and life support systems, if any, should be used and under what conditions.

Long-term care facilities   Institutions that provide long-term care to individuals, including the elderly and people with disabilities; state and federal regulations have established specific requirements that facilities must meet to be classified as long-term care facilities.

Lower criminal courts   Courts with the power to decide minor cases and to conduct pretrial proceedings.

Macrosystem level   The level of social environment that incorporates societal factors affecting an individual, including cultural ideologies, assumptions, and social policies that define and organize a given society.

Managed care   Health-care delivery that limits the use and costs of services and measures performance.

Managed care system   A system of health-care delivery that limits the use and costs of services and measures performance.

Market basket concept   A way of measuring the number of people in poverty based on a formula that includes the estimated costs a family spends to provide a minimum nutritional diet, with adjustments for family size, and a set proportion of income families generally spend for food; families spending less than this proportion of their income are considered below the poverty line.

Mediation   Intervention to reconcile differences and reach compromises; often takes place between a divorcing or divorced couple to promote settlement of child custody and property issues; mediation teams usually include an attorney and a social worker.

Mediator   Person who helps factions experiencing conflict work out their differences.

Medicaid   Public assistance program funded by the federal and state governments that provides health care to low-income individuals and families based on a means test using strict eligibility guidelines.

Medical model   A model that considers those with physical or emotional problems as sick; focuses on deficits and dysfunction of client and family rather than their strengths, with little attention given to environmental aspects; and promotes a hierarchy between the "expert" providing the diagnosis and treatment and the patient receiving it.

Medical social work   The practice of social work in medical settings.

Medical social workers   Social workers who are employed in some type of a medical setting.

Medicare   Federal health insurance program for the elderly.

Membership Assistance Programs (MAP)   Employee support services for union members under the auspices of labor unions.

Mental health   A state of emotional and psychological well-being resulting in productive activities, fulfilling relationships with other people, and the ability to adapt to change and to cope with adversity.

Mental health courts   Courts comprised of specific dockets dedicated to individuals with mental illness. The purpose of mental health courts is to divert persons with mental illness away from jail or prison in lieu of community-based treatment services.

Mental health services   Range of services provided in the community or in an institutional setting to persons with mental health problems.

Mental illness   Term that refers collectively to all diagnosable mental disorders.

Mesosystem level   The level of social environment that incorporates interactions and interrelations among the persons, groups, and settings that comprise an individual's microsystem.

Microsystem level   The level of social environment that encompasses the individual, including intrapsychic characteristics and past life experiences, and all the persons and groups in his or her day-to-day environment.

Migrant workers   People engaged in jobs, such as crop harvesting, that require workers and their families to move from place to place to secure employment.

Millennium Development Goals (MDGs)   Specific targets by the United Nations to address extreme poverty and hunger, child and maternal mortality, and HIV/AIDS and other diseases, while promoting universal primary education, gender equality, environmental sustainability, and a global partnership for development by the year 2015.

Minority group   A category of people distinguished by physical or cultural traits that are used by the majority group to single them out for differential and unequal treatment.

Mobilizer   Person who identifies and convenes resources to address unmet community needs.

Moral treatment   A philosophy among professionals and advocates working with the mentally ill in the late 1700s and early 1800s that advocated a caring, humane approach, as opposed to a punitive, repressive environment.

Multidisciplinary team   A group of professionals from a variety of disciplines working with clients.

Multidisciplinary team approach   An approach to working with clients that involves the shared expertise of professionals from a variety of disciplines, such as social workers, health professionals, educators, attorneys, and psychologists.

NAMH   *See* National Association of Mental Health.

Narcotics   Drugs such as opium and its derivatives, morphine, and heroin that dull the senses, relieve pain, and induce profound sleep.

NASW   *See* National Association of Social Workers.

National Association of Mental Health (NAMH)   A national association of professionals, individuals with mental health problems and their families, and organizations concerned about mental health issues and care of persons with mental health problems; provides education, advocacy, and research.

National Association of Social Workers (NASW)   The major national professional organization for social workers, which promotes ethics and quality in social work practice; stimulates political participation and social action; and maintains eligibility standards for membership.

National Institute of Mental Health (NIMH)   A federal agency created by the U.S. Congress in 1949 to address mental health concerns; now a part of the U.S. Department of Health and Human Services.

National Institute of Occupational Safety and Health (NIOSH)   Federal government program housed within the U.S. Department of Health and Human Services that addresses research and technology issues relating to occupational health and safety and sets federal standards for safe storage, use, and disposal of hazardous materials.

Natural group   A group in which members participate as a result of common interests, shared experiences, similar backgrounds and values, and personal satisfactions derived from interaction with other group members.

Natural helping networks   An informal system of support available to individuals as opposed to a professional service delivery system; includes individuals such as family members, friends, neighbors, coworkers, and members of organizations in which an individual may be involved, such as a church or synagogue; also called *natural support systems.*

Natural support systems   Informal systems of support available to individuals in contrast to professional service delivery systems; examples of natural support systems include family members, friends, neighborhoods, coworkers, and members of organizations in which an individual may be involved, such as a church or synagogue; also called *natural helping networks.*

Negotiator   Intermediary who helps to achieve agreement between factions who have different positions on an issue.

Neighborhood and community organizing   Process designed to develop the capacity of community members to organize around quality-of-life issues in the community such as air quality and noise pollution.

New Deal   Emergency legislation created after the Depression that provided assistance for the jobless and poor; this legislation marked the first time in history that the federal government became engaged directly in providing relief and also provided an interpretation of the health and welfare provisions of the Constitution that established a historical precedent mandating the federal government to assume health and welfare responsibility for its citizens. This policy opened the door for later federal legislation in the areas of civil rights, fair employment practices, school busing, public assistance, and a variety of other social programs.

NIMH   *See* National Institute of Mental Health.

NIOSH   *See* National Institute of Occupational Safety and Health.

Nonorganic failure to thrive   A medical condition that results when a child is three percentiles or more below the normal range for height and weight and no organic reason can be determined; placing a child in a hospital and providing an adequate diet and nurturing will cause the child to gain height and weight, suggesting a lack of parental care as the cause.

Occupational Safety and Health Act   Sets health and safety standards in industrial workplaces through on-site inspections and citations for violations.

Occupational Safety and Health Administration (OSHA)   Federal agency that oversees workplace health and safety.

Occupational social work   Social work services provided through the workplace.

Official poverty   A way of measuring poverty that provides a set of income thresholds adjusted for household size, age of household head, and number of children under 18 years old.

Old Age and Survivors Disability Insurance (OASDI)   A Social Security insurance program established as part of the Social Security

Act of 1935 that provides limited payments to those eligible elderly persons and/or their dependents who have been employed and have had taxes deducted from their wages matched by their employer and paid into a funding pool.

Omnibus Budget Reconciliation Act of 1987 (OBRA) Federal legislation that mandated major nursing home reforms, including increased rights for residents, written care plans, training for staff, and the employment of certified social workers.

Omnibus Health Care Rescue Act of 1989 (HB 18) Legislation designed to provide additional health-care resources with emphasis on rural areas.

Open system A system whose boundaries are permeated easily.

Opportunities Factors within the environment that encourage an individual to meet his or her needs and to develop as a healthy, well-functioning person.

Opportunity structure The accessibility of opportunities for an individual within that individual's environment, including personal and environmental factors such as physical traits, intelligence, family, and availability of employment.

Oppression Unjust use of power against nondominant groups by the dominant group.

Organizing functional communities Community organizing technique in which the scope of concern is advocacy for a specific issue or population, such as marriage rights for gays, and the system targeted for change is the general public and government institutions.

OSHA *See* Occupational Safety and Health Administration.

Outdoor relief Cash or in-kind assistance given to persons in need, allowing them to remain in their own homes (e.g., public assistance payments for food and fuel).

Outsourcing The practice by U.S. businesses of having some or all of their production carried out outside of the United States and its territories.

Own-home services *See* Home-based, family-centered services.

Paradigm Commonly accepted or established way of thinking about things.

Pastoral counselor A person who provides counseling service under the auspices of a religious organization, which usually includes an emphasis on spiritual well-being; typically a member of the clergy.

Patient Protection and Affordable Care Act of 2009 Landmark health-care legislation signed into law by President Obama in March 2010 that provides for quality affordable health care for all Americans.

Permanency planning An idea stating that all child welfare services provided for a child should be centered around a plan directed toward a permanent, nurturing home for that child.

Personal Responsibility and Work Opportunity Budget Reconciliation Act of 1996 (PRWOA) Landmark welfare reform legislation that made sweeping changes to the system for providing welfare benefits to low-income women with dependent children.

Person-environment fit The fit between a person's needs, rights, goals, and capacities and the physical and social environment within which the person functions.

Physical child abuse A physical act of harm or threatened harm against a child by a caretaker that results in physical injury to a child, including beating, hitting, slapping, burning, shaking, or throwing.

Physician-assisted suicide Term used to describe the process whereby terminally-ill patients obtain and use prescriptions from their physicians for self-administered, lethal medications.

Planned change An orderly approach to addressing client needs based on assessment, knowledge of the client system's capacity for change, and focused intervention.

Plea bargaining Negotiations among the prosecutor, the defendant, and the defendant's counsel that lead to the defendant entering a guilty plea in exchange for a reduction in charges or the prosecutor's promise to recommend a more lenient sentence.

Policy research Research that focuses on evaluating the effects of proposed or existing social policy on constituent populations.

Political and social action Community organizing in which the scope of concern is to build political power and institutional change (get the message to those who can do something about the issue or problem).

Poly-trauma injuries Damage to more than one part of the body or organ system, one or more of which may be life-threatening.

Populations at risk Groups that are vulnerable to negative physical, social, or economic outcomes as a result of prejudice, discrimination, and oppression by the dominant group.

Positive youth development Framework that emphasizes providing services and opportunities to support young people in developing a sense of competence, usefulness, belonging, and empowerment.

Post-traumatic stress disorder (PTSD) An anxiety disorder that can develop after exposure to an event in which grave physical harm occurred or was threatened.

Poverty A determination that a household's income is inadequate, judged by a specific standard.

Prejudice An irrational attitude of bias directed against an individual, a group, a race, a country, or other entity or their supposed characteristics; often results in hostility and oppression.

Pre-retirement planning Process of planning for retirement in advance of the actual retirement date.

Primary prevention A program targeted at the total population to prevent a problem from occurring.

Primary setting A setting in which the types of services a professional provides match the primary goals of the setting (e.g., a hospital is a primary setting for a nurse but a secondary setting for a social worker).

Private health insurance Health insurance available to individuals and families through the workplace or through purchase of policies with private insurance companies.

Private nonprofit agency Nongovernmental agencies that provide social services, spending all of their funds to meet the goals of the agency with no financial profit earned by agency owners, directors, or employees.

Private practice In social work, the delivery of client services for pay on an independent, autonomous basis rather than under the auspices of an agency; social workers in most states must have a Master's of Social Work (MSW) degree, receive supervision by an advanced practitioner, and pass a licensing or certification examination before establishing a private practice.

Private sector/private voluntary sector Includes programs and agencies funded and operated by nonpublic entities (for instance, voluntary and proprietary agencies and private businesses).

Probation   Replaces incarceration, in which those convicted face supervised release into the community.

Problem-solving approach   A common intervention used by social workers, based on client's motivation and capacity for change and opportunities available to the client to facilitate the change. The client and worker assess needs, identify problems and needs to be addressed, develop a plan to address problems and needs, and implement and monitor the plan, revising as necessary.

Pro bono   Provision of services at no cost to the recipient; professionals such as lawyers and social workers do pro bono work with low-income clients for the public good.

Program development and community liaison   A form of community organizing in which the desired outcome is the expansion or redirection of agency programs and the system targeted for change consists of agency funding sources and beneficiaries of agency services.

Problem-solving courts   Community justice partnerships that include public agencies and nonprofit or for-profit social service providers. Participants in problem-solving courts are given access to a broad array of treatment services and incentives if they achieve positive outcomes; they also are subject to sanctions for noncompliance if they fail to participate in required services.

Psychiatry   A branch of medicine that deals with mental, emotional, and behavioral disorders.

Psychoanalysis   A method of dealing with emotional problems that focuses on inter-psychic functioning (internal conflicts with the individual).

Psychobiology   A term describing the interactions between biological and environmental factors in understanding human behavior.

Psychological maltreatment/emotional maltreatment   Acting out against a person emotionally or psychologically, such as verbally belittling or attacking a person constantly; or failing to meet emotional needs through acts of omission, such as not providing love, attention, and/or emotional support to a person.

Psychological parent   A person viewed by a child as being his or her parental figure from a psychological or emotional standpoint rather than a birth relationship; if a boy were raised by his grandparents and rarely saw his mother, his grandparents would be his psychological parents. Many court decisions are being made based on the concept of a psychological parent.

Psychology   A science based on the study of mind and behavior; involves many subspecialties.

Psychologist   Individual who practices psychology.

Psychosocial aspects   Impact of interactions between internal psychological processes and the environment.

Psychometric instruments   Tests used to measure psychological functioning.

Psychotic behavior   A mental state often described as involving a loss of contact with reality (e.g., hallucinations, delusions, and impaired insight).

Psychotropic drug   A type of drug used in the treatment of mental health problems, including depression and psychoses, that has resulted in major reductions in numbers of individuals with emotional problems needing long-term hospitalization.

Public assistance   Programs that provide income, medical care, and social services to individuals and families based on economic need; Temporary Assistance to Needy Families (TANF), Supplemental Nutrition Assistance Program (SNAP, formerly food stamps), and Medicaid are public assistance programs.

Public health insurance   Insurance, such as Medicaid, provided by the public sector to those in need who are not covered by private insurance programs and meet eligibility requirements.

Public sector   Programs and agencies funded and operated by government entities, including public schools, agencies, and hospitals.

Racial profiling   Practice of law enforcement officers or others in which a person is treated as a suspect because of his or her race.

Reactive depressive behavior   Behavior resulting from depression, often due to a loss, that can affect the ability to parent and may lead to child neglect.

Reality therapy   An intervention, based on the assumption that people are responsible for their own behavior, that effects change by confronting individuals about irresponsible behaviors and encouraging them to accept responsibility for their behaviors and to develop positive self-worth through positive behavior.

Recidivism   Return to previous behaviors; for example, when persons released from prison commit new crimes.

Recreation group   A group of individuals who engage in recreational activities in a monitored environment.

Recreation skill group   A group designed to promote development of a skill within a recreational or enjoyment context.

Refugee   A person who flees to a foreign country or power to escape danger or persecution.

Rehabilitation   Philosophy of punishment that aims at preventing future crimes by changing individual offenders.

Relative poverty   Poverty measured by comparing the unit being measured (e.g., individuals or families) to a set standard for that unit, such as income, with those falling below that standard identified as being in poverty.

Residential treatment   Treatment provided in 24-hour care facilities for persons with mental health or substance use problems or developmental disabilities; such programs are usually considered less restrictive than psychiatric hospitals.

Resilience   Ability to recover or adapt successfully to adversity.

Retirement   Leaving paid employment, usually because of advanced age; retirees may receive pensions or Social Security benefits depending on their work history and eligibility for such programs.

Richmond, Mary   A major contributor to the Charity Organization Society movement and considered by many to be the founder of the professional clinical social work movement. Richmond inaugurated the first training program for social workers at the New York School of Applied Philanthropy, the forerunner of schools of social work, and formulated the concept of social casework.

Risks   Direct threats to healthy development, or the absence of opportunities that should facilitate healthy individual development.

Root causes   Underlying cause of a social problem.

Rural   A social, occupational, and cultural way of life for persons living in communities with fewer than 2,500 persons.

Rural social work   Social work provided in rural areas usually based on a generalist practice model that involves the actual provision of many services rather than linking individuals with other social service resources.

Same-sex marriage   Legal union between couples of the same sex.

School social work   A social work approach that involves working with children, youth, and their families within a school setting; school social workers deal directly with children, youth, and their families as well as teachers, school administrators, and other community resources.

Secondary prevention   Targeted at specified groups within a larger population that are determined to be "at risk" or more likely to experience a specific problem than the larger population to prevent the problem from occurring, for example, intervention to prevent alcoholism targeted at teens with a parent who is an alcoholic.

Secondary setting   A setting in which the types of services a professional provides differ from the primary focus of the setting (e.g., a social worker in a hospital works in a secondary setting, while a social worker in a social services agency works in a primary setting).

Selective enforcement   The use of discretion to enforce some laws sometimes against some people.

Self-care   Decisions and actions an individual can take to cope with stress, such as taking the time to relax, receiving adequate rest, and maintaining a healthy diet.

Self-concept   The image a person has of herself or himself in relation to appearance, ability, motivation, and capacity to react to the environment; derived primarily through feedback from others.

Self-help group   A group of individuals with similar problems that meets for the purpose of providing support and information to each other and for mutual problem solving—for example, Parents Anonymous and Alcoholics Anonymous.

Settlement house   Physical structure where community-based services and advocacy for the poor and disenfranchised are carried out.

Sexism   Discrimination against an individual because of gender.

Sexual abuse   The use of a child by an adult for sexual or emotional gratification in a sexual way, such as fondling, exposure, sexual intercourse, and exploitation, including child pornography.

Sexual harassment   Unwelcome sexual advances, requests for sexual favors, and other verbal or physical conduct of a sexual nature when submission to or rejection of this conduct explicitly or implicitly affects an individual's employment, unreasonably interferes with an individual's work performance, or creates an intimidating or hostile or offensive work environment.

Sexual inequality   Inequality between men and women based on gender attributes.

Sexual orientation   An enduring emotional, romantic, sexual, or affectional attraction either to persons of the opposite sex or gender as the individual, the same sex or gender as the individual, or to persons of either sex or gender as the individual . Persons may express their sexual orientation through feelings, behaviors, and identity.

Single-case/single-subject designs   Research designs that evaluate the impact of interventions or policy changes on a single client or case.

SNAP (Supplemental Nutrition Assistance Program)   In-kind benefit designed to address food insecurity (formerly the Food Stamp Program); see also *Supplemental Nutrition Assistance Program.*

Social action   A social work approach to working with communities that stresses organization and group cohesion in confrontational approaches geared to modify or eliminate institutional power bases that negatively impact the community.

Social agencies   Organizations whose primary focus is to address social problems.

Social and economic justice   Fairness and equity with regard to basic civil and human rights protections, resources, and opportunities and social benefits.

Social casework   A social work method involving face-to-face contact with individuals, families, groups, or organizations, by which the social worker provides services directly to clients for the purpose of addressing unmet needs; also referred to as *direct practice.*

Social emotional selectivity theory   Theory relating to persons in later stages of life that suggests that positive relationships often increase longevity of life, and that as people age, they narrow their social emotional relationships to those that are most meaningful.

Social group work   A social work method involving intervention with groups of individuals that uses structured interaction to promote individual and group functioning and well-being.

Social inequality   Unequal treatment of social groups based on factors such as economic and social status, age, ethnicity, sexual preference, or gender.

Social insurance   Financial assistance for those whose income has been curtailed because of retirement, death, or long-term disability of the family breadwinner; paid to former working persons or their dependents through a tax on earned income.

Social justice   Fairness and equity in the protection of civil and human rights, the treatment of individuals, the distribution of opportunity, and the assurance of personal and economic opportunity.

Social movements   Form of community organizing in which the desired outcome is action for social justice and the system targeted for change is the general public or political systems.

Social planning   A social work approach to working with communities that emphasizes modification of institutional practices through the application of knowledge, values, and theory; a practical, rational approach.

Social Security   An insurance program established as part of the Social Security Act that provides limited payments to eligible older adults who have been employed (or their dependents) and have had taxes deducted from their wages, matched by their employers, and paid into a funding pool.

Social Security Act   Major social welfare legislation passed by the U.S. Congress in 1935, establishing social insurance programs based on taxes paid by working persons; public assistance programs to provide for those who do not qualify for social insurance programs and cannot provide for themselves or their families financially; and health and welfare services for children, families, the disabled, and the aged such as child welfare services, maternal and child health services, and services for the disabled.

Social study The process of obtaining relevant information about the client system and perceived needs.

Social welfare Efforts organized by societies to facilitate the well-being of their members, usually focused on activities that seek to prevent, alleviate, or contribute to the solution of a selected set of social problems.

Social welfare policy A specific course of actions taken to address an identified social problem, with emphasis on the decisions and choices that help determine those actions.

Social welfare theory A type of theory in which the area of concern in social welfare.

Social work The major profession that implements planned change activities prescribed by social welfare institutions through intervention with individuals, families, and groups or at community, organizational, and societal levels to enhance or restore social functioning.

Social worker A member of the social work profession who works with individuals, families, groups, organizations, communities, or societies to improve social functioning.

Socialization The process of learning to become a social being; the acquisition of knowledge, values, abilities, and skills that are essential to function as a member of the society within which the individual lives.

Socialization group A group of individuals whose goal is to help participants develop socially acceptable behavior and behavioral competency.

Sociologist An individual who studies society, its organization and demographic structure, and patterns of human interaction, including norms, values, and behavior.

Solution-focused therapy Short-term cognitive behavioral intervention that emphasizes the present situation rather than events in the client's past; strategies focus on very specific situations and tasks that are assigned to clients to work on between sessions.

Specialization Practice of social work focused on a specific population or field of practice requiring specialized knowledge and skill; contrasts with *generalist practice.*

Specific deterrent A program or sentence targeted at an individual to discourage him or her from repeating inappropriate/illegal behavior.

Spillover effect A term describing the situation when feelings, attitudes, and behaviors from one domain in a person's life have a positive or a negative impact on other domains (such as from the workplace to the family).

SSI *See* Supplemental Security Income.

Steady state Constant adjustment of a system moving toward its goal while maintaining order and stability within.

Stepfamilies *See* Blended families.

Stereotype A standardized mental picture of a group attributed to all group members.

Stereotypes Beliefs that members of certain groups behave in specific ways.

Stimulants Drugs that stimulate the central nervous system, creating a sense of heightened euphoria.

Strengths perspective An approach to social work that focuses on the strengths of the client system and the broader environment within which it functions rather than on the deficiencies.

Substance use disorder Term used to describe a brain-based disease that involves the misuse of mood-altering substances such alcohol and/or other drugs that results in detrimental effects on an individual's personal life, including school, job, family, friends, health, spiritual life, or the law.

Substitute care Out-of-home care provided for children when parents are unwilling or unable to provide care in their own homes; types of substitute care include foster care, group home care, and residential treatment and are determined based on the child's needs.

Suicide The act or instance of taking one's own life voluntarily and intentionally.

Supplemental Nutrition Assistance Program (SNAP) In-kind assistance program funded by the U.S. Department of Agriculture designed to supplement the food-purchasing power of eligible low-income households to allow families to maintain nutritious diets and to expand the market for agricultural goods (replaced the federal Food Stamp Program in 2008).

Supplemental Security Income (SSI) A program administered in conjunction with the Social Security Program to provide cash assistance to older adults, persons with vision impairments, and persons with other permanent and total disabilities who meet certain eligibility standards established by state and federal regulations.

Support services Services that provide support to individuals and families, such as health care, legal assistance, housing, and social services.

Synergy The combined energy of smaller parts of a larger system that is greater than the sum of the energy of those parts if they functioned separately.

System A social unit consisting of interdependent, interacting parts.

Systems/ecological framework A major framework used by social workers to understand individual, family, community, organizational, and societal events and behaviors that emphasizes the interactions and interdependence between individuals and their environments; also referred as *ecological/systems framework.*

Task-centered method A short-term therapeutic approach to intervention that stresses the selection of specific tasks to be worked on within a limited time frame to address the needs of a client system.

Telecommunications A way of communicating electronically that allows remote sites to have access to information and consultation.

Telemedicine The use of telecommunications by medical health practitioners to gain access to large medical centers where consultation is available for both diagnostic and treatment regimens; increased use of telemedicine is occurring in rural areas.

Temporary Assistance to Needy Families (TANF) A public assistance program that provides cash assistance to families (primarily single-parent women) with children in need because of the loss of financial support as a result of death, disability, or the continued absence of a second parent from the home; assistance is available on a time-limited basis and requires participation in programs that prepare adults in the family for participation in the workforce; TANF replaced the Aid to Families with Dependent Children (AFDC) program.

Tertiary prevention Efforts targeted at individuals who have already experienced a specific problem to prevent that problem from reoccurring.

Testable The ability of a theory to be measured accurately and validly.

Theory A way of organizing facts or sets of facts to describe, explain, or predict events.

Therapeutic group Group requiring skilled professional leaders who assist group members in addressing intensive personal and emotional problems.

Traditional communities Communities in which members attempt to maintain their separateness, uniqueness, cultural integrity, and historical identity (e.g., Amish, Native Americans, Hasidic Jews, and aborigines).

Traumatic Brain Injury A trauma that causes damage to the brain when a person's head is hit suddenly and violently by an object, an object pierces the skull and enters the brain, and/or the person experiences sudden rapid movement that in turn causes rapid movement within the brain cavity.

Trial courts Courts with the power to conduct pre-trial and trial proceedings in all criminal cases.

Underclass The lowest socioeconomic group in society, characterized by chronic poverty and the inability to pull themselves out of their condition, often due to barriers and societal obstacles including oppression.

Under-employment Work in a job for which one's qualifications exceed those established for the position.

Unemployment compensation A program established by the Social Security Act that is funded by taxes assessed by employers and is available to eligible unemployed workers.

United Nations Children's Fund (UNICEF) An organization dedicated to assisting developing countries of the world in creating permanent child health and welfare services.

(Office of) United Nations High Commissioner for Refugees (UNHCR) A United Nations (UN) agency mandated to protect and support refugees at the request of a government or the UN itself and to assist in their voluntary repatriation, local integration or resettlement to a third country.

Universal Declaration of Human Rights A common standard of achievement adopted by Member States of the United Nations in 1948 designed to promote respect for the basic human rights and freedoms among the peoples of Member States and of territories under their jurisdiction.

Universal health care Access to health care by all citizens.

Urban Term used by the U.S. Bureau of the Census to designate cities of a certain size, usually characterized by high population density.

U.S. Children's Bureau Established in 1912, was the first department set up by the federal government to address the needs of children and families; federal programs addressing problems of abuse and neglect, runaway youth, adoption and foster care, and other child welfare services are currently housed within the U.S Department of Health and Human Services.

U.S. Department of Agriculture (USDA) A federal department that oversees the Supplemental Nutrition Assistance Program (SNAP, formerly the food stamp program) and houses the Agricultural Extension Service, which provides services targeted to rural areas.

U.S. Department of Health and Human Services A federal department that oversees the implementation of legislation relating to health and human services, including public assistance programs, child welfare services, and services for older adults.

Values Assumptions, convictions, or beliefs of a person or group in which they have an emotional investment; values influence opinions about the ways people should behave and the principles that should govern behavior.

Voluntary sector A third sector of society, along with the public and for-profit proprietary sectors, that includes private, nonprofit social agencies.

War on Poverty Programs put in place under the Economic Opportunities Act of 1964, an effort led by President Lyndon Baines Johnson to eradicate poverty in the United States.

Welfare devolution Transfer of responsibility for public welfare programs from the federal government to individual states and localities.

Welfare reform Reform of the public welfare system by policy makers and legislators who believe that it is ineffective in achieving its stated goals.

Workers' compensation An insurance program that is funded by taxes assessed to employers and is available to eligible workers who are injured on the job or who experience job-related injuries or illnesses.

Working poor Persons who maintain regular employment but fall below the federal poverty level because of low wages.

Workplace violence (WPV) Acts of violence, including harassment by family members, that occur in the workplace.

World citizenship People accepting responsibility in this interdependent world by thinking and acting as citizens of that world.

World Health Organization (WHO) An organization that provides leadership on global health matters, shaping the health research agenda, setting norms and standards, articulating evidence-based policy options, providing technical support to countries and monitoring and assessing health trends.

Worldview One's perspective on the way the world works.

Index